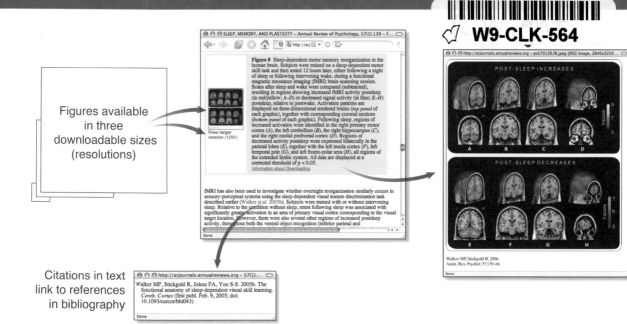

Figures available in three downloadable sizes (resolutions)

Citations in text link to references in bibliography

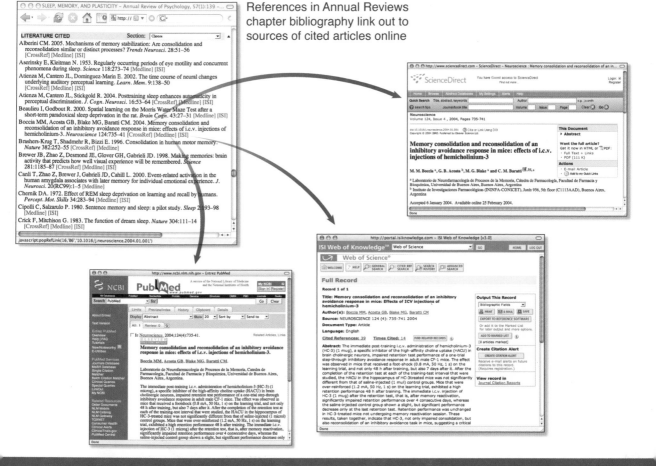

References in Annual Reviews chapter bibliography link out to sources of cited articles online

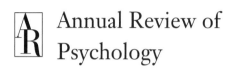

Annual Review of
Psychology

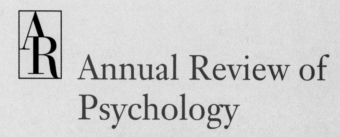

Annual Review of Psychology

Volume 58, 2007

Susan T. Fiske, *Editor*
Princeton University

Alan E. Kazdin, *Associate Editor*
Yale University

Daniel L. Schacter, *Associate Editor*
Harvard University

www.annualreviews.org • science@annualreviews.org • 650-493-4400

Annual Reviews
4139 El Camino Way • P.O. Box 10139 • Palo Alto, California 94303-0139

Annual Reviews
Palo Alto, California, USA

International Standard Serial Number: 0066-4308
International Standard Book Number: 0-8243-0258-3
Library of Congress Catalog Card Number: 50-13143

⊗ The paper used in this publication meets the minimum requirements of American National Standards for Information Sciences—Permanence of Paper for Printed Library Materials, ANSI Z39.48-1992.

TYPESET BY TECHBOOKS, FALLS CHURCH, VIRGINIA
PRINTED AND BOUND BY MALLOY INCORPORATED, ANN ARBOR, MICHIGAN

Preface

Readers of the *Annual Review of Psychology* may appreciate a periodic update regarding how this series operates. We take the liberty of reprinting part of our preface from seven years back, which contains editorial policy useful for authors interested in submitting articles and for readers curious about how the articles get here:

> The *Annual Review of Psychology* resembles conventional review journals, in its goal to represent current knowledge in the field, in all its varieties. The *Annual Review of Psychology* differs, however, in its goal to provide timely perspectives by planful request, rather than by spontaneous submissions. Instead of waiting for submitted snapshots, and holding a contest, the AR commissions landscapes from different perspectives and different styles. Not every area is recorded every year, but over time, we hope to cover the territory. Choices of chapters are guided by a Master Plan of topics in psychology (just revised at the end of the previous team's watch, for which the current team is thankful). Topics come up in rotation, and the editorial committee assembles every spring to issue invitations. The joy of this job is that 90% of the invited authors accept, and 90% of those then deliver.
>
> The *Annual Review of Psychology* holds a unique position for another reason. Its intended audience includes not only one's immediate colleagues expert in the same specialized subarea, but also other psychology colleagues catching up, graduate students coming in, adjacent scientists stopping by, undergraduates exploring around, and teachers keeping up. As such, we aim for articles that people want to read, accessible at several levels, with a lively point-of-view, as well as a scholarly respect for the range of evidence.

Today we still adhere to these guidelines, reflecting the continuity of the series, its mandate, and format. The established process allows for recognizing and responding to new areas of work and areas that have evolved or taken special advantages of conceptual or technological breakthroughs. With seven years' accumulated wisdom, we would add that yes, sometimes, rarely, we do accept submissions of ideas for article topics. Authors with an idea can submit a one- to two-page proposal, including a description of previous reviews on the topic and evidence of its timely quality. We also need an abbreviated curriculum vitae. Note that the editorial committee accepts perhaps 10% of these proposals. Note also that reviews of one's own research program or theory are not appropriate. That being said, sometimes volunteer proposals are accepted at our annual editorial committee meeting in March, and we need those materials by a month in advance.

Finally, we want to reiterate our gratitude to authors, editorial committee members (listed opposite the title page), Production Editor Lisa Dean, and Editor-in-Chief

Samuel Gubins, all of whom contribute to the level of scholarship of the final product. What's more, working with these individuals is a joy, and this too reflects the continuity of the Annual Review.

Susan T. Fiske, Princeton
Alan E. Kazdin, New Haven
Daniel L. Schacter, Cambridge

**Annual Review of
Psychology**

Volume 58, 2007

Contents

Research Methodology

Indexes

Errata

An online log of corrections to *Annual Review of Psychology* chapters (if any, 1997 to the present) may be found at http://psych.annualreviews.org/errata.shtml

Related Articles

Research on Attention Networks as a Model for the Integration of Psychological Science

Michael I. Posner and Mary K. Rothbart[1]

Psychology Department, University of Oregon, Eugene, Oregon 97403-1291; email: mposner@darkwing.uoregon.edu, maryroth@darkwing.uoregon.edu

Annu. Rev. Psychol. 2007. 58:1–23

First published online as a Review in Advance on October 9, 2006

The *Annual Review of Psychology* is online at http://psych.annualreviews.org

This article's doi: 10.1146/annurev.psych.58.110405.085516

[1]We appreciate the invitation of the editors of the *Annual Review of Psychology* to submit a prefatory essay to this year's volume. We have taken the opportunity to propose a unified basis for psychological science based upon an effort to combine experimental and differential approaches to the field. This article is an improved and expanded version of an earlier one along these lines (Posner & Rothbart 2004), and its developmental aspects are further expanded in a book (Posner & Rothbart 2007).

Key Words

attention, candidate genes, orienting, neural networks, temperament

Abstract

As Titchener pointed out more than one hundred years ago, attention is at the center of the psychological enterprise. Attention research investigates how voluntary control and subjective experience arise from and regulate our behavior. In recent years, attention has been one of the fastest growing of all fields within cognitive psychology and cognitive neuroscience. This review examines attention as characterized by linking common neural networks with individual differences in their efficient utilization. The development of attentional networks is partly specified by genes, but is also open to specific experiences through the actions of caregivers and the culture. We believe that the connection between neural networks, genes, and socialization provides a common approach to all aspects of human cognition and emotion. Pursuit of this approach can provide a basis for psychology that unifies social, cultural, differential, experimental, and physiological areas, and allows normal development to serve as a baseline for understanding various forms of pathology. D.O. Hebb proposed this approach 50 years ago in his volume *Organization of Behavior* and continued with introductory textbooks that dealt with all of the topics of psychology in a common framework. Use of a common network approach to psychological science may allow a foundation for predicting and understanding human behavior in its varied forms.

Contents

INTRODUCTION

Can psychology be a unified science, or must it remain fragmented and subject to transient research interests rather than cumulative development? Is psychology teachable or must psychology textbooks remain encyclopedias of often unrelated findings? In this article, we examine research on attention to suggest ways of looking at psychological questions and findings that might lead to hopeful answers to these questions. We offer a model based on Hebbian psychology that reaches out from biological roots to tackle questions of emotion and thought as well as behavior. We, with many of our colleagues, see different levels of analysis in psychology as informing each other, with each level of equal scientific validity. Bridging these levels can allow a higher level of understanding and prediction.

We argue that D.O. Hebb (see **Figure 1**), beginning with his monograph in 1949 and continuing through a series of introductory textbooks (1958, 1966), has convincingly presented the basis for such integration. This integration lies in understanding how genes and experience shape neural networks underlying human thoughts, feelings, and actions.

At the time Hebb wrote his monograph, relatively little was known about how the structure and organization of the central nervous system contribute to the functions observed in psychological studies. This led Hebb to talk in terms of the conceptual nervous system, that is, ideas about its structure that might be imagined or inferred from psychological studies. We suggest that the methods available to Hebb, mostly animal research and behavioral human experiments, were not sufficient to provide empirical methods for linking his conceptual nervous system to real events in the human brain. This methodology has now been provided by neuroimaging. Although Hebb also recognized the importance of studying individual differences in intelligence and affect, at that time there were no methods for exploring the specific genes that are an important source of these differences. The human genome project has provided new methods for exploring this issue.

In Hebb's time, the idea of a network (cell assembly or phase sequence) was a rather vague verbal abstraction that did not allow for models that could produce specific predictions. As a result of the rapid changes in cellular biology (Bullock et al. 2005) and in the mathematics of multilevel networks, this too has changed (Rumelhart & McClelland 1986). Although early versions of these networks were inspired by simple versions of neurons as all-or-none elements, more recent versions (O'Reilly & Munakata 2000) have begun to use the details of neuroanatomy and cellular structure as provided by imaging and cellular studies to develop networks that take more realistic advantage of the structure of the human brain. Hebb's basic idea, together with the new methodological tools and new disciplines (e.g., cognitive, affective, and social neuroscience), all based on network views, give abundant evidence of the value of employing the converging operations strategy advocated by Sternberg (Sternberg 2004).

It is important to recognize the need for integrating cognitive, affective, and social neuroscience with psychology because many of

Attention: the regulating of various brain networks by attentional networks involved in maintaining the alert state, orienting, or regulation of conflict

Neural networks: a number of brain areas that when orchestrated carry out a psychological function

Figure 1
Photograph of Professor Donald O. Hebb.

the theoretical questions that need to be addressed by neuroimaging and genetic studies are exactly those that a century of psychologists have explored. The neuroscience approach provides crucial constraints for psychological theories, but it also benefits when a closer connection is made with the psychological level of analysis.

HEBB'S NETWORK APPROACH

In 1949, D.O. Hebb published his epic work, *The Organization of Behavior*. His book was immediately recognized as providing the potential for an integrated psychology. One reviewer (Attneave 1950, p. 633) wrote:

> I believe *The Organization of Behavior* to be the most important contribution to psychological theory in recent years. Unlike those of his contemporaries who are less interested in psychology than in some restricted aspect thereof to which their principles confine them, Hebb has made a noteworthy attempt to take the experimentally determined facts of behavior, as they are, and account for them in terms of events within the central nervous system.

The most important basic idea that Hebb presented was the cell assembly theory outlined in chapters 4 and 5 of his book (Goddard 1980, Harris 2005). Hebb argued that every psychological event, sensation, expectation, emotion, or thought is represented by the flow of activity in a set of interconnected neurons. Learning occurs by a change in synaptic strength when a synapse conducts excitation at the same time the postsynaptic neuron discharges. This provided a basis for the modification of synapses and showed how neural networks might be organized under the influence of specific experiences. The Hebb synapse plays a central role in modern neuroscience (see Kolb 2003, Milner 2003, Sejnowski 2003). There are important new developments in the study of synapses and in the discovery of other influences among neu-

rons and between neurons and other brain cells (Bullock et al. 2005). These developments have reduced the gap between networks revealed in imaging studies and the complex intracellular activity that underlies them. In particular, they show that learning may reflect the activity of interactions at many time scales and may be modified by aspects of the organism's overall state.

Hebb also introduced the concept of the phase sequence involved in the coordination of multiple cell assemblies. He recognized the importance of the temporal correspondence between assemblies. In recent years these ideas have been supported by studies showing that synchronization of brain areas may be critical to detecting stimuli (Womelsdorf et al. 2006) and for transfer of information between remote areas (Nikolaev et al. 2001). In later years, Hebb (1958) developed an introductory psychology textbook that integrated much of psychology using the framework provided by his 1949 theory. He applied his network theory to heredity, learning and memory, motivation, perception, thought, and development. In later editions, he extended his approach to emotions in their social contexts, individual differences in intelligence, and abnormal psychology.

Despite his efforts and those of his followers at McGill and elsewhere, Hebb's work was unsuccessful in providing a fully integrative psychology, and many still seek to develop such an integration (Sternberg 2004, Sternberg & Grigorenko 2001). One of the major problems with Hebb's framework was that it left no clear empirical path for the acquisition of new knowledge about how human brain networks develop, how they differ among individuals, why they break down, and how they can be restored to functioning. Most of the research by Hebb and his associates was performed on nonhuman animals, while most of psychology concerns human behavior, brain, and mind.

In 1955, Hebb argued for the utility of a conceptual nervous system inferred from psychological studies of motivation. This idea remains of key importance. Despite our growing understanding of the function and structure of the nervous system, psychological knowledge needs to be used to propose hypotheses about how the central nervous system (CNS) works to support feelings, thoughts, and behaviors. We argue that only within an integrated field of psychology can knowledge at all levels be used to develop and constrain these hypotheses.

New Tools

Several major late-twentieth century events give improved prospects for an integration of psychological science around the ideas introduced by Hebb. Cell assemblies and phase sequences are names for aspects of neural networks. Now, thanks to work on the computational properties of neural networks (i.e., Rumelhart & McClelland 1986), we are in a much better position to develop detailed theories integrating information from physiological, cognitive, and behavioral studies.

In addition, new neuroimaging methods now allow us to examine neuronal activity in terms of localized changes in blood flow or metabolism in positron emission tomography (PET) or changes in blood oxygenation by functional magnetic resonance imaging (fMRI). By using tracers that bind to different transmitters, PET can also be used to examine transmitter density. By measuring electrical (electroencephalogram, or EEG) and magnetic (magnetoencephalogram) signals outside the skull, the time course of activation of different brain areas localized by fMRI can be measured (Dale et al. 2000). Pathways of activation can also be imaged by use of diffusion tensor imaging, a form of MRI that traces white matter tracts. In addition to the study of naturally occurring lesions, interrupting information flow by transcranial magnetic stimulation (TMS) can produce temporary functional lesions of pathways (see Toga & Mazziotta 1996 for a review of these and other methods). These methods provide a toolkit that can be used either alone or together to make human brain networks accessible for detailed physiological study.

Some have thought that the influence of imaging has been merely to tell us where in the brain things have happened (Utall 2001). Certainly many, perhaps even most, imaging studies have been concerned with anatomical issues. As **Figure 2** illustrates, several functions of attention have been shown to involve specific anatomical areas that carry out important functions. However, imaging also probes neural networks that underlie all aspects of human thought, feelings, and behavior. The full significance of imaging for (a) viewing brain networks, (b) examining their computation in real time, (c) exploring how they are assembled in development, and (d) their plasticity following physical damage or training is a common theme in current research that is just beginning to reach its potential.

A third development, the mapping of the human genome (Venter et al. 2001), offers the potential for an increased understanding of the physical basis for individual differences, including individual differences in temperament and personality. Many genes exhibit a number of relatively high-frequency variants (polymorphisms) that can code for different physical configurations. These in turn can alter the efficiency of a network. For example, different types of genes (alleles) forming dopamine receptors can lead to different efficiency in binding to dopamine and thus differences in underlying neural networks. In a number of cases, it has been possible to relate these genetic differences to individual performance in tasks involving the network (see Fossella & Posner 2004 for a review). Genetics-based research also provides an important approach to the development of characteristics of neural networks common to all members of the species.

We recognize that not all topics of psychology have been sufficiently explored to illustrate this framework and that limitations in our knowledge prevent us from exploring all of the areas where these developments can be applied. However, attention and

PET: positron emission tomography

fMRI: functional magnetic resonance imaging

Temperament: relatively enduring biological characteristics of individuals that include both reactive and self-regulatory (attentional) aspects

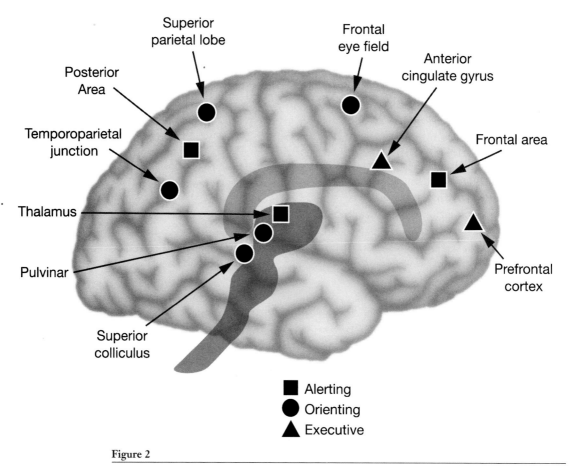

Figure 2

Anatomy of three attentional networks: alerting, orienting, and executive attention (from Posner & Rothbart 2007).

temperament, areas of our study, can be used to consider how a large number of psychological questions can be explored using the neural network framework outlined by Hebb. Attention serves as a basic set of mechanisms that underlie our awareness of the world and the voluntary regulation of our thoughts and feelings. The methods used to understand attentional networks in terms of anatomy, individual differences, development, and plasticity can be applied readily to explore networks related to other aspects of human behavior.

Any approach based on neural networks raises the issue of crude reductionism. Many agree that all human behavior must ultimately be traceable to brain activity, but correctly argue for the importance of cogni-

tive experiments, behavioral observations, and self-report as important elements of psychological science. We hope to illustrate in this article how important such psychological methods are and how they can be integrated within a brain network framework, as Hebb (1955) illustrated in his *Textbook of Psychology*.

IMAGING ATTENTION NETWORKS

Functional neuroimaging has allowed many cognitive tasks to be analyzed in terms of the brain areas they activate, and studies of attention have been among those most often examined (Corbetta & Shulman 2002, Driver et al. 2004, Posner & Fan 2007). Imaging data have supported the presence of three networks related to different aspects of attention (Fan et al. 2005). These networks carry out the functions of alerting, orienting, and executive attention (Posner & Fan 2007). A summary of the anatomy and chemical modulators involved in the three networks is shown in **Table 1**.

Alerting is defined as achieving and maintaining a state of high sensitivity to incoming stimuli; orienting is the selection of information from sensory input; and executive attention involves mechanisms for monitoring and resolving conflict among thoughts, feelings, and responses. The alerting system has been associated with thalamic as well as frontal and parietal regions of the cortex (Fan et al. 2005). A particularly effective way to vary alertness has been to use warning signals prior to targets. The influence of warning signals on the level of alertness is thought to be due to modulation of neural activity by the neurotransmitter norepinephrine (Marrocco & Davidson 1998).

Orienting involves aligning attention with a source of sensory signals. This may be overt, as when eye movements accompany movements of attention, or may occur covertly, without any eye movement. The orienting system for visual events has been associated with posterior brain areas, including the superior parietal lobe and temporal parietal junction, and in addition, the frontal eye fields (Corbetta & Shulman 2002). Orienting can be manipulated by presenting a cue indicating where in space a target is likely to occur, thereby directing attention to the cued location (Posner 1980). It is possible to determine the anatomy influenced by the cue separately from that influenced by the target by using MRI to trace changes in the blood that specifically follow the cue. This method is called event-related functional magnetic resonance imaging, and its use has suggested that the superior parietal lobe is associated with orienting following the presentation of a cue (Corbetta & Shulman 2002). The superior parietal lobe in humans is closely related

Table 1 A summary of the anatomy and chemical modulators involved in the alerting, orienting, and executive attention networks.

Function	Structures	Modulator
Orient	Superior parietal Temporal parietal junction Frontal eye fields Superior colliculus	Acetylcholine
Alert	Locus coeruleus Right frontal Parietal cortex	Norepinephrine
Executive attention	Anterior cingulate Lateral ventral Prefrontal Basal ganglia	Dopamine

to the lateral intraparietal area (LIP) in monkeys, which is involved in the production of eye movements (Andersen 1989). When a target occurs at an uncued location and attention has to be disengaged and moved to a new location, there is activity in the temporal parietal junction (Corbetta & Shulman 2002). Lesions of the temporal parietal junction lobe and superior temporal lobe have been consistently related to difficulties in orienting (Karnath et al. 2001).

Executive control of attention is often studied by tasks that involve conflict, such as various versions of the Stroop task. In the Stroop task, subjects must respond to the color of ink (e.g., red) while ignoring the color word name (e.g., blue) (Bush et al. 2000). Resolving conflict in the Stroop task activates midline frontal areas (anterior cingulate) and lateral prefrontal cortex (Botvinick et al. 2001, Fan et al. 2005). There is also evidence for the activation of this network in tasks involving conflict between a central target and surrounding flankers that may be congruent or incongruent with the target (Botvinick et al. 2001, Fan et al. 2005).

Recently, the role of the anterior cingulate in modulating sensory input has been demonstrated experimentally by showing enhanced connectivity between the anterior cingulate cortex and the sensory modality to which the

Orienting: the interaction of a brain network with sensory systems designed to improve the selected signal

ANT: attention network test

RT: reaction time

ACT-R: adaptive control of thought-rational

person is asked to attend (Crottaz-Herbette & Menon 2006). This finding supports the general idea that anterior cingulate cortex activity regulates other brain areas, at least for sensory areas. Experimental tasks may also provide a means of fractionating the contributions of different areas within the executive attention network (MacDonald et al. 2000). In accord with the findings in recent neuroimaging studies (Beauregard et al. 2001, Ochsner et al. 2001), we have argued that the executive attention network is involved in self-regulation of positive and negative affect as well as a wide variety of cognitive tasks underlying intelligence (Duncan et al. 2000). This idea suggests an important role for attention in moderating the activity of sensory, cognitive, and emotional systems.

Simulating Attention Networks

Quantification has had a high value in psychological research. An advantage of the network approach is that it lends itself to the development of precise computer models that allow both summarization of many findings in the field and prediction of new findings. Currently, symbolic models, such as rule-based systems (Newell 1990), appear to be a good way to capture data from reaction time and other psychological findings. In these models, cognitive functions are represented as chains of production rules and can be identified with the mental operations postulated by cognitive studies. On the other hand, subsymbolic models, such as connectionist models (e.g., O'Reilly & Munakata 2000), permit a more biologically realistic implementation of the operations and closer links to imaging studies.

We have developed the attention network test (ANT) to examine individual differences in the efficiency of the brain networks of alerting, orienting, and executive attention discussed above (Fan et al. 2002, Rueda et al. 2004). The ANT uses differences in reaction time (RT) between conditions to measure the efficiency of each network. Each trial begins with a cue (or a blank interval, in the no-cue

condition) that informs the participant either that a target will occur soon or where it will occur, or both. The target always occurs either above or below fixation, and consists of a central arrow, surrounded by flanking arrows that can point either in the same direction (congruent) or in the opposite direction (incongruent). Subtracting RTs for congruent from incongruent target trials provides a measure of conflict resolution and assesses the efficiency of the executive attention network. Subtracting RTs obtained in the double-cue condition that provides information on when but not where the target will occur from RTs in the no-cue condition gives a measure of alerting due to the presence of a warning signal. Subtracting RTs to targets at the cued location (spatial cue condition) from trials using a central cue gives a measure of orienting, since the spatial cue, but not the central cue, provides valid information about where a target will occur.

The attention network task has now been simulated in the framework of the adaptive control of thought-rational (ACT-R) theory (Wang et al. 2004). The ANT task is divided into subroutines. Cue processing involves switching of attention to the cued location. Target processing involves detection of the direction of the arrow in the center and involves an attention switch and response initiation. Each of these operations is implemented by a chain of production rules. The operations are similar to those discussed in most psychological studies and localized in neurological studies. For example, the switching of attention based on the peripheral cue or target is thought to be implemented by the temporal parietal junction (Corbetta & Shulman 2002).

A connectionist simulation of the ANT (H. Wang & J. Fan, manuscript in preparation) is based upon a local error-driven and associative, biologically realistic algorithm (LEABRA) (O'Reilly & Munakata 2000). The subroutines of ACT-R are now replaced by specific connections between hypothesized neurons. These neurons are somewhat realistic, and are designed to represent the known properties of specific brain areas. Thus, the orienting network can be designed to reflect the known properties of the frontal eye fields, superior parietal lobe, and temporal parietal junction, and they can be connected within the simulation. As shown in **Figure 3**, simulations do a reasonable job of fitting with the known ANT data, although improvement can be expected in the future. The symbolic model makes contact with the mental operations related to imaging, whereas the connectionist framework allows a strong treatment of the underlying biology. Together they illustrate how network views provide a computational means for summarizing many findings within psychology, allowing novel predictions reflecting properties of the network.

INDIVIDUAL EFFICIENCY

Psychology is often divided into two approaches that are almost completely separate in the literature (but see Gardner 1983 for an effort at integration). The discussion above focused on general features of the human mind, such as the ability to attend. Another approach deals with differences among individuals. These differences may involve cognition, as in the measurement of intelligence, or they may involve temperamental differences, many of which relate to energetic factors such as the expression and control of the emotions. Almost all studies of attention have been concerned either with the general abilities involved or with effects of brain injury or pathology on attention. However, it is clear that normal individuals differ in their ability to attend to sensory events, and it is even clearer that they differ in their ability to concentrate for long periods on internal trains of thought.

We used the attention network task to examine the individual efficiency of the alerting, orienting, and executive networks (Fan et al. 2002). In a sample of 40 normal persons, each of these scores was reliable over repeated presentations. In addition, we found no correlation among the orienting, alerting, and executive scores.

The ability to measure differences in attention among adults raises the question of the degree to which attention is heritable. To explore this issue, the ANT was used to assess attention in monozygotic and dizygotic same-sex twins (Fan et al. 2001). Strong heritability was found for the executive network, some heritability for the orienting network, and no apparent heritability for the alerting network. These data support a search for genes in executive attention and in orienting of attention.

We then used the association of the executive network with the neuromodulator dopamine (see **Table 1**) as a way of searching for candidate genes that might relate to the efficiency of the networks (Fossella et al. 2002). To do this, 200 persons performed the ANT and were genotyped to examine frequent polymorphisms in genes related to dopamine. We found significant association of the dopamine 4 receptor and monoamine oxidase A genes. We then conducted a neuroimaging experiment in which persons with different alleles of these two genes were compared while they performed the ANT (Fan et al. 2003). Groups with different alleles of these genes showed differences in performance on the ANT and also produced significantly different activations in the anterior cingulate, a major node of the executive attention network.

Recent studies have confirmed and extended these observations to other dopamine genes and to the orienting network. In two different studies employing other conflict tasks, the catecholamine-O-methyltransferase gene was linked to the mental operations related to resolving conflict (Blasi et al. 2005, Diamond et al. 2004). Different alleles of cholinergic genes were also related to performance on orienting tasks such as visual search (Parasuraman et al. 2005), thus confirming the link between orienting and the neuromodulator acetylcholine (see **Table 1**).

Hebb (1955) thought that most of the networks involved in higher functions were shaped primarily through experience. We now know that there is a great deal in common

Candidate genes: genes that may be involved in the development of utilization of attentional networks

	ALERT	ORIENT	CONFLICT
EXPERIMENTAL RESULTS	47	51	84
ACT-R SIMULATION	55	45	86
LEABRA SIMULATION	70	33	67

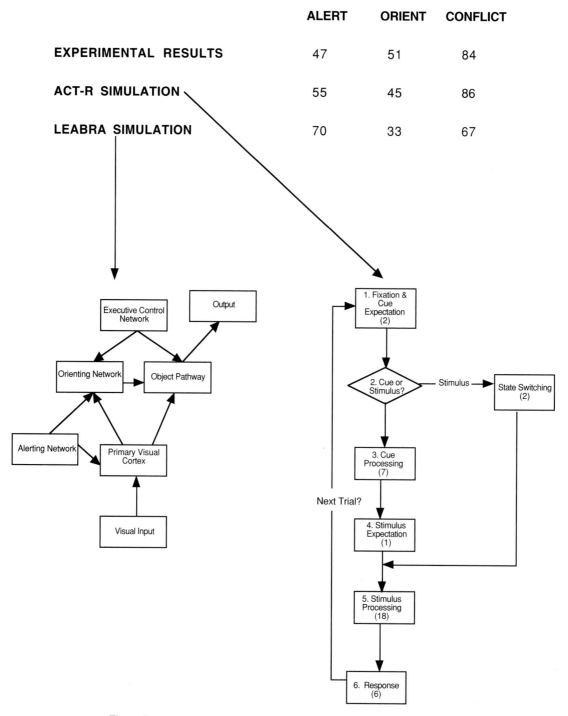

Figure 3

Experimental results compared with simulations of attention networks from ACT-R (Wang et al. 2004) and from a connectionist model (H. Wang & J. Fan, manuscript in preparation). The network scores are in milliseconds.

among humans in the anatomy of these high-level networks, and thus that they must have a basis within the human genome. It seems likely that the same genes that are related to individual differences in attention are also important in the development of the attentional networks that are common among people. Some of these networks are also common to nonhuman animals. By examining these networks in animals, it should be possible to test these assumptions further and to understand the role of genes in shaping networks.

Of importance for this effort is the development of methods to manipulate relevant genes in specific anatomical locations that are important nodes of a particular network. Usually genes are expressed at multiple locations so that changes (e.g., gene knockouts) are not specific to one location. However, using subtractive genomics, a method is currently being developed to do this (Dumas et al. 2005). We believe that this kind of genetic analysis of network development will become a very productive link between genes and both normal and pathological psychological function.

NETWORK DEVELOPMENT

Every parent of more than one child recognizes that from birth, infants are individuals with their own distinct characteristics and dispositions. These include reactive traits such as emotionality, activity level, and orienting to sensory events, and regulatory traits like attention focusing and shifting and inhibitory control. We believe that these early developing temperamental differences reflect the maturation of particular neural networks. We have studied individual differences in attention and related these differences to emotional and behavioral control (Rothbart & Rueda 2005, Ruff & Rothbart 1996).

A major advantage of viewing attention as an organ system is to trace the ability of children and adults to regulate their thoughts and feelings. Over the early years of life, the regulation of emotion is a major issue of development. The ability of attention to control dis-

tress can be traced to early infancy (Harman et al. 1997). Early in life, most regulation depends on the caregiver providing ways to control infant reactions. In our study, we first induced a mild level of distress, and then showed how attentional orienting calms that distress while the infant remains engaged with the object. When the orienting is broken, distress returns to the level present prior to the introduction of the object. It is likely that the distress remains present and is held by networks in the amygdala. Parents often use manipulation of the infant's orienting to control distress, and the infant also exhibits coping behaviors involving orienting to form the basis for one aspect of early self-regulation (Rothbart et al. 1992).

Developmental changes in executive attention found during the third year of life are correlated with parent reports of temperamental effortful control (Gerardi-Caulton 2000). Effortful control is a broad variable identified in temperament research; it includes the ability to inhibit a dominant response in order to produce subdominant response and to detect and correct errors (Rothbart & Rueda 2005). Because children of this age do not read, the location and identity rather than the word meaning and ink color served as the dimensions in a spatial conflict task. In one study (Gerardi-Caulton 2000), children sat in front of two response keys, one located to the child's left and one to the right. Each key displayed a picture, and on every trial, a picture identical to one of the pair appeared on either the left or right side of the screen. Children were rewarded for responding to the identity of the stimulus, regardless of its spatial compatibility with the matching response key. Reduced accuracy and slowed reaction times for spatially incompatible trials relative to spatially compatible trials reflected the effort required to resist the dominant response and to resolve conflict between these two competing dimensions. Performance on this task produces a clear interference effect in adults and activates the anterior cingulate (Fan et al. 2003). Children 24 months of age tended to perseverate on a

Table 2

Flanker task for children: Behavioral results

 Congruent

 Incongruent

Age	Overall RT	Overall %errors	Conflict effect	
			RT (ms)	%errors
4.4	1443	6.8	273	8.9
6	930	13	95	15.6
7	835	5.6	70	0.5
8	811	4.8	70	-0.2
9	740	2.4	67	1.6
10	643	2.2	72	2.1
adults	492	1.2	63	1.6

single response, whereas 36-month-old children performed at high accuracy levels, but like adults, responded more slowly and with reduced accuracy to incompatible trials.

We have traced the development of executive attention into the preschool and primary school periods (Rueda et al. 2004) by using a version of the ANT adapted for children (**Table 2**). In some respects, results were remarkably similar to those found for adults using the adult version of the task. Reaction times for the children were much longer, but they showed similar independence among the three networks. Children had much larger scores for conflict and alerting, suggesting that they have trouble in resolving conflict and in maintaining the alert state when not warned of the new target. Rather surprisingly, the ability to resolve conflict in the flanker task, as measured by the ANT, remains about the same from age eight to adulthood (see **Table 2**).

There is considerable evidence that the executive attention network is of great importance in the acquisition of school subjects such as literacy (McCandliss et al. 2003) and in a wide variety of other subjects that draw upon general intelligence (Duncan et al. 2000). It has been widely believed by psychologists that training involves only specific domains, and that more general training of the mind, for example, by formal disciplines like mathematics or Latin, does not generalize beyond the specific domain trained (Thorndike 1903, Simon 1969). However, attention may be an exception to this idea. Attention involves specific brain mechanisms, as we have seen, but its function is to influence the operation of other brain networks (Posner & Rothbart 2007). Anatomically, the network involving resolution of conflict overlaps with brain areas related to general intelligence (Duncan et al. 2000). Training of attention either explicitly or implicitly is sometimes a part of the school curriculum (Posner & Rothbart 2007), but additional studies are needed to determine exactly how and when attention training can best be accomplished and its long-lasting importance.

Socialization and Culture

Cognitive measures of conflict resolution have been linked to aspects of children's self-control in naturalistic settings. Children who are relatively less affected by spatial conflict also received higher parental ratings of temperamental effortful control and higher scores on laboratory measures of inhibitory control (Gerardi-Caulton 2000). Questionnaires have shown that the effortful control factor, defined in terms of scales measuring attentional focusing, inhibitory control, low intensity pleasure, and perceptual sensitivity (Rothbart & Rueda 2005), is inversely related to negative affect. This is in keeping with the notion that attentional skill may help attenuate negative affect while also serving to constrain impulsive approach tendencies.

Empathy is strongly related to effortful control, with children high in effortful control showing greater empathy (Rothbart et al.

1994). To display empathy toward others requires that we interpret their signals of distress or pleasure. Imaging work shows that sad faces activate the amygdala. As sadness increases, this activation is accompanied by activity in the anterior cingulate as part of the attention network (Blair et al. 1999). It seems likely that the cingulate activity represents the basis for our attention to the distress of others.

Developmental studies find two routes to successful socialization. A strongly reactive amygdala would provide the signals of distress that would easily allow empathic feelings toward others and a hesitancy to perform behaviors that might cause harm related to fear. These children are relatively easy to socialize. In the absence of this form of control, development of the cingulate would allow appropriate attention to the signals provided by amygdala activity. Consistent with its influence on empathy, effortful control also appears to play a role in the development of conscience. The internalization of moral principles appears to be facilitated in fearful preschool-aged children, especially when their mothers use gentle discipline (Kochanska 1995). In addition, internalized conscience is facilitated for children high in effortful control (Kochanska et al. 1996). Two separable control systems, one reactive (fear) and one self-regulative (effortful control), appear to regulate the development of conscience.

Individual differences in effortful control are also related to some aspects of metacognitive knowledge, such as theory of mind, which is the knowledge that people's behavior is guided by their beliefs, desires, and other mental states (Carlson & Moses 2001). Tasks that require the inhibition of a prepotent response are related to theory of mind tasks even when other factors, such as age, intelligence, and working memory, are factored out (Carlson & Moses 2001). The mechanisms of self-regulation and of theory of mind share a similar developmental time course, with advances in both areas between the ages of 2 and 5.

Efforts to determine the neural network involved in theory of mind tasks reveal some of the reasons for the common developmental time course in self-regulation. Theory of mind tasks activate a network that includes areas of the anterior cingulate that are also involved in self-regulation, as well as temporal lobe areas (Gallagher & Frith 2003). These anatomical links provide further support for efforts to integrate psychological topics at a network level.

Emotion, thought, and behavior form a cluster of temporally associated processes in specific situations as experienced by the child. Single and repeated life experiences can thus shape connections between elicited emotion, conceptual understanding of events, and use of coping strategies to deal with these events. Several theorists have made contributions to this approach (e.g., Epstein 1998, Mischel & Ayduk 2004), but the overall framework is in keeping with the idea of Hebbian learning through network activation. Mischel and his colleagues have recently developed a cognitive affective personality theory, making use of cognitive affective units (CAUs) seen to operate within a connectionist network (Mischel & Ayduk 2004). In their model, CAUs are variables encoding the features of situations, which include environmental features as well as self-initiated thoughts.

When they are repeatedly exercised, temporally linked clusters of thoughts, emotions, and action tendencies to a particular situation can become highly likely to reoccur and difficult to change. Some of the processes may be conscious and others unconscious; in most cases, the thoughts about affectively significant material will be self-referent. Research on the distinction between conscious and unconscious processes has shown that special networks are active only when items are conscious (Dehaene et al. 2003). Studies of self-reference have also suggested activation of specific networks of neural areas (Gusnard et al. 2001).

In applying this approach to the control of distress, one basic question is how to weaken the mental connection between the situation and its component reactions. In the eastern tradition, this is done partly through meditation, when ideas can be brought up in a context of calmness and safety, and partly through changing the view of the self so that situations will become less threatening. Links between thoughts and emotions or action tendencies are also weakened. Western therapy similarly works through the client's patterns of reaction, attempting to rework previously consolidated patterns and to provide new frameworks for meaning. From a developmental view, one would attempt to give the child the kinds of experiences that will form favorable and non-injurious mental habits.

Clusters of reactions are found within the young child's temperament. Later clusters of thought, emotion, and behavior will also be based on individual differences in personality, including emotions, expectancies, beliefs, values, goals, self-evaluations, appraisals, and thoughts about the situation, self, and/or others. These clusters will be influenced by temperamental predispositions, but they will also be influenced by socialization and experience. Coping and the application of effortful control operate when "the subjective meaning of the situation, including its self-relevance and personal importance, are appraised. The appraisal itself activates a cascade of other cognitive-affective representations within the system—expectations and beliefs, affective reactions, values and goals" (Mischel & Ayduk 2004, p. 105).

Different coping strategies follow and may be consolidated or rejected in the future, depending in part on their consequences. To develop this idea, Mischel & Ayduk (2004) give the example of individual differences in rejection sensitivity. When persons are particularly prepared to perceive rejection from others, attention is likely to be narrowly focused on this possibility, and it has been demonstrated that rejection by a social group can influence areas of the anterior cingulate related to executive attention and pain (Eisenberger et al. 2003). Defensive behaviors such as anger or preventative rejection of the other may serve to fend off feelings of rejection. These strategies in turn can also provide further support for the idea that the self is unworthy of positive social relationships. Different levels of generality of these clusters are possible. Rejection sensitivity, for example, might extend to a wide range of human relationships, but the sensitivity may also be more specific, so that only rejection by the child's peers, but not by adults, is sensitized. The reaction may in fact be limited to a single person in a single kind of situation, in which case a particular person, but not other persons, elicits rejection sensitivity.

Socialization in western cultures strongly emphasizes the individual, promoting the pursuit of individual security, satisfaction of individual desires, and achievement of a positive self-concept. In other cultures, the shaping of the child's experienced world can be quite different. Mascolo et al. (2003) suggest, for example, that the biological systems on which pride and shame are based are the same across cultures, yet can be shaped in quite different directions. In the United States, pride reactions develop as parents and others praise the child's accomplishments; shame reactions occur when there is self-referent failure. In China, however, parents downplay or criticize children's performance while other adults praise it, leading to more moderate prideful affect. Shame, on the other hand, is directly encouraged by parents and others when children do not fulfill their obligations to family.

The biological equipment or temperament is thus similar across cultures, but the mental habits and representation of self created as a result of the child's actions varies from culture to culture (Ahadi et al. 1993). By the time a child is a well-socialized member of the society, biologically based responses will have been shaped into a set of values, goals, and representations of the self and others. These representations specify what is good and bad for the person. Even for the child who is not well socialized, cultural socialization may have an effect. In the United States,

for example, a child may pursue a positive view of the self even when achievements result from following goals and values that are not socially acceptable.

PATHOLOGY OF ATTENTION NETWORKS

Much of modern psychology is involved in the diagnosis and treatment of mental illness or disturbance, and the network framework may be an ideal one for incorporating ideas related to clinical remediation. An excellent example of this approach has been in the recent studies of Mayberg (2003) on clinical interventions for depression based upon a neural network model. Treatments involved drugs or cognitive behavioral therapy and both forms of therapy were about equally effective, based on the percentage of persons showing improvement. Imaging data, however, indicated that the two therapies involved very different brain networks. The drugs remediated a largely subcortical network of brain areas that might be difficult to control voluntarily. The cognitive-behavioral therapy affected cortical networks, including areas involved in attention that would be more easily subject to voluntary control. These findings show how important network approaches are likely to be in evaluating the outcome of clinical trials.

A similar story may emerge in the study of dyslexia. Many forms of dyslexia involve a difficulty in phonological processing that can be remediated by an intervention targeting the ability to convert visual letters to sound (McCandliss et al. 2003). Following remediation, there is normal activation of a brain region at the boundary between the temporal and parietal lobes related to phonology. However, although these students can now decode words, they do not show fluent reading. This may require development of the visual word form system, which involves an extrastriate visual region (fusiform gyrus) quite distinct from the phonological areas (McCandliss et al. 2003). It is likely that time spent reading is one way to develop

Table 3 Disorders that have been related to attentional networks (from Rothbart & Posner 2006)

Alerting
Normal aging
Attention deficit disorder
Orienting
Autism
Executive control
Alzheimer's
Borderline personality disorder
Schizophrenia
22Q11 deletion syndrome

this brain area, but it may also be possible to create special training exercises that target the area, as has been done for phonological intervention.

The possibility that aspects of brain networks involved in depression and dyslexia might be remediated by therapies based on training illustrates the close connection between therapeutic interventions designed to correct deficits and education designed to improve the performance of people in general. From the perspective of improving neural networks through specific training, therapy and education can represent similar approaches to improving network efficiency.

The ANT has been applied to a number of forms of pathology in adults, the aging, adolescents, and children. **Table 3** presents classification of a number of disorders that have been related to specific nodes of attentional network; a review by Rothbart & Posner (2006) provides a fuller account.

Plasticity

Executive attention as measured by the ANT and other conflict-related tasks provides a basis for the ability of children to regulate their behavior through the use of effortful control. Executive attention has a well-defined neuroanatomy, and much is known about the role of genes in modulating its efficiency. Difficulties in effortful control provide the basis for problems in child socialization and in a

number of disorders of children and adults (Rothbart & Bates 2006). Executive attention represents a neurodevelopmental process in children and adolescents, the alteration of which could affect the propensity for the development of a number of disorders.

It is thus important to link efforts at remediation to the training of underlying brain networks. A central aspect of the executive attention network is the ability to deal with conflict. We used this feature to design a set of exercises for children adapted from efforts to train monkeys to perform tasks during space missions (Rumbaugh & Washburn 1995), which resulted in training monkeys to resolve conflict in a Stroop-like task (Washburn 1994).

Our exercises began by training the child to control the movement of a cat on a computer screen by using a joystick and to predict where an object would move on the screen, given its initial trajectory. Other exercises emphasized the use of working memory to retain information for a matching-to-sample task and the resolution of conflict.

We have tested the efficacy of a very brief five days of attention training with groups of 4- and 6-year-old children (Rueda et al. 2005). The children were brought to the laboratory for seven days for sessions lasting approximately 40 minutes, conducted over a two- to three-week period. The first and last days involved assessment of the effects of training by use of the ANT, a general test of intelligence (the K-BIT; Kaufman & Kaufman 1990), and a temperament scale (the Children's Behavior Questionnaire or CBQ; Rothbart et al. 2001). During administration of the ANT, we recorded 128 channels of EEG to observe the amplitude and time course of activation of brain areas associated with executive attention in adult studies (Rueda et al. 2005).

Five days is of course a minimal amount of training to influence the development of networks that develop over many years. Nonetheless, we found a general improvement in intelligence in the experimental group as measured by the K-BIT. This was due to improvement of the experimental group in performance on the nonverbal portion of the IQ test. Our analysis of the brain networks using EEG recording further suggested that the component most closely related to the anterior cingulate in prior adult studies changed significantly in the trained children to more closely resemble what is found in adults (Rueda et al. 2005).

We also found evidence that prior to training, performance on the ANT, as well as activity of the underlying network, appeared to be related to differences in at least one dopamine gene (Rueda et al. 2005). As the number of children who undergo our training increases, we can examine aspects of their temperament and genotype to help us understand who might most benefit from attention training. Since those with the poorest initial attention seemed to show the most benefit, it is possible that better results will be obtained with children who have more severe attentional disorders.

We are beginning to examine the precursors of executive attention in even younger children, less than one year of age, with the goal of understanding the origin of executive attention. We are also genotyping children in an effort to examine the candidate genes found previously to be related to the efficiency of the executive attention networks. There is already some evidence in the literature with older children who suffer from attention deficit hyperactivity disorder (ADHD) that using attention training methods can produce improvement in the ability to concentrate and in general intelligence (Kerns et al. 1999, Klingberg et al. 2002, Shavlev et al. 2003). As a result, we are also working with other groups to carry out attention training in children with learning-related problems such as ADHD and autism. These projects will test whether the programs are efficacious with children who have special difficulties with attention as part of their disorder. We also hope to have some preschools adopt attention training as a specific part of their preschool curriculum. This would allow training over more extensive periods and testing of other forms of training such as those designed for social groups (Mills & Mills 2000).

We believe that the evidence we have obtained for the development of specific brain networks during early childhood provides a strong rationale for sustained efforts to see if we can improve the attentional abilities of children. In addition, it will be possible to determine how well such methods might generalize to the learning of the wide variety of skills that must be acquired during school.

INTEGRATION OF PSYCHOLOGICAL SCIENCE

In this article, we have tried to cover topics from many areas of psychology, including cognitive, physiological, developmental, individual differences, social, clinical, and quantitative areas. Each of these areas can be shown to be involved as we examine attention networks. Below we argue that most, if not all, of the topics of psychological science can also benefit from a common network approach.

Generality

Fifteen years of cognitive studies using neuroimaging have laid out large-scale networks underlying many cognitive and emotional tasks (see **Table 4** for a partial list). In several fields of research, each area of activity (node) can be associated with a particular function or mental operation (see Posner 2004 for a review). A number of these nodes are active during a given task. The organization of these nodes in real time constitutes a network roughly like Hebb's cell assembly, but involving brain areas rather than individual cells. Of course, not all authors agree on exactly what the function of each node is, and some feel that parts of the brain (e.g., frontal lobes or subcortical areas) are more likely to carry out a number of functions.

We have also attempted to show that the study of attention involves all the branches of psychology. Attention has a detailed anatomy

Table 4 Some networks studied by neuroimaging*

Function	Selected references
Arithmetic	Dehaene (1997, figure 8.5)
Autobiographical memory	Fink et al. 1996
Faces	Ochsner et al. (2006)
Fear	Haxby (2004)
Music	Levitin (2006)
Object perception	Grill-Spector (2004)
Reading and listening	Posner & Raichle (1996)
Reward	Knutson (2003)
Self reference	Johnson et al. 2005
Spatial navigation	Shelton & Gabreli (2002)
Working memory	Smith et al. 1998, Ungerleider et al. 1998

*References cited are illustrative and are not meant to be comprehensive.

that involves large-scale brain areas and details of cellular structure. Nevertheless, the functions of attention are best studied at the cognitive level, which reveals their role in tasks that approximate those of daily life. Networks develop under the influence of social and cultural factors and of genes. The networks support not only the general functions of attention common to all people, but also the individual differences that relate to aspects of temperament and intelligence. We argue that what is true of attention is also true of the many other networks that have now been studied by imaging.

The network approach is general in that it covers the topics of cognitive and emotional mechanisms, and as we have shown above for attention, it allows an approach to issues of socialization and cultural influence, genetics, clinical diagnosis and remediation and their relative individual differences—in short, to all of the traditional areas of psychology.

Results of neuroimaging research also provide an answer to the old question of whether thought processes are localized. Although the network that carries out cognitive tasks is distributed, the mental operations that constitute the elements of the task are localized. A good example is the orienting network. This network carries out a very simple function of providing a priority to a particular source of

sensory input, for example, to the particular location at which a visual event will occur. To carry out this function, the superior parietal lobe, temporal parietal junction, frontal eye fields, superior colliculus, and thalamus are all involved. However, they carry out quite different functions, not all of which are fully understood. For example, the temporal parietal junction is involved in interrupting a focus of attention while the superior colliculus and frontal eye fields appear to move the index of attention, with or without eye movements. Building upon the idea of localization of underlying operations, imaging methods are now being applied to studies of the circuitry, plasticity, and individual development of neural networks. Working together with cellular and genetic methods, there is movement toward a more unified view of the role of the human brain in supporting the human mind.

Another general distinction separates conscious and unconscious processes central to psychological thinking. It has been shown that special networks are active only when items are conscious (Dehaene et al. 2003). Studies of self-reference have also suggested activation of specific networks of neural areas when the self is the object of thought (Gusnard et al. 2001).

The study of human and animal genetics is also illuminating the basis for individuality. A view of brain networks developing under combined genetic and experiential control provides a systematic basis for understanding how common networks can be linked through the study of genetic polymorphisms and the socialization of individual differences. By relating task performance to self- and other report questionnaires, as we have done in our work, it is possible to examine the role of cultural and other social processes in the development of these networks.

Hebb provided a basis for viewing brain activity in terms of networks that could compute the various functions underlying human thoughts and feelings. He also attempted to treat all the issues that would normally be included in elementary psychology textbooks in terms of this common framework. With the addition of new methods, we believe that the task of integrating all aspects of scientific psychology in a common framework is even more feasible than when Hebb undertook it.

At a scientific level, Hebb's dream of an integrated psychology is coming about. Sternberg & Grigorenko (2001) laid out the political and social impediments that any effort at an integrated psychology faces, such as identifications of scholars with psychological subdisciplines (e.g., clinical, social) rather than with the phenomena they study, creating unnecessary boundaries. These factors may unfortunately lead to a failure to realize the old dream of an integrated science, but the opportunities are clearly there. New tools are helping, and Hebb's efforts have led the way.

ACKNOWLEDGMENTS

We acknowledge the support and aid of many people at the University of Oregon, the Sackler Institutes, and Washington University in this work. Grant support was provided by NIMH and the McDonnell and Dana Foundations.

LITERATURE CITED

Ahadi SA, Rothbart MK, Ye R. 1993. Children's temperament in the U.S. and China: similarities and differences. *Eur. J. Personal.* 7:359–78

Andersen RA. 1989. Visual eye movement functions of the posterior parietal cortex. *Annu. Rev. Neurosci.* 12:377–403

Attneave F. 1950. Book review of D.O. Hebb's *Organization of Behavior*. *Am. J. Psychol.* 63:633–35

Beauregard M, Levesque J, Bourgouin P. 2001. Neural correlates of conscious self-regulation of emotion. *J. Neurosci.* 21(RC165)1–6

Blair RJR, Morris JS, Frith CD, Perrett DI, Dolan RJ. 1999. Dissociable neural responses to facial expression of sadness and anger. *Brain* 1222:883–93

Blasi G, Mattay GS, Bertolino A, Elvevåg B, Callicott JH, et al. 2005. Effect of catechol-*O*-methyltransferase $val^{158}met$ genotype on attentional control. *J. Neurosci.* 25(20):5038–45

Botvinick MM, Braver TS, Barch DM, Carter CS, Cohen JD. 2001. Conflict monitoring and cognitive control. *Psychol. Rev.* 108:624–52

Bullock TH, Bennett MVL, Johnston D, Josephson R, Marder E, Fields RD. 2005. The neuron doctrine, redux. *Science* 310:791–93

Bush G, Luu P, Posner MI. 2000. Cognitive and emotional influences in the anterior cingulate cortex. *Trends Cogn. Sci.* 4(6):215–22

Carlson ST, Moses LJ. 2001. Individual differences in inhibitory control in children's theory of mind. *Child Dev.* 72:1032–53

Corbetta M, Shulman GL. 2002. Control of goal-directed and stimulus-driven attention in the brain. *Nat. Neurosci. Rev.* 3:201–15

Crottaz-Herbtte S, Menon V. 2006. Where and when the anterior cingulate cortex modulates attentional response: combined fMRI and ERP evidence. *J. Cogn. Neurosci.* 18:766–80

Dale AM, Liu AK, Fischi BR, Buckner R, Beliveau JW, et al. 2000. Dynamic statistical parameter mapping: combining fMRI and MEG for high-resolution cortical activity. *Neuron* 26:55–67

Dehaene S. 1997. *The Number Sense*. Oxford, UK: Oxford Univ. Press

Provides an excellent review of the neural areas involved in orienting of attention.

Dehaene S, Artiges E, Naccache L, Martelli C, Viard A, et al. 2003. Conscious and subliminal conflicts in normal subjects and patients with schizophrenia: the role of the anterior cingulate. *Proc. Natl. Acad. Sci. USA* 100(23):13722–27

Diamond A, Briand L, Fossella J, Gehlbach L. 2004. Genetic and neurochemical modulation of prefrontal cognitive functions in children. *Am. J. Psychiatry* 161:125–32

Driver J, Eimer M, Macaluso E. 2004. Neurobiology of human spatial attention: modulation, generation, and integration. See Kanwisher & Duncan 2004, pp. 267–300

Dumas T, Hostick U, Wu H, Spaltenstein J, Ghatak C, et al. 2005. Maximizing the anatomical specificity of native neuronal promoters by a subtractive transgenic technique. *Soc. Neurosci. Abstr.*

Duncan J, Seitz RJ, Kolodny J, Bor D, Herzog H, et al. 2000. A neural basis for general intelligence. *Science* 289:457–60

Eisenberger NI, Lieberman MD, Williams KD. 2003. Does social rejection hurt? An fMRI study of social exclusion. *Science* 302:290–92

Epstein S. 1998. Cognitive-experiential self-theory: a dual process personality theory with implications for diagnosis and psychotherapy. In *Empirical Perspectives on the Psychoanalytic Unconscious*, ed. RF Bornstein, JM Masling, 7:99–140. Washington, DC: Am. Psychol. Assoc.

Fan J, Flombaum JI, McCandliss BD, Thomas KM, Posner MI. 2002. Cognitive and brain mechanisms of conflict. *Neuroimage* 18:42–57

Fan J, Fossella JA, Summer T, Posner MI. 2003. Mapping the genetic variation of executive attention onto brain activity. *Proc. Natl. Acad. Sci. USA* 100:7406–11

Fan J, McCandliss BD, Fossella J, Flombaum JI, Posner MI. 2005. The activation of attentional networks. *Neuroimage* 26:471–79

Fan J, McCandliss BD, Sommer T, Raz M, Posner MI. 2002. Testing the efficiency and independence of attentional networks. *J. Cogn. Neurosci.* 3(14):340–47

Fan J, Wu Y, Fossella J, Posner MI. 2001. Assessing the heritability of attentional networks. *BMC Neurosci.* 2:14

Fink GR, Markowitsch HJ, Reinkemeier H, Bruckbauer T, Kessler J, Heiss WD. 1996. Cerebral representation of one's own past: neural networks involved in autobiographical memory. *J. Neurosci.* 16(13):4275–82

Fossella J, Posner MI. 2004. Genes and the development of neural networks underlying cognitive processes. *The Cognitive Neurosciences III*, ed. MS Gazzaniga, pp. 1255–66. Cambridge, MA: MIT Press. 3rd ed.

Fossella J, Sommer T, Fan J, Wu Y, Swanson JM, et al. 2002. Assessing the molecular genetics of attention networks. *BMC Neurosci.* 3:14

Gallagher HL, Frith CD. 2003. Functional imaging of "theory of mind." *Trends Cogn. Sci.* 7:77–83

Gardner F. 1983. *Frames of Mind*. New York: Basic Books

Gerardi-Caulton G. 2000. Sensitivity to spatial conflict and the development of self-regulation in children 24–36 months of age. *Dev. Sci.* 3(4):397–404

Goddard GV. 1980. Component properties of the memory machine: Hebb revisited. In *The Nature of Thought: Essays in Honor of D.O. Hebb*, ed. PW Jusczyk, RM Klein, pp. 231–47. Hillsdale, NJ: LEA

Grill-Spector K. 2004. The functional organization of the visual ventral pathway and its relation to object recognition. See Kanwisher & Duncan 2004, pp. 169–93

Gusnard DA, Akbudak E, Shulman GL, Raichle ME. 2001. Medial prefrontal cortex and self-referential mental activity: relation to a default mode of brain function. *Proc. Natl. Acad. Sci. USA* 98:4259–64

Describes the brain areas activated for each of the three attention networks using fMRI data.

Harman C, Rothbart MK, Posner MI. 1997. Distress and attention interactions in early infancy. *Motiv. Emot.* 21:27–43

Harris KD. 2005. Neural signatures of cell assembly organization. *Nat. Neurosci. Rev.* 6:399–407

Haxby JV. 2004. Analysis of topographically organized patterns of response in fMRI data: distributed representation of objects in the ventral temporal cortex. See Kanwisher & Duncan 2004, pp. 83–97

Hebb DO. 1949. *Organization of Behavior*. New York: Wiley.

Hebb DO. 1955. Drives and the C.N.S. (conceptual nervous system). *Psychol. Rev.* 62:243–54

Hebb DO. 1958. *A Textbook of Psychology*. Philadelphia, PA: Saunders

Hebb DO. 1966. *A Textbook of Psychology*. Philadelphia, PA: Saunders. 2nd ed.

Johnson SC, Schmitz TW, Kawahara-Baccus TN, Rowley HA, Alexander AL, et al. 2005. The cerebral response during subjective choice with and without self-reference. *J. Cogn. Neurosci.* 17(12):1897–906

Kanwisher N, Duncan J, eds. 2004. *Attention and Performance XX: Functional Brain Imaging of Visual Cognition*. London: Oxford Univ. Press

Karnath HO, Ferber S, Himmelbach M. 2001. Spatial awareness is a function of the temporal not the posterior parietal lobe. *Nature* 411:950–53

Kaufman AS, Kaufman NL. 1990. *Kaufman Brief Intelligence Test Manual*. Circle Pines, MN: Am. Guidance Serv.

Kerns KA, Esso K, Thompson J. 1999. Investigation of a direct intervention for improving attention in young children with ADHD. *Dev. Neuropsychol.* 16:273–95

Klingberg T, Forssberg H, Westerberg H. 2002. Training of working memory in children with ADHD. *J. Clin. Exp. Neuropsychol.* 24:781–91

Knutson B, Fong GW, Bennett SM, Adams CM, Homme D. 2003. A region of mesial prefrontal cortex tracks monetarily rewarding outcomes: characterization with rapid event-related fMRI. *Neuroimage* 18(2):263–72

Kochanska G. 1995. Children's temperament, mothers' discipline, and security of attachment: multiple pathways to emerging internalization. *Child Dev.* 66:597–615

Kochanska G, Murray K, Jacques TY, Koenig AL, Vandegeest KA. 1996. Inhibitory control in young children and its role in emerging internationalization. *Child Dev.* 67:490–507

Kolb B. 2003. The impact of the Hebbian learning rule on research in behavioural neuroscience. *Can. Psychol.* 44:14–16

Levitin D. 2006. *This Is Your Brain on Music*. London: Penguin. In press

MacDonald AW, Cohen JD, Stenger VA, Carter CS. 2000. Dissociating the role of the dorsolateral prefrontal and anterior cingulate cortex in cognitive control. *Science* 288:1835–38

Marrocco RT, Davidson MC. 1998. Neurochemistry of attention. In *The Attentive Brain*, ed. R Parasuraman, pp. 35–50. Cambridge, MA: MIT Press

Mascolo MR, Fischer KW, Li J. 2003. Dynamic development of component systems of emotions: pride, shame and guilt in China and the United States. In *Handbook of Affective Sciences*, ed. RJ Davidson, KR Scherer, HH Goldsmith, pp. 375–408. New York: Oxford Univ. Press

Mayberg HS. 2003. Modulating dysfunctional limbic-cortical circuits in depression: towards development of brain-based algorithms for diagnosis and optimized treatment. *Br. Med. Bull.* 65:193–207

McCandliss BD, Beck IL, Sandak R, Perfetti C. 2003. Focusing attention on decoding for children with poor reading skill: design and preliminary test of the word building intervention. *Sci. Stud. Read.* 7(1):75–104

McCandliss BD, Cohen L, Dehaene S. 2003. The visual word form area: expertise for reading in the fusiform gyrus. *Trends Cogn. Sci.* 7:293–99

Presents the original theory of how cell assemblies and phase sequences relate to psychological functions.

Mills D, Mills C. 2000. *Hungarian Kindergarten Curriculum Translation*. London: Mills

Milner P. 2003. The relevance of D.O. Hebb's neural network learning rule to today's psychology. *Can. Psychol.* 44:5–9

Mischel W, Ayduk O. 2004. Willpower in a cognitive-affective processing system: the dynamics of delay of gratification. In *Handbook of Self-Regulation: Research, Theory, and Applications*, ed. RF Baumeister, KD Vohs, pp. 99–129. New York: Guilford

Newell A. 1990. *Unified Theories of Cognition*. Cambridge, MA: Harvard Univ. Press

Nikolaev AR, Ivanitsky GA, Ivanitsky AM, Abdullaev YG, Posner MI. 2001. Short-term correlation between frontal and Wernicke's areas in word association. *Neurosci. Lett.* 298:107–10

Ochsner KN, Ludlow DH, Knierim K, Hanelin J, Ramachandran T, et al. 2006. Neural correlates of individual differences in pain-related fear and anxiety. *Pain* 129(1–2):69–77

Ochsner KN, Kossyln SM, Cosgrove GR, Cassem EH, Price BH, et al. 2001. Deficits in visual cognition and attention following bilateral anterior cingulotomy. *Neuropsychologia* 39:219–30

O'Reilly RC, Munakata Y. 2000. *Computational Explorations of Cognitive Neuroscience*. Cambridge, MA: MIT Press

Parasuraman R, Greenwood PM, Kumar R, Fossella J. 2005. Beyond heritability—neurotransmitter genes differentially modulate visuospatial attention and working memory. *Psychol. Sci.* 16:200–7

Posner MI. 1980. Orienting of attention. The seventh Sir F.C. Bartlett Lecture. *Q.J. Exp. Psychol.* 32:3–25

Posner MI. 2004. The achievements of brain imaging: past and present. See Kanwisher & Duncan 2004, pp. 505–28

Posner MI, Fan J. 2007. Attention as an organ system. In *Neurobiology of Perception and Communication: From Synapse to Society. De Lange Conference IV*, ed. J Pomerantz. London: Cambridge Univ. Press. In press

Posner MI, Raichle ME. 1996. *Images of Mind*. New York: Sci. Am.

Posner MI, Rothbart MK. 2004. Hebb's neural networks support the integration of psychological science. *Can. Psychol.* 45:265–78

Posner MI, Rothbart MK. 2007. *Educating the Human Brain*. Washington, DC: Am. Psychol. Assoc.

Rothbart MK, Ahadi SA, Hershey KL. 1994. Temperament and social behavior in childhood. *Merrill-Palmer Q.* 40:21–39

Rothbart MK, Ahadi SA, Hershey KL, Fisher P. 2001. Investigations of temperament at three to seven years: The Children's Behavior Questionnaire. *Child Dev.* 72(5):1394–408

Rothbart MK, Bates JE. 2006. Temperament in children's development. In *Handbook of Child Psychology: Vol. 3, Social, Emotional, and Personality Development*, book ed. W Damon, R Lerner, vol. ed. N Eisenberg, pp. 99–166. New York: Wiley. 6th ed.

Rothbart MK, Posner MI. 2006. Temperament, attention, and developmental psychopathology. In *Handbook of Developmental Psychopathology, Revised*, ed. D Cicchetti, DJ Cohen, pp. 167–88. New York: Wiley

Rothbart MK, Rueda MR. 2005. The development of effortful control. In *Developing Individuality in the Human Brain: A Festschrift Honoring Michael I. Posner*, ed. U Mayr, E Awh, SW Keele, pp. 167–88. Washington, DC: Am. Psychol. Assoc.

Rothbart MK, Ziaie H, O'Boyle CG. 1992. Self-regulation and emotion in infancy. In *Emotion and Its Regulation in Early Development: New Directions for Child Development No. 55: The Jossey-Bass Education Series*, ed. N Eisenberg, RA Fabes, pp. 7–23. San Francisco: Jossey-Bass

Provides an overview of neuroimaging in relation to psychological concepts.

Relates the implications of neural network development for issues of educating children.

Comprehensively reviews temperament research.

Describes the effortful control temperament variable and how it relates to behavior and underlying networks.

Rueda MR, Fan J, McCandliss BD, Halparin JD, Gruber DB, et al. 2004. Development of attentional networks in childhood. *Neuropsychologia* 42:1029–40

Rueda MR, Rothbart MK, McCandliss BD, Saccomanno L, Posner MI. 2005. Training, maturation, and genetic influences on the development of executive attention. *Proc. Natl. Acad. Sci. USA* 102(41):14931–36

Ruff HA, Rothbart MK. 1996. *Attention in Early Development: Themes and Variations*. New York: Oxford Univ. Press

Rumbaugh DM, Washburn DA. 1995. Attention and memory in relation to learning: a comparative adaptation perspective. In *Attention, Memory and Executive Function*, ed. GR Lyon, NA Krasengor, pp. 199–219. Baltimore, MD: Brookes

Rumelhart DE, McClelland JL. 1986. *Parallel Distributed Processing*. Cambridge, MA: MIT Press

Sejnowski TJ. 2003. The once and future Hebb synapse. *Can. Psychol.* 44:17–20

Shavlev L, Tsal Y, Mevorach C. 2003. Progressive attentional training program: effective direct intervention for children with ADHD. *Proc. Cogn. Neurosci. Soc. NY*, pp. 55–56

Shelton AL, Gabrieli JDE. 2002. Neural correlates of encoding space from route and survey perspectives. *J. Neurosci.* 22(7):2711–17

Simon HA. 1969. *The Sciences of the Artificial*. Cambridge, MA: MIT Press

Smith EE, Jonides J, Marshuetz G, Koeppe RA. 1998. Components of verbal working memory. *Proc. Natl. Acad. Sci. USA* 95:876–82

Sternberg RJ, ed. 2004. *Unity in Psychology: Prospect or Pipedream?* Washington, DC: APA Books

Sternberg RJ, Grigorenko EL. 2001. Unified psychology. *Am. Psychol.* 56(12):1069–79

Thorndike EL. 1903. *Educational Psychology*. New York: Teachers College

Toga AW, Mazziotta JC, eds. 1996. *Brain Mapping: The Methods*. San Diego: Academic

Ungerleider LG, Courtney SM, Haxby HV. 1998. A neural system for human visual working memory. *Proc. Natl. Acad. Sci. USA* 95:883–90

Utall WR. 2001. *The New Phrenology*. Cambridge, MA: MIT Press

Venter JC, Adams MD, Myers EW, Li PW, Mural RJ, et al. 2001. The sequence of the human genome. *Science* 291:1304–35

Wang H, Fan J, Johnson TR. 2004. A symbolic model of human attentional networks. *Cogn. Syst. Res.* 5:119–34

Wang H, Fan J. 2006. Human attentional networks: a connectionist model. Manuscript in preparation

Washburn DA. 1994. Stroop-like effects for monkeys and humans: processing speed or strength of association? *Psychol. Sci.* 5(6):375–79

Womelsdorf T, Fries P, Mitra PP, Desimone R. 2006. Gamma-band synchronization in visual cortex predicts speed of change detection. *Nature* 439:733–36

The Representation of Object Concepts in the Brain

Alex Martin

Laboratory of Brain and Cognition, National Institute of Mental Health, Bethesda, Maryland 20892-1366; email: alexmartin@mail.nih.gov

Annu. Rev. Psychol. 2007. 58:25–45

First published online as a Review in Advance on September 1, 2006

The *Annual Review of Psychology* is online at http://psych.annualreviews.org

This article's doi: 10.1146/annurev.psych.57.102904.190143

0066-4308/07/0203-0025$20.00

Key Words

semantic memory, fusiform gyrus, temporal lobes, category specificity

Abstract

Evidence from functional neuroimaging of the human brain indicates that information about salient properties of an object—such as what it looks like, how it moves, and how it is used—is stored in sensory and motor systems active when that information was acquired. As a result, object concepts belonging to different categories like animals and tools are represented in partially distinct, sensory- and motor property–based neural networks. This suggests that object concepts are not explicitly represented, but rather emerge from weighted activity within property-based brain regions. However, some property-based regions seem to show a categorical organization, thus providing evidence consistent with category-based, domain-specific formulations as well.

Contents

INTRODUCTION

Semantic memory refers to a major division of declarative memory that includes knowledge of the meaning of objects and words. This review focuses on one aspect of the functional neuroanatomy of semantic memory: the representation of the meaning of concrete objects and their properties. The motivation for many of the studies to be discussed comes from reports of patients with category-specific knowledge disorders—specifically, patients with relatively selective knowledge impairments for animals and other animate objects, and those with relatively selective impairments for manmade, inanimate objects such as tools (for review, see Capitani et al. 2003). The studies to be re-

Semantic memory: a large division of long-term memory containing knowledge about the world including facts, ideas, beliefs, and concepts

viewed here were motivated by an appreciation of the importance of these clinical cases for understanding the organization of conceptual knowledge, object recognition, and storage of long-term memories.

For well over one hundred years, thinking about the representation of object concepts in the brain has been dominated by sensory-motor property models (dating from Lissauer 1890 and Freud 1891 to recent accounts by many investigators; for review, see Humphrey & Forde 2001). The central idea is that object knowledge is organized by sensory features (e.g., form, motion, color) and motor properties associated with the object's use (and in some models, other functional/verbally mediated properties such as where an object is typically found, its social significance, etc.). In this view, category-specific knowledge disorders occur when a lesion disrupts information about a particular property or set of properties critical for defining that object category and for distinguishing among its members. Thus, damage to regions that store information about object form will produce a disorder for animals because visual appearance is assumed to be a critical property for defining animals and because the distinction between different animals is assumed to be heavily dependent on knowing about subtle differences in their visual form. In a similar fashion, damage to regions that store information about how an object is used should produce a category-specific disorder for tools and other objects defined by how they are manipulated (see, e.g., Warrington & McCarthy 1987 and Warrington & Shallice 1984). Information is organized in the brain by property, not by conceptual category.

The alternative to property-based models is domain-specific models (Caramazza & Shelton 1998). On this account, evolutionary history, not sensory and motor systems, provides the major constraint on the organization of conceptual knowledge. Specifically, the theory proposes that selection pressures have resulted in dedicated neural machinery for solving, quickly and efficiently, computationally complex survival problems. Likely candidate domains offered are animals, conspecifics, plant life, and possibly tools. These systems, in turn, could be organized by property (Mahon & Caramazza 2003) (see Caramazza 1998 for detailed discussion of models proposed to explain category-selective knowledge deficits). The neuroimaging findings reviewed here provide strong support for sensory-motor property-based models by revealing considerable overlap in the neural circuitry supporting perceiving, acting on, and knowing about objects. Thus, consistent with the idea of embodied cognition, these findings suggest that object concepts are grounded in perception and action (e.g., Allport 1985, Barsalou 1999, Gallese & Lakoff 2005, Martin 1998). However, consistent with domain-specific accounts, these studies also reveal that some of the regions for representing object properties may be organized by category.

The review concentrates on two broad domains of knowledge: animate agents—living things that move on their own, and tools—manmade manipulable objects for which there is a direct relationship between how an object is manipulated and its function. The review is divided into three major sections. First, I discuss functional brain imaging studies of normal subjects that indicate that the posterior regions of the temporal lobes play a prominent role in conceptual processing. This is followed by a review of studies showing that different regions of posterior temporal cortex, as well as other areas of the brain, are involved in perceiving and knowing about specific properties. In the third section, I review studies suggesting that object concepts are represented in at least partially distinct property-based neural circuits.

CONCEPTUAL PROCESSING AND POSTERIOR TEMPORAL CORTEX

Functional brain imaging studies on conceptual and semantic/lexical processing (i.e., using word stimuli) have consistently isolated

two key brain regions: left ventrolateral prefrontal cortex (VLPFC) and the ventral and lateral regions of posterior temporal cortex—typically stronger in the left than in the right hemisphere (**Figure 1**, see color insert) (for reviews, see Bookheimer 2002, Martin 2001, Martin & Chao 2001, Thompson-Schill 2003). Activity in VLPFC has been strongly associated with top-down control of semantic memory; specifically, guiding retrieval and postretrieval selection of conceptual information stored in posterior temporal and perhaps other cortical areas. The role of left VLPFC in retrieving and selecting among competing alternatives has been confirmed by studies of patients with left VLPFC damage (e.g., Thompson-Schill et al. 1998) and most recently by applying transcranial magnetic stimulation (TMS) to left inferior frontal cortex to produce a local, transient disruption in processing (Gough et al. 2005). Recent evidence also suggests that there may be two anatomically distinct mechanisms within left VLPFC; one for retrieving, the other for selecting among competing alternatives (Badre et al. 2005). Although the details of the role of left VLPFC in conceptual processing remain a matter of debate, there is agreement that its main function is controlling and modulating access to information stored elsewhere (e.g., Gold et al. 2005; see Thompson-Schill et al. 2005 for a discussion of VLPFC functioning in the context of other frontal lobe mechanisms for cognitive control).

A large body of functional neuroimaging evidence has implicated the temporal lobes, particularly the posterior region of the left temporal lobe, as a critical site for stored representations, especially about concrete objects. Neuropsychological investigations have linked focal damage to left posterior temporal cortex to a loss of conceptual object knowledge (e.g., Hart & Gordon 1990). Early functional neuroimaging studies provided evidence for this link using a wide variety of tasks with object pictures and their written names (see previously cited reviews). Demonstrating that a common neural

Object concept: memory representations of a class or category of objects. Necessary for numerous cognitive functions including identifying an object as a member of a specific category and drawing inferences about object properties

Category-specific disorder: a relatively greater impairment in retrieving information about members of one superordinate object category (e.g., animals) as compared with other categories following brain injury or disease

TMS: transcranial magnetic stimulation

Repetition suppression: decreased neural response associated with repeated presentation of an identical, or a semantically/conceptually related, stimulus

LO: lateral occipital cortex

substrate was active regardless of whether objects were represented by pictures or words provided support for interpretations appealing to conceptual and/or lexical processes rather than visual feature processing per se.

Recent studies have provided additional support for this view by demonstrating that regions of left posterior temporal cortex known to be active during conceptual processing of pictures and words (fusiform gyrus and inferior and middle temporal gyri) (**Figure 1**) were also active during auditory sentence comprehension (e.g., Davis & Johnsrude 2003, Giraud et al. 2004, Rodd et al. 2005). In these studies, activity was modulated by speech intelligibility (Davis & Johnsrude 2003, Giraud et al. 2004) and semantic ambiguity (Rodd et al. 2005). As comprehension increased, so did activity in left posterior temporal regions.

Another recent approach to investigating the functional neuroanatomy of conceptual processing has been to use stimulus repetition tasks. It has been well established that prior experience with a stimulus results in more efficient processing (repetition priming) and a reduced hemodynamic response— typically referred to as repetition suppression, but also as adaptation, neural priming, and repetition attenuation—when that stimulus is encountered at a later time (Henson 2003, Schacter et al. 2004; see Grill-Spector et al. 2006 for a recent review of neural models of repetition suppression). Recent studies have documented the usefulness of using repetition paradigms—also referred to as adaptation paradigms—for evaluating the processing characteristics of select brain regions (Grill-Spector & Malach 2001).

Using object repetition paradigms, van Turennout et al. (2000) and Vuilleumier et al. (2002) reported that although repeating nonmeaningful (nonsense) and meaningful (real, nameable) objects produced repetition suppression in occipital cortex, more anterior regions of the visual object processing stream, specifically, the fusiform gyrus on the ventral surface of the temporal lobes, showed repetition suppression only to real objects. This finding was consistent with earlier studies showing that while the lateral region of occipital cortex (area LO; **Figure 1**) responded robustly and with equivalent strength to real and nonsense objects (Kanwisher et al. 1997, Malach et al. 1995, Martin et al. 1996), the fusiform gyrus showed a preferential response to real objects (e.g., Martin et al. 1996).

Schacter and colleagues used an object repetition paradigm to provide a stronger link between the fusiform gyrus and conceptual processing (Koutstaal et al. 2001, Simons et al. 2003). In both studies, repetition suppression in the left fusiform gyrus was found not only for repetition of previously seen objects, but also, to a lesser extent, for different exemplars of previously seen objects (i.e., objects with the same basic level name, but with a different visual form than the object previously presented). In contrast, area LO and the right fusiform gyrus showed repetition suppression to only identical objects. Because different exemplars share conceptual and lexical, but not shape, representations, the finding that repetition suppression in the left fusiform gyrus survived an exemplar change provided additional evidence that neural responses in this region are related to conceptual and/or lexical processes, rather than stimulus features per se. However, it is possible that repetition suppression could have been driven by overlap in features in the pictures of the two exemplars of the same object concept. This possibility has been addressed by priming studies using the written names of objects rather than object pictures. These word-based priming studies also provide evidence against the view that activation of the ventral object-processing stream is solely due to the explicit generation of visual object images after the meaning of the stimulus has been established by neural systems located elsewhere.

Dissociating Conceptual Processing from Explicit Visual Image Generation

An important piece of evidence for the idea that information about visual object form is stored in ventral temporal cortex comes from studies showing that regions active when objects are visually recognized are also active when subjects generate visual images of those objects (e.g., Ishai et al. 2000, O'Craven & Kanwisher 2000). These findings, which support the idea that visual object information is stored in this region of the brain, also offer an alternative to interpretations based on appeals to conceptual processing: specifically, that posterior temporal activity simply reflects the explicit retrieval of visual object imagery that accompanies task performance. Thus, within this view, stimuli denoting concrete objects, either pictures or words, trigger visual imagery, which then recruits posterior ventral temporal cortex indirectly; this area does not do any conceptual work. This view is further strengthened by studies showing that activity in the fusiform gyrus is associated with word imageability and concreteness (Sabsevitz et al. 2005, Wise et al. 2000) and visual property verification (Kan et al. 2003, although Kan et al. directly challenge the idea that their findings were due to explicit visual image generation).

Wheatley et al. (2005) addressed this issue by using an automatic semantic priming paradigm in which word pairs were presented using a short stimulus onset asynchrony (SOA; the time from the onset of the first word in a pair to the onset of the second word). Each word was presented for 150 msec, with a 250-msec SOA. The authors reasoned that modulations of cortical activity associated with automatic semantic priming would occur too quickly to be ascribed to explicit visual image generation. Thus, finding repetition suppression in the fusiform gyrus when reading briefly presented semantically related word pairs, relative to unrelated pairs, would add considerable weight to the claim that this region is involved in conceptual processing. Repetition-related reductions in hemodynamic responses (repetition suppression) were observed, in fact, in several regions, including the left fusiform gyrus. Activity was greatest for unrelated pairs (e.g., apple-lion), less for semantically related pairs (dog-horse), and least for same word repetitions (table-table), mirroring the pattern of behavioral performance (slowest for unrelated, faster for related, and fastest for reading identical words; Wheatley et al. 2005). Thus, the fusiform gyrus was sensitive to object meaning. Because of the extremely short duration between words, these data seem to rule out the possibility that fusiform activity was due to the explicit generation of visual object images (see Gold et al. 2006 for a replication using a lexical decision task).

These findings do not argue against the association of fusiform activity with retrieval of visual object information. To the contrary, it is likely that fusiform gyrus activity during automatic semantic priming is a direct reflection of accessing this information. However, given the processing time constraints imposed by the automatic semantic priming paradigm, retrieving this information may be best thought of as reflecting the implicit generation of visual images that occurs as an obligatory component of reading for meaning, not a nonobligatory, explicit generation of visual images occurring after the word's meaning had been determined.

Semantic priming: a short-lasting facilitation in processing a stimulus due to the prior presentation of a semantically related stimulus

Strengthening the Link Between Posterior Temporal Cortex and Conceptual Processing

Three recent neuroimaging studies have provided evidence suggesting that the posterior temporal cortex plays a direct role in conceptual processing. Two of the studies tested patients with semantic deficits due to cortical lesions, and the third used TMS to disrupt conceptual processing in normal individuals. The damaged or disrupted (via TMS) brain

SEMANTIC DEMENTIA AND THE ANTERIOR TEMPORAL LOBES

Semantic dementia (SD) is a progressive neurological disorder that produces a profound impairment of semantic memory, including impaired object naming and degraded knowledge of specific object properties (Hodges et al. 1992). Early neuropathological and structural brain-imaging studies showed that SD was associated with severe atrophy of the anterior temporal lobes (Hodges & Patterson 1996). As a result, this brain region has featured prominently in many neuropsychological and computational models of object semantics (e.g., Rogers et al. 2004, Tyler & Moss 2001). However, the specific functions of anterior temporal regions have not been clearly delineated. This has been due, in part, to difficulty obtaining reliable functional imaging data because of artifacts that decrease signal in this area of the brain. Characterizing the role of the anterior temporal lobes is further complicated by the fact that it is not a homogeneous structure, but rather contains numerous anatomically discrete regions, each of which may play a distinct role in the acquisition, storage, and manipulation of conceptual information. In addition, recent advances in structural neuroimaging have further complicated the picture by showing that the cortical atrophy in SD is not limited to anterior temporal regions, but rather extends more posteriorly than previously appreciated (Gorno-Tempini et al. 2004, Mummery et al. 2000, Williams et al. 2005). In fact, the amount of atrophy in ventral occipitotemporal cortex, including the fusiform gyrus, is as strongly related to semantic impairments in SD patients as is atrophy in the most anterior regions of the temporal lobes (Williams et al. 2005). Improved functional neuroimaging of anterior temporal structures resulting from recent technological advances (Bellgowan et al. 2005) should help to clarify the role(s) of this brain region in conceptual and semantic processing.

Voxel-based structural morphometry revealed marked atrophy in left polar and anterolateral, but not posterior, regions of the left temporal lobe. Nevertheless, functional imaging during performance on picture- and word-based semantic association tasks showed that the patients failed to activate posterior temporal regions that were active in normal subjects (while also overactivating left VLPFC and the atrophic anterior temporal cortex; Mummery et al. 1999).

A similar action-at-a-distance effect was observed in patients with impaired auditory processing due to a focal lesion in the left superior temporal gyrus (Sharp et al. 2004). Although sentence comprehension was impaired, performance was normal on the same visually based semantic association task used in the SD study by Mummery et al. (1999), thus indicating that the network needed for conceptual processing of visual stimuli was intact. However, scanning during an auditory version of the semantic association task revealed that, relative to normal subjects, the patients showed markedly reduced activity in the left fusiform gyrus. Moreover, left fusiform activity was also reduced in normal subjects when comprehension was impaired by degrading the auditory speech signal (Sharp et al. 2004). Taken together, these findings provide compelling evidence that posterior temporal cortex, and especially the left fusiform gyrus, is a critical node in a network of regions involved in conceptual and semantic processing. Moreover, involvement of the fusiform gyrus is independent of stimulus modality (visual, auditory) and format (pictures, words).

The data from the SD patients also indicate that posterior temporal regions can be activated top-down by higher-order processing regions (polar and anterior temporal cortices). As reviewed above, VLPFC has been strongly associated with the top-down control of posterior temporal cortices. Neuroimaging evidence for this top-down influence during conceptual processing comes from a study that combined TMS with functional brain

region was distant from posterior temporal cortex in each study. As a result, the effects on neural responses in posterior temporal cortex from a disturbance in another brain region could be directly evaluated.

The first study evaluated patients with semantic dementia (SD; Mummery et al. 1999). As typically found in SD, the patients performed poorly on object naming and other conceptual and semantic processing tasks.

SD: semantic dementia

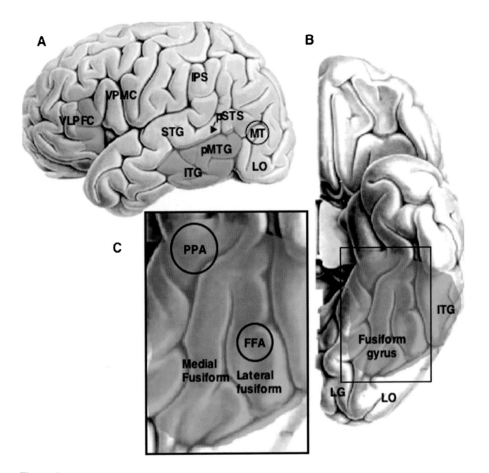

Figure 1

Schematic lateral view of the left hemisphere (*A*) and ventral view of the right temporal and frontal lobes (*B*). The fusiform gyrus is shown in greater detail in (*C*). Regions in red show approximate location of areas typically involved in conceptual processing tasks, especially with concrete objects. ITG, inferior temporal gyrus; LG, lingual gyrus. See text for other abbreviations.

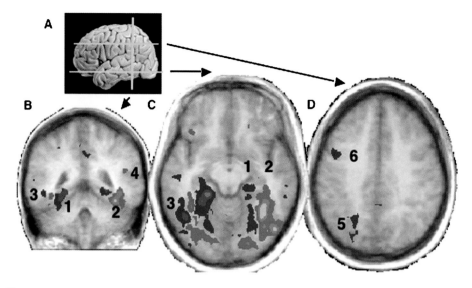

Figure 2

Group fMRI activation map showing the location of hemodynamic activity associated with naming pictures of animals (red-yellow spectrum) and pictures of tools (blue-green spectrum). *Yellow lines* on lateral view of the brain (*A*) indicate location of the coronal (*B*) and axial (*C, D*) slices. (*1*) Medial region of the fusiform gyrus; (*2*) lateral region of the fusiform gyrus; (*3*) middle temporal gyrus; (*4*) superior temporal sulcus; (*5*) left intraparietal sulcus; (*6*) left ventral premotor cortex. Adapted from Chao et al. 2002.

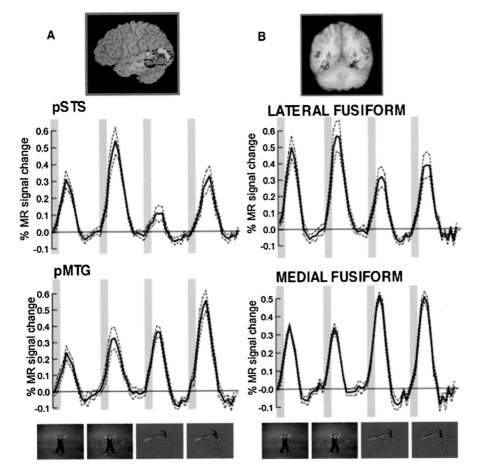

Figure 3

(*A*) Lateral view of the left hemisphere showing location of enhanced activity for identifying static and moving images of people in superior temporal sulcus (*yellow*) and tools in the middle temporal gyrus (*blue*). (*B*) Coronal view showing location of enhanced activity for identifying static and moving images of people in lateral portion of the fusiform gyrus (*yellow*), and tools in the medial fusiform gyrus (*blue*). Beneath each brain view are group-averaged hemodynamic responses showing differential activity for static and moving images in each of these regions. Note that lateral cortical areas (*A*) show category and motion effects. Ventral regions (*B*) show only category effects. Vertical gray bars indicate stimulus presentation (2 sec). *Dashed lines* indicate ±1 SEM. Adapted from Beauchamp et al. 2002.

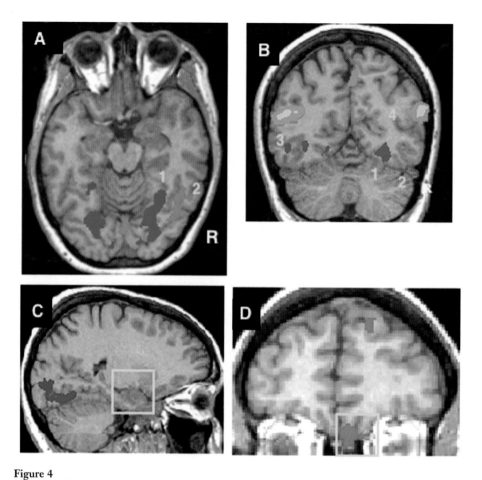

Figure 4

Group fMRI activation map showing axial view (*A*) and coronal view (*B*) of regions with greater activity associated with social (*red*) and mechanical (*blue*) interpretations of moving geometric shapes. (*1*) Medial fusiform gyrus; (*2*) lateral fusiform gyrus; (*3*) middle temporal gyrus; and (*4*) superior temporal sulcus (compare to **Figure 2**). *Yellow squares* indicate right amygdala (*C*) and ventromedial prefrontal region (*D*) more active for social than mechanical vignettes. Adapted from Martin & Weisberg 2003.

imaging (Wig et al. 2005). TMS was applied to left VLPFC and to a nearby control site while subjects engaged in a conceptual processing task (making living/nonliving judgments about object pictures). Functional imaging many minutes later showed a normal pattern of repetition suppression in left VLPFC, posterior temporal cortex, and LO for pictures of objects initially encoded during TMS to the control site. However, for pictures initially encoded during VLPFC TMS, repetition suppression was eliminated not only in VLPFC, but also in posterior temporal cortex, while being maintained in the occipital lobe (area LO) (Wig et al. 2005). These data provide direct evidence for a top-down effect of left VLPFC on posterior temporal cortex during conceptual processing and add further evidence to the processing distinction between LO and adjacent, more anterior regions of the ventral object processing stream.

RETRIEVING INFORMATION ABOUT OBJECT PROPERTIES

The underlying logic of the studies reviewed above was to contrast neural activity associated with performing conceptual and nonconceptual processing tasks (typically requiring low-level perceptual processing) using the same stimuli. When tasks are equated for difficulty, this strategy is ideal for revealing brain regions supporting conceptual processing. However, these designs are not informative about the representational content of the brain regions they identify. The studies reviewed below use a different strategy to address this issue. A single processing task—property production or property verification—is used to evaluate knowledge about different kinds of properties. As a result, questions concerning the possibility that different object properties are stored in different brain regions can be addressed.

For example, Martin et al. (1995) used property production to probe knowledge of object-associated colors and actions. Subjects were presented with achromatic object pictures (in one experiment) or the written names of objects (in the other experiment) and were required to generate words denoting an action (e.g., "pull" in response to a child's wagon) or a color ("red" for the child's wagon) associate. In both experiments, the type of information retrieved modulated activity in posterior temporal cortex. Relative to color word generation, action words elicited heightened activity in several brain regions, including a posterior region of the left lateral temporal cortex, centered on the middle temporal gyrus (pMTG) just anterior to the primary visual motion processing area, MT (**Figure 1**). In contrast, relative to action word generation, color word generation activated the fusiform gyrus anterior to regions associated with color perception (e.g., Zeki et al. 1991) and object perception (LO; e.g., Malach et al. 1995).

Activation of ventral temporal cortex when retrieving color information, relative to other properties, has been replicated several times using property production (Wiggs et al. 1999; Chao & Martin 1999) and property verification tasks (Goldberg et al. 2006, Oliver & Thompson-Schill 2003, Simmons et al. 2006). In addition, numerous reports confirm an association between action word generation and activation of the posterior lateral temporal cortex (reviewed in Martin 2001). Most recently, Tranel et al. (2005b) strengthened the association between left pMTG and action concepts by using a noun-verb homonym production task. Subjects produced a single word in response to pictures of objects (saying "saw" to a picture of a saw) and actions (saying "saw" to a picture of a person sawing). Although both tasks activated left pMTG relative to a baseline task, left pMTG was more active when noun-verb homonyms like "hammer" and "comb" were generated to name actions than when used to name objects, thereby also eliminating concerns related to producing different words in different property production conditions (Tranel et al. 2005b).

Left unanswered by these studies is the question of whether the same neural system

pMTG: posterior middle temporal gyrus

active when retrieving a property like color is also active when colors are perceived. Chao & Martin (1999) addressed this question by evaluating both processes in the same experiment. Color word generation activated posterior ventral temporal cortex as previously reported, but not sites in occipital cortex active during passive viewing of colored stimuli (lingual gyrus; **Figure 1**).

This finding was consistent with studies of color imagery in normal subjects (Howard et al. 1998) and in color-word synethestes who experience vivid color imagery when hearing words (Paulesu et al. 1995). In both of those studies, color imagery was associated with activity in the same ventral temporal sites as found in the color word generation studies discussed above, but not in occipital sites active during color perception (e.g., Zeki et al. 1991). Coupled with neuropsychological reports of a double dissociation between color perception and color imagery (De Vreese 1991, Shuren et al. 1996), these data suggest that information about object color is stored in ventral temporal cortex and that the critical site is close to, but does not include, sites in occipital cortex that selectively respond to the presence of color.

This claim, however, is at odds with the assertion that the same neural systems are involved, at least in part, in perceiving and knowing about specific object properties. However, Chao & Martin (1999) found that naming the color of colored objects (saying "red" in response to a picture of a red wagon), relative to naming colored objects (e.g., say "wagon" in response to the same picture), not only elicited activity in occipital regions active when passively viewing colored displays, but also in the more anterior site in the fusiform gyrus active during color word generation. Thus, this finding suggests that there may be partial overlap in the neural systems supporting perception and storage of specific object properties.

Recent fMRI evidence has provided more direct evidence for this claim. Beauchamp et al. (1999) replicated previous studies showing that neural activity is limited to the occipital lobes when color perception was tested by passive viewing. However, when the task was made more demanding by requiring subjects to judge subtle differences in hue, activity associated with perceiving color now extended from occipital cortex into the fusiform gyrus in ventral temporal cortex. Using this attention-demanding task to evaluate color perception, and a verbal property verification task to assess property knowledge, Simmons and colleagues found that retrieving information about object color—but not object motion—did, in fact, activate the same region in the fusiform gyrus active when color is perceived (Simmons et al. 2006). Thus, these data provide strong evidence that information about a particular object property, like its typical color, is stored in the same neural system active when that property is perceived. Therefore, although detection of color (color sensation) may be mediated by occipital cortical regions located early in the visual processing stream, active color perception seems to require more extensive neural activity extending anteriorly into the fusiform gyrus. One function of this region may be to provide a neural substrate for acquiring new object-color associations and representing those associations in the service of conceptual processing.

These studies suggest that retrieving other sensory- and motor-based properties should elicit activity in the corresponding sensory and motor processing systems. Goldberg et al. (2006) addressed this possibility using property verification tasks. Answering written questions concerning object-associated visual, sound, touch, and taste properties activated regions involved in sensory processing in each of these modalities (Goldberg et al. 2006; see also Kellenbach et al. 2001). Overlap between the neural systems for representing motor action concepts and action production has also been observed. In perhaps the most impressive demonstration in support of this claim, Pulvermuller and colleagues showed that simply reading words denoting specific tongue (lick), finger (pick), and leg (kick) actions activated regions in premotor cortex that were also active when subjects actually made tongue, finger, and leg movements, respectively (Hauk et al. 2004).

REPRESENTING OBJECT CATEGORIES

The studies reviewed above suggest that information about different types of object properties are stored in different brain regions. Moreover, evidence suggests that sensory- and motor-based object properties are stored within sensory and motor systems, respectively. I now turn to studies that forge a closer link between these property-based networks, perceptual and motor processes, and object concepts. These studies show that the regions associated with representing object properties are differentially engaged as a function of object category membership.

Converging evidence from monkey neurophysiology, neuropsychology, and functional brain imaging has established that object recognition is critically dependent on the ventral occipitotemporal processing stream (see Grill-Spector & Malach 2004 for review). In addition, functional brain imaging studies of object recognition have provided compelling evidence that occipitotemporal cortex is not a homogeneous object-processing system, but rather has a fine-grained structure that appears to be related to object category. The most studied categories have been human faces, houses, animals, and tools (see reviews by Kanwisher et al. 2001, Martin 2001). Direct comparison of one object category with another has revealed distinct clusters of activity (e.g., the fusiform face area, FFA; parahippocampal place area, PPA) (**Figure 1**). In addition, pattern analysis techniques have identified distinct object category-related patterns of activity that discriminate between relatively large numbers of object categories (Cox & Savoy 2003, Haxby et al. 2001, Spiridon & Kanwisher 2002). These object category-related patterns extend over a large expanse of occipitotemporal cortex, are stable both within and between subjects, and can be identified even when subjects freely view complex scenes (i.e., while watching a movie; Bartels & Zeki 2004, Hasson et al. 2004).[1]

Chao et al. (1999) provided evidence that category-related clusters of activity in occipitotemporal cortices associated with viewing object pictures are also seen when subjects engage in a verbal conceptual processing task. Perceptual processing was evaluated using passive viewing and delayed match-to-sample with pictures of animals, tools, faces, and houses; conceptual processing was evaluated using silent picture naming and a property verification task probing knowledge of animals and tools denoted by their written names. The main findings were that perceiving animals (as well as faces) showed heightened, bilateral activity in the more lateral region of the fusiform gyrus (see Grill-Spector 2003 for additional evidence that faces and animals selectively activate the lateral region of the fusiform gyrus including the FFA, and Grill-Spector et al. 2004 for evidence that this activity is significantly correlated with identifying faces and birds but not other objects). In contrast, tools showed heightened bilateral activity in the medial region of the fusiform gyrus (**Figure 2**, see color insert). Importantly, the same lateral/medial fusiform gyrus distinction between animals and tools was observed for the property verification task. For example, a region in the lateral portion of the fusiform gyrus that was more active when verifying properties of animals than tools was also more active when viewing pictures of animals than tools (Chao et al. 1999). Thus, consistent with the property production data reviewed above,

---

[1]The significance of this widespread activity has been the subject of considerable debate. In one view, information about a single category like faces or houses is restricted to relatively discrete areas. In the other view, information about faces, houses, and all other objects is distributed throughout the ventral occipitotemporal object-processing stream. Discussion of this important topic is outside the scope of this review (see Haxby et al. 2001, Spiridon & Kanwisher 2002).

pSTS: posterior superior temporal sulcus

these data provide support for an overlap between perceptual and conceptual neural processing systems.

Direct comparison of animals and faces revealed fine-grained differences between them, as well (see Chao et al. 1999 for details). For example, viewing pictures of animals produced more widespread activity than did viewing pictures of faces. This is not surprising given that different human faces are much more homogeneous in visual form than animals. Moreover, faces denote a single basic-level concept, whereas stimuli used to denote animals contain multiple exemplars, each with a specific basic-level name. Nevertheless, relative to manmade objects, activity was focused on the lateral region of the fusiform gyrus for both faces and animals (Chao et al. 1999). Thus, although every object concept must have a distinct neural representation, there appears a broad distinction between animate agents and manmade manipulable objects in the lateral and medial portions of the fusiform gyrus, respectively. The recent demonstration that human bodies are represented adjacent to the representation of faces in the lateral portion of the fusiform gyrus is consistent with this view (Peelen & Downing 2005, Schwarzlose et al. 2005; see also Cox et al. 2004).

Chao et al. (1999) also reported category-related differences in lateral temporal cortex associated with retrieving action properties as reviewed above. Specifically, viewing and naming pictures, and word reading during property verification, elicited enhanced activity in left pMTG for tools and in the posterior region of superior temporal sulcus (pSTS) for animals, stronger in the right than left hemisphere (**Figure 2**).

Similar patterns of object category-related activity in ventral and lateral regions of posterior temporal cortex have now been observed using a range of stimuli (pictures, written names, object-associated sounds, heard names). In ventral temporal cortex, enhanced activity in the lateral region of the fusiform gyrus (including the FFA) has been found

using naming, basic level categorization, or semantic decision tasks with animal pictures and/or their written names by Chao et al. (2002), Devlin et al. (2005), Mechelli et al. (2006), Okada et al. (2000), Price et al. (2003), Rogers et al. (2005), and Wheatley et al. (2005). Enhanced activity in the medial fusiform gyrus using tool pictures and/or their written names has been reported by Chao et al. (2002), Devlin et al. (2005), Mechelli et al. (2006), Noppeney et al. (2006; also in response to spoken names), and Whatmough et al. (2002).

In posterior lateral temporal cortex, enhanced activity in pMTG in response to pictures and/or the written names of tools was reported by Chao et al. (2002), Creem-Regehr & Lee (2005; also when imagining tools), Devlin et al. (2005), Kable et al. (2005), Kellenbach et al. (2003), Mechelli et al. (2006), Noppeney et al. (2005, 2006; also in response to spoken names), Phillips et al. (2002), and Tranel et al. (2005a,b). Finally, Lewis et al. (2004, 2005) and Tranel et al. (2005a) have reported increased activity in left pMTG for naming tool sounds relative to naming sounds associated with specific animals, and Noppeney et al. (2005) reported increased activity in right pSTS for making semantic judgments about spoken words referring to whole body movements (e.g., swimming, climbing) versus answering questions probing knowledge of hand movements.

Compelling evidence that these patterns of neural activity reflect retrieval of object information comes from a recent study of object learning and free recall (Polyn et al. 2005). Subjects learned lists composed of labeled photographs of famous people, places, and common manipulable objects. Pattern classifier techniques based on neural activity during learning revealed distinct patterns of category-related activity that occurred several seconds prior to recall. Moreover, and in agreement with the studies reviewed above, activity in the lateral fusiform (as well as right pSTS) best predicted recall of famous people, activity in left pMTG and left posterior parietal cortex (see below) best predicted recall of manipulable objects, and activity in the PPA best predicted recall of famous places. These findings suggest that accessing a particular item from memory depends on reactivating the pattern of neural activity that occurred during learning. In posterior temporal cortex, the pattern of activity is dependent on, or at least is a reflection of, the item's category membership.

The locations of the category-related activations reported in these studies show a remarkable degree of intersubject consistency despite marked differences in processing task, stimulus format (verbal, nonverbal), and modality of presentation (visual, auditory). However, these factors are clearly relevant. Indeed, studies by Price and colleagues show that category-related neural activity in posterior temporal cortex can be modulated by a host of stimulus and task-related variables (Mechelli et al. 2006; Noppeney et al. 2005, 2006; Price et al. 2003; Rogers et al. 2005). Nevertheless, although neural activity is modulated by these contextual factors, the spatial arrangement of the category-related regions does not change. It is, however, important to note that the organization principles that determine the between-subject consistency of this spatial arrangement remain to be determined (Martin 2006).

Linking Category-Related Representations to Form and Motion Perception

One interpretation of these findings is that differential activity in the fusiform gyrus and other regions of ventral temporal cortex reflects category-related differences in stored representations of form (and form-related properties like color), while differential activity in lateral temporal areas reflect category-related differences in the representation of motion properties (Chao et al. 1999; Kable et al. 2005; Martin et al. 1995, 1996).

Evidence for these claims was provided by Beauchamp and associates in a series of studies using static and moving depictions of biological motion (people performing identifiable movements such as sitting, jumping, walking) and manipulable objects (typical tools like a hammer, saw, or scissors, moving in their characteristic way when being used) (Beauchamp et al. 2002, 2003). As in the studies reviewed above, different patterns of category-related activity were noted in the fusiform gyrus, with the lateral portion more responsive to images of people and the medial portion more responsive to tools. However, these regions of ventral temporal cortex responded similarly to moving and static objects. Thus, ventral temporal cortex showed strong category effects, but these effects were not modulated by motion (**Figure 3**, see color insert).

In contrast, lateral temporal areas responded more strongly to moving than to static images, supporting the hypothesis that lateral temporal cortex is the cortical locus of complex motion processing. Moreover, category-related differences were also observed. pSTS showed a stronger response to people in motion compared with tools in motion, consistent with a large number of monkey neurophysiological (e.g., Oram & Perrett 1994) and human functional brain imaging studies of biological motion (e.g., Grossman & Blake 2001, Pelphrey et al. 2005, Puce et al. 1998). In contrast, pMTG showed a stronger response to tool than to human motion, thus suggesting that these motion-sensitive regions of lateral temporal cortex may have a category-based organization (**Figure 3**).

Category-related activity in ventral (fusiform gyrus) and lateral temporal cortex was also found using more abstract motion stimuli of people and tool motion (point-light displays) (Beauchamp et al. 2003). pSTS and the lateral fusiform gyrus responded more to point-light depictions of people than tools (see also Grossman & Blake 2001, 2002), whereas pMTG and the medial portion of the fusiform gyrus (as well as left parietal and ventral premotor cortices) responded more to tools than to people. Importantly, responses in lateral temporal regions were nearly

Biological motion: motion of animate agents characterized by highly flexible, fully articulated motion vectors, in contrast to the rigid, unarticulated motion vectors associated with most tools.

IPS: intraparietal
sulcus

VPMC: ventral
premotor cortex

equivalent to real object and point-light displays, suggesting that visual motion, not color or form, is a key determinant of activity in lateral temporal cortex. In contrast, in ventral temporal cortex, the response to the point-light displays was significantly reduced relative to real object videos (Beauchamp et al. 2003).

Taken together, these studies provide evidence for both category- and property-related differences in ventral and lateral temporal cortices. Adding motion to depictions of tools and people had little effect on the category-related responses in the fusiform gyrus, but markedly increased responses in lateral temporal cortex (Beauchamp et al. 2002). Eliminating form and color from moving stimuli (point-light displays) had little effect on the category-related responses in lateral temporal regions, but markedly reduced the response in ventral temporal cortex (Beauchamp et al. 2003). These findings suggest that category-related effects may reflect, at least in part, differences in object form (ventral temporal cortex) and object motion (lateral temporal cortex). In lateral temporal cortex, pSTS was selectively responsive to the fully articulated, flexible motion associated with animate entities; pMTG was selectively responsive to the rigid, unarticulated motion associated with manmade objects (Beauchamp et al. 2002, Beauchamp & Martin 2006).

Beyond Form and Motion: Representing Higher-Order Concepts

In 1944, Heider and Simmel showed that simple geometric shapes in motion are readily interpreted as depicting causal interactions, goals, intentions, and the like (Heider & Simmel 1944). Several studies (Castelli et al. 2000, Martin & Weisberg 2003, Schultz et al. 2003) have used displays similar to those of Heider and Simmel to show that the category-related neural activity can be elicited depending on how these stimuli are interpreted. Animations interpreted as depicting social interactions (e.g., hide-and-seek, Schultz et al. 2003; sharing, Martin & Weisberg 2003) or mental states (e.g., persuading, mocking; Castelli et al. 2000) elicited activity in regions linked to perceiving and knowing about the form (lateral fusiform gyrus) and motion (pSTS) of animate agents, and in regions associated with detecting emotional and biologically salient stimuli (the amygdala; see Phelps 2006 for review) and understanding mental states (medial prefrontal cortex; see Frith & Frith 2006 for review). In contrast, animations interpreted as depicting mechanical interaction (e.g., billiard balls, pinball machine) elicited heightened activity in regions linked to representing the form (medial fusiform gyrus) and motion (pMTG) of manipulable objects (Martin & Weisberg 2003) (**Figure 4**, see color insert). Thus, different patterns of activity were associated with the meaning assigned to the stimuli. Moreover, because the same geometric forms were used in both the social and mechanical animations, these results cannot be due to bottom-up processing of the visual stimuli. They must reflect top-down influences.

Linking the Representation of Tools to Motor Systems

The relationship between activity in the dorsal stream—particularly in left posterior parietal cortex centered on intraparietal sulcus (IPS) and left ventral premotor cortex (VPMC)—and the representation of manmade, manipulable objects has been an active field of investigation (for reviews, see Culham & Valyear 2006, Johnson-Frey 2004). Naming photographs of tools, or even simply viewing these pictures, has been shown to elicit enhanced activity in left VPMC and IPS, relative to viewing animals, houses, and faces, and relative to naming pictures of animals (Chao & Martin 2000). These findings are consistent with data from monkey neurophysiology showing that neurons in ventral premotor and parietal cortices respond both when monkeys grasp objects and when they see objects that they have had experience manipulating (e.g., Jeannerod et al. 1995). Recent functional brain imaging studies in humans have shown that these dorsal regions, along with pMTG, are active when subjects perform a wide range of tasks probing knowledge about tools and their related actions (see Tranel et al. 1997, 2003 for evidence that damage to either left pMTG, IPS, or VPMC results in impaired knowledge about tools and their action).

Enhanced activity in left IPS has been reported for judging object similarity based on how objects are manipulated (are a keyboard and a piano manipulated in the same way?) versus similarity based on more verbally mediated functional information (do a cigarette lighter and a match serve the same function?) (Boronat et al. 2005; see Buxbaum & Saffran 2002 for patient data, and Kellenbach et al. 2003 for related neuroimaging data). Other reports have shown enhanced activity in left IPS and VPMC for viewing and imagining grasping common tools versus novel, graspable objects (Creem-Regehr & Lee 2005), making semantic decisions about tool-related actions (Noppeney et al. 2005), holding manipulable, but not nonmanipulable, objects in working memory (Mecklinger et al. 2002), naming tools versus animals (Chao et al. 2002; see Kan et al. 2006 for evidence that left VPMC activity when naming tools varies with motor experience using those tools) and for naming tool-associated sounds versus animal sounds (Lewis et al. 2004, 2005). These findings show that retrieving information about object function engages regions of the cortex that are also active when objects are used. Moreover, as with the previously reviewed studies of object categories, this information is automatically accessed when these objects are identified, regardless of stimulus modality (visual, auditory) or format (verbal, nonverbal).

Learning About Object Properties

The findings reviewed above suggest that it should be possible to predict where in the brain learning-related changes occur when subjects acquire property information about novel objects. Weisberg et al. (2006) addressed this possibility by giving subjects extensive training using novel objects to perform specific, tool-like tasks. Subjects were scanned while performing a simple visual matching task with pictures of these objects. Prior to training, neural activity during object matching was limited to the ventral occipitotemporal object-processing stream, consistent with previous reports on viewing nonmeaningful objects (e.g., van Turennout et al. 2000). However, after training, activations in ventral temporal cortex became more focal. Specifically, whereas activity prior to training was widespread in the fusiform gyrus, after training activity was markedly reduced in the more lateral parts of the fusiform (i.e., regions preferring animate objects like animals and faces), and markedly increased in the medial portion of the fusiform gyrus associated with identifying common tools. In addition, after training, new activations emerged in the network of left hemisphere regions previously linked to naming and retrieving information about tools and their related actions. Specifically, robust activity was now seen in the left pMTG, IPS, and premotor cortices. These changes occurred even though the task during scanning was purely perceptual. Thus, hands-on experience with the objects seemed to have augmented their representations with detailed information about their appearance (supported by changes in the fusiform gyrus), and with information about the motion (pMTG) and motor-related properties (left IPS, premotor cortex) associated with their use.

Grossman et al. (2004) reported a similar type of learning-related change for perceptual learning about animate objects. As noted above, viewing point-light displays of human forms elicits activity in the lateral fusiform gyrus (FFA) and pSTS. Subjects received extensive training that enabled them to accurately perceive point-light displays embedded in visual noise. After training, enhanced activity was observed in the FFA and pSTS relative to pretraining levels. These activations were seen in response to trained items and novel noise-embedded point-light displays, indicating that learning had generalized to new exemplars (see also Weisberg et al. 2006). Moreover, the amount of activity in these regions was directly related to behavioral performance (Grossman et al. 2004).

Whereas in these studies subjects were trained on visuomotor (Weisberg et al. 2006) and perceptual (Grossman et al. 2004) tasks, James & Gauthier (2003) showed that similar learning-related effects can be achieved through verbal learning. Subjects were trained to associate verbal labels referring to auditory properties (e.g., squeaks, roars) and action properties (hops, jumps) to novel animate-like stimuli ("greebles"). After training, viewing greebles associated with auditory properties elicited enhanced activity in a region involved in the early stages of auditory processing (i.e., in the superior temporal gyrus, as defined by an auditory localizer task), and viewing greebles associated with actions elicited enhanced activity in pSTS (defined by viewing point-light displays) (James & Gauthier 2003).

Taken together, these studies demonstrate that the locus of learning-related cortical plasticity is highly constrained by the nature of the information to be learned. Learning to associate novel objects with specific tool-like functions produced enhanced activity in regions associated with the form, motion, and use of common tools (Weisberg et al. 2006), learning to perceive moving dot patterns as people in motion resulted in enhanced activity in regions associated with the form and motion of animate objects, and learning to associate verbal information denoting auditory and motion properties elicited enhanced activity in auditory and biological motion processing areas. These changes occurred even though the tasks during scanning required only visual matching of static images. There was no requirement to explicitly retrieve information about how novel objects were manipulated (Weisberg et al. 2006) or about the auditory and motion properties associated with greebles (James & Gauthier 2003), thus indicating that these newly acquired object-property associations were automatically retrieved when the objects were seen again.

CONCLUSION

The evidence reviewed in this chapter indicates that object properties are stored throughout the brain, with specific sensory and motor-based information stored in their corresponding sensory and motor systems. The evidence further suggests the possibility of dedicated neural circuitry for perceiving and knowing about animate objects and common tools. For animate objects, this circuitry includes two regions in posterior temporal cortex: the lateral portion of the fusiform gyrus and pSTS for representing their visual form and motion, respectively. In addition, evidence is mounting that the amygdala also plays a prominent role in this circuitry, perhaps as a means of alerting the organism to a potentially threatening predator or prey (e.g., Whalen 1998). Indeed, recent studies suggest that the human amygdala responds more to stimuli denoting animals than tools, irrespective of stimulus type (pictures, written words, associated sounds, and heard words; Yang et al. 2005). Other regions, such as medial prefrontal cortex, may also be prominently involved, especially when retrieving information about the mental states of others (e.g., Mitchell et al. 2002). For common tools, the neural circuitry includes the medial portion of the fusiform gyrus as well as pMTG, IPS, and VPMC, all within the left hemisphere, assumed to represent their visual form and action properties (motion and manipulation).

In addition to the findings discussed in this chapter, evidence for other object category-related neural circuits has also been reported. In particular, a large number of studies have shown that the PPA is selectively responsive to depictions of places, buildings (see Kanwisher et al. 2001 for review), and on a more conceptual level, to objects strongly associated with environmental contexts (e.g., traffic light, beach chair; Bar & Aminoff 2003). Other studies have linked number concepts to neural circuitry that includes a discrete region of the left IPS (reviewed in Dehaene et al. 2003, but see Shuman & Kanwisher 2004). Finally, representations of food (especially high-caloric food) have been associated with circuitry that includes areas involved in taste perception (insula), reward (posterior orbital frontal cortex), and affective response (amygdala) (Killgore et al. 2003, Simmons et al. 2005).

Many questions remain to be resolved. These include an understanding of how the nodes of the neural circuitry described here are bound together (Damasio 1989) and how activity within the network is coordinated in the service of conceptual processing (Kraut et al. 2002). Also needed is a better understanding of how object conceptual and lexical representations are linked (Damasio et al. 2004). Equally important will be to identify the neural systems that house our vast store of nonsensory-motor, verbally mediated, encyclopedic knowledge about objects. Finally, specifying how object property-based circuits interact with prefrontal cortex to create highly flexible and novel categories is an important topic for future investigations (Freedman et al. 2003).

ACKNOWLEDGMENT

This work was supported by the Intramural Research Program of the NIMH.

LITERATURE CITED

Allport DA. 1985. Distributed memory, modular subsystems and dysphasia. In *Current Perspectives in Dysphasia*, ed. SK Newman, R Epstein, pp. 207–44. New York: Churchill Livingstone

Badre D, Poldrack RA, Pare-Blagoev EJ, Insler RZ, Wagner AD. 2005. Dissociable controlled retrieval and generalized selection mechanisms in ventrolateral prefrontal cortex. *Neuron* 47:907–18

Bar M, Aminoff E. 2003. Cortical analysis of visual context. *Neuron* 38:347–58

Barsalou LW. 1999. Perceptual symbol systems. *Behav. Brain Sci.* 22:637–60

Bartels A, Zeki S. 2004. Functional brain mapping during free viewing of natural scenes. *Hum. Brain Mapp.* 21:75–85

Beauchamp MS, Haxby JV, Jennings JE, DeYoe EA. 1999. An fMRI version of the Farnsworth-Munsell 100-Hue test reveals multiple color-selective areas in human ventral occipitotemporal cortex. *Cereb. Cortex* 9:257–63

Beauchamp MS, Lee KE, Haxby JV, Martin A. 2002. Parallel visual motion processing streams for manipulable objects and human movements. *Neuron* 34:149–59

Beauchamp MS, Lee KE, Haxby JV, Martin A. 2003. fMRI responses to video and point-light displays of moving humans and manipulable objects. *J. Cogn. Neurosci.* 15:991–1001

Beauchamp MS, Martin A. 2006. Grounding object concepts in perception and action: evidence from fMRI studies of tools. *Cortex.* In press

Bellgowan PSF, Bandettini PA, van Gelderen P, Martin A, Bodurka J. 2006. Improved BOLD detection in the medial temporal region using parallel imaging and voxel volume reduction. *Neuroimage* 29:1244–51

Bookheimer S. 2002. Functional MRI of language: new approaches to understanding the cortical organization of semantic processing. *Annu. Rev. Neurosci.* 25:151–88

Boronat CB, Buxbaum LJ, Coslett HB, Tang K, Saffran EM, et al. 2005. Distinctions between manipulation and function knowledge of objects: evidence from functional magnetic resonance imaging. *Cogn. Brain Res.* 23:361–73

Buxbaum LJ, Saffran EM. 2002. Knowledge of object manipulation and object function: dissociations in apraxic and nonapraxic subjects. *Brain Lang.* 82:179–99

Capitani E, Laiacona M, Mahon B, Caramazza A. 2003. What are the facts of semantic category-specific deficits? A critical review of the clinical evidence. *Cogn. Neuropsychol.* 20:213–61

Caramazza A. 1998. The interpretation of semantic category-specific deficits: What do they reveal about the organization of conceptual knowledge in the brain? Introduction. *Neurocase* 4:265–72

Caramazza A, Shelton JR. 1998. Domain-specific knowledge systems in the brain the animate-inanimate distinction. *J. Cogn. Neurosci.* 10:1–34

Castelli F, Happe F, Frith U, Frith C. 2000. Movement and mind: a functional imaging study of perception and interpretation of complex intentional movement patterns. *Neuroimage* 12:314–25

Chao LL, Haxby JV, Martin A. 1999. Attribute-based neural substrates in temporal cortex for perceiving and knowing about objects. *Nat. Neurosci.* 2:913–19

Chao LL, Martin A. 1999. Cortical representation of perception, naming, and knowledge of color. *J. Cogn. Neurosci.* 11:25–35

Chao LL, Martin A. 2000. Representation of manipulable man-made objects in the dorsal stream. *Neuroimage* 12:478–84

Chao LL, Weisberg J, Martin A. 2002. Experience-dependent modulation of category-related cortical activity. *Cereb. Cortex* 12:545–51

Cox DD, Meyers E, Sinha P. 2004. Contextually evoked object-specific responses in human visual cortex. *Science* 304:115–17

Cox DD, Savoy RL. 2003. Functional magnetic resonance imaging (fMRI) "brain reading": detecting and classifying distributed patterns of fMRI activity in human visual cortex. *Neuroimage* 19:261–70

Creem-Regehr SH, Lee JN. 2005. Neural representations of graspable objects: Are tools special? *Cogn. Brain Res.* 22:457–69

Culham JC, Valyear KF. 2006. Human parietal cortex in action. *Curr. Opin. Neurobiol.* 16:205–12

Damasio AR. 1989. Time-locked multiregional retroactivation: a systems-level proposal for the neural substrates of recall and recognition. *Cognition* 33:25–62

Damasio H, Tranel D, Grabowski T, Adolphs R, Damasio A. 2004. Neural systems behind word and concept retrieval. *Cognition* 92:179–229

Davis MH, Johnsrude IS. 2003. Hierarchical processing in spoken language comprehension. *J. Neurosci.* 23:3423–31

De Vreese LP. 1991. Two systems for color-naming defects: verbal disconnection vs. color imagery disorder. *Neuropsychologia* 29:1–18

Dehaene S, Piazza M, Pinel P, Cohen L. 2003. Three parietal circuits for number processing. *Cogn. Neuropsychol.* 20:487–506

Devlin JT, Rushworth MFS, Matthews PM. 2005. Category-related activation for written words in the posterior fusiform is task specific. *Neuropsychologia* 43:69–74

Freedman DJ, Riesenhuber M, Poggio T, Miller EK. 2003. A comparison of primate prefrontal and inferior temporal cortices during visual categorization. *J. Neurosci.* 23:5235–46

Freud S. 1891 (1953). *On Aphasia*. Transl. E Stengel. New York: Int. Univ. Press

Frith CD, Frith U. 2006. How we predict what other people are going to do. *Brain Res.* 1079:36–46

Gallese V, Lakoff G. 2005. The brain's concepts: the role of the sensory-motor system in conceptual knowledge. *Cogn. Neuropsychol.* 22:455–79

Giraud AL, Kell C, Thierfelder C, Sterzer P, Russ MO, et al. 2004. Contributions of sensory input, auditory search and verbal comprehension to cortical activity during speech processing. *Cereb. Cortex* 14:247–55

Gold BT, Balota DA, Kirchhoff BA, Buckner RL. 2005. Common and dissociable activation patterns associated with controlled semantic and phonological processing: evidence from fMRI adaptation. *Cereb. Cortex* 15:1438–50

Gold BT, Balota DA, Jones SA, Powell DK, Smith CD, Andersen AH. 2006. Functional magnetic resonance imaging evidence for differing roles of multiple frontotemporal regions. *J. Neurosci.* 26:6523–32

Goldberg RF, Perfetti CA, Schneider W. 2006. Perceptual knowledge retrieval activates sensory brain regions. *J. Neurosci.* 26:4917–21

Gorno-Tempini ML, Dronkers NF, Rankin KP, Ogar JM, Phengrasamy L, et al. 2004. Cognition and anatomy in three variants of primary progressive aphasia. *Ann. Neurol.* 55:335–46

Gough PM, Nobre AC, Devlin JT. 2005. Dissociating linguistic processes in the left inferior frontal cortex with transcranial magnetic stimulation. *J. Neurosci.* 25:8010–16

Grill-Spector K. 2003. The neural basis of object perception. *Curr. Opin. Neurobiol.* 13:159–66

Grill-Spector K, Henson R, Martin A. 2006. Repetition and the brain: neural models of stimulus-specific effects. *Trends Cogn. Sci.* 10:14–23

Grill-Spector K, Knouf N, Kanwisher N. 2004. The fusiform face area subserves face perception, not generic within-category identification. *Nat. Neurosci.* 7:555–62

Grill-Spector K, Malach R. 2001. fMR-adaptation: a tool for studying the functional properties of human cortical neurons. *Acta Psychol.* 107:293–321

Grill-Spector K, Malach R. 2004. The human visual cortex. *Annu. Rev. Neurosci.* 27:649–77

Grossman ED, Blake R. 2001. Brain activity evoked by inverted and imagined biological motion. *Vis. Res.* 41:1475–82

Grossman ED, Blake R. 2002. Brain areas active during visual perception of biological motion. *Neuron* 35:1167–75

Grossman ED, Blake R, Kim CY. 2004. Learning to see biological motion: brain activity parallels behavior. *J. Cogn. Neurosci.* 16:1669–79

Hart J, Gordon B. 1990. Delineation of single-word semantic comprehension deficits in aphasia, with anatomical correlation. *Ann. Neurol.* 27:226–31

Hasson U, Nir Y, Levy I, Fuhrmann G, Malach R. 2004. Intersubject synchronization of cortical activity during natural vision. *Science* 303:1634–40

Hauk O, Johnsrude I, Pulvermuller F. 2004. Somatotopic representation of action words in human motor and premotor cortex. *Neuron* 41:301–7

Haxby JV, Gobbini MI, Furey ML, Ishai A, Schouten JL, Pietrini P. 2001. Distributed and overlapping representations of faces and objects in ventral temporal cortex. *Science* 293:2425–30

Heider F, Simmel M. 1944. An experimental study of apparent behavior. *Am. J. Psychol.* 57:243–49

Henson RN. 2003. Neuroimaging studies of priming. *Prog. Neurobiol.* 70:53–81

Hodges JR, Patterson K. 1996. Nonfluent progressive aphasia and semantic dementia: a comparative neuropsychological study. *J. Int. Neuropsychol. Soc.* 2:511–24

Hodges JR, Patterson K, Oxbury S, Funnell E. 1992. Semantic dementia. Progressive fluent aphasia with temporal lobe athrophy. *Brain* 115:1783–806

Howard RJ, ffytche DH, Barnes J, McKeefry D, Ha Y, et al. 1998. The functional anatomy of imagining and perceiving color. *Neuroreport* 9:1019–23

Humphreys GW, Forde EM. 2001. Hierarchies, similarity, and interactivity in object recognition: "category-specific" neuropsychological deficits. *Behav. Brain Sci.* 24:453–509

Ishai A, Ungerleider LG, Haxby JV. 2000. Distributed neural systems for the generation of visual images. *Neuron* 28:979–90

James TW, Gauthier I. 2003. Auditory and action semantic features activate sensory-specific perceptual brain regions. *Curr. Biol.* 13:1792–96

Jeannerod M, Arbib MA, Rizzolatti G, Sakata H. 1995. Grasping objects: the cortical mechanisms of visuomotor transformation. *Trends Neurosci.* 18:314–20

Johnson-Frey SH. 2004. The neural bases of complex tool use in humans. *Trends Cogn. Sci.* 8:71–78

Kable JW, Kan IP, Wilson A, Thompson-Schill SL, Chatterjee A. 2005. Conceptual representations of action in the lateral temporal cortex. *J. Cogn. Neurosci.* 17:1855–70

Kan IP, Barsalou LW, Solomon KO, Minor JK, Thompson-Schill SL. 2003. Role of mental imagery in a property verification task: fMRI evidence for perceptual representations of conceptual knowledge. *Cogn. Neuropsychol.* 20:525–40

Kan IP, Kable JW, Van Scoyoc A, Chatterjee A, Thompson-Schill SL. 2006. Fractionating the left frontal response to tools: dissociable effects of motor experience and lexical competition. *J. Cogn. Neurosci.* 18:267–77

Kanwisher N, Downing P, Epstein R, Kourtzi Z. 2001. Functional neuroimaging of visual recognition. In *Handbook of Functional NeuroImaging of Cognition*, ed. R Cabeza, A Kingstone, pp. 109–52. Cambridge, MA: MIT Press

Kanwisher N, Woods RP, Iacoboni M, Mazziotta JC. 1997. A locus in human extrastriate cortex for visual shape analysis. *J. Cogn. Neurosci.* 9:133–42

Kellenbach ML, Brett M, Patterson K. 2001. Large, colourful or noisy? Attribute- and modality-specific activations during retrieval of perceptual attribute knowledge. *Cogn. Affect. Behav. Neurosci.* 1(3):207–21

Kellenbach ML, Brett M, Patterson K. 2003. Actions speak louder than functions: the importance of manipulability and action in tool representation. *J. Cogn. Neurosci.* 15:20–46

Killgore WDS, Young AD, Femia LA, Bogorodzki P, Rogowska J, Yurgelun-Todd DA. 2003. Cortical and limbic activation during viewing of high- versus low-calorie foods. *Neuroimage* 19:1381–94

Koutstaal W, Wagner AD, Rotte M, Maril A, Buckner RL, Schacter DL. 2001. Perceptual specificity in visual object priming: functional magnetic resonance imaging evidence for a laterality difference in fusiform cortex. *Neuropsychologia* 39:184–99

Kraut MA, Kremen S, Segal JB, Calhoun V, Moo R, Hart J. 2002. Object activation from features in the semantic system. *J. Cogn. Neurosci.* 14:24–36

Lewis JW, Brefczynski JA, Phinney RE, Janik JJ, DeYoe EA. 2005. Distinct cortical pathways for processing tool versus animal sounds. *J. Neurosci.* 25:5148–58

Lewis JW, Wightman FL, Brefczynski JA, Phinney RE, Binder JR, DeYoe EA. 2004. Human brain regions involved in recognizing environmental sounds. *Cereb. Cortex* 14:1008–21

Lissauer H. 1890/1988. A case of visual agnosia with a contribution to theory. Transl. M Jackson. *Cogn. Neuropsychol.* 5:157–92

Mahon BZ, Caramazza A. 2003. Constraining questions about the organisation and representation of conceptual knowledge. *Cogn. Neuropsychol.* 20:433–50

Malach R, Reppas JB, Benson RR, Kwong KK, Jiang H, et al. 1995. Object-related activity revealed by functional magnetic resonance imaging in human occipital cortex. *Proc. Natl. Acad. Sci. USA* 92:8135–39

Martin A. 1998. The organization of semantic knowledge and the origin of words in the brain. In *The Origins and Diversification of Language*, ed. N Jablonski, L Aiello, pp. 69–98. San Francisco: Calif. Acad. Sci.

Martin A. 2001. Functional neuroimaging of semantic memory. In *Handbook of Functional NeuroImaging of Cognition*, ed. R Cabeza, A Kingstone, pp. 153–86. Cambridge, MA: MIT Press

Martin A. 2006. Shades of Dejerine: forging a causal link between the visual word form area and reading. *Neuron* 173–75

Martin A, Chao LL. 2001. Semantic memory and the brain: structure and processes. *Curr. Opin. Neurobiol.* 11:194–201

Martin A, Haxby JV, Lalonde FM, Wiggs CL, Ungerleider LG. 1995. Discrete cortical regions associated with knowledge of color and knowledge of action. *Science* 270:102–5

Martin A, Weisberg J. 2003. Neural foundations for understanding social and mechanical concepts. *Cogn. Neuropsychol.* 20:575–87

Martin A, Wiggs CL, Ungerleider LG, Haxby JV. 1996. Neural correlates of category-specific knowledge. *Nature* 379:649–52

Mechelli A, Sartori G, Orlandi P, Price CJ. 2006. Semantic relevance explains category effects in medial fusiform gyri. *Neuroimage* 30:992–1002

Mecklinger A, Gruenewald C, Besson M, Magnie M, Von Cramon YD. 2002. Separable neuronal circuitries for manipulable and nonmanipulable objects in working memory. *Cereb. Cortex* 12:1115–23

Mitchell JP, Heatherton TF, Macrae CN. 2002. Distinct neural systems subserve person and object knowledge. *Proc. Natl. Acad. Sci. USA* 99:15238–43

Mummery CJ, Patterson K, Price CJ, Ashburner J, Frackowiak RSJ, Hodges JR. 2000. A voxel-based morphometry study of semantic dementia: relationship between temporal lobe atrophy and semantic memory. *Ann. Neurol.* 47:36–45

Mummery CJ, Patterson K, Wise RJS, Vandenberghe R, Price CJ, Hodges JR. 1999. Disrupted temporal lobe connections in semantic dementia. *Brain* 122:61–73

Noppeney U, Josephs O, Kiebel S, Friston KJ, Price CJ. 2005. Action selectivity in parietal and temporal cortex. *Cogn. Brain Res.* 25:641–49

Noppeney U, Price CJ, Penny WD, Friston KJ. 2006. Two distinct neural mechanisms for category-selective responses *Cereb. Cortex* 16:437–45

O'Craven KM, Kanwisher N. 2000. Mental imagery of faces and places activates corresponding stimulus-specific brain regions. *J. Cogn. Neurosci.* 12:1013–23

Okada T, Tanaka S, Nakai T, Nishizawa S, Inui T, et al. 2000. Naming of animals and tools: a functional magnetic resonance imaging study of categorical differences in the human brain areas commonly used for naming visually presented objects. *Neurosci. Lett.* 296:33–36

Oliver RT, Thompson-Schill SL. 2003. Dorsal stream activation during retrieval of object size and shape. *Cogn. Affect. Behav. Neurosci.* 3:309–22

Oram MW, Perrett DI. 1994. Responses of anterior superior temporal polysensory (STPa) neurons to "biological motion" stimuli. *J. Cogn. Neurosci.* 6:99–116

Paulesu E, Harrison J, Baron-Cohen S, Watson JD, Goldstein L, et al. 1995. The physiology of coloured hearing. A PET activation study of color-word synaesthesia. *Brain* 118:661–76

Peelen MV, Downing PE. 2005. Selectivity for the human body in the fusiform gyrus. *J. Neurophysiol.* 93:603–8

Pelphrey KA, Morris JP, Michelich CR, Allison T, McCarthy G. 2005. Functional anatomy of biological motion perception in posterior temporal cortex: an fMRI study of eye, mouth and hand movements. *Cereb. Cortex* 15:1866–76

Phelps EA. 2006. Emotion and cognition: insights from studies of the human amygdala. *Annu. Rev. Psychol.* 57:27–53

Phillips JA, Noppeney U, Humphreys GW, Price CJ. 2002. Can segregation within the semantic system account for category-specific deficits? *Brain* 125:2067–80

Polyn SM, Natu VS, Cohen JD, Norman KA. 2005. Category-specific cortical activity precedes retrieval during memory search. *Science* 310:1963–66

Price CJ, Noppeney U, Phillips J, Devlin JT. 2003. How is the fusiform gyrus related to category-specificity? *Cogn. Neuropsychol.* 20:561–74

Puce A, Allison T, Bentin S, Gore JC, McCarthy G. 1998. Temporal cortex activation in humans viewing eye and mouth movements. *J. Neurosci.* 18:2188–99

Rodd JM, Davis MH, Johnsrude IS. 2005. The neural mechanisms of speech comprehension: fMRI studies of semantic ambiguity. *Cereb. Cortex* 15:1261–69

Rogers TT, Hocking J, Mechelli A, Patterson K, Price C. 2005. Fusiform activation to animals is driven by the process, not the stimulus. *J. Cogn. Neurosci.* 17:434–45

Rogers TT, Ralph MAL, Garrard P, Bozeat S, McClelland JL, et al. 2004. Structure and deterioration of semantic memory: a neuropsychological and computational investigation. *Psychol. Rev.* 111:205–35

Sabsevitz DS, Medler DA, Seidenberg M, Binder JR. 2005. Modulation of the semantic system by word imageability. *Neuroimage* 27:188–200

Schacter DL, Dobbins IG, Schnyer DM. 2004. Specificity of priming: a cognitive neuroscience perspective. *Nat. Rev. Neurosci.* 5:853–62

Schultz RT, Grelotti DJ, Klin A, Kleinman J, Van der Gaag C, et al. 2003. The role of the fusiform face area in social cognition: implications for the pathobiology of autism. *Philos. Trans. R. Soc. Lond. B Biol. Sci.* 358:415–27

Schwarzlose RF, Baker CI, Kanwisher N. 2005. Separate face and body selectivity on the fusiform gyrus. *J. Neurosci.* 25(47):11055–59

Sharp DJ, Scott SK, Wise RJS. 2004. Retrieving meaning after temporal lobe infarction: the role of the basal language area. *Ann. Neurol.* 56:836–46

Shuman M, Kanwisher N. 2004. Numerical magnitude in the human parietal lobe: tests of representational generality and domain specificity. *Neuron* 44:557–69

Shuren JE, Brott TG, Schefft BK, Houston W. 1996. Preserved color imagery in an achromatopsic. *Neuropsychologia* 34:485–89

Simmons WK, Martin A, Barsalou LW. 2005. Pictures of appetizing foods activate gustatory cortices for taste and reward. *Cereb. Cortex* 15:1602–8

Simmons WK, Ramjee V, McRae K, Martin A, Barsalou LW. 2006. fMRI evidence for an overlap in the neural bases of color perception and color knowledge. *Neuroimage.* 31:S182 (Abstr.)

Simons JS, Koutstaal W, Prince S, Wagner AD, Schacter DL. 2003. Neural mechanisms of visual object priming: evidence for perceptual and semantic distinctions in fusiform cortex. *Neuroimage* 19:613–26

Spiridon M, Kanwisher N. 2002. How distributed is visual category information in human occipito-temporal cortex? An fMRI study. *Neuron* 35:1157–65

Thompson-Schill SL. 2003. Neuroimaging studies of semantic memory: inferring "how" from "where." *Neuropsychologia* 41:280–92

Thompson-Schill SL, Bedny M, Goldberg RF. 2005. The frontal lobes and the regulation of mental activity. *Curr. Opin. Neurobiol.* 15:219–24

Thompson-Schill SL, Swick D, Farah MJ, D'Esposito M, Kan IP, Knight RT. 1998. Verb generation in patients with focal frontal lesions: a neuropsychological test of neuroimaging findings *Proc. Natl. Acad. Sci. USA* 95:15855–60

Tranel D, Damasio H, Damasio AR. 1997. A neural basis for the retrieval of conceptual knowledge. *Neuropsychologia* 35:1319–27

Tranel D, Grabowski TJ, Lyon J, Damasio H. 2005a. Naming the same entities from visual or from auditory stimulation engages similar regions of left inferotemporal cortices. *J. Cogn. Neurosci.* 17:1293–305

Tranel D, Kemmerer D, Adolphs R, Damasio H, Damasio AR. 2003. Neural correlates of conceptual knowledge for actions. *Cogn. Neuropsychol.* 20:409–32

Tranel D, Martin C, Damasio H, Grabowski TJ, Hichwa R. 2005b. Effects of noun-verb homonymy on the neural correlates of naming concrete entities and actions. *Brain Lang.* 92:288–99

Tyler LK, Moss HE. 2001. Towards a distributed account of conceptual knowledge. *Trends Cogn. Sci.* 5:244–52

van Turennout M, Ellmore T, Martin A. 2000. Long-lasting cortical plasticity in the object naming system. *Nat. Neurosci.* 3:1329–34

Vuilleumier P, Henson RN, Driver J, Dolan RJ. 2002. Multiple levels of visual object constancy revealed by event-related fMRI of repetition priming. *Nat. Neurosci.* 5:491–99

Warrington EK, McCarthy RA. 1987. Categories of knowledge—further fractionations and an attempted integration. *Brain* 110:1273–96

Warrington EK, Shallice T. 1984. Category-specific semantic impairments. *Brain* 107:829–54

Weisberg J, van Turrennout M, Martin A. 2006. A neural system for learning about object function. *Cereb. Cortex.* In press. doi: 10.1093/cercr/bhj176

Whalen PJ. 1998. Fear, vigilance, and ambiguity: initial neuroimaging studies of the human amygdala. *Curr. Dir. Psychol. Sci.* 7:177–88

Whatmough C, Chertkow H, Murtha S, Hanratty K. 2002. Dissociable brain regions process object meaning and object structure during picture naming. *Neuropsychologia* 40:174–86

Wheatley T, Weisberg J, Beauchamp MS, Martin A. 2005. Automatic priming of semantically related words reduces activity in the fusiform gyrus. *J. Cogn. Neurosci.* 17:1871–85

Wig GS, Grafton ST, Demos KE, Kelley WM. 2005. Reductions in neural activity underlie behavioral components of repetition priming. *Nat. Neurosci.* 8:1228–33

Wiggs CL, Weisberg J, Martin A. 1999. Neural correlates of semantic and episodic memory retrieval. *Neuropsychologia* 37:103–18

Williams GB, Nestor PJ, Hodges JR. 2005. Neural correlates of semantic and behavioural deficits in frontotemporal dementia. *Neuroimage* 24:1042–51

Wise RJS, Howard D, Mummery CJ, Fletcher P, Leff A, et al. 2000. Noun imageability and the temporal lobes. *Neuropsychologia* 38:985–94

Yang JJ, Francis N, Bellgowan PSF, Martin A. 2005. Object concepts and the human amygdala: enhanced activity for identifying animals independent of in-put modality and stimulus format. Presented at *12th Annu. Meet. Cogn. Neurosci. Soc.*, New York

Zeki S, Watson JD, Lueck CJ, Friston KJ, Kennard C, Frackowiak RS. 1991. A direct demonstration of functional specialization in human visual cortex. *J. Neurosci.* 11:641–49

Perception of Human Motion

Randolph Blake[1] and Maggie Shiffrar[2]

[1]Department of Psychology, Vanderbilt University, Nashville, Tennessee 37203

[2]Department of Psychology, Rutgers University-Newark, Newark, New Jersey 07102;
email: randolph.blake@vanderbilt.edu, mag@psychology.rutgers.edu

Annu. Rev. Psychol. 2007. 58:47–73

First published online as a Review in
Advance on August 11, 2006

The *Annual Review of Psychology* is online at
http://psych.annualreviews.org

This article's doi:
10.1146/annurev.psych.57.102904.190152

0066-4308/07/0110-0047$20.00

Key Words

biological motion, visual perception, point-light animation,
action-perception linkage, posterior superior temporal sulcus

Abstract

Humans, being highly social creatures, rely heavily on the ability to
perceive what others are doing and to infer from gestures and expressions what others may be intending to do. These perceptual skills are
easily mastered by most, but not all, people, in large part because human action readily communicates intentions and feelings. In recent
years, remarkable advances have been made in our understanding
of the visual, motoric, and affective influences on perception of human action, as well as in the elucidation of the neural concomitants
of perception of human action. This article reviews those advances
and, where possible, draws links among those findings.

Contents

chologists and cognitive neuroscientists have intensively studied the visual analysis of human action. Some studies have focused on the kinematics specifying different activities and emotional states, others have examined the role of motor involvement in action perception, and still others have sought to uncover the brain mechanisms mediating action perception. In this review, we survey that work, highlighting studies that have employed point-light (PL) animations to isolate human kinematics. Our survey is necessarily selective, for the literature on this topic is quite large. Interested readers can consult other available publications that review material on human action and social perception (Allison et al. 2000, Blakemore & Decety 2001, Knoblich et al. 2006, Puce & Perrett 2003).

The perception of human action depends upon multiple sources of information including sensory, motor, and affective processes. We begin with an overview of the behavioral research supporting the contributions of each of these processes to the analysis of human movement. We give greater weight to the role of visual processes since more research has been conducted in that area. We conclude with an introduction to the neural circuitry underlying action perception.

INTRODUCTION

Perceiving the actions, moods, and intentions of other people is one of most important social skills we possess, and vision provides a particularly rich source of information in support of this skill. Although we can discern a person's affective state from static pictures, motion provides even more reliable and compelling information. As Darwin (1872) noted in his seminal work, *The Expression of Emotions in Man and Animals*, actions speak louder than pictures when it comes to understanding what others are doing and feeling.

In recognition of the importance of action in everyday human social discourse, psy-

Kinematics:
analysis of the motions of objects without regard to the forces producing them

Point-light animations:
biological activity portrayed by small light tokens (point lights) placed on the major body parts of an actor

Perceiving Human Form and Action from Kinematics

Imagine seeing a woman on a golf course, poised over a golf ball with a putter in her hands. You expect to see her smoothly strike the ball, and when she does, you are not surprised. But could you recognize what the person was doing based solely on the dynamics of the body movements in the absence of all other clues? And if you did perceive that the person was a golfer executing a putt, could kinematics alone tell you that it was Annika Sörenstam and not Tiger Woods? The answer to both questions turns out to be "yes." What accounts for this impressive perceptual ability?

Creating Human Motion

First to tackle this technical problem was the French physiologist and physician Etienne-Jules Marey (1884). His lifelong passion to understand movement led him to develop "chronophotography," a high-speed photographic technique that captured multiple successive images on a single photographic plate. To highlight the kinematics of gait, for example, Marey filmed a person walking while wearing a black suit with small markers attached to the joints. The resulting photograph embodied a space/time record of the changing positions of the joints (**Figure 1A**).

The modern-day instantiation of Marey's technique was realized by Swedish psychologist Gunnar Johansson (1973), who devised the technique known as PL animation of biological motion. With this technique, the activity of a human is portrayed by the relative motions of a small number of markers positioned on the head and the joints of the body (**Figure 1B**). Following Marey's lead, Johansson filmed an actor wearing small lights attached to the joints of his body. The resulting video clips depicted only the patterns of motion of the lights and not the rest of the body. In recent years, more refined PL animation techniques have been developed through the use of computer animation (Cutting 1978) and motion-capture technology paired with animation software (Ma et al. 2006, Vanrie & Verfaillie 2004). With all of these techniques, static frames of the resulting animation typically appear as meaningless assemblages of dots, with little hint of an underlying configuration. But when the successive PL frames are shown in rapid succession, naïve observers experience compelling apparent motion depicting a human form engaged in a specific activity. Several laboratories have created Web-based archives containing examples of human motion, available as movie files and/or 3D coordinate files. See Blake & Shiffrar (2006) for a Website showing demonstration PL animations and listing URL addresses for accessing and downloading sets of stimuli.

To be sure, there are techniques other than PL animation for examining the perception of human motion, and these tend to add form information to the kinematics. For example, one can connect the points in PL animations with visible line segments to create stick figures (Hodgins et al. 1998). Partial occlusion of these line segments provides a measure of motion integration across the limbs of human actors (e.g., Shiffrar et al. 1997, Sinha & Poggio 1996). Motion capture systems also have been used to obtain precise measurements of human action upon which bodily and facial forms can be superimposed to create "embodied" actors (e.g., Hill & Johnston 2001) presented within virtual reality displays (e.g., Morris et al. 2005). Displays depicting the whole bodies (e.g., Knoblich & Flach 2001) and body outlines (Ambady et al. 1999) in motion have been successfully used to measure visual sensitivity to human action, even under conditions where the observer himself is engaged in motor activity (Chartrand & Bargh 1999). Action perception can also be studied by systematically exaggerating the actions from statistically defined action prototypes (Pollick et al. 2001a) or by morphing between PL animations depicting different categories of activity (Giese & Lappe 2002). Finally, human motion perception can be studied with displays that are completely devoid of physical motion. For example, two static frames can be pulled from a movie of a simple human action (**Figure 1C**). When these static images are sequentially presented at temporal rates consistent with the amount of time normally required to perform the depicted action, observers perceive biomechanically plausible paths of apparent human action (Heptulla-Chatterjee et al. 1996, Shiffrar & Freyd 1990).

VISUAL ANALYSIS OF HUMAN MOTION

Observers have no trouble identifying what an actor is doing in a given PL display (e.g., Dittrich 1993, Norman et al. 2004),

Apparent motion: perception of smooth motion from brief, successive exposures of static images

A

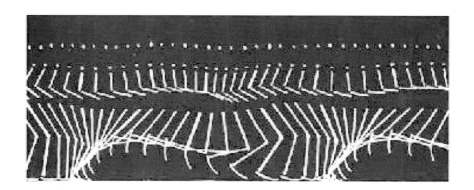

B

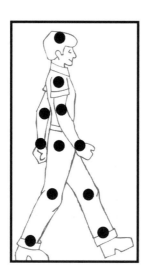 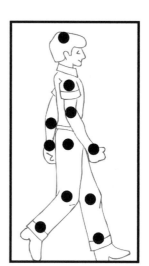

C

even when the number of possible activities is quite large. Observers also readily perceive the identity (Cutting & Kozlowski 1977, Fani et al. 2005, Troje et al. 2005) and sex (Kozlowski & Cutting 1977, 1978; Mather & Murdoch 1994; Sumi 2000; Troje 2002) of a PL-defined walker, although recognition performance is not perfect (Pollick et al. 2005). People can also easily discern activities (e.g., dancing) involving two or more individuals (Mass et al. 1971), and they can judge the emotional implication of an action when viewing PL animations of the whole body (Clarke et al. 2005, Dittrich et al. 1996, Walk & Homan 1984) or even the movements of individual limbs (Pollick et al. 2001b). Facial expressions, too, can be portrayed using PL animation, and people viewing PL faces can identify the facial expression being executed (Bassili 1978) as well as the sex of the actor (Hill et al. 2003). Viewing a PL animation of a talker's face makes it easier to understand what the talker is saying when the vocalizations are heard in noise (Rosenblum et al. 1996). Also of practical relevance, reflective markers worn on the joints of the body make pedestrians walking at night much more conspicuous to drivers (e.g., Wood et al. 2005).

As expected, sensitivity to human motion increases with the number of illuminated joints as well as with the exposure duration of the animation (Neri et al. 1998, Poom & Olsson 2002, Thornton et al. 1998). But even under impoverished or potentially ambiguous conditions, perception of human motion is remarkably robust. Thus observers can recognize human activity when a PL animation is presented for less than one-tenth of a second (Johansson 1973), when the dots are blurred or randomized in contrast polarity over time (Ahlström et al. 1997; but see Mather et al. 1992), or when stereoscopic depths of the dots marking the joint positions of a PL walker are scrambled such that the 3D locations of the dots are unrelated to their implied depth orderings for the human figure (Ahlström et al. 1997, Bülthoff et al. 1998, Lu et al. 2006). Also testifying to the robustness of human motion, observers can easily recognize a walking person when the PL animation is embedded in an array of dynamic noise dots that far outnumber the dozen or so dots defining the person (Bertenthal & Pinto 1994, Cutting et al. 1988, Ikeda et al. 2005). At least for PL walkers, the points defining the wrists and ankles are crucially important when judging the direction of walking (Mather et al. 1992), while the points defining the mid-limb joints (elbow and knees) and the torso (shoulder and hips) contribute significantly to detection of PL walkers embedded within noise (Pinto & Shiffrar 1999). Human action is most compelling when the PL tokens are placed on the joints of the body, but observers can still detect PL human figures when tokens are placed on positions other than the joints, such as intermediate positions on the limbs (Bertenthal & Pinto 1994). Perception of human motion is seriously disrupted by perturbations in the temporal relations of the PL tokens (Bertenthal & Pinto 1993). Introducing spatiotemporal jitter into the phase relations of the moving dots disturbs the quality of human motion (e.g., Grossman & Blake

Dynamic noise: an array of randomly positioned dots that can camouflage perception of PL animations when the noise dots are sufficiently dense

Spatiotemporal jitter: means of degrading perception of PL animations, where the relative timing and positions of the moving dots are perturbed

Figure 1

Examples of animation techniques used to study perception of human motion. (*A*) Photograph produced by prolonged film exposure while a person outfitted with small metallic markers walked from left to right. The resulting image highlights the kinematics of this action. [Photograph from Marey (1884), now in the public domain.] (*B*) Two frames from an animation of a point-light walker. In the actual animation, only the dots are visible—the outline of the human figure is shown here only to make obvious the fixed positions of the dots on the human body. (*C*) Two frames showing a person moving her arm from one position to another. When the two frames are briefly shown in succession with an adequately long blank interval between the two presentations, one sees the arm move in the only direction mechanically plausible for this event.

1999) and seriously impairs detection of human motion embedded in noise (e.g., Hiris et al. 2005a). Likewise, PL animations depicting abnormally slow walking movements produce perception of rotation in depth about a vertical axis, not perception of slow human gait (Beintema et al. 2006).

One of the hallmark characteristics of human motion perception is its vulnerability to inversion: Human action is difficult to perceive in inverted PL animations (e.g., Sumi 1984). In this respect, bodily motion perception resembles face perception, which is also highly susceptible to inversion (Valentine 1988). This orientation dependence operates in egocentric, not environmental, coordinates: PL animations shown upright with respect to gravity are nonetheless difficult to perceive when the observer's head is turned so that the retinal image of those animations is no longer upright with respect to head position (Troje 2003). Prior knowledge cannot counteract this inversion effect: Informing observers ahead of time that they'll be seeing upside-down people does not help them identify what they've seen, which implies that they cannot mentally rotate the images (Pavlova & Sokolov 2000). With practice, observers can learn to detect inverted human motion (Hiris et al. 2005b, Shiffrar & Pinto 2002), but in so doing observers are relying on detection of conspicuous clusters of dots, not on global impression of a human figure.

Besides its vulnerability to inversion, visual sensitivity to human motion (indexed by susceptibility to noise dot motion) is also compromised when a PL figure is imaged in the visual periphery, and this impairment is not simply attributable to the periphery's reduced visual resolution—increasing the sizes of the PL dots and the overall size of the human figure cannot compensate for this loss in sensitivity (Ikeda et al. 2005). Perception of human motion is also impaired when PL animations are viewed under dim light conditions (Grossman & Blake 1999).

Observers can use kinematics information to infer properties of objects with which PL actors are interacting. Thus, for example, people can accurately estimate the weight of a lifted object from observing the lifting motion alone (Bingham 1993), and they can judge the elasticity of a support surface by watching a PL person walking on that surface (Stoffregen & Flynn 1994). There is disagreement whether observers are directly perceiving kinetic object properties from human kinematics information (Runeson & Frykholm 1981) or, instead, are deploying heuristics to infer object properties from kinematics (e.g., Gilden & Proffitt 1994). In either event, however, there is no doubt that kinematics can accurately specify the act of lifting and, moreover, the effort required to do so (Shim et al. 2004).

Accurate perception of PL figures is not limited to human activity. Mather & West (1993) demonstrated that people could identify animals, such as a camel, goat, baboon, horse, and elephant, whose movements were represented by PL animations. People found this task impossible, however, when viewing a single, static frame from the PL sequence. Bellefeuille & Faubert (1998) showed that observers could identify the shape of an animal as accurately when using PL animations as they could when viewing animal shapes defined by luminance contrast. Jokisch & Troje (2003) showed that human observers viewing PL animations of striding dogs could accurately recover the size of the dog using just the stride frequency depicted by the moving dots. For that matter, humans are not the only biological creatures that can perceive animal motion with PL stimuli. Successful discrimination has also been demonstrated in cats (Blake 1993), pigeons (Dittrich et al. 1998, Omori & Watanabe 1996), and newly hatched chicks (Regolin et al. 2000).

The ability to perceive PL depictions of human motion arises early in life, as evidenced by preferential looking studies: Infants four months old will stare at human motion sequences for longer durations than they will at the same number of dots undergoing random motions, a preference not exhibited when infants view an inverted PL person

(Bertenthal 1993, Fox & McDaniel 1982). Sensitivity to human motion is also evidenced in eight-month-old infants by differences in amplitude of event-related potentials (ERPs) to upright versus scrambled PL animations (Hirai & Hiraki 2005) and to upright versus inverted PL animations (Reid et al. 2006). At these young ages, however, children are not yet completely adult-like in their sensitivity to human motion (Bertenthal & Pinto 1993, Pinto 2006). Using behavioral testing, Pavlova et al. (2001) have shown that young children between the ages of three and five steadily improve in their ability to identify human and nonhuman forms portrayed by PL animations, with adult levels of performance achieved by age five. At the other end of the development time scale, observers older than 60 years are quite good at discriminating among various forms of human motion even when the PL sequences are brief in duration or the dots are partially occluded (Norman et al. 2004). This preservation of the ability to perceive human motion stands in contrast to age-related deficits in speed discrimination (Norman et al. 2003), coherent motion detection (Gilmore et al. 1992), detection of low-contrast moving contours (Sekuler et al. 1980), and perception of self-motion from optic flow (Warren et al. 1989). In sum, the human visual system appears to be especially well adapted for the perception of other people's actions.

Top-down and Bottom-up Influences on Human Motion Perception

The decreased sensitivity to inverted displays of human movement described above suggests that low-level visual mechanisms may not be sufficient to account for action perception. There is debate in the literature about the involvement of top-down influences in perception of human motion, where top-down means conceptually driven processing. As with so many of these kinds of debates, the emerging resolution entails a synthesis of bottom-up and top-down determinants

(Kroustallis 2004, Thornton et al. 1998). Still, it is useful to consider the kinds of evidence that favor one view or the other, which we do here.

Evidence for the role of low-level visual processes in the perception of human movement comes from several lines of research. Johansson (1973), the inventor of the PL technique, thought that perceptual process underlying human motion sequences involved vector analysis of the component body parts (defined by pairs of dots), with those vectors then incorporated into a single structured percept. Similar theories built around different assumptions were subsequently advanced by Webb & Aggarwal (1982) and by Hoffman & Flinchbaugh (1982). Construed in this way, the problem boils down to a variant of the structure from motion problem encountered in other aspects of motion perception and solved using bottom-up, data-driven information supplemented by assumptions about the nature of objects (Ullman 1979).

To determine whether low-level motion analyses underlie the perception of human movement, Mather et al. (1992) inserted blank intervals between successive frames of a PL animation, reasoning that low-level motion analysis is restricted to very brief interstimulus intervals (ISIs), whereas high-level motion favors longer ISIs. On direction discrimination tasks involving a PL walker, Mather et al. found that perception of human gait was best at the shortest ISIs and deteriorated with longer ISIs. Mather et al. concluded that the perception of human motion relies on signals arising within low-level visual mechanisms whose response properties are constrained to operate over short spatial and temporal intervals.

Subsequent work showed, however, that higher-level visual processes also support perception of human motion. Thornton and colleagues (1998) found that human gait can be perceived with PL animations over a range of temporal display rates that exceed the value typically associated with low-level, local motion analysis (e.g., Baker & Braddick 1985).

Event-related potential (ERP): electrical brain activity registered from the scalp

More recently, several studies have shown that perception of human motion, under some circumstances, requires focused visual attention. Cavanagh et al. (2001) used a visual search paradigm to show that imposition of an attentional load made it more time consuming for observers to pick out an "oddball" PL walker among an array of PL figures. Similarly, Thornton et al. (2002) found that when a PL sequence is embedded among dynamic noise dots, attention is crucial for perceiving the human figure at long ISIs but not at short ISIs. The same pattern of results was found when Thornton et al. used a very brief ISI but varied the type of masking noise. To perceive a human figure in a mask of scrambled dots (i.e., dot motions with vectors identical to the PL dots), observers had to attend to the animation. Conversely, in random noise mask (i.e., dots randomly replaced each frame), distracted attention had no effect on walker detection. Still, when PL stimuli are designed to render such top-down processes ineffective, bottom-up processes guide the perception of PL animations. For example, ignored PL walkers are processed at a level sufficient to impact the perception of attended PL walkers (Thornton & Vuong 2004). Thus, both bottom-up and top-down processes are employed during the perceptual analysis of PL animations of human motion.

Human motion itself can also exert a top-down influence on other aspects of perception. For example, Watson et al. (2004) found that dichoptically viewed PL walkers differing in color and in heading direction produced binocular rivalry, meaning that observers saw one PL walker or the other over time. Based on this and related results, Watson and colleagues concluded that dominance during rivalry resulted from the integration of high-level perceptual organization (responsible for perception of human motion) with lower-level inhibition between cortical representations of input from the two eyes. Human motion can also influence the perceived direction of translational motion. Thus, when a coherent PL person walks in front of a counterphase flickering grating with no net directional energy, the grating appears to translate in the direction opposite the walker's heading, just as the physical environment flows past us when we walk (Fujimoto 2003). In a similar vein, the global motion engendered by a PL walker provides an effective reference frame for judging whether or not local dot motions are coherent (Tadin et al. 2002). All of these studies imply that human motion exerts a significant influence on putatively low-level motion processing.

Visual Form Influences Perception of Human Motion

PL animations of human activity seemingly contain little form information about the human body, yet people can easily detect PL figures appearing within a cloud of moving "noise" dots whose local motions are identical to those defining the PL figures. Based on motion alone, detection of a PL figure should be extraordinarily difficult under these conditions. Evidently, the visual analysis of human motion is constrained by the hierarchical structure of the human body, for otherwise it would be hopelessly difficult to segregate moving "body" dots from moving "noise" dots and, therefore, to track given body dots over time. Indeed, when PL animations contain motion vectors that violate the hierarchical structure of the human body, observers experience great difficulty detecting the presence of a PL body part (Pinto & Shiffrar 1999).

Several lines of evidence underscore the importance of bodily form. For one thing, sequential presentation of two static pictures of a person performing some action is sufficient for the perception of human action, even though such displays contain minimal motion information (e.g., Heptulla-Chatterjee et al. 1996). For another, there is evidence that the changing positions of the moving points in a PL animation convey sufficient form cues for the detection of a PL walker. To dissociate position and motion, Beintema & Lappe (2002) designed a variant of the point-light

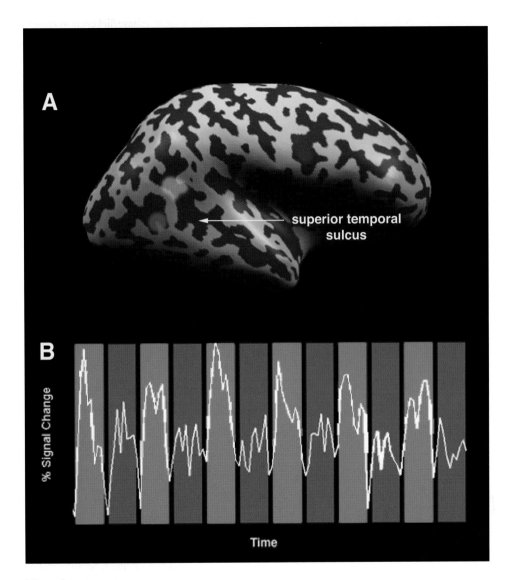

Figure 2

fMRI activation of the posterior portion of the superior temporal sulcus (STSp) upon viewing PL animations. (*A*) Lateral view of the inflated surface of the right hemisphere of the human brain; inflation reveals gyri (*light areas*) and sulci (*dark areas*). The region shown in *yellow* toward the posterior end of the superior temporal sulcus is strongly activated when an observer views PL animations relative to viewing scrambled PL animations. For purposes of reference, motion-sensitive, visual area MT+ is shown in *red*; MT+ responds strongly to both PL and scrambled PL animations. (*B*) Variations over time in fMRI BOLD signal from STSp associated with viewing PL animations (*olive-colored bars*) and with viewing scrambled PL animations (*gray bars*). (Redrawn from data collected by Emily Grossman and Chai-Youn Kim.)

animation in which the positions of the dots are not confined to the joint but instead can appear anywhere along the limbs. Moreover, the dots change their positions along the limbs unpredictably from frame to frame. While these two manipulations should not disrupt specification of body shape, they make it virtually impossible to perceive coherent motion of the dots defining an activity. Nonetheless, observers viewing these displays can judge with reasonable accuracy the direction (left versus right) in which a PL figure is walking. In fact, detection performance measured using these special PL animations is well predicted by the total number of points seen in a trial, irrespective of the distribution of these points over time (Beintema et al. 2006). This result is consistent with a simple template-matching model in which the positions of the stimulus dots in each single frame are matched to the posture of a human body template (Lange & Lappe 2006). This model suggests that human movements can be discriminated by an accumulation of evidence for the body postures indicated by the positions of stimulus dots.

Additional evidence for the importance of bodily form in the perception of human motion comes from Hiris and colleagues (2005a). They created "arbitrary" motion sequences by relocating the dots from a PL walker. Thus, for example, a wrist dot might be placed at the location of the shoulder dot and the shoulder dot relocated to the position of the knee, and so on. The resulting arbitrary figure comprised the same dot motions as the walker in the absence of a human form. Following the design of studies with masked PL walkers, the arbitrary figures were presented within a mask of dynamic dots. With practice, observers learned to discriminate whether or not the arbitrary figure was presented in a mask, with performance eventually approaching that achieved with an ordinary PL walker. However, observers described performing this task by looking for a characteristic cluster of dots at a given location, a strategy very dissimilar from that used with upright PL walkers in noise. Moreover, inverting the arbitrary figure had no effect on detection performance, in stark contrast to the effect of inversion on detection of PL walkers. When a display change forced observers to detect the global pattern of motion in the arbitrary figures, performance hovered near chance levels regardless of practice (Hiris et al. 2005a). Thus, the human form is important for the perception of human motion, especially when it is impossible to rely on local motion regularities. Such results further suggest that different processes are employed during the analyses of human motion and object motion (Shiffrar & Pinto 2002).

Taken together, then, current research indicates that both form and motion play critical roles in the perception of human action. This interplay between form and motion information in the visual specification of human action has been formalized in a computational model developed by Giese & Poggio (2003). Their model is based on bottom-up visual signals analyzed in parallel in a form pathway and a motion pathway, which they identify with the ventral stream and dorsal stream pathways, respectively. The core principle of their model is that human motion is represented as learned sequences or "snapshots" of human shapes and optic flow patterns. Inhibition insures that the neural instantiations of these snapshots are activated only in the correct temporal sequence as incorrect sequences are inhibited. This renders the model highly sensitive to disturbances in the normal temporal relationships among the motions of PL tokens (recall Bertenthal & Pinto 1993, Hiris et al. 2005a). Through successive transformations within the model, more global aspects of the human form and its resulting kinematics are extracted, with size and position invariance embodied at higher levels. In both pathways, representations are stored as 2D, view-dependent patterns; this aspect of the model dovetails with the known view dependence of perception of human motion (e.g., Bülthoff et al. 1998, Sumi 1984). As Giese and Poggio acknowledge, their model remains incomplete in that it does not incorporate top-down

Template-matching model: theory that perception of biological motion results from concatenation of static views of the body

Common coding
principle: theory
that perceiving and
acting share
common mental
representations

influences such as attention (e.g., Thornton et al. 2002). Still, this ambitious model makes a number of testable predictions, some of which have since been confirmed (Peuskens et al. 2005).

MOTORIC CONTRIBUTIONS TO PERCEPTION OF HUMAN MOTION

So far, we have focused on visual sensitivity to human motion. But what are the origins of that sensitivity? Converging lines of evidence strongly suggest that our keen ability to perceive the actions of other people results, in part, from the massive experience we have accumulated over the years in planning and executing self-produced activities. Prinz (1997) and Hommel et al. (2001) have formalized this idea as the common coding principle and the theory of event coding, respectively. According to both of these accounts, sensory representations used during action perception overlap with the motor representations used during action planning. This section summarizes converging lines of evidence supporting this view as it applies to perception of human motion (but see Decety & Grèzes 1999).

First, if action perception and action production share common representations, then an observer's own activities should influence that observer's perception of the activities of other people. This, in fact, happens. For example, an observer is better able to notice a change in the limb position of an actor when the observer, too, is moving the corresponding limb (Reed & Farah 1995). Similarly, an observer's ability to discriminate the gait speeds of a PL walker depends upon whether the observer is standing or walking (Jacobs & Shiffrar 2005), and the ability to judge the size of a box being lifted by an actor depends on the weight of a box being lifted by the observer (Hamilton et al. 2004).

Second, if motor experience does indeed affect visual sensitivity to human action, then observers should demonstrate maximum sensitivity to actions most familiar to them and

reduced sensitivity to actions unfamiliar to them. These predictions, too, have been confirmed. Consider, for example, a study by Knoblich & Flach (2001) in which movies were made of individuals throwing darts at a board. Returning to the laboratory one week later, these individuals viewed short video sequences showing an arm throwing a dart that always stopped at the moment the dart was released. Participants then predicted where the dart would hit the board. Prediction accuracy was highest when participants viewed sequences of their own dart throws. In a similar vein, an observer is especially good at judging whether a pair of PL animations portrays the same actor when those animations were produced by filming the observer himself several months earlier (Loula et al. 2005). In contrast, observers are relatively poor at discriminating the gait speed of a PL walker when the spatiotemporal characteristics of the gait fall outside the range of physically possible human gaits or when the gait was produced by someone other than the observer (Jacobs et al. 2004). Interestingly, people can improve their ability to discriminate unusual action styles simply by repeatedly executing that action style themselves, and this improvement occurs even when people practice while blindfolded (Casile & Giese 2006). Motor learning, in other words, influences visual perception of the learned motor behavior.

A third category of evidence bearing on the action perception/production linkage comes from studies of patients with congenital or disease-related disorders that affect proprioceptive mechanisms and/or motor behavior. Here, too, the results are revealing. One study (Bosbach et al. 2005) assessed action perception in two individuals with no sense of cutaneous touch or proprioception, a condition arising from sensory neuropathy. Unlike normal, control volunteers, both of these individuals had difficulty deducing whether or not another person was surprised at the weight of a lifted object, based on viewing the kinematics of that person's lifting activity. In another study (Funk et al. 2005), an individual born without hands perceived biomechanically impossible hand rotations under stimulus conditions where normally limbed individuals see hand rotations that conform to natural limb trajectories. Importantly, this individual with hand aplasia also experienced no phantom sensation of the congenitally missing hands. Evidently, the ability to represent executable actions constrains the ability to perceptually interpret similar actions performed by other people (Shiffrar 2006). In another patient study (Pavlova et al. 2003), human motion perception was assessed in teenage adolescents who varied in terms of their locomotion ability—the subject population ranged from normal to those with congenital walking disability resulting from spastic cerebral palsy. Sensitivity to human motion was unrelated to severity of motor disorder, implying that the ability to plan a body movement is sufficient for the development of human motion perception. This does not mean that perception and production arise from different brain areas, but rather that a common coding network does not require fine motor execution for utilization in perception.

In summary, converging lines of evidence indicate that one's own actions can affect one's perception of the actions of others. Indeed, some have argued that observers' motor constraints influence their percepts of all moving stimuli (Viviani 2002, Viviani & Stucchi 1992). For that matter, the causal arrow can point in the opposite direction: action perception can influence action execution. Thus, for example, participants in one study were asked to make arm movements while viewing another person (biological) or a robot (nonbiological) execute arm movements (Kilner et al. 2003). Participants' own arm movements exhibited significantly more variability when they viewed human arm movements than when they viewed robot arm movements. This and other results implicate a tight coupling between observation and performance of action. All of these results are consistent with the idea that observers spontaneously simulate, in their motor planning system, the ac-

tions that they observe (Blakemore & Decety 2001, Jeannerod 2004). Moreover, there is reason to believe that this spontaneous simulation occurs at an unconscious level. For example, when a seated observer views another person running on a treadmill, the observer's own respiration rate increases with treadmill speed and hence runner exertion (Paccalin & Jeannerod 2000). When observers view different poses of a moving person, perceptual priming, as assessed by reaction time in a body-pose discrimination task, is restricted to body views that satisfy the biomechanical limitations on human movement (Kourtzi & Shiffrar 1999), a finding that indicates the existence of implicit visual representations of human movement. Likewise, judgments of gait direction are facilitated whenever the previously viewed PL person walks in the same direction, a finding that implies that implicit knowledge of gait dynamics influences visual sensitivity to human motion (Verfaillie 2000). Finally, people tend to mimic the actions of other people without even realizing it, a tendency dubbed the chameleon effect (Chartrand & Bargh 1999). Here, too, we see evidence for tight perception-action coupling operating at an unconscious level.

SOCIAL DETERMINANTS OF PERCEPTION OF HUMAN MOTION

Visual comprehension of human actions promotes effective social interaction. It is natural to assume, therefore, that the sensori-motor analyses underlying perception of human action should incorporate our social needs, and this assumption is supported by evidence. Observers can perceive a wide range of socially relevant characteristics from highly degraded depictions of human action including an actor's identity (Loula et al. 2005), sex (Barclay et al. 1978), sexual orientation (Ambady et al. 1999), dancing ability (Brown et al. 2005), openness (Brownlow et al. 1997), social dominance (Montepare & Zebrowitz-McArthur 1988), vulnerability to attack (Gunns et al.

Chámeleon effect: tendency for people to mimic the actions of others without even knowing it

2002), and intent to deceive (Runeson & Frykholm 1983). Face perception, too, is facilitated by dynamic information such as shifts in eye gaze, lip movements and changes in expression (Haxby et al. 2000, O'Toole et al. 2002). These diverse findings imply that the human visual system is tuned for the pickup of socially relevant information.

One particularly salient characteristic conveyed by human activity is the emotional states of observed individuals. It is well established, for example, that observers can readily identify the emotion being portrayed by a PL actor (e.g., Atkinson et al. 2004). Pollick and colleagues (2001b) have shown that an action as simple as the movements of a PL arm knocking against a door are sufficient for observers to discriminate the emotion of the individual executing the arm movements.

Given this keen sensitivity to socially relevant kinematics, it is reasonable to expect that social processes, per se, should influence action perception. Recent evidence implies that this is so. For example, when observers are asked to detect the presence of a PL walker in a complex PL mask, their performance depends upon the emotion conveyed by the PL walker: Observers detect the presence of angry PL walkers more accurately than they detect neutral, happy, sad, or fearful PL walkers (Chouchourelou et al. 2006). In another study (Clarke et al. 2005), PL animations were created depicting two people engaged in an emotional interaction (i.e., the emotions conveyed included sadness, anger, and disgust). Observers viewing these animations were better able to judge the emotion being expressed when they could see both PL actors, not just one or the other. Social context, in other words, aided perception of emotion. Evidence for the importance of social processes in action perception also comes from the chameleon effect, wherein individuals unconsciously mimic the actions of other people. Social mimicry may serve to increase rapport between individuals, since mimicked individuals express greater liking for those who mimic their actions (Chartrand & Bargh

1999) and since individuals who bring feelings of social exclusion into an interaction are more likely to mimic the other person (Lakin & Chartrand 2003). Such evidence suggests that social processes constrain and are constrained by connections between action perception and action production.

NEURAL BASES OF PERCEPTION OF HUMAN MOTION

The visual and functional importance of human motion perception is instantiated in a specialized neural network. In this final section, we review some of the evidence for the existence of these neural mechanisms for the analysis and interpretation of human motion, including mechanisms responsible for the influences of emotion and motor programming. This section is necessarily brief; for more thorough coverage, see Decety & Grèzes (1999), Puce & Perrett (2003), and Grossman (2006).

Single-Cell Recording Studies

The first neurophysiological evidence for the existence of a brain area visually coding human movement came from the work of Perrett et al. (1982, 1985). Recording from single cells in macaque cortex, these researchers discovered neurons in the superior temporal sulcus (STS) selectively responsive to human forms and motions within an observer-centered coordinate system (Oram & Perrett 1994). The STS represents a point of convergence for the dorsal and ventral visual streams (Felleman & Van Essen 1991), befitting STS's ability to integrate form and motion information arising from the same person (Oram & Perrett 1996, Shiffrar 1994). Although STS neurons are largely visual, their activity can be modulated by the motor system (Hietanen & Perrett 1996) and by the amygdala (Aggleton et al. 1980).

More recently, another remarkable category of visually activated neurons was identified in both the ventral premotor cortex and the inferior parietal cortex of the alert, behaving monkey (Rizzolatti et al. 2001, Rizzolatti & Craighero 2004). Called mirror neurons, these brain cells respond when an animal performs a visually guided activity (e.g., grasping) and, significantly, when the animal observes another individual executing that activity. These unique neurons respond only when an activity involves primate motion, not motion of, say, a mechanical device that simulates the action. Moreover, these neurons also respond to sounds associated with a given action. Significantly, they only respond when the action is goal-directed, as specified by the context in which the action occurs (Fogassi et al. 2005).

These groundbreaking neurophysiological studies paved the way for investigations of human brain mechanisms involved in the perception of human action, investigations to which we now turn.

Neuropsychological Studies

The first clues implicating specialized neural machinery for the analysis of human action in the human brain came from neuropsychological studies revealing selective visual deficits in individuals with focal brain lesions. Schenk & Zihl (1997) identified two patients with parietal lobe lesions who experienced difficulty perceiving a PL walker in noise but had no problem discriminating direction of coherent motion of dots. In a similar vein, patient AF (Vaina et al. 1990), who had bilateral lesions within the posterior visual pathway, had great difficulty perceiving coherent motion in random-dot cinematograms but could easily recognize human activities presented in point-light animations. Conversely, patient AL (Cowey & Vaina 2000) could not recognize PL depictions of human motion even though she could detect movement of the dots and could see that not all were moving in the same direction. These case studies and others (e.g., Battelli et al. 2003) point to the occipito-parietal region for the analysis of the complex kinematics characteristic of human motion.

Recently, Heberlein and colleagues (2004) studied the abilities of brain-damaged patients to judge the emotionality and personality characteristics of actors portrayed by PL animations. Some patients were impaired on one task but not the other, which implied the existence of distinct neural mechanisms for perception of emotion and perception of personality. By analyzing regions of lesion overlap in these patients, Heberlein et al. (2004) concluded that damage to the somatosensory cortex in the right hemisphere was associated with deficits in judging emotion, and damage to the left frontal opercular cortex was associated with deficits in judging personality traits. The cerebellum, a structure traditionally associated with skilled motor behavior, seems to be uninvolved in perception of PL animations of human motion: Patients with cerebellar damage can readily detect a PL walker in masking noise, but have difficulty judging the direction of coherent dot motion in masking noise (Jokisch et al. 2005a).

Deficits in perception of human motion have been described in several other patient populations. In one study, young autistic children, unlike their age-matched cohorts, made more errors on a visual task requiring discrimination of normal PL actors from scrambled PL sequences; these same autistic children performed normally on a comparably difficult visual grouping task involving discrimination of nonbiological shapes (Blake et al. 2003). This is consistent with the association between autism and STS abnormalities (Waiter et al. 2004). Adult schizophrenic individuals also experience difficulties discriminating normal from scrambled point-light animations (Kim et al. 2005). Children with Down syndrome have difficulties differentiating PL displays of moving objects and people (Virji-Babul et al. 2006). Also exhibiting deficits in perception of PL animations are adolescents suffering periventricular leukomalacia, a form of brain damage associated with premature birth (Pavlova et al. 2006).

Mirror neurons: brain cells responsive when an animal engages in an activity or when it watches another animal engaged in that activity

Individuals in several of these patient populations, including those with autism, schizophrenia, and periventricular leukomalacia, can exhibit social and emotional deficits. It is tempting to wonder whether their deficits in perception of human motion might contribute to their stunted social skills and their inability to perceive and respond appropriately to emotional signals expressed by other people (e.g., Hobson et al. 1988).

Human motion perception is also disrupted by formation of temporary "lesions" in normal individuals, with the "lesion" being induced by transcranial magnetic stimulation (TMS). Grossman et al. (2005) applied repetitive TMS to a region of the scalp overlying posterior brain regions including the superior temporal sulcus. (As mentioned above, the STS is involved in the analysis of human motion in the macaque monkey brain.) For a short time following TMS, observers had more difficulty recognizing PL sequences in noise, but only when sequences were shown in their upright orientation; sensitivity to inverted sequences, although generally poorer, was unaffected by TMS. Nor did TMS applied over motion-sensitive area MT+ have any effect on perception of PL actors, a finding that underscores the unique involvement of the STS in perception of human motion.

Brain Imaging: Visual Processes

In recent years, brain imaging studies have revealed an array of brain areas selectively responsive to human action. In the following sections we focus on brain activations measured using either positron emission tomography (PET) or functional magnetic resonance imaging (fMRI). Action perception studies using magnetic encephalography and event-related potentials can be found in Pavlova et al. (2004, 2006), Hirai et al. (2003), Jokisch et al. (2005b), and Wheaton et al. (2001).

In many of the imaging studies summarized here, investigators contrasted brain activation produced when observers viewed animations of point-light-defined people with activations produced when viewing scrambled versions of the same animations. Both kinds of sequences comprise identical individual dot trajectories and, therefore, differ only in the global, spatiotemporal coherence of the dots portraying human action. Differences in activation to the two kinds of animations, therefore, would constitute evidence for specific processing of the kinematics defining human motion (with the stipulation that a perceptually demanding task was used to insure that sustained attention was maintained for both categories of animations). What is found in brain imaging studies?

Using PET, Bonda et al. (1996) identified regions along the posterior portions of the superior temporal sulcus (STSp) that were activated when people viewed coherent, but not scrambled, point-light actions. Subsequently, Grossman et al. (2000) pinpointed activation sites in this same STSp area using fMRI (**Figure 2**, see color insert). These investigators also found that point-light actions activated the human MT/V5+ complex, but no more so than did scrambled point-light sequences (see also Howard et al. 1996 and Peuskens et al. 2005). In a follow-up study, Grossman & Blake (2001) found that STSp activation was stronger to upright human motion than to inverted sequences that, as pointed out above, are more difficult to discern as biological. Using a perceptual learning paradigm paired with brain scanning, Grossman et al. (2004) found that STSp activation varied depending on whether observers were able to recognize a given PL sequence as human. In this study, PL human figures were embedded in enough noise to mask recognition to near-chance levels. When viewed prior to training, these masked sequences yielded no selective responses within STSp. But following extensive practice with these masked sequences, observers' recognition performance improved substantially and, moreover, the previously unrecognizable sequences also readily evoked selective responses to human PL sequences in noise. Significantly, the improvements in recognition performance and in STSp responsiveness generalized to novel PL sequences embedded in noise, which implies neural plasticity within STSp.

In a recent study, Peuskens et al. (2005) found that it was primarily the STSp in the right hemisphere that responds strongly to human motion, a trend evident in the results of others as well (Beauchamp et al. 2003, Grossman et al. 2000, Santi et al. 2003). There is also relatively crude retinotopy within STSp in that a given cluster of voxels can be activated by human action sequences appearing anywhere within five degrees or so of visual angle on either side of central fixation (Grossman et al. 2000). This observation befits the relatively large receptive fields of individual neurons in the homologue of STSp in monkey visual cortex.

STSp is also robustly activated when one views whole-body motions rather than PL sequences (Pelphrey et al. 2003), as well as when one views motion confined to specific limbs or to the eyes, hand, and mouth (Calvert et al. 1997, Grèzes et al. 1998, Puce et al. 1998). Interestingly, brain areas including STSp in the right hemisphere also respond robustly when people view humanly impossible movements (Costantini et al. 2005). Complex motion sequences portraying rigid rotation produce little, if any, activation of STSp (Beauchamp et al. 2002, Grossman & Blake 2002, Pelphrey et al. 2003), and a single static human figure is similarly insufficient to produce STSp activation (Peuskens et al. 2005).

Santi et al. (2003) used fMRI to dissociate brain areas responsive to whole-body actions portrayed in PL animations from brain areas responsive to visible speech rendered using PL animations. While there were a few overlapping activation areas, the speech animations selectively activated the left hemisphere STSp, portions of auditory cortex, and a network of motor regions including Broca's area; the whole-body PL animations, besides activating STSp in the right hemisphere, selectively activated the fusiform gyrus bilaterally and a network of more rostrally lo-cated cortical areas that Santi et al. (2003) believe are involved in the mirror-neuron system discussed above. It is noteworthy that in STSp, speech, PL human motion, and whole-body human motion activations do not overlap (Beauchamp 2005).

Several studies have identified robust STSp activation associated with viewing complex, natural events involving human activity. To give a few examples, Schürmann et al. (2005) measured increased BOLD signals in STSp while people viewed videotapes of another person yawning, a notoriously contagious activity. Activations in STSp were found regardless of whether observers themselves felt compelled to yawn. In a particularly clever study, Hasson et al. (2004) measured whole-brain fMRI activations in observers while they viewed a continuous audiovisual movie segment containing diverse subject matter and a complex, exciting storyline (*The Good, The Bad, and The Ugly*). Hasson and colleagues used intersubject correlation analysis to find brain regions that responded in a reliable fashion across all observers during the movie. Relevant for our purposes, consistent activations in STSp were associated with movie sequences depicting human activity, relative to sequences devoid of human activity, and these activations were reliably seen in all observers.

Area STSp is also activated when one hears footstep sounds produced by people walking, but not when one hears unstructured noise (Bidet-Caulet et al. 2005). In the monkey, STSp neurons respond strongly to species-specific, emotionally charged vocalizations (Gil-da-Costa et al. 2004). Such auditory sensitivity indicates that portions of this specialized brain area receive multimodal input, and further substantiates the idea that STSp is importantly involved in recognition of human activity (Wheaton et al. 2004).

Over the past few years, the chart of brain territories activated by human motion has enlarged significantly. PL animations have been shown to selectively activate regions on the

Extrastriate body area (EBA): brain region activated when a person views a human body or body parts

ventral surface of the temporal lobe (Vaina et al. 2001), on the lateral fusiform gyrus (Beauchamp et al. 2002), and in functionally identified areas including the fusiform face area and the occipital face area (Grossman & Blake 2002). Some of those activation regions, however, may be responsive to the implied presence of a human body and not to the dynamics of the PL sequences per se (Peelen & Downing 2005, Peelen et al. 2006). Michels et al. (2005) showed that ventral stream activations could also be evoked using the modified PL animations designed by Beintema and Lappe, animations in which the dots provide position, but not local motion, information.

In an fMRI study using whole-body motion, Bartels & Zeki (2004) found robust activations in the fusiform gyrus of observers while they were viewing action segments of a James Bond movie. The fusiform gyrus is a brain region often associated with face perception (e.g., Kanwisher 2000, Kanwisher et al. 1997), so it is not clear whether results of Bartels & Zeki reflect face perception, body perception, or both. A related fMRI study that overcomes this limitation was performed by Peelen & Downing (2005). They found areas within the fusiform gyrus that were indeed activated when people viewed human bodies without faces or viewed stick figures depicting stylized human bodies without facial features. Careful, individual analyses of these activated areas revealed that they are contiguous with, but not overlapping, foci of activation produced when viewing faces (the conventional "fusiform face area").

We also should mention the existence of the extrastriate body area (EBA). Situated at the junction of the occipital and temporal lobes, the EBA is activated when one views human bodies or isolated body parts; unlike the STSp, EBA activation does not require bodily activity, although body movements can produce strong responses in the EBA (Downing et al. 2001). A recent fMRI study found that the EBA also responds to self-produced body movements, even if the actor cannot see the movements of his/her limbs (Astafiev et al.

2004). This finding implies that the EBA receives inputs from motor areas responsible for the generation of actions; these endogenous signals could contribute to the specification of agency in actions, i.e., identification of whether an action is self-produced or attributable to another. Such a signaling capacity would implicate the EBA as a critical component in the social interpretations of self and others (Jeannerod 2004), likely in conjunction with the STS, since it responds to the motion of others and not the self (Hietanen & Perrett 1996), and the premotor cortex, since it responds differentially to self and other generated movements (Calvo-Merino et al. 2005, Grèzes et al. 2004).

Considered together, these brain imaging studies imply that cortical regions within the so-called ventral stream pathway are importantly involved in perception of the human body and its activities. Such an involvement is broadly consistent with theories that attribute perception of human motion to a confluence of activity from dorsal and ventral stream brain areas, with the STSp representing a lynchpin within this distributed network (Giese & Poggio 2003, Shiffrar 1994).

Brain Imaging: Social-Emotional Processes

The STS constitutes part of a large neural circuit including the amygdala, the orbitofrontal cortex, and the motor system via the parietal system. These areas are key for the perception of and response to objects and events of social and emotional relevance. Indeed, several recent fMRI studies suggest that STSp is involved in the perception of intention from action. For example, Zacks et al. (2001) found that STSp activation was stronger when an observer viewed an actor switching from one activity to another, as if the goal structure of the action were relevant. Even more compelling are the results of Saxe et al. (2004), in which the same visible action was seen in different contexts that changed the implied intentions of the actor. The associated hemodynamic responses differed depending on the inferred, not directly visualized, intentions of the actor. Saxe et al. (2004) speculate that previous fMRI studies contrasting full-body point-light sequences with scrambled sequences may have unwittingly been localizing neural areas registering perception of intentional action, not just perception of articulate body motions.

Evidence suggests that STS also is activated when an individual attempts to infer the mental states of another behaving agent (Frith & Frith 1999, Morris et al. 2005). For example, STS activation is found when participants make social judgments about other people (e.g., trustworthiness) in the absence of bodily motion (Winston et al. 2002). Furthermore, STS activation is more strongly coupled to the analysis of expressive gestures than to instrumental gestures (Gallagher & Frith 2004). In any case, it is clear that the STS plays a fundamental role in the perceptual analysis of social cues (e.g., Allison et al. 2000), of which body postures and actions are particularly powerful examples. Indeed, it has been proposed that the STS serves to determine the social significance of actions (Iacoboni et al. 2004).

Given the extensive interconnections between the limbic system, particularly the amygdala, and the STS (Adolphs 1999), one could predict that STS modulation should vary as a function of the emotional content of an action. Consistent with this prediction, STS activity increases during the perception of potentially threatening fear-inducing actions (Wheaton et al. 2001). Converging psychophysical measures indicate that observers are best able to detect the presence of angry people (Chouchourelou et al. 2006). Furthermore, STS activity is strongly modulated by dynamic expressions of emotion (LaBar et al. 2003).

Brain Imaging: Motor Processes

Visual perception of human action is also accompanied by activation in the constellation of brain areas involved in motor planning, including both premotor and primary motor cortex (Grèzes et al. 1998, Hamilton et al. 2006, Raos et al. 2004, Santi et al. 2003). Thus, for example, primary motor cortex, M1, is activated when one person observes another person's hand and arm movements (Decety et al. 1997, Hari et al. 1998), but only when those bodily movements are biomechanically possible (Stevens et al. 2000). This association between sensory and motor activation dovetails nicely with the work in nonhuman primates on mirror neurons described above. Indeed, a correlate of this mirror system has been investigated in human observers (see review by Blakemore et al. 2005), including observers viewing PL animations (Tai et al. 2004), and there is some debate over the extent to which such a system could serve as a basis for social cognition (Jacob & Jeannerod 2005). Regardless how this debate plays out, there is little doubt that the perception of another person's actions involves activation of human brain circuits involved in the generation of such actions by the observer (see reviews by Buccino et al. 2004 and Wilson & Knoblich 2005). For example, premotor cortex is activated by PL animations of human action (Saygin et al. 2004). Furthermore, when ballet and Capoeira dancers watch movies of other people performing these two types of dances, premotor (and left STSp) activation is found when they watch their own dance style (Calvo-Merino et al. 2005). Such evidence substantiates the idea that what we see depends, in part, on what we can do.

CONCLUSION

Humans are highly social creatures, and for that reason it is crucial that we be able to perceive what others are doing and to infer from their gestures and expressions what they may be intending to do. Fortunately, perception of these characteristics is easy because human action readily communicates intentions and feelings. So compelling is the information conveyed by activity that we even perceive human-like characteristics in nonhuman animals whose behaviors resemble our own.[1] The overarching message of this review—human actions visually radiate social cues to which we are exquisitely sensitive—is not new and can be traced to Darwin's writings (1872). As documented in this article, remarkable advances have been made in our understanding of the perceptual, motoric, affective, and neural concomitants of the perception of human action. These advances, in turn, may offer deeper insights into the etiology of disorders such as autism and schizophrenia, in which core symptoms include deficits in social interactions.

_____

[1]This strong tendency to anthropomorphize is vividly demonstrated by the visually conspicuous mood states—joyful, sorrowful, fearful, and amorous—we perceive in the emperor penguins in the movie *The March of the Penguins*.

FUTURE ISSUES

1. How does the analysis of human movement diverge from the analysis of nonhuman, animal movement?

2. How do the various neural areas associated with the analysis of human movement interact?

3. Faces and bodies are necessarily connected. How does the perception of one affect the perception of the other?

4. How does motor and social learning modify the perceptual analysis of human action?

5. To what extent can the visual system be understood as an inherently communal mechanism that evolved for the analysis of socially relevant information?

ACKNOWLEDGMENTS

Emily Grossman, Uri Hasson, Eric Hiris, Markus Lappe, Cathy Reed, Jim Thompson, Naznin Virji-Babul, and Tamara Watson provided helpful comments on an earlier draft of this review. David Bloom provided invaluable help with the references. RB and MS are supported by NIH grants EY07760 and EY12300, respectively.

LITERATURE CITED

Adolphs R. 1999. Social cognition and the human brain. *Trends Cogn. Sci.* 3:469–79

Aggleton JP, Burton MJ, Passingham RE. 1980. Cortical and subcortical afferents to the amygdala of the rhesus monkey (*Macaca mulatta*). *Brain Res.* 190:347–68

Ahlström V, Blake R, Ahlström U. 1997. Perception of biological motion. *Perception* 26:1539–48

Allison T, Puce A, McCarthy G. 2000. Social perception from visual cues: role of the STS region. *Trends Cogn. Sci.* 4:267–78

Ambady N, Hallahan M, Conner B. 1999. Accuracy of judgments of sexual orientation from thin slices of behavior. *J. Personal. Soc. Psychol.* 77:538–47

Astafiev SV, Stanley CM, Shulman GL, Corbetta M. 2004. Extrastriate body area in human occipital cortex responds to the performance of motor actions. *Nat. Neurosci.* 7:542–48

Atkinson AP, Dittrich WH, Gemmell AJ, Young AW. 2004. Emotion perception from dynamic and static body expressions in point-light and full-light displays. *Perception* 33:717–46

Baker CLJ, Braddick OJ. 1985. Temporal properties of the short-range process in apparent motion. *Perception* 14:181–92

Barclay C, Cutting J, Kozlowski L. 1978. Temporal and spatial factors in gait perception that influence gender recognition. *Percept. Psychophys.* 23:145–52

Bartels A, Zeki S. 2004. Functional brain mapping during free viewing of natural scenes. *Hum. Brain Mapp.* 21:75–85

Bassili JN. 1978. Facial motion in the perception of faces and of emotional expression. *J. Exp. Psychol.: Hum. Percept. Perform.* 4:373–79

Battelli L, Cavanagh P, Thornton IM. 2003. Perception of biological motion in parietal patients. *Neuropsychologia* 41:1808–16

Beauchamp MS, Lee KE, Haxby JV, Martin A. 2002. Parallel visual motion processing streams for manipulable objects and human movements. *Neuron* 34:149–59

Beauchamp MS, Lee KE, Haxby JV, Martin A. 2003. fMRI responses to video and point-light displays of moving humans and manipulable objects. *J. Cogn. Neurosci.* 15:991–1001

Beauchamp MS. 2005. See me, hear me, touch me: multisensory integration in lateral occipital-temporal cortex. *Curr. Opin. Neurobiol.* 15:145–53

Beintema JA, Lappe M. 2002. Perception of biological motion without local image motion. *Proc. Natl. Acad. Sci. USA* 99:5661–63

Beintema JA, Georg K, Lappe M. 2006. Perception of biological motion from limited lifetime stimuli. *Percept. Psychophys.* In press

Beintema JA, Oleksiak A, van Wezel RJA. 2006. The influence of biological motion perception on structure-from-motion interpretations at different speeds. *J. Vis.* 6:712–26

Bellefeuille A, Faubert J. 1998. Independence of contour and biological-motion cues for motion-defined animal shapes. *Perception* 27:225–35

Bertenthal BI. 1993. Perception of biomechanical motions by infants: intrinsic image and knowledge-based constraints. In *Carnegie Symposium on Cognition: Visual Perception and Cognition in Infancy*, ed. C Granrud, pp. 175–214. Hillsdale, NJ: Erlbaum

Bertenthal BI, Pinto J. 1993. Complementary processes in the perception and production of human movement. In *Dynamic Approaches to Development: Vol. 2 Approaches*, ed. LB Smith, E Thelen, pp. 209–39. Cambridge, MA: MIT Press

Bertenthal BI, Pinto J. 1994. Global processing of biological motions. *Psychol. Sci.* 5:221–25

Bidet-Caulet A, Voisin J, Bertrand O, Fonlupt P. 2005. Listening to a walking human activates the temporal biological motion area. *NeuroImage* 28:132–39

Bingham GP. 1993. Scaling judgments of lifted weight: lifter size and the role of the standard. *Ecol. Psychol.* 5:31–64

Blake R. 1993. Cats perceive biological motion. *Psychol. Sci.* 4:54–57

Blake R, Shiffrar M. 2006. Biological motion resource page. **http://www.psy.vanderbilt.edu/faculty/blake/AR/AR06BM.html**

Blake R, Turner LM, Smoski MJ, Pozdol SL, Stone WL. 2003. Visual recognition of biological motion is impaired in children with autism. *Psychol. Sci.* 14:151–57

Blakemore SJ, Bristow D, Bird G, Frith C, Ward J. 2005. Somatosensory activations during the observation of touch and a case of vision-touch synesthesia. *Brain* 128:1571–83

Blakemore SJ, Decety J. 2001. From the perception of action to the understanding of intention. *Nat. Rev. Neurosci.* 2:561–66

Bonda E, Petrides M, Ostry D, Evans A. 1996. Specific involvement of human parietal systems and the amygdala in the perception of biological motion. *J. Neurosci.* 16:3737–44

Bosbach S, Cole J, Prinz W, Knoblich G. 2005. Inferring another's expectation from action: the role of peripheral sensation. *Nat. Neurosci.* 8:1295–97

Brown WM, Cronk L, Grochow K, Jacobson A, Liu CK, et al. 2005. Dance reveals symmetry especially in young men. *Nature* 438:T148–50

Brownlow S, Dixon AR, Egbert CA, Radcliffe RD. 1997. Perception of movement and dancer characteristics from point-light displays of dance. *Psychol. Rec.* 47:411–21

Buccino G, Binkofski F, Riggio L. 2004. The mirror neuron system and action recognition. *Brain Lang.* 89:370–76

Bülthoff I, Bülthoff H, Sinha P. 1998. Top-down influences on stereoscopic depth-perception. *Nat. Neurosci.* 1:254–57

Calvert GA, Bullmore ET, Brammer MJ, Campbell R, Williams SC, et al. 1997. Activation of auditory cortex during silent lipreading. *Science* 276:593–96

Calvo-Merino B, Glaser DE, Grèzes J, Passingham RE, Haggard P. 2005. Action observation and acquired motor skills: an fMRI study with expert dancers. *Cereb. Cortex* 15:1243–49

Casile A, Giese MA. 2006. Non-visual motor learning influences the recognition of biological motion. *Curr. Biol.* 16:69–74

Cavanagh P, Labianca AT, Thornton IM. 2001. Attention-based visual routines: sprites. *Cognition* 80:47–60

Chartrand TL, Bargh JA. 1999. The chameleon effect: the perception-behavior link and social interaction. *J. Personal. Soc. Psychol.* 76:893–910

Chouchourelou A, Matsuka T, Harber K, Shiffrar M. 2006. The visual analysis of emotional actions. *Soc. Neurosci.* 1:63–74

Clarke TJ, Bradshaw MF, Field DT, Hampson SE, Rose D. 2005. The perception of emotion from body movement in point-light displays of interpersonal dialogue. *Perception* 34:1171–80

Costantini M, Galati G, Ferretti A, Caulo M, Tartaro A, et al. 2005. Neural systems underlying observation of humanly impossible movements: an fMRI study. *Cereb. Cortex* 15:1761–67

Cowey A, Vaina LM. 2000. Blindness to form from motion despite intact static form perception and motion detection. *Neuropsychologia* 38:566–78

Cutting JE. 1978. A program to generate synthetic walkers as dynamic point-light displays. *Behav. Res. Methods Instrum.* 1:91–94

Cutting JE, Kozlowski LT. 1977. Recognition of friends by their walk: gait perception without familiarity cues. *Bull. Psychon. Soc.* 9:353–56

Cutting JE, Moore C, Morrison R. 1988. Masking the motions of human gait. *Percept. Psychophys.* 44:339–47

Darwin C. 1872. *The Expression of the Emotions in Man and Animals.* London: John Murray

Decety J, Grèzes J. 1999. Neural mechanisms subserving the perception of human actions. *Trends Cogn. Sci.* 3:172–78

Decety J, Grèzes J, Costes N, Perani D, Jeannerod M, et al. 1997. Brain activity during observation of actions: influence of action content and subject's strategy. *Brain* 120:1763–77

Dittrich WH. 1993. Action categories and the perception of biological motion. *Perception* 22:15–22

Dittrich WH, Lea SEG, Barrett J, Gurr PR. 1998. Categorization of natural movements by pigeons: visual concept discrimination and biological motion. *J. Exp. Anal. Behav.* 70:281–99

Dittrich WH, Troscianko T, Lea SEG, Morgan D. 1996. Perception of emotion from dynamic point-light displays represented in dance. *Perception* 25:727–38

Downing P, Jiang Y, Shuman M, Kanwisher N. 2001. A cortical area selective for visual processing of the human body. *Science* 293:2470–73

Fani L, Prasad S, Harber K, Shiffrar M. 2005. Recognizing people from their movements. *J. Exp. Psychol.: Hum. Percept. Perform.* 31:210–20

Felleman DJ, van Essen DC. 1991. Distributed hierarchical processing in the primate cerebral cortex. *Cereb. Cortex* 1:1–47

Fogassi L, Ferrari PF, Gesierich B, Rozzi S, Chersi F, Rizzolatti G. 2005. Parietal lobe: from action organization to intention understanding. *Science* 308:662–67

Fox R, McDaniel C. 1982. The perception of biological motion by human infants. *Science* 218:486–87

Frith CD, Frith U. 1999. Interacting minds—a biological basis. *Science* 286:1692–95

Fujimoto K. 2003. Motion induction from biological motion. *Perception* 32:1273–77

Funk M, Shiffrar M, Brugger P. 2005. Hand movement observation by individuals born without hands: phantom limb experience constrains visual limb perception. *Exp. Brain Res.* 164:341–46

Gallagher HL, Frith CD. 2004. Dissociable neural pathways for the perception and recognition of expressive and instrumental gestures. *Neuropsychologia* 42:1725–36

Giese MA, Lappe M. 2002. Measurement of generalization fields for the recognition of biological motion. *Vis. Res.* 42:1847–58

Giese MA, Poggio T. 2003. Neural mechanisms for the recognition of biological movements. *Nat. Rev. Neurosci.* 4:179–92

Gil-da-Costa R, Braun A, Lopes M, Hauser MD, Carson RE, et al. 2004. Toward an evolutionary perspective on conceptual representation: species-specific calls activate visual and affective processing systems in the macaque. *Proc. Natl. Acad. Sci. USA* 101:17516–21

Gilden DL, Proffitt DR. 1994. Heuristic judgment of mass ratio in two-body collisions. *Percept. Psychophys.* 56:708–20

Gilmore GC, Wenk HE, Baylor LA, Stuve TA. 1992. Motion perception and aging. *Psychol. Aging* 7:654–60

Grèzes J, Costes N, Decety J. 1998. Top-down effect of strategy on the perception of human biological motion: a PET investigation. *Cogn. Neuropsychol.* 15:553–82

Grèzes J, Frith CD, Passingham RE. 2004. Inferring false beliefs from the actions of oneself and others: an fMRI study. *NeuroImage* 21:744–50

Grossman E, Donnelly M, Price R, Pickens D, Morgan V, et al. 2000. Brain areas involved in perception of biological motion. *J. Cogn. Neurosci.* 12:711–20

Grossman ED. 2006. Evidence for a network of brain areas involved in perception of biological motion. In *Human Body Perception from the Inside Out*, ed. G Knoblich, IM Thornton, M Grosjean, M Shiffrar, pp. 361–84. New York: Oxford Univ. Press

Grossman ED, Battelli L, Pascual-Leone A. 2005. Repetitive TMS over STSp disrupts perception of biological motion. *Vis. Res.* 45:2847–53

Grossman ED, Blake R. 1999. Perception of coherent motion, biological motion and form-from-motion under dim-light conditions. *Vis. Res.* 39:3721–27

Grossman ED, Blake R. 2001. Brain activity evoked by inverted and imagined biological motion. *Vis. Res.* 41(10–11):1475–82

Grossman ED, Blake R. 2002. Brain areas active during visual perception of biological motion. *Neuron* 35:1157–65

Grossman ED, Blake R, Kim CY. 2004. Learning to see biological motion: brain activity parallels behavior. *J. Cogn. Neurosci.* 16:1669–79

Gunns RE, Johnston L, Hudson S. 2002. Victim selection and kinematics: a point-light investigation of vulnerability to attack. *J. Nonverbal Behav.* 26:129–58

Hamilton A, Wolpert DM, Frith U. 2004. Your own action influences how you perceive another person's action. *Curr. Biol.* 14:493–98

Hamilton A, Wolpert DM, Frith U, Grafton ST. 2006. Where does your own action influence your perception of another person's action in the brain? *NeuroImage* 29:524–35

Hari R, Forss N, Avikainen S, Kirveskari W, Salenius S, Rizzolatti G. 1998. Activation of the human primary motor cortex during action observation: a neuromagnetic study. *Proc. Natl. Acad. Sci. USA* 95:15061–65

Hasson U, Nir Y, Levy I, Fuhrmann G, Malach R. 2004. Intersubject synchronization of cortical activity during natural vision. *Science* 303:1634–40

Haxby JV, Hoffman EA, Gobbini MI. 2000. The distributed human neural system for face perception. *Trends Cogn. Sci.* 4:223–33

Heberlein AS, Adolphs R, Tranel D, Damasio H. 2004. Cortical regions for judgments of emotions and personality traits from point-light walkers. *J. Cogn. Neurosci.* 16:1143–58

Heptulla-Chatterjee S, Freyd J, Shiffrar M. 1996. Configural processing in the perception of apparent biological motion. *J. Exp. Psychol.: Hum. Percept. Perform.* 22:916–29

Hietanen JK, Perrett DI. 1996. Motion sensitive cells in the macaque superior temporal polysensory area: response discrimination between self-generated and externally generated pattern motion. *Behav. Brain Res.* 76:155–67

Hill H, Johnston A. 2001. Categorizing sex and identity from biological motion of faces. *Curr. Biol.* 11:880–85

Hill H, Jonno Y, Johnston A. 2003. Comparing solid-body with point-light animations. *Perception* 32:561–66

Hirai M, Fukushima H, Haraki K. 2003. An event-related potentials study of biological motion perception in humans. *Neurosci. Lett.* 344:41–44

Hirai M, Hiraki K. 2005. An event-related potentials study of biological motion perception in human infants. *Cogn. Brain Res.* 22:301–4

Hiris E, Humphrey D, Stout A. 2005a. Temporal properties in masking of biological motion. *Percept. Psychophys.* 67:435–43

Hiris E, Krebeck A, Edmonds J, Stout A. 2005b. What learning to see arbitrary motion tells us about biological motion perception. *J. Exp. Psychol.: Hum. Percept. Perform.* 31:1096–106

Hobson RP, Ouston J, Lee A. 1988. Emotion recognition in autism: coordinating faces and voices. *Psychol. Med.* 18:911–23

Hodgins JK, O'Brien JF, Tumblin J. 1998. Perception of human motion with different geometrical models. *IEEE Trans. Vis. Comput. Graph.* 4:307–17

Hoffman DD, Flinchbaugh BE. 1982. The interpretation of biological motion. *Biol. Cybern.* 42:195–204

Hommel B, Musseler J, Aschersleben G, Prinz W. 2001. The theory of event coding (TEC): a framework for perception and action planning. *Behav. Brain Sci.* 24:849–937

Howard RJ, Brammer M, Wright I, Woodruff PW, Bullmore ET, Zeki S. 1996. A direct demonstration of functional specialization within motion-related visual and auditory cortex of the human brain. *Curr. Biol.* 6:1015–19

Iacoboni M, Lieberman M, Knowlton B, Molnar-Szakacs I, Moritz M, et al. 2004. Watching social interactions produces dorsomedial prefrontal and medial parietal BOLD fMRI signal increases compared to a resting baseline. *NeuroImage* 21:1167–73

Ikeda H, Blake R, Watanabe K. 2005. Eccentric perception of biological motion is unscalably poor. *Vis. Res.* 45:1935–43

Jacob P, Jeannerod M. 2005. The motor theory of social cognition: a critique. *Trends Cogn. Sci.* 9:21–25

Jacobs A, Pinto J, Shiffrar M. 2004. Experience, context, and the visual perception of human movement. *J. Exp. Psychol.: Hum. Percept. Perform.* 30:822–35

Jacobs A, Shiffrar M. 2005. Walking perception by walking observers. *J. Exp. Psychol.: Hum. Percept. Perform.* 31:157–69

Jeannerod M. 2004. Visual and action cues contribute to self-other distinction. *Nat. Neurosci.* 7:422–23

Johansson G. 1973. Visual perception of biological motion and a model for its analysis. *Percept. Psychophys.* 14:195–204

Jokisch D, Daum I, Suchan B, Troje NF. 2005b. Structural encoding and recognition of biological motion: evidence from event-related potentials and source analysis. *Behav. Brain Res.* 157:195–204

Jokisch D, Troje NF. 2003. Biological motion as a cue for the perception of size. *J. Vis.* 3:252–64

Jokisch D, Troje NF, Koch B, Schwarz M, Daum I. 2005a. Differential involvement of the cerebellum in biological and coherent motion perception. *Eur. J. Neurosci.* 21:3439–46

Kanwisher N. 2000. Domain specificity in face perception. *Nat. Neurosci.* 3:759–63

Kanwisher N, McDermott J, Chun MM. 1997. The fusiform face area: a module in human extrastriate cortex specialized for face perception. *J. Neurosci.* 17:4302–11

Kilner JM, Paulignan Y, Blakemore SJ. 2003. An interference effect of observed biological movement on action. *Curr. Biol.* 13:522–25

Kim J, Doop ML, Blake R, Park S. 2005. Impaired visual recognition of biological motion in schizophrenia. *Schizophr. Res.* 77:299–307

Knoblich G, Flach R. 2001. Predicting the effects of actions: interactions of perception and action. *Psychol. Sci.* 2:467–72

Knoblich G, Thornton IM, Grosjean M, Shiffrar M, eds. 2006. *Human Body Perception from the Inside Out.* New York: Oxford Univ. Press

Kourtzi Z, Shiffrar M. 1999. Dynamic representations of human body movement. *Perception* 28:49–62

Kozlowski LT, Cutting JE. 1977. Recognizing the sex of a walker from a dynamic point light display. *Percept. Psychophys.* 21:575–80

Kozlowski LT, Cutting JE. 1978. Recognizing the gender of walkers from point-lights mounted on ankles: some second thoughts. *Percept. Psychophys.* 23:459

Kroustallis B. 2004. Biological motion: an exercise in bottom-up vs top-down processing. *J. Mind Behav.* 25:57–74

LaBar KS, Crupain M, Voyvodic J, McCarthy G. 2003. Dynamic perception of facial affect and identity in the human brain. *Cereb. Cortex* 13:1023–33

Lakin JL, Chartrand TL. 2003. Using nonconscious behavioral mimicry to create affiliation and rapport. *Psychol. Sci.* 14:334–39

Lange J, Lappe M. 2006. A model of biological motion perception from configural form cues. *J. Neurosci.* 26:2894–906

Loula F, Prasad S, Harber K, Shiffrar M. 2005. Recognizing people from their movement. *J. Exp. Psychol.: Hum. Percept. Perform.* 31:210–20

Lu H, Tjan B, Liu Z. 2006. Shape recognition alters sensitivity in stereoscopic depth discrimination. *J. Vis.* 6:75–86

Ma Y, Paterson HM, Pollick FE. 2006. A motion-capture library for the study of identity, gender, and emotion perception from biological motion. *Behav. Res. Methods* 38:134–41

Marey EJ. 1884. Analyse cinématique de la marche [chronophotograph]. *C.R. Séances Acad. Sci.*, p. 2

Mass JB, Johansson G, Janson G, Runeson S. 1971. Motion perception I and II [film]. Boston: Houghton Mifflin

Mather G, Murdoch L. 1994. Gender discrimination in biological motion displays based on dynamic cues. *Proc. R. Soc. Lond. B Biol. Sci.* 258:273–79

Mather G, Radford K, West S. 1992. Low level visual processing of biological motion. *Proc. R. Soc. Lond. B Biol. Sci.* 249:149–55

Mather G, West S. 1993. Recognition of animal locomotion from dynamic point-light delays. *Perception* 22:759–66

Michels L, Lappe M, Vaina LM. 2005. Visual areas involved in the perception of human movement from dynamic form analysis. *NeuroReport* 16:1037–41

Montepare JM, Zebrowitz-McArthur LA. 1988. Impressions of people created by age-related qualities of their gaits. *J. Personal. Soc. Psychol.* 55:547–56

Morris JP, Pelphrey K, McCarthy G. 2005. Regional brain activation evoked when approaching a virtual human on a virtual walk. *J. Cogn. Neurosci.* 17:1744–52

Neri P, Morrone MC, Burr D. 1998. Seeing biological motion. *Nature* 395:894–96

Norman JF, Payton SM, Long JR, Hawkes LM. 2004. Aging and perception of biological motion. *Psychol. Aging* 19:219–25

Norman JF, Ross HE, Hawkes LM, Long JR. 2003. Aging and the perception of speed. *Perception* 32:85–96

Omori E, Watanabe S. 1996. Discrimination of Johansson's stimuli in pigeons. *Int. J. Comp. Psychol.* 9:92

Oram MW, Perrett DI. 1994. Responses of anterior superior temporal polysensory (STPa) neurons to "biological motion" stimuli. *J. Cogn. Neurosci.* 6:99–116

Oram MW, Perrett DI. 1996. Integration of form and motion in the anterior superior temporal polysensory area (STPa) of the macaque monkey. *J. Neurophysiol.* 76:109–29

O'Toole AJ, Roark DA, Abdi H. 2002. Recognizing moving faces: a psychological and neural synthesis. *Trends Cogn. Sci.* 6:261–66

Paccalin C, Jeannerod M. 2000. Changes in breathing during observation of effortful actions. *Brain Res.* 862:194–200

Pavlova M, Birbaumer N, Sokolov A. 2006. Attentional modulation of cortical neuromagnetic gamma response to biological motion. *Cereb. Cortex* 16:321–27

Pavlova M, Krägeloh-Mann I, Sokolov A, Birbaumer N. 2001. Recognition of point-light biological motion displays by young children. *Perception* 30:925–33

Pavlova M, Lutzenberger W, Sokolov A, Birbaumer N. 2004. Dissociable cortical processing of recognizable and nonrecognizable biological movement: analyzing gamma MEG activity. *Cereb. Cortex* 14:181–88

Pavlova M, Sokolov A. 2000. Orientation specificity in biological motion perception. *Percept. Psychophys.* 62:889–98

Pavlova M, Sokolov A, Birbaumer N, Krägeloh-Mann I. 2006. Biological motion processing in adolescents with early periventricular brain damage. *Neuropsychologia* 44:586–93

Pavlova M, Staudt M, Sokolov A, Birbaumer N, Krägeloh-Mann I. 2003. Perception and production of biological movement in patients with early periventricular brain lesions. *Brain* 126:692–701

Peelen MV, Downing PE. 2005. Selectivity for the human body in the fusiform gyrus. *J. Neurophys.* 93:603–8

Peelen MV, Wiggett AJ, Downing PE. 2006. Patterns of fMRI activity dissociate overlapping functional brain areas that respond to biological motion. *Neuron* 49:815–22

Pelphrey KA, Mitchell TV, McKeown MJ, Goldstein J, Allison T, McCarthy G. 2003. Brain activity evoked by the perception of human walking: controlling for meaningful coherent motion. *J. Neurosci.* 23:6819–25

Perrett DI, Rolls ET, Caan W. 1982. Visual neurons responsive to faces in the monkey temporal cortex. *Exp. Brain Res.* 47:329–42

Perrett DI, Smith P, Mistlin A, Chitty A, Head A, et al. 1985. Visual analysis of body movements by neurons in the temporal cortex of the macaque monkey: a preliminary report. *Behav. Brain Res.* 16:153–70

Peuskens H, Vanrie J, Verfaillie K, Orban GA. 2005. Specificity of regions processing biological motion. *Eur. J. Neurosci.* 21:2864–75

Pinto J. 2006. Developing body representations: a review of infants' responses to biological-motion displays. In *Human Body Perception from the Inside Out*, ed. G Knoblich, IM Thornton, M Grosjean, M Shiffrar, pp. 305–22. New York: Oxford Univ. Press

Pinto J, Shiffrar M. 1999. Subconfigurations of the human form in the perception of biological motion displays. *Acta Psychol.* 102:293–318

Pollick FE, Fidopiastis C, Braden V. 2001a. Recognising the style of spatially exaggerated tennis serves. *Perception* 30:323–38

Pollick FE, Kay JW, Heim K, Stringer R. 2005. Gender recognition from point-light walkers. *J. Exp. Psychol.: Hum. Percept. Perform.* 31:1247–65

Pollick FE, Paterson HM, Bruderlin A, Sanford AJ. 2001b. Perceiving affect from arm movement. *Cognition* 82:B51–61

Poom L, Olsson H. 2002. Are mechanisms for perception of biological motion different from mechanisms for perception of nonbiological motion? *Percept. Mot. Skills* 95:1301–10

Prinz W. 1997. Perception and action planning. *Eur. J. Cogn. Psychol.* 9:129–54

Puce A, Allison T, Bentin S, Gore JC, McCarthy G. 1998. Temporal cortex activation in humans viewing eye and mouth movements. *J. Neurosci.* 18:2188–99

Puce A, Perrett D. 2003. Electrophysiology and brain imaging of biological motion. *Philos. Trans. R. Soc. Lond. B Biol. Sci.* 358:435–45

Raos V, Evangeliou MN, Savaki HE. 2004. Observation of action: grasping with the mind's hand. *NeuroImage* 23:193–201

Reed CL, Farah MJ. 1995. The psychological reality of the body schema: a test with normal participants. *J. Exp. Psychol.: Hum. Percept. Perform.* 21:334–43

Regolin L, Tommasi L, Vallortigara G. 2000. Visual perception of biological motion in newly hatched chicks as revealed by an imprinting procedure. *Anim. Cogn.* 3:53–60

Reid VM, Hoehl S, Striano T. 2006. The perception of biological motion by infants: an event-related potential study. *Neurosci. Lett.* 395:211–14

Rizzolatti G, Craighero L. 2004. The mirror-neuron system. *Annu. Rev. Neurosci.* 27:169–92

Rizzolatti G, Fogassi L, Gallese V. 2001. Neurophysiological mechanisms underlying the understanding and imitation of action. *Nat. Rev. Neurosci.* 2:661–70

Rosenblum LD, Johnson JA, Saldana HM. 1996. Point-light facial displays enhance comprehension of speech in noise. *J. Speech Hear. Res.* 39:1159–70

Runeson S, Frykholm G. 1981. Visual perception of lifted weight. *J. Exp. Psychol.: Hum. Percept. Perform.* 7:733–40

Runeson S, Frykholm G. 1983. Kinematic specification of dynamics as an informational bias for person-and-action perception: expectation, gender recognition, and deceptive intent. *J. Exp. Psychol. Gen.* 112:585–615

Santi A, Servos P, Vatikiotis-Bateson E, Kuratate T, Munhall K. 2003. Perceiving biological motion: dissociating visible speech from walking. *J. Cogn. Neurosci.* 15:800–9

Saxe R, Xiao DK, Kovacs G, Perrett DI, Kanwisher N. 2004. A region of right posterior superior temporal sulcus responds to observed intentional actions. *Neuropsychologia* 42:1435–46

Saygin AP, Wilson SM, Hagler DJ, Bates E, Sereno MI. 2004. Point-light biological motion perception activates human premotor cortex. *J. Neurosci.* 24:6181–88

Schenk T, Zihl J. 1997. Visual motion perception after brain damage: II. Deficits in form-from-motion perception. *Neuropsychologia* 35:1299–310

Schürmann M, Hesse MD, Stephan KE, Saarela M, Zilles K, et al. 2005. Yearning to yawn: the neural basis of contagious yawning. *NeuroImage* 24:1260–64

Sekuler R, Hutman LP, Owsley CJ. 1980. Human aging and spatial vision. *Science* 209:1255–56

Shiffrar M. 1994. When what meets where. *Curr. Dir. Psychol. Sci.* 3:96–100

Shiffrar M. 2006. Body-based views of the world: an introduction to body representations. In *Human Body Perception from the Inside Out*, ed. G Knoblich, IM Thornton, M Grosjean, M Shiffrar, pp. 135–46. New York: Oxford Univ. Press

Shiffrar M, Freyd JJ. 1990. Apparent motion of the human body. *Psychol. Sci.* 1:257–64

Shiffrar M, Lichtey L, Heptulla C. 1997. The perception of biological motion across apertures. *Percept. Psychophys.* 59:51–59

Shiffrar M, Pinto J. 2002. The visual analysis of bodily motion. In *Common Mechanisms in Perception and Action: Attention and Performance, Vol. XIX*, ed. W Prinz, B Hommel, pp. 381–99. Oxford: Oxford Univ. Press

Shim J, Carlton LG, Kim J. 2004. Estimation of lifted weight and produced effort through perception of point-light display. *Perception* 33:277–91

Sinha P, Poggio T. 1996. The role of learning in 3-D form perception. *Nature* 384:460–63

Stevens JA, Fonlupt P, Shiffrar M, Decety J. 2000. New aspects of motion perception: selective neural encoding of apparent human movements. *NeuroReport* 11:109–15

Stoffregen TA, Flynn SB. 1994. Visual perception of support-surface deformability from human body kinematics. *Ecol. Psychol.* 6:33–64

Sumi S. 1984. Upside-down presentation of the Johansson moving light-spot pattern. *Perception* 13:283–86

Sumi S. 2000. Perception of point-light walker produced by eight lights attached to the back of the walker. *Swiss J. Psychol.* 59:126–32

Tadin D, Lappin JS, Blake R, Grossman ED. 2002. What constitutes an efficient reference frame for vision? *Nat. Neurosci.* 5:1010–15

Tai Y, Scherfler C, Brooks D, Sawamoto N, Castiello U. 2004. The human premotor cortex is "mirror" only for biological actions. *Curr. Biol.* 14:117–20

Thornton IM, Pinto J, Shiffrar M. 1998. The visual perception of human locomotion. *Cogn. Neuropsychol.* 15:535–52

Thornton IM, Rensink RA, Shiffrar M. 2002. Active versus passive processing of biological motion. *Perception* 31:837–53

Thornton IM, Vuong QC. 2004. Incidental processing of biological motion. *Curr. Biol.* 14:1084–89

Troje NF. 2002. Decomposing biological motion: a framework for analysis and synthesis of human gait patterns. *J. Vis.* 2:371–87

Troje NF. 2003. Reference frames for orientation anisotropies in face recognition and biological-motion perception. *Perception* 32:201–10

Troje NF, Westhoff C, Lavrov M. 2005. Person identification from biological motion: effects of structural and kinematic cues. *Percept. Psychophys.* 67:667–75

Ullman S. 1979. *The Interpretation of Visual Motion*. Cambridge: MIT Press

Vaina LM, Lemay M, Bienfang DC, Choi AY, Nakayama K. 1990. Intact "biological motion" and "structure from motion" perception in a patient with impaired motion mechanisms: a case study. *Vis. Neurosci.* 5:353–69

Vaina LM, Solomon J, Chowdhury S, Sinha P, Belliveau JW. 2001. Functional neuroanatomy of biological motion perception in humans. *Proc. Natl. Acad. Sci. USA* 98:11656–61

Valentine T. 1988. Upside-down faces: a review of the effect of inversion upon face recognition. *Br. J. Psychol.* 79(Pt. 4):471–91

Vanrie J, Verfaillie K. 2004. Perception of biological motion: a stimulus set of human point-light actions. *Behav. Res. Methods Instrum. Comput.* 36:625–29

Verfaillie K. 2000. Perceiving human locomotion: priming effects in direction discrimination. *Brain Cogn.* 44:192–213

Virji-Babul N, Kerns K, Zhou E, Kapur A, Shiffrar M. 2006. Perceptual-motor deficits in children with Down syndrome: implications for intervention. *Downs Syndr. Res. Pract.* 10:74–82

Viviani P. 2002. Motor competence in the perception of dynamic events: a tutorial. In *Common Mechanisms in Perception and Action: Attention and Performance, Vol. XIX*, ed. W Prinz, B Hommel, pp. 406–42. Oxford: Oxford Univ. Press

Viviani P, Stucchi N. 1992. Biological movements look uniform: evidence of motor-perceptual interactions. *J. Exp. Psychol.: Hum. Percept. Perform.* 18:603–23

Waiter GD, Williams JHG, Murray AD, Gilchrist A, Perrett DI, Whiten A. 2004. A voxel based investigation of brain structure in male adolescents with autistic spectrum disorder. *Neuroimage* 22:619–25

Walk RD, Homan CP. 1984. Emotion and dance in dynamic light displays. *Bull. Psychon. Soc.* 22:437–40

Warren WHJ, Blackwell AW, Morris MW. 1989. Age differences in perceiving the direction of self-motion from optical flow. *J. Gerontol.* 44:P147–53

Watson TL, Pearson J, Clifford CWG. 2004. Perceptual grouping of biological motion promotes binocular rivalry. *Curr. Biol.* 14:1670–74

Webb JA, Aggarwal JK. 1982. Structure from motion of rigid and jointed objects. *Artif. Intell.* 19:107–30

Wheaton KJ, Pipingas A, Silberstein RB, Puce A. 2001. Human neural responses elicited to observing the actions of others. *Vis. Neurosci.* 18:401–6

Wheaton KJ, Thompson J, Syngeniotis A, Abbott D, Puce A. 2004. Viewing the motion of human body parts activates different regions of premotor, temporal, and parietal cortex. *NeuroImage* 22:277–88

Wilson M, Knoblich G. 2005. The case for motor involvement in perceiving conspecifics. *Psychol. Bull.* 131:460–73

Winston JS, Strange BA, O'Doherty J, Dolan RJ. 2002. Automatic and intentional brain responses during evaluation of trustworthiness of faces. *Nat. Neurosci.* 5:277–83

Wood JM, Tyrrell RA, Carberry TP. 2005. Limitations in drivers' ability to recognize pedestrians at night. *Hum. Factors* 47:644–53

Zacks JM, Braver TS, Sheridan MA, Donaldson DI, Snyder AZ, et al. 2001. Human brain activity time-locked to perceptual event boundaries. *Nat. Neurosci.* 4:651–55

Visual Object Recognition: Do We Know More Now Than We Did 20 Years Ago?

Jessie J. Peissig and Michael J. Tarr

Department of Cognitive and Linguistic Sciences, Brown University, Providence, Rhode Island 02912; email: jpeissig@fullerton.edu, Michael_tarr@brown.edu

Annu. Rev. Psychol. 2007. 58:75–96

First published online as a Review in Advance on August 11, 2006

The *Annual Review of Psychology* is online at http://psych.annualreviews.org

This article's doi: 10.1146/annurev.psych.58.102904.190114

Key Words

structural descriptions, view-based, neural codes, visual features, category-selectivity

Abstract

We review the progress made in the field of object recognition over the past two decades. Structural-description models, making their appearance in the early 1980s, inspired a wealth of empirical research. Moving to the 1990s, psychophysical evidence for view-based accounts of recognition challenged some of the fundamental assumptions of structural-description theories. The 1990s also saw increased interest in the neurophysiological study of high-level visual cortex, the results of which provide some constraints on how objects may be represented. By 2000, neuroimaging arose as a viable means for connecting neurons to behavior. One of the most striking fMRI results has been category selectivity, which provided further constraints for models of object recognition. Despite this progress, the field is still faced with the challenge of developing a comprehensive theory that integrates this ever-increasing body of results and explains how we perceive and recognize objects.

Contents

INTRODUCTION

At a functional level, visual object recognition is at the center of understanding how we think about what we see. Object identification is a primary end state of visual processing and a critical precursor to interacting with and reasoning about the world. Thus, the question of how we recognize objects is both perceptual and cognitive, tying together what are often treated as separate disciplines. At the outset, we should state that in spite of the best efforts of many to understand this process, we believe that the field still has a long way to go toward a comprehensive account of visual object recognition. At the same time, we do believe that progress has been made over the past 20 years. Indeed, visual object recognition is a poster child for a multidisciplinary approach to the study of the mind and brain: Few domains have utilized such a wide range of methods, including neurophysiology, neuroimaging, psychophysics, and computational theory. To illustrate this progress, we review the state of the art circa 1985 and contrast this with the state of the art today (2006). We note that some problems have been solved, some have evolved, some have become extinct, and new ones have arisen.

Although there were clearly many neuroscientific and behavioral antecedents (e.g., Konorski 1967, Rock 1973, Selfridge 1959) to Marr & Nishihara's (1978; popularized in Marr's 1982 book) seminal paper, it, more than any other single publication, is arguably the spark for what we think of as the modern study of visual object recognition. Interestingly, although it was heavily motivated by neuropsychological data and behavioral intuition, Marr and Nishihara's theory was purely computational, with no attempt at empirical validation. Colleagues of Marr took a similar approach, identifying in principle problems with then state-of-the-art theories of recognition, but presenting little in the way of concrete data to validate, invalidate, or extend such theories (Pinker 1984).

One reason for this hesitancy to step into the fray may have been the enormous level of flexibility exhibited by the primate visual system—an issue that remains with us today and challenges all would-be accounts of recognition. If anything, the more we have learned about our recognition abilities, the more daunting the problem has become. For example, results regarding the incredible rapidity with which successful recognition is achieved have imposed significant new constraints on current theories. Consider the study by Thorpe et al. (1996), in which they allowed observers only 20 ms to determine whether an animal was present in a natural scene. Event-related potentials (ERPs) measured during performance of this task reveal, approximately 150 ms after stimulus onset, a significant difference between the neural responses for trials in which there is an animal and trials in which there is not. Such data indicate that the primate visual system processes complex natural scenes quite rapidly and with only the briefest of inputs. Interestingly, this result and many more from the past two decades have not been integrated into any extant theory. Thus, although we have made significant empirical progress, as discussed in the next two sections, theoretical models have lagged behind. In future model building, it behooves the field to consider the breadth of psychophysical, neurophysiological, neuropsychological, and neuroimaging data that form the basis of this progress.

CIRCA 1985—STRUCTURAL DESCRIPTION MODELS

Marr & Nishihara (1978) introduced the idea of part-based structural representations based on three-dimensional volumes and their spatial relations. In particular, they proposed that object parts come to be mentally represented as generalized cones (or cylinders) and objects as hierarchically organized structural models relating the spatial positions of parts to one another. To some extent, this proposal was motivated by 1970s-era models from computer vision and computer graphics, but also by the desire of Marr and Nishihara to have their scheme satisfy several computational criteria. First, representations should be accessible. That is, the necessary information to recover a representation in a computationally efficient manner should be available in the visual image. Second, representations should be unique. That is, objects that seem psychologically different from one another should be representationally discriminable from one another. At the same time, representations should be generic, so that the same representational predicates are sufficient to capture the wide variability of objects we encounter. Third, representations should be both stable and sensitive. That is, the wide range of two-dimensional images generated by a single object seen under different combinations of object pose, configuration, and lighting should map to a common object representation (i.e., it is the same object), but the representation should also be sufficiently detailed to make discriminations between visually similar objects (i.e., those are two different objects).

One of the most challenging issues for Marr and Nishihara was the fact that, when rotated in depth, three-dimensional objects change their two-dimensional retinal projection (the problem of viewpoint invariance);

stable object representations require addressing this problem. Thus, in their theory, object parts encoded as generalized cones are represented in an object-centered manner, that is, in a coordinate system that decouples the orientation of the object from the position of the viewer. The significance of this assumption is that the same generalized cones can be recovered from the image regardless of the orientation of the object generating that image. Consequently, object recognition performance should be independent of both observer position and object orientation. Thus, at least for changes in viewing position—the most daunting problem in the eyes of Marr and Nishihara (and much of the field, as we discuss below)—the many-to-one mapping called for by the stability constraint is satisfied. Conversely, the sensitivity constraint is satisfied by two properties of the proposed representation. First, generalized cones—a two-dimensional cross-section of any shape swept along an axis of that shape—can capture an infinite number of part shapes. Clearly, such powerful representational units have the potential to discriminate between objects having only subtle shape differences. Second, these object parts are related to one another by metrically precise spatial relations at multiple scales. That is, a given representation can be refined down to the shape and configural details necessary to distinguish it from other objects of similar coarse shape. For example, two different faces might have subtly different relations between the angles of their noses and eyes as well as subtly different generalized cones representing the shapes of the noses. However, as mentioned above, Marr and Nishihara offered no empirical support for this model.

By far the most well-received structural-description model is recognition by components (RBC; Biederman 1985). RBC is quite similar to Marr and Nishihara's model, but has been refined in important ways. First and foremost is the psychophysical support for the model presented by Biederman (1985; Biederman & Cooper 1991, 1992; Biederman

RBC: recognition by components

& Gerhardstein 1993).[1] Second, Biederman included two important properties to make the model more tractable: (*a*) a restricted set of three-dimensional volumes to represent part shape—Geons—defined by properties, including whether the edge is straight or curved, whether the object is symmetrical or not, if the cross-section is of constant size or expands or contracts, and whether the axis is straight or curved;[2] and (*b*) a single layer of qualitatively specified spatial relations between parts—for example, "above" or "beside." At the same time, Biederman retained the idea of view-invariant representations, but modified it to be based on three-dimensional shape properties that project to stable local contour configurations—so-called viewpoint-invariant properties (Lowe 1985). Critically, Geons are specified by the co-occurrence of multiple instances of these properties in the image. For example, a brick Geon might project to three arrow junctions, three L junctions, and a Y junction that remain visible over many different rotations in depth. RBC assumes that these sets of contour features are identified in the image and used as the basis for inferring the presence of one of the 30 or so Geons that constitute RBC's building blocks for representing part shapes. Because these features are themselves viewpoint invariant (up to occlusion), the recovery of parts is also viewpoint invariant. Object representations are simply assemblies of such parts—deemed "Geon-structural descriptions," and are constructed by inferring the qualitative spatial relations between recovered parts. Because these relations are viewpoint invariant across rotations in depth, the recognition process is likewise viewpoint invariant (but not for picture-plane rotations; e.g., the relation

"above" is perturbed when an object is turned upside down).

A final issue raised by Biederman in the RBC model is the default level of object recognition. That is, there is really no claim that all of object recognition is accomplished as outlined above. Rather, Biederman suggests that typical object recognition tasks occur at the basic level (Rosch et al. 1976) or entry level (Jolicoeur et al. 1984). More specifically, the first and fastest label applied to most objects is their category label (e.g., bird), the exception being visually idiosyncratic category exemplars (e.g., penguin). RBC only explains how observers recognize objects at this level, making no attempt to account for how we arrive at either superordinate labels (e.g., animal—probably more cognitive than visual) or subordinate labels (e.g., species labels such as fairy-wren or individual labels such as Tweety Bird). Thus, even given RBC as a plausible model of basic-level recognition circa 1985, there is no particular theory for how a wide variety of visual recognition tasks are accomplished.

So Where are We?

The late 1970s and early 1980s harbored significant changes in how the field thought about the mind and brain. In particular, accounts of recognition and categorization tasks shifted from purely cognitive problems to, at least in part, perceptual problems. Shepard & Cooper's (1982) and Kosslyn's (1980) empirical investigations into mental imagery brought home the idea that vision is more than an input system. That is, considerable mental work is accomplished before we ever invoke symbolic modes of processing (Fodor 1975) or semantics. Building on this transformation, theorists such as Marr and Biederman formulated theories of visual recognition that postulated high-level visual representations for recognition and categorization. Their models reflected the emerging bodies of both empirical data and work in computational vision. The elder author of this article remembers the excitement

---

[1] Although the bulk of these results were published during the early 1990s, similar empirical designs and results are outlined in the original 1985 paper, as well as in several technical reports.

[2] Geons constitute a highly restricted subset of generalized cones.

surrounding this time—solutions to problems as complex as visual object recognition were just around the corner (e.g., Pinker 1984).

At the same time, this excitement was tempered by clear gaps in knowledge, not the least of which was the relatively small amount of behavioral and neuroscientific data on how humans and other primates actually recognize objects. Although hindsight is 20/20, it appears that many of us underestimated both the extreme complexity of cortical areas past V4 (Van Essen 1985), the flexibility and complexity of the visual recognition tasks we routinely solve, and the computational intricacies of building an artificial vision system. In the sections below, we review some, but certainly not all, of the results that emerged from 1985 to present—not in small part due to the excitement generated during these seminal years.

CIRCA 1990—VIEW-BASED MODELS

As discussed above, one of the core characteristics (and appeals) of structural-description models is their viewpoint invariance. Such models predict that faced with a novel view of a familiar object, observers should be able to recognize it and should do so with no additional cost.[3] That is, response times and errors should be equivalent regardless of viewpoint. Interestingly, despite being one of the core tenets of these models, this assumption had not been tested. This omission may have been in part due to the strong intuition we have that object recognition is effortless even when faced with novel viewing conditions. Even Shepard & Cooper (1982), who ex-

plored extensively the nature of mental rotation in making handedness judgments, argued on logical grounds that this viewpoint-dependent process was not used for object recognition.

At nearly the same time that structural-description models became popular, several groups undertook empirical studies of invariance in visual object recognition.[4] Jolicoeur (1985) simply asked observers to view picture-plane misoriented line drawings of common objects and then to name them as quickly as possible. He found that the time to name a given object was related to how far it was rotated from the upright, revealing a systematic response pattern similar to that found by Shepard and Cooper. However, Jolicoeur also found that this effect was relatively small and diminished quite rapidly with repeated presentations of the objects. Thus, it remained an open question as to whether the effect was due to viewpoint-dependent representations or to more transient viewpoint-dependent processes elicited by the task. Building on this ambiguity, Tarr & Pinker (1989) argued that the critical question was not how observers recognize familiar objects—which potentially had already been encountered in multiple viewpoints—but rather how observers recognize novel objects when viewpoint has been controlled during learning.

Tarr & Pinker (1989) studied this proposal by teaching observers to name several novel shapes appearing at select orientations. They found that observers exhibited a significant cost—in both response times and error rates—when recognizing trained shapes in new orientations and that these costs were systematically related to the distance from a trained view. Interestingly, the pattern looked a good deal like

---

[3]In Marr and Nishihara's model, this prediction is predicated on the successful recovery of the axes and cross sections describing the generalized cones representing parts. In Biederman's model, the same prediction is predicated on the successful recovery of the same Geons from different viewpoints—due to self-occlusions within objects, some rotations in depth will obscure Geons that are part of the representation; in such instances, recognition will become viewpoint dependent.

---

[4]This increased interest was of course due to the theoretical excitement discussed above. However, it also may have been spurred on in part by the new availability of desktop personal computers (PCs) that were sufficiently powerful to both display images and to record response times (the first IBM PC appeared in 1981 and the first Apple Macintosh™ in 1984).

that seen in mental rotation tasks. These and related results were taken as powerful evidence for viewpoint-dependent object representations—sometimes called views—and the use of a continuous mental transformation process to align images of objects in novel viewpoints with familiar views in visual memory (e.g., Shepard & Cooper 1982, Ullman 1989). Bolstering these claims, Tarr (1995) found similar results for three-dimensional objects rotated in depth. That is, the same relationship between familiar and unfamiliar viewpoints holds, even when depth rotation changes the visible surfaces in the image.

More recent results suggest that the viewpoint dependencies seen in object recognition tasks do not arise as a consequence of mental transformation processes. In a study that demonstrates how neuroimaging can inform functional models, Gauthier et al. (2002) explored whether viewpoint-dependent object recognition and viewpoint-dependent handedness judgments (i.e., mental rotation) recruit the same or overlapping neural substrates. Using fMRI, they found that localized regions of the dorsal pathway responded in a viewpoint-dependent manner during mental rotation tasks, while, in contrast, localized regions of the ventral pathway responded in a viewpoint-dependent manner during object recognition tasks. That is, although the behavioral data were nearly identical for the two tasks, the neural bases of the behaviors were qualitatively different, being subserved by entirely different brain areas. This finding strongly suggests that Tarr & Pinker's (1989, Tarr 1995) hypothesis regarding shared mechanisms for mental rotation and object recognition is incorrect. As such, alternative models as to how disparate views of the same object are matched must be considered.

The early 1990s not only saw several studies that supported the hypothesis that objects are represented in a viewpoint-dependent manner, but also offered new ideas as to how unfamiliar views are matched with familiar views. At the same time, these studies

helped to reinforce the overall picture of a significant role for viewpoint-dependent recognition processes (e.g., Lawson et al. 1994). Most notably, Poggio & Edelman (1990) developed both a computational framework and a supporting collection of empirical results (Bülthoff & Edelman 1992, Edelman & Bülthoff 1992) that reinforced the idea of view-based recognition. Their model offers one possible mechanism for matching inputs and representations without mental rotation, proposing that the similarity between input and memory is computed using a collection of radial basis functions, each centered on a meaningful feature in the image. Object representations are view-based in that they are encoded with respect to a particular set of viewing parameters, and matching such representations to novel views of known objects produces errors proportional to the dissimilarity between the two. Thus, larger rotations are likely to produce larger errors, but no mental transformation is used. Another important implication of their model is that similarity is computed with reference to all known views. Therefore, a novel view centered between two known views will be better recognized (interpolation in the model's representational space) as compared to a novel view an equivalent distance away from only one known view (extrapolation in the model's representational space). This model was tested by Bülthoff & Edelman (1992; also Edelman & Bülthoff 1992). Consistent with the specific predictions of the model, Bülthoff and Edelman found the best recognition performance for unfamiliar viewpoints between trained views; poorer performance for viewpoints outside of trained views, but along the same axis; and the poorest performance for viewpoints along the orthogonal axis.

Models based on principles similar to those originally proposed by Poggio and Edelman are still popular today (Riesenhuber & Poggio 1999). Lending empirical support to this framework, Jiang et al. (2006) used an fMRI adaptation paradigm to examine the neural responses to target faces and face morphs between the target face and a nontarget face. Consistent with similarity-based recognition models, they found that adaptation increased as the similarity between target faces and morphed faces increased, indicating a larger degree of overlap in the neural populations coding for the two stimuli.

Jiang et al. (2006) also computationally tested whether their exclusively feature-based model can account for recognition behaviors that appear to be configurally based. Surprisingly, they found that their model was sensitive to configural manipulations (e.g., Rotshtein et al. 2005). Thus, a simple view-dependent, featural model is able to account for a significant number of behavioral and neural findings. At the same time, the large majority of studies supporting this approach speak only to the issue of the nature of the features used in object representations, not to whether structural information, independent of the particular features, is used (Barenholtz & Tarr 2006). Put another way, demonstrations of viewpoint dependence only implicate viewpoint-dependent features; not how those features are related to one another. At the same time, the fact that feature-based models are able to produce configural effects does not rule out, in and of itself, the possibility that such effects are a consequence of structural information. In particular, although configural coding may be realized through larger view-based features (Zhang & Cottrell 2005), the same coding may take the form of explicit relations between features. In the end, it is unclear whether the large body of work focused on view-based models is compatible with, incompatible with, or just orthogonal to structural models of object representation such as RBC (Biederman 1985).

CIRCA 1995—WHAT'S HAPPENING IN THE BRAIN?

Well before most cognitive scientists were thinking about the problem, neurophysiologists were studying visual object recognition by mapping the responses of single neurons in primate visual cortex. In two landmark studies, Gross and colleagues (Gross & Bender 1969, Gross et al. 1972) reported that neurons in the inferotemporal (IT) cortex of macaques responded most strongly to complex visual stimuli, such as hands and faces. As a measure of the times, this result was met with great skepticism and it was years before the field accepted the idea of such strong stimulus selectivity for single neurons. Much of this conservatism stemmed from the fact that prior to this study, recordings from single units in the visual system typically employed simple stimuli, such as light spots and bars. Moreover, most recordings were made in early visual areas such as V1 and V2, not the higher-level regions investigated by Gross and Bender. Interestingly, Gross and Bender found that cells in these higher-level areas of IT showed very little response to simple stimuli, but great sensitivity to complex stimuli. The logical conclusion is that this and related areas of IT are critical to complex visual processing and, presumably, visual object recognition. As reviewed below, this study was the first of many to come, with neurophysiological results coming to play an important role in how we understand the object recognition process.

Before we discuss more recent results from neurophysiology, it is worth stepping back and considering some of the assumptions that make single-unit recording a viable tool for the study of visual object recognition. Because most neurophysiological results are based on the responses of single neurons, it is quite possible that years of neuron-by-neuron probing will reveal almost nothing. Consider a plausible neural architecture in which the representation of objects is wholly distributed: A good proportion of the neural population available for object representation participates in the encoding of each known object. Moreover, this particular population code is distributed across all of IT cortex, and active neurons are interleaved with inactive neurons. Such a coding scheme would render single-unit responses all but useless: The neural firing patterns produced by the perception and

IT: inferotemporal cortex

STS/AMTS:
superior temporal
sulcus/anterior
medial temporal
sulcus

recognition of different objects or object classes would mostly look alike. And when different patterns were found within the small populations recorded in most studies, they would not be particularly diagnostic relative to the overall code. Conversely, it is also possible that only a tiny proportion of the neural population available for object representation participates for any one object. In this case, a neuroscientist might die, still never having managed to find even one neuron selective for any of the particular subset of objects used as stimuli. Happily, neither extreme appears to hold. That is, neuroscientists find object- and class-selective visual neurons in short order— usually in about 10% to 20% of the neurons from which they record. At the same time, they do not find uniform selectivity; different objects produce different and consistent patterns of firing across the measured neural populations. These basic facts suggest a sparse, distributed code that, when uncovered by neurophysiology, is capable of providing constraint on how objects come to be both represented and recognized.

Gross and Bender's discovery of neuronal selectivity for complex stimuli eventually came to be the de facto model of how objects are processed in IT. For example, Perrett et al. (1984) proposed that IT is organized into anatomical groupings of neurons labeled as columns and minicolumns (one cell wide!) that encode for visually similar high-level features. A host of similar findings by Perrett and many other groups (e.g., Desimone et al. 1980; nice reviews are provided by Gross 1994 and Rodman 1994) helped paint a picture of IT as a highly organized structure in which single units appear to code for individual objects or object classes. Of course, such data were rightly taken only as evidence for an orderly cortex, not one in which single units uniquely code for specific objects (e.g., "grandmother" cells). At the same time, the actual neural code for objects seemed (and seems!) elusive. Familiar objects must be represented in the brain somewhere; thus, it is not surprising to find evidence for this. The

problem is that simply enumerating the selectivity of hundreds or even thousands of single units does not tell us much about how such exquisite selectivity arises in the first place or what role it plays in object recognition.

Studies exploring neural learning take us beyond such simplistic cortical mapping and give us some insight into one of the most salient characteristics of object recognition, its flexibility. In a study motivated by Bülthoff & Edelman's (1992) psychophysical results and Poggio & Edelman's (1990) model, Logothetis & Pauls (1995) trained monkeys to recognize paper clip and blob objects at a small number of specific viewpoints. Over the course of training, the experimenters added new views of the objects that were generated by rotations in depth. As with humans, behaviorally the monkeys showed better generalization to views that were closer to the trained, familiar views. Again similar to humans, further experience with these novel views eventually led the monkeys to exhibit invariant performance across a wide range of viewpoints. The questions at the neural level are, how did they accomplish generalization in the first place, and what did they learn to achieve invariance?

To address this question, Logothetis & Pauls (1995) recorded from IT neurons in superior temporal sulcus (STS) and anterior medial temporal sulcus (AMTS) while the monkeys were presented with the familiar objects in familiar viewpoints. About 10% of the neurons recorded from (71 out of 773) responded selectively to particular wire-frame objects at specific trained views. In contrast, they found only eight neurons (~1%) that responded to a specific object in a view-invariant manner. Critically, Logothetis and Pauls found no neurons that were preferentially selective for unfamiliar object views. Invariant recognition performance was apparently achieved by pooling across the generalization gradients of the neurons found to be selective for familiar views. The finding of view-tuned neurons is highly consistent with and provides a neural mechanism for the behaviorally based argument that observers represent objects at multiple viewpoints (Bülthoff & Edelman 1992, Tarr & Pinker 1989). That is, neural selectivity emerges as a consequence of specific visual experiences, whether these experiences be new objects or new views of familiar objects. Moreover, it does not appear that the primate visual system is "recovering" an invariant object representation. Rather, it is relying on the specific representation of many different examples to efficiently cover image space in a manner that supports robust generalization.

Although the results of Logothetis & Pauls (1995) are compelling, some groups voiced concern that overtraining with static, specific viewpoints of objects leads to idiosyncratic object representations that are more view-selective than one might expect to arise from real-world experiences where both observers and objects interact dynamically (the same critique may be applied to the majority of the human psychophysical findings on view sensitivity). To address this concern, Booth & Rolls (1998) recorded from single neurons in the STS of monkeys that had experienced novel objects by playing with them in their cages. However, actual neurophysiological recordings were done with a fixed observer and with static images depicting photographs of the objects at different viewpoints. Of the neurons that were recorded from, Booth and Rolls found that 49% (75 out of 153) responded to specific views and only 14% (21 out of 153) showed view-invariant responses. However, using an information theoretic analysis, they found that the combined firing rates of the view-invariant cells alone were sufficient to discriminate one object from another. That is, the pattern of firing rates across the population of 21 view-invariant neurons differed more for different objects than it did for different views of the same object. This discriminatory power was not feature dependent in that it was observed for different views of the same object that shared no visible features and for grayscale versions of the object images (e.g., discrimination was not based on color features). Critically, Booth and Rolls also demon-

strated that the view-invariant neurons were selective for the particular objects with which the monkeys had played and not for similar objects they had not previously seen. Thus, Booth and Rolls were able to both reinforce and elaborate on the results of Logothetis and Pauls. Specifically, view-invariant neurons are intermingled with view-tuned neurons, and it is theorized that the pooling of the responses of collections of the view-tuned neurons in the population enables invariance in the view-invariant neurons. Finally, such neurons appear capable of supporting recognition in the sense that their responses, considered together, were sufficient to discriminate one familiar object from another.

Further demonstrating the explanatory power of using neural population codes to represent objects, Perrett et al. (1998) demonstrated that collections of feature-selective neurons coding for different parts of an object produce, when their responses are considered together, patterns of viewpoint dependency in object recognition tasks. This finding is based on two facts: (a) each feature-sensitive neuron is highly viewpoint dependent, and (b) the overall rate at which the population will reach a response threshold sufficient for recognition is dependent on its cumulative responses. That is, recognition is a function of the similarity between known local features and their appearance in the input image. As such, the overall neural response pattern is consistent with that observed behaviorally in many different object recognition studies (e.g., Bülthoff & Edelman 1992, Tarr 1995), suggesting a neural basis for the similarity computations proposed by Poggio & Edelman (1990; also Riesenhuber & Poggio 1999).

Further evidence for population codes in the neural representation of objects comes from the work of Kobatake et al. (1998). As in the studies discussed above, a learning paradigm was used to examine how the selectivity of IT neurons in TE change with experience with novel objects. Monkeys were overtrained in a match-to-sample task with

28 simple two-dimensional shapes. Following this training, Kobatake et al. (1998) recorded the responses of IT neurons in five anesthetized monkeys: two trained with the shapes and three controls that had not seen the shapes. A total of 131 neurons were recorded from in the trained animals, while a total of 130 neurons were recorded from in the controls. Not surprisingly, Kobatake et al. (1998) found significantly more neurons selective for the familiar test shapes in the trained group as compared to the control group (although there were some neurons selective for the test shapes in this group as well). More interestingly, they found that the similarity distances between the shape-selective neurons—computed by placing the neural pattern best selective for each trained shape in a location in a high-dimensional response space equal to the total number of recorded neurons—were larger for the trained group as compared to the control. Such results provide additional constraints on how objects come to be coded in IT cortex: With experience, a larger population of neurons is likely to be selective for the familiar objects (a point we return to in the discussion of neuroimaging below), and the responses of these neurons are likely to become more selective (corresponding to larger distances in neural response-defined feature space).

A somewhat different approach to how neurons come to represent complex stimuli was developed by Sigala (2004, Sigala & Logothetis 2002). They trained monkeys to recognize diagrammatic drawings of faces or simple fish composed of separable features that could be systematically altered. For example, it was possible to change the eye height, eye separation, nose length, and mouth height of the faces. Likewise, the fish also had four changeable parameters: the shape of the dorsal fin, the tail, the ventral fins, and the mouth. For both sets, each parameter could independently have three different values. For this discrimination, two of the four parameters were task relevant (the remaining two parameters varied randomly), and maximal per-

formance required attending to the values of both relevant parameters simultaneously. Monkeys were trained to perform this classification task with 10 objects per stimulus set (fish or faces) and then were given the task of classifying 24 new objects, which were also instances of the two trained classes. Following this training regimen, Sigala recorded from anterior IT neurons while the monkeys performed the same categorization task. At issue is whether neural selectivity occurs at the level of the class, the object, or diagnostic features. Sigala (2004) found that a large number of the class-selective neurons responded differentially to at least one parameter value for both faces (45.8%) and fish (43.1%). Of those cells, a large percentage were selective only for those diagnostic parameters (i.e., not to class-irrelevant features; 72.7% for faces, 75% for the fish). Thus, although it is tempting to associate highly selective neural responses with the representation of complete objects, these data suggest that object-selective neurons in IT may be coding for particular task-relevant diagnostic features rather than for objects as a whole.

Some of the most striking evidence with regard to how object features are represented in IT comes from the work of Tanaka (1996). Recording within the TE region of IT, Tanaka uncovered a highly structured pattern of feature selectivity. These results were built on a novel method for determining the best stimulus for a given neuron. Tanaka used an image-reduction technique on a neuron-by-neuron basis to determine which combination of minimal image features maintains the same firing rate as that measured in response to a complex object image for which a given neuron is preferential. These single-neuron object preferences were established by rapidly presenting a large number of common objects to anesthetized monkeys. Once an object was found that produced a strong response in the neuron being recorded, features in the image of this object were systematically manipulated and reduced in a direction that continued to drive the neuron to the same degree as the original image. However, the particular features identified by these methods were not what one might have expected: They tended to be moderately complex two-dimensional shapes depicting lollipops, stars, etc. That is, despite a high degree of organization in area TE, the particular neural code being used to represent objects is not at all obvious. Indeed, Tanaka's (1996) results have proven to be something of a Rorschach test for the field—almost everyone can find something here that seems consistent with their pet theory.

Tanaka also found that TE neurons are neuroanatomically organized according to this feature selectivity. That is, adjacent neurons tended to be selective for the same minimal features. In addition, recordings along electrode penetrations perpendicular to the surface of the cortex revealed neurons that tended to exhibit a maximal response to visually similar objects. For example, within a perpendicular penetration, neurons might respond to small variations in the frontal view of a face, suggesting that area TE is also organized into minicolumns. Tanaka (1996) also used a technique known as optical imaging, which measures the presence of deoxidized hemoglobin, to examine these findings at a more macro scale. Again using faces as the example, he found that adjacent areas (corresponding to several minicolumns) all responded to faces, but at slightly different views. That is, one region might have its highest activation for a frontal view, while adjacent areas might have their highest activations to rotations varying from the frontal view in a systematic manner. Such findings also help to reinforce the hypotheses of Logothetis & Pauls (1995) and Booth & Rolls (1998) regarding the use of view-tuned neurons to achieve viewpoint invariance.

Interestingly, Tanaka himself has argued that these feature columns provide the visual object recognition system with two of the desiderata identified by Marr & Nishihara (1978): sufficient sensitivity to support discrimination among very similar objects, but sufficient stability to generalize across changes in viewpoint, lighting, and size. Tanaka suggests that objects represented by a large population of neuroanatomically adjacent neurons with overlapping selectivities are best able to realize these properties.

Finally, a recent study has gained notoriety for revealing "Jennifer Aniston" cells in the human brain (Quiroga et al. 2005). The nominal question addressed here is how neuron activity is organized into visual representations. The remarkable specificity of the neurons recorded in humans with epilepsy—some neurons responded to Jennifer Aniston alone, but not to Jennifer Aniston with Brad Pitt—seems to hark back to grandmother cells. Yet, it seems clear that if we know something, it must be encoded somewhere in the brain. Thus, it should not be surprising that knowing about Jennifer Aniston (apparently the subjects read *People*) is reflected in neural responses. Moreover, the actual locations of these responses were all in the medial temporal lobe, in regions typically considered to be nonvisual and often implicated in generic memorial processes. Similarly, strong neural responses were prompted by both visual and verbal stimuli. Thus, although it is nice to know that semantic knowledge about things is indeed represented independent of modality, this does not speak to how invariance is achieved within a modality—that is, how the visual system compensates for the infinite variations in size, viewpoint, lighting, and configuration that we encounter every day.

CIRCA 1890/1990— NEUROPSYCHOLOGY REDUX

Neuropsychology—the study of human subjects with brain lesions—is one of the oldest sources of evidence regarding the mechanisms underlying visual object recognition (e.g., Lissauer 1890). Although there has been a steady stream of neuropsychological research over the past century (e.g., Warrington & James 1967), arguably, it was the publication of Farah's (1990) monograph, *Visual*

Visual agnosia: impaired visual recognition abilities, with a preservation of low-level visual functions

Prosopagnosia: impaired visual face recognition, with the relative preservation of visual recognition of other object categories

Double dissociation: a neuropsychological framework in which one type of brain injury impairs Function 1 while sparing Function 2, while a second type of brain injury impairs Function 2 while sparing Function 1

Agnosia, that rekindled interest in the use of neuropsychological case studies. Specifically, she reviewed almost every published case study of visual agnosia—disorders of visual recognition—to gain a clearer picture of what they tell us, in toto, about the process of object recognition in unimpaired subjects. Broadly speaking, Farah's argument is that there exist two independent recognition systems: one that is part-based and one that is holistic. Put another way, one route to recognition is to parse an object into its constituent features or parts and then to use these parts— possibly in a configural manner (which would make such part-based representations truly structural; see Barenholtz & Tarr 2006)—as the match to similarly parsed input images. The other route assumes no such parsing: Objects are represented as undifferentiated images, and recognition proceeds by matching these holistic representations to input images.

Note that it may seem logical to associate the former with structural-description models (e.g., Biederman 1985) and the latter with view-based models (e.g., Poggio & Edelman 1990, Tarr & Pinker 1989). This would be wrong in that the question of view specificity is orthogonal to whether object representations are structural or not (Barenholtz & Tarr 2006). What Farah proposes speaks only to the structural nature of object recognition, her conclusion being that structure is used for some, but not all, recognition tasks. Farah (1990, 1992) proposed this division of labor to account for three major types of neuropsychological deficits that emerged from her review: (*a*) prosopagnosia, a profound deficit in recognizing faces; (*b*) object agnosia, a deficit in recognizing at least some classes of objects; and (*c*) alexia, a deficit in reading written text. She suggests that all three deficits can be explained in the context of damage to these two basic systems. For example, damage to the holistic system is likely to severely impact face recognition (to the extent we believe face recognition is holistic, a hypothesis supported by results such as Tanaka & Farah

1993). Conversely, damage to the part-based system is likely to severely impact text reading (to the extent we believe that reading requires structural representations; a hypothesis supported by results such as those of Pelli et al. 2003). Somewhere in between, damage to either system is also likely to impair the recognition of some objects, depending on the degree to which the recognition of a particular class relies more on structural or holistic mechanisms. And perhaps obviously, damage to both systems is likely to impair the recognition of most objects, including faces and words.

The critical neuropsychological prediction of Farah's model concerns the pattern of sparing and loss seen across different cases of agnosia. Specifically, she predicts that both prosopagnosia and alexia will occur with only limited object agnosia. However, there should never be cases of prosopagnosia and alexia with no object agnosia. Across her exhaustive review of the literature, she finds cases of impaired face recognition, impaired reading, and impaired object recognition, the latter often in combination with one of the former, but she finds not a single clear case in which face recognition and reading are impaired but object recognition is spared. Farah's meta-analysis of neuropsychological data provides powerful evidence for a two-system account of object recognition.

Although Farah did not explicitly make the distinction, it is tempting to associate the structural mechanisms with normal object recognition and holistic mechanisms with face recognition. Indeed, much of the field has adopted this particular dichotomy. Although there are certainly apparent dissociations in face and object recognition in both psychophysics (but see Gauthier & Tarr 1997) and neuroimaging (the focus of the next section), perhaps the most compelling piece of evidence for separable mechanisms comes from a single neuropsychological case. The Holy Grail in neuropsychology is a double dissociation, in which two different cases show opposite patterns of sparing and loss across two abilities (Plaut 1995, however, presents a cogent computational argument as to why double dissociations do not necessarily entail separable mechanisms). For face and object recognition, this would manifest as cases in which face recognition abilities are lost, but object recognition abilities are intact, and cases in which face recognition abilities are intact, but object recognition abilities are severely impaired. Cases of the former—prosopagnosia—are quite prevalent in the literature. At the same time, cases of the latter—intact face recognition with severe agnosia—are rare. In fact, there is only one such published case, that of CK (Moscovitch et al. 1997).

Strikingly, CK appears to have acute object agnosia and alexia, but no deficit in face recognition. Moscovitch et al. found that CK's face recognition abilities for upright faces were comparable to that of unimpaired control subjects. This ability extended to Arcimbaldo's highly schematic faces composed of vegetables or two-tone Mooney faces. At the same time, CK was functionally blind at object recognition in that he was unable to perform even basic-level recognition tasks (although he was able to use context to infer the identity of some objects). Thus, CK appears to be the other end of the double dissociation with prosopagnosia. Moscovitch et al. (1997) suggest that this pattern strongly supports separable mechanisms for face and object recognition. It should be noted, however, that CK's face recognition performance is hardly normal. For example, his recognition of inverted faces was significantly worse as compared to control subjects. One interpretation of this result is that CK's recognition of inverted faces defaults to the standard object recognition process (e.g., Farah et al. 1995), for which he is severely impaired. An alternative is that all normal routes to object recognition are impaired, but that CK has developed an idiosyncratic template-like strategy for recognizing upright faces only (other idiosyncratic but successful recognition strategies have been observed in prosopagnosia; e.g., Bukach et al. 2006).

Moscovitch et al. (1997) also investigated whether CK was capable of recognizing overlapping line drawings of faces or objects, as well as two-tone Mooney faces or objects (Moore & Cavanagh 1998), all tasks that presumably require part segmentation for successful object recognition. Not surprisingly, given his severe object recognition deficit, CK was impaired at recognizing either overlapping objects or Mooney objects. However, CK performed at the same level as control subjects when recognizing overlapping faces or Mooney faces. Such findings indicate that CK's impairment is not in the preprocessing components of object recognition, for instance, segmentation of objects into parts, but rather is located downstream, perhaps at the point at which parts are related to one another to form structural representations. This claim is something of a paradox in that most holistic models assume object features are assembled into higher-order configurations (e.g., Maurer et al. 2002); that is, they are not template models in the strict sense. Yet, configural processing is often cited as a core property of face recognition mechanisms. Thus, it is difficult to see how CK could be impaired at "putting things together" to form configural representations, yet could be good at face recognition. As mentioned above, one wonders whether CK has actually lost most of his visual object recognition abilities, but has somehow retained a much more literal template-like process in which undifferentiated representations are matched to face images (possibly as a residual effect of premorbid face expertise).

CIRCA 2000—THE RISE OF A NEW MACHINE

If any single device since the tachistoscope could be said to have revolutionized the study of the mind and brain, it is the functional magnetic resonance imaging (fMRI) scanner.[5]

fMRI: functional magnetic resonance imaging

[5] As experimental devices, computers have mostly been used as fancy tachistoscopes. On the other hand, the idea of a

BOLD: blood oxygen level-dependent

FFA: fusiform face area

Neuroimaging studies have the potential to bridge the gap between human psychophysics and single neuron physiology by allowing us to measure the neural activity at the scale of hundreds of thousands of neurons concurrently with real-time task performance.

As with neurophysiology, before we discuss specific results from fMRI, it is worth stepping back and considering some of the assumptions that make it a viable tool for the study of visual object recognition (and the mind and brain more generally). The dependent measure in fMRI—the blood oxygen level-dependent (BOLD) effect—provides a neuroanatomical location where neural activity (or its signature) occurs. What can location tell us about the functional properties of the brain? Perhaps nothing. Again consider a wholly distributed neural code. Such a representational scheme would render fMRI useless: The neural patterns produced by the perception and recognition of different objects or object classes, at the scale of fMRI, would be indistinguishable from one another. Again, luckily for us, this sort of encoding does not seem to be the norm. As hinted at by single-unit neurophysiology studies, regions of IT appear to be organized into columns based on visual similarity—the defining characteristic of object classes. That is, hundreds of thousands of adjacent visual neurons tend to be selective for the same object or variations on that object. Thus, there is every reason to expect that fMRI should be able to resolve differential object processing across stimuli and tasks.

One of the most robust and oft-studied results regarding object processing to come out of the neuroimaging is that of category-selectivity. This phenomenon is roughly analogous to the object selectivity seen at the single-unit level: as revealed by fMRI, clusters of hundreds of thousands to millions of adjacent neurons show a selectively higher level of activity in response to objects within

a visually similar class. As with single-unit selectivity, the most well-known finding of this sort is with reference to faces. That is, if subjects view a series of faces and the resultant pattern of activity is compared to the pattern measured when viewing a series of nonface objects, one finds higher activity in a small region of the fusiform gyrus located within the ventral-temporal pathway (actually first revealed using PET; Sergent et al. 1992; replicated by Puce et al. 1995, and later Kanwisher et al. 1997). This face-selective region—dubbed the fusiform face area or FFA—has attained a level of notoriety that is arguably far out of proportion relative to its potential to inform us about the nature of object recognition. That being said, there has been a great deal of interest in both uncovering the computational principles underlying the FFA and exploring whether it is truly exclusive to faces or can be recruited by nonface stimuli.

This latter question is central to the issue of modularity in visual processing (and in the brain more generally). That is, one model of how the brain works is that it is divided into functional modules, each specialized for a particular task (Fodor 1983). Although this is certainly true at some level of analysis—for instance, there are clearly separable areas for vision and language—the jury is still out on whether more specific processing mechanisms within such systems are domain-general or domain-specific. To some extent, fMRI plays into domain-specific arguments. A subject performs a particular task with particular stimuli, and a small area of the brain selectively "lights up" in response. It is certainly tempting to label each such spot as a module and give it a good acronym. Hence we hear about modules for all sorts of things, including, recently, love (Aron et al. 2005) (see **http://www.jsmf.org/badneuro/**). Thus, interpreting neuroimaging results requires some degree of caution—a putative module may be nothing more than an artifactual peak that is potentially neither necessary nor sufficient for the associated task.

---

computer certainly has had dramatic impact on how we think about the mind and brain (e.g., Turing 1950).

Returning to the question of category selectivity in IT, two chief issues have emerged. First, do category-selective regions occur for stimuli other than faces? And, if so, do they rely on the same neural substrates? Second, what are the origins of category selectivity; that is, why does it occur in the first place? Kanwisher (2000) has been the strongest proponent of the view that the FFA is a "face module" and, as such, is face exclusive. At one level, her arguments are weakened by the ever-growing list of putatively category-selective regions in IT: We have the parahippocampal place area (PPA; Epstein & Kanwisher 1998), the extrastriate body area (EBA; Downing et al. 2001), as well as areas for cars (Xu 2005), birds (Gauthier et al. 2000), chess boards (Righi & Tarr 2004), cats, bottles, scissors, shoes, chairs (Haxby et al. 2001), and novel objects called "Greebles" (Gauthier et al. 1999). Category selectivity ceases to have any explanatory power if a new functional module is postulated for each new object class that results in category selective activity (**Figure 1**).

Clearly, the answer to the first question raised above is yes—category selectivity occurs for many nonface objects. As to whether the same neural substrates used for faces are recruited in these cases, the answer is that it depends on whom you ask. There is certainly strong evidence that, up to the resolution of fMRI, the selective responses seen for Greebles (Gauthier et al. 1999), birds (Gauthier et al. 2000), and cars (Xu 2005) appear to colocate with the responses seen for faces. At the same time, it has been argued that better resolution might reveal separable neural populations for each object class, for example, columns similar to those found by Perrett and Tanaka. On the other hand, one might argue that colocalization at this scale is irrelevant. The functional architecture of the visual system is often thinly sliced with regard to selectivity—for example, the tuning to different orientations in adjacent regions of V1—yet the overall picture is one of a common computational basis (no

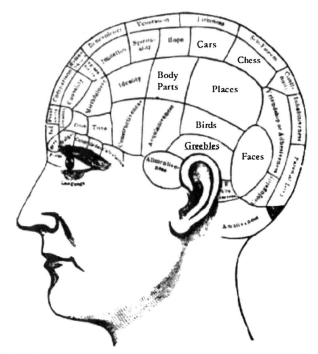

Figure 1

The new phrenology. fMRI reveals numerous category-selective regions in the brain. Simply labeling each as exclusively "for" a particular category provides no explanatory power regarding the functional properties of high-level vision. Please note that the depicted neuroanatomical locations in this figure are arbitrary, but it would not add much more information if they were correct! Adapted from the original drawing by Franz Joseph Gall.

one would reasonably argue that the different orientation columns in V1 were distinct modules). What is more telling is that the large majority of category-selective areas in IT seem to occur nearly on top of one another or quite close to one another. Thus, the best current evidence suggests that they form a single functional subsystem within object processing.

A more informative question is why this functional architecture occurs at all. Efforts to simply map out category selectivity entirely miss this point. In contrast, there has been significant effort by Gauthier and her colleagues to better understand the specific factors that contribute to the origins of this phenomenon. In particular, they have found that the concatenation of a visually homogeneous object class with the learned ability to quickly

Category selectivity: a phenomenon in neurophysiology and neuroimaging where a single neuron or small brain region shows higher responses for a particular object category relative to all other object categories and accurately discriminate between members within this class—perceptual expertise—leads to a shift in the default level of processing and category-selective regions as measured by fMRI (Gauthier et al. 1999, 2000; see also Xu 2005). Critically, these same properties are true for face recognition in almost all humans: we are experts at recognizing individual faces and do so automatically when we encounter a face (Tanaka 2001). Thus, the same explanation applies to why we see category selectivity for faces (we all become face experts during development) and nonface objects (subjects were birdwatchers, car buffs, or were trained in the laboratory to individuate visually similar objects). As such, this account undermines any need to postulate category-exclusive modules.

Different computational principles have been used to account for other divisions of category selectivity. In particular, the explanation offered above would not seem to apply to the place area. Instead, Levy et al. (2001) have suggested that these separable functional regions arise due to the way in which we usually see faces (and objects) as compared to places/buildings. Faces are typically perceived centrally, that is, using one's fovea, whereas places are typically perceived peripherally. Such differences in the eccentricity of viewing are preserved throughout the visual system, so that object representations in IT come to be organized with respect to retinal eccentricity. Again, a putative modular difference based on category (faces versus places) can be accounted for by functional properties arising from the way in which a given object category is typically processed.

As alluded to at the beginning of this section, one issue in interpreting fMRI data is understanding how the measured activity of millions of neurons within a single voxel relates to single neuron responses. To explore this question, Sawamura et al. (2005) used an fMRI adaptation paradigm in both monkeys and humans to measure localized neural activity in the ventral pathway in response to changing object size. At issue was how the

primate brain achieves invariance over image variation—in this case, over changes in the size of an image on the retina. In contrast to an earlier study that suggested minimal size dependency (Grill-Spector et al. 1999), Sawamura et al. found the greatest decrease in neural responses for repetitions of the same object at the same size, intermediate levels of response for repetitions of the same object at different sizes, and lowest response levels for repetition of different objects. Critically, such size dependency at the voxel level is consistent with single-neuron physiology that suggests changes in size result in systematic decreases in the response rate (Ashbridge et al. 2000). A similar correspondence across levels may be seen in the viewpoint-dependent patterns revealed by behavioral, neuroimaging, and neurophysiology studies reviewed above. Overall, such data suggest that it is possible to make connections between methodologies operating at different scales so long as similar methods and stimuli are used at all levels. Unfortunately, corresponding studies are still relatively rare, leaving open many questions regarding the nature of the neural code as understood at different levels of analysis.

Finally, perhaps mirroring errors of the field itself, in this section we have emphasized a particular subset of results at the expense of others. Although the interpretation of fMRI results remains problematic, the past decade has seen a wealth of new findings in this area, many of them speaking to issues that have been with us for far longer. For example, Bar et al. (2006) used fMRI (as well as magnetoencephalography) to study top-down connections within the visual recognition system—clearly an understudied problem relative to its probable importance in visual processing. Bar et al. propose that quite early during the recognition process the orbitofrontal cortex uses low spatial frequencies to determine the coarse shape of objects. This information is then fed back to the temporal cortex as a means for narrowing the candidate object search space. The fMRI results of Bar et al.

(2006) support the existence of this feedback pathway, and their magnetoencephalography results support the claim that these prefrontal areas actually respond more quickly than do early ventral areas during object processing. These results provide one possible mechanism for how the visual system achieves the incredible recognition speeds demonstrated by Thorpe et al. (1996).

CIRCA 2006—TOO MUCH DATA/TOO FEW MODELS

Our review touches upon only a small portion of the huge body of data that has been collected over the past two decades. This explosion of new data is due in large part to innovative methods—for example, computer graphics, psychophysics, ERP, and fMRI—that have invigorated the field, attracting new generations of scientists. We hope we have conveyed at least some of the significant theoretical and empirical progress that has been achieved. The huge successes of the Workshop on Object Perception and Memory (in its thirteenth year) and the Annual Meeting of the VisionSciences Society (in its sixth year) serve as barometers for how far the field has come.

At the same time, we should not get too self-congratulatory. One of the touchstones of the early 1980s was the integration of computational theory with empirical data (e.g., Marr 1982). For the most part, this promise has not come to pass. The wealth of data that has been accrued is almost overwhelming in its complexity, and there are few, if any, overarching models of the complete recognition process. Conversely, of the many computational theories that have been developed over the past two decades, few, if any, are strongly grounded in what we currently know about the functional and neural underpinnings of the primate visual system. Yet, there are reasons for optimism. In particular, within the empirical domain, methods such as fMRI have begun to forge tighter connections between single neurons and functional models of the mind. Similarly, computational theories have matured to the point where simple task completion (e.g., recognizing an object) is not a goal in itself; models have become more tied to neural architectures and to behaviorally based metrics of performance. Thus, we look forward to the next two decades and anticipate the new findings and integrative models that will bring us closer to the goal of explaining how we perceive and recognize objects.

SUMMARY POINTS

1. In the 1980s, structural-description models dominated the thinking about visual object recognition. These models proposed that visual recognition was based on "object-centered" three-dimensional parts. Consequently, recognition performance is predicted to be more or less independent of viewpoint.

2. In the 1990s, view-based models arose as an alternative to structural-description models. Such models propose that visual recognition relies on representations tied to an object's original viewing conditions. Critically, several behavioral studies found that visual recognition was strongly viewpoint dependent.

3. During this same period, neurophysiological researchers found that visual neurons are organized into columns that encode similar visual features. More recently, several studies have found that, with experience, neurons become progressively more selective for trained objects or their component features. However, individual neurons are not sufficient for discriminating between objects; rather, populations of neurons are used.

4. Neuropsychological research has found many cases of visual agnosia that appear to be face-specific. At the same time, there is one reported case of a general object agnosia with spared face recognition abilities. This double dissociation is intriguing regarding the independence of face and object recognition; however, more-detailed analyses suggest that such patterns may occur without separation of these processes.

5. fMRI has dramatically altered the landscape of how we study visual object recognition. Perhaps the most enduring finding from this new methodology has been that of category selectivity, that is, localized neural activity in response to a particular object category, for example, faces. Recent evidence suggests that this phenomenon is a consequence of the task requirements associated with face processing: expertise in individuating members of a homogeneous object category. Thus, similar category selectivity may be found for Greebles, cars, birds, etc.

6. For all of the recent progress in this area, we still have a long way to go. Behavioral and neuroscientific research must become better grounded in well-specified models of object recognition (as opposed to diagrams of boxes with arrows), and computational models must become better grounded in the rich set of constantly growing empirical data.

ACKNOWLEDGMENTS

The authors were supported by a grant from the James S. McDonnell Foundation to the Perceptual Expertise Network, and by National Science Foundation Award #0339122

LITERATURE CITED

Aron A, Fisher H, Mashek DJ, Strong G, Li H, Brown LL. 2005. Reward, motivation, and emotion systems associated with early-stage intense romantic love. *J. Neurophysiol.* 94(1):327–37

Ashbridge E, Perrett DI, Oram MW, Jellema T. 2000. Effect of image orientation and size on object recognition: responses of single units in the macaque monkey temporal cortex. *Cogn. Neuropsychol.* 17:13–34

Bar M, Kassam KS, Ghuman AS, Boshyan J, Schmid AM, et al. 2006. Top-down facilitation of visual recognition. *Proc. Nat. Acad. Sci. USA* 103:449–54

Barenholtz E, Tarr MJ. 2006. Reconsidering the role of structure in vision. *The Psychology of Learning and Motivation*, Vol. 47, ed. A Markman, B Ross B. In press

Biederman I. 1985. Human image understanding: recent research and a theory. *Comp. Vis. Graph. Imag. Process.* 32:29–73

Biederman I, Cooper EE. 1991. Priming contour-deleted images: evidence for intermediate representations in visual object recognition. *Cogn. Psychol.* 23(3):393–419

Biederman I, Cooper EE. 1992. Size invariance in visual object priming. *J. Exp. Psychol.: Hum. Percept. Perform.* 18(1):121–33

Biederman I, Gerhardstein PC. 1993. Recognizing depth-rotated objects: evidence and conditions for three-dimensional viewpoint invariance. *J. Exp. Psychol.: Hum. Percept. Perform.* 19(6):1162–82

Booth MCA, Rolls ET. 1998. View-invariant representations of familiar objects by neurons in the inferior temporal visual cortex. *Cereb. Cortex* 8(6):510–23

A widely cited paper proposing a specific structural-description theory of human object recognition.

Bukach CM, Bub DN, Gauthier I, Tarr MJ. 2006. Perceptual expertise effects are NOT all or none: spacially limited perceptual expertise for faces in a case of prosopagnosia. *J. Cogn. Neurosci.* 18:48–63

Bülthoff HH, Edelman S. 1992. Psychophysical support for a two-dimensional view interpolation theory of object recognition. *Proc. Natl. Acad. Sci. USA* 89:60–64

Desimone R, Albright TD, Gross CG, Bruce C. 1984. Stimulus-selective properties of inferior temporal neurons in the macaque. *J. Neurosci.* 4:2051–62

Downing PE, Jiang Y, Shuman M, Kanwisher N. 2001. A cortical area selective for visual processing of the human body. *Science* 293:2470–73

Edelman S, Bülthoff HH. 1992. Orientation dependence in the recognition of familiar and novel views of three-dimensional objects. *Vis. Res.* 32(12):2385–400

Epstein R, Kanwisher N. 1998. A cortical representation of the local visual environment. *Nature* 392:598–601

Farah MJ. 1990. *Visual Agnosia: Disorders of Object Recognition and What They Tell Us About Normal Vision.* Cambridge, MA: MIT Press

Farah MJ. 1992. Is an object an object an object? Cognitive and neuropsychological investigations of domain-specificity in visual object recognition. *Curr. Dir. Psychol. Sci.* 1(5):164–69

Farah MJ, Tanaka JW, Drain HM. 1995. What causes the face inversion effect? *J. Exp. Psychol.: Hum. Percept. Perform.* 21(3):628–34

Fodor JA. 1975. *The Language of Thought.* Cambridge, MA: Harvard Univ. Press

Fodor JA. 1983. *The Modularity of Mind.* Cambridge, MA: MIT Press

Gauthier I, Hayward WG, Tarr MJ, Anderson AW, Skudlarski P, Gore JC. 2002. BOLD activity during mental rotation and viewpoint-dependent object recognition. *Neuron* 34(1):161–71

Gauthier I, Skudlarski P, Gore JC, Anderson AW. 2000. Expertise for cars and birds recruits brain areas involved in face recognition. *Nat. Neurosci.* 3(2):191–97

Gauthier I, Tarr MJ. 1997. Becoming a "Greeble" expert: exploring mechanisms for face recognition. *Vis. Res.* 37(12):1673–82

Gauthier I, Tarr MJ, Anderson AW, Skudlarski P, Gore JC. 1999. Activation of the middle fusiform "face area" increases with expertise in recognizing novel objects. *Nat. Neurosci.* 2(6):568–73

Grill-Spector K, Kushnir T, Edelman S, Avidan G, Itachak Y, Malach R. 1999. Differential processing of objects under various viewing conditions in the human lateral occipital complex. *Neuron* 24:187–203

Gross CG. 1994. How inferior temporal cortex became a visual area. *Cereb. Cortex* 4(5):455–69

Gross CG, Bender DB, Rocha-Miranda CE. 1969. Visual receptive fields of neurons in inferotemporal cortex of the monkey. *Science* 166:1303–6

Gross CG, Rocha-Miranda CE, Bender DB. 1972. Visual properties of neurons in inferotemporal cortex of the macaque. *J. Neurophysiol.* 35:96–111

Haxby JV, Gobbini MI, Furey ML, Ishai A, Schouten JL, Pietrini P. 2001. Distributed and overlapping representations of faces and objects in ventral temporal cortex. *Science* 293:2425–30

Jiang X, Rosen E, Zeffiro T, VanMeter J, Blanz V, Riesenhuber M. 2006. Evaluation of a shape-based model of human face discrimination using fMRI and behavioral techniques. *Neuron* 50:159–72

Jolicoeur P. 1985. The time to name disoriented natural objects. *Mem. Cogn.* 13:289–303

Jolicoeur P, Gluck M, Kosslyn SM. 1984. Pictures and names: making the connection. *Cogn. Psychol.* 16:243–75

Kanwisher N. 2000. Domain specificity in face perception. *Nat. Neurosci.* 3(8):759–63

An innovative study demonstrating that category selectivity, as revealed by neuroimaging, emerges with expertise with nonface homogeneous object categories.

The first paper to demonstrate that visual neurons can be selective for complex stimuli, such as hands.

Kanwisher N, McDermott J, Chun MM. 1997. The fusiform face area: a module in human extrastriate cortex specialized for face perception. *J. Neurosci.* **17(11):4302–11**

Kobatake E, Wang G, Tanaka K. 1998. Effects of shape-discrimination training on the selectivity of inferotemporal cells in adult monkeys. *J. Neurophysiol.* 80(1):324–30

Konorski J. 1967. *Integrative Activity of the Brain: An Interdisciplinary Approach*. Chicago, IL: Univ. Chicago Press

Kosslyn SM. 1980. *Image and Mind*. Cambridge, MA: Harvard Univ. Press

Lawson R, Humphreys GW, Watson DG. 1994. Object recognition under sequential viewing conditions: evidence for viewpoint-specific recognition procedures. *Perception* 23(5):595–614

Levy I, Hasson U, Avidan G, Hendler T, Malach R. 2001. Center-periphery organization of human object areas. *Nat. Neurosci.* 4(5):533–39

Lissauer H. 1890. Ein fall von seelenblindheit nebst einem Beitrage zur Theori derselben. *Arch. Psychiatr. Nervenkr.* 21:222–70

Logothetis NK, Pauls J. 1995. Psychophysical and physiological evidence for viewer-centered object representations in the primate. *Cereb. Cortex* 5(3):270–88

Lowe DG. 1985. *Perceptual Organization and Visual Recognition*. Boston, MA: Kluwer Acad.

Marr D. 1982. *Vision: A Computational Investigation into the Human Representation and Processing of Visual Information*. San Francisco: Freeman

Marr D, Nishihara HK. 1978. Representation and recognition of the spatial organization of three-dimensional shapes. *Proc. R. Soc. Lond. B Biol. Sci.* **200:269–94**

Maurer D, Le Grand R, Mondloch CJ. 2002. The many faces of configural processing. *Trends Cogn. Sci.* 6(6):255–60

Moore C, Cavanagh P. 1998. Recovery of 3D volume from 2-tone images of novel objects. *Cognition* 67(1–2):45–71

Moscovitch M, Winocur G, Behrmann M. 1997. What is special about face recognition? Nineteen experiments on a person with visual object agnosia and dyslexia but normal face recognition. *J. Cogn. Neurosci.* 9:555–604

Pelli DG, Farell B, Moore DC. 2003. The remarkable inefficiency of word recognition. *Nature* 423(6941):752–56

Perrett DI, Oram MW, Ashbridge E. 1998. Evidence accumulation in cell populations responsive to faces: an account of generalisation of recognition without mental transformations. *Cognition* 67(1–2):111–45

Perrett DI, Smith PAJ, Potter DD, Mistlin AJ, Head AS, et al. 1984. Neurones responsive to faces in the temporal cortex: studies of functional organization, sensitivity to identity and relation to perception. *Hum. Neurobiol.* 3:197–208

Pinker S. 1984. Visual cognition: an introduction. *Cognition* 18:1–63

Plaut DC. 1995. Double dissociation without modularity: evidence from connectionist neuropsychology. *J. Clin. Exp. Neuropsychol.* 17:291–321

Poggio T, Edelman S. 1990. A network that learns to recognize three-dimensional objects. *Nature* 343:263–66

Puce A, Allison T, Gore JC, McCarthy G. 1995. Face-sensitive regions in human extrastriate cortex studied by functional MRI. *J. Neurophyschol.* 74:1192–99

Quiroga RQ, Reddy L, Kreiman G, Koch C, Fried I. 2005. Invariant visual representation by single neurons in the human brain. *Nature* 435:1102–7

Riesenhuber M, Poggio T. 1999. Hierarchical models of object recognition in cortex. *Nat. Neurosci.* 2(11):1019–25

Righi G, Tarr MJ. 2004. Are chess experts any different from face, bird, or Greeble experts? *J. Vis.* 4(8):504 (Abstr.)

Rock I. 1973. *Orientation and Form*. New York: Academic

Rodman HR. 1994. Development of inferior temporal cortex in the monkey. *Cereb. Cortex* 4(5):484–98

Rosch E, Mervis CB, Gray WD, Johnson DM, Boyes-Braem P. 1976. Basic objects in natural categories. *Cogn. Psychol.* 8:382–439

Rotshtein P, Henson RNA, Treves A, Driver J, Dolan RJ. 2005. Morphing Marilyn into Maggie dissociates physical and identity face representations in the brain. *Nat. Neurosci.* 8:107–13

Sawamura H, Georgieva S, Vogels R, Vanduffel W, Orban GA. 2005. Using functional magnetic resonance imaging to assess adaptation and size invariance of shape processing by humans and monkeys. *J. Neurosci.* 25:4294–306

Selfridge OG. 1959. *Pandemonium: a paradigm for learning*. Presented at Symp. Mechanisation Thought Proc., London

Sergent J, Ohta S, MacDonald B. 1992. Functional neuroanatomy of face and object processing: a positron emission tomography study. *Brain* 115:15–36

The first neuroimaging paper to demonstrate category-selective neural responses for face stimuli.

Shepard RN, Cooper LA. 1982. *Mental Images and Their Transformations*. Cambridge, MA: MIT Press

Sigala N. 2004. Visual categorization and the inferior temporal cortex. *Behav. Brain Res.* 149(1):1–7

Sigala N, Logothetis NK. 2002. Visual categorization shapes feature selectivity in the primate temporal cortex. *Nature* 415:318–20

Tanaka JW. 2001. The entry point of face recognition: evidence for face expertise. *J. Exp. Psychol.: Gen.* 130(3):534–43

Tanaka JW, Farah MJ. 1993. Parts and wholes in face recognition. *Q. J. Exp. Psychol.* 46A:225–45

Tanaka K. 1996. Inferotemporal cortex and object vision. *Annu. Rev. Neurosci.* 19:109–39

Tarr MJ. 1995. Rotating objects to recognize them: a case study of the role of viewpoint dependency in the recognition of three-dimensional objects. *Psychon. Bull. Rev.* 2(1):55–82

Tarr MJ, Pinker S. 1989. Mental rotation and orientation-dependence in shape recognition. *Cogn. Psychol.* 21:233–82

An empirical paper that provides evidence in support of view-based object representations.

Thorpe S, Fize D, Marlot C. 1996. Speed of processing in the human visual system. *Nature* 381:520–22

Turing AM. 1950. Computing machinery and intelligence. *Mind* 49:433–60

Ullman S. 1989. Aligning pictorial descriptions: an approach to object recognition. *Cognition* 32:193–254

Van Essen DC. 1985. Functional organization of primate visual cortex. *Cereb. Cortex* 3:259–329

Warrington EK, James M. 1967. An experimental investigation of facial recognition in patients with unilateral cerebral lesion. *Cortex* 3:317–26

Xu Y. 2005. Revisiting the role of the fusiform face area in visual expertise. *Cereb. Cortex* 15:1234–42

Zhang L, Cottrell GW. 2005. Holistic processing develops because it is good. In *Proc. 27th Annu. Cogn. Sci. Conf.*, ed. BG Bara, L Barsalou, M Bucciarelli, pp. 2428–33. Mahwah, NJ: Erlbaum

RELATED RESOURCES

Web sites with relevant information include:
http://www.psy.vanderbilt.edu/faculty/gauthier/PEN/
http://www.tarrlab.org/
http://web.mit.edu/bcs/sinha/
http://web.mit.edu/bcs/nklab/expertise.shtml/
http://www.jsmf.org/badneuro/

Causal Cognition in Human and Nonhuman Animals: A Comparative, Critical Review

Derek C. Penn and Daniel J. Povinelli

Cognitive Evolution Group, University of Louisiana, Lafayette, Louisiana 70504; email: ceg@louisiana.edu

Annu. Rev. Psychol. 2007. 58:97–118

First published online as a Review in Advance on October 9, 2006

The *Annual Review of Psychology* is online at http://psych.annualreviews.org

This article's doi: 10.1146/annurev.psych.58.110405.085555

Key Words

causal reasoning, animal cognition, causal learning, contingency learning, causal Bayes nets, causal power, associationism

Abstract

In this article, we review some of the most provocative experimental results to have emerged from comparative labs in the past few years, starting with research focusing on contingency learning and finishing with experiments exploring nonhuman animals' understanding of causal-logical relations. Although the theoretical explanation for these results is often inchoate, a clear pattern nevertheless emerges. The comparative evidence does not fit comfortably into either the traditional associationist or inferential alternatives that have dominated comparative debate for many decades now. Indeed, the similarities and differences between human and nonhuman causal cognition seem to be much more multifarious than these dichotomous alternatives allow.

Contents

INTRODUCTION

Animals of all taxa have evolved cognitive mechanisms for taking advantage of causal regularities in the physical world. Many are also quite adept at using and manufacturing simple tools. But the way that human subjects cognize causal regularities is clearly a good deal more sophisticated than that of any other animal on the planet. This much, at least, seems indisputable. Which specific cognitive mechanisms human beings share with other animals, however, and which—if any—are uniquely human is an age-old question that is still very much unresolved (see, for example, Castro & Wasserman 2005, Chappell 2006, Clayton & Dickinson 2006, Reboul 2005, Vonk & Povinelli 2006).

In our opinion, substantive progress on this fundamental question has been greatly hindered by the dichotomous debate between "associationist" and "inferential" theories of causal cognition that has dominated comparative research for many decades and still holds sway in some parts of town (see Shanks 2006 for a review). Associationists have long argued that all of nonhuman causal cognition and most of human causal cognition as well can be reduced to a kind of contingency learning based on stimulus-bound, associative mechanisms similar to those that govern Pavlovian conditioning (for reviews, see Dickinson 2001, Pearce & Bouton 2001, Shanks 1995, Wasserman & Miller 1997). More generous comparative researchers, on the other hand, claim that even nonhuman animals are capable of reasoning about "causal-logical" relations in a human-like fashion (Call 2004) and employ "controlled and effortful inferential reasoning processes" to do so (Beckers et al. 2006).

In this article, we review some of the most provocative experimental results to have emerged from comparative labs in recent years. We start with experiments focusing on contingency learning and finish with research that explores nonhuman animals' understanding of unobservable causal mechanisms and causal-logical relations. The theoretical explanation for these provocative results is often inchoate at best. Nevertheless, a clear pattern emerges. The available comparative evidence does not fit comfortably into either the traditional associationist or classically inferential alternatives. Indeed, the similarities and differences between human and nonhuman causal cognition seem to be much more multifarious and fascinating than these dichotomous alternatives allow (for similar suggestions, see Chappell 2006, Clayton & Dickinson 2006, Gallistel 2003, Heyes & Papineau 2005, Povinelli 2000, Shettleworth 1998).

LEARNING ASSOCIATIONS
Retrospective Revaluation Effects

We begin our bottom-up review of the recent comparative literature on causal cognition with a phenomenon that has challenged associationist theory from within. "Retrospective revaluation" is an umbrella term that associationist researchers use to refer to contingency learning scenarios in which the associative strength between a conditioned stimulus (CS) and an unconditioned stimulus (US) changes even though the CS in question is absent on the relevant training episodes. The paradigmatic example of a retrospective revaluation effect is backward blocking.

In the case of forward blocking, a cue is first paired with a US (e.g., A+) and then the first cue is presented in compound with a target cue and the US (e.g., AX+). Kamin (1969) showed that rats presented with A+ and then AX+ trials subsequently exhibited a weaker response to X than did rats who were only exposed to AX+ trials—as if learning that the reward was contingent on A "blocked" the rats from subsequently learning that the reward might also be contingent on X. The venerable Rescorla-Wagner (1972) model of associative learning was developed, in large part, to account for cue competition effects such as forward blocking.

In the case of backward blocking, the compound cue is trained first (AX+) and then the competing cue is presented alone (A+). As in forward blocking, the response to X alone is "blocked" on subsequent trials. This time, however, the blocking effect has occurred even though the X stimulus was absent on the critical A+ trials. There is compelling evidence for a variety of retrospective revaluation effects in nonhuman as well as human subjects (e.g., Balleine et al. 2005, Blaisdell &

Miller 2001, Denniston et al. 2003, Dickinson & Burke 1996, Miller & Matute 1996, Shanks 1985, Shevill & Hall 2004, Wasserman & Berglan 1998, Wasserman & Castro 2005).

Theoretical Accounts of Retrospective Revaluation Effects

Traditional associationist theories, such as the Rescorla-Wagner model, cannot account for retrospective revaluation effects because they assume that only cues present on a given trial can undergo a change in their response-eliciting potential (see discussions in Dickinson 2001, Shanks 2006, Wasserman & Castro 2005). Thus, there have been numerous attempts to revise associationist models in order to account for retrospective revaluation effects (e.g., Chapman 1991, Dickinson & Burke 1996, Van Hamme & Wasserman 1994). These revised associationist models postulate that subjects form within-compound associations between CSs that have occurred together in addition to associations between a CS and a US.

One common characteristic of these revised models is that the associative strength of an absent CS can be updated only if it has previously been associated with a CS that is actually present on the given trial. Recently, however, researchers have shown that the conditioned response to a US is also sensitive to the relation between stimuli that have never actually co-occurred but are only indirectly linked to each other through a web of intermediary associations (e.g., De Houwer & Beckers 2002a,b; Denniston et al. 2001, 2003; Macho & Burkart 2002). For example, Denniston et al. (2003) presented rats with AX+ trials and then with XY+ trials. Rats who subsequently received A- extinction trials responded less strongly to the Y cue than did rats who received no such extinction trials even though the A and Y stimuli never occurred together. As Wasserman & Castro (2005) point out, none of the revised associative models is able to account for higher-order effects such as these since the relevant cues never actually occurred together.

Within-compound associations: associations formed between cues that occur in close physical and/or temporal proximity as distinct from associations that form between cues and outcomes

To inferentially minded researchers, higher-order retrospective revaluation looks like it requires "higher-order reasoning processes" and "conscious propositional knowledge" (De Houwer et al. 2005). According to an inferential account, after the A-extinction trials, the rats in Denniston et al.'s (2003) experiment learned that A was not the true cause. Given this "propositional knowledge," the rats deduced that X, not A, was the actual causal stimulus in the AX+ pairing and then, by further deductive inference, that Y must not have been the true causal stimulus in the XY+ pairing (De Houwer et al. 2005).

A higher-order reasoning account of retrospective revaluation certainly provides one possible explanation for the rats' behavior and has undeniable appeal from a folk psychological point of view. However, it is not the only possible explanation. Denniston et al. (2001), for example, propose an alternative hypothesis that does not require propositional representations or inferential reasoning (see also Blaisdell et al. 1998; Denniston et al. 2003; Stout & Miller, manuscript submitted).

According to this "extended comparator hypothesis," the response to a given CS results from a comparison between the representation of the US directly activated by the target CS and the representation of the US indirectly activated by other CSs with which the target CS has been directly or indirectly associated in the past. For example, in Denniston et al.'s (2003) experiment, the extended comparator hypothesis suggests that the rats' response to Y was modulated by the second-order association between Y and A as well as the first-order associations between Y and X and between X and A (see Denniston et al. 2001 for a detailed exposition).

The extended comparator hypothesis is based firmly on traditional associative principles like spatio-temporal contiguity and "semantically transparent associations" (Fodor 2003, cited by Shanks 2006). However, contrary to traditional associationist theories, the comparator hypothesis posits that cues do not compete for associative strength when they are learned; rather, they compete for control over the subject's behavior when they are evaluated. Indeed, colloquially speaking, the extended comparator hypothesis proposes that a subject's response to a target cue is diminished by the extent to which it is able to "think" of an alternative cause or predictor of the outcome in question (Stout & Miller, manuscript submitted). In short, in order to explain the effects of higher-order retrospective revaluation, the extended comparator hypothesis posits the kind of performance-focused, structured information-processing capabilities that associationists have traditionally eschewed.

The Debate Between Associationist and Inferential Accounts

Which hypothesis best explains higher-order retrospective revaluation effects in human and nonhuman animals is a matter of vigorous debate (Aitken & Dickinson 2005; Beckers et al. 2005; De Houwer et al. 2005; Denniston et al. 2003; Melchers et al. 2004; Wasserman & Castro 2005). Unfortunately, only the associative side of the dispute has provided a formal specification of its claims. Van Overwalle & Timmermans (2001), for example, have proposed a connectionist implementation of Dickinson & Burke's (1996) model of first-order retrospective revaluation. And Stout & Miller (manuscript submitted) have submitted a formal computational specification of the extended comparator hypothesis. Higher-order reasoning accounts of retrospective revaluation, on the other hand, have only been formulated in a "verbal manner rather than formalized mathematically" (De Houwer et al. 2005). As De Houwer et al. (2005) frankly admit, "The most troubling implication of this lack of precision is that it becomes difficult to refute higher-order reasoning accounts." Obviously, an important future challenge for advocates of inferential accounts is to provide a formal, computational specification of their claims.

Regardless of which theoretical account prevails, the existing evidence has already demonstrated that nonhuman animals are capable of feats of causal learning once denied them by traditional associationist theory. Even cognitively minded researchers may need to revise their assessment of nonhuman causal cognition upwards. Visalberghi & Tomasello (1998), for example, once argued that nonhuman primates are unable to understand the "web of possibilities" that connects causes and effects. "Associative learning," Visalberghi & Tomasello (1998) went on to explain, "does not involve a web of possible connections, but only a one-to-one connection between antecedent and consequent." Evidence of higher-order retrospective revaluation in rats demonstrates that at least some nonhuman animals are, in fact, sensitive to higher-order associations between absent cues. And the extended comparator hypothesis demonstrates that the principles of associative learning can, in fact, be revised to take this web of possible connections into account.

ESTIMATING CAUSAL POWER

Ceiling Effects

If an effect, E, always occurs at its maximal level in a given context, regardless of whether a particular cause, C, is present or not, it is impossible to draw any inferences about whether the given cause has the power to produce the effect or not (Cheng 1997, Cheng & Holyoak 1995). The rational response to this state of affairs is for the subject to remain agnostic as to the causal power of the candidate cause in question. A subject interested in evaluating whether or not C prevents E, however, could infer that C is indeed noncausal. Ceiling effects are not symmetrical for generative and preventive causes (Cheng et al. 2006). It has now been well established that both human and nonhuman subjects are sensitive to ceiling effects when learning about contingen-

cies and treat generative and preventive cases differently (see Cheng 1997 for a detailed discussion).

Researchers have recently shown that both human and nonhuman subjects are also sensitive to outcome maximality and additivity effects (Beckers et al. 2005, 2006; De Houwer et al. 2002; Lovibond et al. 2003; Vandorpe et al. 2005). For example, Lovibond et al. (2003) showed that human subjects exhibit significantly stronger blocking when the candidate causes are described as having an additive effect. And Beckers et al. (2006) have shown that forward blocking in rats is attenuated when the intensity of the US presented during test trials is the same as the maximum intensity of the US experienced during prior training trials.

The Power PC Model of "Causal Power"

The traditional model for computing the statistical contingency between two cues is the ΔP model (Jenkins & Ward 1965, Rescorla 1968),

$$\Delta P = p(E|C) - p(E \mid \sim C),$$

where $p(E \mid C)$ is the probability of observing the effect given the presence of the candidate cause, and $p(E \mid \sim C)$ is the probability of observing the effect in the absence of the candidate cause.

The ΔP model of statistical contingency does not account for ceiling effects or the asymmetry between generative and preventive causes. Cheng (1997) showed that the normative model for estimating the contingency between a cause and an effect must consider the base rate probability of the effect in the absence of the candidate cause. In the case of binary causes and effects (i.e., causes and effects that are either present or absent), and assuming that the candidate cause is independent of any alternative causes in the subject's "focal set," Cheng's model for generative

Causal power: the probability with which a candidate cause, when present, actually produces or prevents an effect in question as distinct from the frequency with which the cause and the effect happen to co-occur

Preventive cause: a cause that has the power to prevent (or reduce the probability of) the occurrence of a given effect

Outcome maximality: the highest previous level at which a given outcome has been experienced by the subject

Candidate cause: of all the possible causes for a given effect, the one that is currently being evaluated by the subject

Base rate: the rate at which a given effect occurs in the absence of the candidate cause

Focal set: the set of events that a subject selects as relevant for computing the causal power of a candidate cause in a given context

Outcome additivity: a characteristic of cues that produce a greater intensity outcome when combined with other additive cues than when presented alone

causes is given by

$$q = \frac{\Delta P}{1 - p(E \mid \sim C)},$$

where ΔP is the standard model of statistical contingency described above, $p(E \mid \sim C)$ is the probability of observing the effect in the absence of the candidate cause, and q is an estimate of the unobservable "causal power" of the candidate cause in question.

In principle, the Power PC theory provides a normative model of causal induction in the absence of prior domain-specific causal knowledge that can handle both ceiling effects and the asymmetry between generative and preventive causes. It also handles retrospective revaluation effects by positing that subjects calculate causal power over the appropriate "focal set" of cases as specified by the theory (Cheng & Holyoak 1995).

To be sure, whether or not human causal intuitions actually conform to the Power PC model's predictions for intermediate base-rate probabilities is a matter of some dispute (Allan 2003, Buehner et al. 2003, Griffiths & Tenenbaum 2005, Lober & Shanks 2000, Perales & Shanks 2003). Worse, at least from a comparative point of view, there still have been no experiments testing the Power PC model's central predictions about the interaction between ΔP and base-rate probabilities on nonhuman subjects. In the absence of such evidence, it is still too soon for advocates of the Power PC theory to rest on their laurels.

Do Ceiling Effects Require an Inferential Explanation?

Regardless of whether or not the Power PC theory winds up being an appropriate model of causal induction for human or nonhuman subjects, the evidence for outcome maximality and additivity effects suggests that both human and nonhuman animals are not simply learning about observable contingencies but are sensitive to the unobservable constraints specific to causal inference. Both human and nonhuman animals appear to understand tacitly that covariation only implies causation under special circumstances.

But does ruling out associationist explanations and acknowledging a profound similarity between human and nonhuman causal induction mean that rats necessarily employ "controlled and effortful inferential reasoning processes" and "conscious propositional knowledge" (Beckers et al. 2006, De Houwer et al. 2005)?

Beckers et al. (2006) do not present any computational arguments to justify their propositional attributions. Instead, they argue by analogy to human psychology: i.e., in human causal learning, sensitivity to outcome additivity and maximality seems to involve conscious propositional inferences, so nonhuman animals who exhibit a similar sensitivity must be employing similar mental processes (for an extended critique of this venerable argument, see Povinelli et al. 2000).

There are numerous reasons to be skeptical of this particular analogy. Almost all of the evidence cited in support of the role of conscious inferential processes in human causal cognition has no parallel in nonhuman studies. For example, Vandorpe et al. (2005) showed that the "verbal self-reports" of human subjects are consistent with an inferential account of blocking; blocking in human subjects is sensitive to secondary task difficulty (De Houwer & Beckers 2003, Vandorpe et al. 2005); and verbal information provided to human subjects after all learning trials have concluded nevertheless influences blocking effects (De Houwer 2002). These results certainly suggest a role for "controlled and effortful inferential reasoning" and "propositional knowledge" in human causal cognition. But there is no comparable evidence for nonhuman subjects. Moreover, such verbal reports in human beings may sometimes be just posthoc redescriptions of effects initially generated through implicit nonpropositional mechanisms (Povinelli et al. 2000). It is worth noting, in this respect, that Cheng (1997) has consistently argued that subjects "implicitly" use a "qualitative" version of her model.

Beckers et al. (2005) do not present a formal specification of their hypothesis, so it is difficult to know exactly what they mean when they claim that outcome maximality and additivity effects in rats reflect the operation of "symbolic causal reasoning processes." Certainly, Beckers et al.'s (2005) evidence suggests that rats are able to manipulate representations that stand in for objective properties of stimuli in the world (e.g., the maximum intensity level of a given US) and are able to compute numeric operations over these values (e.g., updating the strength of a "blocked" cue as a function of the actual versus expected outcome). There are good reasons for believing that such information-processing operations require the ability to manipulate symbols and variables (see Marcus 2001 for a lucid discussion). Indeed, Buehner et al. (2003) make a similar claim with respect to the Power PC model. So if this is what Beckers et al. (2005) mean by "symbolic causal reasoning" processes, they seem to be on solid ground.

On the other hand, if what Beckers et al. (2005) mean by "symbolic causal reasoning" is equivalent to the kind of higher-order propositional inferences they attribute to humans, their claim is much more tendentious. In other domains—such as foraging, spatial cognition, and instrumental learning—comparative researchers have proposed a variety of information-processing architectures that could account for the observed outcome maximality and additivity effects in rats without positing the need for higher-order inferential reasoning or propositional representations (e.g., Clayton et al. 2001, Dickinson & Balleine 2000, Gallistel 2003, Shettleworth 1998). Given the species-specific evidence for conscious higher-order inferential reasoning in human cue competition effects (e.g., De Houwer et al. 2005), the suggestion that "parallel processes" are operating in humans and rodents (Beckers et al. 2006) appears premature.

INTERVENING ON CAUSAL STRUCTURES

Causal Bayes Nets

An increasingly influential approach to causal induction proposes that subjects solve causal reasoning problems in a manner consistent with the "causal Bayes net" formalism originally developed in computer science and statistics (Pearl 2000, Spirtes et al. 2001). The mathematical details of the causal Bayes net approach are far beyond the scope of the present review (but see Glymour 2003 for a short, nontechnical introduction). The basic idea, however, can be expressed easily enough in nonmathematical terms.

Causal Bayes nets represent causal structures as directed acyclic graphs in which nodes represent events or states of the world, and the connections between nodes (called "edges") represent causal relations. Some simple examples of possible causal structures include common-cause, common-effect, and causal chain models (see **Figure 1**).

The causal Bayes net formalism is predicated on a set of core assumptions. The most important of these assumptions is the causal Markov condition. The causal Markov condition says that if one holds all the direct causes of a given variable constant, then that variable will be statistically independent of all other variables in the causal graph that are not its effects. For example, in a simple common-cause model in which two effects occur with a certain probability given a particular value of C, the state of the two effects is independent of each other if the value of C is fixed.

The causal Bayes net formalism places special importance on the distinction between interventional and observational predictions (Danks 2006, Hagmayer et al. 2007, Pearl 2000, Spirtes et al. 2001, Woodward 2003). Interventions are formally modeled as an external independent cause that fixes the value of a given node, thereby "cutting off" all other causal influences on that manipulated node. Pearl (2000) has aptly baptized

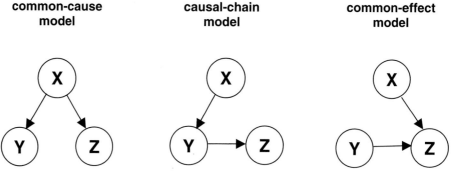

common-cause model   **causal-chain model**   **common-effect model**

Figure 1

Three basic causal structures represented as directed acyclic graphs. In a common-cause structure, X is the common cause of Y and Z. In a causal-chain structure, X influences Y, which influences Z. And in a common-effect structure, X and Y both influence a common effect, Z.

this procedure "graph surgery." Causal Bayes nets provide a formal, computational specification for how to derive interventional predictions from observational learning and vice-versa.

Different versions of the causal Bayes net approach propose different learning algorithms for inferring the causal structure underlying a given set of covariation data. Bottom-up models focus on providing algorithms for inferring causal structures based on statistical data in the absence of any other cues (e.g., Gopnik et al. 2004, Spirtes et al. 2001). The "causal model" approach emphasizes the role of top-down domain-general assumptions that constrain and inform the induction process (Waldmann 1996, Waldmann & Hagmayer 2001, Waldmann & Holyoak 1992). The "theory-based" approach focuses on the influence of domain-specific prior knowledge (Tenenbaum & Griffiths 2003, Tenenbaum et al. 2006).

The causal Bayes net formalism is arguably the most powerful formal account of human causal inference available today (see, for example, Danks 2005, Gopnik et al. 2004, Hagmayer et al. 2007, Lagnado et al. 2005, Tenenbaum & Griffiths 2003). Whether or not it is a psychologically accurate description of causal cognition in any nonhuman subject is another matter.

Intervention Versus Observation in a Nonhuman Subject

To our knowledge, only a single published experimental paper has explicitly claimed that nonhuman animals reason about causal relations in a manner consistent with a causal Bayes net approach. In the crucial experiment in this paper, Blaisdell et al. (2006) presented rats with stimuli whose conditional dependencies purportedly corresponded to one of two alternative causal structures. Rats presented with a common-cause model were given pairings of a light, L, followed by a tone, T, and, then separately, the same light, L, followed by a food reward, F. Rats presented with a causal-chain model were given pairings of T followed by L and then, separately, L followed by F.

During the test phase, each of the two groups of rats was divided randomly into one of two test conditions, and a lever that had not been previously present was inserted into the test chamber. Rats in condition intervene-T received a presentation of T each time they pressed the lever. Rats in condition observe-T observed presentations of T independently of their own actions on the lever. The experimenters recorded the number of nose pokes that the rats made into the magazine where F had been delivered during the training phase (there was no actual food in the magazine during the test phase).

The authors found that rats in condition intervene-T who had witnessed the common-cause model made fewer nose pokes than did rats in condition observe-T. In contrast, there was no significant difference between the intervene-T and observe-T conditions for rats in the causal-chain group. Based on these results, the authors concluded:

> Rats made correct inferences for instrumental actions on the basis of purely observational learning, and they correctly differentiated between common-cause models, causal-chains and direct causal links. These results contradict the view that causal learning in rats is solely driven by associative learning mechanisms, but they are consistent with causal Bayes net theories. The core competency of reasoning with causal models seems to be already in place in animals, even when elaborate physical knowledge may not yet be available. (Blaisdell et al. 2006)

Analysis of Blaisdell et al.'s (2006) Results

We are not surprised that nonhuman causal induction is consistent with at least some predictions of a causal Bayes net approach. How could it not be? The causal Bayes net formalism provides an exceptionally powerful *lingua franca* that can give posthoc explanations for nearly any nonpathological causal inference (Danks 2006). The question of whether human or nonhuman learning is consistent with a causal Bayes net approach is meaningless unless one specifies the particular model at stake. Thus, what is most intriguing about Blaisdell et al.'s results is the particular assumptions that one must make in order to claim that the rats' behavior is consistent with a causal Bayes net approach.

For example, during the initial training phase, the rats in the common-cause group were never presented with L followed by both T and F as would happen if both cues were actually effects of a common cause. Instead, the L → T pairings were perfectly negatively

correlated with the L → F pairings: i.e., every instance of L was followed by either L or T but never both. In other words, rats purportedly presented with a common-cause model were, in fact, never shown covariation information consistent with a common-cause model. The fact that the rats, nevertheless, acted as if they had inferred a common-cause structure should give causal Bayes net enthusiasts reason to pause.

Adopting a simple common-cause model based solely on the observed data would violate the causal Markov condition since T and F are not independent conditional on the state of L. In order for the rats' behavior to be consistent with the causal Markov condition, one must posit that the rats had some sort of prior bias that influenced their causal judgments. One possibility is that the rats were working under the tacit assumption that simpler causal structures (e.g., a simple common-cause model) are more likely than complex causal structures (e.g., a common-cause model with inhibitory edges between effects). Such a prior bias would be consistent with those causal Bayes net approaches that allow for the influence of top-down, domain-general assumptions such as the causal model approach advocated by Waldmann and colleagues (Waldmann 1996, Waldmann & Hagmayer 2001, Waldmann & Holyoak 1992), but it would not be consistent with any causal Bayes net account that generates causal inferences in a purely bottom-up fashion based solely on observed covariations. To be sure, while Waldmann and colleagues have provided extensive evidence in support of their causal model hypothesis with respect to human subjects, the evidence for extending this hypothesis to rats is much more tenuous.

Blaisdell et al.'s (2006) own explanation for why the rats inferred a common-cause structure given the anomalous data is not based on Waldmann et al.'s causal model hypothesis. Instead, the authors proposed that rats who have observed L → T pairings and then observe an L → F pairing "conservatively treat the absent but expected events [i.e., T] as possibly present but missed" (Blaisdell et al. 2006). Given the fact that the T stimulus was a highly salient tone or noise of 10 seconds in duration, the claim that the rats assumed they had somehow "missed" this cue cries out for further experimental corroboration.

Indeed, Blaisdell et al. (2006) provide very little evidence that rats inferred a common-cause model from the data using a causal Bayes net approach at all. Since the pairings were deterministic, the only information a subject could use to distinguish a common-cause structure from a causal-chain structure was the temporal ordering of the cues: i.e., T and F both appeared 10 seconds after L. While some causal Bayes net theorists have emphasized the importance of temporal information for causal learning (see Lagnado et al. 2005 for an example), the use of temporal information to distinguish between alternative causal structures is certainly not unique to the causal Bayes net formalism.

This said, the most critical finding in Blaisdell et al.'s (2006) experiment clearly undermines a traditional associationist account of the rats' behavior (see also Clayton & Dickinson 2006). Rats in the intervene-T condition of the common-cause group were less interested in F than rats in the observe-T condition. Blaisdell et al.'s provocative results challenge any theory of causal cognition that cannot explain how subjects derive novel interventional predictions from purely observational learning. But ruling out a traditional associationist explanation of the rats' behavior does not necessarily mean that rats tacitly cognize their own interventions in a human-like fashion or use the causal Markov condition to do so.

There is an abundance of evidence demonstrating that human subjects are able to use their own interventions in a deliberately epistemic fashion (Danks 2006; Hagmayer et al. 2007; Lagnado & Sloman 2002, 2004; Povinelli & Dunphy-Lelii 2001; Steyvers et al. 2003; Waldmann & Hagmayer 2005; Woodward 2003). Steyvers et al. (2003), for example, showed that human subjects do

not intervene randomly when the number of interventions they are allowed to make is constrained; instead, they choose their interventions in order to provide the most diagnostic test of their initial hypotheses. Indeed, human subjects seem to plan their interventions like quasi-experiments in order to eliminate confounds and distinguish between possible causal structures when observational data alone are ambiguous (Lagnado et al. 2005).

Blaisdell et al.'s (2006) results are consistent with Pearl's concept of graph surgery if one interprets this term as meaning nothing more than implicitly treating two associated events as independent once the subject has intervened on the consequent event (Michael Waldmann, personal communication). Crucially, however, Blaisdell et al.'s (2006) results do not provide any evidence that rats tacitly cognize their own interventions in an epistemic fashion, are sensitive to the causal Markov condition, or plan their own interventions in a quasi-experimental fashion to elucidate ambiguous causal relations as human subjects do. If what the rats did in the results reported by Blaisdell et al. (2006) counts as graph surgery, it is graph surgery by an accidental surgeon.

REASONING ABOUT CAUSAL MECHANISMS

The Role of "Intuitive Theories" in Human Causal Cognition

All of the theories reviewed to this point have focused on causal induction and the part played by domain-general causal assumptions. Researchers who focus on the problems of causal induction—whether from an associationist, causal power, or causal Bayes net perspective—have largely tabled any discussion of domain-specific prior knowledge. Many have explicitly stipulated that the nettlesome problem is outside the scope of their models (e.g., Cheng 1997, Dickinson 2001). Even those theorists who argue for the importance of top-down knowledge have largely focused on tightly canalized, domain-general assumptions rather than learned domain-specific representations (e.g., Lagnado et al. 2005, Waldmann 1996).

Nevertheless, nearly everyone admits that prior domain-specific knowledge is an integral aspect of human causal cognition outside of the laboratory. Human subjects almost always use their prior domain-specific knowledge to evaluate novel causal relations rather than bootstrap their way up from observed covariation information and domain-general assumptions alone (Tenenbaum & Griffiths 2003, Tenenbaum et al. 2006). Indeed, human subjects often seek out and prefer information about underlying mechanisms rather than rely solely on information about covariation (Ahn et al. 1995).

Many cognitively minded researchers claim that human children possess abstract, coherent, rule-governed representations about the unobservable causal mechanisms at work in specific domains such as physics, biology, and psychology. Some theorists argue that this "core knowledge" is highly canalized due to heritable mechanisms (Carey 1985, Keil 1989, Spelke 1994), whereas others posit that it is largely learned on the fly (Gopnik & Meltzoff 1997). In either case, it is widely agreed that a child's causal knowledge is "theory-like" in the sense that it provides principled, allocentric, coherent, abstract explanations for the unobservable causal mechanisms that govern a given domain.

We use the term "intuitive theory" to refer to a subject's coherent domain-specific knowledge about unobservable causal mechanisms (Gopnik & Schulz 2004, Tenenbaum et al. 2006). By "unobservable," we mean that these causal mechanisms are based on the structural or functional relation between objects rather than on perceptually based exemplars (cf. Vonk & Povinelli 2006). One of the salient characteristics of unobservable causal mechanisms, such as gravity and support, is that they can be generalized freely to disparate concrete

examples that share little to no perceptually based featural similarity

We have no doubt that intuitive theories about unobservable causal mechanisms play a formative role in human causal cognition. In the remainder of this article, we review the comparative evidence to ascertain to what extent this is true of nonhuman animals as well (see also Povinelli 2000, Vonk & Povinelli 2006).

Nonhuman Animals' Understanding of Tools, Support, and Gravity

To date, the strongest positive claims concerning nonhuman animals' intuitive theories about the physical world have come from a series of seminal experiments carried out by Hauser and colleagues on nonhuman primates' understanding of tools (Hauser 1997; Hauser et al. 1999, 2002a,b; Santos et al. 2003, 2006).

Hauser (1997) showed that adult tamarin monkeys reliably preferred cane-like tools whose shape is the same as a previously functional tool to cane-like tools with a novel shape but familiar color and texture. Based on these results, Hauser (1997) claimed that tamarin monkeys can distinguish causally relevant from causally irrelevant properties of a tool and thus possess a "functional concept of artifacts." Similar results have been documented for infant tamarin monkeys with minimal prior exposure to manipulable objects (Hauser et al. 2002a) as well as rhesus macaques, vervet monkeys, and lemurs (see Hauser & Santos 2006 for a review). Analogous results have been shown in the domain of food (Santos et al. 2001, 2002), where the sets of relevant and irrelevant features are reversed.

These results add to the growing body of evidence that nonhuman animals indeed do possess evolved domain-specific predispositions that bias how they perceive and manipulate objects in the world in the absence of observed covariation information or direct instrumental learning (see Shettleworth 1998 for a review). On the other hand, a heritable discriminative bias is not the same thing as an intuitive theory. Nothing in Hauser et al.'s results suggests that monkeys possess any insight into why one set of features is more relevant to tools than to food. Nor is there any evidence that their discriminatory biases are abstract, allocentric, or theory-like in the sense attributed to human children. All of Hauser's results to date are consistent with a more modest hypothesis; i.e., nonhuman primates are predisposed to perceive certain clusters of features as more salient than others when selecting among potential tools without understanding anything about the underlying causal mechanisms involved.

There is not simply an absence of evidence that nonhuman primates possess an intuitive theory about tools, there is also consistent evidence of an absence. Povinelli and colleagues have performed an extensive series of tests on chimpanzees' understanding of physical causal mechanisms (see Povinelli 2000). The general conclusion of these experiments is that when tool-use tasks are carefully construed to tease apart observable and unobservable relations, chimpanzees consistently focus solely on the observable relations and fail to cognize the unobservable causal mechanisms at stake (see also Vonk & Povinelli 2006).

In one of these experiments, for example, Povinelli (2000, Chapter 10) replicated Piaget's (1952) cloth-pulling experiment, in which subjects are asked to pull a piece of cloth toward them in order to obtain a reward that is lying on the cloth but out of reach. Hauser et al. (1999) had previously reported that tamarin monkeys successfully distinguished between rewards lying on or off the cloth and understood the support relation "at an abstract level, tolerating all featural transformations." Povinelli and colleagues, however, systematically varied the featural cues available to the chimpanzees and found that they were only sensitive to certain perceptual relations—such as the degree of surface contact between the cloth and the reward—and were insensitive to the actual structural rela-

tion casually relevant to obtaining the reward. In particular, the chimpanzees appeared to be oblivious to whether or not the cloth was actually supporting the reward as opposed to simply being in contact with it.

A series of seminal experiments by Visalberghi et al. provides further evidence for the absence of any intuitive theory among nonhuman primates about purely abstract causal mechanisms such as gravity and support (Limongelli et al. 1995, Visalberghi et al. 1995, Visalberghi & Limongelli 1994, Visalberghi & Trinca 1989). For example, Visalberghi & Limongelli (1994) tested capuchin monkeys' ability to retrieve a piece of food placed inside a transparent tube using a straight stick. In the middle of the tube, there was a highly visible hole with a small transparent cup attached. If the subject pushed the food over the hole, the food fell into the cup and was inaccessible. After about 90 trials, only one out of the four capuchin monkeys learned to push the food away from the hole; and even this one learned the correct behavior through trial and error. Worse, once Visalberghi et al. rotated the tube so that the trap-hole was now facing up and causally irrelevant, the only successful capuchin still persisted in treating the hole as if it needed to be avoided—making it obvious that even this subject did not understand the causal relation between the trap hole and the retrieval of the reward. By way of comparison, it should be noted that children as young as three years of age successfully solve the trap-tube task after only a few trials (Visalberghi & Tomasello 1998).

Povinelli (2000, Chapter 4) replicated Visalberghi's trap-tube setup with seven chimpanzees. Only a single chimp performed above chance on the normal trap tube condition. When tested on the inverted trap condition, this chimp—like the single successful capuchin in Visalberghi's original experiment—failed to take the position of the trap into account. More recently still, Santos et al. (2006) has replicated many of Povinelli's (2000) experiments with tamarin and vervet monkeys and found convergent results. Based on these experiments, Santos et al. (2006) now conclude that nonhuman primates' comprehension of tools "is more limited than previously stated."

The failure to understand unobservable causal mechanisms such as support and gravity in an abstract fashion is not limited to nonhuman primates. Seed et al. (2006) recently presented eight rooks, a species of corvid, with a clever modification to the traditional trap-tube task. Seven out of eight rooks learned the initial version of the modified trap-tube task quite rapidly. Nevertheless, when presented with a series of transfer tasks in which the visual cues that predicted success in the initial task were absent or confounded, only one of the seven subjects passed. In a separate follow-up experiment (Tebbich et al. 2006), none of the rooks passed the transfer task.

Seed et al.'s (2006) results add to the growing evidence that corvids are quite adept at using stick-like tools, perhaps even more adept than nonhuman primates (see, for example, Chappell & Kacelnik 2002, 2004; Weir et al. 2002). But as Seed et al. (2006) point out, these results also suggest that rooks, like nonhuman primates, do not have a species-universal understanding of "unobservable causal properties" like gravity and support. Instead, they appear to solve tool-use problems based on the observable features of the task and evolved, task-specific expectations about what features are likely to be most salient (see also Chappell 2006 on the importance of interindividual differences).

The Case for Diagnostic Causal Reasoning in Nonhuman Apes

Until recently, there has been a consensus that nonhuman animals do not seek out diagnostic causal explanations (Povinelli 2000, Povinelli & Dunphy-Lelii 2001, Premack & Premack 1994, Visalberghi & Tomasello 1998). Breaking with this comparative consensus, Call (2004, 2005) has recently argued that nonhuman apes are, in fact, quite good at seeking out diagnostic causal explanations based on "causal-logical relations" and "quite bad at associating arbitrary stimuli and responses." These tendentious claims are based on a set of experiments testing apes' inferences about the location of food (Call 2004).

In these experiments, Call (2004) presented 4 bonobos, 12 chimpanzees, 6 orangutans, and 8 gorillas with two opaque cups, one of which was baited with a food reward. In the first experiment, the experimenter either showed the contents of both cups to the subjects or shook both of the cups. Unsurprisingly, subjects strongly preferred the cup in which they had seen the reward. Of the 27 original subjects, 9 also preferred the cup in which the shaking motion was associated with a noise.

In the second experiment, the 9 successful subjects from experiment 1 were retested in a condition in which only one of the two cups was shaken. In some trials, the baited cup was shaken; in other trials, the empty cup was shaken. Out of the 9 subjects, 3 were above chance on the crucial condition in which only the empty cup was shaken and the ape had to infer "by exclusion" that the food was in the other cup.

In subsequent experiments, Call (2004) tested a number of arbitrary noises (such as tapping on the cup or playing the recorded sound of a shaking noise) against the actual noise produced by shaking the cup. The apes chose the baited cup more frequently on "causal" conditions than on "arbitrary" ones. Based on this evidence, Call (2004) argued that the apes had understood the "causal-logical relation between the cup movement, the food, and the auditory cue" and understood that "the food causes the noise."

There are numerous problems with Call's interpretation. We do not know enough about the learning history of the subjects involved in these experiments to rule out the alternative hypothesis that they were simply responding on the basis of previously learned contingencies. It seems quite plausible, for example, that these captive apes had previously learned that a shaking noise (N) combined with a shaking motion (M) is jointly indicative of a reward (NM+), whereas a shaking noise without a shaking motion (N-) or a shaking motion without a shaking noise (M-) is not. Positive patterning of this kind is a well-documented phenomenon in the animal conditioning literature (see Wasserman & Miller 1997 for a discussion). None of Call's numerous manipulations ruled out this obvious alternative hypothesis. As we discussed above, there is ample evidence that nonhuman animals often reason about causal relations in a fashion that is inexplicable in associationist terms. Ironically, though, a quite traditional associative explanation suffices in this particular case.

Indeed, Call's (2004) claim that the apes understood the contingencies in a "causal-logical" fashion appears to be refuted by Call's own results. In experiment 3, Call presented the apes with an empty "shaken silent cup" and an empty "rotated silent cup" (i.e., turned upside down and then right side up again). In experiments 1 and 2, the same shaking motion produced an audible rattling noise when the cup contained food. Nevertheless, the subjects strongly preferred the silent shaken cup to the silent rotated cup. If the apes had in fact understood the causal-logical relationship involved, they would have inferred that neither cup contained food and would have chosen randomly between the two cups or, if anything, would have preferred the rotated cup. Call provides no "causal-logical" explanation for why the apes would strongly prefer a shaken silent cup to a rotated silent cup. Once again, an explanation based on simple associative conditioning seems to fit the bill.

CONCLUSIONS, PROBLEMS, SUGGESTIONS

We hope that the comparative evidence we have reviewed over the course of this article has demonstrated why the venerable dichotomy between associationist and inferential explanations of nonhuman causal cognition is both specious and unproductive. We

agree with Chappell (2006): The real situation seems to be much more complicated, multifarious, and fascinating.

Many aspects of both human and nonhuman causal learning are parsimoniously explained in terms of some form of associative conditioning. On the other hand, both human and nonhuman animals are also sensitive to constraints specific to causal relations *sensu strictu*—such as ceiling effects and the asymmetry between generative and preventive causes. This implies that causal induction is not simply reducible to contingency learning in either human or nonhuman subjects. Even nonhuman animals employ cognitive mechanisms that distinguish between causality and covariation.

With respect to nonhuman animals' understanding of their own instrumental actions, the evidence again suggests that nonhuman causal cognition lies somewhere outside the associationist and inferential alternatives. On the one hand, nonhuman animals' capacity for flexible goal-directed actions suggests that they explicitly represent the causal relation between their own action and its consequences as well as the value of the expected outcome (see Dickinson & Balleine 2000). Moreover, Blaisdell et al.'s (2006) provocative results suggest that rats tacitly differentiate between the consequences of interventions on different kinds of causal structures. On the other hand, there is still no convincing evidence that nonhuman animals of any taxa seek out diagnostic explanations of anomalous causal relations or deliberately use their own interventions in order to elucidate ambiguous causal dependencies. For the moment, such diagnostic, inferential reasoning abilities appear to be uniquely human.

Most importantly, there appears to be a fundamental discontinuity between human and nonhuman animals when it comes to cognizing the unobservable causal mechanisms underlying a given task or state of affairs. While many species (including humans) have a tacit understanding that some events have the unobservable "power" to cause other events (Cheng 1997), nonhuman animals' causal beliefs appear to be largely content-free; that is, their causal beliefs do not incorporate an abstract representation of the underlying generative mechanisms involved (Dickinson & Balleine 2000). Reasoning about the unobservable causal-logical relation between one particular causal belief and another appears to be a uniquely human trait.

This is not to say that all nonhuman animals are uniform in their cognitive abilities or that human subjects always reason in abstract, inferential terms. Evolution has clearly sculpted cognitive architectures to serve specific functions in specific species (Shettleworth 1998). The remarkable tool-using abilities of corvids stand as a stark reminder that the humanist notion of a *scala naturae* in causal cognition is wishful thinking. Our hypothesis is simply that in the panoply of animal cognition, the ability to reason about unobservable, domain-specific causal mechanisms in a causal-logical fashion is a specifically human specialization (see also Povinelli 2000, 2004; Vonk & Povinelli 2006).

Why is it that only human animals are able to acquire and use representations about unobservable causal mechanisms? Unfortunately, answering this comparative explanandum is hampered by the fact that our understanding of how intuitive theories work in human subjects is inchoate at best.

Causal Bayes net models are often touted as the way to reconcile bottom-up causal induction and top-down causal knowledge (Danks 2005, Gopnik et al. 2004, Gopnik & Schulz 2004). Upon closer inspection, however, it is clear that causal Bayes nets are not up to the task. As Tenenbaum et al. (2006) point out, any formal specification of intuitive causal theories of human causal cognition must be able to account for the hierarchical coherence among causal relations at various levels of abstraction. Lien & Cheng (2000), for example, showed that human subjects are more likely to judge a candidate cause to be genuinely causal if it is "hierarchically consistent" with their prior knowledge about superordinate causal relations. Unfortunately, the edges and nodes of the causal Bayes net formalism are not "sufficiently expressive" to evaluate what makes a given concrete causal relation more or less coherent with superordinate mechanisms at different levels of abstraction (Tenenbaum et al. 2006).

In the absence of any well-established formal account of intuitive theories in human causal cognition, it is well nigh impossible to give a formal explanation for the discontinuity between human and nonhuman abilities in this area. Nevertheless, in the interests of provoking future research and debate, we close by proposing a preliminary hypothesis.

Our hypothesis is that abstract causal reasoning—i.e., causal cognition that involves reasoning about the relation between causal predicates at various levels of generality—is intimately bound up with the dynamics of analogical reasoning. It is well known that human subjects often learn about novel and unobservable causal relations by analogy to known and/or observable ones: The structure of the atom, for example, is often described by analogy to the solar system; electricity is conceived of as analogous to a flowing liquid; gravity is like a physical force. As Lien & Cheng (2000) suggest, the process of acquiring and predicating abstract causal relations seems akin to analogical inference; i.e., novel causal relations are often learned "by analogy" to known superordinate relations, and superordinate causal schemas are often learned by systematically abstracting out the functional elements common to superficially disparate causal regularities. If this hypothesis is right, computational models of analogical inference may provide the missing link between bottom-up and top-down processes in human causal cognition (French 2002, Gentner et al. 2001, Holyoak & Thagard 1997).

Our hypothesis provides a computational explanation for why human and nonhuman abilities differ so dramatically when it comes to reasoning about unobservable and abstract causal mechanisms. With the exception of a single unreplicated experiment on one language-trained chimp (i.e., Gillan et al. 1981), there is no evidence that any nonhuman animal is capable of analogical reasoning. *Ex hypothesi*, the reason why only human subjects can reason about unobservable domain-specific causal mechanisms is because only humans have the representational architecture necessary to reason by analogy.

SUMMARY POINTS

1. The evidence suggests that nonhuman causal cognition is significantly more sophisticated than can be accounted for by traditional associationist theories. In particular, both human and nonhuman animals do not simply learn about observable contingencies; they appear to be sensitive to the unobservable constraints specific to causal inference.

2. On the other hand, there is a lack of compelling evidence that nonhuman animals pursue diagnostic explanations of anomalous causal relations or deliberately use their own interventions in order to elucidate ambiguous causal dependencies.

3. Nonhuman animals do not appear capable of the kinds of causal-logical inferences employed by human subjects when reasoning about abstract causal relations.

4. Nonhuman casual cognition is not well served by either the traditional associationist or classically inferential alternatives that have dominated comparative debate for many decades.

FUTURE ISSUES

1. Can the new generation of associationist models—such as the extended comparator hypothesis—account for the richness of nonhuman causal cognition without giving up the representational-level parsimony that has been the hallmark of traditional associationist theory?

2. Can advocates of a higher-order inferential account of causal cognition provide a formal, computational specification of their claims?

3. Are nonhuman animals sensitive to the effects of intermediate base-rate probabilities as predicted by the Power PC theory?

4. To what extent can nonhuman animals use their own interventions in a deliberately diagnostic manner? For example, can they use their interventions to elucidate ambiguous causal structures?

5. Can nonhuman animals infer the presence of hidden and/or unobservable causes? Are causal Bayes nets a useful formalism for describing the cognitive processes responsible for nonhuman causal cognition?

6. What representational-level limitations account for the inability of nonhuman animals to reason about unobservable causal relations?

7. What is the computational role of analogical inference in human causal cognition?

ACKNOWLEDGMENTS

We are grateful to the many researchers who provided us with preprints of their papers to review. We would particularly like to thank Aaron Blaisdell, Patricia Cheng, Keith Holyoak, and Michael Waldmann for many invaluable discussions as well as their critical comments and suggestions on early drafts. This work was supported in part by a Centennial Fellowship from the James S. McDonnell Foundation to DJP.

LITERATURE CITED

Ahn W, Kalish CW, Medin DL, Gelman SA. 1995. The role of covariation versus mechanism information in causal attribution. *Cognition* 54:299–352

Aitken MR, Dickinson A. 2005. Simulations of a modified SOP model applied to retrospective revaluation of human causal learning. *Learn. Behav.* 33:147–59

Allan LG. 2003. Assessing Power PC. *Learn. Behav.* 32:192–204

Balleine BW, Espinet A, Gonzalez F. 2005. Perceptual learning enhances retrospective revaluation of conditioned flavor preferences in rats. *J. Exp. Psychol.: Anim. Behav. Process.* 31:341–50

Beckers T, De Houwer J, Pineno O, Miller RR. 2005. Outcome additivity and outcome maximality influence cue competition in human causal learning. *J. Exp. Psychol.: Learn. Mem. Cogn.* 31:238–49

Beckers T, Miller RR, De Houwer J, Urushihara K. 2006. Reasoning rats: forward blocking in Pavlovian animal conditioning is sensitive to constraints of causal inference. *J. Exp. Psychol.: Gen.* 135:92–102

Blaisdell AP, Bristol AS, Gunther LM, Miller RR. 1998. Overshadowing and latent inhibition counteract each other: support for the comparator hypothesis. *J. Exp. Psychol.: Anim. Behav. Process.* 24:335–51

Blaisdell AP, Miller RR. 2001. Conditioned inhibition produced by extinction-mediated recovery from the relative stimulus validity effect: a test of acquisition and performance models of empirical retrospective revaluation. *J. Exp. Psychol.: Anim. Behav. Process.* 27:48–58

Blaisdell AP, Sawa K, Leising KJ, Waldmann MR. 2006. Causal reasoning in rats. *Science* 311:1020–22

Buehner MJ, Cheng PW, Clifford D. 2003. From covariation to causation: a test of the assumption of causal power. *J. Exp. Psychol.: Learn. Mem. Cogn.* 29:1119–40

Call J. 2004. Inferences about the location of food in the great apes (*Pan paniscus, Pan troglodytes, Gorilla gorilla,* and *Pongo pygmaeus*). *J. Comp. Psychol.* 118:232–41

Call J. 2006. Descartes' two errors: reason and reflection in the great apes. In *Rational Animals?*, ed. S Hurley, M Nudds, pp. 219–34. Oxford, UK: Oxford Univ. Press

Carey S. 1985. *Conceptual Change in Childhood.* Cambridge, MA: MIT Press

Castro L, Wasserman EA. 2005. *Associative learning in animals and humans.* Presented at Online Conf. Causality, organized by Inst. Cogn. Sci., Lyon and Univ. Geneva. **http://www.interdisciplines.org/causality/**

Chapman GB. 1991. Trial order affects cue interaction in contingency judgment. *J. Exp. Psychol.: Learn. Mem. Cogn.* 17:837–54

Chappell J. 2006. Avian cognition: understanding tool use. *Curr. Biol.* 16:244–45

Chappell J, Kacelnik A. 2002. Tool selectivity in a nonprimate, the New Caledonian crow (*Corvus Moneduloides*). *Anim. Cogn.* 5:71–78

Chappell J, Kacelnik A. 2004. Selection of tool diameter by New Caledonian crows. *Anim. Cogn.* 7:121–27

This important paper shows that rats are sensitive to outcome additivity and maximality effects.

A provocative and seminal experiment suggesting that the causal Bayes net formalism may be appropriate for nonhuman as well as human subjects.

The author presents evidence that nonhuman apes are able to reason diagnostically in a "causal-logical" fashion.

Cheng PW. 1997. From covariation to causation: a causal power theory. *Psychol. Rev.* 104:367–405

Cheng PW, Holyoak KJ. 1995. Complex adaptive systems as intuitive statisticians: causality, contingency and prediction. In *Comparative Approaches to Cognition*, ed. JA Meyer, HL Roitblat, pp. 271–302. Cambridge, MA: MIT Press

Cheng PW, Novick LR, Liljeholm M, Ford C. 2006. Explaining four psychological asymmetries in causal reasoning: implications of causal assumptions for coherence. In *Topics in Contemporary Philosophy (Vol. 4): Explanation and Causation*, ed. M O'Rourke. Cambridge, MA: MIT Press

Clayton NS, Dickinson A. 2006. Rational rats. *Science* 9:472–74

Clayton NS, Griffiths DP, Emery NJ, Dickinson A. 2001. Elements of episodic-like memory in animals. *Philos. Trans. R. Soc. Lond. B Biol. Sci.* 356:1483–91

Danks D. 2006. Causal learning from observations and manipulations. In *Thinking with Data*, ed. M Lovett, P Shah. Mahwah, NJ: Erlbaum. In press

Danks D. 2005. The supposed competition between theories of human causal inference. *Philos. Psychol.* 2:259–72

De Houwer J. 2002. Forward blocking depends on retrospective inferences about the presence of the blocked cue during the elemental phase. *Mem. Cogn.* 30:24–33

De Houwer J, Beckers T. 2002a. Higher-order retrospective revaluation in human causal learning. *Q. J. Exp. Psychol. B* 55:137–51

De Houwer J, Beckers T. 2002b. Second-order backward blocking and unovershadowing in human causal learning. *Exp. Psychol.* 49:27–33

De Houwer J, Beckers T. 2003. Secondary task difficulty modulates forward blocking in human contingency learning. *Q. J. Exp. Psychol. B* 56:345–57

De Houwer J, Beckers T, Glautier S. 2002. Outcome and cue properties modulate blocking. *Q. J. Exp. Psychol. A* 55:965–85

De Houwer J, Beckers T, Vandorpe S. 2005. Evidence for the role of higher order reasoning processes in cue competition and other learning phenomena. *Learn. Behav.* 33:239–49

Denniston JC, Savastano HI, Blaisdell AP, Miller RR. 2003. Cue competition as a retrieval deficit. *Learn. Motiv.* 34:1–31

Denniston JC, Savastano HI, Miller RR. 2001. The extended comparator hypothesis: learning by contiguity, responding by relative strength. In *Handbook of Contemporary Learning Theories*, ed. RR Mowrer, SB Klein, pp. 65–117. Mahwah, NJ: Erlbaum

Dickinson A. 2001. Casual learning: an associative analysis. *Q. J. Exp. Psychol.* 54B:3–25

Dickinson A, Balleine B. 2000. Causal cognition and goal-directed action. In *The Evolution of Cognition*, ed. CM Heyes, L Huber, pp. 185–204. Cambridge, MA: MIT Press

Dickinson A, Burke J. 1996. Within-compound associations mediate the retrospective revaluation of causality judgements. *Q. J. Exp. Psychol. B* 49:60–80

Fodor JA. 2003. *Hume Variations*. Oxford, UK: Oxford Univ. Press

French RM. 2002. The computational modeling of analogy-making. *Trends Cogn. Sci.* 6:200–5

Gallistel CR. 2003. Conditioning from an information processing perspective. *Behav. Process.* 61:1–13

Gentner D, Holyoak KJ, Kokinov BN, eds. 2001. *The Analogical Mind: Perspectives from Cognitive Sciences*. Cambridge, MA: MIT Press

Gillan DJ, Premack D, Woodruff G. 1981. Reasoning in the chimpanzee: I. Analogical reasoning. *J. Exp. Psychol.: Anim. Behav. Process.* 7:1–17

Glymour C. 2003. Learning, prediction and causal Bayes nets. *Trends Cogn. Sci.* 7:43–48

Gopnik A, Glymour C, Sobel D, Schulz L, Kushnir T, Danks D. 2004. A theory of causal learning in children: causal maps and Bayes nets. *Psychol. Rev.* 111:1–31

Gopnik A, Meltzoff AN. 1997. *Words, Thoughts, and Theories.* Cambridge, MA: MIT Press

Gopnik A, Schulz L. 2004. Mechanisms of theory formation in young children. *Trends Cogn. Sci.* 8:371–77

Griffiths A, Tenenbaum JB. 2005. Structure and strength in causal induction. *Cogn. Psychol.* 51:334–84

Hagmayer Y, Sloman SA, Lagnado DA, Waldmann MR. 2007. Causal reasoning through intervention. In *Causal Learning: Psychology, Philosophy and Computation,* ed. A Gopnik, L Schulz. Oxford, UK: Oxford Univ. Press. In press

Hauser MD. 1997. Artifactual kinds and functional design features: what a primate understands without language. *Cognition* 64:285–308

Hauser MD, Kralik J, Botto-Mahan C. 1999. Problem solving and functional design features: experiments on cotton-top tamarins, *Saguinus oedipus oedipus. Anim. Behav.* 57:565–82

Hauser MD, Pearson H, Seelig D. 2002a. Ontogeny of tool use in cottontop tamarins, *Saguinus oedipus*: innate recognition of functionally relevant features. *Anim. Behav.* 64:299–311

Hauser MD, Santos LR. 2006. The evolutionary ancestry of our knowledge of tools: from percepts to concepts. In *Creations of the Mind: Essays on Artefacts and Their Representation,* ed. E Margolis, S Lawrence. Oxford, UK: Oxford Univ. Press. In press

Hauser MD, Santos LR, Spaepen GM, Pearson HE. 2002b. Problem solving, inhibition and domain-specific experience: experiments on cotton-top tamarins, *Saguinus oedipus. Anim. Behav.* 64:387–96

Heyes CM, Papineau D. 2005. Rational or associative? Imitation in Japanese quail. In *Rational Animals?,* ed. M Nudds, S Hurley, pp. 187–196. Oxford, UK: Oxford Univ. Press

Holyoak KJ, Thagard P. 1997. The analogical mind. *Am. Psychol.* 52:35–44

Jenkins HM, Ward WC. 1965. Judgment of contingency between responses and outcomes. *Psychol. Monog.* 79(Suppl. 1):1–17

Kamin LJ. 1969. Selection association and conditioning. In *Fundamental Issues in Associative Learning,* ed. NJ Mackintosh, pp. 42–64. Halifax, Nova Scotia: Dalhousie Univ. Press

Keil F. 1989. *Concepts, Kinds and Cognitive Development.* Cambridge, MA: MIT Press

Lagnado DA, Sloman SA. 2002. Learning causal structure. In *Proceedings of the Twenty-Fourth Annual Conference of the Cognitive Science Society,* ed. B Bel, I Marlien, pp. 560–65. Mahwah, NJ: Erlbaum

Lagnado DA, Sloman SA. 2004. The advantage of timely intervention. *J. Exp. Psychol.: Learn Mem. Cogn.* 30:856–76

Lagnado DA, Waldmann MR, Hagmayer Y, Sloman SA. 2007. Beyond covariation: cues to causal structure. In *Causal Learning: Psychology, Philosophy and Computation,* ed. A Gopnik, L Schultz. New York: Oxford Univ. Press

Lien Y, Cheng PW. 2000. Distinguishing genuine from spurious causes: a coherence hypothesis. *Cogn. Psychol.* 40:87–137

Limongelli L, Boysen ST, Visalberghi E. 1995. Comprehension of cause-effect relations in a tool-using task by chimpanzees (*Pan troglodytes*). *J. Comp. Psychol.* 109:18–96

Lober K, Shanks DR. 2000. Is causal induction based on causal power? Critique of Cheng 1997. *Psychol. Rev.* 107:195–212

Lovibond PF, Been SL, Mitchell CJ, Bouton ME, Frohardt R. 2003. Forward and backward blocking of causal judgment is enhanced by additivity of effect magnitude. *Mem. Cogn.* 31:133–42

Macho S, Burkart J. 2002. Recursive retrospective revaluation of causal judgments. *J. Exp. Psychol.: Learn. Mem. Cogn.* 28:1171–86

Marcus GF. 2001. *The Algebraic Mind: Integrating Connectionism and Cognitive Science.* Cambridge, MA: MIT Press

Melchers KG, Lachnit H, Shanks DR. 2004. Within compound associations in retrospective revaluation and in direct learning: a challenge for comparator theory. *Q. J. Exp. Psychol.* 57B:25–53

Miller RR, Matute H. 1996. Biological significance in forward and backward blocking: resolution of a discrepancy between animal conditioning and human causal judgment. *J. Exp. Psychol.: Anim. Behav. Process.* 18:251–64

Pearce JM, Bouton ME. 2001. Theories of associative learning in animals. *Annu. Rev. Psychol.* 52:111–39

Pearl J. 2000. *Causality*. London: Cambridge Univ. Press

Perales JC, Shanks DR. 2003. Normative and descriptive accounts of the influence of power and contingency on causal judgment. *Q. J. Exp. Psychol.* 56A:977–1007

Piaget J. 1952. *The Origins of Intelligence in Children*. New York: Norton

Povinelli DJ. 2000. *Folk Physics for Apes*. New York: Oxford Univ. Press

Povinelli DJ. 2004. Behind the apes' appearance: escaping anthropomorphism in the study of other minds. *Daedalus: J. Am. Acad. Arts Sci.* Winter, pp. 29–41

Povinelli DJ, Bering JM, Giambrone S. 2000. Toward a science of other minds: escaping the argument by analogy. *Cogn. Sci.* 24:509–41

Povinelli DJ, Dunphy-Lelii S. 2001. Do chimpanzees seek explanations? Preliminary comparative investigations. *Can. J. Exp. Psychol.* 55:185–93

Premack D, Premack AJ. 1994. Levels of causal understanding in chimpanzees and children. *Cognition* 50:347–62

Reboul A. 2005. *Similarities and differences between human and nonhuman causal cognition*. Presented at Online Conf. Causality, organized by Inst. Cogn. Sci., Lyon and Univ. Geneva. **http://www.interdisciplines.org/causality/**

Rescorla RA. 1968. Probability of shock in the presence and absence of CS in fear conditioning. *J. Comp. Physiol. Psychol.* 66:1–5

Rescorla RA, Wagner AR. 1972. A theory of Pavlovian conditioning: variations in the effectiveness of reinforcement and nonreinforcement. In *Classical Conditioning II: Current Research and Theory*, ed. AH Black, WF Prokasy, pp. 64–99. New York: Appleton-Century-Crofts

Santos LR, Hauser MD, Spelke ES. 2001. Recognition and categorization of biologically significant objects by rhesus monkeys (*Macaca mulatta*): the domain of food. *Cognition* 82:127–55

Santos LR, Hauser MD, Spelke ES. 2002. Domain-specific knowledge in human children and nonhuman primates: artifacts and food. In *The Cognitive Animal*, ed. M Bekoff, C Allen, GM Burghardt, pp. 269–81. Cambridge, MA: MIT Press

Santos LR, Miller CT, Hauser MD. 2003. Representing tools: how two nonhuman primate species distinguish between the functionally relevant and irrelevant features of a tool. *Anim. Cogn.* 6:269–81

Santos LR, Pearson H, Spaepen G, Tsao F, Hauser M. 2006. Probing the limits of tool competence: experiments with two nontool-using species (*Cercopithecus aethiops* and *Saguinus oedipus*). *Anim. Cogn.* 9:94–109

Seed AM, Tebbich S, Emery NJ, Clayton NS. 2006. Investigating physical cognition in rooks (*Corvus frugilegus*). *Curr. Biol.* 16:697–701

Shanks DR. 1985. Forward and backward blocking in human contingency judgment. *Q. J. Exp. Psychol.* 37B:1–21

Shanks DR. 1995. *The Psychology of Associative Learning*. London: Cambridge Univ. Press

Shanks DR. 2006. Associationism and cognition: human contingency learning at 25. *Q. J. Exp. Psychol.* 59:In press

Researchers present nontool-using monkeys with tasks designed to mirror those that had previously challenged chimpanzees.

The authors present an exceedingly clever twist on the traditional trap-tube task to seven rooks, a nontool-using species of corvid.

Shettleworth SJ. 1998. *Cognition, Evolution and Behavior*. New York: Oxford Univ. Press

Shevill I, Hall G. 2004. Retrospective revaluation effects in the conditioned suppression procedure. *Q. J. Exp. Psychol.* 57B:331–47

Spelke E. 1994. Initial knowledge: six suggestions. *Cognition* 50:433–47

Spirtes P, Glymour C, Scheines R, eds. 2001. *Causation, Prediction, and Search*. Cambridge, MA: MIT Press

Steyvers M, Tenenbaum JB, Wagenmakers EJ, Blum B. 2003. Inferring causal networks from observations and interventions. *Cogn. Sci.* 27:453–89

Stout SC, Miller RR. 2006. Sometimes competing retrieval (SOCR): a formalization of the comparator hypothesis. *Psychol. Rev.* Manuscr. submitted

Tebbich S, Seed AM, Emery NJ, Clayton NS. 2006. Non-tool-using rooks (*Corvus frigilegus*) solve the trap-tube task. *Anim. Cogn.* In press

Tenenbaum JB, Griffiths TL. 2003. Theory-based causal induction. In *Advances in Neural Information Processing Systems*, ed. S Becker, S Thrun, K Obermayer, pp. 35–42. Cambridge, MA: MIT Press

Tenenbaum JB, Griffiths TL, Niyogi S. 2006. Intuitive theories as grammars for causal inference. In *Causal Learning: Psychology, Philosophy, and Computation*, ed. A Gopnik, L Schulz. Oxford, UK: Oxford Univ. Press. In press

Van Hamme LL, Wasserman EA. 1994. Cue competition in causality judgments: the role of nonpresentation of compound stimulus elements. *Learn. Motiv.* 25:127–51

Van Overwalle F, Timmermans B. 2001. Learning about an absent cause: discounting and augmentation of positively and independently related causes. In *Connectionist Models of Learning, Development and Evolution: Proceedings of the Sixth Neural Computation and Psychology Workshop*, ed. RM French, JP Sougne, pp. 219–28. London: Springer-Verlag

Vandorpe S, De Houwer J, Beckers T. 2005. Further evidence for the role of inferential reasoning in forward blocking. *Mem. Cogn.* 33:1047–56

Visalberghi E, Fragaszy DM, Savage-Rumbaugh ES. 1995. Performance in a tool-using task by common chimpanzees (*Pan troglodytes*), bonobos (*Pan paniscus*), an orangutan (*Pongo pygmaeus*), and capuchin monkeys (*Cebus apella*). *J. Comp. Psychol.* 109:52–60

Visalberghi E, Limongelli L. 1994. Lack of comprehension of cause-effect relations in tool-using capuchin monkeys (*Cebus apella*). *J. Comp. Psychol.* 108:15–22

Visalberghi E, Tomasello M. 1998. Primate causal understanding in the physical and psychological domains. *Behav. Process.* 42:189–203

Visalberghi E, Trinca L. 1989. Tool use in capuchin monkeys: distinguishing between performance and understanding. *Primates* 30:511–21

Vonk J, Povinelli DJ. 2006. Similarity and difference in the conceptual systems of primates: the unobservability hypothesis. In *Comparative Cognition*, ed. T Zentall, EA Wasserman, pp. 363–87. Oxford, UK: Oxford Univ. Press

Waldmann MR. 1996. Knowledge-based causal induction. In *The Psychology of Learning and Motivation*, ed. DR Shanks, KJ Holyoak, DL Medin, pp. 47–88. San Diego, CA: Academic

Waldmann MR, Hagmayer Y. 2001. Estimating causal strength: the role of structural knowledge and processing effort. *Cognition* 82:27–58

Waldmann MR, Hagmayer Y. 2005. Seeing versus doing: two modes of accessing causal knowledge. *J. Exp. Psychol.: Learn. Mem. Cogn.* 31:216–27

Waldmann MR, Holyoak KJ. 1992. Predictive and diagnostic learning within causal models: asymmetries in cue competition. *J. Exp. Psychol.: Gen.* 121:222–36

Wasserman EA, Berglan LR. 1998. Backward blocking and recovery from overshadowing in human causal judgement: the role of within-compound associations. *Q. J. Exp. Psychol. B* 51:121–38

Wasserman EA, Castro L. 2005. Surprise and change: variations in the strength of present and absent cues in causal learning. *Learn. Behav.* 33:131–46

Wasserman EA, Miller RR. 1997. What's elementary about associative learning? *Annu. Rev. Psychol.* 48:573–607

Weir AAS, Chappell J, Kacelnik A. 2002. Shaping of hooks in New Caledonian crows. *Science* 297:981

Woodward J. 2003. *Making Things Happen: A Theory of Causal Explanation.* Oxford, UK: Oxford Univ. Press

The Development of Coping

Ellen A. Skinner[1] and
Melanie J. Zimmer-Gembeck[2]

[1]Department of Psychology, Portland State University, Portland, Oregon 97221;
email: skinnere@pdx.edu,

[2]School of Psychology, Griffith University, Gold Coast, Queensland, 9726 Australia;
email: m.zimmer-gembeck@griffith.edu.au

Annu. Rev. Psychol. 2007. 58:119–44

First published online as a Review in
Advance on August 11, 2006

The *Annual Review of Psychology* is online
at http://psych.annualreviews.org

This article's doi:
10.1146/annurev.psych.58.110405.085705

Key Words

stress, resilience, children, adolescence, regulation

Abstract

Research on coping during childhood and adolescence is distinguished by its focus on how children deal with actual stressors in real-life contexts. Despite burgeoning literatures within age groups, studies on developmental differences and changes have proven difficult to integrate. Two recent advances promise progress toward a developmental framework. First, dual-process models that conceptualize coping as "regulation under stress" establish links to the development of emotional, attentional, and behavioral self-regulation and suggest constitutional underpinnings and social factors that shape coping development. Second, analyses of the functions of higher-order coping families allow identification of corresponding lower-order ways of coping that, despite their differences, are developmentally graded members of the same family. This emerging framework was used to integrate 44 studies reporting age differences or changes in coping from infancy through adolescence. Together, these advances outline a systems perspective in which, as regulatory subsystems are integrated, general mechanisms of coping accumulate developmentally, suggesting multiple directions for future research.

Contents

Coping: the study of how people deal with actual stressors in real-life contexts and how the effects of these episodes accumulate

INTRODUCTION

Children's lives are filled with challenges and problems, ranging from traumatic insults (e.g., death of a parent) to major chronic stressors (e.g., poverty) to more normative difficulties (e.g., peer rejection) to daily hassles (e.g., sibling conflict) (Garmezy, 1983). Theories and research depicting the impact of these stressors likewise originate from many sources and levels. At a macro level, work on risk and resilience maps the effects of childhood adversity onto the development of children's competence and psychopathology (Masten et al. 1999). At a micro level, researchers document infants' and children's reactions to specific stressors (e.g., novelty, restraint, delay, noncontingency), tracing the effects on their neural, hormonal, attentional, emotional, behavioral, and cognitive functioning.

In the middle of these streams of research is coping. Coping research is distinguished by its focus on what children actually do (their profile of emotional, cognitive, and behavioral responses) in dealing with specific difficulties in real-life contexts, and how these episodes both unfold and accumulate across time. As described by Lois Murphy (1974), the first researcher to study its development systematically, coping captures "the child's way of getting along—with whatever equipment he ha[s] at his developmental stage—and his own individual makeup, as he face[s] the particular external and internal problems of his situation" (p. 71). Coping is essential to a full understanding of the effects of stress on children and adolescents because it not only depicts the individual's active role in the transactional process of dealing with the demands that adversity actually brings into a child's life, but also has the potential to consider how these ongoing encounters shape development.

A great deal has been learned since the appearance of seminal publications urging the study of coping in children and adolescents (Compas 1987, Garmezy & Rutter 1983, Murphy & Moriarity 1976) or across the lifespan (Aldwin 1994). Much of that research has been summarized in recent review articles and handbooks (Compas et al. 2001, Frydenberg 1997, Seiffge-Krenke 1995, Wolchik & Sandler 1997). As with research on adults, research on children and adolescents largely focuses on individual differences, examining the links between different strategies and a range of outcomes in an attempt to identify adaptive and maladaptive patterns. Many ways of coping have been considered—including problem-solving, support-seeking, escape, rumination, positive restructuring, distraction, negotiation, direct action, social withdrawal, and helplessness—and they have been assessed using a number of methodologies, most commonly open-ended interviews, observations, reports from parents or teachers, and, for older children and adolescents, self-report questionnaires. Research on coping during childhood has also examined its links to early temperament and ongoing parental practices as well as the continuity of specific ways of coping over time.

However, despite widespread agreement that development shapes every aspect of how people deal with stress, it has proven surprisingly difficult to realize a developmental agenda for the study of coping (Compas 1998, Skinner & Edge 1998). The field faces many challenges. No overarching developmental framework for the study of coping currently exists. Definitions of coping, largely borrowed from work with adults, are not always explicitly developmental. Research is typically segregated by age and is further fragmented by the kind of stressors children face, such as divorce, illness, or parental conflict (Wolchik & Sandler 1997). A serious obstacle, and one that bedevils research at every age, is the proliferation of ways of coping (Skinner et al. 2003); literally hundreds of responses are measured by current assessments. As a result, work on coping does not always seem well integrated with other research that examines children's reactions to adversity and stress (Compas et al. 1999, Eisenberg et al. 1997).

Goals of the Review

Despite these challenges, there continues to be keen interest in stress and coping during childhood, and recent advances promise to reinvigorate and reorient research. In this review, we first identify key issues in current work on coping that may help guide developmental research. Second, we use a developmental framework based on these issues to structure the review and integration of current research on age differences and changes in coping from infancy to late adolescence.[1] Third, from a selective review of the contributors to coping, we suggest some general devel-

opmental mechanisms that may explain normative age–graded shifts in patterns of coping across infancy, childhood, and adolescence. Fourth, we enumerate future directions for research, highlighting the complex and substantial developmental questions that remain.

KEY ISSUES IN THE DEVELOPMENTAL STUDY OF COPING

We discuss four important advances, focusing on the core consensus that is emerging, as well as identifying important points of contention. The advances are (*a*) the convergence of developmental conceptualizations of coping on constructs of regulation, (*b*) descriptions of the structure of coping using a set of hierarchically organized families, (*c*) suggestions for the outlines of broad developmental levels of coping, and (*d*) the identification of multiple subsystems underlying coping that suggest a set of explanatory mechanisms contributing to normative age changes and differential pathways of development.[2]

Issue One: Developmental Conceptualizations of Coping

Twenty years ago, conceptualizations of coping in children were based almost exclusively on definitions from adulthood, which typically consider coping as "constantly changing cognitive and behavioral efforts to manage specific external and/or internal demands that are appraised as taxing or exceeding the resources of the person" (Lazarus & Folkman 1984, p. 141). Such conceptualizations are not particularly "developmentally friendly" in that they do not provide clear theoretical links to other developing subsystems, such as cognition or language. Without such links, research cannot determine how the development of the components underlying coping

Ways of coping: basic descriptive units that are designed to capture how people actually respond to stress as they contend with real life problems. Common ways of coping include instrumental action, problem-solving, support-seeking, distraction, escape, opposition, and social withdrawal

Developmentally friendly definitions of coping: conceptualizations that provide theoretical links to other developing subsystems, guiding investigation of how development of components underlying coping combine to shape emergence of new coping abilities at successive ages

---

[1]Although development is a lifelong process, we could not include research on age changes across adulthood and old age (but see Aldwin 1994).

[2]The seeds of many of these advances were sown in a series of meetings on the development of coping sponsored by the Coping Consortium (2001) and hosted by Irwin Sandler and Bruce Compas.

ER: emotional
regulation

combine to shape the emergence of new coping capacities (or liabilities) at successive ages.

Although heterogeneity remains (see Compas et al. 2001 for a review), over the past ten years developmental researchers have increasingly converged on conceptualizations that build on the idea of coping as "regulation under stress" (Compas et al. 1997, Eisenberg et al. 1997, Rossman 1992, Skinner 1999). Compas and colleagues (1997, 2001) define coping as "conscious and volitional efforts to regulate emotion, cognition, behavior, physiology, and the environment in response to stressful events or circumstances" (2001, p. 89). Eisenberg and colleagues (1997) view coping as "involving regulatory processes in a subset of contexts—those involving stress" (p. 42). Our own definition of coping as "action regulation under stress" (Skinner 1999, Skinner & Wellborn 1994) refers to "how people mobilize, guide, manage, energize, and direct behavior, emotion, and orientation, or how they fail to do so" (1994, p. 113) under stressful conditions. Collectively, these definitions forge links between coping and work on the regulation of basic psychological and physiological processes, including emotion, behavior, attention, and cognition, as well as the effects of regulatory efforts on social partners and the environment.

Emotion regulation and coping. The affinity between coping and regulation is clearest for emotion regulation (ER) (Barrett & Campos 1991, Bridges & Grolnick 1995, Eisenberg et al. 1997, Folkman & Moskowitz 2004, Kopp 1989, Rossman 1992). Kopp (1989), a pioneer in work on the development of ER, argues that "Emotion regulation is a term used to characterize the processes and characteristics involved in coping with heightened levels of positive and negative emotions" (p. 343). As pointed out by Rossman (1992), "Models for both stress/coping and the ER process include an appraisal of the significance of the environmental circumstance, the attendant emotional experience, the selection of some action to regulate the heightened emo-

tion and perhaps alter the environment, and some kind of feedback regarding the success of the regulation attempt" (p. 1375). Eisenberg and colleagues (1997) make a cogent case for a close connection, noting that not only is coping "motivated by the presence or expectation of emotional arousal (generally resulting from stress or danger)," but "many forms of coping are very similar to types of regulation discussed in the emotion regulation literature" (p. 288). In fact, all strategies of ER can be considered ways of coping (Bridges & Grolnick 1995), and when studying young children (whose capacities to change the environment are limited) or emotion-focused coping at any age, ER and coping become virtually synonymous.

The centrality of emotion to coping is highlighted by functionalist theories, which view emotion as "a kind of radar and rapid response system," or as "biologically endowed processes that permit extremely quick appraisals of situations and equally rapid preparedness to act to sustain favorable conditions and deal with unfavorable conditions" (Cole et al. 2004, p. 319; see also Barrett & Campos 1991, Lazarus 1999). Emotion is integral to all phases of the coping process, from vigilance, detection, and appraisals of threat to action readiness and coordinating responses during stressful encounters. However, adaptive coping does not rely exclusively on positive emotions nor on constant dampening of emotional reactions. In fact, emotions like anger have important adaptive functions, such as readying a person to sweep away an obstacle, as well communicating these intentions to others. Adaptive coping profits from flexible access to a range of genuine emotions as well as the ongoing cooperation of emotions with other components of the action system (Holodynski & Friedlmeier 2006).

Coping as a coordinating concept. Coping is both more and less than emotion regulation. On the one hand, coping refers to only a subset of self-regulatory processes—those that take place under stressful circumstances

(Compas et al. 2001, Eisenberg et al. 1997, Gianino & Tronick 1998, Skinner & Wellborn 1994). On the other hand, coping includes more than the regulation of emotion. When confronted with stress, individuals attempt not only to deal with emotional experience, expression, and physiological reactions, but also to coordinate motor behavior, attention, cognition, and reactions from the social and physical environments (Compas et al. 2001, Eisenberg et al. 1997, Lazarus & Folkman 1984). Correspondingly, researchers have made connections from coping to behavioral self-regulation (e.g., Metcalfe & Mischel 1999), attention deployment (e.g., Wilson & Gottman 1996), ego control and resiliency (Block & Block 1980), and to self-regulation more generally (Aspinwall & Taylor 1997 ; Carver & Scheier 1998 ; Kopp 1982, 1989). Collectively, these forms of regulation can be considered regulatory subsystems that work together to shape the actions that are described by coping (Compas et al. 1997, Eisenberg et al. 1997, Holodynski & Friedlmeier 2006, Skinner 1999). The focus of coping research is on how all of these features of action work together, synergistically or antagonistically, for example, how attempts to regulate behavior can have a negative effect on emotional reactions under stress.

Dual-process models of coping. Most models of regulation conceptualize two processes—one describing the target to be regulated, such as an emotion or impulse, and the other describing the set of processes that regulate it. In work on emotion, these are referred to as emotion and emotion regulation (Cole et al. 2004); in work on temperament, "reactivity" and "regulation" (Rothbart et al. 1994); in work on willpower, the "hot" emotional and the "cool" cognitive systems (Metcalfe & Mischel 1999); in work on motivation, "intrinsic" and "extrinsic" motivation (Deci & Ryan 1985).

In general, the targets of regulation are the result of a fast, reactive, emotionally driven, impulsive "hot" system that appraises and reacts to external stimuli or situations relatively automatically and with little conscious control. Sometimes described as "go" responses, reactions can be of many types: fear reactions to novelty, anger to restraint, approach to people, attention to a threatening object, or grabbing a forbidden treat. "Go" responses refer not to an approach response per se, but to action readiness—the hot system brings the organism into a state of readiness to act in accordance with the emotional urge, whether that be to flee, protest, or approach. The hot system has strong temperamental bases but also incorporates experiences through conditioning and learning. It is adaptive for dealing with stress: Not only is it more flexible and differentiated than innate reflexes, it also triggers environmentally tuned actions faster than a more cognitively mediated system.

In contrast, regulatory processes are given the job of working with the hot system to guide, redirect, boost, interfere with, organize, and/or sequence the actions it urges. Although some of the most effective strategies are cognitive and deliberate, there seem to be many regulatory processes, including neurophysiological, habitual, attentional, and social, that operate already in neonates and infants (e.g., Kopp 1989). Regulatory processes are also adaptive: They allow actions to be more informed and flexible and less determined by local conditions.

Consistent with most models of regulation, coping researchers posit dual-process models. Compas and colleagues (1997, 1999) distinguish between involuntary stress responses, which describe immediate and automatic reactions to stressful situations, and coping, which refers to "regulatory efforts that are volitionally and intentionally enacted specifically in response to stress" (Compas et al. 2001, p. 89). In our work (Skinner 1999), we refer to these two processes as "action tendencies," defined "in terms of their joint properties in creating an 'urge,' 'desire,' 'want,' or 'impulse' that is redundantly experienced as a motor program (e.g., the urge to get out of the way or hide), an emotion (e.g., fear or shock),

Dual-process models of coping: conceptualizations that incorporate stress reactions and action regulation

Stress reactions: immediate and automatic responses to stressful situations

Action regulation: efforts to mobilize, manage, and direct physiology, emotion, attention, behavior, and cognition in response to stress and a goal orientation (e.g., the desire to become small or disappear)" (p. 479) and "action regulation."

As in other areas of regulation, there is active discussion about how stress reactions and regulation work together. Some researchers suggest that they are parallel processes—in that a reaction can be described as either a stress reaction or a coping response (Compas et al. 1997, 1999); some suggest that they are sequential, with the regulation following and modifying reactivity (Cole et al. 2004); and some argue that they are simultaneous and continuous (Campos et al. 2004). Researchers generally agree that they mutually influence each other over time (Compas et al. 2001, Eisenberg et al. 1997, Skinner 1999). For example, an extreme reaction to stress elicits many coping responses. Or, conversely, proactive coping allows a person to avoid situations in which they would be overwhelmed (Aspinwall & Taylor 1997). Some researchers suggest that any given response reflects a balance between the two subsystems (Metcalfe & Mischel 1999). In terms of coping, this implies that "unregulated" involuntary responses could reflect a strong stress reaction and/or a weak (immature or disabled) regulatory system, whereas volitional coping attempts reflect a weak stress response and/or a well-developed action regulation system.

The effects of stress on these regulatory subsystems are receiving widespread empirical attention. Although no definitive answers are available, a common working hypothesis is that moderate levels of stress may create a zone of heightened regulation, during which subsystems are likely to become more cooperative and integrated, and during which regulatory capacities are practiced and consolidated (e.g., Kopp 1989). In contrast, high levels of stress may disrupt, disorganize, or overwhelm regulatory processes.

Summary. Built on constructs of regulation, overarching definitions of coping now have an explicit role for the emotional, behavioral, motivational, attentional, cognitive, and social processes that have long been implicated: Coping focuses on how these multiple regulatory subsystems work together when dealing with stress. Most importantly, these advances open the door to conceptualizations that are developmental. For example, dual-process models suggest that the major components of coping, namely, stress reactions and action regulation, likely have different underlying temperamental bases and different developmental timetables (Compas et al. 2001, Eisenberg et al. 1997, Metcalfe & Mischel 1999, Rothbart et al. 1994). In fact, a few strands of research on regulatory processes directly examine age-graded developmental changes (Holodynski & Friedlmeier 2006; Kopp 1982, 1989; Mischel & Mischel 1983), which should help to identify major landmarks in coping's development. Moreover, emphasis on the constitutional and social bases of regulation points researchers to an analysis of temperament and social relationships as contributors to the differential development of coping.

Issue Two: Families of Coping

"Ways of coping" are basic descriptive units designed to capture how people actually respond to stress as they contend with real-life problems. The empirical examination of actual coping categories, such as problem-solving, support-seeking, rumination, or escape, distinguishes research on coping from closely related work on stress, adaptation, risk, resilience, and competence. The consideration of a profile of responses distinguishes the study of coping from the disparate programs of research focusing on each of the individual categories. Hence, constructing category systems to conceptualize and measure coping have been central endeavors.

However, this task is made challenging by the complexity of coping. Coping responses, because they are suited to specific demands and shaped by the resources and contexts in which they unfold, are virtually infinite in their variety; a recent review collected more than 400 different category labels (Skinner et al. 2003). Moreover, ways of coping are multidimensional and can serve many different functions. They can be used to solve external problems or to deal with one's own emotions (Lazarus & Folkman 1984); to change the environment or to accommodate to it (Brandtstädter & Renner 1990, Rudolph et al. 1995); to engage in stressful interactions or to disengage from them (Connor-Smith et al. 2000).

Hierarchical models of coping. Over the past decade, researchers have put enormous effort into conceptualizing and assessing hierarchical models that use higher-order categories or families to organize multiple lower-order ways of coping (Ayers et al. 1996, Connor-Smith et al. 2000, Ryan-Wenger 1992, Walker et al. 1997). Despite differences in theoretical approaches and dimensions, conceptual and empirical analyses have converged on a small number of families of coping, perhaps a dozen or so, that can be used to classify most if not all of the ways of coping identified in previous research (see **Table 1**; Skinner et al. 2003). These include problem-solving, support-seeking, escape, distraction, cognitive restructuring, rumination, helplessness, social withdrawal, emotional regulation, information-seeking, negotiation, opposition, and delegation.

However, each family includes more than the lower-order way of coping from which it takes its name—each includes all the ways of coping that serve that same set of functions (see **Table 1**). For example, "problem-solving" as a higher-order category includes not only generating solutions to a problem, but also other ways of coping that are designed to coordinate actions with available contingencies to produce desired or prevent undesired outcomes, such as instrumental actions, effort exertion, planning, decision making, and repair. Moreover, some of the families have complementary adaptive functions (see **Table 1**). For example, both support-seeking and self-reliance allow people to coordinate

their reliance on others with the social resources available; and both negotiation and accommodation allow people to coordinate their goals with the options available. [Similar functional analyses have been suggested by other researchers for ways of coping (Lazarus 1999, White 1974), emotions (Barrett & Campos 1991, Sroufe 1996), and action tendencies (Holodynski & Friedlmeier 2006), as well as for individual ways of coping, such as proximity-seeking (Bowlby 1969/1973)].

Developmentally friendly families. The identification of these higher-order families helps clarify the complex structure of coping and encourages renewed discussions of its adaptive functions (Coelho et al. 1974, Lazarus & Folkman 1984). Most importantly for developmentalists, the families offer a way to incorporate the spectrum of age-graded ways of coping by posing the question, "How do the ways of coping in each family manifest themselves at different developmental levels?" To answer this question, researchers first note the functions served by a higher-order family and then trace how those functions are fulfilled by different patterns of action at different ages.

For some families, such analyses have already begun. For example, young children use behavioral strategies to distract themselves (like playing with something fun), whereas older children can use cognitive strategies (like thinking about something pleasant), leading reviewers to note that cognitive secondary control coping strategies emerge in late childhood (Band & Weisz 1990, Compas 1998). By moving the analysis vertically downward in age, it is possible to identify functionally similar coping strategies during the toddler period, when children who cannot actively distract themselves can nevertheless be distracted by others, and even into infancy, when infants turn their heads away from worrisome stimuli to fasten their gaze on other interesting objects. These strategies of attention redeployment can also be seen at older ages, for example, when adolescents plan to

Developmentally graded members of coping families: different ways of coping that serve the same set of functions at different ages

Table 1 Links between higher-order families of coping and adaptive processes

Family of coping	Family function in adaptive process	Adaptive process	Also implicated
Problem-solving Strategizing Instrumental action Planning	Adjust actions to be effective	Coordinate actions and contingencies in the environment	Watch and learn Mastery Efficacy
Information-seeking Reading Observation Asking others	Find additional contingencies		Curiosity Interest
Helplessness Confusion Cognitive interference Cognitive exhaustion	Find limits of actions		Guilt Helplessness
Escape Behavioral avoidance Mental withdrawal Denial Wishful thinking	Escape noncontingent environment		Drop and roll Flight Fear
Self-reliance Emotion regulation Behavior regulation Emotional expression Emotion approach	Protect available social resources	Coordinate reliance and social resources available	Tend and befriend Pride
Support-seeking Contact-seeking Comfort-seeking Instrumental aid Social referencing	Use available social resources		Proximity-seeking Yearning Other alliance
Delegation Maladaptive help-seeking Complaining Whining Self-pity	Find limits of resources		Self-pity Shame
Social isolation Social withdrawal Concealment Avoiding others	Withdraw from unsupportive context		Duck and cover Freeze Sadness
Accommodation Distraction Cognitive restructuring Minimization Acceptance	Flexibly adjust preferences to options	Coordinate preferences and available options	Pick and choose Secondary control
Negotiation Bargaining Persuasion Priority-setting	Find new options		Compromise
Submission Rumination Rigid perseveration Intrusive thoughts	Give up preferences		Disgust Rigid perseverance
Opposition Other-blame Projection Aggression	Remove constraints		Stand and fight Anger Defiance

Adapted from Skinner et al. (2003).

bring a favorite book to distract themselves while they wait for a painful medical procedure. If analyses of the ways of coping in other families uncover parallel age-graded patterns, they may suggest major developmental shifts, for example, toward the increasing use of cognitive means of coping during late childhood.

Summary. Ways of coping are building blocks in the coping area, describing people's actual behavioral, emotional, and cognitive responses to stress. Recent conceptual and empirical analyses have identified approximately a dozen core families of coping; they can be depicted by a small number of dimensions but encompass a wide variety of ways of coping. Each of these families serves multiple functions in dealing with stress, and the discovery of how those functions can be achieved through different ways of coping at different developmental levels may allow the identification and study of age-graded ways of coping within a family and eventually of normative developmental shifts across families.

Issue Three: Developmental Shifts in Coping

Although studies have examined age differences and changes in ways of coping, few reviews are available (Aldwin 1994, Fields & Prinz 1997, Losoya et al. 1998). These studies, because they utilize a wide variety of partially overlapping coping categories and a wide variety of largely unselected age groups and gaps, have proven difficult to integrate (Compas et al. 2001). Hence, a central goal was to construct a framework to organize the research on the normative development of coping during childhood and adolescence (for the complete review, see Zimmer-Gembeck & Skinner 2006). To do so, we relied on (*a*) conceptualizations of coping as regulation to suggest landmarks indicating key ages at which coping might show developmental shifts, and (*b*) notions of hierarchical families to clarify the ways of coping that should be distinguished at each age. We identified studies,

coded the ways of coping they assessed according to the families, and arrayed findings for each family along the axis of age, looking for regular patterns of age changes.

Retrieval of studies. Studies were included if they explicitly used a measure of coping in response to stress.[3] In total, 44 studies reported age differences (or changes) in coping responses prior to or during late adolescence (only 3 studies for children under age 5; 28 for children between ages 5 and 13; and 13 for adolescents age 12 to 18+). Much of the research on developmental changes in children's reactions to stress prior to age five is likely contained in studies of stress physiology, temperament, and regulation (Derryberry et al. 2003; Holodynski & Friedlmeier 2006; Kopp 1982, 1989).

Although research is limited, there was little difficulty in summarizing the studies of very young children; all studies relied on laboratory observations in distressing situations— background interpersonal conflict, stranger-infant interactions, or arm restraint and toy removal. It was more challenging to summarize studies of older children due to the heterogeneity in ages and measures included; age ranges varied from a minimum of 4–10 years to a maximum of 6–32 years, and assessments included interviews, standardized questionnaires, written open-ended responses, observations, and teacher reports.

Families of coping and developmental levels. We abstracted details of study design and measurement and (based on descriptions of

---

[3] It was a difficult decision to exclude studies that examined phenomena we felt tapped coping but were not so labeled by their authors. The inclusion of some studies would likely not be controversial, for example, studies of emotional self-regulation that examine avoidance, distraction, and support-seeking strategies in preschoolers. However, once the terminological condition is removed, it is difficult to know exactly where to stop, given the many phenomena closely allied with coping, such as attachment, mastery, helplessness, problem-solving, delay of gratification, and many kinds of regulation (Compas 1987).

subscale content and sample items provided) systematically coded for families of coping. Unfortunately, coping subscales often contained a mix of coping families. For example, "support-seeking" subscales sometimes combined seeking support from parents and peers, sometimes combined seeking help with seeking guidance and emotional comfort, sometimes distinguished among all these kinds of support-seeking, and sometimes combined support-seeking with other constructive ways of coping like problem-solving. In these cases, we assigned multiple codes and, in a few cases, included the findings multiple times. Because coping strategies can be dependent upon features of the stressful encounter, we also noted whether coping was assessed in response to self-identified stressors, within a particular domain, or with regard to a wide variety of stressors.

Particular times of developmental transition were underscored. Theory and evidence from studies of children's cognitive, emotional, language, memory, and other aspects of development (e.g., brain development) have pointed to particular points during which structure, organization, and flexibility in coping processes are likely to undergo significant qualitative and quantitative shifts. Although there may be others, the most conclusive evidence points to transitions during the following age periods: (*a*) infancy to toddlerhood; (*b*) ages 5 to 7; (*c*) late childhood to early adolescence (about ages 10 to 12); (*d*) early and middle adolescence (about ages 12 to 16); and (*e*) middle and late adolescence (about ages 16 to 22).

Translating these into terms of coping suggests several broad developmental phases characterized by different mechanisms of regulation and different kinds of participation by social partners. Infancy would begin with stress reactions governed by reflexes, soon to be supplemented by coordinated action schema; during this period, caregivers would carry out coping actions based on the expressed intentions of their infants (interpersonal coregulation). During toddlerhood and preschool age, coping would increasingly be carried out using direct actions, including those to enlist the participation of social partners; this would be the age at which voluntary coping actions would first appear (intrapersonal self-regulation). During middle childhood, coping through cognitive means would solidify, as described in work on distraction, delay, and problem-solving; children would be increasingly able to coordinate their coping efforts with those of others. By adolescence, coping through meta-cognitive means would be added, in which adolescents are capable of regulating their coping actions based on future concerns, including long-term goals and effects on others. Throughout the review, we highlight evidence for the development of coping during these transitional age periods.

Ways of coping. Although there were intermittent references to other strategies, 12 coping strategies appeared most often (listed here in order of prevalence of use): support-seeking (sometimes encompassing information-seeking or help-seeking), escape (cognitive and/or behavioral), distraction (cognitive and/or behavioral), problem-solving and instrumental action, accommodation, opposition and denial, self-reliance, aggression, social isolation, negotiation, helplessness, and positive cognitive reappraisal. We provide detailed findings for the four most common strategies, followed by a summary of results for the remaining families.

Support-seeking. Support-seeking and help-seeking, assessed in 32 studies, are among the most commonly used strategies across all ages. However, support-seeking is a complex, multidimensional tactic, with conclusions about development dependent on age, source of support (e.g., parents, peers, teachers), domain (e.g., medical, academic), kind of support sought (e.g., contact, comfort, guidance, instrumental aid), and means of seeking support (e.g., expressions of distress, bids and appeals, social referencing, proximity-seeking, verbal requests).

In the first years of life, young children become better able to seek the aid of attachment figures when distressed. About mid-first year, infants direct their facial responses in ways that elicit support or shape instrumental actions of others (also see Barrett & Campos 1991). Other adaptive strategies also emerge around this time, such as seeking eye contact with caregivers when soothing or other forms of assistance are desired (Kopp 1989; see also Bridges & Grolnick 1995, Holodynski & Friedlmeier 2006, Sroufe 1996).

Age differences in support-seeking were reported in about half of the 29 studies of children and adolescents, with an almost equal number reporting increases and decreases. After examining subscale content, we concluded that there are declines in seeking support from adults, especially from about age 4 to 12, and increases in seeking support from peers into middle adolescence. Further, there is evidence that much of this occurs because of a decline in seeking support from adults during two periods—the age 5 to 7 shift and the adolescent transition (age 9 to 12). Moreover, the pattern of developmental changes in support-seeking between the ages of about 4 and 12 differed as a function of domain of the stressor (e.g., aggression by peers, medical). When in situations that are uncontrollable or in which adults have authority, young people seek support from adults more as they get older. Hence, children are increasingly able to identify situations in which adult support is appropriate and helpful. As children move into adolescence, especially between the ages of about 10 and 16, they become more effective in determining the best source of support for particular problem domains.

Finally, we expected that reasons for support-seeking, such as comfort, instrumental assistance with a problem, advice, or simply to talk about a problem, would change with age. In particular, there should be increasing differentiation among the many reasons to seek support, which would appear as declines in some forms of support-seeking and increases in others. A pattern of increasing differentiation could not be discerned, however, primarily because most subscales included a mix of types of support-seeking as well as items from other coping families.

Problem-solving. Across 28 studies, patterns of age differences depended on whether subscales focused on instrumental actions to change the stressful situation, more complex forms of problem-solving, or, for younger children, some combination that included help- or support-seeking (usually from adults). In studies of children under age 8 (which utilized observer or teacher-report scales focusing on instrumental actions or combinations), children showed modest or low levels of problem-solving as a coping strategy, and age differences were not apparent. Among studies of children 6 and older, when subscales included cognitive problem-solving (e.g., working out other ways of dealing with the problem), this strategy was used much more often, especially by older children and adolescents; in fact, problem-solving was used as often (or more often) than support-seeking and distraction. However, when subscales contained items referring to specific instrumental behaviors or included items concerning self-criticism or taking responsibility, these combinations of coping strategies were not as frequently endorsed.

When it was assessed as cognitive activity to master the problem, problem-solving showed age-related increases, and these increases were found between mid-childhood and early, middle, and late adolescence, and between adolescence and young adulthood. Specifically, increases were reported in 11 studies of children within the age range of 4 to 18, and these findings were specific to the measurement of problem-solving coupled with items that tap self-reliance, cognitive decision-making strategies, and/or have a majority of items tapping practical and mastery-type problem-solving. Similarly, higher levels of problem-solving were found between the ages of 20 and 25 compared with between the ages of 14 and 17. In addition, one study found lower problem-solving at age 11–12 in comparison with younger and older children, which suggests that a focus on the adolescent transition might yield important information about the development of problem-solving and instrumental action as ways of coping with stress.

Conversely, when age-related decreases or no age differences were found, subscales with problem-solving items also included items tapping a range of other families of coping. For example, age-related decreases were found when subscales combined problem-solving and support-seeking from parents or help-seeking. Age-related declines were also found for subscales that combined cognitive and behavioral problem-solving, plus planning, making lists, and reflecting on emotional responses to stress; in addition, declines were found for a subscale that combined problem-solving with commitment, ambition, and hard work.

Taken together, the findings suggest that instrumental action to change the stressful situation (sometimes called approach or primary control engagement coping) comes on-line as a potential stress response as soon as children gain motor control, but that it can be supplemented and replaced by more self-regulated and cognitive activities, such as problem-solving and going to others for advice and help. Even more cognitively advanced forms that extend instrumental actions proactively, such as planning, list making, reflection, commitment, and ambition, may emerge in later adolescence or early adulthood.

Distraction. Twenty-five studies included distraction as a way to cope with stress. Fortunately, behavioral and cognitive forms were often measured separately, making age differences clearer. Surprisingly, however, this distinction was not utilized in studies of adolescents age 14 and over; all of these studies either measured behavioral distraction alone or mixed behavioral and cognitive distraction items.

Behavioral distraction tactics, such as keeping busy or playing games, were among the most common strategies reported by or observed in children, and adolescents reported using these strategies about as often as they used support-seeking. Regarding age differences, there were increases in behavioral distraction during infancy. As would be expected from increasing abilities to locomote and coordinate behaviors, infants' use of escape via gaze aversion declined while distraction by turning to other objects increased between 6 months and 12 months. In contrast, little age-related change in the use of behavioral distraction was found from about age 4 to 6, but behavioral distraction increased between about age 6 and early adolescence. It should be noted, however, that some of these studies included behavioral distraction items in multiple subscales, producing mixed results.

There was little evidence of age differences in behavioral distraction between the ages of 12 to 18. Yet, as was found with support-seeking, features of the stressors were important considerations; age-related increases in behavioral distraction were found when participants reported how they would deal with inescapable and uncontrollable stressors (dental, school report, cancer) or when adolescents identified their own recent problem.

Cognitive distraction, which was assessed separately from behavioral distraction only up to age 14, was most often described as some form of diversionary thinking, such as thinking about other things, thinking about something fun, or trying to forget the stressor. These were used more often as children got older, regardless of whether the age range was from 6 to 9, 5/6 to 11/12, 8 to 14, or 10 to 13. However, these subscales often contained items assessing strategies other than cognitive distraction. Nevertheless, the bulk of the evidence suggested increases in the use of cognitive distraction between childhood and adolescence.

Taken together, the mixed results likely reflect the variety of distraction tactics drawn upon to cope with particular stressors. As children add strategies, they also increasingly comprehend how to apply this expanding repertoire to specific adverse situations, and, as their use becomes more conscious and regulated, young people can more easily shift from behavioral to cognitive distraction and back again.

Escape. Twenty-seven studies examined escape—attempts to leave the distressing environment or to avoid direct action. However, the use of mixed subscales made it challenging to draw conclusions. When we isolated nine studies with the "purest" escape measures, age differences between 4 and 12 years were typically found. Although evidence was not balanced across all age periods, three transitional periods were especially important for identifying changes—ages 5 to 7, ages 9 to 12, and ages 12 to 14. Developmental patterns depended upon whether coping was assessed in response to a specific (recent) stressor or as a general "coping style." When participants, especially adolescents, identified their own stressors or focused on uncontrollable and specific stressors, slight age declines in the use of escape were typically revealed. Unfortunately, findings were too nonspecific and contradictory to test expectations about developmental shifts from behavioral to cognitive forms of escape.

Other families. Because there were so few studies and subscales were nonspecific, there was little evidence of age differences in the coping strategies of social isolation, negotiation, and helplessness. There were some age differences in six categories that appeared more frequently: rumination (part of submission), aggression in response to problems, accommodation (e.g., focus on the positive, acceptance), opposition (e.g., blaming others), denial, and self-reliance (e.g., accepting responsibility for solving the problem, self-regulation of emotions). Of these strategies, children and adolescents reported high lev-els of rumination and worry, accommodation, and self-reliance.

With regard to developmental patterns, age differences were found in two stress responses—rumination and aggression. Rumination was more common among adolescents as compared with preadolescents, and this escalated across the adolescent years. Aggression was relatively uncommon, but was higher in adolescence as compared with late childhood. The transition period between childhood and adolescence also brought with it more use of cognitive restructuring, higher rates of blaming others for problems, and more self-reliance, including managing the practical and emotional aspects of stress. During adolescence, young people increasingly relied on positive self-talk to cope with stress (i.e., accommodation), and self-reliance became a more frequent response.

Summary. Organizing ways of coping into sets of broader families and focusing on certain ages as likely to mark developmental transitions allowed some trends to be detected, especially in comparison with earlier reviews (which included fewer than half of these studies). Despite the hundreds of ways of coping that have been identified, children and youth seem to favor four families—support-seeking, problem-solving (and instrumental action), escape, and, when escape is not possible, distraction. Studies that combined these families or failed to distinguish developmentally appropriate members within them (e.g., behavioral versus cognitive) were unlikely to reveal clear developmental trends.

Interestingly, behavioral forms of these ways of coping, which are common at all ages, may decrease across middle childhood, but they do not disappear. Instead, they tend to be partially replaced or supplemented at older ages, becoming more differentiated in both form and application. Among preschool children, coping shows little differentiation: Young children primarily seek support from caregivers, intervene directly in stressful situations, withdraw, or use behavioral activities to

Temperament:
inborn physiological differences in patterns of responding to environmental stimulation (such as novelty, restraint, or other people)

Temperamental reactivity:
individual differences in arousability or the amount of stimulation required to produce positive and negative reactions

Temperamental regulation:
constitutional differences in the ease with which infants can modulate their reactivity, either facilitating or inhibiting their affective, motor, and attentional responses

distract themselves. As children start school, these strategies become more differentiated: More cognitive strategies are added to both problem-solving and distraction tactics, and children begin to rely on additional sources of support. Moreover, developmental patterns of support-seeking suggest increasing understanding of contextual specificity—in comparison with younger children, older children and adolescents become more selective about sources of support within different stressful situations. Distraction tactics also become more diverse and flexible; as they get older, young people increasingly draw upon both behavioral and cognitive strategies. Further, with age, young people are more self-reliant and can more intentionally monitor and modulate their own internal emotional states through positive self-talk and cognitive reframing. The capacity to focus on the future may also lead to more anxiety and rumination as well.

Our focus on particular transitional periods also revealed that the earliest years of life, as well as the years between ages 5 to 7 and during the transition to adolescence (about ages 8 to 12), are important periods when coping develops rapidly. Yet, as would be expected from recent research on adolescent brain development and knowledge of other important developmental tasks undertaken during adolescence, the capacity to use particular cognitive strategies under stress (such as strategizing, decision making, planning, and reflection) may not fully emerge until late adolescence or early adulthood.

Such a progression is consistent with the picture painted in major reviews of coping during childhood and adolescence (Compas et al. 2001, Fields & Prinz 1997, Losoya et al. 1998). Yet, it was difficult to confirm all the developmental shifts suggested by previous narrative reviews. The current literature on age differences in coping strategies provides important information, but many studies were not designed to capture development, resulting in unclear or incomplete findings; only six were longitudinal. Future studies should use

more differentiated subscales and target specific age periods; there is no reason to believe that all strategies included in mixed subscales show the same developmental trajectories or that coping evinces major, uniform, or linear shifts across all age gaps. More fine-grained analyses within age groups will also be informative, perhaps incorporating information on normative development of emotion and behavioral self-regulation strategies, broadly defined. There is clearly much work to be done in order to investigate how coping strategies become more differentiated, organized, and flexible while they may also be changing in form and function.

Issue Four: Contributors to the Development of Coping

Most of the research on predictors during childhood and adolescence, like research in adulthood, examines concurrent correlates of coping strategies. Recent developmental analyses have pointed out the need to go beyond such research (Aldwin 1994, Bridges 2003, Compas 1998, Compas et al. 1992, Eisenberg et al. 1997, Fields & Prinz 1997, Skinner & Edge 1998) to integrate individual differences and developmental perspectives by examining the constitutional and social contributors to differential developmental pathways of coping; at the same time, studies need to begin to identify underlying developmental changes (e.g., in cognition, communication, and attachment) that contribute to normative developmental shifts in the coping process.

Temperament and coping. Although coping theorists have long pointed out potential connections (Compas 1987, Maccoby 1983, Rutter 1983), research linking dimensions of temperament to specific ways of coping is thin, involving a handful of studies at preschool age (e.g., Eisenberg et al. 1994) and middle childhood (e.g., Lengua & Sandler 1996). However, rich conceptual and empirical literatures on physiologically based differences in susceptibility to stress and stress reactivity in infants would seem to hold particular promise for identifying the constitutional underpinnings of children's coping (Derryberry et al. 2003, Eisenberg et al. 1997). As suggested by Derryberry and colleagues (2003), "temperamental systems can be viewed as coping mechanisms" (p. 1050), some of which "constitute motivational systems that have evolved to detect and respond to stimuli that are crucial to the survival of our species" (p. 1052).

At the most general level, temperament refers to inborn physiological differences in patterns of responding to environmental stimulation (such as novelty, restraint, or other people). A set of dimensions particularly relevant to coping focuses on reactivity, which describes individual differences in arousability or the amount of stimulation required to produce positive and negative reactions. Although all human infants come with species-general capacities and motivations to detect and respond to psychological and bodily threats (Gunnar & Cheatham 2003), the systems of some infants seem to be tuned to a lower threshold and a narrower range of reactions. For example, highly inhibited children tend to react to novelty with fearfulness and withdrawal (Fox et al. 2005), and some children are predisposed to react to mild stressors (e.g., restraint or delay) with anger and frustration (e.g., Calkins et al. 2002). In general, children with high negative reactivity seem particularly vulnerable to the disorganizing effects of stress.

A second broad set of temperamental dimensions relevant to coping refers to regulatory processes and describes constitutional differences in the ease with which infants can modulate their reactivity, either facilitating or inhibiting their affective, motor, and attentional responses. Infants higher in dispositional regulation are better able to govern their attention and behavior, for example, disengaging attention from distressing stimuli, in ways that return arousal to manageable levels (Rothbart et al. 1994). In general, regulation should provide a buffer to reactivity, allowing

children more flexibility and adaptability in their reactions to stress (Eisenberg & Fabes 1992).

Other dimensions, particularly ones describing an "easy" temperament, have also been implicated in coping (Rutter 1983). Children who are more active, sociable, and emotionally positive have been found to be more resistant to the effects of stress, and this may in part be due to the advantages such predispositions confer on coping (Eisenberg et al. 1997). Moreover, infants higher in mastery motivation (i.e., more active, attentive to contingencies, and persistent in the face of challenge) are likely to show more constructive problem-solving and information-seeking.

Empirical studies of children during preschool age and middle childhood are beginning to show that temperament shapes coping processes in many ways, contributing to individual differences in environmental sensitivity, stress reactivity, threat appraisals, initial emotional reactions, preferred ways of coping, and ease of modifying coping strategies in the face of changing demands (e.g., Eisenberg et al. 1994, Lengua & Sandler 1996). Moreover, temperamental dimensions, such as sociability or impulsivity, may also influence coping by shaping other people's reactions, thus making some children more likely to be targets of social stressors, such as criticism or rejection, as well as differential recipients of social support (Maccoby 1983).

Most interesting for developmental research on coping are findings showing that stress reactivity and dispositional regulation are not fixed at birth. Both show regular developmentally graded changes and are shaped by social relationships and experiences of dealing with stress. For example, maturation of the central nervous system during infancy allows for normative improvements in the capacity to maintain behavioral and physiological organization in the face of distressing events (Kopp 1982, Maccoby 1983). Regulation of behavioral, attentional, and emotional reactions have their own interrelated developmental timetables, with the general suggestion that high reactivity interferes with or slows the development of regulatory capacities (Eisenberg & Fabes 1992, Kopp 1989, Rothbart et al. 1994). Moreover, even the physiologically based processes of reactivity and regulation can be dampened or exacerbated by the quality of caregiving and attachments (Fox et al. 2005, Gunnar & Cheatham 2003) and their functioning shaped by cognitive expectancies and developments (Derryberry et al. 2003).

Socialization of coping. Research in adulthood is often accused of considering coping as an individual affair, but research in childhood, from its inception, recognized that coping is shaped by social relationships and contexts (Compas 1987, Maccoby 1983, Murphy & Moriarity 1976, Rutter 1983). Consistent with that perspective, research on attachment, social support, parenting, family processes, peer relationships, teaching, and parent-child interactions have all shown links between availability of support and quality of relationships, on the one hand, and children's physiological and psychological stress reactivity, regulation, and coping, on the other. Social partners, especially sensitive and responsive caregivers, seem to be a fundamental part of the stress reactivity system of infants, influencing not just how they respond but whether they even physiologically register an event as stressful (Gunnar et al. 1996).

It is difficult to overstate the importance of social partners, especially parents, to children's coping (Kliewer et al. 1994, Power 2004, Skinner & Edge 2002, Zimmer-Gembeck & Locke 2006). Parents play a role in determining the stressors, both chronic and acute, to which children are exposed; parents' problems can themselves become stressors for children; parents contribute to the development of children's coping resources, such as their self-efficacy or social skills; parents participate in children's coping through their own emotions and actions; and parents help children learn from bad experiences, including planning proactive coping to prevent their re

occurrence. Beyond the general conclusion that good relationships accompany good coping, specific findings suggest that parents can also be too protective; for example, if they completely shield their highly reactive children from stress, they may also prevent children from developing effective coping strategies (e.g., Fox et al. 2005). These findings suggest that an important function of parents may be to "dose" children, grading their exposure to stress, while providing sufficient supports so that they can learn to manage it well (Power 2004).

Although multiple pathways have been suggested, research is just beginning to explore the precise mechanisms through which social forces shape children's coping (Eisenberg et al. 1997, Power 2004, Skinner & Edge 2002). Of special import are studies examining the ways in which parents socialize coping, either explicitly, for example, through modeling, teaching, and coaching (Kliewer et al. 1994), or implicitly, through comforting, soothing, and helping (Holodynski & Friedlmeier 2006, Sroufe 1996). Theories and methods adapted from work on the socialization of children's emotional reactivity and expression, as well as their behavioral and emotional self-regulation, promise to enrich these avenues of research on coping (Eisenberg et al. 1997, Power 2004). Two intriguing suggestions from this work are that the kinds of parenting that promote the development of coping depend on children's temperamental characteristics (Eisenberg & Valiente 2004) and are likely to change as children develop (Power 2004).

Developments underlying shifts in coping. Perhaps the greatest challenge to the developmental study of coping is to discover how developments in the processes underlying children's reactions and responses to stress lead to age-graded changes in children's coping (Compas et al. 1992, Compas 1998). As noted in previous reviews, the development of coping is affected by changes in physiology, perception, memory, cognition, language, emotion, self-perceptions, motivation, social comparison, and social relationships (Derryberry et al. 2003, Eisenberg et al. 1997, Fields & Prinz 1997, Maccoby 1983, Murphy & Moriarity 1976, Rutter 1983).

Up to now, there has been a narrow focus on specific underlying developments. For example, the development of social referencing allows infants long-distance access to information from their caregivers about danger and safety. The development of mobility opens up a whole range of coping through physical interactions with the environment, such as reaching, withdrawal, and proximity-seeking. Cognitive developments contribute to improvements in problem-solving, internalization of behavioral standards, and perspective taking, all of which allow more constructive and effective coping. During adolescence, improvements in meta-cognitive skills and the recognition of emotions facilitate planning and the use of cognitive strategies to regulate complex emotions. Although many of these developments signal improvements, reviewers also point out developmental increases in vulnerabilities. For example, adolescents are less likely to be overwhelmed by emotional arousal, but they may also be more likely to experience threats to their self-concepts, to worry about social relationships, to internalize negative experiences, or to ruminate (Eisenberg et al. 1997).

At this point, the underlying mechanisms that have been suggested are numerous, heterogeneous, and follow differing yet intertwined timetables. Useful studies will continue to describe age differences, but will also directly examine how coping changes as a function of developments in specific underlying processes (Compas et al. 1992). For example, studies that directly assess cognitive development and then examine whether certain coping strategies are more likely at different levels (e.g., Band & Weisz 1990) provide a firmer foundation for inferences about the basis of age differences. Mapping out these interrelated changes and figuring out how they interact to produce quantitative and qualitative shifts in coping are among the greatest challenges to the area (Compas 1998).

Summary. A broader integrative framework allows for a consideration of how temperament, socialization, and normative developments shape differential pathways of coping. According to this framework, the first "coping" subsystem is physiological, including individual differences such as temperament (Derryberry et al. 2003). These subsystems have their own checks and balances, including social ones, in the form of caregivers who fulfill all the functions of a coping system, such as monitoring and detecting threats, protecting, removing stressors, soothing, and comforting (Barrett & Campos 1991, Holodynski & Friedlmeier 2006). From birth, infants are active participants in these processes, communicating their distress reactions and preferences through their motor behaviors and emotions in social interactions. All these subsystems are shaped by objective stressors, that is, the actual dangers, threats, losses, pleasures, and challenges faced by children and their families on an ongoing basis. Key developmental questions involve how, as children age, the development of new capacities, such as language, voluntary behavior, and cognition, changes both the structure of the coping system and how it functions when encountering such stressors.

FUTURE RESEARCH ON THE DEVELOPMENT OF COPING

Traditional research on the development of coping, including most of the research reviewed above, tends to focus on a single facet, like appraisals, stress reactivity, or ways of coping, and examine how it changes with age or can be predicted from earlier personal or social factors. The next generation of coping research will build on the advances just described, but will focus on individual differences in developmental pathways of coping and on coping episodes as mechanisms of development. Moreover, studies will frame developmental issues as not only increases or decreases in particular components, but also as potential reorganizations of the entire coping system over time. These three important sets of questions, as guides to a developmental agenda to the study of coping, are described below (see also Compas 1998).

What Are the Different Developmental Pathways of Coping and What Shapes Them?

The descriptive strand of this research involves longitudinal studies tracing different pathways from early forms of coping to later forms. For example, if negotiation emerges as an interpersonal coping strategy at about age three, then longitudinal research could trace whether it is more likely to emerge from earlier interpersonal coping via aggression, submission, or some other way of coping. This research could also uncover whether certain early forms of coping or reactivity are "developmental dead ends" in that they interfere with the emergence of later forms.

The explanatory strand of this research examines how profiles of coping emerge as the long-term effect of different combinations of stressors and social relationships on children with differing temperaments. It would be especially important to include markers of previous experiences with aversive events and of the resources or liabilities these experiences engendered, such as stress tolerance or learned helplessness. Studies could also probe possible explanations for why children fail to transform from one means of coping to another (e.g., temperamental vulnerabilities, too much stress, insecure attachments, or repeated failure experiences).

What Are the Effects of Coping on Development?

This research focuses on how coping influences development. Children's reactions and ways of dealing with stress likely shape their social relationships, the subsequent stressors

they encounter, and eventually, even their own stress physiology and development. Studies would investigate how certain patterns of coping contribute to the accumulation of resources and liabilities that shape future stressful encounters, such as a sense of autonomy or close friendships. Eventually, research may explore how coping marks a site of developmental significance—a zone of struggle, practice, or experience—that cumulatively shapes major developments (Skinner & Edge 1998).

How Does Coping (Potentially) Get Better and How Can It Be Promoted?

This research investigates aspects of coping suggested (but not really specified) by terms like flexible, differentiated, appropriate, selective, reflective, considered, organized, constructive, measured, modulated, sturdy, and autonomous. These terms imply a system that potentially progresses from diffuse to differentiated, from uncoordinated to integrated, from egocentric to cooperative, and from reactivity to proactive autonomous regulation. These developmental potentials depict a system that can increasingly monitor and appropriately appraise more (current and future) demands using its own and others' "radar"; maintain composure under higher levels of appraised threat with more capacity to withstand multiple demands and better "fallbacks"; respond increasingly in measured socially competent ways that reflect integration of ongoing emotional, attentional, and motivational reactions; more flexibly adjust actions to meet changing environmental demands without losing sight of genuine priorities; recover more quickly from setbacks; and at the same time, take more away from stressful encounters, learning how to prevent and deal with future challenges and how to deploy coping in line with future goals.

Because not all adolescents (or adults) reach these potentials, the refinement of interventions that promote more adaptive coping is a high priority for developmental research

(Sandler et al. 1997). To the extent that such programs take into account the constraints and opportunities created by children's dispositions and developmental levels and by the configuration of stressors and supports present in their daily lives, these interventions will be more effective in helping children develop their long-term coping resources and capacities.

CONCLUSION

As it becomes clear that the development of coping cannot be understood without considering the multiple physiological, emotional, behavioral, attentional, and interpersonal processes that give rise to it and the larger social ecological contexts within which it unfolds, more researchers have suggested conceptualizing coping as part of a complex adaptive system that includes stress, resilience, and competence (Haggerty et al. 1994, Masten 2006). Although no consensus exists about the specifics of such a perspective, it seems clear that coping operates at multiple levels and across several different time scales. As graphically depicted in **Figure 1**, coping can be considered an adaptive process on the scale of developmental time, an episodic process across days and months, and an interactive process in real time (Coping Consortium 2001).

Currently, most research focuses on coping as an episodic process (middle portion of **Figure 1**): Coping is recruited in response to demands (environmental or intrapsychic) and is shaped by the individual's appraisals and by social and individual resources. From this perspective, the primary questions involve how coping functions with the other components during an episode: How do particular social contexts, demands, social factors, and individual characteristics shape coping? Up to now, these are the main questions that have preoccupied coping researchers.

As important as these questions are, coping research needs to grow and change if it is to benefit from and contribute to other work on stress, adversity, and development. At a more

micro level, studies will need to consider coping as an interactional process, as it operates at the level of interactions with the social and physical context (bottom of **Figure 1**), and as captured by observations or daily diaries. Such research would need to include the multiple components of reactions to stress evoked in real time and should specify how they work together in interactions. Studies may use new conceptualizations of coping as regulation under stress to build on what is known about temperament and stress physiology and to create a place for behavior, emotion, attention, cognition, motivation, and social relationships (Derryberry et al. 2003, Gunnar & Cheatham 2003, Holodynski & Friedlmeier 2006).

At a more macro level, coping has the potential to contribute to research on adversity, competence, and resilience if studies can document its function as part of the adaptive processes through which exposure to adversity has a long-term impact on individual functioning and development (Grant et al. 2003, Masten et al. 1999). At this level (top portion of **Figure 1**), coping can be considered a set of proximal processes depicting how children actually react to and deal with the specific stressors to which they have been exposed.

This article summarizes challenges to research on the development of coping as well as recent advances that promise progress in charting developmental shifts in coping patterns and in capturing the many constitutional, psychological, and social factors that interact to shape those developments. We suggest future research directions that focus on differential pathways of development and on the power of coping episodes to shape short- and long-term developments. As a subtext throughout this article runs the conviction that research on coping is critical to an understanding of stress and adversity in the real lives of children and adolescents. We believe that as an organizational construct, it has the potential to provide an integrative link from the physiological processes of stress reactions to the sociocultural forces that

Coping as a multi-level adaptive system: models of coping as a system operating at multiple embedded levels

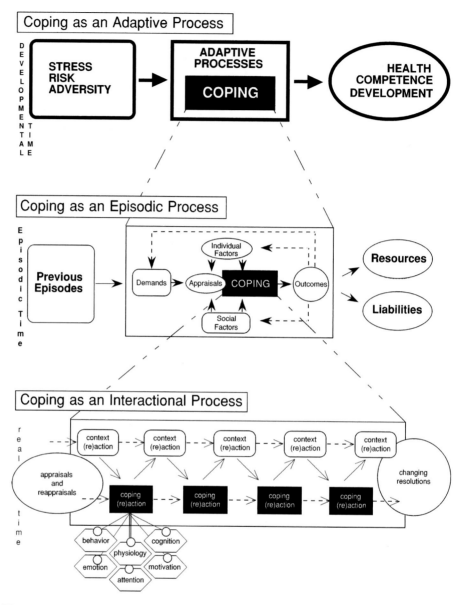

Figure 1

A model of coping as a multi-level adaptive system operating (*a*) as an adaptive process across developmental time, (*b*) as an episodic process across episodic time, and (*c*) as an interactional process across real time.

determine the stressors that societies allow into children's lives. To the extent that work on coping can make developmental progress, it may not only guide research across the age-graded literatures on coping within childhood and adolescence, but may also begin to create meaningful theoretical and empirical links to other important literatures currently attempting to chart the effects of childhood stress and adversity.

SUMMARY POINTS

1. Although development shapes every aspect of how people deal with stress, it has been very difficult to realize a developmental agenda for the study of coping.

2. Two recent theoretical advances promise to orient and invigorate research. First, conceptualizations of coping as regulation under stress establish links between coping and the normative development of emotional, attentional, and behavioral self-regulation. They also suggest constitutional underpinnings and social factors that shape the development of coping. Second, functional analyses of about a dozen hierarchically organized core families of coping can be used to identify how those functions can be achieved through different ways of coping at different ages, allowing the study of developmentally graded ways of coping within a family.

3. The research on age differences and age changes in coping from early childhood to early adulthood can be organized using a framework that relies on the families of coping to map ways of coping and the developmental course of regulation to identify key ages at which coping might show developmental shifts.

4. General mechanisms of coping may accumulate developmentally, starting with stress responses guided by reflexes during the neonatal period, and adding regulation via action schemes during infancy, supplemented by coping through direct action during preschool age, coping using cognitive means during middle childhood, and coping using meta-cognitive means during adolescence.

5. A broad integrative framework considers how temperament, socialization, and normative developments shape differential pathways of coping. Accordingly, the first coping subsystem is physiological, including individual differences such as temperament. These subsystems have their own checks and balances, including social ones, in the form of caregivers who fulfill all the functions of a coping system, such as monitoring and detecting threats, protecting, removing stressors, soothing, and comforting.

6. The greatest challenge to the developmental study of coping is to discover how, as children and adolescents age, the development of new capacities, such as language, voluntary behavior, and meta-cognition, changes both the structure of the coping system and how it functions when encountering stressors.

7. Future research may be guided by multilevel systems perspectives on the development of coping as including both the successive differentiation of responses to different demands (e.g., novelty, failure, delay, separation) and the integration of regulatory subsystems, potentially allowing coping to become more flexible, organized, cooperative, and autonomous across childhood and adolescence.

FUTURE ISSUES

1. How do ways of coping differ and change with age? Studies should use core families to organize ways of coping into more differentiated subscales and focus on certain ages as likely to mark developmental transitions. More fine-grained analyses within age groups should incorporate information on the normative development of emotion, attention, and behavioral self-regulation.

2. How does temperament shape the development of coping? Research can explore the many ways that individual differences in underlying constitutional differences (as well as developmental changes in these physiological processes) contribute to how children deal with stress.

3. How do social partners and social contexts shape the development of coping? Studies should continue to examine the role parents and other social partners play in the development of coping, including the ways in which this role changes as children develop new capacities (and liabilities).

4. How does coping change as a function of developments in specific underlying processes? Research would explore how changes in underlying developmental processes (such as cognition, communication, attachment) interact to produce quantitative and qualitative shifts in coping.

5. What are the different pathways of coping, and what contributes to their development? Research would examine how profiles of coping emerge as the long-term effects of different combinations of stressors and social relationships on children with differing temperaments. This research would include longitudinal studies tracing different pathways from early forms of coping to later forms.

6. What are the effects of coping on development? Research would examine how certain patterns of coping contribute to the accumulation of resources and liabilities that shape future stressful encounters. Eventually research may explore how coping marks a site of developmental significance, a zone of struggle, practice, or experience, that cumulatively shapes major developments.

7. How does coping (potentially) get better and how can it be promoted? Research will continue to refine interventions that promote more adaptive coping. To the extent that such programs take into account the constraints and opportunities created by children's dispositions and developmental levels and by the configuration of stressors and supports present in their daily lives, these interventions will be more effective in helping children develop their long-term coping resources and capacities.

ACKNOWLEDGMENTS

We are pleased to acknowledge the contributions of Danielle Sutton and Glen Richardson in preparing this article. We appreciate Wolfgang Friedlmeier, Ann Masten, and Bruce Compas for their willingness to review earlier drafts. We salute the other members of the Coping Consortium—Irwin Sandler, Bruce Compas, Nancy Eisenberg, Pat Tolan, and Tim Ayers—for the inspiration they provide.

One of the few books that covers the lifespan. Last three chapters review developmental research from birth to death.

LITERATURE CITED

Aldwin CM. 1994. *Stress, Coping, and Development: An Integrative Perspective*. **New York: Guilford**

Aspinwall LG, Taylor SE. 1997. A stitch in time: self-regulation and proactive coping. *Psychol. Bull.* 121:417–36

Ayers TS, Sandler IN, West SG, Roosa MW. 1996. A dispositional and situational assessment of children's coping: testing alternative models of coping. *J. Personal.* 64:923–58

Band EB, Weisz JR. 1990. Developmental differences in primary and secondary control coping and adjustment to juvenile diabetes. *J. Clin. Child Psychol.* 19:150–58

Barrett KC, Campos JJ. 1991. A diacritical function approach to emotions and coping. In *Life-Span Developmental Psychology: Perspectives on Stress and Coping*, ed. EM Cummings, AL Greene, KH Karraker, pp. 21–41. Hillsdale, NJ: Erlbaum

Block JH, Block J. 1980. The role of ego-control and ego-resiliency in the organization of behavior. In *Development of Cognition, Affect, and Social Relations*, ed. WA Collins, Minnesota Symposium on Child Psychology, 13:39–101. Hillsdale, NJ: Erlbaum

Bowlby J. 1969/1973. *Attachment and Loss.* Vols. 1 and 2. New York: Basic Books

Brandtstädter J, Renner G. 1990. Tenacious goal pursuit and flexible goal adjustment: explication and age-related analysis of assimilative and accommodative strategies of coping. *Psychol. Aging* 5:58–67

Bridges LJ. 2003. Coping as an element of developmental well-being. *Well-Being: Positive Development Across the Life Course.* ed. M Bornstein, L Davidson, CL Keyes, KA Moore, pp. 155–66. Mahwah, NJ: Erlbaum

Bridges LJ, Grolnick WS. 1995. The development of emotional self-regulation in infancy and early childhood. In *Review of Personality and Social Psychology.* ed. N Eisenberg, 15:185–211. Thousand Oaks, CA: Sage

Calkins SD, Dedmon SE, Gill KL, Lomax LE, Johnson LM. 2002. Frustration in infancy: implications for emotion regulation, physiological processes, and temperament. *Infancy* 3:175–97

Campos JJ, Frankel CB, Camras L. 2004. On the nature of emotion regulation. *Child Dev.* 75:377–94

Carver CS, Scheier MF. 1998. *On the Self-Regulation of Behavior.* Cambridge, UK: Cambridge Univ. Press

Coelho GV, Hamburg DA, Adams JE, eds. 1974. *Coping and Adaptation.* New York: Basic Books

Cole PM, Martin SE, Dennis TA. 2004. Emotion regulation as a scientific construct: methodological challenges and directions for child development research. *Child Dev.* 75:317–33

Compas BE. 1987. Coping with stress during childhood and adolescence. *Psychol. Bull.* 101:393–403

Compas BE. 1998. An agenda for coping research and theory: basic and applied developmental issues. *Int. J. Behav. Dev.* 22:231–37

Compas BE, Connor J, Osowiecki D, Welch A. 1997. Effortful and involuntary responses to stress: implications for coping with chronic stress. In *Coping with Chronic Stress*, ed. BH Gottlieb, pp. 105–30. New York: Plenum

Compas BE, Connor JK, Saltzman H, Thomsen AH, Wadsworth M. 1999. Getting specific about coping: effortful and involuntary responses to stress in development. In *Soothing and Stress*, ed. M Lewis, D Ramsay, pp. 229–56. Mahwah, NJ: Erlbaum

Compas BE, Connor-Smith JK, Saltzman H, Thomsen AH, Wadsworth ME. 2001. Coping with stress during childhood and adolescence: problems, progress, and potential in theory and research. *Psychol. Bull.* 127:87–127

Compas BE, Malcarne VL, Banez GA. 1992. Coping with psychosocial stress: a developmental perspective. In *Personal Coping: Theory, Research, and Application*, ed. BN Carpenter, pp. 47–63. London: Praeger

Connor-Smith JK, Compas BE, Wadsworth ME, Thomsen AH, Saltzman H. 2000. Responses to stress in adolescence: measurement of coping and involuntary stress responses. *J. Consult. Clin. Psychol.* 68:976–92

First identified disparate strands of research as directly relevant to study of coping. This is the article that defined the field.

State-of-the-art review of theories and research on childhood and adolescent coping. Includes many insights on development although major focus is individual differences.

Coping Consortium (Sandler I, Compas B, Ayers T, Eisenberg N, Skinner E, Tolan P, organizers). 1998, 2001. *New Conceptualizations of Coping.* Workshop sponsored by Arizona State Univ. Prev. Res. Cent., Tempe, AZ

Deci EL, Ryan RM. 1985. *Intrinsic Motivation and Self-Determination in Human Behavior.* New York: Plenum

Derryberry D, Reed MA, Pilkenton-Taylor C. 2003. Temperament and coping: advantages of an individual differences perspective. *Dev. Psychopathol.* 15:1049–66

Eisenberg N, Fabes RA. 1992. Emotion, regulation, and the development of social competence. In *Emotion and Social Behavior. Review of Personality and Social Psychology*, ed. MS Clark, 14:119–50. Thousand Oaks, CA: Sage

Eisenberg N, Fabes RA, Guthrie IK. 1997. Coping with stress: the roles of regulation and development. In *Handbook of Children's Coping: Linking Theory and Intervention*, ed. SA Wolchik, IN Sandler, pp. 41–70. New York: Plenum

Eisenberg N, Fabes RA, Nyman M, Bernzweig J, Pinuelas A. 1994. The relations of emotionality and regulation to children's anger-related reactions. *Child Dev.* 65:109–28

Eisenberg N, Valiente C. 2004. Elaborations on a theme: beyond main effects in relations of parenting to children's coping and regulation. *Parenting Sci. Pract.* 4:319–23

Fields L, Prinz RJ. 1997. Coping and adjustment during childhood and adolescence. *Clin. Psychol. Rev.* 17:937–76

Folkman S, Moskowitz JT. 2004. Coping: pitfalls and promise. *Annu. Rev. Psychol.* 55:745–74

Fox NA, Henderson HA, Marshall PJ, Nichols KE, Ghera MA. 2005. Behavioral inhibition: linking biology and behavior within a developmental framework. *Annu. Rev. Psychol.* 56:235–62

Frydenberg E. 1997. *Adolescent Coping: Theoretical and Research Perspectives.* New York: Routledge

Garmezy N. 1983. Stressors of childhood. In *Stress, Coping, and Development in Children*, ed. N Garmezy, M Rutter, pp. 43–84. Baltimore, MD: Johns Hopkins Univ. Press

Garmezy N, Rutter M, eds. 1983. *Stress, Coping, and Development in Children.* Baltimore, MD: Johns Hopkins Univ. Press

Gianino A, Tronick E. 1998. The mutual regulation model: the infant's self and interactive regulation and coping and defensive capacities. In *Stress and Coping Across Development*, ed. T Field, P McCabe, N Schneiderman, pp. 47–68. Hillsdale, NJ: Erlbaum

Grant KE, Compas BE, Stuhlmacher AF, Thurm AF, McMahon SD, Halpert JA. 2003. Stressors and child and adolescent psychopathology: moving from markers to mechanisms of risk. *Psychol. Bull.* 129:447–66

Gunnar MR, Cheatham CL. 2003. Brain and behavior interface: stress and the developing brain. *Infant Mental Health J.* 24:195–211

Gunnar MR, Brodersen L, Nachmias M, Buss K, Rigatuso J. 1996. Stress reactivity and attachment security. *Dev. Psychobiol.* 29:191–204

Haggerty RJ, Sherrod LR, Garmezy N, Rutter M, eds. 1994. *Stress, Risk, and Resilience in Children and Adolescents: Processes, Mechanisms, and Interventions.* New York: Cambridge Univ. Press

Holodynski M, Friedlmeier W. 2006. *Development of Emotions and Emotion Regulation.* New York: Springer

Kliewer W, Sandler I, Wolchik S. 1994. Family socialization of threat appraisal and coping: coaching, modeling, and family context. In *Social Networks and Social Support in Childhood and Adolescence*, ed. K Hurrelman, F Nestmann, pp. 271–91. Berlin: de Gruyter

Kopp CB. 1982. Antecedents of self-regulation: a developmental perspective. *Dev. Psychol.* 18:199–214

Provocative research-based essay on the implications of considering the basic motivational and attentional subsystems involved in temperament as constituting early coping mechanisms.

Empirical review, guided by a broad heuristic model, that examines roles of emotion regulation, temperament, and socialization in development of coping through adolescence.

Excellent review and integration of research, including age-group comparisons and links between coping and adjustment. Outstanding section on developmental differences.

Describes developmental and clinical perspectives on coping and summarizes an extensive body of empirical research on adolescents.

Shaped and foreshadowed research over subsequent decades in a seminal volume written by experts in subspecialties ranging from

Kopp CB. 1989. Regulation of distress and negative emotions: a developmental view. *Dev. Psychol.* 25:343–54

Lazarus RS. 1999. *Stress and Emotion: A New Synthesis.* New York: Springer

Lazarus RS, Folkman S. 1984. *Stress, Appraisal, and Coping.* New York: Springer

Lengua LJ, Sandler IN. 1996. Self-regulation as a moderator of the relation between coping and symptomatology in children of divorce. *J. Abnorm. Child Psychol.* 24:681–701

Losoya S, Eisenberg N, Fabes RA. 1998. Developmental issues in the study of coping. *Int. J. Behav. Dev.* 22:287–313

Maccoby EE. 1983. Social-emotional development and response to stressors. See Garmezy & Rutter 2003, pp. 217–34

Masten AS. 2006. Developmental psychopathology: pathways to the future. *Int. J. Behav. Dev.* 30:47–54

Masten AS, Hubbard JJ, Gest SD, Tellegen A, Garmezy N, Ramirez ML. 1999. Competence in the context of adversity: pathways to resilience and maladaptation from childhood to adolescence. *Dev. Psychopathol.* 11:143–69

Metcalfe J, Mischel W. 1999. A hot/cool-system analysis of delay of gratification: dynamics of willpower. *Psychol. Rev.* 106:3–19

Mischel HN, Mischel W. 1983. The development of children's knowledge of self-control strategies. *Child Dev.* 54:603–19

Murphy LB. 1974. Coping, vulnerability, and resilience in childhood. In *Coping and Adaptation*, ed. GV Coelho, DA Hamburg, JE Adams, pp. 47–68. New York: Basic Books

Murphy LB, Moriarity A. 1976. *Vulnerability, Coping, and Growth: From Infancy to Adolescence.* New Haven, CT: Yale Univ. Press

Power TG. 2004. Stress and coping in childhood: the parents' role. *Parenting Sci. Pract.* 4:271–317

Rossman BBR. 1992. School-age children's perceptions of coping with distress: strategies for emotion regulation and the moderation of adjustment. *J. Child Psychol. Psychiatry Allied Discipl.* 33:1373–97

Rothbart MK, Derryberry D, Posner MI. 1994. A psychobiological approach to the development of temperament. In *Temperament: Individual Differences at the Interface of Biology and Behavior*, ed. JE Bates, TD Wachs, pp. 83–116. Washington, DC: Am. Psychol. Assoc.

Rudolph KD, Dennig MD, Weisz JR. 1995. Determinants and consequences of children's coping in the medical setting: conceptualization, review, and critique. *Psychol. Bull.* 118:328–57

Rutter M. 1983. Stress, coping, and development: some issues and some questions. See Garmezy & Rutter 1983, pp. 1–41

Ryan-Wenger NM. 1992. A taxonomy of children's coping strategies: a step toward theory development. *Am. J. Orthopsychiatry* 62:256–63

Sandler IN, Wolchik SA, MacKinnon D, Ayers TS, Roosa MW. 1997. Developing linkages between theory and intervention in stress and coping processes. In *Handbook of Children's Coping: Linking Theory, Research, and Intervention*, ed. SA Wolchik, IN Sandler, pp. 3–40. New York: Plenum

Seiffge-Krenke I. 1995. *Stress, Coping, and Relationships in Adolescence.* Hillsdale, NJ: Erlbaum

Skinner EA. 1999. Action regulation, coping, and development. In *Action and Self-Development*, ed. JB Brandtstädter, RM Lerner, pp. 465–503. Thousand Oaks, CA: Sage

Skinner EA, Edge K. 1998. Reflections on coping and development across the lifespan. *Int. J. Behav. Dev.* 22:357–66

biochemistry to public policy.

Reviews research on the physiology of the stress system and how its development is shaped by temperament and social relationships.

Describes the first comprehensive longitudinal study of the development of children's coping from infancy to adolescence.

A developmental and process-oriented review of how parents shape children's coping.

Good example of how to study coping as a developmental process. Reports on studies of a developmental model of stress, coping, and outcomes during adolescence.

Skinner EA, Edge K. 2002. Parenting, motivation, and the development of children's coping. In *Agency, Motivation, and the Life Course: Vol. 48 of the Nebraska Symposium on Motivation*, ed. RA Dienstbier, LJ Crockett, pp. 77–143. Lincoln, NE: Nebraska Univ. Press

Skinner EA, Edge K, Altman J, Sherwood H. 2003. Searching for the structure of coping: a review and critique of category systems for classifying ways of coping. *Psychol. Bull.* 129:216–69

Skinner EA, Wellborn JG. 1994. Coping during childhood and adolescence: a motivational perspective. In *Life-Span Development and Behavior*, ed. D Featherman, R Lerner, M Perlmutter, 12: 91–133. Hillsdale, NJ: Erlbaum

Sroufe LA. 1996. *Emotional Development: The Organization of Emotional Life in the Early Years.* New York: Cambridge Univ. Press

Walker LS, Smith CA, Garber J, Van Slyke DA. 1997. Development and validation of the pain response inventory for children. *Psychol. Assess.* 9:392–405

White RW. 1974. Strategies of adaptation: an attempt at systematic description. In *Coping and Adaptation*, ed. GV Coelho, DA Hamburg, JE Adams, pp. 47–68. New York: Basic Books

Wilson BJ, Gottman JM. 1996. Attention—the shuttle between emotion and cognition: risk, resiliency, and physiological bases. In *Stress, Coping, and Resiliency in Children and Families*, ed. EM Hetherington, EA Blechman, pp. 189–228. Hillsdale, NJ: Erlbaum

Wolchik SA, Sandler IN, eds. 1997. *Handbook of Children's Coping: Linking Theory and Intervention.* New York: Plenum

Zimmer-Gembeck MJ, Locke EM. 2006. The socialization of adolescent coping: relationships at home and school. *J. Adolesc.* In press

Zimmer-Gembeck MJ, Skinner EA. 2006. *The development of coping across childhood and adolescence: An integrative review and critique of research.* Unpubl. manuscr., Portland State Univ., Griffith Univ.

Tackles the problem of constructing core higher-order families of coping.

Definitive compendium of theory, research, and interventions on coping during childhood and adolescence.

The Neurobiology of Stress and Development

Megan Gunnar and Karina Quevedo

Institute of Child Development, University of Minnesota, Minneapolis, Minnesota
55455; email: Gunnar@umn.edu, queve001@umn.edu

Annu. Rev. Psychol. 2007. 58:145–73

First published online as a Review in
Advance on August 11, 2006

The *Annual Review of Psychology* is online
at http://psych.annualreviews.org

This article's doi:
10.1146/annurev.psych.58.110405.085605

0066-4308/07/0110-0145$20.00

Key Words

HPA axis, psychopathology

Abstract

Stress is a part of every life to varying degrees, but individuals differ
in their stress vulnerability. Stress is usefully viewed from a biological
perspective; accordingly, it involves activation of neurobiological systems that preserve viability through change or allostasis. Although
they are necessary for survival, frequent neurobiological stress responses increase the risk of physical and mental health problems,
perhaps particularly when experienced during periods of rapid brain
development. Recently, advances in noninvasive measurement techniques have resulted in a burgeoning of human developmental stress
research. Here we review the anatomy and physiology of stress responding, discuss the relevant animal literature, and briefly outline
what is currently known about the psychobiology of stress in human
development, the critical role of social regulation of stress neurobiology, and the importance of individual differences as a lens through
which to approach questions about stress experiences during development and child outcomes.

Contents

INTRODUCTION

Threats to well-being, whether physical or psychological, are components of life experience. Individuals differ markedly, however, in the frequency with which they experience stressful life events and their vulnerability or resilience to stressful challenges (Akil & Morano 1995). Stress, although often studied as a psychological construct, may be viewed from a biological perspective (Dantzer 1991). Accordingly, stress responses are composed of the activation of neurobiological systems that help preserve viability through change or allostasis (McEwen & Seeman 1999). Although necessary for survival, the effects of frequent physiological stress responses may increase the risk of future physical and mental health problems. The impact of physiological stress reactions on the developing brain may be of particular note, helping to explain how adverse rearing experiences heighten the risk of behavioral and emotional problems in children and adolescents (Gunnar 2000, Heim & Nemeroff 2001, Sanchez et al. 2001). In the past 20 years, advances in measurement techniques have allowed developmental researchers to assess physiological stress responses in children both in the laboratory and under naturalistic conditions (Gunnar & Talge 2006). Consequently, the field of developmental stress research has burgeoned. In the following review, we outline the anatomy and physiology of stress, discuss the animal literature relevant to the study of stress in human psychobiological research, and briefly outline what is currently known about the development of stress reactivity and regulation, the social regulation of stress in human development, the impact of maltreatment on stress neurobiology, and the importance of individual differences as a lens through which to approach questions about stress and experience during development.

NEUROANATOMY AND PHYSIOLOGY

Stress responses in mammals are effected by two distinct but interrelated systems:

the sympathetic-adrenomedullary (SAM; Frankenhaeuser 1986) system and the hypothalamic-pituitary-adrenocortical (HPA; Stratakis & Chrousos 1995) system. The SAM system is a component of the sympathetic division of the autonomic nervous system, releasing epinephrine (adrenaline) from the medulla or center of the adrenal gland. Increases in circulating epinephrine facilitate rapid mobilization of metabolic resources and orchestration of the fight/flight response (Cannon 1929). The HPA system, in contrast, produces glucocorticoids (cortisol in humans, corticosterone in rodents; hereafter GCs) which are steroid hormones. Unlike epinephrine, which does not cross the blood-brain barrier to a significant degree, the brain is a major target of GCs (Bohus et al. 1982). Also unlike epinephrine, GCs production takes some time (approximately 25 minutes to peak levels), and many of its impacts on the body and brain occur through the changes in gene expression (de Kloet 1991). Consequently, the impacts of GCs are slower to develop and continue for longer periods (de Kloet et al. 1996). As discussed more fully below, the role of the HPA system in stress is complex, and its functions are not fully captured by reference to the fight/flight response (Sapolsky et al. 2000). Regulation of both the SAM and HPA systems converges at the level of the hypothalamus, which integrates autonomic and endocrine functions with behavior (Palkovits 1987). Furthermore, inputs to the hypothalamic nuclei that orchestrate HPA and SAM responses to psychosocial stressors involve cortico-limbic pathways (Gray & Bingaman 1996). Each system is described in detail below.

The Sympathetic Adrenomedullary System

The chromaffin cells of the adrenal medulla are secretor cells developmentally and functionally related to postganglionic sympathetic neurons and are considered part of the sympathetic nervous system (see **Figure 1**) (Vollmer 1996). They are innervated by sympathetic preganglionic neurons residing in the intermediolateral gray matter of the spinal cord (Tasaptsaris & Breslin 1989). Sympathetic preganglionic neurons send axons through the ventral root of the spinal cord and form cholinergic synapses with the chromaffin cells. When these cells are stimulated, they secrete catecholamines, predominantly epinephrine (Epi) but also some norepinephrine (NE) (Vollmer 1996). Epi and NE bind to various adrenoreceptors in multiple target organs and thus play multiple roles in fight/flight reactions (Tasaptsaris & Breslin 1989). For example, they both increase heart rate and stroke volume (and hence, cardiac output) and cause vasodilatation in muscles and constriction of blood vessels in the skin and gut. These changes ensure blood supply to the brain and muscles. Critically, Epi stimulates glycogenolysis in the liver, resulting in increased serum levels of glucose and therefore energy to fuel defensive responses. Although neither Epi nor NE cross the blood-brain barrier, the peripheral actions of these catecholamines are paralleled in the brain by NE produced by the locus coeruleus (Morilak et al. 2005). Its role in response to psychosocial threats is to support vigilance, arousal, and narrowing of attention, along with participating in processes that activate the other arm of the mammalian stress system, the HPA axis.

The Limbic Hypothalamic-Pituitary-Adrenocortical Axis

The cascade of events that leads to the production of glucocorticoids by the adrenal cortex begins with the release of corticotrophin-releasing hormone (CRH) and arginine vasopressin (AVP) by cells in the paraventricular nuclei of the hypothalamus (see **Figure 2**; reviewed in Gunnar & Vazquez 2006). CRH and AVP travel through small blood vesicles to the anterior pituitary, where they stimulate the release of adrenocorticotropic hormone (ACTH) (Stratakis & Chrousos 1995).

Stress: psychological condition in which the individual perceives or experiences challenges to physical or emotional well-being as overwhelming their ability and resources for coping

SAM: sympathetic adrenomedullary (system)

Hypothalamic-pituitary-adrenocortical (HPA) system: describes the complex chain of physiological events that characterizes one of the stress response systems

Glucocorticoids (GCs): a family of steroid hormones (such as or cortisol in humans and corticosterone in rodents) produced by the adrenal cortex

Cortico-limbic pathways: interconnected group of cortical and subcortical structures in the human brain that constitute the neural substrate for emotion, motivation, emotional learning, and regulation

Epi: epinephrine

NE: norepinephrine

CRH: corticotrophin-releasing hormone

ACTH: adrenocorticotropic hormone

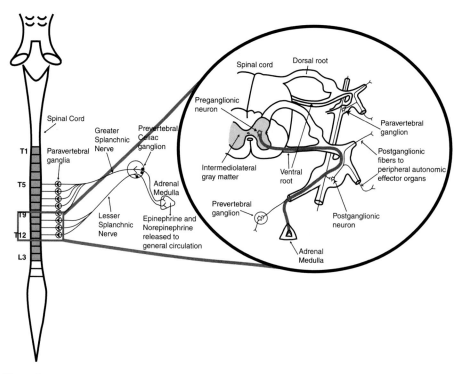

Figure 1

Anatomy of the sympathetic adrenomedullary (SAM) system. The SAM system is a component of the sympathetic nervous system. Its cell bodies (preganglionic neurons) are located in the interomediolateral (IML) cell column and exit the spinal cord via the ventral root to form cholinergic direct synapses on the chromaffin cells of the medulla of the adrenal glands. When stimulated, these chromaffin cells secrete catecholamines, epinephrine (80%), and norepinephrine (20%). The chromaffin cells of the adrenal medulla thus are equivalent to postganglionic sympathetic neurons. Secreted into general circulation, they act as hormones, affecting organs and tissues via adrenergic receptors (alpha and beta) that are activated at lower levels of epinephrine than norepinephrine. Adrenomedullary output greatly enhances sympathetic neural activity.

Sympathetic-adrenomedullary system: a primary biological system controlling stress response. Outflow of sympathetic autonomic nervous system that triggers rapid physiological and behavioral reactions to imminent danger or stressors

MRs: mineralocorticoid receptors

GRs: glucocorticoid receptors

ACTH interacts with receptors on the cortex of the adrenal gland to stimulate the production and release of GCs into general circulation. GCs enter into the cytoplasm of cells throughout the body and the brain, where they interact with their receptors (de Kloet 1991). The activated receptors then enter the nucleus of the cell, where they regulate the transcription of genes with GC-responsive regions. The action of GCs on target tissues involves changes in gene transcription, which explains why the effects of elevated GCs may take many minutes to hours to be produced and may continue to exert effects on physiology and behavior for prolonged periods (Sapolsky et al. 2000).

The effect of GCs depends upon the receptors with which they bind. There are two GC receptors: mineralocorticoid receptor (MR) and glucocorticoid receptor (GR) (de Kloet 1991). Outside the brain, GCs operate through GRs because of the presence of an enzyme, 11-beta hydroxysteroid dehydrogenase (11β-HSD), that prevents GCs from binding to MRs. In the brain, where 11β-HSD is minimally expressed, GCs bind to both MR and GR. Indeed, GCs have higher affinity (i.e., bind more readily) to MRs than to GRs, a fact that is critical in the regulation of both basal and stress responses of the HPA system (reviewed in Gunnar & Vazquez 2006). Because of their differential affinities

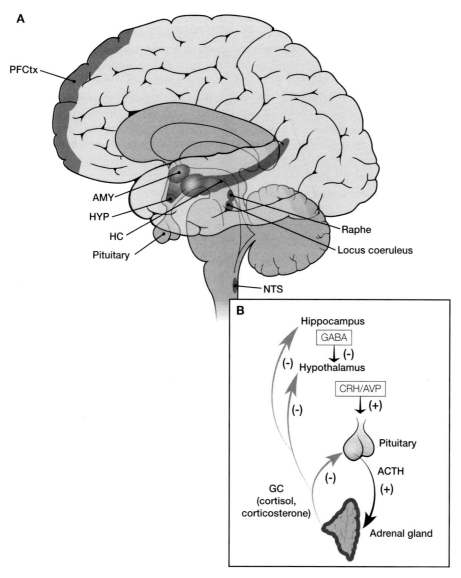

Figure 2

The anatomy of the hypothalamic-pituitary-adrenocortical (HPA) system and the structures that are important in its regulation. Also depicted is the activation (+) and negative feedback inhibition (−) pathways of the HPA system. Increases in glucocorticoids (GCs) are initiated by the release of corticotropin-releasing hormone/arginine vasopressin (CRH/AVP) from the medial parvocellular region of the paraventricular nucleus (PVN) in the hypothalamus. Negative feedback inhibition operates through GCs acting at the level of the pituitary, hypothalamus (HYP), and hippocampus (HC). ACTH, adrenocorticotropic hormone; AMY, amygdala; GABA, gamma aminobutyric acid; HC, hippocampus; HYP, hypothalamus; NTS, nucleus of the tractus solitarius; PFCtx, prefrontal cortex. Reprinted with permission from Gunnar & Vazquez 2006.

for GCs, MRs are 80%–90% occupied when GCs are in basal ranges (de Kloet 1991). By contrast, GRs are occupied only at the peak of the circadian cycle or when stressors stimulate GC elevations over basal concentrations. GRs mediate most of the stress effects of glucocorticoids, whereas MRs tend to mediate most basal effects, which include effects such as maintaining responsiveness of neurons to their neurotransmitters, maintaining the HPA circadian rhythm (highest at wakening and lowest 30 minutes after the onset of the long sleep period each day), and maintaining blood pressure (Sapolsky et al. 2000). Although these basal effects are often considered distinct from stress effects of GCs, they play a permissive role in stress. Basal levels allow effective fight/flight responses by allowing NE and Epi to have maximal impacts on their target tissues.

GR-mediated effects often oppose the ones effected through MR, leading some researchers to argue that stress resilience and vulnerability involve the ratio of MR-to-GR activation (de Kloet 1991). For example, GRs impair neural plasticity and the processes involved in learning and memory as evidenced by their impact on hippocampal neurons. By contrast, basal levels of GCs acting via MRs enhance synaptic plasticity as evidenced by a reduction of the refractory period of hippocampal neurons. MRs facilitate cerebral glucose availability, whereas GRs inhibit glucose utilization throughout the brain, thus endangering cell survival. GRs also activate pathways back to the PVN, which results in inhibition of CRH production (negative feedback) and thus a termination of the HPA stress response. It has long been a mystery why GRs, which are activated during stress responses of the HPA system, should operate to produce such deleterious effects. Why would this system have evolved to impair functioning under conditions of threat? One argument is that the suppressive effects mediated by GRs are necessary to reverse acute response to stressors and ultimately facilitate the recovery of cellular homeostasis (Sapolsky et al. 2000).

Only when stress is prolonged do the costs of suppressive effects begin to outweigh their benefits.

Maintaining viability through activation of SAM and HPA reactions has been termed allostasis, or the maintenance of stability through change (McEwen & Seeman 1999). The costs imposed by frequent or prolonged stress responses are described as allostatic load. In addition, the opposing effects of MRs and GRs combined with the differential affinity of GCs for these receptors explains why the relationship between GCs and adaptive functioning frequently takes an inverted-U function (Sapolsky 1997). Both chronically low and high levels of GCs are associated with nonoptimal adaptation. In contrast, moderate (or controlled elevations) are associated with physical and behavioral health.

Psychosocial Stressors: The Role of Corticotrophin-Releasing Hormone

Both the SAM and HPA systems are centrally modulated by limbic brain circuits that involve the amygdala, hippocampus, and orbital/medial prefrontal cortex [see **Figure 3** (as reviewed in Gunnar & Vazquez 2006)]. These structures/circuits allow psychological stressors to activate stress responses. The fast, SAM-mediated, fight/flight response utilizes CRH-producing neurons located in the central nucleus of the amygdala, the noradrenergic neurons located in the locus coeruleus, and other aminergic cells in the brain stem (Morilak et al. 2005). The locus coeruleus regulates the SAM response through its projecting NE neurons. These pathways, flowing through the lateral hypothalamus, activate sites in the brain stem, which in turn directly activate the sympathetic preganglionic neurons unleashing the release of Epi from the adrenal medulla. The central nucleus of the amygdala and CRH-mediated changes are also involved in activating the HPA response to psychosocial stressors (Shekhar et al. 2005). Here, however, pathways to hypothalamic CRH-producing cells that stimulate the HPA

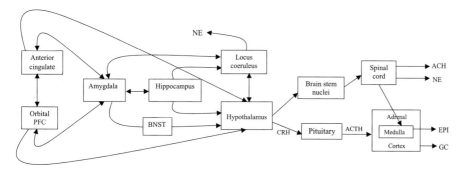

Figure 3

Three levels of neurobiological organization of the stress system responsive to psychological stressors. The cortico-limbic level of organization involves the anterior cingulate (ACC) and orbital frontal cortex (OFC), which relay information to subcortical structures involved in the stress response. The ACC and OFC are reciprocally interconnected with each other and with the amygdala, which has connections with the hippocampus and bed nucleus of the stria terminalis (BNST). The hypothalamic–brain stem level of organization involves the hippocampus and brain stem structures such as the locus coeruleus (LC), which releases norepinephrine (NE) to brain areas involved in alerting. The BNST provides pathways into the paraventricular nucleus (PVN) of the hypothalamus, which produces corticotrophin-releasing hormone (CRH) and arginine vasopressin (AVP), while the hippocampus and regions in the medial frontal cortex (e.g., ACC) maintain feedback control of the PVN. Considering the neural-to-adrenal level of analysis, nuclei in the lateral hypothalamus activate highly interconnected nuclei in the brain stem, including the parabrachial nuclei, that regulate the sympathetic (NE and epinephrine, Epi) and parasympathetic (acetylcholine, Ach) nervous systems via pathways traveling through the spinal cord to preganglionic nuclei or to target organs (e.g., the adrenal medulla). The production of CRH and AVP by the PVN regulates activity of the hypothalamic-pituitary-adrenocortical (HPA) axis and the production of glucocorticoids (GCs) as depicted more fully in **Figure 2**. Adapted with permission from Gunnar & Davis 2003.

cascade are indirect, operating through multisynaptic pathways via the bed nucleus of the stria terminalis that converge on the paraventricular nuclei in the hypothalamus (Herman & Cullinan 1997, Herman et al. 2002). These multiple, converging pathways allow modulation of the strength of the HPA responses in relation to the state of the body, time of day, and current levels of circulating hormone.

Because of the critical role of amygdalar CRH in the activating pathways for both SAM and HPA responses, there is increasing attention to the role of amygdalar CRH and its family of receptors in orchestrating stress reactions (Heinrichs et al. 1995, Nemeroff 1996, Swiergiel et al. 1993). Reacting to psychological stressors requires appraisal by higher brain structures such as the cingulate cortex and the orbital/medial prefrontal cortex (Barbas 1995, Diorio et al. 1993). Threat appraisal also involves subcortical structures

such as the bed nucleus of the stria terminalis and the hippocampus, as well as the further integration by hypothalamic and brain stem structures (Davis et al. 1997). CRH receptors in all of these regions affect components of stress responding (Bale & Vale 2004). For example, CRH infused into the locus coeruleus in rodents intensifies anxiety-related behaviors, and neurons in the locus coeruleus are sensitized to CRH after being exposed to psychological stressors (Butler et al. 1990). As with GCs, there are two prominent CRH receptors (CRH-1 and CRH-2), which tend to mediate opposing actions (Bale & Vale 2004). CRH-1 appears to mediate many of the anxiety-related actions of CRH, while CRH-2 mediates more of the stress effects on vegetative functions. Consistent with this distinction, CRH-1 receptors are more abundant in cortico-limbic pathways that mediate fear and anxiety-related behaviors, whereas CRH-2 receptors are found predominantly in sub-cortical brain regions (Sanchez et al. 2000, Vythilingam et al. 2002). It is unfortunate for students of human development that CRH cannot be noninvasively measured. Further-more, although CRH can be assayed in samples of cerebral spinal fluid (CSF), CSF concentrations do not allow differentiation of the brain locus of production.

Summary

The neuroanatomy and neurophysiology of the stress system involves the SAM and HPA systems. Both systems involve the adrenal gland and its secretions that are released into the bloodstream. Both also are orchestrated by activity in the central nervous system. Unlike the SAM system, however, the brain is a major target organ for the steroid hormones produced by the HPA axis. Also, unlike the SAM system, whose role in stress can be fairly simply described as "fight/flight," the role of the HPA system is more complex. Its basal activity appears to support or permit acute fight/flight responses, while its response to stressors serves to suppress the impact of fight/flight reactions. Over prolonged periods of chronic activation, the suppressive effects of the elevated GCs and the wear and tear of frequent SAM responses can have deleterious effects on physical and mental health. However, in the short term, robust, well-orchestrated activations of these systems tend to support adaptive functioning. This, plus the well-described inverted U-shaped functions relating SAM and HPA stress responses to a variety of adaptive functions, should caution researchers against thinking of increases in SAM and HPA activity as necessarily indexing risk of poor outcomes. Finally, our increasing understanding of the role of amygdalar CRH in orchestrating responses to psychosocial threats suggests that in many cases it is the activity of CRH that should be tracked by researchers studying links between emotional behavior and physiological responses to stressors. Unfortunately, CRH cannot be nonin-vasively measured and thus is not a part of the toolbox for researchers studying psychosocial stress and development in humans.

ANIMAL STUDIES OF EARLY EXPERIENCE AND STRESS NEUROBIOLOGY

More than a decade of research using animal models has shown that in many mammalian species, early experiences shape the neuro-biological systems involved in stress reactivity and regulation, and some of these effects appear permanent. The results of these studies have shaped the formulation of questions about early experiences and stress vulnerability in human development; thus, it is useful to outline the findings of the animal models here.

The Rodent Model

The rat has been the focus of much of this research (Sanchez et al. 2001). In the rat, the period between 4 and 14 days after birth is one during which it is difficult to produce elevations in ACTH and GCs to stressors that provoke responses in older animals (Rosenfeld et al. 1992). Termed the relative stress hyporesponsive period (SHRP), it has been assumed that this period evolved to protect the developing brain from potentially deleterious effects of elevated GCs and the other neurochemicals associated with the mammalian stress response (de Kloet et al. 1988). The SHRP appears to be maintained by very specific stimuli that pups receive from the dam. If the dam is removed for 12 to 24 hours, marked activation of the HPA system and elevated brain levels of CRH are noted (Suchecki et al. 1993). However, if during this time maternal stimulation is mimicked by stroking the pup with a wet paintbrush and infusing milk into its stomach via a cannula, HPA and central (brain) CRH responses are controlled (Cirulli & Alleva 2003).

We now know that not only deprivation of maternal care but also normal variations in rat mothering impact the developing neurobiology of stress (see review by Meaney & Szyf 2005). Dams vary in how much they lick and groom their pups. In comparison with low-licking and -grooming dams, high-licking and -grooming dams have pups that, as adults, are less fearful and better able to contain and terminate stress reactions of the HPA axis (Caldji et al. 1998). The molecular events set into motion by maternal care are increasingly understood. Particularly during the first week of the life in the rat, maternal licking and grooming regulate the extent to which GR genes in the hippocampus become methylated (Weaver et al. 2001). Methylation effectively silences genes. Licking and grooming reduce methylation of hippocampal GR genes. GR genes determine how many hippocampal glucocorticoid receptors an animal will have. Because hippocampal GRs are involved in terminating stress responses of the HPA system, high levels of hippocampal GRs mean efficient control of HPA stress response, whereas low levels mean poor or sluggish regulation, more prolonged stress reactions, and vulnerability to allostatic load over the animal's lifetime (Meaney & Szyf 2005, Weaver et al. 2001). These epigenetic effects of maternal care are potentially irreversible, except through pharmacological manipulations that induce widespread demethylation (Weaver et al. 2005). This is a powerful example of how stress neurobiology can be programmed by social experiences during sensitive periods of development.

The impact of early social stimulation becomes obvious when typical caregiving patterns are disrupted (for reviews, see Cirulli & Alleva 2003, Sanchez et al. 2001). Two closely related paradigms have been studied most: daily separations extending over the period of the SHRP that last for 3 to 15 minutes and similar daily separations that last for several (typically 3) hours. Strikingly, 15 minutes has a markedly different consequence than does 180 minutes of separation daily. In comparison with nonmanipulated dams and pups, the pups who experience 15 minutes of separa-

tion daily (termed "handling") become more stress resilient, whereas those experiencing 180 minutes of separation daily (termed "maternally separated") become more stress vulnerable. Relevant findings include evidence that separated animals, compared with control and handled animals, exhibit larger air-puff startle responses, greater freezing and anxiety behaviors to cat odor, and two- to threefold greater ACTH and glucocorticoid responses to restraint stress as adults (Cirulli & Alleva 2003). In addition, they also display evidence of anhedonia; mild cognitive impairments, especially on hippocampally mediated tasks; and greater consumption of alcohol (Sanchez et al. 2001). These behaviors correspond to increased CRH expression in the amygdala and bed nucleus of the stria terminalis, decreased GR in the hippocampus and consequently impaired negative feedback regulation of the HPA axis, increased NE in the locus coeruleus, and down-regulation of adrenergic receptors, among other changes that reflect shaping of hyperstress reactivity at multiple levels of the central nervous system (Ladd et al. 2000).

The difference between 15 minutes and 180 minutes of maternal separation appears to be conferred via differences in maternal behavior. After brief separations, dams increase their licking and grooming, whereas repeated three-hour separations appear to disorganize the dam, reducing licking and grooming of her pups. Some of the effects of maternal separation appear to be relatively permanent. However, some effects appear to be responsive to postinfancy modification by placing the juvenile animal in complex environments that stimulate exploration and expose the animal to high levels of social stimulation and novelty (Francis et al. 2002). Such enrichment experiences do not increase the previously maternally separated animal's hippocampal GR, but the experiences do appear to reduce activation of cortico-limbic fear circuits in response to novelty and threat in adulthood. Whether the continued deficit in hippocampal GR confers a risk for stress vulnerability in response to

Sensitive periods of development: periods during which an experience (or its absence) has a more marked impact on the neural organization underlying a particular skill or competence

chronic, rather than acute, stressors later in life is not yet known.

Attachment:
psychosocial process resulting in strong emotional bond with a particular person and deriving security from physical and psychological contact with that attachment figure

Early Adverse Experience in Nonhuman Primates

It is generally assumed that events, whether they are positive or negative, have less of an effect on structures and circuits that are already well developed than on those that are rapidly developing (Dobbing 1981). Nonhuman primates are born more mature than are rats; thus, we would expect that postnatal experiences would have somewhat different effects in the primate (for reviews, see Gunnar & Vazquez 2006, Sanchez et al. 2001). This appears to be true, despite the fact that, as in rats, disruptions of parental care in nonhuman primates also affect the neural substrates of stress vulnerability and resilience.

Nonhuman primates form specific attachments to caregivers (Suomi 1995). Separation from the attachment figure provokes acute behavioral distress and increases activity of the HPA and SAM systems (Levine & Wiener 1988). Behavioral distress, however, does not necessarily mirror physiological stress reactions. For example, if the infant monkey can see and call to its mother, vocal distress and behavioral agitation are much greater than if it is isolated from any contact. Nonetheless, physiological stress responses, particularly of the HPA system, are much greater under conditions of isolation (Bayart et al. 1990, Smotherman et al. 1979). Studies of the impact of different pharmacological manipulations during separation also demonstrate that behavioral distress and physiological stress responses are dissociable (Kalin et al. 1988, 1989). Critically, increases in HPA activity appear to correspond more closely with activity of amygdalar CRH and activation of fear circuits (Kalin et al. 1989). Notably, infant primates can gain some reduction in both distress vocalizations and physiological stress reactions when they are provided with surrogate caregivers during separation (reviewed in Levine & Wiener

1988). Consistent with the principles of attachment theory (Bowlby 1969), access to a secure base provided by the attachment figure or attachment surrogate reduces the probability of HPA/CRH stress reactions that could have long-term consequences on brain development.

Studies of nonhuman primates also demonstrate that poor rearing conditions, including peer-only rearing, isolation rearing, repeated separations, and conditions that disrupt responsive maternal care can have long-term impacts on the neurobiology of stress and negative emotionality (reviewed in Sanchez et al. 2001). For example, variable foraging paradigms that result in neglectful maternal care also produce offspring who as adults are more fearful, low in dominance, high in brain levels of CRH, and who exhibit persistent alterations in somatostatin and metabolites of serotonin, dopamine, and NE (Coplan et al. 1996, Rosenblum & Andrews 1994, Rosenblum et al. 1994). However, the long-term effects of social deprivation on the HPA axis are unclear (Mason 2000). For example, 2.5-year-old monkeys reared in isolation for the first year of life exhibited no differences in hypothalamic-CRH expression when compared with maternally reared animals (Sanchez et al. 1999). Similarly, unlike in the rat, no one has yet to demonstrate changes in hippocampal GR. Rather, the levels of stress neurobiology that are disturbed appear to involve the cortico-limbic circuits that evaluate and regulate responses to psychosocial threat, circuits that are still rapidly developing after birth in the monkey as they are in the human child.

POSTNATAL HUMAN DEVELOPMENT AND STRESS BIOLOGY

Neurobiological systems involved in stress include genetic, organ, behavioral, and emotional components that mature and become more organized as children develop. Below is an overview of the development of the components of the stress system, with particular emphasis on the HPA axis.

Infancy and Early Childhood

In adults, cortisol is usually bound to proteins (e.g., corticosteroid-binding globulin; CBG) (Rosner 1990). However, CBGs in newborns are initially low, although they increase over the first six months after birth (Hadjian et al. 1975). As a result, unbound levels of cortisol decrease slightly over the initial months after birth, while plasma or total cortisol increases. Only free cortisol can bind to its receptors and have biological effects; therefore, despite low plasma levels of cortisol at birth, the levels of biologically active cortisol in newborns are enough to have clear physiological effects (Gunnar 1992). Newborns can mount physiologically significant cortisol and ACTH responses to aversive medical procedures (blood draws, physical examinations, and circumcision) (reviewed in Gunnar 1992). Newborns, however, do not show the typical adult rhythm in cortisol production, characterized by higher levels in the morning at wake-up that decrease toward the afternoon and evening. They show two peaks, 12 hours apart, that do not depend upon the time of day (Klug et al. 2000). But by three months, a qualitative shift in physiological development takes place, and the single early morning cortisol peak and evening nadir (lowest level) are generally established (Matagos et al. 1998). The diurnal rhythm also continues to develop over infancy and early childhood, reflecting changes in daytime sleep patterns (Watamura et al. 2004). Specifically, until children give up their daytime naps, decreases in cortisol from mid-morning to mid-afternoon are not observed; after this, the diurnal rhythm of children is consistent with that of adults.

As in the newborn period, two-month-old babies increase cortisol significantly to medical examinations and also fuss and cry when they are examined (Larson et al. 1998). Around three months, there is a diminishing of the HPA response to stressors such as physical examinations, but this does not extend to decreased behavioral distress (Larson et al. 1998). Furthermore, across the first year of life it becomes increasing difficult to provoke cortisol increases to many mild stressors (stranger approach, strange events, 3- to 30-minute separations, and inoculations; reviewed in Gunnar & Donzella 2002). Indeed, by one year of age many infants show no evidence of increases in cortisol to stressors that typically provoke significant behavioral distress reactions. Both physiological changes in the system, such as improved negative feedback regulation of the axis, and decreased sensitivity of the adrenal cortex to ACTH may partially account for the diminution of the HPA stress response (Lashansky et al. 1991). In addition, as described below, the child's access to supportive adult care plays an increasingly salient role in buffering the activity of the HPA component of the stress system. Indeed, by the end of the first year of life, infants in supportive caregiving relationships appear to have entered the human functional equivalent of the rodent stress-hyporesponsive period (reviewed in Gunnar 2003).

As in the primate and rodent, behavioral distress is an unreliable index of HPA activation in young children. In the first weeks of life, this is demonstrated strikingly through studying infants with colic (White et al. 2000). Infants with colic, who by definition exhibit markedly high levels of crying, tend to exhibit low basal levels of cortisol and produce changes similar to those of noncolic babies in cortisol and heart rate in response to distressing events. By the time infants have formed attachment relationships to one or a few caregivers, the presence and history of responsiveness of the attachment figure both influences whether infants exhibit cortisol increases to stressors and whether behavioral distress correlates with these increases (reviewed in Gunnar & Donzella 2002). In secure attachment relationships (Nachmias et al. 1996) and with responsive surrogate caregivers (Gunnar et al. 1992), infants exhibit crying directed at soliciting care but do not exhibit elevations in

Cortisol: arguably the most powerful human glucocorticoid. Essential for regulation and support of vital functions including metabolism, immune response, vascular tone, and general homeostasis

cortisol. Conversely, in insecure relationships or with unsupportive caregivers, stressors continue to be capable of producing elevations in cortisol and distress, and heart rate increases tend to more closely approximate activations of the HPA system (Spangler & Schieche 1998). This generalization tends to hold for acutely stressful experiences, but may not be accurate for more prolonged periods of stress such as those experienced when toddlers enter full-time child care. Here it has been noted that the security of the child's attachment relationship does not determine the magnitude of the cortisol increase as the child adjusts to repeated daily separations, and over time it is the securely attached children whose behavioral distress corresponds to their increases in cortisol during these prolonged periods of separation (Ahnert et al. 2004).

Changes in other stress-sensitive systems are also observed over the early months of life. Notably, corresponding to the diminution of HPA responses to stressors, there is an increase in vagal tone (parasympathetic input to the heart) that may allow more nuanced cardiac and behavioral responses to psychosocial threat (Porges 1992, Porges et al. 1994). Whether changes in vagal tone are related to the emergence of secure-base attachment relationships has not been clearly demonstrated (although see Izard et al. 1991). However, there is evidence that emotion-related patterns of brain electrical activity measured over the frontal cortex are related to the infant's history of sensitive and responsive care. Specifically, infants of mothers who are highly sensitive and responsive exhibit greater left frontal brain electrical (electroencephalogram, or EEG) activity patterns associated with positive emotionality and approach, whereas those with low-responsive mothers exhibit greater right frontal EEG patterns associated with negative emotionality and fearful, inhibited temperament (Hane & Fox 2006). In nonhuman primates, greater left frontal EEG asymmetry has been shown to correlate with lower cortisol reactivity to stressors (Kalin et al. 1998). Higher vagal

tone, lower cortisol reactivity to stressors, and greater left frontal EEG patterns suggest that, at least under conditions of supportive care, the human child enters a period of relative stress hyporesponsivity by the latter part of the first year that may buffer or protect the developing brain and result in a more stress-resilient child.

Later Childhood and Adolescence

There is increasing evidence that the period of relative stress hyporesponsivity or buffering does not end with infancy but extends over most of the childhood years. As is the case with toddlers, it is difficult to find laboratory situations that provoke large increases in cortisol throughout childhood (reviewed in Gunnar & Fisher 2006). Although many children may be largely buffered from stress during infancy and childhood, there is also increasing evidence that this period of relative stress buffering draws to a close as children transition into adolescence. In addition to the psychosocial changes associated with the adolescent transition, biological processes associated with puberty may shift the child's stress neurobiology to adult-responsive patterns (Spear 2000). It is now clear that the increasing level of basal cortisol shown in children between the ages of 6 and 17 years is remarkably similar to that of the rodent, which exhibits increases in basal GC levels at the close of the stress-hyporesponsive period (Kiess et al. 1995, Legro et al. 2003, Netherton et al. 2004, Shirtcliff 2003). Some studies suggest that the increases in basal GCs peak between 10 and 14 years or at around Tanner stage three (Elmlinger et al. 2002, Netherton et al. 2004), whereas others show a more gradual increase with age (Jonetz-Mentzel & Wiedenmann 1993). In addition to increases in basal cortisol levels, there also is increasing evidence that cortisol responses to laboratory stressors may increase with age and pubertal status over the adolescent transition (Klimes-Dougan et al. 2001, Walker et al. 2001, Wewerka et al. 2005). Not all studies have demonstrated such increases in stress responsivity over the transition into adolescence (for review, see Gunnar & Vazquez 2006), but the weight of the evidence is beginning to suggest that an adolescent emergence out of a period of relative stress hyporesponsivity or buffering is real and may have implications for the heightened risk of psychopathology noted among adolescent-aged children (Spear 2000).

SOCIAL REGULATION OF STRESS NEUROBIOLOGY IN HUMANS

The Role of Caregivers

Children's development takes place within the close social relationships with adult caregivers. One of the functions of the caregiving system is to modulate and enable control of physiological and behavioral responses to stressors. In humans, social modulation of physiological stress responses may lay the foundation for the development of emotion regulation competencies (Stansbury & Gunnar 1994). Patterns of social relatedness in infancy can be characterized, in part, by the security of the infant-caregiver attachment relationship (Ainsworth et al. 1978), and physiological stress responses have been found to be mediated by attachment security (Gunnar et al. 1996, Spangler & Schieche 1998, Sroufe & Waters 1979). In the presence of the attachment figure, toddlers who are in secure attachment relationships do not show elevations in cortisol to distress-eliciting events, whereas toddlers in insecure attachment relationships do (reviewed in Gunnar & Donzella 2002). The power of secure attachment relationships to buffer or prevent elevations in cortisol to otherwise mildly stressful events has been demonstrated in both laboratory and naturalistic situations. In comparison to organized but insecure attachment relationships, disorganized/disordered attachment may signal even greater stress vulnerability. Disorganized attachment relationships are believed to arise, in part, from the infant's experience of frightening behavior and episodes of dissociation in the caregiver (Lyons-Ruth et al. 1995). Children in disorganized/disoriented attachment relationships are characterized by their inability to organize or regulate affect and behavior toward their caregiver in stressful situations (van Ijzendoorn et al. 1999). These children are also most likely to exhibit disturbances in HPA axis activity (Hertsgaard et al. 1995, Spangler & Grossmann 1997) and are most at risk for behavioral and emotional problems (van Ijzendoorn et al. 1999).

There is also evidence that family dynamics, beyond attachment security/insecurity, influence cortisol reactivity in developing children. Naturalistic observations from households of typically developing children (ages 2 month to 17 years) yield evidence that traumatic family events (conflict, punishment, shaming, serious quarrelling, and fighting) are strongly associated with periods of elevated cortisol levels when the child's response to acutely traumatic events is compared with their own levels on less traumatic days in the family (Flinn & England 1995). There is also evidence that early disruptions in the parent-child relationship may produce increased levels of cortisol by the preschool years and that these heightened levels predict increased behavioral and emotional problems in the school-aged child (Essex et al. 2002). Likewise, social adversity that results in high maternal expression of depressive symptoms, including disrupted patterns of parenting, has been shown to be related to higher and less-regulated cortisol activity in school-aged children and adolescents (Halligan et al. 2004, Lupien et al. 2000). Additionally, in clinical populations of children with behavior problems, cortisol increases during a parent-child conflict-discussion task have been found to be associated with dysfunctional parenting attitudes and symptoms of anxiety and depression in the child (Granger et al. 1996). In summary, adult caregivers and family influences are powerful regulators of the HPA system.

Caregivers can prevent elevations in cortisol for infants and children even during threatening external events. Responsive caregiving allows children to elicit help by expressing negative emotions, without triggering the endocrine component of the stress response. Conversely, when the parenting is inadequate and/or is the source of threat, relationships can be a major source of physiological stress for children (Repetti et al. 2002).

Peers and Early Socialization Experiences

As children mature, their social circle expands to include other children and adults, particularly in the context of school and daycare centers. This entails the entrance into a complex and challenging environment that demands the emergence of social skills including control of inappropriate behaviors, adapting communication to the listener point of view, interpreting emotional cues, and maintaining play themes over transitions (Rubin et al. 1998). The social challenges posited by peer groups may explain reported cortisol increases over the day in full-day child-care settings (Dettling et al. 1999, 2000; Tout et al. 1998; Watamura et al. 2002a, 2002b, 2003). In such child-care settings, the majority of 2- to 4-year-old children showed increases in cortisol production over the day, whereas this is not observed for the same children at home on days they do not go to child care. As a group, children 5 to 8 years of age do not show increases in cortisol in group-care settings, although individually some children do. It has been suggested that increases in cortisol at child care emerges at the age when peer relations become salient. The challenge of managing interactions with others for children whose social skills are just emerging may tax the young child's coping abilities and, combined with long hours of care, may tax the child's capacity to maintain basal cortisol levels (also reviewed in Gunnar & Donzella 2002). This hypothesis is strengthened by evidence that children with the largest increases in cortisol over the child-care day have been rated by multiple adult observers as less socially competent and less capable of regulating negative emotions and aggression (Dettling et al. 1999, 2000). However, consistent with the argument that support from adults is critical to psychosocial regulation of stress in early childhood, elevations in cortisol in child-care settings are not observed when the child receives individualized, supportive care from care providers (Dettling et al. 2000).

Aside from normative developmental trends and variations associated with social competence, cortisol levels measured when children are in peer group settings also reflect peer acceptance or rejection (Gunnar et al. 1997, 2003). As early as the preschool years, peer-rejected children produce higher levels of cortisol in the preschool classroom in comparison to average or popular children. Peer rejection is associated with poor social skills and poor emotion regulation (Coie et al. 1990). This is often expressed as poorly contained aggression and inability to regulate negative emotions, all of which is associated with poorer peer relations and higher cortisol levels (Gunnar et al. 2003). Interestingly, in studies of preschool-aged children, there is little evidence that children who few others nominate as either liked or disliked (i.e., peer-neglected children) exhibit elevated levels of cortisol (Gunnar et al. 2003). By contrast, at least by early as adolescence, children who are socially neglected and who consequently spend hours alone even when they are with peers (i.e., at school) do exhibit higher levels of cortisol production (Adam 2006). The psychosocial pathways through which peer-rejected and peer-neglected children experience stress related to their social status are not yet understood, although it seems likely that social threats, disappointments, and other aversive interactions are likely involved. In addition, pathways from poor family relationships to poor peer and friendship relations need to be considered.

STRESS NEUROBIOLOGY AND ADVERSE EXPERIENCE: PARENTAL NEGLECT AND ABUSE

Maltreatment during development has been repeatedly linked to maladaptive outcomes (Cicchetti 1996). Adult survivors of childhood maltreatment reveal greater prevalence of psychiatric disorders, including affective disorders, eating disorders, somatic complaints, sexual dysfunction, and substance abuse. Alterations in stress-sensitive neurobiological systems, including regulation of GCs and CRH, have been posited as mechanisms through which adverse experience increases the likelihood of psychopathology (see reviews by Bremner & Vermetten 2001, De Bellis 2001, Heim & Nemeroff 2001, Teicher et al. 2002).

The Stress Neurobiology of Adult Survivors

Researchers studying the impact of maltreatment during childhood are dealing with a still-developing neural system in which developmental change and effects of maltreatment can be difficult to disentangle (Cicchetti & Tucker 1994). It is helpful, therefore, to consider first what is known about the stress neurobiology of adult survivors of childhood maltreatment. Much of the adult survivor research has focused on adults with depression and/or posttraumatic stress disorder (PTSD) pursuant to their maltreatment histories (Glaser 2000, Heim & Nemeroff 2001, Heim et al. 2004). Many of these studies lack appropriate controls. For example, adult survivors of childhood maltreatment who have PTSD may be compared to healthy controls so that differences associated with PTSD and impacts of childhood abuse cannot be disentangled. Nonetheless, the general pattern of findings suggest that severe, early maltreatment may have neurobiological consequences that last into adulthood and that increase the risk of psychopathology. To understand the findings, it is important to briefly describe alterations in stress neurobiology noted for adults with these disorders who do not have childhood maltreatment histories.

PTSD and depression appear to share hyperactivity of CRH at hypothalamic and extrahypothalamic levels (Bremner et al. 1997, Heim et al. 2004). Chronic CRH drive on the pituitary in both disorders appears to result in counter-regulatory down-regulation at the level of the pituitary, leading to blunted ACTH in response to pharmacological CRH challenge tests (Heim et al. 2004). However, these disorders differ in the sensitivity of feedback regulation of the HPA axis. Depression among adults is often associated with reduced negative feedback regulation (e.g., Young et al. 1991), whereas PTSD appears to be associated with increased negative feedback (e.g., Yehuda 2000). As a result, adults with depression often hypersecrete cortisol and exhibit prolonged cortisol elevations, whereas adults with PTSD often hyposecrete cortisol and rapidly return to baseline concentrations following perturbation. The question is whether childhood maltreatment alters these patterns.

Studies using pharmacological challenge tests provide evidence that pituitary down-regulation of ACTH is comparable in adults with depression and PTSD regardless of their childhood maltreatment histories (for a review, see Heim et al. 2004). At the level of the adrenal and with regard to negative feedback regulation, the picture is more complex. There is some suggestion that depression plus early childhood maltreatment may be associated with an exaggerated negative feedback in comparison with what is observed in depression without childhood abuse (Newport et al. 2004). However, this may reflect unmeasured PTSD in the adult maltreatment survivors (Rinne et al. 2002). The picture changes when psychological stressor tests are used. Here hyper-responsiveness of ACTH and in some instances cortisol has been noted, particularly among adult survivors with depression compared with depressed adults without childhood abuse histories (Heim et al.

2000, 2002). Unlike pharmacological challenges, psychological stressors depend on recruitment of cortico-limbic activation pathways. Thus, hyperactivation for psychological as opposed to pharmacological challenge suggests that adult survivors of maltreatment who have PTSD and/or depression may have even more hyper-responsive threat/stress systems at the cortico-limbic level than do nonmaltreated adults with these disorders.

Critically, however, a very different picture emerges when one studies adult survivors of childhood maltreatment who are free from psychopathology (Gunnar & Fisher 2006). By definition, such individuals are resilient. Given their resilience, perhaps it is not surprising to find that across various studies these adults show evidence of reduced activity of stress neurobiology. For example, the CRH challenge test, which produces blunted ACTH responses in individuals with PTSD and/or depression, produces larger-than-average responses in resilient adult survivors of childhood maltreatment (Heim et al. 2001). Because the magnitude of the ACTH response is inversely proportional to the pituitary's chronic or trait-like exposure to CRH (Newport et al. 2003), these results suggest chronic low CRH production in resilient adult survivors. Similar ACTH results have been obtained in response to psychosocial stressors combined with normal to low cortisol and cardiac responses among resilient adult survivors (Girdler et al. 2003). Finally, the adrenals of resilient adult survivors also show lower-than-expected production of cortisol to ACTH challenge tests (Heim et al. 2001). What is not clear is whether this pattern of low stress responding is a risk factor for subsequent physical and mental disorders or is a reflection of individual differences in stress reactivity that may have protected the developing brain from adverse impacts of maltreatment. Both possibilities exist, and the latter should alert developmental researchers to the importance of considering individual differences and their genetic substrate in pursuing questions about the impact of childhood experiences on stress and emotion reactivity and regulation.

Child Maltreatment and Stress Neurobiology

It has been hypothesized that traumatized children initially exhibit complex environmentally induced developmental disorders that later branch toward more specific and adult-like pathologies such as depression and anxiety (Cicchetti 1996). This complexity is evidenced in the data on the stress physiology of abused children, which are often challenging to interpret. For example, sexually abused girls evidence blunted ACTH response in reaction to CRH injections, similar to adult survivors of childhood abuse with depression or PTSD (De Bellis et al. 1994). However, enhanced ACTH responses and normal cortisol levels to CRH challenges have also been reported for depressed, abused children if they are still experiencing adverse home lives (Kaufman et al. 1997). As it does in adults, concurrent psychopathology contributes to the heterogeneous presentation of stress functioning in maltreated children. For example, in one study, maltreated externalizing boys at a summer camp had higher cortisol levels relative to nonmaltreated boys with externalizing problems; however, they did not have elevated cortisol levels relative to nondisordered nonmaltreated boys (Cicchetti & Rogosch 2001b). Indeed, hyporesponsiveness of both the SAM and HPA systems has been related to externalizing symptomatology (McBurnett & Lahey 1994, McBurnett et al. 2000, van Goozen et al. 2000). In a study of maltreated preschool-aged children compared with SES controls, maltreated children exhibited less cortisol reactivity and produced even lower cortisol levels on days when there were high levels of conflict and aggression in their classrooms (Hart et al. 1995). Furthermore, although adults with PTSD and adult survivors of child maltreatment may exhibit low levels of basal cortisol activity, in several studies, children with PTSD pursuant to severe childhood maltreatment exhibited elevated cortisol levels relative to controls (Carrion et al. 2002, De Bellis et al. 1999) and higher urinary excretion of Epi relative to nonmaltreated clinically anxious and nonanxious children (De Bellis et al. 1999). Researchers have argued that the adult PTSD-cortisol pattern may emerge with development and/or time since the trauma exposure (e.g., De Bellis 2001). In addition to the HPA and SAM systems, there is also evidence that cortico-limbic structures involved in emotions and stress are affected by early childhood maltreatment. Prepubertal children with PTSD secondary to maltreatment evidence smaller cerebral volumes, smaller corpus callosa relative to brain volume, and less asymmetry of the prefrontal cortex than do matched controls (reviewed in De Bellis 2001).

Not only physical and sexual maltreatment have an impact on the developing neurobiology of stress. There is increasing evidence that severe neglect also alters the stress neuraxis (De Bellis 2005). Children living in orphanages serve as an example. Cortisol levels in orphanage-reared infants and toddlers tend to be low in the early morning and lack the normal diurnal rhythm (Carlson & Earls 1997 and Kroupina et al. 1997, as reviewed in Gunnar 2000). Similar low early-morning levels have also been noted for domestically neglected children soon after placement in foster care (Dozier et al. 2006, Gunnar & Fisher 2006). There is increasing evidence that severe early neglect affects the development of cortico-limbic circuits involved in emotion and stress responding (Glaser 2000). For example, postinstitutionalized children have been found to have larger amygdala volumes, and amygdala size and function (fMRI findings) correspond to duration of institutional care (Tottenham et al. 2006). It is not clear whether neglect and abuse have different effects on the neurobiological systems that regulate stress and emotional function or whether these effects are comparable. One challenge in answering this question is that many abused children also suffer from neglect (Cicchetti &

Toth 1995). Indeed, there is some evidence that neglect and various types of abuse, along with exposure to violence, have cumulative effects; the most profound effects on stress reactivity and regulation are noted for children with the largest cumulative exposures (Cicchetti & Rogosch 2001a).

INDIVIDUAL DIFFERENCES: CONTRIBUTIONS FROM TEMPERAMENT AND GENETICS

As discussed above, adverse early experiences produce different patterns of stress responding in different individuals; hyperreactivity in some and seemingly hyporeactivity in others. Although the nature and timing of adverse or maltreating experience may partly explain these differences, it is likely that to some extent they also reflect individual differences that have a genetic contribution. Studies of both temperament as a reflection of genetic dispositions and, more recently, candidate genes have begun to flesh out this hypothesis. Most of the temperament work has focused on behavioral dispositions, particularly extreme shyness or behavioral inhibition, that may increase the risk of anxiety and depressive disorders (Kagan et al. 1987). Kagan has argued that the extreme 5% to 10% of behaviorally inhibited children are at risk for developing anxiety disorders, and recent studies have demonstrated that as adults, these individuals do show evidence of exaggerated amygdala responses to social stimuli (i.e., unfamiliar faces; Schwartz et al. 2003). In comparison with extremely noninhibited children, these extremely inhibited children also exhibit heightened vigilance, higher heart rates, lower heart-rate variability or vagal tone, and greater right-frontal EEG activity (Fox et al. 2001, Kagan et al. 1988).

Several researchers have suggested that the transition from extreme temperamental shyness or inhibition to pathological anxiety may involve hyperactivity of the HPA axis and its capacity to increase amygdalar CRH activity, thus orchestrating larger fear and stress reactions with less provocation (Rosen & Schulkin 1998). This would seem to require evidence of greater HPA reactivity to stressors among temperamentally inhibited children, something that has not been reliably found. Researchers have reported higher early-morning basal cortisol levels among more extremely inhibited children (Kagan et al. 1987, Schmidt et al. 1997). But few studies have found higher cortisol increases to psychological stressors such as entering a new play group, starting a new school year, or being exposed to laboratory stressors (for review, see Gunnar 2001). One problem may be that researchers have been searching for main effects of inhibited temperament, while temperament may more often moderate effects of stressors or operate in relation to the social support available to the child. Thus, as noted above, children with more negative emotional temperaments are at risk for larger increases in cortisol when they are in child-care settings, but this is only observed when the care provider is low in supportive and responsive care (Dettling et al. 2000).

The need to consider temperament in relation to the supportiveness of the care children receive is mirrored by recent findings regarding genes that may increase the risk of emotional disorders. Thus, a common regulatory variant (5-HTTLPR) in the serotonin transporter gene (SLC6A4) has received attention because it may increase the risk for anxiety and depression (Lesch 2001). However, several studies have now shown that individuals carrying alleles that result in altered transcription and transporter availability are not at increased risk for depression unless they have experienced more stressful life events, including childhood maltreatment (Caspi et al. 2003, Kaufman et al. 2004). Similarly, among temperamentally inhibited children there is now evidence that this gene variant is not associated with increasing levels of behavioral inhibition with development unless the child also experiences less social support and supportive care during early child-

hood (Fox et al. 2005). These findings are of note because there is evidence that a functionally equivalent gene variant in rhesus monkeys is associated with larger HPA responses to stressors, but only among animals that grow up in less-supportive care conditions (Barr et al. 2004). This is not the only genetic variation that likely makes important contributions to individual differences in stress reactivity and regulation; however, as with the work on shy, inhibited temperament and on the serotonin transporter allele, it is very possible that their consequences need to be considered in the context of the supportiveness of the child's social relationships.

CONCLUSIONS AND FUTURE DIRECTIONS

In the past 20 years, a tremendous amount has been learned about the development of stress reactivity and regulation during human development. Stress reactivity is better understood as the result of intertwined biological and psychological processes that ultimately ensure an organism's survival. Adjusting to external challenges through adaptive internal changes is a universal mechanism through which live organisms interface with their environment. However there is a cost to frequent physiological adjustments (allostatic load). Frequent activation of neurobiological stress responses increases the risk of physical and mental disorders, perhaps particularly while organisms are developing. As such, one of the most interesting findings emerging from the research on the psychobiology of stress is that in the absence of supportive care, stressors experienced during sensitive periods of development can in fact leave permanent imprints in the neural substrate of emotional and cognitive processes. Stress that is chronic, severe, and delivered during vulnerable periods of neural development will ripple through all levels of an organism's vital activity—be it a rat's inability to find its way through a maze or a maltreated child's hypersensitive response to angry faces. It would not be an overstatement to say that the nervous system of mammals carries their singular epigenetic history and expresses it in unique but lawful (i.e. predictable) ways. This is manifested both in the way organisms react to environmental challenges and in the way their neural structures are organized. The negative effects of stress, however, are not always irreversible. The psychobiology of stress reflects both epigenesis and current life circumstances. Improved living conditions and enriched environments have the potential of correcting the impact of early adverse stressors. For example, exposing juvenile rats to complex environments can reverse the neurobiological effects of rearing by a low-licking and -grooming mother. Similarly, maltreated preschool children placed in an early intervention foster care program (which promoted positive parenting strategies) showed both improved behavioral adjustment and more normative regulation of the HPA axis in comparison with children in typical foster care settings (Fisher et al. 2000). Intervention at other levels of the organism's functioning may also correct the long-term effects of early stressors. Antidepressants and CRH antagonists, for example, eliminate many of the behavioral disturbances that animals suffer due to early adverse experience; other pharmacologic agents also may be found to improve stress resilience among at-risk children.

A common theme in stress research is that, consistent with other mammals, during human development social relationships play critical roles in regulating physiological stress reactions and protecting the developing brain from potentially deleterious effects of the hormones and neurochemicals associated with stress reactions. Disturbances in supportive care and care environments that are themselves threatening appear to rob children of an effective stress buffer and expose them to the consequences of biological stress responses that can have deleterious effects for later development. Caregivers and close relatives in a child's life are both potentially the strongest sources of stress and the most pow-

erful defense against harmful stressors. Complex patterns of social stimulation may be part of the critical experiential input that (in interaction with genetic predispositions) shapes children's emotional and biological reactivity. Children's stress responses are also sensitive to social experiences beyond the context of the family. Negotiating peer interactions in school settings is a potent challenge to the stress system, particularly at the stage in development when social skills are just emerging. Above and beyond these normative challenges, children who are less socially competent and/or rejected might be at risk for more frequent and prolonged activation of the stress response. One of the areas that need integration into models of developmental health and psychopathology is how stress activation that is related to social status may affect children's later adaptation and health.

Despite tremendous advances in our understanding of stress neurobiology and development, there is still a great deal that is not understood. Principle among our lacunae is an adequate understanding of the genetic variations among children that moderate the reactivity, regulation, and impact of stress responses. However, numerous candidate genes are being identified whose impacts are now available for study. Integrating genetic studies into work on temperament, social experiences, stress responses, and behavioral outcomes will likely be an increasing focus of future research. Likewise, the emerging field of developmental affective neuroscience has a great deal to offer researchers concerned with understanding how the activity of stress-sensitive systems affects the development of brain systems involved in learning, memory, and emotion (Pollak 2005). Together, these foci of future research on stress should provide developmental researchers with a richer understanding of both normal and pathological development along with increased targets for interventions that will improve outcomes for children at risk for behavioral and emotional problems.

SUMMARY POINTS

1. Stressors trigger the activation of physiological systems designed to ensure the survival of the organism to the temporal detriment of systems controlling growth, reproduction, and replenishment. Although these adaptations through internal changes are desirable, under conditions of chronic stress they are deleterious. Chronic stress can cause inhibition of neurogenesis, disruption of neuronal plasticity, and neurotoxicity. Frequent activation of the stress response tilts the organism toward consuming resources without sufficient recovery and increases the risk for physical and behavioral problems. This has been termed "allostatic load."

2. Glucocorticoids regulate gene expression in multiple brain structures, thus simultaneously affecting central regulation of organic processes. The physiological and molecular events cascading from the activation of the stress systems have a powerful impact on neural tissues and the functions they support at any stage of development. However, these effects may be profound during periods of development, when the brain is undergoing rapid change. Sensitive periods and stages of enhanced brain plasticity are particularly vulnerable to the long-term effects of stress hormones. Chronic elevations of stress hormones can affect synaptic connectivity and neurogenesis and can increase cellular death, effectively altering the typical pathways and organization of the young brain.

3. Stress neurobiology can be shaped by the social environment experienced by young organisms, and adult patterns of stress reactivity can be permanently imprinted by key social influences (whether positive or negative) early in development. Of the various social influences that mammals experience, caregivers are by far the most powerful source of stress and the most effective defenseagainst harmful stressors. Disruption of the mother-infant relationship or failure of the caregiver to provide adequate care contributes to individual differences in physiological and behavioral responses to environmental challenges.

4. Maternal behavior can effectively change gene-controlled patterns of stress responsivity. Genetic information linked to neuroendocrine reactivity can be programmed by early maternal stimulation. In rodent models, highly responsive maternal behavior actually promotes a stress neurobiology that is less reactive and more resilient to challenges. The mechanisms are highly specific and involve relatively permanent modification of DNA controlling the expression of glucocorticoid receptors. However, these effects can be temporarily reversed by pharmacological intervention and in some cases by interventions that dramatically alter the care received by young mammals. The fact that DNA structure can be environmentally programmed posits both a mechanism for the impact of social stimulations and the molecular basis for intervention and healing.

5. The neurobiology of stress changes with development. Normative changes in the neurobiology of stress provide windows of opportunity and risks that are specific to that developmental stage. Reorganization of the stress response is species specific and seems to be tied to maturational changes in nervous system activity. For example, it is likely that with the onset of puberty, the relative low-stress responsivity of childhood ends and is marked by an increase in basal cortisol levels and heightened

neurobiological responses to stressors. If the onset of puberty indeed is characterized by enhanced stress reactivity, this would place adolescents at a heightened risk for psychopathology and could partly explain why there is an increase in the incidence of emotional disorders during adolescence.

6. Stress neurobiology is highly responsive to changes in the environment. Stress neurobiology, although very sensitive to early social contexts, is not a fixed or inflexible system. It reflects both the organism's epigenetic history and its new circumstances. Improved living conditions, enriched environments, and corrective emotional experiences can reverse the adverse consequences of early adversity.

7. Genes and environment interact in stress neurobiology. Constitutional predispositions intertwine with environmental influences to steer the developing stress neurobiology. Certain alleles of genes involved in neurotransmitter activity, neuronal connectivity, and differentiations seem to place children and adults at risk for a wide array of mental and physical disorders, especially when paired with adverse environments and multiple stressors such as those experienced in neglectful and abusive homes. Similarly, temperamentally inhibited children seem to be at risk for higher stress reactivity and behavioral inhibition in the context of lack of supportive care during childhood.

LITERATURE CITED

Adam EK. 2006. Transactions among trait and state emotion and adolescent diurnal and momentary cortisol activity in naturalistic settings. *Psychoneuroendocrinology* 31:664–79

Ahnert L, Gunnar MR, Lamb ME, Barthel M. 2004. Transition to child care: associations with infant-mother attachment, infant negative emotion, and cortisol elevations. *Child Dev.* 75:639–50

Ainsworth MD, Blehar MC, Waters E, Wall S. 1978. *Patterns of Attachment: A Psychological Study of the Strange Situation*. Hillsdale NJ: Erlbaum

Akil H, Morano M. 1995. Stress. In *Psychopharmacology: The Fourth Generation of Progress*, ed. F Bloom, D Kupfer, pp. 773–85. New York: Raven

Bale TL, Vale WW. 2004. CRF and CRF receptors: role in stress responsivity and other behaviors. *Annu. Rev. Pharmacol. Toxicol.* 44:525–57

Barbas H. 1995. Anatomic basis of cognitive-emotional interactions in the primate prefrontal cortex. *Neurosci. Biobehav. Rev.* 19:499–510

Barr CS, Newman TK, Shannon C, Parker C, Dvoskin RL, et al. 2004. Rearing condition and rh5-HTTLPR interact to influence limbic-hypothalamic-pituitary-adrenal axis response to stress in infant macaques. *Biol. Psychol.* 55:733–38

Bayart F, Hayashi KT, Faull KF, Barchas JD, Levine S. 1990. Influence of maternal proximity on behavioral and physiological responses to separation in infant rhesus monkeys (*Macaca mulatta*). *Behav. Neurosci.* 104:98–107

Bohus B, de Kloet ER, Veldhuis HD. 1982. Adrenal steroids and behavioral adaptation: relationship to brain corticoid receptors. In *Current Topics in Neuroendocrinology*, ed. D Granten, DW Pfaff, pp. 107–48. Berlin: Springer-Verlag

Bowlby J. 1969. *Attachment and Loss: Attachment*. New York: Basic Books

Bremner JD, Licino J, Darnell A, Krystal JH, Owens MJ, et al. 1997. Elevated CSF corticotropin-releasing factor concentrations in posttraumatic stress disorder. *Am. J. Psychiatry* 154:624–29

Bremner JD, Vermetten E. 2001. Stress and development: behavioral and biological consequences. *Dev. Psychopath.* 13:473–90

Butler PD, Weiss JM, Stout JC, Nemeroff CB. 1990. Corticotropin-releasing factor produces fear-enhancing and behavioral activating effects following infusion into the locus coeruleus. *J. Neurosci.* 10:176–83

Caldji C, Tannenbaum B, Sharma S, Francis D, Plotsky PM, Meaney MJ. 1998. Maternal care during infancy regulates the development of neural systems mediating the expression of fearfulness in the rat. *Proc. Natl. Acad. Sci. USA* 95:5335–40

Cannon WB. 1929. *Bodily Changes in Pain, Hunger, Fear, and Rage.* Boston: Branford

Carlson M, Earls F. 1997. Psychological and neuroendocrinological sequelae of early social deprivation in institutionalized children in Romania. *Ann. NY Acad. Sci.* 807:419–28

Carrion VG, Weems CF, Ray RD, Glaser B, Hessl D, Reiss AL. 2002. Diurnal salivary cortisol in pediatric posttraumatic stress disorder. *Biol. Psychol.* 51:575–82

Caspi A, Sugden K, Moffit T, Taylor A, Craig IW, et al. 2003. Influence of life stress on depression: moderation by a polymorphism in the 5-HTT gene. *Science* 301:386–89

Cicchetti D. 1996. Child maltreatment: implications for developmental theory and research. *Hum. Dev.* 39:18–39

Cicchetti D, Rogosch FA. 2001a. The impact of child maltreatment and psychopathology on neuroendocrine functioning. *Dev. Psychopathol.* 13:783–804

Cicchetti D, Rogosch FA. 2001b. Diverse patterns of neuroendocrine activity in maltreated children. *Dev. Psychopathol.* 13:677–93

Cicchetti D, Toth SL. 1995. A developmental psychopathology perspective on child abuse and neglect. *J. Am. Acad. Child Adolesc. Psychol.* 34:541–65

Cicchetti D, Tucker D. 1994. Development and self-regulatory structures of the mind. *Dev. Psychopathol.* 6:533–49

Cirulli F, Alleva BE. 2003. Early disruption of the mother-infant relationship: effects on brain plasticity and implications for psychopathology. *Neurosci. Biobehav. Rev.* 27:73–82

Coie JD, Dodge KA, Kupersmidt JB. 1990. Peer group behavior and social status. In *Peer Rejection in Childhood*, ed. SR Asher, JD Coie, pp. 17–59. New York: Cambridge Univ. Press

Coplan JD, Andrews MW, Rosenblum LA, Owens MJ, Friedman S, et al. 1996. Persistent elevations of cerebrospinal fluid concentrations of corticotropin-releasing factor in adult nonhuman primates exposed to early-life stressors: implications for the pathophysiology of mood and anxiety disorders. *Proc. Natl. Acad. Sci. USA* 93:1619–23

Dantzer R. 1991. Stress and disease: a psychobiological perspective. *Ann. Behav. Med.* 13:205–10

Davis M, Walker DL, Lee Y. 1997. Roles of the amygdala and bed nucleus of the stria terminalis in fear and anxiety measured with the acoustic startle reflex. *Ann. NY Acad. Sci.* 821:305–31

De Bellis MD. 2001. Developmental traumatology: the psychobiological development of maltreated children and its implications for research, treatment, and policy. *Dev. Psychopathol.* 13(3):539–64

De Bellis MD. 2005. The psychobiology of neglect. *Child Maltreat.* 10:150–72

De Bellis MD, Baum AS, Birmaher B, Keshavan MS, Eccard CH, et al. 1999. Developmental traumatology, part 1: biological stress systems. *Biol. Psychol.* 9:1259–70

De Bellis MD, Chrousos GP, Dorn LD, Burke L, Helmers K, et al. 1994. Hypothalamic-pituitary-adrenal axis dysregulation in sexually abused girls. *J. Clin. Endocrinol. Metab.* 78:249–55

Provides empirical evidence on how adverse rearing environment results in emotional and endocrine dysregulation.

Reviews evidence in rodent model that demonstrates the basic neurobiological mechanisms through which brain development is under exquisite maternal regulation.

de Haan M, Nelson CA, Gunnar MR, Tout K. 1998. Hemispheric differences in brain activity related to the recognition of emotional expressions by 5-year-old children. *Dev. Neuropsychol.* 14:495–518

de Kloet ER. 1991. Brain corticosteroid receptor balance and homeostatic control. *Front. Neuroendocrinol.* 12:95–164

de Kloet ER, Rosenfeld P, van Eekelen JA, Sutanto W, Levine S. 1988. Stress, glucocorticoids and development. *Prog. Brain Res.* 73:101–20

de Kloet ER, Rots NY, Cools AR. 1996. Brain-corticosteroid hormone dialogue: slow and persistent. *Cell. Mol. Neurobiol.* 16:345–56

Dettling AC, Gunnar MR, Donzella B. 1999. Cortisol levels of young children in full-day childcare centers: relations with age and temperament. *Psychoneuroendocrinology* 24:505–18

Dettling AC, Parker SW, Lane S, Sebanc A, Gunnar MR. 2000. Quality of care and temperament determine whether cortisol levels rise over the day for children in full-day childcare. *Psychoneuroendocrinology* 25:819–36

Diorio D, Viau V, Meaney MJ. 1993. The role of the medial prefrontal cortex (cingulate gyrus) in the regulation of hypothalamic-pituitary-adrenal responses to stress. *J. Neurosci.* 13:3839–47

Dobbing J. 1981. The later development of the brain and its vulnerability. In *Scientific Foundations of Pediatrics*, ed. JA Davis, J Dobbing, pp. 744–59. London: Heinemann Med. Books

Dozier M, Peloso E, Gordon MK, Manni M, Gunnar MR, et al. 2006. Foster children's diurnal production of cortisol: an exploratory study. *Child Maltreat.* 11:189–97

Elmlinger MW, Kuhnel W, Ranke MB. 2002. Reference ranges for serum concentrations of lutropin (LH), follitropin (FSH), estradiol (E2), prolactin, progesterone, sex hormone binding globulin (SHBG), dehydroepiandrosterone (DHEAS), cortisol, and ferritin in neonates, children, and young adults. *Clin. Chem. Lab. Med.* 40:1151–60

Essex MJ, Klein M, Cho E, Kalin NH. 2002. Maternal stress beginning in infancy may sensitize children to later stress exposure: effects on cortisol and behavior. *Biol. Psychiatry* 52:776–84

Fisher PA, Gunnar R, Chamberlain P, Reid JB. 2000. Preventive intervention for maltreated preschool children: impact on children's behavior, neuroendocrine activity, and foster parent functioning. *J. Am. Acad. Child Adolesc. Psychol.* 39:1356–64

Flinn MV, England BG. 1995. Childhood stress and family environment. *Curr. Anthropol.* 36:854–66

Fox NA, Henderson HA, Rubin KH, Calkins SD, Schmidt LA. 2001. Continuity and discontinuity of behavioral inhibition and exuberance: psychophysiological and behavioral influences across the first four years of life. *Child Dev.* 72:1–21

Fox NA, Nichols K, Henderson H, Rubin K, Schmidt L, et al. 2005. Evidence for a gene-environment interaction in predicting behavioral inhibition in middle childhood. *Psychol. Sci.* 16:921–26

Francis D, Diorio J, Plotsky PM, Meaney MJ. 2002. Environmental enrichment reverses the effects of maternal separation on stress reactivity. *J. Neurosci.* 22:7840–43

Frankenhaeuser M. 1986. A psychobiological framework for research on human stress and coping. In *Dynamics of Stress: Physiological, Psychological, and Social Perspectives*, ed. MH Appley, R Trumbull, pp. 101–16. New York: Plenum

Girdler SS, Sherwood A, Hinderliter A, Leserman J, Costello N, et al. 2003. Biologic correlates of abuse in women with premenstrual dysphoric disorder and healthy controls. *Psychol. Med.* 65:849–56

Glaser D. 2000. Child abuse and neglect and the brain—a review. *J. Child Psychol. Psychiatry* 41:97–116

Summarizes evidence pertaining to how life experience steers brain development by influencing how genetic predispositions are expressed.

Granger DA, Weisz JR, McCracken JT. 1996. Reciprocal influences among adrenocortical activation, psychosocial processes, and the behavioral adjustment of clinic-referred children. *Child Dev.* 67:3259–60

Gray TS, Bingaman EW. 1996. The amygdala: corticotropin-releasing factor, steroids, and stress. *Crit. Rev. Neurobiol.* 10:155–68

Gunnar M. 1992. Reactivity of the hypothalamic-pituitary-adrenocortical system to stressors in normal infants and children. *Pediatrics* 90:491–97

Gunnar M. 2000. Early adversity and the development of stress reactivity and regulation. In *The Effects of Adversity on Neurobehavioral Development. The Minnesota Symposia on Child Psychology*, ed. CA Nelson, pp. 163–200. Mahwah, NJ: Erlbaum

Gunnar M. 2001. The role of glucocorticoids in anxiety disorders: a critical analysis. In *The Developmental Psychopathology of Anxiety*, ed. MW Vasey, M Dadds, pp. 143–59. New York: Oxford Univ. Press

Gunnar M. 2003. Integrating neuroscience and psychosocial approaches in the study of early experiences. In *Roots of Mental Illness in Children*, ed. JA King, CF Ferris, II Lederhendler, pp. 238–47. New York: NY Acad. Sci.

Gunnar M, Brodersen L, Nachmias M, Buss KA, Rugatuso J. 1996. Stress reactivity and attachment security. *Dev. Psychobiol.* 29:191–204

Gunnar M, Davis EP. 2003. The developmental psychobiology of stress and emotion in early childhood. In *Comprehensive Handbook of Psychology: Volume 6. Developmental Psychology*, ed IB Weiner, RM Lerner, MA Easterbrooks, J Mistry, pp. 113–43. New York: Wiley

Gunnar M, Donzella B. 2002. Social regulation of the cortisol levels in early human development. *Psychoneuroendocrinology* 27:199–220

Gunnar M, Fisher PA. 2006. Bringing basic research on early experience and stress neurobiology to bear on preventive interventions for neglected and maltreated children. *Dev. Psychopathol.* In press

Gunnar M, Larson M, Hertsgaard L, Harris M, Brodersen L. 1992. The stressfulness of separation among 9-month-old infants: effects of social context variables and infant temperament. *Child Dev.* 63:290–303

Gunnar M, Sebanc AM, Tout K, Donzella B, van Dulmen MMH. 2003. Temperament, peer relationships, and cortisol activity in preschoolers. *Dev. Psychobiol.* 43:346–58

Gunnar M, Talge NM. 2006. Neuroendocrine measures in developmental research. In *Developmental Psychophysiology*, ed. LA Schmidt, S Segalowitz. New York: Cambridge Univ. Press. In press

Gunnar M, Tout K, de Haan M, Pierce S, Stansbury K. 1997. Temperament, social competence, and adrenocortical activity in preschoolers. *Dev. Psychobiol.* 31:65–85

Gunnar M, Vazquez D. 2006. Stress neurobiology and developmental psychopathology. In *Developmental Psychopathology: Developmental Neuroscience*, ed. D Cicchetti, D Cohen, pp. 533–77. New York: Wiley

Hadjian AJ, Chedin M, Cochet C, Chambaz EM. 1975. Cortisol binding to proteins in plasma in the human neonate and infant. *Pediatr. Res.* 9:40–45

Halligan SL, Herbert J, Goodyer IM, Murray L. 2004. Exposure to postnatal depression predicts elevated cortisol in adolescent offspring. *Biol. Psychol.* 55:376–81

Hane AA, Fox NA. 2006. Natural variations in maternal caregiving of human infants influence stress reactivity. *Psychol. Sci.* 17:550–56

Hart J, Gunnar M, Cicchetti D. 1995. Salivary cortisol in maltreated children: evidence of relations between neuroendocrine activity and social competence. *Dev. Psychopathol.* 7:11–26

Extensively reviews role of stress reactivity and neuroendocrine regulation in onset and presentation of mental disorders; emphasizes manifestations of dysregulated LHPA function.

Heim C, Nemeroff CB. 2001. The role of childhood trauma in the neurobiology of mood and anxiety disorders: preclinical and clinical studies. *Biol. Psychol.* 49:1023–39

Heim C, Newport DJ, Bonsall R, Miller AH, Nemeroff CB. 2001. Altered pituitary-adrenal axis responses to provocative challenge tests in adult survivors of childhood abuse. *Am. J. Psychiatry* 158:575–81

Heim C, Newport DJ, Heit S, Graham YP, Wilcox MBR, et al. 2000. Pituitary-adrenal and autonomic responses to stress in women after sexual and physical abuse in childhood. *J. Am. Med. Assoc.* 284:592–97

Heim C, Newport J, Wagner D, Wilcox MM, Miller AH, Nemeroff CB. 2002. The role of early adverse experience and adulthood stress in the prediction of neuroendocrine stress reactivity in women: a multiple regression analysis. *Depress. Anxiety* 15:117–25

Heim C, Plotsky P, Nemeroff CB. 2004. The importance of studying the contributions of early adverse experiences to the neurobiological findings in depression. *Neuropsychopharmacology* 29:641–48

Heinrichs SC, Menzaghi F, Pich EM, Britton KT, Koob GF. 1995. The role of CRF in behavioral aspects of stress. *Ann. NY Acad. Sci.* 771:92–104

Herman JP, Cullinan WE. 1997. Neurocircuitry of stress: central control of the hypothalamo-pituitary-adrenocortical axis. *Trends Neurosci.* 20:78–84

Herman JP, Tasker JG, Ziegler DR, Cullinan WE. 2002. Local circuit regulation of paraventricular nucleus stress integration glutamate-GABA connections. *Pharmacol. Biochem. Behav.* 71:457–68

Hertsgaard L, Gunnar MR, Erickson M, Nachmias M. 1995. Adrenocortical responses to the strange situation in infants with disorganized/disoriented attachment relationships. *Child Dev.* 66:1100–6

Izard CE, Porges SW, Simons RF, Haynes OM, Parisi M, Cohen B. 1991. Infant cardiac activity: developmental changes and relations with attachment. *Dev. Psychol.* 27:432–39

Jonetz-Mentzel L, Wiedenmann G. 1993. Establishment of reference ranges for cortisol in neonates, infants, children and adolescents. *Eur. J. Clin. Chem. Clin. Biochem.* 31:525–29

Kagan J, Reznick JS, Snidman N. 1987. The physiology and psychology of behavioral inhibition in children. *Child Dev.* 58:1459–73

Kagan J, Reznick JS, Snidman N. 1988. Biological bases of childhood shyness. *Science* 240:167–71

Kalin NH, Larson C, Shelton SE, Davidson RJ. 1998. Asymmetric frontal brain activity, cortisol, and behavior associated with fearful temperament in rhesus monkeys. *Behav. Neurosci.* 112:286–92

Kalin NH, Shelton SE, Barksdale CM. 1988. Opiate modulation of separation-induced distress in nonhuman primates. *Brain Res.* 440:856–62

Kalin NH, Shelton SE, Barksdale CM. 1989. Behavioral and physiologic effects of CRH administered to infant primates undergoing maternal separation. *Neuropsychopharmacology* 2:97–104

Kaufman J, Birmaher B, Perel J, Dahl RE, Moreci P, et al. 1997. The corticotropin-releasing hormone challenge in depressed abused, depressed nonabused, and normal control children. *Biol. Psychiatry* 42:669–79

Kaufman J, Yang BZ, Douglas-Palumberi H, Houshyar S, Lipschitz DKJH, Gelernter J. 2004. Social supports and serotonin transporter gene moderate depression in maltreated children. *Proc. Natl. Acad. Sci. USA* 101:17316–21

Kiess W, Meidert RA, Dressensorfer K, Schriever U, Kessler A, et al. 1995. Salivary cortisol levels throughout childhood and adolescence: relation with age, pubertal stage, and weight. *Pediatr. Res.* 37:502–6

Argues that childhood maltreatment may be associated with gross detrimental changes in brain structures such as decreased cerebral and intracranial volumes.

Klimes-Dougan B, Hastings PD, Granger DA, Usher BA, Zahn-Waxler C. 2001. Adreno-cortical activity in at-risk and normally developing adolescents: individual differences in salivary cortisol basal levels, diurnal variation, and responses to social challenges. *Dev. Psychol.* 13:695–719

Klug I, Dressendorfer RA, Strasburger C, Kuhl GP, Reiter A, et al. 2000. Cortisol and 17-hydroxyprogesterone in saliva of healthy neonates: normative data and relation to body mass index, arterial cord blood pH and time of sampling after birth. *Biol. Neonat.* 78:22–26

Kroupina M, Gunnar M, Johnson D. 1997. *Report on salivary cortisol levels in a Russian baby home.* Minneapolis, MN: Inst. Child Dev., Univ. Minn., Minneapolis

Ladd CO, Huot RL, Thrivikraman KV, Nemeroff CB, Meaney MJ, Plotsky PM. 2000. Long-term behavioral and neuroendocrine adaptations to adverse early experience. *Prog. Brain Res.* 122:81–103

Larson M, White BP, Cochran A, Donzella B, Gunnar MR. 1998. Dampening of the cortisol response to handling at 3 months in human infants and its relation to sleep, circadian cortisol activity, and behavioral distress. *Dev. Psychobiol.* 33:327–37

Lashansky G, Saenger P, Kishman K, Gautier T, Mayes D, et al. 1991. Normative data for adrenal steroidogenesis in a healthy pediatric population: age- and sex-related changes after adrenocorticotropin stimulation. *J. Clin. Endocrin. Metab.* 76:674–86

Legro RS, Lin HM, Demers LM, Lloyd T. 2003. Urinary free cortisol increases in adolescent Caucasian females during perimenarche. *J. Clin. Endocrin. Metab.* 88:215–19

Lesch KP. 2001. Variation of serotonergic gene expression: neurodevelopment and the complexity of response to psychopharmacologic drugs. *Eur. Neuropsychopharmacol.* 11:457–74

Levine S, Wiener SG. 1988. Psychoendocrine aspects of mother-infant relationships in non-human primates. *Psychoneuroendocrinology* 13:143–54

Lupien SJ, King S, Meaney MJ, McEwen BS. 2000. Child's stress hormone levels correlate with mother's socioeconomic status and depressive state. *Biol. Psychiatry* 48:976–80

Lyons-Ruth K, Easterbrooks MA, Cibelli CD. 1995. *Disorganized attachment strategies and mental lag in infancy: prediction of externalizing problems at age seven.* Presented at Soc. Res. Child Dev., Indianapolis, Ind.

Mason WA. 2000. Early developmental influences of experience on behavior, temperament, and stress. In *Biology of Animal Stress: Basic Principles and Implications for Animal Welfare*, ed. GP Moberg, JA Mench, pp. 269–90. Wallingford, UK: CAB Int.

Matagos S, Moustogiannis A, Vagenakis AG. 1998. Diurnal variation in plasma cortisol levels in infancy. *J. Pediatr. Endocrin. Metab.* 11:549–53

McBurnett K, Lahey BB. 1994. Psychophysiological and neuroendocrine correlates of conduct disorder and antisocial behavior in children and adolescents. *Prog. Exp. Pers. Psychopathol. Res.* 1994:199–213

McBurnett K, Lahey BB, Rathouz PJ, Loeber R. 2000. Low salivary cortisol and persistent aggression in boys referred for disruptive behavior. *Arch. Gen. Psychiatry* 57:38–43

McEwen BS, Seeman T. 1999. Protective and damaging effects of mediators of stress: elaborating and testing the concepts of allostasis and allostatic load. *Ann. NY Acad. Sci.* 896:30–47

Meaney M, Szyf M. 2005. Environmental programming of stress responses through DNA methylation: life at the interface between a dynamic environment and a fixed genome. *Dialogues Clin. Neurosci.* 7:103–23

Morilak DA, Barrera G, Echevarria J, Garcia AS, Hernandez A, et al. 2005. Role of brain nore-pinephrine in the behavioral response to stress. *Prog. Neuropsychopharmacol. Biol. Psychiatry* 29:1214–24

Delves into molecular basis for how maternal behavior "gets under the skin" and permanently alters behavior and physiology of offspring.

Nachmias M, Gunnar MR, Mangelsdorf S, Parritz R, Buss KA. 1996. Behavioral inhibition and stress reactivity: moderating role of attachment security. *Child Dev.* 67:508–22

Nemeroff CB. 1996. The corticotropin-releasing factor (CRF) hypothesis of depression: new findings and new directions. *Mol. Psychiatry* 1:336–42

Netherton C, Goodyer I, Tamplin A, Herbert J. 2004. Salivary cortisol and dehydroepiandrosterone in relation to puberty and gender. *Psychoneuroendocrinology* 29:125–40

Newport DJ, Heim C, Bonsall R, Miller AH, Nemeroff CB. 2004. Pituitary-adrenal responses to standard and low-dose dexamethasone suppression tests in adult survivors of child abuse. *Biol. Psychiatry* 55:10–20

Newport DJ, Heim C, Owen MJ, Ritchie JC, Ramsey CH, et al. 2003. Cerebral spinal fluid corticotropin-releasing factor (CRF) and vasopressin concentrations predict pituitary responses to the CRF stimulation test: a multiple regression analysis. *Neuropsychopharmacology* 28:569–76

Palkovits M. 1987. Organization of the stress response at the anatomical level. In *Progress in Brain Research*, ed. ER de Kloet, VM Wiegant, D de Wied, pp. 47–55. Amsterdam: Elsevier Sci.

Pollak SD. 2005. Early adversity and mechanisms of plasticity: integrating affective neuroscience with developmental approaches to psychopathology. *Dev. Psychopathol.* 17:735–52

Porges SW. 1992. Vagal tone: a physiological marker of stress vulnerability. *Pediatrics* 90:498–504

Porges SW, Doussard-Roosevelt JA, Portales AL, Suess PE. 1994. Cardiac vagal tone: stability and relation to difficultness in infants and 3-year-olds. *Dev. Psychobiol.* 27:289–300

Repetti R, Taylor SE, Seeman T. 2002. Risky families: family social environments and the mental and physical health of offspring. *Psychol. Bull.* 128:330–66

Rinne T, de Kloet ER, Wouters L, Goekoop JG, DeRijk RH, van den Brink W. 2002. Hyperresponsiveness of hypothalamic-pituitary-adrenal axis to combined dexamethasone/corticotropin releasing hormone challenge in female borderline personality disorder subjects with a history of sustained child abuse. *Biol. Psychiatry* 52:1102–12

Rosen JB, Schulkin J. 1998. From normal fear to pathological anxiety. *Psychol. Rev.* 105:325–50

Rosenblum LA, Andrews MW. 1994. Influences of environmental demand on maternal behavior and infant development. *Acta Paediat. Suppl.* 397:57–63

Rosenblum LA, Coplan JD, Friedman S, Bassoff T, Gorman JM, Andrews MW. 1994. Adverse early experiences affect noradrenergic and serotonergic functioning in adult primates. *Biol. Psychiatry* 35:221–27

Rosenfeld P, Suchecki D, Levine S. 1992. Multifactorial regulation of the hypothalamic-pituitary-adrenal axis during development. *Neurosci. Biobehav. Rev.* 16:553–68

Rosner W. 1990. The function of corticosteroid-binding globulin and sex hormone–binding globulin: recent advances. *Endocr. Rev.* 11:80–91

Rothbart MK, Evans DE, Ahadi SA. 2000. Temperament and personality: origins and outcomes. *J. Personal. Soc. Psychol.* 78:122–35

Rubin K, Bukowski W, Parker JG. 1998. Peer interactions, relationships, and groups. In *Handbook of Child Psychology, Volume 3*, ed. W Damon, N Eisenberg, pp. 619–700. New York: Wiley

Sanchez MM, Ladd CO, Plotsky PM. 2001. Early adverse experience as a developmental risk factor for later psychopathology: evidence from rodent and primate models. *Dev. Psychopathol.* 13:419–50

Provides empirical evidence in humans for how constitutional predispositions interact with attachment quality to yield individual differences in stress reactivity.

Argues that family dynamics powerfully influence children's neuroendocrine functioning and behavioral adaptation.

Sanchez MM, Young LJ, Plotsky PM, Insel TR. 1999. *Different rearing conditions affect the development of corticotropin-releasing hormone (CRF) and arginine vasopressin (AVP) systems in the nonhuman primate.* Presented at 29th Annu. Meet. Soc. Neurosci., Miami Beach, FL

Sanchez MM, Young LJ, Plotsky PM, Insel TR. 2000. Distribution of corticosteroid receptors in the rhesus brain: relative absence of glucocorticoid receptors in the hippocampal formation. *J. Neurosci.* 20:4657–68

Sapolsky RM. 1997. McEwen-induced modulation of endocrine history: a partial review. *Stress* 2:1–12

Sapolsky RM, Romero LM, Munck AU. 2000. How do glucocorticoids influence stress responses? Integrating permissive, suppressive, stimulatory, and preparative actions. *Endocr. Rev.* 21:55–89

Schmidt LA, Fox NA, Rubin KH, Sternberg EM, Gold PW, et al. 1997. Behavioral and neuroendocrine responses in shy children. *Dev. Psychobiol.* 30:127–40

Schwartz CE, Wright CI, Shin LM, Kagan J, Rauch SL. 2003. Inhibited and uninhibited infants "grown up": adult amygdalar response to novelty. *Science* 300:1952–53

Shekhar A, Truitt W, Rainnie D, Sajdyk T. 2005. Role of stress, corticotrophin-releasing factor (CRF) and amygdala plasticity in chronic anxiety. *Stress* 8:209–19

Shirtcliff E. 2003. *Low salivary cortisol levels and externalizing behavior problems: a latent state trait model in normally developing youth.* PhD thesis. Penn. State Univ., Univ. Park

Smotherman WP, Hunt LE, McGinnis LM, Levine S. 1979. Mother-infant separation in group-living rhesus macaques: a hormonal analysis. *Dev. Psychobiol.* 12:211–17

Spangler G, Grossmann K. 1997. Individual and physiological correlates of attachment disorganization in infancy. In *Attachment Disorganization*, ed. J Solomon, C George, pp. 95–126. New York: Guilford

Spangler G, Schieche M. 1998. Emotional and adrenocortical responses of infants to the strange situation: the differential function of emotional expression. *Int. J. Behav. Dev.* 22:681–706

Spear LP. 2000. The adolescent brain and age-related behavioral manifestations. *Neurosci. Biobehav. Rev.* 24:417–63

Sroufe LA, Waters E. 1979. Heart rate as a convergent measure in clinical and developmental research. *Merrill-Palmer Q.* 23:3–27

Stansbury K, Gunnar M. 1994. Adrenocortical activity and emotion regulation. *Monogr. Soc. Res. Child Dev.* 59(2–3):108–34

Stratakis CA, Chrousos GP. 1995. Neuroendocrinology and pathophysiology of the stress system. In *Stress: Basic Mechanisms and Clinical Implications*, ed. GP Chrousos, R McCarty, K Pacak, G Cizza, E Sternberg, PW Gold, R Kvetsnansky, pp. 1–18. New York: NY Acad. Sci.

Suchecki D, Rosenfeld P, Levine S. 1993. Maternal regulation of the hypothalamic-pituitary-adrenal axis in the rat: the roles of feeding and stroking. *Dev. Brain Res.* 75:185–92

Suomi SJ. 1995. Influence of attachment theory on ethological studies of biobehavioral development in nonhuman primates. In *Attachment Theory: Social, Developmental, and Clinical Perspectives*, ed. S Goldberg, R Muir, J Kerr, pp. 185–201. Hillsdale, NJ: Analytic Press

Swiergiel AH, Takahashi LK, Kalin NH. 1993. Attenuation of stress-induced behavior by antagonism of corticotropin-releasing factor receptors in the central amygdala in the rat. *Brain Res.* 623:229–34

Tasaptsaris NP, Breslin DJ. 1989. Physiology of the adrenal medulla. *Urol. Clin. North Am.* 16:439–45

Teicher MH, Andersen SL, Polcarri A, Anderson CM, Navalta CP. 2002. Developmental neurobiology of childhood stress and trauma. *Psychiatr. Clin. North Am.* 25:397–426

Tottenham NH, Hare TA, Quinn BT, McCarry TW, Nurse M, et al. 2006. Amygdala volume and sensitivity to emotional information following orphanage rearing. Manuscr. under review

Tout K, de Haan M, Campbell EK, Gunnar MR. 1998. Social behavior correlates of cortisol activity in child care: gender differences and time-of-day effects. *Child Dev.* 69:1247–62

van Goozen SH, Matthys W, Cohen-Kettenis PT, Buittelaar JK, van Engeland H. 2000. Hypothalamic-pituitary-adrenal axis and autonomic nervous system activity in disruptive children and matched controls. *J. Am. Acad. Child Adolesc. Psychiatry* 39:1438–45

van Ijzendoorn HW, Schuengel C, Bakersmans-Kranenburg MJ. 1999. Disorganized attachment in early childhood: meta-analysis of precursors, concomitants, and sequelae. *Dev. Psychopathol.* 11:225–49

Vollmer RR. 1996. Selective neural regulation of epinephrine and norepinephrine cells in the adrenal medulla—cardiovascular implications. *Clin. Exp. Hypertens.* 18:731–51

Vythilingam M, Heim C, Newport J, Miller AH, Anderson E, et al. 2002. Childhood trauma associated with smaller hippocampal volume in women with major depression. *Am. J. Psychiatry* 159:2072–80

Walker EF, Walder DJ, Reynolds R. 2001. Developmental changes in cortisol secretion in normal and at-risk youth. *Dev. Psychopathol.* 13:721–32

Watamura S, Donzella B, Kertes DA, Gunnar MR. 2004. Developmental changes in baseline cortisol activity in early childhood: relations with napping and effortful control. *Dev. Psychobiol.* 45:125–33

Watamura S, Sebanc A, Donzella B, Gunnar M. 2002a. Naptime at childcare: effects on salivary cortisol levels. *Dev. Psychobiol.* 40:33–42

Watamura SE, Donzella B, Alwin J, Gunnar M. 2003. Morning to afternoon increases in cortisol concentrations for infants and toddlers at child care: age differences and behavioral correlates. *Child Dev.* 74:1006–20

Watamura SE, Sebanc AM, Gunnar MR. 2002b. Rising cortisol at childcare: relations with nap, rest, and temperament. *Dev. Psychobiol.* 40:33–42

Weaver IC, Champagne FA, Brown SE, Dymov S, Sharma S, et al. 2005. Reversal of maternal programming of stress responses in adult offspring through methyl supplementation: altering epigenetic marking later in life. *J. Neurosci.* 25:11045–54

Weaver IC, La Plante P, Weaver S, Parent A, Sharma S, et al. 2001. Early environmental regulation of hippocampal glucocorticoid receptor gene expression: characterization of intracellular mediators and potential genomic target sites. *Mol. Cell. Endocrinol.* 185:205–18

Wewerka S, Madsen NJ, Wiik K. 2005. *Developmental physiologic and neuroendocrine responses to a stressor in 9-, 11-, and 13-year-old children.* Presented at Soc. Res. Child Dev., Atlanta, GA

White BP, Gunnar MR, Larson MC, Donzella B, Barr RG. 2000. Behavioral and physiological responsivity, sleep and patterns of daily cortisol in infants with and without colic. *Child Dev.* 71:862–77

Yehuda R. 2000. Biology of posttraumatic stress disorder. *J. Clin. Psychiatry* 61(Suppl. 7):15–21

Young EA, Haskett RF, Murphy-Weinberg V, Watson SJ, Akil H. 1991. Loss of glucocorticoid fast feedback in depression. *Arch. Gen. Psychiatry* 48:693–99

An Interactionist Perspective on the Socioeconomic Context of Human Development

Rand D. Conger[1] and M. Brent Donnellan[2]

[1]The Family Research Group, Department of Human and Community Development, University of California, Davis, Davis, California 95616; email: rdconger@ucdavis.edu

[2]Department of Psychology, Michigan State University, East Lansing, Michigan 48823; email: donnel59@msu.edu

Annu. Rev. Psychol. 2007. 58:175–99

First published online as a Review in Advance on August 11, 2006

The *Annual Review of Psychology* is online at http://psych.annualreviews.org

This article's doi: 10.1146/annurev.psych.58.110405.085551

Key Words

socioeconomic status, social causation, social selection

Abstract

This article addresses the relationship between socioeconomic status (SES), family processes, and human development. The topic is framed as part of the general issue of health disparities, which involves the oft-observed positive relationship between SES and the cognitive, social, emotional, and physical well-being of adults and children. A review of recent research and theory identifies three general theoretical approaches that provide possible explanations for the association between SES and individual development: the social causation, social selection, and interactionist perspectives. Empirical evidence demonstrates support for the social causation view that SES affects families and the development of children in terms of both family stress processes (the family stress model) and family investments in children (the family investment model). However, there also is empirical support for the social selection argument that individual characteristics lead to differences in SES. Especially important, recent research is consistent with an interactionist approach, which proposes a dynamic relationship between SES and developmental change over time. Drawing on the combined set of research findings, the article concludes with the description of an interactionist model that serves as a heuristic for future studies of the links among SES, parenting behaviors, and child development.

Contents

INTRODUCTION

The present report provides a selective review of research and theory related to the impact of socioeconomic status (SES) on human development, with a special emphasis on the proposition that the family acts as a conduit for socioeconomic influences on the development of children and adolescents (e.g., Repetti et al. 2002, but see Rowe & Rodgers 1997). Given the tremendous recent growth in this literature, we focus on work during the past decade or so (e.g., Bornstein & Bradley 2003, Bradley

& Corwyn 2002, Conger & Conger 2002). In particular, we consider and critically evaluate two dominant perspectives on the causal relation between SES and the development of children: the social causation explanation and the social selection explanation. In the latter sections of this review, we propose a new integrative model designed to guide future investigations of the association between SES and human development.

Important Developmental Correlates of Socioeconomic Circumstances

There is a long history of research on the influence of SES on human development, dating back to the middle of the past century (e.g., Davis & Havighurst 1946, Sears et al. 1957). Economic changes in the United States and other countries during the past two decades (e.g., increasing income inequality) have enhanced this ongoing interest in how social position and economic resources affect families and the development of children (e.g., Conger & Conger 2002, Duncan & Brooks-Gunn 1997, Keating & Hertzman 1999, Prior et al. 1999, Schoon et al. 2002). This research by developmental scholars joins with research in social epidemiology on health disparities, or the general trend that more socially and economically disadvantaged adults and children are at increased risk for physical, emotional, and behavioral problems (Berkman & Kawachi 2000, Bradley & Corwyn 2002, McLeod & Shanahan 1996, Oakes & Rossi 2003). With respect to the influence of SES on children and adolescents, there is evidence for an association between poverty and mental health (e.g., Ackerman et al. 2004, Dearing et al. 2001, McLeod & Shanahan 1996), SES and cognitive development (e.g., Ackerman et al. 2004, Dearing et al. 2001, Hoff 2003, Mezzacappa 2004), and social class position and physical well-being (e.g., Evans & English 2002, McLoyd 1998).

SES: socioeconomic status

Social causation: the argument that social and economic conditions influence individual functioning and development

There are several reasons to suggest that the influence of SES on children and adolescents may result, in large part, from the actions of parents. For example, lower-SES compared with middle-SES parents are more likely to use a harsher, more authoritarian, parenting style as indicated by physical punishment and the absence of reasoning with children about the consequences of their behavior (e.g., Hoffman 2003, Hoff et al. 2002). These parenting practices have been linked to less competent social and emotional development for children and adolescents (e.g., Steinberg 2001). With regard to cognitive functioning, middle- compared with lower-SES parents are more likely to use richer vocabularies and to engage in cognitively stimulating activities with their children. Thus, current evidence suggests that SES is associated with important family socialization practices and with the health and well-being of children. However, there is disagreement over the causal interpretation of these observed relations, as we describe in a subsequent section. Prior to describing this controversy, we consider in some detail the concept of SES and its measurement.

The Multifaceted Nature of Socioeconomic Status

SES is a construct that captures various dimensions of social position, including prestige, power, and economic well-being (Hoff et al. 2002, Liu et al. 2004, Oakes & Rossi 2003). Most contemporary investigators agree that three quantitative indicators provide reasonably good coverage of the domains of interest: income, education, and occupational status (Bradley & Corwyn 2002, Ensminger & Fothergill 2003). Despite the fact that these indicators of social position are positively correlated (Ensminger & Fothergill 2003), there also is general agreement that they should not be combined into simple composite scores. Duncan & Magnuson (2003), for example, suggest that each of these markers of social

status demonstrates different levels of stability across time and differentially predicts family processes and child adjustment. Thus, income, education, and occupational status are not interchangeable indicators of SES: Only by including each of them as a separate variable in data analyses can investigators begin to understand their unique and combined contributions to human development.

Indeed, education, occupation, and income represent separate yet related personal, social, and economic resources that have important implications for the health and well-being of both parents and children. These resources can be thought of as "capital" that differentiates persons, households, and neighborhoods (Bradley & Corwyn 2002, Hoff et al. 2002, Oakes & Rossi 2003). As an illustration, Oakes & Rossi (2003) draw on Coleman (1990) to propose that SES should be defined in terms of material or financial capital (economic resources), human capital (knowledge and skills), and social capital (connections to and the status and power of individuals in one's social network). Income and other forms of wealth obviously relate to material or financial capital and education to human capital. Although the connection is not as straightforward for occupational status, it can be considered a marker of social capital inasmuch as people in higher-status occupations are more likely to associate with others who have higher-than-average occupational status, advanced skills, and economic resources (Bradley & Corwyn 2003, Oakes & Rossi 2003). Our main point is that each aspect of SES may have an important independent influence on how children are raised and on how they develop over time. As such, researchers should separately measure income, education, and occupational status and use analytic techniques that are capable of identifying the potentially unique associations each has with human development. The connection between social status and human development may be quite complex, however, an issue we next consider.

Social selection: the argument that attributes of individuals influence the quality of their social and economic environments

Socioeconomic status: an individual's location in multiple environmental hierarchies, usually involving economic resources, educational achievement, and occupational status

Health disparities: the well-established empirical relationship between higher social and economic status and better health for adults and children

Interactionist perspective: the argument that individual attributes influence a person's social and economic position in a reciprocal process within and across generations

Family stress model (FSM): a framework that links socioeconomic disadvantage to a family stress process that increases parents' emotional distress and jeopardizes the healthy development of children

Family investment model (FIM): an explanatory framework that links parents' socioeconomic advantage to children's physical, emotional, cognitive, and social well-being

Moving from a Static to an Interactionist Model of Socioeconomic Status and Development

The majority of research on SES and human development proposes that social position influences the lives of individuals across time and that socioeconomic disadvantage has negative consequences for adults and children (e.g., Conger et al. 2002). This perspective represents an instance of the social causation argument, which predicts that social conditions lead to variations in social, emotional, cognitive, and physical functioning. The antithesis to this viewpoint is the social selection argument, which proposes that the traits and dispositions of parents influence their social status and the health and well-being of their children (see, e.g., Mayer 1997). According to an interactionist perspective, the actual processes through which SES and a person's health and well-being come to be associated with one another are far more complex than suggested by either the social causation or social selection point of view. From this integrative perspective, the association between SES and human development involves a dynamic interplay between social causation and social selection. That is, the interactionist view of human development proposes an ongoing reciprocal relationship between the characteristics of individuals and the broader socioeconomic environments in which they live (e.g., Magnusson & Stattin 1998). In this review, we consider evidence related to social causation, social selection, and the more dynamic interactionist argument, which only recently has been subjected to empirical evaluation.

A SOCIAL CAUSATION VIEW OF SOCIOECONOMIC INFLUENCE

In this section, we describe two major theoretical approaches consistent with the social causation perspective and evaluate empirical evidence related to each of the approaches. The first theoretical paradigm, the family stress model (FSM) of economic hardship, proposes that financial difficulties have an adverse effect on parents' emotions, behaviors, and relationships, which in turn negatively influence their parenting strategies (Conger & Conger 2002). As reflected in its name, this model focuses on the means by which economic disadvantage exacerbates family stresses that ultimately imperil the healthy development of children and adults. The second perspective, which we title the family investment model (FIM), takes a different approach to SES effects by drawing attention to the ways that parents invest financial, social, and human capital to promote the talents and well-being of their children.

Major Theoretical Perspectives

The family stress model of economic hardship. This model focuses on the economic dimension of SES, consistent with evidence that low income is associated with significant developmental difficulties for children, especially when poverty is severe or persistent (Dearing et al. 2001, Duncan & Magnuson 2003, Magnuson & Duncan 2002, McLoyd 1998). The model builds on a tradition of research dating back to the Great Depression years of the 1930s, when a series of studies indicated that severe hardship undermined family functioning, which in turn negatively affected the lives of both parents and children (e.g., Angell 1936, Cavan & Ranck 1938, Komarovsky 1940; see also Elder 1974, Elder & Caspi 1988). These themes have been carried forward in contemporary investigations that both support and modify many of the conclusions reached in these earlier studies (Leventhal & Brooks-Gunn 2003, McLoyd 1998). Consistent with this line of research, Conger and his colleagues developed the FSM to help explain how financial problems influenced the lives of Iowa families going through a severe downturn in the agricultural economy during the 1980s (Conger & Conger 2002, Conger & Elder 1994, Conger et al. 2002).

As shown in **Figure 1**, the FSM proposes that economic hardship leads to economic pressure in the family. Markers of hardship include low income, high debts relative to assets, and negative financial events (e.g., increasing economic demands, recent income loss, and work instability). These indicators of hardship are consistent with the concept of economic or material capital, which includes both accumulated wealth and current income. These hardship conditions are expected to affect family functioning and individual adjustment primarily through the economic pressures they generate. The FSM proposes that economic pressures include (*a*) unmet material needs involving necessities such as adequate food and clothing, (*b*) the inability to pay bills or make ends meet, and (*c*) having to cut back on even necessary expenses (e.g., health insurance and medical care). According to this model, the experience of these kinds of pressures or strains gives psychological meaning to economic hardship (Conger & Conger 2002; Conger & Elder 1994; Conger et al. 1992, 1993, 1994, 2002).

In addition, the model predicts that when economic pressure is high, parents are at increased risk for emotional distress (e.g., depression, anxiety, anger, and alienation) and for behavioral problems (e.g., substance use and antisocial behavior; Conger 1995, Conger et al. 2002). According to the model, these emotional or behavioral problems predict increased marital conflict and reduced marital warmth, and this process diminishes nurturing and involved parenting. That is, parents distracted by their own personal problems and marital distress are expected to demonstrate less affection toward their children, to be less involved in their children's daily activities, and to be more irritable, harsh, and inconsistent in their disciplinary practices. The last step in the FSM indicates that parental nurturance and involvement lead to greater emotional, behavioral, cognitive, and physical well-being for children. Thus, when this type of child-rearing is threatened by the hypothesized economic stress process, successful development of the child is placed in jeopardy.

According to the model, when families experience economic hardship, children are at risk for suffering both decreases in positive adjustment (e.g., cognitive ability, social competence, school success, and attachment to parents) and increases in internalizing (e.g., symptoms of depression and anxiety) or externalizing (e.g., aggressive and antisocial behavior) problems. The model also proposes, however, that these economic effects indirectly influence children through their impact on the lives of parents. For single-parent families, caregiver conflicts with one another may be omitted from the model or conflicts with an ex-spouse or current romantic partner might be substituted, as economic problems are expected to affect these relationships as well (Conger et al. 2002). Moreover, when children are raised by caregivers other than parents (e.g., grandparents), the same stress process is expected to operate. Although elaborations of the FSM include factors that promote resilience or exacerbate vulnerability to these mediating pathways, the model in **Figure 1** provides the basic tenants of this theoretical framework (Conger & Conger 2002, Conger et al. 2002).

The family investment model. The FIM is rooted in economic principles of investment and builds on the notion that higher-SES compared with lower-SES parents have greater access to financial (e.g., income), social (e.g., occupational status), and human (e.g., education) capital. According to this model, the investment of these resources by families is associated with the successful development of children and adolescents. In terms of financial capital, the FIM proposes that families with greater economic resources are able to make significant investments in the development of their children, whereas more disadvantaged families must invest in more immediate family needs (Becker & Thomes 1986, Bradley & Corwyn 2002, Corcoran & Adams 1997, Duncan & Magnuson 2003, Haveman

Economic pressure: a syndrome of events or conditions that give psychological meaning to the stressful experience of economic hardship

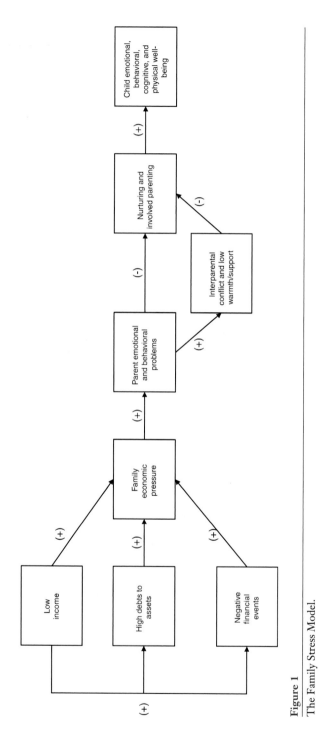

Figure 1

The Family Stress Model.

& Wolfe 1994, Linver et al. 2002, Mayer 1997). These investments involve several different dimensions of family support, including (a) learning materials available in the home, (b) parent stimulation of learning both directly and through support of advanced or specialized tutoring or training, (c) the family's standard of living (adequate food, housing, clothing, medical care, etc.), and (d) residing in a location that fosters a child's competent development. For example, wealthier parents are expected to reside in areas that promote a child's association with conventional friends, access to good schools, and involvement in a neighborhood or community environment that provides resources for the developing child such as parks and child-related activities. According to the theory, then, economic well-being will be positively related to parental material investments and child-rearing activities expected to foster the academic and social success of a child (see **Figure 2**).

Although the traditional investment model from economics is limited to the influence of economic resources on families and children, we extend the basic model by proposing that the educational achievements and occupational positions of parents and other caregivers will be similarly related to investments in children. For example, parents with greater education would be expected to place a priority on activities, goods, and services that foster academic and social competence, a prediction consistent with the idea that the human capital of parents will tend to promote the development of human capital in their children. With regard to occupational position, sociologists have long argued that greater occupational status affects parents' values and priorities in a fashion that positively influences their strategies of child rearing (Kohn 1959, 1963, 1969, 1995). Consistent with these ideas, the model proposes that parents with more prestigious and higher paying work roles will tend to invest in their children in at least two important ways. First, they should provide social capital by increasing access to employment and other career-related activities. Second, they should

provide human capital by guiding their children toward activities that will promote their eventual career success. Thus, the FIM proposes that parents with greater resources are likely to invest their economic, educational, and occupational capital in ways that facilitate the well-being of their offspring from childhood into the adult years.

Empirical Evidence for the Social Causation Perspective

The family stress model of economic hardship. We located seven published reports that both evaluated the FSM in studies of child or adolescent development and also used the same labels for constructs as described in **Figure 1**. These studies represent a rich array of ethnic or national groups, geographic locations, family structures, children's ages, and research designs. The first two reports involved the Iowa Youth and Families Project and provided the first tests of the full FSM. The two separate analyses involved 205 rural, white, seventh-grade boys from two-parent families (Conger et al. 1992) and 220 rural, white, seventh-grade girls from two-parent families (Conger et al. 1993). The third study was of African American families and involved 422 male and female fifth graders living with two caregivers in urban and rural locations (Conger et al. 2002). The fourth study, of 419 boys and girls ranging in age from 5 to 12 years, involved a poor urban sample of primarily ethnic minority (57% African American, 28% Hispanic) families headed by a single parent (83%) (Mistry et al. 2002). The fifth study was based on a nationally representative sample of families and included 753 preschool boys and girls, ages 3–5 years (Yeung et al. 2002). The sixth research report involved 527 early-adolescent boys and girls living in two-parent families in Finland (Solantaus et al. 2004). Finally, the seventh study included European American ($N = 111$) and Mexican American ($N = 167$) families of male and female fifth graders living in urban areas of Southern California (Parke et al. 2004).

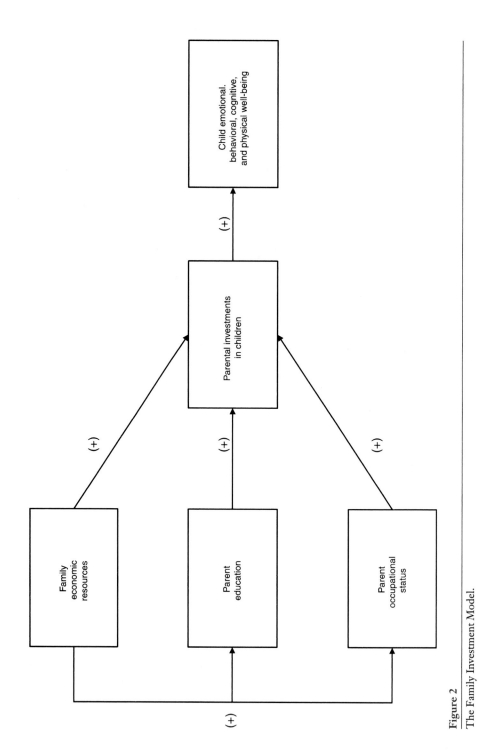

Figure 2

The Family Investment Model.

Given the diversity among these samples, the degree of replication of findings across studies was quite remarkable. With regard to the connection between economic hardship (i.e., low income, debts relative to assets, and/or negative financial events) and economic pressure (see **Figure 1**), the median path or multiple correlation coefficient was 0.68 across these investigations. Also consistent with the model, for all of the reports the link between economic hardship and other variables in the model was indirect through economic pressure. For all of the studies, economic pressure significantly predicted parents' emotional and behavioral problems (median path coefficient = 0.42). Also consistent with the FSM, for the five studies that included information about caregiver relationships, each of the model tests found that parent emotional distress was directly related to interparental conflict after economic pressure was taken into account (median path coefficient = 0.33). Emotional distress also predicted conflicts between caregivers when either one or both of the caregivers were not biological parents of the focal child (Conger et al. 2002). For six out of the seven reports, emotional distress also was either negatively related to positive parenting practices or positively associated with negative parenting behaviors. In most instances, parents' emotional and behavioral problems did not directly predict child or adolescent development once parenting behavior was taken into account, a finding that is consistent with the FSM.

For four of the five reports that included a measure of interparental conflict, this measure was related in the expected direction with parenting behaviors (median path coefficient = 0.45). That is, conflict was positively related to indicators of harsh or rejecting parenting and negatively related to indicators of nurturing and involved parenting. Interparental conflicts had the same effect when one or both caregivers were not the biological parent of the focal child. Moreover, for almost all the studies, interparental conflict was not directly related to measures of child or adolescent development. The major exception was the Mexican American families in the Parke et al. (2004) study, in which interparental conflict demonstrated a substantial direct path to child adjustment problems (standardized path coefficient = 0.53). We believe this finding may result from the high value Mexican American parents and children place on the family unit. Because threats to the family itself engendered by interparental conflict may be especially distressing for Mexican American children, interparental conflict may directly affect the emotional and behavioral problems of these children independently of styles of parenting (Parke et al. 2004). Future research is needed to see if this finding replicates in other samples of Mexican American families.

Finally, all of the studies provided some support for the FSM hypothesis that parenting behavior is significantly associated with child or adolescent well-being. Four of the reports included a measure of child or adolescent positive adjustment, and eight of the nine estimated path coefficients were statistically significant (median path coefficient = 0.31 when parenting is scored in a positive direction). All of the studies included measures of poor child or adolescent adjustment, and 17 of the 21 estimated relationships were statistically significant (median path coefficient = −0.44 when parenting is scored in a positive direction). These results provide substantial evidence that the child-rearing strategies of parents provide the most proximal mechanism through which the economic fortunes of the family affect the development of children and adolescents, consistent with the FSM.

Other studies also indicate that specific aspects of the FSM apply to diverse racial and ethnic groups and to families living in countries outside of the United States (e.g., Borge et al. 2004, Dodge et al. 1994, Gutman et al. 2005, Prior et al. 1999, Robila & Krishnakumar 2005, Wickrama et al. 2005, Zevalkink & Riksen-Walraven 2001). Support for the FSM also comes from studies that use

HOME: home observation for measurement of the environment

the concept of economic strain rather than economic pressure as a key explanatory construct (e.g., Mistry et al. 2004). Even studies that omit these constructs altogether provide support for the basic underlying economic stress process (e.g., Brody et al. 2002, Linver et al. 2002). Moreover, in an interesting extension of the model, Sobolewski & Amato (2005) found that the economic stress processes proposed in the FSM influence the psychological well-being of children grown to adulthood.

Especially exciting are recent experimental, quasi-experimental, or longitudinal studies conducted over significant periods of time that also report results consistent with the FSM. For instance, Costello and her colleagues (2003) reported findings from a quasi-experimental study. The results demonstrated that increased employment in a poor community that resulted from the opening of a casino increased family income, decreased problems in parenting, and reduced externalizing problems for children in the study. Experimental research on income supplementation for poor families or on moving poor families to more economically advantaged neighborhoods also has produced evidence that these programs can have a positive influence on parents' well-being and on developmental outcomes for children and adolescents. Although these findings are quite complex and tend to be contingent on a number of factors, such as the age of the child, a growing body of evidence suggests that improvements in family income may have beneficial effects on parents and children consistent with predictions from the FSM (Gennetian & Miller 2002, Huston et al. 2005, Leventhal & Brooks-Gunn 2003, Leventhal et al. 2005, Morris et al. 2005).

Finally, consistent with evidence reported by Conger and his colleagues showing that the FSM predicts change over time (Conger et al. 1994, 1999 a,b), recent longitudinal studies have shown that increases in family income reduced children's symptoms of depression and antisocial behavior (Strohschein 2005) and

that poverty, and especially chronic poverty, disrupted family functioning, inhibited cognitive development, and exacerbated children's behavior problems across a several-year period (National Institute of Child Health and Human Development Early Child Care Research Network 2005). Collectively, the studies reviewed in this section suggest that the FSM is a useful model for helping to understand how the economic aspects of SES may influence family members, child-rearing practices, and the adjustment of children and adolescents.

The family investment model. Unlike the extensive literature on the FSM and variations of the FSM, only a limited amount of recent research is focused specifically on the parameters included in the proposed FIM (**Figure 2**). In part, this paucity of findings results from the fact that these demographic measures typically are treated as control variables in developmental research rather than as phenomena of theoretical interest in their own right (Hoff et al. 2002, Hoffman 2003). However, a small number of recent studies are specifically related to each of the exogenous constructs in the model involving income, education, and occupational status. In terms of family income, a number of studies have confirmed the most basic propositions of the investment model; that is, family income affects the types of investments parents make in the lives of their children (Bradley & Corwyn 2002, Davis-Kean 2005, Mayer 1997), and family income during childhood and adolescence is positively related to academic, financial, and occupational success during the adult years (Bradley & Corwyn 2002, Corcoran & Adams 1997, Mayer 1997, Teachman et al. 1997).

With regard to the proposed association between income and investments, a seminal study by Bradley and his associates (2001) demonstrated the pervasiveness of this connection. These researchers used data from several waves of the National Longitudinal Survey of Youth to evaluate differences in parental investments and parental behavior, as measured by the Home Observation for Measurement of the Environment (HOME; Bradley & Caldwell 1980), for several thousand children ranging in age from infancy to early adolescence. For three major ethnic groups (European American, African American, and Hispanic American), the study showed that widespread differences existed between the child-rearing contexts of families above the official poverty line in comparison with families below the poverty line. Parents who were more economically advantaged were more likely to engage their children in conversation, provide enriching learning activities for their children, demonstrate affection and respect for their children, and avoid physical punishment or restraint. Likewise, children in more financially secure families also had greater access to books, magazines, toys, and games that stimulate learning; cultural events and activities; special lessons that encourage particular talents in domains such as music and sports; and homes that tended to be safer, cleaner, and roomier. Taken together, the results of this study of a large-scale, nationally representative, multiethnic sample of families demonstrate a clear link between family income and the investments that are made in the human capital of children.

Despite the noted evidence for the connection between family income and the long-term well-being of children grown to adulthood, and between income and a variety of parental investments in children, a significant limitation in most of this earlier research is that the full mediating process proposed by the investment model (**Figure 2**) has not been evaluated. That is, the central concern of the model involves the degree to which parental investments account for the connection between family income and the long-term development of children. A series of recent studies, however, have provided evidence that is reasonably consistent with the full set of empirical relationships proposed by the model.

In a large-scale, multiethnic study of children from birth to five years of age at the time of their analysis, Linver and her colleagues (2002) found an association between family income and child cognitive development at ages 3 and 5 years (standardized intelligence test scores, $b = 0.70$ without control variables and 0.52 with control variables). Consistent with the mediating hypothesis, this association was significantly reduced ($b = 0.36$) when the investment mediator, items from the HOME scale, was introduced into the analyses. The investigators also found that the measure of parental investment completely mediated the association between income and child behavior problems at three and five years of age. Thus, the model tested in this study partially explained how SES influenced both child competence and maladjustment. A particularly important feature of the Linver et al. (2002) study is that the investigators controlled for the influence of parent education and intelligence in the analyses, as well as other social-demographic characteristics. These controls reduced the likelihood that the results could be attributed simply to the educational attainment and intelligence of the parent, which might indicate a direct genetic effect on the child's cognitive abilities.

In a similar set of analyses using data from the Panel Study of Income Dynamics, Yeung et al. (2002) also controlled for parent personal and demographic characteristics in a test of the investment model. Even with these controls, they found evidence that family income had an influence on child outcomes at least in part through parental investments in the competent development of children. In a separate study of 868 eight- to twelve-year-old children, Davis-Kean (2005) showed that family income is positively associated with parents' expectations that their children will experience significant educational achievement. These expectations predicted parental investments that promote learning, for example, by spending more time reading to their children. Taken together, the findings from this set of studies provide substantial support for the link between income and investments and between income and child well-being, as proposed by the FIM. They also provide preliminary support for the FIM proposition that family income will affect the successful development of children primarily through such investments.

Returning to **Figure 2**, the FIM proposes that parent education will have an influence on parental investments similar to that of income, and that these investments, in turn, will have a positive relationship with competent development. Presumably, a better-educated parent will acquire more knowledge about child and adolescent development, have a greater understanding of strategies for encouraging academic and social competence, and will generally be more skillful and effective in teaching children to negotiate the many environments to which they must adapt (Bornstein et al. 2003). Despite the reasonableness of this hypothesized mediating process, there are no specific empirical tests of this proposition cast in terms of the FIM. However, there is some evidence consistent with these ideas.

To begin with, several studies demonstrate that parental education predicts competent child development even when a number of other variables are controlled, such as family income and occupational status, parent's cognitive ability and emotional well-being, and family structure (Dearing et al. 2001, Duncan & Magnusson 2003, Han 2005, Huston & Aronson 2005, Kohen et al. 2002, Tamis-LeMonda et al. 2004). Moreover, recent research is consistent with a long history of empirical findings that relate parent education to socialization practices and priorities (Hoff et al. 2002). For example, in a study of 1053 families from the National Institute of Child Health and Human Development Study of Early Child Care, Huston & Aronson (2005) found that maternal education was positively correlated with maternal sensitivity toward the focal child at 36 months and also with parental investments involving a more enriched and positive home environment as assessed by the HOME. These positive relationships still existed after controlling for a variety of other maternal, child, and family characteristics. Similarly, Tamis-LeMonda and colleagues (2004) found that maternal and paternal education were positively associated with sensitivity, positive regard, and cognitive stimulation of a young child.

In addition to this more general evidence for the plausibility of education as an important part of the investment process, three recent studies provide credible tests of a mediating pathway. First, in an intensive study of 63 families, Hoff (2003) found that more highly educated parents create a richer, more complex language environment for their children, and their children demonstrate greater language skills. Especially important for the investment hypothesis, the richness of maternal speech completely mediated the association between parent education and child productive vocabulary. In an analysis of data from the National Longitudinal Survey of Youth involving children ranging from 3 to 15 years of age, Bradley & Corwyn (2003) found that parental education was positively related to a child's vocabulary, reading, and mathematical skills and negatively related to behavioral problems. Moreover, the association between education and child development was substantially mediated by the parent's stimulation of learning. Finally, using data from the Panel Study of Income Dynamics for 8- to 12-year-old children, Davis-Kean (2005) found that the connection between parent education and child academic achievement was mediated by parental expectations for and investments in academic ability. These three studies provide preliminary evidence consistent with the mediating process proposed by the FIM.

The final exogenous variable in the FIM involves parent or caregiver occupational status (**Figure 2**). Unfortunately, there is very little evidence regarding the role of parents' occupation in the proposed family investment process. The Bradley & Corwyn (2003) paper reporting evidence that learning stimulation (as measured by the HOME) mediated the relationship between parents' educational attainment and child competence also reported a similar mediating process for occupation, as assessed by the Socioeconomic Index of Occupations. In another study, Gottfried et al. (2003) followed a cohort of 130 one-year-old children and their parents for almost two decades. They found that occupational status of fathers (rated from laborer to professional) reliably predicted an enriched cultural, intellectual, and learning environment for children, as measured by the HOME and by the Family Environment Scale (correlations from 0.27 to 0.52). The occupation of mothers also predicted these markers of parental investment, but not as frequently, or at the same level, as the occupation of fathers. The investigators also found that the father's occupation predicted children's cognitive ability, academic achievement, and social-emotional well-being, but in most instances, the mother's occupational status did not. The lack of mother influence may reflect the fact that these were generally traditional two-parent families, in which fathers were most likely to be the primary breadwinners. Unfortunately, the authors did not directly examine the mediating role of parental investments in explaining the association between occupation and child outcomes; however, the pattern of reported correlations suggests that a mediating process was likely.

To summarize, there is general empirical support for the social causation perspective and for several of the specific predictions generated by the FSM and the FIM. Nonetheless, many investigators have noted the limitations of drawing causal inferences from the predominantly nonexperimental studies that have addressed these issues (e.g., Rutter et al. 2001). Indeed, true randomized experiments are the best method for establishing causality (Shadish et al. 2002) and the dilemma facing researchers in this area is that true experiments are often not feasible or are gravely unethical. As such, there are alternative explanations for the observed associations between SES and life course development, as we describe in the following section of this review.

SOCIAL SELECTION AND SOCIOECONOMIC CIRCUMSTANCES

The Social Selection Perspective

The major alternative explanation to the social causation argument is that the connections between parental SES and child development result from a process of social selection (e.g., Becker 1981, Lerner 2003, Mayer 1997, Rowe & Rodgers 1997). To understand this viewpoint better, it is useful to first conceptualize SES as a constellation of outcomes that are potentially influenced by individual differences in traits such as intelligence and personality. According to the social selection perspective, these individual differences both facilitate the accumulation of social advantages and are transmitted from parents to children. The most commonly invoked mode of transmission is genetic (e.g., Rowe & Rodgers 1997), but the exact mechanism is not essential to this argument. What is critical is the proposition that the observed associations between parental SES and child and adolescent outcomes are spurious because they are caused by a third variable. That is, both parental SES and children's development are hypothesized to emanate from certain parental characteristics. For example, Mayer (1997) proposed that "parental characteristics that employers value and are willing to pay for, such as skills, diligence, honesty, good health, and reliability, also improve children's life chances, independent of their effect on parents' income. Children of parents with these attributes do well even when their parents do not have much income" (pp. 2–3). Corcoran & Adams (1997) have called this the "noneconomic parental resources" perspective.

If the social selection perspective is correct, then the FSM and the FIM are not valid causal accounts of the role that SES plays in child development. For instance, returning to **Figure 1**, the social selection argument proposes that positive characteristics of parents, such as those described by Mayer (1997), will reduce exposure to economic hardship and pressure, decrease the likelihood of parent emotional distress and interparental conflict, foster nurturing and involved parenting, and lead to greater child well-being. This proposition leads to the statistical expectation that the connections among the economic variables, family stress processes, and child well-being predicted by the FSM will be greatly reduced or eliminated once these positive parental characteristics are included in data analyses. The same social selection arguments would apply to the connections among SES, parental investments, and child outcomes as proposed by the FIM (see **Figure 2**).

Empirical Evidence for the Social Selection Perspective

There is evidence from longitudinal studies that early emerging individual differences in personality, aggressiveness, and cognitive ability predict SES-relevant outcomes in adulthood such as income, occupational status, and bouts of unemployment (e.g., Caspi et al. 1998, Feinstein & Bynner 2004, Judge et al. 1999, Kokko & Pulkkinen 2000, McLeod & Kaiser 2004, Shiner et al. 2003). Indeed, Judge et al. (1999) noted that "knowledge about one's personality and intelligence early in life proved to be an effective predictor of one's later career success" (p. 643). Moreover, these sorts of traits have been shown to be heritable to a significant degree (e.g., Bouchard 2004). Thus, consistent with the social selection perspective, there are individual differences that seem to influence SES and that can be passed to offspring.

The study of individual differences also raises other specific challenges to some of the pathways specified by the FSM and the FIM. One possibility is that characteristics of children evoke certain parental responses (see, e.g., Bell 1968), thereby clouding the direction of effect proposed by these models. For example, child characteristics might create economic difficulties for parents in a manner that contradicts the causal sequence im-

plied by the FSM. Suggestive evidence for this proposition comes from Hyde and her associates (2004), who found that preschool children with a difficult temperament exacerbated feelings of parental incompetence and depressed affect for mothers. These maternal characteristics, in turn, diminished the quality of the mother's work life. It is plausible that this sort of process could decrease the mother's success in work and the family's overall SES when played out over a significant span of time. Evocative child effects likewise apply to the FIM, given that certain talents and proclivities of children might cause parents to invest certain kinds of resources in their offspring. For example, an academically talented youngster might evoke investments in educational domains, whereas an athletically talented youngster might evoke investments in athletic domains.

Other evidence that individual differences might influence specific causal associations proposed by the FSM was provided by Conger & Conger (2002), who showed that parents who were high in generalized self-efficacy (mastery) actually reduced their level of economic pressure over time. Thus, this trait likely helped the adults cope with economic problems, which should help maintain or even improve family SES in the future. In terms of the FIM, individual differences in parenting skill might moderate the effectiveness of parental investments. Thus, consistent with the broad theme of the social selection argument, there is evidence that individual differences are relevant factors for understanding the relation between parental SES and the development of children and adolescents.

In sum, empirical support exists for both the social causation and social selection perspectives. To be sure, the tension between these two competing explanations for the association between SES and human development is similar to the debates over nature versus nurture or person versus situation that exist in psychology and related disciplines. All three debates are variations on a common theme where the causes of behavior are attributed to either internal or external causes (Turkheimer 2004). To our minds, however, such extreme positions do not capture the complexities of human development, as is illustrated by the often-cited cross-fostering study reported by Capron & Duyme (1989), who found evidence of main effects for both the SES of adoptive parents and the SES of biological parents on the IQs of a sample of French children adopted at birth. The fact that the IQs of these children were influenced by their adopted parents' SES reflected social causation (see also van IJzendoorn et al. 2005 for a review of adoption studies), and similarly, the fact that the IQs of these children were influenced by their biological parents' SES is consistent with the thrust of the social selection argument. Thus, it appears that the truth lies with the well-worn cliché that both intrinsic and extrinsic factors influence the course of human development.

THE INTERACTIONIST APPROACH

Taking the Long View of Life-Course Dynamics

We believe that strict social selection or social causation explanations are unlikely to reflect the complexities of human development as it is played out over time and across generations. On the one hand, the social selection perspective tends to minimize the role that socioeconomic circumstances such as economic catastrophes and windfalls may play in the lives of parents and children. On the other hand, the social causation explanation places too little emphasis on the role of individual differences and human agency. Thus, a comprehensive model that incorporates both social causation and social selection processes seems to hold the most promise for guiding future research. There appears to be an emerging body of evidence for this viewpoint, given that three recent studies have generated findings

suggesting a dynamic interplay between social position and life-course development.

Using data from two national birth cohort studies in Britain, Schoon et al. (2002) showed that low SES in a child's family of origin predicted lower academic achievement and continuing life stress across the years of childhood and adolescence. Children's lower academic competence and higher life stress, in turn, were associated with lower SES when the children reached their adult years. In the second study, Wickrama and his colleagues (2005) found that low SES in the family of origin predicted adverse economic and related life circumstances for adolescents. These events increased risk for both mental and physical health problems during the transition to adulthood, which in turn predicted economic problems and poorer social circumstances during the early adult years. Thus, consistent with the interactionist perspective, both studies suggest a reciprocal process in which early SES predicts personal characteristics of children that influence their SES in adulthood. A problem with both of these studies, however, is that the traits and dispositions of parents may have led to SES in the family of origin and to the course of children's development, consistent with the social selection argument.

Further consideration of this alternative explanation for these findings requires information about the interplay between SES and personal characteristics within a single generation. Support for this type of reciprocal process was provided in a study by Miech and his colleagues (1999), who showed that antisocial youths experience lower educational attainment, which in turn increases their risk for further antisocial behavior as young adults. Presumably, both the SES and ongoing behaviors of these young adults would affect the development of their children. All told, this combined set of studies provides preliminary but important support for the interactionist approach. We next turn to consideration of a model that applies these ideas by proposing a process that begins with a future parent's characteristics during childhood and adolescence and, through a series of intervening mechanisms, eventually influences the development of the next generation of children.

An Interactionist Model of SES and Human Development

Figure 3 depicts our interactionist perspective on SES, family interaction processes, and child development. The model systematically incorporates social selection and social causation processes into an overarching framework. To address the social selection approach, the model begins with the positive characteristics of future parents (G1) during childhood and adolescence. These positive characteristics include attributes such as cognitive abilities, social competence, persistence, planfulness, and ambition. The selection framework proposes that these characteristics will be positively related to G1 SES in adulthood and will be positively related to the investments that parents make in their children (G2). The model also proposes a direct, positive path from G1 personal characteristics to G2 child well-being. This direct pathway could occur biologically (e.g., through genes or the intrauterine environment) or via social learning processes whereby offspring emulate G1 characteristics that demonstrate continuity from childhood to the adult years. Finally, G1's social and cognitive skills are expected to reduce the occurrence of SES-related family stressors, as proposed by the FSM.

The social causation aspects of the integrated model are reflected in pathways from family stress processes to G2 child outcomes along the lines specified by the FSM and in pathways from family SES to parental investments in their offspring along the lines proposed by the FIM. The interactionist model indicates that, although social selection will play a role in determining an adult's social position, socioeconomic circumstances will have an additive influence on eventual outcomes independent of original G1 characteristics. That is, although adult SES is affected by earlier G1 characteristics, the model depicted in **Figure 3** proposes that G1 SES will have an additional and independent impact on parental investments and family stress processes, consistent with both the FIM and FSM. Moreover, family stress processes are expected to decrease parental investments and have a negative impact on G2 development above and beyond the influence of G1 characteristics.

Simply put, the model in **Figure 3** describes a reciprocal dynamic according to which G1 attributes affect SES and SES affects G1 functioning as a parent and spouse, even after controlling for earlier G1 characteristics. According to the model, this reciprocal process ultimately affects the development of the next generation of children. Empirical evaluation of the model will clarify the degree to which this hypothesized dynamic actually occurs. For example, if careful intergenerational studies demonstrate that SES has little influence on family processes or investments after G1's characteristics are taken into account, then the weight of the evidence would favor a social selection argument. On the other hand, if G1 characteristics play only a limited role in predicting either SES or the later constructs in the model after SES is taken into account, then the evidence would favor a social causation view. However, we expect that all of the elements in the model will prove to be important, consistent with the interactionist perspective.

Tests of the model depicted in **Figure 3** require very special types of studies conducted over long periods of time. Data must be collected during childhood or adolescence on future parents, and this G1 generation must be followed long enough into adulthood to evaluate the competing theoretical processes proposed in **Figure 3**. Fortunately, an increasing number of such studies are now available (e.g., Capaldi et al. 2003). Although the demands and costs of such research are quite

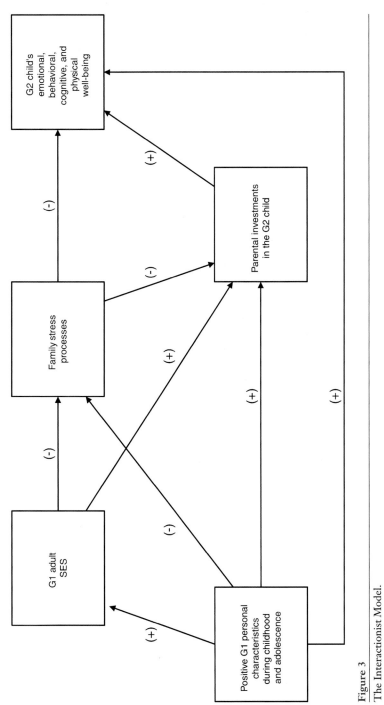

Figure 3

The Interactionist Model.

high, without such long-term investigations it will be impossible to disentangle the degree to which the relationships among SES, family interactions, and child development represent processes of social selection, social causation, or a combination of the two. Nonetheless, many existing datasets can be used to provide preliminary evaluations of aspects of the model described in **Figure 3**, and we hope that researchers will pursue such investigations.

LOOKING TO THE FUTURE

This review was broadly concerned with how SES influences developmental outcomes for children via family processes. We initially framed this discussion within the context of health disparities, given the consistent evidence that lower-SES children are at risk for higher-than-average rates of physical illness and reduced life expectancies, as well as for truncated life opportunities and behavioral or emotional problems. We presented two broad explanations for these findings: a social causation perspective and a social selection perspective. Our final conclusion, however, is that neither perspective is satisfactory on its own, and both explanations can be incorporated into an interactionist model that more accurately captures how SES influences human development over time and across generations. The major take-home message of this review is that researchers should design studies that can evaluate both perspectives simultaneously. To help facilitate the next generation of research, we proposed an interactionist model as a heuristic for future studies of the links among SES, parenting behaviors, and child development. The following brief comments explore future research needs in more detail.

First, it is important to evaluate all of the models we have described using diverse families in terms of their structure, ethnicity, and nationality. These kinds of samples strengthen inferences about the generalizability of the proposed models and identify the boundary conditions for particular models. Results from these kinds of studies often suggest important avenues for future research. For example, Parke et al. (2004) reported that certain aspects of the FSM might operate differently for Mexican American than for European American families. Likewise, Mistry et al. (2002) and Yeung et al. (2002) found that parent emotional distress was directly related to problems in parenting for single-parent families, whereas research with two-parent families suggested that emotional distress usually relates indirectly to parenting problems through interparental conflict. These studies indicate that there are both common and unique pathways that characterize the processes linking SES to child development in diverse types of families and that future work is needed to clarify these processes. Second, it is important to incorporate neighborhood or community effects into discussions of the impact of SES on human development (Leventhal & Brooks-Gunn 2000). We have addressed this issue only tangentially in the present review, but it remains an important issue for future investigations. Third, genetically informed longitudinal studies can be very useful for addressing questions about the interplay between individuals and environmental circumstances (Moffitt et al. 2005). For instance, Kim-Cohen and her associates (2004; but see Turkheimer et al. 2005) found that children's resilience to low SES was in part genetic and in part a function of environmental influences such as parental warmth and stimulating activities.

Finally, a crucial direction for future research is the design of experiments and quasi-experiments that can more powerfully address questions of causality with respect to the models we have considered. As noted earlier, some evaluations of income supplementation or residential relocation programs have shown positive effects (e.g., Gennetian & Miller 2002, Leventhal & Brooks-Gunn 2003). These effects appear to be relatively limited, however, and we suspect these findings result from the fact that planned interventions do not fundamentally alter a family's socioeconomic standing. To be sure, more substantial effect sizes have been reported, but consistent with our argument, these seem to be tied to more substantial boosts in income (see, e.g., Costello et al. 2003). Thus, researchers should have appropriate expectations regarding effect sizes and design studies with adequate power. It is also imperative that all effect sizes are interpreted in the context of these concerns, both for the sake of the scientific literature and for policy makers who may use such findings for making important decisions about programs for families and children. Evaluation studies also should examine the effects of interventions that address other aspects of the models discussed in this article, such as mental health services relevant to family stress processes or supplemental learning programs consistent with the FIM.

All told, researchers from a wide range of disciplines and subdisciplines are using a number of research strategies to tackle the formidable challenge of understanding how SES and family contexts influence individual lives. We anticipate that the next decade or so will provide broad support for interactive models that incorporate aspects of both social causation and social selection. Moreover, we predict that attention to the sort of interactionist model we have outlined in this article will lead to the design of more effective prevention and intervention programs when compared with models that are built exclusively on one tradition or the other. In closing, we note that SES-related health disparities are a reality for both adults and children (Berkman & Kawachi 2000, Repetti et al. 2002), and there is a fundamental need to improve scientific understanding of the reasons for this relationship so that appropriate steps can be taken to improve the lives of families, parents, and children.

SUMMARY POINTS

1. Health disparities are pervasive and demonstrate that lower socioeconomic status is associated with less healthy physical, emotional, behavioral, and cognitive functioning of adults and children.

2. The relationship between SES and healthy development is likely complex.

3. Empirical evidence suggests that low SES may have an adverse influence on child development by exacerbating family stresses that reduce the effective functioning of parents.

4. Empirical evidence suggests that high SES may promote successful child development through the many investments that higher-SES parents are able to make in their children's well-being.

5. Empirical evidence suggests that the earlier attributes of individuals may play a crucial role in their eventual social and economic successes and failures.

6. Empirical evidence indicates that social and economic position and individual attributes may be reciprocally interrelated over time, providing support for an interactionist perspective that argues for both social causes and social selection.

7. Future research on SES and human development would benefit by testing predictions from the interactionist perspective both within and across generations in the same families.

ACKNOWLEDGMENTS

Work on this review was supported by grants from the National Institute of Child Health and Human Development (HD047573, HD051746), the National Institute of Mental Health (MH51361), and the National Institute on Drug Abuse (DA017902, HD047573).

LITERATURE CITED

Ackerman BP, Brown ED, Izard CE. 2004. The relations between persistent poverty and contextual risk and children's behavior in elementary school. *Dev. Psychol.* 40:367–77

Angell RC. 1936. *The Family Encounters the Depression.* New York: Scribner's

Becker GS. 1981. *A Treatise on the Family.* Cambridge, MA: Harvard Univ. Press

Becker GS, Thomes N. 1986. Human capital and the rise and fall of families. *J. Labor Econ.* 4:S1–139

Bell RQ. 1968. A reinterpretation of the direction of effects in studies of socialization. *Psychol. Rev.* 75:81–95

Berkman LF, Kawachi I. 2000. *Social Epidemiology.* New York: Oxford Univ. Press

Borge AIH, Rutter M, Cote S, Tremblay RE. 2004. Early childcare and physical aggression: differentiating social selection and social causation. *J. Child Psychol. Psychiatry* 45:367–76

Bornstein MH, Bradley RH, eds. 2003. *Socioeconomic Status, Parenting, and Child Development.* Mahwah, NJ: Erlbaum

Bornstein MH, Hahn CS, Suwalsky JTD, Haynes OM. 2003. Socioeconomic status, parenting, and child development: the Hollingshead Four-Factor Index of Social Status and the Socioeconomic Index of Occupations. See Bornstein & Bradley 2003, pp. 29–82

Bouchard TJJ. 2004. Genetic influence on human psychological traits: a survey. *Curr. Dir. Psychol. Sci.* 13:148–51

Bradley RH, Caldwell BM. 1980. The relation of the home environment, cognitive competence, and IQ among males and females. *Child Dev.* 51:1140–48

Bradley RH, Corwyn RF. 2002. Socioeconomic status and child development. *Annu. Rev. Psychol.* 53:371–99

Bradley RH, Corwyn RF. 2003. Age and ethnic variations in family process mediators of SES. See Bornstein & Bradley 2003, pp. 161–88

Bradley RH, Corwyn RF, McAdoo HP, García Coll C. 2001. The home environments of children in the United States: part I. Variations by age, ethnicity, and poverty status. *Child Dev.* 72:1844–67

Brody GH, Murry V, Kim S, Brown AC. 2002. Longitudinal pathways to competence and psychological adjustment among African American children living in rural single-parent households. *Child Dev.* 73:1505–16

Capaldi DM, Conger RD, Hops H, Thornberry TP. 2003. Introduction to special section on three-generation studies. *J. Abnorm. Child Psychol.* 31:123–25

Capron C, Duyme M. 1989. Assessment of effects of socio-economic status on IQ in a full cross-fostering study. *Nature* 340:552–54

Caspi A, Wright BRE, Moffitt TE, Silva PA. 1998. Early failure in the labor market: childhood and adolescent predictors of unemployment in the transition to adulthood. *Am. Sociol. Rev.* 63:424–51

Cavan RS, Ranck KH. 1938. *The Family and the Depression: A Study of One Hundred Chicago Families.* Chicago: Univ. Chicago Press

This important study clearly demonstrates the association between SES and a range of parental investments in children. Based on a diverse, national sample of several thousand participants, the results show that in comparison with lower-SES children, higher-SES children experience advantages in terms of more effective and affectionate parenting, enriched learning environments, and safer and more pleasing physical environments.

Coleman JS. 1990. *The Foundations of Social Theory*. Cambridge, MA: Harvard Univ. Press

Conger RD. 1995. Unemployment. In *Encyclopedia of Marriage and the Family*, ed. D Levinson, pp. 731–35. New York: MacMillan

Conger RD, Conger KJ. 2002. Resilience in Midwestern families: selected findings from the first decade of a prospective, longitudinal study. *J. Marriage Fam.* 64:361–73

Conger RD, Conger KJ, Elder GHJ, Lorenz FO, Simons RL, Whitbeck LB. 1992. A family process model of economic hardship and adjustment of early adolescent boys. *Child Dev.* 63:526–41

Conger RD, Conger KJ, Elder GHJ, Lorenz FO, Simons RL, Whitbeck LB. 1993. Family economic stress and adjustment of early adolescent girls. *Dev. Psychol.* 29:206–19

Conger RD, Conger KJ, Matthews LS, Elder GHJ. 1999a. Pathways of economic influence on adolescent adjustment. *Am. J. Community Psychol.* 27:519–40

Conger RD, Elder GHJ. 1994. *Families in Troubled Times: Adapting to Change in Rural America*. Hawthorne, NY: de Gruyter Aldine

Conger RD, Ge X, Elder GHJ, Lorenz FO, Simons RL. 1994. Economic stress, coercive family process, and developmental problems of adolescents. *Child Dev.* 65:541–61

Conger RD, Rueter MA, Elder GHJ. 1999b. Couple resilience to economic pressure. *J. Personal. Soc. Psychol.* 76:54–71

Conger RD, Wallace LE, Sun Y, Simons RL, McLoyd VC, Brody G. 2002. Economic pressure in African American families: a replication and extension of the family stress model. *Dev. Psychol.* 38:179–93

Corcoran M, Adams T. 1997. Race, sex, and the intergenerational transmission of poverty. See Duncan & Brooks-Gunn 1997a, pp. 461–517

Costello EJ, Compton SN, Keeler G, Angold A. 2003. Relationships between poverty and psychopathology: a natural experiment. *JAMA* 290:2023–29

Davis A, Havighurst RJ. 1946. Social class and color differences in child-rearing. *Am. Sociol. Rev.* 11:698–710

Davis-Kean PE. 2005. The influence of parent education and family income on child achievement: the indirect role of parental expectations and the home environment. *J. Fam. Psychol.* 19:294–304

Dearing E, McCartney K, Taylor BA. 2001. Change in family income-to-needs matters more for children with less. *Child Dev.* 72:1779–93

Dodge KA, Pettit GS, Bates JE. 1994. Socialization mediators of the relation between socioeconomic status and child conduct problems. *Child Dev.* 65:649–65

Duncan GJ, Brooks-Gunn J, eds. 1997a. *Consequences of Growing Up Poor*. New York: Russell Sage Found.

Duncan GJ, Brooks-Gunn J. 1997b. Income effects across the life span: integration and interpretation. See Duncan & Brooks-Gunn 1997a, pp. 596–610

Duncan GJ, Magnuson KA. 2003. Off with Hollingshead: socioeconomic resources, parenting, and child development. See Bornstein & Bradley 2003, pp. 83–106

Elder GHJ. 1974. *Children of the Great Depression: Social Change in Life Experience*. Chicago: Univ. Chicago Press

Elder GHJ, Caspi A. 1988. Economic stress in lives: developmental perspectives. *J. Soc. Issues* 44:25–45

Ensminger ME, Fothergill K. 2003. A decade of measuring SES: what it tells us and where to go from here. See Bornstein & Bradley 2003, pp. 13–27

Evans GW, English K. 2002. The environment of poverty: multiple stressor exposure, psychophysiological stress, and socioemotional adjustment. *Child Dev.* 73:1238–48

This report provides an elaborated version of the family stress model, which includes predictions regarding resilience and vulnerability to hypothesized family stress processes. Empirical findings are reviewed that relate to the basic and extended versions of the model.

This study provides groundbreaking evidence that community improvements in family income reduce risk for child psychopathology. The findings from this quasi-experiment demonstrated that new employment opportunities that increased family income on average led to lower rates of children's psychiatric disorder.

Feinstein L, Bynner J. 2004. The importance of cognitive development in middle childhood for adulthood socioeconomic status, mental health, and problem behavior. *Child Dev.* 75:1329–39

Gennetian LA, Miller C. 2002. Children and welfare reform: a view from an experimental welfare program in Minnesota. *Child Dev.* 73:601–20

Gottfried AW, Gottfried AE, Bathurst K, Guerin DW, Parramore MM. 2003. Socioeconomic status in children's development and family environment: infancy through adolescence. See Bornstein & Bradley 2003, pp. 189–207

Gutman LM, McLoyd VC, Tokoyawa T. 2005. Financial strain, neighborhood stress, parenting behaviors, and adolescent adjustment in urban African American Families. *J. Res. Adolesc.* 15:425–49

Han WJ. 2005. Maternal nonstandard work schedules and child cognitive outcomes. *Child Dev.* 76:137–54

Haveman RH, Wolfe BS. 1994. *Succeeding Generations: On the Effects of Investments in Children.* New York: Sage

Hoff E. 2003. The specificity of environmental influence: Socioeconomic status affects early vocabulary development via maternal speech. *Child Dev.* 74:1368–78

Hoff E, Laursen B, Tardif T. 2002. Socioeconomic status and parenting. In *Handbook of Parenting Volume 2: Biology and Ecology of Parenting*, ed. MH Bornstein, pp. 231–52. Mahwah, NJ: Erlbaum. 2nd ed.

Hoffman LW. 2003. Methodological issues in the studies of SES, parenting, and child development. See Bornstein & Bradley 2003, pp. 125–43

Huston AC, Aronson SR. 2005. Mothers' time with infant and time in employment as predictors of mother-child relationships and children's early development. *Child Dev.* 76:467–82

Huston AC, Duncan GJ, McLoyd VC, Crosby DA, Ripke MN, et al. 2005. Impacts on children of a policy to promote employment and reduce poverty for low-income parents: New Hope after 5 years. *Dev. Psychol.* 41:902–18

Hyde JS, Else-Quest NM, Goldsmith HH, Biesanz JC. 2004. Children's temperament and behavior problems predict their employed mothers' work functioning. *Child Dev.* 75:580–94

Judge TA, Higgins CA, Thoresen CJ, Barrick MR. 1999. The Big Five personality traits, general mental ability, and career success across the life span. *Pers. Psychol.* 52:621–52

Keating DP, Hertzman C. 1999. *Developmental Health and the Wealth of Nations.* New York: Guilford

Kim-Cohen J, Moffitt TE, Caspi A, Taylor A. 2004. Genetic and environmental processes in young children's resilience and vulnerability to socioeconomic deprivation. *Child Dev.* 75:651–68

Kohen DE, Brooks-Gunn J, Leventhal T, Hertzman C. 2002. Neighborhood income and physical and social disorder in Canada: associations with young children's competencies. *Child Dev.* 73:1844–60

Kohn ML. 1959. Social class and parental values. *Am. J. Sociol.* 64:337–51

Kohn ML. 1963. Social class and parent-child relationships: an interpretation. *Am. J. Sociol.* 68:471–80

Kohn ML. 1969. *Class and Conformity: A Study in Values.* Oxford: Dorsey

Kohn ML. 1995. Social structure and personality through time and space. In *Examining Lives in Context: Perspectives on the Ecology of Human Development*, ed. P Moen, GH Elder Jr, K Lüscher, pp. 141–68. Washington, DC: Am. Psychol. Assoc.

Kokko K, Pulkkinen L. 2000. Aggression in childhood and long-term unemployment in adulthood: a cycle of maladaptation and some protective factors. *Dev. Psychol.* 36:463–72

Komarovsky M. 1940. *The Unemployed Man and His Family: The Effect of Unemployment Upon the Status of the Man in Fifty-nine Families.* New York: Dryden

Lerner RM. 2003. What are SES effects effects of? A developmental systems perspective. See Bornstein & Bradley 2003, pp. 231–55

Leventhal T, Brooks-Gunn J. 2000. The neighborhoods they live in: the effects of neighborhood residence on child and adolescent outcomes. *Psychol. Bull.* 126:309–17

Leventhal T, Brooks-Gunn J. 2003. Moving on up: neighborhood effects on children and families. See Bornstein & Bradley 2003, pp. 209–30

Leventhal T, Fauth RC, Brooks-Gunn J. 2005. Neighborhood poverty and public policy: a 5-year follow-up of children's educational outcomes in the New York City Moving to Opportunity demonstration. *Dev. Psychol.* 41:933–52

Linver MR, Brooks-Gunn J, Kohen D. 2002. Family processes as pathways from income to young children's development. *Dev. Psychol.* 38:719–34

Liu WM, Ali SR, Soleck G, Hopps J, Dunston K, Pickett TJ. 2004. Using social class in counseling psychology research. *J. Counsel. Psychol.* 51:3–18

Magnuson KA, Duncan GJ. 2002. Parents in poverty. In *Handbook of Parenting: Volume 4. Social Conditions and Applied Parenting*, ed. MH Bornstein, pp. 95–121. Mahwah, NJ: Erlbaum. 2nd ed.

Magnusson D, Stattin H. 1998. Person-context interaction theories. In *Handbook of Child Psychology: Theoretical Models of Human Development*, ed. W Damon, RM Lerner, pp. 685–759. New York: Wiley. 5th ed.

Mayer S. 1997. *What Money Can't Buy: Family Income and Children's Life Chances.* Cambridge, MA: Harvard Univ. Press

McLeod JD, Kaiser K. 2004. Childhood emotional and behavioral problems and educational attainment. *Am. Sociol. Rev.* 69:636–58

McLeod JD, Shanahan MJ. 1996. Trajectories of poverty and children's mental health. *J. Health Soc. Behav.* 37:207–20

McLoyd VC. 1998. Socioeconomic disadvantage and child development. *Am. Psychol.* 53:185–204

Mezzacappa E. 2004. Alerting, orienting, and executive attention: developmental properties and sociodemographic correlates in an epidemiological sample of young, urban children. *Child Dev.* 75:1373–86

Miech RA, Caspi A, Moffitt TE, Wright BRE, Silva PA. 1999. Low socioeconomic status and mental disorders: a longitudinal study of selection and causation during young adulthood. *Am. J. Sociol.* 104:1096–131

Mistry RS, Biesanz JC, Taylor LC, Burchinal M, Cox MJ. 2004. Family income and its relation to preschool children's adjustment for families in the NICHD Study of Early Child Care. *Dev. Psychol.* 40:727–45

Mistry RS, Vandewater EA, Huston AC, McLoyd VC. 2002. Economic well-being and children's social adjustment: the role of family process in an ethnically diverse low income sample. *Child Dev.* 73:935–51

Moffitt TE, Caspi A, Rutter M. 2005. Strategy for investigating interactions between measured genes and measured environments. *Arch. Gen. Psychiatry* 62:473–81

Morris P, Duncan GJ, Clark-Kauffman E. 2005. Child well-being in an era of welfare reform: the sensitivity of transitions in development to policy change. *Dev. Psychol.* 41:919–32

Natl. Inst. Child Health Human Dev. Early Child Care Res. Netw. 2005. Duration and developmental timing of poverty and children's cognitive and social development from birth through third grade. *Child Dev.* 76:795–810

In this paper, the authors report results from a large, multiethnic study of young children. They find support for predictions from both family stress and family investment models in terms of SES influences on children. The analyses include important controls for maternal characteristics that reduce the likelihood that the results represent processes of social selection rather than social causation.

This book lays out various models for evaluating income effects on children's development and provides a particularly helpful description of the investment perspective. The author questions whether income really has an influence on children's development and provides a number of analyses that are consistent her argument.

Miech et al. reports that mental disorders during adolescence can influence eventual SES, and

Oakes JM, Rossi PH. 2003. The measurement of SES in health research: current practice and steps toward a new approach. *Soc. Sci. Med.* 56:769–84

Parke RD, Coltrane S, Duffy S, Buriel R, Dennis J, et al. 2004. Economic stress, parenting, and child adjustment in Mexican American and European American families. *Child Dev.* 75:1632–56

Prior M, Sanson A, Smart D, Oberklaid F. 1999. Psychological disorders and their correlates in an Australian community sample of preadolescent children. *J. Child Psychol. Psychiatry* 40:563–80

Repetti RL, Taylor SE, Seeman TE. 2002. Risky families: family social environments and the mental and physical health of offspring. *Psychol. Bull.* 128:330–66

Robila M, Krishnakumar A. 2005. Effects of economic pressure on marital conflict in Romania. *J. Fam. Psychol.* 19:246–51

Rowe DC, Rodgers JL. 1997. Poverty and behavior: Are environmental measures nature and nurture? *Dev. Rev.* 17:358–75

Rutter M, Pickles A, Murray R, Eaves LJ. 2001. Testing hypotheses on specific environmental causal effects on behavior. *Psychol. Bull.* 127:291–324

Schoon I, Bynner J, Joshi H, Parsons S, Wiggins RD, Sacker A. 2002. The influence of context, timing, and duration of risk experiences for the passage from childhood to midadulthood. *Child Dev.* 73:1486–504

Sears RR, Maccoby EE, Levin H. 1957. *Patterns of Child Rearing.* Oxford: Peterson

Shadish WR, Cook TD, Campbell DT. 2002. *Experimental and Quasi-Experimental Designs for Generalized Causal Inference.* New York: Houghton Mifflin

Shiner RL, Masten AS, Roberts JM. 2003. Childhood personality foreshadows adult personality and life outcomes two decades later. *J. Personal.* 71:1145–70

Sobolewski JM, Amato PR. 2005. Economic hardship in the family of origin and children's psychological well-being in adulthood. *J. Marriage Fam.* 67:141–56

Solantaus T, Leinonen J, Punamäki RL. 2004. Children's mental health in times of economic recession: replication and extension of the family economic stress model in Finland. *Dev. Psychol.* 40:412–29

Steinberg L. 2001. We know some things: parent-adolescent relationships in retrospect and prospect. *J. Res. Adolesc.* 11:1–19

Strohschein L. 2005. Household income histories and child mental health trajectories. *J. Health Soc. Behav.* 46:359–75

Tamis-LeMonda CS, Shannon JD, Cabrera NJ, Lamb ME. 2004. Fathers and mothers at play with their 2- and 3-year-olds: contributions to language and cognitive development. *Child Dev.* 75:1806–20

Teachman JD, Paasch KM, Day RD, Carver KP. 1997. Poverty during adolescence and subsequent educational attainment. See Duncan & Brooks-Gunn 1997a, pp. 382–418

Turkheimer E. 2004. Spinach and ice cream: why social science is so difficult. In *Behavior Genetics Principles: Perspectives in Development, Personality, and Psychopathology*, ed. LF DiLalla, pp. 161–89. Washington, DC: Am. Psychol. Assoc.

Turkheimer E, D'Onofrio BM, Maes HH, Eaves LJ. 2005. Analysis and interpretation of twin studies including measures of the shared environment. *Child Dev.* 76:1217–33

Van IJzendoorn MH, Juffer F, Klein Poelhuis CW. 2005. Adoption and cognitive development: a meta-analytic comparison of adopted and nonadopted children's IQ and school performance. *Psychol. Bull.* 131:301–16

Wickrama KAS, Conger RD, Abraham WT. 2005. Early adversity and later health: the intergenerational transmission of adversity through mental disorder and physical illness. *J. Gerontol.* 60B:125–29

that SES during early adulthood can influence later mental disorders. The article provides important preliminary support for an interactionist perspective on SES and human development.

Parke and his colleagues provide fascinating findings suggesting that the family stress model might operate differently for European compared with Mexican American families. In particular, economic pressures that increase conflicts in the marital relationship may be especially distressing for children of Mexican origin.

Rowe & Rodgers question whether studies that relate SES to child development have adequately controlled for possible genetic influences. This paper provides an important orientation regarding possible genetic pathways in social selection effects.

Yeung WJ, Linver MR, Brooks-Gunn J. 2002. How money matters for young children's development: parental investment and family processes. *Child Dev.* 73:1861–79

Zevalkink J, Riksen-Walraven JM. 2001. Parenting in Indonesia: inter- and intracultural differences in mothers' interactions with their young children. *Int. J. Behav. Dev.* 25:167–75

Solantaus et al. provide an important cross-national replication in Finland of results related to the family stress model. The findings are quite comparable to tests of the model conducted in the United States, and thus provide cross-cultural support for predictions from the model.

Race, Race-Based Discrimination, and Health Outcomes Among African Americans

Vickie M. Mays,[1,3,4] Susan D. Cochran,[2,3] and Namdi W. Barnes[3,4]

Departments of [1]Health Services and [2]Epidemiology, University of California, Los Angeles, School of Public Health; [3]UCLA Center for Research, Education, Training and Strategic Communication on Minority Health Disparities; and [4]Department of Psychology, UCLA, Los Angeles, California 90095-1563; email: mays@ucla.edu, cochran@ucla.edu, nbarnesn@ucla.edu

Annu. Rev. Psychol. 2007. 58:201–25

First published online as a Review in Advance on September 5, 2006

The *Annual Review of Psychology* is online at http://psych.annualreviews.org

This article's doi: 10.1146/annurev.psych.57.102904.190212

Key Words

racism, Blacks, allostatic load, social exclusion, brain, residential segregation, social cognition, cognitive appraisal, self-regulation

Abstract

Persistent and vexing health disadvantages accrue to African Americans despite decades of work to erase the effects of race discrimination in this country. Participating in these efforts, psychologists and other social scientists have hypothesized that African Americans' continuing experiences with racism and discrimination may lie at the root of the many well-documented race-based physical health disparities that affect this population. With newly emerging methodologies in both measurement of contextual factors and functional neuroscience, an opportunity now exists to cleave together a comprehensive understanding of the ways in which discrimination has harmful effects on health. In this article, we review emerging work that locates the cause of race-based health disparities in the external effects of the contextual social space on the internal world of brain functioning and physiologic response. These approaches reflect the growing interdisciplinary nature of psychology in general, and the field of race relations in particular.

Contents

RACE, RACE-BASED DISCRIMINATION, AND HEALTH OUTCOMES AMONG AFRICAN AMERICANS

The ways in which race, racial prejudice, and race discrimination shape the human experience have long been of interest in psychology and the other social sciences. The purpose of this review is threefold. First, we briefly examine the disconcerting evidence for increasing Black/White disparities in health despite the radical changes over the past 50 years in race-based civil rights in the United States (Walker et al. 2004). Next, we explore the notion that African Americans' continuing experiences with racism, discrimination, and possibly social exclusion may account for some proportion of these health disparities (Clark & Adams 2004; Everson-Rose & Lewis 2005; Guyll et al. 2001; Harrell et al. 2003; Massey 2004; Walker et al. 2004; Williams et al. 1997, 2003). Finally, we focus on three emerging perspectives that locate health disparities in the external influences of social space and the internal effects of body and brain functioning. These latter approaches reflect the growing interdisciplinary nature of research models that attempt to explain the continuing legacy of physical health disparities that harmfully affect African Americans. Our aim is to raise several important questions about the ways in which psychology can engage in a plan of research to address health disparities from race-based discrimination and also take a leadership role in informing the development of social policies that will help American society to accelerate its pace of changing negative race-based attitudes and associated social policies.

HEALTH DISPARITIES—THE BLACK/WHITE DIVIDE

In 1985, with the release of the Heckler report, America was put on notice that the health status of African Americans was significantly worse than that of their White counterparts (Heckler 1985). Unfortunately, since then, racial disparities in health have worsened in many ways. In 1990, for example, McCord and Freeman shocked the world by reporting that a Black male in Harlem had less of a chance of reaching the age of 65 than did the average male resident of Bangladesh—one of the poorest countries in the world. At the time of McCord & Freeman's study, African American men fell behind men from Bangladesh in survival rates starting at age 40 (McCord & Freeman 1990, Sen 1993). In the United States, life expectancy for African American males experienced an unprecedented drop every year from 1984 to1989, while all other combinations of Black/White male/female comparisons either remained the same or increased (NVSS 2004).

Today, African Americans still bear a disproportionate burden in disease morbidity, mortality, disability, and injury (MMWR 2005, Williams 1995). This continuing health disadvantage is seen particularly in the age-adjusted mortality rates: African Americans remain significantly and consistently more at risk for early death than do similar White Americans (Geronimus et al. 1996, Kochanek et al. 2004, Levine et al. 2001, MMWR 2005, Smith et al. 1998, Williams & Jackson 2005). Indeed, the overall death rate of African Americans in the United States today is equivalent to that of Whites in America 30 years ago (Levine et al. 2001, Williams & Jackson 2005).

These premature deaths arise from a broad spectrum of disorders. Diabetes, cardiovascular heart disease, hypertension, and obesity disproportionately affect African Americans (Davis et al. 2003; Krieger 1990; Mensah et al. 2005; USDHHS 1990, 2000, 2005). For example, in deaths due to heart disease, the rate per 100,000 persons for African Americans (321.3) is higher than for any other racial/ethnic group, including Asian/Pacific Islanders (137.4), American Indian/Alaska Natives (178.9), Hispanics (188.4), and Whites (245.6) (NCCDPHP 2004). This same pattern for African Americans in comparison with Asian/Pacific Islanders, American Indians/Alaska Natives, Hispanics, and Whites is repeated in deaths due to diabetes (49.9 versus 16.9, 45.3, 36.3, and 22.1, respectively) and strokes (80.0 versus 51.2, 46.1, 44.0, and 55.9, respectively). Even prevalence of hypertension per 100,000 is far greater among African Americans (34.2) than among the other major racial/ethnic groups (16.2, 25.8, 18.9, 25.8, respectively) (NCCDPHP 2004).

Furthermore, these health disadvantages occur in the context of increasing disparities in rates of disease. For example, Williams & Jackson (2005) examined Black/White health disparities using data from the National Center for Health Statistics for the years 1950 to 2000, and found that although rates of heart disease were similar for Blacks and Whites in 1950, by the year 2000, African Americans had a rate of heart disease 30% higher than that of Whites. Similarly, in 1950, African Americans had a lower cancer rate than Whites, but by the year 2000, their rate was 30% higher.

Poverty alone cannot fully explain these differences; even when socioeconomic status (SES) is controlled for, there is still an excess of 38,000 deaths per year or 1.1 million years of life lost among African Americans in the United States (Franks et al. 2005). Simple differences in skin color that might be the basis for the occurrence of discrimination also appear to be an inadequate explanation. For example, in the recent National Survey of American Life (Jackson et al. 2004), comparisons of 6000 Americans who reported being either Black of Caribbean ancestry, African American, or White revealed that of the three groups, African Americans evidenced the worst self-reported physical health status, including higher rates of hypertension, diabetes, and stroke).

DISCRIMINATION AND HEALTH

The continuing legacy of poor health in African Americans, despite the overall improved conditions of their lives, is one compelling reason to take a closer look at the role discrimination may play. The health disparities that affect African Americans in this country arise from many sources, including cultural differences in lifestyle patterns, inherited health risks, and social inequalities that are reflected in discrepancies in access to health care, variations in health providers' behaviors, differences in socioeconomic position (Fiscella & Williams 2004; Krieger 1991, 1999; Krieger & Moss 1996; Krieger et al. 1997; Subramanian et al. 2005), and residential segregation (Massey 2004, Schulz et al. 2000). The extent to which these health disparities are also shaped by the pernicious effects of race-based discrimination is of growing interest (Clark 2003, Clark et al. 1999, Cochran & Mays 1994, Everson-Rose & Lewis 2005, Geronimus et al. 1996, Guyll et al. 2001, Harrell et al. 2003, Hertzman 2000, Krieger & Sidney 1996, Massey 2004, Mays 1995, Mays & Cochran 1998, Mays et al. 1996, McEwen 2000, Mechanic 2005, Morenoff & Lynch 2004, Walker et al. 2004, Williams et al. 2003).

From the perspective of discrimination models, the causal mechanism linking racial/ethnic minority status and health disadvantage is thought to lie in the harmful effects of chronic experiences with race-based discrimination, both actual and perceived. These experiences are thought to set into motion a process of physiological responses (e.g., elevated blood pressure and heart rate, production of biochemical reactions, hypervigilance) that eventually result in disease and mortality.

In attempting to elucidate the negative health outcome mechanisms of race-based discrimination, the effects of both overt and anticipated or perceived experiences of race-based discrimination have been examined. Studies of overt or manifest discrimination typically measure events occurring at the individual level by asking respondents if they have been "treated badly or unfairly," "differently," or are somehow "disadvantaged" relative to others based on their racial or ethnic background (Krieger et al. 2005). The foundation of this work came from the earlier stress research paradigm, where individual differences in vulnerability to stress were seen as key to the development of mental health morbidity (Kessler et al. 1999). Factors that were thought to predispose individuals to negative mental health outcomes included unfair treatment and social disadvantage as well as other social stressors, such as inadequate levels of social support, neuroticism, the occurrence of life events, and chronic role strain (Adler et al. 1994, Brown & Harris 1989, Henderson et al. 1981, Kanner et al. 1991, Lazarus 1993, Pearlin et al. 1981, Thoits 1983). Later studies examining the possible consequences of perceived discrimination began to document that simply the anticipation of being treated badly or unfairly had as powerful an impact on individuals as objectively measured experiences (Kessler et al. 1999). Both of these developments helped move the field toward hypothesizing that chronic experiences with perceived discrimination can have wide-ranging effects on individuals.

Several studies have now documented health effects of discrimination. In one study, experiences of perceived race-based discrimination were positively associated with raised blood pressure and poorer self-rated health (Krieger & Sidney 1996). Perceived race-based discrimination was also found to be the best predictor of smoking among African American adults in two studies (Landrine & Klonoff 2000). Moreover, smokers, as compared with nonsmokers, reported finding the experience of discrimination as subjectively more stressful. In fact, this appraisal of discrimination as stressful was a better predictor of smoking than was the measured status variables of education, gender, income, and age. Landrine & Klonoff (2000) have suggested that perceived race discrimination and the appraisal process may be key factors in explaining the Black-White differential in smoking prevalence, where smoking possibly acts as a means of coping with stress. The issue gains even greater relevance when one considers that the Black-White differential exists not only in smoking prevalence, but also in smoking-related morbidity, mortality (MMWR 1996, Rivo et al. 1989), and death from respiratory cancers (CDC 1994, USDHHS 1998). Similar findings in research on alcohol consumption among African Americans indicate that internalized racism (i.e., a belief that African Americans are inferior) is positively associated with alcohol use as well as psychological distress (Taylor & Williams 2003).

In the 1990s, the perspective in this field shifted somewhat to emphasize the importance of chronicity of discrimination exposure in negative mental health outcomes (Kessler et al. 1999). At the same time, interest in the effects of discrimination on health outcomes strengthened as the federal government released the Healthy People 2000 and Healthy People 2010 objectives, the yearly National Health Care Disparities Report (USDHHS 2005), and reports from the Institute of Medicine on Unequal Burden (Haynes & Smedley1999) and Unequal Treatment (Smedley et al. 2003). Experts in health, social cognition, epidemiology, biology, neuroscience, and clinical psychology began to use new methodologies to study prejudice, discrimination, and racism (Everson-Rose & Lewis 2005; Karlamangala et al. 2005; Krieger 1990; Krieger & Sidney 1996; McEwen 1998, 2005; Morenoff & Lynch 2004). These studies focused on the perspective of the person being targeted (Eberhardt 2005, Everson-Rose & Lewis 2005, Golby et al. 2001, Harrell et al. 2003, Mays & Cochran 1998, Meyer 2003) as well as on the characteristics of persons who target others (Eberhardt et al. 2003, 2004; Phelps et al. 2000, 2003).

The result has been a great melding of disciplines, tools, and perspectives to identify the important components of the pathways linking race-based discrimination and negative health outcomes. For example, human brain imaging is now used to observe cognitive processing of experiences of social exclusion (Eisenberger & Lieberman 2004). Biological measures of race-based stress (allostatic load) reveal intricate relationships among the brain, immune system, autonomic nervous system, and the hypothalamic-pituitary-adrenal (HPA) axis (McEwen & Seeman 1999), as well as the ways in which unhealthy environmental stimuli can "get under the skin" of individuals to cause negative health outcomes (Massey 1985, Taylor et al. 1997). Political scientists interested in racial inequalities of criminal behavior and in a number of other areas are looking at the interaction between environmental exposures and brain chemistry (Masters 2001).

NEW APPROACHES TO OLD ISSUES

Across the disparate fields of psychology, sociology, and neuroscience, work is converging on "candidate" variables (e.g., social processes, functional neuroscience, contextual effects) that might be essential to understanding underlying processes associated with racial discrimination and negative health outcomes in African Americans. The challenge, at this point, is to cleave together the literatures examining the upstream side of discrimination and health with its focus on behavioral, social, and psychological factors to those studying the downstream biological pathways and molecular events that are proximal causes of the high rates of disease and disability (Kaplan 1999, Schillinger et al. 2005). In the past decade, particularly, the number of models proposed to account for the relationship between race-based experiences and poor physical and mental health have exploded (Clark 2003, Clark et al. 1999, Everson-Rose & Lewis 2005, Hertzman 2000, House 2002, House & Williams 2000, Kuh & Ben-Sholmo 1997, Massey 2004, McEwen 2000, Morenoff & Lynch 2004, Smedley et al. 2003). Several of the race-discrimination-health pathway models posit connections among environmental stimuli including conditions of violence, poor education, and negative social connectedness or early childhood exposure to these conditions, and resulting changes in brain functioning and bodily psychophysiological responses (Clark 2003, Clark et al. 1999, Everson-Rose & Lewis 2005, Hertzman 2000, House 2002, House & Williams 2000, Kuh & Ben-Sholmo 1997, Massey 2004, McEwen 2000, Morenoff & Lynch 2004, Smedley et al. 2003). Across these many models, three elements consistently emerge: (*a*) an emphasis on the importance of unhealthy social spaces in which racial stratification (particularly in the form of residential segregation) serves as a structural lattice for maintaining discrimination; (*b*) intergenerational and life-span effects of race discrimination that result in pernicious effects on health despite increasingly better opportunities and better environments; and (*c*) chronicity and magnitude of race-based discrimination (e.g., major life events, everyday hassles, and reduced opportunities) as an allostatic load factor in negative health outcomes. We discuss below three emerging areas where contributions to elucidating the candidate variables in the race-discrimination-health pathway arise in the context of new methodologies.

Social Place, Unhealthy Environments, Racial Stratification, and Health Outcomes

In recent years, the concept of place, particularly social place (e.g., geographic location, local context, neighborhood), has emerged as an important construct in understanding the contributions of discrimination in fostering ill health and health risks (Diez Roux 2002, Ellen et al. 2001, Morenoff & Lynch 2004). Traditionally, research on the health of African Americans focused on individual-level risk factors, with ownership for change residing in individual-level strategies. But the newer work argues for casting a broader net that will capture more complex and multilevel factors in the environment. These are hypothesized to play a significant role in the health status and health outcomes of individuals (Acevedo-Garcia et al. 2003; Diez Roux 2001, 2002, 2003; Diez Roux et al. 1997; Krieger 1999; O'Campo et al. 1997; Pickett & Pearl 2001; Williams & Harris-Reid 1999). For example, a number of sociologists and epidemiologists have made the case that neighborhood is a critical variable in mediating access to economic opportunities, social connections, and

social capital (Diez Roux 2003, Massey 2000, O'Campo et al. 1997, Oliver & Shapiro 1995, Wilson 1987), all of which are components that mediate health status. Integrating neighborhood level effects into models of individual risk represents an intriguing new methodology for psychologists.

When neighborhoods work well, they are a place where individuals derive many social benefits. However, when neighborhoods are characterized by persistently low SES and residential segregation, often linked to ethnic/racial minority population concentrations (Acevedo-Garcia 2000, 2001; Lester 2000; O'Campo et al. 1997; Peterson & Krivo 1999), then African Americans living in those neighborhoods have higher rates of morbidity and mortality. Residential segregation that creates concentrated neighborhoods where residents are predominantly poor, racial/ethnic minority, or of immigrant status are social spaces with concentrated social problems. This increases the chances that residents, whatever their individual backgrounds, will experience greater exposure to stressful environments while also having fewer resources with which to cope with these exposures (Boardman 2004; Roberts 1997, 1999; Macintyre et al. 2002).

Roberts (1997, 1999) presents three different pathways by which poor and often racial/ethnic minority–inhabited neighborhoods can have an effect on individual health. First, poorer communities are less likely to have adequate health and social services, creating a problem of access and timely use. Also, the physical environments are more likely to expose the residents to health hazards (e.g., air pollution, lead, dust, dirt, smog, and other hazardous conditions). Finally, the concentration of poverty and its related characteristics (e.g., exposure to drugs, crime, gangs, and violence; unemployment, stress, and anxiety; substandard housing and schools; and lack of green space or fresh fruits and vegetables) often creates social environments that lessen social connectedness and provide fewer social benefits for residents.

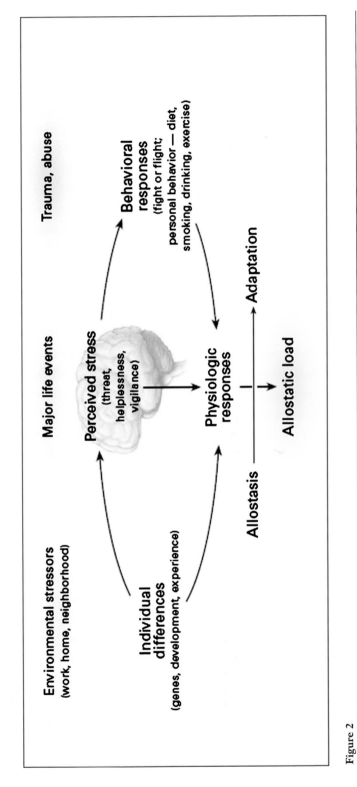

Figure 2

McEwen's (1998) model of stress response and development of allostatic load. Reprinted from McEwen (1998), copyright © 1998 MMS.

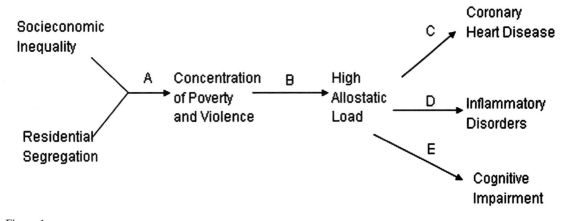

Figure 1

Massey's (2004) biosocial model of racial stratification. Reprinted from Massey 2004.

Although the perspective that some neighborhoods are less fostering of health than others is not new, researchers who are linking this idea to biological responses that might arise from chronic neighborhood stressors are gaining new insights. In **Figure 1**, we depict sociologist Douglas Massey's (2004) model of the upstream/downstream process of risk for specific disease states for African Americans. The pathway begins with two correlated factors: residential segregation and social economic inequality. These factors work to concentrate social stressors, which in turn set into motion high allostatic loads that are associated with increased risk for coronary heart disease, chronic inflammation, and cognitive impairment. In racially segregated, poor neighborhoods, both chronic and acute daily stressors (e.g., violence, unemployment, personal safety concerns) repeatedly invoke a biological challenge similar to the flight/fight response. According to Massey, an African American living in this unhealthy environment responds at a biological level with persistently elevated levels of cortisol and other glucocorticoid hormones. The effect of the chronic stress response is a premature wearing down of the body and a greater tendency to develop specific disease processes.

One of the issues in current work in the area is identifying the core elements in an un-healthy environment that activate a sense of danger or, conversely, protect against harmful effects of chronic neighborhood stressors. Some of the pertinent work has examined the consequences of negative social interactions and has discovered positive associations between perceptions of being treated badly, lacking social support, and an absence of emotional warmth and closeness and patterns of physiological arousal associated with cardiovascular, sympathetic nervous system reactivity (Repetti et al. 2002; Seeman et al. 1993, 1995; Ursa et al. 2003). For example, Kiecolt-Glaser and colleagues found that 30 minutes of conflict between a married couple was associated with changes in norepinephrine, cortisol, and adrenocorticotropic (ACTH) levels, with both husbands and wives showing decreased immunologic responsiveness during the conflictual communication (Kiecolt-Glaser et al. 1997, Robles & Kiecolt-Glaser 2003).

Intergenerational and Developmental Perspectives

Researchers are also making a strong empirical case for the importance of positive emotions and positive relationships as critical ingredients in healthy children and healthy adults. Seeman and her colleagues investigated the relationship between social environments and the activation of biological responses (Repetti et al. 2002, Seeman et al. 1993). Their findings show that when children are exposed to environments characterized by conflict and low levels of nurturance, they are more likely to present dysregulated cortisol activity and show greater cardiovascular and sympathetic nervous system reactivity in the face of stress-related challenges. Similarly, Taylor and colleagues, working with Seeman in reviewing the literature in this area, identified three characteristics of children and young adults' family social environments that contribute to negative mental and physical health in later adult years (Taylor et al. 1997). These are (*a*) social environments that are conflictual, angry, violent, or abusive; (*b*) parenting styles that are highly domineering or controlling; and (*c*) parent-child relationships that are unresponsive and lack the characteristics of warmth, social cohesiveness, and emotional support. Furthermore, a growing number of studies indicate that positive social interactions, positive expectations in the form of optimism, positive illusions, and hopeful outlooks are associated with physiological arousal patterns and biological responses (e.g., lower ambulatory blood pressures) to stress challenges that are consistent with long-term positive physical and mental health outcomes (Fredrickson 2000; Ryff & Singer 2000, 2001; Seeman & McEwen 1996; Taylor & Brown 1994; Taylor et al. 1997).

Identification of candidate psychosocial variables that strongly influence health disparities in this country offers the possibility of developing more highly tailored and efficacious interventions, particularly if these interventions began in childhood. In the United States, one in five children grow up in neighborhoods characterized as poor, and for racial/ethnic minorities, particularly African Americans, the rates are even higher (Mather & Rivers 2006). Children who grow up in these poor neighborhoods are at higher risk than their counterparts in more affluent neighborhoods for a number of health challenges, including teen pregnancy, substance abuse, obesity, smoking, limited exercise, and poor dietary habits, as well as early departure from formal education activities, all of which are risk factors for premature mortality, morbidity, or disability (Mather & River 2006, Messer et al. 2005). Unfortunately, there is also strong evidence that individuals who live in poor neighborhoods as children are more likely to end up as adults living in poor neighborhoods with extended families that also live in similar neighborhoods (Mather & River 2006). Concentrations of families within higher-risk neighborhoods increase individual burden, especially when there is a local catastrophe, as occurred during Hurricane Katrina.

Efforts such as those of Seeman, Repetti, Taylor, Ryff, and others move beyond descriptive epidemiology into the realm of elucidating possible social psychological processes that mediate connections between the conditions in poor neighborhoods and the experience of the individual. This work is important to identifying the ways in which social context influences health disparities in African Americans. Nevertheless, little of the literature cited above examined the specific experiences of African Americans. Some studies have shown a negative health impact of repeated experiences with race discrimination in African Americans, particularly when the response is one of a passive coping style (Krieger 1990, Krieger & Sidney 1996). These results suggest that repeated experiences with race-based discrimination are associated with higher resting systolic blood pressure levels (Armstead et al. 1989, Clark 1992, Clark et al. 1999, Harrell et al. 2003, James et al. 1984, McNeilly et al. 1996) and more frequent reports of being diagnosed with hypertension (Krieger 1990, Krieger & Sidney 1996). Drawing from a larger body of work in this area, one can hypothesize that living in neighborhoods characterized by concentrations of poverty and violence may have harmful effects on both the immune system and neuroendocrine responses. But further study is needed to quantify the nature of these effects.

Allostatic Load: A Physiological Approach to Understanding the Effects of Race-Based Discrimination

Another model developed by neuroscientist Bruce McEwen to explain the effects of stress on the human body is allostatic load. This model can also be used to conceptualize the possible deleterious effects of race-based discrimination. In McEwen's model, the emphasis is on the interaction between cognitive processes and physiologic response (see **Figure 2**, see color insert). In this model, race-based discrimination could be viewed as creating a chronic biological challenge to the human regulatory systems. According to this model, homeostasis is the internal processes of the body that regulate its response to challenges and demands. Allostasis, on the other hand, is the process of the body's response to those challenges (McEwen 1998, 2004, 2005; McEwen & Stellar 1993). The simplest example of the allostasis process is the flight/fight response that occurs when one experiences a challenge, demand, or perceived danger. This response operates through the engagement of the sympathetic nervous system, the HPA axis, and the immune system. McEwen argues that when chronic and/or excessive demands are placed on the body's regulatory systems, these systems over time will exhibit "wear and tear," losing their ability to efficiently and effectively respond to demands (McEwen 2004, 2005). One possible consequence is overt disease pathology. Invoking McEwen's model extends the scope of stressors (challenges) in Massey's model to include environmental stressors of work, home, social relationships, major life events, traumas, and abuses (McEwen 2000). McEwen's model could include racially discriminatory behavior in social interactions as stressors that send the body into allostasis (Brondolo et al. 2005, Mays & Cochran 1998, Mays et al. 1996).

Although increased physiological and psychological arousal during an acute stress response is temporarily and evolutionarily advantageous, continuous bouts of stress such as those daily hassles of race-based discrimination along with frequency of exposure to stressful life events (Jackson 2004, Kessler et al. 1999) could significantly alter physiological responses of African Americans (Benschop & Schedlowski 1999.) Indeed, McEwen finds that moderate challenges to the cardiovascular system actually mobilize energy through the activation of the sympathetic nervous system and enhance immune response. This can be seen in the positive role of exercise in maintaining health. However, when the stress challenge to the cardiovascular system is prolonged and excessive to the point of allostasis, immunity is suppressed, blood pressure increases, and, over time, atherosclerosis can develop (McEwen 2002), resulting in coronary vascular disease.

Although McEwen's model is not specific to African Americans, like Massey's model (2004), it identifies a number of downstream health effects that are expected to result from race-based discriminatory stress challenges that Massey has identified as more prevalent among African Americans. Together, these two models offer perspectives on the ways in which chronic experiences with racial discrimination might exert harmful effects on African Americans' health. Recent studies have shown, for example, that the experience of stressful racial discrimination places African Americans at an increased risk of developing hypertension (Din-Dzietham et al. 2004) and carotid plaque (Troxel et al. 2003), both of which are related to the development of atherosclerosis and other cardiovascular diseases

These models might also facilitate an understanding of one of the important health paradoxes among African Americans: African American women, regardless of socioeconomic status, consistently exhibit the highest rates of preterm birth, and their offspring have the lowest birth weights of any group of

American women (Dole et al. 2004; MMWR 1999, 2002). Furthermore, African American women as compared with White women have a threefold higher rate of very-low-birth-weight babies, secondary to preterm births (Carmichael & Iyasu 1998). The extent to which experiences with discrimination underlie this health disparity is not fully known, but in one study, African American mothers who scored high on a measure of perceived racial discrimination were twice as likely to deliver low-birth-weight infants (Ellen 2000). In a second longitudinal study of 6000 pregnant women, blood samples were taken through the first and second trimesters of pregnancy. Results suggest a correlation between high placental levels of the stress hormone corticotrophin-releasing hormone and preterm delivery (Rich-Edwards et al. 2001). Finally, in a third study, abnormally high levels of corticotrophin-releasing hormone were shown to have a strong correlation with long-term stress (Pike 2005). Although the evidence is still being accumulated, it points to a plausible set of links in a pathway model connecting race-based discrimination, stress, and negative preterm birth outcomes in African American women. In his model of racism and negative health effects, Hertzman (2000) makes the further distinction that the negative health outcomes occur not only at the time of preterm birth, but also in later life because preterm birth increases the risk of eventual coronary heart disease, high blood pressure, diabetes and other chronic diseases in offspring.

Problems with preterm and low-birth-weight babies do not disappear with improving socioeconomic conditions. College-educated African American women as compared with college-educated White American women still are more likely to deliver infants with low birth weight (Schoendorf et al. 1992). Indeed, in comparison with White American women, second-generation high-SES African American women continue to be at higher risk for low-birth-weight deliveries (Foster et al. 2000). A study of second-generation high-SES African American female college graduates and their mothers was compared with a similar cohort at Yale on rates of low birth weight and preterm delivery. Results from this study found that despite two generations of increasing SES in the African American college students, they still had the higher rates of low-birth-weight and preterm delivery, with only modest improvement over the generations (Foster et al. 2000). Furthermore, African American women born in the United States and Caribbean-born women in the United States differ in their risk for low-birth-weight deliveries, with African American women being more likely to give birth to lower-birth-weight babies (Cabral et al. 1990, Fuentes-Afflick et al. 1998, Guendelman & English 1996, Hummer et al. 1999, Pallotto et al. 2000).

EXAMINING REAL-TIME RACE-BASED PROCESSES OF DISCRIMINATION IN THE BRAIN

In the past, studying the brain directly required waiting until death to perform an autopsy or using methods too indirect to capture the subtleties of brain function. Now, with the use of methods to map the human brain, we can map hallucinations as they occur or elucidate the complex circuits and structures in the brain associated with emotions such as sadness, joy, anger, pain, or even the brain's role in helping us to read human emotions in facial expressions (Panksepp & Gordon 2003). The tools of functional magnetic resonance imaging (fMRI), positron emission tomography, dense-array electroencephalograph technology, and the measurement of evoked potentials combined with the methods of psychoneuroimmunology offer exciting opportunities to link the occurrence of everyday social inequalities to brain function and physiologic reactions.

Exciting research that melds the study of social cognition with the techniques of brain mapping have begun to allow direct examination of the functional effects of social inequalities based on social exclusion (Eisenberger et al. 2003) interracial Black/White race contact responses (Baron & Banaji 2006; Cunningham et al. 2004; Eberhardt 2005; Golby et al. 2001; Lieberman et al. 2005; Phelps et al. 2000, 2004), and social pain (Brown et al. 2003, Macdonald & Leary 2005) in brain function. These recent studies have expanded the opportunity to study the relationship between external events and internal brain processes as well as to elucidate the factors that make up the pathways of downstream health effects. In their examinations of how the brain processes social information during functional scans, researchers have shown that neural activity occurs in the brain structures that are directly responsible for activation of stress and the allostatic load responses. In particular, two brain structures, the amygdala and anterior cingulate cortex (ACC), show activation in response to social stresses (Baron & Banaji 2006; Lieberman et al. 2005; Macdonald & Leary 2005; Phelps et al. 2000, 2004). In addition to examining the role of these brain structures in response to social stresses, it is also useful to consider what contributions the processes of cognitive appraisal, self regulation, and social exclusion may play in the effects of race-based discrimination on the health of African Americans.

The Amygdala and Race Imaging

The amygdala plays a key role in the processing of emotions, including anger and fear. It is also the neural structure of the brain that is involved in forming and storing memories for emotional events. Historically, the amygdala was studied in relation to fear conditioning primarily in experiments that used rats. Recently, fMRI studies have demonstrated real-time effects in the amygdala when humans view fearful and threatening imagery (Delgado et al. 2006, Phelps 2006, Phelps et al. 2004). These studies show that as the amygdala responds to a fearful image, it initi-

ates the stress response, in which the body recruits energy while it decides whether to fight or to take flight. Thus, the amygdala is key to understanding the process of allostatic load, or overactivation of the stress response.

In a series of recent studies, all from different labs, results indicate that for both White and Black participants, the viewing of Black faces, as compared with White faces, results in higher measurable levels of implicit brain activity in the amygdala (Cunningham et al. 2004, Lieberman et al. 2005, Phelps et al. 2003). This amygdala activation associated with race-related processing has been interpreted as representing fear conditioning to "culturally learned negative associations regarding African Americans" (Lieberman et al. 2005). Not so surprisingly, it also suggests that implicitly learned negative racial stereotypes about African Americans can be learned and encoded as a response by African Americans as well as White Americans (Olsson et al. 2005). Viewed from Massey's model of racial stratification and poor health outcomes in African Americans, these findings suggest that implicitly learned fearful racial stereotypes may function to make the experience of living in race-segregated and poor neighborhoods a continuing source of chronic stress. This is not to say that racially/ethnically concentrated neighborhoods may not also be a source of providing social support, social connectedness, and a sense of belonging among African Americans (Cutrona et al. 2000). Both sets of conditions can occur simultaneously. But these laboratory findings hint that highly segregated, highly dense neighborhoods, plagued by high rates of crime and poverty, may create a social context in which chronic activation of fear responses leads to greater occurrence of the experience of allostatic load.

The Anterior Cingulate Cortex and Race

Another structure of the brain that is important to consider in examining real-time processes in race-based discrimination is the ACC. Recent studies have described the ACC as a discrepancy detector that monitors and regulates brain processes directed toward achieving goals. It is believed that the ACC functions at the subconscious level by being vigilant to conflicts to our goal attainments. In the case of conflict, the ACC engages conscious cognitive processes of the prefrontal cortex (PFC) to assist in either accommodating to or reducing the conflict (Eisenberger et al. 2003). Cognitive processes used by the ACC in its discrepancy-detector role include reasoning, decision making, motivation, and emotional regulation (Botvinick et al. 2004). These processes can facilitate an adaptive change to bodily states, such as altering heart rate, through mediation by the sympathetic nervous system (Critchley 2005; Critchley et al. 2000, 2001, 2003). The PFC also has the ability to reduce activation of the ACC (thus reducing discrepancies in goals) as well as to increase activation of the ACC, resulting in hypervigilance. Put succinctly, the actual "function of the ACC is to integrate motivationally important information, with appropriate bodily responses" (Critchley et al. 2001). In this context, the ACC emerges as a brain structure with the ability to not only recruit cognitive function to reason and to assess race-based discrimination, but also to play a role in the mediation of aspects of the physiological downstream reactions to race-based discrimination.

Those who have studied discrepancy detection view the ACC as a critical monitoring system (Botvinick et al. 2001, 2004; Eisenberger et al. 2005). When the ACC experiences any inconsistencies between desired goals and impediments or conflicts, its activation acts as a neural alarm to the body that something has gone wrong (Botvinick et al. 2001, 2004; Braver et al. 2001; Carter et al. 1998; Eisenberger et al. 2005; Weissman et al. 2003). The result is a greater demand on conscious cognitive processes with the goal to minimize the discrepancies in current ac-

tions so actions can once again lead to desired goals (Carver & Scheier 1990). As discrepancies resulting from goal conflicts are reduced, so too is activation in the ACC, quieting the alarm and returning the body to homeostasis.

In addition to activation issues with the ACC, Thayer & Friedman (2004) suggest that in a situation where a threat is ever-present, as is the case for possible experiences with race-based discrimination, inhibition of the limbic system by the prefrontal cortex PFC is also partially released. The result is a state of compromise by the brain that allows hypervigilance and perseverative thought to decrease heart rate variability and increase the allostatic load indicators of blood pressure and cortisol through the amygdala and HPA axis activation (Winters et al. 2000). Expectations of race-based discrimination might result in hypervigilance, which would then result in a greater tendency to perceive conflict discrepancies, in spite of behavior that to some may appear not to be overtly discriminatory.

A key topic in understanding the possible role of the ACC, and collaterally the PFC, in linking African Americans' experiences with race-based discrimination and downstream health effects may be that of social exclusion. Social exclusion is a general term used by social policy makers and social scientists to refer both to the consequence of being excluded or marginalized from desired social groups as well as the processes by which this occurs (Macdonald & Leary 2005). Social exclusion may be a consequence of discrimination and prejudice, as well as a mechanism by which discrimination and prejudice can be enacted. Social exclusion is actually best thought of as a dynamic concept in which it is related to social processes that can lead to social isolation of specific groups and individuals when they are marginalized by organizations, groups, or institutions within society. For those who are socially excluded, there is the psychological experience of loss in both a sense of belonging to a desired group and denial of opportunity to participate in certain social, political, cultural, educational, or economical opportunities and rights (Tezanos 2001). For many, this description of social exclusion parallels that of discrimination, or social rejection. Underwood et al. (2004) find not only that social exclusion and social rejection are similar, but also that both create a common pathway in relationship to pain (Baumeister & Leary 1995). Indeed, it has been argued that "being excluded from social groups ranks among the most aversive of human experiences" (Labonte 2004).

In fMRI neuroimaging studies of social exclusion, Eisenberger et al. (2003) found that the anterior cingulate cortex acts as a "neural alarm system or conflict monitor" that is sensitive to the experiences of social pain when social exclusion occurs (Eisenberger & Lieberman 2004, Macdonald & Leary 2005). Social pain is described as a unique form of aversive distress that is felt specifically when rejection or social exclusion occurs (Eisenberger & Lieberman 2004, Macdonald & Leary 2005).

To the extent that experiences of race-based discrimination are perceived similarly to experiences of social exclusion, perceived discrimination too might share—at the level of brain functioning—properties similar to those of social exclusion. This may explain a second paradox in African American health: rates of psychological distress are typically higher as compared with rates for White Americans, but rates of many common, stress-sensitive major mental disorders such as major depression and most anxiety disorders are lower (MMWR 2004, USDHHS 1999). Higher distress levels may reflect chronic activation of unpleasant feelings of anger, hypervigilance, or being on edge. Perceived racial discrimination, with its implied obstruction in access to both belonging to a group and access to social resources, may result in social pain. This may draw the body away from homeostasis and possibly result in the activation of stress-related allostatic responses.

Self-Regulation, Social Acceptance, and Cognitive Appraisal in Race-Based Discrimination

The brain is not a passive recipient of stimulation. Self-regulation and cognitive appraisal are processes that allow individuals to achieve and maintain personal and social goals, including social relationships (Lieberman 2007). Self-regulation has been proposed as indispensable for the maintenance of social acceptance (Baumeister et al. 2005, Carver & Scheier 1981). Self-regulation refers to such functions as executive and cognitive control, emotion and affect regulation, and maintenance of motivational drive (Baumeister & Vohs 2004, Beauregard et al. 2001, Levesque et al. 2004, Muraven et al. 1998, Ochsner & Gross 2005, Ownsworth et al. 2002, Posner & Rothbart 1998, Ylvisaker & Feeney 2002). Self-regulation of emotion maps onto the structures of the amygdala, ACC, and PFC, and thus may be related to the processes of race-based discrimination. In response to social stressors, individuals self-regulate in complex ways that might strengthen social bonds (Higgins 1996, Leary et al. 2006, Williams et al. 2000, Williams & Sommer 1997) or lead instead to increased levels of aggression, depression, and unhealthy behaviors such as tobacco smoking and alcohol and drug use or abuse. An examination of the role that cognitive appraisal and self-regulation play in race-based discrimination and health outcomes in African Americans may provide some useful insights into the pathways of the upstream/downstream discrimination and health relationship.

Self-regulation has been shown to increase the retention of social information about events surrounding an individual's experience of social rejection (Gardner et al. 2000). For example, in an experiment examining the selective retention of socially relevant events, subjects experiencing social rejection had a greater recall of the events than did subjects who experienced social acceptance (Gardner et al. 2000). In addition, a main effect for negative-event recall was greater than for positive events. In particular, the negative aspects of social rejection are consolidated to memory for the individual as a source of potential future harm and avoidance. These findings raise interesting issues to consider in the dynamics of the cognitive appraisal process in race-based discrimination. For example, individuals who have been rejected as the result of perceived racial discrimination may be more likely to have a heightened surveillance for negative social cues that resemble race-based discrimination and social rejection in comparison with individuals who are commonly accepted.

The ability of the appraisal system to self-regulate emotional control can be achieved through the lateral PFC. But, Wheeler & Fiske (2005) have also found that the emotional response to race-related imagery can be altered at the level of the amygdala. For example, studies (Cunningham et al. 2004, Lieberman et al. 2005, Phelps et al. 2003) have demonstrated that presentation of Black faces as compared with White faces results in greater activation of the amygdala. This activation was thought to lie in a process in which simply viewing Black faces stimulated negative stereotypes and prejudicial amygdala activation to outgroup members. However, Wheeler & Fiske (2005) demonstrated that a differential response of the amygdala to White and Black faces could not be achieved by visual inspection alone. Instead, a face must be cognitively processed to a level at which it achieves some social relevance before differential amygdala activation occurs. This suggests that cognitive appraisal of race-based discrimination occurs at multiple levels in the brain. Indeed, the ACC in many ways acts as a social monitor by responding to stressors of social rejection (Eisenberger et al. 2003). If the processes that occur in the brain for race-based discrimination are the same or very similar to those documented in ACC activation in the study of Eisenberger et al. (2003), we would then speculate that the ACC plays an intermediary role in the process of cogni-

tive appraisal as it directs the recruitment of higher cognitive and emotional processing in the actual appraisal process.

A puzzling dilemma is posed to African Americans with regard to self-regulation. The authors of self-regulation and social rejection studies have pointed to a role of self-regulation to achieve social goals and acceptance. But the challenge may be for African Americans to quiet a regulatory system that is stimulated toward hypervigilance. Race-based discrimination may exact a chronic toll on the self-regulatory system and shape cognitive appraisals in ways that have yet to be studied.

NEXT STEPS IN A RESEARCH, INTERVENTION, AND PREVENTION AGENDA

Although there is growing support for the importance of a relationship between experiences with race-based discrimination and various physical health outcomes in African Americans, full understanding of the phenomenon is still a long way off. Indeed, in the next couple of decades, work from other fields, such as the genetic bases of mental and physical health morbidities, promises to complicate attempts to fully capture the complex causal pathways that link the effects of discrimination in the social environment to health at an individual level. But the emerging methodological tools and the increasingly interdisciplinary nature of health-related research offer the promise of articulating how social unfairness works to harm individual health. The work that we have reviewed here merely highlights new directions in the research in this area.

If these methodologies succeed in reliably identifying insidious neighborhood effects on health or specific areas of the brain that are damaged by discrimination, psychologists will face new challenges. What are our social responsibilities to change or alter the conditions that harm health? How do we develop interventions to alter neighborhood structure? If the effects of discrimination are such that early experiences with being treated badly or unfairly alter brain function toward greater sensitivity, quicker reactivity, and greater vulnerability to the impact of later experiences, would we then assign less blame or responsibility to either the behavior of individuals who experience discrimination or the behavior of perpetrators of discrimination on individuals who themselves have had early exposures to discrimination? What will be our societal response if science establishes that discrimination is a brain assault with tangible harmful effects on both quality of life and physical health?

A number of important areas could be more fully explored to help us gain insights into the pathways that may account for the relationship of experiences of race-based discrimination to negative health status in African Americans. Because of page constraints in this review, we could not fully address all of the areas, and for some areas that we discussed above, there was a need for brevity. However, we have presented a number of concepts, many of which are still only possibilities that remain in need of further study to explain upstream/downstream health effects in African Americans.

Psychology is unique as a discipline in being located with one foot solidly in the science of upstream effects and the other in the direct examination of downstream effects. That places us in an enviable position to study the effects of racial discrimination and negative health outcomes in African Americans in a comprehensive manner. In doing so, we honor our long tradition of efforts to use the scientific method to pursue social justice and fairness (Deutsch 1975, Lewin 1997). Much of America's ability to dialogue dispassionately about race had its birth in the early research done by social psychologists on racial attitudes and symbolic racism (Bobo 1983; Bobo & Fox 2003; Sears 1998; Sears & Henry 2003, 2005). This work has also informed the justice system. With these emerging methods, approaches, and collaborative relationships, psychology as a discipline has even greater opportunities to shape our understanding of the ways in which race, racism, and race-based discrimination affect the health of African Americans.

ACKNOWLEDGMENTS

Work on this review was supported by funding from the National Institute of Drug Abuse (DA 15539) and an EXPORT grant from the National Center for Minority Health and Health Disparities (MD P60–000508). We thank our colleagues who read various parts of this manuscript or discussed ideas with us, particularly Teresa Seeman and Jason Woods, though we take full responsibility for the ideas presented.

LITERATURE CITED

Acevedo-Garcia D. 2000. Residential segregation and the epidemiology of infectious diseases. *Soc. Sci. Med.* 51:1143–61

Acevedo-Garcia D. 2001. Zip code level risk factors for tuberculosis: neighborhood environment and residential segregation, New Jersey, 1985–1992. *Am. J. Public Health* 91:734–41

Acevedo-Garcia D, Lochner KA, Ospuyk TL, Subramanian SV. 2003. Future directions in residential segregation and health research: a multilevel approach. *Am. J. Public Health* 93:215–21

Adler N, Boyce T, Chesney M, Cohen S, Folkman S, et al. 1994. Socioeconomic status and health: the challenge of the gradient. *Am. Psychol.* 9:15–24

Armstead C, Lawler K, Gordon G, Cross J, Gibbons J. 1989. The relationship of racial stressors to blood pressure responses and anger expressions in black college students. *Health Psychol.* 8:541–56

Baron AS, Banaji MR. 2006. The development of implicit attitudes. Evidence of race evaluations from ages 6 and 10 and adulthood. *Psychol. Sci.* 17:53–58

Baumeister RF, DeWall CN, Ciarocco NJ, Twenge JM. 2005. Social exclusion impairs self-regulation. *J. Personal. Soc. Psychol.* 88:589–604

Baumeister RF, Leary MR. 1995. The need to belong: desire for interpersonal attachments as a fundamental human motivation. *Psychol. Bull.* 117:497–529

Baumeister RF, Vohs KD. 2004. *Handbook of Self-Regulation: Research, Theory, and Applications.* New York: Guilford

Beauregard M, Levesque J, Bourgouin P. 2001. Neural correlates of conscious self-regulation of emotion. *J. Neurosci.* 21:RC165

Benschop RJ, Schedlowski M. 1999. Acute psychological stress. *Psychoneuroimmunology: An Interdisciplinary Introduction,* ed. M Schedlowski, U Tuwes, pp. 293–306. New York: Kluwer Acad./Plenum

Boardman JD. 2004. Stress and physical health: the role of neighborhoods as mediating and moderating mechanisms. *Soc. Sci. Med.* 58:2473–83

Bobo L. 1983. Whites' opposition to busing: symbolic racism or realistic group conflict? *J. Personal. Soc. Psychol.* 45:1196–210

Bobo L, Fox C. 2003. Race, racism and discrimination: bridging problems, methods, and theory in social psychological research. *Soc. Psychol. Q.* 66:319–32

Botvinick MM, Carter CS, Braver TS, Barch DM, Cohen. 2001. Conflict monitoring and cognitive control. *Psychol. Rev.* 108:624–52

Botvinick MM, Cohen JD, Carter CS. 2004. Conflict monitoring and anterior cingulate cortex: an update. *Trends Cogn. Sci.* 8:539–46

Braver TS, Barch DM, Gray JR, Molfese DL, Snyder A. 2001. Anterior cingulate cortex and response conflict: effects of frequency, inhibition and errors. *Cereb. Cortex* 11:825–36

Brondolo E, Thompson S, Brady N, Appel R, Cassells A, et al. 2005. The relationship of racism to appraisals and coping in a community sample. *Ethnicity Dis.* 15:S5–10

Brown GW, Harris TO. 1989. *Life Events and Illness.* New York: Guilford

Brown JL, Sheffield D, Leary MR, Robinson ME. 2003. Social support and experimental pain. *Psychosom. Med.* 65:276–83

Cabral H, Fried LE, Levenson S, Amaro H, Zuckerman B. 1990. Foreign-born and US-born black women: differences in health behaviors and birth outcomes. *Am. J. Public Health* 80:70–72

Carmichael SL, Iyasu S. 1998. Changes in the black-white infant mortality gap from 1983 to 1991 in the United States. *Am. J. Prevent. Med.* 15:220–27

Carter CS, Braver TS, Barch DM, Botvinick MM, Noll D, Cohen JD. 1998. Anterior cingulate cortex, error detection, and the online monitoring of performance. *Science* 280:747–49

Carver CS, Scheier MF. 1981. The self-attention-induced feedback loop and social facilitation. *J. Exp. Soc. Psychol.* 17:545–68

Carver CS, Scheier MF. 1990. Origins and functions of positive and negative affect: a control-process view. *Psychol. Rev.* 97:19–35

Centers for Disease Control (CDC). 1994. *Advance Report of Final Mortality Statistics, 1992.* Hyattsville, MD: US Dep. Health Human Serv., Public Health

Clark R. 2003. Self-reported racism and social support predict blood pressure reactivity in blacks. *Ann. Behav. Med.* 25:127–36

Clark R, Adams JH. 2004. Moderating effects of perceived racism on John Henryism and blood pressure reactivity in black female college students. *Ann. Behav. Med.* 28:126–31

Clark R, Anderson NB, Clark VR, William DR. 1999. Racism as a stressor for African Americans: a biopsychosocial model. *Am. Psychol.* 54:805–16

Clark WA. 1992. Residential preferences and residential choices in a multiethnic context. *Demography* 29:451–66

Cochran SD, Mays VM. 1994. Depressive distress among homosexually active African American men and women. *Am. J. Psychiatry* 151:524–29

Critchley HD. 2005. Neural mechanisms of autonomic, affective, and cognitive integration. *J. Comp. Neurol.* 493:154–66

Critchley HD, Corfield DR, Chandler MP, Mathias CJ, Dolan RJ. 2000. Cerebral correlates of autonomic cardiovascular arousal: a functional neuroimaging investigations in humans. *J. Physiol.* 523:250–70

Critchley HD, Mathias CJ, Dolan RJ. 2001. Neural activity in the human brain relating to uncertainty and arousal during anticipation. *Neuron* 29:537–45

Critchley HD, Mathias CJ, Josephs O, O'Doherty J, Zanini S, et al. 2003. Human cingulate cortex & autonomic control: converging neuroimaging & clinical evidence. *Brain* 126:2139–52

Cunningham WA, Johnson MK, Rave CL, Gatenby J, Gore JC, Banaji MR. 2004. Separable neural components in the processing of black and white faces. *Psychol. Sci.* 12:806–13

Cutrona CE, Russell DW, Hessling RM, Brown PA, Murry V. 2000. Direct and moderating effect of community context on the psychological well-being of African-American women. *J. Personal. Soc. Psychol.* 79:1088–101

Davis SK, Liu Y, Gibbons GH. 2003. Disparities in trends of hospitalization for potentially preventable chronic conditions among African Americans during the 1990s: implications and benchmarks. *Am. J. Public Health* 93:447–55

Delgado MR, Olsson A, Phelps EA. 2006. Extending animal models of fear conditioning to humans. *Biol. Psychol.* [Epub ahead of print]

Deutsch M. 1975. Equity, equality and need: what determines which value will be used as a basis for distributive justice. *J. Soc. Issues* 31:137–50

Diez Roux AV. 2001. Investigating neighborhood and area effects on health. *Am. J. Public Health* 91:1783–89

Diez Roux AV. 2002. Invited commentary: places, people, and health. *Am. J. Epidemiol.* 155:516–19

Diez Roux AV. 2003. Residential environments and cardiovascular risk. *J. Urban Health* 90:569–89

Diez Roux AV, Nieto FJ, Muntaner C, Tyroler HA, Comstock GW, et al. 1997. Neighborhood environments and coronary heart disease: a multilevel analysis. *Am. J. Epidemiol.* 146:48–63

Din-Dzietham R, Nembhard WN, Collins R, Davis SK. 2004. Perceived stress following race-based discrimination at work is associated with hypertension in African-Americans. The metro Atlanta heart disease study, 1999–2001. *Soc. Sci. Med.* 58:449–61

Dole N, Savitz DA, Siega-Riz AM, Hertz-Picciotto I, McMahon MJ, Buekens P. 2004. Psychosocial factors and preterm birth among African American and white women in central North Carolina. *Am. J. Public Health* 94:1358–65

Duan YF, Winters R, McCabe PM, Green EJ, Huang Y, Schneiderman N. 1996. Behavioral characteristics of defense and vigilance reactions elicited by electrical stimulation of the hypothalamus in rabbits. *Behav. Brain Res.* 81:33–41

Eberhardt JL. 2005. Imaging race. *Am. Psychol.* 60:181–90

Eberhardt JL, Goff PA, Purdie VJ, Davies PG. 2004. Seeing black: race, crime, and visual processing. *J. Personal. Soc. Psychol.* 87:876–93

Eberhardt JL, Dasgupta N, Banaszynki TL. 2003. Believing is seeing: the effects of racial labels and implicit beliefs on face perception. *Personal. Soc. Psychol. Bull.* 29:360–70

Eisenberger NI, Lieberman MD. 2004. Why rejection hurts: a common neural alarm system for physical and social pain. *Trends Cogn. Sci.* 8:294–300

Eisenberger NI, Lieberman MD, Satpute AB. 2005. Personality from a controlled processing perspective: an fMRI study of neuroticism, extraversion, and self-consciousness. *Cogn. Affect. Behav. Neurosci.* 5:169–81

Eisenberger NI, Lieberman MD, Williams KD. 2003. Does rejection hurt? An fMRI study of social exclusion. *Science* 302:237–39

Ellen IG. 2000. Is segregation bad for your health? The case of low birth weight. In *Brookings-Wharton Papers on Urban Affairs*, ed. WG Gale, JR Rothenberg Pack, pp. 203–29. Washington, DC: Brookings Inst. Press

Ellen IG, Mijanovich T, Dillman KN. 2001. Neighborhood effects on health: exploring the links and assessing the evidence. *J. Urban Affairs* 23:391–408

Everson-Rose SA, Lewis TT. 2005. Psychosocial factors and cardiovascular disease. *Annu. Rev. Public Health* 26:469–500

Fiscella K, Williams DR. 2004. Health disparities based on socioeconomic inequities: implications for urban health care. *Acad. Med.* 79:1139–47

Foster HW, Wu L, Bracken MB, Semenya K, Thomas J, Thomas J. 2000. Intergenerational effects of high socioeconomic status on low birthweight and preterm birth in African Americans. *J. Natl. Med. Assoc.* 92:213–21

Franks P, Muennig P, Lubetkin E, Jia H. 2006. The burden of disease associated with being African-American in the United States and the contribution of socio-economic status. *Soc. Sci. Med.* 62(10):2469–78

Fredrickson BL. 2000. Extracting meaning from past affective experiences: the importance of peaks, ends, and specific emotions. *Cogn. Emot.* 14:577–606

Fuentes-Afflick E, Hessol NA, Perez-Stable EJ. 1998. Maternal birthplace, ethnicity, and low birth weigh in California. *Arch. Pediatr. Adolesc. Med.* 152:1105–12

Gardner WL, Pickett CL, Brewer MB. 2000. Social exclusion and selective memory: how the need to belong affects memory for social information. *Personal. Soc. Psychol. Bull.* 26:486–96

Geronimus AT, Bound J, Wadimann TA, Hillemeier MM, Burns PB. 1996. Excess mortality among blacks and whites in the United States. *N. Engl. J. Med.* 35:1552–58

Golby AJ, Gabrieli JDE, Chiao JY, Eberhardt JL. 2001. Differential responses in the fusiform region to same-race and other race faces. *Nat. Neurosci.* 4:845–50

Guendelman S, English PB. 1995. Effect of United States residence on birth outcomes among Mexican immigrants: an exploratory study. *Am. J. Epidemiol.* 142(9 Suppl.):S30–38

Guyll M, Matthews KA, Bromberger JT. 2001. Discrimination and unfair treatment: relationship to cardiovascular reactivity among African American and European American women. *Health Psychol.* 20:315–25

Harrell JP, Halls S, Taliaferro J. 2003. Physiological responses to racism and discrimination: an assessment of the evidence. *Am. J. Public Health* 93:243–48

Haynes MA, Smedley BD. 1999. *The Unequal Burden of Cancer: An Assessment of NIH Research and Programs for Ethnic Minorities and the Medically Underserved.* Washington, DC: Natl. Acad. Press

Heckler MM. 1985. U.S. Task Force on Black and Minority Health. *Report of the Secretary's Task Force on Black and Minority Health.* Washington, DC: U.S. Dep. Health Human Serv.

Henderson S, Byrne DG, Duncan-Jones P. 1981. *Neurosis and the Social Environment.* Sydney: Academic

Hertzman C. 2000. The biological embedding of early experiences and its effects on health in adulthood. *Ann. NY Acad. Sci.* 896:85–95

Higgins ET. 1996. The "self-digest": self-knowledge serving self-regulatory functions. *J. Personal. Soc. Psychol.* 71:1062–83

House JS. 2002. Understanding social factors and inequalities in health: twentieth century progress and twenty-first century prospects. *J. Health Soc. Behav. Res.* 43:125–42

House JS, Williams D. 2000. Understanding and reducing socioeconomic and racial/ethnic disparities in health. In *Promoting Health: Intervention Strategies from Social and Behavioral Research*, ed. BD Smedley, SL Syme, pp. 81–124. Washington, DC: Natl. Acad. Press

Hummer RA, Beigler M, DeTurk PB, Forbes D, Frisbie WP, et al. 1999. Race, ethnicity, nativity, and infant mortality in the United States. *Soc. Forces* 77:1083–118

Jackson JS. 2004. The National Survey of American Life, data and tables. Prog. Res. Black Am. **http://www.rcgd.isr.umich.edu/prba/rta/index.htm.** Accessed Jan. 15, 2006

Jackson JS, Neighbors HW, Neese RM, Trierweiler SJ, Torres M. 2004. Methodological innovations in the National Survey of American Life. *Int. J. Methods Psychiatr. Res.* 13:288–98

James SA, LaCroix AZ, Kleinbaum DG, Strogatz DS. 1984. John Henryism and blood pressure differences among black men. II. The role of occupational stressors. *J. Behav. Med.* 7:259–75

Kanner AD, Feldman SS, Weinberger DA, Ford ME. 1991. Uplifts, hassles, and adaptational outcomes in early adolescents. In *Stress and Coping: An Anthology*, ed. A Monet, RS Lazarus, pp. 158–82. New York: Columbia Univ. Press

Kaplan GA. 1999. Part III Summary: What is the role of the social environment in understanding inequalities in health? In *Socioeconomic Status and Health in Industrialized Nations.* ed. NE Adler, M Marmot, B McEwen, J Stewart, Vol. 896, pp. 116–19. New York: NY Acad. Sci.

Karlamangala AS, Singer BH, Williams DR, Schwartz JE, Matthews KA, et al. 2005. Impact of socioeconomic status on longitudinal accumulation of cardiovascular risk in young adults: the CARDIA study (USA). *Soc. Sci. Med.* 60:999–1015

Kessler RC, Mickelson KD, Williams DR. 1999. The prevalence, distribution, and mental health correlates of perceived discrimination in the United States. *J. Health Soc. Behav.* 40:208–30

Kiecolt-Glaser J, Glaser R, Cacioppo J, MacCallum R, Snydersmith M, et al. 1997. Marital conflict in older adults: endocrinological and immunological correlates. *Psychosomatic Med.* 59:339–49

Kochanek KD, Murphy SL, Anderson RN, Scott C. 2004. Deaths: final data for 2002. *Natl. Vital Statis. Rep.* 53:1–116

Krieger N. 1990. Racial and gender discrimination: risk factors for high blood pressure? *Soc. Sci. Med.* 30:1273–81

Krieger N. 1991. Women and social class: a methodological study comparing individual, household, and census measures of black/white differences in reproductive history. *J. Epidemiol. Comm. Health* 45:35–42

Krieger N. 1999. Embodying inequality: a review of concepts, measures, and methods for studying health consequences of discrimination. *Int. J. Health Serv.* 29:295–352

Krieger N, Moss N. 1996. Accounting for the public's health: an introduction to selected papers from a U.S. conference on "measuring social inequalities in health." *Int. J. Health Serv.* 26:383–90

Krieger N, Sidney S. 1996. Racial discrimination and blood pressure. The CARDIA study of young black and white women and men. *Am. J. Public Health* 6:1370–78

Krieger N, Smith K, Naishadham D, Hartman C, Barbeau EM. 2005. Experiences of discrimination: validity and reliability of a self-report measure for population health research on racism and health. *Soc. Sci. Med.* 61:1576–96

Krieger N, Williams DR, Moss NE. 1997. Measuring social class in U.S. public health research: concepts, methodologies, and guidelines. *Annu. Rev. Public Health* 18:341–78

Kuh D, Ben-Sholmo Y. 1997. *A Life Course Approach to Chronic Disease Epidemiology.* Oxford, UK: Oxford Univ. Press

Labonte R. 2004. Social inclusion/exclusion: dancing the dialectic. *Health Promot. Int.* 19:115–21

Landrine H, Klonoff EA. 2000. Racial discrimination and cigarette smoking among blacks: finding from two studies. *Ethnicity Dis.* 10:195–202

Lazarus RS. 1993. From psychological stress to the emotions: a history of changing outlooks. *Annu. Rev. Psychol.* 44:1–21

Leary MR, Twenge JM, Quinlivan E. 2006. Interpersonal rejection as a determinant of anger and aggression. *Personal. Soc. Psychol. Rev.* 10:111–32

Lester D. 2000. Does residential segregation in cities predict African-American suicide rates? *Percept. Mot. Skills* 91:870

Levesque J, Joanette Y, Mensour B, Beudoin G, Leroux JM, et al. 2004. Neural basis of emotional self-regulation in childhood. *Neuroscience* 129:361–69

Levine RS, Foster JE, Fullilove RE, Fullilove MT, Briggs NC, et al. 2001. Black-white inequalities in mortality and life expectancy, 1933–1999: implications for Healthy People 2010. *Public Health Rep.* 116:474–83

Lewin K. 1997. *Resolving Social Conflicts and Field Theory in Social Science.* Washington, DC: Am. Psychol. Assoc.

Lieberman MD. 2007. Social cognitive neuroscience: a review of core processes. *Annu. Rev. Psychol.* 58:259–89

Lieberman MD, Hariri A, Jarcho JM, Eisenberger NI, Bookheimer SY. 2005. An fMRI investigation of race-related amygdala activity in African-American and Caucasian-American individuals. *Nat. Neurosci.* 6:720–22

Macdonald G, Leary MR. 2005. Why does social exclusion hurt? The relationship between social and physical pain. *Psychol. Bull.* 131:202–23

Macintyre S, Ellaway A, Cummins S. 2002. Place effects on health: How can we conceptualize, operationalize and measure them? *Soc. Sci. Med.* 55:125–39

Massey DS. 1985. Residential segregation and neighborhood conditions in U.S. metropolitan areas. In *America Becoming Racial: Trends and Their Consequences.* ed. N Smesler, WJ Wilson, F Mitchell, pp. 391–434. Washington, DC: Natl. Acad. Press

Massey DS. 2000. Housing discrimination 101. *Popul. Today* 28:1–4

Massey DS. 2004. Segregation and stratification: a biosocial perspective. *DuBois Rev. Soc. Sci. Rev. Race* 1:7–25

Masters RD. 2001. Biology and politics: linking nature and nurture. *Annu. Rev. Polit. Sci.* 4:345–69

Mather M, Rivers KL. 2006. *City Profiles of Child Well-Being: Results from the American Community Survey.* Washington, DC: Annie E. Casey Found.

Mays VM. 1995. Black women, work stress, and perceived discrimination: the Focused Support Group Model as an intervention for stress reduction. *Cult. Divers. Ment. Health* 1:53–65

Mays VM, Cochran SD. 1998. Racial discrimination and health outcomes in African Americans. *Proc. 27th Public Health Conf. Records Stat. Natl. Committee Vital Health Stat. 47th Annu. Symp.* Washington, DC: US Dep. Health Human Serv.

Mays VM, Coleman LS, Jackson JS. 1996. Perceived race-based discrimination, employment status, and job stress in a national sample of black women: implication for health outcomes. *J. Occup. Health Psychol.* 3:319–29

McCord C, Freeman HP. 1990. Excess mortality in Harlem. *N. Engl. J. Med.* 322:1606–67

McEwen BS. 1998. Protective and damaging effects of stress mediators. *N. Engl. J. Med.* 338:171–79

McEwen BS. 2000. Allostasis and allostatic load: implications for neuropsychopharmacology. *Neuropsychopharmacology* 22:108–24

McEwen BS. 2002. Protective and damaging effects of stress mediators: the good and bad sides of the response to stress. *Metabolism* 51(6 Suppl. 1):2–4

McEwen BS. 2004. Protection and damage from acute and chronic stress, allostasis and allostatic load overload and relevance to the pathophysiology of psychiatric disorders. *Ann. NY Acad. Sci.* 1032:1–7

McEwen BS. 2005. Stressed or stressed out: What is the difference? *J. Psychiatry Neurosci.* 30:315–18

McEwen BS, Seeman T. 1999. Protective and damaging effects of mediators of stress. Elaborating and testing the concepts of allostasis and allostatic load. *Ann. NY Acad. Sci.* 896:30–47

McEwen BS, Stellar E. 1993. Stress and the individual: mechanisms leading to disease. *Arch. Intern. Med.* 153:2093–101

McNeilly A, Anderson NB, Armstead CA, Clark R, Corbett MO, et al. 1996. The Perceived Racism Scale: a multidimensional assessment of the perceptions of white racism among African Americans. *Ethnicity Dis.* 6:154–66

Mechanic D. 2005. Policy challenges in addressing racial disparities and improving population health. *Health Affairs* 24:335–38

Mensa GA, Mokdad AH, Ford ES, Greenlund KJ, Croft JB. 2005. State of disparities in cardiovascular health in the United States. *Circulation* 111:1233–41

Messer LC, Kaufman JS, Dole N, Savitz DA, Laraia BA. 2005. Neighborhood crime, deprivation, and preterm birth. *Ann. Epidemiol.* 16(6):455–62

Meyer IH. 2003. Prejudice, social stress, and mental health in lesbian, gay, and bisexual populations: conceptual issues and research evidence. *Psychol. Bull.* 129:674–97

MMWR. 1996. State-specific prevalence of cigarette smoking—United States, 1995. *Morb. Mortal. Weekly Rep.* 45:962–66

MMWR. 1999. Preterm singleton births—United States, 1989–1996. *Morb. Mortal. Weekly Rep.* 48:185–89

MMWR. 2002. Infant mortality and low birth weight among black and white infants—United States, 1980–2000. *Morb. Mortal. Weekly Rep.* 51:589–92

MMWR. 2004. Self-reported frequent mental distress among adults—United States, 1993–2001. *Morb. Mortal. Weekly Rep.* 53:963–66

MMWR. 2005. Health disparities experienced by black or African Americans—United States. *Morb. Mortal. Weekly Rep.* 54:1–3

Morenoff JD, Lynch JW. 2004. What makes a place healthy? Neighborhood influences on racial/ethnic disparities in health over the life course. In *Critical Perspectives on Racial and Ethnic Difference in Health in Late Life*, ed. NB Anderson, AB Rodolfo, B Cohen, pp. 406–49. Washington, DC: Natl. Acad. Press

Muraven M, Tice DM, Baumeister RF. 1998. Self-control as limited resource: regulatory depletion patterns. *J. Personal. Soc. Psychol.* 74:774–89

Natl. Cent. Chronic Dis. Prevent. Health Promot. (NCCDPHP). 2004. *The Burden of Chronic Diseases and Their Risk Factors. National and State Perspectives 2004.* Atlanta, GA: USDHHS. **http://www.cdc.gov/nccdphp/burdenbook2004/**

Natl. Vital Stat. Rep. (NVSS). 2004. Deaths: final data for 2002. *Natl. Vital Stat. Rep.* 53:1–116

O'Campo P, Xue X, Wang MC, Caughy M. 1997. Neighborhood risk factors for low birthweight in Baltimore: a multilevel analysis. *Am. J. Public Health* 87:1113–18

Ochsner KN, Gross JJ. 2005. The cognitive control of emotion. *Trends Cogn. Sci.* 9:242–49

Oliver ML, Shapiro TM. 1995. *Black Wealth/White Wealth: A New Perspective on Racial Inequality.* New York: Routledge

Olsson A, Ebert JP, Banaji MR, Phelps EA. 2005. The role of social groups in the persistence of learned fear. *Science* 5735:785–87

Ownsworth TL, McFarland K, Young RM. 2002. The investigation of factors underlying deficits in self-awareness and self-regulation. *Brain Injury* 16:291–309

Pallotto EK, Collins JWJ, David RJ. 2000. Enigma of maternal race and infant birth weight: a population-based study of US-born black and Caribbean-born black women. *Am. J. Epidemiol.* 151:1080–85

Panksepp J, Gordon N. 2003. The instinctual basis of human affect: affective imaging of laughter and crying. *Conscious. Emot.* 4:197–205

Pearlin LI, Lieberman MA, Menaghan EG, Mullan JT. 1981. The stress process. *J. Health Soc. Behav.* 22:337–56

Peterson ED, Krivo LJ. 1999. Racial segregation, the concentration of disadvantage, and black and white homicide victimization. *Soc. Forum* 14:465–93

Phelps EA. 2006. Emotion and cognition: insights from studies of the human amygdala. *Annu. Rev. Psychol.* 57:27–53

Phelps EA, Cannistraci CJ, Cunningham WA. 2003. Intact performance on an indirect measure of race bias following amygdala damage. *Neuropsychologia* 41:203–8

Phelps EA, Delgado MR, Nearing KI, LeDoux JE. 2004. Extinction learning in humans: role of the amygdala and vmPFC. *Neuron* 43:897–905

Phelps EA, O'Connor KJ, Cunningham WA, Funayama ES, Gatenby JC, et al. 2000. Performance on indirect measures of race evaluation predicts amygdala activation. *J. Cogn. Neurosci.* 12:729–38

Pickett KE, Pearl M. 2001. Multilevel analyses of neighborhood socioeconomic context and health outcomes: a critical review. *J. Epidemiol. Commun. Health* 55:111–22

Pike IL. 2005. Maternal stress and fetal responses: evolutionary perspectives on preterm delivery. *Am. J. Hum. Biol.* 17:55–65

Posner MI, Rothbart MK. 1998. Attention, self-regulation and consciousness. *Philos. Trans. R. Soc. Lond. Ser. B Biol. Sci.* 353:1915–27

Repetti RL, Taylor SE, Seeman TE. 2002. Risky families: family social environments and the mental and physical health of offspring. *Psychol. Bull.* 128:330–66

Rich-Edwards JW, Krieger N, Majzoub J, Zierler S, Lieberman E, Gillman M. 2001. Maternal experiences of racism and violence as predictors of preterm birth: rationale and study design. *Paediatr. Perinat. Epidemiol.* 15(Suppl. 2):124–35

Rivo ML, Kofie V, Schwartz E, Levy ME, Tuckson RV. 1989. Comparisons of black and white smoking-attributable mortality, morbidity, and economic costs in the District of Columbia. *J. Natl. Med. Assoc.* 81:1125–30

Roberts EM. 1997. Neighborhood social environments and the distribution of low birthweight in Chicago. *Am. J. Public Health* 87:597–603

Roberts SA. 1999. Socioeconomic position and health: the independent contribution of community socioeconomic context. *Annu. Rev. Sociol.* 25:489–516

Robles TF, Kiecolt-Glaser JK. 2003. The physiology of marriage: pathways to health. *Physiol. Behav.* 79:409–16

Ryff C, Singer B. 2000. Interpersonal flourishing: a positive health agenda for the new millennium. *Personal. Soc. Psychol. Rev.* 4:30–44

Ryff C, Singer B. 2001. From social structure to biology: integrative science in pursuit of human health and well-being. In *Handbook of Positive Psychology*, ed. CR Snyder, SJ Lopez, pp. 541–55. New York: Oxford Univ. Press

Schillinger M, Exner M, Mlekusch W, Sabeti S, Amighi J, et al. 2005. Inflammation and Carotid Artery Risk for Atherosclerosis Study (ICARAS). *Circulation* 111:2203–9

Schoendorf KC, Hogue CJ, Kleinman JC, Rowley D. 1992. Mortality among infants of black as compared with white college-educated parents. *N. Engl. J. Med.* 326:1522–26

Schulz A, Williams D, Israel B, Becker A, Parker E, et al. 2000. Unfair treatment, neighborhood effects, and mental health in the Detroit metropolitan area. *J. Health Soc. Behav.* 41:314–32

Sears DO. 1988. Symbolic racism. In *Eliminating Racism: Profiles in Controversy, Perspectives in Social Psychology*, ed. PA Katz, DA Taylor, pp. 53–84. New York: Plenum

Sears DO, Henry JP. 2003. The origins of symbolic racism. *J. Personal. Soc. Psychol.* 85:259–75

Sears DO, Henry JP. 2005. Over thirty years later: a contemporary look at symbolic racism. In *Advances in Experimental Social Psychology*, ed. MP Zanna, pp. 95–150. San Diego, CA: Academic

Seeman TE, Berkman LF, Gulanski BI, Robbins RJ, Greenspan SL, et al. 1995. Self-esteem and neuroendocrine response to challenge: MacArthur studies of successful aging. *J. Psychosom. Res.* 39:69–84

Seeman TE, Berkman LF, Kohout F, LaCroix A, Glynn R, Blazer D. 1993. Intercommunity variations in the association between social ties and mortality in the elderly: a comparative analysis of three communities. *Ann. Epidemiol.* 3:325–35

Seeman TE, McEwen BS. 1996. Impact of social environment characteristics on neuroendocrine regulation. *Psychosom. Med.* 58:459–71

Sen A. 1993. The economics of life and death. *Sci. Am.* 268:40–47

Smedley BD, Smith AY, Nelson AR. 2003. *Unequal Treatment: Confronting Racial and Ethnic Disparities in Health Care*. Washington, DC: Natl. Acad. Press

Smith GD, Neaton JD, Wentworth D, Stamler R, Stamler J. 1998. Mortality differences between black and white men in the USA: contribution of income and other risk factors among men screened for the MRFIT. *Lancet* 51:934–39

Subramanian SV, Chen JT, Rehkopf DH, Waterman PD, Krieger N. 2005. Racial disparities in context: a multilevel analysis of neighborhood variations in poverty and excess mortality among black populations in Massachusetts. *Am. J. Public Health* 95:260–65

Taylor SE, Brown JD. 1994. Positive illusions and well-being revisited: separating fact from fiction. *Psychol. Bull.* 116:21–27

Taylor SE, Repetti RL, Seeman T. 1997. Health psychology: What is an unhealthy environment and how does it get under the skin? *Annu. Rev. Psychol.* 48:411–47

Tezanos JF. 2001. La Sociedad divida. Estructuras de clases y desigualdades en las sociedades tecnologicas. Madrid: Biblioteca Nueva

Thayer JF, Friedman BH. 2004. A neurovisceral integration model of health disparities in aging. In *Critical Perspectives on Racial and Ethnic Differences in Health in Late Life*, ed. NB Anderson, RA Bulatao, B Cohen, pp. 567–603. Washington, DC: Natl. Acad. Press

Thoits PA. 1983. Dimensions of life events that influence psychological distress: an evaluation and synthesis of the literature. In *Psychosocial Research: Trends in Theory and Research*, ed. HB Kaplan, pp. 33–103. New York: Academic

Troxel WM, Matthews KA, Bromberger JT, Sutton-Tyrrell K. 2003. Chronic stress burden, discrimination, and subclinical carotid artery disease in African American and Caucasian women. *Health Psychol.* 22:300–9

Underwood MK, Scott BL, Galperin MB, Bjornstad GJ, Sexton AM. 2004. An observational study of social exclusion under varied conditions: gender and developmental differences. *Child Dev.* 75:1538–55

Ursu S, Stenger VA, Shear MK, Jones MR, Carter CS. 2003. Overactive action monitoring in obsessive-compulsive disorder: evidence from functional magnetic resonance imaging. *Psychol. Sci.* 14:347–53

US Dep. Health Human Serv. 1990. *Healthy People 2000: National Health Promotion and Disease Prevention.* Washington, DC: USDHHS

US Dep. Health Human Serv. 1998. *Tobacco Use Among U.S. Racial/Ethnic Minority Groups— African Americans, American Indians and Alaska Natives, Asian Americans and Pacific Islanders, and Hispanics: a Report of the Surgeon General.* Atlanta, GA: USDHHS

US Dep. Health Human Serv. 1999. *Mental Health: Culture, Race and Ethnicity. A Supplement to Mental Health: A Report of the Surgeon General.* Washington, DC: U.S. Public Health Serv.

US Dep. Health Human Serv. 2000. *Healthy People 2010: Understanding and Improving Health.* Washington, DC: USDHHS. 2nd ed.

US Dep. Health Human Serv. 2005. *Health, United States, 2005, with Chartbook on Trends in the Health of Americans.* Hyattsville, MD: US GPO

US Dep. Health Human Serv. 2005. *National Health Care Disparities Report.* Rockville, MD: Agency Healthc. Res. Qual. **http://www.qualitytools.ahrq.gov/disparitiesreport/**

Walker B, Mays VM, Warren R. 2004. The changing landscape for the elimination of racial/ethnic health status disparities. *J. Health Care Poor Underserved* 15:506–21

Weissman DH, Giesbrecht B, Song AW, Mangun GR, Woldorff MG. 2003. Conflict monitoring in the human anterior cingulate cortex during selective attention to global and local object features. *Neuroimage* 19:1361–68

Wheeler ME, Fiske ST. 2005. Controlling racial prejudice: social-cognitive goals affect amygdala and stereotype activation. *Psychol. Sci.* 16:56–63

Williams DR. 1995. African American mental health: persisting questions and paradoxal findings. *Afr. Am. Res. Perspect.* 2:2–6

Williams DR, Harris-Reid M. 1999. Race and mental health: emerging patterns and promising approaches. In *A Handbook for the Study of Mental Health: Social Contexts, Theories, and Systems*, ed. AV Horwitz, TL Schneid, pp. 295–314. New York: Cambridge Univ. Press

Williams DR, Jackson PB. 2005. Social sources of racial disparities in health. *Health Affairs* 24:325–34

Williams DR, Neighbors HW, Jackson JS. 2003. Racial/ethnic discrimination and health: findings from community studies. *Am. J. Public Health* 93(2):200–8

Williams DR, Yu Y, Jackson JS, Anderson NB. 1997. Racial differences in physical and mental health: socioeconomic status, stress, and discrimination. *J. Health Psychol.* 2:335–51

Williams KD, Cheung CK, Choi W. 2000. Cyberostracism: effects of being ignored over the Internet. *J. Personal. Soc. Psychol.* 79:748–62

Williams KD, Sommer KL. 1997. Social ostracism by coworkers: Does rejection lead to loafing or compensation? *Personal. Soc. Psychol. Bull.* 23:693–706

Wilson WJ. 1987. *The Truly Disadvantaged: The Inner City, the Underclass, and Public Policy.* Chicago: Univ. Chicago Press

Winters EW, McCabe PM, Green EJ, Schneiderman N. 2000. Stress responses, coping, and cardiovascular neurobiology: central nervous system circuitry underlying learned and unlearned affective responses to stressful stimuli. In *Stress, Coping, and Cardiovascular Disease*. ed. PM McCabe, N Schneiderman, T Field, AR Wellens, pp. 1–49. Hillsdale, NJ: Erlbaum

Ylvisaker M, Feeney T. 2002. Executive functions, self-regulation, and learned optimism in pediatric rehabilitation: a review and implications for intervention. *Pediatr. Rehab.* 5:51–70

Assessment and Diagnosis of Personality Disorder: Perennial Issues and an Emerging Reconceptualization

Lee Anna Clark

Department of Psychology, University of Iowa, Iowa City, Iowa 52242;
email: la-clark@uiowa.edu

Annu. Rev. Psychol. 2007. 58:227–57

First published online as a Review in
Advance on August 11, 2006

The *Annual Review of Psychology* is online
at http://psych.annualreviews.org

This article's doi:
10.1146/annurev.psych.57.102904.190200

Key Words

personality disorder, assessment, comorbidity, diagnosis, stability

Abstract

This chapter reviews recent (2000–2005) personality disorder (PD) research, focusing on three major domains: assessment, comorbidity, and stability. (*a*) Substantial evidence has accrued favoring dimensional over categorical conceptualization of PD, and the five-factor model of personality is prominent as an integrating framework. Future directions include assessing dysfunction separately from traits and learning to utilize collateral information. (*b*) To address the pervasiveness and extent of comorbidity, researchers have begun to move beyond studying overlapping pairs or small sets of disorders and are developing broader, more integrated common-factor models that cross the Axis I–Axis II boundary. (*c*) Studies of PD stability have converged on the finding that PD features include both more acute, dysfunctional behaviors that resolve in relatively short periods, and maladaptive temperamental traits that are relatively more stable—similar to normal-range personality traits—with increasing stability until after 50 years of age. A new model for assessing PD—and perhaps all psychopathology—emerges from integrating these interrelated reconceptualizations.

Contents

PD: personality disorder

DSM: diagnostic and statistical manual

Comorbidity: co-occurrence of two diagnoses in an individual

INTRODUCTION

Personality disorder (PD) is defined in the *Diagnostic and Statistical Manual of Mental Disorders-Fourth Edition, Text Revision* (DSM-IV-TR; Am. Psychiatr. Assoc. 2000) as sets of traits (stable, longstanding, and pervasive patterns of affectivity, cognition, interpersonal functioning, and impulse control with onset by early adulthood) that are inflexible and maladaptive, deviate markedly from cultural expectations, and cause either significant functional impairment or subjective distress. Based generally on this conceptualization, knowledge about PD has ballooned in the past 20 years, and in a recent editorial in the *American Journal of Psychiatry*, Gabbard (2005) proclaimed that PD had "come of age" (p. 833).

However, conceptual difficulties and controversies have persisted (Clark et al. 1997, Livesley 2003, Widiger & Samuel 2005), there is widespread dissatisfaction in the field, and articles critiquing the domain are common (Jablensky 2002, Livesley 2003, Millon 2002). Widiger et al. (2002) declared, "Official diagnoses are substantially arbitrary, often unreliable, overlapping, and incomplete and have only a limited utility for treatment planning" (p. 435), and Tyrer et al. (2006) stated bluntly, "The assessment of personality disorder is currently inaccurate, largely unreliable, frequently wrong, and in need of improvement."

However, with the turn of the century, the field also seems to have turned a corner, as research findings have (*a*) led to new assessment approaches based on convincing evidence that the structure of PD is dimensional (Trull & Durrett 2005), (*b*) compelled researchers to think more deeply about the theoretical implications of PD comorbidity both within and between axes (Krueger 2005), and (*c*) challenged a simplistic view of PD as unchanging (Clark 2005a, Shea & Yen 2003, Tyrer et al. 2006). Together, these results are moving the field toward a more sophisticated understanding of PD and its relation to Axis I disorders. In this context, this review's goals are (*a*) to analyze how recent (particularly 2000–2005) research is gradually clarifying these three domains—assessment, comorbidity, and stability; (*b*) to describe the growing consensus in each; and (*c*) to articulate the reconceptualization that is emerging and the major directions in which future research should focus.

TOPICS NOT REVIEWED

This review is necessarily focused, so I simply mention here three broad topics and five specific ones not covered, to give the reader a sense of the breadth and depth of PD research. Psychopathy research has run parallel with that on DSM antisocial PD, and not only has survived, but has thrived, with active literatures on its assessment, structure, core nature—including relations with antisocial PD and behavior—and universality across age, gender, and culture. Schizotypy research often is biologically oriented due to its relation to schizophrenia, examining that disorder's full range of neurocognitive deficits; also, several studies have investigated the structure of self-reported dimensions of schizotypy. Focal assessment topics that deserve mention include gender bias, ethnicity/cultural issues, depressive PD (as a possible addition), taxometric analyses [somewhat supportive of schizotypal and antisocial PD categories; mixed, but more suggesting dimensional constructs for borderline personality disorder (BPD), narcissistic PD, and psychopathy; Edens et al. 2006, Fossati et al. 2005, Haslam 2003, Rothschild et al. 2003, Vasey et al. 2005], and the utility of brief screening instruments.

BPD is the most widely researched single-PD domain (Blashfield & Intoccia 2000), encompassing biological, psychosocial, and cognitive factors in etiology and maintenance, functioning, and health care utilization. Related research examines relevant dimensions, including impulsivity, aggression, affective dyscontrol, suicidality, dissociation, traumatic memories and attentional control, as well as attachment and parental rearing style. Because BPD is more likely dimensional than taxonic, and because of poor convergence between BPD measures (Clark et al. 1997), these latter approaches likely will yield more fruitful results.

HOW SHALL I ASSESS THEE? LET ME COUNT THE WAYS

Progress in conceptualizing PD continues to be hampered by limitations in its assessment. Simultaneously, improvement in assessing PD is limited by inadequate conceptualization (Clark et al. 1997). In this section, I discuss the current state of—and emerging directions in—both assessment approaches and related conceptual issues, including planning for DSM-V, the role of the five-factor model (FFM) of personality in shaping the field, increasing interest in the critical component of dysfunction, and nonself-report-based assessment.

TOWARD DIMENSIONS AND AWAY FROM CATEGORIES IN DSM-V?

A late-2004 research-planning workshop sponsored jointly by the American Psychiatric Association, World Health Organization, National Institute of Mental Health, National Institute on Alcohol Abuse and Alcoholism, and National Institute on Drug Abuse focused on models of PD, both what is known and what needs to be determined for a dimensional model to be adopted in DSM-V. The presented papers and ensuing discussion examined dimensional models from multiple perspectives, from behavior genetics and neurobiology to childhood antecedents and cultural factors, from alternative dimensional structures to clinical utility (Widiger et al. 2005), but the overarching theme and consensus were clear: The current categorical system is scientifically untenable (Widiger & Simonsen 2005), and as Allen Frances declared almost 15 years ago with regard to implementing a dimensional system for PD in the DSM, "Not whether, but when and which" (Frances 1993, p. 110).

Focusing on Frances's "which," Widiger & Simonsen (2005) described 18 candidate dimensional systems for PD. Arguing that simply selecting one is scientifically unacceptable

Stability: the degree of consistency in a diagnosis or personality trait over time

BPD: borderline personality disorder

FFM: five-factor model

Dimensional versus categorical: debate regarding whether diagnostic categories or personality trait dimensional characteristics should represent the personality disorder domain

because each has strengths and weaknesses, they presented a common integrative, hierarchical model topped by two "superfactors" (essentially Digman's 1997 alpha and beta factors or Block's 2001 ego resiliency and control), with middle layers of three to seven broad dimensions, which in turn are composed of facets (basic personality traits), all anchored at yet lower levels in specific affects, behaviors, and cognitions. Such a model has its detractors (Block 2001) and limitations in describing personality comprehensively (Hooker & McAdams 2003), and would need further specification to have clinical utility (Verheul 2005), but the common model presented emerges from substantial research and represents a solid base around which to develop a reliable, valid, and scientifically and clinically useful dimensional system.

Often-voiced concerns about dimensional systems regard whether and how they can inform clinical decision-making, and that their complexity complicates clinical communication. Verheul (2005), however, turned the complexity argument around, noting that dimensions provide diagnostic richness and subtlety not afforded by the DSM categories, which are criticized for oversimplicity. Moreover, he argued that the current diagnostic system does not direct either treatment selection or planning; rather, severity is the primary determinant of the decision to treat (see also Tyrer 2005). Moreover, dimensions provide more information for predicting the effectiveness of different treatment options at both the "macro" (e.g., in- versus outpatient, session frequency/duration) and "micro" (e.g., targeting self-harm for initial intervention) levels (Verheul 2005, pp. 293–294). Trull (2005) further discussed the need to determine the most appropriate cut scores on relevant dimensions for various clinical decisions. For example, empirically developed, nonarbitrary cutpoints on trait aggression or self-harm could guide clinical decisions to implement anger-management training or a therapeutic contract regarding suicidal intentions, respectively. Even those who argue

for retaining categories (Paris 2005) acknowledge that they will be replaced eventually, most likely by a still developing comprehensive and consensual dimensional system: "Not whether, but when and which" (Frances 1993, p. 110).

Personality Disorder Diagnosis and the FFM

In the last half of the twentieth century, researchers of normal-range personality made tremendous progress in understanding trait structure. By the turn of the century, there was widespread (though not universal; Block 2001) agreement that the Big Five—neuroticism (negative affectivity/emotionality/temperament; N/NA), extraversion (positive affectivity/ emotionality/temperament; E/PA), agreeableness (A), conscientiousness (C), and culture/openness to experience (O)—that is, a five-factor model (FFM)—reflected the bulk of personality trait variance. Widiger & Simonsen (2005) tapped the FFM as the framework for organizing the 18 extant dimensional models of PD. Research studies examining relations between the DSM PDs and measures of normal-range personality, including the FFM, have revealed that the domains of normal and abnormal personality are largely overlapping (O'Connor 2002). More specifically, the DSM PDs can be characterized with the FFM conceptually—by both clinical researchers (Widiger et al. 2002) and practicing clinicians (Samuel & Widiger 2004, 2006; Sprock 2002, 2003)—and empirically (O'Connor 2005, Saulsman & Page 2004).

Whereas extant normal-range FFM measures may be limited in differentiating among individuals with more severely maladaptive traits, the FFM per se is not, which has been shown using questionnaire items (Haigler & Widiger 2001), semistructured interviews (Bagby et al. 2005a), and adjective descriptors (Coker et al. 2002). Furthermore, the FFM has been related to PD in translation (De Clercq & De Fruyt 2003); in adolescent samples (De Clercq & De Fruyt 2003, Lynam et al. 2005); as conceptualized in the ICD-10 (Brieger et al. 2000); and in relation to other psychopathologies including psychopathy (Lynam et al. 2005), depressive PD (Bagby et al. 2004, Huprich 2003), and dependency (Bornstein & Cecero 2000). Lower-order (facet-level) characterizations differentiate better among individuals with PD than do higher-order (domain-level) ones (Bagby et al. 2005a, Morey et al. 2002, Reynolds & Clark 2001). Moreover, practicing clinicians rated facets as more useful clinically than domain scores (Sprock 2002).

Clinicians preferred the FFM to the DSM for describing actual cases and did so reliably (Samuel & Widiger 2006). When rating vignettes of prototypic and nonprototypic cases, interrater reliability was acceptable for all cases using the FFM, but only for prototypic cases (which are rare in actuality) using categories (Sprock 2003). Yet, clinicians' confidence in their (unreliable) diagnostic and (reliable) FFM ratings of the nonprototypic cases was nearly identical. Thus, the FFM—especially the facet level—appears to have broadband applicability in assessing PD-relevant traits, as well as superior psychometric properties. However, education to familiarize clinicians with using dimensions to diagnose PD will be important when a dimensional system is eventually implemented.

Prototype method of diagnosis. Both to demonstrate that the FFM "possesses the language necessary for the description of the personality disorders" (p. 402) and to utilize clinicians' familiarity with the DSM diagnoses, Lynam & Widiger (2001) developed a prototype method of diagnosing PD with the FFM. Specifically, expert clinical researchers rated "the prototypic case" (p. 403) of each DSM-IV PD using the 30 facets of the Revised NEO Personality Inventory (NEO PI–R; Costa & McCrae 1992). Their ratings were aggregated, yielding an FFM profile for each PD, which diagnoses PD using similarity scores, intraclass coefficients that assess how closely

an individual's FFM profile matches the prototype profiles.

Miller and colleagues (2004) found good agreement ($r = 0.75$) between these expert prototypes and actual FFM facet-PD score correlations using the Structured Interview for DSM-IV Personality (SIDP-IV; Pfohl et al. 1995) to diagnose PD. Similarity scores were stable (median $rs \geq 0.80$) at 6- and 12-month follow-up, and similarity scores based on the NEO-PI-R and Structured Interview for the Five-Factor Model (SIFFM; Trull et al. 2001) converged (median $r = 0.68$) (Miller et al. 2005b).

Miller et al. (2004, 2005b) then correlated FFM similarity scores and actual PD scores in the three samples, obtaining moderate convergence (mean rs in the 0.40s; ranges = 0.02–0.68) using the SIDP-IV or Structured Clinical Interview for DSM-IV Personality Disorders Questionnaire (SCID-II; First et al. 1997) to diagnose PD, and both the NEO-PI-R and SIFFM to assess the FFM. Ranges were anchored consistently by obsessive-compulsive PD (OCPD) and avoidant PD (low and high rs, respectively). Higher mean convergence ($r = 0.64$) was found with the Schedule for Nonadaptive and Adaptive Personality (SNAP; Clark 1993) diagnostic scale scores, perhaps due in part to shared, self-report method variance. Predictive validity of intake similarity scores for consensus diagnoses based on DSM PD criterion ratings was modest: range = 0.33 (intake) to 0.44 (one year later). Finally, Miller et al. (2005a) demonstrated that a simple sum of component FFM facets performed as well as the prototype method (average convergence = 0.39).

Notably, the convergence of similarity and interview-based scores in these five samples is quite similar to the 0.39 reported in a meta-analysis of self-report and interview convergence (Clark et al. 1997). Thus, these results support the FFM's claim as a contender in PD assessment, but also demonstrate that the FFM does not surpass the typically moderate convergence between PD measures.

OCPD:
obsessive-compulsive personality disorder

Furthermore, it is critically important to emphasize that diagnosis-by-prototype is not itself an end—the DSM diagnoses are much too flawed to warrant emulation, especially only moderately convergent emulation. The FFM has great value in PD assessment, but it lies in the dimensions themselves and their potential for deepening our understanding of PD traits, not in their ability to approximate demonstrably inadequate categories. The field will be little advanced by additional studies using this approach, its purpose already having been fulfilled.

Limitations and implications for future directions. These findings indicate that a lower-level FFM personality trait structure could supplant the current categorical system for diagnosing PD, but that—just as with extant measures—certain limitations must be overcome. First, the NEO PI-R is the only existing faceted FFM measure, so the extent to which its particular facets comprehensively cover and validly represent lower-order levels of the FFM domains is unknown. Moreover, even when facets are used to predict DSM PD, as noted with profile-similarity data, substantial unexplained variance remains. Recent studies using multiple regression, maximizing predictive power, confirm this finding: Bagby et al. (2005a), Reynolds & Clark (2001), and Furnam & Crump (2005) all reported moderate R^2s with various combinations of self-report and interview for assessing PD and personality.

Importantly, this limitation is not unique to FFM measures: The SNAP had incremental predictive power over the FFM (mean $\Delta R^2 = 0.22$ and 0.08 for domain and facet scores, respectively), but the reverse also was true (NEO-PI-R scores' mean $\Delta R^2 = 0.04$ and 0.10 for domains and facets, respectively) (Reynolds & Clark 2001). When three questionnaires were used to predict PD scores, each had incremental predictive power over the others (Bagby et al. 2005b). Conversely, Trobst et al. (2004) found the NEO-PI-R had

widely varying predictive power depending on how PD was assessed.

The point is not the limitations of these measures for predicting DSM PD per se—as stated above, those diagnoses are too flawed to be a gold standard. Rather, the diagnoses encompass important clinical problems that comprehensively valid PD measures should assess. Trull (2005) terms this "coverage"—"the extent to which a model or system of personality pathology adequately represents those conditions or symptoms that are frequently encountered by clinicians and studied by psychopathologists" (p. 263)—and frames his discussion in terms of content and construct validity.

Thus, an important challenge facing the DSM-V PD work group will be determining how best to capitalize on the strengths of existing measures of the overall personality–PD space—both those developed specifically to assess either PD diagnoses or traits, and those that target normal-range traits with relevance to PD—to provide a maximally comprehensive yet efficient assessment of adaptive and maladaptive personality traits. Put concretely, whereas the FFM generally characterizes the PD domain space as well as do measures specifically designed for that purpose [e.g., the Dimensional Assessment of Personality Pathology–Basic Questionnaire (DAPP-BQ; Livesley & Jackson 2006) and SNAP], other measures also contribute unique, clinically important variance. Because it is impractical to assess PD traits by administering multiple dimensional-system interviews and questionnaires just to ensure that as much valid variance as possible is tapped, identifying and including this additional variance in more comprehensive future PD trait measures is critical to increase both validity and clinical utility of PD-domain assessment.

Alternative Conceptualizations

SWAP-200. The Shedler-Westen Assessment Procedure (SWAP-200; Westen & Shedler 1999a) is a Q-sort procedure designed to quantify the richness of clinical description. Westen & Shedler (1999b) reported it had seven factors, which they matched to six DSM PDs (paranoid, schizoid, antisocial, histrionic, narcissistic, and obsessional) plus dysphoric, the largest factor, which yielded five subfactors that both matched (avoidant) and did not match (hostile-external) DSM categories. They also used the SWAP-200 to create DSM prototypes and a high-functioning prototype (Westen & Shedler 1999a). A later factor analysis of the same item pool, however, yielded 12 "clinically relevant personality dimensions" (Shedler & Westen 2004, p. 1743), but neither its relation to the 7-factor analysis nor the motivation for refactoring the instrument was discussed. Moreover, many items marked different factors (e.g., "antisocial-psychopathic PD" in the 7-factor, but "schizoid orientation" in the 12-factor solution) or marked a factor in one solution and no factor in the other. Furthermore, an adolescent version yielded a partially overlapping set of "11 dimensions of adolescent personality" (Westen et al. 2005, p. 227), the Big Five can be found in a subset of SWAP-200 items (Shedler & Westen 2004), and the 11 adolescent dimensions relate systematically to a brief adjective measure of the FFM (Westen et al. 2005).

However, it is not clear how these sets of SWAP-200 factors are related. For example, the 12-factor solution's "dissociation" dimension does not appear elsewhere; "histrionic sexualization" in the 11- and 12-factor solutions may map onto the DSM and/or factor-analytic histrionic diagnoses, but these empirical relations are not reported. Although a few small-sample studies have reported promising results with the seven factors (Diener & Hilsenroth 2004) or DSM prototypes (Martin-Avellan et al. 2005), additional studies of the 12 factors have not been reported. Accordingly, whether the SWAP-200 structure is robust or relatively sample-dependent, or why different structures have emerged, is unknown.

Currently, therefore, the contribution of the SWAP-200 lies in its demonstration that clinical language and judgment can provide useful, elaborated, and systematic descriptions of the PD space, which underscores the earlier observation of the importance of identifying and including in future PD measures the PD-relevant variance that may not be well represented in extant FFM and other measures.

Temperament and Character Inventory. Cloninger (1987) proposed a theoretical model linking three "temperament" dimensions (harm avoidance, novelty seeking, and reward dependence, from which persistence was split off later) to underlying neural substrates and specific PDs. Tests of the model have yielded mixed results: Predictions regarding the relations between PD and the Temperament and Character Inventory (TCI) have received more support than those concerning neural substrates (Mitropoulou et al. 2003, Mulder & Joyce 2002). Cloninger et al. (1993) added three "character" dimensions (self-directedness, cooperativeness, and self-transcendence), said to develop from experience, to the three (or four) "innate" temperament dimensions.

Low self-directedness consistently marks a wide range of psychopathology, not limited to PD, as does low cooperativeness, although less consistently and less strongly (Daneluzzo et al. 2005, Mulder et al. 1999). Harm avoidance marks subjective distress, and its correlation pattern parallels that of FFM N/NA, being most strongly and consistently high in cluster C (avoidant, dependent, and OCPD) (Farabaugh et al. 2005, Maggini et al. 2000, Mulder et al. 1999). Novelty seeking, like FFM A and C, marks "externalizing" disorders (Krueger et al. 2002, 2005) including substance abuse (Ball 2004, Fassino et al. 2004) and cluster B (antisocial, borderline, histrionic, and narcissistic) PD (Farabaugh et al. 2005, Mulder et al. 1999). Reward dependence is associated with cluster A (paranoid, schizoid, schizotypal) PD in some studies (Farabaugh et al. 2005, Mulder et al. 1999), as is self-transcendence with schizotypal PD (Daneluzzo et al. 2005).

The TCI is one of the more widely used measures outside the United States, so it has the potential to test the cross-cultural generalizability of PD-relevant constructs. However, O'Connor (2002) investigated the structural robustness of widely used personality and psychopathology measures across clinical and nonclinical samples. Most measures exhibited structural invariance across sample types, whereas the TCI had unstable factor structures both across and within sample types, which may explain its literature's inconsistencies. Nonetheless, the instrument also may contain clinically relevant variance that a comprehensive PD-domain measure should assess.

Assessing Dysfunction

Like all psychopathology, PD requires either subjective distress or functional impairment, but researchers paid comparatively little attention to the latter until recently. Hill and colleagues (2000) examined the extent to which trait abnormality was separable from dysfunction, and concluded that their two measures assessed similar constructs. Johnson and colleagues (2000b) reported that PD at baseline predicted levels of—and increases in—interpersonal and global dysfunction at one-year follow-up, controlling for HIV status and Axis I disorders. An epidemiological study (Hong et al. 2005) found that all but two PD dimensional scores predicted global functioning 13–18 years later, and half still did so controlling for current Axis I disorder. Another study (Johnson et al. 2005) reported that dysfunction was as strongly predicted by PD–not otherwise specified (PD-NOS) as it was by any other PD. Two reviews found PD was associated with reduced quality of life (Narud & Dahl 2002) and dysfunction "in nearly every realm of concern to healthcare providers" (Smith & Benjamin 2002, p. 135).

The Collaborative Longitudinal Personality Disorders Study (CLPS) examined func-

tioning in four PD groups and in no-PD depressed controls. At intake, patients with schizotypal and BPD had significantly poorer functioning in social relationships and at work and recreation than did those with OCPD or depression only; functioning of those with avoidant PD was intermediate (Skodol et al. 2002). However, at two-year follow-up, despite decreases in PD symptomatology (Shea et al. 2002, Shea & Yen 2003), significant functional improvement had occurred in only three of seven domains—spouse/partner relationships, recreation, and global social adjustment—and that was due largely to changes in the depressed-only group (Skodol et al. 2005d). Notably, patients with BPD or OCPD had no change in dysfunction over the two-year period, except those whose BPD symptoms had improved during the first year. CLPS researchers (Skodol et al. 2005d) concluded that functional impairment might be a more enduring component of PD than the diagnostic criteria per se.

Furthermore, CLPS researchers (Skodol et al. 2005c) examined functioning in patients who had baseline PD and three-year follow-up depression, and compared those with and without persistent PD to depressed patients seen as part of a Medical Outcomes Study (MOS). Functioning was highest in the MOS group, intermediate in those with depression and baseline-only PD, and lowest in those with persistent PD. Dimensional diagnostic scores correlated more strongly with functioning measured at baseline than did scores on higher-order dimensions—either the FFM or the three maladaptive dimensions (negative temperament, positive temperament, and disinhibition versus constraint) of the SNAP (Skodol et al. 2005b), but the SNAP's lower-order dimensions of maladaptive personality consistently predicted functioning more strongly, up to four-year follow-up (Morey et al. 2006).

However, Mulder (2002) reviewed the literature relating personality and PD to treatment outcome in depression and found mixed results, with the least PD effect in the best-designed studies. Nonetheless, high FFM-N/NA consistently predicted worse outcome, and PD was never related to better response. Mulder also noted that depressed patients with PD may receive less adequate treatment in some studies. Putting these findings together, it appears that PD has both current and longer-lasting effects on functioning (related CLPS findings: Grilo et al. 2000, 2005); some of these effects may be through relations with Axis I disorders (Hong et al. 2005), and the effects may be attenuated with adequate treatment (Bajaj & Tyrer 2005, Reich 2003).

Noting that assessment of criteria and functioning often are confounded in PD diagnoses, Parker and colleagues (2002) advocated separating their assessment. They reviewed the literature to identify markers of dysfunction, consolidated them into 17 constructs, and developed a 67-item self-report measure of dysfunction with 11 intercorrelated scales representing 2 correlated ($r = 0.64$) higher-order dimensions, noncoping and noncooperativeness (Parker et al. 2004). Factor scales (created from the 10 highest-loading items on each) correlated moderately ($r = 0.56$), and both primary and factor scales correlated moderately (mean $r = 0.50$) with dimensional scores of DSM and ICD-10 diagnoses, suggesting either that measures based on current PD-category concepts tap combinations of traits and dysfunction, or that extremes of personality dimensions are inherently dysfunctional. Research testing these two possibilities is needed.

Self-reported dysfunction correlated with ratings made by a close informant ($r = 0.61$ and 0.41 for noncoping and noncooperativeness, respectively) but not with clinician ratings of functioning across five domains ($rs = 0.16$–0.18). Ratings by two independent interviewers correlated strongly with each other ($rs = 0.70$s), but not with either patient ($rs = 0.33$–0.34) or informant ($rs = 0.25$–0.36) ratings, suggesting that valid ratings of dysfunction may require in vivo life experience with a person (Parker et al. 2004; see also

Milton et al. 2005). Testing dysfunction and PD scores together in a regression analysis, noncoping and self-defeating PD scores best differentiated patients from controls, with no other scales adding predictive power (Parker et al. 2004). These results are encouraging steps toward a two-component diagnostic process, but validation samples were small and the findings need replication.

Alternative Sources of Information

Consideration of who (or what) can provide the most reliable and valid information for assessing PD began no later than the middle 1980s and remains an important open question. Recent research has transcended simple studies of agreement—which typically is modest and variable (Klonsky et al. 2002, Walters et al. 2004)—to ask more sophisticated questions, such as what factors influence self-informant agreement and who is the best informant for what information.

A review of 17 PD self-informant studies (Klonsky et al. 2002) found no systematic variance by assessment instrument type (questionnaire versus interview), sample (patient versus nonclinical), or informant (except higher agreement with spouses), nor did selves or informants report more overall pathology. Interinformant agreement is generally higher than self-informant agreement, which varies positively by age, degree of acquaintance, and trait/disorder "visibility" (e.g., aggression and BPD are more visible than mistrust and narcissistic PD), and negatively with sample size. Agreement is higher for dimensional ratings and personality problems assessed outside the DSM framework, perhaps because DSM disorders are less internally consistent.

Oltmanns & Turkheimer (2006) summarized multiple studies systematically exploring self-informant agreement. Important findings include: (*a*) when asked to rate themselves as they thought others would rate them (meta-perceptions), self-informant agreement increased; (*b*) target- and investigator-selected informants provided similar ratings, although target-selected informants underrated traits associated with clusters A and B and over-rated cluster C traits; (c) selves and informants provided complementary data (for example, self-rated suspiciousness was rated as "cold" by informants, whereas other-rated suspiciousness was rated as "angry" by selves); and (d) self-ratings of internalizing problems and informant ratings of externalizing problems each added independent predictive power to functional outcomes. Furthermore, when interview- and informant-based ratings were discrepant on narcissism, blind raters of nonverbal behavior in videotaped interviews showed increased agreement with informants. Thus, interviewer ratings may be more accurate if based on all behavior—not just verbal responses—although unreliability is a concern and must be examined.

Utilizing written-record data is a long-standing tradition in psychopathy research, but otherwise has been used rarely in PD assessment. Tyrer et al. (2006) demonstrated that most traits could be rated from records as reliably as from interviews, and convergence with consensus diagnoses was promising in a pilot study. Based on a comprehensive review, Meyer (2002) found that diagnostic agreement correlated with the extent of measures' source-information overlap, and multiple-source measurement had greater reliability and validity than did single-source measurement.

In sum, although not without their own weaknesses, other-source data have distinct advantages over self-reports. Moreover, informant studies have revealed how self-reports may be improved. The field should consider seriously how not only informant data but also meta-perceptions, nonverbal behavior, and written records might be incorporated systematically into PD assessment.

Focusing Future PD Assessment Research

Adoption of a dimensional conceptualization of PD inevitably lies ahead, and several key is-sues must be addressed to arrive at that future. First, the higher-order structure of adaptive and maladaptive personality is well mapped, but lower-order structure remains largely uncharted territory. Because the higher-order dimensions are too broad to capture personality's rich complexity, they have limited utility in clinical settings, and better understanding of more focal traits is critically needed. Furthermore, PD diagnosis is incomplete if only traits are assessed: Personality function also must be evaluated. Extreme personality traits are linked empirically with dysfunction and may be inherently maladaptive, but to investigate this issue, we need dysfunction measures not (or at least less) confounded by personality-trait content. Thus, exploring the nature of dysfunction also should be a field priority.

Finally, it is clear that personality—both adaptive and maladaptive—is too complex to be assessed fully from a single perspective. More comprehensive understanding of PD will require integration of the common and unique information that can be provided by self-report, well-known informants, clinicians who have an objective view contextualized by a broad understanding of the PD landscape, written records of behavior, and eventually laboratory data. Learning how information from these various sources can be integrated most validly and usefully likely will challenge researchers for some years to come.

COMORBIDITY

Comorbidity—with its implication of co-occurring but independent disorders—is now widely recognized as a misnomer for the pervasive phenomenon of two or more mental disorders co-occurring; however, the mislabel has stuck and I, too, use it. PD comorbidity has been investigated so much that one would think the topic exhausted, but it is such a fundamental issue that PD-comorbidity research is still increasing. A simple PsycINFO search crossing "personality disorder(s)" and "comorbidity/co-occurrence" yielded more than 1500 citations from 1985 through 2005: 269 in the first 10 years, 477 in the second five years, and 756 beginning in 2000. Part of the increase stems from an ever-widening sphere of investigation revealing PD comorbidity with, for example, ADHD (Davids & Gastpar 2005) and kleptomania (Grant 2004).

Many studies are purely descriptive, reporting the rates of comorbidity within Axis II and/or with Axis I disorders (typically 50% or more in each case in clinical samples), with discussion of methodological factors that may increase rates artifactually, common features, or putative underlying shared etiology [Zimmerman et al. (2005) reported on a particularly large outpatient sample]. Most see PD comorbidity as a problem for the current categorical system, some as its nemesis: "A categorical approach to PDs, resulting in a list of diagnoses, appears useless in psychiatric practice" (Marinangeli et al. 2000, p. 69). The high prevalence of PD-NOS (Verheul & Widiger 2004) may reflect the same fundamental phenomenon as comorbidity—that personality pathology is rarely confined to a single diagnostic entity. Therefore, I focus on new findings and perspectives that add substantially to our understanding. I begin with general consequences of comorbidity, examine results involving particular disorders, and conclude with implications for nosology.

Complications of Comorbidity

Whereas there may be increased prevalence of comorbid PD in samples seeking treatment for Axis I disorders, comorbidity is sufficiently prevalent in population studies that selection bias alone cannot account for it. There is a strong association of PD comorbidity with earlier age of onset (Brieger et al. 2002, Ozkan & Altindag 2005); greater clinical severity (Ozkan & Altindag 2005); poorer treatment outcome (Farabaugh et al. 2005, Ogrodniczuk et al. 2001); longer time to remission (Grilo et al. 2005, Massion et al. 2002); lower long-term social, cognitive, and occupational functioning (Bank & Silk 2001,

Denys et al. 2004, Smith & Benjamin 2002, Tyrer et al. 2003); greater medical utilization (Smith & Benjamin 2002); suicide attempts and completion (Garno et al. 2005, Hawton et al. 2003); and greater risk of psychopathology in offspring (Abela et al. 2005). However, worse outcome—including increased time to remission—is not inevitable (Grilo et al. 2000), varies by PD (Grilo et al. 2005), and to some extent may reflect methodological flaws rather than true effects (Mulder 2002).

Comorbidity with Depression and Anxiety Disorders

Two reviews and the results of several large studies paint a coherent picture of relations among depression and anxiety disorders and maladaptive personality. The National Epidemiologic Survey on Alcohol and Related Conditions (NESARC) assessed more than 43,000 individuals and found both pervasive comorbidity among PDs (Grant et al. 2005a) and PDs (especially avoidant and dependent PD) with mood and anxiety disorders (Grant et al. 2005b). Moreover, anxiety/depression and PD each predict the onset of the other (Goodwin et al. 2005, Hettema et al. 2003) and share genetic variance both with each other and with trait N/NA (Bienvenu & Stein 2003). These relations are unaffected by comorbidity with substance use disorders (Verheul et al. 2000).

A 12-year longitudinal study showed that "cothymia" (mixed anxiety-depressive symptoms), higher baseline self-reported anxiety/depression, plus premorbid PD predicted the least favorable outcome, whereas initial Axis I diagnosis per se did not predict outcome, and "instability of [Axis I] diagnosis over time was much more common than consistency" (Tyrer et al. 2004, p. 1385). Tyrer et al. (2003) suggest that splitting the traditional category of neurosis into specific disorders [e.g., generalized anxiety disorder (GAD), social phobia, dysthymia] was neither helpful nor warranted because of their extensive comorbidity. They argue provocatively that their results demonstrate "a failed classification system," that much comorbidity is really "consanguinity," and that current diagnostic concepts have little impact and "are relatively useless" (p. 136).

Within this picture of general overlap, specific patterns do occur. For example, two studies comparing PD comorbidity in unipolar versus bipolar depression converged on the finding that BPD, OCPD, and avoidant/dependent PD were more common in unipolar patients, and narcissistic PD was more common in bipolar patients (Brieger et al. 2003, Schiavone et al. 2004). Smith et al. (2005), however, found BPD features—especially suicidality and impulse-anger dyscontrol—were more characteristic of bipolar disorder. BPD also has been linked to PTSD (Axelrod et al. 2005). Avoidant/dependent PD predicted reduced remission in GAD (both PDs) and social phobia (avoidant PD only) but not in panic disorder (Massion et al. 2002). Furthermore, some anxiety disorders may be heterogeneous, with different subtypes having differential relations with PD. For example, Lee & Telch (2005) divided OCD obsessions into autogenous obsessions—highly aversive and threatening (e.g., sexual, aggressive, blasphemous, or repulsive) thoughts, images, or impulses—and reactive obsessions—thoughts, doubts, or concerns in which the perceived threat is the possible negative consequence (e.g., of contamination, mistakes, accidents, asymmetry, or disarray). Only the former was associated with schizotypal PD.

Comorbidity with Substance Abuse and Addictive Behavior

The general picture emerging from PD/substance abuse comorbidity research has been fairly consistent over the years: (a) The overlap is strong, especially with cluster B PDs (Ball 2005). (b) Severity moderates comorbidity; for example, comorbidity with antisocial PD increases about twofold (~30% to 60%) from mild to severe drug abuse/dependence (Flynn et al. 1996). (c) Comorbidity is associated with worse treatment outcome that may be attenuated with enhanced treatment, and substance abusers with PD have earlier substance use, have more legal and family problems, and are more susceptible to relapse in the presence of cravings, negative physical and emotional states, and interpersonal conflict (Ball 2005, Westermeyer & Thuras 2005). (d) Substance abuse and antisocial PD likely share a genetically based etiological factor (e.g., Jang et al. 2000, Kendler et al. 2003, Krueger et al. 2002)—temperamental "externalizing"—which likely also underlies other cluster B PDs, particularly BPD (Bornovalova et al. 2005, Trull et al. 2000) and narcissistic PD (Kelsey et al. 2001), as well as pathological gambling (Pietrzak & Petry 2005) and ADHD (Dowson et al. 2004). This broad factor is characterized in large part by impulsivity, a term that has come under increasing scrutiny as evidence has accrued that it is used to denote several unrelated constructs, some measured by self-report and others via laboratory tasks, each of which has some research support (Bornovalova et al. 2005, Looper & Paris 2000, Whiteside & Lynam 2001). (e) Suicidality and other expressions of negative affectivity may also play a role in PD/substance use comorbidity, although not uniquely so (Bornovalova et al. 2005, Casillas & Clark 2002).

Although much research is conducted on various disorders in the externalizing spectrum from biological perspectives, there is little research, other than behavior genetic studies, examining substance abuse/PD relations from these perspectives, perhaps in part because of limitations in PD measurement, and also because research has tended to be disorder centered (e.g., substance abuse research, BPD research). With growing awareness that diverse externalizing disorders share common biological substrates, we may expect an increase in integrated studies from cognitive-affective neuroscience, and neuropsychological and other biological perspectives that are dimensionally based rather than diagnosis centered.

Comorbidity with Eating Disorders

Eating disorders (EDs)—particularly anorexia nervosa (AN) and bulimia nervosa (BN)—comprise the only diagnostic group besides anxiety/depression and externalizing disorders with a sizeable PD-comorbidity literature. A meta-analysis (Sansone et al. 2005) of four ED groups—AN-restricting (AN-R), AN-bingeing (AN-B), BN, and binge eating disorder (BED)—revealed interesting comorbidity patterns with PDs in all three clusters. Avoidant PD was comorbid with all types of ED, whereas BN showed the strongest comorbidity across the PD domain. Of note, the highest comorbidity rate for both AN-R and BED was with OCPD, and BED also overlapped with cluster A PDs more than other EDs. Severe eating disorders with bingeing were associated with BPD, and BN also overlapped with antisocial and narcissistic PD more than did other EDs. Finally, PD traits were largely absent in obese patients (van Hanswijck de Jonge et al. 2003).

A recent review of personality traits and EDs (Cassin & von Ranson 2005) reported generally complementary findings: Both AN and BN were associated with avoidant PD traits, plus traits that commonly characterize most PDs (e.g., FFM N/NA), whereas AN and BN related to opposite ends of a constraint-disinhibition dimension (see Favaro et al. 2005 for a detailed study of impulsive behaviors in ED). Interestingly, BN as well as AN patients score high on perfectionism and related OC traits (Halmi 2005), which suggests that OC traits are not simply facets of constraint, as is often assumed.

These findings provide a generally coherent picture of ED-PD overlap, but in a special issue of *Eating Disorders: The Journal of Treatment & Prevention* that focused on ED-PD comorbidity, Vitousek & Stumpf (2005) caution against assessing personality traits and disorders in ED individuals until after the initial treatment phase because of assessment difficulties (e.g., "state" effects of semistarvation and chaotic eating, denial/distortion in self report, and instability of ED subtypes). Furthermore, CLPS data suggest that ED-PD comorbidity rates reflect disorder base rates rather than meaningful associations (Grilo et al. 2003), and in a general-population twin sample, correlations of PD traits and ED symptoms were modest and nonspecific (Livesley et al. 2005). Thus, observed relations may reflect general associations (e.g., between N/NA and subjective distress) more than specific etiologies, and the large PD/ED comorbidity literature may be "much ado about nothing."

The Meaning of Comorbidity Patterns

Over the years, writers have offered various theoretical possibilities for explaining comorbidity (Clark 2005b), but rarely have these hypotheses been tested directly. Recently, researchers have begun to analyze comorbidity data in ways that can inform psychopathological theory. For example, regarding the validity of the Axis I–Axis II distinction, CLPS data have revealed both convergences and disjunctions between concurrent and longitudinal co-occurrence (McGlashan et al. 2000, Shea et al. 2004). Specifically, both at baseline and longitudinally up to two years follow-up, avoidant PD was associated with social phobia, and BPD with PTSD (Axelrod et al. 2005 also found bidirectional BPD-PTSD relations in combat veterans). However, BPD/substance abuse and avoidant PD/OCD associations were observed only at baseline, whereas a specific BPD/depression association was found longitudinally, but not at baseline. Others who have found concurrent BPD/depression relations (Bellino et al. 2005) typically have not examined association specificity. OCPD and OCD were not associated concurrently or longitudinally.

Concurrent, but not longitudinal, associations suggest artifactual overlap (e.g., due to shared criteria, such as impulsive substance use, or "state" common factors), whereas longitudinal associations more likely reflect shared underlying pathological structures or processes. For example, Klein & Schwartz (2002) tested several etiologic models and found that a common factor best accounted for longitudinal associations between BPD and early onset dysthymia.

Clark (2005b) analyzed parallels between the literatures examining (*a*) comorbidity both within-axis and between-axes and (*b*) relations of personality dimensions to both Axis I and Axis II disorders. Regarding comorbidity, its pervasiveness and extent demonstrated the need to move beyond study of overlapping pairs or small sets of disorders to a broader, more integrated focus. Regarding personality-disorder relations, the data indicated, surprisingly, that personality traits do not have a "privileged" relation with PD, but are equivalently correlated with Axis I and II disorders. Accordingly, Clark (2005b) outlined a general framework to explain both comorbidity and personality-psychopathology relations, suggesting that both domains have common roots in basic temperamental dimensions.

This view is highly congruent with that of Rothbart & Posner (2006), whose comprehensive review of the temperament and developmental psychopathology literature—including their own central contributions linking temperament and attention to neural networks—discusses how temperament and environment act separately and in combination to increase or decrease risk for psychopathology. Relatedly, taxonomies of personality and trait-related symptoms in children and adolescents both strongly suggest they are precursors of the adult FFM dimensions (e.g., De Clercq et al. 2006, Mervielde et al. 2005, Shiner 2005). This work should be required reading for all PD researchers.

STABILITY

A definitional assumption has been that PD is enduring. Some have argued that stability is the sole province of PD, that the inclusion on Axis I of "early onset, chronic impairments that characterize everyday functioning" and the absence of a clear distinction between the two types of disorder reflects inadequate conceptualization (Widiger 2003, p. 90). Moreover, questions about PD diagnostic stability began as early as 1985 (Barasch et al. 1985), when a longitudinal BPD study reported a stability of 77%, termed "relatively stable" (p. 1486). However, they did not compute the statistic kappa (κ)—new at that time—which was a low-moderate 0.46.

Dimensional PD criterion counts proved more stable than diagnoses (Loranger et al. 1991), and Zimmerman's (1994) review found average $\kappa = 0.56$ for both short- and long-term retest stabilities for "any PD." These findings implicated measurement error in diagnostic instability, with underlying personality pathology more stable. That is, if no more diagnostic change occurs over longer compared with shorter intervals, then the observed change likely is artifactual, due to measurement error (e.g., resulting from minor change across diagnostic boundaries). Otherwise, longer interval coefficients should be lower, reflecting either greater measurement error over longer time spans or both error and true change. Interestingly, for individual diagnoses, shorter interval studies did have higher κs (Zimmerman 1994).

Stability Revisited: Set in Clay, not Like Plaster

Recently, findings from four major studies and several more focused ones have stimulated reconsideration of PD stability. The CLPS reported significant diagnostic and criterion-level change over two years (Grilo et al. 2004, Shea et al. 2002): Only 44% of patients met criteria every month during year one, and baseline-to-two-years κs (corrected for rater unreliability) were in the low 0.50s. Remission rates (fewer than two criteria throughout the past year) averaged around 20% at year one and ranged from 20% to 40% at year two. Mean criterion levels for their four target diagnoses dropped, from baseline, an average of 22% (six months), 33% (one year), and 41% (two years).

The Longitudinal Study of Personality Disorders (LSPD), a four-year college student study, found statistically significant mean decreases of 1.4 PD criteria per year, ranging from near 0 in women without baseline PD to just over 2.5 in males with baseline PD, with considerable individual variation (Lenzenweger et al. 2004). The large Children in the Community (CIC) study, examining PD traits three times from an average age of 14 to 22, found steady declines, with overall PD trait levels decreasing 28% (Johnson et al. 2000a).

Finally, Durbin & Klein (2006) reported on a follow-along sample of depressed outpatients who were assessed every 30 months for 10 years. The median κ for any PD meeting full criteria for the four 2.5-year periods, the three 5-year periods, the two 7.5-year periods, and the full 10 years were 0.34, 0.47, 0.42, and 0.23, whereas including cases with one criterion fewer than threshold yielded somewhat higher κs of 0.51, 0.37, 0.46, and 0.29, which suggests the arbitrariness of the DSM's diagnostic thresholds. Specific PD diagnoses were notably more unstable. It is unclear whether the lower 10-year values represent lasting or transient change, given the notably higher 7.5-year stabilities.

The McLean Study of Adult Development (MSAD), an intensive, longitudinal study of BPD, reported similar change rates and patterns (Zanarini et al. 2005). Two smaller studies examined two-year PD stability in adolescents. One obtained similar results (significantly lower scores at reassessment; Grilo et al. 2001), whereas the other found diagnostic stability only in antisocial PD, and mod-erate stability in dimensional PD scores, with no overall decline (Chanen et al. 2004).

Despite diagnostic and criterial instability, all these studies found notably stronger rank-order stability of criterion counts. For example, even given the very restricted range of the DSM PD's 7- to 9-point scales, and the fact that all patients were above diagnostic threshold at baseline (limiting range still further), the CLPS stability coefficients in the PD groups from baseline were 0.74 (six months), 0.67 (one year), and 0.59 (two years) (Grilo et al. 2004). For the total sample, the six-month and one-year stabilities were impressively high: 0.90 and 0.86, respectively (Shea et al. 2002). Similarly, two- to three-year and nine-year rank-order stabilities of any PD in the CIC were 0.69 and 0.52, respectively (Johnson et al. 2000a), whereas average two-year stability in another adolescent sample was 0.50 (Chanen et al. 2004). Durbin & Klein (2006) reported a median intraclass coefficient of 0.59 over 10 years for the three clusters, and 0.49 for specific PDs [range = 0.23 (antisocial) to 0.61 (avoidant)].

How are we to interpret these data? For example, the CLPS met the DSM general diagnostic criteria for PD, including having a longstanding, enduring trait pattern. The CLPS protocol specifically examined "the prior two years, but traits must be characteristic of the person for most of his or her adult life in order to be counted toward a diagnosis" (Shea et al. 2002, p. 2037). Because of this two-year window, if patients were judged not to have enduring patterns of behavior at one-year follow-up, then traits judged at baseline to be enduring either were validly judged enduring at baseline but were not evident at all during the ensuing year, or were not validly judged at either baseline or one-year follow-up—indicating measurement error. That is, either patients changed their story at reassessment and/or interviewers changed their judgment about traits being characteristic of the patients' adult lives and also manifest in the past two years.

In considering these possibilities, given that the DSM definition of personality disorder builds on personality traits, PD stability and change must be evaluated in the context of a broader literature. In 1980, when DSM-III introduced a separate axis for PD, there were few good data on personality stability, and the prevailing notion was that of William James (1950/1890) who claimed that "by the age of 30, the character has set like plaster, and will never soften again" (p. 121). In the intervening 25 years, however, research has challenged this notion, and a more sophisticated understanding of normal-range personality stability and change has emerged.

The main findings can be summarized briefly: Mean-level trait change is moderate through adolescence and well into early adulthood, with increasing levels of positive traits (e.g., A and C) and decreasing levels of negative traits (e.g., N/NA) (Robins et al. 2001, Vaidya et al. 2002). Furthermore, characteristic affect levels are less stable than broad personality dimensions, at least in part because they have stronger relations with positive and negative life events (Vaidya et al. 2002). Rank-order stability is moderate in childhood ($M = 0.31$) and continues to increase through adolescence and adulthood, not peaking ($M = 0.74$) until considerably later, between ages 50 and 70 (Roberts & DelVecchio 2000). Personality structure is quite stable as early as adolescence, whereas individual profile stability is moderate, with more change in level and scatter (spread) than in profile shape (Robins et al. 2004, Vaidya et al. 2002). Thus, change in basic personality configuration is more quantitative than qualitative, and quantitative change is not insignificant.

Given these normative data, there may be yet another possibility in evaluating the observed stability/change in PD besides simply true change and measurement error, and that is that interviewers applied normative standards to their judgments of whether a trait is enduring and characteristic, with the result that the observed level of PD stability closely parallels that of normal traits. For example, CLPS two-year criterion stability in specific diagnoses for patients (initial $M_{age} = 33$) is 0.59, whereas normal-range trait stability for ages 30–39 is 0.62 (Roberts & DelVecchio 2000). Durbin & Klein (2006) provided a more direct comparison by assessing personality with the Eysenck Personality Questionnaire-Revised (EPQ-R; Eysenck et al. 1985). In comparison with the median 0.59 for PD scored dimensionally, median stability for personality was highly similar: 0.65. Thus, these recent studies do not actually challenge the definition of PD traits as stable and longstanding. Rather, they inform us that our intuitive sense of personality stability corresponds to lower numbers than we might have predicted a priori, which concerns the level of our ability to quantify subjective experience rather than the phenomenon per se. Nonetheless, modifying James, it isn't until past the age of 50 that character may set like plaster; before then, it's more like being set in clay—change can occur, but gradually and with effort.

Further Considerations

There are several other issues to consider before drawing final conclusions about PD stability. First is the important theoretical question of whether maladaptive personality may be expected to have more, less, or the same stability as normal-range personality. PD is defined as inflexible, possibly suggesting more stability, but this term likely is intended instead to indicate lack of situational adaptivity. On the other hand, given the strong affective component in most PD (Trobst et al. 2004, Widiger et al. 2002) and the lower stability of trait affect, PD may be less stable than normal-range personality. This issue deserves further consideration, but absent compelling reason to hypothesize otherwise, it is reasonable to assume that the empirical results are face valid—PD has comparable stability to normal-range personality.

Second, recalling that PD diagnoses are less stable than their component traits, it also is important to consider PD stability in the context of Axis I disorder stability. A comparison of remission rates from four longitudinal studies found PD more stable than mood disorders, but generally less so than anxiety disorders (Shea & Yen 2003): Median 1- and 2-year remission rates, respectively, were 0.78 and 0.87 for mood disorders, 0.31 and 0.45 for PD, and 0.14 and 0.20 for anxiety disorders (except 0.40/0.60 in nonagoraphobic panic). Similarly, the Nottingham Study of Neurotic Disorder (Tyrer et al. 2004) found considerable specific-diagnosis instability, but only 36% overall remission after 12 years in patients with GAD, panic disorder, or dysthymia (either with—cothymia—or without comorbid anxiety disorder). Remission was even lower in patients with cothymia and/or PD. Given the close correspondence of anxiety disorder and N/NA, basic temperament dimensions likely undergird the observed diagnostic stability. Durbin & Klein (2006), on the other hand, found comparable stabilities between PD and anxiety disorders overall (10-year κ for any anxiety disorder $= 0.24$), with panic disorder and obsessive-compulsive disorders more stable (10-year $\kappa = 0.32$ and 0.39, respectively) than social or simple phobia (0.07 and -0.02, respectively).

Third, recall that CLPS researchers found high two-year stability of maladaptive functioning (Skodol et al. 2005c; see also Tyrer et al. 2004). Taken together, these three points indicate that whereas PD features (i.e., traits) have the same stability as normal-range personality and PD diagnoses are only moderately stable, PD-based dysfunctionality is relatively more stable, which may contribute to "the commonly held belief that PDs persist" (Skodol et al. 2005d, p. 444). That is, persistent dysfunction may be interpreted as a persistent diagnosis.

Fourth, as noted almost 15 years ago (Shea 1992), the PD diagnostic criteria are qualitatively variable. Some (e.g., sense of entitlement) directly assess their target construct(s) (i.e., a particular enduring trait pattern defining that PD), whereas others (e.g., uncom-

fortable or helpless when alone) assess not the target construct itself (attachment, in this example), but rather "manifestations of an underlying construct" (Shea 1992, p. 37). Among the latter, a further distinction is the degree to which criteria tap acute, dysfunctional behaviors that more closely resemble Axis I symptoms (e.g., recurrent suicidal behavior) that resolve in shorter periods than do maladaptive traits per se (Clark 2005a, Shea et al. 2002).

In the CLPS, examples of more changeable criteria were odd behavior and constricted affect (schizotypal PD), self-injury and behaviors to avoid abandonment (BPD), avoiding interpersonal jobs and potentially embarrassing situations (avoidant PD), and miserly and strict moral behaviors (OCPD). Examples of more stable criteria were paranoid ideation (schizotypal PD), affective instability and anger (BPD), feeling inadequate and socially inept (avoidant PD), and rigidity and difficulty delegating (OCPD) (McGlashan et al. 2005).

The MSAD (Zanarini et al. 2005) provided additional evidence of this distinction, linking BPD's moderately high remission rates to acute symptoms (e.g., suicidal/self-mutilating behaviors) that diminished with treatment, maturation, or stress resolution, whereas basic temperament dimensions (e.g., chronic anger, stress reactivity) changed more slowly—perhaps at the rate of normal-range affective trait change, which is less stable still than nonaffective traits.

Fifth, given that dimensional PD scores are more stable than diagnoses and that PDs are composed of traits (manifested in specific criteria), how do personality traits relate to PD diagnoses when assessed independently of PD diagnoses? In the CLPS, latent longitudinal models demonstrated significant cross-lagged relations between year-one FFM traits and year-two PD diagnoses (but not baseline—year one) for three PDs (not OCPD), beyond the considerable trait and PD diagnostic (rank-order) stability, whereas the reverse was not observed (Warner et al.

2004). Thus, change in personality traits predicted PD change, but not vice versa.

The lack of the effect from baseline to year one likely is because early PD change primarily reflects amelioration of the Axis I–like symptoms that led the patient to seek treatment, rather than trait-level change. The longitudinal associations of certain Axis I disorders with PD discussed above provide some support for this hypothesis. In particular, all significant change occurred between baseline and month 6, with no significant change between 6 and 12 months for any of the PD groups (Shea et al. 2004; see also Grilo et al. 2005).

Sixth and finally, different amounts of information are available at baseline, 6, and 12 months, which means that they are necessarily somewhat different assessment methods with increasing reliability and, concomitantly, validity, based on the principle of aggregation. Specifically, at baseline, only retrospective information is available, whereas at later assessments, 6 or 12 months of prospective data also are available. Assuming even modest consistency, aggregation of more observations increases measurement reliability, with a decreasing rate of change as more and more observations accrue (thus, greater change in the first versus second 6 months of observations). This suggests that initial single-point-in-time PD assessment should be considered "provisional," and that a "definite" diagnosis of PD requires multimodal (self- and informant-report and documentary) evidence of temporal duration of individuals' particular personality trait sets.

RECONCEPTUALIZING PERSONALITY DISORDER

The picture that emerges from joint consideration of these issues is one of change within relative stability. More specifically, personality and PD reflect similarly structured trait combinations (O'Connor 2002, 2005) and have moderate long-term stability, but differ in extremity, maladaptivity, and consequential

behavior. Importantly, PD is defined further by acute symptoms that are linked directly to maladaptive traits (e.g., avoiding interpersonal occupational activity with social inhibition), and/or develop as defensive or compensatory behaviors (e.g., self-mutilation) to cope with stress—both exogenous and self-created by one's own maladaptivity (Skodol et al. 2005a). These more changeable symptoms, together with the inherent lesser reliability of single-observation assessment, largely account for observed diagnostic instability, while patients' personality traits change at the "normal" rate, and being more extreme and maladaptive, account for persistent dysfunction.

This emerging view of PD is consistent with (*a*) the current view of personality as reflecting longstanding—but not immutable—characteristics that are based in genetic inheritance as well as both early and ongoing life experiences (Caspi et al. 2005) and (*b*) empirical data showing that PD diagnoses are, at most, moderately stable. Importantly, this model suggests that PD diagnosis should be approached differently from the current symptom/criterion method, distinguishing assessment of more acute symptoms from that of patients' basic temperament.

Additionally, in this conceptualization, traditional, single-point-in-time and single-source-of-information assessment cannot and should not be expected to yield entirely valid PD diagnoses. We know this intuitively with regard to normal personality, understanding that first impressions only partially capture a person's true nature, that to know someone well, we must interact with them in a variety of situations, discussing a range of topics. PD is no different. The very nature of personality and PD demands longitudinal and multimodal assessment for validity.

New Models for Assessing PD

Reconceptualizing PD must be accompanied by new assessment models; four strikingly similar ones have been offered. Livesley et al.

(1994), ahead of the field, first proposed that all disorders be on Axis I, with personality traits on Axis II. PD diagnosis would have two components (Livesley & Jang 2000). (*a*) Diagnosing disorder—determining dysfunction and assessing acute dysfunctional behaviors (e.g., ideas of reference, aggression, suicidality, hyperperfectionism). Diagnosis would entail determining personality's functional failure to solve major life tasks: developing an integrated sense of self, adaptive interpersonal relationships, and adaptive social functioning. (*b*) Describing the individual's personality traits, organized in four (FFM minus O) broad dimensions (Livesley 2005), but with particular focus on lower-order dimensions. Parker et al. (2000) replicated Livesley's dimensions with an independent set of descriptors and, as noted above, reported promising results for a two-component (dysfunction, traits) diagnostic process (Parker et al. 2002, 2004). Both Livesley and Parker drew parallels between their models of functioning and Freud's definition of psychological health, "*lieben und arbeiten*" (to love and to work).

Widiger et al. (2002) proposed a four-stage model: Assess (*a*) individuals' higher- and lower-order FFM personality profiles, (*b*) specific impairments secondary to extreme traits, (*c*) whether dysfunction is clinically significant (e.g., GAF score), and (*d*) if possible, profile match to a particular PD prototype. They emphasized that some situations might not require all four steps (e.g., a counseling setting where formal diagnosis was unnecessary). Tyrer et al. (2006) advocated assessing (*a*) clinically important personality dysfunction severity (versus PD per se) (Tyrer 2005) and (*b*) four broad dimensions (also FFM minus O), with greater reliability than the DSM's narrower categories and more historical continuity than three or five dimensions, (*c*) using multiple information sources, including written records, and (*d*) longitudinal assessment.

These models differ in order, emphasis, and detail, and each has particular strengths: Livesley's conceptualization has the most theoretical emphasis, linking a PD diagnosis to the functional failure of personality to solve the major life tasks for which it is designed (Wakefield 2006). Parker et al. (2000) developed a promising measure of functioning. Widiger et al.'s model is the most well specified, providing both an established assessment instrument and detailed descriptions of potential problems associated with each facet's extremes. Tyrer et al.'s (2006) model affords the broadest assessment, incorporating multiple information sources and longitudinal assessment.

The models' similarities, however—particularly distinguishing dysfunction and trait assessment, and essential agreement on four of five broad dimensions—are far more important than their differences, and an integrated model could incorporate each models' strengths: A diagnosis of PD—focused on personality-based dysfunctionality—would be recorded on Axis I, whereas individuals' relevant personality traits, that is, the relatively stable characteristics that underlie the Axis I PD diagnosis, would be recorded on Axis II. Initially, diagnosis would be provisional, pending confirmation of the assessed traits' stability and their validity via multiple-source assessment. Rather than the DSM/ICD system, which requires meeting a small number of criteria (currently a mixture of trait manifestations and trait-dysfunction blends), existing psychometrically sound trait assessment measures would be used, and new ones developed, taking advantage of advances in personality theory and assessment, including understandings of personality structure and process (Mroczek & Cooper 2006), cross-cultural generalizability of personality constructs (Ashton & Lee 2005), informant measures (Oltmanns & Turkheimer 2006), written records (Tyrer et al. 2006), and computer adaptive testing (Simms & Clark 2005). Thus, PD trait assessment could evolve as the field matured and could incorporate clinical utility as a development criterion. Assessment of dysfunction needs much more development, but promising starts have been made.

This model has theoretical implications for treatment as well. For example, it suggests that dialectical behavior therapy (Robins et al. 2004) may succeed, at least in part, by sequencing its treatment objectives, first targeting Axis I behaviors that are life threatening, interfere with treatment, and lower quality of life, and then shifting focus to Axis II problems—developing adaptive life skills (e.g., anger management, conflict resolution) and resolving longstanding problematic interpersonal dynamics.

Toward a Unified Model of Axis I–Axis II

No doubt the 1980 separation of PD onto its own Axis II was an important stimulus for launching the current PD research enterprise, and substantial progress has been made in the past 25 years through research largely based on the categorical system in the DSMs. However, as findings cumulate, the validity of the current Axis I–Axis II separation is questioned increasingly. Krueger (2005) called for "a unified model of personality, personality disorders, and clinical disorders" (p. 233); Clark (2005b) argued that basic temperament dimensions provide the basis for personality as well as the development of both Axis I and II disorders, proposing, therefore, that the field work toward a single, hierarchical, integrated framework that would bridge the three domains. Both interdisciplinary work (Rothbart & Posner 2006) and multiple research lines focusing on dimensions of psychopathology (e.g., impulsivity/aggression, sleep disturbance, negative affect, and serotonin dysfunction) without regard to specific diagnoses signal a changing paradigm.

Thus, the integrated PD assessment model described above may be a first step toward an even broader integration: Axis II dimensions may underlie the dysfunctionality of both PD and traditional diagnostic symptom groups recorded on Axis I. A paradigm shift toward a dysfunction-dimensional conceptualization appears to lie in the near future, first for PD, but then for psychopathology in general, with the potential to revolutionize our entire field (Widiger et al. 2005). I urge the field to follow Robert Frost and take this road less traveled by, for that will make all the difference.

SUMMARY POINTS

1. On the basis of the weight of the empirical evidence supporting dimensional approaches to personality disorder diagnosis, serious consideration is being given to switching to a dimensional (from the current categorical) system for Axis II in DSM-V.

2. The five-factor model (FFM) of personality is widely accepted as representing the higher-order structure of both normal and abnormal personality traits. Thus, if a dimensional system is implemented for Axis II in DSM-V, most likely it will be based on some variant of the FFM.

3. Because it is recognized that personality disorder cannot be diagnosed based on extreme personality traits alone, there is increasing interest in assessing personality dysfunction and understanding the link(s) between personality traits and dysfunction.

4. Convergence is modest, at best, between self-report and nonself-report-based assessment of personality and personality disorders. Recent research has documented increased reliability and validity of assessment when multiple sources are used to diagnose personality.

5. Comorbidity both within Axis II and between Axes I and II has been well documented; similarly, personality trait dimensions have been shown to relate moderately

to strongly with both Axis I and Axis II disorders. Converging lines of evidence suggest that personality and psychopathology may have common roots in basic temperament.

6. A definitional assumption has been that personality and PD are enduring, but recent findings have stimulated reconsideration of stability. Specifically, research has established that normal personality becomes more stable over time until at least age 50, and the observed degree of change of personality pathology, when measured dimensionally, appears to be highly similar to that of normal personality. Furthermore, PD criteria have been shown to be a mix of more stable trait dimensions (e.g., low self-worth) and less stable symptomatic behaviors (e.g., self-injury). The lower stability of PD diagnoses (compared with dimensions) may not be simply an artifact of the DSM categorical system, but also may reflect the inclusion of this latter type of criteria.

7. Four strikingly similar models for diagnosing PD have emerged and can be integrated as follows: a *diagnosis* of PD, focused on personality dysfunction, would be recorded on Axis I, whereas the relevant personality traits, that is, the relatively stable characteristics underlying the Axis I PD diagnosis, would be recorded on Axis II. Initial diagnosis would be provisional, pending confirmation of the assessed traits' stability via longitudinal assessment and trait levels through multiple information sources.

8. The described integrated PD assessment model may be a first step toward an even broader integration based on Axis I–Axis II comorbidity patterns. As mentioned in Summary Point 5, abnormal temperament may underlie the dysfunctionality of not only PD but also clinical syndromes traditionally recorded on Axis I. Thus, a paradigm shift toward a two-part conceptualization of psychopathology—dysfunction and dimensional assessment—may lie in the future.

FUTURE ISSUES

1. At some point, perhaps as early as DSM-V, the Axis II PDs will be diagnosed using a dimensional conceptualization, but several key issues remain to be addressed. First, for a dimensional system to have utility in clinical settings, a consensually validated lower-order structure of adaptive and maladaptive personality is needed to capture personality's rich complexity.

2. PD diagnosis is incomplete if only traits are assessed: Personality functioning also must be evaluated. Extreme personality traits are linked empirically with dysfunction and may be inherently maladaptive, but measures of dysfunction that are not—or at least are less—confounded by personality trait content are needed. Thus, exploring the nature of dysfunction should be a field priority.

3. Finally, adaptive and maladaptive personalities are too complex to be assessed fully from a single perspective. More comprehensive understanding of PD will require integration of the common and unique information that is obtained from self-report, well-known informants, clinicians who have an objective view contextualized by a broad understanding of the PD landscape, written records of behavior, and, eventually, laboratory data. Integrating information from these various sources for a fuller understanding of PD will challenge researchers for some years to come.

ACKNOWLEDGMENTS

I wish to thank (*a*) Leigh Wensman for her tireless and ever-cheerful help in searching and obtaining hundreds of articles, compiling and organizing their abstracts, and cross-checking all references, (*b*) the too-many-to-name-individually colleagues who provided chapters, in-press papers, and excellent feedback on an earlier draft, and (*c*) Tom Widiger, in particular, for catalyzing me to rethink the entire final section.

LITERATURE CITED

Abela JRZ, Skitch SA, Auerbach RP, Adams P. 2005. The impact of parental borderline personality disorder on vulnerability to depression in children of affectively ill parents. *J. Personal. Disord.* 19:68–83

Am. Psychiatr. Assoc. 1980. *Diagnostic and Statistical Manual of Mental Disorders-Third Edition (DSM-III).* Washington, DC: Am. Psychiatr. Assoc.

Am. Psychiatr. Assoc. 1994. *Diagnostic and Statistical Manual of Mental Disorders-Fourth Edition (DSM-IV).* Washington, DC: Am. Psychiatr. Assoc.

Am. Psychiatr. Assoc. 2000. *Diagnostic and Statistical Manual of Mental Disorders-Fourth Edition (DSM-IV).* Washington, DC: Am. Psychiatr. Assoc. Text rev.

Ashton MC, Lee K. 2005. The lexical approach to the study of personality structure: toward the identification of cross-culturally replicable dimensions of personality variation. *J. Personal. Disord.* 19:303–8

Axelrod SR, Morgan CA, Southwick SM. 2005. Symptoms of posttraumatic stress disorder and borderline personality disorder in veterans of Operation Desert Storm. *Am. J. Psychiatry* 162:270–75

Bagby RM, Schuller DR, Marshall MB, Ryder AG. 2004. Depressive personality disorder: rates of comorbidity with personality disorders and relations to the five-factor model of personality. *J. Personal. Disord.* 18:542–54

Bagby RM, Costa PT, Widiger TA, Ryder AG, Marshall M. 2005a. DSM-IV personality disorders and the five-factor model of personality: a multi-method examination of domain and facet-level predictions. *Eur. J. Personal.* 19:307–24

Bagby RM, Marshall MB, Georgiades S. 2005b. Dimensional personality traits and the prediction of DSM-IV personality disorder symptom counts in a nonclinical sample. *J. Personal. Disord.* 19:53–67

Bajaj P, Tyrer P. 2005. Managing mood disorders and comorbid personality disorders. *Curr. Opin. Psychiatry* 18:27–31

Ball SA. 2004. Personality traits, disorders, and substance abuse. In *On the Psychobiology of Personality: Essays in Honor of Marvin Zuckerman*, ed. RM Stelmack, pp. 203–22. New York: Elsevier Sci.

Ball SA. 2005. Personality traits, problems, and disorders: clinical applications to substance use disorders. *J. Res. Personal.* 39:84–102

Bank PA, Silk KR. 2001. Axis I and axis II interactions. *Curr. Opin. Psychiatry* 14:137–42

Barasch A, Frances A, Hurt S, Clarkin J, Cohen S. 1985. Stability and distinctness of borderline personality disorder. *Am. J. Psychiatry* 142:1484–86

Bellino S, Patria L, Paradiso E, Di Lorenzo R, Zanon C, et al. 2005. Major depression in patients with borderline personality disorder: a clinical investigation. *Can. J. Psychiatry* 50:234–38

Bienvenu OJ, Stein MB. 2003. Personality and anxiety disorders: a review. *J. Personal. Disord.* 17:139–51

Blashfield RK, Intoccia V. 2000. Growth of the literature on the topic of personality disorders. *Am. J. Psychiatry* 157:472–73

Block J. 2001. Millennial contrarianism: the five-factor approach to personality description 5 years later. *J. Res. Personal.* 35:98–107

Bornovalova MA, Lejuez CW, Daughters SB, Rosenthal MZ, Lynch TR. 2005. Impulsivity as a common process across borderline personality and substance use disorders. *Clin. Psychol. Rev.* 25:790–812

Bornstein RF, Cecero JJ. 2000. Deconstructing dependency in a five-factor world: a meta-analytic review. *J. Personal. Assess.* 74:324–43

Brieger P, Ehrt U, Marneros A. 2003. Frequency of comorbid personality disorders in bipolar and unipolar affective disorders. *Compr. Psychiatry* 44:28–34

Brieger P, Ehrt U, Bloeink R, Marneros A. 2002. Consequences of comorbid personality disorders in major depression. *J. Nerv. Ment. Disord.* 190:304–9

Brieger P, Sommer S, Blöink R, Marneros A. 2000. The relationship between five-factor personality measurements and ICD-10 personality disorder dimensions: results from a sample of 229 subjects. *J. Personal. Disord.* 14:282–90

Casillas A, Clark LA. 2002. Dependency, impulsivity, and self-harm: traits hypothesized to underlie the association between Cluster B personality and substance abuse disorders. *J. Personal. Disord.* 16:424–36

Caspi A, Roberts BW, Shiner RL. 2005. Personality development: stability and change. *Annu. Rev. Psychol.* 56:453–84

Cassin SE, von Ranson KM. 2005. Personality and eating disorders: a decade in review. *Clin. Psychol. Rev.* 25:895–916

Chanen AM, Jackson HJ, McGorry PD, Allot KA, Clarkson V, et al. 2004. Two-year stability of personality disorder in older adolescent outpatients. *J. Personal. Disord.* 18:526–41

Clark LA. 1993. *Schedule for Nonadaptive and Adaptive Personality*. Minneapolis, MN: Univ. Minnesota Press

Clark LA. 2005a. Stability and change in personality pathology: revelations of three longitudinal studies. *J. Personal. Disord.* 19:525–32

Clark LA. 2005b. Temperament as a unifying basis for personality and psychopathology. *J. Abnorm. Psychol.* 114:505–21

Clark LA, Livesley WJ, Morey LC. 1997. Personality disorder assessment: the challenge of construct validity. *J. Personal. Disord.* 11:205–31

Cloninger CR. 1987. A systematic method for clinical description and classification of personality variants: a proposal. *Arch. Gen. Psychiatry* 44:573–88

Cloninger CR, Przybeck TR, Svrakic DM, Wetzel RD. 1994. *The Temperament and Character Inventory TCI: A Guide to Its Development and Use*. St. Louis, MO: Washington Univ. 1st ed.

Cloninger CR, Svrakic DM, Przybeck TR. 1993. A psychobiological model of temperament and character. *Arch. Gen. Psychiatry* 50:975–90

Coker LA, Samuel DB, Widiger TA. 2002. Maladaptive personality functioning within the Big Five and the FFM. *J. Personal. Disord.* 16:385–401

Costa PTJ, McCrae RR. 1992. *Revised NEO Personality Inventory: Professional Manual*. Odessa, FL: Psychol. Assess. Resour.

Daneluzzo E, Stratta P, Rossi A. 2005. The contribution of temperament and character to schizotypy multidimensionality. *Comp. Psychiatry* 46:50–55

Davids E, Gastpar M. 2005. Attention deficit hyperactivity disorder and borderline personality disorder. *Prog. Neuropsychopharm. Biol. Psychiatry* 29:865–77

De Clercq B, De Fruyt F. 2003. Personality disorder symptoms in adolescence: a five-factor perspective. *J. Personal. Disord.* 17:269–92

De Clercq B, De Fruyt F, Van Leeuwen K, Mervielde I. 2006. The structure of maladaptive personality traits in childhood: a step toward an integrative developmental perspective for *DSM-V. J. Abnorm. Psychol.* 80(4):In press

Denys D, Tenney N, van Megen HJG, de Geus F, Westenberg HGM. 2004. Axis I and II comorbidity in a large sample of patients with obsessive-compulsive disorder. *J. Affect. Disord.* 80:155–62

Diener MJ, Hilsenroth MJ. 2004. Multimethod validity assessment of the SWAP-200 Dysphoric Q-Factor. *J. Nerv. Ment. Dis.* 192:479–86

Digman JM. 1997. Higher-order factors of the big five. *J. Personal. Soc. Psychol.* 73:1246–56

Dowson J, Bazanis E, Rogers R, Prevost A, Taylor P, et al. 2004. Impulsivity in patients with borderline personality disorder. *Comp. Psychiatry* 45:29–36

Durbin C, Klein DN. 2006. Ten-year stability of personality disorders among outpatients with mood disorders. *J. Abnorm. Psychol.* 115:75–84

Edens JF, Marcus DK, Lilienfeld SO, Poythress NGJ. 2006. Psychopathic, not psychopath: taxometric evidence for the dimensional structure of psychopathy. *J. Abnorm. Psychol.* 115:131–44

Eysenck SBG, Eysenck HJ, Barrett P. 1985. A revised version of the psychoticism scale. *Personal. Indiv. Diff.* 6: 21–29

Farabaugh A, Fava M, Mischoulon D, Sklarsky K, Petersen T, et al. 2005. Relationships between major depressive disorder and comorbid anxiety and personality disorders. *Compr. Psychiatry* 46:266–71

Fassino S, DaGa GA, Delsedime N, Rogna L, Baffio S. 2004. Quality of life and personality disorder in heroin abusers. *Drug Alcohol Depend.* 76:73–80

Favaro A, Zanetti T, Tenconi E, Degortes D, Ronzan A, et al. 2005. The relationship between temperament and impulsive behaviors in eating disordered subjects. *Eating Disord. J. Treat. Prevent.* 13:61–70

First MB, Gibbon M, Spitzer RL, Williams JBW, Benjamin LS. 1997. *Structured Clinical Interview for DSM-IV Axis II Personality Disorders Self-Report*. Washington, DC: Am. Psychiatr. Press

Flynn PM, Craddock SG, Luckey JW, Hubbard RL, Dunteman GH. 1996. Comorbidity of antisocial personality and mood disorders among psychoactive substance-dependent treatment clients. *J. Personal. Disord.* 10:56–67

Fossati A, Beauchaine TP, Grazioli F, Carretta I, Cortinovis F, et al. 2005. A latent structure analysis of *Diagnostic and Statistical Manual of Mental Disorders, Fourth Edition*, narcissistic personality disorder criteria. *Comp. Psychiatry* 46:361–67

Frances A. 1993. Dimensional diagnosis of personality: not whether, but when and which. *Psychol. Inquiry* 4:110–11

Furnam A, Crump J. 2005. Personality traits, types, and disorders: an examination of the relationship between three self-report measures. *Eur. J. Personal.* 19:167–84

Gabbard GO. 2005. Editorial: personality disorders come of age. *Am. J. Psychiatry* 162:833–35

Garno JL, Goldberg JF, Ramirez PM, Ritzler BA. 2005. Bipolar disorder with comorbid cluster B personality disorder features: impact on suicidality. *J. Clin. Psychiatry* 66:339–45

Goodwin RD, Brook JS, Cohen P. 2005. Panic attacks and the risk of personality disorder. *Psychol. Med.* 35:227–35

Grant BF, Hasin DS, Stinson FS, Dawson DA, Chou SP, et al. 2005b. Co-occurrence of 12-month mood and anxiety disorders and personality disorders in the U.S.: results from the national epidemiologic survey on alcohol and related conditions. *J. Psychiatr. Res.* 39:1–9

Assessed personality and personality disorder repeatedly over 10-year period and found stability of personality disorder comparable to that of anxiety disorder diagnoses and normal personality traits.

Grant BF, Stinson FS, Dawson DA, Chou SP, Ruan WJ. 2005a. Co-occurrence of DSM-IV personality disorders in the United States: results from the National Epidemiologic Survey on Alcohol and Related Conditions. *Comp. Psychiatry* 46:1–5

Grant JE. 2004. Co-occurrence of personality disorders in persons with kleptomania: a preliminary investigation. *J. Am. Acad. Psychiatry Law* 32:395–98

Grilo CM, Becker DF, Edell WS, McGlashan TH. 2001. Stability and change of DSM-III-R personality disorder dimensions in adolescents followed up 2 years after psychiatric hospitalization. *Compr. Psychiatry* 42:364–68

Grilo CM, McGlashan TH, Skodol AE. 2000. Stability and course of personality disorders: the need to consider comorbidities and continuities between Axis I psychiatric disorders and Axis II personality disorders. *Psychiatr. Q.* 71:291–307

Grilo CM, Sanislow CA, Gunderson JG, Pagano ME, Yen S, et al. 2004. Two-year stability and change of schizotypal, borderline, avoidant, and obsessive-compulsive personality disorders. *J. Consult. Clin. Psychol.* 72:767–75

Grilo CM, Sanislow CA, Gunderson JG, Stout RL, Shea MT, et al. 2003. Do eating disorders co-occur with personality disorders? Comparison groups matter. *Int. J. Eating Disord.* 33:155–64

Grilo CM, Sanislow CA, Shea MT, Skodol AE, Stout RL, et al. 2005. Two-year prospective naturalistic study of remission from major depressive disorder as a function of personality disorder comorbidity. *J. Consult. Clin. Psychol.* 73:78–85

Haigler ED, Widiger TA. 2001. Experimental manipulation of NEO PI-R items. *J. Personal. Assess.* 77:339–58

Halmi KA. 2005. Obsessive-compulsive personality disorder and eating disorders. *Eat. Disord. J. Treat. Prevent.* 13:85–92

Haslam N. 2003. The dimensional view of personality disorders: a review of taxometric evidence. *Clin. Psychol. Rev.* 23:75–93

Hawton K, Houston K, Haw C, Townsend E, Harriss L. 2003. Comorbidity of axis I and axis II disorders in patients who attempted suicide. *Am. J. Psychiatry* 160:1494–500

Hettema JM, Prescott CA, Kendler KS. 2003. The effects of anxiety, substance use and conduct disorders on risk of major depressive disorder. *Psychol. Med.* 33:1423–32

Hill J, Fudge H, Harrington R, Pickles A, Rutter M. 2000. Complementary approaches to the assessment of personality disorder: the Personality Assessment Schedule and Adult Personality Functioning Assessment compared. *Br. J. Psychiatry Suppl.* 17:434–39

Hong JP, Samuels J, Bienvenu OJ, Hsu F, Eaton WW, et al. 2005. The longitudinal relationship between personality disorder dimensions and global functioning in a community-residing population. *Psychol. Med.* 35:891–95

Hooker K, McAdams DP. 2003. Personality reconsidered: a new agenda for aging research. *J. Gerontol. B Psychol. Sci. Soc. Sci.* 58B:P296–304

Huprich SK. 2003. Evaluating facet-level predictions and construct validity of depressive personality disorder. *J. Personal. Disord.* 17:219–32

Jablensky A. 2002. The classification of personality disorders: critical review and need for rethinking. *Psychopathology* 35:112–16

James W. 1950 (1890). *The Principles of Psychology*. New York: Dover

Jang KL, Vernon PA, Livesley WJ. 2000. Personality disorder traits, family environment, and alcohol misuse: a multivariate behavioural genetic analysis. *Addiction* 95:873–88

Johnson JG, Cohen P, Kasen S, Skodol AE, Hamagami F, et al. 2000a. Age-related change in personality disorder trait levels between early adolescence and adulthood: a community-based longitudinal investigation. *Acta Psychiatr. Scand.* 102:265–75

Johnson JG, First MB, Cohen P, Skodol AE, Kasen S, et al. 2005. Adverse outcomes associated with personality disorder not otherwise specified in a community sample. *Am. J. Psychiatry* 162:1926–32

Johnson JG, Rabkin JG, Williams JBW, Remien RH, Gorman JM. 2000b. Difficulties in interpersonal relationships associated with personality disorders and Axis I disorders: a community-based longitudinal investigation. *J. Personal. Disord.* 14:42–56

Kelsey RM, Ornduff SR, McCann CM, Reiff S. 2001. Psychophysiological characteristics of narcissism during active and passive coping. *Psychophysiology* 38:292–303

Kendler KS, Prescott CA, Myers J, Neale MC. 2003. The structure of genetic and environmental risk factors for common psychiatric and substance use disorders in men and women. *Arch. Gen. Psychiatry* 60:929–37

Klein DN, Schwartz JE. 2002. The relation between depressive symptoms and borderline personality disorder features over time in dysthymic disorder. *J. Personal. Disord.* 16:523–35

Klonsky ED, Oltmanns TF, Turkheimer E. 2002. Informant-reports of personality disorder: relation to self-reports and future research directions. *Clin. Psychol. Sci. Pract.* 9:300–11

Krueger RF. 2005. Continuity of Axes I and II: toward a unified model of personality, personality disorders, and clinical disorders. *J. Personal. Disord.* 19:233–61

Krueger RF, Hicks BM, Patrick CJ, Carlson SR, Iacono WG, McGue M. 2002. Etiologic connections among substance dependence, antisocial behavior, and personality: modeling the externalizing spectrum. *J. Abnorm. Psychol.* 111:411–24

Krueger RF, Markon KE, Patrick CJ, Iacono W. 2005. Externalizing psychopathology in adulthood: a dimensional-spectrum conceptualization and its implications for *DSM-V*. *J. Abnorm. Psychol.* 114:537–50

Lee HJ, Telch MJ. 2005. Autogenous/reactive obsessions and their relationship with OCD symptoms and schizotypal personality features. *J. Anxiety Disord.* 19:793–805

Lenzenweger MF, Johnson MD, Willett JB. 2004. Individual growth curve analysis illuminates stability and change in personality disorder features: the longitudinal study of personality disorders. *Arch. Gen. Psychiatry* 61:1015–24

Livesley WJ. 2003. Diagnostic dilemmas in classifying personality disorder. In *Advancing DSM: Dilemmas in Psychiatric Diagnosis*, ed. KA Phillips, MB First, HA Pincus, pp. 153–90. Washington, DC: Am. Psychiatr. Assoc.

Livesley WJ. 2005. Behavioral and molecular genetic contributions to a dimensional classification of personality disorder. *J. Personal. Disord.* 19:131–55

Livesley WJ, Jackson DN. 2006. *Manual for the Dimensional Assessment of Personality Pathology*. Port Huron, MI: Sigma. In press

Livesley WJ, Jang KL. 2000. Toward an empirically based classification of personality disorder. *J. Personal. Disord.* 14:137–51

Livesley WJ, Jang KL, Thordarson DS. 2005. Etiological relationships between eating disorder symptoms and dimensions of personality disorder. *Eat. Disord. J. Treat. Prevent.* 13:25–35

Livesley WJ, Schroeder ML, Jackson DN, Jang KL. 1994. Categorical distinctions in the study of personality disorder: implications for classification. *J. Abnorm. Psychol.* 103:6–17

Looper KJ, Paris J. 2000. What dimensions underlie Cluster B personality disorders? *Comp. Psychiatry* 41:432–37

Loranger AW, Lenzenweger MF, Garner AF, Susman VL. 1991. Trait-state artifacts and the diagnosis of personality disorders. *Arch. Gen. Psychiatry* 48:720–28

Lynam DR, Caspi A, Moffitt TE, Raine A, Loeber R, et al. 2005. Adolescent psychopathy and the big five: results from two samples. *J. Abnorm. Child Psychol.* 33:431–43

Reviews various factors that distinguish Axis I clinical syndromes from Axis II personality disorders; argues that these disorders are more similar than different.

Examines whether personality disorders are distinct from each other and from normal personality; analyzes arguments for placing personality disorders and clinical syndromes on different axes.

Lynam DR, Widiger TA. 2001. Using the five-factor model to represent the *DSM-IV* personality disorders: an expert consensus approach. *J. Abnorm. Psychol.* 110:401–12

Maggini C, Ampollini P, Marchesi C, Gariboldi S, Cloninger CR. 2000. Relationships between Tridimensional Personality Questionnaire dimensions and *DSM-III-R* personality traits in Italian adolescents. *Comp. Psychiatry* 41:426–31

Massion AO, Dyck IR, Shea MT, Phillips KA, Warshaw MG, et al. 2002. Personality disorders and time to remission in generalized anxiety disorder, social phobia and panic disorder. *Arch. Gen. Psychiatry* 59:434–40

Marinangeli MG, Butti G, Scinto A, Di Cicco L, Petruzzi C, et al. 2000. Patterns of comorbidity among *DSM-III-R* personality disorders. *Psychopathology* 33:69–74

Martin-Avellan LE, McGauley G, Campbell C, Fonagy P. 2005. Using the SWAP-200 in a personality-disordered forensic population: Is it valid, reliable and useful? *Crim. Behav. Ment. Health* 15:28–45

McGlashan TH, Grilo CM, Sanislow CA, Ralevski E, Morey LC, et al. 2005. Two-year prevalence and stability of individual DSM-IV criteria for schizotypal borderline avoidant and obsessive-compulsive personality disorders: toward a hybrid model of Axis II disorders. *Am. J. Psychiatry* 162:883–89

McGlashan TH, Grilo CM, Skodol AE, Gunderson JG, Shea MT, et al. 2000. The Collaborative Longitudinal Personality Disorders Study: baseline Axis I/II and II/II diagnostic co-occurrence. *Acta Psychiatr. Scand.* 102:256–64

Mervielde I, De Clercq B, De Fruyt F, Van Leeuwen K. 2005. Temperament, personality, and developmental psychopathology as childhood antecedents of personality disorders. *J. Personal. Disord.* 19:171–201

Meyer GJ. 2002. Implications of information-gathering methods for a refined taxonomy of psychopathology. In *Rethinking the DSM: A Psychological Perspective*, ed. LE Beutler, ML Malik, pp. 69–105. Washington, DC: Am. Psychol. Assoc.

Miller JD, Bagby RM, Pilkonis PA. 2005a. A comparison of the validity of the Five-Factor Model (FFM) personality disorder prototypes using FFM self-report and interview measures. *Psychol. Assess.* 17:497–500

Miller JD, Bagby RM, Pilkonis PA, Reynolds SK, Lynam DR. 2005b. A simplified technique for scoring DSM-IV personality disorders with the Five-Factor Model. *Assessment* 12:404–15

Miller JD, Reynolds SK, Pilkonis PA. 2004. The validity of the Five-Factor Model prototypes for personality disorders in two clinical samples. *Psychol. Assess.* 16:310–22

Millon T. 2002. Assessment is not enough: the SPA should participate in constructing a comprehensive clinical science of personality. *J. Personal. Assess.* 78:209–18

Milton J, McCartney M, Duggan C, Evans C, Collins M, et al. 2005. Beauty in the eye of the beholder? How high security hospital psychopathically disordered patients rate their own interpersonal behavior. *J. Forensic Psychiatry Psychol.* 16:552–65

Mitropoulou V, Trestman RL, New AS, Flory JD, Silverman JM, Siever LJ. 2003. Neurobiologic function and temperament in subjects with personality disorders. *CNS Spectrums* 8:725–30

Morey LC, Gunderson JG, Quigley BD, Shea MT, Skodol AE, et al. 2002. The representation of borderline, avoidant, obsessive-compulsive, and schizotypal personality disorders by the five-factor model. *J. Personal. Disord.* 16:215–34

Morey LC, Hopwood CJ, Gunderson JG, Zanarini MC, Skodol AE, et al. 2006. *Comparison of Diagnostic Models for Personality Disorder*. Submitted

Mroczek DK, Cooper ML. 2006. Overview of the Proceedings of the 2005 Meeting of the Association of Research in Personality. *J. Res. Personal.* 40:1–4

Documents differential stability in PD criteria over two years; formulates notion that personality disorders are hybrids of traits and symptomatic behaviors.

Mulder RT. 2002. Personality pathology and treatment outcome in major depression: a review. *Am. J. Psychiatry* 159:359–71

Mulder RT, Joyce PR. 2002. Relationship of temperament and behavior measures to the prolactin response to fenfluramine in depressed men. *Psychiatry Res.* 109:221–28

Mulder RT, Joyce PR, Sullivan PF, Bulik CM, Carter FA. 1999. The relationship among three models of personality psychopathology: *DSM-III–R* personality disorder, *TCI* scores and *DSQ* defences. *Psychol. Med.* 29:943–51

Narud K, Dahl AA. 2002. Quality of life in personality and personality disorders. *Curr. Opin. Psychiatry* 15:131–33

O'Connor BP. 2002. The search for dimensional structure differences between normality and abnormality: a statistical review of published data on personality and psychopathology. *J. Personal. Soc. Psychol.* 83:962–82

O'Connor BP. 2005. A search for consensus on the dimensional structure of personality disorders. *J. Clin. Psychol.* 61:323–45

Ogrodniczuk JS, Piper WE, Joyce AS, McCallum M. 2001. Using DSM Axis II information to predict outcome in short-term individual psychotherapy. *J. Personal. Disord.* 15:110–22

Oltmanns TF, Turkheimer E. 2006. Perceptions of self and others regarding pathological personality traits. In *Personality and Psychopathology: Building Bridges*, ed. RF Krueger, J Tackett, pp. 71–111. New York: Guilford

Ozkan M, Altindag A. 2005. Comorbid personality disorders in subjects with panic disorder: Do personality disorders increase clinical severity? *Comp. Psychiatry* 46:20–26

Paris J. 2005. The diagnosis of borderline personality disorder: problematic but better than the alternatives. *Ann. Clin. Psychiatry* 17:41–46

Parker G, Both L, Olley A, Hadzi-Pavlovic D, Irvine P, et al. 2002. Defining disordered personality functioning. *J. Personal. Disord.* 16:503–22

Parker G, Hadzi-Pavlovic D, Both L, Kumar S, Wilhelm K, Olley A. 2004. Measuring disordered personality functioning: to love and to work reprised. *Acta Psychiatr. Scand.* 110:230–39

Parker G, Hadzi-Pavlovic D, Wilhelm K. 2000. Modeling and measuring the personality disorders. *J. Personal. Disord.* 14:189–98

Pfohl B, Blum N, Zimmerman M. 1995. *Structured Interview for DSM-IV Personality SIDP-IV.* Iowa City: Univ. Iowa Press

Pietrzak RH, Petry NM. 2005. Antisocial personality disorder is associated with increased severity of gambling, medical, drug and psychiatric problems among treatment-seeking pathological gamblers. *Addiction* 100:1183–93

Reich J. 2003. The effects of Axis II disorders on the outcome of treatment of anxiety and unipolar depressive disorders: a review. *J. Personal. Disord.* 17:387–405

Reynolds SK, Clark LA. 2001. Predicting personality disorder dimensions from domains and facets of the five-factor model. *J. Personal.* 69:199–222

Roberts BW, DelVecchio WF. 2000. The rank-order consistency of personality traits from childhood to old age: a quantitative review of longitudinal studies. *Psychol. Bull.* 126:3–25

Robins CJ, Schmidt H, Linehan MM. 2004. Dialectical behavior therapy: synthesizing radical acceptance with skillful means. In *Mindfulness and Acceptance: Expanding the Cognitive-Behavioral Tradition*, ed. SC Hayes, VM Follette, MM Linehan, pp. 30–44. New York: Guilford

Robins RW, Fraley RC, Roberts BW, Trzesniewski KH. 2001. A longitudinal study of personality change in young adulthood. *J. Personal.* 69:617–40

Summarizes multiple studies systematically exploring self-informant agreement. Contributes to the growing understanding that valid PD assessment must be multimodal.

Rothbart MK, Posner MI. 2006. Temperament, attention, and developmental psychopathology. In *Handbook of Developmental Psychopathology*, ed. D Cicchetti, DJ Cohen, pp. 466–501. New York: Wiley

Rothschild L, Cleland C, Haslam N, Zimmerman M. 2003. A taxometric study of borderline personality disorder. *J. Abnorm. Psychol.* 112:657–66

Samuel DB, Widiger TA. 2004. Clinicians' personality descriptions of prototypic personality disorders. *J. Personal. Disord.* 18:286–308

Samuel DB, Widiger TA. 2006. Clinicians' judgments of clinical utility: a comparison of *DSM-IV* and Five Factor Models. *J. Abnorm. Psychol.* 115:298–308

Sansone RA, Levitt JL, Sansone LA. 2005. The prevalence of personality disorders among those with eating disorders. *Eat. Disord. J. Treat. Prevent.* 13:7–21

Saulsman LM, Page AC. 2004. The five-factor model and personality disorder empirical literature: a meta-analytic review. *Clin. Psychol. Rev.* 23:1055–85

Schiavone P, Dorz S, Conforti D, Scarso C, Borgherini G. 2004. Co-morbidity of DSM-IV personality disorders in unipolar and bipolar affective disorders: a comparative study. *Psychol. Rep.* 95:121–28

Shea MT. 1992. Some characteristics of the Axis II criteria sets and their implications for assessment of personality disorders. *J. Personal. Disord.* 6:377–81

Shea MT, Stout R, Gunderson J, Morey LC, Grilo CM, et al. 2002. Short-term diagnostic stability of schizotypal borderline avoidant and obsessive-compulsive personality disorders. *Am. J. Psychiatry* 159:2036–41

Shea MT, Stout RL, Yen S, Pagano ME, Skodol AE, et al. 2004. Associations in the course of personality disorders and Axis I disorders over time. *J. Abnorm. Psychol.* 113:499–508

Shea MT, Yen S. 2003. Stability as a distinction between Axis I and Axis II disorders. *J. Personal. Disord.* 17:373–86

Shedler J, Westen D. 2004. Dimensions of personality pathology: an alternative to the Five-Factor Model. *Am. J. Psychiatry* 161:1743–54

Shiner RL. 2005. A developmental perspective on personality disorders: lessons from research on normal personality development in childhood and adolescence. *J. Personal. Disord.* 19:202–10

Simms LJ, Clark LA. 2005. Validation of a computerized adaptive version of the Schedule for Nonadaptive and Adaptive Personality (SNAP). *Psychol. Assess.* 17:28–43

Skodol AE, Gunderson JG, McGlashan TH, Dyck IR, Stout RL, et al. 2002. Functional impairment in patients with schizotypal, borderline, avoidant, or obsessive-compulsive personality disorder. *Am. J. Psychiatry* 159:276–83

Skodol AE, Gunderson JG, Shea MT, McGlashan TH, Morey LC, et al. 2005a. The Collaborative Longitudinal Personality Disorders Study (CLPS). *J. Personal. Disord.* 19:487–504

Skodol AE, Oldham JM, Bender DS, Dyck IR, Stout RL, et al. 2005b. Dimensional representations of DSM-IV personality disorders: relationships to functional impairment. *Am. J. Psychiatry* 162:1919–25

Skodol AE, Grilo CM, Pagano ME, Bender DS, Gunderson JG, et al. 2005c. Effects of personality disorders on functioning and well-being in major depressive disorder. *J. Psychiatr. Pract.* 11:363–68

Skodol AE, Pagano ME, Bender DS, Shea MT, Gunderson JG, et al. 2005d. Stability of functional impairment in patients with schizotypal, borderline, avoidant, or obsessive-compulsive personality disorder over two years. *Psychol. Med.* 35:443–51

Smith DJ, Muir WJ, Blackwood DHR. 2005. Borderline personality disorder characteristics in young adults with recurrent mood disorders: a comparison of bipolar and unipolar depression. *J. Affect. Disord.* 87:17–23

Examines temporal stability of PD in naturalistic longitudinal studies and compares it to that of depression and anxiety. Contributes to reconceptualization of PD.

Examines stability of functional impairment in the four CLPS PD diagnoses over the first two years of the study.

Smith TL, Benjamin LS. 2002. The functional impairment associated with personality disorders. *Curr. Opin. Psychiatry* 15:135–41

Sprock J. 2002. A comparative study of the dimensions and facets of the five-factor model in the diagnosis of cases of personality disorder. *J. Personal. Disord.* 16:402–23

Sprock J. 2003. Dimensional versus categorical classification of prototypic and nonprototypic cases of personality disorder. *J. Clin. Psychol.* 59:991–1014

Trobst KK, Ayearst LE, Salekin RT. 2004. Where is the personality in personality disorder assessment? A comparison across four sets of personality disorder scales. *Multivar. Behav. Res.* 39:231–71

Trull TJ. 2005. Dimensional models of personality disorder: coverage and cutoffs. *J. Personal. Disord.* 19:262–82

Trull TJ, Durrett CA. 2005. Categorical and dimensional models of personality disorder. *Annu. Rev. Clin. Psychol.* 1:355–80

Trull TJ, Sher KJ, Minks-Brown C, Durbin J, Burr R. 2000. Borderline personality disorder and substance use disorders: a review and integration. *Clin. Psychol. Rev.* 20:235–53

Trull TJ, Widiger TA, Burr R. 2001. A structured interview for the assessment of the Five-Factor Model of personality: facet-level relations to the Axis II personality disorders. *J. Personal.* 69:175–98

Tyrer P. 2005. The problem of severity in the classification of personality disorder. *J. Personal. Disord.* 19:309–14

Tyrer P, Coombs N, Ibrahimi F, Mathilakath A, Bajaj P, et al. 2006. Critical developments in the assessment of personality disorder. *Br. J. Psychiatry* S49:In press

Tyrer P, Seivewright H, Johnson T. 2003. The core elements of neurosis: mixed anxiety-depression cothymia and personality disorder. *J. Personal. Disord.* 17:129–38

Tyrer P, Seivewright H, Johnson T. 2004. The Nottingham Study of Neurotic Disorder: predictors of 12-year outcome of dysthymic, panic and generalized anxiety disorder. *Psychol. Med.* 34:1385–94

Vaidya JG, Gray EK, Haig J, Watson D. 2002. On the temporal stability of personality: evidence for differential stability and the role of life experiences. *J. Personal. Soc. Psychol.* 83:1469–84

van Hanswijck de Jonge P, van Furth EF, Lacey JH, Waller G. 2003. The prevalence of *DSM-IV* personality pathology among individuals with bulimia nervosa, binge eating disorder and obesity. *Psychol. Med.* 33:1311–17

Vasey MW, Kotov R, Frick PJ, Loney BR. 2005. The latent structure of psychopathy in youth: a taxometric investigation. *J. Abnorm. Child Psychol.* 33:411–29

Verheul R. 2005. Clinical utility of dimensional models for personality pathology. *J. Personal. Disord.* 19:283–302

Verheul R, Kranzler HR, Poling J, Tennen H, Ball S, Rounsaville BJ. 2000. Co-occurrence of Axis I and Axis II disorders in substance abusers. *Acta Psychiatr. Scand.* 101:110–18

Verheul R, Widiger TA. 2004. A meta-analysis of the prevalence and usage of the Personality Disorder Not Otherwise Specified (PDNOS) diagnosis. *J. Personal. Disord.* 18:309–19

Vitousek KM, Stumpf RE. 2005. Difficulties in the assessment of personality traits and disorders in eating-disordered individuals. *Eat. Disord. J. Treat. Prevent.* 13:37–60

Wakefield JC. 2006. Personality disorder as harmful dysfunction: *DSM*'s cultural deviance criterion reconsidered. *J. Personal. Disord.* 20:157–69

Walters P, Moran P, Choudhury P, Lee T, Mann A. 2004. Screening for personality disorder: a comparison of personality disorder assessment by patients and informants. *Int. J. Methods Psychiatr. Res.* 13:34–39

Warner MB, Morey LC, Finch JF, Gunderson JG, Skodol AE, et al. 2004. The longitudinal relationship of personality traits and disorders. *J. Abnorm. Psychol.* 113:217–27

Watson DB, Clark LA. 2006. Clinical diagnosis at the crossroads. *Clin. Psychol. Sci. Practice*. In press

Westen D, Dutra L, Shedler J. 2005. Assessing adolescent personality pathology. *Br. J. Psychiatry* 186:227–38

Westen D, Shedler J. 1999a. Revising and assessing axis II, part I: developing a clinically and empirically valid assessment method. *Am. J. Psychiatry* 156:258–72

Westen D, Shedler J. 1999b. Revising and assessing axis II, part II: toward an empirically based and clinically useful classification of personality disorders. *Am. J. Psychiatry* 156:273–85

Westermeyer J, Thuras P. 2005. Association of antisocial personality disorder and substance disorder morbidity in a clinical sample. *Am. J. Drug Alcohol Abuse* 31:93–110

Whiteside SP, Lynam DR. 2001. The five-factor model and impulsivity: using a structural model of personality to understand impulsivity. *Personal. Indiv. Diff.* 30:669–89

Widiger TA. 2003. Personality disorder and Axis I psychopathology: the problematic boundary of Axis I and Axis II. *J. Personal. Disord.* 17:90–108

Widiger TA, Samuel DB. 2005. Diagnostic categories or dimensions? A question for the *Diagnostic and Statistical Manual of Mental Disorders-Fifth Edition*. *J. Abnorm. Psychol.* 114:494–504

Widiger TA, Simonsen E. 2005. Alternative dimensional models of personality disorder: finding a common ground. *J. Personal. Disord.* 19:110–30

Widiger TA, Simonsen E, Krueger R, Livesley W, Verheul R. 2005. Personality disorder research agenda for the DSM-V. *J. Personal. Disord.* 19:315–38

Widiger TA, Trull TJ, Clarkin JF, Sanderson C, Costa PTJ. 2002. A description of the DSM-IV personality disorders with the five-factor model of personality. In *Personality Disorders and the Five-Factor Model of Personality*, ed. PT Costa Jr, TA Widiger, pp. 89–99. Washington, DC: Am. Psychol. Assoc. 2nd ed.

Zanarini MC, Frankenburg FR, Hennen J, Reich DB, Silk KR. 2005. The McLean Study of Adult Development (MSAD): overview and implications of the first six years of prospective follow-up. *J. Personal. Disord.* 19:505–23

Zimmerman M. 1994. Diagnosing personality disorders: a review of issues and research models. *Arch. Gen. Psychiatry* 51:225–45

Zimmerman M, Rothschild L, Chelminski I. 2005. The prevalence of *DSM-IV* personality disorders in psychiatric outpatients. *Am. J. Psychiatry* 162:1911–18

Reviews 18 dimensional models proposed for Axis II and demonstrates that they could be integrated in a common four- or five-factor framework.

Documents assessment issues that remained unresolved with regard to PD diagnosis, including test-retest reliability and poor convergent validity of PD measures.

RELATED RESOURCES

Costa PT Jr, Widiger TA, eds. 2002. *Personality Disorders and the Five-factor Model of Personality*. Washington, DC: Am. Psychol. Assoc. 2nd ed.

Krueger RF, Tackett JL, eds. 2006. *Personality and Psychopathology*. New York: Guilford

Livesley WJ, ed. 2001. *Handbook of Personality Disorders*. New York: Guilford

Social Cognitive Neuroscience: A Review of Core Processes

Matthew D. Lieberman

Department of Psychology, University of California, Los Angeles, Los Angeles, California 90095-1563; email: lieber@ucla.edu

Annu. Rev. Psychol. 2007. 58:259–89

First published online as a Review in Advance on September 26, 2006

The *Annual Review of Psychology* is online at http://psych.annualreviews.org

This article's doi: 10.1146/annurev.psych.58.110405.085654

Key Words

theory of mind, empathy, emotion regulation, self-control, mirror neurons, social cognition, social neuroscience, automaticity, neuroeconomics

Abstract

Social cognitive neuroscience examines social phenomena and processes using cognitive neuroscience research tools such as neuroimaging and neuropsychology. This review examines four broad areas of research within social cognitive neuroscience: (*a*) understanding others, (*b*) understanding oneself, (*c*) controlling oneself, and (*d*) the processes that occur at the interface of self and others. In addition, this review highlights two core-processing distinctions that can be neurocognitively identified across all of these domains. The distinction between automatic versus controlled processes has long been important to social psychological theory and can be dissociated in the neural regions contributing to social cognition. Alternatively, the differentiation between internally-focused processes that focus on one's own or another's mental interior and externally-focused processes that focus on one's own or another's visible features and actions is a new distinction. This latter distinction emerges from social cognitive neuroscience investigations rather than from existing psychological theories demonstrating that social cognitive neuroscience can both draw on and contribute to social psychological theory.

Contents

INTRODUCTION

Social cognitive neuroscience is a burgeoning interdisciplinary field combining the tools of cognitive neuroscience with questions and theories from various social sciences including social psychology, economics, and political science. Although research on the biological correlates of social processes has been ongoing for decades (Cacioppo & Bernston 1992), this approach has gone through a period of rapid expansion with the advent of functional neuroimaging (Adolphs 2003, Ochsner & Lieberman 2001). Since the time of the first conference on social cognitive neuroscience (the UCLA Conference on Social Cognitive Neuroscience, April 2001) until the present,

there has been an enormous growth in the field as evidenced by increasing numbers of research articles, edited volumes, and academic meetings devoted to social cognitive neuroscience. An Internet search using the words "social cognitive neuroscience" yielded 53 hits in early 2001, whereas today the same search yields more than 30,000 hits. Moreover, in the past year, two new journals have been created (*Social Cognitive and Affective Neuroscience* and *Social Neuroscience*) to provide outlets for this work.

Although selective reviews of social cognitive neuroscience have been written in the past few years (Blakemore et al. 2004, Ochsner 2004), no comprehensive review has captured the breadth of the area. Thus, first and foremost, this review covers the broad themes and main findings across numerous areas of social cognitive neuroscience research. The review is divided into four subsections focusing on (*a*) understanding others, (*b*) understanding oneself, (*c*) controlling oneself, and (*d*) the processes that occur at the interface of self and others. Unfortunately, space constraints prevent this review from covering some topics relevant to social cognitive neuroscience, such as emotion recognition and face processing (see Adolphs 2002, Haxby et al. 2002).

The second goal of this review is to identify core-processing distinctions that may cut across the different domains of social cognition and provide a framework for organizing general principles of social cognitive neuroscience. Two core-processing distinctions are examined throughout this review: (*a*) automatic versus controlled processes and (*b*) internally-focused versus externally-focused processes.

Dual-process models of automatic and controlled social cognition have been proposed in nearly every domain of social psychology (Chaiken & Trope 1999). Controlled processes (e.g., rehearsing a nine-digit number) are associated with awareness, intention, effort, and the capacity for interruption (Wegner & Bargh 1998). In contrast, automatic processes (e.g., "Juliet" spontaneously

Table 1 Features associated with X- and C-systems posited to support reflexive (analogous to automatic) and reflective (analogous to controlled) processes. Adapted from Satpute & Lieberman (2006)

X-System	C-System
Parallel processing	Serial processing
Fast operating	Slow operating
Slow learning	Fast learning
Nonreflective consciousness	Reflective consciousness
Sensitive to subliminal presentations	Insensitive to subliminal presentations
Spontaneous processes	Intentional processes
Prepotent responses	Regulation of prepotent responses
Typically sensory	Typically linguistic
Outputs experienced as reality	Outputs experienced as self-generated
Relation to behavior unaffected by cognitive load	Relation to behavior altered by cognitive load
Facilitated by high arousal	Impaired by high arousal
Phylogenetically older	Phylogenetically newer
Representation of symmetric relations	Representation of asymmetric relations
Representation of common cases	Representation of special cases (e.g., exceptions)
	Representation of abstract concepts (e.g., negation, time)

coming to mind upon hearing "Romeo") lack one or more of these qualities. Consistent with the notion that automatic and controlled processes are supported by distinct systems (Smith & DeCoster 1999), distinct neurocognitive systems have been hypothesized to support these two forms of social cognition.

The X-system, named for the "x" in reflexive (Lieberman et al. 2002, Satpute & Lieberman 2006), corresponds roughly to an automatic social cognition system (see **Table 1**). The neural regions associated with the X-system (see **Figure 1**) are the amygdala, basal ganglia, ventromedial prefrontal cortex (VMPFC), lateral temporal cortex (LTC), and dorsal anterior cingulate cortex (dACC).

The C-system, named for the "c" in reflective, corresponds roughly to a controlled social cognition system. The neural regions associated with the C-system are lateral prefrontal cortex (LPFC), medial prefrontal cortex (MPFC), lateral parietal cortex (LPAC), medial parietal cortex (MPAC), medial temporal lobe (MTL), and rostral anterior cingulate cortex (rACC). For a rationale of each

nomination to the two systems, see Satpute & Lieberman (2006). The automatic and control distinctions are addressed in each section of this review for which relevant data are available.

This review also highlights a second core-processing distinction between internally-focused and externally-focused forms of social cognition. This is not a distinction between self- and other-focused cognition. Rather, internally-focused cognition refers to mental processes that focus on one's own or another's mental interior (e.g., thoughts, feelings, experience), whereas externally-focused cognition refers to mental processes that focus on one's own or another's physical and visible features and actions that are perceived through sensory modalities and are experienced as part of the material world. This distinction emerges as a data-driven finding across numerous domains of social cognitive neuroscience rather than from any existing theories of social cognition. As such, this review hopefully reveals how social cognitive neuroscience can inform social psychological theory, in addition to being informed by it.

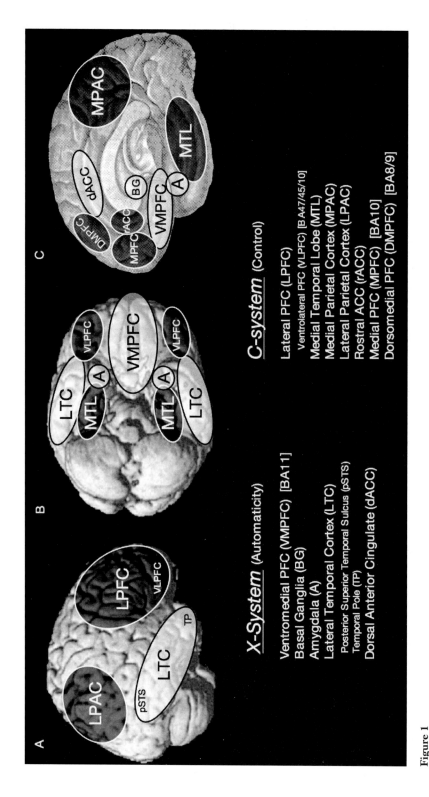

Figure 1

Hypothesized neural correlates of the C-system supporting reflective social cognition (analogous to controlled processing) and the X-system supporting reflexive social cognition (analogous to automatic processing) displayed on a canonical brain rendering from (*A*) lateral, (*B*) ventral, and (*C*) medial views. Note: the basal ganglia and amygdala are subcortical structures that are displayed here on the cortical surface for ease of presentation.

UNDERSTANDING OTHERS

Although social cognition has come to encompass a broad range of mental processes, in the strictest sense, social cognition is about understanding other people. In some ways, other people are like objects that have various physical characteristics, but unlike objects, other people have minds and experiences that are not directly open to inspection. There are at least two ways to try to understand the experience and the mind of another. One of these ways is addressed by work on "theory of mind" (Perner & Wimmer 1985). Theory of mind research examines the ability to propositionally reason from one's theory of how minds operate and how social situations affect mental states in general, in order to represent the mental state of a particular individual given a particular situation. Thus, our knowledge of social rules and norms mediates these insights (Gilbert & Malone 1995). However, there are also times when our insight feels unmediated, when it feels like we are seeing the world directly through another person's eyes and feeling the world through their visceral reactions. In this case, we feel like we have an insider's perspective on what it is like to be that person. The following sections review the neural bases of these two ways of knowing others.

Representing the Minds of Others

Representing psychological states of others. The ability to represent the contents of another's mind consists of two components: (a) the recognition that, unlike other objects in the world, people have minds with thoughts and feelings, and (b) the development of a theory regarding how other people's minds operate and respond to events in their environment. Research on theory of mind (Perner & Wimmer 1985) has found that by age four nearly all children develop the ability to assess the mental states of others. This process may build upon the capacity to recognize biological motion and goal-directed action that emerges by around six months

of age (Woodward 1998). From childhood through adulthood, increasingly complex and domain-specific theories form (Reeder 1993), although this increasing sophistication does not always yield greater accuracy (Gilbert & Malone 1995).

Neuroimaging studies of theory of mind have typically shown activations in DMPFC (BA 8/9), posterior superior temporal sulcus (pSTS) in LTC, and the temporal poles in LTC (for review, see Frith & Frith 2003). Research suggests that pSTS is particularly sensitive to biological motion (Allison et al. 2000) and that the temporal poles may be associated with perception of familiar individuals (Sugiura et al. 2001). Frith & Frith (2003) suggest that unlike LTC, which is sensitive to external visual cues, DMPFC is specifically associated with mentalizing, which is overt thought about the internal mental states of others. Additionally, Saxe et al. (2004) have suggested that the temporoparietal junction in LPAC is distinct from nearby pSTS and is also involved in theory of mind processes. Finally, both neuroimaging and neuropsychological investigations have suggested that right ventrolateral prefrontal cortex (VLPFC), a subregion within LPFC, helps to inhibit one's own experience during the consideration of another's state of mind (Samson et al. 2005, Vogeley et al. 2001). These findings are consistent with developmental research indicating that theory of mind development is linked to advances in general inhibitory control (Carlson & Moses 2001). It is plausible that a failure of this process in adults may play a central role in naïve realism (Griffin & Ross 1991, Pronin et al. 2004), whereby individuals assume that others see the world the same way that they do and have difficulty acknowledging alternative viewpoints (see Lieberman 2005).

Given the early development of sensitivity to biological motion and the fact that adults perceive biological motion without effort, one would expect this to be a relatively automatic process. Alternatively, explicit propositional thought about the content of another's mind would seem to fall squarely within the domain of controlled processes. One study using functional magnetic resonance imaging (fMRI) confirms these intuitions, as cognitive load was found to diminish DMPFC responses, but not pSTS or temporal pole responses, during a mentalizing task (den Ouden et al. 2005). Another study suggests that DMPFC is active during covert mentalizing processes (German et al. 2004); however, the covert condition in this study appears to require more overt mentalizing than does the control condition.

It is also interesting to note that the only medial activation (DMPFC) associated with theory of mind processes is associated with the internally-focused process of considering the contents of another person's mind. Sensitivity to biological motion and person familiarity in lateral regions (pSTS and temporal poles, respectively) are both externally-focused processes that do not require consideration of a target's internal states.

Representing psychological traits of others. Beyond knowing how the typical person would respond psychologically to particular events, individuals are also interested in identifying the enduring psychological traits of others. Individuals use their theories of how people with different kinds of dispositions behave in order to infer targets' dispositions from their behavior (Gilbert 1989). A recent fMRI study of dispositional attribution (Harris et al. 2005) found that when individuals read behavioral descriptions diagnostic for drawing dispositional inferences about a target (Kelley 1967), both DMPFC and pSTS were more active.

Another study (Mitchell et al. 2004) found that trait-relevant action descriptions (e.g., "he refused to loan his extra blanket to the other campers") shown with a target face led to DMPFC activity only when subjects had an explicit goal to form an impression of the target. This is the first study to hold constant the relevance of stimulus information for understanding the mental states or traits of another and instead manipulate whether or not the subject has the goal of understanding another mind.

Given that controlled processes that support trait attribution should only occur when the intention to make sense of another person is present, the study by Mitchell et al. (2004) suggests that DMPFC contributes to controlled processing aspects of trait attribution. Alternatively, pSTS was active in response to the action descriptions regardless of the subject's encoding goal (J.P. Mitchell, personal communication), a finding that suggests that this response reflects automatic social cognition. A similar dissociation has also been observed between DMPFC and the temporal poles (Mason et al. 2004; M.F. Mason, personal communication). Both of these results are consistent with the previously described study by den Ouden et al. (2005) that examined the automatic and controlled components of theory of mind processes. Additionally, these findings are consistent with the internal/external distinction observed in theory of mind research, as DMPFC was associated with encoding the psychological traits of a target (internal), whereas pSTS and the temporal poles were activated in response to descriptions of observable behavior (external).

Experiencing the Mental States of Others

Empathy. This second way of knowing others is far more embodied than logical (Merleau-Ponty 1962) and is more appropriately referred to as empathy than as theory of mind. Empathy has been associated with increased helping and social support (Batson 1991); however, this consequence of empathy requires the individual to maintain an awareness that the emotional response is an embodied simulation of another person's experience, not to be confused with one's own experience. Thus, the two criteria for empathic responses are (*a*) an emotional and experiential response that approximates that of the target and (*b*) an awareness and identification of this emotion as referring to the target's experience.

A number of studies have now addressed the first of these criteria. Wicker et al. (2003) found that two regions associated with affective processing, the anterior insula and dACC, were activated both when individuals smelled disgusting odors themselves and when they watched videoclips of others smelling these odors. Similarly, a number of studies have observed activation in these two regions when individuals either felt physical pain or observed another feeling physical pain (Botvinick et al. 2005, Jackson et al. 2005, Morrison et al. 2004, Singer et al. 2004), and the strength of these responses correlated with self-reported trait empathy (Singer et al. 2004). Alternatively, Farrow et al. (2001) observed greater activity in VMPFC, MPFC, DMPFC, and MPAC when individuals were asked to make empathic judgments relative to other forms of social reasoning. Similarly, Botvinick et al. (2005) found greater VMPFC activity when observing another's pain but not when feeling pain oneself, which suggests that this region might contribute to the additional processes invoked by empathy over direct feeling. Finally, in two neuropsychological investigations of patients with different cortical lesions (Shamay-Tsoory et al. 2003, 2005), VMPFC damage was found to be the strongest predictor of empathic deficits.

Interestingly, unlike theory of mind processes that logically proceed from externally-focused processing of situational information and observed behaviors to internally-focused processing of another's mental state, empathy is focused primarily on the experience of another and is thus internally-focused. Consistent with this distinction, the empathy research reviewed here has typically found medial, rather than lateral, activations. It is also worth noting that in comparison with representing other minds, the sense of experiencing other minds appears to recruit brain regions more closely tied with automatic affective processes, including the dACC and VMPFC.

Issues for empathy research. One open issue for empathy research is whether the pain distress felt while watching another's pain is personal distress or empathic distress. In Batson's (1991) examination of empathy as it relates to altruism, he cites Adam Smith, who wrote about the distinction clearly: "In order to enter into your grief, I do not consider what I, a person of such a character and profession, should suffer if I had a son and if that son was unfortunately to die . . . . I not only change circumstances with you, but I change persons and characters" (1853/1759, p. VII).

In each of the neuroimaging studies of empathy, it is unclear whether subjects are imagining their own experience of pain or truly empathizing (for the study that is most successful at addressing this, see Singer et al. 2006). In the same way that false-belief paradigms were critical in establishing theory of mind because accuracy required children to indicate that a target person had different beliefs from their own, here the study of empathy would seem to require situations in which the subject and the target have different experiential responses. For instance, empathy while watching a masochist receive painful stimulation might be expected to activate reward rather than pain regions.

UNDERSTANDING ONESELF

Given that the self feels hermetically sealed off from others, containing private thoughts and feelings, one might wonder why the self is so heavily researched by social psychologists whose main focus is on social interactions and situational pressures. The playwright Oscar Wilde captured the social psychologist's answer when he wrote, "Most people are other people. Their thoughts are someone else's opinions, their lives a mimicry, their passions a quotation" (Wilde 1905). Social psychologists from Wilde's era (Cooley 1902, Mead 1934) predicated their theories of the self on the notion that the self is formed through social feedback from other people. They believed that what people experience as introspective self-talk is actually a conversation with a simulated other who is an internalized amalgam of our early social learning that comes to serve as a guide for appropriate social behavior. Thus, research on the self is integral to social psychology (Baumeister 1998) and now to social cognitive neuroscience. Here and in the next section, the four topics that have dominated social cognitive neuroscience research on the self (self-recognition, self-reflection, self-knowledge, and self-control) are reviewed.

Recognizing Oneself

Visual self-recognition. The ability for infants to visually recognize themselves in a mirror comes online in the second year of life, with most infants achieving this skill by 21 months of age (Lewis & Ramsay 2004). This contrasts with the ability to recognize one's mother in a mirror by nine months of age (Dixon 1957), suggesting that either more time is needed for the neural machinery supporting self-recognition to mature or more socialization is needed in which parents can teach infants to identify themselves as a self.

Perhaps because self-recognition is one of the few self-processes that can be examined in preverbal humans and animals it has received a great amount of attention. In what is perhaps the first social cognitive neuroscience experiment, self-recognition processes examined in a split-brain patient (Sperry et al. 1979) suggested that each hemisphere of the human brain was independently capable of recognizing the self. One study has replicated this finding (Uddin et al. 2005b), whereas the data in two others have each favored one hemisphere or the other (Keenan et al. 2003, Turk et al. 2002). Other research using different techniques to isolate the processing of each hemisphere has also yielded mixed results (Brady et al. 2004, Keenan et al. 2001).

A half-dozen fMRI studies clarify the neural basis of self-recognition to some extent. Although there is also variability in the fMRI studies examining self-recognition, most have observed greater right LPFC and LPAC activity (Platek et al. 2006; Sugiura 2000, 2005; Uddin et al. 2005a) when individuals identify pictures as themselves compared with when they identify pictures of familiar others. Given the symbolic nature of the self, it is not surprising that the regions involved in self-recognition have been linked with controlled processing.

Agency. In addition to visual recognition of one's face, there is also the recognition of one's body parts and movements as one's own, a process that involves the combined inputs from the visual system and internal proprioception from the muscles. Neuroimaging (Farrer et al. 2003, Farrer & Frith 2002, Leube et al. 2003, Shimada et al. 2005), transcranial magnetic stimulation (MacDonald & Paus 2003), and neuropsychological studies (Sirigu et al. 1999) all suggest that LPAC regions bilaterally, but particularly on the right side, are involved in detecting mismatches between visual and proprioceptive feedback. In these studies, video displays of the subject's own hand movements are shown to the subject either in real time or at short delays such that the visual feedback and proprioceptive feedback are asynchronous. Results indicate that greater LPAC activity is present during mismatches than during matches. In related work, schizophrenics experiencing passivity, a state characterized by a feeling of not owning one's own actions, showed greater activation of right LPAC (Franck et al. 2002, Ganesan et al. 2005, Spence et al. 1997). Similarly, Blanke and colleagues have shown, with a variety of methods, that out-of-body experiences are also associated with right LPAC activity (Blanke et al. 2002). One caveat to these findings is that the LPAC is typically activated when the external visual representation of one's body conflicts with one's internal experience of oneself. Thus, it may be more appropriate to suggest that an absence of LPAC activation is associated with the feeling that one's actions are one's own.

Reflecting on the Self

Reflecting on one's current experience. Although other animals presumably have experiences, humans may be the only living creatures who can reflect upon and explicitly represent the character of those experiences. Having explicit insight into the situations that make one feel good or bad allows an individual to much more efficiently seek out or avoid similar situations in the future. This insight also allows individuals to communicate their preferences and dislikes to others.

Reflecting on one's current experience leads to remarkably consistent activation of MPFC (BA10) across a variety of different tasks. BA10 is the only region of prefrontal cortex that has thus far been found to be disproportionally larger in humans than in other primates (Semendeferi et al. 2001). The studies that most directly isolate the act of self-reflection have examined neural responses occurring when participants indicate their current emotional response to a picture (e.g., "How pleasant do you feel in response to this picture?") compared with when making a non-self-relevant judgment (e.g., "Is the picture of an indoor or outdoor scene?"). In each of these studies (Gusnard et al. 2001, Johnson et al. 2005, Lane et al. 1997, Ochsner et al. 2004), MPFC was more active during self-reflection than during the control task. Two of these studies (Johnson & Schmitz 2005, Ochsner et al. 2004) found additional activation in MPAC. Similarly, Eisenberger et al. (2005) found that greater dispositional self-consciousness was associated with greater MPFC and MPAC activation during a conflict detection task.

Given that cognitive tasks tend to decrease the activity in MPFC (McKiernan et al. 2003), it is possible that results of self-reflection studies are being driven by MPFC changes associated with the control condition rather than by self-reflection per se. However, a neuropsychological study by Beer et al. (2003), which is not susceptible to this alternate explanation, suggests that this is not the case. In their study, patients with extensive damage to MPFC, as well as VMPFC, experienced less self-conscious emotion after engaging in inappropriate behavior compared with controls, suggesting that MPFC is associated with initiating or carrying out self-reflective processes. Surprisingly, patients with MPFC lesions are capable of self-conscious emotions if shown their embarrassing behavior on a video recording (Beer et al. 2006), a process that may rely on externally-focused visual self-recognition mechanisms rather than internally-focused self-reflection. Taylor et al. (2003) also observed increases in MPFC activity, relative to a resting baseline, when participants rated their own emotional reaction to emotional stimuli, also suggesting that the MPFC findings in other studies are not artifacts of the control conditions.

Interestingly, Taylor et al. (2003) found that self-reflection on emotional stimuli was also associated with reduced activity in the amygdala, a region implicated in automatic affective processes (Pasley et al. 2004). Although it seems paradoxical that self-reflection on one's feelings could lead to a reduction in those feelings, this result is consistent with other behavioral research (Silvia 2002, Wilson et al. 2005, Wilson & Schooler 1991) and highlights the fact that feelings themselves and thoughts about feelings are not necessarily isomorphic (Lieberman 2006).

Given that self-reflection feels effortful and resource consuming, it is not surprising that this process relies on neural structures that have undergone recent evolutionary development (Semendeferi et al. 2001) and whose activity is interrupted by cognitive load manipulations (Greicius et al. 2003, McKiernan et al. 2003). Perhaps somewhat more surprising is that the neural correlates of self-reflection are quite distinct from those involved in self-recognition and agency judgments. Self-reflection, an internally-focused process, is strongly associated with activity in a medial frontoparietal network, whereas self-recognition and agency judgments invoke externally-focused processes and are strongly associated with activity in a lateral frontoparietal network. Such a dramatic dissociation between self-reflection and self-recognition processes is not easily accounted for in existing social psychological theories.

Reflecting on past experiences. In addition to being able to reflect upon our current experience, we are also capable of reflecting on our autobiographical past, the events of personal importance that have made up our lives. People do not recall all events from their past equally well. Remembering one's wedding is presumably easier than remembering what one had for breakfast August 21, 2001. Our autobiographical memory tends to be filled with events of personal significance, rather than a linear record of events over time (Lieberman & Eisenberger 2005). Thus, although autobiographical memory and episodic memory bear more than a passing resemblance, their neural correlates are only partially overlapping.

Gilboa (2004) reviewed the prefrontal activations in 14 neuroimaging studies that contained both autobiographical and episodic memory conditions. Gilboa reported that although VLPFC activations are common to retrieving both forms of memory, MPFC (BA10) and VMPFC (BA11) are present only in autobiographical memory retrieval, whereas right DLPFC is present primarily in episodic memory retrieval. The medial activations associated with autobiographical memories may result from these memories being linked to one's internal sense of self and the feelings one had during the events. Multiple studies have also observed MTL activity during both kinds of memory retrieval, but more so during autobiographical retrieval than episodic retrieval (Cabeza et al. 2004, Gilboa et al. 2004).

Reflecting on one's self-concept. Within the study of self-focused processing, reflection upon one's own self-concept in trait terms (e.g., "kind," "smart") has received a great deal of attention (for review, see Lieberman

& Pfeifer 2005). Several studies have examined the neural activity involved in determining whether trait words and sentences are self-descriptive. Most of these studies have included a nonsocial control task, such as determining the number of vowels in the trait words (Johnson et al. 2002). The studies often included a social control task, such as determining whether the trait term describes a close friend (Ochsner et al. 2005, Schmitz et al. 2004), casual acquaintance (Seger et al. 2004), famous politician (Craik et al. 1999, Kelley et al. 2002, Kjaer et al. 2002), or whether the trait is socially desirable (Fossati et al. 2003). Virtually all of these studies report greater MPFC during the self-judgments task than during the nonsocial control task, and several also report greater MPFC during self-judgments than during other social judgments (Craik et al. 1999, Fossati et al. 2003, Kelley et al. 2002, Schmitz et al. 2004). Additionally, a number of these studies also report greater activity in MPAC during self-judgments (Fossati et al. 2003, Johnson et al. 2002, Kelley et al. 2002, Seger et al. 2004). In two other studies, individuals were prompted to think about their own personality characteristics over a period of minutes; greater MPFC and MPAC were observed in this condition than when participants thought about someone else's personality characteristics (D'Argembeau et al. 2005, Kjaer et al. 2002). In addition, in two studies (Fossati et al. 2004, Macrae et al. 2004) that examined the effects of self-referential encoding on memory, it was observed that greater MPFC activity during self-referential encoding is associated with better memory performance for this information (for an analogous study linking DMPFC with memory for social information, see Mitchell et al. 2004). These studies are remarkably consistent in identifying activity in a medial frontoparietal network when individuals reflect on their own psychological make-up, an internally-focused process.

These studies, however, have not disentangled the act of self-reflection (i.e., effortfully trying to think about oneself) from self-knowledge activation (i.e., the knowledge that is reflected upon and retrieved). Although the act of self-reflection is a canonical form of controlled processing, self-knowledge consists of both automatically accessible and effortfully retrieved representations (Klein et al. 1992, 1996; Markus 1977). Lieberman et al. (2004) examined the neural responses of individuals who possessed strong self-schemas (i.e., automatically accessible self-knowledge) for either acting or athletics while they judged the trait descriptiveness of trait words related to acting or athletics. Retrieval of non-schematic self-knowledge was relatively slow and was associated with activity in DMPFC and MTL, whereas automatically accessible schematic self-knowledge was associated with activity in VMPFC, amygdala, ventral striatum in the basal ganglia, LTC, and MPAC. The absence of MPFC in this comparison suggests that the primary role of MPFC is in self-reflection rather than self-knowledge representation (see also J.H. Pfeifer, M.D. Lieberman, & M. Dapretto, under review).

SELF-REGULATION

The capacity for self-regulation is critical to the achievement of both personal and social goals. Self-regulatory skills allow us to act in accordance with long-term goals (e.g., getting a promotion) rather than being slaves to our emotional impulses (e.g., wanting to yell at one's boss). Indeed, individual differences in the ability to delay gratification as a child are highly predictive of achievement decades later (Metcalfe & Mischel 1999). Self-regulation has received a great deal of attention within the social cognitive neuroscience and broader cognitive neuroscience literature. Although the neural regions associated with self-regulation are quite similar across the different forms of self-regulation, there is also a major conceptual distinction between those forms of self-regulation in which the individual has the intention to regulate a response and other forms of self-regulation in which

the regulatory effects occur, but only as an unintended by-product of other processes.

Intentional Self-Regulation

Impulse control. A number of neuroimaging studies have examined the process whereby individuals intentionally override a prepotent response or impulse. The two brain regions that have consistently been associated with this process are dACC and LPFC (MacDonald et al. 2000). A number of studies have implicated the dACC in detecting the conflict between a current goal and the prepotent response rather than in the process of exerting top-down control to facilitate the appropriate response or inhibit the inappropriate response (Botvinick et al. 2004). Alternatively, LPFC has been more closely tied to maintaining the current goal in working memory and to implementing the top-down control needed to produce appropriate responses (Aron et al. 2004). Similar LPFC activations are present when individuals must inhibit beliefs in order to reason correctly (Goel & Dolan 2003).

Reappraising emotional events. Recent studies have built on the impulse control findings by examining self-control of emotional responses and emotional experience (Ochsner & Gross 2005). These studies have examined reappraisal as a strategy for emotional self-control. Reappraisal typically involves reframing a negative emotional event such that the new understanding renders the event less aversive. Reappraisal efforts commonly activate regions of LPFC, most often VLPFC, regardless of whether the reappraisal focuses on trying to reduce the emotional significance of highly aversive images (Ochsner et al. 2002, 2004; Phan et al. 2005), physical pain anticipation (Kalisch et al. 2005), sad films (Levesque et al. 2003), or erotic films (Beauregard et al. 2001). This manipulation also tends to produce decreased activity in the amygdala, with some studies also showing decreased activity in either temporal pole or VMPFC. In one study, Ochsner et al. (2004) manipulated whether individuals reappraised in order to feel more or less negative affect and manipulated whether individuals reappraised in ways that focused on changes in the target's physical situation or in ways that focused on the subject's personal relationship to the target. Reappraising to increase negative affect was associated with activity in DMPFC, MPFC, and posterior cingulate near MPAC, whereas reappraising to decrease negative affect was associated with right lateral orbitofrontal cortex in the vicinity of VLPFC. One can imagine that instructions to increase their negative emotional responses may have led participants to spontaneously engage in internally-focused empathy for the target (resulting in more medial activity), whereas instructions to decrease negative affect may have led participants to engage in externally-focused detachment from the target (resulting in more lateral activity). Similarly, reappraisals focused on one's personal relation to the target activated rACC, whereas situation-focused reappraisal activated left LPFC. Here again, the split between medial and lateral prefrontal activations maps onto internally- versus externally-focused processes, respectively.

Unintentional Self-Regulation

Putting feelings into words. It has long been known that putting feelings into words is an effective strategy for regulating negative emotional responses. Although expressing these feelings is known to have benefits for both mental and physical health (Hemenover 2003, Pennebaker 1997), the benefits seem to occur whether one is intentionally trying to regulate one's emotions or not, and even occur if one writes about an imaginary trauma rather an actual one (Greenberg et al. 1996). A number of neuroimaging studies have shown that merely labeling emotionally evocative visual images with emotional labels (i.e., affect labeling) leads to a reduction in the amygdala activity that would otherwise occur in the presence of these images (Hariri et al. 2000, Lieberman et al. 2006). These studies also show increased

activity in right VLPFC during affect labeling and an inverse relationship between this prefrontal activity and the activity in the amygdala. Thus, the pattern of activity is very similar to the pattern observed during reappraisal processes, suggesting that self-regulation is occurring despite the absence of any intention to self-regulate.

Placebo effects. Expectancy-based placebo effects typically involve a consciously held belief about the effectiveness of a treatment or medication that leads to a reduction in aversive symptoms. Although only a handful of neuroimaging studies have examined placebo effects, the results have been remarkably consistent. Investigations of placebo effects on momentary pain stimulation (Kong et al. 2006, Petrovic et al. 2002, Wager et al. 2004), chronic pain (Lieberman et al. 2004), and the distress associated with aversive images (Petrovic et al. 2005) have almost all observed greater activity in right VLPFC and rACC during placebo compared with control conditions. Placebo effects were also associated with reductions in subjective distress, dACC activity, or amygdala activity, with rACC and LPFC activations predicting the magnitude of these reductions. Interestingly, both rACC and right VLPFC overlap with the opioid network evoked during opioid analgesia (Petrovic et al. 2002). As with putting feelings into words, placebo effects invoke a network similar to that observed during reappraisal, a finding that suggests common processes are at work despite different phenomenologies accompanying reappraisal, placebo, and putting feelings into words.

BEING IN A SOCIAL WORLD

A great deal of our waking lives is spent navigating the social world with others, and many of the processes already reviewed presumably evolved, in part, to facilitate social living (Dunbar 1998). The topics reviewed in this section all link the self and social world together within a single mental act. We coordinate our activity with those around us, use feedback from others to understand ourselves, make sense of others based on our self-theories, and develop personal attitudes about social groups. We also care deeply about being connected to loved ones, not being rejected, and being treated in a fair and trustworthy manner in our interactions with strangers. Together, these processes contribute to a coherent social world in which individuals continuously make adjustments to conform to the norms of other individuals and society more generally.

Mirror Neurons and Imitation

In the early 1990s, di Pellegrino and colleagues discovered a class of neurons in primates that were activated both when primates performed a goal-directed action (e.g., grasping an object) and when they observed the experimenter perform the same action (e.g., grasp the same object). Dubbed mirror neurons, the presence of these neurons suggests that the same motor action representations are activated when performing and observing goal-directed actions (di Pellegrino et al. 1992). This is analogous to Kosslyn's earlier finding that visual perception and visual imagery both rely on the same visual code in visual cortex (for review, see Kosslyn et al. 2001). In humans, activation in regions homologous to those found in primates has also been reported both when participants observe intentional action and when they imitate intentional action (Iacoboni et al. 1999). In particular, regions of LPFC (pars opercularis in BA44) and LPAC have been found to follow this pattern.

It has been widely speculated that mirror neurons represent a basis for understanding the behavior, intentions, and experience of others, but this has not yet been demonstrated empirically. One can imitate without understanding, and to date, no mirror neuron study has assessed whether activity in the mirror neuron system is associated with the experience of understanding the perspec-

tive or experience of another. Based on the earlier section that focused on understanding others, one would expect that if imitation promoted or served as a form of embodied understanding of another's mental states, it would lead to increased activity in the medial frontoparietal network. Instead, imitation is associated with a lateral frontoparietal network consistent with externally-focused understanding of physical action but not with internally-focused processes such as mental state representation or empathy. Indeed, research examining the imitation of emotional facial expressions observed less activity in DMPFC during imitation than observation (Carr et al. 2003), a finding that suggests that imitation may demand externally-focused attention to the actions as actions, rather than as indicators of another's internal states.

It is possible, however, that mirror neurons play an important role in nonverbal communication (i.e., gestures, facial expressions, and posture; see DePaulo 1992). There is evidence for a complex reciprocal nonverbal "dance" that occurs between interaction partners (Word et al. 1974) that can provide the basis for our judgments about an interaction (Chartrand & Bargh 1999). The difficulty in making this link is that whereas a great deal of nonverbal communication occurs without conscious effort (Ambady et al. 2000, Lieberman 2000), the human imaging research on mirror neurons has examined explicit intentions to observe and imitate a single behavior that is presented focally. The connection between mirror neuron work and nonverbal communication could be strengthened if the mirror neuron system were found to be similarly activated by behaviors that are embedded in a larger scene unfolding over time, while participants are not attending to the behavior focally or under cognitive load.

Interactions of Self and Social Understanding

Reflected appraisals (i.e., "what I think you think of me") are thought to be a critical source of self-knowledge throughout development (Cooley 1902, Mead 1934). A single neuroimaging study has examined the neural bases of reflected appraisals. Ochsner et al. (2005) observed that reflected appraisal processes were associated with greater activity in the orbital extension of right VLPFC, MTL, and MPAC, compared with direct appraisals of the self. This pattern of activation is consistent with the notion that overt generation of reflected appraisals is an effortful controlled process.

In contrast to reflected appraisals, which involve consulting one's theory of another person's mind in order to understand oneself, under some conditions, individuals may consult their theories of themselves in order to understand other individuals. The existing evidence suggests that this occurs when the target is a close associate of or is seen as similar to the participant. When individuals judge the psychological traits and states of their mother (Ruby & Decety 2004), close friend (Ochsner et al. 2005), or someone rated as similar to themselves (Mitchell et al. 2005), significant activations are produced in MPFC, the region most typically found in self-reflective processes. Mitchell et al. (2005) also reported an interaction between DMPFC and MPFC activity as a function of similarity between the participant and target, such that DMPFC activity decreased and MPFC activity increased with increasing similarity. This suggests that similarity is promoting understanding the minds of others in terms of one's theory of oneself.

Attitudes and Prejudice

Implicit and explicit attitudes. Attitudes serve a critical function in our social lives as they support and define our social identities. When we share our attitudes with others, we are providing a roadmap to our behavioral proclivities and a promissory note regarding our reactions to different attitude-relevant situations. Neuroimaging work on attitudes has primarily focused on identify-

ing the neural correlates of implicit and explicit attitudes. When individuals express explicit attitudes toward concepts (Cunningham et al. 2004b, Zysset et al. 2002), famous names (Cunningham et al. 2003), geometrical shapes (Jacobson et al. 2006), or paintings (Vartanian & Goel 2004), activation tends to increase in both medial and lateral frontoparietal networks, compared with when nonevaluative judgments are made about the same stimuli. This network includes MPFC, MPAC, VLPFC, and LPAC. These regions have all been associated with controlled processes and are consistent with the notion that the expression of explicit attitudes depends on controlled processing. Additionally, an event-related potential study (Cunningham et al. 2005; see also Cela-Conde et al. 2004) observed that the LPFC activations associated with explicit attitudes appear at least 400 ms after the presentation of the attitude object, also implicating LPFC in controlled processing of attitudes (Neely 1977).

Other studies have identified brain regions associated with implicit attitudes. In these studies, negative- and positive-attitude objects, such as African American and Caucasian American faces, are shown to individuals as they perform a nonevaluative task (e.g., gender judgments). Typically, the amygdala has been found to be more active to negative-attitude objects than to positive-attitude objects (Cunningham et al. 2003, Hart et al. 2000, Wheeler & Fiske 2005; for review of race-related neuroimaging, see Eberhardt 2005; for race-related electroencephalogram research, see Ito et al. 2006). Phelps et al. (2000) observed that the amygdala response of Caucasian Americans to African American faces was correlated with an implicit measure of racial attitudes but not with an explicit attitude measure (cf. Phelps et al. 2003). Lieberman et al. (2005) found that African American subjects also showed greater amygdala activity to African American faces than to Caucasian American faces, consistent with past findings that African Americans have negative implicit attitudes toward African

Americans, in contrast to their positive explicit attitudes toward African Americans (Nosek et al. 2002). Cunningham et al. (2004b) found that the amygdala response to African American faces was stronger when target faces were presented subliminally rather than supraliminally and that the amygdala was the only brain region that showed this pattern of activity. Apart from the amygdala, the only other brain region that has been associated with implicit attitudes is VMPFC. Milne & Grafman (2001) conducted a study of patients with VMPFC damage and observed no implicit gender bias. Similarly, Knutson et al. (2006) found VMPFC activity associated with the automatic activation of political attitudes. These results are consistent with findings from McClure et al. (2004) demonstrating that VMPFC activity was associated with behavioral preferences between Coke and Pepsi when individuals were unaware of the brand they were drinking. Alternatively, when individuals were informed of the brand they were drinking, behavioral preferences were associated with activity in controlled processing regions, DLPFC and MTL.

Regulating prejudicial responses. A number of neuroimaging studies have combined the study of intentional self-regulation with the study of race-related attitudes in order to understand the mechanisms by which people control their prejudicial responses. As with self-control more generally, it appears that the dACC may be involved in detecting that an undesirable attitude is prepotent and about to be revealed (Amodio et al. 2004), whereas LPFC regions tend to be implicated in exerting control and diminishing the activity of the amygdala. Multiple studies have shown that a desire to regulate the expression of a particular attitude is associated with greater activity of right LPFC in the presence of the attitude object (Cunningham et al. 2004a,b; Richeson et al. 2003). Additionally, the magnitude of right LPFC under conditions promoting prejudice regulation is associated with the extent to which amygdala responses are diminished (Cunningham et al. 2004a).

Unintentional self-regulation of prejudicial attitudes has also been demonstrated in fMRI studies. Simply categorizing African American targets in terms of their personal food preferences rather than their group membership was sufficient to reverse the amygdala's response to African American and Caucasian American targets (Wheeler & Fiske 2005). In another study, similar to the affect-labeling studies described above, processing the race of targets verbally rather than perceptually was sufficient to eliminate the amygdala's sensitivity to race, and this reduction was related to increases in right VLPFC activity (Lieberman et al. 2005).

Attitude change. Cognitive dissonance research has established that when individuals perform a behavior or make a choice that conflicts with a previously established attitude, the attitude tends to change in the direction that resolves the conflict with the behavior. From the outside, this process appears to involve rationalization, whereby individuals strategically change their attitudes in order to avoid appearing inconsistent. However, neuropsychological work by Lieberman et al. (2001) demonstrated that this might not always be a conscious strategic process. In one study, anterograde amnesia patients, who had neurological damage affecting the functioning of MTL and were incapable of forming new memories, were compared with healthy controls on a dissonance task. The amnesics had no memory of having performed a behavior that conflicted with their previously established attitudes and thus were not likely to have engaged in conscious strategic attitude change. Nonetheless, the amnesics changed their attitudes to the same extent as controls. These results suggest that, rather than conscious rationalization, cognitive dissonance reduction may sometimes depend on implicit constraint satisfaction processes (Read et al. 1997).

Social Connection and Social Rejection

Social connection. The need for social connection and acceptance are powerful motivators (Baumeister & Leary 1995) that guide human interactions with peers, romantic partners, and family. Although behavioral work in social psychology has emphasized the power of unfamiliar individuals to influence our own behavior (Asch 1956, Sherif 1937), few neuroimaging studies have examined this form of social pressure (Amodio et al. 2006, Berns et al. 2005). Instead, neuroimaging studies have focused primarily on neural responses associated with responses to close others. In these studies, individuals are shown pictures of either their romantic partner or their own infant along with relevant control images. Most often, when individuals see someone they love, they show greater activity in the basal ganglia (Aron et al. 2005; Bartels & Zeki 2000, 2004; Leibenluft et al. 2004; cf. Nitschke et al. 2004). Two of these studies also found a broad network of theory of mind areas to be less active during the presentation of a loved one than a control (Bartels & Zeki 2000, 2004); however, another study found the opposite pattern of activity (Leibenluft et al. 2004). These differences may be attributed to the fact that in the studies showing a decrease in these regions, the images were presented for ~15 seconds, whereas in the study showing an increase in these regions, the images were presented for 1.5 seconds. Thus, there may be differences in the immediate and long-term responses to the presentation of images of loved ones.

Social rejection. Mammals, unlike their reptilian ancestors, form long-term parental bonds with their young. Separation from caregivers typically results in death for young mammals. dACC activity has been associated with the distress of losing social connections. Primates with lesions to this region display a reduced frequency of distress vocalizations (MacLean & Newman 1988), whereas stimulation of this region spontaneously induces distress vocalizations (Robinson 1967, Smith 1945). Additionally, cingulate-lesioned female rodents do not provide effective maternal care, resulting in a 12% survival rate for their offspring compared with 95% for offspring from sham-lesioned rodents (Stamm 1955).

In humans, neuroimaging studies of social exclusion (Eisenberger 2006, Eisenberger et al. 2003) have found that self-reports of social distress are strongly related to dACC activity during exclusion, whereas right VLPFC was associated with downregulating both dACC activity and self-reported social distress. Attachment anxiety is also related to dACC activity when thinking about negative relationship scenarios (Gillath et al. 2005). In related work, the sound of infant cries activated dACC (Lorberbaum et al. 2002) and did so more for parents than nonparents (Seifritz et al. 2003). Finally, a recent study of grief found that activity in dACC, along with a number of theory of mind regions, was greater when bereaved individuals looked at pictures of the recently deceased individual compared with control images (Gundel et al. 2003; cf. Najib et al. 2004).

It has been hypothesized that mammalian social pain may have evolved out of the existing system for physical pain (Eisenberger & Lieberman 2004, MacDonald & Leary 2005, Panksepp 1998), with dACC playing a key role in the emotional distress of physical pain (Rainville et al. 1997). Evidence comes for this, in part, from laboratory findings that feeling socially rejected heightens sensitivity to physical pain (Eisenberger et al. 2006a), whereas social support reduces sensitivity to physical pain (Brown et al. 2003).

Heightened activity in the dACC, amygdala, and periaqueductal gray (another component of the pain matrix; Peyron et al. 2000) during a social rejection episode in the fMRI scanner has also been linked to greater reports of social disconnection in day-to-day life using an experience-sampling methodology (Eisenberger 2006). Finally, dACC reactivity during social rejection has been found to mediate the relationship between a polymorphism in the monoamine oxidase A gene and aggression in males (Eisenberger et al. 2006b), such that this gene may render individuals more sensitive to social threats and lead to greater defensive aggression as a result (Twenge et al. 2001).

Social Decision-Making

Social and moral reasoning. Behavioral research has shown that performance on conditional reasoning tasks is substantially improved if the conditional rules are formulated from real social norms rather than from abstract content (Cheng & Holyoak 1985). Neuroimaging studies investigating domain-specific reasoning effects have found a lateral frontoparietal network that is more active during conditional social reasoning than during conditional abstract reasoning (Canessa et al. 2005, Fiddick et al. 2005), with one group also observing greater activity in DMPFC during social reasoning (Fiddick et al. 2005). It is important to note that the social rules used in these tasks did not require representing mental states (e.g., if a man is drinking beer, he must be over 21), and thus the predominance of lateral frontoparietal activity is consistent with other domains covered in this review.

More attention has been given to the study of moral reasoning. The most common finding across these studies is that moral reasoning activates MPFC to a greater extent than do relevant control tasks (Heekeren et al. 2003; Moll et al. 2002a,b, 2005), with some of these studies also finding greater activation in pSTS and the temporal poles. In the first neuroimaging study of moral reasoning, Greene et al. (2001) compared personal and impersonal moral reasoning. In the personal condition, individuals were induced to focus on their own personal involvement in bringing about a distasteful but utilitarian outcome; in the impersonal condition, individuals were induced to focus primarily on the utilitarian outcome. The personal condition activated a medial frontoparietal network along with

LPAC to a greater degree than did the impersonal condition, consistent with the notion that the personal condition promotes self-reflection on the implications of one's contribution to the outcome. The impersonal condition, in contrast, led to greater activity in lateral frontoparietal regions than did the personal condition, consistent with an external focus on events in the world. A recent study (Mendez et al. 2005) with patients with MPFC damage confirmed these results: The patients were impaired in making personal moral judgments but not impersonal moral judgments.

Fairness and trust in interactions. A new area of research, neuroeconomics (Camerer et al. 2005, Trepel et al. 2005), has combined the study of behavioral economics and cognitive neuroscience. Studies that involve economic exchange with social dynamics are particularly relevant to social cognitive neuroscience. These studies use paradigms such as the ultimatum game (Sanfey et al. 2003), the prisoner's dilemma (Rilling et al. 2002), and the trust game (de Quervain et al. 2004) in order to examine the neural responses associated with cooperation, competition, fairness, and trust. Across these studies, cooperation, trust, and fair play typically activate VMPFC, MPFC, and MPAC (Decety et al. 2004, McCabe et al. 2001, Rilling et al. 2002), whereas unfair and untrustworthy responses activate insula (Sanfey et al. 2003), caudate in the basal ganglia (de Quervain et al. 2004), or DMPFC (Decety et al. 2004). The finding that cooperation, relative to competition, promotes MPFC rather than DMPFC activity is consistent with previously described work by Mitchell et al. (2005), such that cooperation may be associated with seeing the other players as more similar to oneself (see Decety et al. 2004). Cooperation has long been studied as a technique for overcoming intergroup differences and promoting a sense of shared identity (Sherif et al. 1961).

Across these studies of fairness and trust, the fairness of the decision-making process has often been confounded with the material value of the outcome. That is, fair responses from a partner are typically associated with better financial outcomes for the subject. G. Tabibnia, A.B. Satpute, & M.D. Lieberman (under review) recently manipulated the material payoffs and the fairness of the partner's behavior independently. After controlling for material payoffs, fairness still activated an array of motivation- and reward-related regions, including VMPFC, ventral striatum in the basal ganglia, and amygdala, which suggests that fairness is hedonically valued in social interactions.

CORE PROCESSES

Automatic Versus Controlled Processes

Across the different domains of social cognitive neuroscience that allow for an assessment of their automatic and controlled components, a clear pattern of neural activation emerges (see **Figure 2**). Some social psychological processes, by their very nature, appear to consist exclusively of either automatic or controlled processes (e.g., self-reflection, moral decision-making, feeling rejected). Other processes involve task conditions and baseline conditions that intuitively seem to compare controlled processes with spontaneous processes that may be more automatic (e.g., reappraisal, affect labeling). Finally, some processes have been examined with tasks that manipulate whether particular controlled processes of interest are likely to operate or not (e.g., theory of mind, dispositional attribution, self-knowledge, and attitude processes), providing the clearest examination of automaticity and control.

The picture that emerges is consistent with previous work on the neural systems supporting reflective and reflexive social cognition (Lieberman et al. 2002, Satpute & Lieberman 2006). Here, controlled forms of social cognition were consistently associated with ac-

tivations in LPFC, LPAC, MPFC, MPAC, and MTL. Alternatively, automatic forms of social cognition were consistently associated with activations in amygdala, VMPFC, and LTC. Not enough studies of automatic and controlled social cognition have implicated the basal ganglia or rACC one way or another to allow an assessment. Also, the studies were mixed regarding the contribution of dACC. Based on the existing results, dACC could either be (*a*) engaged in active controlled processing or (*b*) responding to goal-related conflict automatically (Bargh 1989) and then triggering other controlled processes as a result. Either alternative would produce dACC activity during tasks that recruit controlled processes in response to conflict.

Although these results must be considered preliminary, they do suggest that differences between automatic and controlled processes may constitute a core-processing distinction in the study of social cognitive neuroscience. Given the importance that this distinction has had over the past 20 years within the field of social cognition (Chaiken & Trope 1999, Wegner & Bargh 1998), it is valuable to identify the neural regions that support this distinction. In the long run, it may be possible to conduct studies in which the extent of automatic and controlled processing can be identified from neuroimaging alone, without the need for cognitive load or subliminal presentations, which would allow for more naturalistic investigations of automatic and controlled social cognition (cf. Poldrack 2006).

Internally-Versus Externally-Focused Processes

Across a number of social psychological domains, a clear division is present between the neural correlates of tasks that focus attention on interior psychological worlds and tasks that focus attention on the exterior social world and the physical social agents in it (see **Figure 3**). Externally-focused processes are

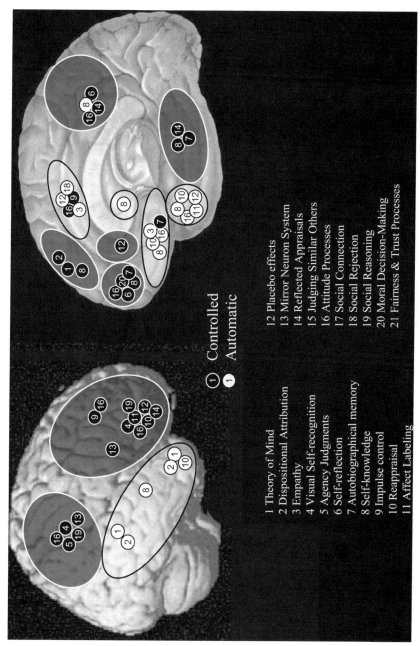

Figure 2

Neural correlates of automatic and controlled processes from multiple domains of social cognition overlaid on to the X-system and C-system regions displayed in **Figure 1**. Controlled/reflective processes are represented by small circles with white text on a black background. Automatic/reflexive processes are represented by small circles with black text on a white background. Small circles are placed schematically within a region and are not meant to indicate a precise location within a region.

The following legend appears within the figure:

○ Controlled
● Automatic

1 Theory of Mind
2 Dispositional Attribution
3 Empathy
4 Visual Self-recognition
5 Agency Judgments
6 Self-reflection
7 Autobiographical memory
8 Self-knowledge
9 Impulse control
10 Reappraisal
11 Affect Labeling

12 Placebo effects
13 Mirror Neuron System
14 Reflected Appraisals
15 Judging Similar Others
16 Attitude Processes
17 Social Connection
18 Social Rejection
19 Social Reasoning
20 Moral Decision-Making
21 Fairness & Trust Processes

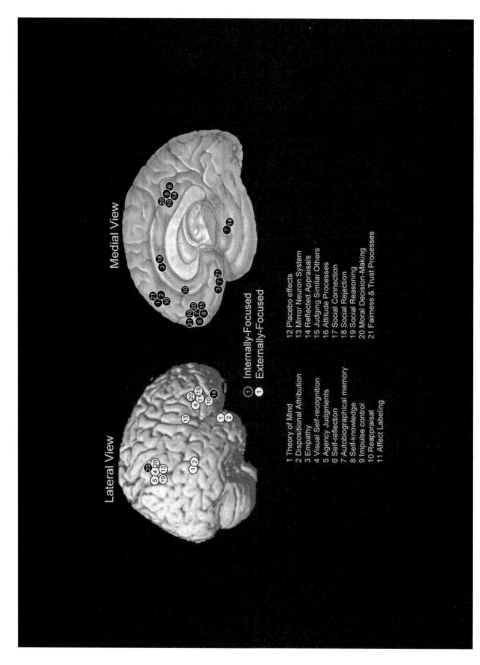

Figure 3

Neural correlates of internally-focused and externally-focused processes from multiple domains of social cognition. Internally-focused processes are represented by small circles with white text on a black background. Externally-focused processes are represented by small circles with black text on a white background. Small circles are placed schematically within a region and are not meant to indicate a precise location within a region.

associated with a lateral frontotemporoparietal network, whereas internally-focused processes are associated with a medial frontoparietal network.

A lateral frontotemporoparietal network is more activated by social-cognitive tasks that focus attention on the external, physical, and most often visual characteristics of other individuals, oneself, or the interaction of the two. This lateral frontotemporoparietal network is activated in tasks involving the nonmentalizing aspects of theory of mind and dispositional attribution tasks, action observation and imitation, visual self-recognition, impersonal moral and social reasoning, reappraisal by focusing on physical events, and labeling the visual displays of affect in the facial expressions of others.

In contrast, a medial frontoparietal network is more activated by social-cognitive tasks that focus attention on the internal, mental, emotional, and experiential characteristics of other individuals or oneself. This medial frontoparietal network is activated by tasks involving the mentalizing aspects of theory of mind and dispositional attribution tasks, empathy, self-reflection on current experiences, autobiographical memory, self-reflection on one's traits, personalized moral reasoning, and reappraisal by focusing on one's personal relation to a target.

It is important to note that this distinction is orthogonal to and cuts across self and other processing. Consequently, this distinction refers to two ways that self and other can each be processed. In the absence of existing neurocognitive data, it is hard to imagine making a case for self-reflection having such a distinct representational basis from self-recognition. However, in the context of the distinction between internally- and externally-focused processes that emerged from this review, these results are entirely sensible.

CONCLUSION

Social cognitive neuroscience is a vibrant young area of research. The amount of research and the number of scientists conducting research at the interface of the social sciences and neuroscience have increased by an order of magnitude since the first review of social cognitive neuroscience (Ochsner & Lieberman 2001). Several exciting lines of social cognitive neuroscience research are providing new discoveries, generating original ideas, and challenging longstanding conceptions of existing social science perspectives. This is exactly what interdisciplinary cross-fertilization should do. Here, I have provided evidence for two broad organizing principles of social cognition within the human brain, one quite old and one that is new. The distinction between automatic and controlled social cognition has long been a contributor to social psychological research. Identifying the neural bases of this distinction will help social cognitive neuroscience research to carve social processes at their joints, just as it has helped social psychologists in the past. In contrast to automaticity and control, the distinction between internally-focused and externally-focused social cognition has no clear theoretical precursor in social psychology, but emerges unmistakably from social cognitive neuroscience research (see also Eisenberger et al. 2005, Ochsner et al. 2004). Hopefully, the identification of this core-processing distinction can contribute to the development of new theories and the enrichment of existing theories within the social sciences, demonstrating that social cognitive neuroscience can be both a science of new techniques and a science of new ideas.

ACKNOWLEDGMENTS

I thank Naomi Eisenberger and the UCLA Social Cognitive Neuroscience laboratory for comments on an earlier draft. This work was supported in part by an NIMH grant (R21MH071521).

LITERATURE CITED

Adolphs R. 2002. Neural systems for recognizing emotion. *Curr. Opin. Neurobiol.* 12:169–77

Adolphs R. 2003. Cognitive neuroscience of human social behavior. *Nat. Rev. Neurosci.* 4:165–78

Allison T, Puce A, McCarthy G. 2000. Social perception from visual cues: role of the STS region. *Trends Cogn. Sci.* 4:267–78

Ambady N, Bernieri F, Richeson J. 2000. Towards a histology of social behavior: judgmental accuracy from thin slices of behavior. *Adv. Exp. Soc. Psychol.* 32:201–72

Amodio DM, Harmon-Jones E, Devine PG, Curtin JJ, Hartley SL, Covert AE. 2004. Neural signals for the detection of unintentional race bias. *Psychol. Sci.* 15:88–93

Amodio DM, Kubota JT, Harmon-Jones E, Devine PG. 2006. Alternative mechanisms for regulating racial responses according to internal vs. external cues. *Soc. Cogn. Affect. Neurosci.* 1:26–36

Aron A, Fisher H, Mashek DJ, Strong G, Li H, Brown LL. 2005. Reward, motivation, and emotion systems associated with early-stage intense romantic love. *J. Neurophysiol.* 94:327–37

Aron AR, Robbins TW, Poldrack RA. 2004. Inhibition and the right inferior frontal cortex. *Trends Cogn. Sci.* 8:170–77

Asch SE. 1956. Studies of independence and conformity: a minority of one against a unanimous majority. *Psychol. Monogr.* 70:416

Bargh JA. 1989. Conditional automaticity: varieties of automatic influence in social perception and cognition. In *Unintended Thought*, ed. JS Uleman, JA Bargh, pp. 3–51. New York: Guilford

Bartels A, Zeki S. 2000. The neural basis of romantic love. *Neuroreport* 11:3829–34

Bartels A, Zeki S. 2004. The neural basis of maternal and romantic love. *Neuroimage* 21:1156–66

Batson CD. 1991. *The Altruism Question: Toward a Social-Psychological Answer*. Hillsdale, NJ: Erlbaum

Baumeister RF. 1998. The self. In *The Handbook of Social Psychology*, ed. DT Gilbert, ST Fiske, G Lindzey, pp. 680–740. Boston, MA: McGraw-Hill

Baumeister RF, Leary MR. 1995. The need to belong: desire for interpersonal attachments as a fundamental human motivation. *Psychol. Bull.* 117:497–529

Beauregard M, Levesque J, Bourgouin P. 2001. Neural correlates of conscious self-regulation of emotion. *J. Neurosci.* 21:RC165

Beer JS, Heerey EA, Keltner D, Scabini D, Knight RT. 2003. The regulatory function of self-conscious emotion: insights from patients with orbitofrontal damage. *J. Personal. Soc. Psychol.* 85:594–604

Beer JS, John OP, Scabini D, Knight RT. 2006. Orbitofrontal cortex and social behavior: integrating self-monitoring and emotion-cognition interactions. *J. Cogn. Neurosci.* 18:871–79

Berns GS, Chappelow J, Zink CF, Pagnoni G, Martin-Skurski ME, Richards J. 2005. Neuro-biological correlates of social conformity and independence during mental rotation. *Biol. Psychol.* 58:245–53

Blakemore SJ, Winston J, Frith U. 2004. Social cognitive neuroscience: Where are we heading? *Trends Cogn. Sci.* 8:215–22

Blanke O, Ortigue S, Landis T, Seeck M. 2002. Stimulating illusory own-body perceptions: the part of the brain that can induce out-of-body experience has been located. *Nature* 419:269–70

Botvinick M, Jha AP, Bylsma LM, Fabian SA, Solomon PE, Prkachin KM. 2005. Viewing facial expressions of pain engages cortical areas involved in the direct experience of pain. *Neuroimage* 25:312–19

Botvinick MM, Cohen JD, Carter CD. 2004. Conflict monitoring and anterior cingulate cortex: an update. *Trends Cogn. Sci.* 8:539–46

Brady N, Campbell M, Flaherty M. 2004. My left brain and me: a dissociation in the perception of self and others. *Neuropsychologia* 42:1156–61

Brown JL, Sheffield D, Leary MR, Robinson ME. 2003. Social support and experimental pain. *Psychosom. Med.* 65:276–83

Cabeza R, Prince SE, Daselaar SM, Greenberg DL, Budde M, et al. 2004. Brain activity during episodic retrieval of autobiographical and laboratory events: an fMRI study photo paradigm. *J. Cogn. Neurosci.* 16:1583–94

Cacioppo JT, Berntson GG. 1992. Social psychological contributions to the decade of the brain. Doctrine of multilevel analysis. *Am. Psychol.* 47:1019–28

Camerer C, Loewenstein G, Prelec D. 2005. Neuroeconomics: how neuroscience can inform economics. *J. Econ. Lit.* 43:9–64

Canessa N, Gorini A, Cappa SF, Piattelli-Palmarini M, Danna M, et al. 2005. The effect of social content on deductive reasoning: an fMRI study. *Hum. Brain Mapp.* 26:30–43

Carlson SM, Moses LJ. 2001. Individual differences in inhibitory control and children's theory of mind. *Child Dev.* 72:1032–53

Carr L, Iacoboni M, Dubeau MC, Mazziotta JC, Lenzi GL. 2003. Neural mechanisms of empathy in humans: a relay from neural systems for imitation to limbic areas. *Proc. Natl. Acad. Sci. USA* 100:5497–502

Cela-Conde CJ, Marty G, Maestu F, Ortiz T, Munar E, et al. 2004. Activation of the prefrontal cortex in the human visual aesthetic perception. *Proc. Natl. Acad. Sci. USA* 101:6321–25

Chaiken S, Trope Y, eds. 1999. *Dual-Process Theories in Social Psychology*. New York: Guilford

Chartrand TL, Bargh JA. 1999. The chameleon effect: the perception-behavior link and social interaction. *J. Personal. Soc. Psychol.* 76:893–910

Cheng PW, Holyoak KJ. 1985. Pragmatic reasoning schemas. *Cogn. Psychol.* 17:391–416

Cooley CH. 1902. *Human Nature and Social Order*. New York: Scribner's

Craik FIM, Moroz TM, Moscovitch M, Stuss DT, Winocur G, et al. 1999. In search of the self: a positron emission tomography study. *Am. Psychol. Sci.* 10:26–34

Cunningham WA, Espinet SD, DeYoung CG, Zelazo PD. 2005. Attitudes to the right- and left: frontal ERP asymmetries associated with stimulus valence and processing goals. *Neuroimage* 28:827–34

Cunningham WA, Johnson MK, Raye CL, Chris Gatenby J, Gore JC, Banaji MR. 2004a. Separable neural components in the processing of black and white faces. *Psychol. Sci.* 15:806–13

Cunningham WA, Johnson MK, Gatenby JC, Gore JC, Banaji MR. 2003. Neural components of social evaluation. *J. Personal. Soc. Psychol.* 85:639–49

Cunningham WA, Raye CL, Johnson MK. 2004b. Implicit and explicit evaluation: fMRI correlates of valence, emotional intensity, and control in the processing of attitudes. *J. Cogn. Neurosci.* 16:1717–29

D'Argembeau AD, Collette F, Van der Linden M, Laureys S, Fiore GD, et al. 2005. Self-referential reflective activity and its relationship with rest: a PET study. *Neuroimage* 25:616–24

de Quervain DJF, Fischbacher U, Treyer V, Schellhammer M, Schnyder U, et al. 2004. The neural basis of altruistic punishment. *Science* 305:1254–59

Decety J, Jackson PL, Sommerville JA, Chaminade T, Meltzoff AN. 2004. The neural basis of cooperation and competition: an fMRI investigation. *Neuron* 23:744–51

den Ouden HE, Frith U, Frith C, Blakemore SJ. 2005. Thinking about intentions. *Neuroimage* 28:787–96

DePaulo BM. 1992. Nonverbal behavior and self-presentation. *Psychol. Bull.* 111:203–43

di Pellegrino G, Fadiga L, Fogassi L, Gallese V, Rizzolatti G. 1992. Understanding motor events: a neurophysiology study. *Exp. Brain Res.* 91:176–80

Dixon JC. 1957. Development of self recognition. *J. Genet. Psychol.* 91:251–56

Dunbar RIM. 1998. The social brain hypothesis. *Evol. Anthropol.* 6:178–90

Eberhardt JL. 2005. Imaging race. *Am. Psychol.* 60:181–90

Eisenberger NI. 2006. Social connection and rejection across the lifespan; a social cognitive neuroscience approach to developmental processes. *Hum. Dev.* In press

Eisenberger NI, Jarcho J, Lieberman MD, Naliboff B. 2006a. An experimental study of shared sensitivity to physical and social pain. *Pain.* In press

Eisenberger NI, Lieberman MD. 2004. Why rejection hurts: a common neural alarm system for physical and social pain. *Trends Cogn. Sci.* 8:294–300

Eisenberger NI, Lieberman MD, Satpute AB. 2005. Personality from a controlled processing perspective: an fMRI study of neuroticism, extraversion, and self-consciousness. *Cogn. Affect. Behav. Neurosci.* 5:169–81

Eisenberger NI, Lieberman MD, Williams KD. 2003. Does rejection hurt? An fMRI study of social exclusion. *Science* 302:290–92

Eisenberger NI, Way B, Taylor SE, Welch W, Lieberman MD. 2006b. MAO-A genetic polymorphism related to dorsal anterior cingulate response during social rejection. *Biol. Psychiatry.* In press

Farrer C, Frith CD. 2002. Experiencing onself vs another person as being the cause of an action: the neural correlates of the experience of agency. *Neuroimage* 15:596–603

Farrer C, Franck N, Georgieff N, Frith CD, Decety J, Jeannerod M. 2003. Modulating the experience of agency: a positron emission tomography study. *Neuroimage* 18:324–33

Farrow TFD, Zheng Y, Wilkinson ID, Spence SA, Deakin JFW, et al. 2001. Investigating the functional anatomy of empathy and forgiveness. *Neuroreport* 12:2849–53

Fiddick L, Spampinato MV, Grafman J. 2005. Social contracts and precautions activate different neurological systems: an fMRI investigation of deontic reasoning. *Neuroimage* 28:778–86

Fossati P, Hevenor SJ, Graham SJ, Grady C, Keightley ML, et al. 2003. In search of the emotional self: an fMRI study using positive and negative emotional words. *Am. J. Psychiatry* 160:1938–45

Fossati P, Hevenor SJ, Lepage M, Graham SJ, Grady C, et al. 2004. Distributed self in episodic memory: neural correlates of successful retrieval of self-encoded positive and negative personality traits. *Neuroimage* 22:1596–604

Franck N, O'Leary DS, Flaum M, Hichwa RD, Andreasen NC. 2002. Cerebral blood flow changes associated with Schneiderian first-rank symptoms in schizophrenia. *J. Neuropsychiatry Clin. Neurosci.* 14:277–82

Frith U, Frith CD. 2003. Development and neurophysiology of mentalizing. *Philos. Trans. R. Soc. Lond. B Biol. Sci.* 358:459–73

Ganesan V, Hunter MD, Spence SA. 2005. Schneiderian first-rank symptoms and right parietal hyperactivation: a replication using fMRI. *Am. J. Psychiatry* 162:1545

German TP, Niehaus JL, Roarty MP, Giesbrecht B, Miller MB. 2004. Neural correlates of detecting pretense: automatic engagement of the intentional stance under covert conditions. *J. Cogn. Neurosci.* 16:1805–17

Gilbert DT. 1989. Thinking lightly about others. Automatic components of the social inference process. In *Unintended Thought*, ed. JS Uleman, JA Bargh, pp. 189–211. New York: Guilford

Gilbert DT, Malone PS. 1995. The correspondence bias. *Psychol. Bull.* 117:21–38

Gilboa A. 2004. Autobiographical and episodic memory—one and the same? Evidence from prefrontal activation in neuroimaging studies. *Neuropsychologia* 42:1336–49

Gilboa A, Winocur G, Grady CL, Hevenor SJ, Moscovitch M. 2004. Remembering our past: functional neuroanatomy of recollection of recent and very remote personal events. *Cereb. Cortex* 14:1214–25

Gillath O, Bunge SA, Shaver PR, Wendelken C, Mikulincer M. 2005. Attachment-style differences in the ability to suppress negative thoughts: exploring the neural correlates. *Neuroimage* 28:835–47

Goel V, Dolan RJ. 2003. Explaining modulation of reasoning by belief. *Cognition* 87:B11–22

Greenberg MA, Wortman CB, Stone AA. 1996. Emotional expression and physical health: revising traumatic memories or fostering self-regulation? *J. Personal. Soc. Psychol.* 71:588–602

Greene JD, Sommerville RB, Nystrom LE, Darley JM, Cohen JD. 2001. An fMRI investigation of emotional engagement in moral judgment. *Science* 293:2105–8

Greicius MD, Krasnow B, Reiss AL, Menon V. 2003. Functional connectivity in the resting brain: a network analysis of the default mode hypothesis. *Proc. Natl. Acad. Sci. USA* 100:253–58

Griffin DW, Ross L. 1991. Subject construal, social inference, and human misunderstanding. In *Advances in Experimental Social Psychology*, ed. MP Zanna, pp. 319–59. San Diego, CA: Academic

Gundel H, O'Connor MF, Littrell L, Fort C, Lane RD. 2003. Functional neuroanatomy of grief: an FMRI study. *Am. J. Psychiatry* 160:1946–53

Gusnard DA, Akbudak E, Shulman GL, Raichle ME. 2001. Medial prefrontal cortex and self-referential mental activity: relation of a default mode of brain function. *Proc. Natl. Acad. Sci USA* 98:4259–64

Hariri AR, Bookheimer SY, Mazziotta JC. 2000. Modulating emotional responses: effects of a neocortical network on the limbic system. *Neuroreport* 11:43–48

Harris LT, Todorov A, Fiske ST. 2005. Attributions on the brain: neuro-imaging dispositional inferences, beyond theory of mind. *Neuroimage* 28:763–69

Hart AJ, Whalen PJ, Shin LM, McInerney SC, Fischer H, Rauch SL. 2000. Differential response in the human amygdala to racial outgroup vs ingroup face stimuli. *Neuroreport* 11:2351–55

Haxby JV, Hoffman EA, Gobbini MI. 2002. Human neural systems for face recognition and social communication. *Biol. Psychiatry* 51:59–67

Heekeren HR, Wartenburger I, Schmidt H, Schwintowski HP, Villringer A. 2003. An fMRI study of simple ethical decision-making. *Neuroreport* 14:1215–19

Hemenover SH. 2003. The good, the bad, and the healthy: impacts of emotional disclosure of trauma on resilient self-concept and psychological distress. *Personal. Soc. Psychol. Bull.* 29:1236–44

Iacoboni M, Woods RP, Brass M, Bekkering H, Mazziotta JC, Rizzolatti G. 1999. Cortical mechanisms of human imitation. *Science* 286:2526–28

Ito TA, Urland GR, Willadsen-Jensen E, Correll J. 2006. The social neuroscience of stereotyping and prejudice: using event-related brain potentials to study social perception. In *Social Neuroscience: People Thinking About People*, ed. JT Cacioppo, PS Visser, CL Pickett. pp 189–208. Cambridge, MA: MIT Press

Jackson PL, Meltzoff AN, Decety J. 2005. How do we perceive the pain of others? A window into the neural processes involved in empathy. *Neuroimage* 24:771–79

Jacobsen T, Schubotz RI, Hofel L, Cramon DY. 2006. Brain correlates of aesthetic judgment of beauty. *Neuroimage* 29:276–85

Johnson SC, Schmitz TW, Kawahara-Baccus TN, Rowley HA, Alexander A, et al. 2005. The cerebral response during subjective choice with and without self-reference. *J. Cogn. Neurosci.* 17:1897–906

Johnson SC, Baxter LC, Wilder LS, Pipe JG, Heiserman JE, Prigatano GP. 2002. Neural correlates of self-reflection. *Brain* 125:1808–14

Kalisch R, Wiech K, Critchley HD, Seymour B, O'Doherty JP, et al. 2005. Anxiety reduction through detachment: subjective, physiological, and neural effects. *J. Cogn. Neurosci.* 17:874–83

Keenan JP, Nelson A, O'Connor M, Pascual-Leone A. 2001. Self-recognition and the right hemisphere. *Nature* 409:305

Keenan JP, Wheeler M, Platek SM, Lardi G, Lassonde M. 2003. Self-face processing in a callosotomy patient. *Eur. J. Neurosci.* 18:2391–95

Kelley HH. 1967. Attribution theory in social psychology. In *Nebraska Symposium on Motivation*, ed. D. Levine. pp. 192–240. Lincoln: Univ. Nebraska Press

Kelley WM, Macrae CN, Wyland CL, Caglar S, Inati S, Heatherton TF. 2002. Finding the self? An event-related fMRI study. *J. Cogn. Neurosci.* 14:785–94

Kjaer TW, Nowak M, Lou HC. 2002. Reflective self-awareness and conscious states: PET evidence for a common midline parietofrontal core. *Neuroimage* 17:1080–86

Klein SB, Loftus J, Kihlstrom JF. 1996. Self-knowledge of an amnesic patient: toward a neuropsychology of personality and social psychology. *J. Exp. Psychol.* 125:250–60

Klein SB, Loftus J, Trafton JG, Fuhrman RW. 1992. Use of exemplars and abstractions in trait judgments: a model of trait knowledge about the self and others. *J. Personal. Soc. Psychol.* 63:739–53

Knutson KM, Wood JN, Spampinato MV, Grafman J. 2006. Politics on the brain: an fMRI investigation. *Soc. Neuro.* 1:25–40

Kong J, Gollub RL, Rosman IS, Webb JM, Vangel MG, et al. 2006. Brain activity associated with expectancy-enhanced placebo analgesia as measured by functional magnetic resonance imaging. *J. Neurosci.* 26:381–88

Kosslyn SM, Ganis G, Thompson WL. 2001. Neural foundations of imagery. *Nat. Rev. Neurosci.* 2:635–42

Lane RD, Fink GR, Chau PM, Dolan RJ. 1997. Neural activation during selective attention to subjective emotional responses. *Neuroreport* 8:3969–72

Leibenluft E, Gobbini MI, Harrison T, Haxby JV. 2004. Mothers' neural activation in response to pictures of their children and other children. *Biol. Psychiatry* 56:225–32

Leube DT, Knoblich G, Erb M, Grodd W, Bartels M, Kircher TT. 2003. The neural correlates of perceiving one's own movements. *Neuroimage* 20:2084–90

Levesque J, Eugene F, Joanette Y, Paquette V, Mensour B, et al. 2003. Neural circuitry underlying voluntary suppression of sadness. *Biol. Psychiatry* 53:502–10

Lewis M, Ramsay D. 2004. Development of self-recognition, personal pronoun use, and pretend play during the second year. *Child. Dev.* 75:1821–31

Lieberman MD. 2000. Intuition: a social cognitive neuroscience approach. *Psychol. Bull.* 126:109–37

Lieberman MD. 2005. Principles, processes, and puzzles of social cognition: an introduction for the special issue on social cognitive neuroscience. *Neuroimage* 28:745–56

Lieberman MD. 2006. D^3-theory: a role for right ventrolateral prefrontal cortex in disruption, disambiguation, and detachment from immediate experience. *Perspect. Psychol. Sci.* In press

Lieberman MD, Eisenberger NI. 2005. Conflict and habit: a social cognitive neuroscience approach to the self. In *On Building, Defending and Regulating the Self: A Psychological Perspective*, ed. A Tesser, JV Wood, DA Stapel, pp. 77–102. New York: Psychol. Press

Lieberman MD, Eisenberger NI, Crockett MJ, Tom S, Pfeifer JH, Way BM. 2006. Putting feelings into words: affect labeling disrupts amygdala activity to affective stimuli. *Psychol. Sci.* In press

Lieberman MD, Gaunt R, Gilbert DT, Trope Y. 2002. Reflection and reflexion: a social cognitive neuroscience approach to attributional inference. *Adv. Exp. Soc. Psychol.* 34:199–249

Lieberman MD, Hariri A, Jarcho JM, Eisenberger NI, Bookheimer SY. 2005. An fMRI investigation of race-related amygdala activity in African-American and Caucasian-American individuals. *Nat. Neurosci.* 8:720–22

Lieberman MD, Jarcho JM, Berman S, Naliboff B, Suyenobu BY, et al. 2004. The neural correlates of placebo effects: a disruption account. *Neuroimage* 22:447–55

Lieberman MD, Jarcho JM, Satpute AB. 2004. Evidence-based and intuition-based self-knowledge: an fMRI study. *J. Personal. Soc. Psychol.* 87:421–35

Lieberman MD, Ochsner KN, Gilbert DT, Schacter DL. 2001. Do amnesics exhibit cognitive dissonance reduction? The role of explicit memory and attention in attitude change. *Psychol. Sci.* 12:135–40

Lieberman MD, Pfeifer JH. 2005. The self and social perception: three kinds of questions in social cognitive neuroscience. In *Cognitive Neuroscience of Emotional and Social Behavior*, ed. A Easton, N Emery, pp. 195–235. Philadephia, PA: Psychol. Press

Lorberbaum JP, Newman JD, Horwitz AR, Dubno JR, Lydiard RB, et al. 2002. A potential role for thalamocingulate circuitry in human maternal behavior. *Biol. Psychiatry* 51:431–45

MacDonald AW, Cohen JD, Stenger VA, Carter CS. 2000. Dissociating the role of the dorsolateral prefrontal and anterior cingulate cortex in cognitive control. *Science* 288:1835–38

MacDonald G, Leary MR. 2005. Why does social exclusion hurt? The relationship between social and physical pain. *Psychol. Bull.* 131:202–23

MacDonald PA, Paus T. 2003. The role of parietal cortex in awareness of self-generated movements: a transcranial magnetic stimulation study. *Cereb. Cortex* 13:962–67

MacLean PD, Newman JD. 1988. Role of midline frontolimbic cortex in production of the isolation call of squirrel monkeys. *Brain Res.* 450:111–23

Macrae CN, Moran JM, Heatherton TF, Banfield JF, Kelley WM. 2004. Medial prefrontal activity predicts memory for self. *Cereb. Cortex* 14:647–54

Markus HR. 1977. Self-schemata and processing information about the self. *J. Personal. Soc. Psychol.* 35:63–78

Mason MF, Banfield JF, Macrae CN. 2004. Thinking about actions: the neural substrates of person knowledge. *Cereb. Cortex* 14:209–14

McCabe K, Houser D, Ryan L, Smith V, Trouard T. 2001. A functional imaging study of cooperation in two-person reciprocal exchange. *Proc. Natl. Acad. Sci. USA* 98:11832–35

McClure SM, Li J, Tomlin D, Cypert KS, Montague LM, Montague PR. 2004. Neural correlates of behavioral preference for culturally familiar drinks. *Neuron* 44:379–87

McKiernan KA, Kaufman JN, Kucera-Thompson J, Binder JR. 2003. A parametric manipulation of factors affecting task-induced deactivation in functional neuroimaging. *J. Cogn. Neurosci.* 15:394–408

Mead GH. 1934. *Mind, Self, and Society.* Chicago: Univ. Chicago Press

Mendez MF, Anderson E, Shapira JS. 2005. An investigation of moral judgement in frontotemporal dementia. *Cogn. Behav. Neurol.* 18:193–208

Merleau-Ponty M. 1962. *Phenomenology of Perception*. London: Routledge

Metcalfe J, Mischel W. 1999. A hot/cool system analysis of delay of gratification: dynamics of willpower. *Psychol. Rev.* 106:3–19

Milne E, Grafman J. 2001. Ventromedial prefrontal cortex lesions in humans eliminate implicit gender stereotyping. *J. Neurosci.* 21:RC150

Mitchell JP, Banaji MR, Macrae CN. 2005. The link between social cognition and self-referential thought in the medial prefrontal cortex. *J. Cogn. Neurosci.* 17:1306–15

Mitchell JP, Macrae CN, Banaji MR. 2004. Encoding-specific effects of social cognition on the neural correlates of subsequent memory. *J. Neurosci.* 26:4912–17

Moll J, de Oliveira-Souza R, Bramati IE, Grafman J. 2002a. Functional networks in emotional moral and nonmoral social judgments. *Neuroimage* 16:696–703

Moll J, de Oliveira-Souza R, Eslinger PJ, Bramati IE, Mourao-Miranda J, et al. 2002b. The neural correlates of moral sensitivity: a functional magnetic resonance imaging investigation of basic and moral emotions. *J. Neurosci.* 22:2730–36

Moll J, de Oliveira-Souza R, Moll FT, Ignacio FA, Bramati IE, et al. 2005. The moral affiliations of disgust: a functional MRI study. *Cogn. Behav. Neurol.* 18:68–78

Morrison I, Lloyd D, di Pellegrino G, Roberts N. 2004. Vicarious responses to pain in anterior cingulate cortex: Is empathy a multisensory issue? *Cogn. Affect. Behav. Neurosci.* 4:270–78

Najib A, Lorberbaum JP, Kose S, Bohning DE, George MS. 2004. Regional brain activity in women grieving a romantic relationship breakup. *Am. J. Psychiatry* 161:2245–56

Neely JH. 1977. Semantic priming and retrieval from lexical memory: roles of inhibitionless spreading activation and limited capacity attention. *J. Exp. Psychol.: Gen.* 106:226–54

Nitschke JB, Nelson EE, Rusch BD, Fox AS, Oakes TR, Davidson RJ. 2004. Orbitofrontal cortex tracks positive mood in mothers viewing pictures of their newborn infants. *Neuroimage* 21:583–92

Nosek BA, Banaji MR, Greenwald AG. 2002. Harvesting implicit group attitudes and beliefs from a demonstration web site. *Group Dyn.* 6:101–15

Ochsner KN. 2004. Current directions in social cognitive neuroscience. *Curr. Opin. Neurobiol.* 14:254–58

Ochsner KN, Beer JS, Robertson ER, Cooper JC, Gabrieli JD, et al. 2005. The neural correlates of direct and reflected self-knowledge. *Neuroimage* 28:797–814

Ochsner KN, Bunge SA, Gross JJ, Gabrieli JD. 2002. Rethinking feelings: an FMRI study of the cognitive regulation of emotion. *J. Cogn. Neurosci.* 14:1215–29

Ochsner KN, Gross JJ. 2005. The cognitive control of emotion. *Trends Cogn. Sci.* 9:242–49

Ochsner KN, Knierim K, Ludlow DH, Henelin J, Ramachandra T, et al. 2004. Reflecting upon feelings: an fMRI study of neural systems supporting the attribution of emotion to self and other. *J. Cogn. Neurosci.* 16:1746–72

Ochsner KN, Lieberman MD. 2001. The emergence of social cognitive neuroscience. *Am. Psychol.* 56:717–34

Ochsner KN, Ray RD, Cooper JC, Robertson ER, Chopra S, et al. 2004. For better or for worse: neural systems supporting the cognitive down- and up- regulation of negative emotion. *Neuroimage* 23:483–99

Panksepp J. 1998. *Affective Neuroscience*. London: Oxford Univ. Press

Pasley BN, Mayes LC, Schultz RT. 2004. Subcortical discrimination of unperceived objects during binocular rivalry. *Neuron* 42:163–72

Pennebaker JW. 1997. Writing about emotional experiences as a therapeutic process. *Psychol. Sci.* 8:162–66

Perner J, Wimmer H. 1985. "John thinks that Mary thinks that. . .": attribution of second-order beliefs by 5- to 10-year-old children. *J. Exp. Child Psychol.* 39:437–71

Petrovic P, Dietrich T, Fransson P, Andersson J, Carlsson K, Ingvar M. 2005. Placebo in emotional processing—induced expectations of anxiety relief activate a generalized modulatory network. *Neuron* 46:957–69

Petrovic P, Kalso E, Petersson KM, Ingvar M. 2002. Placebo and opioid analgesia—imaging a shared neuronal network. *Science* 295:1737–40

Peyron R, Laurent B, Garcia-Larrea L. 2000. Functional imaging of brain responses to pain. A review and meta-analysis. *Neurophysiol. Clin.* 30:263–88

Pfeifer JH, Lieberman MD, Dapretto M. 2006. "I know you are but what am I?" Neural bases of self- and social-knowledge retrieval in children and adults. Under review

Phan KL, Fitzgerald DA, Nathan PJ, Moore GL, Uhde TW, Tancer ME. 2005. Neural substrates for voluntary suppression of negative affect: a functional magnetic resonance imaging study. *Biol. Psychiatry* 57:210–19

Phelps EA, Cannistraci CJ, Cunningham WA. 2003. Intact performance on an indirect measure of race bias following amygdala damage. *Neuropsychologia* 41:203–8

Phelps EA, O'Connor KJ, Cunningham WA, Funayama ES, Gatenby JC, et al. 2000. Performance on indirect measures of race evaluation predicts amygdala activation. *J. Cogn. Neurosci.* 12:729–38

Platek SM, Loughead JW, Gur RC, Busch S, Ruparel K, et al. 2006. Neural substrates for functionally discriminating self-face from personally familiar faces. *Hum. Brain Mapp.* 27:91–8

Poldrack RA. 2006. Can cognitive processes be inferred from neuroimaging data? *Trends Cogn. Sci.* 10:59–63

Pronin E, Gilovich T, Ross L. 2004. Objectivity in the eye of the beholder: divergent perceptions of bias in self versus others. *Psychol. Rev.* 111:781–99

Rainville P, Duncan GH, Price DD, Carrier B, Bushnell MC. 1997. Pain affect encoded in human anterior cingulate but not somatosensory cortex. *Science* 277:968–71

Read SJ, Vanman EJ, Miller LC. 1997. Connectionism, parallel constraint satisfaction processes, and gestalt principles: (re)introducing cognitive dynamics to social psychology. *Personal. Soc. Psychol. Rev.* 1:26–53

Reeder GD. 1993. Trait-behavior relations in dispositional inference. *Personal. Soc. Psychol. Bull.* 19:586–93

Richeson JA, Baird AA, Gordon HL, Heatherton TF, Wyland CL, et al. 2003. An fMRI investigation of the impact of interracial contact on executive function. *Nat. Neurosci.* 6:1323–28

Rilling JK, Gutman DA, Zeh TR, Pagnoni G, Berns GS, Kilts CD. 2002. A neural basis for social cooperation. *Neuron* 35:395–405

Robinson BW. 1967. Vocalization evoked from forebrain in *Macaca mulatta*. *Physiol. Behav.* 2:345–54

Ruby P, Decety J. 2004. How would you feel versus how do you think she would feel? A neuroimaging study of perspective-taking with social emotions. *J. Cogn. Neurosci.* 16:988–99

Samson D, Apperly IA, Kathirgamanathan U, Humphreys GW. 2005. Seeing it my way: a case of selective deficit in inhibiting self-perspective. *Brain* 128:1102–11

Sanfey AG, Rilling JK, Aronson JA, Nystrom LE, Cohen JD. 2003. The neural basis of economic decision-making in the Ultimatum Game. *Science* 300:1755–58

Satpute AB, Lieberman MD. 2006. Integrating automatic and controlled processing into neurocognitive models of social cognition. *Brain Res.* 1079:86–97

Saxe R, Carey S, Kanwisher N. 2004. Understanding other minds: linking developmental psychology and functional neuroimaging. *Annu. Rev. Psychol.* 55:87–124

Schmitz TW, Kawahara-Baccus TN, Johnson SC. 2004. Metacognitive evaluation, self-relevance, and the right prefrontal cortex. *Neuroimage* 22:941–47

Seger CA, Stone M, Kennan JP. 2004. Cortical activations during judgments about the self and another person. *Neuropsychologia* 42:1168–77

Seifritz E, Esposito F, Neuhoff JG, Luthi A, Mustovic H, et al. 2003. Differential sex-independent amygdala response to infant crying and laughing in parents versus nonparents. *Biol. Psychiatry* 54:1367–75

Semendeferi K, Schleicher A, Zilles K, Armstrong E, Van Hoesen GW. 2001. Evolution of the hominoid prefrontal cortex: imaging and quantitative analysis of area 10. *Am. J. Physical Anthropol.* 114:224–41

Shamay-Tsoory SG, Lester H, Chisin R, Isreal O, Bar-Shalom R, et al. 2005. The neural correlates of understanding the other's distress: a positron emission tomography investigation of accurate empathy. *Neuroimage* 27:468–72

Shamay-Tsoory SG, Tomer R, Berger BD, Aharon-Peretz J. 2003. Characterization of empathy deficits following prefrontal brain damage: the role of the right ventromedial prefrontal cortex. *J. Cogn. Neurosci.* 15:324–27

Sherif M. 1937. An experimental approach to the study of attitudes. *Sociometry* 1:90–98

Sherif M, Harvey OJ, White BJ, Hood WR, Sherif CW. 1961. *Intergroup Conflict and Cooperation: The Robber's Cave Experiment.* Norman: Univ. Oklahoma Press

Shimada S, Hiraki K, Oda I. 2005. The parietal role in the sense of self-ownership with temporal discrepancy between visual and proprioceptive feedbacks. *Neuroimage* 24:1225–32

Silvia PJ. 2002. Self-awareness and emotional intensity. *Cogn. Emot.* 16:195–216

Singer T, Seymour B, O'Doherty J, Kaube H, Dolan RJ, Frith CD. 2004. Empathy for pain involves the affective but not sensory components of pain. *Science* 303:1157–62

Singer T, Seymour B, O'Doherty JP, Stephan KE, Dolan RJ, Frith CD. 2006. Empathic neural responses are modulated by the perceived fairness of others. *Nature* 439:466–69

Sirigu A, Daprati E, Pradat-Diehl P, Franck N, Jeannerod M. 1999. Perception of self-generated movement followng left parietal lesion. *Brain* 122:1867–74

Smith ER, DeCoster J. 1999. Associative and rule-based processing: a connectionist interpretation of dual-process models. In *Dual-Process Theories in Social Psychology*, ed. S Chaiken, Y Tropez, pp. 323–36, New York: Guilford

Smith W. 1945. The functional significance of the rostral cingular cortex as revealed by its responses to electrical excitation. *J. Neurophysiol.* 8:241–55

Spence SA, Brooks DJ, Hirsch SR, Liddle PF, Meehan J, Grasby PM. 1997. A PET study of voluntary movement in schizophrenic patients experiencing passivity phenomena. *Brain* 120:1997–2011

Sperry RW, Zaidel E, Zaidel D. 1979. Self recognition and social awareness in the deconnected minor hemisphere. *Neuropsychologia* 17:153–66

Stamm JS. 1955. The function of the medial cerebral cortex in maternal behavior of rats. *J. Comp. Physiol. Psychol.* 47:21–27

Suguira M, Kawashima R, Nakamura K, Okada K, Kato T, et al. 2000. Passive and active recognition of one's own face. *Neuroimage* 11:36–48

Suguira M, Kawashima R, Nakamura K, Sato N, Nakamura A, et al. 2001. Activation reduction in anterior temporal cortices during repeated recognition of faces of personal acquaintances. *Neuroimage* 13:877–90

Suguira M, Watanabe J, Maeda Y, Matsue Y, Fukuda H, Kawashima R. 2005. Cortical mechanisms of visual self-recognition. *Neuroimage* 24:143–49

Tabibnia G, Satpute AB, Lieberman MD. 2006. The neural basis of fairness preference. Under review

Taylor ST, Phan KL, Decker LR, Liberzon I. 2003. Subjective rating of emotionally salient stimuli modulates neural activity. *Neuroimage* 18:650–59

Trepel C, Fox CR, Poldrack RA. 2005. Prospect theory on the brain? Toward a cognitive neuroscience of decision under risk. *Brain Res. Cogn. Brain Res.* 23:34–50

Turk DJ, Heatherton TF, Kelley WM, Funnell MG, Gazzaniga MS, Macrae CN. 2002. Mike or me? Self-recognition in a split-brain patient. *Nat. Neurosci.* 5:841–42

Twenge JM, Baumeister RF, Tice DM, Stucke TS. 2001. If you can't join them, beat them: effects of social exclusion on aggressive behavior. *J. Personal. Soc. Psychol.* 81:1058–69

Uddin LQ, Kaplan JT, Molnar-Szakacs I, Zaidel E, Iacoboni M. 2005. Self-face recognition activates a frontoparietal "mirror" network in the right hemisphere: an event-related fMRI study. *Neuroimage* 15:926–35

Uddin LQ, Rayman J, Zaidel E. 2005. Split-brain reveals separate but equal self-recognition in the two cerebral hemispheres. *Conscious Cogn.* 14:633–40

Vartanian O, Goel V. 2004. Neuroanatomical correlates of aesthetic preference for paintings. *Neuroreport* 15:893–97

Vogeley K, Bussfeld P, Newen A, Herrmann S, Happe F, et al. 2001. Mind reading: neural mechanisms of theory of mind and self-persepctive. *Neuroimage* 14:170–81

Wager TD, Rilling JK, Smith EE, Sokolik A, Casey KL, et al. 2004. Placebo-induced changes in FMRI in the anticipation and experience of pain. *Science* 303:1162–67

Wegner DM, Bargh JA. 1998. Control and automaticity in social life. In *The Handbook of Social Psychology*, ed. DT Gilbert, ST Fiske, G Lindzey, pp. 446–96. New York: McGraw-Hill

Wheeler ME, Fiske ST. 2005. Controlling racial prejudice: social-cognitive goals affect amygdala and stereotype activation. *Psychol. Sci.* 16:56–63

Wicker B, Keysers C, Plailly J, Royet J, Gallese V, Rizzolatti G. 2003. Both of us disgusted in my insula: the common neural basis of seeing and feeling disgust. *Neuron* 40:655–64

Wilde O. 1905. *De Profundis*. Mineola, NY: Dover

Wilson TD, Centerbar DB, Kermer DA, Gilbert DT. 2005. The pleasures of uncertainty: prolonging positive moods in ways people do not anticipate. *J. Personal. Soc. Psychol.* 88:5–21

Wilson TD, Schooler JW. 1991. Thinking too much: introspection can reduce the quality of preferences and decisions. *J. Personal. Soc. Psychol.* 60:181–92

Woodward AL. 1998. Infants selectively encode the goal object of an actor's reach. *Cognition* 69:1–34

Word CO, Zanna MP, Cooper J. 1974. The nonverbal mediation of self-fulfilling prophecies in interracial interaction. *J. Exp. Soc. Psychol.* 10:109–20

Zysset S, Huber O, Ferstl E, von Cramon DY. 2002. The anterior frontomedian cortex and evaluative judgment: an fMRI study. *Neuroimage* 15:983–91

Partitioning the Domain of Social Inference: Dual Mode and Systems Models and Their Alternatives

Arie W. Kruglanski and Edward Orehek

Department of Psychology, University of Maryland, College Park, Maryland
20742-4411; email: arie@psyc.umd.edu, eorehek@psyc.umd.edu

Annu. Rev. Psychol. 2007. 58:291–316

First published online as a Review in
Advance on August 25, 2006

The *Annual Review of Psychology* is online
at http://psych.annualreviews.org

This article's doi:
10.1146/annurev.psych.58.110405.085629

Key Words

judgment, automaticity, rule-following, conditioning, unimodel

Abstract

Recent decades of theorizing about social inference phenomena have
seen a variety of models that partitioned the underlying processes
into two qualitatively distinct types whose specific nature was depicted differently in the different frameworks. The present article
reviews major such partitioning efforts as well as their proposed alternatives, and discusses their unique features, their commonalities,
and the conceptual and empirical issues that they raise.

Contents

INTRODUCTION

The 1986 edition of Webster's dictionary defines inference as "the act of passing from one proposition, or judgment to another whose truth is assumed to follow from that of the former." In this sense, inference constitutes the act of reaching a judgment on the basis of information treated as evidence for its veridicality (Kruglanski & Thomson 1999a). It is, quintessentially, the act of going "beyond the information given" (Bruner 1973) to the conclusion that such information is seen to imply. Whereas in the 1960s, social cognition theorists attempted to model the

mechanisms of inference, e.g., in Bayesian (Edwards et al. 1963), "probabilogical" (McGuire 1960), or quasi-statistical (Kelley 1967) terms, in the 1970s, the focus shifted to demonstrating the shortcomings of human judgment (Nisbett & Ross 1980). In part, the latter were tied to the cognitive miser metaphor, whereby "... people are limited in their capacity to process information... Consequently, errors and biases stem from inherent features of the cognitive system" (Fiske & Taylor 1984, p. 12).

In subsequent decades, social cognition researchers adopted a more nuanced view, guided by the "motivated tactician" metaphor. As Fiske & Taylor (1991, p. 13) characterized it, "the social perceiver... might best be termed the motivated tactician, a fully engaged thinker who has multiple cognitive strategies available and chooses among them based on goals, motives, and needs. Sometimes the motivated tactician chooses wisely, in the interest of adaptability and accuracy, and sometimes the motivated tactician chooses defensively in the interest of speed or self-esteem. ..."

Unlike the cognitive miser model, in which people are viewed as generally unwilling or unable to process information thoroughly, the motivated tactician perspective assumes a flexible process wherein the availability of motivational and cognitive resources may vary across persons and situations. Too, the motivated tactician metaphor implies a dichotomy between suboptimal and optimal inferential modes. This distinction has inspired a variety of dualistic models of judgment that have dominated the field in the past two decades. As a general characterization, these dual-process models draw a distinction between a brief and superficial mode, often assumed to operate under limited resource conditions, and a more thorough, resource-dependent mode.

Following other authors (cf. Gawronski & Bodenhausen 2006), we draw a distinction between dual-mode and dual-systems formulations. The earlier dual-mode formulations were typically domain specific, whereas the dual-systems formulations were more general and assumed to apply across domains. Furthermore, the dual-mode formulations were information focused; they typically coordinated the two proposed modes to two different types of information (e.g., peripheral cues versus message arguments, social categories versus personality attributes). The more recent dual-systems models, in contrast, were process focused, and they didn't relate their binary systems of inference to distinct information types. Critiques of the dualistic formulations have been voiced, and alternative ways of conceptualizing human inference

have been proposed. Our present purpose is to review some of the major dual-process models of social inference and to consider their alternatives.

DUAL-MODE FORMULATIONS

We begin our review of the dual-mode models by considering the influential persuasion models of this type, namely the Elaboration Likelihood Model (ELM; Petty & Cacioppo 1986) and the Heuristic Systematic Model (HSM; Chaiken et al. 1989). Space limitations prevent a more exhaustive review of the dual-mode models; thus, we direct the reader to recent Annual Review articles (Crano & Prislin 2006, Fazio & Olson 2002, Macrae & Bodenhausen 2000, Wood 2000). The ELM and the HSM can be considered information focused because they distinguish between two types of information: information contained in the message and information unrelated to the issue, yet capable of producing persuasion under some circumstances.

The Elaboration Likelihood Model

The ELM's central mode pertains to a thorough processing of message or issue information. A special feature of the ELM is the notion that the same variable is capable of serving different functions. What function will be served is assumed to depend on the elaboration likelihood, i.e., the likelihood that the information will be processed extensively. When the elaboration likelihood is low, a variable (say, source attractiveness) could serve as a cue; when the elaboration likelihood is high, the same variable could serve as a message argument. When the elaboration likelihood is intermediate, this variable could determine the elaboration likelihood itself (e.g., an attractive source may prompt a more extensive processing of her message). Peripheral processing is based on a wide variety of cues whose commonality is not explicitly identified. The ELM accords a major role in this regard to the elaboration likelihood continuum, suggesting that the peripheral route will be taken when the elaboration likelihood is low and the central route when the elaboration likelihood is high. The two modes are assumed to coexist in inverse relation to each other. Thus, as one moves toward the low end of the continuum, one should find an increasing proportion of peripheral relative to central processing and vice versa as one moves toward the high end.

Commentary

The ELM distinguishes between a cue function and a message argument function. However, it does not specify what the cue function is and how it differs from the argument function. Furthermore, the notion of the elaboration continuum has an ambiguous implication. It refers both to the extent of processing and to the type of information processed. Specifically, the low end of the continuum denotes both limited processing and the processing of peripheral information, whereas the high end denotes both extensive processing and the processing of message information. The current notion of the elaboration continuum seems to confound the type of information processed with the way it is processed, namely, briefly versus extensively.

The Heuristic Systematic Model

The HSM's systematic mode pertains to a thorough processing of all the available information, that is, of message as well as of heuristic information. The HSM's "heuristic" mode is defined more precisely in terms of general rules of thumb of the kind "experts are correct" or "friends are to be trusted." The "heuristics-as-rules" notion affords the additional implication that heuristic processing would be more likely to the extent that the heuristic rules were more cognitively accessible. The HSM proposes a "sufficiency threshold" constituting an acceptable level of confidence an individual may require concerning a

given judgment. Moreover, the "least-effort" principle was proposed as a guiding mechanism of inference formation. When the sufficiency threshold is low, the individual is assumed to employ heuristic processing. When it is high, systematic processing is assumed to kick in because the heuristic mode is assumed to afford relatively low levels of confidence. Systematic processing is assumed to take place only if the heuristic mode failed to deliver the desired level of confidence. The heuristic and the systematic modes may interact in three different ways: (*a*) Heuristic and systematic processing may augment each other if they lead to similar conclusions, (*b*) systematic processing may reduce the judgmental impact of heuristic processing when it leads to opposite conclusions, and (*c*) heuristic processing may affect the direction and extent of systematic processing. Finally, the HSM regards heuristics as general knowledge structures that are applied in a top-down manner, whereas systematic processing is assumed to reflect bottom-up responding to arguments presented and a use of the arguments to construct (more abstract) conclusions.

Commentary

The HSM implies that heuristic cues are generally processed first, whereas message and issue information is processed only when the heuristic processing fails to yield a sufficient level of confidence. This reasoning seems to assume that the processing of heuristic information is generally easier and therefore is preferable to the processing of message information. It isn't clear why this should be generally true, unless one defined heuristics as easy-to-process information. Yet, if the latter definition were adopted, this would preempt the definition of heuristics as general beliefs unrelated to the message contents, because heuristics need not be universally easy to process. Such a definition would render problematic the juxtaposition of heuristics to message arguments that might be also quite easy to process.

Models of Categorization and Stereotyping

Two dual-process models addressed person perception: Fiske's continuum model (Fiske & Neuberg 1990, Fiske et al. 1999) and Brewer's (1988) impression formation model. The most fundamental commonality was that both models distinguished between category-based and attribute-based processing and viewed them as qualitatively different. In both models, categorical processing was assumed to proceed in a top-down fashion, whereas attribute processing was assumed to proceed in a bottom-up fashion. Both models assumed that impression formation follows a fixed order, commencing with an automatic identification of the target in terms of some general categories to which it belongs.

Impression Formation Model

Brewer's (1988) model suggested that different stages have distinct types of cognitive representations: The initial stage, automatic identification, was assumed to consist of judgments represented as categories in multidimensional space. The second stage, category-based typing, was assumed to be represented via pictoliteral prototypes. In the third stage, individuation, the representation was assumed to depend on category subtypes. The final stage, personalization, was assumed to depend on the individual's schemata within a verbal, propositional, network. The Brewer model posits different decision rules following each stage of processing.

More recently, Brewer & Harasty Feinstein (1999) offered a re-evaluation of its postulates in light of known evidence. Importantly, Brewer & Harasty Feinstein (1999) denied priority to category-based processing over attribute-based processing. As they put it, "The distinction between the two modes revolves around what information is attended to and what prior knowledge is activated at the time the information is presented" (p. 258). Nor are Brewer & Harasty Feinstein (1999, p. 259) assuming that category-based versus person-based representations are correlated with effortless versus effortful processing modes. "On the contrary, both modes of person perception can be either heuristic or elaborated."

Continuum Model

Fiske's model assumes no qualitative differences in mental representation as a function of processing stages. At both the categorization and the individuation stages, mental representations are assumed to form a network in which both verbal and visual representations may be included. In the Fiske model, an initial interest/relevance judgment and the degree of informational fit apply at each processing stage. "For example a target can be a good or poor fit to an initial category, a good or a poor fit to a subtype, a good or poor fit to an exemplar" (Fiske 1988, p. 70). The Fiske conception emphasizes a continuum. Thus, involvement affects each process along the continuum from confirmatory categorization, through recategorization, to piecemeal integration.

More recently, Fiske et al. (1999) summarized additional evidence for the continuum model. They cited research suggesting that people often use social category information to the extent "that the category is pragmatic in context" (Fiske et al. 1999, p. 236), that is, to the extent to which it is informative about the judgmental dimension of interest. Fiske et al. (1999) also cite evidence that people often recategorize social objects when the objects' attributes do not fit the original categorization, and that motivation increases attention to expectancy disconfirming information. Finally, evidence exists that the motivational effects on impression formation are mediated by attention paid to specific types of information, such as attention to the targets' attributes (Fiske et al. 1999, pp. 241–42).

Commentary

Statements by Fiske et al. (1999) and Brewer & Harasty Feinstein (1999) represent interesting developments in their respective models. Both sets of authors agree that categories will be used to the extent that they are known, accessible, and informative. This conclusion represents an increased flexibility in their perspective and a relaxation of their original assumption of a fixed sequence running from categorization to individuation. In stressing the commonalities of process shared by category and attribute information, the recent theorizing represents less clearly dualistic formulations than did the original models.

DISPOSITIONAL ATTRIBUTIONS

Gilbert (e.g., 1989) and Trope & Alfieri (1997) proposed a pair of attributional dual-mode models.

Gilbert's Correction Model

Gilbert's (1989, p. 193) model of attributional inferences views "causal attributions as the net result of a chain of events." Additionally, Gilbert's model draws qualitative distinctions between informational contents. Specifically, the model suggests that dispositional inferences are arrived at automatically, in a resource-independent mode impervious to disruption, whereas controlled processes that are resource dependent handle situational information. Situational information is considered in a controlled correction process designed to overcome the potential biases induced by the initial, automatic, characterization. Nonetheless, Gilbert allows for a range of automaticity among dispositional inferences. As he states, "all behaviors are not equally easy to analyze, and ... fewer resources might be required to draw dispositional inferences from nonverbal than from verbal behavior" (p. 201). "Thus ... although characterization is in general a relatively automatic process, characterizations from nonverbal behavior may be *more* automatic than characterizations from verbal behavior" (p. 202). Finally, Gilbert's model suggests that dispositional and situational information is processed in a specific order. In this connection, he cites Quattrone (1982) as having "shown that ... perceivers *first* draw dispositional inferences about others and *then* correct these inferences with information about the situational forces" (Gilbert 1989, p. 193).

Commentary

Gilbert's (1989) model involves the assumptions that dispositional attributions are automatic, whereas situational attributions are controlled, and that dispositional judgments typically precede situational judgments. However, cross-cultural research conducted by Nisbett and others (see Nisbett et al. 2001) suggests that participants in collectivist cultures are automatically and initially more likely to make situational rather than dispositional attributions. This is likely due to different cultural norms that place a premium on either dispositional or situational inferences. Moreover, Webster's (1993) work demonstrated that situational requirements may determine whether dispositional or situational inferences come to mind initially or are made only upon subsequent inquiry. Finally, Gilbert suggests that verbal and nonverbal information types are generally processed at different levels of automaticity. However, if attending to verbal communication becomes highly routinized (say by a person with a visual impairment), inferences utilizing verbal information could be more automatic than nonverbal information. Such a claim suggests a continuum of automaticity, as proposed by Bargh (1996), incompatible with a dichotomous separation between controlled and automatic processes (see also Moors & De Houwer 2006). The degree of routinization need not be tied, necessarily, to any informational type or content. Any inference can become highly routinized.

Trope's Integration Model

Trope and colleagues offered a sequential dual-mode model of causal attribution (Trope 1986, Trope & Alfieri 1997, Trope & Liberman 1996). Trope (1986) departed from the assumption that before it can be attributed to the person or the situation, an actor's behavior needs first to be identified. Thus, the stage of behavior identification was assumed to precede that of dispositional attribution. Trope & Alfieri (1997) expanded these notions to a dual-process model wherein contextual constraint information affects behavior identification and dispositional inference in qualitatively distinct ways. At the identification stage, the incorporation of contextual constraints was said to be effortless, automatic, and independent of cognitive resources. By contrast, at the dispositional inference stage, the influence of context was portrayed as controlled, deliberative, and capacity demanding (Trope & Alfieri 1997, p. 663).

Trope & Gaunt (2000) juxtaposed their integration model to Gilbert's (1989) correction model by showing that situational constraint information can exert its subtractive effects (discounted) under load, something denied by Gilbert's formulation, provided it is sufficiently activated and hence is easy to process. Their research demonstrated that the dispositional inference stage can be independent of cognitive load. Finally, Chun et al. (2002) found that behavioral identifications can be undermined by load when the contextual information is nonsalient; hence, its incorporation into the behavior identification is made difficult.

Commentary

Trope & Gaunt's (2000) and Chun et al.'s (2002) findings suggest that the behavior identification stage, even though it logically precedes the dispositional attribution stage, isn't qualitatively distinct from it as far as cognitive resources are concerned. Depending on informational saliency or accessibility, either can be more or less dependent on cognitive resources. This suggests that the need for cognitive resources depends on the difficulty of information processing. The behavior identification and the dispositional attribution stages seem to differ in the contents of the judgmental question (comprising the "what" question in the case of behavior identification and the "why" question in the case of dispositional attribution), but do not seem to differ in their dependence on resources.

DUAL-MODE MODELS OF SOCIAL INFERENCE: CONCLUDING COMMENTS

The dual-mode models of social inference exerted considerable influence on understanding a variety of phenomena in social cognition and made a significant contribution. A general conceptual issue for these formulations has stemmed from the fact that they typically tied the two modes to different contents of information and assumed that these are subject to qualitatively different processing. But insofar as the possible contents or types of information are vast, this approach might lead to an open-ended proliferation of processes. Possibly in recognition of this problem, some of the models (Brewer & Harasty Feinstein 1999, Fiske et al. 1999) relaxed their assumptions concerning differential processing of different information types. These developments are well considered and compelling, yet they reduce somewhat the models' dualistic character that has rested thus far on a differentiation between information types.

DUAL-SYSTEMS MODELS OF SOCIAL INFERENCE

In the category of dual-systems models belong frameworks that highlight the qualitatively distinct judgmental processes whereby social inferences can be reached and downplay the role of distinct informational contents highlighted in the various dual-mode models. Kahneman's (2003) recent framework straddles the divide between the dual-mode and the dual-systems formulations.

Intuitive Versus Rational Systems of Inference

Kahneman (2003) distinguished two modes of cognitive function, labeled System 1 and System 2 processing. Intuitions were defined as "thoughts and preferences that come to mind quickly and without much reflection" (Kahneman 2003). What determines whether a thought or a preference would be considered intuitive is its accessibility. Kahneman further suggested that thoughts and preferences can be made intuitive "by prolonged practice" (Kahneman 2003, p. 699). Indeed, major theories of accessibility (e.g., Higgins 1996) have stressed that construct accessibility is a function of the frequency of activation. As Kahneman (2003, p. 698) described it, "The operations of System 1 are typically fast, automatic, effortless, associative, implicit (not available to introspection), and often emotionally charged; they are also governed by habit and are therefore difficult to control or modify. The operations of System 2 are slower, serial, effortful, more likely to be consciously monitored and deliberately controlled; they are also relatively flexible and potentially rule governed. ...." Kahneman also asserted that the extensional (i.e., rational) and prototypical (i.e., intuitive) judgments are assumed to be "governed by characteristically different logical *rules*" (Kahneman 2003, p. 713, emphasis added), implying that both processes are rule based in fact, albeit mediated by different rules.

Empirical Evidence

A critical aspect of Kahneman's dual-systems framework is that System 2 (versus System 1) operation amounts to a more extensive processing of the information given. For instance, Smith & Levin (1996) showed that framing effects are reduced in a between-subjects design

for participants with high scores on the need for cognition because such participants apparently moved away from the initial framing they were given. LeBoeuf & Shafir (2003) did not replicate the between-participants' effect, but did show that individuals higher on the need for cognition exhibited lesser framing effects in a within-subject design where each respondent encountered two framing versions of a problem. Note, however, that the presence of a usable cue can be thought of as lying on a continuum of accessibility or retrievability. In those terms, individuals with a greater degree of processing motivation may be willing to engage in a more extensive search and ultimately retrieve less accessible items of relevant information than would less motivated individuals.

Commentary

A critical aspect of System 1 operation is that it is based on intuitions, defined as those that are highly accessible. Accessibility, however, "is a continuum, not a dichotomy" (Kahneman 2003, p. 700). In addition, however, System 1 operation is characterized by the use of heuristics that in prior work (e.g., Tversky & Kahneman 1974) was often juxtaposed to the use of statistical rules (e.g., based on base rates or conjunctive probabilities). If the use of the statistical rules characterizes System 2 operation, then the continuum discussed by Kahneman (2003) is characterized both by the degree of processing and the type of information processed, not unlike the confound obtaining in the ELM and the HSM formulations.

Alternatively, one could state that System 1 refers to a highly restricted processing operation in which only the highly accessible information is used, whereas System 2 refers to more extensive processing. More or less processing is a matter of degree; hence, such a framing stresses the continuum aspect of Kahneman's theory and virtually removes the need for a qualitative distinction between two separate systems.

Reflection Versus Reflexion

In a recent paper, Lieberman et al. (2002, p. 205) stated, "The idea that automatic processes are merely faster and quieter versions of controlled processes is theoretically parsimonious, intuitively compelling, and wrong." Their conclusion derives from the notion that different brain structures seem to be activated in automatic versus controlled behavior. More specifically, Lieberman et al. (2002) proposed that (what they refer to as) the X system, which includes the lateral temporal cortex, amygdala, and basal ganglia, is involved in automatic processing. The C system, related to activity in anterior cingulate, prefrontal cortex, and the hippocampus, seems activated when deliberative or controlled processing takes place.

Empirical Evidence

Lieberman et al. (2002, p. 214) cite numerous neuroimaging studies as suggestive evidence that the inferotemporal cortex is involved in automatic categorization. Neuroimaging studies also revealed that "rule-based processing... led to prefrontal, anterior cingulate and hippocampus activation, belonging with the C system" (Lieberman et al. 2002, p. 228). Yet, the fact that different brain structures have been involved in instances of automatic versus controlled processing need not be considered compelling evidence that automatic and controlled processes aren't "faster and quieter versions of controlled processes" (Lieberman et al. 2002, p. 205).

The notion that automatic and controlled processes lie on a continuum is widely accepted (see, e.g., Bargh 1996, Logan 1989, Posner & Rothbart 1989, Schneider & Shiffrin 1977), and the rule-like (if-then) nature of associative as well as controlled inferences also has been noted (Holyoak et al. 1989, Lovibond 2003, Williams 1995). Instead of assuming qualitatively different systems, one might argue that the different brain structures simply respond to processing difficulty such that beyond some threshold of difficulty, processing capability offered by X structures might not suffice, and other brain structures (e.g., those included in the C category) might need to kick in. This is akin to additional muscles getting involved when the weight one tried to lift exceeded a given threshold. In short, involvement of different brain structures in the processing of more versus less practiced (efficient) if-then rules (Bargh 1996, Uttal 2001) might merely indicate that the brain is responsive to resource requirements of different information-processing tasks.

Lieberman et al. (2002) assume that system X is designed to process identity information (e.g., identification of a given behavior as a member of a given category), whereas the C system is assumed to process causality information and hence yield inferences about the behavior's causal origins. Thus, the X system is assumed to be involved both in the processing of identity information and in automatic processing. Similarly, the C system is assumed to be involved both in the processing of causality information and controlled processing. However, there are reasons to believe that not all identity processing is automatic and that not all causality processing is deliberative or controlled. Trope & Gaunt (2000) showed that making the causal attribution task easier eliminated its sensitivity to cognitive load; this would put it in the category of automatic (efficient) processing. Michotte's (1963) classic work illustrates the immediacy with which causal attributions can be made when information about contiguity and temporal precedence is clear and salient, suggesting that causal inferences may be direct and efficient. In addition, Schneider & Shiffrin's (1977) classic task consisted of identifying letters and digits in a grid-like array. This represents an identity task par excellence, yet it took participants months to automatize. Furthermore, Chun et al. (2002) rendered the identification task controlled (and hence resource dependent) by decreasing the saliency of information pertinent to the identity inference.

Commentary

If system X is involved in automatic processing and not in controlled processing, it cannot be generally involved in identity processing because it can be automatic in some circumstances and controlled in others. Similarly, if system C is involved in controlled processing, it could not be involved in causal processing because the latter, too, could be automatic in some circumstances and controlled in others. Therefore, the dichotomy between the X and C systems does not offer strong evidence for a dual-systems model of attributional inferences in which the identification phase is automatic and the causal inference phase is controlled.

Sloman's Two Systems of Reasoning

Sloman (1996) distinguished between associative and rule-based processes of reaching judgments. Sloman (1996) analyzed several examples of phenomenally experienced variation in an attempt to identify a substantial criterion for process distinctiveness. Sloman settled on the one criterion, Criterion S (for simultaneity), that he viewed as satisfactory in warranting a qualitative distinction between systems of reasoning: "A reasoning problem satisfies Criterion S if it causes people to simultaneously believe two contradictory responses."

Commentary

Because of the key importance that Sloman attaches to his Criterion S, it may be well to examine it carefully. Take Sloman's own example, the statement that a whale is a mammal. Whales are commonly perceived to resemble fish more than typical mammals. Thus, a knower may need to deal in this case with two contradictory beliefs, one derived from the whale's outward similarity to fish (assumed to constitute an associative process) and one derived from the "academic" knowledge that

classifies whales as mammals (assumed to illustrate a rule-based process).

Yet, we may have here two distinct rules yielding opposite conclusions. One rule might be based on similarity, or the "representativeness" heuristic (heuristics have been generally defined as rules), e.g., "If the whale looks like a fish, swims like a fish, and lives in water, then the whale is a fish." The other rule may be based on other criteria for classification as a mammal, e.g., "breast-feeding of offspring" or, indeed, the source heuristic: If a biology text claims X (e.g., that whales are mammals), then X is the case.

A similar issue arises in Sloman's discussion of Kahneman et al.'s (1982) Linda problem, whereby the probability that Linda is both a bank teller and a feminist (after being provided evidence that she is likely to be a feminist) is judged more likely than the probability of her being a bank teller, in violation of the conjunction rule in probability calculus. However, intuitive heuristics have been defined as informal rules of thumb. Hence, the contradictory implications of these two rules need not be considered compelling evidence for two qualitatively distinct reasoning processes, in which only one is rule based.

Another of Sloman's (1996) examples concerns the Müller-Lyer illusion. Here, perception provides the answer that the lines are of unequal length, and a ruler demonstrates that they are equally long. Again, it is easy to understand this phenomenon in terms of two rules in which the individual happens to believe strongly and that lead to disparate conclusions. One of these rules is that one's visual perceptions are valid ("If my eyes inform me that X, then X it is"); the other, that application of a ruler yields valid answers.

In summary, Sloman's (1996) Criterion S is compatible with the notion that different rules (major premises) applied to the same evidence (minor premises) may yield different conclusions. Thus, incompatible, strongly held beliefs do not seem to warrant the postulation of a qualitative difference in the reasoning process. From this perspective, associations can be thought of as conditional rules of the "if X then Y" variety that may come to mind very rapidly and effortlessly because of their strength—that is, the degree to which the individual is confident that X attests to Y—and their accessibility (Higgins 1996).

The Two-Memory-Systems Model

Smith & DeCoster (2000) hypothesized the existence of two qualitatively different memory systems: the slow-learning and the fast-learning systems. The slow-learning system is assumed to be associative and to learn general regularities gradually and through the accretion of instances. The fast-learning system is assumed to be rule based and to form representations of novel events quickly. Smith & DeCoster (2000, p. 110) define rules as symbolically represented and structured by language and logic: "Symbolic rules may constitute a formal system such as the laws of arithmetic or of logical inference that is accepted by social consensus in a way that goes beyond its inherent persuasiveness." Note that this definition is narrower than the presently advanced if-then conception of rules (see also Anderson 1983, Holyoak et al. 1989, Rescorla & Wagner 1972, Tolman 1932).

Commentary

Smith & DeCoster's (2000) definition of rules as formal structures has certain implications: If to qualify as a rule a cognitive relation needs to be stated in symbolic terms, and to be part of a formal system of explicit reasoning, then conditioning (animal or human) could not possibly be rule based. This is contrary to recent agreements that it is rule based (see De Hewour et al. 2001, Holyoak et al. 1989). Furthermore, in Smith & DeCoster's (2000) framework, informal heuristics such as "expertise implies correctness" or "careful manner of dressing and persuasive argumentation are typical of lawyers" could not qualify as rules even though they are generally defined as rules of thumb in the social judgment litera-ture. In other words, the widely accepted definition of the rule concept in terms of its conditional if-then structure is broader than Smith & DeCoster's (2000) definition that characterizes the rule concept in terms of its (symbolic or formal) contents as well as in the degree of social consensus it commands.

Beyond definitional matters, the properties of rules proposed by Smith & DeCoster (2000) raise questions as to their generality. Thus, (symbolic) rules are assumed to be learned fast, yet we know from experience how slow and difficult can be the learning of statistical or logical rules (Kahneman 2003). On the other hand, the learning of what Smith & DeCoster (2000) would define as associations could be exceedingly fast. Taste aversion is one striking instance of such rapid learning (Garcia et al. 1968). Furthermore, evidence exists that evaluative conditioning can also occur in a minimal number of trials, even one (Baeyens et al. 1995, Martin & Levey 1994, Stuart et al. 1987). Thus, it is not necessary for associations to be built slowly over time and/or for rules to be acquired quickly. According to Smith & DeCoster (p. 112), "Rule based processing... tends to be analytic, rather than based on overall or global similarity, for example a symbolic rule may single out one or two specific features of an object to be used in categorization, based on conceptual knowledge of the category. In contrast, associative processing categorizes objects nonanalytically on the basis of their overall similarity to category prototypes or known exemplars."

The question, however, is whether phenomena, such as classical conditioning, that have been typically regarded as associative actually are based on perceptions of overall similarity or on specific features that seem to predict a given event (e.g., the onset of the unconditioned stimulus). Holyoak et al. (1989, pp. 320–321) argue that the latter is, in fact, the case: "Unless a feature is included in a candidate rule, nothing can be learned about its relation to other features or to appropriate behaviors... a complex environment may contain many features, few of which are likely to be cues that would help form useful rules. For example, a rat may receive a shock while listening to an unfamiliar tone, scratching itself, looking left, and smelling food pellets. Intuitively, we might expect that the rule 'if tone, then expect shock' will more likely be generated in this situation than the rule 'If looking left, scratching, and smelling pellets, then shock.'"

In summary, the distinction between qualitatively distinct slow associative learning and fast rule learning (Smith & DeCoster 2000) may be questioned on several grounds. What has been traditionally viewed as associations can be learned relatively fast, whereas rules may be acquired slowly and with difficulty. The notion that associations are learned on the basis of global similarity and that rules are based on specific features has also been criticized (Holyoak et al. 1989). Finally, in classical conditioning, associations between the conditioned stimulus and unconditioned stimulus have been thought to represent if-then rules in which some term or category is contingently linked with another (Holyoak et al. 1989).

Unconscious Thought Theory

Recently, Dijksterhuis & Nordgren (2006) proposed a dual-systems model based on the distinction between judgments arrived via unconscious versus conscious modes of information processing. This model, referred to as the Unconscious Thought Theory (UTT), incorporates six basic principles. The first postulates the existence of "two modes of thought: unconscious and conscious. The two modes of thought have different characteristics, making them differentially applicable or differentially appropriate under different circumstances" (Dijksterhuis & Nordgren 2006, p. 96). The second principle asserts that conscious but not unconscious thought is constrained by cognitive capacity. "It follows that conscious thought by necessity often takes into account only a subset of the information it should take into account" (Dijksterhuis & Nordgren 2006, p. 96).

The third principle states that "the unconscious works bottom-up or aschematically, consciousness works top-down or schematically" (p. 97). Moreover, "conscious thought is guided by expectancies and schemas" (p. 97), whereas "unconscious thought slowly integrates information to form an objective summary judgment" (p. 98). The fourth principle states, "The unconscious naturally weights the relative importance of various attributes. Conscious thought often leads to suboptimal weighting because it disturbs this natural process" (Dijksterhuis & Nordgren 2006, p. 99–101).

Principle 5 suggests that "conscious thought can follow strict rules and is precise. Unconscious thought gives rough estimates p. 101." Finally, the sixth principle states, "Conscious thought and memory search during conscious thought is focused and convergent. Unconscious thought is more divergent" (Dijksterhuis & Nordgren 2006, p. 102).

Empirical Evidence

To test the notion that unconscious processing can handle more units of information than conscious processing, Dijksterhuis (2004) had participants complete a judgmental task either immediately after the relevant information was presented, after listing reasons for making their anticipated judgment (conscious thought condition), or after being distracted (unconscious thought condition). In each of five studies, participants were presented with many more pieces of information than conscious thought was thought to be able to handle (based on the notion that conscious thought can handle seven, plus or minus two, pieces of information; Miller 1956). Consistently across studies, participants made more accurate judgments in the unconscious thought condition than in the conscious thought condition.

Dijksterhuis & Bos (manuscript submitted) set out to investigate the hypothesis (derived from UTT's third principle) that conscious processing will lead to a schema-based judgment. Participants were given a "stereotypical expectation" ("You are now going to read information about Mr. Hamoudi, a Moroccan man"), followed by more detailed behavioral information. Some of the behavioral information was congruent with the stereotype, whereas other information was stereotype incongruent. Conscious thinkers judged the targets stereotypically and recalled more stereotype congruent (versus incongruent) information. Unconscious thinkers, however, made neutral judgments and recalled more stereotype-incongruent than stereotype-congruent information. Moreover, conscious thinkers recalled less information overall than did unconscious thinkers.

To test the prediction (derived from principle four) that unconscious (versus conscious) processing results in superior weighting of the available information, Dijksterhuis (2004, Study 3) had participants make judgments about roommates. Beforehand, participants rated how important the various attributes were for them in selecting a roommate. Conscious reasoning weighted the worst, whereas unconscious thinkers weighted the best, though differences between conditions were not statistically significant.

As evidence that the unconscious is not able to follow specific rules, but does integrate information appropriately (derived from principle 5), Betsch and colleagues (Betsch et al. 2001) asked participants to look at ads displayed on a computer screen. Simultaneously, information about the fluctuating prices of five stocks was displayed (75 units of information). Participants were not able to answer accurately specific questions about the stocks, but were able to determine the best and worst stocks.

Finally, Dijksterhuis & Meurs (2006) tested the notion (derived from principle 6) that unconscious thought is more divergent; hence, it affords greater creativity than does conscious thought. Participants were presented with a creativity task (to generate new names for pasta or to generate places starting with "A"). In the pasta experiment, participants were given five examples, each ending in the letter "i." Conscious thinkers almost exclusively listed names ending with "i," whereas unconscious thinkers listed names with other endings. In an experiment where participants were asked to generate Dutch cities and villages starting with "A," conscious thinkers listed highly accessible and obvious names such as Amsterdam, whereas unconscious thinkers listed a greater number of less well-known villages.

Commentary

Dijksterhuis & Nordgren's (2006) findings of wide-ranging differences between conscious and unconscious conditions are intriguing. Yet the underlying processes mediating these results aren't well understood as yet. For instance, the assumption that the conscious process constitutes rule following doesn't necessarily imply that it should lead to inferior judgments. Some rules are quite appropriate to various judgments and are quite warranted (e.g., rules of logic, mathematics). Thus, contrary to the UTT's implication, conscious processes might not universally lead to inferior judgments relative to unconscious processes.

In a certain sense, the UTT model seems contrary in its implications to major dual-process models in realms of persuasion (Chaiken et al. 1989, Petty & Cacioppo 1986), stereotyping (Brewer 1988, Fiske & Neuberg 1990), and judgment under uncertainty (Kahneman 2003, Kruglanski et al. 2006a). The latter models suggest that a high degree of processing motivation leads to a thorough (conscious) consideration of the information given, juxtaposed to the use of accessible heuristics. By contrast, the use of heuristics has been often likened to intuitive, associative, and unconscious processing (Smith & DeCoster 2000).

Above all, even though unconscious processing may require little cognitive capacity, it is unlikely to suffice for solving truly complex problems without the assistance of conscious processing. That may be particularly true if conscious processing is abetted by various capacity-enhancing devices such as writing, printing, and computer programming. It would seem plausible that considerable advances in science and technology were enabled through the foregoing devices, whose implementation seems hardly unconscious. Thus, whereas unconscious processing may be very fast, its results may typically require a careful evaluation in the sobering light of consciousness. Finally, even though it may be quicker and more efficient than conscious processing, unconscious processing may well be carried through the same rule-following process, albeit in a highly routinized form, as conscious processing (James 1890; Kruglanski et al. 2006a,b; Kruglanski & Dechesne 2006; Logan 1992; Schneider & Shiffrin 1977).

The Reflective-Impulsive Model

Strack & Deutsch (2004) recently proposed a dual-process model based on a distinction between the reflective and the impulsive systems. These are depicted as governed by different principles of representation and information processing. Specifically, "... in the reflective system, behavior is elicited as a consequence of a decision process... knowledge about the value and the probability of potential consequences is weighed and integrated to reach a preference for one behavioral option. If a decision is made, the reflective system activates appropriate behavioral schemata through a self-terminating mechanism of *intending*. In contrast, the impulsive system activates behavioral schemata through spreading activation, which may originate from perceptual input or from reflective processes" (Strack & Deutsch 2004, p. 222; emphasis in original).

The reflective-impulsive model suggests that "both systems operate in parallel. However, an asymmetry exists between them such that the impulsive system is *always* engaged in processing (by itself or in parallel to operation of the reflective system) whereas the reflective system may be disengaged" (Strack & Deutsch 2004, p. 223; emphasis added). Engagement of the reflective system requires the allocation of attention to the stimulus. Thus, the investment of effort represents a fundamental difference between the two modes of thinking. Accordingly, "processes of the reflective system are disturbed more easily than those of the impulsive system" (p. 223).

Modes of representing and storing information additionally differ in the two systems. "In the reflective system, elements are connected through semantic relations. In the impulsive system, the relations are associative links between elements and are formed according to the principles of *contiguity* and *similarity*" (Strack & Deutsch 2004, p. 223; emphasis added). The associative links in the impulsive system form "over many learning trials," "bind together frequently co-occurring features and form *associative clusters*" (Strack & Deutsch 2004, p. 223; emphasis added). The associative clusters are conceptualized as "nonpropositional representations," whereas the reflective system is "capable of forming propositional representations by connecting one or more elements through the instantiation of relational schemata to which a truth value is attached" (p. 223).

Associations can be formed in the impulsive system as a result of frequent activation of nodes by the reflective system. "Thus, semantic concepts will emerge in the impulsive system through frequent propositional categorizations... [but] *are not assumed to have any semantic meaning by themselves*" (Strack & Deutsch 2004, p. 224; emphasis in original). Though absent propositional rules, "associative clusters in the impulsive system can be hierarchically structured and can differ in abstractness. As a consequence, *clusters may resemble* either concrete perceptual concepts or abstract *semantic concepts* or schemata" (Strack & Deutsch 2004, p. 224; emphasis in original).

Strack & Deutsch also coordinate the impulsive system to long-term memory and the reflective system to temporary storage in which "the amount of information that can be represented at any given time is limited, and the representation will fade if it is not rehearsed" (p. 225). The impulsive system, Strack & Deutsch (2004) suggest, is limited in its ability to process certain types of information. Specifically, (*a*) it cannot process or store negation and (*b*) it cannot generate a time perspective. It follows that the reflective system "allows individuals to resist immediate rewards and strive for more valuable future outcomes" (Strack & Deutsch 2004, p. 228). From this perspective, judgment is defined as a necessarily reflective process. This assumes that products of impulsive thought must be translated to rule-based logic before they can be articulated.

The reflective-impulsive model incorporates affective, motivational, and cognitive principles ultimately producing behavior. A major motivational principle is that of relative deprivation, and a major informational principle is that of accessibility. Affect and cognition interact to yield behavior: "Positive or negative affect induces motivational orientations, preparing the organism to decrease (approach) or to increase (avoidance) the distance towards an object. Deprivation of a... need activates behavioral schemata that previously were successful in ending the state of deprivation. Therefore, when deprived (e.g., thirsty), need-relevant stimuli (e.g., water) are easier detected, and they are more easily approached. . . ." (Deutsch & Strack 2006, p. 5).

Empirical Evidence

To support the claim that the impulsive system cannot process or store negation, Strack & Deutsch (2004) cite research (Gilbert et al. 1990) in which participants attempted to learn novel vocabulary (e.g., a "waihas" is a fish). Each vocabulary word was tagged as true or false. When participants were distracted during the trials, vocabulary words tagged as false were more often erroneously remembered as true than were words tagged as true being remembered as false.

However, rather than assuming that these findings attest to the essential incapability of the impulsive system to process negation, it is possible that negation is more ambiguous than affirmation (e.g., knowing that "waihas" is not a fish is uninformative as to what "waihas" actually is), hence it is more difficult to learn than affirmation. This might explain why the learning of negation is interfered with under depleted resources. Furthermore, the goal of learning a vocabulary is that of learning affirmations. Participants may have regarded the learning of negations as less important than the learning of affirmations and may not have striven to accomplish it, particularly when doing so required considerable effort.

To support the claim that the impulsive system is incapable of generating a time perspective, Deutsch & Strack (2002) presented participants with a short negative or a short positive picture, followed by a delay in which there came a lengthier presentation of an oppositely valenced picture. It was found that in the absence of load, participants preferred the lengthier and delayed presentation of the positive picture. Under load, participants preferred the shorter and more immediate presentation of the positive picture.

Again, it is unclear whether such data require two qualitatively distinct systems for their explication. Load, after all, is a continuous variable, as is the extent of cognitive resources. It is possible that when the load is high relative to resources, individuals are unable to suppress the temptation of the positive picture or to engage in the kind of cognitive work required for self-control, something that they may be able to accomplish in the absence of load. It should follow that if the individuals had lesser resources they might prefer the immediate positive picture, even in the absence of load. Similarly, if the individuals had greater resources they might prefer the delayed positive picture, even under load.

Commentary

Strack & Deutsch's (2004) reflective-impulsive model (RIM) resembles in several respects alternative dual-systems' frameworks such as those of Sloman (1996), Smith & DeCoster (2000), and Dijksterhuis & Nordgren (2006). In all such models, an associative, efficient process is juxtaposed to a rule-following, resource-exigent process. The alternative dual-systems models differ from the RIM in that they aimed exclusively at the explication of judgments, whereas RIM also includes the explanation of behavior. Furthermore, the systemic alternatives to RIM were mute on the topic of affect, whereas in RIM, affect plays an important part in instigating cognitive and behavioral activity. Thus, the RIM is more of a "grand" psychological theory than are similar alternative dual-system frameworks in that it subsumes nearly all facets of psychological functioning.

The sweep of the RIM formulation, though creative and imaginative, constitutes also its problematic aspect as far as scientific theorizing is concerned. It seems to yield little in the way of unique predictions, and the empirical evidence cited in its support seems open to alternative interpretations.

DUAL-SYSTEMS FRAMEWORKS: CONCLUDING COMMENTS

The dual-systems frameworks leave several questions for consideration:

(*a*) Their fundamental distinction between rule following and associative processes needs to come to terms with the body of evidence suggesting that associations are actually rule-like (Holyoak et al. 1989).

(*b*) Their assumption that the associative process is independent of resources needs to account for the fact that in learning the association an actor must pay attention to a given aspect of the total situation to connect it associatively with another aspect. Presumably, the ability to pay such attention requires attentional resources.

(*c*) Their qualitative distinction between unconscious and conscious processes (assumed to characterize the associative/automatic and the reflective/deliberative processes) seems inconsistent with the notion that automaticity or consciousness lie on a continuum (Bargh 1996, Logan 1992, Posner 1990), that efficiency is a matter of routinization (Schneider & Shiffrin 1977), and that consciousness is removed as a function of routinization (James 1890, p. 496), suggesting that routinization too is continuous rather than discrete.

(*d*) Proponents of the associative/reflective dichotomy (e.g., Strack & Deutsch 2004) assert that contiguity and repetition are causally involved in the formation of associations. However, it is questionable whether repeated contiguity and repetition are necessary and sufficient for "associative clusters" to form. Single-shot associative connections can be formed as well. Additionally, temporal contiguity doesn't seem necessary for the formation of such conceptions. Indeed, "There are many demonstrations of classical and instrumental conditioning in which the delay between events is on the order of many seconds or minutes..." (Holyoak et al. 1989, p. 316).

In short, the dual-systems (versus dual-mode) models do avoid the assumption that some informational contents (peripheral or heuristic cues, social categories, etc.) are processed shallowly or briefly, whereas others are processed deeply or extensively, and they characterize general cognitive processes applicable across informational contents. Nonetheless, evidence-based arguments exist that the two types of processes they characterize as distinct share an important commonality related to the learning of rules and that the processes they address may represent different points on the same quantitative continua (e.g., routinization) rather than representing qualitative dichotomies.

ALTERNATIVES TO THE DUAL-PROCESS MODELS

As the foregoing review illustrates, the dualistic partition between modes or systems of human inference has represented the dominant conceptual approach to this domain of phenomena. However, even though novel dualistic frameworks continue to be advanced (Dijksterhuis & Nordgren 2006, Strack & Deutsch 2004), alternatives to those formulations have been also advanced. Such alternative models either argue that the dualistic frameworks do not draw sufficiently fine distinctions between psychological processes (Conrey et al. 2005, Sherman 2006) or that the qualitative distinctions they make may be effectively reconceptualized in quantitative terms (Erb et al. 2003, Kruglanski et al. 2006a).

The Quad Model

Typically, multiple-process models have distinguished between two judgmental modes, one operating when judgments are made automatically, and another when they are made deliberatively. As an alternative, the Quad Model (Conrey et al. 2005, Sherman 2006) proposes four qualitatively distinct processes: two automatic and two controlled. The automatic processes are referred to as association activation and guessing. The controlled processes are referred to as overcoming bias and discriminability.

The association activation process reflects the likelihood that the stimulus will give rise to an association. The guessing process is derived from memory models in which familiarity is used as a cue only when attempts at recollection fail (e.g., Jacoby 1991, Mandler 1980). The discriminability parameter reflects the likelihood that the "correct" answer can be reached, and that sufficient resources will be available for the kind of controlled processing

needed to arrive at a correct answer. In order to reach a correct answer, appropriate information must be available in memory or the environment. Moreover, sufficient cognitive capacity and motivation are needed to process the stimulus and to retrieve information.

The overcoming-bias process occurs when the automatically activated association is inhibited through controlled endeavors. Therefore, overcoming bias is influenced by motivation and capacity constraints. If bias is overcome, then discriminability determines the judgment, whereas the automatic association determines the judgment when bias is not overcome.

The likelihood that each process will operate is conditionally dependent upon the preceding processes. For example, association activation and discriminability both must occur for bias to be overcome. Similarly, only if neither association activation nor discriminability occurs may guessing take place. Guessing may be the result of automatic or controlled response biases. For example, an automatic tendency to respond with the right hand may occur. Also, a "strategic bias," such as responding positively to black faces, may occur.

Empirical Evidence

In the first test of the Quad Model, participants were presented with a flowers-insects implicit association test (IAT) (Greenwald et al. 1998). Supporting the conceptualization of the association activation (AC) parameter, participants preferred flowers to insects. Discriminability of the stimuli (D) was high, indicating that participants were able to judge accurately the difference between a flower and an insect, as expected. The overcoming-bias (OB) parameter was estimated in a situation where oppositely valenced stimuli were experimentally associated (i.e., flowers with negative words, and insects with positive words). The rate of correct responses in these conditions was significantly greater than zero, indicating that the discriminability parameter plays an important role in judgment.

A second study manipulated the time given participants to respond to each item in a black-white IAT. Time constraints reduced discriminability and overcoming bias. However, they did not affect the automatic processes. The association activation parameter did vary as a function of the attitude measured, but importantly, did not vary as a function of time constraints. Also, right-hand guessing bias was found in both the time-constrained and unconstrained conditions.

In the third experiment, the number of unpleasant versus pleasant words was manipulated to determine the impact on the guessing parameter. A stronger right-hand bias was predicted and obtained when participants had to respond more often with the right-hand key (i.e., more pleasant words) than when they had to respond more often with the left-hand key (i.e., more unpleasant words).

The fourth experiment tested the Quad Model on a standard IAT to determine the relationships between IAT standard scoring and the Quad Model parameters. In accord with predictions, the association activation parameter was positively correlated with the standard IAT scores. Also, there was a negative correlation between overcoming bias and standard IAT scores. Sherman (2006) interprets these findings as suggesting, "to the extent that people have strong implicit associations, they show stronger bias and, to the extent that they are able to overcome their associations, they show weaker bias. This shows that IAT performance is influenced by controlled processes."

In the fifth experiment, Conrey et al. (2005) reanalyzed data reported by Lambert et al. (2003), which showed that an anticipated public context (making participants accountable) increased the extent of bias on the Weapons Identification Task (WIP). The reanalysis showed that D was diminished in the public condition and OB was enhanced. Thus, one type of controlled process was inhibited by an audience and another was enhanced by the audience. Moreover, the analysis showed that the AC parameter did increase in the public condition.

Commentary

The Conrey et al. (2005) data attest to the generative ability of the Quad Model. Nonetheless, at the conceptual level several questions remain. As with the other multi-system models, the Conrey et al. (2005) formulation needs to come to terms with evidence that associative processes may be actually rule based (e.g., Holyoak et al. 1989, Lovibond 2003). For instance, in an IAT-type task, the "association" could be of the form "if flower then good," and the experimentally acquired rule, "if flower then [press] the A key." Following the latter rule may represent the overcoming of bias and the attainment of discriminability, whereas following the former rule could represent a bias. Also, the former rule might be more practiced and automatic, and hence less vulnerable to resource depletion, yet it could be similar to it in form. In other words, exhibiting bias or overcoming bias might simply mean following different rules.

Second, it is unclear that the guessing parameter is qualitatively different from the association activation parameter. Specifically, the association activation parameter would seem to apply to the activation of rules in general, whereas the guessing parameter seems to apply to specific rules, such as "if a name feels familiar then it is famous." Thus, in the same way that associations in general are strengthened through repeated pairing, so may be the "guessing bias." For instance, in work by Conrey et al. (2005, Study 3), the right-hand "guessing" bias was enhanced through the number of instances in which the correct answer required a right-hand response. In present terms, a possible rule that "if stimulus then right response" might have been strengthened in this case by the number of instances in which a reinforcement (positive feedback) followed the pairing of a stimulus with a right-hand response.

Third, the overcoming bias notion carries the implication that previously formed associations were biased or incorrect, whereas the deliberative rule that overcomes those associations led to a correct response. However, there might be instances in which the original association was correct, whereas the deliberative judgment exercised via the application of considerable mental resources was incorrect.

Finally, the overcoming bias notion may be thought of as a clash between two rules, one more routinized than the other. But there could also exist a clash between two routinized rules (e.g., conflicting stereotypes of an Asian and a woman clashing in the example of an Asian Woman), or a clash between two conscious rules. In short, the interesting data of Conrey et al. (2005) could be reinterpreted in ways that do not require the postulation of four qualitatively distinct processes.

The Unimodel

The various multimode models (whether of the process or the system variety) assume that there exist qualitatively distinct ways of reaching judgments. In contrast, the unimodel (e.g., Erb et al. 2003; Kruglanski & Thompson 1999a,b; Kruglanski et al. 1999, 2006a,b; Pierro et al. 2004, 2005) assumes that the basic process of judgment is governed by several orthogonal parameters whose combinations at various values determine whether the information given exerts impact on judgments.

Rule following. The unimodel assumes that the judgmental process is essentially rule based, where rules are defined broadly as if-then contingencies that the organism "knows" (whether explicitly or tacitly). Judgments are based on "evidence," constituting an antecedent term in a conditional if-then premise stored in an individual's memory. For instance, the inference that one's overall life satisfaction is high might be based on one's momentary mood (Schwarz & Clore 2006). This requires that the individual subscribe to the inference "if my mood is good then my life satisfaction is high."

Kruglanski et al. (2006a,b) discuss various prior attempts to distinguish rule-based judgmental processes from putative alternatives processes, such as associative learning (Sloman 1996), pattern recognition (Lieberman et al. 2002), classical conditioning, or evaluative conditioning (Gawronski & Bodenhausen 2006). Drawing on various types of evidence, Kruglanski et al. (2006a,b) conclude that associative learning as well as pattern recognition represent instances of rule following rather than constituting alternatives to rule following. Thus, Holyoak et al. (1989) conclude their review of classical conditioning research by noting that "representations of the environment take the form of (IF THEN) rules that compose mental models (for instance) the rat's knowledge about the relation between tones and shocks might be informally represented by a rule such as "if a tone sounds… then a shock will occur" (p. 320). Also, whereas evaluative conditioning may not constitute signal learning, there are reasons to believe that it does constitute an instance of rule learning, e.g., involving a causal misattribution to the conditioned stimulus of affect engendered by the unconditioned stimulus.

Kruglanski et al. (2006a,b) note that the rules involved in conditioning may be applied with considerable ease and alacrity. The notion that automatic phenomena in the domain (motor or cognitive) skill acquisition involve a routinization of if-then sequences has been central to Anderson's (1983) atomic components of thought (ACT*) model, which Smith and his colleagues (1989, Smith & Branscombe 1988, Smith et al. 1988) generalized to the realm of social judgments. Their research has demonstrated that social judgments represent a special case of procedural learning based on practice that strengthens the if-then components, resulting in increased efficiency (automaticity) (cf. Bargh 1996).

The notion that rule-following behavior can be automatic and unconscious is supported by the notion of perception theorists that vision depends critically on hard-wired inference rules for translating the retinal image into the experienced percept. In this vein, a recent Annual Review article "treats object perception as a visual inference problem" (Kersten et al. 2004) and suggests "the visual system resolves ambiguity through built-in knowledge of... how retinal images are formed and uses this knowledge to automatically and unconsciously *infer* the properties of objects" (p. 273, emphasis added).

Similarly, pattern recognition is compatible with, rather than constituting an alternative to, rule following. A pattern is a configuration of cues that collectively points to some judgment. In this sense, a pattern constitutes a conjunctive antecedent of an if-then rule. In Holyoak et al's. (1989, p. 319) conception, for instance, "configural cues are... multiple-element conditions of rules." Indeed, Lieberman et al. (2002) allow that products of the X system, assumed to operate on the basis of pattern recognition, "can also be described as a result of executing... IF THEN statements" (p. 221).

The judgmental parameters. Based on the general assumption that judgments are rule based, the unimodel identifies a number of continuous parameters whose intersections determine the impact on judgments of the information given.

Subjective relevance. The degree to which the antecedent X implies a consequent Y in the "if X then Y" conditional may vary, constituting a continuous parameter. In some cases, the X-to-Y implication could be strong. If so, an encounter with X would create a strong sense that Y is to be expected. Put differently, knowledge that X is the case constitutes compelling evidence that Y is too. Strong inferences may be afforded by the way our perceptual system is hard-wired (Pizlo 2001). Nonetheless, perceptual learning of some sort may take place. As Bruner (1958, pp. 90–91) observed, "we learn... the probabilistic texture of the world, conserve this learning, use

it as a guide to tuning our perceptual readiness to what is most likely next. It is this that permits us to go beyond the information given."

Some inferential rules may be overlearned to the point of routinization (Schneider & Shiffrin 1977), whereas others may derive from a powerful single-shot experience (Garcia et al. 1968) or from a trusted epistemic authority (Kruglanski et al. 2005). With lesser degree of routinization, an experience with less impact, or a less trusted epistemic authority, the X-to-Y implication may be weaker and more tenuous. In those instances, the confidence in Y given X would be correspondingly feeble.

Gleaning difficulty. Judgmental contexts may vary in the degree of hardship involved in applying a given inference rule by a given individual seeking to answer a given question. Gleaning difficulty may be determined by external task demands and by internal states of the knower.

External task demands. The informational context may determine how easy or difficult it is to detect the specific information from which inferences can be made. The information may be highly complex and lengthy. It may contain considerable noise, and the relevant evidence may be faint or insufficiently salient to attract attention. The informational array may contain several relevant items, each fitting a different inference rule whose implications might clash with one another. The requisite discriminations (e.g., in the perceptual realm) might be exceedingly fine. All these may contribute to judgmental task difficulty. Placement of the relevant information in the sequence may also matter. A front-end placement may make the items easier to process, whereas a later placement may make them more difficult to process due to the depletion of cognitive resources by the early items.

As Kruglanski and colleagues (e.g., Erb et al. 2003; Kruglanski et al. 2006a,b) noted, across a variety of judgmental research some information types (e.g., peripheral/heuristic, categorical) may have been presented to participants in a relatively easy format, whereas other information types (e.g., issue related, individuating) may have been presented to participants in a relatively difficult format. Different types of information are qualitatively distinct because they comprise distinct contents. It is therefore possible that the frequent claims for qualitatively different processes of judgment rest in part on the inadvertent confounding in prior research of information types with task difficulty.

Empirical evidence. Research in the unimodel framework has attempted to control for such confounds and examine how this affects phenomena previously understood from a dual-mode perspective. In the realm of persuasion, Kruglanski and colleagues (Kruglanski & Thompson 1999a,b; Pierro et al. 2005) demonstrated that the difficulty of processing, rather than the type of information processed, interacts with the availability of motivational and cognitive resources to determine persuasion. In the realm of attribution, Chun et al. (2002) found that the difficulty of information processing determines whether the assimilative influence of context on behavior identification requires resources. In the same vain, the claim that the subtractive effect of context on dispositional attributions is resource dependent was contravened by the findings of Trope & Gaunt (2000) such that it doesn't require resources when it is made easier to process.

Chun & Kruglanski (2006) obtained evidence that the well-known phenomenon of base-rate neglect (Kahneman 2003, Tversky & Kahneman 1974) can be partially accounted for by the interaction of difficulty of processing and the availability of processing resources. Both the use of statistical information and that of heuristic information (e.g., representativeness) is greater where such information is easy to process and the resources are restricted, or when it is relatively challenging to process and the resources are plentiful. Thus,

it was found that, ironically, the processing of statistical information was increased under cognitive load (!), provided such information was brief and easy to use, as compared with lengthier and more difficult to process heuristic information.

Finally, Pierro et al. (2004) obtained evidence that the often observed failure to use peripheral/heuristic information under conditions of high-processing resources is due to the fact that, as a category, such information is typically perceived as less relevant to the requisite judgments than is the message argument information. Thus, under high-resource conditions, a "relevance override" may take place such that the more relevant information tends to be relied on, whereas the less relevant information tends to be neglected.

Commentary

Thus far, the empirical research guided by the unimodel has concerned the confounds of processing difficulty and informational contents. The unimodel has not been empirically applied to the distinction between associative and rule-based processing central to the several dual-systems models. According to the unimodel, the so-called associations are if-then rules that humans (and animals) can learn, often to the point of routinization. Such routinization may render them relatively independent of mental resources, which removes the need to exercise conscious attention over their execution (Bargh 1996, Norman & Shallice 1986). The unimodel thus unpacks the "phenotypic" differences between instances of social inference in terms of the underlying if-then "genotypic" structure that they all seem to possess, and the differences in efficiency, consciousness, speed, etc. that they seem to exhibit.

CONCLUDING COMMENTS

The domain of human inference is diverse and multifaceted. First, inferences vary in the domain of content to which they belong.

Secondly, inferences vary in their speed and immediacy. Inferences vary also on the process-awareness dimension. Possibly driven by this multifarious variability, a plethora of models and theories has been advanced to identify the processes and mechanisms underlying human inference. In recent decades, such formulations have preponderantly adopted a partitioning approach distinguishing between qualitatively different manners of reaching inferences.

Our review reveals that in early dual-mode models, the critical partition often hinged on different types of information. Possibly in recognition of the open-ended variety of informational types or contents, the more recent dual-systems models tended to be "content-free." Such models typically adopted two categorical distinctions, namely those between (*a*) automatic versus controlled processes and (*b*) associative versus rule-based processes. The latter categorizations were assumed to coincide such that the associative processes were typically assumed to be automatic, whereas the rule-based processes were assumed to be controlled. The dual-systems models have been closely attuned to the prevalent Zeitgeist in social cognition apparent in their emphasis on automatic processes and their reliance on brain activity findings as evidence for their postulates.

Conceptual departures from the strict dualistic paradigms have also been noted. The Quad Model proposes to partition the basic automatic/controlled distinction further into its more specific subtypes. The unimodel parts ways with qualitative partitions altogether and proposes to account for the phenomena of human inference in terms of a number of intersecting quantitative continua. These latter departures challenge the prevalent dualistic approach to human inference and pose fundamental questions to be resolved, hopefully, via creative new research initiatives (for a recent debate on these issues, see Deutsch & Strack 2006; Kruglanski et al. 2006a,b; Sherman 2006).

ACKNOWLEDGMENT

This work was supported by NSF Grant SBR-9417422.

LITERATURE CITED

Anderson JR. 1983. *The Structure of Cognition*. Cambridge, MA: Harvard Univ. Press

Baeyens F, Crombez G, Hendrickx H, Eelen P. 1995. Parameters of human flavor-flavor conditioning. *Learn. Motiv.* 26:141–60

Bargh JA. 1996. Automaticity in social psychology. See Higgins & Kruglanski 1996, pp. 169–83

Betsch T, Plessner H, Schwieren C, Gutig R. 2001. I like it but I don't know why: a value-account approach to implicit attitude formation. *Personal. Soc. Psychol. Bull.* 27:242–53

Brewer MB. 1988. A dual process model of impression formation. In *Advances in Social Cognition*, ed. TK Srull, RS Wyer, 1:1–36. Hillsdale, NJ: Erlbaum

Brewer MB, Harasty Feinstein AS. 1999. Dual processes in the cognitive representations of persons and social categories. See Chaiken & Trope 1999, pp. 255–70

Bruner JS. 1958. Social psychology and perception. In *Readings in Social Psychology*, ed. EE Maccoby, TM Newcomb, EL Hartley, pp. 85–93. New York: Holt, Rinehart, & Winston

Bruner JS. 1973. *Beyond the Information Given: Studies on the Psychology of Knowing*. Oxford, UK: Norton

Chaiken S, Liberman A, Eagly AH. 1989. Heuristic and systematic information processing within and beyond the persuasion context. In *Unintended Thought*, ed. JS Uleman, JA Bargh, pp. 212–52. New York: Guilford

Chaiken S, Trope Y, eds. 1999. *Dual-Process Theories in Social Psychology*. New York: Guilford

Chun WY, Kruglanski AW. 2006. The role of task demands and processing resources in the use of base-rate and individuating information. *J. Personal. Soc. Psychol.* 91:205–17

Chun WY, Spiegel S, Kruglanski AW. 2002. Assimilative behavior identification can also be resource dependent: a unimodel perspective on personal-attribution phases. *J. Personal. Soc. Psychol.* 83:542–55

Conrey FR, Sherman JW, Gawronsky B, Hugenberg K, Groom CJ. 2005. Separating multiple processes in implicit social cognition: the quad-model of implicit task performance. *J. Personal. Soc. Psychol.* 89:469–87

Crano WD, Prislin R. 2006. Attitudes and persuasion. *Annu. Rev. Psychol.* 57:345–74

De Hewour J, Thomas S, Baeyens F. 2001. Associative learning of likes and dislikes: a review of 25 years of research on human evaluative conditioning. *Psychol. Bull.* 127:853–69

Deutsch R, Strack E. 2002. *Evaluative learning with delayed gratification. Impulsive and reflective processes*. Unpubl. manuscr., Univ. Wurzburg

Deutsch S. 2006. Duality models in social psychology: from dual processes to interacting systems. *Psychol. Inq.* In press

Dijksterhuis A. 2004. Think different: the merits of unconscious thought in preference development and decision making. *J. Personal. Soc. Psychol.* 87:586–98

Dijksterhuis A, Bos MW. 2006. I am thinking about you... when I shouldn't: the dangers of conscious thought during impression formation. Manuscr. submitted

Dijksterhuis A, Meurs T. 2006. Where creativity resides: the generative power of unconscious thought. *Conscious. Cogn.* 15:135–46

Dijksterhuis A, Nordgren LF. 2006. A theory of unconscious thought. *Perspect. Psychol. Sci.* 1:95–180

Edwards W, Lindman H, Savage LJ. 1963. Bayesian statistical research in psychological research. *Psychol. Rev.* 70:193–242

Erb HP, Kruglanski AW, Chun WY, Pierro A, Mannetti L, Spiegel S. 2003. Searching for commonalities in human judgment: the parametric unimodel and its dual mode alternatives. *Eur. Rev. Soc. Psychol.* 14:1–47

Fazio RH, Olson MA. 2002. Implicit measures in social cognition research: their meaning and use. *Annu. Rev. Psychol.* 54:297–327

Fiske ST. 1988. Compare and contrast: Brewer's dual process model and Fiske et al's continuum model. In *A Dual Process Model of Impression Formation*, ed. TK Srull, RS Wyer, pp. 65–76. Hillsdale, NJ: Erlbaum

Fiske ST, Lin M, Neuberg SL. 1999. The continuum model: ten years later. See Chaiken & Trope 1999, pp. 231–54

Fiske ST, Neuberg SL. 1990. A continuum model of impression formation, from category-based to individuating processes: influences of information and motivation on attention and interpretation. In *Advances in Experimental Social Psychology*, ed. MP Zanna, 23:1–74. New York: Academic

Fiske ST, Taylor SE. 1984. *Social Cognition*. New York: Random House

Fiske ST, Taylor SE. 1991. *Social Cognition*. New York: Random House. 2nd ed.

Garcia J, McGowan BK, Ervin FR, Koelling RA. 1968. Cues: their relative effectiveness as a function of the reinforcer. *Science* 160:794–95

Gawronski B, Bodenhausen GV. 2006. Associative and propositional processes in evaluation: an integrative review of implicit and explicit attitude change. *Psychol. Bull.* In press

Gilbert DT. 1989. Thinking lightly about others: automatic components of the social inference process. In *Unintended Thought*, ed. JS Uleman, JA Bargh, pp. 189–211. New York: Guilford

Gilbert DT, Krull DS, Malone PS. 1990. Unbelieving the unbelievable: some problems with the rejections of false information. *J. Personal. Soc. Psychol.* 59:601–13

Greenwald AG, McGhee DE, Schwartz JLK. 1998. Measuring individual differences in implicit cognition: the implicit association test. *J. Personal. Soc. Psychol.* 74:1464–80

Higgins ET. 1996. Knowledge activation: accessibility, applicability and salience. See Higgins & Kruglanski 1996, pp. 133–68

Higgins ET, Kruglanski AW, eds. 1996. *Social Psychology: Handbook of Basic Principles.* New York: Guilford

Holyoak KJ, Kohl K, Nisbett RE. 1989. A theory of conditioned reasoning: inductive learning within rule-based hierarchies. *Psychol. Rev.* 96:315–40

Jacoby LL. 1991. A process dissociation framework: separating automatic from intentional uses of memory. *J. Mem. Lang.* 30:513–41

James W. 1890. *The Principles of Psychology.* New York: Henry Colt

Kahneman D. 2003. A perspective on judgment and choice: mapping bounded rationality. *Am. Psychol.* 58:697–720

Kahneman D, Slovic P, Tversky A. 1982. *Judgment Under Uncertainty: Heuristics and Biases.* New York: Cambridge Univ. Press

Kelley HH. 1967. Attribution theory in social psychology. *Nebraska Symp. Motiv.* 15:192–238

Kersten D, Mamassian P, Yuille A. 2004. Object perception and Bayesian inference. *Annu. Rev. Psychol.* 55:271–304

Kruglanski AW, Dechesne M, Erb HP, Pierro A, Mannetti L, Chun WY. 2006a. Modes, systems and the sirens of specificity: the issues in gist. (Authors' response to commentaries.) *Psychol. Inq.* In press

Kruglanski AW, Dechesne M. 2006. Are associative and propositional processes qualitatively distinct? A comment on Gawronski & Bodenhausen 2006. *Psychol. Bull.* In press

Kruglanski AW, Pierro A, Mannetti L, Erb HP, Spiegel S. 2006b. Persuasion according to the unimodel. *J. Comm.* In press

Kruglanski AW, Raviv A, Bar-Tal D, Raviv A, Sharvit K, et al. 2005. Says who? Epistemic authority effects in social judgment. In *Advances in Experimental Social Psychology*, ed. MP Zanna, 37:345–92. New York: Academic

Kruglanski AW, Thomson EP. 1999a. Persuasion by a single route: a view from the unimodel. *Psychol. Inq.* 10:83–109

Kruglanski AW, Thomson EP. 1999b. The illusory second mode or, the cue is the message. *Psychol. Inq.* 10:182–93

Kruglanski AW, Thomson EP, Spiegel S. 1999. Separate or equal? Bimodal notions of persuasion and a single process "unimodel." See Chaiken & Trope 1999, pp. 293–313

Lambert AJ, Payne BK, Jacoby LL, Shaffer LM, Chasteen AL, Khan SR. 2003. Stereotypes as dominant responses: on the "social facilitation" of prejudice in anticipated public contexts. *J. Personal. Soc. Psychol.* 84:277–95

LeBoeuf RA, Shafir E. 2003. Deep thoughts and shallow frames: on the susceptibility to framing effects. *J. Behav. Decis. Mak.* 16:77–92

Lieberman MD, Gaunt R, Gilbert TD, Trope Y. 2002. Reflection and reflexion: a social cognitive neuroscience approach to attributional inference. In *Advances in Experimental Social Psychology*, ed. MP Zanna, 34:199–249. New York: Academic

Logan GD. 1989. Automaticity and cognitive control. In *Unintended Thought*, ed. JS Uleman, JA Bargh, pp. 52–74. New York: Guilford

Logan GD. 1992. Attention and preattention in theories of automaticity. *Am. J. Psychol.* 105:317–39

Lovibond PF. 2003. Causal beliefs and conditioned responses: retrospective revaluation induced by experience and by instruction. *J. Exp. Psychol.: Learn. Mem. Cogn.* 29:97–106

Macrae CN, Bodenhausen GV. 2000. Social cognition: thinking categorically about others. *Annu. Rev. Psychol.* 51:93–120

Mandler G. 1980. Recognizing: the judgment of previous occurrence. *Psychol. Rev.* 87:252–71

Martin I, Levey AB. 1994. The evaluative response: primitive but necessary. *Behav. Res. Ther.* 32:301–5

McGuire WJ. 1960. A syllogistic analysis of cognitive relationships. In *Attitude Organization and Change: An Analysis of Consistency Among Attitude Components*, ed. CI Hovland, MJ Rosenberg, pp. 65–111. Oxford, UK: Yale Univ. Press

Michotte A. 1963. *The Perception of Causality*. Oxford, UK: Basic Books

Miller GA. 1956. Information theory. *Sci. Am.* 195:42–46

Moors A, De Houwer J. 2006. Problems with dividing the realm of cognitive processes. *Psychol. Inq.* In press

Nisbett RE, Peng K, Choi I, Norenzayan A. 2001. Culture and systems of thought: holistic versus analytic cognition. *Psychol. Rev.* 108:291–310

Nisbett R, Ross L. 1980. *Human Inference: Strategies and Shortcomings of Social Judgment*. Englewood Cliffs, NJ: Prentice Hall

Norman DA, Shallice T. 1986. Attention to action: willed and automatic control of behavior. In *Consciousness and Self Regulation: Advances in Research and Theory*, ed. JR Davidson, GE Schwartz, D Shapiro, 4:1–18. New York: Plenum

Petty RE, Cacioppo JT. 1986. The elaboration likelihood model of persuasion. In *Advances in Experimental Social Psychology*, ed. L Berkowitz, 19:123–205. San Diego, CA: Academic

Pierro A, Mannetti L, Erb HP, Spiegel S, Kruglanski AW. 2005. Informational length and order of presentation as determinants of persuasion. *J. Exp. Soc. Psychol.* 41:458–69

Pierro A, Mannetti L, Kruglanski AW, Sleeth-Keppler D. 2004. Relevance override: on the reduced impact of "cues" under high motivation conditions of persuasion studies. *J. Personal. Soc. Psychol.* 86:251–64

Pizlo Z. 2001. Perception viewed as an inverse problem. *Vis. Res.* 41:3145–61

Posner MI. 1990. Hierarchical distributed networks in the neuropsychology of selective attention. In *Cognitive Neuropsychology and Neurolinguistics: Advances in Models of Cognitive Function and Impairment*, ed. A Caramaxxa, pp. 187–210. Hillsdale NJ: Erlbaum

Posner MI, Rothbart MK. 1989. Intentional chapters on unintended thoughts. In *Unintended Thought*, JS Uleman, JA Bargh, pp. 450–70. New York: Guilford

Quattrone G. 1982. Overattribution and unit formation: when behavior engulfs the person. *J. Personal. Soc. Psychol.* 42:593–607

Rescorla RA, Wagner AR. 1972. A theory of Pavlovian conditioning: variations in the effectiveness of reinforcement and nonreinforcement. In *Classical Conditioning II: Current Theory and Research*, ed. AH Black, WF Procasy, pp. 64–99. New York: Appleton-Century-Crofts

Schneider W, Shiffrin RM. 1977. Controlled and automatic human information processing: I. Detection, search, and attention. *Psychol. Rev.* 84:1–66

Schwarz N, Clore GL. 2006. Feelings and phenomenal experiences. In *Social Psychology: Handbook of Basic Principles*, ed. ET Higgins, AW Kruglanski. New York: Guilford. 2nd ed. In press

Sherman JW. 2006. On building a better process model: it's not only how many, but which ones and by which means? *Psychol. Inq.* In press

Sloman SA. 1996. The empirical case of two systems of reasoning. *Psychol. Bull.* 119:3–22

Smith ER. 1989. Procedural efficiency: general and specific components and effects on social judgment. *J. Exp. Soc. Psychol.* 25:500–23

Smith ER, Branscombe NR. 1988. Category accessibility as implicit memory. *J. Exp. Soc. Psychol.* 24:490–504

Smith ER, Branscombe NR, Bormann C. 1988. Generality of the effects of practice on social judgment tasks. *J. Personal. Soc. Psychol.* 54:385–95

Smith ER, DeCoster J. 2000. Dual process models in social and cognitive psychology: conceptual integration and links to underlying memory systems. *Personal. Soc. Psychol. Rev.* 4:108–31

Smith SM, Levin IP. 1996. Need for cognition and choice framing effects. *J. Behav. Decis. Mak.* 9:283–90

Strack F, Deutsch R. 2004. Reflective and impulsive determinants of social behavior. *Personal. Soc. Psychol. Rev.* 8:220–47

Stuart EW, Shimp TA, Engle RW. 1987. Classical conditioning of consumer attitudes: four experiments in an advertising context. *J. Consum. Res.* 14:334–49

Tolman EC. 1932. *Purposive Behavior in Animals and Men.* New York: Appleton-Century-Crofts

Trope Y. 1986. Identification and inferential processes in dispositional attribution. *Psychol. Rev.* 93:239–57

Trope Y, Alfieri T. 1997. Effortfulness and flexibility of dispositional judgment processes. *J. Personal. Soc. Psychol.* 73:662–74

Trope Y, Gaunt R. 2000. Processing alternative explanations of behavior: correction of integration? *J. Personal. Soc. Psychol.* 79:344–54

Trope Y, Liberman A. 1996. Social hypothesis testing: cognitive and motivational mechanisms. See Higgins & Kruglanski 1996, pp. 239–70

Tversky A, Kahneman D. 1974. Judgment under uncertainty: heuristics and biases. *Science* 185:1124–30

Uttal WR. 2001. *The New Phrenology: The Limits of Localizing Cognitive Processes in the Brain.* Cambridge, MA: MIT Press

Webster DM. 1993. Motivated augmentation and reduction of the overattribution bias. *J. Personal. Soc. Psychol.* 65(2):261–71

Williams DA. 1995. Forms of inhibition in animal and human learning. *J. Exp. Psychol.: Anim. Behav. Process.* 29:129–42

Wood W. 2000. Attitude change: persuasion and social influence. *Annu. Rev. Psychol.* 51:539–70

Motivational and Emotional Aspects of the Self

Mark R. Leary

Department of Psychology and Neuroscience, Duke University, Durham,
North Carolina 27708; email: leary@duke.edu

Annu. Rev. Psychol. 2007. 58:317–44

First published online as a Review in
Advance on September 5, 2006

The *Annual Review of Psychology* is online at
http://psych.annualreviews.org

This article's doi:
10.1146/annurev.psych.58.110405.085658

0066-4308/07/0203-0317$20.00

Key Words

self-awareness, self-enhancement, self-verification, self-expansion,
self-conscious emotions, motivation, emotion, guilt, shame, pride,
self-evaluation

Abstract

Recent theory and research are reviewed regarding self-related motives (self-enhancement, self-verification, and self-expansion) and
self-conscious emotions (guilt, shame, pride, social anxiety, and embarrassment), with an emphasis on how these motivational and emotional aspects of the self might be related. Specifically, these motives
and emotions appear to function to protect people's social well-being.
The motives to self-enhance, self-verify, and self-expand are partly
rooted in people's concerns with social approval and acceptance, and
self-conscious emotions arise in response to events that have real or
imagined implications for others' judgments of the individual. Thus,
these motives and emotions do not operate to maintain certain states
of the self, as some have suggested, but rather to facilitate people's
social interactions and relationships.

Contents

MOTIVATIONAL AND EMOTIONAL ASPECTS OF THE SELF

Many of the philosophers, psychologists, and sociologists who founded the social and behavioral sciences were keenly interested in topics related to self and identity. James, Cooley, Mead, Blumer, and others viewed self-thought and self-representation as a bridge between the social events that occurred outside of the individual (including both interpersonal interactions and society more broadly) and the individual's own thoughts, behaviors, and emotions. This interest dwindled with the advent of behaviorism and, with the exception of work by the humanistic psychologists, the scientific study of the self lay dormant for nearly 50 years. Then, in the 1970s and 1980s, the study of self and identity regained respectability, fueled partly by the cognitive revolution, which led to cognitive models of self-awareness, self-conceptualization, and self-regulation (e.g., Carver & Scheier 1981, Duval & Wicklund 1972, Markus 1977).

Following this resurgence of interest, research on self-processes proceeded along two relatively distinct lines. One line focused primarily on "cold," cognitive aspects of the self such as self-construals, self-schematic processing, self-organization, self-categorization, self and memory, self-reference effects, and executive processes. Although some of this work examined emotions and motives as well, the processes under investigation were primarily cognitive. The other line of research focused on "hot" motivational and emotional self-processes such as those involved in self-esteem, self-enhancement, self-verification, and self-conscious emotions. These two literatures on self-processes are both huge and burgeoning, so the focus of this review is limited to recent work on motivational and emotional aspects of the self. The reader is referred to previous reviews by Banaji & Prentice (1994) and Ellemers et al. (2002), as well as to Leary & Tangney (2003a), for coverage of other areas.

Much of the popularity of the self as an explanatory construct stems from theories that attribute people's thoughts or behaviors to "self-motives" such as motives for self-enhancement, self-verification, self-expansion, or self-assessment. Although differing in specifics, these approaches assume that human thought and action are affected by motives to maintain or promote certain kinds of self-images. At the same time, psychologists have long known that people's self-thoughts are strongly linked to their emotions. Researchers who study self-processes have been particularly interested in the so-called self-conscious emotions—shame, guilt, embarrassment, social anxiety, and pride—although, as I discuss below, virtually every emotion, not only self-conscious emotions, can be evoked by self-reflection.

Motives and emotions are inextricably linked. Fulfilled and unfilled motives usually evoke emotional reactions, and emotions are often reactions to fulfilled or thwarted motives (Johnson-Laird & Oatley 1992). Yet, the literatures on self-related motives and emotions have developed independently, with little discussion of the relationships between them. I try to rectify this situation at the end of the article. However, I begin by examining the three self-motives that have garnered the most attention, followed by a look at the self-conscious emotions.

SELF-MOTIVES

Theorists have posited the existence of a number of self-motives, including motives for self-enhancement, self-verification, self-expansion, self-appraisal, self-improvement, self-actualization, and self-transcendence. Unfortunately, progress in studying self-processes, including self-relevant motives, has been hampered by vagueness and inconsistency in how writers have used the term "self." "Self" has been used to refer to several distinct phenomena, including aspects of personality, the cognitive processes that underlie self-awareness, a person's mental representation of him- or herself, an executive control center that mediates decision-making and self-regulation, and the whole person (for discussions of problems with the definition of self, see Leary & Tangney 2003b, Olson 1999).

In the case of self-motives, some concepts refer to mechanisms by which people create or maintain certain self-images, self-beliefs, or self-evaluations in their own minds. For example, self-enhancement involves the desire to maintain the positivity of one's self-concept, and self-verification is the desire to confirm one's existing self-views. In contrast, other terms refer to motives involving the individual as a person. For example, self-improvement is not a motive to improve the psychological self but rather a tendency toward increasing the person's capabilities. Likewise, self-actualization involves the hypothesized movement toward becoming a fully functioning person. Neither self-improvement nor self-actualization are aimed toward changing the self per se (as opposed to the person), although the self may indeed be involved.

In my view, a "self-motive" is an inclination that is focused on establishing or maintaining a particular state of self-awareness, self-representation, or self-evaluation. Thus, self-enhancement and self-verification might qualify as self-motives because they involve a tendency for the psychological self to maintain a certain state (of positivity or consistency). However, self-improvement and self-actualization would not be regarded as self-motives because, although they may involve self-reflection, they are not about the self. And, to complicate matters further, at least one concept, self-expansion, has been used to refer both to a motive to expand one's behavioral efficacy (which is not a self-motive according to my definition) and to expand the breadth of one's self-concept (which does seem to qualify as a self-motive).[1]

SELF-ENHANCEMENT

By far, the greatest amount of research on self-motives has involved self-enhancement—the desire to maintain or increase the positivity (or decrease the negativity) of one's self-concept or, alternatively, the desire to maintain,

---

Self-motive: any inclination that is aimed toward establishing or maintaining a particular state of self-awareness, self-representation, or self-evaluation

Self-enhancement: the desire to maintain or increase the positivity (or decrease the negativity) of one's self-concept; the desire to maintain, protect, and enhance one's self-esteem

---

[1]A lesser studied self-motive is self-assessment—the desire to have objective, accurate, and diagnostic information about oneself. This effect is shown in experimental studies when people prefer receiving information about themselves that is highly diagnostic in the sense that it measures aspects of themselves accurately (e.g., Brown 1990, Sedikides 1993, Strube 1990, Trope 1986). Although people clearly desire accurate feedback under certain circumstances, the fact that this effect is stronger when the potential information is likely to be positive suggests that self-assessment often takes a backseat to self-enhancement (Sedikides 1993).

protect, and enhance one's self-esteem. A large number of phenomena have been explained with reference to the motive to self-enhance. Self-enhancement has been identified as underlying people's tendency to believe that they have improved relative to the past and that their personal improvement has been greater than other people's (Wilson & Ross 2001), self-handicap in order to provide an attribution for failure that does not implicate their ability (McCrae & Hirt 2001), seek information that supports their self-esteem (Ditto & Lopez 1993), take more personal responsibility for success than failure (Blaine & Crocker 1993), idiosyncratically define their traits in ways that cast them in a positive light (Dunning & Cohen 1992), overvalue people, places, and things with which they are associated (Pelham et al. 2002), interpret other people's behaviors and traits in ways that reflect well on them personally (Dunning & Beauregard 2000), believe that they are better than they actually are (Alicke & Govorum 2006), compare themselves with others who are worse than they are (Wood et al. 1999), derogate others in order to feel good about themselves (Fein & Spencer 1997), distance themselves from those who outperform them (Tesser 1988), and deny that they possess these sorts of self-enhancing tendencies (Pronin et al. 2002). Space does not permit a full review of these literatures, so I focus on four phenomena that have been attributed to the self-enhancement motive—self-serving attributions, the better-than-average effect, implicit egotism, and the bias blind spot.

Self-Serving Attributions

The earliest programmatic research on self-enhancement focused on self-serving attributions (for early discussions, see Bradley 1978, Snyder et al. 1978). Since then, hundreds of studies have shown that people tend to attribute positive events to their own personal characteristics but attribute negative events to factors beyond their control, presumably in an effort to maintain a positive self-image and

self-esteem (Blaine & Crocker 1993). Self-serving attributions are also seen when people work together in groups. When a group performs well, each member tends to feel that he or she was more responsible for the group's success than most of the other members were. When the group performs poorly, however, each member feels less responsible for the outcome than does the average member (Mullen & Riordan 1988, Schlenker & Miller 1977). In addition, group members sometimes make group-serving attributions. Members of groups tend to attribute favorable group outcomes to the group itself but conclude that bad things that befall the group are due to factors outside the group or beyond its control (Ellemers et al. 1999, Sherman & Kim 2005). If group members are led to affirm their personal sense of self, group-serving attributions are reduced (Sherman & Kim 2005), presumably because self-affirmation lowers the motive to self-enhance through group-serving attributions.

Most researchers have explained self-serving attributions in terms of people's efforts to protect or enhance their self-esteem (Blaine & Crocker 1993). Not only does claiming responsibility for positive events and denying responsibility for negative events appear inherently self-enhancing, but experimental manipulations that threaten or boost self-esteem influence self-serving attributions (Sherman & Kim 2005). However, from the beginnings of research on self-serving attributions, other explanations have been offered. First, Miller & Ross (1975) argued that such effects might occur because people accept greater personal responsibility for expected than unexpected outcomes, and people are more likely to expect success than failure. Second, events that implicate the individual might influence the salience of the self as a judgmental anchor so that self-serving and group-serving attributions reflect the degree to which various plausible causes are cognitively available (Cadinu & Rothbart 1996, Otten 2002, Sherman & Kim 2005). Third, self-serving attributions sometimes reflect self-presentational efforts to maintain a positive image in the eyes of other people rather than intrapsychic efforts to buttress self-esteem (Bradley 1978, Leary 1995). I return to explanations of self-enhancing biases below, but, for now, the safest conclusion after more than 30 years of research is that self-serving patterns of attributions may reflect self-enhancement motives, logical inferences about the causes of one's successes and failures, the salience of factors affecting one's outcomes, and self-presentational processes.

The Better-than-Average Effect

Many studies have shown that people tend to evaluate themselves more positively than objective information warrants, as well as more positively than third-party observers do (Colvin et al. 1995, Dunning et al. 1989, Robins & Beer 2001, Zuckerman et al. 2004). In fact, people tend to evaluate themselves more positively than they rate the average person on virtually every dimension that has been studied (for a review, see Alicke & Govorum 2006). In one study (Alicke et al. 1995), participants rated themselves and the average college student on 20 positive traits and 20 negative traits. Results showed that the average participant rated him- or herself more positively than did the average student on 38 of the 40 traits. The better-than-average effect is quite robust and has been obtained in a number of cultures (Alicke & Govorum 2006; Brown & Kobayashi 2002; Hoorens 1993; Sedikides et al. 2003, 2005). Interestingly, the psychological processes that underlie the better-than-average effect have not been directly examined, possibly because researchers have assumed that it arises from the motive for self-enhancement.

Implicit Self-Enhancement

Researchers have explored the possibility that people may self-enhance not only by evaluating themselves favorably but also by positively evaluating things that are associated with them. Implicit egotism is the tendency for people's positive, self-enhancing evaluations of themselves to spill over into their evaluations of objects, places, and people that are associated with them (Greenwald & Banaji 1995). For example, research on the endowment effect shows that people come to evaluate things they own more positively than they did prior to owning them (Beggan 1992, Kahneman et al. 1990). Implicit egotism may also underlie people's tendency to evaluate the groups to which they belong favorably (Gramzow & Gaertner 2005). Similarly, research has shown that people tend to evaluate the letters of the alphabet that appear in their own names more positively than the letters that are not in their names, and the effect is particularly strong for people's initials (Hodson & Olson 2005, Kitayama & Karasawa 1997, Koole et al. 2001).

This case of implicit egotism has intriguing implications. If people evaluate the letters in their own names particularly positively, perhaps they also like things that also have those letters. In support of this idea, Pelham et al. (2002) found that people live in states that start with the same letter as their own names at higher-than-chance levels. Furthermore, people whose names match a city that begins with "Saint," such as St. Louis, are disproportionately likely to live in a namesake city (Pelham et al. 2002). Perhaps more startling, people are disproportionately likely to have jobs that start with their own initials (owners of hardware stores were more likely to have names starting with "H" than one would expect, for example) and to marry people whose names resemble their own, and this effect is not simply due to ethnic matching (Jones et al. 2004, Pelham et al. 2002).

Controlled experiments have demonstrated the name letter effect as well. People prefer bogus brands of tea, crackers, and candy that resemble their own names to brands that do not resemble their names (Brendl et al. 2004). Other research showed that participants liked other participants whose arbitrary experimental number resembled their own

Better-than-average effect: the tendency for people to evaluate themselves more positively than they rate the average person

birth date and whose surnames shared letters with their own names (Jones et al. 2004). Interestingly, the biases to rate name letters and birthdates positively are correlated, suggesting the existence of individual differences in implicit self-enhancement (Koole et al. 2001).

Bias blind spot: the tendency for people to think that they are less biased than most other people are

Although the name letter effect has been replicated in at least 14 countries, questions have been raised about its strength and generalizability (Gallucci 2003, Pelham et al. 2003). For example, in four experiments, Hodson & Olson (2005) obtained the name letter effect when participants rated letters and brand names but not when they rated generic attitude objects involving foods, animals, national groups, or leisure activities. Hodson & Olson suggested that the effect might occur primarily for objects and activities that serve a value-expressive function by communicating one's beliefs, values, or identity.

Although implicit egotism effects are robust, the psychological mechanisms that underlie them are not clear. We do know that implicit self-enhancement operates automatically and without conscious reflection. When people are induced to think deliberately, these automatic effects reduce or disappear, but when people are placed under cognitive load, positive self-evaluations increase (Koole et al. 2001, Paulhus & Levitt 1987).

The Bias Blind Spot

Ironically, people's tendency to self-enhance also leads them to think they are not self-enhancing. Pronin et al. (2004) explored the "bias blind spot"—the tendency for people to think that they are less susceptible to biases than other people are. In one study, participants rated how much they personally showed eight biases in perception and judgment, including the better-than-average effect and self-serving attributional bias, and also rated how much the average American shows each bias. Results showed that participants thought that they were affected less by all eight biases than the average American (Pronin et al. 2002).

Two Debates Regarding Self-Enhancement

Although people show strong self-enhancing patterns, this topic has been subject to two particularly interesting and generative debates involving cultural differences and whether self-enhancement is a benefit or a liability.

Cultural differences. Most studies of self-enhancement have been conducted in the United States, Europe, and Australia, leaving open the question of whether people in other cultures, particularly in east Asia, also self-enhance and whether self-enhancement is related to psychological outcomes similarly in the East and West. On one side of the debate, researchers have suggested that people in certain cultures, such as Japan, do not show the same self-enhancing tendencies as people in the United States (Heine et al. 1999, Markus & Kitayama 1991). Several studies show that Japanese participants more readily accept negative feedback about themselves, are not as unrealistically optimistic about their futures, and tend to be modest rather than self-enhancing, leading some to conclude that they are not motivated to maintain a positive view of themselves (Heine et al. 2001, Heine & Lehman 1995). People who are raised in collectivistic cultures may avoid self-enhancement because it brings attention to them and may foster friction among group members (Heine 2001). Furthermore, East Asian societies tend to emphasize self-improvement over self-enhancement, which may promote self-criticism (Heine et al. 2001).

Other researchers have argued that all people prefer to feel good rather than bad about themselves and behave in self-enhancing ways that promote self-esteem (Sedikides et al. 2003). However, because different characteristics are valued in different cultures, people promote their self-esteem in culturally defined ways. Ironically, either self-criticism or self-enhancement can make people feel good about themselves, depending on what their culture values. In most Western societies, characteristics such as confidence, individualism, autonomy, and superiority are valued, so people want to see themselves (and for others to see them) in these ways. In other societies, greater value may be placed on modesty, interdependency, harmony, and self-criticism, so that people prefer to possess these kinds of collectivist characteristics.

In support of this hypothesis, Sedikides et al. (2003) found that both American and Japanese participants self-enhanced but used different tactics to do so. American participants self-enhanced primarily on individualistic attributes (such as independence and uniqueness), whereas Japanese participants self-enhanced primarily on collectivist attributes (such as agreeableness and cooperation). Similarly, meta-analyses by Sedikides et al. (2005) showed that Western participants self-enhance on attributes that are relevant to individualism, whereas Eastern participants self-enhance on attributes relative to collectivism. This and other research (Chang & Asakawa 2003, Chang et al. 2001, Kurman 2001) suggest that differences in self-enhancement between American and Japanese participants are more nuanced than a general East-West model would suggest and that self-enhancement does occur in non-Western cultures (see, however, Heine 2005.) Even so, European Americans may be more prone to self-enhancement than East Asians, depending on the domain under investigation (Sedikides et al. 2003, Yik et al. 1998), and members of both cultural groups sometimes show the other pattern (with East Asians showing more self-enhancement) under certain circumstances (Chang & Asakawa 2003, Chang et al. 2001, Sedikides et al. 2003). In addition, it is not yet clear whether the cultural differences reflect differences in self-enhancement per se or some other process, such as the ease with which memories of positive and negative events are primed (see Chang & Asakawa 2003) or self-presentational differences in the desire to be seen as enhancing versus modest by others (Kudo & Numazaki 2003, Kurman 2003).

The healthy illusion debate. A second debate involves whether self-enhancement is beneficial or detrimental to people's well-being. One argument is that self-enhancing biases promote well-being, more effective behavior, and greater success (Taylor & Brown 1988). Advocates of this hypothesis point out that self-esteem tends to be associated with positive outcomes, such as lower anxiety, higher confidence, lower stress, and greater success, whereas low self-esteem tends to be associated with problems such as anxiety, drug abuse, delinquency, and depression (Taylor & Brown 1988, 1994; Taylor et al. 2003a,b). For example, a study of people who were in or near the World Trade Center towers at the time of the September 11 attacks showed that self-enhancement was associated with better resilience and adjustment (Bonanno et al. 2005). Similarly, more positive self-evaluations predicted better adjustment among civilians who were coping with the aftermath of civil war in Bosnia and among people whose spouses had died (Bonanno et al. 2002).

Other researchers question whether self-enhancement is wholly beneficial (Block & Colvin 1994, Colvin et al. 1995, Robins & Beer 2001). They point out that the relationships between high self-esteem and positive outcomes are weak and that research has revealed several drawbacks of having high self-esteem (Baumeister et al. 2003). For example, efforts to self-enhance may lead people, particularly those with high trait self-esteem, to make risky decisions, treat others shabbily, and react aggressively (Baumeister et al. 1993a, 1996; Heatherton & Vohs 2000; Johnson et al. 1997). Furthermore, processing information in a self-serving manner is associated with greater unethical behavior (von Hippel et al. 2005).

In addition, self-enhancement leads people to conclude that their perceptions of themselves are more accurate than other people's perceptions of themselves, that their own

Self-verification:
the tendency for
people to prefer and
seek out information
that is consistent
with their existing
views of themselves

perceptions of other people are more accurate than others' impressions of them, and that other people are less objective and fair than they are (Pronin et al. 2002, 2004). Thus, when others disagree with their perceptions and opinions, people tend to assume that the others are deluded, biased, or ignorant, leading to a good deal of interpersonal conflict. Furthermore, people view self-enhancing individuals more negatively (Bonanno et al. 2002, 2005; Colvin et al. 1995; Leary et al. 1997; Robins & John 1997; however, see Joiner et al. 2003 for a possible gender difference in this effect). For example, in studies of the relationship between self-esteem and coping, people who experienced terrorist attacks, civil war, or death of a spouse were judged more negatively by others despite being more psychologically resilient (Bonanno et al. 2002, 2005). Although self-enhancing biases often make people feel good about themselves and have other short-term benefits, they can undermine people's interpersonal relationships and well-being in the long run (Colvin et al. 1995, Paulhus 1998, Robins & Beer 2001). Crocker & Park (2004) provide an exceptional overview of the various costs of self-enhancement.

Part of the difficulty in resolving the healthy illusion debate stems from the fact that many studies that purport to demonstrate beneficial effects of self-enhancement do not actually assess whether people's positive self-views are "illusory" or "self-enhancing" as opposed to justifiably positive (Kwan et al. 2004, Taylor & Armor 1996). In many studies, self-enhancement has been operationalized in terms of the positivity of participants' self-reports (e.g., Taylor et al. 2003a) or in terms of differences between participants' ratings of themselves versus their ratings of others (e.g., Alicke 1985), neither of which necessarily reflects whether the individual's perceptions are accurate or self-enhancing. Recently, studies that assessed self-enhancement independently of the mere absolute or relative positivity of people's self-evaluations have shown self-enhancement to have both beneficial and detrimental effects (Kwan et al. 2004, Paulhus et al. 2003).

Furthermore, people who self-enhance may also tend to report excessively favorable well-being and adjustment, leading to spurious correlations between self-enhancement and self-reported well-being (Shedler et al. 1993). And, the effects of self-enhancement may depend on whether one examines the effects of self-enhancement on subjective experience, interpersonal relationships, task performance, or physical health. Altogether, as Paulhus (1998, p. 1207) observed, "self-enhancement is best viewed as a mixed blessing."

SELF-VERIFICATION

Swann's discovery that people sometimes prefer to receive negative rather than positive feedback challenged the notion that self-enhancement is the predominant self-relevant motive. In several studies, participants were found to choose feedback that was consistent with their current self-views even when those self-views were negative (e.g., Hixon & Swann 1993; Swann & Pelham 2002; Swann & Read 1981; Swann et al. 1989, 1992a). According to self-verification theory (Swann 1983, 1990), people are motivated to verify, validate, and sustain their existing self-concepts. Self-verifying information leads to stability in people's self-concepts and makes people feel that they understand themselves, thereby providing a reliable guide to thought and action that facilitates smooth, effective, and enjoyable interactions (Swann et al. 1992a).

Self-verification processes appear to influence behavior in at least three ways. First, the motive to self-verify leads people to interact with those who confirm their self-concepts. Experiments have shown that people prefer to interact with strangers who see them as they see themselves (Swann et al. 1989) and, in ongoing relationships, people are more committed to spouses whose views of them are consistent with their own self-concepts. In both cases, these effects occur even when the person's self-concept is negative, demonstrating that people sometimes sacrifice self-enhancing positivity for self-verifying consistency (Burke & Stets 1999; Swann et al. 1992a, 1994). Similarly, students whose self-views more closely coincided with others' appraisals of them felt more connected to their groups and performed more successfully in them (Swann et al. 2000). Self-verification also occurs with respect to people's collective self-definitions—those aspects of people's self-concepts that involve memberships in social groups. People prefer to interact with others who see the groups to which they belong as they see them; again, this pattern occurs whether people's views of their groups are positive or negative (Chen et al. 2004). Although exceptions of the self-verifying pattern have been found, studies suggest that people gravitate toward interactions and relationships with people who verify their self-images.

Second, people tend to behave in ways that elicit self-verifying feedback from others. People tend to solicit feedback about themselves that is consistent with their self-concepts (Robinson & Smith-Lovin 1992, Swann et al. 1992b). Particularly when others have inaccurate impressions of them, people go out of their way to affirm their view of what they are like (Swann & Read 1981). Third, people look for, see, and remember information that verifies their view of themselves (Swann & Read 1981). That is, people's interpretations of self-relevant feedback are biased in ways that confirm their existing self-images. People not only sometimes misinterpret information in ways that are consistent with their self-views, but they also dismiss inconsistent but accurate feedback as inaccurate (Doherty et al. 1990).

Self-enhancement and self-verification motives may either coincide or conflict. In cases in which people have a positive self-view, both self-enhancement and self-verification lead them to seek positive information about themselves. However, when people's self-views are negative, self-enhancement leads them to seek positive feedback, whereas self-verification leads them to seek negative feedback. Studies have explored how people with negative self-views reconcile these pressures toward enhancement versus verification. For example, Swann et al. (1989) found that people prefer receiving positive rather than negative information about themselves, as self-enhancement theorists predict. However, when people explicitly seek information about attributes on which their existing self-views are negative, they tend to seek unfavorable feedback.

Bernichon et al. (2003) suggested that the apparent conflict between self-enhancement and self-verification may also be reduced by distinguishing global self-esteem (how people generally feel about themselves) from specific self-views (people's appraisals of particular characteristics). Their research suggested that people with high self-esteem self-verified specific negative self-views but that people with low self-esteem did not, preferring instead positive feedback even if it was inconsistent with how they saw themselves (and, thus, not self-verifying). Along the same lines, Swann et al. (2002) examined how people balance their desires for self-enhancement and self-verification in the context of romantic relationships. They found that people desired to be perceived in highly positive ways on dimensions that were essential to attracting a romantic partner, such as physical attractiveness, but preferred to be seen in self-confirming ways on other dimensions.

There seems to be little question that people prefer a coherent, predictable self-image and often engage in behaviors that evoke reactions from other people that coincide with how they see themselves. Furthermore, these preferences sometimes lead people to prefer self-verifying information, even when it is negative. However, the data are less clear that all self-verification effects arise from the motive to verify and sustain one's existing self-concept per se. An alternative explanation traces self-verification effects to interpersonal concerns involving social acceptance.

Although people undoubtedly like others to perceive them positively, relating to people whose views of us are more favorable than our views of ourselves poses certain interpersonal risks. As nice as it is to be perceived positively, the love and social acceptance we receive from people who see us more positively than we see ourselves feels tenuous. If and when others learn that we are not what they thought, disillusionment, disappointment, and accusations of deceit may result. The worrisome threat of falling from grace may be enough to lead people toward self-verifying interactions and partners. Ironically, then, people may feel more comfortable being accepted by those who see them less positively but accurately. Indeed, there's a great deal of confidence inherent in being loved by someone who accurately sees one's flaws.

This interpersonal explanation might account for why self-verification strivings are strongest when people's self-views are confidently held (Swann & Ely 1984, Swann & Pelham 2002). People are likely to assume that confident self-images are accurate and, thus, will eventually be perceived by others. It might also explain why self-verification is more pronounced in established relationships, such as marriages (Swann et al. 1994). Early in a relationship, the risks of being seen inaccurately are not particularly serious. However, as a relationship deepens, suddenly being "found out" has greater consequences.

SELF-EXPANSION

The self-expansion model (Aron & Aron 1996, 1997) proposes that people possess a central motivation for self-expansion—a motive to increase the "physical and social resources, perspectives, and identities that facilitate achievement of any goal that might arise" (Aron et al. 2001, p. 478). The model is based on the notion, first articulated by James (1890), that people include other individuals in their sense of self. People who have incorporated others into their sense of self not only treat those individuals preferen-

tially (Aron et al. 1991) but also process information about them differently (Aron et al. 1991, Aron & Fraley 1999, Maschek et al. 2003, Smith et al. 1996). For example, when people include others as part of the self, social comparisons with those individuals become less self-serving (Gardner et al. 2002), and people seem to confuse themselves with the other when making judgments (Aron & Fraley 1999). However, the self-expansion model goes beyond the idea that people merely incorporate others into their self-concept to assert that people are motivated to do so in the service of self-expansion.

Much of the research on self-expansion has dealt with its role in close relationships. The model suggests that developing an interpersonal relationship "expands the self" via several routes. For example, a new partner may perceive and validate aspects of the person that were previously ignored, or the individual may try out new or suppressed identities that are well received by the partner. Furthermore, to the extent that the individual includes the partner within his or her own view of him- or herself, he or she has access to new characteristics, resources, and perspectives. In a longitudinal study, Aron et al. (1995) asked university students to describe themselves ("Who are you today?") and answer other questions over a 10-week period. Their results showed that students who reported falling in love during this period showed a greater increase in the diversity of the domains that they used to describe themselves. In a second study, students who fell in love during the study showed greater increases in self-efficacy and self-esteem than students who did not fall in love. These changes were observed in both within-participants analyses (before versus after falling in love) and between-participants analyses (those who did and did not fall in love) and were not merely due to changes in mood.

Although a good deal of research has shown that people are attracted to those who are similar to them, people may also be attracted to those who are different because dissimilar others provide a greater potential to expand one's self-concept (Aron et al. 2002). Along these lines, Amodio & Showers (2005) found that, for people in less committed relationships, greater perceived dissimilarity predicted greater liking. Because lower similarity implies a greater possibility of self-expansion, people who are less similar to oneself are sometimes liked better in the early stages of relationship development.

Consistent with the notion that self-expansion has a motivational quality, behaviors that expand people's self-concepts are affectively positive (Aron et al. 2000, Reissman et al. 1993). However, the positive emotions associated with rapid self-expansion early in a relationship wane as the process of self-expansion slows over time, which may account for the decline in relationship satisfaction in long-term relationships. If so, giving couples new opportunities for self-expansion may reignite positive affect. In support of this hypothesis, laboratory and field experiments showed that couples who participated in involving, self-expanding activities reported increases in relationship satisfaction (Aron et al. 2000, Reissman et al. 1993).

People also expand the self by identifying with groups (Smith et al. 1996, Smith & Henry 1996). In an extension of the self-expansion model, Wright et al. (2002) proposed that in-group identification is partly the result of the self-expansion motive. In their words, "we seek to include groups in the self because doing so increases our confidence that we can meet the demands of our world and achieve goals" (p. 350). Tropp & Wright (2001) showed that the cognitive representations of oneself and one's in-group are more strongly interconnected among people who identify highly with their in-groups, suggesting that people's self-concepts have expanded to include the group.

As noted above, authors have used the word "self" to refer to several different phenomena, and this problem has befallen the study of self-expansion in particular. Researchers interested in self-expansion have used "self" in two distinct ways that are synonymous with "person" and with "self-concept." In one usage, self-expansion is conceptualized as a process of improving one's potential efficacy for achieving one's goals by increasing one's resources, perspectives, and identities (a process that Aron et al. 2001 compare to self-improvement; see Taylor et al. 1995). The other usage of self-expansion refers to people broadening their beliefs about themselves and their potential to act effectively—an expansion of the self-concept (Gardner et al. 2002). These two elements of self-expansion obviously coincide (e.g., expanding one's capabilities should be reflected in self-beliefs regarding one's potential effectiveness), yet they should be regarded as distinct. Research clearly supports the notion that people's self-concepts expand and diversify when they enter relationships and have other novel experiences and that people seek experiences and relationships that increase their efficacy. However, there is less evidence to support the broader hypothesis that people are motivated to expand their sense of self per se or that they engage in interpersonal behavior with the goal of expanding their self-image.

THE THEORETICAL VIABILITY OF SELF-MOTIVES

The general assumption has been that these inclinations to seek self-enhancing, self-verifying, and self-expanding experiences and feedback reflect inherent motives of the self (Aron et al. 2001, Gaertner et al. 2002, Sedikides 1993, Sedikides & Strube 1997, Swann 1990). Although no one could doubt that people act in ways that enhance, verify, and expand their current views of themselves, one can reasonably ask whether these effects reflect a motivational feature of the self as opposed to the use of the self to satisfy other (nonself) motives. To put it differently, does the self actually have motives to sustain certain states of the self-concept, or is the self, as the cognitive mechanism that underlies self-awareness and self-relevant thought, merely

Terror management theory: traces a great deal of human behavior to people's efforts to reduce existential anxiety caused by knowledge of their own mortality

Sociometer theory: conceptualizes self-esteem as a component of a psychological system that monitors the social environment for cues that indicate one's relational value to other people

involved in satisfying other, perhaps more basic, motives? This is a difficult question—one for which no easy answer currently exists—but theorists are beginning to entertain the possibility that these effects do not arise out of any inherent motivational properties of the self. Attention has been directed most intently to alternative explanations of the self-enhancement motive; because of space limitations, I mention only two perspectives—terror management theory and sociometer theory—to show how certain self-motives are being reconceptualized as operating in the service of other, nonself motives.

Terror management theory (Solomon et al. 1991) proposes that people self-enhance because self-esteem buffers them against the existential anxiety caused by knowledge that they will someday die. According to the theory, awareness of one's own mortality creates paralyzing terror unless people construct views of their worlds and themselves that convince them that they are valuable participants in a meaningful world. People experience anxiety when their worldview is undermined (for example, by threats to important beliefs or institutions) or when they believe that they are not meeting their culture's standards (and, thus, have low self-esteem). However, people who have high self-esteem are buffered against terror because they believe that they are living up to important cultural values and, thus, will achieve either literal immortality (in terms of going to heaven, being reincarnated, or whatever) or symbolic immortality (in that their impact, good works, and memory will live on after they die). In either case, this assurance, buttressed by high self-esteem, protects them against the anxiety they would otherwise feel. Put simply, terror management theory suggests that people self-enhance to keep terror at bay.

Research has supported many predictions of terror management theory. Studies have shown that people who are reminded of their own mortality defend their cultural worldviews (Florian & Mikulincer 1997, Greenberg et al. 1992a, Rosenblatt et al. 1989), people

with high versus low self-esteem react differently to reminders of mortality and other threatening stimuli (Greenberg et al. 1992b, Harmon-Jones et al. 1997), and making death salient increases people's desire to have high self-esteem (Greenberg et al. 1992b). However, it is not certain that the primary function of self-enhancement is to assuage existential terror (see Leary 2002).

A second approach to self-enhancement suggests that many effects that have been attributed to self-motives arise in the service of promoting one's social acceptance by other people. Sociometer theory (Leary & Baumeister 2000, Leary & Downs 1995) suggests that self-esteem is part of a sociometer that monitors people's relational value in other people's eyes. Because people's well-being requires that they be valued and accepted by other people, people must be attuned to indications that other people do not value them as social interactants, group members, and relationship partners. When people detect cues that other people may reject them, they are alerted by an aversive loss of self-esteem. Thus, events that lower self-esteem—such as failure, rejection, humiliating events, and immoral actions—do so because these events may result in the person being devalued or rejected (Leary et al. 1995). According to sociometer theory, people do not self-enhance for its own sake but rather because they are trying to increase their value and acceptance in others' eyes, an idea that is consistent with early explanations that stressed the interpersonal functions of self-enhancement (e.g., Bradley 1978).

Research supports sociometer theory's description of the role of self-esteem in monitoring relational value. In laboratory experiments, manipulations that convey rejection, disapproval, or disinterest consistently lower participants' state self-esteem (Leary et al. 1995, 1998, 2001; Nezlek et al. 1997), and rejecting events in everyday life are associated with negative self-feelings as well (Baumeister et al. 1993b, Leary et al. 1995, Murray et al. 2003). Furthermore, the effects of performing certain actions on people's self-esteem parallel how they believe those behaviors will affect the degree to which others will accept or reject them (Leary et al. 1995), and longitudinal research shows that perceived relational value predicts changes in self-esteem over time (Srivastava & Beer 2005). Even people who claim to be unconcerned with others' approval show declines in self-esteem when they are rejected (Leary et al. 2003).

Overall, research on self-related motives has reached a point where researchers are increasingly asking whether people are motivated to maintain certain states of the self as has been assumed or whether these phenomena actually reflect the role of the self in other interpersonal motives. As Leary & Tangney (2003b) suggested, "it may be more parsimonious to conclude that emotional and motivational systems are intimately linked to the self but are not an inherent part of it" (p. 11).

THE SELF AND EMOTION

Animals that lack self-awareness nonetheless experience a wide array of emotional states (Masson & McCarthy 1994), as do infants before they acquire the ability to self-reflect, indicating that self-awareness is not necessary for emotion. Even so, the capacity for self-relevant thought renders human beings' emotional lives more complex than those of selfless animals. The ability to think about oneself over time (the extended self) allows emotions to arise from thoughts about oneself in the past and future, the ability to reflect on one's own subjective reactions (private self) allows emotions to arise from self-evaluation and inferences about others' judgments, and the ability to conceptualize oneself in abstract and symbolic ways (conceptual self) allows emotions to arise from abstract and arbitrary self-judgments (see Leary & Buttermore 2003, Neisser 1988).

Self-Conscious Emotions

Researchers have designated a distinct family of "self-conscious emotions" that includes guilt, shame, embarrassment, social anxiety, and pride, but the basis of this designation has been a matter of debate. Some theorists have conceptualized self-conscious emotions as emotions that emerge from self-reflection and self-evaluation. For example, Mascolo & Fischer (1995) traced emotions such as pride, shame, and guilt to people's evaluations of their own value, worth, or wrongdoing, and Tracy & Robins (2004a) proposed that people experience self-conscious emotions "when they become aware that they have lived up to, or failed to live up to, some actual or ideal self-representation" (p. 105). However, the self-conscious emotions are not unique in being elicited by self-reflection or self-evaluation. For example, an athlete who worries about playing in an upcoming game is anxious as a result of self-reflection and self-evaluation, yet we do not characterize anxiety as a "self-conscious" emotion. In fact, virtually every emotion can be elicited purely by self-reflection, so this criterion cannot serve as a means of distinguishing self-conscious emotions from other emotional states.

Other theorists have suggested that self-conscious emotions involve inferences about other people's evaluations of the individual. When people feel ashamed, guilty, embarrassed, socially anxious, or proud, they are assessing themselves from the perspectives of real or imagined other people. Thus, several researchers have proposed that self-conscious emotions involve reactions to social-evaluative events or transgressions of social standards (see Dickerson et al. 2004, Keltner & Beer 2004). In some cases, the reaction is in response to the judgments of specific individuals, whereas in other cases, it is a reaction to an internalized standard of some "generalized other" (Mead 1934).

Evidence that self-conscious emotions fundamentally involve drawing inferences about other people's evaluations rather than simply comparing one's behavior to personal self-representations or standards comes from several sources. First, we do not see evidence of self-conscious emotions in young children

Self-conscious emotions: emotions such as guilt, shame, embarrassment, social anxiety, and pride that arise from people's inferences about others' evaluations of them, particularly with respect to their social acceptability

until they have internalized knowledge of others' standards and judgments and can take others' perspectives (Barrett 1995, Harter 1999, Lewis 1994, Stipek 1995, Stipek et al. 1992). Furthermore, self-conscious emotions are much more strongly tied to what people think other people think of them than to what people think of themselves. For example, people may become embarrassed when other people perceive them in an undesired fashion even when they know that those people's perceptions of them are inaccurate (Miller 1996), and other people can make us feel guilty or ashamed even though we know that we did nothing wrong. Likewise, people may feel proud while knowing that they did nothing exemplary, as when people bask in the reflected glory of others who excel (Cialdini et al. 1976). People experience self-conscious emotions not because of how they evaluate themselves but rather because of how they think they are being evaluated or might be evaluated by others.

Consensus is emerging that self-conscious emotions are involved in the self-regulation of interpersonal behavior. Successfully relating to other people requires that an individual abide by social and moral standards and occasionally subordinate one's own interests in favor of those of the group or other people. Self-conscious emotions play a central role in guiding behavior, motivating people to adhere to norms and morals, affectively punishing misbehaviors, and promoting appropriate remediative responses when needed (Baumeister et al. 1994, Beer & Keltner 2004, Keltner & Beer 2005, Keltner & Buswell 1997, Miller & Leary 1992, Tangney 2002, Tangney et al. 2007). In fact, people who do not experience self-conscious emotions mismanage their interpersonal relationships in situations that would produce embarrassment, guilt, or shame in most other people (Beer et al. 2003, Keltner et al. 1995, Tangney & Dearing 2002). Furthermore, people with damage to the orbitofrontal cortex, known to be a center for executive and self-regulatory control, show both deficits in self-conscious emotions and inappropriate social behavior (Beer et al. 2003).

Of course, people can experience emotions simply from thinking about or evaluating themselves in their own minds, creating happiness, anger, anxiety, sadness, guilt, pride, and other emotions. People internalize others' values, then use those values to judge themselves. Importantly, the emotional consequences of these imagined reactions help to regulate people's behavior even in the absence of explicit feedback from others. Yet, the necessary and sufficient cause of self-conscious emotions is the real or imagined appraisals of other people, even if those appraisals are in one's mind (see Baldwin & Baccus 2004).

In addition, the expressive features of self-conscious emotions appear to serve as social signals that influence the inferences and behavior of onlookers (Keltner 1995; Keltner & Buswell 1996, 1997; Leary et al. 1992). In particular, the negative self-conscious emotions—guilt, shame, and embarrassment—include behavioral features that are seen in the appeasement displays of many other species, including gaze aversion, nervous smiling, reduced physical size, and a downward movement of the head (Keltner & Buswell 1997, Leary et al. 1992). Behaviors associated with pride, on the other hand, seem to convey a sense of accomplishment or superiority (Lazarus 1991, Tracy & Robins 2004c).

Guilt and Shame

For many years, the consensus was that people felt guilty when they violated their own personal standards but ashamed when they violated social standards. However, Lewis (1971), Tangney (1992), and others have shown that the distinction between guilt and shame lies not in the nature of the standards being violated but rather in the degree to which the person views the violation as a reflection upon his or her behavior (which produces guilt) or upon his or her global character (which produces shame) (Tangney 1992; Tangney et al. 1994, 1996a). Put simply, people feel guilty when they think they did a bad thing but feel ashamed when they think they are a bad person (Niedenthal et al. 1994, Tangney & Dearing 2002).

People also experience vicarious guilt and shame due to the actions of other people who are associated with them (Branscombe & Doosje 2004, Lickel et al. 2005). For example, when in-group members engage in negative behaviors that are relevant to the identity of the group, other members may experience vicarious guilt or shame even though they personally did nothing wrong (Lickel et al. 2004). Participants who identified strongly with their national or ethnic group reported shame when other group members behaved prejudicially (Johns et al. 2005, Schmader & Lickel 2006).

Guilt and shame have different cognitive, subjective, and behavioral features. Shame is a more painful emotion that is accompanied by feelings of worthlessness, efforts to deny the transgression or escape the situation, defensiveness, and anger (Gramzow & Tangney 1992, Tangney et al. 1996b). When ashamed, people focus on themselves rather than the people they have hurt (Leith & Baumeister 1998, Tangney 1992, Tangney et al. 1994). In contrast, guilt is less painful, presumably because the person's negative self-judgment applies to a specific behavior rather than to his or her character. When people experience guilt, they typically feel regret regarding their transgression, are empathic toward those they have hurt, and try to correct the situation through apology and reparation (Baumeister et al. 1994, Leith & Baumeister 1998, Tangney et al. 1994). Guilt also seems to involve a lower degree of self-focused attention than shame, possibly because guilty people focus primarily on those they have harmed, whereas ashamed people focus primarily on themselves (Arndt & Goldenberg 2004).

These differences have led theorists to suggest that guilt is a more adaptive emotion than shame from both an interpersonal and psychological perspective (Baumeister et al. 1994, Tangney 2002, Tangney et al. 1996a). Not only is guilt more strongly associated with

empathy and behaviors that redress undesired situations, but individual differences in guilt-proneness are associated with better psychological adjustment than individual differences in shame-proneness (for a review, see Tangney et al. 1995). Furthermore, contrary to the assumption that shame deters people from engaging in undesirable behaviors, people who are high in shame-proneness are actually more likely to commit immoral and illegal actions than are those low in shame-proneness. In contrast, guilt-proneness is associated with more socially acceptable behaviors (Tangney 1994, Tangney & Dearing 2002).[2]

Social Anxiety and Embarrassment

Social anxiety and embarrassment involve people's concerns with how they are being perceived and evaluated by others. Social anxiety arises when people are motivated to make a particular impression on others but doubt that they will be able to do so, and embarrassment occurs when people believe that others have already formed an undesired impression of them (Leary & Kowalski 1995, Miller 1996, Schlenker & Leary 1982). Experiments that raise and lower people's concerns with others' impressions of them cause changes in their social anxiety (DePaulo et al. 1990, Leary 1986), and people's beliefs in their ability to make desired impressions predict how socially anxious they feel in real and imagined encounters (Alden & Wallace 1991, Leary et al. 1988, Patterson & Ritts 1997). Social anxiety is clearly an interpersonal emotion that is involved in detecting and responding to events that have implications for the degree to which people are valued and accepted by others (see Leary 2001).

Likewise, embarrassment is caused by events that might lead others to draw negative inferences about the individual (Miller 1995).

---

[2] The uniformly maladaptive nature of the reactions that accompany shame raises the question of why shame might have evolved in the first place. This question goes beyond the focus of the current review but is addressed by Tangney (2003).

Thus, people report feeling embarrassed as a result of pratfalls (e.g., falling down), cognitive shortcomings (e.g., forgetting something important), loss of bodily control (e.g., belching), failure to maintain their own or another's privacy (e.g., unexpectedly being seen naked or seeing others naked), and stilted social interactions that connote interpersonal ineptitude (e.g., awkward silences in conversations) (Miller 1992). In addition, people may be teased into embarrassment when others point out their undesired characteristics or behaviors (Keltner & Buswell 1997, Miller 1992).

Pride

Pride has received less theoretical and empirical attention than guilt, shame, embarrassment, or social anxiety. Pride appears to arise when people believe that they are responsible for a socially valued outcome or that they are a socially valued person (Barrett 1995, Mascolo & Fischer 1995). Although pride typically involves outcomes for which the individual was personally responsible, it may also arise from the outcomes of others with whom one is associated and even from possession of a valued object (Lazarus 1991).

Researchers have suggested that two forms of pride reflect pride in one's behavior versus pride in one's personal characteristics, a distinction that parallels that between guilt and shame (Lewis 1992, Tangney 2003, Tracy & Robins 2006). Preliminary evidence suggests that pride in one's actions is more adaptive than pride in who one is, which tends to be hubristic and egocentric (Lewis 1992, Tracy & Robins 2006). Evidence also suggests that some instances of pride are defensive reactions to threat rather than reasonable responses to one's own actions or outcomes (McGregor et al. 2005). Although research supports the distinction between two forms of pride and the more adaptive nature of pride-in-behavior (Tracy & Robins 2003, 2006), it is not clear whether these ought to be regarded as two types of pride or as two distinct emotions (as guilt and shame are).

The functions of pride have not been deeply investigated, but they may involve motivating socially valued behaviors (i.e., people may behave in socially valued ways to experience the pleasant feeling of pride) or bringing one's positive accomplishments or attributes to other people's attention. The fact that pride has a distinct nonverbal expression that is recognized by both children and adults cross-culturally (Tracy & Robins 2004c, Tracy et al. 2005) suggests that its expression may serve some interpersonal function such as conveying success, competence, or status.

THE LINK BETWEEN SELF-MOTIVES AND EMOTIONS

As noted, motives and emotions are closely linked. Achieving or not achieving the goal that is associated with a motivational state results in affective reactions, and emotions typically imply the existence of a motive that was or was not fulfilled (see Johnson-Laird & Oatley 1992, Zurbriggen & Sturman 2002). This consideration raises a previously unexplored question regarding the relationship between self-motives and self-conscious emotions. Why are particular motives and emotions linked to the self, and what relationship, if any, do these motives and emotions have to each other? There may be two answers to this question—one that may be broadly applied to a number of motives and emotions, and another that is more specific to the particular motives and emotions discussed in this article.

The Co-option of Self-Awareness for Motivation and Emotion

The broad answer is that, once human beings acquired self-awareness during their evolutionary past, self-reflection came into play in a wide array of motivated actions and emotional responses that previously operated nonconsciously (as they do in animals without a self). For example, using the extended self to contemplate the past or future could create motivational and emotional states under conditions that would have not done so prior to the emergence of self-awareness. Thus, once human beings became self-aware, self-thought created cognitive and emotional states that previously arose only from the tangible satisfaction of particular needs or goals. [See Leary & Buttermore (2003) for a discussion of the effects of the evolution of self-awareness.]

Most relevant to the current article, cognitively construing the causes or meaning of events in particular self-relevant ways could lead to feelings of success, satisfaction, and self-approval in the absence of actual success. Through cognitively self-enhancing, people could reap the emotional benefits of doing well or being a good person without actually having performed in an exemplary manner. Similarly, by interpreting feedback in a self-verifying way, people could promote certainty regarding their self-image. In addition, the emergence of self-awareness permitted people to develop self-concepts and to evaluate themselves in their own minds, setting the stage for an array of phenomena that involve self-evaluation, self-verification, and self-expansion. These innovations in the cognitive self presaged the beginnings of modern human life, including deliberate self-regulation, symbolic collective identities, and deliberate conformity to arbitrary cultural standards, as well as an array of emotions elicited solely by self-reflection, such as prolonged worry (Leary 2004).

Although the self is undoubtedly involved in motives and emotions in this fashion, we may ask whether it is most parsimonious to regard the self's role in these sorts of cognitive-emotional reactions as reflecting one or more "self-motives" as opposed to the use of self-thought in the service of fostering positive affect or pursuing other motives. Stated differently, is the self actually motivated to maintain certain kinds of self-enhancing, self-verifying, or self-expanding thoughts, or do people simply use their powers of self-reflection to think about themselves in ways that lead to desired emotions and outcomes? Contrary to the impression that one gets from much of the existing literature, there is relatively little evidence that the self is inherently motivated to promote certain self-images or that certain self-images reliably produce self-conscious emotions in the absence of real or imagined interpersonal implications.

Interpersonal Motives and Emotions

The second answer to the question of how self-motives relate to self-conscious emotions assumes that the ability to self-reflect functions primarily to promote people's actual physical and social well-being rather than merely to sustain certain self-images or to produce self-related emotions. As we have seen, the so-called self-motives typically reflect concerns with real or imagined interpersonal relations, and the self-conscious emotions arise from concerns with what others are thinking about the individual. Both require the individual to imagine him- or herself from the perspectives of other people and, thus, involve the self. In fact, the ability to think consciously about oneself may be necessary in order to draw inferences about other people's perceptions of oneself and may have evolved for just that purpose (Humphrey 1986).

Viewed in this way, the majority of reactions involving self-motives and self-conscious emotions are not fundamentally about the psychological self but rather are inclinations toward and reactions to interpersonal relationships. That is, human beings are not inherently motivated to create or sustain certain mental images or feelings about themselves (i.e., they may have no self-motives per se) but rather are motivated to create and sustain certain kinds of interpersonal relationships for which these motives and emotions are relevant. As Lazarus (1991) observed, "Although emotions can seem to arise privately and without others being around … they always involve other persons" (p. 241) (see also Keltner & Haidt 1999).

This is not to say that people never use their powers of self-reflection to create psychological states to reduce anxiety, promote feelings of accomplishment, or make themselves feel good when situational conditions would not otherwise elicit such states naturally. But self-relevant rationalizations, illusions, biases, and other cognitive shenanigans are not likely to be the fundamental purpose of the self-motives and self-conscious emotions discussed here. Fundamental motives are aimed toward satisfying fundamental needs, and emotions appear to serve the dual functions of alerting people to certain conditions and prompting them to respond to those conditions (Oatley & Jenkins 1996). The outcomes toward which motives and emotions are pointed are situated in the individual's social and physical environment and not merely in the individual's own mind.

CONCLUSION

The appearance of self-awareness led to dramatic changes in human thought, emotion, and behavior (Leary 2004). Among other things, self-awareness allowed people to think about how they were perceived and evaluated by others and to regulate their behavior to bring about desired interpersonal outcomes. Many, although by no means all, of the "hot" self-relevant processes investigated by behavioral researchers, including those discussed in this article, directly or indirectly involve this interest in being perceived and treated in desired ways by other people. The motives to self-enhance, self-verify, and self-expand are partly rooted in people's pervasive concerns with approval and acceptance, and self-conscious emotions are reactions to events that involve people's real or potential standing in the eyes of other people. Because people can think about themselves in their own minds, they sometimes conjure up these motives and emotions in the absence of real interpersonal events, yet these phenomena appear to be fundamentally rooted in the vitally important need for social connection.

SUMMARY POINTS

1. Psychologists have ascribed a good deal of human behavior and emotion to self-enhancement, self-verification, self-expansion, and other self-relevant motives.

2. Although people undoubtedly self-enhance (for example, through self-serving attributions, the better-than-average effect, implicit self-enhancement, and the bias blind spot), self-verify (by seeking information that is consistent with their self-views), and self-expand (by seeking experiences that broaden their resources, perspectives, and identities), questions may be raised regarding whether these are motives to maintain particular states of the psychological self.

3. Rather than serving intrapsychic motives, self-enhancement, self-verification, and self-expansion may reflect efforts to obtain material or interpersonal outcomes, such as to establish, maintain, and protect one's relationships with other people.

4. The capacity for self-awareness renders human beings' emotional experiences quite different from those of self-less animals by allowing people to generate emotion purely though self-relevant thought and by permitting people to imagine how they are being perceived by other people.

5. The so-called self-conscious emotions—guilt, shame, embarrassment, social anxiety, and pride—are reactions to inferences about other people's evaluations of the

individual, playing a role in guiding behavior, motivating people to adhere to norms and morals, affectively punishing misbehaviors, and promoting corrective actions following misdeeds.

ACKNOWLEDGMENTS

I wish to thank Eleanor Tate, Ashley Batts Allen, and Teresa Hill for their help with this review.

LITERATURE CITED

Alden LE, Wallace ST. 1991. Social standards and social withdrawal. *Cogn. Ther. Res.* 15:85–100

Alicke MD. 1985. Global self-evaluation as determined by the desirability and controllability of trait adjectives. *J. Personal. Soc. Psychol.* 49:1621–30

Alicke MD, Govorum O. 2006. The better-than-average effect. In *The Self in Social Judgment*, ed. MD Alicke, ML Klotz DA Dunning, JI Krueger. Philadelphia, PA: Psychol. Press. In press

Alicke MD, Klotz ML, Breitenbecher DL, Yurak TJ, Vredenburg DS. 1995. Personal contact, individuation, and the better-than-average effect. *J. Personal. Soc. Psychol.* 68:804–25

Amodio DM, Showers CJ. 2005. "Similarity breeds liking" revisited: the moderating role of commitment. *J. Soc. Pers. Relat.* 22:817–36

Arndt J, Goldenberg JL. 2004. From self-awareness to shame-proneness: evidence of causal sequence among women. *Self Ident.* 3:27–37

Aron A, Aron EN. 1996. Self- and self-expansion in relationships. In *Knowledge Structures in Close Relationships: A Social Psychological Approach*, ed. GJO Fletcher, J Fitness, pp. 325–44. Mahwah, NJ: Erlbaum

Aron A, Aron EN. 1997. Self-expansion motivation and including others in the self. In *Handbook of Personal Relationships*, ed. S Duck, 1:251–70. London: Wiley. 2nd ed.

Aron A, Aron EN, Norman C. 2001. Self-expansion model of motivation and cognition in close relationships and beyond. In *Blackwell Handbook of Social Psychology: Interpersonal Processes*, ed. GJO Fletcher, MS Clark, pp. 478–501. Malden, MA: Blackwell

Aron A, Aron E, Tudor M, Nelson G. 1991. Close relationships as including others in the self. *J. Personal. Soc. Psychol.* 60:241–53

Aron A, Fraley B. 1999. Relationship closeness as including others in the self: cognitive underpinnings and measures. *Soc. Cogn.* 17:140–60

Aron A, Norman CC, Aron EN, McKenna C, Heyman R. 2000. Couple's shared participation in novel and arousing activities and experienced relationship quality. *J. Personal. Soc. Psychol.* 78:273–84

Aron A, Paris M, Aron EN. 1995. Falling in love: prospective studies of self-concept change. *J. Personal. Soc. Psychol.* 69:1102–12

Aron A, Steele J, Kashdan T. 2002. *Attraction to others with similar interests as moderated by perceived opportunity for a relationship*. Unpubl. manuscr., State Univ. N.Y., Stony Brook

Baldwin MW, Baccus JR. 2004. Maintaining a focus on the social goals underlying self-conscious emotions. *Psychol. Inq.* 15:139–44

Banaji MR, Prentice DA. 1994. The self in social contexts. *Annu. Rev. Psychol.* 45:297–332

Barrett KC. 1995. A functionalist approach to guilt and shame. In *Self-Conscious Emotions*, ed. JP Tangney, KW Fischer, pp. 25–63. New York: Guilford

Provides an overview of self-expansion theory and its supporting evidence.

Comprehensively reviews the literature on the benefits and liabilities of high self-esteem.

Baumeister RF, Campbell JD, Krueger JI, Vohs KD. 2003. **Does high self-esteem cause better performance, interpersonal success, happiness, or healthier lifestyles?** *Psychol. Sci. Public Interest* **4**:1–44

Baumeister RF, Heatherton TF, Tice DM. 1993a. When ego threats lead to self-regulation failure: negative consequences of high self-esteem. *J. Personal. Soc. Psychol.* 64:141–56

Baumeister RF, Smart L, Boden JM. 1996. Relation of threatened egotism to violence and aggression: the dark side of high self-esteem. *Psychol. Rev.* 103:5–33

Baumeister RF, Stillwell AM, Heatherton TF. 1994. Guilt: an interpersonal approach. *Psychol. Bull.* 115:243–67

Baumeister RF, Wotman SR, Stillwell AM. 1993b. Unrequited love: on heartbreak, anger, guilt, scriptlessness, and humiliation. *J. Personal. Soc. Psychol.* 64:377–94

Beer JS, Heerey EA, Keltner D, Scabini D, Knight RT. 2003. The self-regulatory function of self-conscious emotion: insights from patients with orbitofrontal damage. *J. Personal. Soc. Psychol.* 85:594–604

Beer JS, Keltner D. 2004. What is unique about self-conscious emotions? *Psychol. Inq.* 15:126–28

Beggan JK. 1992. On the social nature of nonsocial perception: the mere ownership effect. *J. Personal. Soc. Psychol.* 62:229–37

Bernichon T, Cook KE, Brown JD. 2003. Seeking self-evaluative feedback: the interactive role of global self-esteem and specific self-views. *J. Personal. Soc. Psychol.* 84:194–204

Blaine B, Crocker J. 1993. Self-esteem and self-serving biases in reactions to positive and negative events: an integrative review. In *Self-Esteem: The Puzzle of Low Self-Regard*, ed. RF Baumeister, pp. 55–85. New York: Plenum

Block J, Colvin CR. 1994. Positive illusion and well-being revisited: separating fiction from fact. *Psychol. Bull.* 116:28

Bonanno GA, Field NP, Kovacevic A. 2002. Self-enhancement as a buffer against extreme adversity: civil war in Bosnia and traumatic loss in the United States. *Personal. Soc. Psychol. Bull.* 28:184–96

Bonanno GA, Rennicke C, Dekel S. 2005. Self-enhancement among high-exposure survivors of the September eleventh terrorist attack: resilience or social maladjustment? *J. Personal. Soc. Psychol.* 88:984–98

Bradley GW. 1978. Self-serving biases in the attribution process: a reexamination of the fact or fiction question. *J. Personal. Soc. Psychol.* 36:56–71

Branscombe NR, Doojse B, eds. 2004. *Collective Guilt: International Perspectives*. Cambridge, UK: Cambridge Univ. Press

Brendl M, Chattopadhyay A, Pelham BW, Carvallo M. 2004. *The Name Letter Effect in Choice*. Manuscr. submitted, State Univ. N.Y., Buffalo

Brown JD. 1990. Evaluating one's abilities: shortcuts and stumbling blocks on the road to self-knowledge. *J. Exp. Soc. Psychol.* 26:149–67

Brown JD, Kobayashi C. 2002. Self-enhancement in Japan and America. *Asian J. Soc. Psychol.* 5:145–67

Burke PJ, Stets JE. 1999. Trust and commitment through self-verification. *Soc. Psychol. Q.* 62:347–97

Cadinu MR, Rothbart M. 1996. Self-anchoring and differentiation processes in the minimal group setting. *J. Personal. Soc. Psychol.* 70:661–77

Carver CS, Scheier MF. 1981. *Attention and Self-Regulation: A Control-Theory Approach to Human Behavior*. New York: Springer-Verlag

Chang EC, Asakawa K. 2003. Cultural variations on optimistic and pessimistic bias for self versus a sibling: Is there evidence for self-enhancement in the West and self-criticism in the East when the referent group is specified? *J. Personal. Soc. Psychol.* 84:569–81

Chang EC, Asakawa K, Sanna LJ. 2001. Cultural variations in optimistic and pessimistic bias: Do Easterners really expect the worst and Westerners really expect the best when predicting future life events? *J. Personal. Soc. Psychol.* 81:476–91

Chen S, Chen KY, Shaw L. 2004. Self-verification motives at the collective level of self-definition. *J. Personal. Soc. Psychol.* 86:77–94

Cialdini RB, Borden RJ, Thorne A, Walker MR, Freeman S, Sloan LR. 1976. Basking in reflected glory: three (football) field studies. *J. Personal. Soc. Psychol.* 34:366–75

Colvin CR, Block J, Funder DC. 1995. Overly positive self-evaluations and personality: negative implications for mental health. *J. Personal. Soc. Psychol.* 68:1152–62

Crocker J, Park LE. 2004. The costly pursuit of self-esteem. *Psychol. Bull.* 130:392–414

DePaulo BM, Epstein JA, LeMay CS. 1990. Responses of the socially anxious to the prospect of interpersonal evaluation. *J. Personal.* 48:623–40

Dickerson SS, Gruenewald TL, Kemeny ME. 2004. When the social self is threatened: shame, physiology, and health. *J. Personal.* 72:1189–216

Ditto PH, Lopez DA. 1993. Motivated skepticism: use of differential decision criteria for preferred and nonpreferred conclusions. *J. Personal. Soc. Psychol.* 63:568–84

Doherty K, Weigold MF, Schlenker BR. 1990. Self-serving interpretations of motives. *Personal. Soc. Psychol. Bull.* 16:485–95

Dunning D, Beauregard KS. 2000. Regulating others to affirm images of the self. *Soc. Cogn.* 18:198–222

Dunning D, Cohen GL. 1992. Egocentric definitions of traits and abilities in social judgment. *J. Personal. Soc. Psychol.* 63:341–55

Dunning D, Meyerowitz JA, Holzberg A. 1989. Ambiguity and self-evaluation: the role of idiosyncratic trait definitions in self-serving assessments of ability. *J. Personal. Soc. Psychol.* 57:1082–90

Duval S, Wicklund RA. 1972. *A Theory of Objective Self-Awareness.* New York: Academic

Ellemers N, Kortekaas P, Ouwerkerk JW. 1999. Self-categorisation, commitment to the group, and group self-esteem as related but distinct aspects of social identity. *Eur. J. Soc. Psychol.* 29:371–89

Ellemers N, Spears R, Doosje B. 2002. Self and social identity. *Annu. Rev. Psychol.* 53:161–86

Fein S, Spencer SJ. 1997. Prejudice as self-image maintenance: affirming the self through derogating others. *J. Personal. Soc. Psychol.* 73:31–44

Florian V, Mikulincer M. 1997. Fear of death and the judgment of social transgressions: a multidimensional test of terror management theory. *J. Personal. Soc. Psychol.* 73:369–80

Gaertner L, Sedikides C, Vevea JL, Iuzzini J. 2002. The "I," the "we," and the "when": a meta-analysis of motivational primacy in self-definition. *J. Personal. Soc. Psychol.* 83:574–91

Gallucci M. 2003. I sell seashells by the seashore and my name is Jack: comment on Pelham, Mirenberg, and Jones 2002. *J. Personal. Soc. Psychol.* 85:789–99

Gardner WL, Gabriel S, Hochschild L. 2002. When you and I are "we," you are not threatening: the role of self-expansion in social comparison. *J. Personal. Soc. Psychol.* 82:239–51

Gramzow RH, Gaertner L. 2005. Self-esteem and favoritism toward novel in-groups: the self as an evaluative base. *J. Personal. Soc. Psychol.* 88:801–15

Gramzow RH, Tangney JP. 1992. Proneness to shame and the narcissistic personality. *Personal. Soc. Psychol. Bull.* 18:369–76

Examines the negative consequences of seeking self-esteem.

Greenberg J, Simon L, Pyszczynski T, Solomon S, et al. 1992a. Terror management and tolerance: Does mortality salience always intensify negative reactions to others who threaten one's worldview? *J. Personal. Soc. Psychol.* **63:212–20**

Greenberg J, Solomon S, Pyszczynski T, Rosenblatt A, Burling J, et al. 1992b. Assessing the terror management analysis of self-esteem: converging evidence of an anxiety-buffering function. *J. Personal. Soc. Psychol.* 63:913–22

Greenwald AG, Banaji MR. 1995. Implicit social cognition: attitudes, self-esteem, and stereotypes. *Psychol. Rev.* 102:4–27

Harmon-Jones E, Simon L, Greenberg J, Pyszczynski T, Solomon S, McGregor H. 1997. Terror management and self-esteem: evidence that self-esteem reduces mortality salience effects. *J. Personal. Soc. Psychol.* 72:24–26

Harter S. 1999. *The Construction of the Self*. New York: Guilford

Heatherton TF, Vohs KD. 2000. Interpersonal evaluations following threats to self: role of self-esteem. *J. Personal. Soc. Psychol.* 78:725–36

Heine SJ. 2001. Self as cultural product: an examination of East Asian and North American selves. *J. Personal.* 69:881–906

Heine SJ. 2005. Where is the evidence for pancultural self-enhancement? A reply to Sedikides, Gaertner, and Toguchi 2003. *J. Personal. Soc. Psychol.* 89:531–38

Heine SJ, Kitayama S, Lehman DR. 2001. Cultural differences in self-evaluation: Japanese readily accept negative self-relevant information. *J. Cross-Cult. Psychol.* 32:434–43

Heine SJ, Kitayama S, Lehman DR, Takata T, Ide E, et al. 2001. Divergent consequences of success and failure in Japan and North America: an investigation of self-improving motivations and malleable selves. *J. Personal. Soc. Psychol.* 81:599–615

Heine SJ, Lehman DR. 1995. Cultural variation in unrealistic optimism: Does the West feel more invulnerable than the East? *J. Personal. Soc. Psychol.* 68:595–607

Heine SJ, Lehman DR, Markus HR, Kitayama S. 1999. Is there a universal need for positive self-regard? *Psychol. Rev.* 106:766–94

Hixon JG, Swann WB Jr. 1993. When does introspection bear fruit? Self-reflection, self-insight, and interpersonal choices. *J. Personal. Soc. Psychol.* 64:35–43

Hodson G, Olson JM. 2005. Testing the generality of the name letter effect: name initials and everyday attitudes. *Personal. Soc. Psychol. Bull.* 31:1099–111

Hoorens V. 1993. Self-enhancement and superiority biases in social comparison. In *European Review of Social Psychology*, ed. W Strobe, M Hewstone, pp. 113–39. Chichester, UK: Wiley

Humphrey N. 1986. *The Inner Eye*. London: Faber & Faber

James W. 1890. *The Principles of Psychology*. New York: Holt

Johns M, Schmader T, Lickel B. 2005. Ashamed to be an American? The role of identification in predicting vicarious shame for anti-Arab prejudice after 9–11. *Self Ident.* 4:331–48

Johnson EA, Vincent N, Ross L. 1997. Self-deception versus self-esteem in buffering the negative effects of failure. *J. Res. Personal.* 31:385–405

Johnson-Laird PN, Oatley K. 1992. Basic emotions, rationality, and folk theory. *Cogn. Emot.* 6:201–23

Joiner Jr TE, Vohs KD, Katz J, Kwon P, Kline JP. 2003. Excessive self-enhancement and interpersonal functioning in roommate relationships: her virtue is his vice? *Self Ident.* 2:21–30

Jones JT, Pelham BW, Carvallo M, Mirenberg MC. 2004. How do I love thee? Let me count the Js: implicit egotism and interpersonal attraction. *J. Personal. Soc. Psychol.* **87:665–83**

Kahneman D, Knetch J, Thaler R. 1990. Experimental tests of the endowment effect and the coase theorem. *J. Polit. Econ.* 98:1325–48

One of many intriguing and important articles by Greenberg, Pyszczynski, and Solomon in which aspects of terror management theory are inspected.

Presents research showing that people's positive evaluations of the letters in their own names have implications for the course of their lives.

Keltner D. 1995. The signs of appeasement: evidence for the distinct displays of embarrassment, amusement, and shame. *J. Personal. Soc. Psychol.* 68:441–54

Keltner D, Beer JS. 2005. Self-conscious emotion and self-regulation. In *On Building, Defending, and Regulating the Self: A Psychological Perspective*, ed. A Tesser, JV Wood, DA Stapel, pp. 197–215. New York: Psychol. Press

Keltner D, Buswell BN. 1996. Evidence for the distinctiveness of embarrassment, shame, and guilt: a study of recalled antecedents and facial expressions of emotion. *Cogn. Emot.* 10:155–72

Keltner D, Buswell BN. 1997. Embarrassment: its distinct form and appeasement functions. *Psychol. Bull.* 122:250–70

Keltner D, Haidt J. 1999. Social functions of emotions at four levels of analysis. *Cogn. Emot.* 13:505–21

Keltner D, Moffit T, Stouthamer-Loeber M. 1995. Facial expression and psychopathology in adolescent boys. *J. Abnorm. Psychol.* 104:644–52

Kitayama S, Karasawa M. 1997. Implicit self-esteem in Japan: name-letters and birthday numbers. *Personal. Soc. Psychol. Bull.* 23:736–42

Koole SL, Dijksterhuis A, van Knippenberg A. 2001. What's in a name: implicit self-esteem and the automatic self. *J. Personal. Soc. Psychol.* 80:669–85

Kudo E, Numazaki M. 2003. Explicit and direct self-serving bias in Japan: reexamination of the self-serving bias for success and failure. *J. Cross-Cult. Psychol.* 34:511–21

Kurman J. 2001. Self-enhancement: Is it restricted to individualistic cultures? *Personal. Soc. Psychol. Bull.* 12:1705–16

Kurman J, 2003. Why is self-enhancement low in certain collectivist cultures? An investigation of two competing explanations. *J. Cross-Cult. Psychol.* 34:496–510

Kwan VSY, John OP, Kenny DA, Bond MH, Robins RW. 2004. Reconceptualizing individual differences in self-enhancement bias: an interpersonal approach. *Psychol. Rev.* 111:94–111

Lazarus AS. 1991. *Emotion and Adaptation*. Oxford, UK: Oxford Univ. Press

Leary MR. 1986. The impact of interactional impediments on social anxiety and self-presentation. *J. Exp. Soc. Psychol.* 22:122–35

Leary MR. 1995. *Self-Presentation: Impression Management and Interpersonal Behavior*. Boulder, CO: Westview

Leary MR. 2001. Social anxiety as an early warning system: a refinement and extension of the self-presentation theory of social anxiety. In *From Social Anxiety to Social Phobia: Multiple Perspectives*, ed. SG Hofmann, PN DiBartolo, pp. 321–34. Boston, MA: Allyn & Bacon

Leary MR. 2002. The interpersonal basis of self-esteem: death, devaluation, or deference? In *The Social Self: Cognitive, Interpersonal, and Intergroup Perspectives*, ed. J Forgas, KD Williams, pp. 143–59. New York: Psychol. Press

Leary MR. 2004. *The Curse of the Self: Self-Awareness, Egotism, and the Quality of Human Life*. New York: Oxford Univ. Press

Leary MR, Baumeister RF. 2000. The nature and function of self-esteem: sociometer theory. In *Advances in Experimental Social Psychology*, ed. MP Zanna, 32:1–62. San Diego: Academic

Leary MR, Bednarski R, Hammon D, Duncan T. 1997. Blowhards, snobs, and narcissists: interpersonal reactions to excessive egotism. In *Aversive Interpersonal Behaviors*, ed. RM Kowalski, pp. 111–31. New York: Plenum

Leary MR, Britt TW, Cutlip WD, Templeton JL. 1992. Social blushing. *Psychol. Bull.* 112:446–60

Leary MR, Buttermore N. 2003. The evolution of the human self: tracing the natural history of self-awareness. *J. Theory Soc. Behav.* 33:365–404

Reviews evidence in support of the sociometer theory of self-esteem, which conceptualizes self-esteem as a psychological gauge of social acceptance and rejection.

Leary MR, Cottrell CA, Phillips M. 2001. Deconfounding the effects of dominance and social acceptance on self-esteem. *J. Personal. Soc. Psychol.* 81:898–909

Leary MR, Downs DL. 1995. Interpersonal functions of the self-esteem motive: the self-esteem system as a sociometer. In *Efficacy, Agency, and Self-Esteem*, ed. M Kernis, pp. 123–44. New York: Plenum

Leary MR, Gallagher B, Fors EH, Buttermore N, Baldwin E, et al. 2003. The invalidity of disclaimers about the effects of social feedback on self-esteem. *Personal. Soc. Psychol. Bull.* 29:623–36

Leary MR, Haupt A, Strausser K, Chokel J. 1998. Calibrating the sociometer: the relationship between interpersonal appraisals and state self-esteem. *J. Personal. Soc. Psychol.* 74:1290–99

Leary MR, Kowalski RM. 1995. *Social Anxiety.* New York: Guilford

Leary MR, Kowalski RM, Campbell C. 1988. Self-presentational concerns and social anxiety: the role of generalized impression expectancies. *J. Res. Personal.* 22:308–21

Leary MR, Tambor ES, Terdal SK, Downs DL. 1995. Self-esteem as an interpersonal monitor: the sociometer hypothesis. *J. Personal. Soc. Psychol.* 68:518–30

Leary MR, Tangney JP, eds. 2003a. *Handbook of Self and Identity.* New York: Guilford

Leary MR, Tangney JP. 2003b. The self as an organizing construct in the self and behavioral sciences. In *Handbook of Self and Identity*, ed. MR Leary, JP Tangney, pp. 3–14. New York: Guilford

Leith KP, Baumeister RF. 1998. Empathy, shame, guilt, and narratives of interpersonal conflicts: Guilt-prone people are better at perspective taking. *J. Personal.* 66:1–37

Lewis HB. 1971. *Shame and Guilt in Neurosis.* New York: Int. Univ. Press

Lewis M. 1992. *Shame: The Exposed Self.* New York: Free Press

Lewis M. 1994. Myself and me. In *Self-Awareness in Animals and Humans: Developmental Perspectives*, ed. ST Parker, RW Mitchell, ML Boccia, pp. 20–34. New York: Cambridge Univ. Press

Lickel B, Schmader T, Barquissau M. 2004. The evocation of moral emotions in intergroup contexts: the distinction between collective guilt and collective shame. In *Collective Guilt: International Perspectives*, ed. N Branscombe, B Doojse, pp. 35–55. Cambridge, UK: Cambridge Univ. Press

Lickel B, Schmader T, Curtis M, Ames DR. 2005. Vicarious shame and guilt. *Group Process. Intergr. Relat.* 8:145–47

Markus H. 1977. Self-schemata and processing information about the self. *J. Personal. Soc. Psychol.* 35:63–78

Markus H, Kitayama S. 1991. Culture and the self: implications for cognition, emotion, and motivation. *Psychol. Rev.* 98:224–53

Maschek D, Aron A, Boncimino M. 2003. Confusions of self with close others. *Personal. Soc. Psychol. Bull.* 29:382–92

Mascolo MF, Fischer KW. 1995. Developmental transformation in appraisals for pride, shame, and guilt. In *Self-Conscious Emotions: The Psychology of Shame, Guilt, Embarrassment, and Pride*, ed. JP Tangney, KW Fischer, pp. 64–113. New York: Guilford

Masson JM, McCarthy S. 1994. *When Elephants Weep: The Emotional Lives of Animals.* London: Cape

McCrae SM, Hirt ER. 2001. The role of ability judgments in self-handicapping. *Personal. Soc. Psychol. Bull.* 27:1378–89

McGregor I, Nail PR, Marigold DC, Kang S. 2005. Defensive pride and consensus: strength in imaginary numbers. *J. Personal. Soc. Psychol.* 89:978–96

Mead GH. 1934. *Mind, Self, and Society.* Chicago: Univ. Chicago Press

Miller DT, Ross M. 1975. Self-serving biases in the attribution of causality: fact or fiction? *Psychol. Bull.* 82:213–25

Miller RS. 1992. The nature and severity of self-reported embarrassing circumstances. *Personal. Soc. Psychol. Bull.* 18:190–98

Miller RS. 1995. On the nature of embarrassability: shyness, social evaluation, and social skill. *J. Personal.* 63:315–39

Miller RS. 1996. *Embarrassment: Poise and Peril in Everyday Life*. New York: Guilford

Miller RS, Leary MR. 1992. Social sources and interactive functions of emotion: the case of embarrassment. In *Emotion and Social Behavior*, ed. MS Clark, pp. 202–21. Beverly Hills, CA: Sage

Mullen R, Riordan CA. 1988. Self-serving attributions for performance in naturalistic settings: a meta-analytic review. *J. Appl. Soc. Psychol.* 18:3–22

Murray SL, Griffin DW, Rose P, Bellavia GM. 2003. Calibrating the sociometer: the relational contingencies of self-esteem. *J. Personal. Soc. Psychol.* 85:63–84

Neisser U. 1988. Five kinds of self-knowledge. *Philos. Psychol.* 1:35–59

Nezlek JB, Kowalski RM, Leary MR, Blevins T, Holgate S. 1997. Personality moderators of reactions to interpersonal rejection: depression and trait self-esteem. *Personal. Soc. Psychol. Bull.* 23:1235–44

Niedenthal PM, Tangney JP, Gavanski I. 1994. "If only I weren't" versus "if only I hadn't": distinguishing shame and guilt in counterfactual thinking. *J. Personal. Soc. Psychol.* 67:585–95

Oatley K, Jenkins JM. 1996. *Understanding Emotions*. Cambridge, MA: Blackwell

Olson ET. 1999. There is no problem of the self. In *Models of the Self*, ed. S Gallagher, J Shear, pp. 49–61. Thorverton, UK: Imprint Acad.

Otten S. 2002. "Me and us" or "us and them"? The self as heuristic for defining minimal ingroups. *Eur. Rev. Soc. Psychol.* 13:1–33

Patterson ML, Ritts V. 1997. Social and communicative anxiety: a review and meta-analysis. In *Communication Yearbook 20*, ed. BR Burleson, pp. 263–303. Thousand Oaks, CA: Sage

Paulhus DL. 1998. Interpersonal and intrapsychic adaptiveness of trait self-enhancement: a mixed blessing? *J. Personal. Soc. Psychol.* 74:1197–208

Paulhus DL, Harms PD, Bruce MN, Lysy DC. 2003. The overclaiming technique: measuring self-enhancement independent of ability. *J. Personal. Soc. Psychol.* 84:890–904

Paulhus DL, Levitt K. 1987. Desirable responding triggered by affect: automatic egotism? *J. Personal. Soc. Psychol.* 52:245–59

Pelham BW, Carvallo M, DeHart T, Jones JT. 2003. Assessing the validity of implicit egotism: a reply to Gallucci 2003. *J. Personal. Soc. Psychol.* 85:800–7

Pelham BW, Mirenberg MC, Jones JT. 2002. Why Susie sells seashells by the seashore: implicit egoism and major life decisions. *J. Personal. Soc. Psychol.* 82:469–87

Pronin E, Gilovich T, Ross L. 2004. Objectivity in the eye of the beholder: divergent perceptions of bias in self versus others. *Psychol. Rev.* 3:781–99

Pronin E, Lin DY, Ross L. 2002. The bias blind spot: perceptions of bias in self versus others. *Personal. Soc. Psychol. Bull.* 28:369–81

Reissman C, Aron A, Bergen MR. 1993. Shared activities and marital satisfaction: causal direction and self-expansion versus boredom. *J. Soc. Personal. Relat.* 10:243–54

Robins RW, Beer JS. 2001. Positive illusions about the self: short-term benefits and long-term costs. *J. Personal. Soc. Psychol.* 80:340–52

Robins RW, John OP. 1997. The quest for self-insight: theory and research on accuracy and bias in self-perception. In *Handbook of Personality Psychology*, R Hogan, JA Johnson, SR Briggs, pp. 649–79. New York: Academic

Robinson DT, Smith-Lovin L. 1992. Selective interaction as a strategy for identity maintenance: an affect control model. *Soc. Psychol. Q.* 55:12–28

Rosenblatt A, Greenberg J, Solomon S, Pyszczynski T, Lyon D. 1989. Evidence for terror management theory: I. The effects of mortality salience on reactions to those who violate or uphold cultural values. *J. Personal. Soc. Psychol.* 57:681–90

Schlenker BR, Miller RS. 1977. Egotism in groups: self-serving bias or logical information processing. *J. Personal. Soc. Psychol.* 35:755–64

Schlenker MR, Leary MR. 1982. Social anxiety and self-presentation: a conceptualization and model. *Psychol. Bull.* 92:641–69

Schmader T, Lickel B. 2006. Stigma and shame: emotional responses to the stereotypic actions of one's ethnic in-group. In *Stigma and Group Inequality: Social Psychological Approaches*, ed. S Levin, C van Laar. Hillsdale, NJ: Erlbaum. In press

Sedikides C. 1993. Assessment, evaluation, and verification determinants of the self-evaluation process. *J. Personal. Soc. Psychol.* 65:317–38

Sedikides C, Gaertner L, Toguchi Y. 2003. Pancultural self-enhancement. *J. Personal. Soc. Psychol.* 84:60–79

Sedikides C, Gaertner L, Vevea JL. 2005. Pancultural self-enhancement reloaded: a meta-analytic reply to Heine 2005. *J. Personal. Soc. Psychol.* 89:539–51

Sedikides C, Strube MJ. 1997. Self-evaluation: to thine own self be good, to thine own self be sure, to thine own self be true, and to thine own self be better. *Adv. Exp. Soc. Psychol.* 29:209–69

Shedler J, Mayman M, Manis M. 1993. The illusion of mental health. *Am. Psychol.* 48:1117–31

Sherman DK, Kim HS. 2005. Is there an "I" in "team?" The role of the self in group-serving judgments. *J. Personal. Soc. Psychol.* 88:108–20

Smith ER, Henry S. 1996. An in-group becomes part of the self: response time evidence. *Personal. Soc. Psychol. Bull.* 22:635–42

Snyder ML, Stephan WG, Rosenfield D. 1978. Egotism and attribution. In *New Directions in Attribution Research*, ed. JH Harvey, W Ickes, RF Kidd, Vol. 2, pp. 91–120. Hillsdale, NJ: Erlbaum

Solomon S, Greenberg J, Pyszczynski T. 1991. A terror management theory of social behavior: the psychological functions of self-esteem and cultural worldviews. In *Advances in Experimental Social Psychology*, ed. M Zanna, 24:91–159. Orlando, FL: Academic

Srivastava S, Beer JS. 2005. How self-evaluations relate to being liked by others: integrating sociometer and attachment perspectives. *J. Personal. Soc. Psychol.* 89:966–77

Stipek D. 1995. The development of pride and shame in toddlers. In *Self-Conscious Emotions: The Psychology of Shame, Guilt, Embarrassment, and Pride*, ed. JP Tangney, KW Fischer, pp. 237–52. New York: Guilford

Stipek D, Recchia S, McClintic S. 1992. Self-evaluation in young children. *Monogr. Soc. Res. Child Dev.* 57:1–84

Strube MJ. 1990. In search of self: balancing the good and the true. *Personal. Soc. Psychol. Bull.* 16:699–704

Swann WB Jr. 1983. Self-verification: bringing social reality into harmony with the self. In *Psychological Perspectives on the Self*, ed. J Suls, AG Greenwald, 2:33–66. Hillsdale, NJ: Erlbaum

Swann WB Jr. 1990. To be adored or to be known: the interplay of self-enhancement and self-verification. In *Handbook of Motivation and Cognition*, ed. RM Sorrentino, ET Higgins, 2:408–48. New York: Guilford

Swann WB Jr, Bosson J, Pelham BW. 2002. Different partners, different selves: strategic verification of circumscribed identities. *Personal. Soc. Psychol. Bull.* 28:1215–28

Reports an exceptional program of research dealing with the question of whether the motive for self-enhancement is universal.

Swann WB Jr, De La Ronde C, Hixon JG. 1994. Authenticity and positivity strivings in marriage and courtship. *J. Personal. Soc. Psychol.* 66:857–69

Swann WB Jr, Ely RJ. 1984. A battle of wills: self-verification versus behavioral conformation. *J. Personal. Soc. Psychol.* 46:1287–302

Swann WB Jr, Milton L, Polzer J. 2000. Creating a niche or falling in line: identity negotiation and small group effectiveness. *J. Personal. Soc. Psychol.* 79:238–50

Swann WB Jr, Pelham B. 2002. Who wants out when the going gets good? Psychological investment and preference for self-verifying college roommates. *Self Ident.* 1:219–33

Swann WB Jr, Pelham BW, Krull DS. 1989. Agreeable fancy or disagreeable truth? Reconciling self-enhancement and self-verification. *J. Personal. Soc. Psychol.* 57:782–91

Swann WB Jr, Read SJ. 1981. Self-verification processes: how we sustain our self-conceptions. *J. Exp. Soc. Psychol.* 17:351–72

Swann WB Jr, Stein-Seroussi A, Giesler RB. 1992a. Why people self-verify. *J. Personal. Soc. Psychol.* 62:392–401

Swann WB Jr, Wenzlaff RM, Krull DS, Pelham BW. 1992b. The allure of negative feedback: self-verification strivings among depressed persons. *J. Abnorm. Psychol.* 101:293–306

Tangney JP. 1992. Situational determinants of shame and guilt in young adulthood. *Personal. Soc. Psychol. Bull.* 18:199–206

Tangney JP. 2002. Self-conscious emotions: the self as a moral guide. In *Self and Motivation: Emerging Psychological Perspectives*, ed. A Tesser, D Stapel, JV Wood, pp. 97–117. Washington, DC: Am. Psychol. Assoc.

Tangney JP. 2003. Self-relevant emotions. In *Handbook of Self and Identity*, ed. MR Leary, JP Tangney, pp. 384–400. New York: Guilford

Tangney JP, Burggraf SA, Wagner PE. 1995. Shame-proneness, guilt-proneness, and psychological symptoms. In *Self-Conscious Emotions: The Psychology of Shame, Guilt, Embarrassment, and Pride*, ed. JP Tangney, KW Fischer, pp. 343–67. New York: Guilford

Tangney JP, Dearing RL. 2002. *Shame and Guilt.* New York: Guilford

Tangney JP, Marschall DE, Rosenberg K, Barlow DH, Wagner EE. 1994. *Children and adults' autobiographical accounts of shame, guilt, and pride experiences: a qualitative analysis of situational determinants and interpersonal concerns.* Unpubl. manuscr., George Mason Univ., Fairfax, VA

Tangney JP, Miller RS, Flicker L, Barlow DH. 1996a. Are shame, guilt, and embarrassment distinct emotions? *J. Personal. Soc. Psychol.* 70:797–809

Tangney JP, Stuewig J, Mashek DJ. 2007. Moral emotions and moral behavior. *Annu. Rev. Psychol.* 57:In press

Tangney JP, Wagner PE, Hill-Barlow DH, Marschall DE, Gramzow RH. 1996b. Relations of shame and guilt to constructive versus destructive responses to anger across the lifespan. *J. Personal. Soc. Psychol.* 70:797–809

Taylor SE, Armor DA. 1996. Positive illusions and coping with adversity. *J. Personal.* 64:873–98

Taylor SE, Brown JD. 1988. Illusion and well-being: a social psychological perspective on mental health. *Psychol. Bull.* 103:193–210

Taylor SE, Brown JD. 1994. Positive illusions and well-being revisited: separating fact from fiction. *Psychol. Bull.* 116:21–27

Taylor SE, Lerner JS, Sherman DK, Sage RM, McDowell NK. 2003a. Are self-enhancing cognitions associated with healthy or unhealthy biological profiles? *J. Personal. Soc. Psychol.* 85:605–15

Taylor SE, Lerner JS, Sherman DK, Sage RM, McDowell NK. 2003b. Portrait of the self-enhancer: well adjusted and well liked or maladjusted and friendless? *J. Personal. Soc. Psychol.* 84:165–76

Describes one of Swann's long-standing programs of studies on self-verification.

Offers a clear picture of the similarities and differences among shame, guilt, and embarrassment.

Taylor SE, Neter E, Wayment HA. 1995. Self-evaluative processes. *Personal. Soc. Psychol. Bull.* 21:1278–87

Tesser A. 1988. Toward a self-evaluation model of social behavior. *Adv. Exp. Soc. Psychol.* 21:181–227

Tracy JL, Robins RW. 2003. Death of a (narcissistic) salesman: an integrative model of fragile self-esteem. Comment. *Psychol. Inq.* 14:57–62

Tracy JL, Robins RW. 2004a. Putting the self into self-conscious emotions: a theoretical model. *Psychol. Inq.* 15:103–25

Tracy JL, Robins RW. 2004c. Show your pride: evidence for a discrete emotional expression. *Psychol. Sci.* 15:194–97

Tracy JL, Robins RW. 2006. The psychological structure of pride: a tale of two facets. *J. Personal. Soc. Psychol.* In press

Tracy JL, Robins RW, Lagattuta KH. 2005. Can children recognize the pride expression? *Emotion* 5:251–57

Trope Y. 1986. Self-enhancement and self-assessment in achievement behavior. In *Handbook of Motivation and Cognition: Foundations of Social Behavior*, ed. RM Sorrentino, ET Higgins, 1:350–78. New York: Guilford

Tropp LR, Wright SC. 2001. Ingroup identification and inclusion of ingroup in the self. *Personal. Soc. Psychol. Bull.* 27:585–600

Von Hippel W, Lakin JL, Shakarchi RJ. 2005. Individual differences in motivated social cognition: the case of self-serving information processing. *Personal. Soc. Psychol. Bull.* 31:1347–57

Wilson AE, Ross M. 2001. From chump to champ: people's appraisals of their earlier and present selves. *J. Personal. Soc. Psychol.* 80:572–84

Wood JV, Giordano-Beech M, Ducharme MJ. 1999. Compensating for failure through social comparison. *Personal. Soc. Psychol. Bull.* 25:1370–86

Wright SC, Aron A, Tropp LR. 2002. Including others (and groups) in the self: self-expansion and intergroup relations. In *The Social Self: Cognitive, Interpersonal, and Intergroup Perspectives*, ed. JP Forgas, KD Williams, pp. 343–63. New York: Psychol. Press

Yik MSM, Bond MH, Paulhus DL. 1998. Do Chinese self-enhance or self-efface? It's a matter of domain. *Personal. Soc. Psychol. Bull.* 24:399–406

Zuckerman M, Knee CR, Kieffer SC, Gagne M. 2004. What individuals believe they can and can not do: explorations of realistic and unrealistic control beliefs. *J. Personal. Assess.* 82:215–32

Zurbriggen EL, Sturman TS. 2002. Linking motives and emotions: a test of McClelland's hypothesis. *Personal. Soc. Psychol. Bull.* 28:521–35

Presents groundbreaking research on the nature of pride.

Moral Emotions and Moral Behavior

June Price Tangney,*,[1] Jeff Stuewig,[1]
and Debra J. Mashek[2]

[1]Department of Psychology, George Mason University, Fairfax, Virginia 22030;
email: jtangney@gmu.edu, jstuewig@gmu.edu

[2]Department of Humanities and Social Sciences, Harvey Mudd College,
Claremont, California 91711; email: mashek@hmc.edu

Annu. Rev. Psychol. 2007. 58:345–72

First published online as a Review in
Advance on September 5, 2006

The *Annual Review of Psychology* is online at
http://psych.annualreviews.org

This article's doi:
10.1146/annurev.psych.56.091103.070145

0066-4308/07/0203-0345$20.00

*Corresponding author

Key Words

shame, guilt, pride, elevation, gratitude

Abstract

Moral emotions represent a key element of our human moral apparatus, influencing the link between moral standards and moral behavior. This chapter reviews current theory and research on moral
emotions. We first focus on a triad of negatively valenced "self-
conscious" emotions—shame, guilt, and embarrassment. As in previous decades, much research remains focused on shame and guilt. We
review current thinking on the distinction between shame and guilt,
and the relative advantages and disadvantages of these two moral
emotions. Several new areas of research are highlighted: research
on the domain-specific phenomenon of body shame, styles of coping with shame, psychobiological aspects of shame, the link between
childhood abuse and later proneness to shame, and the phenomena
of vicarious or "collective" experiences of shame and guilt. In recent
years, the concept of moral emotions has been expanded to include
several positive emotions—elevation, gratitude, and the sometimes
morally relevant experience of pride. Finally, we discuss briefly a
morally relevant emotional process—other-oriented empathy.

Contents

OVERVIEW

What confluence of factors foster a moral life lived to the benefit of self and others? This review summarizes current theory and research on moral emotions, offering a framework for thinking about the ways in which morally relevant emotions may moderate the link between moral standards and moral decisions, and ultimately moral behavior.

Living a moral, constructive life is defined by a weighted sum of countless individual, morally relevant behaviors enacted day in and day out (plus an occasional particularly self-defining moment). As imperfect human beings, however, our behavior does not always bear a one-to-one correspondence to our moral standards.

Many potential explanations exist for the discrepancy between behavioral decisions (intentions) and actual behavior in both moral and nonmoral domains. Historically, much social psychological theory and research was devoted to understanding the imperfect link between intentions (e.g., moral decisions) and behavior. Field theory, the very foundation of social psychology, highlights the variability of individual behavior as a function of situational context (Lewin 1943); interpersonal negotiation can undermine the link between intention and behavior (DeVisser & Smith 2004); and diffusion of responsibility can undermine one's ability to act on deeply held beliefs (see, e.g., Latane & Darley 1968). Ajzen's (1991) theory of planned behavior offers a well-integrated model of the ways in which attitudes, norms, and perceived control feed into behavioral intentions and subsequent behavior.

As with the link between intentions and behaviors in general, the link between moral intentions and moral behaviors is likewise an important issue. However, owing to space limitations, this chapter focuses on the processes further upstream from intentions: the less widely studied factors that strengthen (or disrupt) linkages between moral standards and moral intentions (which we refer to throughout this article as moral decisions), and thus moral behaviors. In our view, the link between moral standards and moral decisions and/or moral behavior is influenced in important ways by moral emotions.

Moral standards represent an individual's knowledge and internalization of moral norms and conventions. People's moral standards are dictated in part by universal moral laws, and in part by culturally specific proscriptions. The current review emphasizes cognitive and emotional processes relevant to the more cross-culturally invariant moral standards. Of primary interest are prohibitions against behaviors likely to have negative consequences for the well-being of others and for which there is broad social consensus that such behaviors are "wrong" (e.g., interpersonal violence, criminal behavior, lying, cheating, stealing).

Naturally, people do, on occasion, lie, cheat, and steal, even though they know such behavior is deemed wrong by moral and societal norms. Individual differences in people's anticipation of and experience of moral emotions likely play key roles in determining actual moral choices and behavior in real-life contexts.

Moral emotions represent an important but often overlooked element of our human moral apparatus. Moral emotions may be critically important in understanding people's behavioral adherence (or lack of adherence) to their moral standards. Haidt (2003) defines moral emotions as those "that are linked to the interests or welfare either of society as a whole or at least of persons other than the judge or agent" (p. 276). Moral emotions provide the motivational force—the power and energy—to do good and to avoid doing bad (Kroll & Egan 2004).

In this article, we focus on a triad of morally relevant, negatively valenced "self-conscious" emotions—shame, guilt, and embarrassment. We also consider several positively valenced moral emotions—elevation, gratitude, and the sometimes morally relevant experience of pride. In addition, we discuss briefly a morally relevant emotional process—empathy.

SELF-CONSCIOUS EMOTIONS: ANTICIPATORY AND CONSEQUENTIAL REACTIONS TO THE SELF

Shame, guilt, embarrassment, and pride are members of a family of "self-conscious emotions" that are evoked by self-reflection and self-evaluation. This self-evaluation may be implicit or explicit, consciously experienced or transpiring beneath the radar of our awareness. But importantly, the self is the object of these self-conscious emotions.

As the self reflects upon the self, moral self-conscious emotions provide immediate punishment (or reinforcement) of behavior. In effect, shame, guilt, embarrassment, and pride function as an emotional moral barometer, providing immediate and salient feedback on our social and moral acceptability. When we sin, transgress, or err, aversive feelings of shame, guilt, or embarrassment are likely to ensue. When we "do the right thing," positive feelings of pride and self-approval are likely to result.

Moreover, actual behavior is not necessary for the press of moral emotions to have effect. People can anticipate their likely emotional reactions (e.g., guilt versus pride/self-approval) as they consider behavioral alternatives. Thus, the self-conscious moral emotions can exert a strong influence on moral choice and behavior by providing critical feedback regarding both anticipated behavior (feedback in the form of anticipatory shame, guilt, or pride) and actual behavior (feedback in the form of consequential shame, guilt, or pride). In our view, people's anticipatory emotional reactions are typically inferred based on history—that is, based on their past consequential emotions in reaction to similar actual behaviors and events.

Thus far, we have been discussing situation-specific experiences of consequential and anticipatory feelings of shame, guilt, embarrassment, and pride. In the realm of moral emotions, researchers are also interested in dispositional tendencies to experience these self-conscious emotions (e.g., shame-proneness, guilt-proneness). An emotion disposition is defined as the propensity to experience that emotion across a range of situations (Tangney 1990). From this perspective, shame-prone individuals would be more susceptible to both anticipatory and consequential experiences of shame, relative to their less shame-prone peers. That is, a shame-prone person would be inclined to anticipate shame in response to a range of potential behaviors and outcomes. In turn, such an individual also would be inclined to experience shame as a consequence of actual failures and transgressions.

Shame and Guilt

The vast majority of research on moral emotions has focused on two negatively valanced, self-conscious emotions—shame and guilt.

Many individuals, including clinicians, researchers, and lay people, use the terms "shame" and "guilt" synonymously. Nonetheless, a number of attempts have been made to differentiate between shame and guilt over the years.

What's the difference between shame and guilt? Attempts to differentiate between shame and guilt fall into three categories: (*a*) a distinction based on types of eliciting events, (*b*) a distinction based on the public versus private nature of the transgression, and (*c*) a distinction based on the degree to which the person construes the emotion-eliciting event as a failure of self or behavior.

Research indicates that type of event has surprisingly little to do with the distinction between shame and guilt. Analyses of personal shame and guilt experiences provided by children and adults revealed few, if any, "classic" shame-inducing or guilt-inducing situations (Keltner & Buswell 1996, Tangney 1992, Tangney et al. 1994, Tracy & Robins 2006). Most types of events (e.g., lying, cheating, stealing, failing to help another, disobeying parents) are cited by some people in connection with feelings of shame and by other people in connection with guilt. Some researchers claim that shame is evoked by a broader range of situations including both moral and nonmoral failures and transgressions, whereas guilt is more specifically linked to transgressions in the moral realm (Ferguson et al. 1991, Sabini & Silver 1997, Smith et al. 2002). In our view (Tangney et al. 2006b), like its sibling guilt, shame qualifies as a predominantly moral emotion, once one moves beyond narrowly conceptualizing the domain of morality in terms of the ethic of autonomy (Shweder et al. 1997). Of the "Big Three" ethics of morality—autonomy, community, and divinity (Shweder et al. 1997)—shame may be more closely tied to violations of the ethics of community (e.g., violations of the social order) and divinity (e.g., actions that remind us of our animal nature), but violations of particular ethics do not bear a one-to-one correspondence to particular situations or events. As demonstrated by Shweder et al. (1997), most failures and transgressions are experienced as relevant to a mix of moral ethics. In short, from this broader cultural perspective, shame and guilt are emotions each primarily evoked by moral lapses.

Another frequently cited distinction between shame and guilt focuses on the public versus private nature of transgressions (e.g., Benedict 1946). From this perspective, shame is viewed as the more "public" emotion arising from public exposure and disapproval of some shortcoming or transgression. Guilt, on the other hand, is conceived as a more "private" experience arising from self-generated pangs of conscience. As it turns out, empirical research has failed to support this public/private distinction in terms of the actual structure of the emotion-eliciting situation (Tangney et al. 1994, 1996a). For example, a systematic analysis of the social context of personal shame- and guilt-eliciting events described by several hundred children and adults (Tangney et al. 1994) indicated that shame and guilt are equally likely to be experienced in the presence of others. Solitary shame experiences were about as common as solitary guilt experiences. Even more to the point, the frequency with which others were aware of the respondents' behavior did not vary as a function of shame and guilt, in direct contradiction to the public/private distinction. Similarly, in a study of personal emotion narratives, Tracy & Robins (2006) found that, relative to guilt, shame was elicited somewhat more frequently by achievement events and personal events, which are each more private than relational and familial events.

Where does the notion that shame is a more public emotion come from? Although shame- and guilt-inducing situations are equally public (in terms of the likelihood that others are present and aware of the failure or transgression) and equally likely to involve interpersonal concerns, there appear to be systematic differences in the nature of those interpersonal concerns. Tangney et al. (1994)

found that when describing shame-inducing situations, respondents expressed more concern with others' evaluations of the self. In contrast, when describing guilt experiences, respondents were more concerned with their effect on others. This difference in "egocentric" versus "other-oriented" concerns isn't surprising given that shame involves a focus on the self, whereas guilt relates to a specific behavior. A shamed person who is focusing on negative self-evaluations would naturally be drawn to a concern over others' evaluations. It's a short leap from thinking what a horrible person one is to thinking about how one might be evaluated by others. On the other hand, a person experiencing guilt is already relatively "decentered"—focusing on a negative behavior somewhat separate from the self. In focusing on a bad behavior, rather than a bad self, a person in the middle of a guilt experience is more likely to recognize (and have concerns about) the effects of that behavior on others rather than on others' evaluations. Several subsequent studies (Smith et al. 2002) provide ample evidence that shame is associated with such concerns. For example, participants primed to focus on public exposure of a moral transgression attributed equivalent levels of shame and guilt to story protagonists, but when the public versus private dimension was not highlighted, participants attributed less shame (guilt was uniformly high across conditions). However, taken together, Smith et al.'s findings are consistent with the notion that people focus on others' evaluations because they are feeling shame, not vice versa. When participants were asked to think of a situation in which they had felt bad because an inferior aspect of themselves "*was revealed or publicly exposed* to another person or to other people" (p. 154; emphasis added), the majority spontaneously described the resulting feeling as one of embarrassment—only 6.7% identified the feeling as shame (twice as many identified the feeling as guilt). Similarly, in the moral condition (feeling bad because "something wrong" that they did was exposed), the modal emotion term was embarrassment—three times more

common than shame (which was no more frequent than guilt). In short, when experiencing shame, people may feel more exposed—more aware of others' disapproval—but the reality is that situations causing both shame and guilt are typically social in nature. More often than not, our failures and transgressions do not escape the notice of others.

The currently most dominant basis for distinguishing between shame and guilt—focus on self versus behavior—was first proposed by Helen Block Lewis (1971) and more recently elaborated by Tracy & Robins's (2004a) appraisal-based model of self-conscious emotions. According to Lewis (1971), shame involves a negative evaluation of the global self; guilt involves a negative evaluation of a specific behavior. Although this distinction may, at first glance, appear rather subtle, empirical research supports that this differential emphasis on self ("*I* did that horrible thing") versus behavior ("I *did* that horrible *thing*") sets the stage for very different emotional experiences and very different patterns of motivations and subsequent behavior.

Both shame and guilt are negative emotions and as such, both can cause intrapsychic pain. Nonetheless, shame is considered the more painful emotion because one's core self—not simply one's behavior—is at stake. Feelings of shame are typically accompanied by a sense of shrinking or of "being small" and by a sense of worthlessness and powerlessness. Shamed people also feel exposed. Although shame does not necessarily involve an actual observing audience present to witness one's shortcomings, there is often the imagery of how one's defective self would appear to others. Lewis (1971) described a split in self-functioning in which the self is both agent and object of observation and disapproval. Guilt, on the other hand, is typically a less devastating, less painful experience because the object of condemnation is a specific behavior, not the entire self. Rather than needing to defend the exposed core of one's identity, people in the throes of guilt are drawn to consider their behavior and its consequences. This focus leads to tension, remorse, and regret over the "bad thing done."

Empirical support for Lewis's (1971) distinction between shame and guilt comes from a range of experimental and correlational studies employing a range of methods including qualitative case study analyses, content analyses of shame and guilt narratives, participants' quantitative ratings of personal shame and guilt experiences, analyses of attributions associated with shame and guilt, and analyses of participants' counterfactual thinking (for a review, see Tangney & Dearing 2002). Most recently, for example, Tracy & Robins (2006) employed both experimental and correlational methods showing that internal, stable, uncontrollable attributions for failure were positively related to shame, whereas internal, unstable, controllable attributions for failure were positively related to guilt.

Shame and guilt are not equally "moral" emotions. One of the consistent themes emerging from empirical research is that shame and guilt are not equally "moral" emotions. On balance, guilt appears to be the more adaptive emotion, benefiting individuals and their relationships in a variety of ways (Baumeister et al. 1994, 1995a,b; Tangney 1991, 1995a,b), but there is growing evidence that shame is a moral emotion that can easily go awry (Tangney 1991, 1995a,b; Tangney et al. 1996b).

In this section, we summarize research in five areas that illustrates the adaptive functions of guilt, in contrast to the hidden costs of shame. Specifically, we focus on the differential relationship of shame and guilt to motivation (hiding versus amending), other-oriented empathy, anger and aggression, psychological symptoms, and deterrence of transgression and other risky, socially undesirable behavior.

Hiding versus amending Research consistently shows that shame and guilt lead to contrasting motivations or "action tendencies" (Ketelaar & Au 2003, Lewis 1971, Lindsay-Hartz 1984,

Tangney 1993, Tangney et al. 1996a, Wallbott & Scherer 1995, Wicker et al. 1983). On the one hand, shame corresponds with attempts to deny, hide, or escape the shame-inducing situation. Physiological research has linked the shame experience with elevated levels of proinflammatory cytokine and cortisol (Dickerson et al. 2004a), which can trigger postural signs of deference and self-concealment (see New Directions in Research on Shame and Guilt: Physiological Correlates of Shame). Guilt, on the other hand, corresponds with reparative actions including confessions, apologies, and undoing the consequences of the behavior. On the whole, empirical evidence evaluating the action tendencies of people experiencing shame and guilt suggests that guilt promotes constructive, proactive pursuits, whereas shame promotes defensiveness, interpersonal separation, and distance.

Other-oriented empathy versus self-oriented distress Second, shame and guilt are differentially related to empathy. Specifically, guilt goes hand in hand with other-oriented empathy. Feelings of shame, in contrast, apparently disrupt individuals' ability to form empathic connections with others. This differential relationship of shame and guilt to empathy is apparent both at the level of emotion disposition and at the level of emotional state. Research on emotional dispositions (Joireman 2004; Leith & Baumeister 1998; Tangney 1991, 1995b; Tangney & Dearing 2002) demonstrates that guilt-proneness consistently correlates with measures of perspective-taking and empathic concern. In contrast, shame-proneness is (depending on assessment method) negatively or negligibly correlated with other-oriented empathy and positively linked with the tendency to focus egocentrically on one's own distress. Similar findings arise in research on emotional states—feelings of shame and guilt "in the moment." In describing personal experiences of guilt, people convey greater empathy for others than when describing shame experiences (Leith & Baumeister 1998, Tangney et al. 1994). Marschall (1996) found that people induced to feel shame subsequently reported less empathy for a disabled student, especially among low-shame-prone individuals.

Why might shame, but not guilt, interfere with other-oriented empathy? Shame's inherently egocentric focus on the "bad self" (as opposed to the bad behavior) derails the empathic process. Individuals in the throes of shame turn tightly inward, and are thus less able to focus cognitive and emotional resources on the harmed other (Tangney et al. 1994). In contrast, people experiencing guilt are specifically focused on the bad behavior, which in turn highlights the negative consequences experienced by others, thereby fostering an empathic response and motivating people to "right the wrong."

Constructive versus destructive reactions to anger
Third, research indicates a robust link between shame and anger, again observed at both the dispositional and state levels. In her earlier clinical case studies, Helen Block Lewis (1971) observed the peculiar dynamic between shame and anger (or humiliated fury), noting that clients' feelings of shame often preceded expressions of anger and hostility in the therapy room. More recent empirical research has supported her claim. Across individuals of all ages, proneness to shame is positively correlated with anger, hostility, and the propensity to blame factors beyond the self for one's misfortunes (Andrews et al. 2000, Bennett, et al. 2005, Harper & Arias 2004, Paulhus et al. 2004, Tangney & Dearing 2002).

In fact, compared with those who are not shame-prone, shame-prone individuals are more likely to engage in externalization of blame, experience intense anger, and express that anger in destructive ways, including direct physical, verbal, and symbolic aggression, indirect aggression (e.g., harming something important to the target, talking behind the target's back), all manner of displaced aggression, self-directed aggression, and anger held in (a ruminative unexpressed anger). Finally, shame-prone individuals report awareness that their anger typically results in negative long-term consequences for both themselves and for their relationships with others.

Guilt-proneness, in contrast, is consistently associated with a more constructive constellation of emotions, cognitions, and behaviors. For example, proneness to "shame-free" guilt is positively correlated with constructive intentions in the wake of wrongdoing and consequent constructive behaviors (e.g., nonhostile discussion, direct corrective action). Compared with their nonguilt-prone peers, guilt-prone individuals are less likely to engage in direct, indirect, and displaced aggression when angered. And they report positive long-term consequences to their anger (Tangney et al. 1996a). Consistent with these findings, Harper et al. (2005) recently evaluated the link between shame-proneness and perpetration of psychological abuse in the dating relationships by heterosexual college men. Shame proneness was significantly correlated with perpetration of psychological abuse, and men's anger mediated this relationship.

Shame and anger have been similarly linked at the situational level, too (Tangney et al. 1996a, Wicker et al. 1983). For example, in a study of anger episodes among romantically involved couples, shamed partners were significantly more angry, more likely to engage in aggressive behavior, and less likely to elicit conciliatory behavior from their perpetrating significant other (Tangney 1995b). Taken together, the results provide a powerful empirical example of the shame-rage spiral described by Lewis (1971) and Scheff (1987), with (*a*) partner shame leading to feelings of rage, (*b*) and destructive retaliation, (*c*) which then sets into motion anger and resentment in the perpetrator, (*d*) as well as expressions of blame and retaliation in kind, (*e*) which is then likely to further shame the initially shamed partner, and so forth—without any constructive resolution in sight.

Recently, Stuewig et al. (2006) examined mediators of the link between moral emotions and aggression in four samples. We theorized that negative feelings associated with shame lead to externalization of blame, which in turn leads shame-prone people to react aggressively. Guilt, on the other hand, should facilitate empathic processes, thus reducing outward directed aggression. As anticipated, we found that across all samples, externalization of blame mediated the relationship between shame-proneness and both verbal and physical aggression. Guilt-proneness, on the other hand, continued to show a direct inverse relationship to aggression in three of the four samples. In addition, the link between guilt and low aggression was partially mediated through other-oriented empathy and a propensity to take responsibility.

In short, shame and anger go hand in hand. Desperate to escape painful feelings of shame, shamed individuals are apt to turn the tables defensively, externalizing blame and anger outward onto a convenient scapegoat. Blaming others may help individuals regain some sense of control and superiority in their life, but the long-term costs are often steep. Friends, coworkers, and loved ones are apt to become alienated by an interpersonal style characterized by irrational bursts of anger.

Psychological symptoms When considering the domain of social behavior and interpersonal adjustment, empirical research suggests that guilt, on balance, is the more moral or adaptive emotion. Guilt appears to motivate reparative action, foster other-oriented empathy, and promote constructive strategies for coping with anger. But are there intrapersonal or intrapsychic costs for those individuals who are prone to experience guilt? Does guilt-proneness lead to anxiety, depression, and/or a loss of self-esteem? Conversely, is shame perhaps less problematic for intrapersonal as opposed to interpersonal adjustment?

The answer is clear in the case of shame. Research over the past two decades consistently indicates that proneness to shame is related to a wide variety of psychological symptoms. These run the gamut from low self-esteem, depression, and anxiety to eating disorder symptoms, posttraumatic stress disorder (PTSD), and suicidal ideation (Andrews et al. 2000, Ashby et al. 2006, Brewin et al. 2000, Crossley & Rockett 2005, Feiring & Taska 2005, Feiring et al. 2002, Ferguson et al. 2000, Ghatavi et al. 2002, Harper & Arias 2004, Henderson & Zimbardo 2001, Leskela et al. 2002, Mills 2003, Murray et al. 2000, Orsillo et al. 1996, Sanftner et al. 1995, Stuewig & McCloskey 2005; see also review in Tangney & Dearing 2002). The negative psychological implications of shame are evident across measurement methods, diverse age groups, and populations. Both the clinical literature and empirical research agree that people who frequently experience feelings of shame about the self are correspondingly more vulnerable to a range of psychological problems.

Although the traditional view is that guilt plays a significant role in psychological symptoms, the empirical findings have been more equivocal. Clinical theory and case studies make frequent reference to a maladaptive guilt characterized by chronic self-blame and obsessive rumination over one's transgressions (Blatt 1974, Ellis 1962, Freud 1924/1961, Hartmann & Loewenstein 1962, Rodin et al. 1984, Weiss 1993). Recently, however, theorists and researchers have emphasized the adaptive functions of guilt, particularly for interpersonal behavior (Baumeister et al. 1994, 1995a; Hoffman 1982; Tangney 1991, 1994, 1995b; Tangney et al. 1992; Tangney & Dearing 2002).

In an effort to reconcile these perspectives, Tangney (1996) argued that earlier work failed to take into account the distinction between guilt and shame. Once one conceptualizes guilt as a negative emotion in response to a specific failure or transgression, there's no compelling reason to expect guilt to be associated with poor psychological adjustment. Instead, guilt is most likely to be maladaptive when it becomes fused with shame. The advantages of guilt are lost when a person's guilt experience ("Oh, look at what a horrible *thing* I have *done*") is magnified and generalized to the self ("...and aren't I a horrible *person*"). Ultimately, it's the shame component of this sequence—not the guilt component—that poses the problem, as the person becomes saddled with feelings of contempt and disgust for a bad, defective self.

Moreover, such painful feelings of shame are difficult to resolve. Shame—and, shame-fused guilt—offers little opportunity for redemption. It is a daunting challenge to transform a self that is defective at its core. Thus, guilt with an overlay of shame is most likely the source of the painful self-castigation and rumination so often described in the clinical literature. In contrast, there are typically a multitude of paths to redemption in the case of uncomplicated guilt focused on a specific behavior. A person (*a*) often has the option of changing the objectionable behavior; (*b*) or even better yet, has an opportunity to repair the negative consequences; (*c*) or at the very least, can extend a heartfelt apology. And when it is not possible to make these external amends, one can resolve to do better in the future.

Consistent with this conceptual analysis, empirical studies that fail to take into account the distinction between shame and guilt, or that employ adjective checklist-type (and other globally worded) measures that are ill-suited to distinguish between shame and guilt, report that guilt-proneness is associated with psychological symptoms (Boye et al. 2002, Fontana & Rosenbeck 2004, Ghatavi et al. 2002, Harder 1995, Jones & Kugler 1993, Meehan et al. 1996). For example, using the Interpersonal Guilt Questionnaire (O'Connor et al. 1997), Berghold & Locke (2002) found that solely the "self-hate" guilt scale differentiated between a control group and adolescents diagnosed with anorexia nervosa. (The authors concluded that, in fact, shame—not guilt—is more important to a clinical understanding of this eating disorder.)

On the other hand, measures sensitive to Lewis's (1971) distinction between shame about the self versus guilt about a specific behavior (e.g., scenario-based methods assessing shame and guilt with respect to specific situations) show that the propensity to experience "shame-free" guilt is essentially unrelated to psychological symptoms. Numerous independent studies converge: guilt-prone children, adolescents, and adults are not at increased risk for depression, anxiety, low self-esteem, etc. (Gramzow & Tangney 1992; Leskela et al. 2002; McLaughlin 2002; Quiles & Bybee 1997; Schaefer 2000; Stuewig & McCloskey 2005; Tangney 1994; Tangney & Dearing 2002; Tangney et al. 1991, 1992, 1995).

It is worth noting, however, that in most scenario-based measures of shame and guilt (including the Test of Self-Conscious Affect, or TOSCA), the majority of situations are relatively ambiguous regarding responsibility or culpability. For the negatively valenced (but not positively valenced) situations, respondents are asked to imagine events in which they clearly failed or transgressed in some way. Problems are likely to arise when people developed an exaggerated or distorted sense of responsibility for events beyond their control or for which they have no personal involvement (Ferguson et al. 2000, Tangney & Dearing 2002, Zahn-Waxler & Robinson 1995). Survivor guilt is a prime example of such a problematic guilt response that has been consistently linked to psychological maladjustment (Kubany et al. 1995, 2004; O'Connor et al. 2002). In an experimental study of elementary school–aged children, Ferguson et al. (2000) varied the degree to which situations in a scenario-based measure were ambiguous with respect to responsibility. They found a positive relationship between internalizing symptoms (e.g., depression) and proneness to guilt specifically in situations where responsibility was ambiguous.

In short, the benefits of guilt are evident when people acknowledge their failures and transgressions and take appropriate responsibility for their misdeeds. In such situations, the interpersonal benefits of guilt do not appear to come at a cost to the individual. The propensity to experience "shame-free" guilt in response to clear transgressions is generally unrelated to psychological problems, whereas shame is consistently associated with maladaptive processes and outcomes at multiple levels.

Linking moral emotions to risky, illegal, and otherwise inadvisable behavior Because shame and guilt are painful emotions, it is often assumed that they motivate individuals to avoid doing wrong. From this perspective, anticipated shame and guilt should decrease the likelihood of transgression and impropriety. But what exactly do the data show?

Empirical studies of diverse samples, employing a range of measures, clearly indicate that guilt-proneness is inversely related to antisocial and risky behavior. In a study of college undergraduates (Tangney 1994), guilt-proneness was associated with endorsing such items as "I would not steal something I needed, even if I were sure I could get away with it." Similarly, Tibbetts (2003) found that college students' guilt-proneness was inversely related to self-reported criminal activity. Among adolescents, proneness to shame-free guilt has been negatively correlated with delinquency (Merisca & Bybee 1994, Stuewig & McCloskey 2005; although Ferguson et al. 1999 found a negative relationship between guilt-proneness and externalizing symptoms among boys, the opposite was true for girls). The moral emotions appear to be well established by middle childhood and have implications for moral behavior for years to come (Tangney & Dearing 2002). Children prone to shame-free guilt in the fifth grade were, in adolescence, less likely to be arrested, convicted, and incarcerated. They were more likely to practice safe sex, and they were less likely to abuse drugs. Importantly, these findings held when controlling for family income and mothers' education. Guilt-prone college students, too, are less likely to abuse drugs

and alcohol (Dearing et al. 2005). Even among adults already at high risk, guilt-proneness appears to serve a protective function. In a longitudinal study of jail inmates, guilt-proneness assessed shortly after incarceration negatively predicted recidivism and substance abuse during the first year post-release (Tangney et al. 2006).

The pattern of results for shame is quite different, with virtually no evidence supporting the presumed adaptive nature of shame. In studies of children, adolescents, college students, and jail inmates, shame does not appear to serve the same inhibitory functions as guilt (Dearing et al. 2005, Stuewig & McCloskey 2005, Tangney et al. 1996b). To the contrary, research suggests that shame may even make things worse. In a study of children, Ferguson et al. (1999) found that shame-proneness was positively correlated with externalizing symptoms on the Child Behavior Checklist. In a sample of college students, Tibbetts (1997) found a positive relationship between shame-proneness and intentions toward illegal behavior. Shame-proneness assessed in the fifth grade predicted later risky driving behavior, earlier initiation of drug and alcohol use, and a lower likelihood of practicing safe sex (Tangney & Dearing 2002). Similarly, proneness to problematic feelings of shame has been positively linked to substance use and abuse in adulthood (Dearing et al. 2005, Meehan et al. 1996, O'Connor et al. 1994, Tangney et al. 2006).

The differential link of shame and guilt to moral behavior may not generalize across all populations with respect to all behaviors. Harris (2003) assessed event-specific experiences of shame and guilt among drunk-driving offenders following their appearance in court or at a restorative justice conference. In contrast to most extant studies, Harris found no evidence that shame and guilt form distinct factors. It's important to note that this study focused on a unique, homogeneous sample (convicted drunk drivers, many of whom have substance abuse problems) and a single type of transgression. Harris's findings raise the intriguing possibility that individuals with substance abuse problems may not have well-differentiated experiences of shame and guilt. Alternatively, guilt and its attendant empathic focus on the harmed other may be less relevant to transgressions, such as drunk driving, that typically do not result in objective physical harm to others. (That is, the magnitude of consequences of an automobile accident is potentially huge, whereas the probability of its occurrence on any given occasion is rather small. Most drunk-driving offenders are arrested for erratic driving, not at the scene of an accident involving actual harm to another person.)

In sum, empirical results converge, indicating that guilt but not shame is most effective in motivating people to choose the moral paths in life. The capacity for guilt is more apt to foster a lifelong pattern of moral behavior, motivating individuals to accept responsibility and take reparative action in the wake of the occasional failure or transgression. In contrast, research has linked shame with a range of illegal, risky, or otherwise problematic behaviors. Thus, when considering the welfare of the individual, his or her close relationships, or society, feelings of guilt represent the moral emotion of choice.

New directions in research on shame and guilt.

Context- or domain-specific shame and guilt Some clinicians have lamented the research literature's heavy focus on dispositional shame (Leeming & Boyle 2002). Andrews (1998) notes that at least three different conceptualizations of the high-shame individual are implicit in the range of current dispositional measures of shame. Some researchers conceptualize shame-proneness as the propensity to experience shame across a range of situations (operationalized by scenario-based measures such as the TOSCA-3). Others conceptualize high-shame individuals as those who frequently or continuously experience global shame, an affect not necessarily con-

nected to particular events (operationalized by global adjective checklists, such as the PFQ-2, and by the Internalized Shame Scale). A third and more recent conceptualization of "high shame" is explicitly domain specific—individuals who are chronically shamed about particular circumscribed behaviors or personal characteristics (e.g., physical appearance, level of education, race/ethnicity, and stuttering).

A number of researchers have developed measures to assess shame and guilt with respect to specific domains. For example, researchers concerned with the psychology of eating disorders and those exploring hypotheses drawn from the Objectification Theory of Frederickson & Roberts (1997) have assessed feelings of shame specifically in reference to one's body. "Body shame" has been consistently associated with self-objectification and eating disorder symptoms (Hallsworth et al. 2005). Andrews (1995, 1998) has examined the link between childhood abuse and body shame (see below).

Regarding guilt, researchers have begun to examine the nature and implications of domain-specific feelings of guilt associated with trauma. Trauma-related guilt cognitions, such as false beliefs about responsibility or pre-outcome knowledge, are reliably associated with symptoms of depression among diverse samples of trauma survivors (Blacher 2000; Kubany et al. 1995, 2004; Lee et al. 2001). Moreover, cognitive processing therapy and prolonged exposure interventions appear to be effective at reducing trauma-related guilt cognitions (Nishith et al. 2005, Resick et al. 2002).

Styles of coping with the shame (and guilt) experience Most theory and research on shame and guilt has focused on the events that lead up to these emotional experiences, the phenomenology of these emotions, or the consequences of these emotions for motivation and behavior. Less attention has been directed toward how people cope with aversive feelings of shame and guilt. Drawing on

Nathanson's (1992) Compass of Shame theory, Elison et al. (2006a) developed a measure of individual differences in coping with shame. The Compass of Shame Scale (COSS-4) consists of four 10-item scales representing the poles of Nathanson's Compass of Shame plus a fifth assessing adaptive responses. More specifically:

- "Attack Self" assesses inward-directed anger and blame (e.g., self-disgust)
- "Withdrawal" assesses the tendency to hide or withdraw when shamed (e.g., avoid others)
- "Avoidance" assesses disavowal and emotional distancing or minimization (e.g., minimizing the importance of a failing grade)
- "Attack Other" assesses outward-directed anger and blame (e.g., blaming someone else for the failure or transgression)
- "Adaptive" assesses acknowledgment of shame and motivation to apologize and/or make amends

Some clear parallels exist between the scales of the COSS-4 and the scales of the TOSCA. Attack Self and Withdrawal bear a close resemblance to the two types of items that comprise the TOSCA Shame scale—negative self-appraisals and avoidance. The Adaptive Responses scale bears a close resemblance to the TOSCA Guilt scale. Attack Other bears considerable resemblance to the TOSCA Externalization of Blame scale. And Avoidance resembles the TOSCA Detachment scale (although the TOSCA Detachment scale appears less internally consistent than the COSS-4 Avoidance scale). The use of different terms to describe similar types of response most likely reflects differences in theoretical formulation. Nathanson (1992) draws on modern psychoanalytic theory, Tomkin's (1963) emotion theory, and associated attachment theory. The TOSCA measures were informed by social-cognitive theories of emotion, with much influence from Lewis (1971). As one might expect, of the four scales of the COSS-4, the Withdrawal and Attack Self scales are most highly correlated with shame, as well as measures of more general psychological adjustment (Elison et al. 2006a,b).

In a sample of undergraduates, Campbell & Elison (2005) found that both subscales of the Self-Report Psychopathy Scale (SRPS) were negatively related to the guilt-like Adaptive Response to Shame scale and positively related to Attack Others and Avoidance scales. The SRPS subscale assessing antisocial lifestyle paralleling Hare's (1991) Factor 2 on the Psychopathy Checklist-Revised was positively correlated with Attack Self and Withdrawal scales—scales that assess shame much as defined by Lewis (1971) and Tangney (1996). But the Primary Psychopathy subscale, assessing psychopathic personality features akin to Hare's (1991) Factor 1, was negatively or negligibly related to shame per se—the Attack Self and Withdrawal scales. Future research examining how correlates of the COSS-4 parallel or differ from the TOSCA is needed.

Psychobiological correlates of shame Researchers have recently begun to evaluate psychobiological markers of shame, examining biological responses to laboratory manipulations designed to threaten the social self (Dickerson et al. 2004b, Gruenewald et al. 2004; see Dickerson et al. 2004a for a review). Dickerson et al. found that participants who wrote about incidents wrought with self-blame, in contrast to participants who wrote about daily activities, evidenced increased levels of self-reported shame (and guilt) from pretest to post-test. More importantly, these same participants evidenced increased proinflammatory cytokine activity from pretest to post-test, and this response was significantly predicted by increases in self-reported shame. Consistent with theory differentiating shame and guilt, shame uniquely predicted this immune-related response; changes in neither guilt nor general negative affect significantly predicted changes in the cytokine response. Recent applied research is equally suggestive: Among people with HIV, persistent feelings of shame predicted t-cell decline, an indicator of compromised immune function (Weitzman et al. 2004).

Gruenewald et al. (2004) examined cortisol responses of individuals performing stressful speaking and arithmetic tasks with and without an audience. Individuals in the social evaluation condition reported more shame (and lower self-esteem) than did individuals in the nonevaluative condition. Moreover, those individuals in this shame-eliciting condition also evidenced significant increases in cortisol levels. Similarly, among children, nonverbal expressions of shame and embarrassment during laboratory tasks were associated with greater cortisol changes during the session, relative to other nonverbal behavioral styles (Lewis & Ramsay 2002).

Considering these patterns of immunoresponse in toto, Dickerson et al. (2004a) note, "...shame may be experienced particularly in conditions characterized by negative social evaluation and rejection. The cortisol and proinflammatory cytokine systems also appear to be responsive to social-evaluative threat. While tentative, there is support for the notion that the activation of these systems under the very specific condition of threat to the social self may hinge on the experience of shame and related emotions" (p. 1205).

Cardiovascular reactivity seems likewise associated with experiences of shame. For example, in addition to evaluating cortisol response, Gruenewald et al. (2004) also evaluated heart rate and blood pressure changes in response to the stressful speaking and arithmetic tasks. Although heart rate and systolic blood pressure increased in both the social evaluative and nonevaluative conditions, the response was somewhat more marked in the social evaluative condition. Extending this work with a clever laboratory manipulation of experienced emotions, Herrald & Tomaka (2002) evaluated cardiovascular reactivity in the wake of pride, shame, and anger. They found that the negatively valenced emotions of shame and anger resulted in higher levels of cardiovascular reactivity than pride; im-

portantly, participants in the shame condition showed higher peripheral resistance (associated with hypertension) and participants in the anger condition showed higher cardiac contractility (associated with coronary disease).

In sum, there seems to be distinct physiological correlates corresponding to the experience of shame. Such physiological markers may prove to be useful as a measurement tool in future research on situation-specific states of shame.

Childhood abuse and the propensity to experience shame Clinicians have long reported that victims of abuse or trauma are often haunted by feelings of shame. This may especially be true in cases of child maltreatment because of its secretive and hidden nature (Deblinger & Runyon 2005). The experience of abuse at a young age may instigate and reinforce shame-inducing thoughts (Andrews 1998). Also, severely punitive parenting practices may engender in children feelings of helplessness and self-blame, which may then lead to a globalized sense of shame. Although child maltreatment in its different forms (physical abuse, sexual abuse, neglect, harsh parenting) has long been theorized to engender a vulnerability to shame, systematic empirical research has been conducted only recently.

A number of studies have found a relationship between childhood physical and sexual abuse and specific forms of shame, including body shame (Andrews 1995, Andrews & Hunter 1997) and shame about a traumatic event (Andrews et al. 2000). In addition, Murray & Waller (2002) found a relationship between unwanted sexual experience of any sort and internalized shame. Although Hoglund & Nicholas (1995) reported no relationship between a history of physical abuse and shame-proneness, they did find a link between shame-proneness and history of emotional abuse. In this same vein, Gilbert et al. (1996) found that put-downs and shaming practices by parents were associated with adult children's shame-proneness. Each of these studies, however, was based on retrospective reports of maltreatment and parenting practices, which have known weaknesses (Widom et al. 2004).

Nonetheless, when considering studies using prospective or observational designs, the results for nonsexual abuse and shame are similar. Bennett et al. (2005) report an association between physical abuse and nonverbal shame, although there was not a significant relationship for neglect. In addition, Alessandri & Lewis (1996) found girls coded as maltreated to have higher nonverbal shame. More generally, negative or harsh parenting has been associated with the propensity to experience shame (Alessandri & Lewis 1993, 1996; Ferguson & Stegge 1995; Mills 2003). Stuewig & McCloskey (2005) report a relationship between harsh parenting in childhood and shame-proneness in adolescence, a relationship that was mediated by rejecting parenting practices also measured in adolescence.

The relationship between sexual abuse and shame seems to be less straightforward. In research studies of individuals who have experienced sexual abuse, shame has been consistently implicated in poor outcomes such as depression and PTSD symptoms (Feiring & Taska 2005; Feiring et al. 1996, 2002; Talbot et al. 2004). Feiring & Taska (2005) have also found abuse-specific shame to be moderately stable across time.

However, neither Alessandri & Lewis (1996), using observational measures of shame, nor Stuewig & McCloskey (2005), using self-reports of shame-proneness, found a relationship between history of sexual abuse and shame, but both studied small samples of sexually abused individuals. Another reason for these null findings may be that complex emotions surround not only the abusive act but also how the individual copes with the experience. Using facial coding data for shame, Bonanno et al. (2002) found that individuals with a documented history of sexual abuse who did not disclose the abuse in an interview had higher levels of observed shame than those individuals who did disclose their sexual abuse history. There was no difference in shame between those who did disclose and a nonabused comparison group. In a follow-up (Negrao et al. 2005), individuals who did disclose their sexual abuse history were higher on shame coded from narratives compared with those who did not disclose and those in a nonabused comparison group. In other words, individuals who disclosed their abuse histories expressed more shame verbally, whereas those who did not disclose expressed more shame nonverbally, relative to control participants.

In sum, the findings regarding the relationship between childhood abuse and subsequent difficulties with shame are mixed, no doubt due in part to the fact that studies have employed different measures and conceptualizations of both maltreatment and shame (Berliner 2005). Nonetheless, taken together, the weight of evidence suggests that people who experience maltreatment in childhood are somewhat more vulnerable to shame issues later in life.

Vicarious or "collective" shame and guilt: group-based self-conscious emotion Thus far, this review has focused almost exclusively on shame and guilt experienced in reaction to one's own misdeeds. In recent years, a number of investigators have substantially expanded the literature on self-conscious emotions by considering "vicarious" or "group-based" shame and guilt—feelings experienced in response to the transgressions and failures of other individuals. This research represents an exciting integration of self-conscious emotions theory with the social psychological literature on social identity, group, and intergroup processes. To the extent that the self is, in part, defined by our interpersonal relations and group memberships, it is possible to construe the behavior of an in-group member as reflecting on the self. Thus, personal causality is not always a prerequisite for the experience of shame or guilt.

In many ways, the phenomena of vicarious shame and guilt parallel personal shame and guilt experiences. Lickel, Schmader, and colleagues (Lickel et al. 2004, 2005) have developed a process model linking specific types of appraisals with vicarious experiences of shame and guilt, respectively. They present compelling evidence that group-based shame is most likely elicited when a threatened shared identity is salient—that is, when concerns about maintaining a positive group identity arise. Vicarious guilt, on the other hand, is more likely when one's interpersonal dependence with the perpetrator is salient, and when relational-based concerns are highlighted by a focus on harm to another group or individual. For example, Lickel et al. (2005) found that vicarious shame (but not guilt) experiences were positively related to their ratings of the relevance of an offending behavior to the identity shared by the respondent and the perpetrator. The link between identity concerns and vicarious or group-based shame are evident in both correlational and experimental studies (Iyer et al. 2006, Schmader & Lickel 2006).

Degree of interdependence with the perpetrator appears to be uniquely related to vicarious guilt (Lickel et al. 2005). However, identification with the perpetrating group can also have implications for vicarious, group-based guilt as well (Branscombe & Doosje 2004, Doosje et al. 1998), especially when individuals are prompted to focus on the harm done (Iyer et al. 2003)

Of particular applied relevance to current international conflicts, when people are provided with ambiguous information about group members' transgressions, those who are highly identified with the group appear to capitalize on the ambiguity, reporting less vicarious shame (Johns et al. 2005) and group-based guilt (Doosje et al. 1998) relative to those who are less identified, and whose self is presumably less threatened.

As with personal guilt experiences, group-based guilt has been associated with empathy (Zebel et al. 2004) and a motivation to repair or make amends (Iyer et al. 2003, Lickel et al. 2005, Swim & Miller 1999, Zebel et al. 2004).

And as with personal shame experiences, vicarious group-based shame (but not guilt) has been linked to a desire to distance oneself from the shame-eliciting event (Johns et al. 2005, Lickel et al. 2005). Furthermore, the link between anger and shame is evident when considering vicarious shame (Iyer et al. 2006, Johns et al. 2005, Schmader & Lickel 2006). Nonetheless, there are some indications that vicarious or group-based shame may have a kinder, gentler side than personal shame. For example, under some circumstances, group-based shame appears to motivate a desire to change the image of the group in a proactive fashion (Lickel et al. 2006).

Embarrassment

Embarrassment appears to be less centrally relevant to the domain of morality than are shame and guilt. For example, adults' ratings of personal shame-, guilt-, and embarrassment-eliciting events indicate that when people feel embarrassed, they are less concerned with issues of morality than when they feel shame or guilt (Tangney et al. 1996a). Nonetheless, certain conditions exist under which embarrassment may support or undermine people's efforts to live life in a manner consistent with their moral standards.

Miller (1995) defines embarrassment as "an aversive state of mortification, abashment, and chagrin that follows public social predicaments" (p. 322). Embarrassment accounts from hundreds of high school students and adults (Miller 1992) indicate that the most common causes of embarrassment are "normative public deficiencies"—situations in which a person behaves in a clumsy, absent-minded, or hapless way (tripping in front of a crowd, forgetting someone's name, unintended bodily-induced noises). Other common embarrassment-inducing situations include awkward social interactions and being conspicuous (e.g., during the "birthday" song). Generally, events causing embarrassment seem to signal that something is amiss— some aspect of the self or one's behavior needs to be carefully monitored, hidden, or changed.

The motivations prompted by embarrassment, however, may have implications for moral behavior. Research indicates that embarrassed people are inclined to behave in conciliatory ways in order to win approval and (re)inclusion from others (Cupach & Metts 1990, 1992; Leary et al. 1996; Miller 1996; Sharkey & Stafford 1990). In other words, upon feeling embarrassment (or to avoid embarrassment), people are inclined to conform and curry favor. Thus, depending on the local norms of the immediate social environment, embarrassment may prompt adherence to broadly accepted moral standards or to locally endorsed deviant acts.

As with shame and guilt, there are individual differences in the degree to which people are prone to experience embarrassment. Research has shown that embarrassability is associated with neuroticism, high levels of negative affect, self-consciousness, and a fear of negative evaluation from others (Edelmann & McCusker 1986, Leary & Meadows 1991, Miller 1995b). To the extent that embarrassment-prone individuals are highly aware of and concerned with social rules and standards, they may be especially vulnerable to the influence of peer pressure.

Moral Pride

Thus far, this chapter has focused on negatively valenced moral emotions. We turn now to one of the long-neglected positively valenced moral emotions—morally relevant experiences of pride. Of the self-conscious emotions, pride is the neglected sibling. Mascolo & Fischer (1995) define pride as an emotion "generated by appraisals that one is responsible for a socially valued outcome or for being a socially valued person" (p. 66). From their perspective, pride serves to enhance people's self-worth and, perhaps more importantly, to encourage future behavior that conforms to social standards of worth or merit (see also Barrett 1995).

Most theoretical and empirical research on pride emphasizes achievement-oriented pride (Tracy & Robins 2004b). Although pride may most often arise in response to scholastic, occupational, or athletic achievement, self-conscious experiences of pride in moral contexts may be an important component of our moral emotional apparatus. Feelings of pride for meeting or exceeding morally relevant standards (and for inhibiting impulses to behave immorally) may serve important motivational functions, rewarding and reinforcing one's commitment to ethics of autonomy, community, and divinity.

In parallel to the self-versus-behavior distinction of guilt and shame, it may be useful to distinguish between two types of pride. Along similar lines, Tangney (1990) distinguished between "alpha" pride (pride in self) and "beta" pride (pride in behavior), M. Lewis (1992) distinguished between hubris (pridefulness) and pride (experienced in reference to a specific action or behavior), and Tracy & Robins (2004b) distinguished between hubris and more event-specific achievement-oriented pride. Tracy & Robins (2006), drawing on multiple methods, present compelling empirical evidence for these two types of pride.

Little empirical research has been conducted on individual differences in proneness to pride in self (or pride in behavior, for that matter). The Tests of Self-Conscious Affect (e.g., Tangney et al. 1989; see Tangney & Dearing 2002 for details) each contain measures of the propensity to experience alpha pride and beta pride, respectively. These subscales, however, have very modest reliabilities, largely because they draw on only a few items. Thus, we and other investigators have made little use of these ancillary scales. Lewis (1992) views hubris as largely maladaptive, noting that hubristic individuals are inclined to distort and invent situations to enhance the self, which can lead to interpersonal problems. It remains to be seen how individual differences in pride or hubris relate to the capacity to self-regulate or to choose the moral path in life.

One possibility is that pride and hubris represent the flip side of guilt and shame—one the "modern," adaptive moral emotion and the other, its evil twin.

OTHER-FOCUSED MORAL EMOTIONS

Thus far, our review of theory and research on moral emotion has focused on the self-conscious emotions of shame, guilt, embarrassment, and pride. These emotions vary in valence and in attributions regarding the particular source of offense (e.g., self versus self's behavior). But these self-conscious emotions are similar in that in each case, the emotion is elicited when some aspect of the self is scrutinized and evaluated with respect to moral standards. Recently, Haidt (2000, 2003) added importantly to our thinking about the nature of "moral emotions." In his work, Haidt focuses primarily on the emotions of elevation and gratitude—emotions that are experienced when observing the admirable deeds of others, and that then motivate observers to engage in admirable deeds themselves.

In fact, by crossing the two dimensions of focus (self versus other) and valence (positive versus negative), one can conceptualize four categories of moral emotion (see Haidt 2003, following Ortony et al. 1988). To date most theory and research on moral affect has emphasized the negatively valenced self-conscious quadrant. With the advent of the positive psychology movement and Haidt's groundbreaking work, we anticipate that the next decade will see exciting new developments in our understanding of the moral functions of negatively and positively valenced other-directed emotions.

Righteous Anger, Contempt, and Disgust

Anger is a negatively valenced, other-focused emotion not typically considered in the morally relevant sphere. People may experience anger for a very broad range of situations—e.g., when insulted, frustrated, in-convenienced, or injured in any one of a number of ways. According to appraisal theorists (Lazarus 1991, Roseman 1991, Smith & Ellsworth 1985), people typically feel angry when they appraise an event as personally relevant, inconsistent with their goals, and when the event appears to be caused (often intentionally) by a responsible other. The emphasis is on perceptions of actual or potential self-harm (e.g., a personally relevant goal has been thwarted or frustrated, a valued possession has been threatened or harmed) in conjunction with attributions of intentionality and/or responsibility on the part of the offending other.

Righteous anger, however, arises in response to a special class of anger-eliciting events, those in which the perpetrator's behavior represents a violation of moral standards. In such cases, the harm need not be personally experienced. One can feel anger upon witnessing morally repulsive behavior aimed at a third party. Rozin et al. (1999) presented evidence that righteous anger tends to occur more specifically in response to violations of the ethic of autonomy—the ethic most familiar in Western culture. Righteous anger can serve moral functions in that it can motivate "third-party" bystanders to take action in order to remedy observed injustices.

The emotions of contempt and disgust also stem from negative evaluations of others, but seem somewhat less apt than righteous anger to motivate morally corrective action. Among participants in both the United States and Japan, Rozin et al. (1999) found that feelings of contempt were differentially linked to violations of the ethic of community (e.g., violations of social hierarchy), whereas feelings of disgust were linked to violations of the ethic of divinity (e.g., actions that remind us of our animal nature, such as defecation, problems with hygiene, etc., as well as assaults on human dignity, such as racism and abuse).

Elevation

Just as disgust is the moral emotion people experience when observing violations of the ethic of divinity, elevation is the positive emotion elicited when observing others behaving in a particularly virtuous, commendable, or superhuman way (Haidt 2000). In a study of college students, Haidt et al. (2002) explored the phenomenology of elevation, asking participants to recall "a manifestation of humanity's 'higher' or 'better' nature." Participants reported warm, pleasant, "tingling" feelings in their chest, they felt open to other people as their attention turned outward, and they felt motivated to help others and to become better people themselves. In this respect, elevation appears to be the quintessential positive emotion, especially apt to foster a "broaden and build" (Frederickson 2000) orientation to the world.

Gratitude

Gratitude is another example of an other-oriented, positively valenced moral affect. People are inclined to feel gratitude specifically in response to another person's benevolence—that is, when they are the recipient of benefits provided by another, especially when those benefits are unexpected and/or costly to the benefactor. Gratitude is a pleasant affective state, distinct from indebtedness, which implies an obligation and is often experienced as a negative state.

McCullough et al. (2001) classify gratitude as a moral affect, not because the experience and expression of gratitude is in and of itself "moral," but because feelings of gratitude (a) result from moral (e.g., prosocial, helping) behavior of the benefactor, and (b) engender subsequent moral motivation on the part of recipients. They observe that grateful people are often motivated to respond prosocially—both to their benefactor and toward others not involved in the gratitude-eliciting act. Moreover, expressions of gratitude can serve as a moral reinforcer, encouraging benefactors' helping behavior in the future (Bennett et al. 1996, Clark et al. 1988, Goldman et al. 1982).

Gratitude not only benefits benefactors and relationships. Those who benefit most from the experience and expression of gratitude are grateful people themselves. In a series of experimental studies, feelings of gratitude enhanced psychological resilience, physical health, and the quality of daily life (Emmons & McCullough 2003). In fact, both dispositional and situation-specific episodes of gratitude have been linked to psychological well-being and adaptive behavior in nonclinical samples (Emmons & Shelton 2002; Frederickson et al. 2003; Kendler et al. 2003; McCullough et al. 2001, 2002) and among combat veterans with PTSD (Kashdan et al. 2006).

EMPATHY: A MORAL EMOTIONAL PROCESS

Finally, we discuss briefly a morally relevant emotional process—other-oriented empathy. (For a more complete review, see Eisenberg et al. 2004, 2006.) In contrast to the other moral emotions discussed in this review, empathy is not a discrete emotion. Rather it is an emotional process with substantial implications for moral behavior. Current conceptualizations of empathy integrate both affective and cognitive components. Feshbach (1975), for example, defines empathy as a "shared emotional response between an observer and a stimulus person." She suggests that empathic responsiveness requires three interrelated skills or capacities: (a) the cognitive ability to take another person's perspective, (b) the cognitive ability to accurately recognize and discriminate another person's affective experience, and (c) the affective ability to personally experience a range of emotions (since empathy involves sharing another person's emotional experience). Similarly, Coke and colleagues (1978) proposed a two-stage model of empathic responding, whereby perspective-taking facilitates empathic concern, which in turn leads to a desire to help.

Some researchers have made a distinction between "true" empathy and sympathy. Eisenberg (1986) explains that sympathy involves feelings of concern for the emotional state of another, but does not necessarily involve the vicarious experience of the other person's feelings or emotions (e.g., emotional matching). Thus, one may feel concern (sympathy) for an angered individual without being vicariously angered oneself (an empathic reaction).

Others have distinguished between other-oriented empathy and self-oriented personal distress (Batson 1990, Batson & Coke 1981, Davis 1983). Other-oriented empathy involves taking another person's perspective and vicariously experiencing similar feelings. These responses often involve feelings of sympathy and concern for the other person, and often lead to helping behavior. Importantly, the empathic individual's focus remains on the experiences and needs of the other person, not on his or her own empathic response. In contrast, self-oriented personal distress involves a primary focus on the feelings, needs, and experiences of the empathizer. Empirical research underscores the importance of this distinction. Empathic concern for others has been linked to altruistic helping behavior, whereas self-oriented personal distress is unrelated to altruism (Batson et al. 1988) and may in fact interfere with prosocial behavior (Davis & Oathout 1987; Eisenberg et al. 1990, 1993; Estrada 1995).

Empathy and its close cousin sympathy have been cited as central to the human moral affective system for at least three reasons (Eisenberg et al. 2004, 2006). First, empathic reactions to others' distress often elicit feelings of concern for the distressed other (Feshbach 1975). Second, such empathic concern often prompts behavior aimed at helping the distressed other (Batson 1991, Eisenberg & Miller 1987, Feshbach 1987). Third, feelings of empathy are apt to inhibit aggression and other behaviors that are harmful to oth-

ers (Feshbach & Feshbach 1969, Miller & Eisenberg 1988).

SUMMARY AND FUTURE DIRECTIONS FOR RESEARCH

This review has considered the implications of moral standards and moral emotion for moral decisions and moral behavior. In this sense, the structure of this review reflects the current state of the field. Little research has examined the relation between moral standards and moral emotional factors, much less their interactive influence in moderating the link between moral standards and people's moral behavior. Our hope is that this framework will encourage integrated research along such exciting lines. Future directions for research include evaluating the relative importance of cognitive and emotional factors in various domains of morality, as well as the degree to which particular emotional factors are differentially more important in influencing behavior among particular subpopulations (e.g., corporate managers, criminal offenders) and at different points in development.

In addition, this review may help clarify several points of conceptual confusion evident in portions of the literature. For example, in the guilt literature, some theory and associated measures have confounded proneness to guilt with moral standards or other related attitudes and beliefs (e.g., Mosher 1966; see Tangney 1996 for discussion). Although feelings of guilt generally arise from some failure or violation of moral standards, proneness to guilt (an affective disposition) is conceptually distinct from moral standards (a set of beliefs guiding one's evaluation of behavior). With the advantage of greater conceptual clarity, future researchers can address many questions about the functions and costs of various forms of moral emotion. Such research has potential to pay off substantially, informing educational, judicial, and social policies that foster adaptive moral processes and ultimately moral behavior that benefits all.

ACKNOWLEDGMENTS

This research was supported by grant #RO1 DA14694 to the first author from the National Institute on Drug Abuse. Many thanks to Laura Harty, Walt Swenson, and members of the Human Emotions Research Lab for their assistance.

LITERATURE CITED

Ajzen I. 1991. The theory of planned behavior. *Org. Behav. Hum. Decis. Process.* 50:179–211

Alessandri S, Lewis M. 1993. Parental evaluation and its relation to shame and pride in young children. *Sex Roles* 29:335–43

Alessandri S, Lewis M. 1996. Differences in pride and shame in maltreated and nonmaltreated preschoolers. *Child Dev.* 67:1857–69

Andrews B. 1995. Bodily shame as a mediator between abusive experiences and depression. *J. Abnorm. Psychol.* 104:277–85

Andrews B. 1998. Shame and childhood abuse. In *Shame: Interpersonal Behavior, Psychopathology, and Culture. Series in Affective Science*, ed. P Gilbert, B Andrews, pp. 176–90. New York: Oxford Univ. Press

Andrews B, Brewin CR, Rose S, Kirk M. 2000. Predicting PTSD symptoms in victims of violent crime: the role of shame, anger, and childhood abuse. *J. Abnorm. Psychol.* 109:69–73

Andrews B, Hunter E. 1997. Shame, early abuse, and course of depression in a clinical sample: preliminary study. *Cogn. Emot.* 11(4):373–81

Ashby JS, Rice KG, Martin JL. 2006. Perfectionism, shame, and depressive symptoms. *J. Couns. Dev.* 84(2):148–56

Barrett KC. 1995. A functionalist approach to shame and guilt. See Tangney & Fischer 1995, pp. 25–63

Batson CD. 1990. How social an animal? The human capacity for caring. *Am. Psychol.* 45:336–46

Batson CD. 1991. *The Altruism Question.* Hillsdale, NJ: Erlbaum

Batson CD, Coke JS. 1981. Empathy: a source of altruistic motivation for helping? In *Altruism and Helping Behavior: Social, Personality, and Developmental Perspectives*, ed. JP Rushton, RM Sorrentino, pp. 167–87. Hillsdale, NJ: Erlbaum

Batson CD, Dyck JL, Brandt JR, Batson JG, Powell AL, et al. 1988. Five studies testing two new egoistic alternatives to the empathy-altruism hypothesis. *J. Personal. Soc. Psychol.* 55:52–77

Baumeister RF, Stillwell AM, Heatherton TF. 1994. Guilt: an interpersonal approach. *Psychol. Bull.* 115:243–67

Baumeister RF, Stillwell AM, Heatherton TF. 1995a. Interpersonal aspects of guilt: evidence from narrative studies. See Tangney & Fischer 1995, pp. 255–73

Baumeister RF, Stillwell AM, Heatherton TF. 1995b. Personal narratives about guilt: role in action control and interpersonal relationships. *Basic Appl. Soc. Psychol.* 17:173–98

Benedict R. 1946. *The Chrysanthemum and the Sword.* Boston: Houghton Mifflin

Bennett DS, Sullivan MW, Lewis M. 2005. Young children's adjustment as a function of maltreatment, shame, and anger. *Child Maltreat.* 10(4):311–23

Bennett L, Ross MW, Sunderland R. 1996. The relationship between recognition, rewards, and burnout in AIDS caregiving. *AIDS Care* 8:145–53

Berghold K, Locke J. 2002. Assessing guilt in adolescents with anorexia nervosa. *Am. J. Psychother.* 56(3):378–90

Berliner L. 2005. Shame in child maltreatment: contributions and caveats. *Child Maltreat.* 10:387–90

Blacher R. 2000. "It isn't fair": postoperative depression and other manifestations of survivor guilt. *Gen. Hosp. Psychiatry* 22(1):43–48

Blatt S. 1974. Levels of object representation in anaclitic and introjective depression. *Psychoanal. Study Child.* 29:107–57

Bonanno G, Keltner D, Noll J. 2002. When the face reveals what words do not: facial expressions of emotions, smiling, and the willingness to disclose childhood sexual abuse. *J. Personal. Soc. Psychol.* 83(1):94–110

Boye, Bentson, Malt. 2002. Does guilt proneness predict acute and long-term distress in relatives of patients with schizophrenia? *Acta Psychiatr. Scand.* 106:351–57

Branscombe NR, Doojse B. 2004. *Collective Guilt: International Perspectives*. New York: Cambridge Univ. Press

Brewin CR, Andrews B, Rose S. 2000. Fear, helplessness, and horror in posttraumatic stress disorder: investigating DSM-IV criterion A2 in victims of violent crime. *J. Trauma. Stress* 13:499–509

Campbell JS, Elison J. 2005. Shame coping styles and psychopathic personality traits. *J. Personal. Assess.* 84:96–104

Clark HB, Northrop JT, Barkshire CT. 1988. The effects of contingent thank-you notes on case managers' visiting residential clients. *Educ. Treat. Child.* 11:45–51

Coke JS, Batson CD, McDavis K. 1978. Empathic mediation of helping: a two-stage model. *J. Personal. Soc. Psychol.* 36:752–66

Crossley D, Rockett K. 2005. The experience of shame in older psychiatric patients: a preliminary enquiry. *Aging Mental Health* 9:368–73

Cupach WR, Metts S. 1990. Remedial processes in embarrassing predicaments. In *Communication Yearbook 13*, ed. J Anderson, pp. 323–52. Newbury Park, CA: Sage

Cupach WR, Metts S. 1992. The effects of type of predicament and embarrassability on remedial responses to embarrassing situations. *Commun. Q.* 40:149–61

Davis MH. 1983. Measuring individual differences in empathy: evidence for a multidimensional approach. *J. Personal. Soc. Psychol.* 44:113–26

Davis MH, Oathout HA. 1987. Maintenance of satisfaction in romantic relationships: empathy and relational competence. *J. Personal. Soc. Psychol.* 53:397–410

Dearing RL, Stuewig J, Tangney JP. 2005. On the importance of distinguishing shame from guilt: relations to problematic alcohol and drug use. *Addict. Behav.* 30:1392–404

Deblinger E, Runyon M. 2005. Understanding and treating feelings of shame in children who have experienced maltreatment. *Child Maltreat.* 10(4):364–76

DeVisser RO, Smith AMA. 2004. Which intention? Whose intention? Condom use and theories of individual decision making. *Psychol. Health Med.* 9:193–204

Dickerson SS, Gruenaewald TL, Kemeny ME. 2004a. When the social self is threatened: shame, physiology, and health. *J. Personal.* 72:1191–216

Dickerson SS, Kemeny ME, Aziz N, Kim KH, Fahey JL. 2004b. Immunological effects of induced shame and guilt. *Psychosom. Med.* 66:124–31

Doojse B, Branscombe NR, Spears R, Manstead ASR. 1998. Guilty by association: when one's group has a negative history. *J. Personal. Soc. Psychol.* 75:872–86

Edelmann RJ, McCusker G. 1986. Introversion, neuroticism, empathy, and embarrassability. *Personal. Individ. Differ.* 7:133–40

Eisenberg N. 1986. *Altruistic Cognition, Emotion, and Behavior*. Hillsdale, NJ: Erlbaum

Eisenberg N, Fabes RA, Carlo G, Speer AL, Switzer G, et al. 1993. The relations of empathy-related emotions and maternal practices to children's comforting behavior. *J. Exp. Child Psychol.* 55:131–50

Eisenberg N, Fabes RA, Miller PA, Shell R, Shea C, Mayplumlee T. 1990. Pre-schoolers' vicarious emotional responding and their situational and dispositional prosocial behavior. *Merrill-Palmer Q.* 36:507–29

Eisenberg N, Miller PA. 1987. Empathy, sympathy, and altruism: empirical and conceptual links. In *Empathy and Its Development*, ed. N Eisenberg, J Strayer, pp. 292–316. New York: Cambridge Univ. Press

Eisenberg N, Spinrad TL, Sadovsky A. 2006. Empathy-related responding in children. In *Handbook of Moral Development*, ed. M Killen, JG Smetana, pp. 517–49. Hillsdale, NJ: Erlbaum

Eisenberg N, Valiente C, Champion C. 2004. Empathy-related responding: moral, social, and socialization correlates. In *The Social Psychology of Good and Evil*, ed. AG Miller, pp. 386–415. New York: Guilford

Elison J, Lennon R, Pulos S. 2006a. Investigating the compass of shame: the development of the compass of shame scale. *Soc. Behav. Personal.* 34:221–38

Elison J, Pulos S, Lennon R. 2006b. Shame-focused coping: an empirical study of the Compass of Shame. *Soc. Behav. Personal.* 34:161–68

Ellis A. 1962. *Reason and Emotion in Psychotherapy*. New York: Lyle Stuart

Emmons RA, McCullough ME. 2003. Counting blessings versus burdens: an experimental investigation of gratitude and subjective well-being in daily life. *J. Personal. Soc. Psychol.* 84:377–89

Emmons RA, Shelton CS. 2002. Gratitude and the science of positive psychology. In *Handbook of Positive Psychology*, ed. CR Snyder, SJ Lopez, pp. 459–71. New York: Oxford Univ. Press

Estrada P. 1995. Adolescents' self-reports of prosocial responses to friends and acquaintances: the role of sympathy-related cognitive, affective, and motivational processes. *J. Res. Adolesc.* 5:173–200

Feiring C, Taska L. 2005. The persistence of shame following sexual abuse: a longitudinal look at risk and recovery. *Child Maltreat.* 10:337–49

Feiring C, Taska L, Lewis M. 1996. A process model for understanding adaptation to sexual abuse: the role of shame in defining stigmatization. *Child Abuse Neglect* 20:767–82

Feiring C, Taska L, Lewis M. 2002. Adjustment following sexual abuse discovery: the role of shame and attributional style. *Dev. Psychol.* 38:79–92

Ferguson TJ, Stegge H. 1995. Emotional states and traits in children: the case of guilt and shame. See Tangney & Fischer 1995, pp. 174–97

Ferguson TJ, Stegge H, Damhuis I. 1991. Children's understanding of guilt and shame. *Child Dev.* 62:827–39

Ferguson TJ, Stegge H, Eyre HL, Vollmer R, Ashbaker M. 2000. Context effects and the (mal)adaptive nature of guilt and shame in children. *Genet. Soc. Gen. Psychol. Monogr.* 126:319–45

Ferguson TJ, Stegge H, Miller ER, Olsen ME. 1999. Guilt, shame, and symptoms in children. *Dev. Psychol.* 35:347–57

Feshbach ND. 1975. Empathy in children: some theoretical and empirical considerations. *Couns. Psychol.* 5:25–30

Feshbach ND. 1987. Parental empathy and child adjustment/maladjustment. In *Empathy and Its Development*, ed. N Eisenberg, J Strayer, pp. 271–91. New York: Cambridge Univ. Press

Feshbach ND, Feshbach S. 1969. The relationship between empathy and aggression in two age groups. *Dev. Psychol.* 1:102–7

Fontana A, Rosenbeck R. 2004. Trauma, change in strength of religious faith, and mental health service use among veterans treated for PTSD. *J. Nerv. Ment. Dis.* 192:579–84

Frederickson BL. 2000. Cultivating positive emotions to optimize well-being and health. *Prevent. Treat.*, vol. 3, article 0001a

Frederickson BL, Roberts T. 1997. Objectification theory: toward understanding women's lived experiences and mental health risks. *Psychol. Women Q.* 21:173–206

Frederickson BL, Tugade MM, Waugh CE, Larkin GR. 2003. What good are positive emotions in crises? A prospective study of resilience and emotions following the terrorist attacks on the United States on September 11, 2001. *J. Personal. Soc. Psychol.* 84:365–76

Freud S. 1961/1924. The dissolution of the Oedipus complex. In *The Standard Edition of the Complete Psychological Works of Sigmund Freud*, ed. and transl. J Strachey, 19:173–82. London: Hogarth

Ghatavi K, Nicolson R, MacDonald C, Osher S, Levitt A. 2002. Defining guilt in depression: a comparison of subjects with major depression, chronic medical illness and healthy controls. *J. Affect. Disord.* 68:307–15

Gilbert P, Allan S, Goss K. 1996. Parental representations, shame, interpersonal problems, and vulnerability to psychopathology. *Clin. Psychol. Psychother.* 3:23–24

Goldman M, Seever M, Seever M. 1982. Social labeling and the foot-in-the-door effect. *J. Soc. Psychol.* 117:19–23

Gramzow R, Tangney JP. 1992. Proneness to shame and the narcissistic personality. *Personal. Soc. Psychol. Bull.* 18:369–76

Gruenewald TL, Kemeny ME, Aziz N, Fahey JL. 2004. Acute threat to the social self: shame, social self-esteem, and cortisol activity. *Psychosom. Med.* 66:915–24

Haidt J. 2000. The positive emotion of elevation. *Prevent. Treat.*, Vol. 3. ISSN: 1522-3736

Haidt J. 2003. Elevation and the positive psychology of morality. In *Flourishing: Positive Psychology and the Life Well-Lived*, ed. CL Keyes, J Haidt, pp. 275–89. Washington, DC: Am. Psychol. Assoc.

Haidt J, Algoe S, Meijer Z, Tam A. 2002. *Elevation: An Emotion That Makes People Want to Do Good Deeds.* Unpubl. manuscr., Univ. Virginia, Charlottesville

Hallsworth L, Wade TD, Tiggemann M. 2005. Individual differences in male body image: an examination of self-objectification in recreational body builders. *Br. J. Health Psychol.* 10:453–65

Harder DW. 1995. Shame and guilt assessment, and relationships of shame- and guilt-proneness to psychopathology. See Tangney & Fischer 1995, pp. 368–92

Hare RD. 1991. *The Hare Psychopathy Checklist-Revised.* Toronto: Multi-Health Syst.

Harper FWK, Arias I. 2004. The role of shame in predicting adult anger and depressive symptoms among victims of child psychological maltreatment. *J. Fam. Violence* 19(6):367–75

Harper FWK, Austin AG, Cercone JJ, Arias I. 2005. The role of shame, anger, and affect regulation in men's perpetration of psychological abuse in dating relationships. *J. Interpers. Violence* 20:1648–62

Harris H. 2003. Reassessing the dimensionality of the moral emotions. *Br. J. Psychol.* 94:457–73

Hartmann E, Loewenstein R. 1962. Notes on the superego. *Psychoanal. Study Child* 17:42–81

Henderson L, Zimbardo P. 2001. Shyness as a clinical condition: the Stanford model. In *International Handbook of Social Anxiety: Concepts, Research and Interventions Relating to the Self and Shyness*, ed. WR Crozier, LE Alden, pp. 431–47. New York: Wiley

Herrald MM, Tomaka J. 2002. Patterns of emotion-specific appraisal, coping, and cardiovascular reactivity during an ongoing emotional episode. *J. Personal. Soc. Psychol.* 83:434–50

Hoffman ML. 1982. Development of prosocial motivation: empathy and guilt. In *Development of Prosocial Behavior*, ed. N Eisenberg-Berg, pp. 281–313. New York: Academic

Hoglund C, Nicholas K. 1995. Shame, guilt, and anger in college students exposed to abusive family environments. *J. Fam. Violence* 10:141–57

Iyer A, Leach CW, Crosby FJ. 2003. White guilt and racial compensation: the benefits and limits of self-focus. *Personal. Soc. Psychol. Bull.* 29:117–29

Iyer A, Schmader T, Lickel B. 2006. Predicting American and British opposition to the occupation of Iraq: the role of group-based anger, shame, and guilt. Unpubl. manuscr.

Johns M, Schmader T, Lickel B. 2005. Ashamed to be an American? The role of identification in predicting vicarious shame for anti-Arab prejudice after 9–11. *Self Ident.* 4:331–48

Joireman J. 2004. Empathy and the self-absorption paradox II: self-rumination and self-reflection as mediators between shame, guilt, and empathy. *Self Ident.* 3:225–38

Jones WH, Kugler K. 1993. Interpersonal correlates of the Guilt Inventory. *J. Personal. Assess.* 61:246–58

Kashdan TB, Uswatte G, Julian T. 2006. Gratitude and hedonic and eudaimonic well-being in Vietnam War veterans. *Behav. Res. Therapy* 44:177–99

Keltner D, Buswell BN. 1996. Evidence for the distinctness of embarrassment, shame, and guilt: a study of recalled antecedents and facial expressions of emotion. *Cogn. Emot.* 10:155–71

Kendler KS, Liu X, Gardner CO, McCullough ME, Larson D, Prescott CA. 2003. Dimensions of religiosity and their relationship to lifetime psychiatric and substance use disorders. *Am. J. Psychiatry* 160:496–503

Ketelaar T, Au WT. 2003. The effects of feelings of guilt on the behavior of uncooperative individuals in repeated social bargaining games: an affect-as-information interpretation of the role of emotion in social interaction. *Cogn. Emot.* 17:429–53

Kroll J, Egan E. 2004. Psychiatry, moral worry, and moral emotions. *J. Psychiatr. Pract.* 10:352–60

Kubany ES, Abueg FR, Owens JA, Brennan JM, Kaplan AS, Watson SB. 1995. Initial examination of a multidimensional model of trauma-related guilt: applications to combat veterans and battered women. *J. Psychopathol. Behav. Assess.* 17(4):353–76

Kubany ES, Hill EE, Owens JA, Iannce-Spencer C, McCaig MA, et al. 2004. Cognitive trauma therapy for battered women with PTSD (CTT-BW). *J. Consult. Clin. Psychol.* 72(1):3–18

Latane B, Darley JM. 1968. Group inhibition of bystander intervention. *J. Personal. Soc. Psychol.* 10:215–21

Lazarus RS. 1991. *Emotion and Adaptation*. New York: Oxford Univ. Press

Leary MR, Landel JL, Patton KM. 1996. The motivated expression of embarrassment following a self-presentational predicament. *J. Personal.* 64:619–37

Leary MR, Meadows S. 1991. Predictors, elicitors, and concomitants of social blushing. *J. Personal. Soc. Psychol.* 60:254–62

Lee D, Scragg P, Turner S. 2001. The role of shame and guilt in traumatic events: a clinical model of shame-based and guilt-based PTSD. *Br. J. Med. Psychol.* 74:451–66

Leeming D, Boyle M. 2004. Shame as a social phenomenon: a critical analysis of the concept of dispositional shame. *Psychol. Psychother. Theory Res. Pract.* 77:375–96

Leith KP, Baumeister RF. 1998. Empathy, shame, guilt, and narratives of interpersonal conflicts: guilt-prone people are better at perspective taking. *J. Personal.* 66:1–37

Leskela J, Dieperink M, Thuras P. 2002. Shame and posttraumatic stress disorder. *J. Trauma. Stress* 15:223–26

Lewin K. 1943. Defining the "filed at a given time." *Psychol. Rev.* 50:292–310

Lewis HB. 1971. *Shame and Guilt in Neurosis*. New York: Int. Univ. Press

Lewis M. 1992. *Shame: The Exposed Self*. New York: Free Press

Lewis M, Ramsay D. 2002. Cortisol response to embarrassment and shame. *Child Dev.* 73:1034–45

Lickel B, Schmader T, Barquissau M. 2004. The evocation of moral emotions in intergroup contexts: the distinction between collective guilt and collective shame. In *Collective Guilt: International Perspectives*, ed. NR Branscombe, B Doosje, pp. 35–55. New York: Cambridge Univ. Press

Lickel B, Schmader T, Spanovic M. 2006. Group-conscious emotions: the implications of others' wrongdoings for identity and relationships. In *The Self-Conscious Emotions: Theory and Research*, ed. R Robins, J Tracy, JP Tangney. New York: Guilford. In press

Lickel B, Schmader T, Curtis M, Scarnier M, Ames DR. 2005. Vicarious shame and guilt. *Group Process. Intergroup Relat.* 8:145–47

Lindsay-Hartz J. 1984. Contrasting experiences of shame and guilt. *Am. Behav. Sci.* 27:689–704

Marschall DE. 1996. *Effects of induced shame on subsequent empathy and altruistic behavior*. Unpubl. thesis, George Mason Univ., Fairfax, VA

Mascolo MF, Fischer KW. 1995. Developmental transformations in appraisals for pride, shame, and guilt. See Tangney & Fischer 1995, pp. 64–113

McCullough ME, Emmons RA, Tsang J. 2002. The grateful disposition: a conceptual and empirical topography. *J. Personal. Soc. Psychol.* 82:112–27

McCullough ME, Kilpatrick S, Emmons RA, Larson D. 2001. Is gratitude a moral effect? *Psychol. Bull.* 127:249–66

McLaughlin DE. 2002. Posttraumatic stress disorder symptoms and self-conscious affect among battered women. *Diss. Abstr. Int. B Sci. Eng.* 62:4470

Meehan MA, O'Connor LE, Berry JW, Weiss J, Morrison A, Acampora A. 1996. Guilt, shame, and depression in clients in recovery from addiction. *J. Psychoactive Drugs* 28:125–34

Merisca R, Bybee JS. 1994. *Guilt, not moral reasoning, relates to volunteerism, prosocial behavior, lowered aggressiveness, and eschewal of racism*. Poster presented at Annu. Meet. East. Psychol. Assoc., Providence, RI

Miller PA, Eisenberg N. 1988. The relation of empathy to aggressive and externalizing/antisocial behavior. *Psychol. Bull.* 103:324–44

Miller RS. 1992. The nature and severity of self-reported embarrassing circumstances. *Personal. Soc. Psychol. Bull.* 18:190–98

Miller RS. 1995a. Embarrassment and social behavior. See Tangney & Fischer 1995, pp. 322–39

Miller RS. 1995b. On the nature of embarrassability: shyness, social-evaluation, and social skill. *J. Personal.* 63:315–39

Miller RS. 1996. *Embarrassment: Poise and Peril in Everyday Life*. New York: Guilford

Mills R. 2003. Possible antecedents and developmental implications of shame in young girls. *Infant Child Dev.* 12:329–49

Mosher DL. 1966. The development and multitrait-multimethod matrix analysis of three measures of three aspects of guilt. *J. Consult. Clin. Psychol.* 30:25–29

Murray C, Waller G. 2002. Reported sexual abuse and bulimic psychopathology among non-clinical women: the mediating role of shame. *Int. J. Eat. Disord.* 32:186–91

Murray C, Waller G, Legg C. 2000. Family dysfunction and bulimia psychopathology: the mediating role of shame. *Int. J. Eat. Disord.* 28:84–89

Nathanson DL. 1992. *Shame and Pride: Affect, Sex, and the Birth of Self*. New York: Norton

Negrao C, Bonanno GA, Noll JG, Putnam FW, Trickett PK. 2005. Shame, humiliation, and childhood sexual abuse: distinct contributions and emotional coherence. *Child Maltreat.* 10(4):350–63

Nishith P, Nixon R, Resick P. 2005. Resolution of trauma-related guilt following treatment of PTSD in female rape victims: a result of cognitive processing therapy targeting comorbid depression? *J. Affect. Disord.* 86:259–65

O'Connor LE, Berry JW, Inaba D, Weiss J. 1994. Shame, guilt, and depression in men and women in recovery from addiction. *J. Subst. Abuse Treat.* 11:503–10

O'Connor LE, Berry JW, Weiss J. 1997. Interpersonal guilt: the development of a new measure. *J. Clin. Psychol.* 53:73–89

O'Connor LE, Berry JW, Weiss J. 2002. Guilt, fear, submission, and empathy in depression. *J. Affect. Disord.* 71:19–27

Orsillo SM, Heimburg RG, Juster HR, Garrett J. 1996. Social phobia and PTSD in Vietnam veterans. *J. Trauma. Stress* 9:235–52

Ortony A, Clore GL, Collins A. 1988. *The Cognitive Structure of Emotions.* Cambridge, UK: Cambridge Univ. Press

Paulhus DL, Robins RW, Trzesniewski KH, Tracy JL. 2004. Two replicable suppressor situations in personality research. *Multivar. Behav. Res.* 39:303–28

Quiles ZN, Bybee J. 1997. Chronic and predispositional guilt: relations to mental health, prosocial behavior and religiosity. *J. Personal. Assess.* 69:104–26

Resick PA, Nishith P, Weaver TL, Astin MC, Feuer CA. 2002. A comparison of cognitive-processing therapy with prolonged exposure and a waiting condition for the treatment of chronic posttraumatic stress disorder in female rape victims. *J. Consult. Clin. Psychol.* 70(4):867–79

Rodin J, Silberstein L, Striegel-Moore R. 1984. Women and weight: a normative discontent. In *Nebraska Symposium on Motivation*, ed. TB Sonderegger 32:267–307. Lincoln: Univ. Nebraska Press

Roseman IJ. 1991. Appraisal determinants of discrete emotions. *Cogn. Emot.* 5:161–200

Rozin P, Lowery L, Imada S, Haidt J. 1999. The CAD triad hypothesis: a mapping between three moral emotions (contempt, anger, disgust) and three moral codes (community, autonomy, divinity). *J. Personal. Soc. Psychol.* 76:574–86

Sabini J, Silver M. 1997. In defense of shame: shame in the context of guilt and embarrassment. *J. Theory Soc. Behav.* 27:1–15

Sanftner JL, Barlow DH, Marschall DE, Tangney JP. 1995. The relation of shame and guilt to eating disorders symptomatology. *J. Soc. Clin. Psychol.* 14:315–24

Schaefer DA. 2000. The difference between shame-prone and guilt-prone persons on measures of anxiety, depression and risk of alcohol abuse. *Diss. Abstr. Int. B Sci. Eng.* 60:2389

Scheff TJ. 1987. The shame-rage spiral: a case study of an interminable quarrel. In *The Role of Shame in Symptom Formation*, ed. HB Lewis, pp. 109–49. Hillsdale, NJ: Erlbaum

Schmader T, Lickel B. 2006. Stigma and shame: emotional responses to the stereotypic actions of one's ethnic ingroup. In *Stigma and Group Inequality: Social Psychological Approaches*, ed. S Levin, C van Laar, pp. 261–85. Mahwah, NJ: Erlbaum

Sharkey WF, Stafford L. 1990. Responses to embarrassment. *Hum. Commun. Res.* 17:315–42

Shweder RA, Much NC, Mahapatra M, Park L. 1997. The "Big Three" of morality (autonomy, community, divinity) and the "Big Three" explanation of suffering. In *Morality and Health*, ed. A Brandt, P Rozin, pp. 119–69. New York: Routledge

Smith CA, Ellsworth PC. 1985. Patterns of cognitive appraisal in emotion. *J. Personal. Soc. Psychol.* 48:813–38

Smith RH, Webster JM, Parrot WG, Eyre HL. 2002. The role of public exposure in moral and nonmoral shame and guilt. *J. Personal. Soc. Psychol.* 83:138–59

Stuewig J, McCloskey L. 2005. The impact of maltreatment on adolescent shame and guilt: psychological routes to depression and delinquency. *Child Maltreat.* 10:324–36

Stuewig J, Tangney JP, Heigel C, Harty L. 2006. Re-examining the relationship between shame, guilt, and aggression. Manuscr. in prep.

Swim JK, Miller DL. 1999. White guilt: its antecedents and consequences for attitudes toward affirmative action. *Personal. Soc. Psychol. Bull.* 25:500–14

Talbot J, Talbot N, Tu X. 2004. Shame-proneness as a diathesis for dissociation in women with histories of childhood sexual abuse. *J. Traum. Stress* 17(5):445–48

Tangney JP. 1990. Assessing individual differences in proneness to shame and guilt: development of the Self-Conscious Affect and Attribution Inventory. *J. Personal. Soc. Psychol.* 59:102–11

Tangney JP. 1991. Moral affect: the good, the bad, and the ugly. *J. Personal. Soc. Psychol.* 61:598–607

Tangney JP. 1992. Situational determinants of shame and guilt in young adulthood. *Personal. Soc. Psychol. Bull.* 18:199–206

Tangney JP. 1993. Shame and guilt. In *Symptoms of Depression*, ed. CG Costello, pp. 161–80. New York: Wiley

Tangney JP. 1994. The mixed legacy of the superego: adaptive and maladaptive aspects of shame and guilt. In *Empirical Perspectives on Object Relations Theory*, ed. JM Masling, RF Bornstein, pp. 1–28. Washington, DC: Am. Psychol. Assoc.

Tangney JP. 1995a. Recent empirical advances in the study of shame and guilt. *Am. Behav. Sci.* 38:1132–45

Tangney JP. 1995b. Shame and guilt in interpersonal relationships. See Tangney & Fischer 1995, pp. 114–39

Tangney JP. 1996. Conceptual and methodological issues in the assessment of shame and guilt. *Behav. Res. Ther.* 34:741–54

Tangney JP, Burggraf SA, Wagner PE. 1995. Shame-proneness, guilt-proneness, and psychological symptoms. See Tangney & Fischer 1995, pp. 343–67

Tangney JP, Dearing R. 2002. *Shame and Guilt.* New York: Guilford

Tangney JP, Fischer KW, eds. 1995. *Self-Conscious Emotions: The Psychology of Shame, Guilt, Embarrassment, and Pride.* New York: Guilford

Tangney JP, Marschall DE, Rosenberg K, Barlow DH, Wagner PE. 1994. *Children's and Adults' Autobiographical Accounts of Shame, Guilt and Pride Experiences: An Analysis of Situational Determinants and Interpersonal Concerns.* Unpubl. manuscr. George Mason Univ., Fairfax, VA

Tangney JP, Mashek D, Stuewig J. 2006. Working at the social-clinical-community-criminology interface: the GMU inmate study. *J. Soc. Clin. Psychol.* In press

Tangney JP, Miller RS, Flicker L, Barlow DH. 1996a. Are shame, guilt and embarrassment distinct emotions? *J. Personal. Soc. Psychol.* 70:1256–69

Tangney JP, Stuewig J, Mashek D. 2006b. An emotional-cognitive framework for understanding moral behavior. Unpubl. manuscr. George Mason Univ., Fairfax, VA

Tangney JP, Wagner PE, Burggraf SA, Gramzow R, Fletcher C. 1991. *Children's shame-proneness, but not guilt-proneness, is related to emotional and behavioral maladjustment.* Poster presented meet. Am. Psychol. Soc., Washington, DC

Tangney JP, Wagner PE, Fletcher C, Gramzow R. 1992. Shamed into anger? The relation of shame and guilt to anger and self-reported aggression. *J. Personal. Soc. Psychol.* 62:669–75

Tangney JP, Wagner P, Gramzow R. 1989. *The Test of Self-Conscious Affect (TOSCA).* Fairfax, VA: George Mason Univ.

Tangney JP, Wagner PE, Hill-Barlow D, Marschall DE, Gramzow R. 1996b. Relation of shame and guilt to constructive versus destructive responses to anger across the lifespan. *J. Personal. Soc. Psychol.* 70:797–809

Tibbetts SG. 1997. Shame and rational choice in offending decisions. *Crim. Justice Behav.* 24:234–55

Tibbetts SG. 2003. Self-conscious emotions and criminal offending. *Psychol. Rep.* 93:101–26

Tomkins SS. 1963. *Affect, Imagery, Consciousness. Volume 2. The Negative Affects.* New York: Springer

Tracy JL, Robins RW. 2004a. Putting the self into self-conscious emotions: a theoretical model. *Psychol. Inq.* 15:103–25

Tracy JL, Robins RW. 2004b. Show your pride: evidence for a discrete emotion expression. *Psychol. Sci.* 15(3):194–97

Tracy JL, Robins RW. 2006. Appraisal antecedents of shame, guilt, and pride: support for a theoretical model. *Personal. Soc. Psychol. Bull.* In press

Wallbott HG, Scherer KR. 1995. Cultural determinants in experiencing shame and guilt. See Tangney & Fischer 1995, pp. 465–87

Weiss J. 1993. *How Psychotherapy Works.* New York: Guilford

Weitzman O, Kemeny ME, Fahey JL. 2004. *HIV-related Shame and Guilt Predict CD4 Decline.* Manuscr. submitted

Wicker FW, Payne GC, Morgan RD. 1983. Participant descriptions of guilt and shame. *Motiv. Emot.* 7:25–39

Widom C, Raphael K, DuMont K. 2004. The case for prospective longitudinal studies in child maltreatment research: commentary on Dube, Williamson, Thompson, Felitti and Anda 2004. *Child Abuse Neglect* 28:175–722

Zahn-Waxler C, Robinson J. 1995. Empathy and guilt: early origins of feelings of responsibility. See Tangney & Fischer 1995, pp. 143–73

Zebel S, Doosje B, Spears R. 2004. It depends on your point of view: implications of perspective-taking and national identification for Dutch collective guilt. In *Collective Guilt: International Perspectives*, ed. NR Branscombe, B Doosje, pp. 148–68. New York: Cambridge Univ. Press

The Experience of Emotion

Lisa Feldman Barrett,[1] Batja Mesquita,[2]
Kevin N. Ochsner,[3] and James J. Gross[4]

[1] Department of Psychology, Boston College, Chestnut Hill, Massachusetts 02467 and
Psychiatric Neuroimaging Research Program, Massachusetts General Hospital,
Harvard Medical School, Charlestown, Massachusetts 02129; email: barretli@bc.edu

[2] Department of Psychology, Wake Forest University, Winston-Salem, North
Carolina 27109; email: mesquita@wfu.edu

[3] Department of Psychology, Columbia University, New York, New York 10027;
email: kochsner@paradox.psych.columbia.edu

[4] Department of Psychology, Stanford University, Stanford, California 94305;
email: james@psych.stanford.edu

Annu. Rev. Psychol. 2007. 58:373–403

First published online as a Review in
Advance on September 26, 2006

The *Annual Review of Psychology* is online
at http://psych.annualreviews.org

This article's doi:
10.1146/annurev.psych.58.110405.085709

Key Words

emotion, affect, consciousness

Abstract

Experiences of emotion are content-rich events that emerge at the
level of psychological description, but must be causally constituted
by neurobiological processes. This chapter outlines an emerging scientific agenda for understanding what these experiences feel like and
how they arise. We review the available answers to what is felt (i.e.,
the content that makes up an experience of emotion) and how neurobiological processes instantiate these properties of experience. These
answers are then integrated into a broad framework that describes, in
psychological terms, how the experience of emotion emerges from
more basic processes. We then discuss the role of such experiences
in the economy of the mind and behavior.

Contents

INTRODUCTION

As psychology transformed from the science of the mind (James 1890, Wundt 1897) into the science of behavior (Skinner 1953, Watson 1919), an important topic slipped from scientific view: the subjective experience of emotion. Recently, scientific discourse on this topic has reemerged (Barrett 2006b, Frijda 2005, Lambie & Marcel 2002, Sabini & Silver 2005), but the prevailing wisdom remains that "emotion researchers need to figure out how to escape from the shackles of subjectivity if emotion research is to thrive" (LeDoux 2000, p. 156). Our current, impoverished understanding of emotion experience is due not only to American psychology's behaviorist legacy, but also to a view of the mind that eschews phenomenology and characterizes mental states as nothing but their causes. Consequently, knowing the causes of emotion is presumed sufficient to answer the question of what the experience is. While expedient, this scientific approach leaves out an important aspect of reality: people feel something when they experience emotion. Describing how emotion experiences are caused does not substitute for a description of what is felt, and in fact, an adequate description of what people feel is required so that scientists know what to explain in the first place.

In this chapter, we frame an emerging scientific agenda for understanding what an experience of emotion feels like and how such feelings arise. We begin by reviewing the place of experience in existing models of emotion that largely define the mind as nothing but the processes that produce it. Next, drawing on the writings of philosopher John Searle (1992, 2000, 2004), we argue that experiences of emotion are content-rich events that emerge at the level of psychological description, but are instantiated by neurobiological processes, and any theory of emotion experience must address both content and process. We then review the available answers to what is felt (i.e., the content that makes up an experience of emotion) and how neurobiological processes account for these properties of experience. These answers are then integrated into a broad framework that describes, in psychological terms, how the experience of emotion emerges from more basic processes. Specifically, we suggest that the experience of emotion emerges from both a continuous stream of evolving affect and conceptual processing (much like the seeing "red" is a discrete experience of color that derives from a continuous spectrum of reflected light; Barrett 2006b). Affect, perceptions of the world, and conceptual knowledge about emotion are bound together at a moment in time, producing an intentional state where affect is experienced as having been caused by some object or situation. Finally, we briefly address several insights deriving from our view that have the potential to shape a scientific agenda for the study of emotion experience.

SCIENTIFIC ACCOUNTS OF EMOTION EXPERIENCE

Traditional Theories of Emotion

Most influential scientific accounts of emotion assume that experiences of emotion—like other mental events—are entailed or instantiated by physical processes in the brain or body and thus can be explained by events in the physical world. In principle, this assumption must be correct, but materialist accounts (as they are called) often go one step further by assuming that experiences can be redefined as nothing but these causes, and therefore must be understood solely in terms of them (cf. Searle 1992, 2000, 2004). Materialist theories differ greatly in the specifics of how emotions are caused and manifest, but they share a common assumption that an explanation of emotion experience requires only an explication of causes or effects.

Behaviorist models of emotion, the extreme version of this view, define experience out of existence, or at least out of bounds for the scientific study of emotion (e.g., LeDoux 1996, 2000) by characterizing emotion as nothing but behavior. In this view, understanding emotion means understanding the causes of emotional behavior. Identity approaches to emotion redefine ex-

periences of emotion as bodily states (James 1890), or, as in basic emotion models, as activity in brain circuits, neurochemical systems, so-called affect programs, or action plans (Buck 1999; Ekman 1972, 1992; Izard 1977, 1993; Oatley & Johnson-Laird 1987; Panksepp 1998; Plutchik 1980), or some combination of the body and the brain (Damasio 1994, 1999).[1] Functionalist approaches to emotion, such as some appraisal models, define emotion by its immediate causal relations; two experiences are of the same type (e.g., anger) if they are evoked by the same psychological situation (e.g., unpleasant, another person is to blame, controllable), are defined by the same behavioral consequences (e.g., antagonistic behavior), or some combination thereof (e.g., Arnold 1960; Frijda 1986; Lazarus 1966, 1991; Leventhal & Scherer 1987; Power 1997; Roseman et al. 1990, 1996; Scherer 1984).[2]

Materialist theories: theories rooted in the assumption that mental contents are caused by and therefore can be redefined as nothing but physical processes

---

[1] Identity theories reduce mental states, such as emotion experiences, to states of the nervous system. Type-type identity theories of emotion experience (e.g., the basic emotion theories) are grounded in the assumption that for every kind of emotion experience (e.g., the experience of anger), there is only one type of neurophysiological state. Token-token identity theories of emotion experience (e.g., James 1890, 1894) argue that every instance of emotion characterized by a distinctive feeling will be identical with a distinctive physical state (e.g., different experiences of anger will be instantiated by different neurophysiological states). The current trend in some neuroscience papers to refer to emotion as increased activity in certain brain areas relies on identity assumptions about emotion.

[2] Appraisal models began as an attempt to account for the mentalistic aspects of emotion experience in all its variety, but several prominent theories came to view the situation as the eliciting factor that produces emotional responses and in so doing, took on functionalist assumptions that reduce the experience of emotion to its immediate causal relations. Functionalist approaches assume that it is the function, rather than the brain or body, that makes an experience the type it is. In input-output functionalism, two instances of experience are tokens (exemplars) of the same type of emotion (e.g., anger) because they were evoked by the same stimuli (situations with certain kinds of meaning), because they were caused by the same sorts of cognitive mechanisms (typically called "appraisals"), or because of their relation to behavior (or tendencies to behave). A second form of functionalism offers a more distal or teleological approach to understanding why emotion evolved and what specific and adaptive functional roles it serves in the lives of the individuals and/or species, so that two experiences are

Biological Naturalism

Biological naturalism: John Searle's approach to the mind-body problem that challenges both dualist and materialist views of the mind. Consciousness is treated as a biological phenomenon that is part of the natural world (like photosynthesis or digestion). Conscious states are defined as ontologically subjective (i.e., exist only as experienced by human or animal), content-rich (i.e., they feel like something), primarily intentional events (i.e., they are about or refer to something) that are ultimately constituted by, but not redefined as, neurobiological events

"It is a mistake to confuse the evidence that we have about a subject matter for the subject matter itself. The subject matter of psychology is the human mind, and human behavior is evidence for the existence and features of the mind, but is not itself the mind" (Searle 2004, pp. 52–53).

Biological naturalism is a philosophical framework that stands in opposition to traditional materialist views of the mind (Searle 1992, 2000, 2004) and in so doing offers three novel tenets for the scientific study of emotion experience. First, an adequate account of emotion experience requires more than a specification of cause; it also requires a description of content (i.e., of what is felt) that is common to all experiences of emotion and that which distinguishes one experience from another. Descriptions of phenomenological content need not convey an experience of emotion in all its richness and complexity to have scientific utility and value (i.e., describing is not experiencing) (Edelman & Tononi 2000).[3]

Second, content cannot be entirely reduced to its causes. The experience of emotion, like any conscious state, is a system-level

property of the brain (which can be explained by neuronal activity), much as digestion is a system-level property of the gastrointestinal system (which can be explained causally by the chemistry of the body) or solidity is a property of the material world (which can be explained causally by the behavior of the molecules). To conflate these different levels of analysis would be to make what Ryle (2000) called a category error. Experiences of emotion can be entirely explained in terms of the neurobiological (material) features of the brain (i.e., they can be causally reduced to brain activity), but they cannot be exclusively equated with any single element or feature such as neural circuitry, biochemical properties of synaptic changes, and so on (i.e., they cannot be ontologically reduced to any material cause). Any conscious event has both neurobiological and phenomenological features. Therefore, knowing about brain activity (or, at another level of analysis, mental processes) alone will not provide a full scientific account of emotion experience. The job of science is to work out the "bridging laws" that link different levels of analysis (Nagel 1961).

Third, conscious states exist only from a first-person point of view. They are ontologically subjective, meaning they only exist when experienced by a conscious agent and cannot be redefined independently of the experiencer. Consequently, they cannot be eliminated in favor of third-person references to instrument-based measures of behavior, physiological activation, or neural events. It is not possible to measure more easily observable aspects of emotion (e.g., facial movements, vocal acoustics, voluntary behaviors, peripheral physiology) to learn something about its subjective aspect. To know what emotion feels like, it is necessary to ask people what they experience. The role of science is to study these subjective events in an epistemologically objective manner.

From the vantage point of biological naturalism, then, scientists must ask questions about subjectively experienced content to understand emotion experience; questions

tokens of the same emotion because they perform the same function in the life of the person feeling them. By characterizing specific contents of what is experienced (e.g., in anger, people experience their goals as being blocked by another person or by the structure of the situation) in terms of the cognitive processes that produce the content (e.g., in anger, people engage a literal cognitive mechanism for deciding whether or not their goals are blocked), these models are (perhaps unintentionally) reductionistic. Moreover, they stand in contrast to other appraisal models that define appraisals as dimensions of situated meaning that constitute an experience of emotion, rather than cause it.

[3] Scientists sometimes make the mistake of assuming that a scientific description of emotion experience must represent what an emotion feels like with perfect fidelity. No description, however precise, can fully account for the experience of emotion, or for the experience of any conscious content, for that matter. Just as no description will ever allow a color-blind person to experience a color (no matter how much they read descriptions of the content), no scientific description of color instantiates the experience of color. Yet it is possible to study color perception and color experience from a scientific point of view.

about the material underpinnings of experience will never reveal the entire story. The question "What is the experience of emotion?" is really the question "What do people feel when they feel an emotion?" This is the question of content. What are the correct concepts for capturing or describing the psychological features of the system? Lambie & Marcel (2002) drew attention to the importance of this question in their recent conceptual analysis of emotion experience. The question "How does the brain instantiate these experiences?" is the straightforward (but difficult) question of how neurophysiological events constitute phenomenological contents. Although science is far from understanding how the brain produces conscious experience, it is possible to sketch the neural circuitry that becomes active during certain types of content. In the next two sections, we address each of these questions in turn. Answers to these two questions are then situated in a psychological framework that describes how experiences of emotion emerge from more basic processes.

THE PHENOMENOLOGICAL CONTENTS OF EMOTION EXPERIENCE

Not all mental states are conscious, but conscious mental states are mental representations that can, in principle, be reported (Frith et al. 1999), although at any given time they may not be (for a different view, see Lambie & Marcel 2002). To say that a person is consciously experiencing emotion is to say that he or she has a mental representation of emotion: past feelings (memories), hypothetical feelings (imaginings), or feelings that are occurring in the moment (on-line experiences). The most direct way to measure the contents of a mental representation of emotion is to examine people's verbal behaviors regarding their own mental state, in the form of self-reports (e.g., narratives or simple ratings of emotion words using Likert-type scales). The use of specific words does not directly reveal

the contents of the specific mental states to which they refer, but self-reports are a type of communicative act, and communicative acts carry information about a person's internal state that can be inferred by a listener (Wilson & Sperber 2003), whether the listener is a friend, a therapist, or a scientist. Although self-reports are often not useful to explain why people experience what they do (i.e., self-reports do not reveal causal processes; Nisbett & Wilson 1977, Wilson & Dunn 2004), they are useful—and indeed essential—for revealing the ontological structure of consciousness (assuming that you have a willing and able respondent).

One way that scientists can infer the content in mental states such as experiences of emotion is by treating self-reports as verbal behaviors and examining how people use words to represent those experiences.[4] Self-report studies, where participants characterize their experiences using emotion words, reveal that states of pleasure or displeasure comprise mental representations of emotion and point to several contents of experience in addition to valence.

Core Affect

At its core, a mental representation of emotion is a contentful state of pleasure or displeasure (Barrett 2006b,c; Russell 2003; Russell & Barrett 1999), termed "core affect." The word "core" signifies a form of affective responding that functions as a kind of core knowledge about whether objects or events are helpful or harmful, rewarding or threatening, calling for acceptance or rejection (for a discussion of core knowledge, see Spelke 2000). States of pleasure and displeasure are termed core affect because (a) the capacity to experience pleasure and displeasure is universal to all humans (Mesquita 2003,

---

[4]Other ways to infer a mental representation of emotion, such as observing a person's face or body, may be adequate at times (cf. Frith et al. 1999, Lambie & Marcel 2002), but they generally do not capture the full content of experience (Barrett 2006a, Ortony & Turner 1990, Russell, 2003).

The experience of emotion: affect, perceptions of meaning in the world, and conceptual knowledge about emotion are bound together at a moment in time, producing an intentional state where affect is experienced as having been caused by some object or situation

Core affect: information about the external world is translated into an internal affective code or state that indicates whether an object or situation is helpful or harmful, rewarding or threatening, requiring approach or withdrawal. With awareness, core affect is experienced as feelings of pleasure or displeasure that are to some extent arousing or quieting. Core affect may be constituted by a constantly changing stream of transient alterations in an organism's neurophysiological state that represents its immediate relationship to the flow of changing events

Russell 1983, Scherer 1997b);[5] (*b*) experiences of pleasure and displeasure are present at birth (Emde et al. 1976, Spitz 1965, Sroufe 1979); (*c*) all instrument-based measures of emotion give evidence of a person's pleasant and unpleasant state or its intensity [e.g., peripheral nervous system activation (Bradley & Lang 2000; Cacioppo et al. 1997, 2000); facial electromyographic activity (Cacioppo et al. 1997, 2000; Messinger 2002); vocal acoustics (Bachorowski 1999); expressive behavior (Cacioppo & Gardner 1999); and neural activations (Wager et al. 2003); for a review, see (Barrett 2006a)]; (*d*) pleasure and displeasure constitute a neuropsychologic barometer of the individual's relationship to an environment at a given point in time (Nauta 1971), such that (*e*) they form the core of consciousness (Edelman & Tononi 2000; Searle 1992, 2004; see A Psychological Framework for Understanding Emotion Experience section below).

There is mounting empirical evidence that mental representations of emotion have pleasure or displeasure at their core. People are able to give an explicit account of pleasant and unpleasant feelings using a variety of self-rating scales (Barrett & Russell 1998; Bradley & Lang 1994; Carroll et al. 1999; Frijda et al. 1989; Kitayama et al. 2000; Lang et al. 1993; Roseman et al. 1996; Russell et al. 1989; Scherer 1997b; Smith & Ellsworth 1985, 1987; Yik et al. 1999). Scales that are explicitly built to measure discrete emotions such as fear, anger, or sadness also provide strong evidence of a common core of pleasant and unpleasant feelings (Barrett & Russell 1998; Boyle 1986; Feldman 1993, 1995a; Mayer & Gaschke 1988; Russell 1980; Watson & Clark 1994; Watson & Tellegen 1985; Zuckerman & Lubin 1985) (for reviews, see Barrett 2006c, Barrett & Russell 1999, Russell & Barrett 1999, Watson et al. 1999). A large experience-sampling project involving idiographic analyses of experiences that were sampled in natural settings over many weeks verified that all participants (approximately 700 American college students) implicitly represented feelings of pleasure and displeasure (Barrett 2006c). This valenced content did not reflect the artificial influence of language (for evidence, see Barrett 2004, 2006b) or social desirability (Barrett 1996), but rather constituted an intrinsic content in mental representations of emotion.

Although core affect is ubiquitous, there are individual and group differences in the degree to which people characterize their experience in terms of pleasure and displeasure. Individuals who are sensitive to the evaluative properties of their surroundings implicitly emphasized the hedonics of their experience (Barrett 2006c). Furthermore, Japanese (compared with American) respondents more often report that they have not experienced any emotional content whatsoever, which suggests that people in these cultures less readily foreground their affective state (Mesquita & Kawasaka 2002).

---

[5]Considerable evidence shows that people can represent their experience in a dialectic fashion (Bagozzi et al. 1999, Kitayama et al. 2000, Schimmack et al. 2002, Scollon et al. 2005), and this has led some to wonder whether pleasure and displeasure really configure as a bipolar dimension of experience. This debate is easily remedied by remembering that a person cannot be aware of two scenes, or objects, or percepts within the same modality at exactly the same moment in time (as illustrated by a Necker cube, Gestalt images such as the young-lady/old-lady ambiguous figure, and incongruent inputs into two eyes in studies of binocular rivalry). So it is with pleasure and displeasure. Conscious experience can move at great speed (estimated at 100–150 ms per conscious moment; Edelman & Tononi 2000, Gray 2004), so that it is easy to shift back and forth between alternative experiences very quickly, and to summarize both experiences in a memory-based judgment. In fact, research that specifically limits the time window to momentary experience does not find dialectic representations at single moments in time (Leu et al. 2006, Scollon et al. 2005, Yik 2006). As a result, it very unlikely that pleasure and displeasure co-occur in real time, although people can quickly shift experience contents from one moment to the next, and summarize all of the experienced contents in memory. As usual, it all comes down to precision in scientific language, namely, what one means by "at once" in the sentence, "People can (or cannot) feel two things at once." The same argument can be made about emotional complexity, or feeling more than one emotion at once (Charles 2005).

From Core Affect to Complex Mental Representations of Emotion

Core affect is not, in and of itself, sufficient for a mental representation of emotion. An experience of emotion is an intentional state—it is an affective state that is about something. Consequently, any description of emotion experience must go beyond pleasure and displeasure to give a systematic account of the phenomenological differences between emotions that we take to be psychologically distinct, such as anger, sadness, fear, pride, awe, and joy. Studies that focus on emotion words (e.g., angry, sad, afraid, guilty) to describe emotion experiences and studies of appraisals (i.e., the meaning of situations) reveal something about the content of these phenomenological differences. There is still much to be learned about the additional content that constitutes mental representations of emotion, but a brief review of the literature makes clear that mental representations of emotion include representations of arousal as well as relational and situational contents (Fitness & Fletcher 1993, Mesquita & Frijda 1992, Shaver et al. 1987, Shweder 1993).

Arousal content. Mental representations of emotion often, but not always, include some arousal-based content (i.e., feeling as if the mind or body is active, as in aroused, attentive, or wound-up, versus feeling that the mind or body is still, as in quiet, still, or sleepy). Felt activation is typically related to, but does not have a one-to-one correspondence with, actual physiologic activity (for a review, see Barrett et al. 2004, Wiens 2005). Cross-sectional studies examining how Western participants self-report their experiences using common English emotion words often give evidence of arousal-based content (for a review, see Russell & Barrett 1999). It is not yet clear, however, whether arousal is a property of a core affective state (as claimed by Russell 2003, Russell & Barrett 1999; also see The Neurobiology of Core Affect section below) because idiographic studies of emotion experience indicate that many, but not all, participants in Western samples represent feelings of activation and deactivation in experiences of emotion (Barrett 1998, 2004; Barrett & Fossum 2001; Feldman 1995b). In comparison with those who are not very aware of their somatovisceral states, individuals who are interoceptively sensitive emphasize arousal as an aspect of their emotion experience (Barrett et al. 2004) and rate evocative stimuli as more arousing (Pollatos et al. 2005). One possibility is that a person's core affective state can be characterized by arousal (associated with the uncertainty regarding whether a stimulus will predict threat or reward, the need to pay more attention to a stimulus of importance, or an urgency to engage in active coping), but that people vary in their ability or propensity to attend to this property of their core affective state so as to experience it as a feeling.

Arousal content: an experience of feeling active, aroused, attentive, or wound-up, versus feeling still, as in quiet, still, or sleepy. Does not have a simple one-to-one relationship to objectively measured physical states of arousal

AROUSAL AND THE EXPERIENCE OF EMOTION

It is often assumed that arousal is essential to the experience of emotion because people perceive emotional feelings in their bodies. William James and later Antonio Damasio proposed that the experience of specific emotions results from the perception of specific and unique patterns of somatovisceral arousal. Schachter and Singer, in contrast, argued that the experience of emotion was due to the direct and explicit experience of a generalized autonomic arousal. Decades of research, however, suggest that neither of these views is correct in the strong sense (for a review, see Barrett et al. 2004). First, little support has been obtained for the idea that different categories of emotion are consistently associated with unique sets of visceral sensations. Second, different measures of autonomic, somatic, or cortical arousal tend not to correlate highly with one another, such that "arousal" is not a unitary phenomenon, suggesting that there is no single accepted definition of arousal. Third, people do not have automatic, immediate, and explicit access to autonomic and somatic activity. As a result, the exact role of bodily feelings in the experience of emotion is still an open scientific question.

Relational content:
the content in an
emotion experience
that represents the
emoter's relationship
to another person. In
many cases, a mental
representation of
emotion
incorporates the
proximity or status of
an individual with
respect to other
individuals present
or imagined.
Cultural models of
relating tend to
influence relational
content

Situational content:
the meaning of a
situation, particularly
as it relates to the
perceived cause of
core affect.
Situational content
has been mapped
using several
appraisal dimensions
but likely goes
beyond these
dimensions to
reference cultural
meanings and
practices

Relational content. In self-report studies using emotion words, people report experiencing content related to dominance or submission (Russell & Mehrabian 1977). A number of studies in which American and Japanese samples rated their experience on English and Japanese words (and their translations) have yielded a dimension of social engagement versus disengagement (e.g., Kitayama et al. 2000, Markus & Kitayama 1991). Although dominance and social engagement are not synonymous, both are consistent with the relational models in a particular cultural context: Dominance would be the high end of autonomy that is valued in North American cultures, and social engagement would be the high end of harmony or symbiosis that is normative in Japanese cultural contexts (Rothbaum et al. 2000).

Situational content. Mental representations of emotion are intentional states in that they contain some experience of a psychological situation that is perceived by the person to be causally linked to core affective feelings. Appraisals, when they are treated as descriptions (rather than causes) of situated meaning (e.g., Clore & Ortony 2000, Frijda 2006, Smith & Ellsworth 1985), provide the best available evidence for mapping the experience of a situation that occurs in a mental representation of emotion. Situational events are experienced as (*a*) novel or unexpected, (*b*) conducive or obstructive to some goal, and (*c*) compatible (or not) with norms and values (*d*) for which a person has (or does not have) some responsibility or agency. A situation is also experienced as calling for some maintenance or change in the behavioral stance (action readiness) where the parameters for actual action are probabilistically certain to some degree. These abstract dimensions of situational meaning show a remarkable degree of convergence across different appraisal models (see Table 29.1 in Ellsworth & Scherer 2003) and, together with core affect, account for a little less than half of the variance that differentiates categories of emotion experience (e.g.,

Frijda et al. 1989; Roseman 1991; Roseman et al. 1990, 1996; Scherer 1997b; Smith & Ellsworth 1985, 1987) (for reviews, see Mesquita & Ellsworth 2001, Scherer 1997a). These dimensions of experience also show a remarkable degree of consistency across cultures, although there is variability (e.g., Frijda et al. 1995, Mauro et al. 1992, Mesquita 2001).

Beyond appraisal dimensions. Despite their descriptive value for understanding mental representations of emotion, appraisal dimensions alone do not provide a sufficient account of what people feel when they experience an emotion. First, instances of experience that are categorized as the same emotion, such as anger, are constituted by a variety of experiences of both the physical surroundings and the sociocultural context (Mesquita & Leu 2006). An experience of anger might indeed involve an insult, where the situation is experienced as obstructing a person's goals, incompatible with his or her identity, and so on, but these abstract descriptions aggregate important phenomenological details that distinguish one feeling of anger from another. You might feel insulted when your friend violates a deeply held belief and you calmly explain your views; when someone cuts you off on the highway and you speed up, yell, or shake your fist; or when someone calls your intelligence into question, causing you to withdraw and quickly leave. The goal for the science of experience is to discover a parsimonious way to describe these variations in anger feelings, but in a fashion that conserves what is meaningfully different about them.

Second, although it is true that respondents across the world can describe emotion experiences in terms of the appraisal dimensions proposed by Western researchers, it is not clear that these dimensions are in fact the most salient aspects of non-Western emotion experiences (Mesquita & Leu 2006, Shweder & Haidt 2000). Contentful states of emotion will involve the cultural meanings and practices of self and relating (Markus & Kitayama

1994, Shweder & Haidt 2000). In an attempt to capture some of the sociocultural content of experience, a number of studies have added appraisal dimensions that reflect more salient meanings in non-Western cultural contexts (Mesquita & Ellsworth 2001). For example, esteem by others (status, honor) was an important experience for Surinamese and Turkish immigrants in the Netherlands, but not for Dutch indigenous people (Mesquita 2001).

Third, the appraisal approach to mapping mental contents is currently limited by the paucity of evidence that appraisal dimensions are adequate representations of emotion as they are experienced in the moment (Parkinson 1997; but see Mesquita & Kawaska 2002). The overwhelming majority of studies using an appraisal approach ask people to remember or imagine emotion experiences, and self-reports in this context tend to engage semantic knowledge or beliefs about emotion that have an uncertain relationship to the content of emotion experience in real time (Barrett 1997, Robinson & Clore 2002). As a result, these studies are best understood as measuring the contents that describe a prototypic experience of anger, sadness, fear, and the like, rather than on-line instances of emotion experience per se (for a discussion, see Barrett 2006b).

THE NEURAL REFERENCE SPACE FOR THE EXPERIENCE OF EMOTION

Ontologically, experiences of emotion are pleasant or unpleasant states that contain additional experiential contents, such as felt arousal, and relational or situational meaning. At present, it is not possible to causally reduce these experiences to neurobiological processes and explain how neural activity instantiates specific emotional contents (or any conscious contents for that matter). It is possible, however, to offer a preliminary sketch of the brain areas that are active during experiences of emotion (i.e., a neural reference space for mental representations of emotion), and we do so in **Figure 1** (see color insert).

This neural reference space is derived from neuroanatomical studies of the human brain and from neuroimaging studies of emotion experience, including an ongoing meta-analytic effort conducted by Barrett, Wager, and their students. A summary of studies that have imaged the experience of emotion (anger, sadness, fear, disgust, and happiness) and core affective feelings (pleasant and unpleasant affects) in normal participants using a number of different induction techniques (visual, auditory, olfactory, imagery, and memory) has produced a summary activation map (**Figure 2**; see color insert) that is similar to the neural reference space for mental representations of emotion hypothesized in **Figure 1**.[6] Many of the brain areas depicted in this neural reference space are part of the larger circuitry that entails consciousness more generally, because experiences of emotion are just one type of conscious content.

As we discuss in this section, the reference space includes circuitry in a ventral system at the front of the brain that is broadly related (although likely not specific) to core affective feelings of pleasure and displeasure. It is currently not possible to specify the brain areas that correspond to the other conscious contents found in mental representations of anger, sadness, fear, and so on (i.e., arousal-, relational-, and situation-based content).[7]

Neural reference space: brain areas that show increased activity during a certain type of mental event, and presumably instantiate that mental content

---

[6]The question of how the brain gives rise to emotion (and the experience of it) is often understood and answered (e.g., LeDoux 1996, Panksepp 1998) as a quest for "essential nodes" or brain systems dedicated to generating specific emotions, such as anger, sadness, fear, and so on. However, research guided by this quest has thus far produced little support for consistency and specificity in the circuitry that supports the experience and perception of emotion in humans, as evidenced by two recent meta-analyses (Murphy et al. 2003, Phan et al. 2002) summarizing the first decade of neuroimaging (fMRI and PET) research on emotion (for a review, see Barrett & Wager 2006). Although it may be premature to reject the idea of essential nodes for discrete emotions in the brain, it is not prudent to accept that idea too quickly, either.

[7]It is difficult to assess the brain structures associated with arousal-related content because studies typically tend to confound three different types of arousal (i.e., the intensity of a stimulus, feelings of bodily activity, and feelings of alertness).

OFC: orbitofrontal
cortex

VMPFC:
ventromedial
prefrontal cortex

ACC: anterior
cingulate cortex

However, research suggests that mental representations of emotion routinely involve a more dorsal medial prefrontal system that may support the cognitive processes involved with generating at least some of these contents, specifically conceptualizations of situational cause. Similar ventral and dorsal systems have been discussed previously as the circuitry supporting the generation and regulation of an emotional reaction (Ochsner & Gross 2005, Yamasaki et al. 2002) or affective state (Phillips et al. 2003).

The Neurobiology of Core Affect

Figure 2 indicates that mental representations of emotion are consistently associated with increased activation involving a broad swath of the temporal lobe (including the amygdala), orbitofrontal cortex (OFC), and the ventromedial prefrontal cortex (VMPFC) (for definitions, see **Figure 1**). Together, these areas form a distributed, functional circuit in the ventral portion of the human brain that is involved in establishing the threat or reward value of a stimulus. Value is established by linking sensory information about the stimulus with a representation of how the stimulus affects the person's somatovisceral state (Barbas et al. 2003, Ghashghaei & Barbas 2002, Kringelbach & Rolls 2004, Ongur et al. 2003, Ongur & Price 2000). Neuroanatomical studies of both primates and humans, along with neuroimaging and lesion evidence in humans, suggest that this ventral system creates a context-sensitive neural representation of an object's value by influencing a person's core affective state to resemble that which has resulted from prior experiences with the object. This view has elements in common with the somatic marker hypothesis (e.g., Bechara et al. 2000) and is consistent with the evidence that OFC plays a role in reinforcement and reversal learning (Kringelbach 2005, Kringelbach & Rolls 2004).

Although the details remain to be specified, the available evidence suggests that neural representations of sensory information about a stimulus and its somatovisceral impact are entailed by two related functional circuits that make up the ventral system for core affect (for reviews, see Carmichael & Price 1996, Elliott et al. 2000, Ongur & Price 2000). The first functional circuit involves connections between the basolateral (BL) complex of the amygdala, which indelibly codes the original value of a stimulus (Bouton 2005), the central and lateral aspects of the OFC, which is necessary to a flexible, experience- or context-dependent representation of an object's value (Elliott et al. 2000, Kringelbach 2005, Kringelbach & Rolls 2004, Morris & Dolan 2004), and the anterior insula, which is involved in representing interoceptive cues (Craig 2002, 2003; Dunkley et al. 2005; Wiens 2005). Both the BL and lateral OFC have robust connections with cortical representations of every sensory modality and have strong reciprocal connections (Ghashghaei & Barbas 2002, Kringelbach & Rolls 2004, McDonald 1998, Stefanacci & Amaral 2002), so that they form a functional circuit that integrates sensory (including somatovisceral) information. This information is needed to establish (at least initially) a value-based representation of an object that includes both external sensory features of the object along with its impact on the homeostatic state of the body. One recent formulation argues that the BL complex formulates the predictive value of a stimulus, whereas the OFC participates in generating a response based on that prediction (Holland & Gallagher 2004).

The second circuit, entailing a neural representation that guides visceromotor control, involves reciprocal connections between the ventromedial prefrontal cortex (VMPFC), including the closely related subgenual anterior cingulate cortex (ACC) and the amygdala, which together modulate the visceromotor (i.e., autonomic, chemical, and behavioral) responses that are part of the value-based representations of an object (Koski & Paus 2000). VMPFC, in particular, may help to link sensory representations of stimuli and

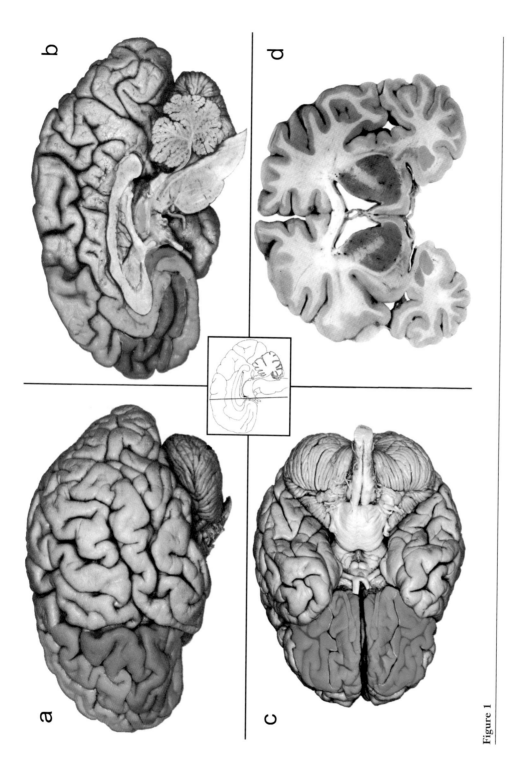

Figure 1

Figure 1

Key brain areas in the neural reference space for mental representations of emotion. The ventral system for core affect includes two closely connected circuits that are anchored in the orbitofrontal cortex (the entire ventral surface of the front part of the brain lying behind the orbital bone above the eye; Figure 1*c*). The sensory system involves the lateral sector of the orbitofrontal cortex (OFC) and includes the lateral portions of BA 11 and 13, BA 47/12 (*a, c, purple*). It is closely connected to the anterior insula (*d, yellow*) and the basolateral (BL) complex in the amygdala (*d, rose*, ventral aspect). The visceromotor circuitry includes the ventral portion of the ventromedial prefrontal cortex (VMPFC), which lies in the medial sector of the OFC (*a, b, c, blue*) and includes medial BA 11 and 13 ventral portions of BA 10, as well as BA 14, where the medial and lateral aspects of OFC connect; VMPFC is closely connected to the amygdala (including the central nucleus, *d, rose*, dorsal aspect) and the subgenual parts of the anterior cingulate cortex involving the anterior aspects of BA 24, 25, and 32 on the medial wall of the brain (ACC; *b, copper* and *tan*). The dorsal system is associated with mental state attributions including the dorsal aspect of the VMPFC corresponding to the frontal pole in BA 10 (*b, maroon*), the anterior ACC (*peach*), and the dorsomedial prefrontal cortex (DMPFC) corresponding to the medial aspects of BA 8, 9, and 10 (*a, b, green*). Ventrolateral prefrontal cortex (VLPFC) is shown in *red* (*a*). Also shown for reference are the thalamus (*b, light pink*), the ventral striatum (*d, green*), and the middle frontal gyrus in the dorsolateral prefrontal cortex (*a, orange*). Photographs adapted from DeArmond et al. (1989, pp. 5, 7, 8, and 43).

a

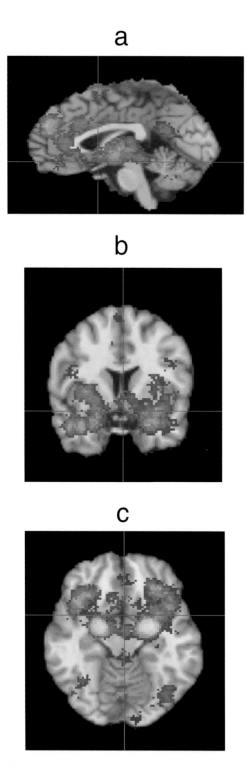

b

c

Figure 2

Figure 2

Preliminary summary of neuroimaging studies of core affective and emotion experiences. Activation foci were registered to a common stereotaxic brain atlas (Talairach & Tournoux 1988) where x = distance in millimeters to the right (+) or left (−) of midline; y = distance anterior (+) or posterior (−) to the anterior commissure; and z = distance superior (+) or inferior (−) to a horizontal plane through the anterior and posterior commissures. Midsagital (a, x = 0), coronal (b, y = 7), and horizontal (c, z = −13) images are presented. Significant areas of activation include OFC, insula, amygdala, ACC, and DMPFC (as well as VLPFC; not shown). VMPFC activations were also observed, but it is not clear that they extend down to the ventral surface, c, probably owing to problems with imaging that area of the brain. Lighter colors indicate a larger number of studies reported significant peak activations at that location (summary corrected for false discovery rate).

their associated visceromotor (i.e., core affective) outcomes and provides an "affective working memory" whose contents inform choices and judgments contingent upon an assessment of affective value (as computed by the BL and lateral OFC). This conclusion fits with the finding that VMPFC (particularly the medial sector of the OFC) is important for altering simple stimulus-reinforcer associations via extinction (Milad et al. 2005, Phelps et al. 2004, Quirk et al. 2000) or reversal learning (Fellows & Farah 2003) and is preferentially activated by somatovisceral or interoceptive information (Hurliman & Parlo 2005) more generally. The representations encoded in VMPFC may also be useful for decisions based on intuitions and feelings rather than on explicit rules (Goel & Dolan 2003, Shamay-Tsoory et al. 2005), including guesses and familiarity-based discriminations (Elliott et al. 1999, 2000; Schnider et al. 2000; Schnyer et al. 2005).

By virtue of a series of cascading routes, this ventral circuitry projects directly and indirectly (via ventral striatum) to hypothalamus and brainstem areas involved in computing value quickly and efficiently to influence the autonomic, chemical, and behavioral responses that help to establish an affective representation of an object.[8] The resulting perturbations of the organism's somatovisceral state (or internal milieu) translate information about the external world into an internal affective code or representation (Damasio 1994, 1999; Nauta 1971). These representations make up a person's core affective reaction to an object or stimulus, directing the body to prepare for some behavioral response toward that object. A neural representation that entails core affect not only musters attention toward an object (via the brainstem and basal forebrain) (Mesulam 2000, Parvizi & Damasio 2001), but also enhances visual processing of the object (Amaral et al. 2003, Freese & Amaral 2005; for a recent review, see Phelps 2006). This core affective state is also available to be experienced and can contribute directly to the contents of conscious experience. Furthermore, the circuitry is not only responsible for entailing a pleasant or unpleasant feeling, but it also may be involved in feelings of arousal, as it controls the degree of cortical arousal associated with feelings of alertness as well as the degree of physiologic arousal that is, at times, associated with feelings of activity and energy.

Although neural representations of core affect provide the substrates for experience, the contents of conscious experience may not directly reflect the operation of any single neural component involved in core affect computations. Consider, for example, that individuals with amygdala lesions do not report alterations in the experience of emotion (Anderson & Phelps 2002). This might mean that amygdala activity influences experience indirectly by influencing the perception of and memory for emotional events, rather than directly modulating experience per se (Anderson & Phelps 2001). Alternatively, the amygdala's impact on experience may have been missed by the memory-based measures of emotion used in this study, because such measures rely on semantic knowledge (Barrett 1997, Robinson & Clore 2002) that is preserved in those with amygdala lesions (Anderson & Phelps 2000), unless lesions take place during early development (Adolphs et al. 1997). However, many emotion induction experiments do not show increased amygdala activation, and those that do show it find that the increase occurs only early in the emotion induction process, when the stimulus is still being viewed, which suggests that the amygdala activity may not produce core affective

---

[8]The VMPFC, OFC, and both the BL complex and central nucleus of the amygdala project to the ventral striatum (particularly the nucleus accumbens or NAcc shell), which is involved in orchestrating motor control (Grillner et al. 2005) and effortful behavior (Salamone & Correa 2002; Salamone et al. 2006). There is considerable debate about whether the NAcc dopamine system specifically supports rewarding outcomes, with some arguing that dopamine specifically supports reward behaviors (e.g., Schultz 2004, Schultz et al. 2000) or pleasant, high-arousal affective states (Knutson & Bhanjim 2006), and with others arguing against the dopamine-reward hypothesis (see Salamone et al., 2005).

experience but rather may be a neural pre-condition that allows for it.

Furthermore, there are mixed findings regarding the emotion experience of patients with OFC lesions, who report experiencing guilt, shame, and pride, although they do tend to report experiences of embarrassment that are dysregulated from the social context (Beer 2006). Other studies, however, indicate that individuals with OFC lesions report decreased affective reactions involved in empathy (Shamay-Tsoory et al. 2004), decreased regret (Camille et al. 2004), and alterations in experiences of anger and happiness (Berlin et al. 2004); individuals with bilateral OFC lesions report large alterations in emotion experience (Hornak et al. 2003).

The Neurobiology of Emotional Contents Beyond Core Affect

Today, we know little about the contents that make up experiences of emotion beyond the abstract properties described by appraisal dimensions, and we know even less about the specific neural referents for these experienced contents. We do know, however, that humans are equipped both by nature and by culture with the mechanisms for making mental state attributions of the sort likely to be necessary for producing such contents.

Presumably, during a mental representation of emotion, a person makes an attribution about his or her own core affective state. Recent theoretical treatments have argued that mental representations of emotion emerge when core affective feelings are bound to conceptions of the situation and, in so doing, allow an attribution about the cause of one's core affective state (cf. Barrett 2006b, Frijda 2006, Russell 2003). The word "attribution" usually implies that affect has some priority as being real, while perceived causes about affect are not real, or that affect comes first, with attributions of cause coming later, perhaps via a set of rules that people use in an intentional fashion to figure out why they feel some affective state (Schachter & Singer

1962). A mental representation of emotion, however, is better thought of as a state of mind that instantaneously emerges when core affective feelings are experienced as causally linked to the psychological situation as it is perceived by the person. This view is consistent with recent evidence from social psychology indicating that perceptions of behavior do not occur independently from inferences about cause, but rather both processes proceed in parallel (Kunda & Thagard 1996, Lieberman et al. 2002, Reed et al. 1997, Smith & DeCoster 2000) and likely constrain one another, rendering perceptions of physical actions instantly into psychologically meaningful acts.

As illustrated in **Figures 1** and **2**, experiences of emotion activate two cortical regions that play a role in mental state attributions: medial prefrontal cortex (MPFC), including both the dorsomedial prefrontal cortex (DMPFC) aspect and the more dorsal extension of the VMPFC aspect, and the ACC. The consistent activation of these areas during experiments that involve the experience of emotion (but not necessarily its report) support the hypothesis that mental state attributions are involved in establishing a mental representation of emotion.

The functional contributions of the MPFC have yet to be precisely determined, but recent research and theorizing suggest that these brain areas jointly contribute to making mental state attributions (for reviews, see Adolphs 2001, Allman et al. 2001, Blakemore et al. 2004, Gallagher & Frith 2003, Lane & Garfield 2005, Lane & McRae 2004, Ochsner & Gross 2006), such as when a person makes judgments about or infers the psychological (including emotional) states of another person, or monitors, introspects, or makes inferences about his or her own moment-to-moment feelings (for a summary of studies, see Ochsner et al. 2004; also see Goldin et al. 2005; Mitchell et al. 2005b,c; Ochsner et al. 2005). Similar activations are observed when individuals process the affective connotations of words (Beauregard et al. 1997; Cato et al.

2004; Crosson et al. 1999, 2002), or pictures (for review, see Ochsner et al. 2004), or simulate the mental states (e.g., Mitchell et al. 2005a) and empathize with others (Shamay-Tsoory et al. 2003), presumably because these skills require mental state attributions. Several other lesion studies further suggest that damage to these areas changes the experience of both positive and negative affective feelings (e.g., Bechara et al. 1994, 1996; but see Camille et al. 2004, Dunn et al. 2006, Hornak et al. 1996), as well as the experience of emotion (e.g., Hornak et al. 2003, Weniger & Irle 2002). However, the measurement methods adopted in those studies do not allow for strong conclusions regarding the specific roles that various brain structures play in the experience of emotion.

Figure 2 indicates that both the rostral (so-called affective) and dorsal (or cognitive) ACC (Bush et al. 2000) showed a consistent increase in activation associated with mental representations of emotion. The specific functions of the ACC remain a matter of debate (see Allman 2001, Bush et al. 2000), so that its role in the experience of emotion remains speculative, but the ACC may signal the need to represent mental contents in consciousness so as to reduce conflict or seek greater understanding or control over them (Davidson et al. 2002, Lane & McRae 2004).

In addition to the MPFC and the ACC, a third cortical region identified as active in mental representations of emotion is the left inferior frontal cortex, also called ventrolateral prefrontal cortex (VLPFC). Several studies of response inhibition, response selection, and working memory have shown that the VLPFC is activated in the context of retrieving, maintaining, monitoring, and manipulating conceptual knowledge stored elsewhere in the brain (Gabrieli et al. 1998, Martin & Chao 2001, Poldrack et al. 1999, Wagner et al. 2001). VLPFC may play a supporting role to the MPFC, coming into play to retrieve conceptual knowledge about emotion, particularly when selecting an appropriate label for a core affective feeling. This conclusion is consistent with the fact that experiences of emotion consistently produce increased activation in the inferior aspects of BA 45, thought to be important for resolving competition between retrieved representations that are goal-relevant and -irrelevant competitors (Badre et al. 2005).

Finally, **Figure 2** also indicates a fourth cortical region corresponding to posterior cingulate or retrosplenial cortex (BA 31) was active during mental representations of emotion. Although the function of this area remains unclear (Maddock 1999), it may play a role in episodic memory processes supporting the experience of emotion (see, e.g., Mantani et al. 2005). The adjacent precuneus area is associated with self-related mental representations (Cavanna & Trimble 2006).

A PSYCHOLOGICAL FRAMEWORK FOR UNDERSTANDING EMOTION EXPERIENCE

The evidence from both content-based and neurobiological (i.e., neuroanatomical, neuroimaging, and neuropsychological) analyses of emotion experience indicates that a mental representation of emotion can be (at least minimally) described as pleasure or displeasure experienced in conjunction with other mental contents deriving from mental state attributions (e.g., experiencing the psychological situation in a way that is causally linked to affective feeling). These findings are largely consistent with recent psychological treatments of emotion experience that hypothesize the psychological processes by which mental representations of emotion emerge. The central idea is that a mental representation of emotion on a particular occasion is a continuously changing stream of consciousness in which core affect continuously evolves, interacts with, and mutually constrains construals of the psychological situation (see Barrett 2006b, Barrett et al. 2006, Frijda 2006, Russell, 2003).

VLPFC: ventrolateral prefrontal cortex

Continuously through time, the brain is processing and integrating sensory information from the world, somatovisceral information from the body, and prior knowledge about objects and situations to produce an affective state that is bound to a particular situational meaning, as well as a disposition to act in a particular way. As a result, core affective feelings and construals of the psychological situation very likely are perceptually categorized and experienced as a single unified percept, much like color, depth, and shape are experienced together in object perception. Building on this percept, a mental representation of emotion may be an example of what Edelman (1989) calls "the remembered present."

Across this continuously varying landscape, patterns appear that occasionally constitute the conditions for the experience of emotion. In the view described here, an emotion experience is a conceptual structure stored in memory whose conditions include current perceptions, cognitions, actions, and core affect. A specific emotion conceptualization (e.g., a context-specific conceptualization of anger) is generated via a top-down, multimodel simulation that reinstates how these conditions have been experienced in the past, and this conceptual representation interacts with the existing affect-situation percept to produce the emergence of an emotion experience. In this way, a situated conceptualization (Barsalou 1999, 2003; Barsalou et al. 2003) of emotion (i.e., category knowledge about emotion that is situated in knowledge about the social world and is designed for action; Barsalou et al. 2003, Niedenthal et al., 2005) constrains the emerging perceptual categorization (for a discussion, see Barrett 2006b). In the resulting representation, core affect is foregrounded and bound to conceptions of the situation, and in so doing, transforms affect into an intentional state by allowing an attribution about its cause. The resulting experience is an emergent gestalt that corresponds to the colloquial notion of having an emotion.

As a result, when you sit around a table with others and a colleague argues against a proposal that you have just offered, and you experience an unpleasant feeling with blood pounding in your ears, it is possible to say what the percept is (e.g., an instance of anger), to make reasonable inferences about it (e.g., you are angry because someone interfered with your goal), to predict how best to act on it (e.g., you are in a business meeting so you keep your voice measured and you do not scowl), and to communicate the experience of it to others (e.g., "I was so angry at today's meeting"). It is the content of these acts of categorization that make one feeling of anger distinct from another feeling of anger and different from any feeling of fear.

The general idea, then, is that people have affective information about their current relationship to the world, either at a sensory level via homeostatic feedback from the body or via neural representations of prior instances when an object or event predicted some homeostatic change. The affective information is not delivered as a specific interoceptive readout of autonomic activity or anything so precise. Rather, it is a core affective state that gives rise to feelings of pleasure or displeasure (and perhaps activation) that are linked to (but not completely derived from) ongoing automatic evaluations or primary appraisals of the world. The way that people conceptualize their affective state will depend on the knowledge about emotion that they bring to bear when categorizing it. A person might experience his or her core affective state as a particular sort of sadness, anger, or nervousness, depending on the conceptual knowledge that he or she brings to bear in that situation.

This view—that an experience of emotion is a state of mind whose content is at once affective (pleasant or unpleasant) and conceptual (a representation of your relation to the world around you)—is consistent with recent theoretical insights in the neurobiology of consciousness. There is a growing consensus that a conscious experience emerges when a selection of neuronal groups, coding for specific perceptual properties, fire together to form a temporary coalition or assembly of synchronous neural activity (Crick & Koch 2004, Dehaene & Changeux 2004, Edelman & Tononi 2000, Engel & Singer 2001, Llinas et al. 1998). Reverberating, globally co-ordinated ("reentrant") neural activity of sufficient intensity and duration allows different sensorial features such as color, shape, sound, smell, and interoceptive cues, and, as we now suggest, core affect, as well as other cognitive contents like beliefs or memories, to bind together into a single experience (but for a dissenting view, see Dennett 1991, Zeki 2003).[9] When people perceive some object or situation, they have a mental representation of something in the outside world. When core affect is simultaneously foregrounded (for any number of reasons), pleasure or displeasure and perceptions of the world are bound in a meaningful way, yielding a mental representation of emotion. This mental event stands for a person's inference about how psychologically meaningful events in the world are causally linked to his or her core affective feeling. Thus, we suggest that coordinated re-entrant neural activity of sufficient intensity and duration produces a unified conscious content, one type of which is the experience of an emotion.

IMPLICATIONS FOR A SCIENTIFIC AGENDA

Using the framework provided by Searle's (1992, 2000, 2004) biological naturalism, we have argued that a scientific understanding of emotion experience requires rich, context-sensitive descriptions of what is experienced, the causal explanations of how those contents are implemented in the human brain, and an explanatory framework that neither reduces one to the other, nor confounds the two. In the following section, we briefly touch on six important implications of this framework for the scientific study of emotion experience.

---

[9]Disunity can occur in rare cases of disorder where there are problems with feature binding, such as Balint's syndrome, in patients with commissurotomy, or in some cases of schizophrenia.

A Focus on the Heterogeneity of Emotional Life

By viewing experiences of emotion as conceptual acts, researchers can better map the richness and diversity in mental representations of emotion. Variation in conceptualizing an instance of core affect, whether because of language use, context, culture, or individual differences in prior experience, will produce variation in whether emotions are experienced, which emotions are experienced, and how they are experienced. As a result, it will be important to describe what is constant and what varies in the conceptual system for emotion from one person to the next. We presently know very little about the conceptual system that supports the mental representation of emotion, and we know even less about the neural referents for the conceptual system for emotion.

The Functionality of Perceiving Core Affective Feelings as Emotions

An individual's momentary conceptualization of core affect, like all categorization, serves some function (even if maladaptive in a given instant). Categorization shapes core affect into a meaningful experience, allowing inferences about what caused the state, how to deal with the situation, and how to communicate efficiently their experiences of core affect to others. A better understanding of this categorization process will yield important insights into the functional nature of emotion experiences.

There are individual differences in the extent to which people represent emotional content over and above feelings of pleasure and displeasure. Studies have documented that people differ in emotional granularity, or the extent to which they characterize their experiences in discrete emotional versus broadly affective terms (Barrett 1998, 2004; Barrett et al. 2000, 2001; Lane & Schwartz 1987; Lane et al. 1997). These differences cannot be fully accounted for by verbal intelligence or how well people understand the meaning of emotion words. Individuals high in granularity represent mental contents in addition to valence, whereas those low in granularity represent their experiences primarily as feelings of pleasure or displeasure. Low granularity means that different negative (or different positive) emotion words are used interchangeably to describe the same experience (such that the use of multiple words is not necessarily a sign of the complexity of feelings). Conscious states have high informational value when they can be easily distinguished or differentiated from other different states (Edelman & Tononi 2000), so that a granular representation of emotion will allow a person to be more functionally effective, in part because it will differentiate among a large repertoire of possible causes for the experienced state, which potentially reduces uncertainty and provides information about what to do next (Barrett & Gross 2001).

Core Affect is an Intrinsic Aspect of Consciousness

Those who write about consciousness assume that affect is intrinsic to conscious experience (cf. Edelman & Tononi 2000; Searle 1992, 2004). Pleasure and displeasure are not only mental contents that can be consciously experienced, but also are regulatory factors that play a broader role in selecting the contents of consciousness. Neuroanatomical evidence indicates that the circuitry underlying core affect (see **Figure 1**) entrains sensory processing by virtue of strong reciprocal projections to the brainstem and basal forebrain systems; these areas, in turn, have diffuse, unidirectional afferent projections to the rest of cortex and can influence the probability that neurons will fire throughout the entire cortical mantle (Mesulam 2000, Parvizi & Damasio 2001). In this way, core affect can enhance local sensory processing that is stimulus specific, so that a person can effectively and efficiently assess the relevance or value of the stimulus. Thus, areas involved with establishing a core affective state entrain ongoing processing throughout the rest of the cortex, selecting for neuronal assemblies that maximize reward or minimize threat, thereby influencing which contents are experienced in the moment and which are more likely to be stored in long-term memory (Edelman & Tononi 2000).

Attention and the Experience of Emotion

Experiences of emotion are not sequenced, discriminable, conscious events distinct from nonemotion experiences. Neurobiological models of consciousness imply that incoming sensory information (such as that which entails a core affective state) modulates a preexisting conscious field rather than generating it anew (Llinas et al. 1998). This stream of core affect can be a central or a background feature (figure or ground) of consciousness, depending on where attention is applied. When core affect is in the background, it functions as background feelings (Lane & Garfield 2005) or background emotions (Damasio 1999) that color conscious experience in a less direct fashion but presumably have the potential to influence behavior implicitly (Berridge & Winkielman 2003, Winkielman et al. 2005). Backgrounded core affect is experienced as a property of the external world rather than as the person's reaction to it. We experience some people as nice and others as mean, some foods as delicious but others as distasteful, some pictures as pleasing and others as negative. It may be under these circumstances that core affect directly translates into a behavioral response. When core affect is foregrounded, it can be experienced directly as pleasant or unpleasant content and can serve as information for making explicit judgments and decisions (Clore et al. 2005, Schwarz & Clore 1983), or core affective feelings can be attributed to some situational cause, thereby forming the basis of an emotion experience (cf. Barrett 2006b, Russell 2003; but see Frijda 2005, Lambie & Marcel 2002, who characterize backgrounded affect as emotion experience). Core affective feelings will be foregrounded, either because of their intensity, because of a goal to introspect, or because the situation cues attention. Clearly, a key question for future research is when and how foregrounding happens to produce the experience of "having an emotion."

Common Substrates for Psychopathology

It seems likely at this point that many psychological disorders share a common or "transdiagnostic" (Harvey et al. 2004) disturbance in core affective processing (Barlow 2002) that involves vigilance to threat (Harvey et al. 2004, Quigley & Barrett 1999), is on a continuum with normal personality variability (Weinstock & Whisman 2006), and is linked to the short allele of a serotonin transporter (5-HTT) gene which produces an affective vulnerability to environmental stress (for a review, see Hariri & Holmes 2006). The brain structures and neurotransmitters (such as serotonin and dopamine) associated with the ventral system for core affect are implicated in a range of psychopathologies characterized by affective disturbances, including depression (e.g., Anand et al. 2005, Drevets 2000, Drevets et al. 1997, Hariri et al. 2005, Lacerda et al. 2004, Mayberg 1997, Pezawas et al. 2005), schizophrenia (e.g., Fahim et al. 2005a,b), obsessive-compulsive disorder (e.g., Nakao et al. 2005, Valente et al. 2005), posttraumatic stress disorder (e.g., Bryant et al. 2005; Rauch et al. 2000; Shin et al. 2004, 2005), social anxiety and generalized anxiety disorder (for a review see Stein et al. 2002), and panic disorder (e.g., Kent et al. 2005). Such a transdisorder affective syndrome, if it exists, might also predispose people to health-related problems as well (Gallo & Matthews 2003, Pressman & Cohen 2005).

Furthermore, which emotion is experienced, and how it is experienced, is a matter of intentional focus and interpretation, so that

MORE ON THE FOREGROUNDING OF CORE AFFECT

The mechanisms by which affect is foregrounded or backgrounded remain to be specified, but it is generally accepted that an "attentional matrix" (Mesulam 2000) within the brain foregrounds particular contents of consciousness (whether core affect and/or beliefs about core affect) by modulating the intensity of neural firing in coalitions of neurons. This attentional matrix includes not only the core affect–driven bottom-up form of attention (supported by the brainstem and basal forebrain; Edelman & Tononi 2000, Parvizi & Damasio 2001), but also a top-down form of attention (supported by dorsolateral prefrontal, anterior cingulate, and parietal cortices) that is entrained by sensory stimulation of sufficient intensity or driven by an individual's processing goals (Crick & Koch 2004, Dehaene & Changeux 2004, Maia & Cleeremans 2005, Naghavi & Nyberg 2005). Whatever the mix of attentional factors, each person has one seamless flow of experience that is continually changing and can be more or less infused with some sort of affective content, depending on the focus of attention.

the conceptualization process may also act as a transdisorder vulnerability to mood-related disorders. Conceptualizing core affect might be thought of as a skill, in that some people are better than are others at tailoring conceptual knowledge to meet the needs of socially situated action (Barrett 2006b). This skill for wielding conceptual knowledge about emotion might be considered a core aspect of emotional intelligence (Barrett & Gross 2001) and is a central feature of emotion-focused psychotherapeutic treatments (Greenberg 1993, Moses & Barlow 2006).

Cognition and the Experience of Emotion

Finally, the distinction between cognitive activity and emotion experience is probably better conceptualized as more of a gradient rather than two independent systems that can interact with one another. Although scientists are very used to thinking about cognitive events (such as thoughts, memories, and beliefs) as separate from emotional events, this distinction is probably phenomenological rather than causal and does not seem to be respected by the brain. Brain structures at the heart of the neural circuitry for emotion (e.g., the amygdala) impact cognitive processing from early attention allocation (Holland & Gallagher 1999) through perceptual processing to memory (for a recent review, see Phelps 2006). Similarly, brain structures involved in the neural circuitry for cognition, such as DMPFC and VLPFC, have an intrinsic role in the experience of emotion (see **Figure 2**). Decision-making processes that are traditionally thought of in cognitive terms, such as moral reasoning, seem to have core affect as their basis (Greene et al. 2004, Haidt 2001), and unrelated experiences of emotion can color such diverse outcomes as economic decisions (Loewenstein & Lerner 2003) and stereotyping (e.g., Bodenhausen & Moreno 2000, DeSteno et al. 2004). Consider the distinction between feeling and thinking, compared with other phenomenological boundaries respected by the brain, such as visual and auditory processing. No one would ever mistake seeing for hearing (although one sensory representation might trigger another), but the same cannot be said for feeling and thinking.

SUMMARY

In much scientific writing about emotion, everyday words for emotion, such "anger," "sadness," and "fear," are used as technical terms to refer to both conscious events and to causal (i.e., behavioral, cognitive, or neurological) events, without a detailed exposition about how the two are related, because one is literally redefined in terms of the other. Although this approach has been expedient, it has left emotion experiences, a fundamental centerpiece in human existence, largely underspecified from a scientific standpoint.

In this chapter, we began by locating the study of emotion experience in a philosophical approach to understanding consciousness, because questions about emotion experience are essentially questions about consciousness and discussions about the nature of emotion experience are always grounded in some philosophical perspective, even if implicitly. Using Searle's (1992, 2000, 2004) biological naturalism, we argued that building a scientific model of emotion experience requires both a descriptive psychology of mental contents and a detailed neurobiology that entails them. We believe that words refer to mental states but not to the mechanisms that generated those states (Barrett 2006b, Russell 2003, Sabini & Silver 2005). Thus, we have argued that emotion words are not the names of things—rather they demarcate mental representations that are constituted as feelings of pleasure or displeasure and socially situated conceptualizations of emotion.

We then outlined what is currently known regarding (a) psychological descriptions of the contents of mental representations of emotion and (b) the neural reference space (based on neuroanatomical, neuroimaging, and, to some degree, neuropsychological findings) that is correlated with those contents. In addition, we framed these findings within an emerging psychological model for the experience of emotion that describes mental representations of emotion as emergent phenomena, constructed from more basic affective and conceptual representations, and we discussed how the binding of core affect and conceptual knowledge might arise naturally from the neurobiological processes that allow neural activity to give rise to conscious content. Taken together, this framework sets a scientific agenda that affords several advantages for a psychological understanding of emotion experiences as real, potent, and important aspects of conscious life, as well as for understanding the role of emotion experience in the economy of the mind and behavior.

SUMMARY POINTS

1. A scientific understanding of emotion experience requires a rich, context-sensitive description of what is experienced, a causal explanation of how experienced content is constituted by the human brain, and an explanatory framework that neither reduces one to the other nor confounds the two.

2. At its core, the experience of emotion can be described a contentful state of pleasure or displeasure. Some degree of arousal may also be experienced. Some situation with a specific relational meaning is experienced simultaneously with and as having caused these affective feelings.

3. At present, it is not possible to explain how neural activity instantiates specific emotional contents (or any conscious content, for that matter). It is possible, however, to offer a preliminary sketch of a neural reference space for mental representations of emotion.

4. The available evidence on content and neurobiological accounting of emotion experience can be integrated into a broad framework that describes, in psychological terms, how the experience of emotion emerges from more basic processes. Core affect and construals of the psychological situation are perceptually categorized and experienced as a single unified percept. Conceptual knowledge about emotion constrains perceptual processing to shape the emergence of an experience of emotion.

FUTURE ISSUES

1. Regarding core affect: Is core affect a natural kind category? Are other contents, such as arousal, fundamental properties of core affect? Is there only one kind of pleasure (or displeasure) or many phenomenologically distinct feelings? What are processes by which and conditions for when affect is backgrounded and experienced as a property of the world or foregrounded and experienced as a property of the self?

2. Regarding other aspects of the psychological content of emotion experience: Beyond the abstract properties described by appraisal dimensions, what is the additional content that constitutes mental representations of emotion? Can any cognitive content play a role in shaping an emotion experience?

3. Regarding the neurobiological bases of emotion: Is the neural reference space misspecified, or incomplete? How do neurobiological processes give rise to the contents of emotion experience?

4. Regarding the mental representation of emotion: When and why is core affect conceptualized as emotion? What is the structure and content of the conceptual system that supports the mental representation of emotion and the neural referents that support this conceptual system? What are the individual differences in the content, structure, and function of the conceptual system? Do they relate to observed differences in emotional granularity, and what is their functional consequence? How do affect and conceptual knowledge about emotion constrain one another in real-time processing?

ACKNOWLEDGMENTS

This work was supported by an NSF grant (BCS 0527440) and an NIMH Independent Scientist Research Award (K02 MH001981) to Lisa Feldman Barrett and NIH grants (R01 MH58147 and R01 MH66957) to James Gross. The authors wish to thank William Irwin for preparing **Figure 1**, Tor Wager for his permission to report the preliminary meta-analytic findings presented in **Figure 2**, Larry Barsalou for contributing some of the wording in the description of situated conceptualizations of emotion, as well as Gerald Clore, Chris Wright, Nico Frijda, Tony Marcel, Jeanne Tsai, Seth Duncan, Kristen Lindquist, Eliza Bliss-Moreau, and Jennifer Mize for their comments on earlier drafts of this paper.

LITERATURE CITED

Adolphs R. 2001. The neurobiology of social cognition. *Curr. Opin. Neurobiol.* 11:231–39

Adolphs R, Lee GP, Tranel D, Damasio AR. 1997. Bilateral damage to the human amygdala early in life impairs knowledge of emotional arousal. *Soc. Neurosci. Abstr.* 23:1582

Allman JM, Hakeem A, Erwin JM, Nimchinsky E, Hoff P. 2001. The anterior cingulate cortex: the evolution of an interface between emotion and cognition. *Ann. NY Acad. Sci.* 935:107–17

Amaral DG, Behniea H, Kelly JL. 2003. Topographical organization of projections from the amygdala to the visual cortex in the Macaque monkey. *Neuroscience* 118:1099–120

Anand A, Li Y, Wang Y, Wu J, Gao S, et al. 2005. Activity and connectivity of brain mood regulating circuit in depression: a functional magnetic resonance study. *Biol. Psychiatry* 57:1079–88

Anderson AK, Phelps EA. 2000. Expression without recognition: contributions of the human amygdala to emotional communication. *Psychol. Sci.* 11:106–11

Anderson AK, Phelps EA. 2001. Lesions of the human amygdala impair enhanced perception of emotionally salient events. *Nature* 411:305–9

Anderson AK, Phelps EA. 2002. Is the human amygdala critical for the subjective experience of emotion? Evidence of intact dispositional affect in patients with amygdala lesions. *J. Cogn. Neurosci.* 14:709–20

Arnold M. 1960. *Emotion and Personality*. New York: Columbia Univ. Press

Bachorowski J. 1999. Vocal expression and perception of emotion. *Curr. Dir. Psychol. Sci.* 8:53–56

Badre D, Poldrack RA, Pare-Blagoev EJ, Insler RZ, Wagner AD. 2005. Dissociable controlled retrieval and generalized selection mechanisms in ventrolateral prefrontal cortex. *Neuron* 47:907–18

Bagozzi RP, Wong KS, Youjae Y. 1999. The role of culture and gender in the relationship between positive and negative affect. *Cogn. Emot.* 13:641–72

Barbas H, Saha S, Rempel-Clower N, Ghashghaei T. 2003. Serial pathways from primate prefrontal cortex to autonomic areas may influence emotional expression. *BMC Neurosci.* 4:25

Barlow DH. 2002. *Anxiety and Its Disorders: The Nature and Treatment of Anxiety and Panic*. New York: Guilford

Barrett LF. 1996. Hedonic tone, perceived arousal, and item desirability: three components of affective experience. *Cogn. Emot.* 10:47–68

Barrett LF. 1997. The relationships among momentary emotion experiences, personality descriptions, and retrospective ratings of emotion. *Personal. Soc. Psychol. Bull.* 23:1100–10

Barrett LF. 1998. Discrete emotions or dimensions? The role of valence focus and arousal focus. *Cogn. Emot.* 12:579–99

Barrett LF. 2004. Feelings or words? Understanding the content in self-report ratings of experienced emotion. *J. Personal. Soc. Psychol.* 87:266–81

Barrett LF. 2006a. Emotions as natural kinds? *Perspect. Psychol. Sci.* 1:28–58

Barrett LF. 2006b. Solving the emotion paradox: categorization and the experience of emotion. *Personal. Soc. Psychol. Rev.* 10:20–46

Barrett LF. 2006c. Valence as a basic building block of emotional life. *J. Res. Personal.* 40:35–55

Barrett LF, Fossum T. 2001. Mental representations of affect knowledge. *Cogn. Emot.* 15:333–63

Barrett LF, Gross JJ. 2001. Emotional intelligence: a process model of emotion representation and regulation. In *Emotions: Current Issues and Future Directions*, ed. TJ Mayne, GA Bonanno, pp. 286–310. New York: Guilford

Barrett LF, Gross J, Christensen TC, Benvenuto M. 2001. Knowing what you're feeling and knowing what to do about it: mapping the relation between emotion differentiation and emotion regulation. *Cogn. Emot.* 15:713–24

Barrett LF, Lane RD, Sechrest L, Schwartz GE. 2000. Sex differences in emotional awareness. *Personal. Soc. Psychol. Bull.* 26:1027–35

Barrett LF, Niedenthal PM, Winkielman P, eds. 2005. *Emotion and Consciousness*. New York: Guilford

Barrett LF, Quigley K, Bliss-Moreau E, Aronson KR. 2004. Arousal focus and interoceptive sensitivity. *J. Personal. Soc. Psychol.* 87:684–97

Barrett LF, Russell JA. 1998. Independence and bipolarity in the structure of current affect. *J. Personal. Soc. Psychol.* 74:967–84

Barrett LF, Russell JA. 1999. The structure of current affect: controversies and emerging consensus. *Curr. Dir. Psychol. Sci.* 8:10–14

Barrett LF, Wager T. 2006. The structure of emotion: evidence from the neuroimaging of emotion. *Curr. Dir. Psychol. Sci.* 15:79–85

Barsalou LW. 1999. Perceptual symbol systems. *Behav. Brain Sci.* 22:577–660

Barsalou LW. 2003. Situated simulation in the human conceptual system. *Lang. Cogn. Process. Spec. Issue Concept. Represent.* 18:513–62

Barsalou LW, Niedenthal PM, Barbey A, Ruppert J. 2003. Social embodiment. In *The Psychology of Learning and Motivation*, ed. B Ross, pp. 43–92. San Diego: Academic

Beauregard M, Chertkow H, Bub D, Murtha S, Dixon R, Evans A. 1997. The neural substrate for concrete, abstract, and emotional word lexica: a positron emission tomography study. *J. Cogn. Neurosci.* 9:441–61

Bechara A, Damasio AR, Damasio H, Anderson SW. 1994. Insensitivity to future consequences following damage to human prefrontal cortex. *Cognition* 50:7–15

Bechara A, Damasio H, Damasio AR. 2000. Emotion, decision making and the orbitofrontal cortex. *Cereb. Cortex* 10:295–307

Bechara A, Tranel D, Damasio H, Damasio A. 1996. Failure to respond autonomically to anticipated future outcomes following damage to prefrontal cortex. *Cereb. Cortex* 6:215–25

Beer JS. 2006. The importance of emotion-social cognition interactions for social functioning: insights from orbitofrontal cortex. In *Fundamentals of Social Neuroscience*, ed. EH Jones, P Winkielman. Cambridge, MA: MIT Press. In press

Berlin HA, Rolls ET, Kischka U. 2004. Impulsivity, time perception, emotion and reinforcement sensitivity in patients with orbitofrontal cortex lesions. *Brain* 127:1108–26

Berridge KC, Winkielman P. 2003. What is an unconscious emotion? (The case for unconscious "liking.") *Cogn. Emot.* 17:181–11

Blakemore SJ, Winston J, Frith U. 2004. Social cognitive neuroscience: Where are we heading? *Trends Cogn. Sci.* 8:216–22

Bodenhausen GV, Moreno KN. 2000. How do I feel about them: the role of affective reactions in intergroup perception. In *The Message Within: Subjective Experience in Social Cognition and Behavior*, ed. H Bless, JP Forgas, pp. 283–303. Philadelphia, PA: Psychol. Press

Bouton ME. 2005. Behavior systems and the contextual control of anxiety, fear, and panic. See Barrett et al. 2005, pp. 205–27

Boyle GJ. 1986. Higher-order factors in the Differential Emotions Scale (DES-III). *Personal. Individ. Differ.* 7:305–10

Bradley MM, Lang PJ. 2000. Measuring emotion: behavior, feeling, and physiology. In *Cognitive Neuroscience of Emotion*, ed. RD Lane, L Nadel, GL Ahern, JJB Allen, AW Kaszniak, SZ Rapcsak, GE Schwartz, pp. 242–76. New York: Oxford Univ. Press

Bradley MM, Lang PJ. 1994. Measuring emotion: the self-assessment manikin and the semantic differential. *J. Behav. Therapy Exper. Psychiatry* 22:49–59

Bryant RA, Felmingham KL, Kemp AH, Barton M, Peduto AS, et al. 2005. Neural networks of information processing in posttraumatic stress disorder: a functional magnetic resonance imaging study. *Biol. Psychiatry* 52:111–18

Buck R. 1999. The biological affects: a typology. *Psychol. Rev.* 106:301–36

Bush G, Luu P, Posner MI. 2000. Cognitive and emotional influences in anterior cingulate cortex. *Trends Cogn. Sci.* 4:215–22

Cacioppo JT, Berntson GG, Klein DJ, Poehlmann KM. 1997. The psychophysiology of emotion across the lifespan. *Annu. Rev. Gerontol. Geriatr.* 17:27–74

Cacioppo JT, Berntson GG, Larsen JT, Poehlmann KM, Ito TA. 2000. The psychophysiology of emotion. In *The Handbook of Emotion*, ed. M Lewis, M Haviland-Jones, pp. 173–91. New York: Guilford

Cacioppo JT, Gardner WL. 1999. Emotion. *Annu. Rev. Psychol.* 50:191–214

Camille N, Coricelli G, Sallet J, Pradat-Diehl P, Duhamel JR, Sirigu A. 2004. The involvement of the orbitofrontal cortex in the experience of regret. *Science* 304:1167–70

Carmichael ST, Price JL. 1996. Connectional networks within the orbital and medial prefrontal cortex of macaque monkeys. *J. Comp. Neurol.* 371:179–207

Carroll JM, Yik MSM, Russell JA, Barrett LF. 1999. On the psychometric principles of affect. *Rev. Gen. Psychol.* 3:14–22

Cato MA, Crosson B, Gokcay D, Soltysik D, Wierenga C, et al. 2004. Processing words with emotional connotation: an FMRI study of time course and laterality in rostral frontal and retrosplenial cortices. *J. Cogn. Neurosci.* 16:167–77

Cavanna AE, Trimble MR. 2006. The precuneus: a review of its functional anatomy and behavioral correlates. *Brain* 129:564–83

Charles ST. 2005. Viewing injustice: greater emotional heterogeneity with age. *Psychol. Aging* 20:159–64

Clore GL, Ortony A. 2000. Cognition in emotion: always, sometimes, or never? In *Cognitive Neuroscience of Emotion*, ed. RD Lane, L Nadel, pp. 24–61. London: London Univ. Press

Clore GL, Storbeck J, Robinson MD, Centerbar DB. 2005. Seven sins in the study of unconscious affect. See Barrett et al. 2005, pp. 384–408

Craig AD. 2002. How do you feel? Interoception: the sense of the physiological condition of the body. *Nat. Neurosci.* 3:655–66

Craig AD. 2003. Interoception: the sense of the physiological condition of the body. *Curr. Opin. Neurobiol.* 13:500–5

Crick FC, Koch C. 2004. A framework for consciousness. In *The Cognitive Neurosciences*, ed. MS Gazzaniga, pp. 1133–44. Cambridge, MA: MIT Press

Crosson B, Cato MA, Sadek JR, Gokcay D, Bauer RM, et al. 2002. Semantic monitoring of words with emotional connotation during fMRI: contribution of anterior left frontal cortex. *J. Int. Neuropsychol. Soc.* 8:607–22

Crosson B, Radonovich K, Sadek JR, Gokcay D, Bauer RM, et al. 1999. Left-hemisphere processing of emotional connotation during word generation. *Neuroreport* 10:2449–55

Damasio AR. 1994. *Descartes' Error: Emotion, Reason, and the Human Brain*. New York: Grossett/Putnam

Damasio AR. 1999. *The Feeling of What Happens: Body and Emotion in the Making of Consciousness*. New York: Harcourt Brace

Davidson RJ, Pizzagalli D, Nitschke JB, Putnam K. 2002. Depression: perspectives from affective neuroscience. *Annu. Rev. Psychol.* 53:545–74

DeArmond SJ, Fusco MM, Dewey MM. 1989. Structure of the human brain: a photographic atlas. New York: Oxford Univ. Press. 3rd ed.

Dehaene S, Changeux JP. 2004. Neural mechanisms for access to consciousness. In *The Cognitive Neurosciences*, ed. MS Gazzaniga, pp. 1145–58. Cambridge, MA: MIT Press

Dennett DC. 1991. *Consciousness Explained*. Boston: Little, Brown

DeSteno D, Dasgupta N, Bartlett MY, Cajdric A. 2004. Prejudice from thin air: the effect of emotion on automatic intergroup attitudes. *Psychol. Sci.* 15:319–24

Drevets WC. 2000. Neuroimaging studies of mood disorders. *Biol. Psychiatry* 48:813–29

Drevets WC, Gadde K, Krishman R. 1997. Neuroimaging studies of depression. In *Neurobiology of Mental Illness*, ed. DS Charney, EJ Nestler, BJ Bunney, pp. 461–90. New York: Oxford Univ. Press

Dunkley P, Wise RG, Aziz Q, Painter D, Brooks J, et al. 2005. Cortical processing of visceral and somatic stimulation: differentiating pain intensity from unpleasantness. *Neuroscience* 133:533–42

Dunn BD, Dalgleish T, Lawrence AD. 2006. The somatic marker hypothesis: a critical evaluation. *Neurosci. Biobehav. Rev.* 30:239–71

Edelman GM. 1989. *The Remembered Present*. New York: Basic

Edelman GM, Tononi G. 2000. *A Universe of Consciousness*. New York: Basic

Ekman P. 1972. Universals and cultural differences in facial expressions of emotion. 1971. In *Nebraska Symposium on Motivation*, ed. JR Cole, pp. 207–83. Lincoln: Univ. Nebraska Press

Ekman P. 1992. Are there basic emotions? *Psychol. Rev.* 99:550–53

Elliott R, Dolan RJ, Frith CD. 2000. Dissociable functions in the medial and lateral orbitofrontal cortex: evidence from human neuroimaging studies. *Cereb. Cortex* 10:308–17

Elliott R, Rees G, Dolan RJ. 1999. Ventromedial prefrontal cortex mediates guessing. *Neuropsychologia* 37:403–11

Ellsworth PC, Scherer KR. 2003. Appraisal processes in emotion. In *Handbook of the Affective Sciences*, ed. H Goldsmith, RJ Davidson, KR Scherer, pp. 572–95. New York: Oxford Univ. Press

Emde RN, Gaensbauer TJ, Harmon RJ. 1976. Emotional expression in infancy: a biobehavioral study. *Psychol. Issues* 10:1–200

Engel AK, Singer W. 2001. Temporal binding and the neural correlates of sensory awareness. *Trends Cogn. Sci.* 5:16–25

Fahim C, Stip E, Mancini-Marïe A, Gendron A, Mensour B, Beauregard M. 2005a. Differential hemodynamic brain activity in schizophrenia patients with blunted affect during quetiapine treatment. *J. Clin. Psychopharmacol.* 25:367–71

Fahim C, Stip E, Mancini-Marïe A, Mensour B, Boulay LJ, et al. 2005b. Brain activity during emotionally negative pictures in schizophrenia with and without flat affect: an fMRI study. *Psychiatr. Res. Neuroimag.* 140:1–15

Feldman LA. 1993. Distinguishing depression from anxiety in self-report: evidence from confirmatory factor analysis on nonclinical and clinical samples. *J. Consult. Clin. Psychol.* 69:153–66

Feldman LA. 1995a. Variations in the circumplex structure of mood. *Personal. Soc. Psychol. Bull.* 21:806–16

Feldman LA. 1995b. Valence focus and arousal focus: individual differences in the structure of affective experience. *J. Personal. Soc. Psychol.* 69:153–66

Fellows LK, Farah MJ. 2003. Ventromedial frontal cortex mediates affective shifting in humans: evidence from a reversal learning paradigm. *Brain* 126:1830–37

Fitness J, Fletcher GJO. 1993. Love, hate, anger, and jealousy in close relationships: a prototype and cognitive appraisal analysis. *J. Personal. Soc. Psychol.* 65:942–58

Freese JL, Amaral DG. 2005. The organization of projections from the amygdala to visual cortical areas TE and V1 in the macaque monkey. *J. Comp. Neurol.* 486:295–317

Frijda NH. 1986. *The Emotions.* Cambridge: Cambridge Univ. Press

Frijda NH. 2005. Emotion experience. *Cogn. Emot.* 19:473–97

Frijda NH. 2006. *The Laws of Emotion.* Mahwah, NJ: Erlbaum

Frijda NH, Kuipers P, ter Schure E. 1989. Relations among emotion, appraisal, and emotional action readiness. *J. Personal. Soc. Psychol.* 57:212–28

Frijda NH, Markam S, Sato K, Wiers R. 1995. Emotion and emotion words. In *Everyday Conceptions of Emotion,* ed. JA Russell, J-M Fernandez-Dols, ASR Manstead, JC Wellencamp, pp. 121–43. Boston: Kluwer Acad.

Frith C, Perry R, Lurner E. 1999. The neural correlates of conscious experience: an experimental framework. *Trends Cogn. Sci.* 3:105–14

Gabrieli JD, Poldrack RA, Desmond JE. 1998. The role of left prefrontal cortex in language and memory. *Proc. Natl. Acad. Sci. USA* 95:906–13

Gallagher HL, Frith CD. 2003. Functional imaging of "theory of mind." *Trends Cogn. Sci.* 7:77–83

Gallo LC, Matthews KA. 2003. Understanding the association between socioeconomic status and physical health: Do negative emotions play a role? *Psychol. Bull.* 129:10–51

Ghashghaei HT, Barbas H. 2002. Pathways for emotion: interactions of prefrontal and anterior temporal pathways in the amygdala of the rhesus monkey. *Neuroscience* 115:1261–79

Goel V, Dolan RJ. 2003. Reciprocal neural response within lateral and ventral medial prefrontal cortex during hot and cold reasoning. *Neuroimage* 20:2314–21

Goldin PR, Hutcherson CAC, Ochsner KN, Glover GH, Gabrieli JDE, Gross JJ. 2005. The neural bases of amusement and sadness: a comparison of block contrast and subject-specific emotion intensity regression approaches. *Neuroimage* 27:26–39

Gray JA. 2004. *Consciousness.* New York: Oxford Univ. Press

Greenberg LS. 1993. Emotion and change processes in psychotherapy. In *Handbook of Emotion,* ed. M Lewis, JM Haviland, pp. 499–508. New York: Guilford

Greene JD, Nystrom LE, Engell AD, Darley JM, Cohen JD. 2004. The neural bases of cognitive conflict and control of moral judgment. *Neuron* 44:389–400

Grillner S, Hellgren J, Menard A, Saitoh K, Wilstrom MA. 2005. Mechanisms for selection of basic motor programs—roles for the striatum and pallidum. *Trends Neurosci.* 28:364–70

Haidt J. 2001. The emotional dog and its rational tail: a social intuitionist approach to moral judgment. *Psychol. Rev.* 108:814–34

Hariri AR, Drabant EM, Munoz KE, Kolachana BS, Mattay VS, et al. 2005. A susceptibility gene for affective disorders and the response of the human amygdala. *Arch. Gen. Psychiatry* 62:146–52

Hariri AR, Holmes A. 2006. Genetics of emotional regulation: the role of the serotonin transporter in neural function. *Trends Cogn. Sci.* In press

Harvey AG, Watkins E, Mansell W, Shafran R. 2004. *Cognitive Behavioural Processes Across Psychological Disorders: A Transdiagnostic Approach to Research and Treatment*. New York: Oxford Univ. Press

Holland PC, Gallagher M. 1999. Amygdala circuitry in attentional and representational processes. *Trends Cogn. Sci.* 3:65–73

Holland PC, Gallagher M. 2004. Amygdala-frontal interactions and reward expectancy. *Curr. Opin. Neurobiol.* 14:148–55

Hornak J, Bramam J, Rolls ET, Morris RG, O'Dohery J, et al. 2003. Changes in emotion after circumscribed surgical lesions of the orbitofrontal and cingulate cortices. *Brain* 126:1691–712

Hornak J, Rolls ET, Wade D. 1996. Face and voice expression identification in patients with emotional and behavioural changes following ventral frontal lobe damage. *Neuropsychologia* 34:247–61

Hurliman E, Nagode JC, Pardo JV. 2005. Double dissociation of exteroceptive and interoceptive feedback systems in the orbital and ventromedial prefrontal cortex of humans. *J. Neurosci.* 25:4641–48

Izard CE. 1977. *Human Emotions*. New York: Plenum

Izard CE. 1993. Four systems for emotion activation: cognitive and noncognitive processes. *Psychol. Rev.* 100:68–90

James W. 1890. *The Principles of Psychology*. New York: Holt

Kent JM, Coplan JD, Mawlawi O, Martinez JM, Browne ST, et al. 2005. Prediction of panic response to a respiratory stimulant by reduced orbitofrontal cerebral blood flow in panic disorder. *Am. J. Psychiatry* 162:1379–81

Kitayama S, Markus HR, Kurokawa M. 2000. Culture, emotion and well-being: good feelings in Japan and the United States. *Cogn. Emot.* 14:93–124

Knutson B, Bhanji J. 2006. Neural substrates for emotional traits? In *Biology of Personality Individual Difference*, ed. T Canli, pp. 116–32. New York: Guilford

Koski L, Paus T. 2000. Functional connectivity of the anterior cingulate cortex within the human frontal lobe: a brain-mapping meta-analysis. *Exp. Brain Res.* 133:55–65

Kringelbach ML. 2005. The human orbitofrontal cortex: linking reward to hedonic experience. *Nat. Neurosci.* 6:691–702

Kringelbach ML, Rolls ET. 2004. The functional neuroanatomy of the human orbitofrontal cortex: evidence from neuroimaging and neuropsychology. *Prog. Neurobiol.* 72:341–72

Kunda Z, Thagard P. 1996. Forming impressions from stereotypes, traits, and behaviors: a parallel-constraint-satisfaction theory. *Psychol. Rev.* 103:284–308

Lacerda ALT, Keshavan MS, Hardan AY, Yorbik O, Brambilla P, et al. 2004. Anatomic evaluation of the orbitofrontal cortex in major depressive disorder. *Biol. Psychiatry* 55:353–58

Lambie JA, Marcel AJ. 2002. Consciousness and the varieties of emotion experience: a theoretical framework. *Psychol. Rev.* 109:219–59

Lane RD, Ahern GL, Schwartz GE, Kaszniak AW. 1997. Is alexithymia the emotional equivalent of blindsight? *Biol. Psychiatry* 42:834–44

Lane RD, Garfield DAS. 2005. Becoming aware of feelings: integration of cognitive-developmental, neuroscientific, and psychoanalytic perspectives. *Neuropsychoanalysis* 7:1–66

Lane RD, McRae K. 2004. Neural substrates of conscious emotional experience: a cognitive-neuroscientific perspective. In *Consciousness, Emotional Self-Regulation and the Brain*, ed. M Beauregard, pp. 87–122. Amsterdam: Benjamins

Lane RD, Schwartz GE. 1987. Levels of emotional awareness: a cognitive-developmental theory and its application to psychopathology. *Am. J. Psychiatry* 144:133–43

Lang P, Greenwald M, Bradley M, Hamm A. 1993. Looking at pictures: affective, facial, visceral, and behavioral reactions. *Psychophysiology* 30:261–73

Lazarus RS. 1966. *Psychological Stress and the Coping Process*. New York: McGraw-Hill

Lazarus RS. 1991. *Emotion and Adaptation*. New York: Oxford Univ. Press

Lazarus RS, Folkman S. 1984. *Stress, Appraisal and Coping*. New York: Springer

LeDoux JE. 1996. *The Emotional Brain: The Mysterious Underpinnings of Emotional Life*. New York: Simon & Schuster

LeDoux JE. 2000. Emotion circuits in the brain. *Annu. Rev. Neurosci.* 23:155–84

Leu J, Mesquita B, Ellsworth PC, Yong ZZ, Huijian Y, et al. 2006. Cultural models of emotion regulation in East and West: "dialectical" emotions vs. the pursuit of pleasantness. Manuscr. under review

Leventhal H, Scherer K. 1987. The relationship of emotion to cognition: a functional approach to a semantic controversy. *Cogn. Emot.* 1:3–28

Lieberman MD, Gaunt R, Gilbert DT, Trope Y. 2002. Reflexion and reflection: a social cognitive neuroscience approach to attributional inference. In *Advances in Experimental Social Psychology, Volume 34*, ed. MP Zanna, pp. 199–49. San Diego: Academic

Llinas R, Ribary U, Contreras D, Pedroarena C. 1998. The neuronal basis for consciousness. *Philos. Trans. R. Soc. Lond. B Biol. Sci.* 353:1841–49

Loewenstein G, Lerner JS. 2003. The role of affect in decision making. In *Handbook of Affective Science*, ed. H Goldsmith, R Davidson, K Scherer, pp. 619–42. New York: Oxford Univ. Press

Maddock RJ. 1999. The retrosplenial cortex and emotion: new insights from functional neuroimaging of the human brain. *Trends Neurosci.* 22:310–16

Maia TV, Cleeremans A. 2005. Consciousness: converging insights from connectionist modeling and neuroscience. *Trends Cogn. Sci.* 9:397–404

Mantani T, Okamoto Y, Shirao N, Okada G, Yamawaki S. 2005. Reduced activation of posterior cingulate cortex during imagery in subjects with high degrees of alexithymia: a functional magnetic resonance imaging study. *Biol. Psychiatry* 57:982–90

Markus HR, Kitayama S. 1991. Culture and the self: implications for cognition, emotion, and motivation. *Psychol. Rev.* 98:224–53

Markus HR, Kitayama S. 1994. The cultural construction of self and emotion: implications for social behavior. In *Emotion and Culture: Empirical Studies of Mutual Influence*, ed. S Kitayama, HR Markus, pp. 89–130. Washington, DC: Am. Psychol. Assoc.

Martin A, Chao LL. 2001. Semantic memory and the brain: structure and processes. *Curr. Opin. Neurobiol.* 11:194–201

Mauro R, Sato K, Tucker J. 1992. The role of appraisal in human emotions: a cross-cultural study. *J. Personal. Soc. Psychol.* 62:301–17

Mayberg HS. 1997. Limbic-cortical dysregulation: a proposed model of depression. *J. Neuropsychiatry Clin. Neurosci.* 9:471–81

Mayer JD, Gaschke YN. 1988. The experience and meta-experience of mood. *J. Personal. Soc. Psychol.* 55:102–11

McDonald AJ. 1998. Cortical pathways to the mammalian amygdala. *Prog. Neurobiol.* 55:257–332

Mesquita B. 2001. Emotions in collectivist and individualist contexts. *J. Personal. Soc. Psychol.* 80(1):68–74

Mesquita B. 2003. Emotions as dynamic cultural phenomena. In *Handbook of the Affective Sciences*, ed. H Goldsmith, R Davidson, K Scherer, pp. 871–90. New York: Oxford

Mesquita B, Ellsworth PC. 2001. The role of culture in appraisal. In *Appraisal Processes in Emotion: Theory, Methods, Research*, ed. KR Sherer, SA Schorr, pp. 233–48. New York: Oxford Univ. Press

Mesquita B, Frijda NH. 1992. Cultural variations in emotions: a review. *Psychol. Bull.* 112:179–204

Mesquita B, Leu J. 2006. The cultural psychology of emotion. In *Handbook of Cultural Psychology*, ed. SKD Cohen. New York: Guilford. In press

Mesquita B, Kawasaka M. 2002. Different emotional lives. *Cogn. Emot.* 16:127–41

Messinger DS. 2002. Positive and negative: infant facial expressions and emotions. *Curr. Dir. Psychol. Sci.* 11:1–6

Mesulam MM. 2000. *Principles of Behavioral and Cognitive Neurology*. New York: Oxford Univ. Press

Milad MR, Orr SP, Pitman RK, Rauch SL. 2005. Context modulation of memory for fear extinction in humans. *Psychophysiology* 42:456–64

Mitchell JP, Banaji MR, Macrae CN. 2005a. The link between social cognition and self-referential thought in the medial prefrontal cortex. *J. Cogn. Neurosci.* 17:1306–15

Mitchell JP, Banaji MR, Macrae CN. 2005b. General and specific contributions of the medial prefrontal cortex to knowledge about mental states. *NeuroImage* 28:757–62

Mitchell JP, Macrae CN, Banaji MR. 2005c. Forming impressions of people versus inanimate objects: social-cognitive processing in the medial prefrontal cortex. *NeuroImage* 26:251–57

Morris JS, Dolan RJ. 2004. Dissociable amygdala and orbitofrontal responses during reversal fear conditioning. *Neuroimage* 22:372–80

Moses EB, Barlow DH. 2006. A new unified treatment approach for emotional disorders based on emotion science. *Curr. Dir. Psychol. Sci.* In press

Murphy FC, Nimmo-Smith I, Lawrence AD. 2003. Functional neuroanatomy of emotions: a meta-analysis. *Cogn. Affect. Behav. Neurosci.* 3:207–33

Nagel E. 1961. *The Structure of Science*. London: Routledge & Kegan Paul

Naghavi HR, Nyberg L. 2005. Common fronto-parietal activity in attention, memory, and consciousness: shared demands on integration? *Conscious. Cogn.* 14:390–425

Nakao T, Nakagawa A, Yoshiura T, Nakatani E, Nabeyama M, et al. 2005. Brain activation of patients with obsessive-compulsive disorder during neuropsychological and symptom provocation tasks before and after symptom improvement: a functional magnetic resonance imaging study. *Biol. Psychiatry* 57:901–10

Nauta WJ. 1971. The problem of the frontal lobe: a reinterpretation. *J. Psychiatric Res.* 8:167–87

Niedenthal PM, Barsalou LW, Winkielman P, Krauth-Gruber S, Ric F. 2005. Embodiment in attitudes, social perception, and emotion. *Personal. Soc. Psychol. Rev.* 9:184–211

Nisbett RE, Wilson TD. 1977. Telling more than we can know: verbal reports on mental processes. *Psychol. Rev.* 84:231–59

Oatley K, Johnson-Laird PN. 1987. Towards a cognitive theory of emotions. *Cogn. Emot.* 1:29–50

Ochsner KN, Beer JS, Robertson ER, Cooper JC, Gabrieli JDE, et al. 2005. The neural correlates of direct and reflected self-knowledge. *NeuroImage* 28:797–814

Ochsner KN, Gross JJ. 2005. The cognitive control of emotion. *Trends Cogn. Sci.* 9:242–49

Ochsner KN, Gross JJ. 2007. The functional architecture of emotion regulation. In *The Handbook of Emotion Regulation*, ed. JJ Gross. New York: Guilford. In press

Ochsner KN, Knierim K, Ludlow DH, Hanelin J, Ramachandran T, et al. 2004. Reflecting upon feelings: an fMRI study of neural systems supporting the attribution of emotion to self and other. *J. Cogn. Neurosci.* 16:1746–72

Ongur D, Ferry AT, Price JL. 2003. Architectonic subdivision of the human orbital and medial prefrontal cortex. *J. Comp. Neurol.* 460:425–49

Ongur D, Price JL. 2000. The organization of networks within the orbital and medial prefrontal cortex of rats, monkeys and humans. *Cereb. Cortex* 10:206–19

Ortony A, Turner TJ. 1990. What's basic about basic emotions? *Psychol. Rev.* 97:315–31

Panksepp J. 1998. *Affective Neuroscience: The Foundations of Human and Animal Emotions.* London: Oxford Univ. Press

Parkinson B. 1997. Untangling the appraisal-emotion connection. *Personal. Soc. Psychol. Rev.* 1:62–79

Parvizi J, Damasio A. 2001. Consciousness and the brainstem. *Cognition* 79:135–59

Pezawas L, Meyer-Lindenberg A, Drabant EM, Verchinski BA, Munoz KE, et al. 2005. 5-HTTLPR polymorphism impacts human cingulate-amygdala interactions: a genetic susceptibility mechanism for depression. *Nat. Neurosci.* 8:828–34

Phan KL, Wager T, Taylor SF, Liberzon I. 2002. Functional neuroanatomy of emotion: a meta-analysis of emotion activation studies in PET and fMRI. *Neuroimage* 16:331–48

Phelps EA. 2006. Emotion and cognition: insights from studies of the human amygdala. *Annu. Rev. Psychol.* 57:27–53

Phelps EA, Delgado MR, Nearing KI, LeDoux JE. 2004. Extinction learning in humans: role of the amygdala and vmPFC. *Neuron* 43:897–905

Phillips ML, Drevets WC, Rauch SL, Lane R. 2003. Neurobiology of emotion perception I: the neural basis of normal emotion perception. *Biol. Psychiatry* 54:504–14

Plutchik R. 1980. *Emotion: A Psychoevolutionary Synthesis.* New York: Harper & Row

Poldrack RA, Wagner AD, Prull MW, Desmond JE, Glover GH, Gabrieli JD. 1999. Functional specialization for semantic and phonological processing in the left inferior prefrontal cortex. *Neuroimage* 10:15–35

Pollatos O, Kirsch W, Schandry R. 2005. On the relationship between interoceptive awareness, emotional experience, and brain processes. *Cogn. Brain Res.* 25:948–62

Power MDT. 1997. *Cognition and Emotion: From Order to Disorder.* Mahwah. NJ: Erlbaum

Pressman SD, Cohen S. 2005. Does positive affect influence health? *Psychol. Bull.* 131:925–71

Quigley KS, Barrett LF. 1999. Emotional learning and mechanisms of intentional psychological change. In *Action and Development: Origins and Functions of Intentional Self-Development,* ed. RM Lerner, J Brandtstadter, pp. 435–64. Thousand Oaks, CA: Sage

Quirk GJ, Russo GK, Barron JL, Lebron K. 2000. The role of ventromedial prefrontal cortex in the recovery of extinguished fear. *J. Neurosci.* 20:6225–31

Rauch SL, Whalen PJ, Shin LM, McInerney SC, Macklin ML, et al. 2000. Exaggerated amygdala response to masked facial stimuli in posttraumatic stress disorder: a functional MRI study. *Biol. Psychiatry* 47:769–76

Reed SJ, Vanman EJ, Miller LC. 1997. Connectionism, parallel constraint satisfaction processes, and Gestalt principles: (re)introducing cognitive dynamics to social psychology. *Personal. Soc. Psychol. Rev.* 1:26–53

Robinson M, Clore GL. 2002. Episodic and semantic knowledge in emotional self-report: evidence for two judgment processes. *J. Personal. Soc. Psychol.* 83:198–215

Roseman IJ. 1991. Appraisal determinants of discrete emotions. *Cogn. Emot.* 5:161–200

Roseman IJ, Antoniou AA, Jose PE. 1996. Appraisal determinants of emotions: constructing a more accurate and comprehensive theory. *Cogn. Emot.* 10:241–77

Roseman IJ, Spindel MS, Jose PE. 1990. Appraisals of emotion-eliciting events: testing a theory of discrete emotions. *J. Personal. Soc. Psychol.* 59:899–915

Rothbaum F, Pott M, Azuma H, Miyake K, Weisz J. 2000. The development of close relationships in Japan and the United States: paths of symbiotic harmony and generative tension. *Child Dev.* 71:1121–42

Russell JA. 1980. A circumplex model of affect. *J. Personal. Soc. Psychol.* 39:1161–78

Russell JA. 1983. Pancultural aspects of human conceptual organization of emotions. *J. Personal. Soc. Psychol.* 45:1281–88

Russell JA. 2003. Core affect and the psychological construction of emotion. *Psychol. Rev.* 110:145–72

Russell JA, Barrett LF. 1999. Core affect, prototypical emotional episodes, and other things called emotion: dissecting the elephant. *J. Personal. Soc. Psychol.* 76:805–19

Russell JA, Mehrabian A. 1977. Evidence for a three-factor theory of emotions. *J. Res. Personal.* 11:273–94

Russell JA, Weiss A, Mendelsohn GA. 1989. Affect grid: a single-item scale of pleasure and arousal. *J. Personal. Soc. Psychol.* 57:493–502

Ryle G. 2000. *The Concept of Mind.* Chicago, IL: Univ. Chicago Press

Sabini J, Silver M. 2005. Why emotion names and experiences don't neatly pair. *Psychol. Inq.* 16:1–10

Salamone JD, Correa M. 2002. Motivational views of reinforcement: implications for understanding the behavioral functions of nucleus accumbens dopamine. *Behav. Brain Res.* 137:3–25

Salamone JD, Correa M, Mingote SM, Weber SM. 2005. Beyond the reward hypothesis: alternative functions of nucleus accumbens dopamine. *Curr. Opin. Pharmacol.* 5:34–41

Salamone JD, Correa M, Mingote SM, Weber SM, Farrar AM. 2006. Nucleus accumbens dopamine and the forebrain circuitry involved in behavioral activation and effort-related decision making: implications for understanding anergia and psychomotor slowing in depression. *Curr. Psychiatry Rev.* In press

Schachter S, Singer JE. 1962. Cognitive, social, and physiological determinants of emotional state. *Psychol. Rev.* 69:379–99; errata 121

Scherer KR. 1984. On the nature and function of emotion: a component process approach. In *Approaches to Emotion*, ed. KR Scherer, P Ekman, pp. 293–317. Hillsdale, NJ: Erlbaum

Scherer KR. 1997a. Profiles of emotion-antecedent appraisal: testing theoretical predictions across cultures. *Cogn. Emot.* 11:113–50

Scherer KR. 1997b. The role of culture in emotion-antecedent appraisal. *J. Personal. Soc. Psychol.* 73:902–22

Schimmack U, Oishi S, Diener E. 2002. Cultural influences on the relation between pleasant emotions and unpleasant emotions: Asian dialectic philosophies or individualism-collectivism? *Cogn. Emot.* 19:705–19

Schnider A, Treyer V, Buck A. 2000. Selection of currently relevant memories by the human posterior medial orbitofrontal cortex. *J. Neurosci.* 20:5880–84

Schnyer DM, Nicholls L, Verfaellie M. 2005. The role of VMPC in metamemorial judgments of content retrievability. *J. Cogn. Neurosci.* 17:832–46

Schultz W. 2004. Neural coding of basic reward terms of animal learning theory, game theory, microeconomics and behavioural ecology. *Curr. Opin. Neurobiol.* 14:139–47

Schultz W, Tremblay L, Hollerman JR. 2000. Reward processing in primate orbitofrontal cortex and basal ganglia. *Cereb. Cortex* 10:272–84

Schwarz N, Clore GL. 1983. Mood, misattribution, and judgments of well-being: informative and directive functions of affective states. *J. Personal. Soc. Psychol.* 45:513–23

Scollon CN, Diener E, Oishi S, Biswas-Diener R. 2005. An experience sampling and cross-cultural investigation of the relation between pleasant and unpleasant affect. *Cogn. Emot.* 19:27–52

Searle JR. 1992. *The Rediscovery of the Mind*. Cambridge, MA: MIT Press

Searle JR. 2000. Consciousness. *Annu. Rev. Neurosci.* 23:557–78

Searle JR. 2004. *Mind*. New York: Oxford Univ. Press

Shamay-Tsoory SG, Lester H, Chisin R, Israel O, Bar-Shalom R, et al. 2005. The neural correlates of understanding the other's distress: a positron emission tomography investigation of accurate empathy. *Neuroimage* 27:468–72

Shamay-Tsoory SG, Tomer R, Berger BD, Aharon-Peretz J. 2003. Characterization of empathy deficits following prefrontal brain damage: the role of the right ventromedial prefrontal cortex. *J. Cogn. Neurosci.* 15:324–37

Shamay-Tsoory SG, Tomer R, Goldsher D, Berger BD, Aharon-Peretz J. 2004. Impairment in cognitive and affective empathy in patients with brain lesions: anatomical and cognitive correlates. *J. Clin. Exp. Neuropsychol.* 26:1113–27

Shaver P, Schwartz J, Kirson D, O'Connor C. 1987. Emotion knowledge: further exploration of a prototype approach. *J. Personal. Soc. Psychol.* 52:1061–86

Shin LM, Orr SP, Carson MA, Rauch SL, Macklin ML, et al. 2004. Regional cerebral blood flow in the amygdala and medial prefrontal cortex during traumatic imagery in male and female Vietnam veterans with PTSD. *Arch. Gen. Psychiatry* 61:168–76

Shin LM, Wright CI, Cannistraro PA, Wedig MM, McMullin K, et al. 2005. A functional magnetic resonance imaging study of amygdala and medial prefrontal cortex responses to overtly presented fearful faces in posttraumatic stress disorder. *Arch. Gen. Psychiatry* 62:273–81

Shweder RA. 1993. The cultural psychology of emotions. In *Handbook of Emotion*, ed. M Lewis, M Haviland-Jones, pp. 417–31. New York: Guilford

Shweder RA, Haidt J. 2000. The cultural psychology of emotions: ancient and new. In *Handbook of Emotions*, ed. M Lewis, M Haviland-Jones, pp. 397–414. New York: Guilford

Skinner BF. 1953. *Science and Human Behavior*. New York: Macmillan

Smith CA, Ellsworth PC. 1985. Patterns of cognitive appraisal in emotion. *J. Personal. Soc. Psychol.* 48:813–38

Smith CA, Ellsworth PC. 1987. Patterns of appraisal and emotion related to taking an exam. *J. Personal. Soc. Psychol.* 52:475–88

Smith ER, DeCoster J. 2000. Dual-process models in social and cognitive psychology: conceptual integration and links to underlying memory systems. *Personal. Soc. Psychol. Rev.* 4:108–31

Spelke ES. 2000. Core knowledge. *Am. Psychol.* 55:1233–43

Spitz RA. 1965. *The First Year of Life*. New York: Int. Univ. Press

Sroufe LA. 1979. Socioemotional development. In *Handbook of Infant Development*, ed. JD Osofsky, pp. 462–516. New York: Wiley

Stefanacci L, Amaral DG. 2002. Some observations on cortical inputs to the macaque monkey amygdala: an anterograde tracing study. *J. Comp. Neurol.* 451:301–23

Stein DJ, Westenberg HGM, Liebowitz MR. 2002. Social anxiety disorder and generalized anxiety disorder: serotonergic and dopaminergic neurocircuitry. *J. Clin. Psychiatry* 63:12–19

Talairach J, Tournoux P. 1988. *Co-Planar Stereotaxic Atlas of the Human Brain*. Stuttgart: Thieme

Valente AAJ, Miguel EC, Castro CC, Amaro EJ, Duran FLS, et al. 2005. Regional gray matter abnormalities in obsessive-compulsive disorder: a voxel-based morphometry study. *Biol. Psychiatry* 58:479–87

Wager TD, Phan KL, Liberzon I, Taylor SF. 2003. Valence, gender, and lateralization of functional brain anatomy in emotion: a meta-analysis of findings from neuroimaging. *NeuroImage* 19:513–31

Wagner AD, Maril A, Bjork RA, Schacter DL. 2001. Prefrontal contributions to executive control: fMRI evidence for functional distinctions within lateral prefrontal cortex. *Neuroimage* 14:1337–47

Watson D, Clark LA. 1994. Manual for the positive and negative affect schedule (expanded form). Unpubl. manuscr., Univ. Iowa, Iowa City

Watson D, Tellegen A. 1985. Toward a consensual structure of mood. *Psychol. Bull.* 98:219–35

Watson D, Wiese D, Vaidya J, Tellegen A. 1999. The two general activation systems of affect: structural findings, evolutionary considerations, and psychobiological evidence. *J. Personal. Soc. Psychol.* 76: 820–38

Watson JB. 1919. A schematic outline of the emotions. *Psychol. Rev.* 26:165–96

Weinstock LM, Whisman MA. 2006. Neuroticism as a common feature of the depressive and anxiety disorders: a test of the Revised Integration Hierarchical Model in a national sample. *J. Abnorm. Psychol.* 115:68–74

Weniger G, Irle E. 2002. Impaired facial affect recognition and emotional changes in subjects with transmodal cortical lesions. *Cereb. Cortex* 12:258–68

Wiens S. 2005. Interoception in emotional experience. *Curr. Opin. Neurol.* 18:442–47

Wilson D, Sperber D. 2003. Relevance theory. In *Handbook of Pragmatics*, ed. G Ward, L Horn, pp. 607–32. Oxford, UK: Blackwell Sci.

Wilson TD, Dunn EW. 2004. Self-knowledge: its limits, value and potential for improvement. *Annu. Rev. Psychol.* 55:493–518

Winkielman P, Berridge KC, Wilbarger JL. 2005. See Barrett et al. 2005, pp. 335–62

Wundt WM. 1897. *Outlines of Psychology*. Leipzig: Engelmann

Yamasaki H, LaBar KS, McCarthy G. 2002. Dissociable prefrontal brain systems for attention and emotion. *Proc. Natl. Acad. Sci. USA* 99:11447–51

Yik M. 2006. Culture, gender, and the bipolarity of affect. *Cogn. Emot.* In press

Yik MSM, Russell JA, Barrett LF. 1999. Structure of self-reported current affect: integration and beyond. *J. Personal. Soc. Psychol.* 77:600–19

Zeki S. 2003. The disunity of consciousness. *Trends Cogn. Sci.* 7:214–18

Zuckerman M, Lubin B. 1985. *Manual for the MAACL-R: The Multiple Affect Adjective Checklist Revised*. San Diego, CA: Educ. Ind. Test. Serv.

The Close Relationships of Lesbians and Gay Men

Letitia Anne Peplau and Adam W. Fingerhut

Psychology Department, University of California, Los Angeles,
California 90095-1563; email: lapeplau@ucla.edu, awf@ucla.edu

Annu. Rev. Psychol. 2007. 58:405–24

First published online as a Review in
Advance on August 11, 2006

The *Annual Review of Psychology* is online
at http://psych.annualreviews.org

This article's doi:
10.1146/annurev.psych.58.110405.085701

Key Words

division of household labor, gay-related stressor, power,
second-parent adoption, sexual orientation, homosexuality, social
stigma, social support, stress-related psychological disorders

Abstract

This article reviews empirical studies of same-sex couples in the
United States, highlighting consistent findings, drawing comparisons to heterosexual couples, and noting gaps in available research.
U.S. Census data indicate that there were more than 600,000 same-
sex couples living together in 2000. Research about relationship formation, the division of household labor, power, satisfaction, sexuality,
conflict, commitment, and relationship stability is presented. Next,
we highlight three recent research topics: the legalization of same-
sex relationships through civil unions and same-sex marriage, the
experiences of same-sex couples raising children, and the impact of
societal prejudice and discrimination on same-sex partners. We conclude with comments about the contributions of empirical research
to debunking negative stereotypes of same-sex couples, testing the
generalizability of theories about close relationships, informing our
understanding of gender and close relationships, and providing a
scientific basis for public policy.

Contents

INTRODUCTION

In the past half century, the close relationships of lesbians and gay men have moved from the shadows of society as a "love that dares not speak its name" to center stage in a national and international debate about same-sex marriage. The increasing visibility of same-sex couples has challenged researchers to provide scientific information that can illuminate the relationship experiences of lesbians and gay men. Research findings can also inform legal and policy questions that have been raised by ongoing efforts to achieve equal rights for same-sex couples.

This review focuses on the experiences of same-sex couples in the United States. We begin with up-to-date estimates about the number of same-sex couples. Next, we review the research literature on same-sex couples and

identify major empirical findings. When possible, we compare the experiences of same-sex couples to those of heterosexual couples in order to indicate areas of commonality and of difference. It is noteworthy that research on same-sex couples began slowly in the 1970s, grew in the 1980s, and then diminished as researchers shifted their attention to the impact of the AIDS epidemic on the gay community. Much of the research we review was conducted 10 or 20 years ago.

In the past few years, however, research on same-sex couples has been revitalized and has shifted to a new set of topics. We highlight three recent research directions: the legalization of same-sex relationships through civil unions and same-sex marriage, the experiences of same-sex couples raising children, and the impact of societal prejudice and discrimination on same-sex partners. We conclude with general comments about the role of empirical research in four areas: debunking negative stereotypes about same-sex couples, testing the generalizability of theories about close relationships, informing our understanding of gender and close relationships, and providing a scientific basis for public policy.

COUNTING SAME-SEX COUPLES

Although same-sex couples have a clear and growing presence in American society, several factors make it difficult to provide an accurate estimate of the number of lesbians and gay men who are currently in a same-sex relationship. First, some lesbians and gay men are reluctant to reveal their sexual identity or the nature of their romantic attachments. Second, lacking the equivalent of legal heterosexual marriage and divorce, we have no public records of how many lesbians and gay men are currently in a serious relationship or have experienced the loss of a serious relationship through breakup or the death of a partner. Third, researchers have used differing and noncomparable questions to assess the relationship status of lesbians and gay men, asking, for instance, if an individual is in a romantic/sexual relationship, has a steady partner, has been together with a partner for six months or more, or currently lives with a romantic partner.

Nonetheless, available evidence suggests that many gay men and lesbians are in couple relationships. Recently, the U.S. Census and other national surveys added the category "unmarried partner" to their household roster, making it possible to estimate the number of gay and lesbian adults who live together with a same-sex partner. According to the 2000 Census, there were approximately 600,000 same-sex couples living together in the United States, with roughly equal numbers of men and women (Gates & Ost 2004). Approximately 16% of same-sex couples included at least one Hispanic partner, and 14% included at least one black partner. One estimate is that about 28% of gay men and 44% of lesbians are currently living with a same-sex partner (Black et al. 2000). Although same-sex couples are more common in urban areas, they are located in all parts of the United States.

BASIC FINDINGS ABOUT SAME-SEX COUPLES

In the sections that follow, we review major findings from research on same-sex couples and offer suggestions about areas in need of further investigation. Prior to turning to these findings, it is useful to comment briefly on the sources of data that have been used in research on same-sex couples. Most studies have been conducted in the United States with individuals who self-identify as gay or lesbian, for instance by volunteering to participate in a study about gay and lesbian couples. Like many studies of heterosexual couples, studies of same-sex couples have typically recruited younger, well-educated, middle-class, white volunteers. Many studies have relied on questionnaires and have obtained reports from only one partner in a couple.

In addition to many small-scale studies, there have been a few major research programs focusing on same-sex couples. For example, in a project known as the American Couples Study, Blumstein & Schwartz (1983) obtained responses to lengthy questionnaires from both partners in 957 gay male, 772 lesbian, 653 heterosexual cohabiting, and 3656 heterosexual married couples. A subset of participants also completed an 18-month follow-up questionnaire. More recently, Kurdek conducted two longitudinal studies involving repeated assessments of both partners in same-sex couples and married heterosexual couples (see reviews in Kurdek 1994a, 2004a). Our review encompasses both small-scale studies and larger programs of research.

Relationship Formation

Several studies have compared the qualities that lesbians, gay men, and heterosexuals seek in romantic partners (see review by Peplau & Spalding 2000). Regardless of sexual orientation, most individuals value affection, dependability, shared interests, and similarity of religious beliefs. Men, regardless of sexual orientation, are more likely to emphasize a partner's physical attractiveness; women, regardless of sexual orientation, give greater emphasis to personality characteristics. Like their heterosexual counterparts, lesbians and gay men report that they often meet potential dates through friends, at work, at a bar, or at a social event (e.g., Bryant & Demian 1994). Urban areas with visible gay and lesbian communities provide expanded opportunities to meet potential partners. In addition, the Internet has rapidly become a way for gay men and lesbians to meet each other. There is some evidence that lesbians and gay men, like their heterosexual counterparts, rely on fairly conventional scripts when they go on dates with a new partner (Klinkenberg & Rose 1994).

For lesbians and gay men, the boundaries between friendship and romantic or sexual relationships may be particularly complex (e.g., Diamond & Dube 2002, Nardi 1999).

Rose et al. (1993), for example, found that many lesbian romantic relationships began as a friendship, then developed into a love relationship, and later became sexual. Some women reported difficulties with this pattern of relationship development, such as problems in knowing if a relationship was shifting from friendship to romance and in gauging the friend's possible sexual interest. In addition, lesbians and gay men may be especially likely to remain friends with former sexual partners (Solomon et al. 2004, Weinstock 2004). In a recent study (Harkless & Fowers 2005), lesbians and gay men were more likely than were heterosexuals to agree, "When a relationship is ending, one of my biggest fears is that I will lose the friendship" or that it is important "to remain friends with someone with whom I've had a serious relationship." Lesbians and gay men were also more likely than were heterosexuals to report continued phone calls and social contacts with ex-partners. The factors that encourage same-sex ex-partners to remain friends are not well understood but may include the small size of some gay and lesbian social networks, the norms of particular gay and lesbian communities, and the benefits that can accrue from transforming ties with ex-lovers into friendship (Nardi 1999, Weinstock 2004).

The Division of Household Labor and Power

Traditional heterosexual marriage is organized around two basic principles: a division of labor based on gender and a norm of greater male power and decision-making authority. Researchers have investigated how same-sex couples, who lack biological sex as a basis for assigning tasks and status, organize their lives together (see review by Peplau & Spalding 2000).

Turning first to the division of labor, it is important to emphasize that most gay men and lesbians are in dual-earner relationships, so neither partner is the exclusive breadwinner and each partner has some measure of economic independence. When it comes to housework, same-sex couples are likely to divide chores fairly equitably. For example, Kurdek (1993) compared the division of housework (e.g., cleaning, cooking, and shopping) in cohabiting same-sex couples and married heterosexual couples, none of whom had children. In heterosexual couples, wives typically did most of the housework. In contrast, lesbian and gay couples divided the household tasks more equally (see also Kurdek 2006). Lesbian partners tended to share tasks; gay male partners were more likely to have each partner specialize in certain tasks. In a review of research on this topic, Kurdek (2005, p. 252) concluded that "although members of gay and lesbian couples do not divide household labor in a perfectly equal manner, they are more likely than members of heterosexual couples to negotiate a balance between achieving a fair distribution of household labor and accommodating the different interests, skills, and work schedules of particular partners."

Questionnaire studies may not capture the nuanced complexities of domestic work for cohabiting couples. An in-depth study of dual-earner heterosexual families (Hochschild & Machung 1989) showed that although most wives did the bulk of housework, many couples found ways to characterize their allocation of housework as balanced. Similarly, based on in-depth interviews and home observations, Carrington (1999) suggested that same-sex couples' reports of equal sharing of household activities may reflect their ideals but often mask substantial observable differences between partners' actual contributions. He found that equal sharing of domestic activities was far from universal: It was most common among affluent couples who relied on paid help, and when both partners had less demanding jobs with more flexible schedules.

When researchers assess power in close relationships, they typically try to characterize the overall pattern of dominance to determine whether one partner is more influential than the other is. The lesbians and gay men who participate in psychological research tend to be advocates of power equality in their relationships. In an early study, 92% of gay men and 97% of lesbians defined the ideal balance of power as one in which both partners were "exactly equal" (Peplau & Cochran 1980). In a more recent study, partners in gay and lesbian couples rated power equality as important in an ideal relationship, although lesbians scored significantly higher on the value of equality than did gay men (Kurdek 1995a). This strong endorsement of power sharing may reflect, in some measure, the tendency for researchers to recruit participants who are well educated and generally liberal in their attitudes.

Not all couples who strive for power equality achieve this ideal. Reports of the actual balance of power vary from study to study. For example, when Peplau & Cochran (1980) asked lesbians and gay men "who has more say" in your relationship, only 38% of gay men and 59% of lesbians characterized their current relationship as "exactly equal." Equal power was reported by 59% of the lesbians studied by Reilly & Lynch (1990) and by 60% of the gay men studied by Harry & DeVall (1978).

Social exchange theory predicts that greater power accrues to the partner who has relatively greater personal resources, such as education, money, or social standing. Studies of gay men have supported this hypothesis. For example, Harry found that gay men who were older and wealthier than their partner was tended to have more power (Harry 1984, Harry & DeVall 1978). Blumstein & Schwartz (1983, p. 59) concluded that "in gay male couples, income is an extremely important force in determining which partner will be dominant." For lesbians, research results are less clear-cut, with some studies finding that income is significantly related to power (Caldwell & Peplau 1984, Reilly & Lynch 1990) and others not (Blumstein & Schwartz 1983). Dunne (1997, p. 180) concluded that "lesbian women are comfortable neither with dominating nor with being dominated in their partnerships." Further research on the balance of power is needed to clarify these incon-

sistent results and to broaden our knowledge about correlates of power imbalances.

Love and Satisfaction

Stereotypes depict gay and lesbian relationships as unhappy and dysfunctional, especially in comparison with heterosexual relationships (e.g., Crawford & Solliday 1996, Testa et al. 1987). In fact, empirical research finds striking similarities in the reports of love and satisfaction among contemporary lesbian, gay, and heterosexual couples. Peplau & Cochran (1980) found no significant differences in scores on standardized Love and Liking scales among matched samples of lesbians, gay men, and heterosexuals who were all currently in a romantic/sexual relationship. In a longitudinal study of married heterosexual and cohabiting homosexual couples, Kurdek (1998) found similar results. Controlling for age, education, income, and years cohabiting, the couples did not differ in relationship satisfaction at initial testing. Over the five years of this study, all types of couples tended to decrease in relationship satisfaction, but no differences were found among gay, lesbian, or heterosexual couples in the rate of change in satisfaction. A survey of African American lesbians and gay men in committed relationships (Peplau et al. 1997) also found high levels of relationship satisfaction and closeness. Further, the partner's race was unrelated to relationship satisfaction: Interracial couples were no more or less satisfied, on average, than same-race couples.

Researchers have begun to identify factors that enhance or detract from satisfaction in same-sex relationships. Like their heterosexual counterparts, gay and lesbian couples generally benefit when partners are similar in background, attitudes, and values (Kurdek & Schmitt 1987). Additionally, consistent with social exchange theory, happiness tends to be high when partners perceive many rewards and few costs from their relationship (e.g., Beals et al. 2002, Duffy & Rusbult 1986). A study of lesbian relationships found support for another exchange theory prediction, that satisfaction is higher when partners are equally involved in or committed to a relationship (Peplau et al. 1982). For lesbian couples, greater satisfaction has also been linked to perceptions of greater equity or fairness in the relationship (Schreurs & Buunk 1996). Finally, several studies of lesbians and gay men have found that satisfaction is higher when partners believe they are relatively equal in power and decision-making (reviewed by Peplau & Spalding 2000).

Sexuality

Sexuality has been a popular topic of investigation in studies of gay and lesbian couples. A comprehensive review of this literature is provided by Peplau et al. (2004). Research on the frequency of sex in relationships has identified several consistent patterns. Among same-sex and heterosexual couples, there is wide variability in sexual frequency and a general decline in frequency as relationships continue over time. In the early stages of a relationship, gay male couples have sex more often than do other couples. Further, research consistently finds that lesbian couples report having sex less often than either heterosexual or gay male couples.

Considerable attention has been given to the low frequency of sex reported by lesbians, in part because this pattern may reflect broader issues about female sexuality (Fassinger & Morrow 1995, Peplau & Garnets 2000). One suggestion is that gender socialization leads women to repress and ignore sexual feelings, and this effect is magnified in a relationship with two female partners. Another view is that women have difficulty taking the lead to initiate sexual activities with a partner, resulting in low levels of sexual activity. A third possibility is that men are generally more interested in sex than are women, leading to higher levels of sexual activity in couples that include a male partner. A fourth possibility is that traditional conceptions of sexuality, which equate "sex" with penile penetration, may not adequately capture lesbian women's sexual experiences. Finally, there may be methodological problems with the ways researchers have asked questions about women's sexuality (Rothblum 2000).

In addition to studying sexual frequency, researchers have also investigated sexual satisfaction in gay and lesbian couples. High levels of sexual satisfaction have been reported in studies of students and young adults (e.g., Peplau & Cochran 1981, Peplau et al. 1978), predominantly white adult samples (e.g., Blumstein & Schwartz 1983, Kurdek 1991, McWhirter & Mattison 1984), and samples of African American lesbians and gay men (e.g., Peplau et al. 1997). Not surprisingly, sexual satisfaction and sexual frequency are linked. In the American Couples sample, for example, the correlation between sexual frequency and sexual satisfaction was $r = 0.50$ for gay men and $r = 0.48$ for lesbians (controlling for age and duration of relationship). Sexual satisfaction is also associated with global measures of relationship satisfaction in gay and lesbian as well as heterosexual couples (e.g., Bryant & Demian 1994, Eldridge & Gilbert 1990, Peplau et al. 1997).

Research has documented differences between gay, lesbian, and heterosexual couples concerning the issue of sexual exclusiveness versus openness. First, there are differences in attitudes about monogamy (Bailey et al. 1994). In the American Couples Study, only 36% of gay men indicated that it was important to be sexually monogamous, compared with 71% of lesbians, 84% of heterosexual wives, and 75% of husbands. Second, there are major differences in reports of actual behavior (Bryant & Demian 1994, McWhirter & Mattison 1984). In the American Couples Study, only a minority of lesbians (28%), wives (21%), and husbands (26%) reported having engaged in extradyadic sex, compared with 82% of gay men. Third, among those individuals who had engaged in extradyadic sex, gay men reported having a greater number of sex partners. Finally, Kurdek (1991) found that sexual fidelity was positively related to relationship satisfaction for lesbian and heterosexual couples, but not for gay male couples. This may reflect the norms of the gay male community and the fact that some male couples have agreements that extradyadic sex is acceptable (Hickson et al. 1992).

We know little about possible changes in sexual attitudes and behavior that may have occurred among lesbians and gay men in recent years, both in response to the AIDS epidemic and the greater attention being given to same-sex marriage. Rutter & Schwartz (1996) suggested that from the 1970s to the 1990s gay men's attitudes shifted toward greater endorsement of monogamy but their actual sexual behavior did not undergo a corresponding change.

Conflict and Partner Violence

Few couples avoid occasional disagreements and conflicts. Lesbian, gay male, and heterosexual couples report a similar frequency of arguments and tend to disagree about similar topics, with finances, affection, sex, criticism, and household tasks heading the list (Kurdek 1994a, 2005, 2006; Metz et al. 1994). How well do lesbians and gay men solve problems that arise in their relationships? Available research indicates that their problem-solving skills are at least as good as are those of heterosexual couples. In a study of homosexual and heterosexual couples, Kurdek (1998) found no differences in the frequency of using positive problem-solving styles such as negotiating or compromising. Nor were differences found in the use of poor strategies, such as launching personal attacks or refusing to talk to the partner. A study that observed couples discussing relationship conflicts in a laboratory setting found that gay and lesbian partners used somewhat more positive communication styles than did heterosexual couples (Gottman et al. 2003). Finally, as with heterosexual couples, happy lesbian and gay male couples are more likely than are unhappy couples to use constructive problem-solving approaches (Kurdek 2004, Metz et al. 1994).

Recently, researchers have begun to document the existence and nature of violence in same-sex relationships (see review by Potoczniak et al. 2003). It is impossible to estimate accurately the frequency of same-sex domestic violence, not only because of underreporting to the police but also because research studies have been based on small, unrepresentative samples. Interviews with abused gay and lesbian individuals (e.g., Potoczniak et al. 2003, Renzetti & Miley 1996) have documented a cycle of escalating abuse in some same-sex couples. This pattern, in which one partner uses violence and threats of violence to intimidate and control the other, bears many similarities to violence in heterosexual couples that Johnson (2006) has characterized as "intimate terrorism." We know less about other types of violence in same-sex relationships, including violent resistance to abuse by a partner and situational violence that occurs when a verbal conflict turns physical. We also lack information about the correlates of domestic violence among same-sex couples. In male-female couples, traditional attitudes about gender roles, differences in physical size and strength, and differences in financial resources can all contribute to patterns of abuse. How do these factors affect same-sex couples? In addition, are there other factors unique to lesbians and gay men that contribute to violence, including experiences of discrimination or the stress of belonging to a sexual minority group (Balsam & Szymanski 2005)?

Commitment and Relationship Stability

Three general factors contribute to partners' psychological commitment to each other and to the longevity of their relationship; all three appear to be relevant to same-sex couples (see reviews by Kurdek 2000, Peplau & Spalding 2000). Of obvious importance are positive attraction forces, such as love and satisfaction, that make partners want to stay together. A second factor is the availability of alternatives to the current relationship, most often a more desirable partner. Partners who perceive few alternatives are less likely to leave a relationship. Finally, barriers that make it difficult for a person to leave a relationship also matter (Kurdek 1998, 2000). Barriers include investments that increase the psychological, emotional, or financial costs of ending a relationship, as well as moral or religious feelings of obligation or duty to one's partner. A model including all three predictors of commitment was tested by Beals et al. (2002) using data on lesbian couples from the American Couples Study. Their analyses found that relationship satisfaction, the quality of alternatives, and investments each predicted psychological commitment, which in turn predicted relationship stability.

There is evidence that married heterosexual couples perceive more barriers than do gay, lesbian, or cohabiting heterosexual couples (e.g., Kurdek 1998, Kurdek & Schmitt 1986). A relative lack of barriers may make it less likely that lesbians and gay men will be trapped in miserable and deteriorating relationships. On the other hand, weaker barriers may also allow partners to end relationships that might have improved if given more time and effort. In a longitudinal study, Kurdek (1998) found that barriers to leaving the relationship were a significant predictor of relationship stability over a five-year period. Today, as lesbians and gay men gain greater legal recognition for their relationships, the barriers to ending same-sex relationships may become more similar to those of heterosexuals. The impact of such trends on the stability of same-sex relationships is an important topic for future investigations.

Given the weaker barriers to ending same-sex relationships, we might anticipate that there would be fewer long-term relationships among lesbians and gay men compared with heterosexuals. Unfortunately, we currently know little about the longevity of same-sex relationships. No information comparable to divorce statistics for heterosexual marriages is available. Several studies have documented the existence of very-long-

lasting gay and lesbian relationships (e.g., Johnson 1990, McWhirter & Mattison 1984). Longitudinal studies provide further clues about relationship stability. In a five-year prospective study, Kurdek (1998) reported a breakup rate of 7% for married heterosexual couples, 14% for cohabiting gay male couples, and 16% for cohabiting lesbian couples. Controlling for demographic variables, cohabiting gay and lesbian couples were significantly more likely than were married heterosexuals to break up (see also Kurdek 2004).

In this section, we reviewed empirical research describing basic features of same-sex relationships and comparing them with heterosexual relationships. In the next section, we consider three new directions in research on same-sex couples.

RECENT RESEARCH DIRECTIONS

The twenty-first century has seen renewed interest in research on same-sex couples, spurred by the increasing visibility of lesbians and gay men and by public policy debates about same-sex marriage and gay adoption. A shift has also occurred from viewing same-sex couples through the lens of abnormality and dysfunction toward viewing lesbians and gay men as members of a sexual minority group dealing with social stigma and discrimination.

Legalizing Same-Sex Relationships: Marriage, Civil Unions, and Domestic Partnerships

For heterosexual couples, marriage represents both a public sign of commitment and a legal status affecting many aspects of life. The General Accounting Office (2004) has estimated that marriage affects 1138 federal rights, including taxes, Social Security, and veterans' benefits. Not surprisingly, lesbians and gay men have actively sought to make legal recognition of their relationships a reality. In a national survey (Kaiser Family Foundation 2001), 74% of lesbians and gay men said that if they could legally marry someone of the same sex, they would like to do so someday. In recent decades, advances have been made in achieving formal recognition for same-sex relationships. Within gay and lesbian communities, same-sex couples are holding commitment ceremonies to celebrate their relationships, and some religious groups now perform same-sex wedding ceremonies. Additionally, increasing numbers of employers provide domestic partner benefits to same-sex partners. Despite this progress, the substantial social and legal benefits and protections accorded to legally married couples by state and federal laws are still beyond the reach of most same-sex partners in the United States.

Efforts to legalize same-sex relationships have met with considerable opposition. Reflecting public sentiment, President Clinton signed the Defense of Marriage Act in 1996, clarifying that for the federal government, marriage is defined as "a legal union of one man and one woman as husband and wife" and that spouse should be defined only as "a person of the opposite sex who is a husband or a wife." A majority of state governments have also taken steps to restrict marriage to heterosexual couples (Human Rights Campaign 2006). Recent national poll data indicate that a 53% majority of Americans oppose allowing gay men and lesbians to marry legally, with only 36% in favor of same-sex marriage and 11% uncertain (The Pew Forum on Religion and Public Life 2005). For many Americans, opposition to same-sex marriage is strongly correlated with the belief that homosexuality is immoral (Lewis 2006). Despite opposition to same-sex marriage, an increasing percentage of Americans endorses extending legal rights and protections to lesbians and gay men. In national surveys (e.g., Kaiser Family Foundation 2001), more than two-thirds of Americans support providing inheritance rights, health insurance, and social security benefits to same-sex domestic partners. For the first time in 2005, a 53% majority of those polled favored permitting lesbians and gay men to enter into civil unions that would give

them many of the same rights as married couples (The Pew Forum on Religion and Public Life 2005). Public attitudes and governmental policies differ from state to state. Currently, only Massachusetts offers legal marriage to same-sex couples, and six other states recognize some form of same-sex civil union.

In addition to information about heterosexuals' attitudes toward same-sex marriage, researchers have also gathered information about the attitudes of gay men and lesbians. Lannutti (2005) used an open-ended Web-based survey to examine the attitudes of 288 lesbians and gay men toward same-sex marriage. Her findings revealed complex and nuanced views. Virtually all participants emphasized fairness and equal rights: Legal marriage would be a sign that lesbians and gay men had achieved first-class citizenship. Many positive aspects of same-sex marriage were noted. Marriage would help couples feel closer and strengthen their relationships, in part by creating structural barriers to relationship dissolution. Respondents also suggested that marriage would reduce the stress that same-sex couples experience, by increasing legal rights and benefits, reducing societal prejudice, and diminishing internalized homophobia among lesbians and gay men. At the same time, respondents expressed concerns that the availability of legal unions might put pressure on individuals to get married "for the wrong reasons" or might create status hierarchies within the gay/lesbian community that could stigmatize those who choose not to marry. Another concern was that legalizing same-sex marriage might lead to assimilation into mainstream heterosexual norms and values that would change and harm unique features of the gay/lesbian community.

Currently, we have very little information about American couples who seek civil unions or same-sex marriage. Solomon, Rothblum and colleagues (e.g., Solomon et al. 2004, 2005; Todosijevic et al. 2005) studied the first cohort of couples to obtain civil unions in Vermont. For comparison purposes, the researchers asked gay and lesbian respondents to nominate a married heterosexual sibling and the sibling's spouse as well as a gay or lesbian couple from their friendship circle who were not in a civil union. Results from this research replicated many findings from previous studies concerning sexuality, conflict, and the division of housework and childcare among same-sex couples. Few differences were found among same-sex couples based on their civil union status.

As time goes by, researchers will be able to investigate the impact of civil unions and same-sex marriage on gay and lesbian couples more thoroughly. An important goal will be to identify factors that distinguish same-sex couples who seek legal recognition from those who do not, including their motives and the extent to which couples emphasize the symbolic and psychological meaning of legal recognition or the financial and legal benefits that recognition may confer. A further question concerns the impact of legal recognition itself on the nature and longevity of same-sex relationships. Will legalization increase the stability of same-sex relationships? Data from Norway and Sweden, where registered same-sex partnerships have been available since the 1990s, indicate that the rate of dissolution within five years of entering a legal union is higher among same-sex partnerships than among heterosexual marriages, with lesbian couples having the highest rates of dissolution (Andersson et al. 2006). Unfortunately, the Scandinavian data do not permit comparisons with the longevity of same-sex couples who did not seek legal recognition. Many other questions remain unanswered (Patterson 2004a). For example, do the social and economic benefits of legal recognition affect relationship functioning and satisfaction? Does legal recognition change the way in which couples or their family and friends think about their relationship? Does legalization lead to better physical and mental health for gay and lesbian people (Herdt & Kertzner 2006, Herek 2006, King & Bartlett 2006)? Finally, does the form of legal recognition—

marriage, civil union, domestic partnership—make a difference?

Same-Sex Couples with Children

Based on data from the 2000 U.S. Census (Gates & Ost 2004), it has been estimated that among adults aged 22–55, 34% of lesbian couples who live together and 22% of gay male couples who live together are raising children. Consequently, approximately 250,000 children under the age of 18 are being raised by same-sex couples. Although the experiences of these children are beyond the scope of our review, it is important to note that research has documented that they are comparable to children of heterosexual parents on measures of psychological well-being, self-esteem, cognitive abilities, and peer relations (see reviews by Fulcher et al. 2006, Patterson 2003, Tasker 2005).

Gay- and lesbian-headed families are created in a variety of ways (Patterson 1995a). Some lesbians and gay men, perhaps the majority at present, had children in a previous heterosexual relationship. Growing numbers of lesbians and gay men are choosing to have children within the context of a same-sex relationship. In a national poll, 49% of gay men and lesbians who were not parents said they would like to have or adopt children of their own (Kaiser Family Foundation 2001). Given the obstacles to parenthood faced by self-identified gay men and lesbians, there is a high likelihood that their children are strongly desired and planned.

Several paths to parenthood are available to same-sex couples, each affecting the biological relatedness of the child to the parents. Some couples adopt, in which case neither parent is biologically related to the child. Some gay male couples turn to surrogacy, so that the partner who provides the sperm is biologically related to the child. Some lesbian couples use donor insemination, so that the lesbian who carries the child is biologically related to the child. Other lesbian couples use in vitro fertilization so that one woman contributes the egg and the other woman is the birth mother. There are also differences in the legal relations between parents and children. Some states permit two same-sex partners to be the legal parents of a child, whereas many others do not. In states that do not allow second-parent adoption by a same-sex partner, only one partner in the couple is a legal parent. It is likely that the family experiences of lesbians and gay men differ, depending on how they become parents and the nature of their biological and legal relationship to their children.

Although census data provide basic information about same-sex couples with children, small-scale studies provide richer details about the experiences of these couples. Several studies have investigated relationship satisfaction among lesbian couples with children (see review by Patterson 1995a). There is some evidence that relationship satisfaction may decline shortly after the birth of a child, as is generally true for heterosexual couples. A recent longitudinal study followed lesbian couples from one month before the birth of a child to three months after the birth (Goldberg & Sayer 2006). All couples used donor insemination. For both the biological and nonbiological mother, love for the partner typically declined and conflict increased with the transition to parenthood. Patterns of change were affected by the women's neuroticism, expectations about social support from family, and features of the partners' interaction. Other studies have compared lesbian parenting couples with other couples. In an illustrative study, Flaks et al. (1995) compared 15 lesbian couples to 15 heterosexual couples, all with children between the ages of three and nine who were conceived through donor insemination. No significant differences were found between the lesbian and heterosexual couples on the Dyadic Adjustment Scale, a standard measure of relationship quality.

Does the egalitarian division of household labor typically found among gay and lesbian couples without children hold for those with children? Although limited, available research indicates that parenthood does not change the general pattern of shared household responsibilities for same-sex couples (see review on lesbian parenthood by Parks 1998). This is particularly true for the allocation of household chores and decision-making (e.g., Patterson 1995b, Patterson et al. 2004). The division of childcare responsibilities, on the other hand, is less clear-cut.

Research consistently demonstrates that lesbian couples with children endorse an egalitarian division of childcare as their ideal (Chan et al. 1998, Patterson 1995b, Patterson et al. 2004). This is in contrast to heterosexual couples, who tend to endorse a nonegalitarian division, with the wife ideally doing more childcare than the husband does. Research on the actual division of childcare among lesbian mothers is less consistent. Some studies have reported that lesbian partners share equally in childcare (Hand 1991, Patterson et al. 2004), but others have reported that lesbian couples adopt a less-than-egalitarian division of childcare (Ciano-Boyce & Shelley-Sireci 2002, Patterson 1995b). The reasons for these differences are not understood. They may result from the use of relatively small samples. It seems likely, however, that other factors are also at play. In particular, the biological and legal relationship of each parent to the children may make a difference. It may be, for example, that biological mothers tend to be more involved in childcare than are nonbiological mothers. Research systematically examining these issues is needed.

Currently, research on same-sex couples with children is quite limited. Research on gay fathers is rare (Patterson 2004b). Studies of ethnic minority families and low-income families are also needed. Further, it would be useful for researchers to go beyond studying relationship satisfaction and the division of labor to address a broader set of issues in the lives of same-sex couples raising children and to go beyond description toward specifying underlying mechanisms affecting couples' functioning. Longitudinal approaches to studying same-sex couples as they transition into parenthood may prove especially useful.

Societal Stigma: Stress and Social Support

The stigma of homosexuality affects lesbians, gay men, and their relationships in many ways. Personal experiences of rejection and discrimination are common. In a national survey (Kaiser Family Foundation 2001), 74% of lesbians and gay men reported experiencing discrimination based on sexual orientation, with 23% reporting that discrimination occurred "a lot." Additionally, 34% reported that their family or a family member had refused to accept them because of their sexual orientation. Discrimination often comes in the form of minor daily hassles, such as derogatory remarks or poor service. Swim (2004) utilized daily experience accounts to assess gay and lesbian people's experience with these everyday hassles. Over a one-week period, participants reported experiencing an average of two hassles related to their sexual orientation. Two-thirds of these hassles were verbal, including jokes, comments based on stereotypes, hostile or threatening comments, and comments expressing general dislike of gay men and lesbians. In an experimental study, Jones (1996) demonstrated that same-sex couples requesting a hotel room with a shared bed were denied a room significantly more often than were other-sex couples making an identical request. Lewis et al. (2001) identified several types of gay-related stressors that are specific to lesbians and gay men. One type concerned family reactions and included rejection, lack of support, or ignoring the person's sexual orientation. Other gay-related stressors involved the need to hide one's sexual orientation, fear of being exposed as homosexual, violence and harassment, lack of societal acceptance, and discrimination.

Gay and lesbian couples are also vulnerable to hate crimes based on their sexual orientation. In 2002, a lesbian couple and their infant son barely escaped with their lives when arsonists set their home on fire, only days after the women had sued the University of Montana for failing to provide domestic partner benefits. In 1999, two brothers claiming to be carrying out God's will brutally murdered long-term gay partners Gary Matson, 50, and Winfield Mowder, 40, while they slept in their home. In a national survey, 32% of lesbian and gay respondents reported having been the target of physical violence against them or their property because of their sexual orientation (Kaiser Family Foundation 2001).

Researchers have consistently shown that lesbians and gay men who experience greater levels of discrimination are at greater risk for poor psychological adjustment and stress-related psychological disorders (e.g., Mays & Cochran 2001; Meyer 1995, 2003). Indeed, researchers are now testing the applicability of models of minority stress, first developed with regard to ethnic minorities, to the experiences of lesbian and gay individuals (Meyer 1995, 2003). Unfortunately, we currently have little information about how social stigma and discrimination affect same-sex couples. Research with heterosexual married couples has clearly demonstrated that high levels of stress from sources outside a relationship (e.g., financial difficulties, lack of social support) are associated with lower marital satisfaction and declines in satisfaction over time (Karney & Bradbury 2005). Further, during times of high stress, married couples report experiencing more marital problems.

It is reasonable to assume that discrimination based on sexual orientation places strains on gay and lesbian couples (Mays et al. 1993, Otis et al. 2006). A study of same-sex couples in civil unions (Todosijevic et al. 2005) found a significant association between reports of more gay-specific stressors and lower relationship satisfaction for lesbian couples but not for gay male couples. The effects of gay-related stress on couple functioning may be direct, for example, through limited access to important resources such as jobs and housing, or rejection of the couple or their children by family, neighbors, or peers at work or school. Discrimination may also affect couples indirectly, by diminishing the self-esteem or mental health of the partners or their ability to function effectively in a relationship. Research to determine the ways in which discrimination affects same-sex couples is needed.

Equally important will be studies of the resilience of same-sex couples in the face of prejudice and discrimination. Central to understanding how couples cope with discrimination will be analyses of social support. Research consistently shows that, compared with heterosexuals, lesbians and gay men perceive less social support from their family of origin (Elizur & Mintzer 2003; Kurdek 2004, 2006). Of course, these average differences can be misleading. Some gay men and lesbians have strong and supportive family ties that are undoubtedly a valuable source of aid and comfort in times of need. At the other extreme, some lesbians and gay men have negative relations with their families, ranging from grudging acceptance to outright rejection of them and/or their partner. There is evidence that greater social support from relatives is associated not only with greater personal well-being but also with greater relationship satisfaction in same-sex couples (Kurdek 1988, 1995b). In addition, there may be distinctive types of social support that are of special relevance to lesbians and gay men. Preliminary evidence that support for a woman's lesbian identity may be particularly important to psychological well-being comes from a two-week-long daily experience study of lesbians (Beals & Peplau 2005).

A further consistent finding is that lesbians and gay men may compensate for lower levels of family support by establishing closer ties with friends. Some lesbians and gay men create "families of choice," that is, a network of friends who provide love and support, celebrate holidays and rituals, share leisure activities, and offer assistance in time of need (Carrington 1999). Oswald (2002) referred to the creation of these families as "choosing kin"

and noted commonalities between these flexible family networks and the fictive kinship patterns seen in African American and Latino communities. Studies of the impact of supportive friends on the well-being of same-sex couples would be valuable (Elizur & Mintzer 2003).

Social relations can be a mixed blessing (Rook 1998). On the one hand, supportive relationships are a source of aid and comfort in times of stress. On the other hand, social relations can be powerful sources of conflict, hostility, and disappointment that create stress. Further research on sources of stress and support for same-sex couples is needed, along with explicit analyses of how models of minority stress may apply to same-sex couples.

In this section, we have reviewed three relatively new topics of research about same-sex couples: legal recognition of same-sex relationships, same-sex partners as parents, and the impact of gay-related stress on gay and lesbian couples. An important direction for future research will be to use better and more varied research methodologies. The recent availability of information about same-sex couples gathered from large, representative samples including the U.S. Census and other major surveys has been a major advance. Survey research can fruitfully be augmented with daily experience methods, longitudinal assessments, behavioral observations in controlled settings, and experimental designs. In-depth interviews, participant observations, and ethnographies can provide rich descriptions of the daily lives of same-sex couples within a specific cultural, historical, and social context. Studies specifically focusing on couples from diverse ethnic and social class backgrounds would fill an important gap in existing knowledge.

CONCLUDING COMMENTS

The growing body of research on same-sex couples has contributed to our understanding of close relationships in several important ways. One contribution has been to challenge the accuracy of negative social stereotypes about gay and lesbian relationships and to provide more reliable information (see review by Peplau 1991). For decades, the media have depicted homosexuals as unhappy individuals who are unsuccessful in developing stable romantic ties and so end up frustrated and lonely. Both the women lovers in Radclyffe Hall's popular 1928 novel, *The Well of Loneliness* (Hall 1928), and the male lovers in the recent award-winning film, *Brokeback Mountain*, reflected this theme. Contrary to these media images, research has documented that many contemporary lesbians and gay men establish enduring intimate relationships. Research has also debunked a second stereotype, that gay and lesbian relationships are dysfunctional or inferior in quality to those of heterosexuals. Instead, studies have shown that on standardized measures of love, satisfaction, and relationship adjustment, same-sex and heterosexual couples are remarkably similar. This is not to say that all same-sex relationships are happy and problem-free, but rather that gay and lesbian couples are not necessarily more prone to relationship difficulties than are heterosexuals. A third stereotype, that same-sex relationships universally mimic heterosexual marriages by creating "husband" and "wife" roles, has also been discredited. Historical and anthropological accounts have documented that masculine-feminine distinctions have sometimes been important in structuring same-sex relations, and this may continue to be true among some Americans today (Murray 2000, Peplau 2001, Peplau et al. 1999). However, most contemporary gay and lesbian couples in the United States share homemaking tasks and financial provider responsibilities, rather than dividing them such that one partner is the "husband" and the other partner is the "wife" (Kurdek 2005).

A second contribution of research on gay and lesbian relationships has been to test the generalizability of relationship concepts and theories that were based, implicitly or explicitly, on heterosexual couples. We reviewed research showing the applicability of social exchange models of commitment and stability to same-sex couples. Although same-sex couples may differ from heterosexual couples in their mean level of exchange variables, such as barriers to dissolution, the hypothesized associations among key constructs have been strongly supported. This research provides evidence for the general usefulness of exchange models. It also suggests that researchers studying gay and lesbian relationships can build on the existing theoretical literature about close relationships, rather than having to start anew. We agree with Kurdek (2005, p. 253), who observed that "despite external differences in how gay, lesbian and heterosexual couples are constituted, the relationships of gay and lesbian partners appear to work in much the same way as the relationships of heterosexual partners." A promising new direction is provided by studies applying ideas from adult attachment theory to same-sex couples (e.g., Elizur & Mintzer 2003, Kurdek 2002, Ridge & Feeney 1998).

A third contribution of research on same-sex relationships has been to provide a new way to investigate how gender affects close relationships. For example, by comparing how women behave with male versus female partners, we can begin to disentangle the effects on social interaction of an individual's own sex and the sex of their partner. This comparative research strategy is obviously not identical to an experiment, but can nonetheless be informative. Research on social influence in close relationships is illustrative. Studies of heterosexuals have shown that men and women tend to use somewhat different tactics when trying to influence an intimate partner, but could not clarify if these differences were due to the sex of the influence agent, the sex of the target, or some other factor such as relative power in the relationship. Studies including gay, lesbian, and heterosexual couples (Falbo & Peplau 1980, Howard et al. 1986) have demonstrated that regardless of gender or sexual orientation, partners with relatively less power in a relationship tend to use "weak strategies" such as withdrawal or supplication. In contrast, partners with relatively more power tend to use "strong strategies" including bargaining or bullying.

A fourth contribution of empirical research on same-sex relationships has been to provide a scientific basis for policy and legal decisions. Activities of the American Psychological Association (APA) are illustrative. In July 2004, the APA Council of Representatives issued a resolution on sexual orientation and marriage. It stated, "APA believes that it is unfair and discriminatory to deny same-sex couples legal access to civil marriage and to all its attendant benefits, rights and privileges." The resolution explicitly referred to research on same-sex couples and concluded that research provides no evidence to justify discrimination against same-sex couples. The APA has also submitted research-based legal briefs *amicus curiae* for court cases challenging state marriage laws in Nebraska, New Jersey, New York, Oregon, and Washington (Herek 2006).

As this review suggests, research on same-sex couples has been reinvigorated by the continuing public debate about same-sex marriage, by the availability of improved research methods, and by general theoretical advances in the field of close relationships.

ACKNOWLEDGMENT

We are grateful for advice and assistance provided by David Frederick, Negin Ghavami, Andrew Galperin, Gary Gates, Gregory Herek, Natalya Maisel, Cristina Nguyen, Danny Osborn, Kelly Turner, and Curtis Yee.

LITERATURE CITED

Am. Psychol. Assoc. 2004. Resolution on sexual orientation and marriage. **http://www.apa.org/pi/lgbc/policy/marriage.pdf**

Andersson GT, Noack T, Seierstad A, Weedon-Fekjaer H. 2006. The demographics of same-sex marriages in Norway and Sweden. *Demography* 43:79–98

Bailey JM, Gaulin S, Agyei Y, Gladue BA. 1994. Effects of gender and sexual orientation on evolutionarily relevant aspects of human mating psychology. *J. Personal. Soc. Psychol.* 66:1081–93

Balsam KF, Szymanski DM. 2005. Relationship quality and domestic violence in women's same-sex relationships: the role of minority stress. *Psychol. Women Q.* 29:258–69

Beals KP, Impett EA, Peplau LA. 2002. Lesbians in love: why some relationships endure and others end. *J. Lesbian Stud.* 6:53–63

Beals KP, Peplau LA. 2005. Identity support, identity devaluation, and well-being among lesbians. *Psychol. Women Q.* 29:140–48

Black D, Gates G, Sanders S, Taylor L. 2000. Demographics of the gay and lesbian population in the United States. *Demography* 37:139–54

Blumstein P, Schwartz P. 1983. *American Couples*. New York: Morrow. 656 pp.

Bryant AS, Demian. 1994. Relationship characteristics of American gay and lesbian couples: findings from a national survey. In *Social Services for Gay and Lesbian Couples*, ed. LA Kurdek, pp. 101–17. New York: Haworth

Caldwell MA, Peplau LA. 1984. The balance of power in lesbian relationships. *Sex Roles* 10:587–600

Carrington C. 1999. *No Place Like Home: Relationships and Family Life Among Lesbians and Gay Men*. Chicago: Univ. Chicago Press. 273 pp.

Chan RW, Brooks RC, Raboy B, Patterson CJ. 1998. Division of labor among lesbian and heterosexual parents: associations with children's adjustment. *J. Fam. Psychol.* 12:402–19

Ciano-Boyce C, Shelley-Sireci L. 2002. Who is mommy tonight? Lesbian parenting issues. *J. Homosex.* 43:1–13

Crawford I, Solliday E. 1996. The attitudes of undergraduate college students toward gay parenting. *J. Homosex.* 30:63–77

Diamond LM, Dube EM. 2002. Friendship and attachment among heterosexual and sexual-minority youths. *J. Youth Adolesc.* 31:155–66

Duffy SM, Rusbult CE. 1986. Satisfaction and commitment in homosexual and heterosexual relationships. *J. Homosex.* 12:1–24

Dunne GA. 1997. *Lesbian Lifestyles: Women's Work and the Politics of Sexuality*. Toronto: Univ. Toronto Press. 258 pp.

Eldridge NS, Gilbert LA. 1990. Correlates of relationship satisfaction in lesbian couples. *Psychol. Women Q.* 14:43–62

Elizur Y, Mintzer A. 2003. Gay males intimate relationship quality: the roles of attachment security, gay identity, social support, and income. *Pers. Relat.* 10:411–36

Falbo T, Peplau LA. 1980. Power strategies in intimate relationships. *J. Personal. Soc. Psychol.* 38:618–28

Fassinger RE, Morrow SL. 1995. Overcome: repositioning lesbian sexualities. In *The Psychology of Sexual Orientation, Behavior, and Identity: A Handbook*, ed. L Diamant, RD McAnulty, pp. 197–219. London: Greenwood

Flaks DK, Ficher I, Masterpasqua F, Joseph G. 1995. Lesbians choosing motherhood: a comparative study of lesbian and heterosexual parents and their children. *Dev. Psychol.* 31:105–14

Fulcher M, Sutfin EL, Chan RW, Scheib JE, Patterson CJ. 2006. Lesbian mothers and their children. In *Sexual Orientation and Mental Health: Examining Identity and Development in Lesbian, Gay, and Bisexual People*, ed. AM Omoto, HS Kurtzman, pp. 281–99. Washington, DC: Am. Psychol. Assoc.

Gates G, Ost J. 2004. *The Gay and Lesbian Atlas*. Washington, DC: Urban Inst. Press. 232 pp.

Gen. Account. Off. 2004. Defense of Marriage Act: update to prior report. Document GAO-04-353R. Washington, DC: GAO

Goldberg AE, Sayer A. 2006. Lesbian couples' relationship quality across the transition to parenthood. *J. Marriage Fam.* 68:87–100

Gottman JM, Levenson RW, Swanson C, Swanson K, Tyson R, Yoshimoto D. 2003. Observing gay, lesbian and heterosexual couples' relationships: mathematical modeling of conflict interaction. *J. Homosex.* 45:65–91

Hall R. 1928. *The Well of Loneliness*. New York: Bard Avon. 506 pp.

Hand SI. 1991. *The lesbian parenting couple*. PhD thesis. San Francisco: Prof. School Psychol.

Harkless LE, Fowers BJ. 2005. Similarities and differences in relational boundaries among heterosexuals, gay men, and lesbians. *Psychol. Women Q.* 29:167–76

Harry J. 1984. *Gay Couples*. New York: Praeger. 151 pp.

Harry J, DeVall WB. 1978. *The Social Organization of Gay Males*. New York: Praeger. 223 pp.

Herdt G, Kertzner R. 2006. I do, but I can't: the impact of marriage denial on the mental health and sexual citizenship of lesbians and gay men in the United States. *J. Sex. Res. Soc. Policy* 3(1):33–49, online ISSN 1553-6610

Herek GM. 2006. Legal recognition of same-sex relationships in the United States: a social science perspective. *Am. Psychol.* 61:In press

Hickson FC, Davies PM, Hunt AJ, Weatherburn P, McManus TJ, Coxon AP. 1992. Maintenance of open gay relationships: some strategies for protection against HIV. *AIDS Care* 4:409–19

Hochschild A, Machung A. 1989. *The Second Shift: Working Parents and the Revolution at Home.* New York: Viking

Howard JA, Blumstein P, Schwartz P. 1986. Sex, power, and influence tactics in intimate relationships. *J. Personal. Soc. Psychol.* 51:102–9

Human Rights Campaign. 2006. *Statewide marriage laws.* **http://www.hrc.org/Template. cfm?Section=Center&CONTENTID=2822.5&TEMPLATE=/ContentManage ment/ContentDisplay.cfm**

Johnson MP. 2006. Violence and abuse in personal relationships: conflict, terror, and resistance in intimate partnerships. In *The Cambridge Handbook of Personal Relationships*, ed. A Vangelisti, D Perlman, pp. 557–78. New York: Cambridge Univ. Press

Johnson S. 1990. *Staying Power: Long-Term Lesbian Couples.* Tallahassee, FL: Naiad Press. 333 pp.

Jones DA. 1996. Discrimination against same-sex couples in hotel reservation policies. *J. Homosex.* 31:153–59

Kaiser Family Found. 2001. *Inside-Out: A Report on the Experiences of Lesbians, Gays and Bisexuals in America and the Public's View on Issues and Policies Related to Sexual Orientation*, Menlo Park, CA

Karney BR, Bradbury TN. 2005. Contextual influences on marriage: implications for policy and intervention. *Curr. Dir. Psychol. Sci.* 14:171–74

King M, Bartlett A. 2006. What same-sex civil partnerships may mean for health. *J. Epidemiol. Community Health* 60:188–91

Klinkenberg D, Rose S. 1994. Dating scripts of gay men and lesbians. *J. Homosex.* 26:23–35

Kurdek LA. 1988. Perceived social support in gays and lesbians in cohabiting relationships. *J. Personal. Soc. Psychol.* 54:504–9

Kurdek LA. 1991. Correlates of relationship satisfaction in cohabiting gay and lesbian couples. *J. Personal. Soc. Psychol.* 61:910–22

Kurdek LA. 1993. The allocation of household labor in gay, lesbian, and heterosexual married couples. *J. Soc. Issues* 49(3):127–39

Kurdek LA. 1994a. The nature and correlates of relationship quality in gay, lesbian, and heterosexual cohabiting couples. In *Lesbian and Gay Psychology: Volume 1*, ed. B Greene, GM Herek, pp. 113–55. Thousand Oaks, CA: Sage

Kurdek LA. 1994b. Areas of conflict for gay, lesbian, and heterosexual couples: What couples argue about influences relationship satisfaction. *J. Marr. Fam.* 56:923–34

Kurdek LA. 1995a. Developmental changes in relationship quality in gay and lesbian cohabiting couples. *Dev. Psychol.* 31:86–94

Kurdek LA. 1995b. Lesbian and gay couples. In *Lesbian, Gay, and Bisexual Identities over the Lifespan*, ed. AR D'Augelli, CJ Patterson, pp. 243–61. New York: Oxford

Kurdek LA. 1998. Relationship outcomes and their predictors: longitudinal evidence from heterosexual married, gay cohabiting, and lesbian cohabiting couples. *J. Marr. Fam.* 60:553–68

Kurdek LA. 2000. Attractions and constraints as determinants of relationship commitment: longitudinal evidence from gay, lesbian, and heterosexual couples. *Pers. Relat.* 7:245–62

Kurdek LA. 2002. On being insecure about the assessment of attachment styles. *J. Soc. Personal. Relat.* 19:811–34

Kurdek LA. 2004. Are gay and lesbian cohabiting couples *really* different from heterosexual married couples? *J. Marr. Fam.* 66:880–900

Kurdek LA. 2005. What do we know about gay and lesbian couples? *Curr. Dir. Psychol. Sci.* 14:251–54

Kurdek LA. 2006. Differences between partners from heterosexual, gay, and lesbian cohabiting couples. *J. Marr. Fam.* 68:509–28

Kurdek LA, Schmitt JP. 1986. Relationship quality of partners in heterosexual married, heterosexual cohabiting, and gay and lesbian relationships. *J. Personal. Soc. Psychol.* 51:711–20

Kurdek LA, Schmitt JP. 1987. Partner homogamy in married, heterosexual cohabitating, gay, and lesbian couples. *J. Sex Res.* 23(2):212–32

Lannutti PJ. 2005. For better or worse: exploring the meanings of same-sex marriage within the lesbian, gay, bisexual and transgendered community. *J. Soc. Personal. Relat.* 22:5–18

Lewis GB. 2006. *Thinking about gay marriage: putting the moral condemnation back into morality policy*. Presented at Williams Inst. 5th Annu. Update Sex. Orientation Law Public Policy, Univ. Calif., Los Angeles

Lewis RJ, Derlega VJ, Berndt A, Morris LM, Rose S. 2001. An empirical analysis of stressors for gay men and lesbians. *J. Homosex.* 42(1):63–88

Mays VM, Cochran SD. 2001. Mental health correlates of perceived discrimination among lesbian, gay, and bisexual adults in the United States. *Am. J. Public Health* 91:1869–76

Mays VM, Cochran SD, Rhue S. 1993. The impact of perceived discrimination on the intimate relationships of black lesbians. *J. Homosex.* 25:1–14

McWhirter DP, Mattison AM. 1984. *The Male Couple: How Relationships Develop*. Englewood Cliffs, NJ: Prentice-Hall. 341 pp.

Metz ME, Rosser BRS, Strapko N. 1994. Differences in conflict-resolution styles among heterosexual, gay, and lesbian couples. *J. Sex Res.* 31:1–16

Meyer IH. 1995. Minority stress and mental health in gay men. *J. Health Soc. Behav.* 36:38–56

Meyer IH. 2003. Prejudice, social stress, and mental health in lesbian, gay, and bisexual populations: conceptual issues and research evidence. *Psychol. Bull.* 129:674–97

Murray SO. 2000. *Homosexualities*. Chicago: Univ. Chicago Press. 507 pp.

Nardi PM. 1999. *Gay Men's Friendships*. Chicago: Univ. Chicago Press. 253 pp.

Oswald RF. 2002. Resilience within the family networks of lesbians and gay men: intentionality and redefinition. *J. Marr. Fam.* 64:374–83

Otis MD, Rostosky SS, Riggle EDB, Hamrin R. 2006. Stress and relationship quality in same-sex couples. *J. Soc. Personal. Relat.* 23:81–99

Parks CA. 1998. Lesbian parenthood: a review of the literature. *Am. J. Orthopsychiatry* 68:376–89

Patterson CJ. 1995a. Lesbian mothers, gay fathers, and their children. In *Lesbian, Gay, and Bisexual Identities over the Lifespan: Psychological Perspectives*, ed. AR D'Augelli, CJ Patterson, pp. 262–90. New York: Oxford Univ. Press

Patterson CJ. 1995b. Families of the baby boom: parents' division of labor and children's adjustment. *Dev. Psychol.* 31:115–23

Patterson CJ. 2003. Children of lesbian and gay parents. In *Psychological Perspectives on Lesbian, Gay, and Bisexual Experiences*, ed. LD Garnets, DC Kimmel, pp. 497–548. New York: Columbia Univ. Press. 815 pp. 2nd ed.

Patterson CJ. 2004a. What difference does a civil union make? Changing public policies and the experiences of same-sex couples: comment on Solomon, Rothblum, and Balsam 2004. *J. Fam. Psychol.* 18:287–89

Patterson CJ. 2004b. Gay fathers. In *The Role of the Father in Child Development*, ed. ME Lamb, pp. 397–416. New York: Wiley. 4th ed.

Patterson CJ, Sutfin EL, Fulcher M. 2004. Division of labor among lesbian and heterosexual parenting couples: correlates of specialized versus shared patterns. *J. Adult Dev.* 11:179–89

Peplau LA. 1991. Lesbian and gay relationships. In *Homosexuality: Research Findings for Public Policy*, ed. JC Gonsiorek, JD Weinrich, pp. 177–96. Newbury Park, CA: Sage

Peplau LA, Spalding LR, Conley TD, Veniegas RC. 1999. The development of sexual orientation in women. *Annu. Rev. Sex Res.* 10:70–99

Peplau LA. 2001. Rethinking women's sexual orientation: an interdisciplinary, relationship-focused approach. *Pers. Relat.* 8:1–19

Peplau LA, Cochran SD. 1980. *Sex differences in values concerning love relationships*. Presented at Annu. Meet. Am. Psychol. Assoc., Montreal

Peplau LA, Cochran SD. 1981. Value orientations in the intimate relationships of gay men. *J. Homosex.* 6:1–19

Peplau LA, Cochran SD, Mays VM. 1997. A national survey of the intimate relationships of African American lesbians and gay men: a look at commitment, satisfaction, sexual behavior, and HIV disease. In *Ethnic and Cultural Diversity among Lesbians and Gay Men*, ed. B Greene, pp. 11–38. Thousand Oaks, CA: Sage

Peplau LA, Cochran SD, Rook K, Padesky C. 1978. Women in love: attachment and autonomy in lesbian relationships. *J. Soc. Issues* 34(3):7–27

Peplau LA, Fingerhut AW, Beals KP. 2004. Sexuality in the relationships of lesbians and gay men. In *Handbook of Sexuality in Close Relationships*, ed. J Harvey, A Wenzel, S Sprecher, pp. 350–69. Mahwah, NJ: Erlbaum

Peplau LA, Garnets LD, eds. 2000. Women's sexualities: new perspectives on sexual orientation and gender. *J. Soc. Issues* 56(2):181–364

Peplau LA, Padesky C, Hamilton M. 1982. Satisfaction in lesbian relationships. *J. Homosex.* 8:23–35

Peplau LA, Spalding LR. 2000. The close relationships of lesbians, gay men and bisexuals. In *Close Relationships: A Sourcebook*, ed. C Hendrick, SS Hendrick, pp. 111–24. Thousand Oaks, CA: Sage

Potoczniak MJ, Mourot JE, Crosbie-Burnett M, Potoczniak DJ. 2003. Legal and psychological perspectives on same-sex domestic violence: a multisystemic approach. *J. Fam. Psychol.* 17:252–59

Reilly ME, Lynch JM. 1990. Power-sharing in lesbian partnerships. *J. Homosex.* 19:1–30

Renzetti CM, Miley CH. 1996. *Violence in Gay and Lesbian Domestic Partnerships*. New York: Haworth. 121 pp.

Ridge SR, Feeney JA. 1998. Relationship history and relationship attitudes in gay males and lesbians: attachment style and gender differences. *Aust. NZ J. Psychiatry* 32(6):848–59

Rook KS. 1998. Investigating the positive and negative sides of personal relationships: through a lens darkly? In *The Dark Side of Close Relationships*, ed. BH Spitzberg, WR Cupach, pp. 369–93. Mahwah, NJ: Erlbaum

Rose S, Zand D, Cini M. 1993. Lesbian courtship scripts. In *Boston Marriages: Romantic but Asexual Relationships Among Contemporary Lesbians*, ed. ED Rothblum, KA Brehony, pp. 70–85. Amherst: Univ. Mass. Press

Rothblum ED. 2000. Sexual orientation and sex in women's lives: conceptual and methodological issues. *J. Soc. Issues* 56(2):193–204

Rutter V, Schwartz P. 1996. Same-sex couples: courtship, commitment, context. In *The Diversity of Human Relationships*, ed. AE Auhagen, M von Salisch. pp. 197–223. New York: Cambridge Univ. Press

Schreurs KMG, Buunk BP. 1996. Closeness, autonomy, equity and relationship satisfaction in lesbian couples. *Psychol. Women Q.* 20:577–92

Solomon SE, Rothblum ED, Balsam KF. 2004. Pioneers in partnership: lesbian and gay male couples in civil unions compared with those not in civil unions and heterosexual married siblings. *J. Fam. Psychol.* 18:275–86

Solomon SE, Rothblum ED, Balsam KF. 2005. Money, housework, sex, and conflict: same-sex couples in civil unions, those not in civil unions, and heterosexual married siblings. *Sex Roles* 52:561–75

Swim JK. 2004. *Day to day experiences with heterosexism: heterosexist hassles as daily stressors.* Work. Pap., Dept. Psychol., Penn. State Univ.

Tasker F. 2005. Lesbian mothers, gay fathers, and their children: a review. *J. Dev. Behav. Pediatr.* 26(3):224–40

Testa RJ, Kinder BN, Ironson G. 1987. Heterosexual bias in the perception of loving relationships of gay males and lesbians. *J. Sex Res.* 23:163–72

The Pew Forum on Religion and Public Life. 2005. *Abortion and rights of terror suspects top court issues; strong support for stem cell research.* **http://pewforum.org/docs/index.php?Doc ID=91**

Todosijevic J, Rothblum ED, Solomon SE. 2005. Relationship satisfaction, affectivity, and gay-specific stressors in same-sex couples joined in civil unions. *Psychol. Women Q.* 29:158–66

Weinstock JS. 2004. Lesbian FLEX-ibility: friend and/or family connections among lesbian ex-lovers. *J. Lesbian Stud.* 8(3/4):193–238

Ostracism

Kipling D. Williams

Department of Psychological Sciences, Purdue University, West Lafayette,
Indiana 47907; email: kip@psych.purdue.edu

Annu. Rev. Psychol. 2007. 58:425–52

First published online as a Review in
Advance on August 25, 2006

The *Annual Review of Psychology* is online
at http://psych.annualreviews.org

This article's doi:
10.1146/annurev.psych.58.110405.085641

0066-4308/07/0203-0425$20.00

Key Words

ignoring, social exclusion, rejection, silent treatment

Abstract

In this review, I examine the social psychological research on ostracism, social exclusion, and rejection. Being ignored, excluded,
and/or rejected signals a threat for which reflexive detection in the
form of pain and distress is adaptive for survival. Brief ostracism
episodes result in sadness and anger and threaten fundamental needs.
Individuals then act to fortify or replenish their thwarted need or
needs. Behavioral consequences appear to be split into two general categories: attempts to fortify relational needs (belonging, self-
esteem, shared understanding, and trust), which lead generally to
prosocial thoughts and behaviors, or attempts to fortify efficacy/
existence needs of control and recognition that may be dealt with
most efficiently through antisocial thoughts and behaviors. Available research on chronic exposure to ostracism appears to deplete
coping resources, resulting in depression and helplessness.

Contents

INTRODUCTION

If no one turned round when we entered, answered when we spoke, or minded what we did, but if every person we met "cut us dead," and acted as if we were nonexisting things, a kind of rage and impotent despair would ere long well up in us, from which the cruelest bodily tortures would be a relief; for these would make us feel that, however bad might be our plight, we had not sunk to such a depth as to be unworthy of attention at all. (James 1890/1950, pp. 293–94)

Socially, Mack and the boys were beyond the pale. Sam Malloy didn't speak to them as they went by the boiler. They drew into themselves and no one could foresee how they would come out of the cloud. For there are two possible reactions to social ostracism—either a man emerges determined to be better, purer, and kindlier or he goes bad, challenges the world and does even worse things. This last is by far the commonest reaction to stigma. (Steinbeck 1987/1945, pp. 250–51)

Belonging is a fundamental requirement for security, reproductive success, and mental health (Baumeister & Leary 1995, Smith et al. 1999). The past decade has witnessed a proliferation of research interest on what happens when the person does not belong, through acts of ostracism, social exclusion, and rejection. These interrelated interpersonally aversive phenomena have been woven in our social fabric for eons, practiced not only by humans, but also by other social animals. Indeed, these powerful behavioral strategies provide strength and resiliency to this fabric. The group that ostracizes becomes more cohesive (Gruter & Masters 1986). Thus, it is somewhat perplexing that these powerful and universal processes have only recently attracted attention in social psychology. Perhaps one reason for our current fascination with the processes and consequences of social exclusion is that we are searching for explanations for what appears to be a recent surge in seemingly irrational and socially intolerable behaviors that have appeared worldwide: random acts of monstrous violence. In news reports that we consider almost routine now, we are bombarded with stories of incidences in which individuals, often students in high school, have wielded weapons and, without apparent concern for their own survival, have shot and killed many of their peers and teachers. We have witnessed peoples' willingness to conduct terrorist acts against countless and unknown others, again with plausible certainty that in carrying out these acts, they will perish with the victims. Since 1994, in U.S. schools alone, there have been more than 220 separate shooting incidents in which at least one person was killed and 18 episodes that involved multiple killings (Anderson et al. 2001). Mass shootings (or attempts that have been intercepted by authorities) at schools and other public places are occurring with increasing frequency in the United States as well as in a growing number of other countries (see Newman 2004 for a sociological/ethnographic perspective on school shootings).

Although the reasons for this apparent upsurge in violence are still not clear, a recent line of investigation has linked such incidents with growing social isolation (Twenge 2000), and further evidence is beginning to emerge that experiences of social exclusion may have played a motivating role in the actions of many shooters. In a case analysis of 15 post-1995 U.S. school shootings, Leary et al. (2003) suggest that chronic social rejection in the form of ostracism, bullying, and/or romantic rebuff was a major contributing factor in 87% of cases. Studies of Martin Bryant, who, in 1996, killed 35 people at a popular tourist attraction at Port Arthur, Tasmania, suggest that he felt lonely and isolated (Bingham 2000, Crook 1997). Robert Steinhauser, who killed 16 people at his ex-high school in Erfurt, Germany, in 2002, though not a social outcast (Lemonick 2002), had been greatly upset by a significant act of exclusion—expulsion from his school. In 2005, at Valparaiso High School in Indiana, a 15-year-old boy held hostage and slashed with two sharp-edged blades—one described as a machete—seven of his classmates. When peers were asked about this boy, it was reported, "He was so invisible at Valparaiso High School this fall that students who sat next to him in Spanish class didn't know his name" ("7 Valparaiso High Students Hurt in Stabbing Rampage," *Indianapolis Star*, Nov. 25, 2004). The consequences of being ostracized, either intentionally or unintentionally, seem to be a thread that weaves through case after case of school violence.

But what would drive an individual, or a group of individuals, to violate all laws of instinctual human survival to carry out these most heinous and violent acts? As the following review suggests, ostracism and other forms of social exclusion often lead to changes in behavior that are likely to garner social approval and increase the likelihood of social acceptance and inclusion. But evidence also supports a link between being a target of ostracism and targeting others for acts of violence. Furthermore, under certain conditions, this link may be so strong that it

Ostracism: ignoring and excluding individuals or groups by individuals or groups

Rejection: an explicit declaration that an individual or group is not wanted

Social exclusion: being kept apart from others

Aggression:
intention to harm
other living beings

obliterates concerns for acceptance and liking by others and even for self-preservation, self-regulation, or inevitable future punishment. Ostracism may lead to other maladaptive decisions and behaviors precisely because of a need to belong (Baumeister & Leary 1995) and to be accepted by others. Ostracism can cause such a strong desire to belong, to be liked by someone, perhaps anyone, that individuals' ability to discriminate good from bad may be impaired to the point that they become attracted to any group that will have them, even cults and extremist groups. Political scientist Paul James of Royal Melbourne Institute of Technology indicated in a television interview (on January 14, 2003) that the profile of Australian citizens who had recently joined terrorist groups like Al Qaeda was of individuals who felt isolated, marginalized, or excluded within their society and who were attracted to the intense face-to-face connectedness that these extremist groups have to offer. Joining and following the dictates of extremist groups can also fulfill needs for control and recognition because these groups promise retribution and worldwide attention.

By all accounts, ostracism occurred long before it was named (*ostrakismos*) around 500 B.C., when Athenians cast their votes on shards of clay, *ostraca*, to determine whether a member of the community, usually a former political leader, should be banished for a period of 10 years. Indeed, ostracism, defined here as being ignored and excluded, has been observed in almost all social species (e.g., primates, lions, wolves, buffalos, bees); in anthropological accounts of tribes from around the world; in modern industrialized nations; in governmental, religious, military, penal, and educational institutions; in informal groups and in close relationships (relational ostracism, or the silent treatment); in playgrounds; and by children, adolescents, and adults (see Gruter & Masters 1986; Williams 1997, 2001). It appears that ostracism is pervasive and powerful.

Psychology's interest in ostracism and related phenomena such as social exclusion and rejection was largely implicit for the first century. Schachter's (1951) research on opinion deviance in group discussions found that if those who disagreed with the group did not yield to communicative attempts to conform to the group's opinion, they would face expulsion from the group. Indeed, a common—often untested—theme of all research in social influence, including obedience, conformity, compliance, and social inhibition, was that people caved to the real or imagined pressures of others to avoid rejection and exclusion. Thus, while fear of anticipated rejection and exclusion was tacitly acknowledged as a motive for many social behaviors, there was little direct investigation into the consequences of experiencing rejection and exclusion.

Although a few scattered studies prior to 1990 examined reactions to being ignored, excluded, or rejected, they had little theoretical foundation or impact (cf. Geller et al. 1974; for a review, see Williams 1997, 2001). Subsequent to this, a model and examples of ostracism were put forth that explicated a taxonomy (various types of ostracism, different modes, motives, etc.), the need-threat notion (ostracism threatens belonging, self-esteem, control, and meaningful existence needs), and short-term (attempts to fortify threatened needs) and long-term (giving up) responses. Additionally, a theory of the need to belong was published that elevated interest in inclusion and exclusion (Baumeister & Leary 1995). In the mid 1990s, a Zeitgeist for research on ostracism surfaced, characterized by a confluence of theories and research interests that gave life to a broad-based and extensive examination of how people respond to acts of being ignored, excluded, and rejected.

In this article, I review the empirical literature that has erupted in the past decade in social psychology on ostracism, social exclusion, and rejection. An active research tradition in developmental psychology on peer rejection includes the topics of bullying, relational, and indirect forms of aggression. For an extensive review of this literature, see Crick et al. (2004) and Juvonen & Gross (2005). Additionally, most of the research reported here deals with the effect of being excluded or ostracized. A future issue to be explored is the motives and factors that predict when individuals and groups will choose to ostracize others (Foddy et al. 1999, Williams et al. 2003, Zadro et al. 2005).

DEFINITIONS

Despite the large number of studies and chapters devoted to examining the impact of ostracism, social exclusion, and rejection, little progress has been made in determining whether these terms describe separate phenomena or are essentially interchangeable. Although some have attempted to delineate semantic and psychologically meaningful distinctions between ostracism, social exclusion, and rejection (Leary 2001, 2005), virtually no empirical research has established distinctions that lead to different consequences. Ostracism is typically defined as being ignored and excluded, and it often occurs without excessive explanation or explicit negative attention. Ostracism is often operationalized as a process that is characterized as an unfolding sequence of responses endured while being ignored and excluded. Laboratory research on ostracism examines the consequences of being ignored and excluded over several minutes; but field, diary, and interview studies examine ostracism over days, weeks, and years (Williams et al. 2000, 2001). Social exclusion appears to be defined as being excluded, alone, or isolated, sometimes with explicit declarations of dislike, but other times not (Twenge et al. 2001). Typically, the exclusion manipulation occurs either after interaction and separation from the others or as a hypothetical consequence in the future. Rejection (Leary et al. 2005) is typically operationalized as a declaration by an individual or group that they do not (or no longer) want to interact or be in the company of the individual. Again, rejection does not typically involve a protracted episode, but occurs after interaction and separation. Despite these apparent distinctions, investigators do not appear to be wedded to these operational definitions, nor do they consistently use specific terms for specific operations. Thus, I use these terms interchangeably.

AN EVOLUTIONARY PERSPECTIVE?

Because ostracism has been observed in most social species and across time and cultures, it is appropriate to consider an evolutionary perspective on its function and existence. As argued in a volume on ostracism by Gruter & Masters (1986), groups that ostracized burdensome or deviating members became more cohesive, offering their members more security and reproductive opportunities; ostracized members died. Ostracism was functional and adaptive (Barner-Barry 1986). Likewise, organisms that were especially good at detecting or anticipating ostracism were probably most likely to be able to do something about it that might prevent the inevitable loss of group membership, protection, and reproductive opportunities. An ostracism-detection system, therefore, probably coevolved with the widespread use of ostracism. Such a detection system was probably selectively biased to detect any possibility of ostracism, thus leading to an error management system that favored a bias for false alarms over misses (see Haselton & Buss 2000, Schaller et al. 2006, Spoor & Williams 2006). Misperceiving an event as ostracism when it was not ostracism might incur some psychological costs, but missing ostracism when it was about to happen would likely result in death. Thus, humans would expect that we have evolved to detect ostracism in such a way that it would signal an alarm that would serve to direct attention toward determining if ostracism was in fact occurring, and if so, would direct our resources toward coping with it. A good alarm signal would be pain. An immediate painful response to any hint of ostracism would capture the individual's attention and require an appraisal so that action could be taken to remedy the situation. The research reviewed below supports such strong immediate re-actions to even the most minimal forms of ostracism.

PARADIGMS AND MANIPULATIONS OF OSTRACISM, SOCIAL EXCLUSION, AND REJECTION

Several paradigms have enjoyed frequent use in research on ostracism and related phenom-ena. Undoubtedly, these paradigms them-selves may account for some of the dis-crepant outcomes (i.e., pro- versus antisocial responses), so it is wise to consider each and to note which paradigms are associated with which outcomes.

Ball Tossing

Williams (1997) developed a minimal os-tracism paradigm in which participants are ig-nored and excluded within the context of an emergent ball-tossing game that appears to have no connection with the experiment it-self. Participants (two confederates and one actual participant) are told to wait quietly for the experimenter's return, at which point the experiment will begin. One of the confeder-ates notices a ball and starts to toss it around. Once each person has had a chance to catch and throw a few times, participants randomly assigned to the ostracism condition are never again thrown the ball, nor are they looked at or responded to. The two confederates con-tinue playing enthusiastically for another four or so minutes. In the inclusion condition, par-ticipants continue to receive the ball approxi-mately one-third of the time.

Cyberball

Williams et al. (2000; see also Williams & Jarvis 2006) developed a virtual analogue to the ball-tossing paradigm that was intended to be more efficient (it requires no confeder-ates) and less traumatic. Instead of an emer-gent game that occurs ostensibly outside the experiment, researchers inform participants over the computer that the study involves the effects of mental visualization on a subsequent task, and that a game, Cyberball, has been found to work well in exercising their mental visualization skills. Participants are told they are playing with two (sometimes three) others who connected over the Internet (or Intranet) and that it does not matter who throws or catches, but rather that they use the animated ball-toss game to assist them in visualizing the other players, the setting, the temperature, and so on. This cover story, like the emergent game in the ball-tossing paradigm, is meant to assure participants that not getting the ball has no detrimental effects on their performance in the experiment. As in ball tossing, ostracized participants receive the ball substantially less than did the included participants, usually get-ting only one or two tosses near the beginning of the game. Typically, the game proceeds for 30–50 throws.

Life Alone

Twenge et al. (2001) and Baumeister et al. (2002) developed a personality test, the life-alone prognosis paradigm, in which partici-pants respond to a personality questionnaire, receive accurate introversion/extraversion feedback, and are randomly assigned to one of three additional forms of feedback. In the accepted/high-belonging condition, partici-pants are told that they are the type who has rewarding relationships throughout life; that they will have a long and stable marriage, and have lifelong friendships with people who care about them. In the rejected/low-belonging condition, they are told that they are the type who will end up alone later in life; that al-though they have friends and relationships now, by the time they are in their mid-20s most of these will disappear. They may have multiple marriages, but none of them will last, and they will end up being alone later in life. As a negative-feedback control condition, par-ticipants in the accident-prone condition are told they will endure a lifetime of accidents and injuries.

Get Acquainted

This paradigm, developed by Nezlek et al. (1997), involves the use of a small group of actual participants engaged in a get-acquainted discussion. They are given examples of topics to discuss (e.g., favorite movies, major in college) and take turns talking within the group setting. Following this discussion, they are separated and asked to identify the individual from the group with whom they would most like to work. A few minutes later, they receive one of two types of feedback concerning how the others voted, that either everyone wanted to work with them (inclusion) or that no one wanted to work with them (rejection).

Other Paradigms

Several other ostracism, social exclusion, and rejection paradigms have been used with less frequency. Ostracism, social exclusion, and/or rejection have been manipulated within the context of a continuous public goods dilemma game (Ouwerkerk et al. 2005), chat rooms (Gardner et al. 2000, Williams et al. 2002), face-to-face conversations (Geller et al. 1974), cell phone text messaging (Smith & Williams 2004), role playing (Williams et al. 2000, Zadro et al. 2005), reliving or imagining rejection experiences (Craighead et al. 1979, Pickett et al. 2004, Williams & Fitness 2004), scenario descriptions of rejection and social exclusion (Fiske & Yamamoto 2005, Hitlan et al. 2006), and a variety of virtual reality worlds (K.D. Williams & A.T. Law, unpublished data).

THEORIES OF OSTRACISM, SOCIAL EXCLUSION, AND REJECTION

Whereas many hypotheses have been proposed to explain specific experimental predictions, there are currently three major theories that attempt to explain and predict the impact and consequences of ostracism, social exclusion, and rejection.

A TEMPORAL EXAMINATION OF RESPONSES TO OSTRACISM

Although only a few theorists have emphasized the importance of examining the impact of ostracism over time (Brewer 2005; Williams 1997, 2001), the extant literature supports the utility of such a temporal framework. As with responses to many situational factors, there are automatic reflexive responses to ostracism that are followed by more deliberative reflective reactions. This temporal examination can be taken further to examine (although perhaps not through experiments) the impact of cumulative instances of frequent exposures to ostracism or to long-lasting episodes of ostracism.

Williams (1997, 2001; Williams & Zadro 2005) proposes the following sequence: (*a*) reflexive painful response to any form of ostracism, unmitigated by situational or individual difference factors; (*b*) threats to the need for belonging, self-esteem, control, and meaningful existence, and increases in sadness and anger; and (*c*) a reflective stage that is responsive to cognitive appraisals of the situation, the sources of ostracism, the reasons for ostracism, and predisposing inclinations that reflect individual differences residing within the target of ostracism, all of which guide the individual to fortify the most threatened needs. If relational needs (belonging and self-esteem) are most thwarted, then ostracized individuals will seek to fortify these needs by thinking, feeling, and behaving in a relatively prosocial manner. If, however, efficacy and existence/recognition needs are most thwarted, ostracized individuals will attempt to fortify these needs, which in many instances may result in controlling, provocative, and even antisocial responses. For individuals who encounter multiple episodes (or single long-term episodes) of ostracism, their ability to marshal their resources to fortify threatened needs will be diminished, and feelings of helplessness, alienation, and despair will infuse their thoughts, feelings, and actions.

THE SOCIAL MONITORING SYSTEM AND SOCIOMETER THEORY

Another major theoretical perspective that has gained support focuses primarily on how ostracism, social exclusion, and/or rejection thwart the need to belong, in particular (Gardner et al. 2005, Pickett & Gardner 2005), and how a psychological system—the social monitoring system—helps regulate optimal levels of belongingness. When belonging is threatened, the individual is motivated to attend more carefully to social cues, presumably to achieve success in subsequent social interactions. This approach is consistent with Leary et al.'s (1995 and 1998) sociometer theory, which asserts that self-esteem is a gauge of relational valuation that, when low, signals the individual that changes must be made to improve inclusionary status.

COGNITIVE DECONSTRUCTION AND SELF-REGULATION IMPAIRMENT

A third theoretical framework argues that the blow of social exclusion is much like the blow of a blunt instrument, and it causes a temporary state of cognitive deconstruction (Baumeister et al. 2002), much like the affectively flat stage that precedes suicide attempts. This explanation has been offered especially when socially excluded individuals show no signs of mood impact (see also Baumeister & DeWall 2005). Consistent with this explanation of cognitive impairment is the premise that social exclusion impairs individuals' ability to self-regulate, which inhibits their ability to utilize the cognitive/motivational resources that are necessary to avoid impulsive acts and

to engage in hedonic sacrifice and delayed gratification. This explanation fits nicely with observations of anger and indiscriminant aggression that sometimes follow social exclusion, and with recent evidence showing impaired inhibition against eating nonnutritive foods and avoidance of less tasty, nutritive foods (Baumeister et al. 2006).

REVIEW OF THE EMPIRICAL FINDINGS

I first review the empirical findings by examining how individuals respond immediately during the ostracism episode, referred to as the reflexive stage. I then review the evidence for mediating impact that might direct future thoughts, feelings, and behaviors, referred to as the reflective stage (these terms are used similarly to those used by Lieberman et al. 2002). Finally, I review the research examining the behavioral consequences of ostracism, social exclusion, and rejection.

REFLEXIVE STAGE: IMMEDIATE IMPACT OF OSTRACISM

A considerable number of studies have assessed reactions to ostracism either during or immediately after the ostracism episode. Usually, the measures taken immediately following the ostracism are asked retrospectively, for example, "How did you feel while you were playing the Cyberball game?" Thus, participants are reporting about their feelings and thoughts as the ostracism episode occurred. This distinction becomes important because the available evidence suggests that the reflexive pain/distress signal is quickly followed by appraisals and coping mechanisms that direct the individual toward thoughts and feelings that alleviate the pain. To be included in this section, the assessments must, therefore, have been taken during or immediately following the ostracism experience and must pertain to their responses during the ostracism experience.

Physiological Responses and Brain Activation

A few studies have examined physiological responses during or immediately following ostracism or rejection experiences. In one study, participants were attached to an impedance cardiograph while they played Cyberball (Zadro 2004). Guided by Blascovich & Tomaka's (1996) challenge/threat model, Zadro compared participants' baseline (waiting) levels to their initial inclusion levels, then their levels during ostracism, and finally to inclusion again. A challenge response is characterized as a functional behavioral reaction to situational demands that the individual has the capacity to handle and that has physiological concomitants of increased blood flow with arterial expansion. Threat, however, is a dysfunctional behavioral response that is accompanied by increased blood flow and arterial constriction. Ostracism did not produce a systematic threat response, but there was evidence for increased blood pressure during ostracism.

Similarly, Stroud et al. (2000) developed the Yale InterPersonal Stressor (YIPS) paradigm, which involved several forms of interpersonal rejection (including active derision) and exclusion within a small-group setting. In comparison with participants who had been engaged in a nonsocial task of searching for letter strings, researchers found the rejected/excluded participants to have significant increases in blood pressure and cortisol levels (in addition to higher self-reported levels of tension). It must be noted that because several abusive/rejection/exclusion acts occurred during the social interaction, and the control group had no social interaction at all, it is not clear which of these acts, if any, produced these effects.

Eisenberger et al. (2003) tested participants with a functional magnetic resonance imagery scanner while they played Cyberball over several stages. In Stage 1, called the implicit rejection condition, participants were told they would soon be playing a mental imagery game with two others (who were also in scanners) and who had already begun playing. Participants were told that their computers were not yet hooked up to the other two players' computers, so at first they would simply be watching the other two participants play the game. At some point when their computers were communicating with those of the other two players, they would be thrown the ball, and they could begin playing, too. In Stage 2, they were included. In Stage 3, the other two players apparently intentionally ostracized the participant (explicit rejection). Participants then completed a post-Cyberball questionnaire, which measured the distress during Stage 3. The results of this study showed that regardless of whether the ostracism was unintentional or intentional, it was associated with increased activation of the dorsal anterior cingulate cortex (dACC), a region of the brain that shows activation during exposure to physical pain (and loss of social connections, see Lieberman 2007; but also discrepancy detection, see Miller & Cohen 2001). As support for the pain interpretation, participants' dACC activation in Stage 3 was highly positively correlated with self-reported distress. The right ventral prefrontal cortex showed increased activation, but only during intentional ostracism. This region's function is to moderate the pain response, and consistent with this interpretation, its increased activation was negatively associated with self-reported distress. Additionally, Eisenberger (2006) found that dACC, amygdala, and periaqueductal gray activity during Cyberball-induced ostracism correlated with diary reports of social disconnections (see also MacDonald & Leary 2005).

Dickerson & Kemeny (2004; see also Dickerson et al. 2004) conducted a meta-analysis of studies examining cortisol levels as a function of social-evaluative threat. Social-evaluative threat was defined broadly as any feedback about the self that others could judge negatively. Cortisol is a hormone that is secreted presumably to rally the organism's

dACC: dorsal anterior cingulate cortex

efforts to survive and deal effectively with danger. Gunnar et al. (2003) report higher levels of cortisol levels in children for whom sociometric measures indicated peer rejection.

Self-Reported Distress Levels

Many studies have examined various self-reported levels of distress following ostracism, social exclusion, and rejection. These measures may include assessments of mood (usually sadness and anger), hurt feelings, levels of belonging, self-esteem, control, and meaningful existence, and more direct measures of distress or pain. Several studies have measured self-esteem, finding reductions following temporary or remembered instances of rejection and ostracism (Leary et al. 1995, Sommer et al. 2001, Williams et al. 2000, Zadro et al. 2004). Similarly, a sense of belonging, control, and meaningful existence diminishes following ostracism (Smith & Williams 2004; Williams et al. 2000; Zadro et al. 2004, 2006). At this time, there are few compelling reasons to separate these measures because they usually show high levels of intercorrelation.

Taken together, these studies provide ample evidence that ostracism increases self-reported distress. Williams and his colleagues have shown repeatedly that ostracism increases sadness and anger and lowers levels of belonging, self-esteem, control, and meaningful existence (reviewed by Williams & Zadro 2005). The typical effect size of ostracism on self-reported distress (as measured by moods and need threat) is high, between 1.0 and 2.0. Williams et al. (2000) found a distress pattern that was linearly associated with the amount of ostracism to which the participants were exposed, such that more ostracism (included only twice at the beginning of the game and never again) was more distressing than less ostracism (being included for one-sixth of the throws), which was more distressing than inclusion, which itself was less pleasant than overinclusion. Research has also shown that ostracism increases reports of hurt feelings and pain. When participants were

asked to recall a physically painful event or a socially painful event, levels of currently experienced pain were considerably higher when they relived socially painful events, especially those coded as including ostracism (Williams & Fitness 2004). These pain levels, using the McGill pain inventory, were comparable to pain levels observed in meta-analyses (Wilkie et al. 1990) for chronic back pain and even childbirth.

Furthermore, considerable (but not all) research suggests that ostracism-induced distress is very resilient to moderation by situational factors or individual differences. Ostracism-induced distress emerged regardless of initial levels of trait self-esteem. Similarly, Leary et al. (1998) reported that trait self-esteem did not moderate participants' reactions to interpersonal rejection. Smith & Williams (2004) reported increased psychological distress following ostracism during a cell phone text-messaging interaction, and levels of individualism-collectivism did not moderate this effect. Additional studies find no moderation of ostracism-induced distress by individual-difference variables, including introversion-extraversion (Nadasi 1992), participant gender (Williams & Sommer 1997), loneliness and need for belonging (Carter-Sowell et al. 2006), and social anxiety (Zadro et al. 2006).

Ostracism-induced distress has also been resilient to situational variation, even when the situational manipulations would reasonably be expected to affect appraisals of the importance and threat value of ostracism. For instance, as already discussed, dACC activation occurred for both unintentional and intentional ostracism, although it was greater for intentional ostracism (Eisenberger et al. 2003). Self-reported distress measures show even less influence of situational factors. Self-reported distress levels are no higher when participants believe that other players are acting on their own volition compared with when they are told that other players are simply following a script and ostracizing them. Perhaps more surprisingly, in the same study, self-reported distress was no lower when participants were told they were merely playing with a computer (Zadro et al. 2004). In another study, experimenters convinced participants they were playing Cyberball with similar others (i.e., those holding similar political leanings), rival others (i.e., those leaning toward the views of the major rival political party), or despised others (i.e., those leaning toward the views of the Australian Ku Klux Klan). Despite strong reasons to discount ostracism by an outgroup or, especially, a despised outgroup, the distress of ostracized participants was unmoderated by the psychological closeness of the ostracizing group (Gonsalkorale & Williams 2006). Whether inclusion comes with a cost (50 cents deducted for each throw received) or not, or whether the object being thrown is a ball or bomb (that is expected to explode, "killing off the player with the ball"), participants are still distressed by being ostracized (van Beest & Williams 2006a,b). We have also found that eliminating the human characteristics within a Cyberball-like game, and giving no instructions to mentally visualize the experience, resulted in no distress, but if participants generated agent-volition thoughts, they did show distress (Law & Williams 2006).

In contrast to the evidence reviewed above, several studies show behavioral consequences following the exclusion manipulation, in the absence of personal distress. In particular, the work of Baumeister, Twenge, and their colleagues typically finds no effects of social exclusion on mood, regardless of the type of mood measure employed. These researchers suggest that one consequence of social exclusion is a state of cognitive deconstruction and affective numbness, which may even extend to a lack of physical and social sensitivity (Baumeister et al. 2002, DeWall & Baumeister 2006, Twenge 2005). Although this suggestion is intriguing, there is also evidence by others that ostracism can make individuals more sensitive to social information (Gardner et al. 2000, Pickett et al. 2004). It is important to note that all social exclusion manipulations

may not have the same impact, and in this case, it may be that the life-alone paradigm is particularly strong in inducing a sense of helplessness and inevitability. Compared with other methods of manipulating exclusion or rejection, there would seem to be nothing participants could do about their future aloneness, and this realization may induce a concussed state, as the authors suggest.

Taken as a whole, these studies suggest that the immediate or reflexive reactions to ostracism are painful and/or distressing and are resistant to moderation by individual differences or situational factors. Even if moderation is eventually documented, it appears that an immediate and painful reaction to even the slightest hint of ostracism may be an adaptive response that directs attention to the situation, presumably to assess its threat value and to take actions to ameliorate the situation. Manipulating signals (e.g., stigma, attractiveness) may be the best bet for identifying potential moderators because these factors also have strong survival/reproductive value. Moderation may be more likely when ostracism is manipulated less strongly, as could be achieved with partial ostracism conditions.

REFLECTIVE STAGE: RESPONSES TO OSTRACISM FOLLOWING APPRAISAL

A casual review of these studies could easily suggest that ostracized, socially excluded, and rejected individuals are capable of responding in a variety of ways, many of which appear to be quite contradictory. For example, ostracized individuals can be more helpful, positive, and cooperative. They can also be more mean-spirited and indiscriminately aggressive. They are also capable of cognitive and emotional shut down. Finally, they seem to show evidence for fleeing the situation, if that option is available. We often think of the response to threat as falling into one of three categories, fight, flight, or freeze. Taylor et al. (2000) suggest, however, another reaction to threat is to tend-and-befriend (see also

MacDonald & Kingsbury 2006 for discussion of fight-flight-freeze distinctions related to social exclusion). I review the literature using these general categories of response to the initial pain and threat of ostracism, first focusing on research that examines moderation by individual differences and then by situational factors. I then propose a framework within which to view and understand these apparent disparate findings.

Moderation by Individual Differences on Coping Responses

Although the blunt blow of ostracism appears to overwhelm personality and individual differences during the exclusion episode itself, dispositions that affect individuals' construal of the ostracism episode ought to moderate the meaning and importance they attach to it and guide appropriate coping strategies.

Fight. A great deal of work by Downey and colleagues has shown that despite generally universal needs for acceptance and belonging, important individual differences exist in how people respond to imagined or actual rejection experiences. These researchers proposed a defensive motivational system that influences and guides perceived appropriate responding in the face of rejection (Downey et al. 2004). Rejection sensitivity, Downey posits, emerges from a history of being repeatedly rejected, and generally leads to maladaptive responses to rejection that may perpetuate further rejection. Individuals who score high on rejection sensitivity (RS) (using the RS questionnaire, Downey & Feldman 1996) tend to chronically expect rejection, to see it when it may not be happening, and to respond to it hostilely. Men who score highly on RS and who are highly invested in a romantic relationship are more likely to have a propensity for violence in that relationship (Downey et al. 2000). A link between RS scores and hostile intention toward people they believed did or could reject them has also been found (Downey & Feldman 1996, Feldman & Downey 1994). Similarly,

children scoring high in rejection sensitivity who were presented with an ambiguous rejection scenario (by peers or teachers) were more likely to endorse hostile responses (Downey et al. 1998). In pleasant interactions ending mysteriously without explanation, rejection sensitivity and hostile ideation was strongly linked for females (Ayduk et al. 1999) and males (Ayduk & Downey; reported in Romero-Canyas & Downey 2005). Internet chat partners who abruptly indicated no further interest in interacting were negatively evaluated by high-RS women (Ayduck et al. 1999). Finally, in diary studies, Downey et al. (1998, and reported in Romero-Canyas & Downey 2005) found that following higher reports of rejection, high-RS individuals report higher incidence of relational conflicts.

Individuals who varied in agreeableness were given varying magnitudes of rejection by their partner after they had disclosed information about themselves (Buckley et al. 2004, Study 1). Agreeableness predicted but did not moderate negative reactions to rejection, and any amount of rejection was sufficient to cause increases in sadness, hurt feelings, anger, and antisocial inclinations. In Study 2, these authors used rejection sensitivity as a predictor and manipulated constant or increasing rejection over time. Rejection sensitivity predicted negative reactions but did not moderate the impact of rejection, and increasing rejection was worse than constant rejection.

Jealousy is one response by a partner who is rejected in favor of another. An examination of nonromantic jealousy found that self-esteem played a major role of the rejected partner, mediating the link between the diverted interest of their partner and how much jealousy they expressed, and between jealousy and aggressive responses. When the partner's interest in the rival implied an ego-threat to the participant, the participant's self-esteem dropped and jealousy rose, as did aggression (measured through the allocation of hot sauce) (DeSteno et al. 2006).

One type of fight response is to derogate those who reject and socially exclude.

In a cross-cultural study, it was argued that although members of all cultures negatively experience exclusion, the reaction to exclusion should be culture-specific. For instance, the content of derogation would depend upon the culture's values related to belonging (Fiske & Yamamoto 2005). Specifically, these authors posit that social exclusion violates desires for belonging, control, self-enhancement, trust, and shared understanding. With respect to belonging, they argue that in Western cultures (e.g., the United States) belonging is defined as "belonging widely and loosely," meaning that Westerners have an expectation that their relationships will be more flexible. Because of this, Westerners are more immediately willing to trust and embrace strangers and, therefore, are hurt more by strangers' rejections. Easterners (e.g., Japanese) define belonging as "belonging securely," meaning that they expect their relationship to last for a lifetime; thus, they are more cautious with respect to strangers and have lower expectations and concern for strangers' rejections. Participants from both cultures felt bad after rejection (i.e., negative evaluation from a partner in a scenario study), and about half from each culture reciprocated the rejection of that partner. But, in support of Fiske and Yamamoto's hypothesis, Americans were most trusting of their partners before receiving feedback, and they lowered their impressions of the partner on warmth, competence, and compatibility after rejection. Rejected Japanese participants lowered only their warmth impressions and kept their impressions of competence and compatibility at neutral levels. This research is important in that it is the first to compare cultures with respect to rejection, and it suggests that although rejection is negatively experienced across cultures, it is interpreted and acted upon differently.

Trait self-esteem plays an important role on derogation responses to rejection. Self-esteem played a role in individuals who were somehow mindful of possible acceptance threats from their relationship partners (Murray et al. 2002). For instance, in one study (Murray et al. 2002, Study 3), partners sat back-to-back, presumably writing about one aspect of their partner's character that they disliked. Unbeknownst to the participants, they were actually filling out different forms, and in the acceptance threat condition, the other partner was actually asked to list all the items in their home dwelling, so that it appeared as though the other partner had serious problems with the partner's character. The results indicated that only low-self-esteem partners were likely to exaggerate the problems with their partners and to subsequently derogate their partners and reduce their perceived closeness with them. This suggests that low-self-esteem individuals might be caught in a downward spiral of perceiving rejection when it is not happening and consequently weakening their attachments. Murray's work highlights the importance of rejection experiences within relationships. Other work also examines relational ostracism, also known as the silent treatment, within close relationships. More than two-thirds of Americans surveyed in a national poll indicated that they had given the silent treatment to a loved one, and three-quarters said they had received the silent treatment from a loved one (Faulkner et al. 1997). The silent treatment is characterized by loss of eye contact and communication, and the most common feelings associated with receiving the silent treatment are significant increases in anger and reductions in feelings of belonging, self-esteem, control, and meaningful existence (Williams et al. 1998). Participants asked to write narratives about a time they received (and gave) the silent treatment, how it felt, and how it ended up (Sommer et al. 2001) were shown to respond with self-esteem threat following the silent treatment; low-self-esteem individuals were more likely to reciprocate with the silent treatment.

Researchers found that trait self-esteem (and depression) moderated distress reactions to rejection when rejection was manipulated in the get-acquainted paradigm (Nezlek et al. 1997). Whereas everyone responded with lower temporary feelings of self-esteem after they learned their peers rejected them, the impact was stronger for those lower in trait self-esteem. In another study (Sommer & Baumeister 2002, Study 1), participants were subliminally primed with acceptance or rejection words and found that in comparison with the acceptance prime condition, rejection primes resulted in more negative self-descriptions for those low in self-esteem, whereas individuals with high self-esteem described themselves with more positive self-descriptions even when primed with rejection.

Flight. Another response associated with scoring high in rejection sensitivity is to avoid interactions where rejection is possible. High scores on the RS questionnaire are correlated with higher scores on social avoidance (Downey & Feldman 1996). By avoiding social situations, opportunities for acceptance are simultaneously diminished, as are chances to practice socially appropriate behaviors. Consequently, high-RS individuals who find themselves in social interactions are more likely to behave inappropriately, often hostilely. Men who are not highly invested in a romantic relationship are more likely to avoid romantic opportunities (Downey et al. 2000).

Tend-and-befriend. Gender moderated anonymous group-oriented cooperative behavior, such that females were more likely to socially compensate (i.e., work harder on collective compared with coactive tasks) after they had been ostracized in the ball-tossing paradigm (Williams & Sommer 1997). Males, on the other hand, engaged in social loafing following ostracism, as they did following inclusion. In a study that examined potential moderation of social sensitivity by loneliness, Gardner et al. (2005) found that individuals who were high in need to belong, or who were high in loneliness, were more likely to show improvements on memory for social information. On the other hand, high lonely individuals performed less well on a task that measured accuracy in detecting nonverbal expressions. Participants who were higher in

need for belonging (Leary et al. 2005) were more sensitive to nonverbal cues (Pickett et al. 2004).

Freeze. Once the initial shock and pain of ostracism is experienced, reflected upon, and appraised, it stands to reason that the individual's personality will moderate the appraisal and subsequent impact of the experience and the amount of time necessary to recover from the threat. After exposure to rejection primes (in comparison with acceptance and misfortune primes), low-self-esteem individuals gave up more quickly on an unsolvable anagram task, whereas high-self-esteem individuals were actually more likely to persist (Sommer & Baumeister 2002, Study 2). Similarly, individuals with low (but not high) self-esteem experienced more interference with rejection (but not acceptance) words in a modified Stroop task (Dandeneau & Baldwin 2004). In their second study, Dandeneau & Baldwin (2004) demonstrated that the interference effect by low-self-esteem individuals could be minimized with conditioning.

Zadro et al. (2006), reasoning that socially anxious individuals might be expected to more quickly or strongly react to an ostracism experience than individuals who were less socially anxious, recruited participants in the normal and extreme ranges of social anxiety to participate in a Cyberball study. Immediately following ostracism, socially anxious individuals were no more distressed than were those with normal levels of social anxiety. After several filler tasks that took approximately 45 minutes to complete, general distress was measured again, and this time, those with normal levels of social anxiety had returned to the nondistress levels reported by included participants. Highly socially anxious participants, however, had only partially recovered; still showing significant distress in comparison with their inclusion counterparts. This study demonstrates that individual-difference variables that are theoretically related to being sensitive to ostracism, exclusion, and rejection, like social anxiety, do exert influence, but only after a length of time. Although actual reflection was not assessed, this pattern of data suggests that individual differences were more or less successful in allowing participants to cope with the ostracism.

Summary on Individual Differences as Moderators of Coping Responses

One would expect other individual differences to similarly affect coping and recovery from ostracism. Thus, although previous research has not found moderation by introversion-extraversion, individualism-collectivism, need for belonging, and loneliness, individuals high in particular traits like these or others (self-esteem, rejection sensitivity, narcissism, and attachment style, to name a few) may certainly cope differently once the pain is detected. For instance, lonely people may take longer to recover from ostracism and may evidence helplessness more than individuals who are high in need for belonging (Cacioppo & Hawkley 2005). Certain individuals may generate more sinister attributions, negative self-appraisals, and be more likely to generalize their reactions to other situations that might direct them to be more self-protective or antisocial, whereas others may respond by minimizing and compartmentalizing the episode, attributing the ostracism to the peculiarities of the others in a particular situation, or by trying to make themselves more socially acceptable to others. For instance, high rejection sensitivity predisposes females to depressive symptoms (Ayduk et al. 2001). As Sommer & Rubin (2005) explain, the research on self-esteem and reactions to rejection suggests, "The key to predicting how people cope with rejection may lie with their expectations of future acceptance. Positive social expectancies [characteristic of people higher in self-esteem] lead people to draw closer to others, whereas negative expectancies [characteristic of those low in self-esteem] lead them to distance themselves from others" (p. 182). Whether pro- or antisocial routes are determined specifically by an ex-

pectation of future acceptance as Sommer and Rubin suggest, or by a sense of control over one's environment (Warburton et al. 2006), requires further examination.

Moderation of Situational Influences on Coping with Ostracism

Situational factors such as those already examined and assessed for immediate responses should also play a more central role in directing the appraisal of ostracism and subsequent behavioral responses. Although many studies have examined behavioral responses following ostracism, social exclusion, and rejection, few have measured intervening cognitive appraisals, perhaps because research efforts feared methodological contamination and interference by intervening measures. Thus, most research in this vein manipulates ostracism, social exclusion, or rejection, alone or in concert with other manipulations, and presents the individual with behavioral choices that are assessed either through self-report or directly.

Tend-and-befriend. Numerous studies using a variety of paradigms and measures indicate that one common response to ostracism is to think, feel, and behave in ways that improve the inclusionary status of the individual. That is, individuals will think or do things that ought to help them be more acceptable to others. Thus, I am using "prosocial" in a broad sense, including not only being helpful, but also including behaviors that should strengthen interpersonal bonds. I should also note that many of these so-called prosocial responses are not necessarily in the best interest of the individual who is engaging in them. In many instances, trying to be more socially acceptable can lead individuals down the path of gullibility and social susceptibility, making them easy targets for social manipulation.

For example, in one study, participants first ostracized or included participants using the ball-toss paradigm (there was also a no-ball-toss control group) and then asked them to work on an idea-generation task either coactively, in which individuals efforts could be easily assessed and experimenter evaluations would affect only the individual and no others, or collectively, in which their efforts were unidentifiable and experimenter evaluations would be spread across the group (Williams & Sommer 1997). Participants in the no-ball-toss control group demonstrated the typical social loafing effect (Karau & Williams 1993), working less hard collectively than coactively. When ostracized, males were more likely to make other-blame attributions, whereas females were more likely to make self-denigrating attributions. Across all inclusion/ostracism conditions, male participants socially loafed. Ostracized females, however, socially compensated (worked harder in the collective relative to the coactive condition). The authors interpreted the females' social compensation as a strategy to gain favor by helping the group do well on the task. Thus, ostracized females exerted more effort toward a prosocial goal—to enhance the evaluation of the very group that had ostracized them.

Many other studies have now shown a prosocial response to ostracism, social exclusion, and rejection. Cyberball participants who played over the Internet were more likely to conform to a unanimous incorrect majority (of individuals who were not part of the Cyberball game) on a perceptual judgment task than were participants who were included (Williams et al. 2000, Study 2). Ostracized participants were more likely to comply to the foot-in-the-door and door-in-the-face techniques than were included participants (Carter-Sowell & Williams 2005). Ostracized individuals were more likely to favorably evaluate both a legitimate student group (i.e., one that helped its members prepare for the job market) and an illegitimate group (i.e., one that taught its members to bend forks through mind-control and to walk through walls), a finding that indicates that ostracized individuals see others, regardless of their merits, more positively (Wheaton 2001).

Following ostracism (by Cyberball), participants were more likely to engage in nonconscious mimicry of a person with whom they spoke, especially if that person was an ingroup member (Lakin & Chartrand 2005). Nonconscious mimicry has been shown to increase affiliation and rapport (Lakin & Chartrand 2003). Conscious, strategic mimicry of a good citizen's behavior was more likely to occur following a threat of rejection or actual rejection in a public goods dilemma (Ouwerkerk et al. 2005). And, as mentioned previously, several studies have found that following ostracism, individuals become more socially attentive (Gardner et al. 2000, Pickett & Gardner 2005, Pickett et al. 2004). The authors view enhanced social sensitivity as a means for improving success in subsequent social interactions.

Although the time-out literature is primarily based on case studies, there appears to be common acceptance by educators and parents to use time-out as a method for disciplining and correcting the behavior of children (Heron 1987). Time-out is a short period of time in which the child is ignored and excluded, and it can be seen as a socially acceptable use of ostracism. Admittedly circular, it would seem perplexing that such a form of discipline would be so widely used if it were not at least moderately successful at improving the child's behavior and making it more socially acceptable.

Evidence for tend-and-befriend is also supported by six experiments that showed that socially excluded individuals tried to establish new bonds with others and had more positive impressions of others, as long as the excluded participants anticipated face-to-face interaction with the others and were not themselves high in fear of negative evaluation (Maner et al. 2006).

Finally, some clinical developmental literature deserves a bit of attention. Employing "still face"—a nonresponsive facial expression—on autistic children who ordinarily avoided eye contact and other socially oriented behaviors, Nadel et al. (2005) found that a single episode of still face led to increased eye contact and social attention in the autistic child. This is reminiscent of the use of shock on autistic children by Lovaas et al. (1965) to increase positive social attention by the child to the shock giver. It is as though, for autistic children, the social pain of shock or inattention by an adult is enough to trigger, at least temporarily, a prosocial orientation.

Fight. In the introduction to this review, I propose that the recent surge of interest in ostracism and related phenomena might be linked to its association with horrific violent events. There is now ample evidence that the link is not merely correlational; ostracism, social exclusion, and rejection are causally linked to a reduction in prosocial behaviors (Tice et al. 2002) and an increase in derogation of the excluder (Bourgeois & Leary 2001), and antisocial behaviors to others who may or may not have been the source of exclusion (Gaertner & Iuzzini 2005, Twenge et al. 2001, Warburton et al. 2006).

In a groundbreaking set of five studies, Twenge et al. (2001) manipulated social exclusion through either the life-alone paradigm or the get-acquainted paradigm, and employed a number of measures of aggression, both direct and indirect, toward others who either had or had not insulted the participants. Regardless of method, measure, or presence of provocation, derogation and aggression (in the form of noise blasts) increased following exclusion. The only instance in which socially excluded participants were not more aggressive was when the target had just praised them (Study 3). Twenge et al. (2006) also have found that making salient other friendly connections reduces the social exclusion→aggression link. Other studies indicate that replenishing a sense of belonging can reduce negative and aggressive consequences of social exclusion (Gardner et al. 2005, Twenge et al. 2006).

Reasoning that ostracism would lead to aggression only if it caused or was associated with an excessively strong control threat, Warburton et al. (2006) argued that aggres-

sion was a means to fortify control. Using the ball-toss paradigm, they assigned participants to be either ostracized or included. Afterward, participants were subjected to 10 blasts of highly aversive noise; half of the participants could control the onset of the blasts, the other half could not. Participants were then told through an elaborate cover story that they would be doling out an amount of food to be given to a new participant, whom they learned hated hot sauce. They were also told that the food taster would be required to eat all of the food that the participant doled out. Supporting their hypothesis that control threat underlay the link between ostracism and aggression, a significant increase in hot sauce allocation (their measure of aggression) occurred only in the ostracism-no control condition.

Freeze. Another reaction to stress is to freeze, as we commonly think a deer does when facing a headlight. Such a response could be adaptive in certain circumstances, when fight or flight might be more dangerous, as when predators respond to prey movement. Perhaps a flight or fight reaction to ostracism is similarly unwise, because either response effectively severs one's group membership. Thus, a concussed or affectively numb response may allow an opportunity for a less dysfunctional reaction later. As mentioned above, following the life-alone feedback, participants were more likely to show a reduction in complex cognitive thought. They were, however, more likely to perceive time standing still and to report a sense of meaninglessness, lethargy, and flat emotions (Baumeister et al. 2002, Twenge et al. 2003). Additionally, these authors typically find little or no emotional or mood changes following life-alone feedback, which is consistent with the emotional flatness finding. In further support for this interpretation, participants given the life-alone feedback are more insensitive to physical pain, showing higher thresholds and tolerances (DeWall & Baumeister 2006). They also found reductions in affective forecasting of joy or sadness over a future football outcome, and less empathy for another individual's suffering for either a socially or physically painful experience. Another study found marginally higher rates of self-defeating behavior (inability or unwillingness to practice for an upcoming math test) following life-alone feedback (Oikawa et al. 2004). It should be noted, however, that Eisenberger et al. (2006) report effects opposite to those of DeWall and Baumeister with regard to pain tolerances when using Cyberball-induced ostracism. It may well be that life-alone feedback produces depression-like symptoms, whereas Cyberball induces anxiety (M. Lieberman, personal communication).

Flight? Only a handful of studies appear to allow an opportunity for flight following ostracism. Ostracized participants (using an early version of the ball-tossing paradigm) were less likely to want to continue working with the group that ostracized them, but were about equally likely to prefer to work alone as to working with a new group (Predmore & Williams 1983). In one Internet Cyberball game, participants were permitted to exit the game when they desired (Williams et al. 2000, Study 1). Completely ostracized participants chose to quit playing more quickly than the included participants (but partially ostracized participants remained in the game longer). Rejected individuals not only derogated their rejectors, but expressed no interest in continuing to work with them (Pepitone & Wilpeski 1960). Similarly, excluded participants avoided looking in the mirror (Twenge et al. 2003). After inducing social acceptance or exclusion in the get-acquainted paradigm and then offering participants a choice to either leave the experiment immediately or to help the experimenter on an ancillary task that had nothing to do with the experiment, nearly all of the rejected participants chose to leave, whereas accepted participants were more likely to stay and help (Tice et al. 2002). Although the authors interpreted this study as showing less prosocial behavior following rejection, another interpretation is that rejected

participants took the first opportunity to flee the negatively charged situation.

Summary on Moderation of Situational Factors on Coping with Ostracism

The research to date suggests that situational factors produce a broad arsenal of coping responses to ostracism. As with individual-difference factors, these responses can be characterized as fight, tend-and-befriend, freeze, or flight. Factors such as who is ostracizing (ingroup members or outgroup members) and why, and whether there are options for (or perceived control over) future inclusion, play an important role and deserve further attention. Other factors, such as whether individuals perceive the ostracism to be targeted at them as individuals or at their group memberships, also merit attention as we begin to think of ostracism on a larger scale, when groups, race, culture, religion, and political ideology are the source of ostracism (see, for instance, McCauley 2006).

ACCEPTANCE STAGE: RESPONSES TO CHRONIC OSTRACISM

A third stage of responses to ostracism, social exclusion, and rejection may well be one in which individuals' resources are depleted because they have had to endure long-term ostracism as a result of being continuously or repetitively ignored and excluded by important people in their lives. Whereas there is not much research on this stage yet, there is some supportive evidence.

A review of the literature on depression proposed a social risk theory of depression, which suggests that when individuals have experienced ample social exclusion, they perceive their value to others as low and their presence to others as a burden (Allen & Badcock 2003). In such cases, it becomes especially risky to engage in social interactions because if rejected further, the individual risks total exclusion. Avoiding losing all possible connections, they argue, is critical to fitness from an evolutionary perspective. Thus, chronically excluded individuals will be hypersensitive to signals of social threat and will send signals to others that they do not wish to chance risky interactions. In this sense, depression is viewed as functional, an interesting but controversial proposition. Nevertheless, this argument suggests a strong link between long-term exclusion and depression. A similar argument is made for highly lonely people: rather than attempting to fortify thwarted needs, they appear more likely to exhibit learned helplessness and alienation (Cacioppo & Hawkley 2005).

Zadro (2004) conducted and coded 28 interviews with long-term targets of the silent treatment or ostracism. She reports strong themes that long-term targets had learned to accept what short-term targets fight: rather than seeking belonging, they accepted alienation and isolation; rather than seeking self-enhancement, they accepted low self-worth; rather than seeking control, they expressed helplessness; and rather than provoking recognition by others of their existence, they became depressed and avoided further painful rejection. These themes, of course, are from a sample of individuals who sought to be part of the study, so they should be viewed with caution. Cause and effect are impossible to determine with this study, so it is possible that people who think little of themselves and who withdraw are likely targets for ostracism. Nevertheless, it is important to conduct studies like this to learn how individuals who face continuous isolation from their loved ones, friends, or society cope or fail to cope.

Although speculative, experiments employing the life-alone paradigm, or those that examine highly lonely individuals, may be tapping into this third temporal stage of exposure to ostracism in that the life-alone paradigm projects long-term exposure to ostracism, and loneliness appears to remove motivation to fortify thwarted needs, thus leading to acceptance and helplessness.

A NEED-THREAT/NEED-FORTIFICATION FRAMEWORK

There are several possible explanations for why ostracism might be especially likely to lead to aggression (see also Leary et al. 2006). First, ostracism has been shown to threaten at least four fundamental needs: to belong, to maintain reasonably high self-esteem, to perceive a sufficient amount of personal control over one's social environment, and to be recognized as existing in a meaningful way. Although belonging and self-esteem threats may motivate individuals to please others, control and meaningful existence threats might motivate aggressive and provocative responses. When these motives compete, there may be ambivalent response tendencies (Warburton & Williams 2005). Which tendency surfaces may depend on the method of measurement or the behavior that is measured. Behaviors seen and easily interpreted by others may evoke seemingly positive approach tendencies; but underlying feelings or easily disguised behaviors may reflect antisocial tendencies. For instance, in a study by Echterhoff et al. (2005), a very mild form of exclusion was used through feedback that negated a shared reality with another individual, which threatened another core need, shared understanding (Fiske 2004; see also Pinel et al. 2006 regarding the importance of shared understanding). In that study, participants showed overt signs of connecting with that individual while at the same time covertly rejecting that individual's communication. Similarly, Williams et al. (2003) reported a study in which, following ostracism, participants were no more derogatory toward an oppressed outgroup on explicit measures, but yielded more negative associations to that group (than included participants) when tested with an implicit measure.

The pro- or antisocial response tendency may also depend upon which need or need cluster is most threatened. There may be instances in which the control and meaningful existence desires are so strong that they simply outweigh concerns for belonging and being liked. Existential concerns (e.g., "I exist and I matter") and desires to believe one has an impact on others, when threatened strongly, may supersede desires to fulfill belonging and being liked by self and others. When individuals are unilaterally ignored and excluded, they lose control over the social interaction, which increases frustration and anger. Ostracism is also a painful reminder of one's insignificance that reminds individuals what life would be like if they did not exist. Ostracized individuals report a feeling of invisibility, that their existence is not even recognized. In this case, a desire to be noticed may supplant a desire to be liked. Both control and meaningful existence, if sufficiently threatened by ostracism, might lead to behaviors that garner control and attention from others. In this regard, antisocial behaviors may be as good or better to achieve these goals. Aggression researchers regard aggression as an act of control (Tedeschi 2001). In order to be recognized (either positively or negatively) by the largest audience, it may be far easier to achieve this sole goal by committing a heinous act than by behaving prosocially (consider this thought: How could you become world famous in an hour, with your name splashed across all newspapers and news programs?).

Thus, although speculative, one way to find harmony with the various reactions that people have to ostracism, social exclusion, and rejection is to recognize that these aversive interpersonal behaviors have multiple effects on the individual and can result in an intrapsychic battle between fundamental needs. When belonging and self-esteem are particularly threatened, we might be more likely to observe prosocial responses; that is, responses that serve to increase the individual's inclusionary status. As discussed above, responses that serve this goal might be adaptive in the sense that they may clue individuals into undesirable behaviors in themselves that they can minimize, but they may also be maladaptive in the sense that they may try too hard to please others, becoming vulnerable to manipulation and perhaps even losing a sense of self. If control and meaningful existence are particularly threatened, more antisocial reactions may be expected because antisocial acts achieve control and demand attention. It is perhaps not surprising, then, that certain manipulations that imply inevitability of long-term exclusion and strip away any sense of personal control, like those used in the life-alone paradigm, might yield more antisocial or depressed reactions than do temporary and relatively minimal forms of acute ostracism, like ball tossing and Cyberball. Research is needed to determine whether variations in methods can account for variations in responses.

SUMMARY

The research on ostracism, social exclusion, and rejection has proliferated in the past decade, and we have benefited from a considerable amount of theory and knowledge about these processes and their impact. Of course, there are still more questions than answers. Clearly, even for very brief episodes that have minimal mundane realism, ostracism plunges individuals into a temporary state of abject misery, sending signals of pain, increasing stress, threatening fundamental needs, and causing sadness and anger. It is also clear that exposures to short episodes of ostracism, social exclusion, and rejection lead to robust behavioral consequences, many of which can be characterized as potentially dysfunctional to the individual's well-being, such as becoming socially susceptible to influence and social attention, antisocial and hostile, or temporarily catatonic. But just as clearly, we need to understand better the role of personality variables and situational factors that lead individuals toward these different behavioral paths, and we need to discover whether there are more functional responses that can be or are made by individuals. Ostracism occurs not only in dyads and small groups, but also at the societal and global level, and it is perhaps even more important to discover how groups who are ostracized within their city, nation, or in the world community respond. Groups might be buffered from some threats (e.g., they can seek each others' support to maintain a sense of belonging), but they might also be predisposed to responding provocatively and hostilely, to gain attention and respect (see Hogg 2005 and Jetten et al. 2006 for social identity perspectives on intragroup and intergroup rejection experiences). It is thus also important for researchers to turn their attention to groups that are being ostracized, in order to uncover the complex dynamics by which they respond and cope.

SUMMARY POINTS

1. Ostracism is adaptive for groups because it eliminates burdensome members and maintains their cohesiveness and strength.

2. Ostracism is painful and distressing to those who are ostracized. Detecting ostracism is adaptive for the individual so that corrections can be made in order to increase inclusionary status.

3. Cognitive factors (such as who is ostracizing and why) and personality factors of the ostracized individuals appear to have little influence in determining the detection of ostracism or the pain that it initially brings.

4. With time to reflect on the ostracism experience, cognitive, personality, and situational factors appear to moderate the speed of recovery and the type of coping response chosen (e.g., aggressive or prosocial).

5. Ostracism can lead to a variety of responses, including (*a*) behaviors that reflect the desire to be liked and get re-included, (*b*) antisocial and aggressive behaviors, (*c*) a stunned and affectless state, and (*d*) attempts to flee the situation. Understanding which response path is chosen is the current challenge for researchers.

6. There is the potential for ostracized individuals to be more receptive to extreme groups that show an interest in the individual, and at the same time, if these groups are also ostracized by the dominant society, they may be predisposed to act in such a way to attract recognition and attention, possibly through violence.

FUTURE ISSUES

1. It remains to be demonstrated whether ostracism, social exclusion, and rejection are synonymous psychologically, can be distinguished operationally, and can be shown to have different consequences.

2. More research is needed that determines under what conditions ostracism leads to attempts to be re-included versus attempts to lash out and aggress.

3. More research is needed on the ostracism of small (and large) groups and on how ostracism affects individual and group-related cognitions, emotions, and behaviors.

4. Can ostracism be coped with successfully, without making individuals become aggressive or overly susceptible to social influence?

5. Can therapies be developed to assist individuals who endure frequent or lengthy episodes of ostracism?

ACKNOWLEDGMENTS

The preparation of this chapter was facilitated by grants from the Australian Research Council and the National Science Foundation. The author is indebted to Halina Mathis for her assistance and to Adrienne Carter-Sowell, Zhansheng Chen, Stephanie Goodwin, Ty Law, Eric Wesselmann, and Jim Wirth for their comments.

LITERATURE CITED

Allen NB, Badcock PBT. 2003. The social risk hypothesis of depressed mood: evolutionary, psychosocial, and neurobiological perspectives. *Psychol. Bull.* 129:887–913

Anderson MA, Kaufman J, Simon TR, Barrios L, Paulozzi L, et al. 2001. School-associated violent deaths in the United States. *J. Am. Med. Assoc.* 286:2695–700

Ayduk O, Downey G, Kim M. 2001. Rejection sensitivity and depressive symptoms in women. *Personal. Soc. Psychol. Bull.* 27:868–77

Ayduk O, Downey G, Testa A, Yen Y, Shoda Y. 1999. Does rejection elicit hostility in rejection sensitive women? *Soc. Cogn.* 17:245–71

Barner-Barry C. 1986. Rob: children's tacit use of peer ostracism to control aggressive behavior. *Ethol. Sociobiol.* 7:281–93

Baumeister RF, DeWall CN. 2005. The inner dimension of social exclusion: intelligent thought and self-regulation among rejected persons. See Williams et al. 2005, pp. 53–75

Baumeister RF, DeWall CN, Ciarocco NL, Twenge JM. 2006. Social exclusion impairs self-regulation. *J. Personal. Soc. Psychol.* 88:589–604

Baumeister RF, Leary MR. 1995. The need to belong: desire for interpersonal attachments as a fundamental human motivation. *Psychol. Bull.* 117:497–529

Baumeister RF, Twenge JM, Nuss CK. 2002. Effects of social exclusion on cognitive processes: anticipated aloneness reduces intelligent thought. *J. Personal. Soc. Psychol.* 83:817–27

Bingham M. 2000. *Suddenly One Sunday.* Pymble, NSW: HarperCollins. 2nd ed.

Blascovich J, Tomaka J. 1996. The biopsychosocial model of arousal regulation. In *Advances in Experimental Social Psychology*, Vol. 80, ed. M Zanna, pp. 253–67. New York: Academic

Bourgeois KS, Leary MR. 2001. Coping with rejection: derogating those who choose us last. *Motiv. Emot.* 25:101–11

Brewer MB. 2005. The psychological impact of social isolation: discussion and commentary. See Williams et al. 2005, pp. 333–45

Buckley KE, Winkel RE, Leary MR. 2004. Reactions to acceptance and rejection: effects of level and sequence of relational evaluation. *J. Exp. Soc. Psychol.* 40:14–28

Carter AR, Williams KD. 2005. *Effects of ostracism on social susceptibility.* Presented at 77th Annu. Meet. Midwest. Psychol. Assoc., Chicago

Carter-Sowell AR, Chen Z, Williams KD. 2006. *Loneliness and social monitoring in social interaction.* Presented at 78th Annu. Meet. Midwest. Psychol. Assoc., Chicago

Cacioppo JT, Hawkley LC. 2005. People thinking about people: the vicious cycle of being a social outcast in one's own mind. See Williams et al. 2005, pp. 91–108

An important demonstration that individuals are less able to self-regulate following manipulations of social exclusion.

Social exclusion also impairs complex, but not simple, cognitive processes.

Craighead WE, Kimball WH, Rehak PJ. 1979. Mood changes, physiological responses, and self-statements during social rejection imagery. *J. Consult. Clin. Psychol.* 47:385–96

Crick NR, Ostrov JM, Appleyard K, Jansen EA, Casas JF. 2004. Relational aggression in early childhood: "You can't come to my birthday party unless..." In *Aggression, Antisocial Behavior, and Violence Among Girls: A Developmental Perspective*, ed. M. Putallaz, KL Bierman, pp. 71–89. New York: Guilford

Crook JB. 1997. *Port Arthur: Gun Tragedy, Gun Law Miracle*. Melbourne: Gun Control Australia

Dandeneau SD, Baldwin MW. 2004. The inhibition of socially rejecting information among people with high versus low self-esteem: the role of attentional bias and the effect of bias reduction training. *J. Soc. Clin. Psychol.* 23:584–602

DeSteno D, Valdesolo P, Bartlett MY. 2006. Jealousy and the threatened self: getting to the heart of the green-eyed monster. *J. Personal. Soc. Psychol.* In press

DeWall CN, Baumeister RF. 2006. Alone but feeling no pain: effects of social exclusion on physical pain tolerance and pain threshold, affective forecasting, and interpersonal empathy. *J. Personal. Soc. Psychol.* In press

Dickerson SS, Gruenewald TL, Kemeny ME. 2004. When the social self is threatened: shame, physiology, and health. *J. Personal.* 72:1191–216

Dickerson SS, Kemeny ME. 2004. Acute stressors and cortisol responses: a theoretical integration and synthesis of laboratory research. *Psychol. Bull.* 130:355–91

Downey G, Feldman SI. 1996. Implications of rejection sensitivity for intimate relationships. *J. Personal. Soc. Psychol.* 70:1327–43

Downey G, Feldman SI, Ayduk O. 2000. Rejection sensitivity and male violence in romantic relationships. *Pers. Relat.* 7:45–61

Downey G, Frietas AL, Michaelis B, Khouri H. 1998. The self-fulfilling prophecy in close relationships: rejection sensitivity and rejection by romantic partners. *J. Personal. Soc. Psychol.* 75:545–60

Downey G, Mougios V, Ayduk O, London B, Shoda Y. 2004. Rejection sensitivity and the defensive motivational system: insights from the startle response to rejection cues. *Psychol. Sci.* 15:668–73

Echterhoff G, Higgins ET, Groll S. 2005. Audience-tuning effects on memory: the role of shared reality. *J. Personal. Soc. Psychol.* 89:257–76

Eisenberger NI. 2006. Social connection and rejection across the lifespan; a social cognitive neuroscience approach to developmental processes. *Hum. Devel.* In press

Eisenberger NI, Jarcho J, Lieberman MD, Naliboff B. 2006. *An experimental study of shared sensitivity to physical and social pain*. Work. Pap., Dep. Psychol., Univ. Calif. Los Angeles

Eisenberger NI, Lieberman MD, Williams KD. 2003. Does rejection hurt? An fMRI study of social exclusion. *Science* 302:290–92

Faulkner SJ, Williams KD, Sherman B, Williams E. 1997. *The "silent treatment": Its incidence and impact*. Presented at 69th Annu. Meet. Midwest. Psychol. Assoc., Chicago

Feldman S, Downey G. 1994. Rejection sensitivity as a mediator of the impact of childhood exposure to family violence on adult attachment behavior. *Dev. Psychopathol.* 6:231–47

Fiske ST. 2004. *Social Beings: A Core Motives Approach to Social Psychology*. New York: Wiley

Fiske ST, Yamamoto M. 2005. Coping with rejection: core social motives across cultures. See Williams et al. 2005, pp. 185–98

Foddy M, Smithson M, Hogg M, Schneider S, eds. 1999. *Resolving Social Dilemmas*. New York: Psychol. Press

Gaertner L, Iuzzini J. 2005. Rejection and entitativity: a synergistic model of mass violence. See Williams et al. 2005, pp. 307–20

Pioneering work on an individual-difference variable that predisposes some people to expect rejection and to react to it in ways that perpetuate further rejection.

The first neuroscience evidence that a brief episode of ostracism activates the dorsal anterior cingulate cortex, a region of the brain that is also activated by physical pain.

Gardner WL, Pickett CL, Brewer MB. 2000. Social exclusion and selective memory: how the need to belong influences memory for social events. *Personal. Soc. Psychol. Bull.* 26:486–96

Gardner WL, Pickett CL, Knowles M. 2005. Social snacking and shielding: using social symbols, selves, and surrogates in the service of belonging needs. See Williams et al. 2005, pp. 227–42

Geller DM, Goodstein L, Silver M, Sternberg WC. 1974. On being ignored: the effects of violation of implicit rules of social interaction. *Sociometry* 37:541–56

Gonsalkorale K, Williams KD. 2006. The KKK won't let me play: ostracism even by a despised outgroup hurts. *J. Eur. Soc. Psychol.* In press

Gruter M, Masters RD. 1986. Ostracism: a social and biological phenomenon. *Ethol. Sociobiol.* 7:149–395

Gunnar MR, Sebanc AM, Tout K, Donzella B, van Dulmen MMH. 2003. Peer rejection, temperament, and cortisol activity in preschoolers. *Dev. Psychol.* 43:346–68

Haselton MG, Buss DM. 2000. Error management theory: a new perspective on biases in cross-sex mind reading. *J. Personal. Soc. Psychol.* 78:81–91

Hitlan RT, Kelly KM, Schepman S, Schneider KT, Zaraté MA. 2006. Language exclusion and the consequences of perceived ostracism in the workplace. *Group Dyn. Theor. Res. Pract.* 10:56–70

James W. 1890/1950. *Principles of Psychology, Volume 1.* New York: Dover

Juvonen J, Gross EF. 2005. The rejected and the bullied: lessons about social misfits from developmental psychology. See Williams et al. 2005, pp. 155–70

Heron TE. 1987. Timeout from positive reinforcement. In *Applied Behavior Analysis*, ed. IO Cooper, TE Heron, H Merrill, pp. 439–53. Columbus, OH: Merrill

Hogg MA. 2005. All animals are equal but some animals are more equal than others: social identity and marginal membership. See Williams et al. 2005, pp. 243–61

Jetten J, Branscombe NR, Spears R. 2006. Living on the edge: dynamics of intragroup and intergroup rejection experiences. In *Social Identities: Motivational, Emotional and Cultural Influences*, ed. R Brown, D Capozza. London: Sage. In press

Karau SJ, Williams KD. 1993. Social loafing: a meta-analytic review and theoretical integration. *J. Personal. Soc. Psychol.* 65:681–706

Lakin JL, Chartrand TL. 2003. Using nonconscious mimicry to create affiliation and rapport. *Psychol. Sci.* 14:334–39

Lakin JL, Chartrand TL. 2005. Exclusion and nonconscious behavioral mimicry. See Williams et al. 2005, pp. 279–95

Law AT, Williams KD. 2006. *Minimal world: Responses to minimal representations of ostracism.* Work. Pap., Dep. Psychol. Sci., Purdue Univ., West Lafayette, Ind.

Leary MR. 2001. Toward a conceptualization of interpersonal rejection. In *Interpersonal Rejection*, ed. Leary MR, pp. 3–20. New York: Oxford Univ. Press

Leary MR. 2005. Varieties of interpersonal rejection. See Williams et al. 2005, pp. 35–51

Leary MR, Haupt AL, Strausser KS, Chokel JT. 1998. Calibrating the sociometer: the relationship between interpersonal appraisals and state self-esteem. *J. Personal. Soc. Psychol.* 74:1290–99

Leary MR, Kelly KM, Cottrell CA, Schreindorfer LS. 2005. *Individual differences in the need to belong: mapping the nomological network.* Work. Pap, Dep. Psychol. Wake Forest Univ., Winston-Salem, NC

Leary MR, Kowalski RM, Smith L, Phillips S. 2003. Teasing, rejection, and violence: case studies of the school shootings. *Aggress. Behav.* 29:202–14

Leary MR, Tambor ES, Terdal SK, Downs DL. 1995. Self-esteem as an interpersonal monitor: the sociometer hypothesis. *J. Personal. Soc. Psychol.* 68:518–30

Leary MR, Twenge JM, Quinlivan E. 2006. Interpersonal rejection as a determinant of anger and aggression. *Personal. Soc. Psychol. Rev.* 10:111–32

Lemonick MD. 2002 (May 6). Germany's Columbine. *Time* 159/18:36–39

Lieberman MD. 2007. Social cognitive neuroscience: a review of core processes. *Annu. Rev. Psychol.* 58:259–89

Lieberman MD, Gaunt R, Gilbert DT, Trope Y. 2002. Reflection and reflexion: a social cognitive neuroscience approach to attributional inference. In *Advances in Experimental Social Psychology*, ed. M Zanna, 34:199–249. New York: Academic

Lovaas OI, Schaeffer B, Simmons JQ. 1965. Building social behavior in autistic children by use of electric shock. *J. Exp. Res. Personal.* 1:99–105

MacDonald G, Kingsbury R. 2006. Does physical pain augment anxious attachment? *J. Soc. Pers. Relat.* In press

MacDonald G, Leary MR. 2005. Why does social exclusion hurt? The relationship between social and physical pain. *Psychol. Bull.* 131:202–23

Maner JK, DeWall CN, Baumeister RF, Schaller M. 2006. Does social exclusion motivate interpersonal reconnection? Resolving the "Porcupine Problem." *J. Personal. Soc. Psychol.* In press

McCauley C. 2006. Psychological issues in understanding terrorism and the response to terrorism. In *The Psychology of Terrorism*, ed C Stout. Westport, CT: Greenwood Publ. In press

Miller EK, Cohen JD. 2001. An integrative theory of prefrontal cortex function. *Annu. Rev. Neurosci.* 24:167–202

Murray SL, Rose P, Bellavia GM, Holmes JG, Kusche AG. 2002. When rejection stings: how self-esteem constrains relationship-enhancement processes. *J. Personal. Soc. Psychol.* 83:556–73

Nadasi C. 1992. *The effects of social ostracism on verbal and nonverbal behavior in introverts and extraverts.* Hon. Thesis, Univ. Toledo. 77 pp.

Nadel J, Prepin K, Okanda M. 2005. Experiencing contingency and agency: first step toward self-understanding in making a mind? *Interact. Stud.: Spec. Iss. Making Minds* 6:447–62

Newman KS. 2004. Rampage: the social roots of school shootings. Cambridge, MA: Basic Books. 434 pp.

Nezlek JB, Kowalski RM, Leary MR, Blevins T, Holgate S. 1997. Personality moderators of reactions to interpersonal rejection: depression and trait self-esteem. *Personal. Soc. Psychol. Bull.* 23:1235–44

Oikawa H, Kumagai T, Ohbuchi K. 2004. *Social exclusion and self-defeating behavior.* Presented at 16th Int. Soc. Res. Aggress., Santorini Island, Greece

Ouwerkerk JW, Kerr NL, Gallucci M, van Lange PAM. 2005. Avoiding the social death penalty: ostracism and cooperation in social dilemmas. See Williams et al. 2005, pp. 321–32

Pepitone A, Wilpizeski C. 1960. Some consequences of experimental rejection. *J. Abnorm. Soc. Psychol.* 60:359–64

Pickett CL, Gardner WL. 2005. The social monitoring system: enhanced sensitivity to social clues as an adaptive response to social exclusion. See Williams et al. 2005, pp. 213–26

Pickett CL, Gardner WL, Knowles M. 2004. Getting a cue: the need to belong and enhanced sensitivity to social cues. *Personal. Soc. Psychol. Bull.* 30:1095–107

Pinel EC, Long AE, Landau MJ, Alexander K, Pyszczynski T. 2006. Seeing I to I: a pathway to interpersonal connectedness. *J. Personal. Soc. Psychol.* In press

Predmore SC, Williams KD. 1983. *The effects of social ostracism on affiliation.* Presented at 55th Annu. Meet. Midwest. Psychol. Assoc., Chicago

An important theoretical integration that argues that the social pain system is piggybacked on the physical pain neural architecture and that many similarities exist between physical and social pain.

One of several findings that manipulations of social exclusion can lead to hypersensitivity to social information.

Romero-Canyas R, Downey G. 2005. Rejection sensitivity as a predictor of affective and behavioral responses to interpersonal stress: a defensive motivational system. See Williams et al. 2005, pp. 131–54

Schachter S. 1951. Deviation, rejection, and communication. *J. Abnorm. Soc. Psychol.* 46:190–207

Schaller M, Duncan LA. 2006. The behavioral immune system: its evolution and social psychological implications. In *The Evolution of the Social Mind: Evolutionary Psychology and Social Cognition*, ed. JP Forgas, M Haselton, W von Hippel. New York: Psychol. Press. In press

Smith A, Williams KD. 2004. R U there? Effects of ostracism by cell phone messages. *Group Dyn. Theory Res. Pract.* 8:291–301

Smith ER, Murphy J, Coats S. 1999. Attachment to groups: theory and measurement. *J. Personal. Soc. Psychol.* 77:94–110

Sommer KL, Baumeister RF. 2002. Self-evaluation, persistence, and performance following implicit rejection: the role of trait self-esteem. *Personal. Soc. Psychol. Bull.* 28:926–38

Sommer KL, Rubin YS. 2005. Role of social expectancies in cognitive and behavioral responses to social rejection. See Williams et al. 2005, pp. 171–83

Sommer KL, Williams KD, Ciarocco NJ, Baumeister RF. 2001b. When silence speaks louder than words: explorations into the interpersonal and intrapsychic consequences of social ostracism. *Basic Appl. Soc. Psychol.* 83:606–15

Spoor J, Williams KD. 2006. The evolution of an ostracism detection system. In *The Evolution of the Social Mind: Evolutionary Psychology and Social Cognition*, ed. JP Forgas, M Haselton, W von Hippel. New York: Psychol. Press. In press

Steinbeck J. 1945/1987. *Of Mice and Men/Cannery Row*. New York: Penguin

Stroud LR, Tanofsky-Kraff M, Wilfley DE, Salovey P. 2000. The Yale Interpersonal Stressor (YIPS): affective, physiological, and behavioral responses to a novel interpersonal rejection paradigm. *Ann. Behav. Med.* 22:204–13

Taylor SE, Klein LC, Lewis BP, Gruenewald TL, Gurung RAR, Updegraff JA. 2000. Female responses to stress: tend and befriend, not fight or flight. *Psychol. Rev.* 107:411–29

Tedeschi JT. 2001. Social power, influence, and aggression. In *Social Influence: Direct and Indirect Processes*, ed. JP Forgas, KD Williams, pp. 109–28. New York: Psychol. Press

Tice DM, Twenge JM, Schmeichel BJ. 2002. Threatened selves: the effects of social exclusion on prosocial and antisocial behavior. In *The Social Self: Cognitive, Interpersonal, and Intergroup Perspectives*, ed. JP Forgas, KD Williams, pp. 175–87. New York: Psychol. Press

Twenge JM. 2000. The age of anxiety? The birth cohort change in anxiety and neuroticism. *J. Personal. Soc. Psychol.* 79:1007–21

Twenge JM. 2005. When does social rejection lead to aggression? The influences of situations, narcissism, emotion, and replenishing social connections. See Williams et al. 2005, pp. 201–12

Twenge JM, Baumeister RF, Tice DM, Stucke TS. 2001. If you can't join them, beat them: effects of social exclusion on aggressive behavior. *J. Personal. Soc. Psychol.* 81:1058–69

Twenge JM, Catanese KR, Baumeister RF. 2003. Social exclusion and the deconstructed state: time perception, meaninglessness, lethargy, lack of emotion, and self-awareness. *J. Personal. Soc. Psychol.* 85:409–23

Twenge JM, Zhang L, Catanese KR, Dolan-Pascoe B, Lyche LE, Baumeister RF. 2006. Replenishing connectedness: reminders of social anxiety activity reduce aggression after social exclusion. *Br. J. Soc. Psychol.* In press

van Beest I, Williams KD. 2006a. When inclusion costs and ostracism pays, ostracism still hurts. *J. Pers. Soc. Psychol.* In press

The first demonstration that social exclusion can trigger antisocial and aggressive responses.

Something akin to a concussive state of affective flatness can follow social exclusion.

Van Beest I, Williams KD. 2006b. Cyberbomb: Is it painful to be ostracized from Russian roulette? Work. Pap., Dep. Psychol., Leiden Univ.

Warburton WA, Williams KD. 2005. Ostracism: when competing motivations collide. In *Social Motivation: Conscious and Unconscious Processes*, ed. JP Forgas, KD Williams, SD Laham, pp. 294–313. New York: Cambridge Univ. Press

Warburton WA, Williams KD, Cairns DR. 2006. When ostracism leads to aggression: the moderating effects of control deprivation. *J. Exp. Soc. Psychol.* **42:213–20**

Wheaton A. 2001. *Ostracism and susceptibility to the overtures of socially deviant groups and individuals*. Hon. Thesis. Macquarie Univ., Sydney, Australia. 67 pp.

Wilkie D, Savedra M, Holzemer W, Tesler M, Paul S. 1990. Use of the McGill Pain Questionnaire to measure pain: a meta-analysis. *Nursing Res.* 39:37–40

Williams KD. 1997. Social ostracism. In *Aversive Interpersonal Behaviors*, ed. RM Kowalski, p. 133–70. New York: Plenum

Williams KD. 2001. *Ostracism: The Power of Silence*. New York: Guilford. 282 pp.

Williams KD, Bernieri F, Faulkner S, Grahe J, Gada-Jain N. 2000. The Scarlet Letter Study: five days of social ostracism. *J. Person. Interperson. Loss* **5:19–63**

Williams KD, Case TI, Govan CL. 2003. Impact of ostracism on social judgments and decisions: explicit and implicit responses. In *Social Judgments: Implicit and Explicit Processes*, ed. JP Forgas, KD Williams, W von Hippel, pp. 325–42. New York: Cambridge Univ. Press

Williams KD, Cheung CKT, Choi W. 2000. CyberOstracism: effects of being ignored over the Internet. *J. Personal. Soc. Psychol.* 79:748–62

Williams KD, Fitness J. 2004. Social and physical pain: similarities and differences. Presented at Soc. Exp. Social Psychol., Ft. Worth, TX

Williams KD, Forgas JP, Hippel WV. 2005. *The Social Outcast: Ostracism, Social Exclusion, Rejection, and Bullying*. New York: Psychol. Press

Williams KD, Govan CL, Croker V, Tynan D, Cruickshank M, Lam A. 2002. Investigations into differences between social and cyber ostracism. *Group Dyn. Theory Res. Pract.* 6:65–77

Williams KD, Jarvis B. 2006. Cyberball: a program for use in research on ostracism and interpersonal acceptance. *Behav. Res. Methods Instrum. Comput.* 38:174–80

Williams KD, Shore WJ, Grahe JE. 1998. The silent treatment: perceptions of its behaviors and associated feelings. *Group Process Intergroup Relat.* 1:117–41

Williams KD, Sommer KL. 1997. Social ostracism by one's coworkers: Does rejection lead to loafing or compensation? *Personal. Soc. Psychol. Bull.* 23:693–706

Williams KD, Wheeler L, Harvey J. 2001. Inside the social mind of the ostracizer. In *The Social Mind: Cognitive and Motivational Aspects of Interpersonal Behavior*, ed. JP Forgas, KD Williams, L Wheeler, pp. 294–320. New York: Cambridge Univ. Press

Williams KD, Zadro L. 2005. Ostracism: the indiscriminate early detection system. See Williams et al. 2005, pp. 19–34

Zadro L. 2004. *Ostracism: Empirical studies inspired by real-world experiences of silence and exclusion*. PhD thesis. Univ. New South Wales. 294 pp.

Zadro L, Boland C, Richardson R. 2006. How long does it last? The persistence of the effects of ostracism in the socially anxious. *J. Exp. Soc. Psychol.* In press

Zadro L, Williams KD. 2006. How do you teach the power of ostracism? Evaluating the train ride demonstration. *Soc. Influence* 1:1–24

Even fortification of nonsocial control can decouple the link between ostracism and aggression.

A minimal manipulation of ostracism, being ignored and excluded in a virtual ball toss game (Cyberball), is sufficient to thwart fundamental needs and to increase subsequent acts of conformity.

Zadro L, Williams KD, Richardson R. 2004. How low can you go? Ostracism by a computer lowers belonging, control, self-esteem, and meaningful existence. *J. Exp. Soc. Psychol.* 40:560–67

Zadro L, Williams KD, Richardson R. 2005. Riding the 'O' train: comparing the effects of ostracism and verbal dispute on targets and sources. *Group Process Interperson. Relat.* 8:125–43

The Elaboration of Personal Construct Psychology

Beverly M. Walker[1] and David A. Winter[2]

[1]School of Psychology, University of Wollongong, Wollongong 2522, Australia;
email: bwalker@uow.edu.au

[2]School of Psychology, University of Hertfordshire, Hatfield AL10 9AB and Barnet,
Enfield and Haringey Mental Health NHS Trust, United Kingdom;
email: d.winter@herts.ac.uk

Annu. Rev. Psychol. 2007. 58:453–77

First published online as a Review in
Advance on August 11, 2006

The *Annual Review of Psychology* is online
at http://psych.annualreviews.org

This article's doi:
10.1146/annurev.psych.58.110405.085535

Key Words

George Kelly, personality theory, clinical psychology, repertory
grid, laddering, constructivism

Abstract

More than half a century has passed since the publication of George
Kelly's (1955/1991) *The Psychology of Personal Constructs*. This review
considers the elaboration of personal construct psychology (PCP)
during this time, both by Kelly and by others who developed his
ideas. Advances to the theory have principally concerned implicative relationships between constructs, construing of the self, social
relationships, emotions, links with other approaches, and supporting research. With regard to methods of assessment of construing,
major developments have occurred in both repertory grid and non-
grid techniques, such as laddering. The principal advances in the
applications of PCP have been in the clinical, educational, and organizational fields, but have by no means been limited to these areas.
It can be concluded that PCP has met Kelly's own design specifications for a useful theory and that PCP can perhaps anticipate at least
another half-century of elaboration.

Contents

Personal construct:
a bipolar
discrimination
between elements of
an individual's world

PCP: personal
construct psychology

INTRODUCTION

Although many psychological approaches from 50 years ago have waned in importance, personal construct psychology (PCP) was ahead of its time (Mischel 1980). Subsequent theoretical movements have advocated themes overlapping with the originally radical position George Kelly articulated in *The Psychology of Personal Constructs* (1955/1991).

"Scientometric" studies of PCP indicate that the approach developed "an international base of support enjoyed by few psychological theories" (Neimeyer et al. 1990, p. 17). References to it are made in nearly half of the volumes of the *Annual Review of Psychology* between 1955 and 2005. For example, Tyler (1981) describes the publication of Kelly's book as a "landmark event in the opening toward individuality," remarking, "Although it took a number of years for the full significance of Kelly's theory to become apparent, there is now a worldwide network of com-

municating investigators who are developing and extending Kelly's theory and techniques, applying them in clinical and environmental psychology, anthropology, criminology, urban planning, and many other research areas" (p. 8).

PCP is a position that sees people as adventurers, capable of pushing the boundaries of their lives as they experiment with alternative interpretations of their changing worlds in an attempt to increase predictability. Critical here are the discriminations people make, whereby they see some things as similar to and others as different from others. These discriminations, known as constructs, are bipolar, with both poles necessary for understanding of the discrimination. "Hot" cannot be understood except in relationship to "cold." Our actions reflect the application of these construct poles, as we behave in accordance with our constructions. Contrasts are central to an understanding of change in that the contrast (or opposite pole) to the current way of seeing the world is the most readily available alternative, and changed behavior will reflect this, at least initially.

The processes that relate to the development, application, and modification of this construing are central to understanding differences between individuals and facilitating change, rather than merely the content of construing per se. Critical to the construct system's development are processes such as the Validation Cycle, in which ways of making sense of the world are tested and revised or buttressed, as in Kelly's metaphor of the person as a potential scientist, and the Creativity Cycle, which describes how we can create something new by successively loosening the ways we construe, then tightening up to a defined outcome. The hierarchical nature of construing, with constructs employed more widely being known as superordinate, relative to those with more specific applicability, the subordinate, is also important in determining change. Although Kelly (1955) formally presents some of his theory in a fundamental postulate and 11 corollaries, these do little to convey the spirit of the theory and omit central features, such as the emphasis on constructive alternativism, whereby we can always construe things differently. Concepts they encompass include commonality (shared construing) and individuality, thereby spanning both nomothetic and idiographic approaches, as well as sociality (relationships based on construing others' construing). However, some know PCP best for its methodologies, especially the repertory grid. This method examines the ways a person's constructs apply to aspects of the world, termed "elements."

Our focus is on how Kelly's theory, and associated methodologies and practice, have been elaborated since 1955. Priority has been given among the thousands of publications to developments that are influential, are relevant to psychologists, are relatively recent, and involve a body of work. Because we want to present, as far as possible, a view shared among the personal construct community, we requested from other authors[1] in the field a list of five post-1955 developments in theory, method, and application. They were generous in their responses and this paper benefited from that collective picture.

THEORY

Kelly's Own Elaborations

Kelly's extensions and refocusing of his theory were partly based on others' interpretations of PCP. For example, he was assembling a challenge, reflected in posthumous papers (Maher 1969), to views of the theory as merely cognitive, ignoring life's passions (e.g., Bruner 1956, Rogers 1956).

Kelly's psychology moves beyond the 1955 statement of his position to demonstrating, in the form of the papers themselves, a more radical way of doing psychology—"by the man-

ner and style of his telling, by a rhetoric of humor and disrespect, tradition and innovation, that he employs to speak a *frame of mind* into life" (Mair 1989, p. 4). His papers are full of narratives, both personal (Kelly 1962, 1978) and cultural (Kelly 1969a,d). Today such an approach seems less controversial, as narrative approaches to psychology are increasingly prominent (Mair 1988, 1989).

Although *The Psychology of Personal Constructs* (Kelly 1955) focuses more centrally on problematic construing, subsequent papers explore optimal functioning, arguing that this requires an Experience Cycle involving anticipation, investment, encounter, dis/confirmation, and constructive revision (Kelly 1980).

Kelly (1969b) broadens the consideration of how people depend on others to meet their needs beyond the therapy context to observations about society and its reliance on complex webs of interdependency. Our construing concerning dependencies on others consists of some of our earliest, nonverbal discriminations. Kelly challenges the view that infants are more dependent than adults by arguing that adults have more needs. Infant depending is not problematic because of the amount of dependency entailed but because it is precarious, depending on few to meet all needs. Some people retain such a fragile pattern of undispersed dependency as adults. Broadening his developmental perspective, Kelly links progressive dispersion of dependencies to the child's developing capacity to construe other people's construing ("sociality"). Maturing individuals thus adapt their demands to what others are prepared to give, as well as understanding what others may need from them.

Despite Kelly's PhD thesis on speech and reading, his main mention of language in 1955 is to indicate that construing is not synonymous with the words used to approximate the discriminations made. Subsequently, he focuses on how labels give the illusion of objectivity, or "that a word is beholden to the object it is used to describe. The object

Sociality: the construing of another person's way of viewing their world

Repertory grid: a technique for the assessment of the structure and content of a construct system

[1]We thank R Bell, L Botella, P Caputi, R Cromwell, G Feixas, M Frances, F Fransella, M Fromm, B Gaines, D Jankowicz, D Kalekin-Fishman, J Mancuso, G Neimeyer, R Neimeyer, and J Scheer.

determines it" (Kelly 1969d, p. 73). Kelly (1969e) goes further in alerting us to the ways language channels our stance to the world. We commonly use the indicative mood, implying that the relationship we propose is inherent in the nature of the subject of our sentence, namely that something has certain properties. Kelly suggests adopting an invitational mood, by which the listener is invited to imagine that this is but one possibility, thus fostering the adventurousness that Kelly advocates for scientific thinking and everyday living.

For a clinical psychologist of his era, Kelly (1955) gives surprising emphasis to cultural factors, and in 1962 he extends this to an understanding of shared features of construing within different nationalities. His focus is on how we make choices by using constructs that, being bipolar, provide alternatives for movement. He proposes that we are enmeshed within a cultural decision matrix, which at the same time presents choices and limits the extent of choice available. He highlights the impact of exploring the construing of a different culture—"looking through glasses that are not your own can permanently affect your eyesight" (Kelly 1962, p. 90)—and considers implications of this position for international understanding.

Thus, far from *The Psychology of Personal Constructs* being a bible for future PCP work, Kelly sets an example of active elaboration of his position. We consider below the extent to which that challenge has been grasped.

Theory of Construct Implications

In our survey of PCP contributors, the doctoral dissertation of Kelly's student, Hinkle (1965), exploring why and how people change (and especially why they do not change), figured the most extensively. Hinkle's theory of construct implications concentrates less on the way constructs apply to elements of the person's world and more on how constructs interrelate. It is based on organization, rather than content, of construing. For Hinkle, it is not so much that a superordinate con-

struct encompasses a wider range of elements than the more subordinate, but rather that constructs differ in their range of implications, with those constructs having a larger number of implications (both superordinate and subordinate) considered more meaningful. (For example, for most people the construct of "good-bad" would carry many more implications than a more concrete construct such as "symmetrical-asymmetrical.") Hinkle reworks Kelly's notion of threat, which focuses on awareness of wide-ranging imminent change in core constructs, to awareness of "an imminent comprehensive reduction of the total number of predictive implications of the personal construct system" (p. 25). Similarly, whereas Kelly views anxiety as awareness that occurrences are not able to be accommodated by one's current construct system, Hinkle writes of awareness of the lack of implications for the constructs that one confronts.

Hinkle argues that people choose to see themselves in terms of that pole of a construct they anticipate will be more likely to extend the implications of their system, and thereby the meaning of their lives. Consequently, people resist movement to unelaborated poles (anxiety) or reduced implicativeness (threat). The higher a construct is in the hierarchy, the greater are its implications and its resistance to change from one pole to the other. Hinkle demonstrates findings consistent with this theoretical elaboration.

More recent elaborations of the notion of the hierarchical organization of personal constructs include the clarification of possible types of implicative relationships between constructs (ten Kate 1981) and the development of a model from set and graph theories (Chiari et al. 1990).

The Self

The unitary notion of a self as the essence of the person is rejected by Kelly. He considers that self is one pole of a construct, which in turn is construed. His position entails the relevance of contrast and the view that the construction of self occurs in comparison with others. Additionally, our sense of self is constructed by our understanding of others' views of us (Bannister 1983).

One example of the examination of patterns of construing linking self and others (Adams-Webber 1990) is a research program centering on the "golden section hypothesis," whereby individuals apply the positive poles of their constructs to others and assign themselves and others to the same poles of constructs approximately 62% of the time (Benjafield & Adams-Webber 1976).

Others take a more critical stance on the individualistic approach of Western society and psychology. A "community of selves" metaphor moves away from an interpretation of the person as the intellectual controller, dispensing constructs, to one of "patterned movement," of "a remarkably powerful sense of actions, interactions, transactions and counteractions" (Mair 1977, p. 142). Disparities between different self-constructions, including "self," "ideal self," and "self as others see me," are more predictive of self-esteem (Moretti & Higgins 1990) and neuroticism (Watson & Watts 2001) than are those individual selves.

This multiple-selves perspective is compatible with subsequent approaches, such as social constructionism. Nevertheless, individuals, despite seeing themselves as different depending on the interpersonal context, overwhelmingly report the importance of "being myself," which is only possible in interactions in which they do not feel self-conscious (Butt et al. 1997).

The "multiple self-awareness" group, in which each participant selects one of his or her selves to be part of a joint venture with each other participant's selected self, is an application of this approach (Sewell et al. 1998). The resulting interactions are a powerful vehicle for understanding others' reactions to the selected roles.

PCP as a Social Psychology: Beyond the Individual

Although PCP is commonly classified as a personality theory, a case can be made for it being a social psychology. Consideration of the person-in-relation (Walker 1996) is evident in numerous aspects of Kelly's theorizing, including the importance of "sociality" and "commonality," people being "validating agents" for the testing of constructions, and dependency. (See Kalekin-Fishman & Walker 1996 and Stringer & Bannister 1979 for further elaboration of this area.) Kelly's approach of choosing the alternatives that appear to offer greatest opportunities to extend and define our system can be applied to friendship and partner choices. Duck (1979) proposes that individuals actively assemble validation of their worldview, seeking those with similar constructs. Personal relationships depend on sharing of constructs, and the type of shared construing varies with the process of friendship, with advanced friendships evidencing commonality in less superficial construing than acquaintanceships. This model is supported cross-sectionally, longitudinally, and across different ages and genders.

Holding an apparently identical construct does not ensure similarity in construct use, but such "functional similarity" is greater among dyads who perceive one another more positively (Neimeyer & Neimeyer 1981). Acquaintances use physical constructs most similarly, followed by interactional, then psychological, whereas friends apply psychological constructs most similarly. Evidence that intimate partners have comparably complex construct systems (Adams-Webber 2001) further supports the importance of similarity in the structure as well as content of partners' construing.

The choice of marriage partners may be viewed as a decision to elaborate some aspects of construing relative to others (Neimeyer & Hudson 1985). Marriages involve the development of many construct subsystems, and can be seen "...as a vital form of intimate colleagueship in which two personal scientists develop an enduring collaboration with respect to one another's important life projects" (p. 129). Those marriages with which the partners are satisfied are characterized by partners' similar use of constructs (particularly when these are superordinate) and better capacity to predict each other's use of superordinates. A taxonomy of disordered relationships from a PCP perspective has been proposed (Neimeyer & Neimeyer 1985). At least one disordered relationship cannot be understood readily from other positions: "negative relationships," in which spouses embody their partner's nonpreferred construct poles.

Kelly's (1962) elaboration of construing within a cultural and subcultural matrix provides impetus for one of the most important elaborations, the family construct system (Procter 1981). From this perspective, family members hold shared as well as idiosyncratic ways of making sense of the world. The family's unique system structures how they see their lives, justifies their actions, and governs their interactions. An important difference from other family therapists' formulations is the assumption that this family construct system intrinsically includes contrasts to where the family is currently construed. Formalizing his position in relation to Kelly, Procter (1981) proposes two additional corollaries to those in Kelly's theory. The Group Corollary states that "to the extent that a person can construe the relationships between members of a group, he may take part in a group process with them" (Procter 1981, p. 354). The Family Corollary indicates that "for a group of people to remain together over an extended period of time, each must make a choice, within the limitations of his system, to maintain a common construction of the relationships in the group" (Procter 1981, pp. 354–55). A similar focus on shared construing is evident in applications within organizational psychology concerning corporate construing (e.g., Balnaves & Caputi 2000).

Kelly's distinction between dispersed and undispersed dependency has been operationalized (Walker et al. 1988). Consistent with Kelly's predictions, people with relatively undispersed dependencies have fewer constructs about dependency than those with more dispersed dependencies, and they differ in the type of construing employed. Developmental trajectories of dependency based on Kelly's views concerning transition have also been elaborated (Chiari et al. 1994), and this position has been differentiated from the integration of PCP with attachment theory.

Emotions

In 1955, Kelly redefines emotions in ways challenging our conventional understandings. He rejects the distinction between thought and feeling, using construing to encompass both (Bannister 1977b). He links the experience of emotions to transitions and defines them phenomenologically, from the perspective of the experiencer rather than that of the recipient. However, the repertoire of emotions reinterpreted is limited to aggression, hostility, guilt, anxiety, threat, and fear. An extension of this list interprets positive emotions as indications of validation of construing and negative emotions of invalidation of construing (McCoy 1981). Such an approach views (in)validation as similar to negative and positive reinforcement, a link Kelly (1955) rejects. Confirmation of a view of oneself as worthless is unlikely to be experienced positively, for example, irrespective of its corroboration of our self-construction. The linkage between anger and hostility is also criticized by those concerned to elaborate the concept of anger (Cummins 2003).

Relationship to Other Theories

Considering historical precursors of PCP, Kelly's theory has been argued to represent an approach more usually found in the domain of philosophy, rather than "mere" psychology (Warren 1998, 2003). Kelly's most explicit debt is to pragmatism and Dewey's writing, which emphasize the utility of constructions rather than correspondence to reality. Also relevant is Dewey's rejection of many dualisms often taken for granted and Mead's emphasis on interaction with others as integral to selfhood (Butt 2006). Kelly's position regarding language is related by McWilliams (1996) to Korzybski's (1933) General Semantics approach, which argues for the elimination of the verb "to be" in English, resulting in greater awareness of responsibility for our constructions. Remarks such as "she is X" are replaced by "she behaves like an X," or "she gives the appearance of an X," statements more conducive to the facilitation of change.

Turning to contemporary psychological approaches, despite Kelly (1969f) being at pains to point out that his is not a cognitive theory, frequently he is seen as the precursor of the "cognitive revolution." Several of the references to PCP in the *Annual Review of Psychology* are in the context of it being a pioneering cognitive approach, such as the statement that Kelly was "the first truly cognitive personologist" (Wiggins & Pincus 1992, p. 496). Debts to Kelly are acknowledged by leading cognitive therapists, although personal construct psychotherapy can be differentiated from at least the original "rationalist" versions of these approaches both theoretically and empirically. However, more recent cognitive approaches, showing greater concern with processes (as opposed to the content) of cognition, arguably are more compatible with PCP. Nevertheless, several personal construct theorists (e.g., Epting 1984) consider PCP more aligned with the humanistic tradition, albeit a "rigorous humanism" (Rychlak 1977).

PCP's relationships to postmodernism (Botella 1995) and constructivism (Mahoney 1988) have also been discussed. There are alternative constructions of the latter relationship, with writers proposing differing categories of constructivism. For example, Chiari & Nuzzo (1996) locate different positions on a dimension contrasting realism and idealism;

these positions concern whether or not reality exists independently of our knowing it. Closer to the realist pole is epistemological constructivism, which assumes that there are many differing interpretations of external reality. This contrasts with hermeneutic constructivism, which focuses on subject/object interdependence. Opinions differ on which form of constructivism best characterizes Kelly's theory. Minimum realism, whereby some features of reality are assumed to be independent of our experiences, may be linked to Kelly's views that truth can be approached (Stevens 1998). Others express concern that PCP may "sink without trace" if subsumed under the constructivist umbrella (Fransella 1995, p. 131).

Testing the Theory

Although personal construct theory is relatively abstract, some key assumptions may be formulated in testable ways. Research supportive of the theory is reviewed in other sections of this article (see also Adams-Webber 2003), but we focus here on whether construing should be viewed as bipolar, as this is a key differentiator between PCP and other approaches. In practice (at least in most methods of repertory grid administration), construing is widely treated as dimensional rather than dichotomous. The issue of whether construing is universally bipolar (having two contrasting poles), rather than unipolar (as in a single concept) or multipolar (one pole having a number of opposite poles), is more important since it links to the central issue of change. If a feature of the world, such as oneself, is viewed as lying on one pole of a construct, if one chooses or is forced to change, the opposite pole is the perceived alternative.

Researchers have compared how a set of elements is rated on each pole of a construct, and have found that although such ratings are negatively correlated, they are by no means perfectly dichotomous. One of these studies included the variation of allowing some participants to specify additional contrasts for each of their construct poles and concluded that the results do not contradict Kelly's position of construing as entailing both similarity and contrast, but rather challenge the view of constructs as strictly dichotomous (Riemann 1990). Another study ingeniously overcame methodological problems in previous research by using a lexical decision task to explore construct dichotomy (Millis & Neimeyer 1990). The finding that a construct pole on which a particular priming element was highly rated and its contrast pole both resulted in quicker reaction times than construct poles unrelated to the element provides support for the assumption of construct bipolarity. Further support is provided by Bell's (2000) investigation of the application of supplied constructs to a common set of elements.

The issue of whether bipolarity of construing is universal is not addressed in these studies. Preemptive construing, whereby an element is construed in only one way, does not always appear to be bipolar, having, at best, a nondiscriminating contrast (Walker et al. 1988). Bipolar constructs may be considered more useful (Walker 2003) because they provide alternatives for movement should the application of one pole to an element be invalidated, as in Sewell's (2003) view of unelaborated contrast poles as "Plan B." These positions extend, but do not challenge, the importance of bipolar construing.

METHOD

A variety of assessment techniques has been developed from PCP (Neimeyer 1993); they can be divided into grid- and nongrid-based methods. These techniques may be viewed as ways of structuring conversations and as interventions rather than neutral reflections of reality (Fransella et al. 2004, Jankowicz 2003). However, they are still sometimes applied as if they were standardized, objective tests, perhaps reflecting the divorce of techniques from their theoretical basis.

Grid-Based Methods

Construct-element grids. Kelly is perhaps best known for devising the repertory grid technique, in which a series of elements (e.g., "myself now," "my partner") is sorted in terms of a number of constructs (e.g., "kind-mean"). Indeed, more than 90% of personal construct research employs this technique (Neimeyer et al. 1990). A major reason for the popularity of grids is their flexibility. A wide range of elements has been employed, including not just people matching role titles, as in the original procedure, but also different selves, relationships, parental roles, body parts, life events, pictures, and video clips. Constructs have not only been elicited from the individual, but also have been supplied. When constructs are elicited, this has not always been by Kelly's original procedure, in which, for successive triads of elements, the person is asked in what important way two of the elements are similar and thereby different from the third. Instead, particularly with those who find the triadic procedure too complex, constructs have been elicited by comparison of pairs of elements, description of single elements, or an interview. Finally, in assigning elements to construct poles, Kelly's dichotomous method has been largely replaced by ranking or rating the elements in terms of the constructs, resulting in a matrix of numbers in a grid in which the constructs constitute one axis and the elements the other. There has been considerable research on the effects of such procedural variations on grid scores. For example, various studies, reviewed by Fransella et al. (2004), indicate, consistent with Kelly's theory, that elicited constructs are more meaningful and used more complexly than are supplied constructs. In addition, approximately half of the variance of ratings on personal constructs is unique, in comparison with supplied constructs reflecting the Big Five personality traits (Grice 2004).

Grid versatility can be illustrated by considering two applications. With couples and families, modifications allow exploration of such areas as empathy and power balance in relationships. These include the completion not only of individual grids, but also grids as it is imagined that others will complete them, grids completed together with a partner, and grids using both the individual's and family members' constructs (Feixas et al. 1993). The personal meaning of death has been explored in an extensive research program utilizing a form of grid termed the "threat index," in which death threat is assumed to be indicated by discrepancies in how constructs are applied to the element "death" and to the self and ideal self (Neimeyer & Epting 1992).

A bewildering array of methods of analysis has been developed, accompanied by computer packages, including programs pioneered by Slater (1977) not only for individual grid analysis but also for the comparison of grids and the derivation of "consensus grids" for groups. Computer packages provide measures of properties of constructs and elements and their interrelationships (including hierarchical relationships; Bell 2004), which may be represented visually. They also provide measures of the structure of the construct system. These follow a tradition developed by Bieri (1955) and Crockett (1965) with measures of "cognitive complexity," the former grid-based and the latter not, which generated much research, particularly concerning social prediction. Subsequent measures have been developed of the extent of differentiation and integration in a construct system, of the tightness or looseness of construct relationships, and of logical inconsistencies in construing (Fransella et al. 2004).

Kelly was somewhat dismissive of traditional psychometric requirements of reliability and validity, and indeed, since there is no standard form of grid, general statements about its psychometric properties are not very meaningful. Nevertheless, the literature indicates relatively high test-retest reliability of particular grid measures and their validity, for example, in differentiating between certain groups or predicting behavior (Fransella et al. 2004).

Construct-construct grids. In two procedures linked to Hinkle's (1965) theory of implications, both grid axes are formed by constructs. In the implications grid, individuals are asked, for each construct, if they were to change from one pole to the other, on what other constructs they would be likely to change. A variation involves asking the person, for each construct pole, what other poles would characterize an individual so described (Fransella 1972). Implication grids may be analyzed by mapping the implicative relationships between constructs and counting the number of implications for each construct or in the grid as a whole. In the resistance-to-change grid, individuals are presented with constructs in pairs and asked, if they had to change from the preferred to the nonpreferred pole on one of these, on which constructs they would find this most difficult. The resistance-to-change score for each construct is the number of times the person would prefer not to change on it.

Element-element grids. Kelly's (1955) situational resources repertory test, or dependency grid, involves asking to whom, out of a list of people (resources), a person would turn for help in various difficult situations. Subsequent variations include changes in the situations and resources used and asking who would turn to the individual for help in the situations concerned. The major post-Kellian development is the derivation of quantitative measures of the degree of dispersion of dependencies, which have been found to be reliable and valid (Bell 2001, Walker 1997).

The coordinate grid, in which elements are ranked in terms of their similarity to each other, allows the derivation of measures of integrative complexity and logical inconsistency (Chambers 1983). The perceiver element grid is a qualitative method in which family members indicate how they view each other (Procter 2005).

Nongrid-Based Methods

Laddering: a technique designed to elicit increasingly superordinate constructs

Self-characterization: an assessment method involving the writing of an autobiographical sketch in the third person

Laddering and pyramiding. Laddering technique (Hinkle 1965) is seemingly simple in its description, complex in application, and can be powerful in impact. The interviewer progressively elicits constructs of increasing superordinacy by asking which pole of a construct the respondent prefers and why. When a new construct pole is thus elicited, its contrast pole determined, and preference established, the "why?" question is repeated. This continues until the person cannot or prefers not to respond (Fransella 2003b).

Laddering has been used extensively in marketing to explore construing governing product choice. Reynolds & Gutman (1988) elaborate the laddering process as three stages (means-end analysis). Constructs first elicited are product attributes, which are followed by consequences and finally become end states or values. This tradition of research has experimented with different formats, for example, hard and soft laddering. The former, often conducted by questionnaire or computer, involves the successive production of individual ladders, giving answers within each ladder at increasing levels of abstraction. The latter involves the derivation of ladders from a free-flowing interview. Russell et al. (2004) conclude that the relative utility of the formats depends on the researcher's goals, characterizing soft laddering as the gold standard. The technique's fertility is illustrated by the astonishing range of applications, including perceptions of wrestling (Deeter-Schmelz & Sojka 2004), consumer goals for recycling (Bagozzi & Dabholkar 1994), and food preferences (Zanoli & Naspetti 2002).

Strong evidence of the validity of laddering and related theoretical assumptions is provided by Neimeyer et al. (2001). This includes findings that more concrete constructs, concerning films, lead to longer ladders than do constructs concerning family members; that constructs higher in hierarchies (elicited later in the series of "why" questions) have greater response latency and are more diffi-

cult to articulate; and that more superordinate than subordinate constructs concern existential and moral themes, and fewer concern specific interests and relationships.

The pyramiding technique elicits subordinate constructs (Landfield 1971). It is restricted to exploring three levels of ordination. The questions focused on are "how" or "what," so that starting with a construct pole the interviewer might ask, "How would I know if someone was an X? What would they do?" The interviewer works on each pole of each construct, eliciting both similarity and contrast, resulting in one construct at the first level, two at the second, and four at the third.

ABC technique. The ABC technique highlights impediments to movement (Tschudi 1977). Constructs are elicited at three levels, beginning with the construct on which movement is desired; then why change is desirable, eliciting advantages of the pole to which movement is desired and disadvantages of the current position; and finally the impediments to change, ascertaining advantages of the current situation and disadvantages of the position of movement.

Self-characterization and textual analysis. The self-characterization technique involves writing an autobiographical sketch in the third person (Kelly 1955). More specific character sketches have been proposed and researchers have developed categorical methods of exploring sketches. Jackson's (1988) categories are linked to Kelly's corollaries, reflecting, for example, choice, sociality, commonality, and organization, while Klevjer & Walker's (2002) involve dispositional traits, personal concerns, and narrative.

Longer autobiographical sketches or chapter headings (e.g., "Before the baby was born," "Since I've been in graduate school") and summaries for these (Neimeyer 1985) have also been employed. Constructs and elements may be extracted from such sketches, or indeed any text, which may then be analyzed as a grid (Feixas & Villegas 1991).

Interview methods. Content analysis scales have been applied to verbalizations, generally obtained from open-ended interviews, by Viney & Caputi (2005). Of these scales, which concern a range of emotions, sociality, psychosocial stages, and experiences of control, cognitive anxiety is most closely linked to Kellian concepts. Nevertheless, the overall framework of Viney's research program is informed by PCP, and her approach enables important problems to be explored less intrusively than by more formal techniques.

Interview methods for children have been developed by Ravenette (2003), for example, to explore their "troubles" (in PCP terms, experiences of invalidation). There are also interview procedures for the elicitation of core constructs (Leitner 1985) and to explore the links between family members' constructions of others and their actions (Feixas et al. 1993).

Construct content analysis. Despite PCP's emphasis on process, content has not been ignored, and various methods have been developed to categorize constructs elicited by any of the methods described above (Green 2004). One of the first such systems, consisting of 22 categories (e.g., forcefulness), most with subcategories (e.g., high, low), was provided by Landfield (1971). Problems with this system have been addressed by Feixas et al. (2002) in a scheme for the classification of personal constructs using categories of moral, emotional, relational, personal, intellectual/operational, values/interests, existential, and concrete descriptors, each with subcategories.

Questionnaires. Because of PCP's idiographic emphasis, questionnaires have rarely been used, with two exceptions. The Personal Construct Inventory (Chambers & O'Day 1984) provides measures of processes of construing and has been revised based on its psychometric properties (Watson et al. 1997). Statements from newspapers illustrative of types of construing have been used to develop a questionnaire on economic attitudes that differentiates supporters of different political parties (Theodoulou 1996). This methodology has potential uses in other areas.

Visual techniques. There is increasing awareness that verbal symbols of construing can be supplemented by the nonverbal. Ravenette's (1999) work with children, which pioneers the use of drawings (and their opposites), is influential and may be extended to use with adults, as in the exploration of choices confronting women dealing with the menopause (Foster & Viney 2006).

A procedure in which a person is asked to take a series of photographs to answer the question "Who am I?" provides a measure of the degree of constriction (drawing in of the boundaries of application) of the construct system, reflected in the range of categories of the resulting photographs (Bailey & Walker 2003). Consistent with Kelly's theorizing, depression is associated with a more constricted system (Hanieh & Walker 2007).

APPLICATIONS

Clinical Applications

Kelly's two-volume magnum opus evolved from the handbook of clinical procedures he wrote for his students, and the clinical field is that in which PCP has been most widely used. The primary advances are in the understanding of disorder and of therapy, with the development and evaluation of new approaches to personal construct psychotherapy.

Disorder. Kelly (1955) views disorder as "any personal construction which is used repeatedly in spite of consistent invalidation" (p. 831). His classification of disorders into those of construction and of transition contains several inconsistencies, and it has been suggested that the notion of disorder carries mechanistic implications antithetical to Kelly's philosophy (Walker & Winter 2005).

Kelly's definition of disorder implies a failure to complete the process of experimentation described in his Validation and

Experience Cycle. The earlier the blockage in the Experience Cycle, the more severe the likely resulting disorder (Neimeyer 1985a). The failure to test construing adequately has been termed "nonvalidation" (Walker 2002), and it may be regarded as a strategy to avoid reconstruing. It may be associated with an imbalance in the use of the pairs of processes that Kelly considers central to construing, e.g., loosening versus tightening and dilation versus constriction. Although, optimally, there is a cyclical and balanced interplay of contrasting processes, disorders may involve the virtually exclusive use of one process. However, the distinction between optimal functioning and disorder extends beyond individual processes to such aspects of interpersonal relationships as the "egalitarian outlook," which combines an acceptance of individuality with cooperativeness and lack of oppression (Warren 1992), and "sociality" (Leitner & Pfenninger 1994).

Kelly (1955) and subsequent personal construct theorists (Raskin & Lewandowski 2000) criticize psychiatric nosology for its tendency to lead to preemptive construing, in which a person is seen solely in terms of a diagnostic label. Nevertheless, much post-Kellian clinical research considers clients defined by conventional psychiatric diagnostic categories (Button 1985), partly to facilitate communication with a community steeped in such constructions. One of the first such research programs associated schizophrenic thought disorder with loose construing, specifically when psychological constructs are applied to people (Bannister 1962, Bannister & Salmon 1966). Evidence was provided that this may result from serial invalidation of construing (Bannister 1965), and the Grid Test of Schizophrenic Thought Disorder (Bannister & Fransella 1966) was developed as a diagnostic instrument. Bannister's research spawned numerous studies, and although some proposed alternative explanations for his results, none was entirely convincing (Winter 1992). Schizophrenia has also been explored from a PCP perspective by Lorenzini et al. (1989),

who differentiate it from paranoia in terms of the earlier age at which major invalidation has been experienced, and Gara et al. (1989), who associate it with unelaborated (poorly developed) self-construing.

A single profound invalidation may lead to fragmentation of construing, as indicated in studies associating post-traumatic stress disorder with unelaborated construing of the traumatic event (Sewell 1997). This leads to "constructive bankruptcy" (p. 209), in which the person cannot relate the trauma to other life experiences. Childhood sexual abuse is one trauma that has received considerable attention from a PCP perspective (Erbes & Harter 2002).

In contrast to schizophrenic thought disorder, a pattern of tight construing may characterize individuals with anxiety disorders (Winter 1985). There is evidence that those diagnosed as agoraphobic may constrict their worlds to avoid anxiety associated with interpersonal conflict, the agoraphobic's construing of which tends to be at a low level of awareness (Winter 1989).

In one of Kelly's (1961) own elaborations, he distinguishes different types of suicidal acts. Suicide as a "dedicated act," as in many cases of suicide bombings, is "designed to validate one's life . . . to extend its essential meaning" rather than to terminate it (Kelly 1961, p. 260). Kelly differentiates this from "mere suicide," which may occur in circumstances of realism (certainty) and indeterminacy (chaos). In the former, "the course of events seems so obvious that there is no point in waiting around for the outcome," whereas in the latter, "everything seems so unpredictable that the only definite thing one can do is to abandon the scene altogether" (Kelly 1961, p. 260). This taxonomy has been extended to encompass nonfatal acts of deliberate self-harm (Neimeyer & Winter 2006). Some of this research associates high suicidal intent with constriction of the construct system, although the findings are not entirely consistent.

PCP perspectives have been provided on numerous other clinical problems, including obsessive-compulsive disorder, depression, eating disorders, substance abuse, psychopathy, and psychosexual problems (Winter 1992). Such applications are not limited to the adult mental health setting, but extend to work with children (Butler & Green 1998), older people (Viney 1993), people with learning disabilities (Davis & Cunningham 1985) and autism (Procter 2001), and those with physical illnesses (Viney 1983). They include books aimed at facilitating clients' understanding of their difficulties and of solutions to them (e.g., Rowe 2003).

Psychotherapy. Most personal construct studies of psychotherapy use grid technique, which is an indication of its value as a therapy research measure (Winter 2003). In pioneering work by Landfield (1971) and in subsequent investigations, aspects of construing have been predictive of therapeutic outcome, in some studies differentiating between responses to particular therapies (Winter 1990). For example, there is evidence that tight construing predicts a poor response to exploratory psychotherapy. Studies of the therapeutic process reveal patterns of construing, such as cyclical alternations of loose and tight construing, occurring during therapy, while outcome studies indicate the reconstruction associated with successful therapy.

PCP now views an optimal therapeutic process as involving experiences of invalidation within an overall climate of validation. When invalidation predominates, or threatens core constructs, the client may resist therapy, this being an understandable attempt to preserve the integrity of the construct system (Fransella 1993). Therapists who fail to heed this warning and adjust their approach accordingly may be faced with a therapeutic casualty (Winter 1996). There have been some studies of the process of personal construct psychotherapy, which has been shown to differ significantly from that of rationalist cognitive therapy (Winter & Watson 1999).

In one of the first demonstrations of the relationship between construing and behav-

ior, Fransella (1972) proceeded from evidence that stuttering provides an elaborated "way of life" for people who stutter to develop a therapeutic approach focusing on elaborating an alternative, fluent way of life. Her findings are supported by a study using a text-based measure of the complexity of construct systems (DiLollo et al. 2005). Since Fransella's work, there have been numerous elaborations of personal construct psychotherapeutic approaches for various disorders and types of client, both individually and with their partners or families (Leitner & Dunnett 1993, Neimeyer & Neimeyer 1987, Winter & Viney 2005).

Personal construct psychotherapy is technically eclectic, employing a range of techniques from various orientations but conceptualizing them from a PCP perspective. In Neimeyer's (1988b) view, this has evolved to "theoretically progressive integrationism," allowing not only techniques but also concepts to be borrowed from other approaches sharing PCP's metatheoretical assumptions. There are various reviews of personal construct psychotherapy in the context of more general developments in constructivist therapies (e.g., Neimeyer & Mahoney 1995, Neimeyer & Raskin 2001). One particular integrative direction views psychotherapy as involving reconstruction of narratives, as in Neimeyer's (2001) work on bereavement and loss, which regards meaning reconstruction as central to grieving. PCP has also been influential in the development of other therapeutic approaches, such as cognitive analytic therapy (Ryle 1990).

There have been some adaptations of Kelly's own therapeutic techniques. His fixed-role therapy procedure, in which the client is asked to take on a new role for a limited period, has been modified to include mini fixed roles to tackle particular problems (Epting 1984) and adapted for use in marital therapy (Kremsdorf 1985). Developments in personal construct group psychotherapy have included various structured approaches, notably the Interpersonal Transaction Group (Landfield

& Rivers 1975, Neimeyer 1988a). This involves a phase of rotating dyads in which group members briefly interact with every other member concerning a provided topic, followed by a plenary phase in which members discuss these dyadic experiences. One particular variant of personal construct psychotherapy emphasizing the intimate client-therapist relationship, rather than techniques, is Leitner's (1988) experiential approach. He argues that such relationships pose the danger of invalidation of core constructs and may therefore be terrifying; this is less likely if an optimal therapeutic distance, balancing connection and separateness, is maintained between therapist and client.

Although conventional outcome research has been regarded by some personal construct psychotherapists as incompatible with constructivism, there is a growing evidence base for this form of therapy with a wide range of client groups (Viney et al. 2005). Meta-analysis of the studies concerned, which compare the outcome of personal construct psychotherapy with either no treatment, standard care, or other types of intervention, has indicated effect sizes comparable to those in cognitive-behavioral and psychodynamic therapies (Viney et al. 2005). This research is complemented by numerous uncontrolled, single-case, and/or qualitative studies.

Educational Applications

Another major area of application of PCP is the educational setting. Although Kelly ran a traveling service to schools, he devotes little attention in his writing to the process of the development of construing. However, PCP has subsequently been elaborated as a psychology of personal growth, and both similarities and differences have been noted with Piaget's epistemological position (Salmon 1970, Soffer 1993). For example, both approaches view the individual as an active experimenter, and both focus on structural aspects of development rather than the content of the person's view of the world. It has been suggested,

however, that Piaget's view of reality is more absolutist than is Kelly's.

Personal construct approaches to educational psychology have also been developed, and the implications of PCP for the process of learning have been elaborated.

Children's construing. A series of studies, mostly using grids (Salmon 1976), provides evidence for elaboration of construing during childhood. Mancuso (2003) views child development as the construction of self-guiding anticipatory narratives, essentially stories based on children's self-constructions and determining their actions. He identifies, and provides training in, the characteristics of expert parents, those who most facilitate their children's development. One way in which a parent may attempt to develop a child's construing is by reprimand, which Mancuso considers a possible outcome of rule violation, the invalidation of a person's construction of an event by another. Invalidation by a child of an adult's construction of how a learner should behave may lead to the child being construed preemptively in terms of a diagnosis such as attention deficit/hyperactivity disorder. This is likely to impair the child's ability to develop a construction of self as a competent learner.

Educational psychology and learning. Personal construct educational psychology was pioneered by Ravenette (1999), who developed methods for elicitation of children's construing. These exemplify such features of PCP as the credulous approach (taking the client's views at face value), the emphasis on contrast, and that assessment itself may promote reconstruction. Ravenette stresses that problems in which the educational psychologist is asked to intervene are generally not presented by children themselves but by adults interacting with them. He considers that such problems occur "when a person cannot make sense out of an event, *and feels that he should*" (Ravenette 1988, p. 103; italics in original). Resolution is as likely to require reconstruing by an adult as by the child. For example, he describes how a boy was no longer construed by his teacher as a "problem child" but rather as simply "having reading difficulties" when the teacher understood that the boy's withdrawal from her had invalidated her core construction of herself as a caring person.

Some of Kelly's post-1955 publications indicate the importance of personal meanings in the learning process (Kelly 1970, 1979, 2003), and this theme has been continued (Pope & Denicolo 2001). For example, Thomas & Harri-Augstein (1985) promote self-organized learning, in which people are helped to reflect upon their learning processes by engaging in learning conversations. Others focus on making teachers more aware of the learner's and their own construing (Pope 2003), in some cases using fixed-role therapy and grids (Diamond 1991) or techniques developed to explore constructions of educational progression (Salmon & Claire 1984). In Novak's (1990) approach, the emphasis is on developing a pedagogical relationship that is inviting rather than dictating.

Organizational Applications

An area of application of PCP that has grown with the recognition of the inherently social nature of the theory is its utility in organizational and business settings, extending beyond the construct system of the individual within the organization to that of the organization itself.

The individual within the organization. Personal construct work with individuals in organizations includes personal development, coaching, counseling (Brophy et al. 2003, Fransella et al. 1988), and vocational guidance (Savickas 1997). It relies heavily upon, but is not limited to, the use of grids (Stewart & Stewart 1981).

The organization. Personal construct assessment methods are also used in areas relevant to broader concerns of organizations, including market research, job analysis, se-

lection procedures, employee induction, performance appraisal, facilitation of decision-making, team building exercises, exploration of communication, conflict resolution, and analysis of how managers and employees view a company's work (Brophy et al. 2003, Coopman 1997, Jankowicz 1990). The results are often fed back to participants, allowing the planning of change processes such as retraining programs, which in turn may be evaluated by grids. A particularly helpful outcome may be the facilitation of construing not only of individuals' own construction processes, but also those of other stakeholders in the organization. A personal construct understanding of transitions and resistance to change is central to much of this work (e.g., Fournier 1995).

The range of settings in which such approaches have been applied is considerable. The impact has been extensive in some cases, such as that of an airport authority where a PCP perspective has been applied to every aspect of its work involving people (Brophy et al. 2003).

Other Applications

The work of post-Kellian personal construct theorists shows the theory to have a range of convenience, or of useful application, extending far beyond the clinical, educational, and organizational settings. Other spheres in which it is applied include the forensic setting, politics, sport, the arts, anthropology, religion, accounting, and artificial intelligence (Fransella 2003a, Fransella & Thomas 1988, Horley 2003, Kalekin-Fishman & Walker 1996, Scheer & Sewell 2006).

CONCLUSIONS

A feature of PCP is reflexivity, the ability to turn its concepts upon itself. How, then, has the theory fared in the past half-century when evaluated in personal construct terms?

Kelly (1955, p. 22) sets out a list of "design specifications for a psychological theory of personality," namely that it should have an appropriate focus and range of convenience, be fertile, produce testable hypotheses, be valid, have generality, be amenable to operational definition, be modifiable and ultimately expendable, avoid the problems associated with assumptions of mental energy, be able to account for the choices that people make, and recognize individuality.

The appropriateness of the focus of convenience of PCP on the "psychological reconstruction of life" (Kelly 1955, p. 23) is particularly demonstrated by post-Kellian elaborations of personal construct psychotherapy. The diversity of its other applications indicates that its range of convenience extends throughout human psychology, including areas in which it was initially not well elaborated. These applications, and the new approaches and research programs generated from PCP, also demonstrate its fertility. The theory has produced numerous hypotheses that have been subjected to experimental test, and the support that these have received indicates something of the theory's validity (perhaps a surprising concept for Kelly to employ, but one that essentially refers to predictive efficiency). The abstractness of the theory's constructs enables them to have a generality extending far beyond the clinical realm and the historical context in which they were originally developed. These concepts have also been operationally defined, often using assessment methods developed from PCP. That the theory itself, as opposed to the approaches and techniques devised from it, has been subject to little or no modification may attest to the viability of Kelly's ideas. While there have been attempts to integrate the theory with, or subsume it within, other approaches, there has also been resistance to such developments. This itself supports Kelly's view that people, even personal construct theorists, are threatened by the prospect of their core constructs being expendable. On the other hand, some personal construct theorists regard the assimilation of the theory into other perspectives and disciplines a natural stage in the development of a successful theory, and one to which its followers should aspire (Neimeyer 1985). The lack of concepts of mental energy has not hampered the theory's explanatory power, and its notion of choice has received empirical support and enabled the understanding of the often surprising, and sometimes apparently self-defeating or destructive (Neimeyer & Winter 2006, Winter 2006), choices that people make. Finally, the idiographic application of the theory to such areas as individual choice is complemented by nomothetic applications, such as the derivation and testing of hypotheses concerning the construing of particular groups.

The elaboration of PCP can therefore be considered to demonstrate that the theory meets Kelly's design specifications, perhaps too well in that it has yet to become expendable! He concludes the second volume of his book with the hope that the "unique pair of spectacles" through which the reader has been offered a look will be found to fit (Kelly 1955). The extent of the subsequent fit in extremely diverse fields may be far greater than even Kelly could have anticipated.

SUMMARY POINTS

1. Personal construct psychology anticipated numerous subsequent developments in psychology.

2. It is not, as sometimes described, merely a cognitive psychology of the individual, but is concerned with the whole person, including the person in relation to others.

3. Particular areas in which the theory has been developed include implicative relationships between constructs, self-construing, social relationships, emotions, relationships with other theories, and research testing aspects of the theory.

4. There has been considerable adaptation of Kelly's repertory grid and self-characterization methods for the assessment of construing; several other assessment methods have also been developed.

5. Personal construct psychology has been applied extensively in the clinical, educational, and organizational fields, as well as in a wide range of other areas.

6. There is a growing evidence base for personal construct psychotherapy.

FUTURE ISSUES

1. There should be further elaboration of the position of personal construct psychology in relation to constructivism and other contemporary psychological approaches.

2. Various aspects of personal construct theory, such as Kelly's view of choice, could be subjected to further research investigation.

3. The extensive developments that have occurred in personal construct assessment techniques have focused more on measures of the structure and content of construing than on construing processes. The assessment of the latter should be a priority for further developments in the area.

4. The recent reconsideration of the personal construct psychology view of psychological disorder has scope for further elaboration.

5. There should be development of the evidence base for personal construct interventions in clinical and other settings.

LITERATURE CITED

Adams-Webber J. 1990. Some fundamental asymmetries in the structure of personal constructs. See Neimeyer & Neimeyer 1990, pp. 49–85

Adams-Webber J. 2001. Cognitive complexity and role relationships. *J. Constr. Psychol.* 14:43–50

Adams-Webber J. 2003. Research in personal construct psychology. See Fransella 2003a, pp. 51–58

Bagozzi RP, Dabholkar PA. 1994. Consumer recycling goals and their effect on decisions to recycle: a means-end chain analysis. *Psychol. Market.* 11:313–40

Bailey A, Walker BM. 2003. Using psychophotography as a nonverbal measure of constriction. In *Psychological Constructivism and the Social World*, ed. GC Chiari, ML Nuzzo, pp.306–12. Milan: FrancoAngeli

Balnaves M, Caputi P. 2000. A theory of social action: why personal construct psychology needs a superpattern corollary. *J. Constr. Psychol.* 13:117–34

Bannister D. 1962. The nature and measurement of schizophrenic thought disorder. *J. Ment. Sci.* 108:825–42

Bannister D. 1965. The genesis of schizophrenic thought disorder: retest of the serial invalidation hypothesis. *Brit. J. Psychiatry* 111:377–82

Bannister D, ed. 1970, *Perspectives in Personal Construct Theory*. London: Academic

Demonstrates empirically that a particular type of psychological disorder, schizophrenic thought disorder, is related to features of construing.

Bannister D, ed. 1977a. *New Perspectives in Personal Construct Theory*. London: Academic

Bannister D. 1977b. The logic of passion. See Bannister 1977a, pp. 21–37

Bannister D. 1983. Self in personal construct theory. In *Applications of Personal Construct Theory*, ed. JR Adams-Webber, JC Mancuso, pp. 379–86. Toronto: Academic

Bannister D, Fransella F. 1966. A grid test of schizophrenic thought disorder. *Br. J. Soc. Clin. Psychol.* 5:95–102

Bannister D, Salmon P. 1966. Schizophrenic thought disorder: specific or diffuse? *Br. J. Med. Psychol.* 39:215–19

Bell RC. 2000. A psychometric assessment of the bipolarity of constructs in repertory grid data. See Scheer 2000, pp. 141–49

Bell RC. 2001. Some new measures of dispersion of dependency in a situation-resource grid. *J. Constr. Psychol.* 14:227–34

Bell RC. 2004. Predictive relationships in repertory grid data: a new elaboration of Kelly's Organization Corollary. *J. Constr. Psychol.* 4:281–95

Benjafield J, Adams-Webber J. 1976. The golden section hypothesis. *Br. J. Psychol.* 67:11–15

Bieri J. 1955. Cognitive complexity-simplicity and predictive behavior. *J. Abnorm. Soc. Psychol.* 51:263–86

Bonarius H, Holland H, Rosenberg S, eds. 1981. *Personal Construct Psychology: Recent Advances in Theory and Practice*. London: Macmillan

Botella L. 1995. Personal construct theory, constructivism, and postmodern thought. See Neimeyer & Neimeyer 1995, pp. 3–35

Brophy S, Fransella F, Reed N. 2003. The power of a good theory. See Fransella 2003a, pp. 329–38

Bruner JS. 1956. A cognitive theory of personality. *Contemp. Psychol.* 1:355–57

Butler R, Green D. 1998. *The Child Within: The Exploration of Personal Construct Theory with Young People*. Oxford: Butterworth Heinemann

Butt T. 2006. Personal construct therapy and its history in pragmatism. In *Personal Construct Psychology: New Ideas*, ed. P Caputi, H Foster, LL Viney, pp. 20–34. London: Wiley

Butt T, Burr V, Bell RC. 1997. Fragmentation and the sense of self. *Constr. Hum. Sci.* 2:12–29

Button E, ed. 1985. *Personal Construct Theory and Mental Health*. Beckenham, UK: Croom Helm

Chambers WV. 1983. Circumspection, preemption and personal constructs. *Soc. Behav. Personal.* 11:33–35

Chambers WV, O'Day P. 1984. A nomothetic view of personal construct processes. *Psychol. Rep.* 55:554

Chiari G, Mancini F, Nicolò F, Nuzzo ML. 1990. Hierarchical organization of personal construct systems in terms of their range of convenience. *Int. J. Personal. Constr. Psychol.* 3:281–311

Chiari G, Nuzzo ML. 1996. Psychological constructivisms: a metatheoretical differentiation. *J. Constr. Psychol.* 9:163–84

Chiari G, Nuzzo ML, Alfano V, Brogna P, D'Andrea T, et al. 1994. Personal paths of dependency. *J. Constr. Psychol.* 7:17–34

Coopman SJ. 1997. Personal constructs and communication in interpersonal and organizational contexts. See Neimeyer & Neimeyer 1997, pp. 101–47

Crockett. 1965. Cognitive complexity and impression formation. In *Progress in Experimental Personality Research*, ed. BA Maher, 3:47–90. New York: Academic

Cummins P. 2003. Working with anger. See Fransella 2003a, pp. 83–91

Davis H, Cunningham C. 1985. Mental handicap: people in context. See Button 1985, pp. 246–61

Deeter-Schmelz DR, Sojka JZ. 2004. Wrestling with American values: an exploratory investigation of World Wrestling Entertainment as a product-based subculture. *J Consum. Behav.* 4:132–43

Diamond CPT. 1991. *Teacher Education as Transformation*. Milton Keynes, UK: Open Univ. Press

DiLollo A, Manning WH, Neimeyer RA. 2005. Cognitive complexity as a function of speaker role for adult persons who stutter. *J. Constr. Psychol.* 18:215–36

Duck S. 1979. The personal and the interpersonal in construct theory: social and individual aspects of relationships. See Stringer & Bannister 1979, pp. 279–97

Epting FR. 1984. *Personal Construct Counseling and Psychotherapy*. New York: Wiley

Epting FR, Landfield AW, eds. 1985. *Anticipating Personal Construct Psychology*. Lincoln: Univ. Nebraska Press

Erbes CR, Harter SL. 2002. Constructions of abuse: understanding the effects of childhood sexual abuse. See Raskin & Bridges 2002, pp. 27–48

Feixas G, Geldschläger H, Neimeyer RA. 2002. Content analysis of personal constructs. *J. Constr. Psychol.* 15:1–20

Feixas G, Procter HG, Neimeyer GJ. 1993. Convergent lines of assessment: systemic and constructivist contributions. See GJ Neimeyer 1993, pp. 143–78

Feixas G, Villegas M. 1991. Personal construct analysis of autobiographical texts: a method presentation and case illustration. *Int. J. Personal. Constr. Psychol.* 4:51–83

Foster H, Viney LL. 2007. Nonverbal explorations of construing: drawing menopause. *J. Constr. Psychol.* In press

Fournier V. 1995. Personal change following organizational entry: from a role-person fit model to a PCP framework. See Neimeyer & Neimeyer 1995, pp. 133–89

Fransella F. 1972. *Personal Change and Reconstruction: Research on a Treatment of Stuttering*. London: Academic

Fransella F. 1993. The construct of resistance in psychotherapy. See Leitner & Dunnett 1993, pp. 117–34

Fransella F. 1995. *George Kelly*. London: Sage

Fransella F, ed. 2003a. *International Handbook of Personal Construct Psychology*. Chichester, UK: Wiley

Fransella F. 2003b. Some skills and tools for personal construct practitioners. See Fransella 2003a, pp. 105–21

Fransella F, Bell R, Bannister D. 2004. *A Manual for Repertory Grid Technique*. Chichester, UK: Wiley. 2nd ed.

Fransella F, Jones H, Watson J. 1988. A range of applications of PCP within business and industry. See Fransella & Thomas 1988, pp. 405–17

Fransella F, Thomas L, eds. 1988. *Experimenting with Personal Construct Psychology*. London: Routledge

Gara MA, Rosenberg S, Mueller DR. 1989. Perception of self and others in schizophrenia. *Int. J. Personal. Constr. Psychol.* 2:253–70

Green B. 2004. Personal construct psychology and content analysis. *Personal. Constr. Theory Pract.* 1:82–91. Retrieved from **http://www.pcp-net.org/journal/pct04.pdf**

Grice JW. 2004. Bridging the idiographic-nomothetic divide in ratings of self and others on the Big Five. *J. Personal.* 72:203–41

Hanieh E, Walker BM. 2007. Photography as a measure of constricted construing. *J. Constr. Psychol.* In press

Hinkle DN. 1965. *The change of personal constructs from the viewpoint of a theory of construct implications*. PhD thesis, Ohio State Univ. 113 pp.

Demonstrates the breadth of application of personal construct psychology since 1955.

Describes repertory grid technique and reviews developments in this method and its applications.

Influential thesis because of theoretical insights concerning change and resistance to change and innovative methods for exploring hierarchical relationships between constructs.

Horley J, ed. 2003. *Personal Construct Perspectives on Forensic Psychology*. London: Routledge

Jackson SR. 1988. Self-characterization: dimensions of meaning. See Fransella & Thomas 1998, pp. 223–31

Jankowicz AD. 1990. Applications of personal construct psychology in business practice. See Neimeyer & Neimeyer 1990, pp. 257–87

Jankowicz D. 2003. *The Easy Guide to Repertory Grids*. London: Wiley

Kalekin-Fishman D, Walker BM, eds. 1996. *The Construction of Group Realities: Culture, Society and Personal Construct Psychology*. Malabar, FL: Krieger Publ.

Kelly GA. 1955 (1991). *The Psychology of Personal Constructs*. New York: Norton/London: Routledge

Kelly GA. 1961. Theory and therapy in suicide: the personal construct point of view. In *The Cry for Help*, ed. M Farberow, E Scheidman, pp. 255–80. New York: McGraw-Hill

Kelly GA. 1962. Europe's matrix of decision. In *Nebraska Symposium on Motivation*, ed. RM Jones, pp. 82–123. Lincoln: Univ. Nebraska Press

Kelly GA. 1969a. Hostility. See Maher 1969, pp. 267–80

Kelly GA. 1969b. In whom confide: on whom depend for what? See Maher 1969, pp. 189–206

Kelly GA. 1969c. Man's construction of his alternatives. See Maher 1969, pp. 66–93

Kelly GA. 1969d. Sin and psychotherapy. See Maher 1969, pp. 165–88

Kelly GA. 1969e. The language of hypotheses: man's psychological instrument. See Maher 1969, pp. 147–62

Kelly GA. 1969f. The psychotherapeutic relationship. See Maher 1969, pp. 224–64

Kelly GA. 1970. Behaviour is an experiment. See Bannister 1970, pp. 255–69

Kelly GA. 1978. Confusion and the clock. In *Personal Construct Psychology 1977*, ed. F Fransella, pp. 209–32. London: Academic

Kelly GA. 1979. Social inheritance. See Stringer & Bannister 1979, pp. 4–17

Kelly GA. 1980. A psychology of the optimal man. In *Personal Construct Psychology: Psychotherapy and Personality*, ed. AW Landfield, LM Leitner, pp.18–35. New York: Wiley

Kelly GA. 2003. Teacher-student relations at university level. See Fransella 2003a, pp. 295–301

Klevjer I, Walker BM. 2002. Beyond the "Big Five": a qualitative study of age differences in personality. *Aust. J. Psychol. (Suppl.)* 54:5

Korzybski A. 1933. *Science and Sanity: An Introduction to Non-Aristotelian Systems and General Semantics*. Lancaster, PA: Science

Kremsdorf R. 1985. An extension of fixed-role therapy with a couple. See Epting & Landfield 1985, pp. 216–24

Landfield A. 1971. *Personal Construct Systems in Psychotherapy*. Chicago: Rand McNally

Landfield AW, Rivers PC. 1975. An introduction to interpersonal transaction and rotating dyads. *Psychother. Theory Res. Prac.* 12:365–73

Leitner LM. 1985. Interview methods for construct elicitation: searching for the core. See Epting & Landfield 1985, pp. 292–306

Leitner LM. 1988. Terror, risk and reverence: experiential personal construct psychotherapy. *Int. J. Personal. Constr. Psychol.* 1:25–61

Leitner LM, Dunnett NGM, eds. 1993. *Critical Issues in Personal Construct Psychotherapy*. Malabar, FL: Krieger, Publ.

Leitner LM, Pfenninger DT. 1994. Sociality and optimal functioning. *J. Constr. Psychol.* 7:119–35

Lorenzini R, Sassaroli S, Rocchi MT. 1989. Schizophrenia and paranoia as solutions to predictive failure. *Int. J. Personal. Constr. Psychol.* 2:417–32

Maher B, ed. 1969. *Clinical Psychology and Personality: The Collected Papers of George Kelly*. New York: Wiley

Presents key components of a clinical approach based centrally on sociality, involving diagnosis by diagnostic framework focusing on differing styles of interpersonal relationships.

Contains a collection of engaging papers presented or written by Kelly after his magnum opus was published in 1955; indicates the subsequent development of his ideas.

Mahoney MJ. 1988. Constructive metatheory: I. Basic features and historical foundations. *Int. J. Personal. Constr. Psychol.* 1:1–35

Mair JMM. 1977. The community of self. See Bannister 1977a, pp. 125–49

Mair M. 1988. Psychology as story-telling. *Int. J. Personal. Constr. Psychol.* 1:125–38

Mair M. 1989. Kelly, Bannister, and a story-telling psychology. *Int. J. Personal. Constr. Psychol.* 2:1–14

Mancuso JC. 2003. Children's development of personal constructs. See Fransella 2003a, pp. 275–82

McCoy MM. 1981. Positive and negative emotion: a personal interpretation. See Bonarius et al. 1981, pp. 95–104

McWilliams SA. 1996. Accepting the invitational. In *Personal Construct Theory: A Psychology for the Future*, ed. BM Walker, J Costigan, LL Viney, B Warren, pp. 57–78. Melbourne: Aust. Psychol. Soc.

Millis KK, Neimeyer RA. 1990. A test of the dichotomy corollary: propositions versus constructs as basic cognitive units. *Int. J. Personal. Constr. Psychol.* 3:167–81

Mischel W. 1980. George Kelly's anticipation of psychology. In *Psychotherapy Process: Current Issues and Future Directions*, ed. MJ Mahoney, pp. 85–87. New York: Plenum

Moretti MM, Higgins ET. 1990. Relating self-discrepancy to self-esteem: the contribution of discrepancy beyond actual-self ratings. *J. Exp. Soc. Psychol.* 26:108–23

Neimeyer GJ. 1985. Personal constructs in the counseling of couples. See Epting & Landfield 1985, pp. 201–15

Neimeyer GJ, ed. 1993. *Constructivist Assessment: A Casebook*. London: Sage

Neimeyer GJ, Hudson JE. 1985. Couple's constructs: personal systems in marital satisfaction. In *Issues and Approaches in Personal Construct Theory*, ed. D Bannister, pp. 127–41. London: Academic

Neimeyer GJ, Neimeyer RA. 1981. Personal construct perspectives on cognitive assessment. In *Cognitive Assessment*, ed. T Merluzzi, C Glass, M Genest, pp. 188–232. New York: Guilford

Neimeyer GJ, Neimeyer RA. 1985. Relational trajectories: a personal construct contribution. *J. Soc. Pers. Relat.* 2:325–49

Neimeyer GJ, Neimeyer RA, eds. 1990. *Advances in Personal Construct Psychology*. Vol. 1. Greenwich, CT: JAI

Neimeyer GJ, Neimeyer RA, eds. 1997. *Advances in Personal Construct Psychology*. Vol. 4. Greenwich, CT: JAI

Neimeyer RA. 1985a. Personal constructs in clinical practice. In *Advances in Cognitive-Behavioral Research and Therapy*, ed. PC Kendall, 4:275–339. New York: Academic

Neimeyer RA. 1985b. *The Development of Personal Construct Psychology*. Lincoln: Univ. Nebraska Press

Neimeyer RA. 1988a. Integrative directions in personal construct therapy. *Int. J. Personal. Constr. Psychol.* 1:283–97

Neimeyer RA. 1988b. Clinical guidelines for conducting interpersonal transaction groups. *Int. J. Personal. Constr. Psychol.* 1:181–90

Neimeyer RA. 1993. Constructivist approaches for the measurement of meaning. See GJ Neimeyer 1997, pp. 58–103

Neimeyer RA. 2001. The language of loss: grief therapy as a process of meaning reconstruction. In *Meaning Reconstruction and the Experience of Loss*, ed. RA Neimeyer, pp. 261–92. Washington, DC: Am. Psychol. Assoc.

Neimeyer RA, Anderson A, Stockton L. 2001. Snakes versus ladders: a validation of laddering as a technique as a measure of hierarchical structure. *J. Constr. Psychol.* 14:85–106

Neimeyer RA, Baker KD, Neimeyer GJ. 1990. The current status of personal construct theory: some scientometric data. See Neimeyer & Neimeyer 1990, pp. 3–22

Neimeyer RA, Epting FR. 1992. Measuring personal meanings of death: twenty years of research using the Threat Index. In *Advances in Personal Construct Psychology*, ed. RA Neimeyer, GJ Neimeyer, 2:121–47. Greenwich, CT: JAI

Neimeyer RA, Mahoney MJ, eds. 1995. *Constructivism in Psychotherapy*. Washington, DC: Am. Psychol. Assoc.

Neimeyer RA, Neimeyer GJ, eds. 1987. *Personal Construct Therapy Casebook*. New York: Springer

Neimeyer RA, Neimeyer GJ, eds. 1995. *Advances in Personal Construct Psychology*. Vol. 3. Greenwich, CT: JAI

Neimeyer RA, Raskin JD. 2001. Varieties of constructivism in psychotherapy. In *Handbook of Cognitive-Behavioral Therapies*, ed. KS Dobson, pp. 393–430. New York: Guilford

Neimeyer RA, Winter DA. 2006. To be or not to be: personal construct perspectives on the suicidal choice. In *Cognition and Suicide: The Science of Suicidal Thinking*, ed. T Ellis, pp. 149–69. Washington, DC: Am. Psychol. Assoc.

Novak JM. 1990. Advancing constructive education: a framework for teacher education. See Neimeyer & Neimeyer 1995, pp. 233–55

Pope M. 2003. Construing teaching and teacher education worldwide. See Fransella 2003a, pp. 303–10

Pope ML, Denicolo PM. 2001. *Transformative Education: Personal Construct Approaches to Practice and Research*. London: Whurr

Introduces the notion of the family construct system, with properties similar to individual construct systems.

Procter HG. 1981. Family construct psychology: an approach to understanding and treating families. In *Developments in Family Therapy*, ed. S Walrond-Skinner, pp. 350–66. London: Routledge

Procter HG. 2001. Personal construct psychology and autism. *J. Constr. Psychol.* 14:107–26

Procter H. 2005. Techniques of personal construct family therapy. See Winter & Viney 2005, pp. 94–108

Raskin JD, Lewandowski AM. 2000. The construction of disorder as human enterprise. In *Constructions of Disorder: Meaning-Making Frameworks in Psychotherapy*, ed. RA Neimeyer, JD Raskin, pp. 15–40. Washington, DC: Am. Psychol. Assoc.

Ravenette AT. 1977. Personal construct theory: an approach to the psychological investigation of children and young people. See Bannister 1977a, pp. 251–80

Ravenette AT. 1988. Personal construct psychology in the practice of an educational psychologist. In *Working with People: Clinical Uses of Personal Construct Psychology*, ed. G. Dunnett, pp. 101–21. London: Routledge

Ravenette AT. 1999. *Personal Construct Theory in Educational Psychology: A Practitioner's View*. London: Whurr

Ravenette T. 2003. Constructive intervention when children are presented as problems. See Fransella 2003a, pp 283–93

Reynolds TJ, Gutman J. 1988. Laddering theory, method, analysis, and interpretation. *J. Advert. Res.* 28:11–31

Riemann R. 1990. The bipolarity of personal constructs. *Int. J. Personal. Constr. Psychol.* 3:149–65

Rogers CR. 1956. Intellectualized psychotherapy. *Contemp. Psychol.* 1:357–58

Rowe D. 2003. *Depression: The Way Out of Your Prison*. Hove, UK/New York: Brunner-Routledge. 3rd ed.

Russell CG, Busson A, Flight I, Bryan J, van Lawick van Pabst J, Cox D. 2004. A comparison of three laddering techniques applied to an example of a complex food choice. *Food Qual. Pref.* 15:569–83

Rychlak JF. 1977. *The Psychology of Rigorous Humanism*. New York: Wiley

Ryle A. 1990. *Cognitive-Analytic Therapy: Active Participation in Change: A New Integration in Brief Therapy*. Chichester, UK: Wiley

Salmon P. 1970. A psychology of personal growth. See Bannister 1970, pp. 197–221

Salmon P. 1976. Grid measures with child subjects. In *The Measurement of Intrapersonal Space by Grid Technique. Volume 1. Explorations of Intrapersonal Space*, ed. P Slater, pp. 15–46. Chichester, UK: Wiley

Salmon P, Claire H. 1984. *Classroom Collaboration*. London: Routledge & Kegan Paul

Savickas ML. 1997. Constructivist career counseling: models and methods. See Neimeyer & Neimeyer 1997, pp. 149–82

Scheer JW, Sewell KW, eds. 2006. *Creative Construing: Personal Constructions in the Arts*. Giessen: Psychosozial-Verlag

Sewell KW. 1997. Posttraumatic stress: towards a constructivist model of psychotherapy. See Neimeyer & Neimeyer 1997, pp. 207–35

Sewell KW. 2003. An approach to post-traumatic stress. See Fransella 2003a, pp. 223–31

Sewell KW, Baldwin CL, Moes AJ. 1998. The multiple self awareness group. *J. Constr. Psychol.* 11:59–78

Slater P. 1977. *The Measurement of Intrapersonal Space by Grid Technique. Volume 2. Dimensions of Intrapersonal Space*. Chichester, UK: Wiley

Soffer J. 1993. Jean Piaget and George Kelly: toward a stronger constructivism. *Int. J. Personal. Constr. Psychol.* 6:59–77

Stevens CD. 1998. Realism and Kelly's pragmatic constructivism. *J. Constr. Psychol.* 11:283–308

Stewart V, Stewart A. 1981. *Business Applications of Repertory Grid*. London: McGraw-Hill

Stringer P, Bannister D, eds. 1979. *Constructs of Sociality and Individuality*. London: Academic

ten Kate H. 1981. A theoretical explication of Hinkle's implication theory. See Bonarius et al. 1981, pp. 167–75

Theodoulou S. 1996. Construing economic and political reality. *J. Econ. Psychol.* 17:400–41

Thomas LF, Harri-Augstein S. 1985. *Self-Organised Learning: Foundations of a Conversational Science of Psychology*. London: Routledge

Tschudi F. 1977. Loaded and honest questions: a personal construct view of symptoms and therapy. See Bannister 1977a, pp. 321–50

Tyler LE. 1981. More stately mansions—psychology extends its boundaries. *Ann. Rev. Psychol.* 32:1–20

Viney LL. 1983. *Images of Illness*. Malabar, FL: Krieger

Viney LL. 1993. *Life Stories: Personal Construct Therapy with the Elderly*. Chichester, UK: Wiley

Viney LL, Caputi P. 2005. The origin and pawn, positive affect, psychosocial maturity and cognitive affect scales: using them in counseling research. *Meas. Eval. Couns. Dev.* 34:115–26

Viney LL, Metcalfe C, Winter DA. 2005. The effectiveness of personal construct psychotherapy: a meta-analysis. See Winter & Viney 2005, pp. 347–64

Walker BM. 1996. A psychology for adventurers: an introduction to personal construct psychology from a social perspective. See Kalekin-Fishman & Walker 1996, pp. 7–26

Walker BM. 1997. Shaking the kaleidoscope: dispersion of dependency and its relationships. See Neimeyer & Neimeyer 1997, pp. 63–97

Walker BM. 2002. Nonvalidation vs. (in)validation: implications for theory and practice. See Raskin & Bridges 2002, pp. 49–61

Walker BM. 2003. Identity and traveling. In *Crossing Borders—Going Places*, ed. JW Scheer, pp. 82–92. Giessen: Psychosozial-Verlag

Walker BM, Ramsey FL, Bell RC. 1988. Dispersed and undispersed dependency. *Int. J. Personal. Constr. Psychol.* 1:63–80

Walker BM, Winter DA. 2005. Psychological disorder and reconstruction. See Winter & Viney 2005, pp. 21–33

Warren B. 1998. *The Philosophical Dimensions of Personal Construct Psychology*. London: Routledge

Warren B. 2003. Pragmatism and religion: Dewey's twin influences? See Fransella 2003a, pp. 387–94

Warren WG. 1992. Personal construct theory and mental health. *Int. J. Personal. Constr. Psychol.* 4:223–37

Watson N, Watts R. 2001. The predictive strength of personal constructs versus conventional constructs: self-image disparity and neuroticism. *J. Personal.* 69:121–45

Watson S, Winter D, Rossotti N. 1997. The Personal Construct Inventory: an alternative construction of personal construct methodology, or just another questionnaire? In *Sharing Understanding and Practice*, ed. P Denicolo, M Pope, pp. 177–87. Farnborough, UK: EPCA Press

Wiggins JS, Pincus AL. 1992. Personality: structure and assessment. *Annu. Rev. Psychol.* 43:473–504

Winter DA. 1985. Neurotic disorders: the curse of certainty. See Button 1985, pp. 103–31

Winter DA. 1989. An alternative construction of agoraphobia. In *Agoraphobia: Current Perspectives on Theory and Treatment*, ed. K Gournay, pp. 93–119. London: Routledge

Winter DA. 1990. Therapeutic alternatives for psychological disorder: personal construct psychology investigations in a health service setting. See Neimeyer & Neimeyer 1990, pp. 89–116

Winter DA. 1992. *Personal Construct Psychology in Clinical Practice: Theory, Research and Applications.* **London: Routledge**

Winter DA. 1996. Psychotherapy's contrast pole. In *Empirical Constructivism in Europe: The Personal Construct Approach*, ed. J Scheer, A Catina, pp. 149–59. Giessen: Psychosozial-Verlag

Winter DA. 2003. Repertory grid technique as a psychotherapy research measure. *Psychother. Res.* 13:25–42

Winter DA. 2006. Destruction as a constructive choice. In *Forensic Psychiatry: Influences of Evil*, ed. T Mason, pp. 153–77. Totowa, NJ: Humana

Winter DA, Viney LL. 2005. *Personal Construct Psychotherapy: Advances in Theory, Practice and Research*. London: Whurr

Winter DA, Watson S. 1999. Personal construct psychotherapy and the cognitive therapies: different in theory but can they be differentiated in practice? *J. Constr. Psychol.* 12:1–22

Zanoli R, Naspetti S. 2002. Consumer motivations in the purchase of organic food. *Br. Food J.* 104:643–53

Comprehensively reviews clinical applications of personal construct psychology.

RELATED RESOURCES

Journals

Journal of Constructivist Psychology
Personal Construct Theory and Practice

PCP information site

http://www.pcp-net.de/info/index.html. This site contains the most comprehensive range of information about PCP resources, events, conferences, email lists, constructivist groups, personalities, and more.

Recommended general introductions to PCP

Bannister D, Fransella F. 1986. *Inquiring Man*. London: Croom Helm. 3rd ed.

Dalton P, Dunnett G. 2005. *A Psychology for Living: Personal Construct Theory for Professionals and Clients*. Philadelphia, PA: Whurr. 2nd ed.

Epting FR, Leitner LM, Raskin JD. 2005. George Kelly and personal construct psychology. In *Personality and Personal Growth*, ed. R Frager, J Fadiman, pp. 291–310. Upper Saddle River, NJ: Pearson. 6th ed.

The Internet Encyclopaedia of Personal Construct Psychology, ed. J Scheer, BM Walker. **http://www.pcp-net.org/encyclopaedia/**

Cross-Cultural Organizational Behavior

Michele J. Gelfand,[1] Miriam Erez,[2] and Zeynep Aycan[3]

[1] Department of Psychology, University of Maryland, College Park, Maryland 20742; email: mgelfand@psyc.umd.edu

[2] Technion, Israel Institute of Technology, Technion City, Haifa, Israel 32000; email: merez@ie.technion.ac.il

[3] Department of Psychology, Koc University, Sariyer, Istanbul, Turkey 34450; email: zaycan@ku.edu.tr

Annu. Rev. Psychol. 2007. 58:479–514

First published online as a Review in Advance on October 17, 2006

The *Annual Review of Psychology* is online at http://psych.annualreviews.org

This article's doi: 10.1146/annurev.psych.58.110405.085559

Key Words

culture, management, organizations, work

Abstract

This article reviews research on cross-cultural organizational behavior (OB). After a brief review of the history of cross-cultural OB, we review research on work motivation, or the factors that energize, direct, and sustain effort across cultures. We next consider the relationship between the individual and the organization, and review research on culture and organizational commitment, psychological contracts, justice, citizenship behavior, and person-environment fit. Thereafter, we consider how individuals manage their interdependence in organizations, and review research on culture and negotiation and disputing, teams, and leadership, followed by research on managing across borders and expatriation. The review shows that developmentally, cross-cultural research in OB is coming of age. Yet we also highlight critical challenges for future research, including moving beyond values to explain cultural differences, attending to levels of analysis issues, incorporating social and organizational context factors into cross-cultural research, taking indigenous perspectives seriously, and moving beyond intracultural comparisons to understand the dynamics of cross-cultural interfaces.

Contents

INTRODUCTION

OB: organizational behavior

Broadly construed, cross-cultural organizational behavior (OB) is the study of cross-cultural similarities and differences in processes and behavior at work and the dynamics of cross-cultural interfaces in multicultural domestic and international contexts. It encompasses how culture is related to micro organizational phenomena (e.g., motives, cognitions, emotions), meso organizational phenomena (e.g., teams, leadership, ne-

gotiation), macro organizational phenomena (e.g., organizational culture, structure), and the interrelationships among these levels. In this review, we focus on cross-cultural micro and meso OB, and provide an update to the MH Bond & Smith (1996) *Annual Review of Psychology* chapter. We briefly discuss the history of cross-cultural OB. Next, starting at the micro level, we review research on work motivation, or the factors that energize, direct, and sustain effort in organizations across cultures. We then consider the nature of the relationship between the individual and the organization, and review research on culture and organizational commitment, psychological contracts, organizational justice, organizational citizenship behavior, and person-environment fit. Thereafter, we consider how individuals manage their interdependence in organizations, and review research on culture and negotiation and disputing, teams, and leadership, followed by research on managing across borders and expatriation. We conclude with some observations on the progress that has been made and with a critical assessment of the field.[1]

A BRIEF HISTORY OF CROSS-CULTURAL ORGANIZATIONAL BEHAVIOR

Cross-cultural OB has a long past but a short research history. Some of the earliest accounts of cultural differences at work can be found in writings by the Greek historian Herodotus, who observed differences in work behavior throughout the Persian Empire circa 400 BC (Herodotus et al. 2003). Trade between people of different cultures was also widespread along the Silk Road, which stretched from Rome and Syria in the West to China in the East and to Egypt and Iran in the Middle East dating from the second century BC (Elisseeff 2000). Although globalization in the twenty-first century has certainly increased the ease and scope of cross-cultural interactions at work exponentially, this is clearly an ancient phenomenon.

It is only in the past two decades, however, that cross-cultural theory and research have started to take on a central role in the

DEFINITION OF CULTURE

A wide range of definitions have been used for the term "culture." Culture has been defined as the human-made part of the environment (Herkovits 1955), including both objective and subjective elements (Triandis 1972); as a set of reinforcements (Skinner 1981); as the collective programming of the mind (Hofstede 1991); as a shared meaning system (Shweder & LeVine 1984); as patterned ways of thinking (Kluckhohn 1954); and as unstated standard operating procedures or ways of doing things (Triandis 1994). Although definitions of culture vary, many emphasize that culture is shared, is adaptive or has been adaptive at some point in the past, and is transmitted across time and generations (Triandis 1994). Although culture operates at multiple levels of analysis, this article is concerned primarily with national culture as it relates to organizational behavior.

field of OB. In the 1960s and 1970s, culture was largely ignored in OB (Barrett & Bass 1976), and existing culture research was generally atheoretical, descriptive, and plagued with methodological problems. Most, if not all, OB theories were developed and tested on Western samples, without much regard for their potential global scope. The fact that OB research developed primarily in the United States, a society that historically has supported a melting pot view of cultural differences, also likely contributed to the lack of attention to culture in OB. Later, in the 1980s, with the advent of culture typologies (Hofstede 1980), attention to national culture increased in OB research and began to have more of a theoretical backbone. Research began to uncover the cultural boundaries of some Western OB models, which in some cases were not as applicable to the Far East. Reciprocally, Japanese models, such as quality control circles, were not successfully adopted in the West (Erez & Earley 1993). Nevertheless, cross-cultural research in OB was still more often the exception than the norm and was largely separate from mainstream OB research. It was, in essence, tolerated and not particularly influential or widespread.

Globalization: economic interdependence among countries that develops through cross-national flows of goods and services, capital, know-how, and people

---

[1]This review covers the period of 1996–2005. Literature searches were done through PsycINFO, ABI/INFORM, JSTOR, the Wilson Index, and Business Source Premier, and through calls on international listservers. Given space limitations, we had to omit details on topics and instead give selected exemplars in each area. For other reviews, see Aguinis & Henle 2003, Earley & Erez 1997, Hofstede 2001, Hofstede & Hofstede 2005, Kirkman et al. 2006, Leung et al. 2005, and Sparrow 2006.

EMIC AND ETIC

Emic and etic were originally discussed in linguistics. Phonemics referred to sounds used in a particular language and phonetics referred to sounds that are found across all languages (Pike 1967). These distinctions were later imported into cross-cultural psychology by Berry (1969), who referred to ideas and behaviors that are culture-specific as emics, and ideas and behaviors that are culture-general or universal as etics.

We are, however, entering a new era when culture research is beginning to be embraced in OB. Dramatic changes in the work context in response to globalization have increased the importance of cross-cultural research in OB, and as described below, we have witnessed a large wave of cross-cultural research across all areas of the field. Culture theory is more dynamic (Hong et al. 2000), more attentive to organizational context factors (Aycan et al. 2000), and more rich in what it offers to OB, as evidenced in new taxonomies of cultural values (House et al. 2004, Schwartz 1994, Smith et al. 1996), beliefs (Bond et al. 2004), norms (Gelfand et al. 2006b), and sophisticated ways of combining emic (or culture-specific) with etic (or universal) perspectives on cultural differences (Morris et al. 1999). Developmentally, cross-cultural research in OB is coming of age, and this review reflects this momentum. But as we discuss below, a number of fundamental issues and challenges for research in cross-cultural OB need attention if the field is to thrive in the coming decade.

CULTURE AND WORK MOTIVATION

In this section, we consider both personal (e.g., motives, goals) and situational (e.g., feedback, rewards, job characteristics) factors that predict work motivation across cultures.

Culture and Personal Motives

There is some evidence that motives such as self-efficacy, need for achievement, and

intrinsic needs for competence are universal (Bandura 2002, Erez & Earley 1993). Yet the specific factors that drive such motives vary across cultures. Earley et al. (1999) showed that personal feedback influenced self-efficacy beliefs in individualistic cultures, whereas group feedback also influenced self-efficacy beliefs in collectivistic cultures. Likewise, while the need for control seems to be universal, personal control is critical in individualistic cultures, and collective control is more critical in collectivistic cultures (Yamaguchi et al. 2005). Although some have argued that achievement motivation is stronger in individualistic than in collectivistic cultures (Sagie et al. 1996), the meaning of it varies across cultures. Collectivists believe that positive outcomes result from collective efforts, and not only from individual efforts (Niles 1998).

Intrinsic motives for autonomy, competence, and relatedness are important for well-being across cultures (Ryan & Deci 2000), yet antecedents to such motivation vary cross-culturally. Iyengar & Lepper (1999) found that while personal choice was critical for intrinsic motivation among Anglo Americans, Asian Americans were more intrinsically motivated when trusted authority figures or peers made choices for them. By contrast, exploration, curiosity, and variety seeking are more associated with intrinsic motivation in individualistic cultures than in cultures where conformity is highly valued (Kim & Drolet 2003). Also, the negative effects of extrinsic motivation are weaker in non-Western cultures (Ryan et al. 1999).[2]

Research has also shown that a promotion motive to achieve desired outcomes

---

[2]The authors acknowledge that the terms "Western" and "Eastern" create a superficial dichotomy, which does not reflect the complexity and heterogeneity within each cluster. The terms are used heuristically and for purpose of communication convenience in this article. Likewise, although many studies present findings from one particular sample in a culture, cultures are complex and heterogeneous, and therefore findings might change with other samples and/or in different situations.

motivates employees with independent selves, whereas the prevention motive to avoid negative consequences motivates individuals with interdependent selves (Heine et al. 2001, Lee et al. 2000). Similarly, Lockwood et al. (2005) showed that role models who conveyed a prevention focus of avoiding failures motivated Asian Canadians, whereas role models who highlighted a strategy for promoting success had a stronger impact on Anglo-Canadians. Experiencing shame in organizational contexts had a negative effect on adaptive behavior and performance among Dutch samples who experienced shame as a threat to the independent self, whereas it had a positive effect on outcomes among Philippinos, who experienced shame as a threat to harmony that needed to be restored (Bagozzi et al. 2003; see also Earley 1997).

Culture also affects performance and learning motivational orientations. In Confucian philosophy, there is an emphasis on the need to perfect oneself, and as a result, in the Chinese culture, learning appears more fundamental than achievement per se (Li 2002). Learning and performance orientation were highly correlated and both were associated with performance among Hong Kong students, whereas they were more distinct among American students (Lee et al. 2003).

Culture and Goals

Several studies suggest that elements of goal setting theory do not necessarily generalize across cultures. Kurman (2001) found that in collectivistic and high-power-distance cultures, choosing achievable moderate goals was more highly motivating than choosing difficult goals. Sue-Chan & Ong (2002) found that power distance moderated the effect of assigned versus participative goal setting on goal commitment and performance, with higher commitment and performance for assigned goals in high- rather than low-power-distance cultures. Self-efficacy mediated the goal-assignment commitment, and performance relationships only in low-power-

distance cultures. Lam et al. (2002a) showed that the relationship between participation and individual performance is the highest for idiocentrics with high self-efficacy, and the relationship between participation and group performance is the highest for allocentrics with high collective efficacy.

Culture and Feedback

Feedback giving and feedback seeking are theorized to vary across cultures (De Luque & Sommer 2000). For example, Morrison et al. (2004) showed that individuals from the United States reported more newcomer feedback seeking than did individuals from Hong Kong, which was related to cultural differences in assertiveness and power distance. Culture also influences the effect of feedback sign on behavior. Positive feedback is universally perceived to be of higher quality than negative feedback, and even more so in collectivistic cultures (e.g., Van de Vliert et al. 2004). Japanese had stronger emotional reactions to negative feedback (Kurman et al. 2003), yet were more responsive to it than are Americans, who tended to engage in compensatory self-enhancement (Brockner & Chen 1996, Heine et al. 2001, Kitayama et al. 1997). Van de Vliert et al. (2004) also showed that the target of the feedback matters: Individual versus group performance induced more positive evaluations from individualists and collectivists, respectively. Little research, however, has been done on feedback in intercultural settings. Matsumoto (2004) found that Japanese managers provide implicit and informal feedback, which caused frustration among Americans.

Culture and Rewards

Cultural values shape the preferences for organizational rewards and their implementation across cultures (Erez & Earley 1993). Good pay and bonuses were the most preferred rewards for students in Chile and China, whereas promotion and interesting work were the most preferred rewards for American students, which may be attributable to cultural and economic conditions (Corney & Richards 2005, King & Bu 2005). Regardless of the strength of money as a motivator, work appears to be valued beyond just monetary rewards in developing as well as developed countries (Adigun 1997).

At a more macro level, cultures differ in their dominant reward systems. Brown & Reich (1997) showed that U.S. firms implemented payment-by-result systems, congruent with individualistic values, whereas Japanese firms endorsed seniority-based pay systems, congruent with respect for seniority. Tosi & Greckhamer (2004) found that CEO pay was related to power distance. The market reform in China has strengthened the preference for differential rewards among Chinese who emphasize vertical collectivism but not among those who emphasize horizontal collectivism (Chen et al. 1997). Group-based profit sharing and saving plans are effective motivators for reducing turnover rates in *maquiladoras*—American-owned plants in Mexico—as they fit with the strong collectivistic Mexican culture (Miller et al. 2001). Culture affects incentives in multinationals, with higher incentives in subsidiaries that are culturally close to the headquarters (Roth & O'Donnell 1996).

Culture and Job and Organizational Characteristics

Several studies have shown that the meaning of job content (e.g., autonomy) is similar across cultures (e.g., Sadler-Smith et al. 2003). Frese et al. (1996) found that job autonomy and task complexity increased initiative behaviors in both East and West Germany. Likewise, Roe et al. (2000) found that job characteristics had similar effects on motivation and commitment in the Netherlands, Bulgaria, and Hungary. Yet, autonomy had a more powerful effect on critical psychological states in the Netherlands, an individualistic culture (see also Deci et al. 2001). Em-

powerment resulted in lower performance for individuals from high-power-distance (i.e., Asians) compared with low-power-distance (i.e., Canada) cultures (Eylon & Au 1999) and was negatively associated with satisfaction in India, a high-power-distance culture, in comparison with the United States, Poland, and Mexico (Robert et al. 2000). However, empowering employees to implement change can be effective when it is congruent with values in the cultural context. For example, in Morocco, a successful implementation of Total Quality Management occurred by associating it with Islamic norms and values, and using authority figures as role models. In Mexico, an emphasis on norms and values regarding the family and the community helped to enhance cooperation (d'Iribarne 2002).

Job demands have universal negative effects on employees' health and well-being, yet their effect on intentions to leave was the lowest in Hungary, reflecting lower alternative job opportunities as compared with Italy, the United States, and the United Kingdom (Glazer & Beehr 2005). In China, similar to the West, high job demands and low control increased anxiety and lowered satisfaction (Xie 1996). However, different factors mitigate stress in different cultures. Self-efficacy served as a buffer of job demands for Americans, but collective efficacy served this function in Hong Kong (Schaubroeck et al. 2000).

Culture and Job Satisfaction

Culture significantly influences job and pay satisfaction (Diener et al. 2003). In general, employees in Western and in capitalistic developed cultures have higher job satisfaction than those in Eastern cultures and in socialist developing cultures (Vecernik 2003). Research has shown that the meaning of job satisfaction is equivalent across countries speaking the same language and sharing similar cultural backgrounds, yet its equivalence decreases with increasing cultural distance (Liu et al. 2004).

Positive self-concepts and internal locus of control are related to job satisfaction across cultures (Piccolo et al. 2005, Spector et al. 2002). As well, social comparisons are universally related to pay satisfaction across cultures (Sweeney & McFarlin 2004). Yet the factors that contribute to satisfaction also vary across cultures. A 42-nation study revealed a positive link between satisfaction and self-referent motivation, and a negative link between satisfaction and other-referent motivation, which were pronounced in countries of high income levels, education, and life expectancy (Van de Vliert & Janssens 2002). Work group and job characteristics differentially affect satisfaction across cultures: A warm and congenial work group produced higher satisfaction among collectivists but lower satisfaction among individualists (Hui & Yee 1999). Although extrinsic job characteristics were positively related to job satisfaction across cultures, intrinsic job characteristics were more strongly associated with job satisfaction in rich countries dominated by individualistic and low-power-distance values (Huang & Van de Vliert 2003, Hui et al. 2004). Job level is related to job satisfaction in individualistic cultures but not in collectivistic cultures (Huang & Van de Vliert 2004). Finally, research has also found that culture moderates the impact of job satisfaction on withdrawal behaviors; a stronger relationship exists in individualistic cultures as compared with collectivistic and low-power-distance and high-power-distance cultures (Posthuma et al. 2005, Thomas & Au 2002, Thomas & Pekerti 2003).

CULTURE AND THE NATURE OF THE RELATIONSHIP BETWEEN THE INDIVIDUAL AND ORGANIZATION

Culture and Organizational Commitment

Research has demonstrated that existing measures of organizational commitment (OC) have construct validity in numerous European countries (e.g., Vandenberghe et al. 2001), yet others have questioned the factor validity of OC measures, particularly in East Asian samples (e.g., Ko et al. 1997). A key question is whether differences in factor validity are due to translation problems or to cultural differences in the OC construct. Lee et al. (2001) argued for the former and showed that when using general items that minimize translation problems, factor structures are similar across cultures. Others, however, have shown the importance of developing emic (culture-specific) items when assessing etic (culture-general) OC constructs (e.g., Wasti 2002).

Research has examined whether the antecedents of OC are similar across cultures. A meta-analysis (Meyer et al. 2002) found that normative commitment (NC) was more strongly associated with perceived organizational support and less strongly associated with demographics (e.g., age and tenure) in studies outside versus inside the U.S. By contrast, job-related factors such as role conflict and role ambiguity were stronger predictors of OC within the United States, particularly for affective commitment (AC). Wasti (2003) similarly found that satisfaction with work and promotions were the strongest predictors of OC among individualists, whereas satisfaction with supervisor was an important predictor of OC among collectivists. Across seven nations, Andolsek & Stebe (2004) also found that material job values (e.g., job quality) were more predictive of OC in individualistic societies, whereas postmaterialistic job values (e.g., helping others) were more predictive of OC in collectivistic societies. Others have shown the importance of examining emic predictors of OC, such as in-group opinions (Wasti 2002), subjective norms (Abrams et al. 1998), and the Islamic work ethic (Yousef 2000).

Consequences of OC vary across cultures. A meta-analysis (Meyer et al. 2002) found that AC is a more powerful predictor of job outcomes in the United States, whereas NC was more important for job outcomes in studies outside of the United States (cf. Wasti 2003).

IC: individualism-collectivism

Justice: a multidimensional construct that encompasses distributive justice, procedural justice, and interactional justice

Distributive justice (DJ): the perceived justice of decision outcomes

Procedural justice (PJ): the perceived fairness of processes used to determine outcomes

Equity: outcomes are distributed based on relative contributions

Equality: outcomes are distributed equally, regardless of relative contributions

Dimensions of OC also interact in distinct ways to predict outcomes across cultures. In China, Cheng & Stockdale (2003) found that NC reduced the relationship between continuance commitment and job satisfaction, and Chen & Francesco (2003) found that NC moderated the impact of AC on organizational citizenship behavior and performance, providing further support for the primacy of NC in non-Western cultures.

Culture and Psychological Contracts

The construct of psychological contracts (PCs), or perceptions of the mutual obligations that exist between employers and employees (Rousseau 1989), is applicable across cultures (e.g., Hui et al. 2004), yet the nature of PCs may vary across cultures (see Rousseau & Schalk 2000). Taking a bottom-up approach, Thomas et al. (2003) theorized that individualistic employees form transactional PCs to enhance the independent self, whereas collectivistic employees form relational PCs to enhance the interdependent self. Others take a more macro, top-down approach, suggesting that human resources practices and institutional factors cause divergence in PCs across cultures. Sels et al. (2004) showed that the nature of human resources practices (e.g., participation) and the nature of formal contracts (e.g., blue collar versus white collar) predicted differences in PCs in Belgium (see also King & Bu 2005). Thomas et al. (2003) theorized that employees with collectivistic values have a higher threshold for the perception of PC violations, yet once violations are perceived, they experience more negative affective reactions. Kickul et al. (2004) found that violations to extrinsic contracts (e.g., pay) had more of a negative impact on attitudes among Hong Kong employees, whereas violations to intrinsic contracts (e.g., job autonomy) had more of a negative impact in the United States.

Culture and Organizational Justice

Research on culture and reward allocation preferences has yielded mixed results. On the one hand, a meta-analysis by Sama & Papamarcos (2000) showed that equity was preferred in individualistic cultures, while equality was preferred in collectivistic cultures (particularly in situations with in-group members). However, another meta-analysis by Fischer & Smith (2003) showed that IC at the national level was unrelated to reward allocation preferences. The discrepancy in these findings is likely due to contextual factors, namely the differential role of the allocator across the two meta-analyses. More specifically, Leung (1997) argued that when the allocator was also a recipient of rewards, individuals in collectivistic cultures would prefer equality with in-groups (consistent with the studies reviewed in Sama & Papamarcos). However, if the allocator is *not* a recipient of rewards (i.e., is dividing resources among others), equity would be preferred across individualistic and collectivistic cultures (consistent with the studies reviewed in Fischer & Smith). Interestingly, Fischer & Smith (2003) also showed that power distance is a more important explanatory dimension in situations where the allocator is not a recipient of rewards: Cultures high on power distance and hierarchy preferred equity, whereas cultures low on power distance and with egalitarian values preferred equality (Chen et al. 1997, 1998b). Research has also shown that equity preferences vary depending on industry even within the same cultural context (e.g., He et al. 2004), further illustrating the importance of the situational context in reward allocation preferences across cultures.

Research has shown that even when individuals value the same justice rule (e.g., equity), people in different cultures may use different criteria in implementing these rules (Morris et al. 1999). For example, what counts in terms of contributions or inputs when making reward allocation decisions varies across cultures (Fischer & Smith 2004, Gomez et al. 2000, Hundley & Kim 1997, Zhou & Martocchio 2001). Hundley & Kim (1997) found that Koreans weighed seniority, education, and family size more than Americans in making judgments about pay fairness. Zhou & Martocchio (2001) found that Chinese were more likely than Americans to weigh the relationship that employees had with others when making nonmonetary decisions, and to weigh work performance less and needs more when making monetary decisions. Gomez et al. (2000) found that collectivists valued maintenance contributions of their teammates more than did individualists, whereas individualists valued task contributions of their teammates more than did collectivists. Other research has similarly shown that people in different cultures may weigh their outcomes differently in forming distributive justice (DJ) perceptions. Mueller et al. (1999) found that met expectations about autonomy were more important for perceived distributive justice in the United States, whereas met expectations about advancement were more important in Korea.

Research has found that procedural justice (PJ) has consequences for fairness and trust across numerous cultures (e.g., Lind et al. 1997, Pearce et al. 1998). PJ's effects have consistently been shown to depend on levels of power distance (PD) both at the individual and culture level. Lam et al. (2002b) found that the influence of PJ (as well as DJ) on satisfaction, performance, and absenteeism was stronger for individuals who endorsed low, rather than high, PD values (see also Farh et al. 1997, Fischer & Smith 2006, Lee et al. 2000). Brockner et al. (2001) found that the effect of voice on organizational commitment and performance was more pronounced in low- as compared with high-PD nations; the effect was mediated by individual-level measures of PD (see also Price et al. 2001). PJ and DJ also interact to affect outcomes differently across cultures (Fields et al. 2000). Brockner et al. (2000) showed that a tendency for high PJ to mitigate low DJ is pronounced in cultures that emphasize collectivism, and that interdependent self-construals mediated country effects. Unlike in the DJ literature, however, there is scant attention to contextual moderators (e.g., industry, situational context) in culture and PJ research.

Finally, there is a dearth of research on culture and justice in intercultural contexts. Shared perceptions of justice are critical for the effectiveness of intercultural alliances, especially when cultural distance between the parties is high (Luo 2005). Yet intercultural settings are precisely where there may be conflict due to differences in perceptions of justice (Ang et al. 2003, CC Chen et al. 2002, Leung et al. 2001). Moreover, surprisingly little research has been done on culture and interactional justice. Although this form of justice may be universally important, the specific practices through which it is implemented are likely to vary across cultures (Leung & Tong 2004).

Culture and Organizational Citizenship Behavior

Conceptions of what constitutes extra role (or citizenship) behavior vary across cultures. Lam et al. (1999) found that a five-factor structure of organizational citizenship behaviors (OCBs)—altruism, conscientiousness, civic virtue, courtesy, and sportsmanship—was replicated in Japan, Australia, and Hong Kong. However, Japanese and Hong Kong employees were more likely to define some categories of OCBs (e.g., courtesy, sportsmanship) as part of "in-role" performance as compared with Australian and U.S. employees. Similarly, Farh et al. (1997) developed an indigenous OCB measure in Taiwan and found that although altruism, conscientiousness, and identification qualified as etic dimensions of OCB, sportsmanship and courtesy were not found to be part of the OCB construct in the Taiwanese sample. There were also emic dimensions, such as interpersonal harmony and protecting company resources, that were not previously identified in the West.

Antecedents of OCBs also vary across cultures. Meyer et al. (2002) found that normative commitment was more strongly associated with OCBs in non-Western contexts, whereas affective commitment is

Interactional justice: the perceived fairness of interpersonal treatment

OCB: organizational citizenship behavior

particularly important for OCBs in the United States. Organizational-based self-esteem has been found to mediate the effect of collectivism on OCBs (Van Dyne et al. 2000). Studies have shown that commitment to one's supervisor is a more powerful predictor of OCBs than are organizational attitudes in the Chinese context (ZX Chen et al. 2002, Cheng et al. 2003). Research has also found that fulfillment of psychological contracts predicts OCBs in non-Western cultures such as China (Hui et al. 2004) and Hong Kong (Kickul et al. 2004).

Culture and Person-Environment Fit

Supporting the importance of person-environment fit across cultures, Turban et al.'s (2001) findings show that individuals are attracted to certain organizational characteristics (e.g., state-owned enterprises) based on their personality characteristics (e.g., risk aversion) in China, and Vandenberghe (1999) found that congruence between individual and organizational values predicted turnover in Belgium. Others have focused on the fit between IC at the individual and organizational levels. Parkes et al. (2001) found that individuals who were collectivistic in their orientation who were employed by Asian organizations were more committed as compared with collectivists who were employed by Australian organizations (see also Robert & Wasti 2002). Taking a more contextual perspective, Erdogan et al. (2004) found that value congruence was related to satisfaction in Turkey, yet only when leader-member exchange (LMX) and perceived organization support were low, suggesting that supportive relationships can offset value incongruity. Nyambergera et al. (2001) found that neither congruence with organizational values nor fit of individual preferences with actual human resource management policies had a strong impact on job involvement among Kenyan employees, suggesting that fit may not be as important in developing economies where unemployment is high and/or there are strong norms that suppress individual preferences.

CULTURE AND NEGOTIATION/DISPUTING

Culture and Negotiation

Culture affects negotiators' frames, or cognitive representations of conflicts. Gelfand et al. (2001) found that Americans perceived conflicts to be more about winning and violations to individual rights, whereas Japanese perceived the same conflicts to be about compromise and violations to duties. Research has also examined whether negotiators' judgment biases, which have consistently been found in the West, are found in non-Western cultures. Negotiators in the United States are particularly susceptible to competitive judgment biases, such as fixed pie biases (Gelfand & Christakopolou 1999) and self-serving biases (Gelfand al. 2002, Wade-Benzoni et al. 2002), and are more likely to make internal attributions of other negotiators' behavior (Morris et al. 2004, Valenzuela et al. 2005). Negotiators' judgments in non-Western cultures, by contrast, are more affected by relational concerns. Japanese base their fairness assessments on obligations to others, whereas Americans base their fairness assessments on their alternative economic options (Buchan et al. 2004). Chinese negotiators are more susceptible to the influence of others (e.g., anchoring effects) than are Americans (Liu et al. 2005).

Culture also affects negotiation processes and outcomes (Brett 2001, Gelfand & Brett 2004). Although the stages that negotiators go through may be etic, there is cultural variation in the types of strategies used across different stages (Adair & Brett 2005). U.S. negotiators are more likely to share information directly and achieve high joint gains through this strategy, whereas Japanese, Russian, and Hong Kong negotiators are more likely to share information indirectly through their patterns of offers and achieve high joint gains through this strategy (Adair et al. 2001). Culture also affects persuasion and concession making in negotiations. Emotional appeals are theorized to be more common in collectivistic cultures, whereas rational appeals are more common in individualistic cultures (Gelfand & Dyer 2000). Hendon et al. (2003) showed that preferred concession patterns varied across nine nations. Samples from the United States preferred to concede at the end of negotiations, whereas samples from Latin America and developed Asia preferred "de-escalating" sequences, with generous concessions at first and gradual reductions of concessions with few concessions at later stages. There are also cultural differences in the perceived appropriateness of bargaining tactics. For example, at the national level, Volkema (2004) found that power distance was negatively related to perceived appropriateness of competitive bargaining tactics and that uncertainty avoidance was negatively related to perceived appropriateness of inappropriate information collection and influencing others' professional networks to gain concessions.

The factors that contribute to satisfaction in negotiation also vary across cultures. Satisfaction is related to maximizing economic gains among U.S. samples and to the use of integrative tactics and equalization of outcomes in East Asian samples (Ma et al. 2002, Tinsley & Pillutla 1998). Relational capital is theorized to be critical for the implementation of agreements in cultures where the relational self is highly accessible (Gelfand et al. 2006a).[3]

Situational and personal factors also moderate cultural effects in negotiation. Cultural tendencies in negotiation tend to be exacerbated in conditions of high accountability (Gelfand & Realo 1999), high need for closure (Morris & Fu 2001), and high ambiguity (Morris et al. 2004). Negotiator roles are more important for negotiation outcomes in hierarchical cultures (e.g., Japan) than in egalitarian cultures (Kamins et al. 1998; see also Cai et al. 2000). By contrast, negotiator personality (e.g., extraversion and agreeableness) has a greater impact in the United States than in China (Liu et al. 2005). Competitive processes have been found among collectivistic samples in certain conditions, including intergroup or outgroup negotiations (Chen & Li 2005, Probst et al. 1999, Triandis et al. 2001), negotiations with little external monitoring (Gelfand & Realo 1999), and in situations in which negotiators have strong egoistic motives (Chen et al. 2003).

There has been a dearth of attention to the dynamics of intercultural negotiations. Brett & Okumura (1998) found that joint gains were lower in U.S.-Japanese intercultural negotiations than in either United States or Japanese intracultural negotiations, in part because of lower judgment accuracy and conflicting styles of information exchange in intercultural negotiations (Adair et al. 2001). Cultural incongruence in negotiator scripts has been theorized to lead to less organized social action (Gelfand & McCusker 2002) and high levels of negative affect (George et al. 1998, Kumar 1999) in intercultural negotiations. Little research, however, has examined situational or personal factors that moderate intercultural negotiation effectiveness (cf. Drake 2001).

Culture and Disputing

Kozan (1997) differentiated three models of conflict resolution used across cultures: a direct confrontational model, a regulative model, and a harmony model (see also Tinsley 1998). Consistent with a direct confrontational model, individuals in individualistic nations prefer to resolve conflicts using their own expertise and training (Smith et al. 1998), prefer forcing conflict resolution styles (Holt & DeVore 2005), and tend to focus

---

[3]Relational self: the extent to which individuals regard themselves as connected to other individuals; the relational self has been empirically differentiated from the independent self and the collective self across five nations (Kashima et al. 1995).

on integrating interests (Tinsley 1998, 2001). Germans endorse a regulative model, in part due to values for explicit contracting (Tinsley 1998, 2001). By contrast, individuals in collectivistic cultures prefer styles of avoidance and withdrawal (Holt & DeVore 2005, Ohbuchi et al. 1999), and this preference has been explained in terms of differences in conservation values (Morris et al. 1998), the interdependent self (Oetzel et al. 2001), and/or expectations that avoidance leads to better outcomes (Friedman et al. 2006).

Research has shown, however, that avoidance does not necessarily mean the same thing across cultures. Contrary to Western theory, avoidance can reflect a concern for others rather than a lack of concern for others (Gabrielidis et al. 1997). Tjosvold & Sun (2002) showed that there are a wide range of motives and strategies for avoidance in East Asian cultures, ranging from passive strategies to highly proactive strategies that often involve working through third parties (see also Tinsley & Brett 2001). Situational context is also critical for predicting avoidance. Avoidance and nonconfrontational strategies are preferred in collectivistic cultures in disputes of high intensity (Leung 1997), with ingroup members (Derlega et al. 2002, Pearson & Stephan 1998), and with superiors (Brew & Cairns 2004, Friedman et al. 2006). In all, avoidance is a multifaceted construct and more nuanced in Asia than is typically understood in the West.

CULTURE AND TEAMS

Culture and Attitudes About Teams

Employee values of individualism are associated with general resistance to teams, whereas employee values of high power distance, being-orientation, and determinism are related to resistance to self-management in teams (Kirkman & Shapiro 1997, 2001a). Similarly, at the team level, Kirkman & Shapiro (2001b) found that collectivism and doing-orientation were related to lower resistance to teams and lower resistance to self-management, respectively, which in turn increased team effectiveness. Situational conditions, however, are important moderators of team attitudes across cultures. Americans had particularly negative attitudes toward teams when they perform well individually but their teams perform poorly, whereas Chinese demonstrated more in-group favoritism in these conditions (YR Chen et al. 1998). Ramamoorthy & Flood (2002) found that individualists felt more obligated to teamwork when they had high pay equity (pay related to individual performance), yet collectivists felt less obligated under these conditions. In comparison with Australians, Taiwanese had more negative attitudes when teams had a highly fluid, changing membership, in part due to differences in the perceived importance of maintaining relationships in groups (Harrison et al. 2000).

Culture and Team Processes

With respect to cognitive team processes, research has found that individuals in collectivistic cultures are more likely than are those in individualistic cultures to see groups as "entities" that have agentic qualities and dispositions (e.g., Chiu et al. 2000, Kashima et al. 2005, Morris et al. 2001). Gibson & Zellmer-Bruhn (2001) found that employees in different national cultures construe teamwork through different metaphors (military, sports, community, family, and associates), which leads to divergent expectations of team roles, scope, membership, and team objectives. Schemas for what constitutes "successful" workgroups also vary across cultures. Mexicans perceived that socioemotional behaviors were important for group success, whereas Anglos perceived that high task orientation and low socioemotional behaviors were important for group success (Sanchez-Burks et al. 2000).

Research has shown that culture affects motivational/affective processes in teams. Collectivism predicts self-efficacy for teamwork (Eby & Dobbins 1997) and moderates the impact of group goals and group efficacy on performance. Erez & Somech (1996) found that collectivistic samples in Israel experienced fewer group performance losses regardless of the type of group goal, whereas individualistic samples performed quite poorly when only given a "do your best goal" for their team. In a field study, Gibson (1999) found that when collectivism in teams was high, group efficacy was more strongly related to group effectiveness. Earley (1999) examined the role of power distance and group efficacy. In high-status groups, group efficacy judgments were more strongly tied to higher-status rather than to lower-status group judgments, whereas in low-power-distance cultures, members contributed equally to collective efficacy judgments.

Different conditions create feelings of attraction and trust toward group members in different cultures. Man & Lam (2003) found that job complexity and autonomy were much more important for group cohesiveness in the United States than in Taiwan. Drach-Zahavy (2004) similarly showed that job enrichment (i.e., high task identity and flexibility) had a negative effect on team support in high-power-distance groups. Yuki et al. (2005) showed that trust is developed through different relational bases across cultures: In Japan, an important basis for trust is having indirect personal ties with other group members, whereas in the United States, an important basis for trust is having a strong identification based on a shared category membership (e.g., being from the same school) (see also Yuki 2003 and Doney et al. 1998 for additional discussions of culture and trust).

Culture also affects behavioral team processes. Eby & Dobbins (1997) found that teams with a high percentage of collectivistic members exhibited higher levels of cooperation, which in turn was related to higher performance. Taking a more contextual perspective, CC Chen et al. (1998a) theorized that different situational conditions

lead to cooperation in individualistic and collectivistic cultures. In individualistic cultures, instrumental factors such as high goal interdependence, enhancement of personal identity, and cognitive-based trust foster cooperation, whereas in collectivistic cultures, socioemotional factors such as goal sharing, enhancement of group identity, and affect-based trust foster cooperation.

Finally, social influence processes in teams also vary across cultures. Collectivism affects rates of conformity in groups at the national level (R. Bond & Smith 1996). Values at the individual level also affect influence processes. Ng & Van Dyne (2001) found that decision quality improved for individuals exposed to a minority perspective, yet this was particularly the case for targets that were high on horizontal individualism and low on horizontal collectivism. Influence targets with high vertical collectivism also demonstrated higher-quality decisions, but only when the influence agent held a high-status position in the group. At the team level, Goncalo & Staw (2006) found that individualistic groups were more creative than collectivistic groups, especially when given explicit instructions to be creative.

Multicultural Teams

Several authors have argued that multicultural teams (MCTs) can provide strategic advantages for organizations (see Earley & Gibson 2002, Shapiro et al. 2005). By far, however, most theory and research cites the negative processes that occur in MCTs. Shapiro et al. (2002) argued that characteristics of transnational teams (cultural differences, electronic communication, and lack of monitoring) reduce the salience of team identity, which leads to effort-withholding behaviors. MCTs may have high levels of ethnocentrism (Cramton & Hinds 2005), in-group biases (Salk & Brannon 2000), and high levels of task and/or emotional conflict (Elron 1997, Von Glinow et al. 2004).

MCT: multicultural team

However, some factors help MCTs to be more effective. Culturally heterogeneous teams performed as or more effectively as homogeneous teams when leaders help to prevent communication breakdowns (Ayoko et al. 2002) and help to broker hidden knowledge between culturally diverse members (Baba et al. 2004). Global virtual teams are more effective when they impose formal temporal coordinating mechanisms (Montoya-Weiss et al. 2001), develop temporal rhythms around periods of high interdependence (Maznevski & Chudoba 2000), develop norms for meaningful participation (Janssens & Brett 1997), develop a strong team identity (Van Der Zee et al. 2004), and have an integration and learning perspective (Ely & Thomas 2001).

Attention also needs to be given to when cultural identities become salient in MCTs. Randel (2003) showed that cultural identities were particularly salient when either most or very few of their fellow members had the same country of origin. Moreover, although culturally diverse teams generally have lower performance than homogeneous teams (Thomas 1999), they tend to perform as well as homogeneous teams over time (Harrison et al. 2002, Watson et al. 1998). Highly heterogeneous teams also outperform moderately heterogeneous teams because they avert subgroup fractionalization and faultlines (Earley & Mosakowski 2000).

CULTURE AND LEADERSHIP

Culture as a Main Effect on Leaders and Followers

One of the most influential studies investigating cultural variations in perceptions of what traits are effective was the Global Leadership and Organizational Behavior Effectiveness Project (House et al. 2004). In this project, the relationships between societal culture, organizational culture, and leadership prototypes were investigated in 62 cultural societies involving approximately 17,000 middle managers. Findings revealed that two leadership attributes were universally endorsed: charismatic leadership and team-oriented leadership. Both organizational and societal values, rather than practices, were significantly related to leadership prototypes. For example, power distance was positively associated with self-protective leadership and negatively associated with charismatic and participative leadership. Significant variations in leadership prototypes or behavioral manifestations of the prototypes were found across and within cultural clusters (Brodbeck et. al. 2000) as well as across hierarchical positions (Den Hartog et al. 1999). For example, for top managers, effective leader attributes included being innovative, visionary, and courageous, whereas for lower-level managers effective leader attributes included attention to subordinates, team building, and participation.

Ensari & Murphy (2003) found that in individualistic cultures, perception of charisma is based on recognition-based perceptions (i.e., leadership effectiveness is a perception that is based on how well a person fits the characteristics of a "good" or "effective" leader), whereas in collectivistic cultures, it is based on inference-based perceptions (i.e., leadership effectiveness is an inference based on group/organizational performance outcomes). On the other hand, Valikangas & Okumura (1997) showed that Japanese employees follow a "logic of appropriateness" model, whereas U.S. employees follow a "logic of consequence" model. Other studies on followers' preference of leadership have found that across-country variance accounts for more variance in leadership preferences than within-country variance (e.g., across demographics and occupational grouping) (Zander & Romani 2004).

Beyond culture's influence on leadership prototypes, there are important cross-cultural differences in leadership behaviors and practices. In a study of how middle managers in 47 countries handle work events, Smith et al. (2002) found that cultural values (e.g., high collectivism, power distance, conservatism, and loyal involvement) were related to reliance on vertical sources of guidance (i.e., formal rules and superiors), rather than reliance on peers or tacit sources of guidance. Geletkanycz (1997) compared executives' strategic orientations in 20 countries and showed that individualism, low uncertainty avoidance, low power distance, and short-term orientation were associated with executives' adherence to existing strategy. Similarly, in a study on leaders' goal priorities, Hofstede et al. (2002) found that individualism and long-term orientation correlated positively with importance of profits in upcoming years, and power distance correlated negatively with staying within the law.

Research has shown that culture affects the use of power and influence tactics. Rahim & Magner (1996) found that there is greater emphasis on coercive power in individualistic cultures (e.g., the United States), whereas there is greater emphasis on expert power in collectivistic cultures (e.g., Bangladesh and South Korea; but see Ralston et al. 2001). Rao et al. (1997) showed that Japanese managers were similar to U.S. managers in their use of assertiveness, sanctions, and appeals to third parties, yet Japanese managers also used some culture-specific influence strategies (i.e., appeals to firm's authority, personal development). In an innovative study of 12 nations, Fu et al. (2004) found that the perceived effectiveness of influence strategies is influenced by both individual-level variables (e.g., beliefs) and macro-level variables (e.g., national culture values). For example, individuals who believed in fate control were more likely to use assertive and relationship-based influence strategies, particularly in societies that were high on future orientation, in-group collectivism, and uncertainty avoidance.

Bass (1997) argued that transformational and transactional leadership are universal dimensions, with the former being more effective than the latter (see also Dorfman et al. 1997 and Shenkar et al. 1998). Yet there is evidence for the culture-specific enactment of these dimensions and/or additional lead-ership dimensions in other cultures. For example, Mehra & Krishnan (2005) found that Indian *svadharma* orientation (following one's own dharma, or duty) is an important component of transformational leaders in India. Charismatic leadership is predicted by collectivism and organic organizational structures (Pillai & Meindl 1998), yet the manifestations of charisma vary across cultures. Through a discourse analysis of speeches of global leaders, Den Hartog & Verburg (1997) found that a strong voice with ups and downs was associated with the perception of enthusiasm in Latin American cultures, whereas a monotonous tone was associated with the perception of respect and self-control in Asian cultures. Similarly, although the structure of task- and relationship-oriented leadership behaviors is replicable in China, an additional set of role-related behaviors (i.e., political role) emerged as critical in this context (Shenkar et al. 1998).

Culture as a Moderator of Leadership

Research has shown that culture moderates the relationship between leadership and employees' outcomes. Walumbwa & Lawler (2003) found that collectivism strengthens the effect of transformational leadership on employees' job satisfaction, organizational attitudes, and turnover intentions (Jung & Avolio 1999, Spreitzer et al. 2005; see Pillai et al. 1999). Similarly, Shin & Zhou (2003) found that transformational leadership enhanced creativity in followers with high, rather than low, conservatism values in Korea. Newman & Nollen (1996) found that participative leadership practices improved profitability of work units in countries with relatively low power distance but did not affect profitability in high-power-distance ones. Dorfman & Howell (1997) showed that three leadership behaviors (leader supportiveness, contingent reward, and charismatic) had a positive impact on employee outcomes across five countries, but three leader behaviors

Paternalistic leadership: hierarchical relationship in which a leader guides professional and personal lives of subordinates in a manner resembling a parent, and in exchange expects loyalty and deference

(participation, directive leadership, and contingent punishment) had differential impact. For example, contingent punishment only had a positive effect in the United States, and directive leadership only had a positive effect in Taiwan and Mexico. Elenkov & Manev (2005) showed that level of innovation in Russian culture is facilitated by charisma, demonstration of confidence, and idealized influence as well as active and passive management by exception, whereas in Sweden it is facilitated by inspirational motivation and intellectual stimulation. Finally, Agarwal et al. (1999) found that initiating structure decreased role stress and role ambiguity in the United States but not in India, whereas consideration decreased these negative experiences and enhanced organizational commitment in both cultures.

Emic Dimensions of Leadership and Leadership in a Multicultural Context

During the period examined in this review, scales for paternalistic leadership were developed and validated by two independent groups of researchers: Aycan and colleagues (Aycan et al. 2000, Aycan 2006) and Farh & Cheng (2000), both of whom showed that paternalistic leadership has a positive impact on employee attitudes in collectivistic and high-power-distance cultures (see also Pellegrini & Scandura 2006, Sinha 1997, Westwood 1997). Law et al. (2000) showed that supervisor-subordinate *guanxi*[4] is a concept distinct from LMX and commitment to the supervisor and has explanatory power for supervisory decisions on promotion and reward allocation after controlling for performance (see also Chen et al. 2004).

Research has increasingly compared leadership styles of expatriate and local managers

---

[4]*Guanxi* can be defined as the social connections between people that are based implicitly on mutual interest and benefits. When *guanxi* is established, people can ask a favor from each other with the expectation that the debt incurred will be repaid sometime in the future (Yang 1994, pp. 1–2).

(e.g., Howell et al. 2003, Suutari 1996) and has investigated if and how expatriates change their leadership style to fit to the local context (e.g., Hui & Graen 1997, Smith et al. 1997). Setting cooperative goals and using cooperative conflict management strategies (Chen et al. 2006) and having a leader-follower match in ethnicity (Chong & Thomas 1997) fosters positive leadership outcomes in multicultural work settings.

EXPATRIATE MANAGEMENT

Expatriate Adjustment

Several recent meta-analyses (Bhaskar-Shrinivas et al. 2005, Hechanova et al. 2003) support a tripartite conceptualization of expatriate adjustment: general or cultural adjustment, work adjustment, and interaction adjustment (Black et al. 1991). Factors that predict all facets of adjustment include personal factors, such as learning orientation and self-efficacy (e.g., Palthe 2004), and job and organizational factors, such as support from coworkers, available resources (Bhaskar-Shrinivas et al. 2005, Gilley et al. 1999), and supervisory support, especially when expatriates had prior international experience (Gilley et al. 1999). Among nonwork factors, spousal adjustment is a predictor of all facets of adjustment (e.g., Caligiuri et al. 1998, Takeuchi et al. 2002b). As well, the amount of time spent in the host country affects adjustment. Generally, the U-curve hypothesis received support, but a sideways S (i.e., initial U-curve of adjustment followed by a reverse U-curve) appeared to be a better-fitting model to explain the process of adjustment (Bhaskar-Shrinivas et al. 2005).

In addition, there are unique predictors of each facet of adjustment. Work adjustment was found to be enhanced by low role ambiguity, role conflict, and role novelty (e.g., Gilley et al. 1999, Takeuchi et al. 2002a); high role clarity and discretion (Bhaskar-Shrinivas et al. 2005, Gilley et al. 1999, Palthe 2004); number of months on the assignment and amount of interaction with host nationals (Caligiuri 2000, Hechanova et al. 2003); and openness to new experiences (Huang et al. 2005). Shaffer et al. (1999) reported some interesting moderators; they demonstrated that role discretion had a stronger influence on work adjustment for expatriates at higher versus lower managerial levels. Native-language competence was more useful for nonnative speakers of English going to English-speaking Anglo-Saxon countries than for English speaking expatriates going to non–English speaking countries (Bhaskar-Shrinivas et al. 2005).

Interaction adjustment and general/cultural adjustment were found to be positively correlated with extraversion, agreeableness, openness to new experiences (Huang et al. 2005), and native language competence (Bhaskar-Shrinivas et al. 2005). Psychological barriers (e.g., perceived inability to adjust) and unwillingness to communicate with host nationals hampered both types of adjustment (e.g., Bhaskar-Shrinivas et al. 2005, Russell et al. 2002; see also Aycan 1997). Women expatriates were reported to have better interaction adjustment than men (cf. Hechanova et al. 2003), despite having experienced disadvantages in the selection for overseas assignments (see, e.g., Paik & Vance 2002). Although perceived organizational support was positively associated with general adjustment, cross-cultural training had a low but negative relationship with general adjustment, presumably due to poor quality of cross-cultural trainings (Hechanova et al. 2003). Prior experience with a similar culture moderated the relationship between tenure (i.e., length of time in the current assignment) and general adjustment, whereas culture-general prior experience moderated the relationship between tenure and work adjustment (Palthe 2004, Takeuchi et al. 2005a).

Grounded in the acculturation literature, Aycan's (1997) process theory of expatriate adjustment included another critical dimension of expatriate adjustment: psychological adjustment (i.e., maintaining good mental health

and psychological well-being). Using a social network perspective, Wang & Kanungo (2004) found that expatriates' psychological well-being was associated with their network size, network cultural diversity, and contact frequency. Based on their meta-analysis, Hechanova et al. (2003) concluded that adjustment reduced the strain experienced by expatriates (see also Takeuchi et al. 2005b). In the stress-coping approach to expatriate management, a number of studies have demonstrated the usefulness of a problem-focused as compared with a symptom-focused coping, especially for those who hold lower power positions in the local unit or who work in culturally distant countries (Selmer 2002, Stahl & Caligiuri 2005).

Expatriate Attitudes and Performance

Expatriate job satisfaction is enhanced with increasing task significance, job autonomy, job authority, job similarity, and teamwork (Jackson et al. 2000). Organizational commitment was positively associated with perceived value that organizations attach to international assignments (Gregersen & Black 1996) and low role ambiguity (Kraimer & Wayne 2004). Perceived organizational support to career development enhanced commitment to the parent company, whereas support in financial matters enhanced commitment to the local unit (Kraimer & Wayne 2004). Intention to withdraw from the assignment was negatively associated with job satisfaction, organizational commitment (Shaffer & Harrison 1998), participation in decision making, extraversion, agreeableness, and emotional stability (Caligiuri 2000); perceived organizational support to work-family balance; and low work-family conflict (Shaffer et al. 2001, Shaffer & Harrison 1998). Finally, expatriate performance is positively related to the density and quality of ties with host country nationals (Liu & Shaffer 2005), conscientiousness (Caligiuri 2000), self-monitoring (Caligiuri & Day

2000), and LMX (Kraimer at al. 2001), and negatively related to cultural distance (Kraimer & Wayne 2004).

OVERALL CONCLUSIONS AND RESEARCH DIRECTIONS

As this review illustrates, cross-cultural research in OB is thriving. Once an area that was ignored or largely tolerated, cultural perspectives have infiltrated virtually all of the micro and meso areas of OB. Cross-cultural research has helped to broaden the theories, constructs, and research questions in OB and thus has been critical in making OB more global and less ethnocentric in its focus. It has also been critical to illuminate limiting assumptions and in identifying boundary conditions for previously assumed universal phenomena. And importantly, cross-cultural research in OB provides knowledge that can help individuals navigate in an increasingly global context. In some ways, cross-cultural research is coming of age. However, despite this progress, there remain some fundamental issues and challenges for research in cross-cultural OB if it is to truly thrive in the coming decade.

Moving Beyond Values to Unpack Cultural Differences and Levels of Analysis Issues

Our review illustrates that research is increasingly moving beyond merely documenting descriptive differences across cultures to understanding why cultural differences exist. Yet efforts to unpackage cultural differences in OB are far too narrow, focusing almost exclusively on cultural values, and in particular on IC values, to explain all differences across cultures (Bond 1997), despite the fact that conceptual and empirical confusion on IC abounds in the literature (Brewer & Chen 2006, Oyserman et al. 2002). Future research sorely needs to move beyond the IC obsession to explore other constructs that ex-

plain cultural differences. Cultural differences are also a function of the strength of social norms (Gelfand et al. 2006b), the nature of roles (McAuley et al. 2002, Peterson & Smith 2000), beliefs about the social and physical world (Leung et al. 2002), and/or implicit theories that are domain-specific (Chiu et al. 2000). Sources of cultural differences might be outside of conscious awareness, which suggests that efforts to unpack differences need to also use nonobtrusive measures as well.

Level of analysis confusion also continues to abound in the cross-cultural OB literature. The individual-level bias is still strongly entrenched at both the level of theory and measurement, and research continues to blindly apply culture-level theory to the individual level and vice versa. Future research needs to be explicit in defining the level of analysis being examined in cross-cultural OB studies. Much more precision is needed regarding when and why relationships are expected to be similar across levels. Likewise, unpacking cultural differences at the dyad, team, and work unit levels of analyses with appropriate constructs at each level is critical for future research. For example, compositional models are needed to understand how cultural knowledge and attitudes at the individual level help to explain cultural differences in team-level and unit-level phenomenon. Cultural differences in dispersion are also sorely needed in theories and research in organizational behavior at multiple levels (Gelfand et al. 2006b).

Modeling the Multilevel Context

This review shows that cross-cultural research in OB is increasingly taking contextual factors into account when examining cross-cultural differences. Whether it is motivation, team attitudes, negotiation, justice, or leadership, this review clearly shows that situational factors exert powerful effects within cultures that can exacerbate, reduce, and/or radically change the nature of baseline cultural tendencies. Yet despite this evidence, research in cross-cultural OB still focuses largely on cultural main effects and ignores situational factors as main effects or moderators. Future research in cross-cultural OB needs to examine context from a multilevel perspective. At the culture level, contextual factors include political, economic, and legal factors, educational systems, climate, resources, level of technological advancement, and demographic composition. At the organizational level, contextual factors include industry, size, ownership, life stage, strategy, technology, and workforce characteristics. At the team level, contextual factors include team structure, team member composition, and task characteristics; and at the individual level, contextual factors include personality and demographics, among others. The global context is also yet another contextual level within which organizations and individuals are embedded. The interplay between culture and context is an exciting and critical frontier in cross-cultural OB. For example, cross-level research that examines how cultural values at the national level interact with organizational context factors to predict unit-level processes or outcomes, or how cultural values at the national level interact with individual differences and situational contexts to predict attitudes and behaviors, is a needed wave of the future.

Understanding the Cross-Cultural Interface

Our review clearly illustrates that much of the research in cross-cultural OB is focused on intracultural comparisons—comparing attitudes and behaviors across cultural groups. Far less attention has been paid to the dynamics of culture in intercultural encounters, or what we would refer to as the "cross-cultural interface." Whether it is differences in motives, justice, negotiation, or leadership, the cross-cultural literature rarely focuses on whether and how cultural differences actually affect intercultural encounters. Theory

far outstrips the data even on topics that focus primarily on cultural dynamics, such as in multicultural teams. The next wave of cross-cultural OB research needs to address critical questions regarding cross-cultural interfaces. For example, what are the conditions that help to create third cultures or hybrid cultures in intercultural encounters? Likewise, research is sorely needed on when cultural identities are made salient at the cultural interface and how people negotiate and manage their cultural differences in ways that increase positive outcomes for individuals and organizations. Shifting our attention from intracultural comparisons to the dynamics of cross-cultural interfaces may require a fundamental theoretical and methodological shift in cross-cultural OB (cf. Chao & Moon 2005).

Organizational behavior in an interconnected world also requires new theories in search of understanding not only the interface between national cultures, but also the interface between the new global work context and all nested levels—national, organizational, and individual (Erez & Gati 2004, Shokef & Erez 2006). At the organizational level, research should identify the cultural values of the global work environment, the commonalities across subsidiaries of multinational organizations as they are becoming interconnected, and the balance between the global corporate culture and the national cultures comprising its subsidiaries (Selmer & de Leon 2002). At the individual level, new theories are needed for understanding the processes by which individuals adapt to the global work environment. Cultural intelligence has been identified as an important individual characteristic that facilitates cultural adaptation and performance (Earley & Ang 2003). Further research is needed for understanding the factors that facilitate the emergence of a global identity, how individuals balance their global and local identities, and how the activation of these identities affects behavior in organizations and managing cultural interfaces (Erez & Gati 2004).

Taking Indigenous Research Seriously to Understand Recessive Characteristics

Our review illustrates a number of studies capturing non-Western indigenous concepts of organizational behavior, such as paternalistic leadership and guanxi. In addition, we cite numerous culture-specific manifestations of Western constructs (e.g., transformational leadership) and examples of phenomena in which additional culture-specific dimensions were discovered and certain Western dimensions were found to be less relevant (e.g., OCBs). We witnessed that some organizational behaviors serve different functions in different cultural contexts (e.g., avoidance in conflicts in Asia). Research reviewed in this article also captured numerous variform universals (i.e., general principles hold across cultures but the form or enactment of these principles vary) (e.g., Mehra & Krishnan 2005, Leung & Tong 2004, Wasti 2002) and variform functional universals (i.e., the relationship between variables is always found but the magnitude or direction may change depending on the cultural context) (e.g., Lam et al. 2000a, Eylon & Au 1999, Newman & Nollen 1996).

Indigenous perspectives are critical for organizational behavior and need to be prioritized in future research. They not only contribute to the development of more universal knowledge and more sustainable and appropriate strategies for fostering human resource development and productivity in other cultures (Marsden 1991), but they also help us to understand our own culture (Tinsley 2004). As stated by Pruitt (2004, p. xii), "characteristics that are dominant in one culture tend to be recessive in another, and vice-versa. By studying other societies where these features are dominant, they can develop concepts and theories that will eventually be useful for understanding their own." Future cross-cultural research should invest more in emic or indigenous perspectives to unearth recessive characteristics in other cultures and to build a more comprehensive global science of OB.

CONCLUDING REMARKS

In a world that offers global opportunities as well as global threats, understanding and managing cultural differences have become necessities. In recognition of this need, the production of scientific knowledge in the past decade has increased almost exponentially. We reviewed more than one thousand publications for this article, and all signs indicate that this is only the beginning of a large wave of research on cross-cultural OB. In the next phase of scholarship in this field, the challenge is to develop theories and conduct research that can help us capture the level of sophistication, complexity, and dynamism occurring in cross-cultural phenomena in organizational contexts.

SUMMARY POINTS

1. Cross-cultural research in OB has greatly expanded in the past decade and has broadened and deepened existing theories, has illuminated limiting assumptions and boundary conditions, and has identified new emic constructs in OB.

2. Cultural differences in OB can take various forms. For example, general principles might hold across cultures, but the enactment of these principles can vary (e.g., equity principles). The magnitude or direction of relationships can also vary across cultures (e.g., participative leadership and performance). Additional and/or different dimensions might be needed to understand OB phenomena in other cultures (e.g., guanxi networks, interpersonal harmony components of OCBs).

3. Cross-cultural research in OB still largely focuses on main effects, yet there is increasing evidence that situational factors at multiple levels can exacerbate, reduce, and/or radically change the nature of cultural baseline tendencies.

4. Efforts to explain cultural differences are still too narrow and focus almost exclusively on individualism-collectivism to explain variance in organizational behavior across cultures.

FUTURE ISSUES

New research paradigms are needed in cross-cultural OB to make fundamental shifts from:

1. The study of intracultural comparisons to the study of the dynamics of cultural interfaces in multicultural teams, in negotiations, and in global companies and mergers and acquisitions.

2. The study of one cultural value (individualism-collectivism) to the study of multiple values simultaneously and the examination of neglected sources of cultural differences (e.g., roles, norms, implicit theories, and beliefs).

3. A focus on cultural main effects in cross-cultural organizational behavior to the examination of interactions between cultural variables and contextual factors at multiple levels of analysis.

4. A dearth of attention to levels-of-analysis issues to the development of multilevel theories and research where the level of theory and measurement is adequately developed.

5. A primary emphasis on differences in cultural values and management practices to an additional focus on similarities in values and management practices in the global work context.

ACKNOWLEDGMENTS

This review is dedicated to Harry C. Triandis in honor of his eightieth birthday. The article was supported by National Science Foundation Grant #991076 to the first author. We express our gratitude to Dana Avital (Van Raalte), Selin Derya, Soner Dumani, and Lynn Imai for their help with literature searches and insights.

LITERATURE CITED

Abrams D, Ando K, Hinkle S. 1998. Psychological attachment to the group: cross-cultural differences in organizational identification and subjective norms as predictors of workers' turnover intentions. *Personal. Soc. Psychol. Bull.* 24:1027–39

Adair WL, Brett JM. 2005. The negotiation dance: time, culture, and behavioral sequences in negotiation. *Organ. Sci.* 16:33–51

Adair WL, Okumura T, Brett JM. 2001. Negotiation behavior when cultures collide: the United States and Japan. *J. Appl. Psychol.* 86:317–85

Adigun I. 1997. Orientations to work: a cross-cultural approach. *J. Cross-Cult. Psychol.* 28:352–55

Agarwal S, De Carlo TE, Vyas SB. 1999. Leadership behavior and organizational commitment: a comparative study of American and Indian salespersons. *J. Int. Bus. Stud.* 30:727–43

Aguinis H, Henle CA. 2003. The search for universals in cross-cultural organizational behavior. In *Organizational Behavior: The State of the Science*, ed. J Greenberg, pp. 373–411. Mahwah, NJ: Erlbaum. 2nd ed.

Andolsek DM, Stebe J. 2004. Multinational perspectives on work values and commitment. *Int. J. Cross-Cult. Manage.* 4:181–209

Ang S, Van Dyne L, Begley TM. 2003. The employment relationships of foreign workers versus local employees: a field study of organizational justice, job satisfaction, performance, and OCB. *J. Organ. Behav.* 24:561–83

Aycan Z. 1997. Expatriate adjustment as a multifaceted phenomenon: individual and organizational level predictors. *Int. J. Hum. Resour. Manage.* 8:434–56

Aycan Z. 2006. Paternalism: towards conceptual refinement and operationalization. In *Scientific Advances in Indigenous Psychologies: Empirical, Philosophical, and Cultural Contributions*, ed. KS Yang, KK Hwang, U Kim, pp. 445–66. London: Cambridge Univ. Press

Aycan Z, Kanungo RN, Mendonca M, Yu K, Deller J, et al. 2000. Impact of culture on human resource management practices: a ten country comparison. *Appl. Psychol. Int. Rev.* 49:192–220

Ayoko BO, Hartel CE, Callan VJ. 2002. Resolving the puzzle of productive and destructive conflict in culturally heterogeneous workgroups: a communication accommodation theory approach. *Int. J. Confl. Manage.* 13:165–95

Baba ML, Gluesing J, Ratner H, Wagner KH. 2004. The contexts of knowing: natural history of a globally distributed team. *J. Organ. Behav.* 25:547–87

Bagozzi RP, Verbeke W, Gavino JC. 2003. Culture moderates the self-regulation of shame and its effects on performance: the case of salespersons in the Netherlands and the Philippines. *J. Appl. Psychol.* 88:219–33

Bandura A. 2002. Social cognitive theory in cultural context. *Appl. Psychol.* 51:269–90

Barrett GV, Bass BM. 1976. Cross-cultural issues in industrial and organizational psychology. In *Handbook of Industrial and Organizational Psychology*, ed. MD Dunnette, pp. 1639–86. Chicago: Rand McNally

Bass BM. 1997. Does the transactional-transformational leadership paradigm transcend organizational and national boundaries? *Am. Psychol.* 52:130–39

Berry JW. 1969. On cross-cultural comparability. *Int. J. Psychol.* 4:119–28

Bhaskar-Shrinivas P, Harrison DA, Luk DM, Shaffer MA. 2005. Input-based and time-based models of international adjustment: meta-analytic evidence and theoretical extensions. *Acad. Manage. J.* 48:257–81

Black JS, Mendenhall M, Oddou G. 1991. Toward a comprehensive model of international adjustment: an integration of multiple theoretical perspectives. *Acad. Manage. Rev.* 16:291–317

Bond MH. 1997. Adding value to the cross-cultural study of organizational behavior. See Earley & Erez 1997, pp. 256–75

Bond MH, Leung K, Tong K, de Carrasquel SR, Murakami F, et al. 2004. Culture-level dimensions of social axioms and their correlates across 41 countries. *J. Cross-Cult. Psychol.* 35:548–70

Bond MH, Smith PB. 1996. Cross-cultural social and organizational psychology. *Annu. Rev. Psychol.* 47:205–35

Bond R, Smith PB. 1996. Culture and conformity: a meta-analysis of studies using Asch's (1952b, 1956) line judgment task. *Psych. Bull.* 1:111–37

Brett JM. 2001. *Negotiating Globally: How to Negotiate Deals, Resolve Disputes, and Make Decisions Across Cultural Boundaries*. San Francisco: Jossey-Bass

Brett JM, Okumura T. 1998. Inter- and intracultural negotiation: U.S. and Japanese negotiators. *Acad. Manage. J.* 41:495–510

Brew FP, Cairns DR. 2004. Do culture or situational constraints determine choice of direct or indirect styles in intercultural workplace conflicts? *Int. J. Intercult. Relat.* 28:331–52

Brewer MB, Chen Y-R. 2006. Where (who) are collectives in collectivism? Toward conceptual clarification of individualism and collectivism. *Psychol. Rev.* In press

Brockner J, Ackerman G, Greenberg J, Gelfand MJ, Francesco AM, et al. 2001. Culture and procedural justice: the influence of power distance on reactions to voice. *J. Exp. Soc. Psychol.* 37:300–15

Brockner J, Chen Y. 1996. The moderating roles of self-esteem and self-construal in reaction to a threat to the self: evidence from the People's Republic of China and the United States. *J. Personal. Soc. Psychol.* 71:603–4

Brockner J, Chen Y, Mannix E, Leung K, Skarlicki DP. 2000. Culture and procedural fairness: when the effects of what you do depend on how you do it. *Adm. Sci. Q.* 45:138–59

Brodbeck FC, Frese M, Akerblom S, Audia G, Bakacsi G, et al. 2000. Cultural variation of leadership prototypes across 22 European countries. *J. Occup. Organ. Psychol.* 73:1–29

Brown C, Reich M. 1997. Micro-macro linkages in high-performance employment systems. *Organ. Stud.* 18:765–81

Buchan NR, Croson RTA, Johnson EJ. 2004. When do fair beliefs influence bargaining behavior? Experimental bargaining in Japan and the United States. *J. Consum. Res.* 31:181–90

Cai DA, Wilson SR, Drake LE. 2000. Culture in context of intercultural negotiation: individualism-collectivism and paths to integrative agreements. *Hum. Commun. Res.* 26:591–617

Caligiuri PM. 2000. The big five personality characteristics as predictors of expatriate's desire to terminate the assignment and supervisor-rated performance. *Pers. Psychol.* 53:67–88

Caligiuri PM, Day DV. 2000. Effects of self-monitoring on technical, contextual, and assignment-specific performance: a study of cross-national work performance ratings. *Group Org. Manage.* 25:154–74

Caligiuri PM, Hyland MM, Joshi A, Bross AS. 1998. Testing a theoretical model for examining the relationship between family adjustment and expatriates' work adjustment. *J. Appl. Psychol.* 83:598–614

Chao GT, Moon H. 2005. The cultural mosaic: a metatheory for understanding the complexity of culture. *J. Appl. Psychol.* 90:1128–40

Chen CC, Chen X, Meindl JR. 1998a. How can cooperation be fostered? The cultural effects of individualism-collectivism. *Acad. Manage. Rev.* 23:285–304

Chen CC, Chen YR, Xin K. 2004. Guanxi practices and trust in management: a procedural justice perspective. *Organ. Sci.* 15:200–9

Chen CC, Choi J, Chi S. 2002. Making justice sense of local-expatriate compensation disparity: mitigation by local referents, ideological explanations, and interpersonal sensitivity in China-foreign joint ventures. *Acad. Manage. J.* 45:807–17

Chen CC, Meindl JR, Hui H. 1998b. Deciding on equity or parity: a test of situational, cultural, and individual factors. *J. Organ. Behav.* 19:115–29

Chen CC, Meindl JR, Hunt RG. 1997. Testing the effects of vertical and horizontal collectivism: a study of reward allocation preferences in China. *J. Cross-Cult. Psychol.* 28:44–70

Chen X, Li S. 2005. Cross-national differences in cooperative decision-making in mixed-motive business contexts: the mediating effect of vertical and horizontal individualism. *J. Int. Bus. Stud.* 36:622–36

Chen Y, Su F, Tjosvold D. 2006. Working with foreign managers: conflict management for effective leader relationships in China. *Int. J. Conflict Manage.* In press

Chen YR, Brockner J, Katz T. 1998. Toward an explanation of cultural differences in in-group favoritism: the role of individual versus collective primacy. *J. Personal. Soc. Psychol.* 75:1490–502

Chen YR, Mannix EA, Okumura T. 2003. The importance of who you meet: effects of self- versus other-concerns among negotiators in the United States, the People's Republic of China, and Japan. *J. Exp. Soc. Psychol.* 39:1–15

Chen ZX, Francesco AM. 2003. The relationship between the three components of commitment and employee performance in China. *J. Vocat. Behav.* 62:490–510

Chen ZX, Tsui AS, Farh J. 2002. Loyalty to supervisor vs. organizational commitment: relationships to employee performance in China. *J. Occup. Organ. Psychol.* 75:339–56

Cheng B, Jiang D, Riley JH. 2003. Organizational commitment, supervisory commitment, and employee outcomes in the Chinese context: proximal hypothesis or global hypothesis? *J. Organ. Behav.* 24:313–34

Cheng Y, Stockdale MS. 2003. The validity of the three-component model of organizational commitment in a Chinese context. *J. Vocat. Behav.* 62:465–89

Chiu C, Hong Y, Morris MW, Menon T. 2000. Motivated cultural cognition: the impact of implicit cultural theories on dispositional attribution varies as a function of need for closure. *J. Personal. Soc. Psychol.* 78:247–59

Chong LMA, Thomas DC. 1997. Leadership perceptions in cross-cultural context: Pakeha and Pacific Islanders of New Zealand. *Leadersh. Q.* 8:275–93

Corney WJ, Richards CH. 2005. A comparative analysis of the desirability of work characteristics: Chile versus the United States. *Int. J. Manage.* 22:159–65

Cramton CD, Hinds PL. 2005. Subgroup dynamics in internationally distributed teams: ethnocentrism or cross-national learning? *Res. Organ. Behav.* 26:231–63

Deci EL, Ryan RM, Gagné M, Leone DR, Usunov J, Kornazheva BP. 2001. Need satisfaction, motivation, and well-being in the work organizations of a former Eastern bloc country: a cross-cultural study of self-determination. *Personal. Soc. Psychol. Bull.* 27:930–42

De Luque MFH, Sommer SM. 2000. The impact of culture on feedback-seeking behavior: an integrated model and propositions. *Acad. Manage. Rev.* 25:829–49

Den Hartog DN, House RJ, Hanges PJ, Ruiz-Quintanilla SA, Dorfman PW. 1999. Culture specific and cross-culturally generalizable implicit leadership theories: Are attributes of charismatic/transformational leadership universally endorsed? *Leadersh. Q.* 10:219–56

Den Hartog DN, Verburg RM. 1997. Charisma and rhetoric: the communicative techniques of international business leaders. *Leadersh. Q.* 8:355–91

Derlega VJ, Cukur CS, Kuang JCY, Forsyth DR. 2002. Interdependent construal of self and the endorsement of conflict resolution strategies in interpersonal, intergroup, and international disputes. *J. Cross-Cult. Psychol.* 33:610–25

Diener E, Oishi S, Lucas RE. 2003. Personality, culture, and subjective well-being: emotional and cognitive evaluations of life. *Annu. Rev. Psychol.* 54:403–25

d'Iribarne P. 2002. Motivating workers in emerging countries: universal tools and local adaptations. *J. Organ. Behav.* 23:243–56

Doney PM, Cannon JP, Mullen MR. 1998. Understanding the influence of national culture on the development of trust. *Acad. Manage. Rev.* 23:601–20

Dorfman PW, Howell JP, Hibino S, Lee JK, Tate U, Bautista A. 1997. Leadership in Western and Asian countries: commonalities and differences in effective leadership processes across cultures. *Leadersh. Q.* 8:233–74

Drach-Zahavy. 2004. The proficiency trap: how to balance enriched job designs and the team's need for support. *J. Organ. Behav.* 25:979–96

Drake LE. 2001. The culture-negotiation link: integrative and distributive bargaining through an intercultural communication lens. *Hum. Commun. Res.* 27:317–49

Earley PC. 1997. *Face, Harmony, and Social Structure: An Analysis of Organizational Behaviour Across Cultures.* New York: Oxford Univ. Press

Earley PC. 1999. Playing follow the leader: status-determining traits in relation to collective efficacy across cultures. *Organ. Behav. Hum. Decis. Process.* 80:192–212

Earley PC, Ang S. 2003. *Cultural Intelligence: Individual Interactions Across Cultures.* Stanford, CA: Stanford Univ. Press

Earley PC, Erez M, eds. 1997. *New Perspectives on International Industrial/Organizational Psychology.* San Francisco: New Lexington/Jossey-Bass

Earley PC, Gibson CB. 2002. *Multinational Teams: A New Perspective.* Mahwah, NJ: Erlbaum

Earley PC, Gibson CB, Chao CC. 1999. "How did I do?" versus "How did we do?" *J. Cross-Cult. Psychol.* 30:594–619

Earley PC, Mosakowski E. 2000. Creating hybrid team cultures: an empirical test of transnational team functioning. *Acad. Manage. J.* 43:26–49

Eby LT, Dobbins GH. 1997. Collectivistic orientation in teams: an individual- and group-level analysis. *J. Organ. Behav.* 18:275–95

Elenkov DS, Manev IM. 2005. Top management leadership and influence on innovation: the role of sociocultural context. *J. Manage.* 31:381–402

Elisseeff V. 2000. *The Silk Roads: Highways of Culture and Commerce.* Oxford/New York: UNESCO Publ./Berghahn Books

Elron E. 1997. Top management teams within multinational corporations: effects of cultural heterogeneity. *Leadersh. Q.* 8:393–412

Ely RJ, Thomas DA. 2001. Cultural diversity at work: the effects of diversity perspectives on work group processes and outcomes. *Admin. Sci. Q.* 46:229–73

Ensari N, Murphy SE. 2003. Cross-cultural variations in leadership perceptions and attribution of charisma to the leader. *Organ. Behav. Hum. Decis. Process.* 92:52–66

Erdogan B, Kraimer ML, Liden RC. 2004. Work value congruence and intrinsic career success: the compensatory roles of leader-member exchange and perceived organizational support. *Pers. Psychol.* 57:305–32

Erez M, Earley PC. 1993. *Culture, Self-Identity, and Work.* New York: Oxford Univ. Press

Erez M, Gati E. 2004. A dynamic multi-level model of culture: from the micro level of the individual to the macro level of a global culture. *Appl. Psychol.* 53:583–98

Erez M, Somech A. 1996. Is group productivity loss the rule or the exception? Effects of culture and group-based motivation. *Acad. Manage. J.* 39:1513–37

Eylon D, Au KY. 1999. Exploring empowerment cross-cultural differences among the power distance dimension. *Int. J. Intercult. Relat.* 23:373–85

Farh JL, Cheng BS. 2000. Paternalistic leadership in Chinese organizations: a cultural analysis. *Indig. Psychol. Res. Chinese Soc.* 13:127–80

Farh JL, Earley C, Lin S. 1997. Impetus for action: a cultural analysis of justice and organizational citizenship behavior in Chinese society. *Adm. Sci. Q.* 42:421–44

Fields D, Pang M, Chiu C. 2000. Distributive and procedural justice as predictors of employee outcomes in Hong Kong. *J. Organ. Behav.* 21:547–62

Fischer R, Smith PB. 2003. Reward allocation and culture: a meta-analysis. *J. Cross-Cult. Psychol.* 34:251–68

Fischer R, Smith PB. 2004. Values and organizational justice: performance- and seniority-based allocation criteria in the United Kingdom and Germany. *J. Cross-Cult. Psychol.* 35:669–88

Fischer R, Smith PB. 2006. Who cares about justice? The moderating effect of effect of values on the link between organizational justice and work behavior. *Appl. Psychol. Int. Rev.* In press

Frese M, Kring W, Soose A, Zempel J. 1996. Personal initiative at work: differences between East and West Germany. *Acad. Manage. J.* 39(1):37–63

Friedman R, Chi S, Liu LA. 2006. An expectancy model of Chinese-American differences in conflict-avoiding. *J. Int. Bus. Stud.* 37:76–91

Fu PP, Kennedy J, Tata J, Yukl G, Bond MH, et al. 2004. The impact of societal cultural values and individual social beliefs on the perceived effectiveness of managerial influence strategies: a meso approach. *J. Int. Bus. Stud.* 35:284–305

Gabrielidis C, Stephan WG, Ybarra O, Pearson VM, Villareal L. 1997. Preferred styles of conflict resolution: Mexico and the United States. *J. Cross-Cult. Psychol.* 28:661–77

Geletkanycz MA. 1997. The salience of "culture's consequences": the effects of cultural values on top executive commitment to the status quo. *Strateg. Manage. J.* 18:615–34

Gelfand MJ, Brett JM, eds. 2004. *The Handbook of Negotiation and Culture*. Stanford, CA: Stanford Univ. Press

Gelfand MJ, Christakopoulou S. 1999. Culture and negotiator cognition: judgment accuracy and negotiation processes in individualistic and collectivistic cultures. *Organ. Behav. Hum. Decis. Process.* 79:248–69

Gelfand MJ, Dyer N. 2000. A cultural perspective on negotiation: progress, pitfalls, and prospects. *Appl. Psychol.* 49:62–99

Gelfand MJ, Higgins M, Nishii LH, Raver JL, Dominguez A, et al. 2002. Culture and ego-centric biases of fairness in conflict and negotiation. *J. Appl. Psychol.* 87:833–45

Gelfand MJ, Major VS, Raver JL, Nishii LH, O'Brien K. 2006a. Negotiating relationally: the dynamics of the relational self in negotiations. *Acad. Manage. Rev.* 31:427–51

Gelfand MJ, McCusker C. 2002. Metaphor and the cultural construction of negotiation: a paradigm for theory and research. In *Handbook of Cross-Cultural Management*, ed. M Gannon, KL Newman, pp. 292–314. New York: Blackwell

Gelfand MJ, Nishii LH, Holcombe KM, Dyer N, Ohbuchi KI, Fukuno M. 2001. Cultural influences on cognitive representations of conflict: interpretations of conflict episodes in the United States and Japan. *J. Appl. Psychol.* 86:1059–74

Gelfand MJ, Nishii LH, Raver JL. 2006b. On the nature and importance of cultural tightness-looseness. *J. Appl. Psychol.* In press

Gelfand MJ, Realo A. 1999. Individualism-collectivism and accountability in intergroup negotiations. *J. Appl. Psychol.* 84:721–36

George JM, Jones GR, Gonzalez JA. 1998. The role of affect in cross-cultural negotiations. *J. Int. Bus. Stud.* 49:749–72

Gibson CB. 1999. Do they do what they believe they can? Group efficacy and group effectiveness across tasks and cultures. *Acad. Manage. J.* 42:138–52

Gibson CB, Zellmer-Bruhn ME. 2001. Metaphors and meaning: an intercultural analysis of the concept of teamwork. *Adm. Sci. Q.* 46:274–303

Gilley KM, Harrison DA, Shaffer MA. 1999. Dimensions, determinants, and differences in the expatriate adjustment process. *J. Int. Bus. Stud.* 30:557–81

Glazer S, Beehr TA. 2005. Consistency of implications of three role stressors across four countries. *J. Organ. Behav.* 26:467–87

Gomez C, Kirkman B, Shapiro D. 2000. The impact of collectivism and in-group/out-group membership on the evaluation generosity of team members. *Acad. Manage. J.* 43:1097–106

Goncalo JA, Staw BM. 2006. Individualism-collectivism and group creativity. *Organ. Behav. Hum. Decis. Process.* 100:96–109

Gregersen HB, Black JS. 1996. Multiple commitments upon repatriation: the Japanese experience. *J. Manage.* 22:209–29

Harrison DA, Price KH, Gavin JH, Florey A. 2002. Time, teams, and task performance: changing effects of surface- and deep-level diversity on group functioning. *Acad. Manage. J.* 45:1029–45

Harrison GL, McKinnon JL, Wu A, Chow CW. 2000. Cultural influences on adaptation to fluid workgroups and teams. *J. Int. Bus. Stud.* 31:489–505

He W, Chen CC, Zhang L. 2004. Rewards-allocation preferences of Chinese employees in the new millennium: the effects of ownership reform, collectivism, and goal priority. *Organ. Sci.* 15:221–31

Hechanova R, Beehr TA, Christiansen ND. 2003. Antecedents and consequences of employees' adjustment to overseas assignment: a meta-analytic review. *Appl. Psychol.* 52:213–36

Heine SJ, Kitayama S, Lehman DR, Takata T, Ide E, et al. 2001. Divergent consequences of success and failure in Japan and North America: an investigation of self-improving motivations and malleable selves. *J. Personal. Soc. Psychol.* 81:599–615

Hendon DW, Roy MH, Ahmed ZU. 2003. Negotiation concession patterns: a multicountry, multiperiod study. *Am. Bus. Rev.* 21:75–81

Herskovits MJ. 1955. *Cultural Anthropology.* New York: Knopf

Herodotus, Marincola JM, de Selincourt A. 2003. *The Histories.* London: Penguin

Hofstede G. 1980. *Culture's Consequences: International Differences in Work-Related Values.* Beverly Hills, CA: Sage

Hofstede G. 1991. *Cultures and Organizations.* London: McGraw-Hill

Hofstede G. 2001. *Culture's Consequences: Comparing Values, Behaviors, Institutions, and Organizations Across Nations.* Thousand Oaks, CA: Sage. 2nd ed.

Hofstede G, Hofstede GJ. 2005. *Cultures and Organizations: Software of the Mind.* New York: McGraw-Hill

Hofstede G, Van Deusen CA, Mueller CB, Charles TA. 2002. What goals do business leaders pursue? A study in fifteen countries. *J. Int. Bus. Stud.* 33:785–803

Holt JL, DeVore CJ. 2005. Culture, gender, organizational role, and styles of conflict resolution: a meta-analysis. *Int. J. Intercult. Relat.* 29:165–96

Hong Y, Morris MW, Chiu C, Benet-Martinez V. 2000. Multicultural minds: a dynamic constructivist approach to culture and cognition. *Am. Psychol.* 55:709–20

House RJ, Hanges PW, Javidan M, Dorfman P, Gupta V, eds. 2004. *Culture, Leadership, and Organizations: The GLOBE Study of 62 Societies.* Thousand Oaks, CA: Sage

Howell JP, Romero EJ, Dorfman PW, Paul J, Bautista JA. 2003. Effective leadership in the Mexican maquiladora: challenging common expectations. *J. Int. Manage.* 9:51–73

Huang T, Chi S, Lawler JS. 2005. The relationship between expatriates' personality traits and their adjustment to international assignments. *Int. J. Hum. Resour. Manage.* 16:1656–70

Huang X, Van de Vliert E. 2003. Where intrinsic job satisfaction fails to work: national moderators of intrinsic motivation. *J. Organ. Behav.* 24:159–79

Huang X, Van de Vliert E. 2004. Job level and national culture as joint roots of job satisfaction. *Appl. Psychol.* 53:329–48

Hui C, Graen GB. 1997. Guanxi and professional leadership in contemporary Sino-American joint ventures in mainland China. *Leadersh. Q.* 8:451–65

Hui C, Lee C, Rousseau DM. 2004. Psychological contract and organizational citizenship behavior in China: investigating generalizability and instrumentality. *J. Appl. Psychol.* 89:311–21

Hui CH, Yee C. 1999. The impact of psychological collectivism and workgroup atmosphere on Chinese employees' job satisfaction. *Appl. Psychol.* 48:175–85

Hundley G, Kim J. 1997. National culture and the factors affecting perceptions of pay fairness in Korea and the United States. *Int. J. Org. Anal.* 5:325–42

Iyengar SS, Lepper MR. 1999. Rethinking the value of choice: a cultural perspective on intrinsic motivation. *J. Personal. Soc. Psychol.* 76:349–66

Jackson DW Jr, Naumann E, Widmier SM. 2000. Examining the relationship between work attitudes and propensity to leave among expatriate salespeople. *J. Person. Sell. Sales Manage.* 20:227–41

Janssens M, Brett JM. 1997. Meaningful participation in transnational teams. *Eur. J. Work Organ. Psychol.* 6:153–68

Jung DI, Avolio BJ. 1999. Effects of leadership style and followers' cultural orientation on performance in group and individual task conditions. *Acad. Manage. J.* 42:208–18

Kamins MA, Johnston WJ, Graham JL. 1998. A multi-method examination of buyer-seller interactions among Japanese and American businesspeople. *J. Int. Market.* 6:8–32

Kashima Y, Kashima E, Chiu C, Farsides T, Gelfand MJ, et al. 2005. Culture, essentialism, and agency: Are individuals universally believed to be more real entities than groups? *Eur. J. Soc. Psychol.* 35:147–69

Kashima Y, Yamaguchi S, Kim U, Choi S, Gelpand MJ, Yuki M. 1995. Culture, gender, and self: a perspective from individualism-collectivism research. *J. Personal. Soc. Psychol.* 69:925–37

Kickul J, Lester SW, Belgio E. 2004. Attitudinal and behavioral outcomes of psychological contract breach: a cross cultural comparison of the United States and Hong Kong Chinese. *Int. J. Cross-Cult. Manage.* 4:229–49

Kim HS, Drolet A. 2003. Choice and self-expression: a cultural analysis of variety-seeking. *J. Personal. Soc. Psychol.* 85:373–82

King RC, Bu N. 2005. Perceptions of the mutual obligations between employees and employers: a comparative study of new generation IT professionals in China and the United States. *Int. J. Hum. Resour. Manage.* 16:46–64

Kirkman BL, Lowe KB, Gibson CB. 2006. A quarter century of culture's consequences: a review of empirical research incorporating Hofstede's cultural values framework. *J. Int. Bus. Stud.* 37:285–320

Kirkman BL, Shapiro DL. 1997. The impact of cultural values on employee resistance to teams: toward a model of globalized self-managing work team effectiveness. *Acad. Manage. Rev.* 22:730–57

Kirkman BL, Shapiro DL. 2001a. The impact of cultural values on job satisfaction and organizational commitment in self-managing work teams: the mediating role of employee resistance. *Acad. Manage. J.* 44:557–69

Kirkman BL, Shapiro DL. 2001b. The impact of team members' cultural values on productivity, cooperation, and empowerment in self-managing work teams. *J. Cross-Cult. Psychol.* 32:597–617

Kitayama S, Markus HR, Matsumoto H, Norasakkunkit V. 1997. Individual and collective processes in the construction of the self: self-enhancement in the United States and self-criticism in Japan. *J. Personal. Soc. Psychol.* 72:1245–67

Kluckhohn C. 1954. Culture and behavior. In *Handbook of Social Psychology*, ed. G. Lindzey, vol. 2, pp. 931–76. Cambridge, MA: Addison-Wesley

Ko J, Price JL, Mueller CW. 1997. Assessment of Meyer's and Allen's three-component model of organizational commitment in South Korea. *J. Appl. Psychol.* 82:961–73

Kozan MK. 1997. Culture and conflict management: a theoretical framework. *Int. J. Confl. Manage.* 8:338–60

Kraimer ML, Wayne SJ. 2004. An examination of perceived organizational support as a multidimensional construct in the context of an expatriate assignment. *J. Manage.* 30:209–37

Kraimer ML, Wayne SJ, Jaworski JA. 2001. Sources of support and expatriate performance: the mediating role of expatriate adjustment. *Pers. Psychol.* 54:71–99

Kumar R. 1999. A script theoretical analysis of international negotiating behavior. In *Research in Negotiation in Organizations*, ed. RJ Bies, RJ Lewicki, BH Sheppard, 7:285–311. Greenwich, CT: Elsevier Sci./JAI

Kurman J. 2001. Self-regulation strategies in achievement settings: culture and gender differences. *J. Cross-Cult. Psychol.* 32:491–503

Kurman J, Yoshihara-Tanaka C, Elkoshi T. 2003. Is self-enhancement negatively related to constructive self-criticism? Self-enhancement and self-criticism in Israel and in Japan. *J. Cross-Cult. Psychol.* 34:24–37

Lam SSK, Chen XP, Schaubroeck J. 2002a. Participative decision making and employee performance in different cultures: the moderating effects of allocentrism/idiocentrism and efficacy. *Acad. Manage. J.* 45:905–15

Lam SSK, Hui C, Law KS. 1999. Organizational citizenship behavior: comparing perspectives of supervisors and subordinates across four international samples. *J. Appl. Psychol.* 84:594–601

Lam SSK, Schaubroeck J, Aryee S. 2002b. Relationship between organizational justice and employee work outcomes: a cross-national study. *J. Organ. Behav.* 23:1–18

Law KS, Wong CS, Wang D, Wang L. 2000. Effect of supervisor-subordinate guanxi on supervisory decisions in China: an empirical investigation. *Int. J. Hum. Resour. Manage.* 11:751–65

Lee AY, Aaker JL, Gardner WL. 2000. The pleasures and pains of distinct self-construals: the role of interdependence in regulatory focus. *J. Personal. Soc. Psychol.* 78:1122–34

Lee C, Pillutla M, Law KS. 2000. Power-distance, gender and organizational justice. *J. Manage.* 26:685–704

Lee C, Tinsley C, Bobko P. 2003. Cross-cultural variance in goal orientations and their effects. *Appl. Psychol.* 52:272–97

Lee K, Allen NJ, Meyer JP, Rhee K. 2001. The three-component model of organizational commitment: an application to South Korea. 50:596–614

Leung K. 1997. Negotiation and reward allocations across cultures. See Earley & Erez 1997, pp. 640–75

Leung K, Bhagat RS, Buchan NR, Erez M, Gibson CB. 2005. Culture and international business: recent advances and their implications for future research. *J. Int. Bus. Stud.* 36:357–78

Leung K, Bond MH, de Carrasquel SR, Munoz C, Hernandez M, et al. 2002. Social axioms: the search for universal dimensions of general beliefs about how the world functions. *J. Cross-Cult. Psychol.* 33:286–302

Leung K, Tong K. 2004. Justice across cultures: a three-stage model for intercultural negotiation. See Gelfand & Brett 2004, pp. 313–33

Leung K, Wang Z, Smith PB. 2001. Job attitudes and organizational justice in joint venture hotels in China: the role of expatriate managers. *Int. J. Hum. Resour. Manage.* 12:926–45

Li J. 2002. A cultural model of learning—Chinese "heart and mind for wanting to learn." *J. Cross-Cult. Psychol.* 33:248–69

Lind AE, Tyler TR, Huo YJ. 1997. Procedural context and culture: variation in the antecedents of procedural justice judgments. *J. Personal. Soc. Psychol.* 73:767–80

Liu C, Borg I, Spector PE. 2004. Measurement equivalence of the German Job Satisfaction Survey used in a multinational organization: implications of Schwartz's culture model. *J. Appl. Psychol.* 89:1070–82

Liu LA, Friedman RA, Chi S. 2005. "*Ren qing*" versus the "big five": the role of culturally sensitive measures of individual difference in distributive negotiations. *Manage. Organ. Rev.* 1:225–47

Liu X, Shaffer MA. 2005. An investigation of expatriate adjustment and performance: a social capital perspective. *Int. J. Cross-Cult. Manage.* 5:235–55

Lockwood P, Marshall TC, Sadler P. 2005. Promoting success or preventing failure: cultural differences in motivation by positive and negative role models. *Personal. Soc. Psychol. Bull.* 31:379–92

Luo Y. 2005. How important are shared perceptions of procedural justice in cooperative alliances? *Acad. Manage. J.* 48:695–709

Ma Z, Anderson T, Wang X, Wang Y, Jaeger A, Saunders D. 2002. Individual perception, bargaining behavior, and negotiation outcomes: a comparison across two countries. *Int. J. Cross-Cult. Manage.* 2:171–84

Man CD, Lam SSK. 2003. The effects of job complexity and autonomy on cohesiveness in collectivistic and individualistic work groups: a cross-cultural analysis. *J. Organ. Behav.* 24:979–1001

Marsden D. 1991. Indigenous management. *Int. J. Hum. Resour. Manage.* 2:21–38

Matsumoto T. 2004. Learning to "do time" in Japan: a study of US interns in Japanese organizations. *Int. J. Cross-Cult. Manage.* 4:19–37

Maznevski ML, Chudoba KM. 2000. Bridging space over time: global virtual team dynamics and effectiveness. *Organ. Sci.* 11:473–92

McAuley PC, Bond MH, Kashima E. 2002. Toward defining situations objectively: a culture-level analysis of role dyads in Hong Kong and Australia. *J. Cross-Cult. Psychol.* 33:363–79

Mehra P, Krishnan VR. 2005. Impact of svadharma-orientation on transformational leadership and followers' trust in leader. *J. Indian Psychol.* 23:1–11

Meyer JP, Stanley DJ, Herscovitch L, Topolnytsky L. 2002. Affective, continuance, and normative commitment to the organization: a meta-analysis of antecedents, correlates, and consequences. *J. Vocat. Behav.* 61:20–52

Miller JS, Hom PW, Gomez-Mejia LR. 2001. The high cost of low wages: Does maquiladora compensation reduce turnover? *J. Int. Bus. Stud.* 32:585–95

Montoya-Weiss MM, Massey AP, Song M. 2001. Getting it together: temporal coordination and conflict management in global virtual teams. *Acad. Manage. J.* 44:1251–62

Morris MW, Fu H. 2001. How does culture influence conflict resolution? A dynamic constructivist analysis. *Soc. Cogn.* 19:324–49

Morris MW, Leung K, Ames D, Lickel B. 1999. Views from inside and outside: integrating emic and etic insights about culture and justice judgments. *Acad. Manage. Rev.* 24:781–96

Morris MW, Leung K, Iyengar SS. 2004. Person perception in the heat of conflict: negative trait attributions affect procedural preferences and account for situational and cultural differences. *Asian J. Soc. Psychol.* 7:127–47

Morris MW, Menon T, Ames DR. 2001. Culturally conferred conceptions of agency: a key to social perception of persons, groups, and other actors. *Personal. Soc. Psychol. Rev.* 5:169–82

Morris MW, Williams KY, Leung K, Larrick R, Mendoza MT, et al. 1998. Conflict management style: accounting for cross-national differences. *J. Int. Bus. Stud.* 29:729–47

Morrison EW, Chen Y, Salgado SR. 2004. Cultural differences in newcomer feedback seeking: a comparison of the United States and Hong Kong. *Appl. Psychol.* 53:1–22

Mueller CW, Iverson RD, Jo D. 1999. Distributive justice evaluations in two cultural contexts: a comparison of US and South Korean teachers. *Hum. Relat.* 52:869–93

Newman KL, Nollen SD. 1996. Culture and congruence: the fit between management practices and national culture. *J. Int. Bus. Stud.* 24:753–79

Ng KY, Van Dyne L. 2001. Individualism-collectivism as a boundary condition for effectiveness of minority influence in decision making. *Organ. Behav. Hum. Decis. Process.* 84:198–225

Niles S. 1998. Achievement goals and means: a cultural comparison. *J. Cross-Cult. Psychol.* 29:656–67

Nyambegera SM, Daniels K, Sparrow P. 2001. Why fit doesn't always matter: the impact of HRM and cultural fit on job involvement of Kenyan employees. *Appl. Psychol.* 50:109–40

Oetzel JG, Ting-Toomey S, Matsumoto T, Yokochi Y, Pan X, et al. 2001. Face and facework in conflict: a cross-cultural comparison of China, Germany, Japan, and the United States. *Commun. Monogr.* 68:235–58

Ohbuchi K, Osamu F, Tedeschi JT. 1999. Cultural values in conflict management: goal orientation, goal attainment, and tactical decision. *J. Cross.-Cult. Psychol.* 30:51–71

Oyserman D, Coon HM, Kemmelmeier M. 2002. Rethinking individualism and collectivism: evaluation of theoretical assumptions and meta-analyses. *Psychol. Bull.* 128:3–72

Paik Y, Vance CM. 2002. Evidence of back-home selection bias against US female expatriates. *Women Manage. Rev.* 17:68–79

Palthe J. 2004. The relative importance of antecedents to cross-cultural adjustment: implications for managing a global workforce. *J. Intercult. Relat.* 28:37–59

Parkes LP, Bochner S, Schneider SK. 2001. Person-organisation fit across cultures: an empirical investigation of individualism and collectivism. *Appl. Psychol.* 50:81–108

Pearce JL, Bigley GA, Branyiczki I. 1998. Procedural justice as modernism: placing industrial/organisational psychology in context. *Appl. Psychol.* 47:371–96

Pearson VMS, Stephan WG. 1998. Preferences for styles of negotiation: a comparison of Brazil and the US. *Int. J. Intercult. Relat.* 22:67–83

Pellegrini EK, Scandura TA. 2006. Leader-member exchange (LMX), paternalism, and delegation in Turkish business culture: an empirical investigation. *J. Int. Bus. Stud.* In press

Peterson MF, Smith PB. 2000. Sources of meaning, organizations, and culture. In *Handbook of Organizational Culture and Climate*, ed. N Ashkanasay, CPM Wilderom, MF Peterson, pp. 101–15. Thousand Oaks, CA: Sage

Piccolo RF, Judge TA, Takahashi K, Watanabe N, Locke EA. 2005. Core self-evaluations in Japan: relative effects on job satisfaction, life satisfaction, and happiness. *J. Organ. Behav.* 26:965–84

Pike KL. 1967. *Language in Relation to a Unified Theory of the Structure of Human Behavior.* The Hague: Mouton

Pillai R, Meindl JR. 1998. Context and charisma: a "meso" level examination of the relationship of organic structure, collectivism, and crisis to charismatic leadership. *J. Manage.* 24:643–71

Pillai R, Scandura TA, Williams EA. 1999. Leadership and organizational justice: similarities and differences across cultures. *J. Int. Bus. Stud.* 30:763–79

Posthuma RA, Joplin JR, Maertz J, Carl P. 2005. Comparing the validity of turnover predictors in the United States and Mexico. *Int. J. Cross-Cult. Manage.* 5:165–80

Price KD, Hall TW, Van D Bos K, Hunton JE, Lovett S, Tippett MJ. 2001. Features of the value function for voice and their consistency across participants from four countries:

Great Britain, Mexico, the Netherlands, and the United States. *Organ. Behav. Hum. Decis. Process.* 84:95–121

Probst TM, Carnevale PJ, Triandis HC. 1999. Cultural values in intergroup and single-group social dilemmas. *Organ. Behav. Hum. Decis. Process.* 77:171–91

Pruitt DG. 2004. Foreword. See Gelfand & Brett 2004, pp. xi–xiii

Rahim MA, Magner NR. 1996. Confirmatory factor analysis of the bases of leader power: first-order factor model and its invariance across groups. *Multivar. Behav. Res.* 31:495–517

Ralston DA, Vollmer GR, Srinvasan N, Nicholson JD, Tang M, Wan P. 2001. Strategies of upward influence: a study of six cultures from Europe, Asia, and America. *J. Cross-Cult. Psychol.* 32:728–35

Ramamoorthy N, Flood P. 2002. Employee attitudes and behavioral intentions: a test of the main and moderating effects of individualism-collectivism orientations. *Hum. Relat.* 55:1071–96

Randel AE. 2003. The salience of culture in multinational teams and its relation to team citizenship behavior. *Int. J. Cross-Cult. Manage.* 3:27–44

Rao A, Hashimoto K, Rao A. 1997. Universal and culturally specific aspects of managerial influence: a study of Japanese managers. *Leadersh. Q.* 8:295–312

Robert C, Probst TM, Martocchio JJ, Drasgow F, Lawler JJ. 2000. Empowerment and continuous improvement in the United States, Mexico, Poland, and India: predicting fit on the basis of the dimensions of power distance and individualism. *J. Appl. Psychol.* 85:643–58

Robert C, Wasti SA. 2002. Organizational individualism and collectivism: theoretical development and an empirical test of a measure. *J. Manage.* 28:544–66

Roe RA, Zinovieva IL, Dienes E, Ten Horn L. 2000. A comparison of work motivation in Bulgaria, Hungary, and the Netherlands: test of a model. *Appl. Psychol.* 49:658–87

Roth K, O'Donnell S. 1996. Foreign subsidiary compensation strategy: an agency theory perspective. *Acad. Manage. J.* 39:678–703

Rousseau DM. 1989. Psychological and implied contracts in organizations. *Empl. Responsib. Rights J.* 2:121–39

Rousseau DM, Schalk. 2000. Psychological contracts in employment: cross-national perspectives. Newbury Park, CA: Sage

Russell JEA, Takeuchi R, Yun S. 2002. Antecedents and consequences of the perceived adjustment of Japanese expatriates in the USA. *Int. J. Hum. Resour. Manage.* 13:1224–44

Ryan RM, Chirkov VI, Little TD, Sheldon KM, Timoshina E, Deci EL. 1999. The American dream in Russia: extrinsic aspirations and well-being in two cultures. *Personal. Soc. Psychol. Bull.* 25:1509–24

Ryan RM, Deci EL. 2000. Self-determination theory and the facilitation of intrinsic motivation, social development, and well-being. *Am. Psychol.* 55:68–78

Sadler-Smith E, El-Kot G, Leat M. 2003. Differentiating work autonomy facets in a non-Western context. *J. Organ. Behav.* 24:709–31

Sagie A, Elizur D, Yamauchi H. 1996. The structure and strength of achievement motivation: a cross-cultural comparison. *J. Organ. Behav.* 7:431–44

Salk JE, Brannen MY. 2000. National culture, networks, and individual influence in a multinational management team. *Acad. Manage. J.* 43:191–202

Sama LM, Papamarcos SD. 2000. Hofstede's I-C dimension as predictive of allocative behaviors: a meta-analysis. *Int. J. Value-Based Manage.* 13:173–88

Sanchez-Burks J, Nisbett RE, Ybarra O. 2000. Cultural styles, relational schemas and prejudice against outgroups. *J. Personal. Soc. Psychol.* 79:174–89

Schaubroeck J, Xie JL, Lam SSK. 2000. Collective efficacy versus self-efficacy in coping responses to stressors and control: a cross-cultural study. *J. Appl. Psychol.* 85:512–25

Schwartz SH. 1994. Beyond individualism/collectivism: new cultural dimensions of values. In *Individualism & Collectivism: Theory, Method and Application*, ed. U Kim, HC Triandis, C Kagitcibasi, S Choi, G Yoon, pp. 85–119. Thousand Oaks, CA: Sage

Selmer J. 2002. Coping strategies applied by Western vs overseas Chinese business expatriates in China. *Int. J. Hum. Resour. Manage.* 13:19–34

Selmer J, de Leon CT. 2002. Parent cultural control of foreign subsidiaries through organizational acculturation: a longitudinal study. *Int. J. Hum. Resour. Manage.* 13:1147–65

Sels L, Janssens M, Van den Brande I. 2004. Assessing the nature of psychological contacts: a validation of six dimensions. *J. Organ. Behav.* 25:461–88

Shaffer MA, Harrison DA. 1998. Expatriates' psychological withdrawal from international assignments: work, nonwork, and family influences. *Pers. Psychol.* 51:87–118

Shaffer MA, Harrison DA, Gilley MK. 1999. Dimensions, determinants, and differences in the expatriate adjustment process. *J. Int. Bus. Stud.* 30:557–81

Shaffer MA, Harrison DA, Gilley MK, Luk D. 2001. Struggling for balance amid turbulence: work-family conflict on international assignments. *J. Manage.* 27:99–121

Shapiro DL, Furst S, Spreitzer G, Von Glinow M. 2002. Transnational teams in the electronic age: Are team identity and high performance at risk? *J. Organ. Behav.* 23:455–67

Shapiro DL, Von Glinow M, Cheng JLC. 2005. *Managing Multinational Teams: Global Perspectives.* Oxford: Elsevier Sci.

Shenkar O, Ronen S, Shefy E, Hau-siu Chow I. 1998. The role structure of Chinese managers. *Hum. Relat.* 51:51–73

Shin SJ, Zhou J. 2003. Transformational leadership, conservation, and creativity: evidence from Korea. *Acad. Manage. J.* 46:703–14

Shokef E, Erez M. 2006. Global work culture and global identity as a platform for a shared understanding in multicultural teams. In *Research in Managing Groups and Teams: National Culture and Groups*, ed. B Mannix, M Neale, Y Chen. Oxford: Elsevier Sci. In press

Shweder R, LeVine R. 1984. *Culture Theory: Essays on Mind, Self, and Emotion.* London: Cambridge Univ. Press

Sinha JBP. 1997. Indian perspectives on leadership and power in organizations. In *Asian Perspectives on Psychology*, ed. HSR Kao, D Sinha, pp. 218–35. Thousand Oaks, CA: Sage

Skinner BF. 1981. Selection by consequences. *Science* 213:501–4

Smith PB, Dugan S, Peterson MF, Leung K. 1998. Individualism-collectivism and the handling of disagreement: a 23 country study. *Int. J. Intercult. Relat.* 22:351–67

Smith PB, Dugan S, Trompenaars F. 1996. National culture and the values of organizational employees: a dimensional analysis across 43 nations. *J. Cross-Cult. Psychol.* 27:231–64

Smith PB, Peterson MF, Schwartz SH, Ahmad AH, Akande D, et al. 2002. Cultural values, sources of guidance and their relevance to managerial behaviors: a 47 nation study. *J. Cross-Cult. Psychol.* 33:188–208

Smith PB, Wang ZM, Leung K. 1997. Leadership, decision-making and cultural context: event management within Chinese joint ventures. *Leadersh. Q.* 8:413–31

Sparrow PR. 2006. International management: some key challenges for industrial and organizational psychology. In *International Review of Industrial and Organizational Psychology, Vol. 21*, ed. GP Hodgkinson, JK Ford. Chichester, UK: Wiley. In press

Spector PE, Cooper CL, Sanchez JI, O'Driscoll M, Sparks K, et al. 2002. Locus of control and well-being at work: How generalizable are Western findings? *Acad. Manage. J.* 45:453–66

Spreitzer GM, Perttula KH, Xin K. 2005. Traditionality matters: an examination of the effectiveness of transformational leadership in the United States and Taiwan. *J. Organ. Behav.* 26:205–27

Stahl GK, Caligiuri PM. 2005. The effectiveness of expatriate coping strategies: the moderating role of cultural distance, position level and the time on the international assignment. *J. Appl. Psychol.* 90:603–15

Sue-Chan C, Ong M. 2002. Goal assignment and performance: assessing the mediating roles of goal commitment and self-efficacy and the moderating role of power distance. *Organ. Behav. Hum. Decis. Process.* 89:1140–61

Suutari V. 1996. Variation in the average leadership behavior of managers across countries: Finnish expatriates' experiences from Germany, Sweden, France and Great Britain. *Int. J. Hum. Resour. Manage.* 7:677–707

Sweeney PD, McFarlin DB. 2004. Social comparisons and income satisfaction: a cross-national examination. *J. Occup. Organ. Psychol.* 77:149–54

Takeuchi R, Seokhwa Y, Russell JEA. 2002a. Antecedents and consequences of the perceived adjustment of Japanese expatriates in the USA. *Int. J. Hum. Resour. Manage.* 13:1224–44

Takeuchi R, Tesluk PE, Seokhwa Y, Lepak DP. 2005a. An integrative view of international experience. *Acad. Manage. J.* 48:85–100

Takeuchi R, Tesluk PE, Yun S. 2002b. An examination of crossover and spillover effects of spousal and expatriate cross-cultural adjustment on expatriate outcomes. *J. Appl. Psychol.* 87:655–66

Takeuchi R, Wang M, Marinova SV. 2005b. Antecedents and consequences of psychological workplace strain during expatriation: a cross-sectional and longitudinal investigation. *Pers. Psychol.* 58:925–48

Thomas DC. 1999. Cultural diversity and work group effectiveness: an experimental study. *J. Cross-Cult. Psychol.* 30:242–63

Thomas DC, Au K. 2002. The effect of cultural differences on behavioral responses to low job satisfaction. *J. Int. Bus. Stud.* 33:309–26

Thomas DC, Au K, Ravlin EC. 2003. Cultural variation and the psychological contract. *J. Organ. Behav.* 24:451–71

Thomas DC, Pekerti AA. 2003. Effect of culture on situational determinants of exchange behavior in organizations: a comparison of New Zealand and Indonesia. *J. Cross-Cult. Psychol.* 34:269–81

Tinsley CH. 1998. Models of conflict resolution in Japanese, German, and American cultures. *J. Appl. Psychol.* 83:316–23

Tinsley CH. 2001. How negotiators get to yes: predicting the constellation of strategies used across cultures to negotiate conflict. *J. Appl. Psychol.* 86:583–93

Tinsley CH. 2004. Culture and conflict: enlarging our dispute resolution framework. See Gelfand & Brett 2004, pp. 193–212

Tinsley CH, Brett JM. 2001. Managing workplace conflict in the United States and Hong Kong. *Organ. Behav. Hum. Decis. Process.* 85:360–81

Tinsley CH, Pillutla MM. 1998. Negotiating in the United States and Hong Kong. *J. Int. Bus. Stud.* 29:711–28

Tjosvold D, Sun HF. 2002. Understanding conflict avoidance: relationship, motivations, actions, and consequences. *Int. J. Confl. Manage.* 13:143–64

Tosi HL, Greckhamer T. 2004. Culture and CEO compensation. *Organ. Sci.* 15:657–70

Triandis HC. 1972. *The Analysis of Subjective Culture*. New York: Wiley

Triandis HC. 1994. *Culture and Social Behavior*. New York: McGraw-Hill

Triandis HC, Carnevale P, Gelfand MJ, Robert C, Wasti SA, et al. 2001. Culture and deception in business negotiations: a multilevel analysis. *Int. J. Cross-Cult. Manage.* 1:73–90

Turban DB, Lau CM, Ngo HY, Chow IHS, Si SX. 2001. Organizational attractiveness of firms in the People's Republic of China: a person-organization fit persepective. *J. Appl. Psychol.* 86:194–206

Valenzuela A, Srivastava J, Lee S. 2005. The role of cultural orientation in bargaining under incomplete information: differences in causal attributions. *Organ. Behav. Hum. Decis. Process.* 96:72–88

Välikangas L, Okumura A. 1997. Why do people follow leaders? A study of a US and a Japanese change program. *Leadersh. Q.* 8:313–37

Vandenberghe C. 1999. Organizational culture, person-culture fit, and turnover: a replication in the health care industry. *J. Organ. Behav.* 20:175–84

Vandenberghe C, Stinglhamber F, Bentein K, Delhaise T. 2001. An examination of the cross-cultural validity of a multidimensional model of commitment in Europe. *J. Cross-Cult. Psychol.* 32:322–47

Van der Zee K, Atsma N, Brodbeck F. 2004. The influence of social identity and personality on outcomes of cultural diversity in teams. *J. Cross-Cult. Psychol.* 35:283–303

Van de Vliert E, Janssen O. 2002. "Better than" performance motives as roots of satisfaction across more and less developed countries. *J. Cross-Cult. Psychol.* 33:380–97

Van de Vliert E, Shi K, Sanders K, Wang Y, Huang X. 2004. Chinese and Dutch interpretations of supervisory feedback. *J. Cross-Cult. Psychol.* 35:417–35

Van Dyne L, Vandewalle D, Kostova T, Latham ME, Cummings LL. 2000. Collectivism, propensity to trust and self-esteem as predictors of organizational citizenship in a nonwork setting. *J. Organ. Behav.* 21:3–23

Vecernik J. 2003. Skating on thin ice: a comparison of work values and job satisfaction in CEE and EU countries. *Int. J. Comp. Sociol.* 44:444–71

Volkema RJ. 2004. Demographic, cultural, and economic predictors of perceived ethicality of negotiation behavior: a nine-country analysis. *J. Bus. Res.* 57(1):69–78

Von Glinow M, Shapiro DL, Brett JM. 2004. Can we talk, and should we? Managing emotional conflict in multicultural teams. *Acad. Manage. Rev.* 29:578–92

Wade-Benzoni KA, Brett JM, Tenbrunsel AE, Okumura T, Moore DA, Bazerman MH. 2002. Cognitions and behavior in asymmetric social dilemmas: a comparison of two cultures. *J. Appl. Psychol.* 87:87–95

Walumbwa FO, Lawler JJ. 2003. Building effective organizations: transformational leadership, collectivist orientation, work-related attitudes and withdrawal behaviors in three emerging economies. *Int. J. Hum. Resour. Manage.* 14:1083–101

Wang X, Kanungo RN. 2004. Nationality, social network and psychological well-being: expatriates in China. *Int. J. Hum. Resour. Manage.* 15:775–93

Wasti SA. 2002. Affective and continuance commitment to the organization: test of an integrated model in the Turkish context. *Int. J. Intercult. Relat.* 26:525–50

Wasti SA. 2003. The influence of cultural values on antecedents of organizational commitment: an individual-level analysis. *Appl. Psychol. Int. Rev.* 52:533–54

Watson WE, Johnson L, Kumar K, Critelli J. 1998. Process gain and process loss: comparing interpersonal processes and performance of culturally diverse and nondiverse teams across time. *Int. J. Intercult. Relat.* 22:409–30

Westwood R. 1997. Harmony and patriarchy: the cultural basis for "paternalistic headship" among the overseas Chinese. *Organ. Stud.* 18:445–80

Xie JL. 1996. Karasek's model in the People's Republic of China: effects of job demands, control, and individual differences. *Acad. Manage. J.* 39:1594–618

Yamaguchi S, Gelfand M, Ohashi MM, Zemba Y. 2005. The cultural psychology of control: illusions of personal versus collective control in the United States and Japan. *J. Cross-Cult. Psychol.* 36:750–61

Yang MM. 1994. *Gifts, Favors and Banquets: The Art of Social Relationships in China*. Ithaca, NY: Cornell Univ. Press

Yousef DA. 2000. Organizational commitment as a mediator of the relationship between Islamic work ethic and attitudes toward organizational change. *Hum. Relat.* 53:513–37

Yuki M. 2003. Intergroup comparison versus intragroup relationships: a cross-cultural examination of social identity theory in North American and East Asian cultural contexts. *Soc. Psychol. Q.* 66:166–83

Yuki M, Maddux WW, Brewer MB, Takemura K. 2005. Cross-cultural differences in relationship- and group-based trust. *Personal. Soc. Psychol. Bull.* 31:48–62

Zander L, Romani L. 2004. When nationality matters: a study of departmental, hierarchical, professional, gender and age-based employee groupings' leadership preferences across 15 countries. *Int. J. Cross-Cult. Manage.* 4:291–315

Zhou J, Martocchio J. 2001. Chinese and American managers' compensation award decisions: a comparative policy-capturing study. *Pers. Psychol.* 54:115–45

Work Group Diversity

Daan van Knippenberg
and Michaéla C. Schippers

RSM Erasmus University, Erasmus University Rotterdam, Rotterdam 3000 DR, The Netherlands; email: dvanknippenberg@rsm.nl, mschippers@rsm.nl

Annu. Rev. Psychol. 2007. 58:515–41

First published online as a Review in Advance on August 11, 2006

The *Annual Review of Psychology* is online at http://psych.annualreviews.org

This article's doi: 10.1146/annurev.psych.58.110405.085546

Key Words

group composition, group performance, teams, team effectiveness, organizational behavior

Abstract

Work group diversity, the degree to which there are differences between group members, may affect group process and performance positively as well as negatively. Much is still unclear about the effects of diversity, however. We review the 1997–2005 literature on work group diversity to assess the state of the art and to identify key issues for future research. This review points to the need for more complex conceptualizations of diversity, as well as to the need for more empirical attention to the processes that are assumed to underlie the effects of diversity on group process and performance and to the contingency factors of these processes.

Contents

WORK GROUP DIVERSITY

Diversity: a characteristic of social grouping that reflects the degree to which objective or subjective differences exist between group members

Groups in organizations have become increasingly diverse over the years and will continue to become more diverse in years to come (Jackson et al. 2003, Triandis et al. 1994, Williams & O'Reilly 1998). Organizations have become more diverse in terms of demographic differences between people (e.g., in terms of gender, age, and ethnicity). Moreover, organizations are increasingly adopting work group compositions that incorporate differences in functional or educational background, such as in cross-functional project teams; mergers, acquisitions, and joint ventures also introduce diversity into work groups. Because work group diversity may have positive as well as negative effects on group performance (for reviews, see Jackson et al. 2003, Milliken & Martins 1996, Williams & O'Reilly 1998; also see recent *Annual Review of Psychology* chapters by Guzzo & Dickson 1996, Ilgen et al. 2005, Kerr & Tindale 2004), the questions of which processes underlie these effects of diversity and how to manage these processes pose major challenges to research in organizational behavior. In the present article, we aim to assess the state of the art in this field. In doing so, we strive to answer the question of what we may conclude from the extant research as well as to provide a research agenda for diversity research in years to come.

Although the field is known as "organizational diversity," theory and research focus almost exclusively on the work group level, studying how group composition affects group performance, cohesion, and social interaction, and group members' commitment, satisfaction, and other indicators of subjective well-being. This review, therefore, focuses on work group diversity and how it affects groups and their members. Diversity is a group characteristic, but there is a stream of research on what is called relational demography (Chattopadhyay et al. 2004a, Tsui & O'Reilly 1989) that studies the effects of individuals' similarity to their work group (e.g., Chatman & Flynn 2001, Chatman & O'Reilly 2004, Chattopadhyay 1999, Chattopadhyay & George 2001) or to their leader (Epitropaki & Martin 1999, Tsui et al. 2002) as predictors of individual outcomes. Because greater dissimilarity from the group does not necessarily imply greater work group diversity (e.g., a sole female in an otherwise all-male group is very dissimilar to the group in terms of gender, while at the same time the group is quite gender-homogeneous), results from studies on relational demography cannot be taken to directly reflect diversity effects. Space limitations force us to restrict the current review to studies of diversity as a group characteristic, although we do refer to relational demography studies when they seem relevant to the issue under consideration.

The starting point for our article is a seminal review by Williams & O'Reilly (1998), who examined 40 years of diversity research covering more than 80 studies. The Williams & O'Reilly review is an important milestone not only because it provides a comprehensive review of the diversity literature at the time, but also because it is somewhat of a watershed in diversity research. The state of the field that emerged from the Williams & O'Reilly review is one that has yielded largely inconsistent results, probably in part as a result of a somewhat too simplified approach to diversity. In the years following the review, however, the field moved to more sophisticated conceptualizations of diversity and its effects, and we hope to capture this development in the present review. We take the excellent work done by Williams & O'Reilly as a stepping-stone and review diversity research in the period from 1997 to 2005.

To access the relevant literature, we conducted a PsycInfo search of titles and abstracts covering this period and a manual search of the 2000–2005 volumes of major journals in applied psychology and organizational behavior. We also sent out a mailing to solicit papers in press. We should note, however, that our aim is not an exhaustive coverage of the literature, but rather a more selective review that highlights the developments we judge to be most relevant and important.

In the following sections, we first introduce the research field. Second, we address the issue of the conceptualization and operationalization of diversity, arguing in favor of more complex conceptualizations of diversity than typically have been used in diversity research. Next, we focus on what we may learn about the processes underlying the effects of work group diversity by reviewing studies of the mediators and moderators of the effects of diversity, and we briefly touch on possible curvilinear effects of diversity. We conclude by summarizing what we see as the most im-

portant questions for future research. These questions center around the need to develop conceptualizations of diversity that go beyond mere dispersion as well as the need to pay greater attention to the processes mediating the effects of diversity and to the contingencies of these processes.

WORK GROUP DIVERSITY: AN INTRODUCTION IN BROAD STROKES

Diversity is typically conceptualized as referring to differences between individuals on any attribute that may lead to the perception that another person is different from self (Jackson 1992, Triandis et al. 1994, Williams & O'Reilly 1998). In principle, diversity research may concern any possible dimension of differentiation, but in practice diversity research has primarily focused on differences in gender, age, ethnicity, tenure, educational background, and functional background (Milliken & Martins 1996, Williams & O'Reilly 1998). The key question in diversity research is how differences between work group members affect group process and performance, as well as group member attitudes and subjective well-being. To address this question, diversity research has largely been guided by two research traditions: the social categorization perspective and the information/decision-making perspective (Williams & O'Reilly 1998). This is not to say, however, that these are well-articulated theoretical perspectives in diversity research. Often they represent a more loosely defined emphasis on either the preference to work with similar others or the value of diverse information, knowledge, and perspectives.

The starting point for the social categorization perspective is the notion that similarities and differences between work group members form the basis for categorizing self and others into groups, distinguishing between similar ingroup members and dissimilar outgroup members. In diverse groups, this may mean that people distinguish subgroups

Social categorization perspective: differences between work group members may engender the classification of others as either ingroup/similar or outgroup/dissimilar, categorizations that may disrupt group process

Information/ decision-making perspective: diversity may introduce differences in knowledge, expertise, and perspectives that may help work groups reach higher quality and more creative and innovative outcomes within the work group. People tend to favor ingroup members over outgroup members, to trust ingroup members more, and to be more willing to cooperate with them (Brewer 1979, Brewer & Brown 1998, Tajfel & Turner 1986). The result of such categorization processes may be that work groups function more smoothly when they are homogeneous than when they are more diverse, and that group members are more satisfied with and attracted to the group when it is homogeneous and they are similar to the other group members. This analysis is corroborated by findings of, for instance, higher group cohesion (e.g., O'Reilly et al. 1989), lower turnover (e.g., Wagner et al. 1984), and higher performance (e.g., Murnighan & Conlon 1991) in more homogeneous groups.

The social categorization perspective is complemented by the similarity/attraction perspective (Williams & O'Reilly 1998), which does not concern social groups but rather focuses on interpersonal similarity (primarily in attitudes and values) as determinants of interpersonal attraction (Berscheid & Reis 1998, Byrne 1971). The similarity/attraction perspective arrives at the same basic prediction as the social categorization perspective in diversity research, that people prefer to work with similar others (Jackson 1992).

In contrast to the social categorization (and similarity/attraction) perspective, the information/decision-making perspective emphasizes the positive effects of work group diversity. The starting point for this perspective is the notion that diverse groups are likely to possess a broader range of task-relevant knowledge, skills, and abilities, and members with different opinions and perspectives. This gives diverse groups a larger pool of resources that may be helpful in dealing with nonroutine problems. It may also set the stage for more creative and innovative group performance because the need to integrate diverse information and reconcile diverse perspectives may stimulate thinking that is more creative and prevent groups from moving to premature consensus on issues that need careful consideration (van Knippenberg et al. 2004). Corroborating this analysis, some studies find an association of diversity with higher performance and innovation (e.g., Bantel & Jackson 1989).

In their simplest form (a main effect of diversity), neither analysis is supported. Evidence for the positive effects as well as for the negative effects of diversity is highly inconsistent (Bowers et al. 2000, Webber & Donahue 2001, Williams & O'Reilly 1998) and raises the question of whether, and how, the perspectives on the positive and the negative effects of diversity can be reconciled and integrated. Because the information/decision-making perspective focuses on task performance, whereas the social categorization perspective seems to put the relational aspect more center stage, some scholars have concluded that diversity may be good for group performance while at the same time it is bad for interpersonal relations and attitudes toward the work group (e.g., Triandis et al. 1994). Given the relationship between group interaction and cohesiveness on the one hand and group performance on the other hand (De Dreu & Weingart 2003, Mullen & Copper 1994), however, it is difficult to see how the outcomes described by the social categorization and the information/decision-making perspectives could occur simultaneously. Indeed, there hardly seems to be evidence for both occurring at the same time (but see Keller 2001).

One thing that stands out in this respect is that the field has been dominated by studies focusing on "main effects," testing relationships between dimensions of diversity and outcomes without taking potentially moderating variables into account (Jackson & Joshi 2004, Pelled et al. 1999). Narrative reviews and meta-analyses alike seem to corroborate the conclusions that this main effects approach is unable to account for the effects of diversity adequately (Bowers et al. 2000, Webber & Donahue 2001, Williams & O'Reilly 1998). It seems time to declare the bankruptcy of the main effects approach and to argue for models that are more complex and that consider moderating variables in explaining the effects of diversity. Accordingly, the present review largely disregards studies of potential main effects in favor of studies identifying moderators of the effects of diversity.

This focus on moderators is important not only to identify when diversity may be expected to have positive or negative effects, but also because it is informative about the processes underlying the influence of work group diversity (i.e., moderator effects observed may corroborate conclusions about the processes in operation). Attention to these processes is important, because another major impediment to the advancement of the field is a tendency to assume rather than assess mediating processes. When a social categorization perspective is argued to predict negative effects of diversity and these are observed, the implicit conclusion is that social categorization processes occurred even when no empirical evidence for such processes is provided. In similar vein, often the occurrence of information/decision-making processes is concluded from the observation of positive effects of diversity on group performance without evidence regarding the processes taking place during group interaction. The predicted outcome is not necessarily evidence of the predicted process, however, and relying on outcomes to determine process runs the risk of resulting in misleading conclusions. The field may thus benefit from more attention to the processes translating work group diversity into outcomes, and the current review emphasizes studies that shed light on these mediating processes. First, however, we address another issue that emerged more recently—the possibility that conceptualizations of diversity that are more complex may yield more insight into the effects of diversity.

CONCEPTUALIZING DIVERSITY

Diversity may be seen as a characteristic of a social grouping (i.e., group, organization, so-

ciety) that reflects the degree to which there are objective or subjective differences between people within the group (without presuming that group members are necessarily aware of objective differences or that subjective differences are strongly related to more objective differences). Such a definition and similar definitions coined by others (see above) leave unanswered a couple of important questions about how to deal with diversity conceptually, however, and some of these are quite salient in current research in diversity. Our review of the field suggests that four issues in this respect especially warrant attention: first, the possibility to better understand the effects of diversity by distinguishing between different types of diversity; second, the potential added value of moving beyond the study of demographic and functional diversity; third, the potential added value of conceptualizations of diversity that move beyond simple dispersion; and fourth, the notion that diversity's effects may be better understood if the influence of different dimensions of diversity is studied in interactions rather than as additive effects.

Typologies of Diversity

To introduce some higher-order structure in diversity research, a number of researchers have proposed typologies that may be used to classify different dimensions of diversity. These typologies include the distinction between readily observable demographic attributes (e.g., gender, race/ethnicity, age) that may be less job related and less easily discernable, and more job-related attributes such as differences in educational or functional background (Jackson 1992, Jehn et al. 1999, Milliken & Martins 1996, Pelled et al. 1999, Schneider & Northcraft 1999, Tsui et al. 1992; cf. Harrison et al. 1998). In addition, a number of researchers have argued that it is also important to take into account differences that may not be readily visible but are not always job-related either, such as differences in personality, attitudes, and values (Bowers et al. 2000, Harrison et al. 1998, Jehn et al. 1999).

The question from the current perspective is, Do these typologies help in making sense of the effects of diversity?

Some researchers have proposed that demographic diversity, as well as diversity in personality, values, and attitudes, has negative effects on group performance and affective-evaluative responses to the group, whereas diversity on more information-related dimensions, such as education and functional background, is more likely to have positive effects on group performance (Jehn et al. 1999, Pelled et al. 1999). Although this reasoning makes intuitive sense, it does not seem to be supported by the data. In support of the moderating role of diversity type, Jehn et al. (1999) found that informational diversity was positively related to group performance and commitment, whereas perceived value diversity (which does not necessarily reflect actual value diversity; cf. Harrison et al. 2002) was negatively related to group performance and group member satisfaction, intent to remain, and commitment. Contrary to predictions, however, demographic diversity was unrelated to group performance and was positively related to member satisfaction, intent to remain, and commitment, as well as to perceived work group performance. Pelled et al.'s (1999) hypotheses implied that functional diversity would be positively related to group performance, whereas demographic diversity would be negatively related to group performance, but neither type of diversity was related to group performance.

Other studies incorporating both demographic and informational dimensions of diversity report very similar relationships for, on the one hand, demographic diversity and presumably more job-related dimensions of diversity and, on the other hand, outcomes such as group performance, information use, and learning as well as team member satisfaction and commitment (Dahlin et al. 2005, Schippers et al. 2003, van der Vegt & Bunderson 2005). Bunderson & Sutcliffe (2002) report positive and negative relationships with team process and performance for different forms of informational diversity. In addition, there are also other reports of positive effects of demographic diversity (e.g., Bantel & Jackson 1989) and negative effects of informational diversity (e.g., Simons et al. 1999) that run against the proposed moderating role of diversity type. Together these findings suggest that the distinction between diversity types is not associated with differential relationships with outcome variables. Most importantly, perhaps, meta-analyses do not support the notion of type of diversity as moderator of the positive versus the negative effects of diversity either—although it should be noted that these meta-analyses only covered a subset of the studies that could potentially have been included. In a meta-analysis of 13 studies, Bowers et al. (2000) distinguished gender, personality, attitude, and ability diversity and found no reliable relationship between any form of diversity and group performance. In a meta-analysis of 24 studies, Webber & Donahue (2001) distinguished between highly job-related and less job-related diversity and found no reliable relationships for either form of diversity, neither with group performance nor with group cohesiveness.

An important conclusion to emerge from the current state of the art is that, contrary to what seems popular belief, the positive versus the negative effects of diversity are not associated with job-related informational diversity versus less job-related demographic diversity, neither for group performance nor for more affective/evaluative responses to the group. Interestingly, this means not only that organizations should be a bit more cautious in their enthusiasm for functional diversity, but also that they can be more optimistic about the possibilities to benefit from demographic diversity.

The inability to reliably link the positive and negative effects of diversity to types of diversity has led van Knippenberg et al. (2004) to propose that diversity research abandon attempts to explain the effects of diversity through typologies of diversity. In contrast, they propose that all dimensions of diversity may in principle elicit social categorization processes as well as information/decision-making processes, because all dimensions of diversity in principle both provide a basis for differentiation and may be associated with differences in task-relevant information and perspectives. Following this conclusion, and in deviation from earlier reviews (e.g., Milliken & Martins 1996, Williams & O'Reilly 1998), we do not structure the current review by diversity dimension, but rather we aim to highlight the processes that may be engendered by diversity and the contingencies of these processes.

Beyond Demographic and Functional Diversity

Perhaps understandably, diversity research has mainly focused on demographic and functional/educational diversity. Other dimensions of diversity that may be less easily captured by the existing typologies have received less attention, although they may be equally relevant to our understanding of group functioning. For instance, a growing number of studies link diversity in group member personality (mostly conceptualized in terms of the five-factor model of personality; Costa & Macrae 1992) to group performance and more processes-related measures, such as team social integration (Barrick et al. 1998; Barry & Stewart 1997; Harrison et al. 2002; Mohammed & Angell 2003, 2004; Neuman et al. 1999; Neuman & Wright 1999; Schneider et al. 1998; Van Vianen & De Dreu 2001). So far, the picture emerging from these studies is quite inconsistent for the relationship between personality diversity and group process and performance, and further research addressing the contingencies of these relationships seems in order.

Others have also pointed to diversity in attitudes and values as an influence on group functioning (Hoffman & Maier 1961). Here, too, findings are highly inconsistent. Some studies suggest that diversity in attitudes and values may be associated with negative outcomes (Harrison et al. 1998, 2002; Jehn & Mannix 2001; also see Jehn et al. 1997, 1999). Some of these studies also show, however, that diversity in attitudes and values may be associated with positive outcomes (e.g., social integration) or may be unrelated to these outcomes (Harrison et al. 1998, 2002). The conclusion seems justified that diversity in attitudes and values, too, is worthy of research attention, but that we need more complex models to capture the potential influence of this diversity (cf. Harrison et al. 1998).

Socially shared cognition and affect typically is not considered in diversity research, but it arguably concerns dimensions of diversity. Research in socially shared cognition shows how individuals' understanding of their team and their task (conceptualized as task representations, Tindale et al. 1996; mental models, Cannon-Bowers et al. 1993; team schemas, Rentsch & Hall 1994; or beliefs, Cannon & Edmondson 2001) may be shared among group members to a greater or lesser extent [i.e., group members may be more or less similar in their understanding of the team and the task (Mohammed & Ringseis 2001; also see Colquitt et al. 2002, Klein et al. 2001, Schneider et al. 2002)]. Because the level of sharedness may affect group performance (Mathieu et al. 2005), diversity in such team- and task-relevant cognitions deserves a place on the agenda of diversity research. In a similar vein, affective states (i.e., moods, emotions) may be shared to a greater or lesser extent (George 1990, Totterdell 2000, Totterdell et al. 1998), and the extent to which affect is shared has been shown to be related to group cooperation and conflict (Barsade et al. 2000). Affective diversity thus also warrants further research.

In sum, then, without denying the importance of the study of demographic diversity and diversity in functional and educational background, many other dimensions of diversity may influence group process and performance and therefore deserve research attention. This would seem to hold all the more because an understanding of the effects of demographic diversity seems at least partially to require an understanding of the more psychological dimensions that demographic differences are often presumed to be associated with, such as differences in attitudes, values, and perspectives (Beyer et al. 1997, Chattopadhyay et al. 1999, Cox et al. 1991). That is, analyses of demographic diversity to a certain extent treat demographic differences as proxies for deeper underlying differences (Priem et al. 1999), and investigating this proposed link as well as the processes governing the influence of these underlying differences may increase our understanding of the influence of demographic diversity.

Beyond Dispersion

Diversity research has typically operationalized diversity as the dispersion of group members' positions on a given dimension of diversity. Differences between group members are reflected in indices of the extent to which group members differ from each other, such as the standard deviation, Euclidian distance (Tsui et al. 1992), Blau (1977), and Teachman (1980) indices, and the coefficient of variation (for a detailed discussion of these measures, see Harrison & Klein 2005, Harrison & Sin 2005), or simply by distinguishing groups with high versus low dispersion. Harrison & Klein (2005) note that dimensions of diversity may differ in the extent to which they represent different positions on a continuum (e.g., attitudes), different nominal categories (e.g., gender), or different positions that are associated with greater or lesser power or status (e.g., educational level). Differences between group members on different dimensions may therefore mean different things, and Harrison & Klein urge researchers to be more explicit about their conceptualization of diversity (e.g., whether it associated with status or power differentials), and to choose operationalizations that are commensurate with their conceptualization (also see Sørenson 2002, Williams & Meân 2004).

Moreover, a couple of considerations suggest that there are potential benefits in complementing simple dispersion models with more complex conceptualizations and operationalizations of diversity (cf. Chan 1998, Kozlowski & Bell 2003; also see the discussion of faultlines below). Research on relational demography (i.e., focusing on individual dissimilarity to the work group rather than on diversity) shows that being dissimilar to the work group more negatively affects people who are typically in majority positions in Western organizations (i.e., men, Caucasians) than it does people who are more often in the minority position (i.e., women, members of ethnic minorities; Chatman & O'Reilly 2004, Tsui et al. 1992). To the extent that these outcomes for dissimilar group members affect group functioning and performance (e.g., through lower satisfaction, lower cohesion, and higher turnover), we might expect groups with, for instance, a female minority to function better than groups with a male minority. Whether or not this is the case needs to be tested, but the point is that simple dispersion models do not capture these more subtle effects because they treat a group with a male minority and a group with a comparable female minority (e.g., eight men and two women versus two men and eight women) as equally diverse (cf. Harrison & Klein 2005).

Another consideration is that once a given background or perspective is represented by one or two members (e.g., members with a particular functional background within a cross-functional team), adding additional representatives of this background or perspective to the group might add relatively less to the group's potential to perform well—i.e., sometimes diversity may be more a dichotomy (present versus absent) than a matter of degree. The effects of diversity may also be contingent on the mean level of the diversity dimension, as illustrated in Barsade et al.'s (2000) finding that the relationship of top management team diversity in positive affect with group conflict and cooperation was contingent on the mean level of positive affect in the team.

Such complex conceptualizations of diversity are acknowledged more in theoretical analyses than in empirical research, but they do seem to have the potential to enrich our understanding of the effects of diversity, and research following up on some of these notions should be highly worthwhile. In this respect, it is important to note that organizational surveys typically do not tap into the whole range of potential group compositions (e.g., work groups dominated by ethnic minorities tend to be rare in most samples), and more sophisticated conceptualizations of diversity might suggest that this poses a threat to the conclusions that may be reached on the basis of studies relying on more traditional dispersion models (Harrison & Klein 2005).

Faultlines: Interacting Dimensions of Diversity

Traditionally, diversity research has focused on the effects of different dimensions of diversity in isolation or in additive models, not taking into account the possibility that the effects of a dimension of diversity may be contingent on diversity on other dimensions. Research on the salience of social categorizations (Oakes et al. 1994, Turner et al. 1987) and cross-categorization (Brewer 1995, Crisp et al. 2002) suggests that the correlation between different dimensions of differentiation influences the likelihood that diversity elicits subcategorization processes. It might therefore be better to think of work group diversity as an interaction of differences on different dimensions than to look only at the additive effects of dimensions of diversity.

Lau & Murnighan (1998) coined the term "faultlines" to refer to combinations of correlated dimensions of diversity that yield a clear basis for differentiation between subgroups (i.e., implying both between-group differences and within-group similarity; Turner et al. 1987). A group composition in which all the men are relatively old and all the women

are relatively young, for example, is more likely to elicit subcategorization than is a composition in which gender and age are unrelated. The stronger the diversity faultline, the more likely subcategorizations should be to arise, and the greater the chance of disruptions of group functioning.

In support of this proposition, Li & Hambrick (2005) found that a faultline index was negatively related to self-rated group performance and that this relationship was mediated by relational conflict and behavioral integration (cf. social integration). Sawyer et al. (2005) compared informationally diverse decision-making groups that were ethnically homogeneous (all Caucasian) with groups that had an ethnic minority member present who was either also in the informational minority (i.e., a faultline) or in the informational majority (i.e., crosscutting informational and ethnic diversity), and reported that groups with crosscutting dimensions of diversity outperformed homogeneous and faultline groups. In a similar vein, Homan & van Knippenberg (2003) showed that cross-categorization leads to a more favorable group process than does a faultline dividing the group equally (also see Phillips et al. 2004). More-indirect evidence of the disruptive influence of faultlines was provided by Lau & Murnighan (2005), who found that faultlines are associated with less positive relationships of communication between subgroups with learning, psychological safety, group satisfaction, and expected group performance.

The evidence is less consistent, however, than one would like it to be. Lau & Murnighan (2005) also observed that faultlines were associated with lower relational conflict, and higher satisfaction and psychological safety. Sawyer et al. (2005) did not observe differences between faultline and homogeneous groups, and Phillips et al. (2004) found that a faultline involving a single dissimilar member resulted in better decision-making performance than did a situation in which single-member dissimilarity and informational differences crosscut each other.

Faultlines: when positions on different dimensions of diversity are correlated, the combination of diversity on these dimensions may suggest a clear distinction between subgroups

The possibility that faultlines have a curvilinear relationship with outcomes does not explain the above inconsistencies, but it hints at the possibility that the effects of faultlines are less straightforward than initially conceived. Both Gibson & Vermeulen (2003) and Thatcher et al. (2003) found curvilinear relationships in which moderate faultlines were associated with outcomes that were more positive (team learning, morale, performance, and reduced conflict). However, both studies used faultline measures where moderate faultlines might also be labeled moderate cross-categorization, and it is unclear to what extent these findings point to the benefits of moderate faultlines (i.e., eliciting subgroup categorization) or of crosscutting dimensions of diversity (i.e., diversity without associated subgroup salience).

Earley & Mosakowski (2000) showed that the faultline notion could also be applied to a single dimension of diversity when the dimension has multiple nominal categories. They found that teams with members from two different countries showed greater evidence of subcategorization and performed more poorly than did both nationality-homogeneous teams and teams that consisted of members from several different countries (i.e., the two-nationality composition arguably represents a stronger faultline).

The faultline and cross-categorization concepts have added value in terms of explaining diversity effects, but the relationship between faultlines and outcomes is not clear-cut. In part, this may reflect problems with the operationalization of faultlines. It might be worthwhile, for instance, to consider the possibility that there are asymmetries in the effects of faultlines that are not captured by current faultline measures. For example, along similar lines as discussed in the previous section, a faultline between a male Caucasian minority and a female Asian majority might affect group functioning differently than a faultline between a male Caucasian majority and a female Asian minority. In part, the observed inconsistency in findings may also reflect a need to focus on the contingencies of the effects of faultlines (cf. Gibson & Vermeulen 2003) because, for instance, salient categorizations only under certain circumstances translate into disruptive intergroup biases (van Knippenberg et al. 2004). And clearly, research actually assessing the categorization processes implied by faultline theory (cf. Earley & Mosakowski 2000) is needed to explicitly test predictions about the assumed processes.

PROCESSES UNDERLYING THE INFLUENCE OF DIVERSITY AND THEIR CONTINGENCIES

An important issue is that not much clear evidence exists for the processes implied by the social categorization (and similarity/attraction) and information/decision-making perspectives identified by Williams & O'Reilly (1998). This is due in part to the fact that many studies did not include process measures. A complicating factor in this respect is that neither the social categorization perspective on work group diversity nor the information/decision-making perspective represents a clearly articulated theoretical framework; rather, the perspectives are more like loosely defined applications of social categorization theories and notions about group information processing and decision making.

In the following sections, we address the empirical evidence for the processes underlying the effects of work group diversity and the factors that moderate these processes. Most of the evidence in diversity research is not easily and unambiguously interpreted in terms of social categorization and information/decision-making processes, however, and a substantial part of our discussion concerns studies that may be consistent (to a greater or lesser extent) with the social categorization and information/decision-making perspectives without providing direct evidence to that effect. In that respect, we identify three (sets of) factors that are receiving increased research attention as moderators of the effects of diversity: interdependence, time, and diversity mind-sets.

Social Categorization Processes

Diversity research has typically applied insights from research in social categorization and intergroup relations in a straightforward way, predicting that differences between people may elicit social categorization processes (stereotypic perceptions of dissimilar others, subgroup formation, intergroup biases) that disrupt group functioning and lower affective/evaluative responses to the group. In support of this analysis, there is evidence that diversity may elicit subcategorization. Earley & Mosakowski (2000) assessed subgroup categorization and common group identity (although the latter measure arguably reflects cohesiveness more than social categorization) and found that groups with stronger faultlines had a stronger sense of subgroups and a weaker common identity. Moreover, they found evidence that common identity mediated the relationship between faultlines and satisfaction (but not performance). These findings were not replicated in a second study, though.

Research on relational demography also yields evidence for social categorization processes, although this should be treated more carefully because, as noted above, individual dissimilarity does not necessarily reflect group diversity. Chattopadhyay et al. (2004b) found that dissimilarity to the work group lowered individuals' self-categorization as a member of the group. Randel (2002) found that group gender composition affected the salience of male group members' gender identity (cf. Mehra et al. 1998) and that identity salience moderated the relationship between gender composition and relational conflict (i.e., suggesting a translation of categorization into intergroup bias; also see Randel & Jaussi 2003). Evidence that diversity affects social categorization thus is quite modest, and it would seem important for future research to estab-

lish the validity of this basic tenet of the social categorization perspective on work group diversity.

A second question is whether there is evidence of an association of work group diversity with intergroup bias in perceptions, evaluations, and social interaction. Social categorization processes are presumed to engender more favorable attitudes toward ingroup than outgroup others, more trust, more willingness to cooperate, and generally smoother interaction with ingroup than with outgroup others. In line with this argument, Chatman & Flynn (2001) found that demographic diversity was associated with lower self-rated team cooperativeness. Consistent with the idea that computer-mediated interaction removes social categorization cues (Sproull & Kiesler 1986), Bhappu et al. (1997) found that computer-mediated communication in gender-diverse groups showed fewer signs of intergroup bias (operationalized as differential attention to same-gender versus other-gender communication) than did face-to-face communication. Chattopadhyay (1999) observed in a study of relational demography that trust in peers mediated the negative relationship between individual dissimilarity and organizational citizenship behavior (see also Chattopadhyay & George 2001). None of these studies presented direct evidence of social categorization processes, however, so caution is in order in concluding that these studies provide evidence of intergroup bias.

Research focusing on social/behavioral integration and relational conflict similarly yields evidence that is consistent with a social categorization interpretation. Randel's (2002) findings for the role of identity salience in relational conflict probably provide the most persuasive evidence of social categorization disrupting group process in diverse work groups. Other studies offer evidence that is more indirect because they included no direct measure of categorization (e.g., the association observed between diversity faultlines and behavioral integration by Li & Hambrick 2005). Evidence of negative relationships between diversity and social integration (Harrison et al. 1998, 2002), and positive relationships between diversity and relational conflict (Pelled et al. 1999) that also mediated the relationship with outcomes (Bayazit & Mannix 2003, Jehn et al. 1999, Knight et al. 1999, Mohammed & Angell 2004), is consistent with the social categorization prediction. However, it does not prove that these relationships follow from social categorization processes rather than from other factors associated with diversity.

Complicating matters, evidence also links diversity to higher social integration and group identification (identification reflects self-categorization), and lower relational conflict (Polzer et al. 2002; cf. Swann et al. 2003). Building on research by Swann and colleagues on self-verification (being seen by others as one sees oneself; for an overview, see Swann et al. 2004), Polzer et al. (2002) tested interactions between congruence of group members' self-views and the views other group members have of them (arguably a proxy for self-verification) and demographic and functional diversity. They found that whereas higher diversity tended to be associated with more negative outcome when congruence was low, it actually tended to be associated with more positive outcome when congruence was high. For the social categorization perspective to account for the effects of diversity adequately, it would thus seem that it should also be able to incorporate positive relationships of diversity with group identification and group interaction (cf. van Knippenberg & Haslam 2003).

A number of studies thus yield results that are consistent with a social categorization analysis of the effects of work group diversity. Surprisingly few studies, however, directly assessed social categorization processes, and results are inconsistent enough to raise doubts about the extent to which social categorization processes are in operation. Moreover, without supporting process evidence, some of the negative relationships between diversity and group process may also be interpreted as reflecting the consequences of misunderstanding and disagreement per se (i.e., a more dysfunctional side of information/decision-making processes) rather than social categorization. Empirical attention to the actual categorization processes therefore would be warranted to substantiate the social categorization analysis of work group diversity.

It might also be useful to extend social categorization (and similarity/attraction) analyses with insights from the study of social networks in organizations (Brass et al. 2004). Social network analysis has attempted to capture relationships between group members in terms of the strength and nature of their ties, and has proven useful in capturing the influence of diversity on the relationships formed by group members (Klein et al. 2004, Reagans & Zuckerman 2001). Network analysis may help to paint a more elaborate picture of the social relations within a work group that moves beyond the relatively simple notion of a split in subgroups and thus enable a more fine-grained analysis of social categorization processes. Moreover, it may also prove useful in capturing the external (i.e., outside of the work group) network of group members as it may be affected by diversity (Reagans et al. 2004).

Models that are more sophisticated and that focus on the contingencies of subcategorization and intergroup bias (van Knippenberg et al. 2004) also seem in order. In this respect, research on the salience of social categorizations (Oakes et al. 1994, Turner et al. 1987) shows that there is more to social categorization than just differences between people. As reflected in the notion of diversity faultlines, some combinations of differences (i.e., those that result in high between-group differences and within-group similarities) are more likely to elicit subcategorizations than are others. In this sense, diversity is also context: In more-diverse organizations, work group diversity may be less salient (cf. Martins et al. 2003; also see Brief et al. 2005, Joshi et al. 2005).

In addition, for diversity to elicit a particular categorization, the categorization also has to make sense within individuals' psychological frame of reference (an issue that diversity research so far has hardly touched upon): In order to become salient, a categorization should not only capture similarities and differences between people, but should also be meaningful to the individual (Turner et al. 1987). Moreover, as van Knippenberg et al. (2004) argue, it is intergroup bias (favoring one's own subgroup) that may disrupt group process and not categorization per se (i.e., the perception of subgroups), and categorization only translates into intergroup bias under certain circumstances. Thus, diversity research might benefit from a more fine-grained analysis of the factors that elicit social categorization as well as of the factors that translate social categorization into intergroup bias.

Information/Decision-Making Processes

At the core of the information/decision-making perspectives lies the notion that work group diversity may be associated with differences in information, knowledge, and perspectives, and that this diversity may benefit group performance. These informational differences are not limited to what are often seen as informational or job-relevant dimensions of diversity (Tsui & O'Reilly 1989, van Knippenberg et al. 2004). As van Knippenberg et al. (2004) outline, this implies that at the core of the positive effects of diversity emphasized in the information/decision-making perspective lies elaboration of task-relevant information—the group-level exchange, processing, and integration of diverse information and perspectives (cf. Hinsz et al. 1997). In line with this analysis, Earley & Mosakowski (2000) found that a measure of team communication that seems to be closely aligned with this notion of elaboration mediated the relationship of group diversity and performance (although this finding was not replicated in a second study), and Dahlin et al. (2005) found that (moderate) diversity was associated with greater information use.

Related to the proposed role of elaboration of task-relevant information is the notion that divergent viewpoints may stimulate team reflexivity. Team reflexivity refers to the team's careful consideration and discussion of its functioning and is proposed to result in team learning and improved team performance (Schippers et al. 2005; West 1996, 2002). Just as diversity may stimulate elaboration of task-relevant information, divergent perspectives on the task that may be associated with diversity may invite a team to reflect on its own functioning. In support of this proposition, Schippers et al. (2003) found that team reflexivity mediated the (moderated) relationship between diversity and team performance, commitment, and satisfaction. Providing further support for this perspective, Gibson & Vermeulen (2003) found that diversity may be positively related to team learning behavior (cf. reflexivity), and Van der Vegt & Bunderson (2005) found that team learning behavior partly mediated the relationship between expertise diversity and team performance.

A number of researchers working from a related perspective have pointed to the role of task conflict—disagreements about the task performed (Jehn et al. 1999, Lovelace et al. 2001, Pelled et al. 1999). Diversity is proposed to have the potential to stimulate task conflict through its associated differences in viewpoints, ideas, and opinions, and task conflict is argued to engender more careful consideration of the task at hand. Consistent with this notion, Jehn et al. (1999) found that task conflict mediated the positive relationship between informational diversity and group performance. Inconsistent with this reasoning, however, they also found that perceived value diversity positively correlated with task conflict (cf. Jehn & Mannix 2001), while perceived value diversity was negatively related to performance. Pelled et al. (1999) also found evidence that functional background diversity was positively related to task conflict (as do Lovelace et al. 2001), but found no relationship between diversity and group performance.

Raising further doubts about the proposed role of task conflict, the notion that task conflict mediates the positive influence of diversity on group performance is at odds with the meta-analytic finding that task conflict is negatively related to group performance (De Dreu & Weingart 2003). Indeed, as van Knippenberg et al. (2004) argue, although task conflict might engender elaboration of task-relevant information and thus foster group performance under certain conditions (cf. Lovelace et al. 2001), task conflict does not necessarily do so, nor is task conflict a prerequisite for elaboration of task-relevant information to occur. Accordingly, it may be the elaboration of task-relevant information per se and not task conflict that drives the positive effects of diversity, but studies assessing both task conflict and group-level information processing are required to address this issue.

If positive effects of diversity on performance flow from group information processing, then the positive effects of diversity should be more likely on tasks with stronger information-processing and/or decision-making requirements (van Knippenberg et al. 2004). In support of this proposition, Jehn et al. (1999) found that informational diversity was more positively related to group performance on less-routine tasks, and Bowers et al.'s (2000) meta-analysis showed that diversity was positively related to group performance on more complex tasks but was negatively related on simpler tasks. Although this is no evidence for the actual elaboration of information assumed to underlie this moderating effect, these findings are consistent with the information/decision-making perspective.

There thus is some evidence for the processes implied in the information/decision-making perspective, although studies assessing these processes are generally somewhat lacking. Moreover, there seems to be some controversy about the role of task conflict. It therefore seems that diversity research may benefit from more theoretical as well as empirical attention to the information process-ing and decision-making processes that are presumed to drive the positive effects of diversity. In addition, in view of the lack of support for an overall positive effect of diversity, theoretical models of the contingencies of information/decision-making processes are required. Research on social information processing, for instance, suggests that processing motivation and ability are key determinants of in-depth processing of information (Chaiken & Trope 1999). Motivation and ability have received little attention in diversity research, yet they potentially also are important determinants of groups' use of their diversity of information and perspectives (van Knippenberg et al. 2004).

Social Categorization Processes As Moderator of Information/Decision-Making Processes

The social categorization perspective and the information/decision-making perspective have largely developed along separate lines, and there are few studies considering the interaction between social categorization and information/decision-making processes. Yet, because intergroup bias may render individuals less open to communication from dissimilar others (van Knippenberg 1999), intergroup bias engendered by diversity may disrupt group information processing and thus stand in the way of realizing the potential benefits of diversity (van Knippenberg et al. 2004).

Consistent with this proposition, Jehn et al. (1999) found that higher perceived value diversity and demographic diversity were associated with less-positive relationships between informational diversity and indicators of group performance. In a similar vein, Phillips et al.'s (2004) finding that groups that were split equally along a faultline dealt less successfully with their informational diversity is consistent with this argument (also see Homan & van Knippenberg 2003). Neither study includes measures of social categorization processes, though, so some caution is in order in attributing these findings to the disruptive influence of social categorization processes. Lau & Murnighan's (2005) observation that faultlines disrupted the positive relationship between intersubgroup communication (cf. Bhappu et al. 1997) and positive group outcomes is also in line with this argument. Their finding that faultlines were also associated with less relational conflict and greater psychological safety and satisfaction raises some doubts about a straightforward social categorization interpretation of these findings, however. Although the available evidence thus seems reasonably consistent with the proposition that diversity may disrupt group information processing, the evidence for the actual operation of social categorization and information/decision-making processes is largely missing.

A possibility that has received less attention is that social categorization processes may also stimulate group information processing. A line of research by Phillips and colleagues hints at this possibility, suggesting that informationally diverse groups that contain a member who is dissimilar to the other members of the group are more likely to make effective use of their informational diversity than are more-homogeneous groups, presumably because dissimilarity alerts the group to potential associated differences in information (Phillips 2003; Phillips et al. 2004, 2005; Phillips & Loyd 2005). However, because measures of categorization are missing from these studies, it is not clear whether these effects can be attributed to social categorization processes.

Either way, the work by Phillips and colleagues raises the following questions: Under which conditions is greater diversity beneficial to a group's use of distributed information, and under which conditions is diversity more likely to disrupt group information processing? As Phillips et al. (2004) show, whether social categorization processes point to a solo minority member or to equal-sized subgroups may be one factor (but see Sawyer et al. 2005), but a more comprehensive account of the

contingencies of these effects awaits future research.

Cooperation and Interdependence

Group members may depend to a greater or lesser extent on each other for task performance (i.e., task interdependence; Wageman 1995) and for outcomes that may flow from task performance (i.e., outcome interdependence; Wageman 1995). Moreover, this interdependence may be more cooperative or competitive in nature (i.e., own and others' interests may align or conflict). A number of researchers have proposed that the degree and nature of interdependence between group members moderates the relationship between work group diversity and outcomes. Such a moderating role is consistent with both the social categorization and the information/decision-making perspective. From a social categorization perspective, higher, more cooperative interdependence between group members may focus group members on the common group identity and distract from subgroup categorizations (Gaertner & Dovidio 2000). In addition, interdependence may also facilitate intergroup contact and be conducive to more harmonious relations between different groups (Pettigrew 1998). At the same time, the need to collaborate may also set the stage for group information processing because it may invite information exchange and discussion. From both perspectives, cooperative interdependence would thus be expected to be associated with effects of diversity that are more positive.

In support of this notion, Chatman et al. (1998; also see Chatman & Spataro 2005) in a study of relational demography showed that in groups with collectivistic norms emphasizing cooperation (versus individualistic norms emphasizing competition and independence), dissimilarity is more positively associated with group process and performance. Mohammed & Angell (2004) found that gender diversity was associated with relational conflict only when group members were less concerned with cooperative relations, and that time urgency (an individual difference variable) diversity was positively related to relational conflict when team process was low rather than high in terms of cooperation, communication, and task-oriented leadership. It should be noted, however, that they did not obtain similar relationships for ethnic diversity and extraversion diversity, and that they observed these relationships at time 1 but not at time 2. Schippers et al. (2003) reported that diversity was positively related to team reflexivity (i.e., arguably an indicator of information/decision processes), self-rated group performance, and satisfaction for high-outcome interdependence and negatively for low-outcome interdependence. Jehn et al. (1999) observed that demographic diversity was more positively related to satisfaction and commitment when task interdependence was higher. Van der Vegt & Janssen (2003) found that diversity was only positively related to innovative behavior when both task and outcome interdependence were high, which suggests that it may be worthwhile to consider task and outcome interdependence in combination.

Whereas these studies are generally consistent with the notion that greater cooperative interdependence is associated with more positive relationships between diversity and outcomes, two studies suggest that the issue may be more complex and that interdependence may be a double-edged sword. Ely (2004) found that tenure and age diversity interacted with a team process measure including cooperation, such that higher scores were associated with more negative relationships between diversity and performance. Jehn & Bezrukova (2004) observed that work group cultures that were more cooperative were associated with more positive relationships between diversity and performance for some dimensions of diversity but with more negative relationships for another dimension, while group culture did not affect this relationship for yet other dimensions of diversity.

These findings suggest that the role of cooperation and interdependence may be more complex than is currently conceived, although it is also possible that more mundane explanations in terms of differences in measurement and specific conceptualizations would account for some of these observations. Either way, it would be valuable if future research would focus more on the processes underlying the effects of cooperation and interdependence and develop more-comprehensive accounts of the role of cooperation and interdependence vis-à-vis social categorization and information/decision-making perspectives on the effects of work group diversity.

Time/Team Tenure

Harrison and colleagues in particular have advanced the idea that the effects of diversity may change over time as groups gain extended experience working with each other (Harrison et al. 1998, 2002). Extended tenure may lead group members to find out that initial stereotype-based impressions about fellow group members were wrong (cf. Pettigrew 1998), thus attenuating the effects of social categorization processes. At the same time, extended tenure may also bring to the surface more hidden differences that may negatively affect group process. Extended team tenure may thus be associated with less negative as well as more negative effects of diversity. Harrison et al. (1998) link the first to surface-level demographic dimensions of diversity and the second to deep-level, more hidden dimensions of diversity.

Consistent with Harrison et al.'s (1998) proposition, a number of studies yield evidence that associations between demographic diversity and outcomes may become less negative over time (Chatman & Flynn 2001; Harrison et al. 1998, 2002; Pelled et al. 1999; Watson et al. 1993; cf. Earley & Mosakowski 2000, Sacco & Schmitt 2005), and that the associations between more hidden dimensions of diversity and outcomes may become more negative over time (Harrison et al. 1998,

2002). However, other studies yield evidence inconsistent with Harrison et al.'s (1998) proposition. Watson et al. (1998) found that demographic diversity was more negatively related to outcomes over time. Schippers et al. (2003) observed that more hidden dimensions of diversity were more strongly (and positively) related to group process and performance when team tenure was low rather than high. Mohammed & Angell (2004) found no difference between the correlates of surface-level and deep-level diversity between two measurement points.

Aside from the fact that these inconsistent findings corroborate our earlier claim that typologies of diversity do not explain the differential effects of diversity, these findings underscore that time/team tenure is a factor that may moderate the effects of diversity. Models that are more elaborate would help to predict the exact nature of this moderating effect, however. In this respect, future research may also take into account the possibility that groups need extended tenure to benefit from differences—that is, that the positive effects of diversity need some time to emerge (van Knippenberg et al. 2004).

Diversity Mind-Sets

The notion that people prefer to work with similar others in homogeneous groups features prominently in accounts of the effects of diversity. Perhaps somewhat surprisingly then, only a limited number of studies have actually focused on what people think about diversity, and on the possibility that people's ideas about diversity may influence the effects of diversity. This seems to be changing. On the individual level of analysis, some researchers have examined attitudes toward diversity and beliefs about the value of diversity (Hostager & De Meuse 2002, Strauss et al. 2003, van Knippenberg & Haslam 2003). On the group and organizational levels of analysis, attempts have been made to assess shared cognition about diversity in the form of diversity climates, cultures, or perspectives (Chen & Eastman 1997, Ely & Thomas 2001, Kossek & Zonia 1993, Mor Barak et al. 1998. Although some of these studies merely focus on evaluations of diversity, others also try to capture people's understanding of how to deal with diversity (cf. mental models; Ely & Thomas 2001, van Ginkel & van Knippenberg 2003). To capture these partly overlapping approaches to people's diversity cognitions, van Knippenberg et al. (2005) proposed the label "diversity mind-sets," which refers to people's understanding of how diversity may affect their work group or organization, their understanding of the appropriate way to deal with diversity, and their associated evaluations of diversity.

The general idea driving research on what may be summarized as diversity mind-sets is that the effects of diversity should be more positive in contexts where individuals, groups, and organizations have more favorable beliefs about and attitudes toward diversity, are more focused on harvesting the benefits of diversity, and have a better understanding of how to realize these benefits. Diversity mind-sets favoring diversity may thus be expected to prevent intergroup bias as well as to stimulate the integration of diverse information, viewpoints, and perspectives (Chen & Eastman 1997, Ely & Thomas 2001, van Knippenberg & Haslam 2003). That is, diversity mind-sets may moderate social categorization as well as information/decision-making processes. Rather than testing this moderating role, however, research has largely concentrated on developing measures of aspects of diversity mind-sets and studying their antecedents (Hostager & De Meuse 2002, Kossek & Zonia 1993, Mor Barak et al. 1998, Roberson et al. 2001, Strauss et al. 2003).

Even so, there is some evidence that diversity mind-sets favoring diversity and describing ways of realizing the benefits of diversity may be associated with effects of diversity that are more positive. R.J. Ely & D.A. Thomas (manuscript submitted; also see Ely & Thomas 2001) show that racial diversity is more positively related to performance at bank branches that are focused on learning from diversity (cf. Richard et al. 2003). Homan et al. (2004) show that gender-diverse decision-making groups are more likely to use their informational diversity when they believe in the value of diversity. van Ginkel & van Knippenberg (2003) find that groups reach higher-quality decisions when they have a shared understanding of how to deal with their informational diversity, and van Knippenberg et al. (2003) report more positive relationships between diversity and identification for group members who believe more in the value of diversity. Thus, although research on diversity mind-sets is still at an embryonic stage, it does seem to have promise.

CURVILINEAR RELATIONSHIPS

From notions about the role of group information processing follows the idea that the effects of diversity might be curvilinear. To benefit from the diversity of information, expertise, and perspectives that may be associated with dimensions of differentiation, group members should be able to understand and integrate the contributions of dissimilar others. As group members differ more in background, experience, and expertise, however, it becomes more likely that they do not share a common frame of reference (i.e., "speak the same language") that allows in-depth understanding of diverse others' input. Thus, the potentially positive effects of diversity on group performance may only obtain up to a certain level of diversity, beyond which the lack of a common frame of reference may get in the way of fully appreciating all group members' contributions (van Knippenberg et al. 2004).

In support of this proposition, researchers have reported evidence of curvilinear relationships in which moderate diversity is associated with more positive outcomes than is lower as well as higher diversity (Brodbeck 2003; Dahlin et al. 2005; V. Gonzalez-Roma, M.A. West, & C. Borrill, manuscript submit-

ted; Richard et al. 2004). Contrary to this proposition, however, Richard et al. (2004) and Dahlin et al. (2005) also find evidence for the opposite curvilinear relationship, as do Gibson & Vermeulen (2003). Further complicating matters, Van der Vegt & Bunderson (2005) found, contingent on level of team commitment, both U-shaped (high commitment) and inverted U-shaped (low commitment) relationships for the association between expertise diversity and team learning and performance.

The evidence for curvilinear effects of diversity thus is far from straightforward. Yet, echoing similar conclusions in the previous section, enough indications exist to warrant a closer look at curvilinear relationships in addition to linear relationships (also see the curvilinear effects observed for diversity faultlines). This seems especially important because the notion of curvilinear relationships also hints at the possibility that some of the inconsistent findings in diversity research might be due to restriction of range effects. That is, contingent on which part of the range is sampled, a curvilinear relationship in the population might yield a positive, a null, or a negative relationship between diversity and outcomes.

CONCLUSIONS

How much progress has research in organizational diversity made since Williams & O'Reilly (1998) assessed the state of the art? Clearly, with the increased attention to more complex conceptualizations of diversity, to the processes mediating the effects of work group diversity, and to the contingencies of these processes, our current understanding of the effects of work group diversity on group process and performance goes well beyond the 1998 state of the art. At the same time, however, much is still unclear about the effects of diversity. The increasing attention to the mediators and moderators of diversity's effects is exactly what the field needed, but some important steps still need to be made.

An important issue is that there seems to be too much ad hoc theorizing and too little development of theoretical frameworks that are more widely applied in the study of diversity. Directly related to this is the lack of empirical attention to the processes that are presumed to underlie the effects of diversity. As the current review shows, very few studies actually capture the range of processes that are implied by the reasoning underlying hypotheses and that should ideally be assessed for a proper test of the implied theoretical model. In combination with the inconsistent evidence for most propositions, this seriously impairs the field's progress. Especially when results do not confirm predictions, it would seem important to know whether diversity did not elicit the presumed processes or whether these processes were not associated with the outcomes as predicted. Also, when different perspectives may predict the same outcome through different processes, information about process would seem essential to theory development. Clearer articulation of the theoretical models driving diversity research makes more apparent which processes should be assessed to test these models, and more consistent application of these models will make clearer to what extent they provide valid accounts of the effects of diversity. In similar vein, studies of the moderators of the effects of diversity should work from clear links with the processes predicted by these theoretical models and should assess whether the proposed moderators indeed affect these processes.

To establish the causality implied in theoretical models of diversity, it is also essential that survey research is complemented by controlled experiments. An additional advantage of controlled experiments is that they typically allow for superior assessment of group processes (i.e., by behavioral observation rather than by relying on self-reports; Weingart 1997).

We have identified a number of avenues for future research that we deem to be particularly important. The development of more complex conceptualizations of diversity seems an important step in advancing our understanding of work group diversity. Further application of insights from social categorization research about the salience of social categories would also seem valuable. The emerging attention to diversity faultlines is a promising step in this direction, but this would also include research on the role of the extent to which the categorization makes sense within the individuals' psychological frame of reference and on the role of the wider organizational and societal context in which the group is embedded (e.g., the diversity of the organization as a whole). In similar vein, a focus on the factors that affect the translation of social categorization into intergroup bias would seem important. Diversity research may also benefit from greater application of insights from research on social information processing and group decision making to develop theoretical models of information/decision-making processes. Finally, exploring possible curvilinear effects of diversity in addition to linear effects may lead to important new insights and contribute to explaining some of the inconsistencies in diversity research. Given the value of an understanding of diversity at work for organizations and societies that are becoming ever more diverse, it would seem important to take on these research challenges and invest in the continued progress of this field.

SUMMARY POINTS

1. Typologies of diversity (most commonly differentiating forms of demographic and functional diversity) do not explain the differential effects that work group diversity may have on group process and performance.

2. Diversity research needs to move beyond conceptualizations and operationalizations of diversity simply as dispersion on a single dimension of diversity. Rather, it should conceptualize diversity as a combination of different dimensions of differentiation, take asymmetries into account, and be open to nonlinear effects.

3. Diversity research should pay more theoretical and empirical attention to the social categorization and information/decision-making processes presumed to underlie the effects of diversity on work group performance.

4. Diversity research should pay more attention to the moderators of social categorization, intergroup bias, and information/decision-making processes.

ACKNOWLEDGMENTS

We are grateful to Susan Fiske for her guidance and advice and to Jeremy Dawson, Dave Harrison, Susan Mohammed, Kathy Phillips, Charles O'Reilly, Bill Swann, and Rolf van Dick for their valuable comments on a previous draft of this article.

LITERATURE CITED

Bantel K, Jackson S. 1989. Top management and innovations in banking: Does the composition of the team make a difference? *Strateg. Manage. J.* 10:107–24

Barrick MR, Stewart GL, Neubert MJ, Mount MK. 1998. Relating member ability and personality to work-team processes and team effectiveness. *J. Appl. Psychol.* 83:377–91

Barry B, Stewart GL. 1997. Composition, process, and performance in self-managed groups: the role of personality. *J. Appl. Psychol.* 82:62–78

Barsade SG, Ward AJ, Turner JDF, Sonnenfeld JA. 2000. To your heart's content: a model of affective diversity in top management teams. *Admin. Sci. Q.* 45:802–36

Bayazit M, Mannix EA. 2003. Should I stay or should I go? Predicting team members' intent to remain in the team. *Small Group Res.* 34:290–321

Berscheid E, Reis HT. 1998. Attraction and close relationships. In *The Handbook of Social Psychology*, ed. DT Gilbert, ST Fiske, G Lindzey, pp. 193–281. New York: McGraw-Hill

Beyer JM, Chattopadhyay P, George E, Glick WH, Ogilvie DT, Pugliese D. 1997. The selective perception of managers revisited. *Acad. Manage. J.* 40:716–37

Bhappu AD, Griffith TL, Northcraft GB. 1997. Media effects and communication bias in diverse groups. *Organ. Behav. Hum. Decis. Process.* 70:199–205

Blau PM. 1977. *Inequality and Heterogeneity*. New York: Free Press

Bowers CA, Pharmer JA, Salas E. 2000. When member homogeneity is needed in work teams. a meta-analysis. *Small Group Res.* 31:305–27

Brass DJ, Galaskiewicz J, Greve HR, Tsai W. 2004. Taking stock of networks and organizations: a multilevel perspective. *Acad. Manage. J.* 47:795–817

Brewer MB. 1979. In-group bias in the minimal intergroup situation: a cognitive-motivational analysis. *Psychol. Bull.* 86:307–24

Brewer MB. 1995. Managing diversity: the role of social identities. In *Diversity in Work Teams: Research Paradigms for a Changing Workplace*, ed. S Jackson, MN Ruderman, pp. 47–68. Washington, DC: Am. Psychol. Assoc.

Brewer MB, Brown RJ. 1998. Intergroup relations. In *Handbook of Social Psychology*, ed. DT Gilbert, ST Fiske, pp. 554–94. Boston: McGraw-Hill

Brief AP, Umphress EE, Dietz J, Butz RM, Burrows J, Scholten L. 2005. Community matters: realistic group conflict theory and the impact of diversity. *Acad. Manage. J.* 48:830–44

Brodbeck F. 2003. *Contradiction as an inhibitor and facilitator of group performance*. Presented at Eur. Cong. Work Organ. Psychol., Lisbon

Bunderson JS, Sutcliffe KM. 2002. Comparing alternative conceptualizations of functional diversity in management teams: process and performance effects. *Acad. Manage. J.* 45:875–93

Byrne D. 1971. *The Attraction Paradigm*. New York: Academic

Cannon M, Edmondson A. 2001. Confronting failure: antecedents and consequences of shared beliefs about failure in organizational work groups. *J. Organ. Behav.* 22:161–77

Cannon-Bowers JA, Salas E, Converse S. 1993. Shared mental models in expert team decision making. In *Individual and Group Decision Making: Current Directions*, ed. NJ Castellan, pp. 221–46. Hillsdale, NJ: Erlbaum

Chaiken S, Trope Y. 1999. *Dual Process Theories in Social Psychology*. New York: Guilford

Chan D. 1998. Functional relations among constructs in the same content domain at different levels of analysis: a typology of composition models. *J. Appl. Psychol.* 83:234–46

Chatman JA, Flynn FJ. 2001. The influence of demographic heterogeneity on the emergence and consequences of cooperative norms in work teams. *Acad. Manage. J.* 44:956–74

Chatman JA, O'Reilly CA. 2004. Asymmetric reactions to work group sex diversity among men and women. *Acad. Manage. J.* 47:193–208

Chatman JA, Polzer JT, Barsade SG, Neale MA. 1998. Being different yet feeling similar: the influence of demographic composition and organizational culture on work processes and outcomes. *Admin. Sci. Q.* 43:749–80

Chatman JA, Spataro SE. 2005. Using self-categorization theory to understand relational demography-based variations in people's responsiveness to organizational culture. *Acad. Manage. J.* 48:321–31

Chattopadhyay P. 1999. Beyond direct and symmetrical effects: the influence of demographic dissimilarity on organizational citizenship behavior. *Acad. Manage. J.* 42:273–87

Chattopadhyay P, George E. 2001. Examining the effects of work externalization through the lens of social identity theory. *J. Appl. Psychol.* 86:781–88

Chattopadhyay P, George E, Lawrence SA. 2004b. Why does dissimilarity matter? Exploring self-categorization, self-enhancement, and uncertainty reduction. *J. Appl. Psychol.* 89:892–900

Chattopadhyay P, Glick WH, Miller CC, Huber GP. 1999. Determinants of executive beliefs: comparing functional conditioning and social influence. *Strateg. Manage. J.* 20:763–89

Chattopadhyay P, Tluchowska M, George E. 2004a. Identifying the ingroup: a closer look at the influence of demographic dissimilarity on employee social identity. *Acad. Manage. Rev.* 29:180–202

Chen CC, Eastman W. 1997. Toward a civic culture for multicultural organizations. *J. Appl. Behav. Sci.* 33:454–70

Colquitt JA, Noe RA, Jackson CL. 2002. Justice in teams: antecedents and consequences of procedural justice climate. *Pers. Psychol.* 55:83–109

Costa PTJ, McCrae RR. 1992. *The NEO-PI-R: Revised Personality Inventory (NEO-PI-R)*. Odessa, FL: Assess. Resourc.

Cox T, Lobel S, McLeod P. 1991. Effects of ethnic group cultural differences on cooperative and competitive behavior on a group task. *Acad. Manage. J.* 34:827–47

Crisp RJ, Ensari N, Hewstone M, Miller NW. 2002. A dual-route model of crossed categorization effects. In *European Review of Social Psychology*, ed. W Stroebe, M Hewstone, pp. 35–74. Hove, UK/Philadelphia, PA: Psychol. Press

Dahlin KB, Weingart LR, Hinds PJ. 2005. Team diversity and information use. *Acad. Manage. J.* 48:1107–23

De Dreu CKW, Weingart LR. 2003. Task and relationship conflict, team performance, and team member satisfaction: a meta-analysis. *J. Appl. Psychol.* 88:741–49

Earley PC, Mosakowski E. 2000. Creating hybrid team cultures: an empirical test of transnational team functioning. *Acad. Manage. J.* 43:26–49

Ely RJ. 2004. A field study of group diversity, participation in diversity education programs, and performance. *J. Organ. Behav.* 25:755–80

Ely RJ, Thomas DA. 2001. Cultural diversity at work: the effects of diversity perspectives on work group processes and outcomes. *Admin. Sci. Q.* 46:229–73

Epitropaki O, Martin R. 1999. The impact of relational demography on the quality of leader-member exchanges and employees' work attitudes and well-being. *J. Occup. Organ. Psychol.* 72:237–40

Gaertner SL, Dovidio JF. 2000. *Reducing Intergroup Bias. The Common Ingroup Identity Model.* Philadelphia, PA: Psychol. Press

George JM. 1990. Personality, affect and behavior in groups. *J. Appl. Psychol.* 75:107–16

Gibson C, Vermeulen F. 2003. A healthy divide: subgroups as a stimulus for team learning behavior. *Admin. Sci. Q.* 48:202–39

Guzzo RA, Dickson MW. 1996. Teams in organizations: recent research on performance and effectiveness. *Annu. Rev. Psychol.* 47:307–38

Harrison DA, Klein KJ. 2006. What's the difference? Diversity constructs as separation, variety, or disparity in organizations. *Acad. Manage. Rev.* In press

Harrison DA, Price KH, Bell MP. 1998. Beyond relational demography: time and the effects of surface- and deep-level diversity on work group cohesion. *Acad. Manage. J.* 41:96–107

Harrison DA, Price KH, Gavin JH, Florey AT. 2002. Time, teams, and task performance: changing effects of surface- and deep-level diversity on group functioning. *Acad. Manage. J.* 45:1029–45

Harrison DA, Sin HS. 2005. What is diversity and how should it be measured? In *Handbook of Workplace Diversity*, ed. AM Konrad, P Prasad, JK Pringle, pp. 191–216. Newbury Park, CA: Sage

Hinsz VB, Tindale RS, Vollrath DA. 1997. The emerging conceptualization of groups as information processors. *Psychol. Bull.* 121:43–64

Hoffman LR, Maier NRF. 1961. Quality and acceptance of problem solutions by members of homogeneous and heterogeneous groups. *J. Abnorm. Soc. Psychol.* 62:401–7

Homan AC, van Knippenberg D. 2003. *The beneficial effects of cross-categorizing informational and demographical diversity in groups.* Presented at Eur. Cong. Work Organ. Psychol., Lisbon

Homan AC, van Knippenberg D, Van Kleef GA, De Dreu CKW. 2004. *Managing group diversity beliefs to increase performance in diverse teams: Promoting diversity helps!* Presented at Annu. Meet. Soc. Ind. Organ. Psychol., Chicago, IL

Hostager TJ, De Meuse KP. 2002. Assessing the complexity of diversity perceptions: breadth, depth, and balance. *J. Bus. Psychol.* 17:189–206

Ilgen DR, Hollenbeck JR, Johnson M, Jundt D. 2005. Teams in organizations: from input-process-output models to IMOI models. *Annu. Rev. Psychol.* 56:517–43

Jackson SE. 1992. Team composition in organizational settings: issues in managing an increasingly diverse work force. In *Group Process and Productivity*, ed. S Worchel, W Wood, JA Simpson, pp. 136–80. Newbury Park, CA: Sage

Jackson SE, Joshi A. 2004. Diversity in social context: a multi-attribute, multilevel analysis of team diversity and sales performance. *J. Organ. Behav.* 25:675–702

Provides a thorough analysis of different ways to conceptualize and operationalize diversity, and outlines how the conceptualization adopted may affect conclusions of diversity research.

Jackson SE, Joshi A, Erhardt NL. 2003. Recent research on team and organizational diversity: SWOT analysis and implications. *J. Manage.* 29:801–30

Jehn KA, Bezrukova K. 2004. A field study of group diversity, workgroup context, and performance. *J. Organ. Behav.* 25:703–29

Jehn KA, Chadwick C, Thatcher S. 1997. To agree or not to agree: the effects of value congruence, member diversity, and conflict on workgroup outcomes. *Int. J. Confl. Manage.* 8:287–305

Jehn KA, Mannix EA. 2001. The dynamic structure of conflict: a longitudinal study of intragroup conflict and group performance. *Acad. Manage. J.* 44:238–51

Jehn KA, Northcraft GB, Neale MA. 1999. Why differences make a difference: a field study of diversity, conflict, and performance in workgroups. *Admin. Sci. Q.* 44:741–63

Joshi A, Liao H, Jackson SE. 2005. Cross-level effects of workplace diversity on sales performance and pay. *Acad. Manage. J.* In press

Keller RT. 2001. Cross-functional project groups in research and new product development: diversity, communications, job stress, and outcomes. *Acad. Manage. J.* 44:547–59

Kerr NL, Tindale RS. 2004. Group performance and decision making. *Annu. Rev. Psychol.* 55:623–55

Klein KJ, Conn AB, Smith DB, Sorra JS. 2001. Is everyone in agreement? An exploration of within-group agreement in employee perceptions of the work environment. *J. Appl. Psychol.* 86:3–16

Klein KJ, Lim BC, Saltz JL, Mayer DM. 2004. How do they get there? An examination of the antecedents of centrality in team networks. *Acad. Manage. J.* 47:952–63

Knight D, Pearce CL, Smith KG, Olian JD, Sims HP, et al. 1999. Top management team diversity, group process, and strategic consensus. *Strateg. Manage. J.* 20:445–65

Kossek EE, Zonia SC. 1993. Assessing diversity climate: a field study of reactions to employer efforts to promote diversity. *J. Organ. Behav.* 14:61–81

Kozlowski SWJ, Bell BS. 2003. Work groups and teams in organizations. In *Handbook of Psychology: Industrial and Organizational Psychology*, ed. WC Borman, DR Ilgen, RJ Klimoski, pp. 333–75. London: Wiley

Lau DC, Murnighan JK. 1998. Demographic diversity and faultlines: the compositional dynamics of organizational groups. *Acad. Manage. Rev.* 23:325–40

Lau DC, Murnighan JK. 2005. Interactions within groups and subgroups: the effects of demographic faultlines. *Acad. Manage. J.* 48:645–59

Li J, Hambrick DC. 2005. Factional groups: a new vantage on demographic faultlines, conflict, and disintegration in work teams. *Acad. Manage. J.* 48:794–813

Lovelace K, Shapiro DL, Weingart LR. 2001. Maximizing cross-functional new product teams' innovativeness and constraint adherence: a conflict communications perspective. *Acad. Manage. J.* 44:779–93

Martins LL, Milliken FJ, Wiesenfeld BM, Salgado SR. 2003. Racioethnic diversity and group members' experiences: the role of the racioethnic diversity of the organizational context. *Group Organ. Manage.* 28:75–106

Mathieu JE, Heffner TS, Goodwin GF, Cannon-Bowers JA, Salas E. 2005. Scaling the quality of teammates' mental models: equifinality and normative comparisons. *J. Organ. Behav.* 26:37–56

Mehra A, Kilduff M, Brass DJ. 1998. At the margins: a distinctiveness approach to the social identity and social networks of underrepresented groups. *Acad. Manage. J.* 41:441–52

Milliken FJ, Martins LL. 1996. Searching for common threads: understanding the multiple effects of diversity in organizational groups. *Acad. Manage. Rev.* 21:402–33

Introduced the concept of faultline to diversity research in a way that sparked a still-expanding research interest.

Mohammed S, Angell LC. 2003. Personality heterogeneity in teams: Which differences make a difference for team performance? *Small Group Res.* 34:651–77

Mohammed S, Angell LC. 2004. Surface- and deep-level diversity in workgroups: examining the moderating effects of team orientation and team process on relationship conflict. *J. Organ. Behav.* 25:1015–39

Mohammed S, Ringseis E. 2001. Cognitive diversity and consensus in group decision making: the role of inputs, processes, and outcomes. *Organ. Behav. Hum. Decis. Process.* 85:310–35

Mor Barak ME, Cherin DA, Berkman S. 1998. Organizational and personal dimensions of diversity climate: ethnic and gender differences in employee perceptions. *J. Appl. Behav. Sci.* 31:82–104

Mullen B, Copper C. 1994. The relation between group cohesiveness and performance: an integration. *Psychol. Bull.* 115:210–27

Murnighan JK, Conlon DE. 1991. The dynamics of intense work groups: a study of British string quartets. *Admin. Sci. Q.* 36:165–86

Neuman GA, Wagner SH, Christiansen ND. 1999. The relationship between work-team personality composition and the job performance of teams. *Group Organ. Manage.* 24:28–45

Neuman GA, Wright J. 1999. Team effectiveness: beyond skills and cognitive ability. *J. Appl. Psychol.* 84:376–89

Oakes PJ, Haslam SA, Turner JC. 1994. *Stereotyping and Social Reality*. Malden, MA: Blackwell Sci.

O'Reilly CA, Caldwell DF, Barnett WP. 1989. Work group demography, social integration, and turnover. *Admin. Sci. Q.* 34:21–37

Pelled LH, Eisenhardt KM, Xin KR. 1999. Exploring the black box: an analysis of work group diversity, conflict, and performance. *Admin. Sci. Q.* 44:1–28

Pettigrew TF. 1998. Intergroup contact theory. *Annu. Rev. Psychol.* 49:65–85

Phillips KW. 2003. The effects of categorically based expectations on minority influence: the importance of congruence. *Personal. Soc. Psychol. Bull.* 29:3–13

Phillips KW, Loyd DL. 2006. When surface and deep-level diversity collide: the effects on dissenting group members. *Organ. Behav. Hum. Decis. Process.* 99:143–60

Phillips KW, Mannix EA, Neale MA, Gruenfeld DH. 2004. Diverse groups and information sharing: the effects of congruent ties. *J. Exp. Soc. Psychol.* 40:497–510

Phillips KW, Northcraft GB, Neale MA. 2006. Surface-level diversity and information sharing: When does deep-level diversity help? *Group Process. Intergroup Relat.* In press

Polzer JT, Milton LP, Swann WBJ. 2002. Capitalizing on diversity: interpersonal congruence in small work groups. *Admin. Sci. Q.* 47:296–324

Priem RL, Lyon DW, Dess GG. 1999. Inherent limitations of demographic proxies in top management team heterogeneity research. *J. Manage.* 25:935–53

Randel AE. 2002. Identity salience: a moderator of the relationship between group gender composition and work group conflict. *J. Organ. Behav.* 23:749–66

Randel AE, Jaussi KS. 2003. Functional background identity, diversity, and individual performance in cross-functional teams. *Acad. Manage. J.* 46:763–74

Reagans R, Zuckerman EW. 2001. Networks, diversity, and productivity: the social capital of corporate R&D teams. *Organ. Sci.* 12:502–17

Reagans R, Zuckerman EW, McEvily B. 2004. How to make the team: Social networks versus demography as criteria for designing effective teams. *Admin. Sci. Q.* 49:101–33

Rentsch JR, Hall RJ. 1994. Members of great teams think alike: a model of team effectiveness and schema similarity among team members. In *Advances in Interdisciplinary Studies of Work Teams*, ed. MM Beyerlein, DA Johnson, pp. 223–61. Stamford, CT: JAI

Richard O, McMillan A, Chadwick K, Dwyer S. 2003. Employing an innovation strategy in radically diverse workforce. *Group Organ. Manage.* 28:107–26

Richard OC, Barnett T, Dwyer S, Chadwick K. 2004. Cultural diversity in management, firm performance, and the moderating role of entrepreneurial orientation dimensions. *Acad. Manage. J.* 47:255–66

Roberson L, Kulik CT, Pepper MB. 2001. Designing effective diversity training: Influence of group composition and trainee experience. *J. Organ. Behav.* 22:871–85

Sacco JM, Schmitt N. 2005. A dynamic multilevel model of demographic diversity and misfit effects. *J. Appl. Psychol.* 90:203–31

Sawyer JE, Houlette MA, Yeagley EL. 2006. Decision performance and diversity structure: comparing faultlines in convergent, crosscut, and racially homogeneous groups. *Organ. Behav. Hum. Decis. Process.* 99:1–15

Schippers MC, Den Hartog DN, Koopman P. 2006. Reflexivity in teams: a measure and correlates. *Appl. Psychol. Int. Rev.* In press

Schippers MC, Den Hartog DN, Koopman PL, Wienk JA. 2003. Diversity and team outcomes: the moderating effects of outcome interdependence and group longevity and the mediating effect of reflexivity. *J. Organ. Behav.* 24:779–802

Schneider B, Salvaggio AN, Subirats M. 2002. Climate strength: a new direction for climate research. *J. Appl. Psychol.* 87:220–29

Schneider B, Smith DB, Taylor S, Fleenor J. 1998. Personality and organizations: a test of the homogeneity of personality hypothesis. *J. Appl. Psychol.* 83:462–70

Schneider SK, Northcraft GB. 1999. Three social dilemmas of workforce diversity in organizations: a social identity perspective. *Hum. Relat.* 52:1445–67

Simons T, Pelled LH, Smith KA. 1999. Making use of difference: diversity, debate, and decision comprehensiveness in top management teams. *Acad. Manage. J.* 42:662–73

Sørenson JB. 2002. The use and misuse of the coefficient of variation in organizational demography research. *Sociol. Meth. Res.* 30:475–91

Sproull L, Kiesler S. 1986. Reducing social context cues: electronic mail in organizational communication. *Manage. Sci.* 32:1492–512

Strauss JP, Connerley ML, Ammermann PA. 2003. The "threat hypothesis," personality, and attitudes toward diversity. *J. Appl. Behav. Sci.* 39:32–52

Swann WB, Polzer JT, Seyle DC, Ko SJ. 2004. Finding value in diversity: verification of personal and social self-views in diverse groups. *Acad. Manage. Rev.* 29:9–27

Swann WBJ, Kwan VSY, Polzer JT, Milton LP. 2003. Fostering group identification and creativity in diverse groups: the role of individuation and self-verification. *Personal. Soc. Psychol. Bull.* 29:1396–406

Tajfel H, Turner JC. 1986. The social identity theory of intergroup behavior. In *Psychology of Intergroup Relations*, ed. S Worchel, W Austin, pp. 7–24. Chicago: Nelson-Hall

Teachman JD. 1980. Analysis of population diversity. *Sociol. Meth. Res.* 8:341–62

Thatcher SMB, Jehn KA, Zanutto E. 2003. Cracks in diversity research: the effects of diversity faultlines on conflict and performance. *Group Decis. Negot.* 12:217–41

Tindale RS, Smith CM, Thomas LS, Filkins J, Sheffey S. 1996. Shared representations and asymmetric social influence in small groups. In *Understanding Group Behavior: Consensual Action by Small Groups*, ed. E Witte, JH Davis, pp. 81–83. Mahwah, NJ: Erlbaum

Totterdell P. 2000. Catching moods and hitting runs: mood linkage and subjective performance in professional sport teams. *J. Appl. Psychol.* 85:848–59

Totterdell P, Kellett S, Teuchmann K, Briner RB. 1998. Evidence of mood linkage in work groups. *J. Personal. Soc. Psychol.* 74:1504–15

Triandis HC, Kurowski LL, Gelfand MJ. 1994. Workplace diversity. In *Handbook of Industrial and Organizational Psychology*, Vol. 4, ed. HC Triandis, MD Dunnette, LM Hough, pp. 769–827. Palo Alto, CA: Consult. Psychol. Press. 2nd ed.

Tsui AS, Egan TD, O'Reilly CA. 1992. Being different: relational demography and organizational attachment. *Admin. Sci. Q.* 37:549–79

Tsui AS, O'Reilly CA. 1989. Beyond simple demographic effects: the importance of relational demography in superior-subordinate dyads. *Acad. Manage. J.* 32:402–23

Tsui AS, Porter LW, Egan TD. 2002. When both similarities and dissimilarities matter: extending the concept of relational demography. *Hum. Relat.* 55:899–929

Turner JC, Hogg MA, Oakes PJ, Reicher SD, Wetherell MS. 1987. *Rediscovering the Social Group: A Self-Categorization Theory*. Oxford, UK: Blackwell

Van der Vegt GS, Bunderson JS. 2005. Learning and performance in multidisciplinary teams: the importance of collective team identification. *Acad. Manage. J.* 48:532–47

Van der Vegt GS, Janssen O. 2003. Joint impact of interdependence and group diversity on innovation. *J. Manage.* 29:29–51

van Ginkel WP, van Knippenberg D. 2003. *The role of shared mental models for informational diversity in group decision-making*. Presented at Eur. Assoc. Exp. Soc. Psychol. Small Group Meet. on Small Group Decision Making: Motiv. Cogn., Amsterdam

van Knippenberg D. 1999. Social identity and persuasion: reconsidering the role of group membership. In *Social Identity and Social Cognition*, ed. D Abrams, MA Hogg, pp. 315–31. Oxford, UK: Blackwell Sci.

van Knippenberg D, De Dreu CKW, Homan AC. 2004. Work group diversity and group performance: an integrative model and research agenda. *J. Appl. Psychol.* 89:1008–22

van Knippenberg D, Haslam SA. 2003. Realizing the diversity dividend: exploring the subtle interplay between identity, ideology, and reality. In *Social Identity at Work: Developing Theory for Organizational Practice*, ed. SA Haslam, D van Knippenberg, MJ Platow, N Ellemers, pp. 61–77. New York/Hove: Psychol. Press

van Knippenberg D, Haslam SA, Platow MJ. 2003. *Work group diversity and work group identification: diversity as an aspect of group identity*. Presented at 11th Eur. Congr. Work Organ. Psychol., Lisbon

van Knippenberg D, van Ginkel WP, Homan AC, Kooij-de Bode HJM. 2005. *Diversity mind sets: a new focus in diversity research*. Presented at 12th Eur. Congr. Work Organ. Psychol., Istanbul

Van Vianen AEM, De Dreu CKW. 2001. Personality in teams: its relationship to social cohesion, task cohesion, and team performance. *Eur. J. Work Organ. Psychol.* 10:97–120

Wageman R. 1995. Interdependence and group effectiveness. *Admin. Sci. Q.* 40:140–80

Wagner GW, Pfeffer J, O'Reilly CA. 1984. Organizational demography and turnover. *Admin. Sci. Q.* 29:74–92

Watson W, Johnson L, Merritt D. 1998. Team orientation, self-orientation, and diversity in task groups: their connection to team performance over time. *Group Organ. Manage.* 23:161–88

Watson W, Kumar K, Michaelson L. 1993. Cultural diversity's impact on interaction process and performance: comparing homogeneous and diverse task groups. *Acad. Manage. J.* 36:590–602

Webber SS, Donahue LM. 2001. Impact of highly and less job-related diversity on work group cohesion and performance: a meta-analysis. *J. Manage.* 27:141–62

Weingart L. 1997. How did they do that? The ways and means of studying group process. *Res. Organ. Behav.* 19:189–39

Provides an integrative model bridging and extending the social categorization perspective and the information/decision-making perspective, the two main traditions in diversity research.

West MA. 1996. Reflexivity and work group effectiveness: a conceptual integration. In *Handbook of Work Group Psychology*, ed. MA West, pp. 555–79. Chichester, UK: Wiley

West MA. 2002. Sparkling fountains or stagnant ponds: an integrative model of creativity and innovation implementation in work groups. *Appl. Psychol. Int. Rev.* 51:355–87

Williams HM, Meân LJ. 2004. Measuring gender composition in work groups: a comparison of existing models. *Organ. Res. Methods* 7:456–74

Williams KY, O'Reilly CA. 1998. Demography and diversity in organizations: a review of 40 years of research. *Res. Organ. Behav.* 20:77–140

Reviews diversity research up to 1998. Complements the current article for a full overview of the field.

Work and Vocational Psychology: Theory, Research, and Applications

Nadya A. Fouad

Department of Educational Psychology, University of Wisconsin-Milwaukee,
Milwaukee, Wisconsin 53201-0413; email: nadya@uwm.edu

Annu. Rev. Psychol. 2007. 58:543–64

First published online as a Review in
Advance on August 11, 2006

The *Annual Review of Psychology* is online
at http://psych.annualreviews.org

This article's doi:
10.1146/annurev.psych.58.110405.085713

0066-4308/07/0110-0543$20.00

Key Words

career development, career counseling, career adaptability,
person-environment fit, Holland's theory, career decision-making,
interests, career self-efficacy, social cognitive career theory

Abstract

Work is integral to human functioning, and all psychologists need to
understand the role of work in people's lives. Understanding factors
influencing work choices and helping individuals effectively make
career decisions is the focus of vocational psychologists. However,
external changes, such as shifts in the economy and labor force,
as well as initiatives within the field are challenging the assumptions within vocational psychology. This chapter reviews the empirical work since 1995 in four areas: (*a*) what factors influence career
choices, (*b*) how people make career decisions, (*c*) how context influences career choices, and (*d*) effective interventions for help with
the first three questions. The review focuses first on vocational psychology's rich tradition of theoretically driven research, and then
discusses research in career development that crosses a number of
theoretical approaches, and finally identifies the assumptions in the
field and questions for future examination.

Contents

INTRODUCTION

Understanding the role of work in people's lives is critical for applied psychologists since work is so integral to human functioning. Meta-analyses show that work is positively linked to indices of well-being (Murphy & Athanasou 1999, Parker et al. 2003), whereas underemployment (Friedland & Price 2003) and unemployment (McKee-Ryan et al. 2005) are related to lower levels of psychological well-being. However, greater understanding of the importance of work is occurring at a time that the world of work is adjusting to shifts within the economy and labor force that have influenced who works, how they work, where they work, and the security of their employment. Demographic changes in who works have resulted in a workforce that includes older workers, working mothers, and increasingly culturally diverse workers. Emerging technologies change how individuals work in nearly every occupational area. The global economy has allowed companies to move manufacturing to other countries to take advantage of low wages, a change that both affects where individuals work and with whom they work. Employment security is affected by changes in, or elimination of, retirement pensions and layoffs. The assumption that an individual will work for one company until retirement is no longer valid. Thus, established notions of career and work are dramatically shifting from viewing career as a choice made early in life to viewing career as a series of choices or forced transitions that individuals make over a life span.

Counseling and vocational psychologists must adapt to understand how individuals make choices in, or adjust to, a world of work that is a moving target. They cannot assume that all individuals have work choices, that they will enter a career until they choose to leave it, or that opportunities are open to all. "Work choice," in fact, may be an oxymoron. Within the field, some are advocating adoption of postmodern philosophies to better understand how individuals construct meaning around their careers (Young & Collin 2004). Others have made a strong push to understand how the context of people's lives influence their career and work development, such as socioeconomic status or race/ethnicity (Richardson 2004). Meanwhile, as vocational psychologists learn to accommodate these changes, research in vocational psychology has powerful policy implications. These implications include examining and perhaps helping to ameliorate gender and race/ethnicity inequities in work, identifying mechanisms to support employment for the unemployed, predicting successful reforms to welfare programs, and

Table 1 Framework of major areas of research in vocational psychology

What factors influence career choices?			How do people make career decisions?	How does context influence career decisions?	How are clients effectively helped?
Work personality ●Holland's theory	Development over the life span ●Super's theory	Self-efficacy ●Social cognitive career theory	●Indecision ●Career decision-making self-efficacy	●Gender? ●Race/ethnicity ●Sexual orientation? ●Social class	●Counseling ●Interventions ●Working alliance
●Across cultures ●Relationship to personality measures	●Aspirations ●Exploration ●Transitions				
Cross-theoretical constructs					
Vocational interests	Barriers	Relationships			

developing model programs to support men's and women's work/life balance.

It is interesting to review research in a field that is in the midst of a major transition. This chapter focuses on a selective review of empirical research in vocational psychology since 1995 and strives to integrate new paradigms where appropriate. A database search on 16 critical key words (e.g., vocational psychology, career development, Holland's theory, career counseling) and a manual search of the major journals in which vocational psychology research is published (*Journal of Vocational Behavior*, *Journal of Career Assessment*, *Career Development Quarterly*, *Journal of Counseling Psychology*, and the *Journal of Counseling and Development*) resulted in the identification of approximately 800 articles published since 1995. Only a fraction of the total number is included in this chapter; many good studies or conceptual articles were excluded owing to space limitations. For example, educational achievement, midlife transitions, work/family balance, and retirement planning are not reviewed here, though they are important to the field. Recent edited books have assessed some of these aspects (e.g., Brown & Lent 2005, Walsh & Savickas 2005), and an important new book by Blustein (2006) has more fully explicated an inclusive psychology of working.

The chapter is organized around the major questions (listed in **Table 1**) that vocational psychologists investigate. The four overarching questions in the first row include what factors influence career choices, how people make career decisions, how context influences career choices, and effective interventions for help with the first three questions. The bulleted areas in the other rows represent the research covered in the past 10 years within each question (e.g., researchers in decision-making focused on indecision and decision-making self-efficacy). Researchers examining the factors influencing career choices have focused on support for three theoretical models (Holland's, Super's, and the social cognitive career theory models). Additional research has emphasized specific aspects of Holland's and Super's theories, and these are bulleted in row three of **Table 1**. Finally, row four contains three areas of research that cross several theoretical constructs.

CAREER CHOICES: THE ROLE OF WORK PERSONALITY

The fundamental notion that has driven career development researchers and practitioners for the past 100 years has been Parsons' (1909) premise that in choosing a career, individuals need to know themselves, know the

Person-environment fit: how well an individual's interests, skills/abilities, and values correspond to activities, tasks, and responsibilities at work. Higher level of fit corresponds to greater job satisfaction

RIASEC: themes in Holland's theory (realistic, investigative, artistic, social, enterprising, and conventional) that capture individuals' work personality

Congruence: matching an individual's RIASEC work personality with RIASEC work environment should lead to greater job satisfaction and length of time on job

world of work, and have some "true reasoning" between the two. His original notion of true reasoning was essentially the ability to analyze self in relation to the world of work, and it has become known as the person-environment fit model. The most widely used and researched theoretical person-environment fit model is Holland's theory of vocational personality types (Holland 1997, Spokane et al. 2005). Individuals may be described by one or a combination of six interest themes [realistic, investigative, artistic, social, enterprising, and conventional (RIASEC)]; each theme captures some aspect of work personality (e.g., liking to work with people).

Support for Holland's theory has been demonstrated over many years (Spokane et al. 2005). In the past decade, additional research has demonstrated that individuals in different RIASEC environments indeed are attracted to environments that allow them to work with similar people (Wampold et al. 1995) or allow them to solve problems in preferred ways (Wampold et al. 1995). Personality type appears to develop over the life span and is influenced by the activities in which individuals choose to engage (Reichel & Muchinsky 1995), although this appears to occur in late childhood and adolescence since Holland codes cannot be predicted accurately from second grade interests (Helwig 2003). However, less support has been found for the predicted outcomes of a person-environment fit. Environments, as well as individuals, may be described by RIASEC themes with the match between person and environment known as congruence. Theoretically, a better fit between an individual's work personality and his/her work environment should lead to greater job satisfaction and length of time on the job. In reality, though, the relationship between satisfaction and congruence is small, with congruence explaining less than 5% of the variance in job satisfaction (Spokane et al. 2000, Tsabari et al. 2005).

Holland's Theory: Cross-Cultural Applications

The structure of Holland's theory is hexagonal: the six RIASEC themes are arranged at equal points in a circular order around a hexagon. Adjacent types are predicted to be more similar, whereas opposing types (e.g., R versus S) are hypothesized to be the least similar. This structure of interests is assumed to underlie individuals' perceptions of the world of work and, indeed, is a valuable heuristic of the theory because it helps clients and counselors put an organizational framework on the world of work. However, if the structure differs across cultural groups, the theory may not be applicable across populations and may affect the cross-cultural validity of the model.

Within the United States, studies with racially and ethnically diverse middle school students (Turner & Lapan 2003), high school students (Day & Rounds 1998, Ryan et al. 1996), college students (Fouad 2002; Fouad & Mohler 2004; Hansen et al. 1999, 2000), and professionals (Fouad et al. 1997) have generally found support for Holland's structure, although studies have not demonstrated support for equal distances between themes. Most of the studies cited here found fewer differences across racial/ethnic groups than between genders; however, one study with large samples of men and women did not find sex differences in the structure of interests (Anderson et al. 1997).

The structure of Holland's theory has been investigated in nearly every continent of the world. The RIASEC ordering was found among participants in Korea (Tak 2004), Portugal (Alves Ferreira & Hood 1995), Japan (Tracey et al. 1997), India (Leong et al. 1998), and Singapore (Soh & Leong 2001), but not in South Africa (du Toit & de Bruin 2002, Watson et al. 1998), China (Tang 2001, Yang et al. 2005), Bolivia (Glidden-Tracey & Parraga 1996), or Hong Kong (Farh et al. 1998, Yang et al. 2005). In all countries, men and women's interests were significantly different; moreover, Farh and colleagues' study in Hong Kong found that low acceptance of traditional norms was related to greater fit with Holland's structure.

Many cross-cultural studies used a similar methodology to assess applicability. The first step was to assess whether the pattern of correlations fit the predicted order (e.g., RI correlation greater than that of RS) and how many correlations violated the predicted order. If there were too many violations, researchers concluded that Holland's model did not fit the data; if the model fit, researchers used multidimensional scaling to assess the location of the themes on a circle. Armstrong et al. (2003) assessed group differences with a more stringent approach than was used in the other studies. Using circular unidimensional scaling, they compared each racial/ethnic male and female group with two models; one model allowed unequal distances among themes and the second constrained the distances to be equal. They reanalyzed the large samples from studies by Day & Rounds (1998) and Fouad et al. (1997), and concluded that Holland's theory may be less salient for groups other than Caucasians and Asian Americans. Differences in responses by racial/ethnic minority groups may be due to the measurement of a secondary trait related to culture in addition to interests (Fouad & Walker 2005).

Holland Themes and Other Personality Measures

The past decade has seen a burgeoning interest in the relationship between Holland's theory of vocational personality and personality variables more broadly defined. A meta-analysis of the studies that combined assessment of both interests and personality concluded that there were significant points of convergence between the two domains. Specifically, artistic themes were related to openness to experience, and social and enterprising themes were related to extraversion; smaller relationships were found between in-

vestigative and openness to experience and between conventional and enterprising and conscientiousness (Larson et al. 2002). Sullivan & Hansen (2004) demonstrated that more narrowly focused personality facets could account for these correlations. The association between social and extraversion was accounted for by warmth; the relationship between enterprising and extraversion was accounted for primarily by assertiveness, and the correlation between artistic and openness to experience was accounted for by the relationship between aesthetics and openness to experience.

CAREER CHOICES: DEVELOPMENT

Donald Super's seminal contribution to the field of vocational psychology was the notion that rather than springing forth fully formed, career and occupational choices are actually developed through childhood. Savickas (2002b, 2005) has taken on the mantle of revising and updating Super's theory, incorporating Super's constructs under the meta-theoretical umbrella of social constructionism; this is the first major theoretical integration of postmodern philosophy in vocational psychology. Central to Savickas's formulations are (a) careers are representations of reality, (b) development is better characterized as continuing to adapt to a changing environment rather than as an internal impetus to maturation, (c) careers are constructed by individuals from their past experiences and future dreams into a life theme, and (d) an individual's subjective career "emerges from an active process of making meaning, not discovering preexisting facts" (Savickas 2005, p. 43). Implementation of the self-concept continues to be central to the theory. Self-concepts develop "through the interaction of inherited aptitudes, physical makeup, opportunities to observe and play various roles. . ., and evaluation of the extent to which the results of role-playing meet with the. . .approval [of others]" (p. 46).

Career
constructionism:
careers are viewed as
the representation of
reality that
individuals construct
from their
experiences and
dreams for the future

Career adaptability:
an individual's
readiness and
resources to
complete the
developmental tasks
associated with
career development

Career Aspirations

Examination of children's aspirations influenced the development of several national longitudinal studies in the 1980s in which researchers asked various cohorts of students, "What do you expect to be when you are 30?" As it turns out, teenagers' predictions of future occupational attainment are not very accurate. For example, less than half of the nearly 9000 participants in the Longitudinal Study of the High School Class of 1972 had achieved their occupational expectation by age 30; women tended to work in less prestigious occupations than they had expected, whereas men worked in occupations leading to higher socioeconomic status (Rindfuss et al. 1999).

Nonetheless, researchers have been very interested in understanding children's career dreams and hopes. Children's career aspirations appear to be shaped by a number of factors, including their parents' economic standing and expectations, schooling, and the availability of opportunities. The influence of social class on children's aspirations is not direct. Rather, socioeconomic status is mediated through parents' sense of efficacy in influencing children's academic development and level of parental aspirations (Bandura et al. 2001). Moreover, while parents' social class was important in shaping their aspirations for their children and their ability to provide material support, teenagers' own level of aspiration was found to mediate the effects of social class (Schoon & Parsons 2002).

Career Exploration

During adolescence, children are hypothesized to enter into the exploration phase, in which they are beginning to search how to translate the concept of self into vocational identity. Career construction theory hypothesizes that this stage is accompanied by vocational development tasks that "are experienced as social expectations" (Savickas 2002a, p. 156). Greater exploration is presumed to lead to greater consideration of opportunities and ultimately a better choice of careers. As may be predicted, exploration appears to be fostered by openness to experience, personal growth initiative (Robitschek & Cook 1999), and emotional intelligence (Brown et al. 2003a).

Since children are expected to move closer to a career goal or implementation of a work choice after high school, one question has been whether exploration activities increase with age. Indices of exploration do change with age, such that twelfth graders are doing more exploration of the environment and of themselves than are ninth graders (Jepsen & Dickson 2003, Taviera et al. 1998). Schultheiss et al. (2005) interviewed elementary school students and documented the evolving nature of interaction of sense of self and the external world and the importance of significant others (often parents) in helping to form children's understanding about the world of work.

As students get older, the social support of important others has also been shown to influence exploration. Parents' behavior and support were related to the career exploration of their high school–aged children, regardless of parents' educational level (Kracke 1997). A secure attachment to both parents and peers appears to set a solid base from which children and adolescents can explore independent identities (Felsman & Blustein 1999, Ketterson & Blustein 1997).

Career Transitions

Super and colleagues (1996) conceptualized career maturity as the developmental tasks encountered compared with an individual's chronological age. Savickas (1997, 2002a) offered the construct of career adaptability as a more relativistic alternative that better captures the way individuals construct their careers. Career adaptability is viewed as the readiness and resources an individual has to complete the developmental tasks associated with career development. Resources may be cognitive (knowledge and decision

-making skills), social (including social support of others) and/or psychological (e.g., emotional readiness to make a decision).

The transitions that students make after high school graduation have attracted a great deal of attention, particularly for those not entering postsecondary training or education. Adaptability is clearly a factor in successful school-to-work transitions. For example, those with poor career adaptability skills are more likely to be unemployed; the strongest predictors of unemployment pathways for young adults are number of arrests, low academic achievement, low postsecondary aspirations, and association with deviant friendships (Rojewski & Kim 2003, Wiesner et al. 2003). However, the effects of unemployment are mediated by a strong work and relational identity (Meeus et al. 1997). It has been demonstrated that students' social class helps to shape the way they construct meaning about their work and career choices and also shapes the resources (psychological and social) they bring to the transition process (Blustein et al. 2002, Phillips et al. 2002). Successful transitions are facilitated by the participants' perception of readiness for the transition, support from others, and the ability to use resources.

The transition of youths from school to work has been examined in two longitudinal cohort studies of all babies born during one-week periods in 1958 and in 1970 in Great Britain (Bynner 1997, 1998; Bynner & Parsons 2002). The British employment context was quite different when each cohort reached the age of 21; unemployment, in particular, was quite high for the 1970 cohort. Highlighting the importance of the resources that individuals need to successfully adapt to a career, social and psychological capital was an important factor in predicting successful transitions for both groups, though it was stronger for the 1970 cohort, perhaps because the role of family of origin in determining one's path has loosened in the past 45 years in Britain. Lack of psychological and social capital was critical in identifying those who had never

transitioned to the workplace or to an educational setting.

CAREER CHOICES: SELF-EFFICACY

The role of personal agency in making career decisions was first hypothesized by Hackett & Betz (1981) and then empirically examined by Betz & Hackett (1981). They documented the role of self-efficacy in the career choices of women and demonstrated that women's perceptions of their lack of abilities were powerful predictors that they would preclude math/science careers. Hackett & Betz's application of Bandura's (1997) social cognitive model was later expanded and developed into a full model that predicted career interests, choices, and performance (Lent et al. 2005). Specifically, self-efficacy and outcome expectations predict interests, which predict action steps (choices), and these in turn predict level of performance. Considerable support for the model has been found across racial/ethnic groups (Flores & O'Brien 2002, Fouad & Smith 1996, Gainor & Lent 1998, Tang et al. 1999) and academic and interest areas (Anderson & Betz 2001, Diegelman & Subich 2001, Fouad et al. 2002, Lapan et al. 1996, Nauta et al. 1998, Smith & Fouad 1999). Consistent with Hackett & Betz's (1981) early work, the theoretical framework continues to be useful in identifying factors that predict women's choices of a science/technical/engineering/math career.

Social cognitive career theory has also been significantly expanded in the past years to incorporate the role that the perception of barriers plays in predicting individuals' career choices. Swanson et al. (1996) hypothesized that the perception of barriers may be a significant impediment to optimal career choice. They defined barriers as "external conditions or internal states that make career progress difficult" (p. 237) and suggested that embedding barriers within the social cognitive career theory could be a useful way to link barriers to an existing theoretical model. They raised

Career-related self-efficacy: an individual's confidence in ability to complete tasks necessary to enter an occupational area or to make a career-related decision

School-to-work transition: transitions made after high school graduation, particularly transition for students entering the workforce directly

a number of conceptual concerns about the role of barriers in the model, and Lent et al. (2000) expanded their theoretical framework to incorporate barriers at a point proximal to career choice (e.g., Do I have enough money to go to medical school? Will my family support this choice?) as well as at a distal point. The latter is conceptualized as barriers that stem from one's background, including lack of parental support, impoverished learning environments, or sexism and racism effects that influence schooling and learning opportunities. Two studies provide support for the role of barriers in influencing career choice indirectly through self-efficacy (Lent et al. 2001, 2003). Research related to a broader view of barriers for racial/ethnic minorities is discussed in the Barriers section below.

CROSS-THEORETICAL CONSTRUCTS

Interest Assessment

Assessment of interests has been a major focus of vocational psychologists since E.K. Strong developed the first interest inventory 80 years ago. All three of the theories described above note the central importance of interests in vocational choice. As noted below, valid interpretation of assessment tools is one of the five critical ingredients of effective career counseling (Brown et al. 2003b), and an interest inventory is the most commonly used assessment tool. However, most of the research on interest inventories has focused more on measurement concerns than on application.

How well interest inventories capture the domain of interests has been a topic of debate for well over two decades; the debate has centered on whether interests can be best captured in two dimensions (Prediger & Swaney 2004) or three (Armstrong et al. 2004). The relevance of these arguments is important in the valid construction of an interest inventory. Those advocating for two dimensions suggest that the domain of interests is best characterized by a dimension anchored by people versus

things and a second dimension anchored by data versus ideas. Those proposing three dimensions believe that the domain is captured by persuasion versus problem solving, structured versus dynamic, and social service versus solitary work. It has been suggested that the third dimension is either a prestige dimension (Tracey & Rounds 1996) or a sex-type dimension (Einarsdottir & Rounds 2000). However, when people are asked how they naturally perceive the world of work, they say three dimensions, with prestige being the third dimension (Shivy et al. 1999).

A blend of Holland's theory and social cognitive theory was the impetus for the development of the Skills Confidence Inventory, designed to assess self-efficacy for activities in each RIASEC theme (Betz et al. 2003) and found to be useful for high school students (Betz & Wolfe 2005), college students, and adults (Betz et al. 1998). A meta-analysis of 60 studies that included both self-efficacy and interests showed that the overall correlation between the two constructs was 0.59, with the strongest relationships found between interests and self-efficacy in math- and science-related areas (Rottinghaus et al. 2003b). Self-perception of skills and interests together accounted for more variance in educational aspirations and college major choices than either did alone (Rottinghaus et al. 2003a). Rottinghaus et al. (2003a) also found that individuals who had a high level of interest in gender-nontraditional areas tended to express less confidence in their skills in those areas. Recent work, however, has documented the potential of interventions to increase self-efficacy for women in nontraditional areas (Betz & Schifano 2000).

Factors that influence the development of interests have been investigated to understand the optimal intervention point to prevent children from prematurely narrowing their range of interests or foreclosing options. Interests appear to form early (Lubinski et al. 1995), perceptions of some occupations as only appropriate for one gender is strongest in younger children (Miller & Budd

1999), and those early interests are linked to perceptions of the opportunity structure (Lapan et al. 2000). Clearly, helping young adolescents develop an accurate portrayal of the world of work is critical. The structure of children's interests has been examined in a number of studies (Tracey 2001, 2005; Tracey & Ward 1998), and findings demonstrate that children's perceptions of interests do not fit a circular pattern. However, a better fit to the circular pattern increases with age, and the pattern appears to be somewhat shaped by eighth grade. A longitudinal study showed that adolescents' patterns of interests were stable over their high school years, although the strength of those interests increased over time (Tracey et al. 2005).

Barriers

The role of barriers as an impediment to career choice was initially discussed within the social cognitive model; much of that research focused on explicating barriers for women entering math/science careers. Additional attention has focused on the possible barriers for racial/ethnic minorities in career dreams, career choices, or career options. A meta-analysis of racial/ethnic differences in aspirations, barriers, and decision making found few differences in occupational aspirations, but significant differences between whites and racial/ethnic minorities on perceptions of barriers (Fouad & Byars-Winston 2005). Racial/ethnic minority individuals viewed fewer career opportunities and significantly more barriers to occupational entry than did whites, and perceived more discrimination against racial/ethnic minorities than whites perceived against racial/ethnic minorities (Chung & Harmon 1999). Racial/ethnic minority students had higher expectations of educational barriers than did white students and had lower expectations of coping efficacy (Luzzo & McWhirter 2001). Barriers clearly shape career choices; greater perceptions of barriers appear to differentially prompt racial/ethnic minority stu-

dents to prematurely foreclose career options (Leal-Muniz & Constantine 2005) or lead to greater levels of indecision (Constantine et al. 2005).

Relational Influences

One of the major areas of emphasis in the past decade has been on examining the role of relationships in facilitating or hindering career development. Strong positive relationships help to promote career exploration, set a foundation within which individuals make career decisions, and serve as a motivating force behind exploration (Blustein et al. 2004, Flum 2001). The converse is also true; negative relationships can impede successful career choices. The influence of others has been grouped into three broad categories that include both positive and negative influences: direct actions of others (support, criticism), others recruited to be involved (seeking advice, weighing options), and career decisions shaped by pushing others away (Phillips et al. 2001).

A comprehensive meta-analysis on the role of family of origin in career development concluded that parental attachment influences exploration and decidedness and that the attachment to a parent was more predictive of positive outcomes than was separation from a parent (Whiston & Keller 2004). Kenny & Bledsoe's (2005) study explicated the role that the support of important others (parents, teachers, peers, and close friends) can play in career adaptability: Family support was specifically related to perceptions of barriers and career outcomes expected, teacher support contributed to engagement with school, and peer support contributed to perceptions of barriers and identification with school.

Other researchers have examined the way that relationships may influence women's pursuit of nontraditional careers, particularly powerful others. Girls' relationships with mothers were important in influencing career self-efficacy for nontraditional careers, career orientation, and realism (O'Brien 1996).

Relational influences on career development: strong positive relationships promote career exploration, offer options for exploration, and help to motivate career development. Negative relationships hinder career development

However, girls' perceptions of their parents' and their boyfriends' preferences for them predicted their career orientation; that early career orientation predicted their career behavior 15 years later (Vincent et al. 1998).

DECISION-MAKING

How do people make career decisions? What happens when individuals have trouble making a career decision, and are there factors that are related to helping them make those decisions? Psychologists, driven by the very practical concerns of practitioners coping with students who have decisional problems, have focused on some of these questions. Reviews of research on career decision-making (Krieshok 1998) include the findings that decision-making skills increase with age, decision making is a complex process, and those who have decision-making difficulties also have other difficulties, most typically related to anxiety. Krieshok suggested that, in fact, most decisions are made outside conscious processing.

Gati and colleagues (Gati et al. 1995, 1996) have developed a taxonomy of career decision difficulties, identifying origins of difficulties prior to and during the decision-making process. Gati developed an instrument to assess aspects of the taxonomy, the Career Decision Difficulties Questionnaire. Substantial evidence indicates construct validity for the instrument with college students in the United States (Lancaster et al. 1999, Mau 2001, Osipow & Gati 1998) and China (Jackson & Neville 1998) and with high school students in Israel (Gati & Saka 2001) and Australia (Albion & Fogarty 2002). However, the model fit less well for Taiwanese college students (Mau 2001).

Another area of research in career decision making has focused on individuals' self-efficacy beliefs about their ability to make a career decision. Stemming from the early work of Taylor & Betz (1983), career decision-making self-efficacy has been found to be significantly negatively related to career inde-cision (Betz & Klein 1996, Betz & Voyten 1997, Luzzo 1996) and positively related to career maturity (Anderson & Brown 1997, Luzzo 1996). Duffy & Blustein (2005) found career decision-making self-efficacy to be related to spirituality and religiousness; they suggest that a strong spiritual base may lead to a general sense of confidence in one's decisions.

CONTEXTUAL INFLUENCES

The context in which individuals develop, and the influence of that context on their career decisions, has been a major focus within vocational psychology for the past two decades. Men and women have different interests, socialization patterns, and societal expectations (Cook et al. 2002); women and racial/ethnic minorities have different career expectations and perceptions of barriers (Fouad & Byars-Winston 2005) and are not equally distributed across occupational areas (U.S. Census Bureau 2005). In sum, the occupational landscape is not equal for men and women or racial/ethnic minorities and whites. The influence of gendered expectations, sexism, homophobia, classism, racism, and racial discrimination has a long and pervasive effect on opportunities for individuals, influencing their career histories and decisions.

Gender

Gender influences career development from the very beginning, as girls and boys continue to have aspirations for careers that are gender stereotypic. Although the perception that some jobs should be performed only by one gender decreases over time for females, they continue to want to pursue female-appropriate jobs (Miller & Budd 1999). High school students were more likely to change their career aspirations in the direction of more gender-traditional expectations (Armstrong & Crombie 2000) or to occupations more in keeping with their perceptions of opportunities (Wall et al. 1999).

When girls had high school aspirations of a nontraditional career, they were less likely to persist in that choice (Farmer et al. 1995, Mau 2003), although girls had higher educational and occupational aspirations than boys (Rojewski & Yang 1997). Levine & Zimmerman's (1995) analysis of National Longitudinal Surveys suggests, though, that once women graduate from high school, the probability of entering a female-traditional occupation is much greater for women than is the probability of their entry into a nontraditional field.

More recently, researchers have begun to examine men's career choices, assessing whether men's choices are shaped by stereotypic gender role attributes. As might be predicted from gender differences in career aspirations, males and females cited different reasons for their occupational choice, even when the choice was the same. For example, males were more likely to indicate that interests shaped their decision to choose engineering as a major, whereas females were more likely to cite social or altruistic reasons for choosing engineering (e.g., "I like to help people") (Davey 2001, Farmer et al. 1998). Traditionalism of career choice for men appears to be related to antifeminine attitudes, self-perception of toughness, restrictive emotionality, and homophobic attitudes. However, career-traditional men were not different from career-nontraditional men in valuing power, success, competition, work/family balance, or status (Jome & Tokar 1998). Persistence in nontraditional choices was related to liberal attitudes (Lease 2003). Men's vocational interests mediate masculinity and traditionalism of career choice, such that antifemininity is related negatively to social, artistic, and enterprising interests, whereas status is positively related to enterprising interests (Tokar & Jome 1998).

Race/Ethnicity

Just as career dreams are shaped by gender, they are also shaped by an individual's ethnic minority status; career dreams appear to be related to perceptions of opportunities and the reality of racism in the marketplace. For example, only 13% of African American males at age 18 accurately predicted their eventual occupation (Levine & Zimmerman 1995). By second grade, inner-city African American boys "expect to recreate the systems of class- and race-based occupations" found in the United States (Cook et al. 1996, p. 3375). Acculturation and SES were significantly related to career expectations of Mexican Americans (McWhirter et al. 1998, Reyes et al. 1999).

Several qualitative studies have focused on the construction of meaning for various racial/ethnic minority groups. Five themes emerged from interviews with American Indians: meaning of career (planfulness, goal oriented, traditional ways for American Indians); success as a collective experience; supportive factors, such as family, value on education; obstacles (discrimination, alienation from the tribe, limits on reservation); and their perceptions that they were living in two worlds (American Indian and the majority culture) (Juntunen et al. 2001). Other qualitative studies have focused on Latina professionals (Gomez et al 2001) and African American college or professional women (Jones 1997, Pearson & Bieschke 2001, Richie et al. 1997). Overall, these studies have found that the women were highly career committed, resilient in the face of sexism and racism or ethnocentrism (often viewing these challenges as an opportunity), and that they frequently mentioned the tremendous support they received from others.

Sexual Orientation

Sexual orientation is a contextual factor that has not yet received much empirical examination, although vocational psychologists have issued calls to better understand the role that sexual orientation plays in vocational development and choice. Fassinger (1995, 1996) and Prince (1995) noted that the identification of one as gay or lesbian might impede the career development process. They suggested several ways this might occur. For example, the development of an identity as gay or lesbian may occur at the expense of attention to vocational identity tasks; identifying oneself as gay or lesbian may preclude consideration of some occupations; and the process of coming out may result in loss of parental and family support.

Although this is a new area, two qualitative studies have examined the role of sexual orientation in the construction of careers. Participants reported educational and career delays and the simultaneous development of career and sexual identity. Many participants felt they had lost career opportunities due to homophobia (including the fear of being "outed") and felt their identity had a negative effect on their self-esteem and confidence. On the positive side, some reported more opportunities due to networking and social support from other gays and lesbians within the community (Adams et al. 2005, Boatwright et al. 1996).

Social Class

Very few studies examined social class as a contextual variable. The few studies highlight the relationship between the opportunity structure, relationship support, and the construction of work for low-income individuals (Kenny et al. 2003). Chaves et al. (2004) demonstrated the significance of the perceptions of opportunities (or lack thereof) among low-income urban youths. Their interviews revealed that the students viewed work as a means to an end, rather than viewing the intrinsic reward of working; students reported that the message from their families was that work was a necessary function to earn money.

CAREER COUNSELING AND INTERVENTIONS

The focus of research and conceptual articles on career counseling echoes, in many ways, various directions in the empirical literature elsewhere in vocational behavior. Counselors have been encouraged to incorporate a relational perspective in their career counseling (Schultheiss 2003) and to understand clients as individuals within a context (Richardson 2002). Consistent with social constructionism, Richardson advocated that counselors adopt a meta-perspective that identifies work and relationships cutting across both private and public domains, thus helping clients function better in all contexts. Others have also urged practitioners to focus more holistically on the context of clients' lives in helping them to make career decisions (Cook et al. 2002, Hartung et al. 1998, Spokane et al. 2003).

A meta-analysis that evaluated the effectiveness of career counseling has shown that career interventions are useful and that individual career counseling is the most successful method of intervention (Whiston et al. 1998). A meta-analysis of the effective factors within individual counseling provided evidence that five ingredients were critical (Brown et al. 2003b): written homework given to clients, individualized assessment interpretation, giving clients information about the world of work, providing exposure to models of career exploration, and attending to helping clients build support. These ingredients together accounted for more of the variance in effectiveness than did any of the ingredients individually (Brown et al. 2003b).

Heppner & Heppner (2003) outlined a research agenda for career counseling and advocated for researchers to conduct studies that document the process variables that are effective in career counseling (e.g., working alliance, what leads to effective learning, and the influence of culture in career counseling). Heeding their call, researchers examined the role of the working alliance, documenting its effectiveness in helping to reduce psychological distress (Multon et al. 2001) and in increasing problem-solving ability and adjustment (Heppner et al. 2004).

FUTURE DIRECTIONS

The articles reviewed here indicate that research in vocational psychology has a number of strengths. These strengths include a strong tradition of theory-based research that has helped to contribute to the overall knowledge about influences on the career choices of adolescents, connections to broader psychological science, and a promising start to understanding the contextual influences on individuals' constructions of career. However, as noted in the introduction, the assumptions in the field, listed below, are changing, leading to new questions.

- **Everyone has the ability to make work choices**. All of the theoretical models in vocational psychology are predicated on the assumption of choice, but this assumption is not true for a great many individuals. Some may not have the luxury of time, abilities, or resources to consider options and opportunities; for others, the occupational opportunity structure may be limited. Research needs to examine work in the lives of individuals who do not have choices in where or how they work. Further study is needed to answer the questions of how we can understand the vocational behavior of individuals for whom work is a means to economic survival, and what are effective interventions for those who do not have work choices.

- **Work is a contained part of people's lives**. In fact, however, work is often intertwined with all other domains of life. How one feels about work, or lack of work, affects relationships, family organization and well-being, sense of identity, and self-esteem. It does not make sense for psychologists to study, or intervene, in one aspect of an individual's life without understanding the other interconnecting domains. An important future question is, What role does work play in psychological health?

- **The world of work is predictable**. Globalization, introduction of technology in all occupational areas, changes in corporate structure, and changes in the demographic makeup of the labor force all contribute to an increasingly unpredictable world of work. We do not know, however, how individuals cope with those changes and what factors help to predict which individuals will be most successful in adapting to the changing world of work. Additional questions for psychologists include, How do individuals function as the world of work shifts and changes? Which skills, interests, and values are critical in helping to predict those who will function well in a changing environment? In addition, as technology is increasingly shaping occupations, how can vocational psychologists help those who lack technological skills?

- **An individual will make one decision early in life**. One of the consequences of the labor force changes is that many career transitions will be made throughout the life of an individual. Yet most of the research reviewed in this chapter focused on adolescents and the decisions made early in life. Future questions may include, What psychological, cognitive, and social resources do individuals bring to their work decisions and transitions throughout their work lives, including in midlife and through retirement? How does career adaptability predict successful transitions after adolescence?

- **Career counseling is short term and focused in information giving**. However, as noted above, many career issues overlap with other aspects of life. Heppner & Heppner's (2003) research agenda for career counseling is a promising start for psychologists to begin examining what is effective in the career counseling process. Questions for future research include, What are the critical characteristics of the career counseling process? What contextual variables alter career counseling? What types and formats of career counseling work for what types of clients?

Clearly, there are a number of areas in which vocational psychology research can help to make a difference in people's lives, including the contributions made by psychologists in welfare-to-work reform (Juntunen et al. 2006) and the connection between career development, academic achievement, and educational development that can help to shape educational reform. Additional opportunities for research in vocational psychology to inform public policy include leveling the occupational landscape for men and women as well as for whites and racial/ethnic minorities, and helping to promote healthy work/life balance. It is, indeed, an exhilarating time for vocational psychologists as they contribute to knowledge that has broad psychological, contextual, and policy implications.

SUMMARY POINTS

1. Job satisfaction is more fully explained by variables other than congruence, but other aspects of Holland's theory were supported. Holland's theory appears to be most applicable for cultural groups similar to Caucasians.

2. Children's career dreams and aspirations do not very accurately predict their occupations in adulthood. Those eventual choices are influenced by parental socioeconomic status, schooling, and educational/environmental opportunities. However, aspirations can mediate the effects of an impoverished background.

3. Career exploration is best promoted by an individual's career adaptability, positive relationships, openness to experiences, and social and psychological capital.

4. An individual's beliefs in his/her ability to accomplish career-related tasks are critical predictors of career choice, particularly in nontraditional careers.

5. The context in which an individual lives is shaped by his/her gender, race/ethnicity, social class, and sexual orientation. All of these factors influence an individual's actual and perceived career opportunities and choices.

6. Career decision-making difficulties may be related to an individual's need to continue exploring various options and lack of readiness to make a decision. However, decision-making difficulties also may be related to other types of psychological concerns, such as general anxiety and indecisiveness.

7. Career counseling and interventions are effective. The most effective type of career counseling is individual counseling that contains homework, assessment interpretations, information on the world of work, social support, and exposure to role models.

FUTURE ISSUES

1. What role does work play in psychological health?

2. How can new methodologies and theoretical perspectives (constructivism, social constructionism) help to further our understanding of individuals' meaning of career and work?

3. How can research expand in complexity to better explain career and work behavior?

4. How does context influence the career and work choices of individuals at various developmental points? Are some contexts more salient at certain times than at other stages?

5. Is career counseling that integrates multiple life contexts more effective? Does this effectiveness differ across various groups?

6. How can vocational psychology be integrated with and influence contemporary public policy issues?

ACKNOWLEDGMENTS

The author wishes to thank David Blustein, Jean Carter, Ruth Fassinger, Gail Hackett, Robert Leitheiser, and Stephen Wester for comments on a draft of this manuscript and Mary Fitzpatrick, Sarah Gillis, and Neeta Kantamneni for assistance collecting and organizing the articles reviewed.

LITERATURE CITED

Adams EM, Cahill BJ, Ackerlind SJ. 2005. A qualitative study of Latino lesbian and gay youths' experiences with discrimination and the career development process. *J. Vocat. Behav.* 66:199–218

Albion MJ, Fogarty GJ. 2002. Factors influencing career decision making in adolescents and adults. *J. Career Assess.* 10:91–126

Alves Ferreira JA, Hood AB. 1995. The development and validation of a Holland-type Portuguese vocational interest inventory. *J. Vocat. Behav.* 46:119–30

Anderson MZ, Tracey TJG, Rounds J. 1997. Examining the invariance of Holland's vocational interest model across gender. *J. Vocat. Behav.* 50:349–64

Anderson S, Brown C. 1997. Self-efficacy as a determinant of career maturity in urban and rural high school seniors. *J. Career Assess.* 5:305–15

Anderson SL, Betz NE. 2001. Sources of social self-efficacy expectations: their measurement and relation to career development. *J. Vocat. Behav.* 58:98–117

Armstrong PI, Crombie G. 2000. Compromises in adolescents' occupational aspirations and expectations from grades 8 to 10. *J. Vocat. Behav.* 56:82–98

Armstrong PI, Hubert L, Rounds J. 2003. Circular unidimensional scaling: a new look at group differences in interest structure. *J. Couns. Psychol.* 50:297–308

Armstrong PI, Smith TJ, Donnay DAC, Rounds J. 2004. The Strong Ring: a basic interest model of occupational structure. *J. Couns. Psychol.* 51:299–313

Bandura A. 1997. *Self-Efficacy: The Exercise of Control.* New York: Freeman

Bandura A, Barbaranelli C, Vittorio CG, Pastorelli C. 2001. Self-efficacy beliefs as shapers of children's aspirations and career trajectories. *Child Dev.* 72:187–206

Betz NE, Borgen FH, Kaplan A, Harmon LW. 1998. Gender and Holland type as moderators of the validity and interpretive utility of the Skills Confidence Inventory. *J. Vocat. Behav.* 53:281–99

Betz NE, Borgen FH, Rottinghaus P, Paulsen A, Halper CR, Harmon LW. 2003. The Expanded Skills Confidence Inventory: measuring basic dimensions of vocational activity. *J. Vocat. Behav.* 62:76–100

An empirical examination that shows the influence of parents' self-efficacy on children's aspirations.

Empirical demonstration of the influence of self-efficacy in the considerations of nontraditional careers for women.

Betz NE, Hackett G. 1981. The relationship of career-related self-efficacy expectations to perceived career options in college women and men. *J. Couns. Psychol.* 28:399–410

Betz NE, Klein KL. 1996. Relationships among measures of career self-efficacy, generalized self-efficacy, and global self-esteem. *J. Career Assess.* 4:285–98

Betz NE, Schifano RS. 2000. Evaluation of an intervention to increase realistic self-efficacy and interests in college women. *J. Vocat. Behav.* 56:35–52

Betz NE, Voyten KK. 1997. Efficacy and outcome expectations influence career exploration and decidedness. *Career Dev. Q.* 46:179–89

Betz NE, Wolfe JB. 2005. Measuring confidence for basic domains of vocational activity in high school students. *J. Career Assess.* 13:251–70

Blustein DL. 2006. *Psychology of Working: A New Perspective on Career Development, Counseling, and Public Policy.* Mahweh, NJ: Erlbaum

A qualitative study that demonstrates the influence of social class and career adaptability in career considerations for inner-city youth.

Blustein DL, Chaves AP, Diemer MA, Gallagher LA, Marshall KG, et al. 2002. Voices of the forgotten half: the role of social class in the school-to-work transition. *J. Couns. Psychol.* 49:311–23

Blustein DL, Schultheiss DEP, Flum H. 2004. Toward a relational perspective of the psychology of careers and working: a social constructionist analysis. *J. Vocat. Behav.* 64:423–40

Boatwright KJ, Gilbert MS, Forrest L, Ketzenberger K. 1996. Impact of identity development upon career trajectory: listening to the voices of lesbian women. *J. Vocat. Behav.* 48:210–28

Brown C, George-Curran R, Smith ML. 2003a. The role of emotional intelligence in the career commitment and decision-making process. *J. Career Assess.* 11:379–92

Brown SD, Lent RW. 2005. *Career Development and Counseling: Putting Theory and Research to Work.* New York: Wiley

A meta-analysis that describes five critical ingredients in career counseling: homework, assessment interpretations, information on the work world, social support, and exposure to role models.

Brown SD, Ryan Krane NE, Brecheisen J, Castelino P, Budisin I, et al. 2003b. Critical ingredients of career choice interventions: more analyses and new hypotheses. *J. Vocat. Behav.* 62:411–28

Bynner J. 1997. Basic skills in adolescents' occupational preparation. *Career Dev. Q.* 45:305–21

Bynner J. 1998. Education and family components of identity in the transition from school to work. *Int. J. Behav. Dev.* 22:29–53

Bynner J, Parsons S. 2002. Social exclusion and the transition from school to work: the case of young people not in education, employment, or training (NEET). *J. Vocat. Behav.* 60:289–309

Chaves AP, Diemer MA, Blustein DL, Gallagher LA, DeVoy JE, et al. 2004. Conceptions of work: the view from urban youth. *J. Couns. Psychol.* 51:275–86

Chung YB, Harmon LW. 1999. Assessment of perceived occupational opportunity for black Americans. *J. Career Assess.* 7:45–62

Constantine MG, Wallace BC, Kindaichi MM. 2005. Examining contextual factors in the career decision status of African American adolescents. *J. Career Assess.* 13:307–19

Cook EP, Heppner MJ, O'Brien KM. 2002. Career development of women of color and white women: assumptions, conceptualization, and interventions from an ecological perspective. *Career Dev. Q.* 50:291–305

Cook TD, Church MB, Ajanaku S, Shadish WR, Kim, JR, Cohen R. 1996. The development of occupational aspirations and expectations among inner-city boys. *Child Dev.* 67:3368–85

Davey FH. 2001. The relationship between engineering and young women's occupational priorities. *Can. J. Couns.* 35:221–28

Day SX, Rounds J. 1998. Universality of vocational interest structure among racial and ethnic minorities. *Am. Psychol.* 53:728–36

Diegelman NM, Subich LM. 2001. Academic and vocational interests as a function of outcome expectancies in social cognitive career theory. *J. Vocat. Behav.* 59:394–405

du Toit R, de Bruin GP. 2002. The structural validity of Holland's R-I-A-S-E-C model of vocational personality types for young black South African men and women. *J. Career Assess.* 10:62–77

Duffy RD, Blustein DL. 2005. The relationship between spirituality, religiousness, and career adaptability. *J. Vocat. Behav.* 67:429–40

Einarsdottir S, Rounds J. 2000. Application of three dimensions of vocational interests to the Strong Interest Inventory. *J. Vocat. Behav.* 56:363–79

Farh J, Leong FTL, Law KS. 1998. Cross-cultural validity of Holland's model in Hong Kong. *J. Vocat. Behav.* 52:425–40

Farmer HS, Rotella S, Anderson C, Wandrop J. 1998. Gender differences in science, math, and technology careers: prestige level and Holland interest type. *J. Vocat. Behav.* 53:73–96

Farmer HS, Wardrop JL, Anderson MZ, Risinger R. 1995. Women's career choices: focus on science, math, and technology careers. *J. Couns. Psychol.* 42:155–70

Fassinger RE. 1995. From invisibility to integration: lesbian identity in the workplace. *Career Dev. Q.* 44:148–67

Fassinger RE. 1996. Notes from the margins: integrating lesbian experience into the vocational psychology of women. *J. Vocat. Behav.* 48:160–75

Felsman DE, Blustein DL. 1999. The role of peer relatedness in late adolescent career development. *J. Vocat. Behav.* 54:279–95

Flores LY, O'Brien KM. 2002. The career development of Mexican American adolescent women: a test of social cognitive career theory. *J. Couns. Psychol.* 49:14–27

Flum H. 2001. Relational dimensions in career development. *J. Vocat. Behav.* 59:1–16

Fouad NA. 2002. Cross-cultural differences in vocational interests: between-group differences on the Strong Interest Inventory. *J. Couns. Psychol.* 49:283–89

Fouad NA, Byars-Winston AM. 2005. Cultural context of career choice: meta-analysis of race/ethnicity differences. *Career Dev. Q.* 53:223–33

Fouad NA, Harmon LW, Borgen FH. 1997. Structure of interests in employed male and female members of US racial-ethnic minority and nonminority groups. *J. Couns. Psychol.* 44:339–45

Fouad NA, Mohler CJ. 2004. Cultural validity of Holland's theory and the Strong Interest Inventory for five racial/ethnic groups. *J. Career Assess.* 12:423–39

Fouad NA, Smith PL. 1996. A test of a social cognitive model for middle school students: math and science. *J. Couns. Psychol.* 43:338–46

Fouad NA, Smith PL, Zao KE. 2002. Across academic domains: extensions of the social-cognitive career model. *J. Couns. Psychol.* 49:164–71

Fouad NA, Walker CM. 2005. Cultural influences on responses to items on the Strong Interest Inventory. *J. Vocat. Behav.* 66:104–23

Friedland DS, Price RH. 2003. Underemployment: consequences for the health and well-being of workers. *Am. J. Community Psychol.* 32:33–45

Gainor KA, Lent RW. 1998. Social cognitive expectations and racial identity attitudes in predicting the math choice intentions of black college students. *J. Couns. Psychol.* 45:403–13

Gati I, Krausz M, Osipow SH. 1996. A taxonomy of difficulties in career decision making. *J. Couns. Psychol.* 43:510–26

Gati I, Osipow SH, Givon M. 1995. Gender differences in career decision making: the content and structure of preferences. *J. Couns. Psychol.* 42:204–16

Outlines an argument for the role of relationships in vocational identity development.

Conceptualizes career decision-making difficulties as stemming from lack of information, lack of readiness, or inconsistent information; has been empirically supported.

Gati I, Saka N. 2001. High school students' career-related decision-making difficulties. *J. Couns. Dev.* 79:331–40

Glidden-Tracey CE, Parraga MI. 1996. Assessing the structure of vocational interests among Bolivian university students. *J. Vocat. Behav.* 48:96–106

Gomez MJ, Fassinger RE, Prosser J, Cooke K, Mejia B, Luna J. 2001. Voces abriendo caminos (voices foraging paths): a qualitative study of the career development of notable Latinas. *J. Couns. Psychol.* 48:286–300

Hackett G, Betz NE. 1981. A self-efficacy approach to the career development of women. *J. Vocat. Behav.* 18:326–39

Hansen JIC, Sarma ZM, Collins RC. 1999. An evaluation of Holland's Model of vocational interests for Chicana(o) and Latina(o) college students. *Meas. Eval. Couns. Dev.* 32:2–13

Hansen JIC, Scullard MG, Haviland MG. 2000. The interest structures of Native American college students. *J. Career Assess.* 8:159–72

Hartung PJ, Vandiver BJ, Leong FTL, Pope M, Niles SG, Farrow B. 1998. Appraising cultural identity in career-development assessment and counseling. *Career Dev. Q.* 46:276–93

Helwig AA. 2003. The measurement of Holland types in a 10-year longitudinal study of a sample of students. *J. Employ. Couns.* 40:24–32

Heppner MJ, Heppner PP. 2003. Identifying process variables in career counseling: a research agenda. *J. Vocat. Behav.* 62:429–52

Heppner MJ, Lee D, Heppner PP, McKinnon LC, Multon KD, Gysbers NC. 2004. The role of problem-solving appraisal in the process and outcome of career counseling. *J. Vocat. Behav.* 65:217–38

Holland JL. 1997. *Making Vocational Choices: A Theory of Vocational Personalities and Work Environments.* Odessa, FL: Psychol. Assess. Resour. 3rd ed.

Jackson CC, Neville HA. 1998. Influence of racial identity attitudes on African American college students' vocational identity and hope. *J. Vocat. Behav.* 53:97–113

Jepsen DA, Dickson GL. 2003. Continuity in life-span career development: career exploration as a precursor to career establishment. *Career Dev. Q.* 51:217–33

Jome LM, Tokar DM. 1998. Dimensions of masculinity and major choice traditionality. *J. Vocat. Behav.* 52:120–34

Jones SR. 1997. Voices of identity and difference: A qualitative exploration of the multiple dimensions of identity development in women college students. *J. Coll. Student Dev.* 38:376–86

Juntunen CL, Barraclough DJ, Broneck CL, Seibel GA, Winrow SA, Morin PM. 2001. American Indian perspectives on the career journey. *J. Couns. Psychol.* 48:274–85

Juntunen CL, Cavett AM, Clow RB, Rempel V, Darrow RE, Guilmino A. 2006. Social justice through self-sufficiency: Vocational psychology and the transition from welfare to work. In *Handbook of Social Justice in Counseling Psychology*, ed. RL Toporek, LH Gerstein, NA Fouad, G Roysircar, T Israel, pp. 294–312. Thousand Oaks, CA: Sage

Kenny ME, Bledsoe M. 2005. Contributions of the relational context to career adaptability among urban adolescents. *J. Vocat. Behav.* 66:257–72

Kenny ME, Blustein DL, Chaves A, Grossman JM, Gallagher LA. 2003. The role of perceived barriers and relational support in the educational and vocational lives of urban high school students. *J. Couns. Psychol.* 50:142–55

Ketterson TU, Blustein DL. 1997. Attachment relationships and the career exploration process. *Career Dev. Q.* 46:167–78

Kracke B. 1997. Parental behaviors and adolescents' career exploration. *Career Dev. Q.* 45:341–50

Articulates an agenda for research in career counseling.

Krieshok TS. 1998. An anti-introspectivist view of career decision making. *Career Dev. Q.* 46:210–29

Lancaster BP, Rudolph CE, Perkins TS, Patten TG. 1999. The reliability and validity of the Career Decision Difficulties Questionnaire. *J. Career Assess.* 7:393–413

Lapan RT, Adams A, Turner S, Hinkelman JM. 2000. Seventh graders' vocational interest and efficacy expectation patterns. *J. Career Dev.* 26:215–29

Lapan RT, Shaughnessy P, Boggs K. 1996. Efficacy expectations and vocational interests as mediators between sex and choice of math/science college majors: a longitudinal study. *J. Vocat. Behav.* 49:277–91

Larson LM, Rottinghaus PJ, Borgen FH. 2002. Meta-analyses of Big Six interests and Big Five personality factors. *J. Vocat. Behav.* 61:217–39

Leal-Muniz V, Constantine MG. 2005. Predictors of the career commitment process in Mexican American college students. *J. Career Assess.* 13:204–15

Lease SH. 2003. Testing a model of men's nontraditional occupational choices. *Career Dev. Q.* 51:244–58

Lent RW, Brown SD, Brenner B, Chopra SB, Davis T, et al. 2001. The role of contextual supports and barriers in the choice of math/science educational options: a test of social cognitive hypotheses. *J. Couns. Psychol.* 48:474–83

Lent RW, Brown SD, Hackett G. 2000. Contextual supports and barriers to career choice: a social cognitive analysis. *J. Couns. Psychol.* 47:36–49

Lent RW, Brown SD, Schmidt J, Brenner B, Lyons H, Treistman D. 2003. Relation of contextual supports and barriers to choice behavior in engineering majors: test of alternative social cognitive models. *J. Couns. Psychol.* 50:458–65

Lent RW, Brown SD, Sheu HB, Schmidt J, Brenner BR, et al. 2005. Social cognitive predictors of academic interests and goals in engineering: utility for women and students at historically black universities. *J. Couns. Psychol.* 52:84–92

Leong FTL, Austin JT, Sekaran U, Komarraju M. 1998. An evaluation of the cross-cultural validity of Holland's theory: career choices by workers in India. *J. Vocat. Behav.* 52:441–55

Levine PB, Zimmerman DJ. 1995. A comparison of the sex-type of occupational aspirations and subsequent achievement. *Work Occup.* 22:73–84

Lubinski D, Benbow CP, Ryan J. 1995. Stability of vocational interests among the intellectually gifted from adolescence to adulthood: a 15-year longitudinal study. *J. Appl. Psychol.* 80:196–200

Luzzo DA. 1996. A psychometric evaluation of the Career Decision-Making Self-Efficacy Scale. *J. Couns. Dev.* 74:276–79

Luzzo DA, McWhirter EH. 2001. Sex and ethnic differences in the perception of educational and career-related barriers and levels of coping efficacy. *J. Couns. Dev.* 79:61–67

Mau WC. 2001. Assessing career decision-making difficulties: a cross-cultural study. *J. Career Assess.* 9:353–64

Mau WC. 2003. Factors that influence persistence in science and engineering career aspirations. *Career Dev. Q.* 51:234–43

McKee-Ryan F, Song Z, Wanberg CR, Kinicki AJ. 2005. Psychological and physical well-being during unemployment: a meta-analytic study. *J. Appl. Psychol.* 90:53–76

McWhirter EH, Hackett G, Bandalos DL. 1998. A causal model of the educational plans and career expectations of Mexican American high school girls. *J. Couns. Psychol.* 45:166–81

Meeus W, Dekovic M, Iedema J. 1997. Unemployment and identity in adolescence: a social comparison perspective. *Career Dev. Q.* 45:369–80

Miller L, Budd J. 1999. The development of occupational sex-role stereotypes, occupational preferences and academic subject preferences in children at ages 8, 12 and 16. *Educ. Psychol.* 19:17–35

Multon KD, Heppner MJ, Gysbers NC, Zook C, Ellis-Kalton CA. 2001. Client psychological distress: an important factor in career counseling. *Career Dev. Q.* 49:324–35

Murphy GC, Athanasou JA. 1999. The effect of unemployment on mental health. *J. Occup. Organ. Psychol.* 72:83–99

Nauta MM, Epperson DL, Kahn JH. 1998. A multiple-groups analysis of predictors of higher level career aspirations among women in mathematics, science, and engineering majors. *J. Couns. Psychol.* 45:483–96

O'Brien KM. 1996. The influence of psychological separation and parental attachment on the career development of adolescent women. *J. Vocat. Behav.* 48:257–74

Osipow SH, Gati I. 1998. Construct and concurrent validity of the career decision-making difficulties questionnaire. *J. Career Assess.* 6:347–64

Parker CP, Baltes BB, Young SA, Huff JW, Altmann RA, et al. 2003. Relationships between psychological climate perceptions and work outcomes: a meta-analytic review. *J. Organ. Behav.* 24:389–416

Parsons F. 1909. *Choosing a Vocation.* Garrett Park, MD: Garrett Park Press

Pearson SM, Bieschke KJ. 2001. Succeeding against the odds: an examination of familial influences on the career development of professional African American women. *J. Couns. Psychol.* 48:301–9

Phillips SD, Blustein DL, Jobin-Davis K, White SF. 2002. Preparation for the school-to-work transition: the views of high school students. *J. Vocat. Behav.* 61:202–16

Phillips SD, Christopher-Sisk EK, Gravino KL. 2001. Making career decisions in a relational context. *Couns. Psychol.* 29:193–213

Prediger DJ, Swaney KB. 2004. Work task dimensions underlying the world of work: research results for diverse occupational databases. *J. Career Assess.* 12:440–59

Prince JP. 1995. Influences on the career development of gay men. *Career Dev. Q.* 44:168–77

Reichel LS, Muchinsky PM. 1995. Life-history and developmental antecedents of female vocational preferences. *J. Career Assess.* 3:21–34

Reyes O, Kobus K, Gillock K. 1999. Career aspirations of urban, Mexican American adolescent females. *Hisp. J. Behav. Sci.* 21:366–82

Richardson MS. 2002. A metaperspective for counseling practice: a response to the challenge of contextualism. ***J. Vocat. Behav.*** **61:407–23**

Richardson MS. 2004. The emergence of new intentions in subjective experience: a social/personal constructionist and relational understanding. *J. Vocat. Behav.* 64:485–98

Richie BS, Fassinger RE, Linn SG, Johnson J, Prosser J, Robinson S. 1997. Persistence, connection, and passion: a qualitative study of the career development of highly achieving African American black and white women. *J. Couns. Psychol.* 44:133–48

Rindfuss RR, Cooksey EC, Sutterlin RL. 1999. Young adult occupational achievement: early expectations versus behavioral reality. *Work Occup.* 26:220–63

Robitschek C, Cook SW. 1999. The influence of personal growth initiative and coping styles on career exploration and vocational identity. *J. Vocat. Behav.* 54:127–41

Rojewski JW, Kim H. 2003. Career choice patterns and behavior of work-bound youth during early adolescence. *J. Career Dev.* 30:89–108

Rojewski JW, Yang B. 1997. Longitudinal analysis of select influences on adolescents' occupational aspirations. *J. Vocat. Behav.* 51:375–410

Rottinghaus PJ, Betz NE, Borgen FH. 2003a. Validity of parallel measures of vocational interests and confidence. *J. Career Assess.* 11:355–78

Argues that therapists need to reconceptualize the role of work in client's lives, and that public and private living domains need to be viewed holistically.

Rottinghaus PJ, Larson LM, Borgen FH. 2003b. The relation of self-efficacy and interests: a meta-analysis of 60 samples. *J. Vocat. Behav.* 62:221–36

Ryan JM, Tracey TJG, Rounds J. 1996. Generalizability of Holland's structure of vocational interests across ethnicity, gender, and socioeconomic status. *J. Couns. Psychol.* 43:330–37

Savickas ML. 1997. Career adaptability: an integrative construct for life-span, life-space theory. *Career Dev. Q.* 45:247–59

Savickas ML. 2002a. A developmental theory of vocational psychology. In *Career Choice and Development*, ed. D Brown, pp. 149–205. San Francisco: Jossey-Bass

Savickas ML. 2002b. Reinvigorating the study of careers. *J. Vocat. Behav.* 61:381–85

Savickas ML. 2005. The theory and practice of career construction. See Brown & Lent 2005, pp. 42–70

Schoon I, Parsons S. 2002. Teenage aspirations for future careers and occupational outcomes. *J. Vocat. Behav.* 60:262–88

Schultheiss DEP. 2003. A relational approach to career counseling: theoretical integration and practical application. *J. Couns. Dev.* 81:301–10

Schultheiss DEP, Palma TV, Manzi AJ. 2005. Career development in middle childhood: a qualitative inquiry. *Career Dev. Q.* 53:246–62

Shivy VA, Rounds J, Jones LE. 1999. Applying vocational interest models to naturally occurring occupational perceptions. *J. Couns. Psychol.* 46:207–17

Smith PL, Fouad NA. 1999. Subject-matter specificity of self-efficacy, outcome expectancies, interests, and goals: implications for the social-cognitive model. *J. Couns. Psychol.* 46:461–71

Soh S, Leong FTL. 2001. Cross-cultural validation of Holland's theory in Singapore: beyond structural validity of RIASEC. *J. Career Assess.* 9:115–33

Spokane AR, Cruza-Guet MC, Brown SD, Lent RW. 2005. Holland's theory of vocational personalities in work environments. See Brown & Lent 2005, pp. 24–41

Spokane AR, Fouad NA, Swanson JL. 2003. Culture-centered career intervention. *J. Vocat. Behav.* 62:453–58

Spokane AR, Meir EI, Catalano M. 2000. Person-environment congruence and Holland's theory: a review and reconsideration. *J. Vocat. Behav.* 57:137–87

Sullivan BA, Hansen JIC. 2004. Mapping associations between interests and personality: toward a conceptual understanding of individual differences in vocational behavior. *J. Couns. Psychol.* 51:287–98

Super DE, Savickas ML, Super CM. 1996. The life-span, life-space approach to careers. In *Career Choice and Development*, ed. D Brown, L Brooks, pp. 121–78. San Francisco: Jossey-Bass

Swanson JL, Daniels KK, Tokar DM. 1996. Assessing perceptions of career-related barriers: the Career Barriers Inventory. *J. Career Assess.* 4:219–44

Tak J. 2004. Structure of vocational interests for Korean college students. *J. Career Assess.* 12:298–311

Tang M. 2001. Investigation of the structure of vocational interests of Chinese college students. *J. Career Assess.* 9:365–80

Tang M, Fouad NA, Smith PL. 1999. Asian Americans' career choices: a path model to examine factors influencing their career choices. *J. Vocat. Behav.* 54:142–57

Taviera M, Silva MC, Rodríguez ML, Maia J. 1998. Individual characteristics and career exploration in adolescence. *Br. J. Guid. Couns.* 26:89–104

Taylor KM, Betz NE. 1983. Applications of self-efficacy theory to the understanding and treatment of career indecision. *J. Vocat. Behav.* 22:63–81

Provides a rationale for moving from a career maturity view to career adaptability; first significant modification of Super's developmental theory from a social constructivist perspective.

Tokar DM, Jome LM. 1998. Masculinity, vocational interests, and career choice traditionality: evidence for a fully mediated model. *J. Couns. Psychol.* 45:424–35

Tracey TJG. 2001. The development of structure of interests in children: setting the stage. *J. Vocat. Behav.* 59:89–104

Tracey TJG, Robbins SB, Hofsess CD. 2005. Stability and change in interests: a longitudinal study of adolescents from grades 8 through 12. *J. Vocat. Behav.* 66:1–25

Tracey TJG, Rounds J. 1996. The spherical representation of vocational interests. *J. Vocat. Behav.* 48:3–41

Tracey TJG, Ward CC. 1998. The structure of children's interests and competence perceptions. *J. Couns. Psychol.* 45:290–303

Tracey TJG, Watanabe N, Schneider PL. 1997. Structural invariance of vocational interests across Japanese and American cultures. *J. Couns. Psychol.* 44:346–54

Tsabari O, Tziner A, Meir EI. 2005. Updated meta-analysis on the relationship between congruence and satisfaction. *J. Career Assess.* 13:216–32

Turner SL, Lapan RT. 2003. The measurement of career interests among at-risk inner-city and middle-class suburban adolescents. *J. Career Assess.* 11:405–20

U.S. Census Bureau. 2005. Employed persons by occupation, race, Hispanic or Latino ethnicity, and sex. **http://www.census.gov**

Vincent PC, Peplau LA, Hill CT. 1998. A longitudinal application of the theory of reasoned action to women's career behavior. *J. Appl. Soc. Psychol.* 28:761–78

Wall J, Covell K, MacIntyre PD. 1999. Implications of social supports for adolescents' education and career aspirations. *Can. J. Behav. Sci.* 31:63–71

Walsh WB, Savickas ML. 2005. *Handbook of Vocational Psychology.* Mahweh, NJ: Erlbaum

Wampold BE, Ankarlo G, Mondin G, Trinidad-Carrillo M, Baumler B, Prater K. 1995. Social skills of and social environments produced by different Holland types: a social perspective on person/environment fit models. *J. Couns. Psychol.* 42:365–79

Watson MB, Stead GB, Schonegevel C. 1998. Does Holland's hexagon travel well? *Aust. J. Career Dev.* 7:22–26

Whiston SC, Keller BK. 2004. The influences of the family of origin on career development: a review and analysis. *Couns. Psychol.* 32:493–568

Whiston SC, Sexton TL, Lasoff DL. 1998. Career-intervention outcome: a replication and extension of Oliver and Spokane 1988. *J. Couns. Psychol.* 45:150–65

Wiesner M, Vondracek FW, Capaldi DM, Porfeli E. 2003. Childhood and adolescent predictors of early adult career pathways. *J. Vocat. Behav.* 63:305–28

Yang W, Stokes GS, Hui CH. 2005. Cross-cultural validation of Holland's interest structure in Chinese population. *J. Vocat. Behav.* 67:379–96

Young RA, Collin A. 2004. Introduction: constructivism and social constructionism in the career field. *J. Vocat. Behav.* 64:373–88

Health Psychology: Psychological Adjustment to Chronic Disease

Annette L. Stanton,[1] Tracey A. Revenson,[2] and Howard Tennen[3]

[1] Department of Psychology, University of California, Los Angeles, California 90095-1563; email: astanton@ucla.edu

[2] Program in Psychology, Graduate Center of the City University of New York, New York 10016-4309; email: TRevenson@gc.cuny.edu

[3] Department of Community Medicine and Health Care, University of Connecticut Health Center, Farmington, Connecticut 06030-6325; email: tennen@nso1.uchc.edu

Annu. Rev. Psychol. 2007. 58:565–92

First published online as a Review in Advance on August 24, 2006

The *Annual Review of Psychology* is online at http://psych.annualreviews.org

This article's doi: 10.1146/annurev.psych.58.110405.085615

0066-4308/07/0203-0565$20.00

Key Words

quality of life, coping, cancer, arthritis, cardiovascular disease

Abstract

Chronic diseases carry important psychological and social consequences that demand significant psychological adjustment. The literature is providing increasingly nuanced conceptualizations of adjustment, demonstrating that the experience of chronic disease necessitates adaptation in multiple life domains. Heterogeneity in adjustment is apparent between individuals and across the course of the disease trajectory. Focusing on cancer, cardiovascular disease, and rheumatic diseases, we review longitudinal investigations of distal (socioeconomic variables, culture/ethnicity, and gender-related processes) and proximal (interpersonal relationships, personality attributes, cognitive appraisals, and coping processes) risk and protective factors for adjustment across time. We observe that the past decade has seen a surge in research that is longitudinal in design, involves adequately characterized samples of sufficient size, and includes statistical control for initial values on dependent variables. A progressively convincing characterization of risk and protective factors for favorable adjustment to chronic illness has emerged. We identify critical issues for future research.

Contents

INTRODUCTION

In reflecting on his chronic and life-threatening illness, amyotrophic lateral sclerosis, Stephen Hawking tells his readers, "Apart from being unlucky enough to get ALS...I have been fortunate in almost every other respect. The help and support I received...have made it possible for me to lead a fairly normal life...." (Hawking 1988, p. vii). For decades, psychological theorists and physicians have conjectured about why some people who face the enduring stress of a chronic illness adjust well, whereas others demonstrate significant emotional and inter-personal decline. Research has yielded complex conceptualizations of what it means to adjust to chronic disease, theoretical frameworks to identify the factors that promote or hinder adjustment, and empirical evidence regarding the predictive utility of those constructs.

In this article, we examine psychosocial processes that contribute to people's adjustment to disease, with a focus on three disease clusters that constitute the major causes of death and disability in the United States: cancer, cardiovascular disease, and rheumatic diseases. We offer crosscutting observations about what is known regarding adjustment to these diseases, beginning with a brief discussion of the definition and impact of chronic disease and then considering the concept of adjustment. We review findings across several domains of constructs that predict adjustment and conclude by identifying major contributions of this work and critical issues for continued study.

The empirical literature on adjustment to chronic disease is large; for example, we identified more than 200 longitudinal reports on predictors of adjustment to cancer alone. We were necessarily selective in our review. To address predictors of adjustment, we set boundary conditions for studies to be included as exemplars. They had to pertain to cancer, cardiovascular disease, or rheumatic diseases; be published from 1985 to 2005; be longitudinal in design; include at least 50 participants at baseline; and include adjustment to illness as an outcome. We searched PsycINFO using specified criteria; we also searched specialty medical journals that regularly publish research on disease-related adjustment and that have high impact factors (ISI Web of Knowledge Journal Citation Reports).[1]

---

[1] In addition to medical journals referenced in PsycINFO, we reviewed the following medical journals: (*a*) for cardiovascular disease, *J. Am. Coll. Cardiology*, *Eur. Heart J.*, *Am. Heart J.*, *Chest*, and *Heart*; (*b*) for cancer, *J. Natl. Cancer Inst.*, *J. Clin. Oncol.*, *Cancer Epidem. Biomarkers Prev.*, and *Cancer*; and (*c*) for rheumatic diseases, *Arth. Rheum.*, *Rheumatology*, *Ann. Rheum. Dis.*, *J. Rheumatol.*, and *Lupus*.

In this article, we do not tackle the important topics of adjustment to chronic disease in childhood, predictors of caregiver adjustment, health behavior change and psychosocial interventions[2] in chronic disease, and unique issues in advanced or end-stage disease. Although we selected disease clusters that span levels of life threat, controllability, and treatment demands, we are mindful that other diseases, such as diabetes and acquired immune deficiency syndrome, can pose unique challenges. The literature on psychological processes as causal in disease outcomes was not our focus. However, in the final section we address developments in that body of work.

Definition and Impact of Chronic Disease

Chronic diseases are "illnesses that are prolonged, do not resolve spontaneously, and are rarely cured completely" [Centers for Disease Control and Prevention (CDC) 2003]. Psychologically, however, the definition of chronic disease is complex: Does one stop being a cancer patient when treatment is completed? When one celebrates the five-year anniversary after diagnosis? Although most investigators would agree that the disease process must persist at least several months to constitute chronic disease, the meaning of "chronic" lies in the eye of the beholder (Rabin et al. 2004).

More than 90 million Americans live with chronic diseases, with racial minorities and women disproportionately affected (CDC 2005). Chronic diseases cause 7 of every 10 deaths (1.7 million people each year) in the United States (CDC 2005), and they are the leading cause of disability. Chronic, disabling conditions result in major activity limitations for more than 1 in 10 Americans;

arthritis, the most common cause of disability, affects approximately 43 million people (CDC 2005). Chronic diseases account for 75% of the $1.4 trillion medical care costs in the United States (CDC 2005). As the population ages, increasing numbers of people will live with at least one chronic condition.

Whereas some consequences of chronic disease are abrupt and unmistakable, such as in surgical interventions, others are gradual and subtle, such as losing energy (Thompson & Kyle 2000). Declines in daily activities, vitality, and relationships with friends and family can proceed with an uneven course. This great variation, even among people with the same disease, presents a genuine challenge to any attempt to cull generalizations from the literature on how people adjust to chronic disease.

CONCEPTUALIZATIONS OF ADJUSTMENT TO CHRONIC DISEASE

What does it mean to adjust to chronic disease? Three broad conclusions emerge from the literature: (a) chronic disease requires adjustment across multiple life domains, (b) adjustment unfolds over time, and (c) there is marked heterogeneity across individuals in how they adjust to chronic illness.

Multifaceted Nature of Adjustment

Stanton et al. (2001) identified five related conceptualizations of adjustment to chronic disease: mastery of disease-related adaptive tasks, preservation of functional status, perceived quality of life in several domains, absence of psychological disorder, and low negative affect. Increasingly, researchers are considering positive indicators of adjustment, such as maintaining positive mood and retaining purpose in life. These conceptualizations reveal that adjustment encompasses multiple components that cross interpersonal, cognitive, emotional, physical, and behavioral domains. Components also are interrelated, so that functional status affects and is affected

---

[2]We elaborate on implications of the literature on conceptualizations and predictors of adjustment to chronic illness for the design of psychosocial interventions in Stanton & Revenson (2007).

MI: myocardial
infarction

RA: rheumatoid
arthritis

by depressive symptoms among people with chronic disease (DeVellis et al. 1997), and depression magnifies the risk for nonadherence to medical regimens in chronic disease patients (DiMatteo et al. 2000).

Hamburg & Adams (1967) identified several essential adaptive tasks in adjustment to major life transitions, including serious illness: regulating distress, maintaining personal worth, restoring relations with important others, pursuing recovery of bodily functions, and bolstering the likelihood of a personally and socially acceptable situation once physical recovery is attained. Taylor's (1983) cognitive adaptation theory also highlights self-esteem enhancement and preservation of a sense of mastery, and adds resolution of a search for meaning as an adaptive task. Focusing on physical illness, Moos & Schaefer (1984) added the tasks of managing pain and symptoms, negotiating the health care environment, and maintaining satisfactory relationships with medical professionals. Other conceptualizations (e.g., Spelten et al. 2002) focus on functional status, often operationalized as resumption of paid employment, routine activities, and mobility. Quality of life in physical, functional, social, sexual, and emotional domains also denotes adjustment to chronic disease (Cella 2001, Newman et al. 1996).

Adjustment is most commonly defined as the presence or absence of diagnosed psychological disorder, psychological symptoms, or negative mood. Investigators also have begun to examine positive affect and perceived personal growth as indicators of adjustment, for several reasons. First, many individuals with chronic disease report positive adjustment (e.g., Mols et al. 2005). Second, positive adjustment is not simply the absence of distress. A disease that disrupts life does not preclude the experience of joy (Folkman & Moskowitz 2000a), and individuals who find positive meaning in their illness are not immune to significant distress (Calhoun & Tedeschi 2006). Third, positive and negative

affect represent relatively distinct dimensions (Watson et al. 1999) and potentially have different determinants (e.g., Echteld et al. 2003) and consequences (see Kiecolt-Glaser et al. 2002, Pressman & Cohen 2005 for reviews). Fourth, positive affect may buffer or repair negative mood (Fredrickson 2001). For example, the presence of positive affect appears to reduce the magnitude of the relation between pain and negative affect in rheumatic disease patients (Zautra et al. 2001). Finally, the depiction of chronic disease as guaranteeing unrelenting suffering can provoke inordinate despair in those who face serious disease.

Unbalanced attention to positive adjustment can also have untoward consequences. The expectation of the unfailingly "strong" patient permits the ill person little latitude for having a bad day (or a bad year). Presenting a positive face may become prescriptive, so that one falls prey to the "tyranny of positive thinking" (Holland & Lewis 2000, p. 14) or the notion that any distress or negative thinking will exacerbate chronic disease.

Adjustment as a Dynamic Process

Owing to changing contextual factors, adaptation to chronic illness is neither linear nor lockstep. Twists and turns in disease progression such as cancer recurrence, repeat myocardial infarction (MI), or arthritis flares require readjustment. Although stage theories of adjustment to trauma or disease have been proposed, scant supporting evidence exists (Wortman & Silver 2001). Disease severity and prognosis, the rapidity of health declines, and whether the disease involves symptomatic and asymptomatic periods all shape the adaptive tasks of illness. In individuals with long-standing rheumatoid arthritis (RA), for example, depressive symptoms and quality of life indices are relatively stable over time (e.g., Brown et al. 1989), unless the person is coping with a flare, which involves a sudden increase in pain and disability, or joint replacement surgery (e.g., Fitzgerald et al. 2004).

Evidence for Heterogeneity in Adjustment

Certainly, the experience of chronic illness carries psychological consequences. The strongest evidence that chronic illness provokes life disruption is offered by large-scale, prospective studies in which adjustment is assessed prior to and following disease diagnosis. For example, in the Nurses' Health Study cohort of 48,892 women, 759 were diagnosed with breast cancer during a four-year period (Michael et al. 2000). After control in analyses for multiple covariates, women diagnosed with cancer experienced an increase in pain and declines in physical and social function, vitality, and ability to perform emotional and physical roles, compared to women who did not receive a cancer diagnosis. Group differences remained for four of seven quality-of-life domains up to four years postdiagnosis, although fewer problems were apparent as time since diagnosis increased.

Polsky et al. (2005) examined five biennial waves of the Health and Retirement Study in more than 8000 adults aged 51 to 61 without significant depressive symptoms at study onset. Within two years after an initial diagnosis of cancer, diagnosed individuals had the highest risk of significant depressive symptoms (hazard ratio = 3.55 versus no incident disease), which decreased during the next six years. The risk of onset of depressive symptoms also increased significantly within the first two years of a diagnosis of heart disease or chronic lung disease (but not hypertension, arthritis, diabetes, or stroke), and higher risk for depressive symptoms persisted over the next six years for those with heart disease. Those diagnosed with arthritis had increased risk for depressive symptoms two to four years after diagnosis.

Despite elevated risk for distress, there is considerable variability in adjustment to chronic illness. For example, studies in rheumatic disease reveal large differences in pain, disability, and fatigue among populations with similar clinical parameters (e.g., Stone et al. 1997). Good evidence for heterogeneity in trajectories of adjustment is provided by Helgeson et al. (2004), who identified trajectories of functioning in women with breast cancer from 4 to 55 months after diagnosis. Forty-three percent of the sample evidenced high and stable psychological quality of life, 18% began somewhat lower and improved slightly, 26% evidenced low psychological functioning shortly after diagnosis but showed rapid improvement, and 12% had an immediate and substantial decline in psychological functioning with slight improvement. With regard to heart disease, Dew et al. (2005) identified five groups of heart transplant patients based on their distinct temporal distress profiles over several years: a group with consistently low distress, a group with consistent clinically significant levels of distress, groups with high distress for the first several months or for three years followed by improvement, and a group with fluctuating distress. Boudrez & De Backer (2001) also demonstrated heterogeneity in adjustment. Although most coronary artery bypass graft (CABG) patients evidenced improvement in the first six months after surgery, fully 30% of the sample demonstrated increasing distress, declining well-being, or failure to improve.

Instead of catalyzing global maladjustment, chronic disease typically has more circumscribed effects for most people. Andersen et al. (1989) observed that cancer creates "islands" of disruption in specific life domains and at particular points in the disease trajectory. For example, fear or uncertainty about the future, physical limitations, and pain are common concerns across diseases (e.g., Dunkel-Schetter et al. 1992, Newman et al. 1996); life threat is more relevant in cancer and heart disease. Effects on work and daily activities and the economic impact of treatment can loom large for all three illnesses (i.e., cancer, heart disease, and rheumatic disease). Although commonalities such as these are apparent, considerable variability in concerns exists across persons, time, and contexts. A goal of theoretical frameworks that posit

CABG: coronary artery bypass graft

risk and protective factors is to account for this variation.

SES: socioeconomic status

CONTRIBUTORS TO ADJUSTMENT TO CHRONIC DISEASE

Theories of stress and coping, self-regulation, personality, and social processes have shaped the foundation for identifying determinants of adjustment to chronic disease. Rather than detailing discrete theories, we review predictors that emerge across theories. We discuss socioeconomic variables, culture/ethnicity, and gender-related processes as more distal contributors to adjustment, and interpersonal processes, personality attributes, cognitive appraisals, and coping processes as more proximal determinants. Although these domains capture many of the factors that have received attention as predictors of adjustment, they are embedded in still other contexts not detailed here (Revenson 2003). For example, developmental issues are relevant, including whether the disease is occurring "on time" or "off time" in the life cycle (Neugarten 1979). Acknowledging a complex picture, we characterize a sampling of central contributors to adjustment.

What people think, feel, and do about their health is situated in a wider context. A contextual approach (Ickovics et al. 2001, Revenson 1990) emphasizes the interdependence of individuals' behavior and their life circumstances, and the interplay of distal contexts and proximal mechanisms for influencing health. Macro-level or "upstream" factors (Berkman & Glass 1999) such as culture, socioeconomic status (SES), and social change (e.g., urbanization) affect social network structure, which in turn sets the stage for psychosocial mechanisms (e.g., social support) to influence health through "downstream" behavioral and physiological pathways. Similarly, Taylor et al. (1997), in an analysis of unhealthy environments, suggest that SES affects health indirectly through its influence on key physical and social environments.

Socioeconomic Status

Marked and growing socioeconomic disparities in the United States are disquieting, in part because of the well-documented inverse graded association of SES with morbidity and mortality (e.g., Adler & Ostrove 1999). Reflected in educational attainment, income, occupational status, or some combination of those variables, SES affects health outcomes directly and through environmental and psychosocial mechanisms, including access to health care and risky and protective health behaviors (e.g., smoking, alcohol abuse, and exercise).

Poverty and low-SES environments set the stage for two intertwined phenomena—experiencing more stressful life events of greater magnitude and having fewer social and psychological resources to manage them—that, in turn, contribute to poorer mental and physical health (Gallo & Matthews 2003). Low education and the perception of medical care as being a substantial economic burden predict greater depressive symptoms and poorer functional status among the chronically ill (e.g., Harrison et al. 2005, Havranek et al. 2004, McEntegart et al. 1997, Stommel et al. 2004). Callahan et al. (1996) demonstrated that a sense of helplessness mediated the relation between lower education and early mortality in RA patients.

Although we conceptualize SES as a predictor of adjustment, the pattern is not unidirectional. Chronic, disabling diseases have enormous impact on work disability. Studies of RA show that people often stop working early in the disease process (e.g., Reisine et al. 2001). Such work-related disability can create downward drift in SES.

Culture and Ethnicity

Although the concept of culture applies across standard social categories (e.g., race, gender, and sexual orientation), most research in illness adjustment has focused on race/ethnicity. Ethnic group membership is a marker for many psychological processes—identity, group pride, and discrimination—that are embedded in a sociohistorical context. Thus, race and ethnicity can be considered markers related to differences in exposure to risk factors and resources. In the chronic disease literature, we uncovered few longitudinal studies of how predictors of disease-related adjustment might be conditioned by culture or ethnicity (Alferi et al. 2001, Taylor et al. 2002).

Within– or between–ethnic group cross-sectional studies were more numerous (e.g., Giedzinska et al. 2004). This small literature reveals few pronounced differences in broad indicators of disease-related quality of life, although elevated psychological symptoms or disease-related concerns have been reported in some groups (e.g., low-income Latina cervical cancer patients; Meyerowitz et al. 2000). Group differences in approaches to confronting disease also have emerged, with African American and Latina cancer patients more likely to endorse spiritual practices than white patients, for example (Lee et al. 2000).

Mechanisms for these group differences have not been established. Thus, while we can say that the correlates of mental and physical health in lupus vary across ethnic groups (e.g., Bae et al. 2001), we are hard pressed to understand why. In light of observations that between-group studies do little to illuminate mechanisms for obtained differences and that ethnic categories contain within-group variability, it is clear that very little is known about implications of culture and ethnicity for disease-related adjustment.

Gender-Related Processes

Gender differences in adjustment among individuals with chronic disease mirror differences observed in the general population, such that women report more depressive symptoms than men, for example (DeVellis et al. 1997, Hagedoorn et al. 2000, Stommel et al. 2004). Women also report greater pain, symptoms, and disability in association with rheumatic disease (Katz & Criswell 1996). Beyond the examination of group differences, gender-linked personality orientations and gender roles as they operate in relationships of the chronically ill are two areas that have received attention.

How might gender socialization translate into differentially effective modes of coping with illness? One vehicle involves the development of gender-linked personality orientations, such as agency and communion (see Helgeson 1994, Helgeson & Fritz 1998 for reviews). Agency has been linked to better adjustment across a number of chronic diseases, including coronary heart disease (Helgeson 1993). Unmitigated communion, i.e., overinvolvement with others to the detriment of personal well-being, predicts subsequent greater disease-related distress (Danoff-Burg et al. 2004; Fritz 2000; Helgeson 1993, 1994).

Interpersonal relationships are vital components of women's adjustment to major stressors (Revenson 1994), potentially creating both demands (Wethington et al. 1987) and benefits (Brown et al. 2003). Emery et al. (2004) reported that a sense of companionship enhanced women cardiac patients' emotional quality of life, and this enhancement was over and above benefits bestowed by dispositional optimism. Whether they are the patient or caregiver, women often focus on others and maintain their domestic roles. After a heart attack, men tend to reduce work activities and are nurtured by their partners. In contrast, after returning home from the hospital, women take on household responsibilities more quickly (King 2000, Michela 1987). Studies of cancer, heart disease, and arthritis reveal that women report more distress than men whether they are the patient or the caregiver (Revenson 2003, Tuinstra et al. 2004), and longitudinal research on couples' patterns of adjustment to cancers of the gastrointestinal tract in one spouse suggests that both gender and the patient/partner role affect adjustment (Northouse et al. 2000, Schulz & Schwarzer 2004, Tuinstra et al. 2004). The intersection of biological and environmental influences on gender differences (e.g., Taylor et al. 2000) in adjustment to chronic disease is a promising area for study.

Social Resources and Interpersonal Support

Most adaptive tasks of chronic disease require help from others, including emotional sustenance and practical aid. Social support affects adaptive outcomes through a number of physiological, emotional, and cognitive pathways (see Wills & Fegan 2001). It can help recipients use effective coping strategies by offering a better understanding of the problem and increasing motivation to take action. Support can encourage positive health behaviors or minimize risky behaviors, and it can diminish physiological reactivity to stress. Discussing disease-related concerns in a supportive, uncritical social environment allows people to better address the adaptive tasks of illness.

Most work examining effects of interpersonal ties in chronic disease has focused on their positive effects. Both structural aspects of social ties (e.g., marital status and network size) and functional dimensions (e.g., validating emotions and providing information) can yield benefit (e.g., Carver et al. 2005, Demange et al. 2004). Prospective studies of patients with rheumatic diseases reveal both direct and buffering effects of support on depressive symptoms (Demange et al. 2004), functional status (Fitzgerald et al. 2004), and disease activity (Evers et al. 2003). Daily stressful events are more strongly associated with next-day mood disturbance among RA patients who have lower levels of support (Affleck et al. 1994), and one way that support influences daily pain is through fostering use of specific coping strategies (Holtzman et al. 2004). Moreover, sound social support helps explain trajectories of psychological adjustment in cancer patients (e.g., Helgeson et al. 2004) and heart disease patients (Bennett et al. 2001).

Although social support is typically assessed as a fairly stable characteristic of an individual's social environment, it may change over time. Social support can erode, and greater distress reported by the patient may presage such erosion (Alferi et al. 2001, Moyer & Salovey 1999). Among men who have had an MI or CABG surgery, the beneficial effects of intimacy appear to fade over time as support becomes burdensome or demands of recovery fail to match support providers' expectations (Fontana et al. 1989). Thus, the dynamic nature of adjustment may reflect the unfolding of interpersonal as well as intrapersonal factors.

Just as close relationships can be supportive and caring, they also can be characterized by misunderstanding, disapproval, and antagonism. Well-intended support attempts can go awry, for example, if support is ill timed or does not match the recipient's needs (Cutrona & Russell 1990, Revenson 1993). Pain flares and increases in disease activity in rheumatoid disease tend to be preceded by interpersonal stress (Zautra et al. 1997, Zautra & Smith 2001), and patients who report high spousal support and appraise their illness as a challenge (rather than a threat) are more distressed, perhaps because support does not match their needs (Schiaffino & Revenson 1995). Among individuals hospitalized following their first coronary event, disappointing supportive interactions are a particularly robust predictor of poorer adjustment (Helgeson 1993). Similarly, cancer patients who report communication problems with their medical team evidence increased distress three months later (Lerman et al. 1993). Demonstrating the importance of the absence of support, social isolation prior to a breast cancer diagnosis in the Nurses' Health Study cohort predicted poorer quality of life four years postdiagnosis, explaining greater variance than did treatment- and tumor-related factors (Michael et al. 2002).

Research on couples in which one partner has a chronic illness provides insight into how the transactional nature of social support affects patients' adjustment. Depressive symptoms may elicit feelings of irritation and resentment in the spouse, which leads to increased anger and reduced support provision (Druley et al. 2003, Revenson & Majerovitz 1990). At the same time, patients may (mis)interpret partners' negative comments to mean that they are incompetent or powerless; in a study of older women with osteoarthritis (Martire et al. 2002), this pattern of spousal interaction predicted increased depressive symptoms six months later.

Among women with RA, initial levels of social constraint—feelings that one's partner is unreceptive to hearing about one's experiences—were related to functional outcomes, distress, and pain a year later, though not to changes in those outcomes (Danoff-Burg et al. 2004; see also Stephens et al. 2002). In a study of breast cancer patients and their partners (Manne et al. 2005), perceived unsupportive behavior by the partner, involving both avoidance and criticism, predicted women's distress over time. Low social constraint has been shown to buffer the relation between disease-related intrusive thoughts and subsequent distress among cancer patients (Lepore 2001).

Personality Attributes

Much of the research examining how personality affects adaptation falls into two perspectives: personality as a risk factor (Smith & Gallo 2001) or as a protective factor or stress-resistance resource (Ouellette & DiPlacido 2001). We were surprised to find few longitudinal studies that examined risk factors for psychological adjustment; for example, there is a large literature on type A behavior and hostility predicting heart disease onset and progression (Smith & Gallo 2001), but few studies examining hostility as a risk factor for adjustment to heart disease.

In recent years, dispositional optimism (Scheier & Carver 1985) has been the most frequently examined personality attribute in relation to disease-related adjustment. Among individuals with ischemic heart disease, optimism assessed shortly after hospital discharge predicts fewer depressive symptoms a year later (Shnek et al. 2001). Optimism also predicts faster in-hospital recovery and return to normal life activities for people undergoing CABG surgery (Scheier et al. 1989; cf. Contrada et al. 2004). There is some evidence that optimism and pessimism have distinct effects on adjustment outcomes (Engel et al. 2004). In heart disease patients, low levels of pessimism soon after CABG surgery predicts more positive affect and lower pain 6 to 12 months later (Mahler & Kulik 2000). High optimism, on the other hand, appears to serve as a resource earlier in recovery. Optimism assessed near cancer diagnosis predicts more positive adjustment during the next year (e.g., Carver et al. 1993, Schou et al. 2005; cf. Stanton & Snider 1993), and optimism's benefits have been demonstrated in people with various cancers and at several periods in the disease trajectory (Allison et al. 2000, Carver et al. 2005, Miller et al. 1996, Trunzo & Pinto 2003).

Optimism's emotionally protective effects appear to work by bolstering the use of approach-oriented coping strategies and affective social support, as well as reducing disease-related threat appraisals and avoidant coping (Carver et al. 1993, Scheier et al. 1989, Schou et al. 2005, Trunzo & Pinto 2003). Personality attributes also may interact with other variables to affect adjustment. Thus, interpersonal stress predicts increases in negative affect and disease activity in arthritis patients only for those who show excessive dispositional sensitivity to others' feelings and behavior (Smith & Zautra 2002). Emotionally expressive coping predicts decreased distress and fewer medical appointments for cancer-related morbidities in breast cancer patients high in hope (Stanton et al. 2000).

Health outcomes associated with optimism also are receiving attention. Although there are null findings (Schofield et al. 2004), some evidence suggests that dispositional optimism predicts survival in chronic disease (e.g., Giltay et al. 2004, 2006). In the Normative Aging Study, an optimistic explanatory style halved the risk for cardiac events over ten years (Kubzansky et al. 2001). If a reliable relation is established between optimism and health outcomes, examination of associated biological and behavioral mechanisms will be crucial.

Cognitive Appraisal Processes

Most theories of psychosocial adjustment to illness converge on the point that how individuals view their disease is a fundamental determinant of ensuing coping efforts and adjustment. Lazarus's stress and coping theory (e.g., Lazarus & Folkman 1984) constitutes the foundation for much of the research on disease-related adjustment. In this theory, cognitive appraisal processes are assigned central importance, including primary appraisal, in which one evaluates the situation's potential for harm and benefit, and secondary appraisal, in which one assesses the situation's controllability and one's available coping resources. Perceived threats to health and life goals, disease-related expectancies, and finding meaning in the illness experience are three appraisal processes that have received a good deal of empirical attention.

Perceived threats to life goals. Theorists have considered appraised implications of disease for one's life goals as a key determinant of adjustment. Lazarus's (1991) revised conceptualization of primary appraisal incorporates elements of goal relevance, goal congruence, and personal meaning of the illness. In Carver & Scheier's (1998) self-regulation theory, illness represents an experience that can interfere with plans and activities that bring meaning to life (Scheier & Bridges 1995). To the extent that one perceives illness as impeding treasured goals or intruding on valued activities, psychological pain is likely. Thus, threat and harm/loss appraisals were central predictors of later anxiety and depression in cardiac

patients (Waltz et al. 1988). Perceived goal barriers predict pain and fatigue in fibromyalgia patients (Affleck et al. 2001). Among RA patients, loss of valued activities predicts depressive symptoms in the following year (Katz & Yelin 1995), mediated by unfavorable social comparisons and dissatisfaction with abilities (Neugebauer et al. 2003). Prostate cancer patients who accommodate their illness by altering important life goals appear to be less negatively affected by physical dysfunction than men who do not (Lepore & Eton 2000).

Leventhal's self-regulation theory (e.g., Leventhal et al. 2001) underscores perceived threats to the self-system with regard to disease cause, identity, time line, controllability, and consequences. For example, individuals who view their cancer as chronic or cyclic evidence greater distress than those who conceptualize it as an acute disease, controlling for actual disease stage (Rabin et al. 2004).

Disease-specific expectancies. Expectancies regarding control over the experience of chronic disease and confidence in one's ability to effect a desired outcome, i.e., self-efficacy, contribute to adjustment. Chronic disease can chip away at perceptions of control over bodily integrity, daily planning to engage in valued activities, and life itself. A hallmark of chronic disease is that committed involvement in medical treatments and healthy behaviors cannot ensure control over its outcome, and individuals perceive more control over consequences of disease, e.g., symptom management, than its ultimate outcome (e.g., Affleck et al. 1987b, Thompson et al. 1993).

A sense of general control predicts diminished distress in cancer patients undergoing bone marrow transplant prior to hospital discharge and one year later (Fife et al. 2000) and in cancer patients undergoing radiation (Stiegelis et al. 2003). Thompson & Kyle (2000) concluded that control expectancies need not match realistic opportunities for control to confer benefit, although others have suggested that the utility of control appraisals depends on whether the threat is responsive to control attempts (Christensen & Ehlers 2002). For example, perceived control over RA symptoms as opposed to perceived control over disease course predicts positive affect and better adjustment (Schiaffino & Revenson 1992). A related construct within the arthritis literature is perceived helplessness. Appraisals of helplessness reliably predict increases in depressive symptoms in studies of RA patients (Smith & Wallston 1992). Moreover, perceptions of helplessness affect physical functioning independent of disease severity (Lorish et al. 1991) and may even affect inflammatory processes (Parker et al. 1991).

Control appraisals also affect adjustment to cardiac events and surgical interventions. Among CABG patients, individuals who expect more control over their recovery prior to surgery have briefer hospital stays and report less pre- and postoperative distress (Mahler & Kulik 1990). Consistent with the idea that an untoward experience during chronic illness may be viewed by the patient as a temporary setback rather than a disconfirmation of cherished control beliefs (Taylor 1983), Helgeson (1992) found the perception of control protected patients who were rehospitalized during the study: Rehospitalized patients who reported a strong sense of personal control over their illness had emotional functioning comparable to patients who did not require another hospital stay.

Disease-related self-efficacy expectancies also predict adjustment. Several longitudinal studies document the predictive utility of self-efficacy in adjustment to rheumatic diseases and joint replacement surgery (e.g., Cronan et al. 2002, Culos-Reed & Brawley 2003, Engel et al. 2004). Increases in self-efficacy also predicted less anxiety and more vigor among individuals in cardiac rehabilitation (Blanchard et al. 2002), and self-efficacy expectancies assessed premorbidly predicted subsequent depressive symptoms among older adults with heart disease (van Jaarsveld et al. 2005).

Although self-efficacy is typically considered an intrapersonal phenomenon, Rohrbaugh et al. (2004) demonstrated its potential interpersonal dynamics. Among individuals with congestive heart failure, although both the patient's and the spouse's confidence in the patient's ability to meet challenges associated with the disease predicted survival, only spouse confidence predicted survival when both ratings were included in the predictive equation. We suspect that spouse confidence also affects patient well-being.

Carver et al. (2000) have argued that perceived control is important only to the extent that it contributes to positive outcome expectancies. In two samples of breast cancer patients, the expectancy of remaining cancer free predicted less distress during the following year, whereas perceived control over the disease did not predict distress (Carver et al. 2000). A related construct, response expectancy, e.g., asking patients how fatigued they expect to be after treatment with no reference to perceived control, also predicts outcomes. Response expectancies regarding pain and fatigue assessed prior to breast cancer surgery predict those outcomes postsurgery, controlling for presurgery distress (Montgomery & Bovbjerg 2004; see also Montgomery & Bovbjerg 2001). Folkman & Moskowitz (2000b) and Tennen & Affleck (2000) offered speculations regarding the contexts in which disease-related control and outcome expectancies might affect well-being.

Finding meaning. Finding meaning in chronic illness has been conceptualized in several ways. Janoff-Bulman & Frantz (1997) distinguish "meaning as comprehensibility," i.e., an attempt to determine how an event makes sense, and "meaning as significance." The search for comprehensibility often prompts an awareness of personal vulnerability, which paves the way for creating meaning in life "by generating significance through appraisals of value and worth" (Janoff-Bulman & Berger 2000, p. 33). Thus, "meaning as significance" can lead one to find benefits in the chronic disease experience.

Individuals affected by chronic disease often report personal growth arising from the experience (e.g., Cordova et al. 2001). Finding meaning and benefit in the experience of chronic disease has been examined both as a predictor of subsequent adjustment, which we address here, and as an adaptive outcome in its own right. People with RA who report interpersonal benefit in their illness show improved physical functioning a year later, but not lower distress (Danoff-Burg & Revenson 2005), and patients who perceive more benefits report fewer subsequent days during which their activities are limited by severe pain (Tennen et al. 1992).

In a review of research on benefit finding in cancer patients, Stanton et al. (2006) concluded that the evidence for a relation between benefit finding and adjustment is decidedly mixed. Among the notable positive findings, perceived positive meaning resulting from the breast cancer experience at one to five years after diagnosis predicted an increase in positive affect five years later (Bower et al. 2005), and finding benefit in the year after breast cancer surgery predicted lower distress and depressive symptoms four to seven years later (Carver & Antoni 2004). Assessed earlier in the cancer trajectory, however, benefit finding appears to have no or even a negative relation with positive adjustment (Sears et al. 2003, Tomich & Helgeson 2004); perhaps engagement in finding benefit serves distinct functions over the course of chronic disease (Stanton et al. 2006). Conceptualization, operationalization (e.g., the use of retrospective reports of positive change), and adaptive consequences of finding meaning and benefit require further theoretical and empirical attention (Tennen & Affleck 2002, 2006).

Coping Processes

It is difficult to imagine that the ways that individuals respond to the demands of illness would not affect subsequent adjustment.

Although limited by problems in conceptualization, measurement, and methodology (Folkman & Moskowitz 2004, Somerfield & McCrae 2000), the empirical literature leads us to conclude that coping affects adjustment to chronic illness.

Coping efforts may be directed toward approaching or avoiding the demands of chronic disease (Suls & Fletcher 1985). This approach-avoidance continuum also reflects a fundamental motivational construct (Carver & Scheier 1998, Davidson et al. 2000). Approach-oriented or active coping strategies include information seeking, problem solving, seeking social support, actively attempting to identify benefit in one's experience, and creating outlets for emotional expression. In contrast, avoidance-oriented coping involves cognitive strategies such as denial and suppression, and behavioral strategies such as disengagement. Other coping efforts, such as spiritual coping, potentially can serve either approach or avoidance goals.

The coping strategies people employ and their utility are likely to vary as the adaptive tasks of illness change (Blalock et al. 1993). Minimizing threat, an avoidant strategy, may be useful at acute points of crisis. However, research indicates that avoidance typically predicts maladjustment over time (Roesch et al. 2005, Stanton et al. 2001). For example, in comparison with less avoidant women, breast cancer patients who were high on cognitive avoidance prior to breast biopsy reported more distress at that point, after cancer diagnosis, and after surgery (Stanton & Snider 1993; see also Hack & Degner 2004, Lutgendorf et al. 2002). Similarly, the use of avoidant coping to manage health problems was associated with continued emotional distress during the year following heart transplant (Dew et al. 1994). A strong and consistent finding in studies of rheumatic disease is that passive strategies directed toward disengagement predict poor adjustment over time (Covic et al. 2003, Evers et al. 2003, Felton & Revenson 1984, Smith & Wallston 1992). Coping through avoidance may involve damaging behaviors (e.g., alcohol use), paradoxically prompt intrusion of disease-related thoughts and emotions (Wegner & Pennebaker 1992), or impede more effective coping efforts.

Although findings are not as uniform as those for avoidant coping (Roesch et al. 2005, Stanton et al. 2001), approach-oriented strategies appear to be more effective. Problem-focused coping attempts such as information seeking, cognitive restructuring, and pain control are consistently associated with indicators of positive adjustment in RA patients (Keefe et al. 2002, Young 1992). Day-to-day, relaxation coping strategies and active efforts to reduce pain contribute to reductions in next-day pain as well as enhancement of positive mood (Keefe et al. 1997). The demonstrated values of interventions that encourage the use of approach-oriented strategies such as problem-solving and emotional processing also suggest the utility of approach-oriented coping (e.g., Savelkoul et al. 2003).

Establishing the links between approach-oriented coping and adaptive outcomes is complicated by the fact that some approach-oriented strategies, such as problem solving, are not effective for immutable facets of the disease. In addition, avoidance- and approach-oriented strategies may differentially predict negative and positive outcomes (e.g., Echteld et al. 2003). The exclusion of positive adjustment indicators in many studies may obscure the benefits of approach-oriented coping.

Coping strategies are likely to mediate relations between personality attributes (e.g., optimism), interpersonal support processes, and adjustment, or to moderate the effects of other predictors. For example, the combination of high avoidance-oriented coping and low social support has been identified as a risk factor for distress in individuals with chronic illness (Devine et al. 2003, Jacobsen et al. 2002), and avoidant coping is a mechanism for the relations between unsupportive behaviors by the partner and cancer patients' distress (Manne et al. 2005). Carels et al. (2004) found among heart failure patients that a day

that included efforts to improve symptoms was followed by a day of fewer illness symptoms, whereas a day that included trying to distract oneself from the illness was followed by a day with more symptoms. Rather than focusing solely on coping as a predictor of adjustment, we urge researchers to evaluate mediational and moderational models in longitudinal, daily process, and experimental designs.

PROGRESS AND CRITICAL ISSUES IN RESEARCH

Contributions of the Literature on Adjustment to Chronic Disease

The literature of the past two decades offers a number of vital contributions to the understanding of adjustment to chronic disease. First, it provides increasingly nuanced conceptualizations of adjustment. Empirical evidence now supports the observations that living with chronic disease requires adaptation in multiple life domains; that adaptation is a changing, but not always fluid, process; and that examination of both positive and negative indicators of adjustment enhances understanding of the phenomenon. Although several adaptive tasks are common across diseases, we observed some sharpening of research focus in recent years to concentrate on those domains of adjustment and points in the disease trajectory that are most challenging for individuals with particular diseases. An example is the recent empirical focus on the symptom clusters of fatigue, depression, and pain in cancer, resulting in a National Institutes of Health State-of-the-Science Conference Statement (Patrick et al. 2004).

This focus on prominent psychological risks conferred by chronic disease and its treatments is balanced by research on the experience of chronic illness as an opportunity for finding positive meaning, altering health behaviors, enriching emotional life, and deepening personal relationships. Although the lion's share of the research on adjustment to chronic disease has been centered on the period surrounding diagnosis and medical treatment, research is increasingly focused on adjustment in other phases in the disease trajectory, including the period after major medical treatments are completed, periods of relatively symptom-free quiescence, and, for life-limiting conditions, periods of disease recurrence and end-stage disease. The resulting more complex conceptualization of what it means to live with chronic disease can inform theory development as well as clinical assessment and intervention with affected individuals and loved ones.

A second contribution of the past 20 years of research is its progressively convincing characterization of risk and protective factors for favorable adjustment to chronic illness. Whereas early (and much of the recent) research yielded suggestive evidence regarding correlates of adjustment from cross-sectional studies, the past decade has seen a surge in research that is longitudinal in design, involves adequately characterized samples of sufficient size for reliable analysis, and includes statistical control for initial values on dependent variables to bolster causal inference. Although theoretical frameworks for higher-order constructs as predictors of adjustment to chronic disease have existed for some time (e.g., Moos & Schaefer 1984, Smith & Wallston 1992), we now have a good start on filling in the blanks with regard to specific factors that confer risk or protection. Thus, emotionally supportive relationships set the stage for positive adjustment to chronic disease, whereas criticism, social constraints, and social isolation impart risk. Positive generalized and disease-specific expectancies, general perceived control and mastery, and a sense of control over specific disease-related domains also promote adjustment. Active, approach-oriented coping attempts to manage disease-related challenges often bolster adjustment, whereas concerted attempts to avoid disease-related thoughts and feelings are robust predictors of heightened distress. These findings will allow investigators to hone theories of adjustment to chronic disease and to sharpen psychoso-

cial interventions in order to target specific psychosocial processes shown to influence adaptive outcomes.

We also want to note exciting progress in the development of biopsychosocial models of chronic disease. Research in rheumatic disease suggests that stressful experiences and negative affect might lead to immunologic changes, which in turn affect disease activity (although reverse causation also is possible) (e.g., Peralta-Ramirez et al. 2004, Zautra et al. 1997). In the cancer literature, plausible biological mediators of the potential relations of stress, depression, and lack of social support with disease progression also have been advanced (for a review, see Antoni et al. 2006).

The most convincing evidence is in the area of behavioral cardiology. For example, hostility/aggression, anxiety, depression/hopelessness, interpersonal isolation/conflict, and chronic stress have been reliably linked to the development of heart disease and associated morbidity and mortality (for reviews, see Gallo et al. 2004, Krantz & McCeney 2002, Rozanski et al. 1999, Smith & Ruiz 2002; for evidence on construing benefit as a protective factor, see Affleck et al. 1987a). Nowhere is progress more evident than in the burgeoning literature on the links between depression and cardiovascular disease. Although not entirely consistent (see Stewart et al. 2003 for a review), two lines of evidence are relevant. First are demonstrations that depression predicts the development of heart disease (e.g., Todaro et al. 2003). For example, adjusting for baseline risk factors, individuals with elevated depressive symptoms but without a history of coronary disease were twice as likely as their nondepressed counterparts to have carotid plaque (Haas et al. 2005). Even stronger evidence links depression to cardiac morbidity and mortality among individuals with coronary illness. Even minimal depressive symptoms increase mortality risk after an MI (Bush et al. 2001), and depression doubles the risk of a recurrent cardiac event after CABG surgery (Blumenthal et al. 2003). Carney et al. (2002) reviewed evidence for several behavioral (e.g., treatment nonadherence) and biological (e.g., inflammation) mechanisms that might explain how depression places individuals at risk for cardiac morbidity and mortality. In a review, Frasure-Smith & Lespérance (2005) concluded that adequately powered prospective studies are "remarkably consistent in their support of depression as a risk factor for both the development of and worsening of CHD" (p. 523).

Limitations of the Literature on Adjustment to Chronic Disease

Although we see substantial advances in understanding adjustment to chronic disease over the past decades, progress is uneven, and many questions remain. First, in contrast to the foundation of evidence on proximal variables as risk and protective factors, we know less about implications of specific distal parameters for disease-related adjustment (Link & Phelan 1995). Although relevant research is scant, economic burden and associated factors (e.g., low education) are likely to constitute barriers to positive adaptation, as are rigid and extreme gender roles. Cultural dynamics involving the intersections of ethnic identity, acculturation, socioeconomic status, and experiences of racism as they affect disease-related adjustment have received minimal attention. Community environments and other environmental factors have not been examined. For example, communities that incorporate a high degree of social capital—resources inherent in relationships including mutual trust and a sense of belongingness—might bolster adjustment. Aspects of the built environment, such as hospital spaces where families of surgery patients can spend the night comfortably, might foster a sense of control and facilitate interactions, also promoting adjustment.

By and large, the body of work on adjustment to chronic illness has not included consideration of premorbid biological, environmental, and personal contexts. With few exceptions, research on hazardous or nurturing early environments as setting the stage for later psychological and biological adaptation under stress (e.g., Taylor et al. 1997) and on genetic vulnerability to poor psychological outcomes under adverse conditions (e.g., Caspi et al. 2003) have not been translated into research in disease-related adjustment. And, as the population ages, the presence of comorbid physical illnesses is going to complicate adjustment to chronic disease (e.g., Stommel et al. 2004).

Second, we know little about intersections among and within proximal and distal parameters in their contribution to adjustment, although research is accruing. Interpersonal relationships and personality attributes are likely to moderate the effects of cognitive appraisal and coping processes on adjustment (e.g., Affleck et al. 2001, Lepore 2001, Smith & Zautra 2002). Macro-level factors such as SES, gender, and cultural variables have been examined infrequently in conjunction with other predictors for their potential moderating influences.

Examining moderated relationships in adjustment to chronic disease is important in its implications for intervention. For example, Cameron et al. (2005) recently reported that illness perception-based education for cardiac patients failed to promote cardiac rehabilitation attendance and to reduce disability among MI patients high on negative affectivity (NA). Indeed, the intervention had detrimental effects on high-NA patients' exercise and diet habits six months after MI compared to high-NA patients assigned to standard care. Examination of moderated relations in research on predictors of adjustment can suggest variables on which to target and tailor interventions.

Third, progress on knowledge of mechanisms for the effects of identified predictors of adjustment to chronic disease is uneven. Some mediating processes, such as pathways for the effects of optimism on disease-related adjustment, are relatively well determined, but mechanisms for the influence

NA: negative affectivity

of other factors remain to be established. For example, although frameworks positing mechanisms of the effects of more distal factors such as SES on health-related outcomes have been developed (e.g., Gallo & Matthews 2003), research on such mechanisms for adjustment to chronic disease is just beginning. As mechanisms for ethnic disparities in chronic disease outcomes see increased empirical attention (e.g., Green et al. 2003, Meyerowitz et al. 1998, Tammemagi et al. 2005), a rise in attention to mechanisms for ethnic and cultural differences in adjustment is likely to occur. For example, psychological manifestations of ethnic group membership such as perceived racism may act as a stressor that adversely affects risk factors for cardiovascular health (Brondolo et al. 2003, Clark et al. 1999), but their implications for adaptation to chronic illness are unknown.

Fourth, we found much more attention in the literature to issues surrounding adjustment to chronic disease in some diseases than others and in some populations than others. The majority of existing research was conducted with individuals who are white and of relatively high SES. Cancer, and particularly early-stage breast cancer, yielded the largest body of work on predictors of adjustment. A related issue is that particular constructs received more attention than others in specific diseases. For example, perceptions of helplessness received more study in arthritis than in other conditions, perhaps owing to the demands associated with chronic pain and disability. And some constructs are just being added to models, such as sexuality as an important component of quality of life (e.g., Derogatis 2001) and purpose in life and spirituality as predictors of health-related outcomes (Seeman et al. 2003, Smith & Zautra 2004).

Finally, little of the research identifying predictors of disease-related adjustment has been translated directly into interventions. Exceptions are Folkman and Chesney's coping effectiveness training (Chesney et al. 2003), which capitalizes on findings from stress and coping theory to bolster adjustment to chronic disease, and Keefe et al's. (2002) pain coping interventions for rheumatic disease, which are based on research demonstrating the adverse effects of catastrophizing and the benefits of family support. Moreover, few attempts have been made to target interventions to those who might be in most need of them, such as those who manifest risk factors for poor adjustment.

Directions for Research

Gaps apparent in the existing literature make way for the next decade of research on adjustment to chronic disease. Integration of environmental and sociocultural contexts with more proximal predictors, accompanied by examination of mediators and moderators of their effects on adjustment, will enrich our understanding of adjustment to chronic disease. Relatively neglected populations such as individuals with very advanced disease and ethnically diverse groups merit greater inclusion, along with examination of mechanisms for observed between-group differences.

Now that considerable longitudinal research across chronic diseases is available to generate confidence in the significance of several risk and protective factors for adjustment, greater attention to translation into interventions is warranted. The existing literature can guide psychosocial interventions in at least four ways. First, it can inform the development of interventions through inclusion of processes that predict positive adjustment, for example, specific techniques aimed at bolstering self-efficacy for disease-related tasks (Graves 2003). Second, the research base can promote the specification of how interventions work, for example, through altering coping strategies or illness-related cognitions (e.g., Scheier et al. 2005). Third, the empirical literature on disease-related adjustment can aid in targeting interventions to vulnerable groups. Research on trajectories of adjustment to illness suggests that there is an identifiable group of people who have few personal and social resources and who are at risk for a sharp decline in psychological functioning with the experience of chronic disease (Dew et al. 2005, Helgeson et al. 2004). It is this group that might best be targeted for intervention. Truly prospective research is needed to distinguish among groups that have longstanding poor functioning and those that are specifically affected by the experience of chronic illness to determine whether they need distinct intervention approaches. Finally, existing research can promote consideration of the person-environment fit in interventions (e.g., Antoni et al. 2001, Lepore et al. 2003). The intervention approach required for individuals high on negative affectivity or avoidance-oriented coping processes might differ from that required for less-vulnerable individuals, for example.

Future theoretically guided research to examine both contextual and individual contributors to multifaceted indicators of adjustment in longitudinal designs will require relatively large samples and lengthy time frames. Several additional approaches can be adopted, however. First, although we were impressed with the large body of longitudinal work that has accrued in the past two decades, experimental designs will enhance causal inference regarding risk and protective factors. Experimental research on the effects of social comparison (Stanton et al. 1999, Van der Zee et al. 1998) on adaptive outcomes in chronic disease is an example. In-depth analysis of single contributors to adjustment and specific adaptive outcomes also can be useful. Examples are the research on response expectancies as predictors of adjustment (e.g., Montgomery & Bovbjerg 2004) and on determinants of fatigue (Bower et al. 2003, 2006).

New methodologies and quantitative approaches provide tools to address the next decade of complex questions. Intensive, daily process methodologies can shed light on adjustment to disease within the life context and are particularly suited to diseases for which coping and self-management demands occur daily (Tennen et al. 2000). Hierarchical linear modeling and other approaches allow for sophisticated modeling of change over time between and within persons living with chronic disease.

Research over the past two decades increasingly has illuminated the ingredients of living well in the face of chronic disease. We expect that over the next decade we will continue to see progress in our understanding of adaptational processes. If the past is prologue, we expect that ten years from now, a review article such as this will include more culturally anchored approaches; a greater number of studies that integrate biological, psychological, and social levels of analysis; and a more seamless translation of research findings into clinical interventions.

SUMMARY POINTS

1. Multifaceted conceptualizations of adjustment to chronic disease have been advanced in the literature, indicating that chronic disease necessitates adjustment in multiple life domains across the course of the disease trajectory.

2. Prospective research reveals that the experience of chronic disease provokes significant distress and life disruption; however, many individuals with chronic disease report positive adjustment, and good evidence exists for heterogeneity in trajectories of adjustment across individuals. Further, examination of both positive and negative indicators of adjustment in research can enrich the understanding of adjustment to chronic disease.

3. Socioeconomic and cultural contexts, as well as gender-related processes, influence adaptive outcomes in chronically ill individuals, although these domains have not received as much empirical attention as have more proximal predictors of adjustment.

4. Longitudinal research has revealed a progressively convincing characterization of risk and protective factors for favorable adjustment to chronic illness in the domains of interpersonal relationships, personality attributes, cognitive variables, and coping processes. Progress also is evident in the empirical foundations for biopsychosocial models of some chronic diseases.

5. Future progress in research on adjustment to chronic disease will include integration of environmental, sociocultural, and biological contexts with more proximal predictors, accompanied by examination of mediators and moderators of their effects on adjustment. Translation of research identifying risk and protective factors for adaptive outcomes into interventions to bolster chronic disease-related adjustment also is a promising direction for research.

LITERATURE CITED

Adler NE, Ostrove JE. 1999. Socioeconomic status and health: what we know and what we don't. *Ann. NY Acad. Sci.* 896:3–15

Affleck G, Tennen H, Croog S, Levine S. 1987a. Causal attribution, perceived benefits, and morbidity after a heart attack: an 8-year study. *J. Consult. Clin. Psychol.* 55:29–35

Affleck G, Tennen H, Pfeiffer C, Fifield J. 1987b. Appraisals of control and predictability in adapting to chronic disease. *J. Personal. Soc. Psychol.* 53:273–79

Affleck G, Tennen H, Urrows S, Higgins P. 1994. Person and contextual features of daily stress reactivity: individual differences in relations of undesirable daily events with mood disturbance and chronic pain intensity. *J. Personal. Soc. Psychol.* 66:329–40

Affleck G, Tennen H, Zautra A, Urrows S, Abeles M, Karoly P. 2001. Women's pursuit of personal goals in daily life with fibromyalgia: a value-expectancy analysis. *J. Consult. Clin. Psychol.* 69:587–96

Alferi SM, Carver CS, Antoni MH, Weiss S, Durán RE. 2001. An exploratory study of social support, distress, and life disruption among low-income Hispanic women under treatment for early stage breast cancer. *Health Psychol.* 20:41–46

Allison PJ, Guichard C, Laurent G. 2000. A prospective investigation of dispositional optimism as a predictor of health-related quality of life in head and neck cancer patients. *Qual. Life Res.* 9:951–60

Andersen BL, Anderson B, de Prosse C. 1989. Controlled prospective longitudinal study of women with cancer: II. Psychological outcomes. *J. Consult. Clin. Psychol.* 57:692–97

Antoni MH, Lehman JM, Kilbourn KM, Boyers AE, Culvers JL, et al. 2001. Cognitive-behavioral stress management intervention decreases the prevalence of depression and enhances benefit finding among women under treatment for early-stage breast cancer. *Health Psychol.* 20:20–32

Antoni MH, Lutgendorf SK, Cole SW, Dhabhar FS, Sephton SE, et al. 2006. The influence of bio-behavioural factors on tumor biology: pathways and mechanisms. *Nat. Rev. Cancer* 6:240–48

Bae SC, Hashimoto H, Karlson EW, Liang MH, Daltroy LH. 2001. Variable effects of social support by race, economic status, and disease activity in systemic lupus erythematosus. *J. Rheumatol.* 28:1245–51

Bennett SJ, Perkins KA, Lane KA, Deer M, Brater DC, Murray MD. 2001. Social support and health-related quality of life in chronic heart failure patients. *Qual. Life Res.* 10:671–82

Berkman LF, Glass T. 1999. Social integration, social networks, social support, and health. In *Social Epidemiology*, ed. LF Berkman, T Glass, pp. 137–73. New York: Oxford Univ. Press

Blalock SJ, DeVellis BM, Holt K, Hahn PM. 1993. Coping with rheumatoid arthritis: Is one problem the same as another? *Health Educ. Q.* 21:119–32

Blanchard CM, Rodgers WM, Courneya KS, Daub B, Black B. 2002. Self-efficacy and mood in cardiac rehabilitation: Should gender be considered? *Behav. Med.* 27:149–60

Blumenthal JA, Lett HS, Babyak MA, White W, Smith PK, et al. 2003. Depression as a risk factor for mortality after coronary artery bypass surgery. *Lancet* 362:604–9

Boudrez H, De Backer G. 2001. Psychological status and the role of coping style after coronary artery bypass graft surgery. Results of a prospective study. *Qual. Life Res.* 10:37–47

Bower JE, Ganz PA, Aziz N, Fahey JL, Cole SW. 2003. T-cell homeostasis in breast cancer survivors with persistent fatigue. *J. Natl. Cancer Inst.* 95:1165–68

Bower JE, Ganz PA, Desmond KA, Bernaards C, Rowland JH, et al. 2006. Fatigue in long-term breast carcinoma survivors: a longitudinal investigation. *Cancer* 106:751–58

Bower JE, Meyerowitz BE, Desmond KA, Bernaards CA, Rowland JH, Ganz PA. 2005. Perceptions of positive meaning and vulnerability following breast cancer: predictors and outcomes among long-term breast cancer survivors. *Ann. Behav. Med.* 29:236–45

Brondolo E, Rieppi R, Kelly KP, Gerin W. 2003. Perceived racism and blood pressure: a review of the literature and conceptual and methodological critique. *Ann. Behav. Med.* 25:55–65

Brown GK, Nicassio PM, Wallston KA. 1989. Pain coping strategies and depression in rheumatoid arthritis. *J. Consult. Clin. Psychol.* 57:652–57

Brown SL, Nesse RM, Vinokur AD, Smith DM. 2003. Providing social support may be more beneficial than receiving it: results from a prospective study of mortality. *Psychol. Sci.* 14:320–27

Bush DE, Ziegelstein RC, Tayback M, Richter D, Stevens S, et al. 2001. Even minimal symptoms of depression increase mortality risk after acute myocardial infarction. *Am. J. Cardiol.* 88:337–41

Calhoun LG, Tedeschi RG, eds. 2006. *Handbook of Posttraumatic Growth: Research and Practice.* Mahwah, NJ: Erlbaum

Callahan LF, Cordray DS, Wells G, Pincus T. 1996. Formal education and five-year mortality in rheumatoid arthritis: mediation by helplessness scale scores. *Arthritis Care Res.* 9:463–72

Cameron LD, Petrie KJ, Ellis CJ, Buick D, Weinman JA. 2005. Trait negative affectivity and responses to a health education intervention for myocardial infarction patients. *Psychol. Health* 20:1–18

Carels RA, Musher-Eizenman D, Cacciapaglia H, Perez-Benitez CI, Christie S, O'Brien W. 2004. Psychosocial functioning and physical symptoms in heart failure patients: a within-individual approach. *J. Psychosom. Res.* 56:95–101

Carney RM, Freedland KE, Miller GE, Jaffe AS. 2002. Depression as a risk factor for cardiac mortality and morbidity: a review of potential mechanisms. *J. Psychosom. Res.* 53:897–902

Carver CS, Antoni MH. 2004. Finding benefit in breast cancer during the year after diagnosis predicts better adjustment five to eight years after diagnosis. *Health Psychol.* 23:595–98

Carver CS, Harris SD, Lehman JM, Durel LA, Antoni MH, et al. 2000. How important is the perception of personal control? Studies of early stage breast cancer patients. *Personal. Soc. Psychol. Bull.* 26:139–49

Carver CS, Pozo C, Harris SD, Noriega V, Scheier MF, et al. 1993. How coping mediates the effect of optimism on distress: a study of women with early stage breast cancer. *J. Personal. Soc. Psychol.* 65:375–90

Carver CS, Scheier MF. 1998. *On the Self-regulation of Behavior.* New York: Cambridge Univ. Press

Carver CS, Smith RG, Antoni MH, Petronis VM, Weiss S, Derhagopian RP. 2005. Optimistic personality and psychosocial well-being during treatment predict psychosocial well-being among long-term survivors of breast cancer. *Health Psychol.* 24:508–16

Caspi A, Sugden K, Moffitt TE, Taylor A, Craig IW, et al. 2003. Influence of life stress on depression: moderation by a polymorphism in the 5-HTT gene. *Science* 301:386–89

Cella D. 2001. Quality-of-life measurement in oncology. In *Psychosocial Interventions for Cancer*, ed. A Baum, BL Andersen, pp. 57–76. Washington, DC: Am. Psychol. Assoc.

Cent. Dis. Control Prev. (CDC) Natl. Cent. Chronic Dis. Prev. Health Promot. 2005. *Chronic disease overview*. **http://www.cdc.gov/nccdphp/overview.htm**

Cent. Dis. Control Prev. U.S. Dept. Health Human Serv. 2003. *About chronic disease.* **http://www.cdc.gov/washington/overview/chrondis.htm**

Chesney MA, Chambers DB, Taylor JM, Johnson LM, Folkman S. 2003. Coping effectiveness training for men living with HIV: results from a randomized clinical trial testing a group-based intervention. *Psychosom. Med.* 65:1038–46

Christensen AJ, Ehlers SL. 2002. Psychological factors in end-stage renal disease: an emerging context for behavioral medicine research. *J. Consult. Clin. Psychol.* 70:712–24

Clark R, Anderson NB, Clark VR, Williams DR. 1999. Racism as a stressor for African Americans: a biopsychosocial model. *Am. Psychol.* 54:805–16

Contrada RJ, Goyal TM, Cather C, Rafalson L, Idler EL, Krause TJ. 2004. Psychosocial factors in outcomes of heart surgery: the impact of religious involvement and depressive symptoms. *Health Psychol.* 23:227–38

Cordova MJ, Cunningham LL, Carlson CR, Andrykowski MA. 2001. Posttraumatic growth following breast cancer: a controlled comparison study. *Health Psychol.* 20:176–85

Covic T, Adamson B, Spencer D, Howe G. 2003. A biopsychosocial model of pain and depression in rheumatoid arthritis: a 12-month longitudinal study. *Rheumatology* 42:1287–94

Cronan TA, Serber ER, Walen HR. 2002. Psychosocial predictors of health status and health care costs among people with fibromyalgia. *Anxiety Stress Coping* 15:261–74

Culos-Reed SN, Brawley LR. 2003. Self-efficacy predicts physical activity in individuals with fibromyalgia. *J. Appl. Behav. Res.* 8:27–41

Cutrona CE, Russell DW. 1990. Type of social support and specific stress: toward a theory of optimal matching. In *Social Support: An Interactional View*, ed. BR Sarason, IG Sarason, GR Pierce, pp. 319–66. New York: Wiley

Danoff-Burg S, Revenson TA. 2005. Benefit-finding among patients with rheumatoid arthritis: positive effects on interpersonal relationships. *J. Behav. Med.* 28:91–103

Danoff-Burg S, Revenson TA, Trudeau KJ, Paget SA. 2004. Unmitigated communion, social constraints, and psychological distress among women with rheumatoid arthritis. *J. Personal.* 72:29–46

Davidson RJ, Jackson DC, Kalin NH. 2000. Emotion, plasticity, context, and regulation: perspectives from affective neuroscience. *Psychol. Bull.* 126:890–909

Demange V, Guillemin F, Baumann M, Suurmeiher BM, Moum T, et al. 2004. Are there more than cross-sectional relationships of social support and social networks with functional limitations and psychological distress in early rheumatoid arthritis? *Arthritis Rheum.* 51:782–91

Derogatis LR. 2001. Sexual function and quality of life: endpoints and outcomes. *J. Gend. Specif. Med.* 4:35–42

DeVellis BM, Revenson TA, Blalock S. 1997. Arthritis and autoimmune diseases. In *Health Care for Women: Psychological, Social and Behavioral Issues*, ed. S Gallant, GP Keita, R Royak-Schaler, pp. 333–47. Washington, DC: Am. Psychol. Assoc.

Devine D, Parker PA, Fouladi RT, Cohen L. 2003. The association between social support, intrusive thoughts, avoidance, and adjustment following an experimental cancer treatment. *Psycho-Oncol.* 12:453–62

Dew MA, Myaskovsky L, Switzer GE, DiMartini AF, Schulberg HC, Kormos RL. 2005. Profiles and predictors of the course of psychological distress across four years after heart transplantation. *Psychol. Med.* 35:1215–27

Dew MA, Simmons RG, Roth LH, Schulberg HC, Thompson ME, et al. 1994. Psychosocial predictors of vulnerability to distress in the year following heart transplantation. *Psychol. Med.* 24:929–45

DiMatteo MR, Lepper HS, Croghan TW. 2000. Depression is a risk factor for noncompliance with medical treatment: meta-analysis of the effects of anxiety and depression on patient adherence. *Arch. Intern. Med.* 160:2101–7

Druley JA, Stephens MAP, Martire LM, Ennis N. 2003. Emotional congruence in older couples coping with wives' osteoarthritis: exacerbating effects of pain behavior. *Psychol. Aging* 18:406–14

Dunkel-Schetter C, Feinstein LG, Taylor SE, Falke RL. 1992. Patterns of coping with cancer. *Health Psychol.* 11:79–87

Echteld MA, van Elderen T, Van der Kamp LJT. 2003. Modeling predictors of quality of life after coronary angioplasty. *Ann. Behav. Med.* 26:49–60

Emery CF, Frid DJ, Engebretson TO, Alonzo AA, Fish A, et al. 2004. Gender differences in quality of life among cardiac patients. *Psychosom. Med.* 66:190–97

Engel C, Hamilton NA, Potter PT, Zautra AJ. 2004. Impact of two types of expectancy on recovery from total knee replacement surgery (TKR) in adults with osteoarthritis. *Behav. Med.* 30:113–23

Evers AWM, Kraaimaat FW, Geenen R, Jacobs JWG, Bijlsma JWJ. 2003. Pain coping and social support as predictors of long-term functional disability and pain in early rheumatoid arthritis. *Behav. Res. Ther.* 41:1295–310

Felton BJ, Revenson TA. 1984. Coping with chronic illness: a study of illness controllability and the influence of coping strategies on psychological adjustment. *J. Consult. Clin. Psychol.* 52:343–53

Fife BL, Huster GA, Cornetta KG, Kennedy VN, Akard LP, Broun ER. 2000. Longitudinal study of adaptation to the stress of bone marrow transplantation. *J. Clin. Oncol.* 18:1539–49

Fitzgerald JD, Orav EJ, Lee TH, Marcantonio ER, Poss R, et al. 2004. Patient quality of life during the 12 months following joint replacement surgery. *Arthritis Care Res.* 51:100–9

Folkman S, Moskowitz JT. 2000a. Positive affect and the other side of coping. *Am. Psychol.* 55:647–54

Folkman S, Moskowitz JT. 2000b. The context matters. *Personal. Soc. Psychol. Bull.* 26:150–51

Folkman S, Moskowitz JT. 2004. Coping: pitfalls and promise. *Annu. Rev. Psychol.* 55:745–74

Fontana AF, Kerns RD, Rosenberg RL, Colonese KL. 1989. Support, stress, and recovery from coronary heart disease: a longitudinal causal model. *Health Psychol.* 8:175–93

Frasure-Smith N, Lespérance F. 2005. Reflections on depression as a cardiac risk factor. *Psychosom. Med.* 67(Suppl. 2):S19–25

Fredrickson BL. 2001. The role of positive emotions in positive psychology: the broaden-and-build theory of positive emotions. *Am. Psychol.* 56:218–26

Fritz HL. 2000. Gender-linked personality traits predict mental health and functional status following a first coronary event. *Health Psychol.* 19:420–28

Gallo LC, Ghaed SG, Bracken WS. 2004. Emotions and cognitions in coronary heart disease: risk, resilience, and social context. *Cogn. Ther. Res.* 28:669–94

Gallo LC, Matthews KA. 2003. Understanding the association between socioeconomic status and physical health: Do negative emotions play a role? *Psychol. Bull.* 129:10–51

Giedzinska AS, Meyerowitz BE, Ganz PA, Rowland JH. 2004. Health-related quality of life in a multiethnic sample of breast cancer survivors. *Ann. Behav. Med.* 28:39–51

Giltay EJ, Geleijnse JM, Zitman FG, Hoekstra T, Schouten EG. 2004. Dispositional optimism and all-cause and cardiovascular mortality in a prospective cohort of elderly Dutch men and women. *Arch. Gen. Psychiatry* 61:1126–35

Giltay EJ, Kamphuis MH, Kalmijn S, Zitman FG, Kromhout D. 2006. Dispositional optimism and the risk of cardiovascular death: the Zutphen Elderly Study. *Arch. Intern. Med.* 166:431–36

Graves KD. 2003. Social cognitive theory and cancer patients' quality of life: a meta-analysis of psychosocial intervention components. *Health Psychol.* 22:210–19

Green CR, Anderson KO, Baker TA, Campbell LC, Decker S, et al. 2003. The unequal burden of pain: confronting racial and ethnic disparities in pain. *Pain Med.* 4:277–94

Haas DC, Davidson KW, Schwartz DJ, Rieckmann N, Roman MJ, et al. 2005. Depressive symptoms are independently predictive of carotid atherosclerosis. *Am. J. Cardiol.* 95:547–50

Hack TF, Degner LF. 2004. Coping responses following breast cancer diagnosis predict psychological adjustment three years later. *Psychooncology* 13:235–47

Hagedoorn M, Kuijer RG, Buunk BP, DeJong GM, Wobbes T, et al. 2000. Marital satisfaction in patients with cancer: Does support from intimate partners benefit those who need it most? *Health Psychol.* 19:274–82

Hamburg DA, Adams JE. 1967. A perspective on coping behavior: seeking and utilizing information in major transitions. *Arch. Gen. Psychiatry* 17:277–84

Harrison MJ, Tricker KJ, Davies L, Hassell A, Dawes P, et al. 2005. The relationship between social deprivation, disease outcome measures, and response to treatment in patients with stable, long-standing rheumatoid arthritis. *J. Rheumatol.* 32:2330–36

Havranek EP, Spertus JA, Masoudi FA, Jones PG, Rumsfeld JS. 2004. Predictors of the onset of depressive symptoms in patients with heart failure. *J. Am. Coll. Cardiol.* 44:2333–38

Hawking SW. 1988. *A Brief History of Time: From the Big Bang To Black Holes.* New York: Bantam

Helgeson VS. 1992. Moderators of the relation between perceived control and adjustment to chronic illness. *J. Personal. Soc. Psychol.* 63:656–66

Helgeson VS. 1993. Implications of agency and communion for patient and spouse adjustment to a first coronary event. *J. Personal. Soc. Psychol.* 64:807–16

Helgeson VS. 1994. Relation of agency and communion to well-being: evidence and potential explanations. *Psychol. Bull.* 116:412–28

Helgeson VS, Fritz HL. 1998. A theory of unmitigated communion. *Personal. Soc. Psychol. Rev.* 2:173–83

Helgeson VS, Snyder P, Seltman H. 2004. Psychological and physical adjustment to breast cancer over 4 years: identifying distinct trajectories of change. *Health Psychol.* 23:3–15

Holland JC, Lewis S. 2000. *The Human Side of Cancer: Living with Hope, Coping with Uncertainty.* New York: HarperCollins

Holtzman S, Newth S, DeLongis A. 2004. The role of social support in coping with daily pain among patients with rheumatoid arthritis. *J. Health Psychol.* 9:677–95

Ickovics JR, Thayaparan B, Ethier KA. 2001. Women and AIDS: a contextual analysis. In *Handbook of Health Psychology*, ed. A Baum, TA Revenson, JE Singer, pp. 817–39. Mahwah, NJ: Erlbaum

Jacobsen PB, Sadler IJ, Booth-Jones M, Soety E, Weitzner MA, et al. 2002. Predictors of posttraumatic stress disorder symptomatology following bone marrow transplantation for cancer. *J. Consult. Clin. Psychol.* 70:235–40

Janoff-Bulman R, Berger AR. 2000. The other side of trauma: towards a psychology of appreciation. In *Loss and Trauma: General and Close Relationship Perspectives*, ed. JH Harvey, ED Miller, pp. 29–44. Philadelphia, PA: Taylor & Francis

Janoff-Bulman R, Frantz CM. 1997. The impact of trauma on meaning: from meaningless world to meaningful life. In *The Transformation of Meaning in Psychological Therapies*, ed. M Power. CR Brewin, pp. 91–106. New York: Wiley

Katz PP, Criswell LA. 1996. Differences in symptom reports between men and women with rheumatoid arthritis. *Arthritis Care Res.* 9:441–48

Katz PP, Yelin EH. 1995. The development of depressive symptoms among women with rheumatoid arthritis. *Arthritis Rheum.* 38:49–56

Keefe FJ, Affleck G, Lefebvre JC, Starr K, Caldwell DJ, Tennen H. 1997. Pain coping strategies and coping efficacy in rheumatoid arthritis: a daily process analysis. *Pain* 69:35–42

Keefe FJ, Smith SJ, Buffington ALH, Gibson J, Studts JL, et al. 2002. Recent advances and future directions in the biopsychosocial assessment and treatment of arthritis. *J. Consult. Clin. Psychol.* 70:640–55

Kiecolt-Glaser JK, McGuire L, Robles TF, Glaser R. 2002. Emotions, morbidity, and mortality: new perspectives from psychoneuroimmunology. *Annu. Rev. Psychol.* 53:83–107

King KM. 2000. Gender and short-term recovery from cardiac surgery. *Nurs. Res.* 49:29–36

Krantz DS, McCeney MK. 2002. Effects of psychological and social factors on organic disease: a critical assessment of research on coronary heart disease. *Annu. Rev. Psychol.* 53:341–69

Kubzansky LD, Sparrow D, Vokonas P, Kawachi I. 2001. Is the glass half empty or half full? A prospective study of optimism and coronary heart disease in the Normative Aging Study. *Psychosom. Med.* 63:910–16

Lazarus RS. 1991. *Emotion and Adaptation*. New York: Oxford Univ. Press

Lazarus RS, Folkman S. 1984. *Stress, Appraisal, and Coping*. New York: Springer

Lee MM, Lin SS, Wrensch MR, Adler SR, Eisenberg D. 2000. Alternative therapies used by women with breast cancer in four ethnic populations. *J. Natl. Cancer Inst.* 92:42–47

Lepore SJ. 2001. A social-cognitive processing model of emotional adjustment to cancer. In *Psychosocial Interventions for Cancer*, ed. A Baum, BL Andersen, pp. 99–116. Washington, DC: Am. Psychol. Assoc.

Lepore SJ, Eton DT. 2000. Response shifts in prostate cancer patients: an evaluation of suppressor and buffer models. In *Adaptations to Changing Health: Response Shift in Quality-of-Life Research*, ed. C Schwartz, M Sprangers, pp. 37–51. Washington, DC: Am. Psychol. Assoc.

Lepore SJ, Helgeson VS, Eton DT, Schulz R. 2003. Improving quality of life in men with prostate cancer: a randomized controlled trial of group education interventions. *Health Psychol.* 22:443–52

Lerman C, Daly M, Walsh WP, Resch N, Seay J, et al. 1993. Communication between patients with breast cancer and health care providers: determinants and implications. *Cancer* 72:2612–20

Leventhal H, Leventhal EA, Cameron L. 2001. Representations, procedures, and affect in illness self-regulation: a perceptual-cognitive model. In *Handbook of Health Psychology*, ed. A Baum, TA Revenson, JE Singer, pp. 19–47. Mahwah, NJ: Erlbaum

Link BG, Phelan J. 1995. Social conditions as fundamental causes of disease. *J. Health Soc. Behav.* 36:80–94

Lorish C, Abraham N, Austin J, Bradley LA, Alarcón GS. 1991. Disease and psychosocial factors related to physical functioning in rheumatoid arthritis. *J. Rheumatol.* 18:1150–57

Lutgendorf SK, Anderson B, Ullrich P, Johnsen EL, Buller RE, et al. 2002. Quality of life and mood in women with gynecologic cancer: a one year prospective study. *Cancer* 94:131–40

Mahler HIM, Kulik JA. 1990. Preferences for health care involvement, perceived control and surgical recovery: a prospective study. *Soc. Sci. Med.* 31:743–51

Mahler HIM, Kulik JA. 2000. Optimism, pessimism and recovery from coronary bypass surgery: prediction of affect, pain and functional status. *Psychol. Health Med.* 5:347–58

Manne SL, Ostroff J, Winkel G, Grana G, Fox K. 2005. Partner unsupportive responses, avoidant coping, and distress among women with early stage breast cancer: patient and partner perspectives. *Health Psychol.* 24:635–41

Martire LM, Stephens MAP, Druley JA, Wojno WC. 2002. Negative reactions to received spousal care: predictors and consequences of miscarried support. *Health Psychol.* 21:167–76

McEntegart A, Morrison E, Capell HA, Duncan MR, Porter D, et al. 1997. Effect of social deprivation on disease severity and outcome in patients with rheumatoid arthritis. *Ann. Rheum. Dis.* 56:410–13

Meyerowitz BE, Formenti SC, Ell KO, Leedham B. 2000. Depression among Latina cervical cancer patients. *J. Soc. Clin. Psychol.* 19:352–71

Meyerowitz BE, Richardson J, Hudson S, Leedham B. 1998. Ethnicity and cancer outcomes: behavioral and psychosocial considerations. *Psychol. Bull.* 123:47–70

Michael YL, Berkman LF, Colditz GA, Holmes MD, Kawachi I. 2002. Social networks and health-related quality of life in breast cancer survivors: a prospective study. *J. Psychosom. Res.* 52:285–93

Michael YL, Kawachi I, Berkman LF, Holmes MD, Colditz GA. 2000. The persistent impact of breast carcinoma on functional health status: prospective evidence from the Nurses' Health Study. *Cancer* 89:2176–86

Michela JL. 1987. Interpersonal and individual impacts of a husband's heart attack. In *Handbook of Psychology and Health*, ed. A Baum, JE Singer, 5:255–301. Hillsdale, NJ: Erlbaum

Miller DL, Manne SL, Taylor K, Keates J, Dougherty J. 1996. Psychological distress and well-being in advanced cancer: the effects of optimism and coping. *J. Clin. Psychol. Med. Settings* 3:115–30

Mols F, Vingerhoets AJJM, Coebergh JW, van Poll-Franse LV. 2005. Quality of life among long-term breast cancer survivors: a systematic review. *Eur. J. Cancer* 41:2613–19

Montgomery GH, Bovbjerg DH. 2001. Specific response expectancies predict anticipatory nausea during chemotherapy for breast cancer. *J. Consult. Clin. Psychol.* 69:831–35

Montgomery GH, Bovbjerg DH. 2004. Presurgery distress and specific response expectancies predict postsurgery outcomes in surgery patients confronting breast cancer. *Health Psychol.* 23:381–87

Moos RH, Schaefer JA. 1984. The crisis of physical illness. In *Coping with Physical Illness*, ed. R Moos, pp. 3–26. New York: Plenum

Moyer A, Salovey P. 1999. Predictors of social support and psychological distress in women with breast cancer. *J. Health Psychol.* 4:177–91

Neugarten B. 1979. Time, age and the life cycle. *Am. J. Psychiatry* 136:887–94

Neugebauer A, Katz PP, Pasch LA. 2003. Effect of valued activity disability, social comparison, and satisfaction with ability on depressive symptoms in rheumatoid arthritis. *Health Psychol.* 22:253–62

Newman S, Fitzpatrick R, Revenson TA, Skevington S, Williams G. 1996. *Understanding Rheumatoid Arthritis*. London: Routledge & Kegan Paul

Northouse LL, Mood D, Templin T, Mellon S, George T. 2000. Couples' patterns of adjustment to colon cancer. *Soc. Sci. Med.* 50:271–84

Ouellette SC, DiPlacido J. 2001. Personality's role in the protection and enhancement of health: where the research has been, where it is stuck, how it might move. In *Handbook of Health Psychology*, ed. A Baum, TA Revenson, J Singer, pp. 175–94. Mahwah NJ: Erlbaum

Parker J, Smarr KL, Walker SE, Hagglund KJ, Anderson SK, et al. 1991. Biopsychosocial parameters of disease activity in rheumatoid arthritis. *Arthritis Care Res.* 4:73–80

Patrick DL, Ferketich SL, Frame PS, Harris JJ, Hendricks CB, et al. 2004. National Institutes of Health State-of-the-Science Conference Statement: symptom management in cancer: pain, depression, and fatigue, July 15–17, 2002. *J. Natl. Cancer Inst. Monogr.* (32):9–16

Peralta-Ramírez MI, Jiménez-Alonso J, Godoy-García JF, Perez-García M. 2004. The effects of daily stress and stressful life events on the clinical symptomatology of patients with lupus erythematosus. *Psychosom. Med.* 66:788–94

Polsky D, Doshi JA, Marcus S, Oslin D, Rothbard A, et al. 2005. Long-term risk for depressive symptoms after a medical diagnosis. *Arch. Intern. Med.* 165:1260–66

Pressman SD, Cohen S. 2005. Does positive affect influence health? *Psychol. Bull.* 131:925–71

Rabin C, Leventhal H, Goodin S. 2004. Conceptualizations of disease timeline predicts post-treatment distress in breast cancer patients. *Health Psychol.* 23:407–12

Reisine S, Fifield J, Walsh SJ, Feinn R. 2001. Factors associated with continued employment among patients with rheumatoid arthritis: a survival model. *J. Rheumatol.* 28:2400–8

Revenson TA. 1990. All other things are *not* equal: an ecological perspective on the relation between personality and disease. In *Personality and Disease*, ed. HS Friedman, pp. 65–94. New York: John Wiley

Revenson TA. 1993. The role of social support with rheumatic disease. In *Balliere's Clinical Rheumatology*, ed. S Newman, M Shipley, 7(2):377–96. London: Bailliere Tindal

Revenson TA. 1994. Social support and marital coping with chronic illness. *Ann. Behav. Med.* 16:122–30

Revenson TA. 2003. Scenes from a marriage: examining support, coping, and gender within the context of chronic illness. In *Social Psychological Foundations of Health and Illness*, ed. J Suls, K Wallston, pp. 530–59. Oxford: Blackwell Sci.

Revenson TA, Majerovitz SD. 1990. Spouses' support provision to chronically ill patients. *J. Soc. Personal. Rel.* 7:575–86

Roesch SC, Adams L, Hines A, Palmores A, Vyas P, et al. 2005. Coping with prostate cancer: a meta-analytic review. *J. Behav. Med.* 28:281–93

Rohrbaugh MJ, Shoham V, Coyne JC, Cranford JA, Sonnega JS, Nicklas JM. 2004. Beyond the "self" in self-efficacy: spouse confidence predicts patient survival following heart failure. *J. Fam. Psychol.* 18:184–93

Rozanski A, Blumenthal JA, Kaplan J. 1999. Impact of psychological factors on the pathogenesis of cardiovascular disease and implications for therapy. *Circulation* 99:2192–217

Savelkoul M, de Witte L, Post M. 2003. Stimulating active coping in patients with rheumatic diseases: a systematic review of controlled group intervention studies. *Patient Educ. Couns.* 50:133–43

Scheier MF, Bridges MW. 1995. Person variables and health: personality predispositions and acute psychological states as shared determinants for disease. *Psychosom. Med.* 5:255–68

Scheier MF, Carver CS. 1985. Optimism, coping and health: assessment and implications of generalized outcome expectancies. *Health Psychol.* 4:219–47

Scheier MF, Helgeson VS, Schulz R, Colvin S, Berga S, et al. 2005. Interventions to enhance physical and psychological functioning among younger women who are ending nonhormonal adjuvant treatment for early-stage breast cancer. *J. Clin. Oncol.* 23:4298–311

Scheier MF, Matthews KA, Owens JF, Magovern GJ, Lefebvre RC, et al. 1989. Dispositional optimism and recovery from coronary artery bypass surgery: the beneficial effects on physical and psychological well-being. *J. Personal. Soc. Psychol.* 57:1024–40

Schiaffino KM, Revenson TA. 1992. The role of perceived self-efficacy, perceived control, and causal attributions in adaptation to rheumatoid arthritis: distinguishing mediator vs moderator effects. *Personal. Soc. Psychol. Bull.* 18:709–18

Schiaffino KM, Revenson TA. 1995. Relative contributions of spousal support and illness appraisals to depressed mood in arthritis patients. *Arthritis Care Res.* 8:80–87

Schofield P, Ball D, Smith JG, Borland R, O'Brien P, et al. 2004. Optimism and survival in lung carcinoma patients. *Cancer* 100:1276–82

Schou I, Ekeberg Ø, Ruland CM. 2005. The mediating role of appraisal and coping in the relationship between optimism-pessimism and quality of life. *Psychooncology* 14:718–27

Schulz U, Schwarzer R. 2004. Long-term effects of spousal support on coping with cancer after surgery. *J. Soc. Clin. Psychol.* 23:716–32

Sears SR, Stanton AL, Danoff-Burg S. 2003. The yellow brick road and the emerald city: benefit finding, positive reappraisal coping and posttraumatic growth in women with early-stage breast cancer. *Health Psychol.* 22:487–97

Seeman TE, Dubin LF, Seeman M. 2003. Religiosity/spirituality and health: a critical review of the evidence for biological pathways. *Am. Psychol.* 58:53–63

Shnek ZM, Irvine J, Stewart D, Abbey S. 2001. Psychological factors and depressive symptoms in ischemic heart disease. *Health Psychol.* 20:141–45

Smith BW, Zautra AJ. 2002. The role of personality in exposure and reactivity to interpersonal stress in relation to arthritis disease activity and negative affect in women. *Health Psychol.* 21:81–88

Smith BW, Zautra AJ. 2004. The role of purpose in life in recovery from knee surgery. *Int. J. Behav. Med.* 11:197–202

Smith CA, Wallston KA. 1992. Adaptation in patients with chronic rheumatoid arthritis. *Health Psychol.* 11:151–62

Smith TW, Gallo LC. 2001. Personality traits as risk factors for physical illness. In *Handbook of Health Psychology*, ed. A Baum, TA Revenson, J Singer, pp.139–74. Mahwah, NJ: Erlbaum

Smith TW, Ruiz JM. 2002. Psychosocial influences on the development and course of coronary heart disease: current status and implications for research and practice. *J. Consult. Clin. Psychol.* 70:548–68

Somerfield MR, McCrae R. 2000. Stress and coping research: methodological challenges, theoretical advances, and clinical applications. *Am. Psychol.* 55:620–25

Spelten ER, Sprangers MAG, Verbeek JHAM. 2002. Factors reported to influence the return to work of cancer survivors: a literature review. *Psychooncology* 11:124–31

Stanton AL, Bower JE, Low CA. 2006. Posttraumatic growth after cancer. In *Handbook of Posttraumatic Growth: Research and Practice*, ed. LG Calhoun, RG Tedeschi, pp. 138–75. Mahwah, NJ: Erlbaum

Stanton AL, Collins CA, Sworowski LA. 2001. Adjustment to chronic illness: theory and research. In *Handbook of Health Psychology*, ed. A Baum, TA Revenson, JE Singer, pp. 387–403. Mahwah, NJ: Erlbaum

Stanton AL, Danoff-Burg S, Cameron CL, Bishop MM, Collins CA, et al. 2000. Emotionally expressive coping predicts psychological and physical adjustment to breast cancer. *J. Consult. Clin. Psychol.* 68:875–82

Stanton AL, Danoff-Burg S, Cameron CL, Snider P, Kirk SB. 1999. Social comparison and adjustment to cancer: an experimental examination of upward affiliation and downward evaluation. *Health Psychol.* 18:151–58

Stanton AL, Revenson TA. 2007. Progress and promise in research on adjustment to chronic disease. In *Foundations of Health Psychology*, ed. HS Friedman, RC Silver, pp. 203–33. New York: Oxford Univ. Press

Stanton AL, Snider PR. 1993. Coping with a breast cancer diagnosis: a prospective study. *Health Psychol.* 12:16–23

Stephens MAP, Druly JA, Zautra A. 2002. Older adults' recovery from surgery for osteoarthritis of the knee: psychosocial resources and constraints as predictors of outcomes. *Health Psychol.* 21:377–83

Stewart RA, North FM, West TM, Sharples KJ, Simes RJ, et al. 2003. Depression and cardio-vascular morbidity and mortality: cause or consequence? *Eur. Heart J.* 24:2027–37

Stiegelis HE, Hagedoorn M, Sanderman R, Van der Zee KI, Buunk BP, et al. 2003. Cognitive adaptation: a comparison of cancer patients and healthy references. *Br. J. Psychol.* 8:303–18

Stommel M, Kurtz ME, Kurtz JC, Given CW, Given BA. 2004. A longitudinal analysis of the course of depressive symptomatology in geriatric patients with cancer of the breast, colon, lung, or prostate. *Health Psychol.* 23:564–73

Stone AA, Broderick JE, Porter LS, Kaell AT. 1997. The experience of rheumatoid arthritis pain and fatigue: examining momentary reports and correlates over one week. *Arthritis Care Res.* 10:185–93

Suls J, Fletcher B. 1985. The relative efficacy of avoidant and nonavoidant coping strategies: a meta-analysis. *Health Psychol.* 4:249–88

Tammemagi CM, Nerenz D, Neslund-Dudas C, Feldkamp C, Nathanson D. 2005. Comor-bidity and survival disparities among black and white patients with breast cancer. *JAMA* 294:1765–72

Taylor KL, Lamdan RM, Siegel JE, Shelby R, Hrywna M, et al. 2002. Treatment regimen, sexual attractiveness concerns and psychological adjustment among African American breast cancer patients. *Psychooncology* 11:505–17

Taylor SE. 1983. Adjustment to threatening events: a theory of cognitive adaptation. *Am. Psychol.* 38:1161–73

Taylor SE, Klein LC, Lewis BP, Gruenewald TL, Gurung RAR, Updegraff JA. 2000. Biobe-havioral responses to stress in females: tend-and-befriend, not fight-or-flight. *Psychol. Rev.* 107:411–29

Taylor SE, Repetti R, Seeman TE. 1997. Health psychology: What is an unhealthy environment and how does it get under the skin? *Annu. Rev. Psychol.* 48:411–47

Tennen H, Affleck G. 2000. The perception of personal control: sufficiently important to warrant careful scrutiny. *Personal. Soc. Psychol. Bull.* 26:152–56

Tennen H, Affleck G. 2002. Benefit-finding and benefit-reminding. In *Handbook of Positive Psychology*, ed. CR Snyder, SJ Lopez, pp. 584–97. New York: Oxford Univ. Press

Tennen H, Affleck G. 2006. Positive change following adversity: In search of meticulous meth-ods. In *Positive Life Changes in the Context of Physical Illness*, ed. C Park, S Lechner, AL Stanton, MH Antoni. Washington, DC: Am. Psychol. Assoc. In press

Tennen H, Affleck G, Armeli S, Carney MA. 2000. A daily process approach to coping: linking theory, research, and practice. *Am. Psychol.* 55:626–36

Tennen H, Affleck G, Urrows S, Higgins P, Mendola R. 1992. Perceiving control, construing benefits, and daily processes in rheumatoid arthritis. *Can. J. Behav. Sci.* 24:186–203

Thompson SC, Kyle DJ. 2000. The role of perceived control in coping with the losses associated with chronic illness. In *Loss and Trauma: General and Close Relationship Perspectives*, ed. JH Harvey, ED Miller, pp. 131–45. Philadelphia, PA: Brunner-Routledge

Thompson SC, Sobolew-Shubin A, Galbraith ME, Schwankovsky L, Cruzen D. 1993. Maintaining perceptions of control: finding perceived control in low-control circumstances. *J. Personal. Soc. Psychol.* 64:293–304

Todaro JF, Shen BJ, Niaura R, Spiro A, Ward K, Weiss S. 2003. A prospective study of negative emotions and CHD incidence: the normative aging study. *Am. J. Cardiol.* 92:901–6

Tomich PL, Helgeson VS. 2004. Is finding something good in the bad always good? Benefit finding among women with breast cancer. *Health Psychol.* 23:16–23

Trunzo JJ, Pinto BM. 2003. Social support as a mediator of optimism and distress in breast cancer survivors. *J. Consult. Clin. Psychol.* 71:805–11

Tuinstra J, Hagedoorn M, Van Sonderen E, Ranchor AV, Van den Bos GA, et al. 2004. Psychological distress in couples dealing with colorectal cancer: gender and role differences and intracouple correspondence. *Br. J. Health Psychol.* 9:465–78

Van der Zee K, Buunk B, Sanderman R. 1998. Neuroticism and reactions to social comparison information among cancer patients. *J. Pers.* 66:175–94

van Jaarsveld CHM, Ranchor AV, Sanderman R, Ormel J, Kempen GIJM. 2005. The role of premorbid psychological attributes in short- and long-term adjustment after cardiac disease. A prospective study in the elderly in The Netherlands. *Soc. Sci. Med.* 60:1035–45

Waltz M, Badura B, Pfaff H, Schott T. 1988. Marriage and the psychological consequences of a heart attack: a longitudinal study of adaptation to chronic illness after 3 years. *Soc. Sci. Med.* 27:149–58

Watson D, Weise D, Vaidya J, Tellegen A. 1999. The two general activation systems of affect: structural findings, evolutionary consideration, and psychobiological evidence. *J. Personal. Soc. Psychol.* 76:820–38

Wegner D, Pennebaker J. 1992, eds. *Handbook of Mental Control.* New York: Prentice-Hall

Wethington E, McLeod JD, Kessler R. 1987. The importance of life events for explaining sex differences in mental health. In *Gender and Stress*, ed. RC Barnett, L Biener, GK Baruch, pp. 144–55. New York: Free Press

Wills TA, Fegan MF. 2001. Social networks and social support. In *Handbook of Health Psychology*, ed. A Baum, TA Revenson, JE Singer, pp. 139–73. Mahwah, NJ: Erlbaum

Wortman CB, Silver RC. 2001. The myths of coping with loss revisited. In *Handbook of Bereavement Research: Consequences, Coping, and Care*, ed. MS Stroebe, RO Hansson, W Stroebe, H Schut, pp. 405–29. Washington, DC: Am. Psychol. Assoc.

Young LD. 1992. Psychological factors in rheumatoid arthritis. *J. Consult. Clin. Psychol.* 60:619–27

Zautra AJ, Hoffman J, Potter P, Matt KS, Yocum D, et al. 1997. Examination of changes in interpersonal stress as a factor in disease exacerbations among women with rheumatoid arthritis. *Ann. Behav. Med.* 19:279–86

Zautra AJ, Smith BW. 2001. Depression and reactivity to stress in older women with rheumatoid arthritis and osteoarthritis. *Psychosom. Med.* 63:687–96

Zautra AJ, Smith BW, Affleck G, Tennen H. 2001. Examinations of chronic pain and affect relationships: applications of a dynamic model of affect. *J. Consult. Clin. Psychol.* 69:785–96

Mediation Analysis

David P. MacKinnon, Amanda J. Fairchild,
and Matthew S. Fritz

Department of Psychology, Arizona State University, Tempe, Arizona 85287-1104;
email: david.mackinnon@asu.edu, amanda.fairchild@asu.edu, matt.fritz@asu.edu

Annu. Rev. Psychol. 2007. 58:593–614

First published online as a Review in
Advance on August 29, 2006

The *Annual Review of Psychology* is online at
http://psych.annualreviews.org

This article's doi:
10.1146/annurev.psych.58.110405.085542

Key Words

intervening variable, indirect effect, third variable, mediator

Abstract

Mediating variables are prominent in psychological theory and research. A mediating variable transmits the effect of an independent variable on a dependent variable. Differences between mediating variables and confounders, moderators, and covariates are outlined. Statistical methods to assess mediation and modern comprehensive approaches are described. Future directions for mediation analysis are discussed.

Contents

INTRODUCTION

Mediating variables form the basis of many questions in psychology:

- Will changing social norms about science improve children's achievement in science?

- If an intervention increases secure attachment among young children, do behavioral problems decrease when the children enter school?
- Does physical abuse in early childhood lead to deviant processing of social information that leads to aggressive behavior?
- Do expectations start a self-fulfilling prophecy that affects behavior?
- Can changes in cognitive attributions reduce depression?
- Does trauma affect brain stem activation in a way that inhibits memory?
- Does secondary rehearsal increase image formation, which increases word recall?

Questions like these suggest a chain of relations where an antecedent variable affects a mediating variable, which then affects an outcome variable. As illustrated in the questions, mediating variables are behavioral, biological, psychological, or social constructs that transmit the effect of one variable to another variable. Mediation is one way that a researcher can explain the process or mechanism by which one variable affects another.

One of the primary reasons for the popularity of mediating variables in psychology is the historical dominance of the stimulus organism response model (Hebb 1966). In this model, mediating mechanisms in the organism translate how a stimulus leads to a response. A second related reason for the importance of mediating variables is that they form the basis of many psychological theories. For example, in social psychology, attitudes cause intentions, which then cause behavior (Fishbein & Ajzen 1975), and in cognitive psychology, memory processes mediate how information is transmitted into a response. A newer application of the mediating variable framework is in prevention and treatment research, where interventions are designed to change the outcome of interest by targeting mediating variables that are hypothesized to be causally related to the outcome.

A third reason for interest in mediation is methodological. Mediation represents the consideration of how a third variable affects the relation between two other variables. Although the consideration of a third variable may appear simple, three-variable systems can be very complicated, and there are many alternative explanations of observed relations other than mediation. This methodological and statistical challenge of investigating mediation has made methodology for assessing mediation an active research topic.

This review first defines the mediating variable and the ways in which it differs from other variables, such as a moderator or a confounder. Examples of mediating variables used in psychology are provided. Statistical methods to assess mediation in the single-mediator case are described, along with their assumptions. These assumptions are addressed in sections describing current research on the statistical testing of mediated effects, longitudinal mediation models, models with moderators as well as mediators, and causal inference for mediation models. Finally, directions for future research are outlined.

Definitions

Most research focuses on relations between two variables, X and Y, and much has been written about two-variable relations, including conditions under which X can be considered a possible cause of Y. These conditions include randomization of units to values of X and independence of units across and within values of X. Mediation in its simplest form represents the addition of a third variable to this X → Y relation, whereby X causes the mediator, M, and M causes Y, so X→ M → Y. Mediation is only one of several relations that may be present when a third variable, Z (using Z to represent the third variable), is included in the analysis of a two-variable system. One possibility is that Z causes both X and Y, so that ignoring Z leads to incorrect inference about the relation of X and Y; this would be an example of a confounding variable. In another

situation, Z may be related to X and/or Y, so that information about Z improves prediction of Y by X, but does not substantially alter the relation of X to Y when Z is included in the analysis; this is an example of a covariate. Z may also modify the relation of X to Y such that the relation of X to Y differs at different values of Z; this is an example of a moderator or interaction effect. The distinction between a moderator and mediator has been an ongoing topic of research (Baron & Kenny 1986, Holmbeck 1997, Kraemer et al. 2001). A mediator is a variable that is in a causal sequence between two variables, whereas a moderator is not part of a causal sequence between the two variables. More detailed definitions of these variables in a three-variable system may be found in Robins & Greenland (1992).

The single-mediator model is shown in **Figure 1**, where the variables X, M, and Y are in rectangles and the arrows represent relations among variables. **Figure 1** uses the notation most widely applied in psychology, with *a* representing the relation of X to M, *b* representing the relation of M to Y adjusted for X, and *c′* the relation of X to Y adjusted for M. The symbols e_2 and e_3 represent residuals in the M and Y variables, respectively. The equations and coefficients corresponding to **Figure 1** are discussed below. For now, note that there is a direct effect relating X to Y and a mediated effect by which X indirectly affects

Mediation Model

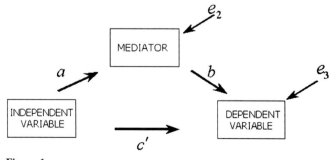

Figure 1

Mediation model.

Table 1 Subject area coverage in current mediation research

Subject area	# Articles cited
Social psychology	98
Clinical psychology	70
Health psychology	29
Developmental psychology	27
IO psychology	24
Cognitive psychology	18
Quantitative psychology (methods)	12
Program evaluation	8
Educational psychology	3
Environmental psychology	1
Evolutionary psychology	1

Y through M. Given that most prior mediation research has applied this single-mediator model, this review starts with this model. Limitations and extensions of the model are described in subsequent sections.

When thinking of mediation, it is helpful to understand that two models exist: One is theoretical, corresponding to unobservable relations among variables, and the other is empirical, corresponding to statistical analyses of actual data (MacCorquodale & Meehl 1948). The challenging task of research is to infer the true state of mediation from observations. There are qualifications even to this simple dichotomy, and in general, it will take a program of research to justify concluding that a third variable is a mediating variable.

Mediation in Psychological Research

In order to ascertain how often mediation is used in psychology, a search was conducted using the *PsycInfo* search engine for articles containing the word "mediation" in the title and citing the most widely cited article for mediation methods, Baron & Kenny (1986). This search yielded 291 references. Of these articles, 80 came from American Psychological Association (APA) journals. Publications

earlier than the year 2000 were primarily APA sources, but there was a surge in non-APA articles after that time. The majority of these sources (239 citations) examined mediation alone, and 52 investigated both mediation and moderation effects. These studies included a mix of cross-sectional and longitudinal data, and ordinary least squares regression and structural equation modeling were the primary analytic methods. The articles covered a wide range of substantive areas, including social psychology (98 articles) and clinical psychology (70); a complete breakdown is listed in **Table 1**.

Mediation studies, such as those discussed above, are of two general but overlapping types. One type consists of investigating how a particular effect occurs. These studies usually occur after an observed X → Y relation is found. This approach stems from the elaboration methodologies outlined by Lazarsfeld (1955) and Hyman (1955). In this framework, a third variable is added to the analysis of an X → Y relation in order to improve understanding of the relation or to determine if the relation is spurious. A mediating variable improves understanding of such a relation because it is part of the causal sequence of X → M → Y. For example, physical abuse in early childhood is associated with violence later in life. One explanation of this pattern is that children exposed to physical violence acquire deviant patterns of processing social information that lead to later violent behavior. Dodge et al. (1990) found evidence for this theoretical mediating process because social processing measures explained the relation between early childhood physical abuse and later aggressive behavior.

The second type of study uses theory regarding mediational processes to design experiments. Some of the best examples of this approach are found in the evaluation of treatment and prevention programs. In this research, an intervention is designed to change mediating variables that are hypothesized to be causally related to a dependent variable. If the hypothesized relations are correct, a prevention or treatment program that substantially changes the mediating variables will in turn change the outcome. Primary prevention programs, such as drug prevention programs, are designed to increase resistance skills, educate, and change norms to reduce drug use. Secondary prevention programs such as campaigns to increase screening rates for serious illness (Murray et al. 1986) educate and change norms regarding health to increase screening rates. In both of these examples, a mediator that transmits the effect of an independent variable on a dependent variable is first identified by theory and later tested in an experiment. Researchers from many fields have stressed the importance of assessing mediation in treatment and prevention research (Baranowski et al. 1998; Donaldson 2001; Judd & Kenny 1981a,b; Kraemer et al. 2002; MacKinnon 1994; Shadish 1996; Weiss 1997). First, mediation analysis provides a check on whether the program produced a change in the construct it was designed to change. If a program is designed to change norms, then program effects on normative measures should be found. Second, mediation analysis results may suggest that certain program components need to be strengthened or measurements need to be improved, as failures to significantly change mediating variables occur either because the program was ineffective or the measures of the mediating construct were not adequate. Third, program effects on mediating variables in the absence of effects on outcome measures suggest that program effects on outcomes may emerge later or that the targeted constructs were not critical in changing outcomes. Fourth, mediation can sometimes be used to discover proximal outcomes that can be used as a surrogate for an ultimate outcome. For example, in medical studies to reduce death owing to a disease, instead of waiting until death, a more proximal outcome such as disease symptoms may be identified. Finally, and most importantly, mediation analysis generates evidence for how a program achieved its effects. Identification of the critical ingredients can streamline and improve these programs by focusing on effective components.

Experimental Approaches to Mediation

Many psychological studies investigating mediation use a randomized experimental design, where participants are randomized to levels of one or more factors in order to demonstrate a pattern of results consistent with one theory and inconsistent with another theory (MacKinnon et al. 2002a, Spencer et al. 2005, West & Aiken 1997). Differences in means between groups are then attributed to the experimental manipulation of the mediator. The results of the randomized study along with the predictions of different theories are used to provide evidence for a mediation hypothesis and suggest further studies to localize and validate the mediating process. For example, a researcher may randomize individuals to conditions that will or will not induce cognitive dissonance. In one such study, Sherman & Gorkin (1980) randomly assigned subjects to solve either (a) a sex-role related brainteaser, or (b) a brainteaser not related to sex roles. The sexist brainteaser condition was designed to evoke cognitive dissonance in the self-identified feminist subjects, while the nonsex-role related condition was not. Participants were then asked to judge the fairness of a legal decision made in an affirmative action trial. The results were consistent with the prediction that participants with strong feminist beliefs were more likely to make extreme feminist judgments in the trial if they failed the sexist brainteaser task, in an attempt to reduce cognitive dissonance. Although results of this experiment were taken as evidence of a cognitive dissonance mediation relation, the mediating variable of cognitive conflict was not measured to obtain more information on the link between the manipulation, cognitive dissonance, and feminist judgments.

Double randomization. In some designs it may be possible to investigate a mediational process by a randomized experiment to investigate the $X \rightarrow M$ relation and a second randomized experiment to investigate the $M \rightarrow Y$ relation (MacKinnon et al. 2002a, Spencer et al. 2005, West & Aiken 1997). Spencer et al. (2005) recently summarized two experiments reported by Word et al. (1974) that executed this design in a study of self-fulfilling prophecy for racial stereotypes. In study 1, white participants were randomly assigned to interview a black or white confederate. Using measures from the participants, black applicants received less immediacy, higher rates of speech errors, and shorter interviews than did white confederates. This part of the study demonstrated that race of applicant (X) significantly affected interview quality (M). In study 2, confederate white interviewers interviewed the participants from study 1. The confederate interviewers either gave interviews like white applicants were given in study 1 or they interviewed applicants with less immediacy, higher rates of speech errors, and shorter amounts of interviewer time, like black applicants. Here the M variable, type of interview, was randomized and the behavior of the applicants, the Y variable, was measured. The results of study 2 indicated that participants treated like blacks in study 1 performed less adequately and were more nervous in the interview than participants treated like whites in study 1. Although this type of experiment does much to reduce alternative explanations of the mediation hypothesis, it may be difficult to implement double randomization in other research contexts. Generally, the most difficult aspect of the design is the ability to randomly assign participants to the levels of the mediator so that the $M \rightarrow Y$ relation can be studied experimentally.

SINGLE-MEDIATOR MODEL

Mediation Regression Equations

Experimental studies in psychology rarely involve both manipulation of the mediator and measurement of mediating variables. If a research study includes measures of a mediating variable as well as the independent and dependent variable, mediation may be investigated statistically (Fiske et al. 1982). In this way, mediation analysis is a method to increase information obtained from a research study when measures of the mediating process are available.

There are three major approaches to statistical mediation analysis: (*a*) causal steps, (*b*) difference in coefficients, and (*c*) product of coefficients (MacKinnon 2000). All of these methods use information from the following three regression equations:

$$Y = i_1 + cX + e_1, \qquad 1.$$
$$Y = i_2 + c'X + bM + e_2, \qquad 2.$$
$$M = i_3 + aX + e_3, \qquad 3.$$

where i_1 and i_2 and i_3 are intercepts, Y is the dependent variable, X is the independent variable, M is the mediator, c is the coefficient relating the independent variable and the dependent variable, c' is the coefficient relating the independent variable to the dependent variable adjusted for the mediator, b is the coefficient relating the mediator to the dependent variable adjusted for the independent variable, a is the coefficient relating the independent variable to the mediator, and e_1, e_2, and e_3 are residuals. Equations 2 and 3 are depicted in **Figure 1**. Note that the mediation equations may be altered to incorporate linear as well as nonlinear effects and the interaction of X and M in Equation 2, as described later in this review.

The most widely used method to assess mediation is the causal steps approach outlined in the classic work of Baron & Kenny (1986; also Kenny et al. 1998) and Judd & Kenny (1981a, 1981b). Four steps are involved in the Baron and Kenny approach to establishing mediation. First, a significant relation of the independent variable to the dependent variable is required in Equation 1. Second, a significant relation of the independent variable to the hypothesized mediating variable is required in Equation 3. Third, the mediating variable must be significantly related to the dependent variable when both the independent variable and mediating variable are predictors of the dependent variable in Equation 2. Fourth, the coefficient relating the independent variable to the dependent variable must be larger (in absolute value) than the coefficient relating the independent variable to the dependent variable in the regression model with both the independent variable and the mediating variable predicting the dependent variable. This causal steps approach to assessing mediation has been the most widely used method to assess mediation. As discussed below, there are several limitations to this approach.

The mediated effect in the single-mediator model (see **Figure 1**) may be calculated in two ways, as either $\hat{a}\hat{b}$ or $\hat{c} - \hat{c}'$ (MacKinnon & Dwyer 1993). The value of the mediated or indirect effect estimated by taking the difference in the coefficients, $\hat{c} - \hat{c}'$, from Equations 1 and 2 corresponds to the reduction in the independent variable effect on the dependent variable when adjusted for the mediator. To test for significance, the difference is then divided by the standard error of the difference and the ratio is compared to a standard normal distribution.

The product of coefficients method, involves estimating Equations 2 and 3 and computing the product of $\hat{a}$ and $\hat{b}$, $\hat{a}\hat{b}$, to form the mediated or indirect effect (Alwin & Hauser 1975). The rationale behind this method is that mediation depends on the extent to which the program changes the mediator, a, and the extent to which the mediator affects the outcome variable, b. To test for significance, the product is then divided by the standard error of the product and the ratio is compared to a standard normal distribution.

The algebraic equivalence of the $\hat{a}\hat{b}$ and $\hat{c} - \hat{c}'$ measures of mediation was shown by MacKinnon et al. (1995) for normal theory ordinary least squares and maximum likelihood estimation of the three mediation regression equations. For multilevel models (Krull & MacKinnon 1999), logistic or probit regres-

sion (MacKinnon & Dwyer 1993), and survival analysis (Tein & MacKinnon 2003), the $\hat{a}\hat{b}$ and $\hat{c} - \hat{c}'$ estimators of the mediated effect are not always equivalent, and a transformation is required for the two to yield similar results (MacKinnon & Dwyer 1993).

Plotting the Mediation Equations

The quantities in Equations 1–3 can also be presented geometrically, as shown in **Figure 2** (MacKinnon 2007; R. Merrill, unpublished dissertation). Artificial data are plotted in **Figure 2**, where the independent variable, X, is dichotomous (to simplify the plot), the mediator, M, is on the horizontal axis, and the dependent variable, Y, is on the vertical axis. The two slanted lines in the plot represent the relation of M to Y in each X group, one line for the control group and one line for the treatment group. The two lines are parallel (note that if there were an XM interaction in Equation 2, then the slopes would not be parallel), with the slope of each line equal to the b coefficient ($\hat{b} = 0.91$, $se_{\hat{b}} = 0.18$). The distance between the horizontal lines in the plots is equal to the overall effect of X on Y, c ($\hat{c} = 1.07$, $se_{\hat{c}} = 0.27$), and the distance between the vertical lines is equal to the effect of X on M, a ($\hat{a} = 0.87$, $se_{\hat{a}} = 0.23$). The mediated effect is the change in the regression line relating M to Y for a change in M of a units as shown in the graph. The indirect effect, $\hat{a}\hat{b}$, is equal to $\hat{c} - \hat{c}'(\hat{c}' = 0.23$, $se_{\hat{c}'} = 0.24$). Plots of the mediated effect may be useful to investigate the distributions of data for outliers and to improve understanding of relations among variables in the mediation model.

Standard Error of the Mediated Effect

Sobel (1982, 1986) derived the asymptotic standard error of the indirect effect using the multivariate delta method (Bishop et al. 1975) in Equation 4. This is the most commonly used formula for the standard error of the

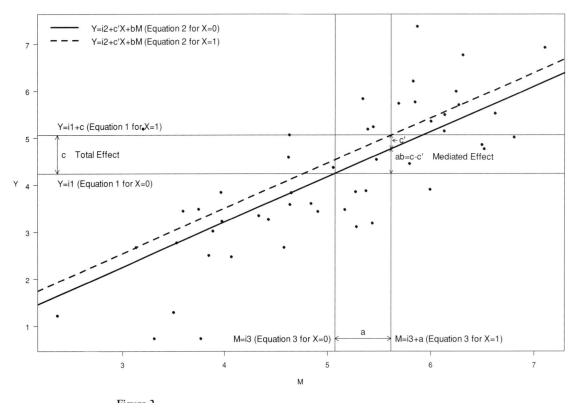

Figure 2

Plot of the mediated effect. To simplify figure, no hats are included above coefficient estimates.

mediated effect.

$$\sigma_{\hat{a}\hat{b}} = \sqrt{\sigma_{\hat{a}}^2 \hat{b}^2 + \sigma_{\hat{b}}^2 \hat{a}^2} \qquad 4.$$

Other formulas for the standard error of $\hat{a}\hat{b}$ and $\hat{c} - \hat{c}'$ are described in MacKinnon et al. (2002a).

Simulation studies indicate that the estimator of the standard error in Equation 4 shows low bias for sample sizes of at least 50 in single-mediator models (MacKinnon et al. 1995, 2002a). In models with more than one mediator, the standard error is accurate for minimum sample sizes of 100–200 (Stone & Sobel 1990). Similar results were obtained for standard errors of negative and positive path values, and larger models with multiple mediating, independent, and dependent variables

(MacKinnon et al. 2002a, 2004; J. Williams, unpublished dissertation).

Confidence Limits for the Mediated Effect

The standard error of $\hat{a}\hat{b}$ can be used to test its statistical significance and to construct confidence limits for the mediated effect as shown in Equation 5:

$$\hat{a}\hat{b} \pm z_{1-\omega/2}{}^* \sigma_{\hat{a}\hat{b}}. \qquad 5.$$

Confidence limits based on the normal distribution for the mediated effect are often inaccurate as found in simulation studies (MacKinnon et al. 1995, 2002a; Stone & Sobel 1990) and from bootstrap analysis of the mediated effect (Bollen & Stine 1990, Lockwood

& MacKinnon 1998). These mediated effect confidence intervals tend to lie to the left of the true value of the mediated effect for positive mediated effects and to the right for negative mediated effects (Bollen & Stine 1990, MacKinnon et al. 1995, Stone & Sobel 1990). Asymmetric confidence limits based on the distribution of the product and bootstrap estimation have better coverage than these tests (MacKinnon et al. 2004).

Significance Testing

A simulation study of 14 methods to assess the mediated effect found that the power to detect mediated effects using the most widely used causal step methods was very low, as were type I error rates (MacKinnon et al. 2002a, 2004). Low power was also observed for tests based on the normal distribution for mediated effect estimators (i.e., $\hat{a}\hat{b}$ and $\hat{c} - \hat{c}'$) divided by their respective standard errors (Hoyle & Kenny 1999). A joint test of the significance of $\hat{a}$ and $\hat{b}$ was a good compromise between type I and type II errors.

There are several explanations for the low power of most tests for mediation. First of all, the requirement that there be a significant X to Y relation in the Baron and Kenny causal steps test severely reduces power to detect mediation, especially in the case of complete mediation (i.e., direct effect is zero). There are many cases where significant mediation exists but the requirement of a significant relation of X to Y is not obtained. A recent study using empirical approaches to determine required sample size for 0.8 power to detect a mediated effect with small effect size values of the a and b path required approximately 21,000 subjects for the causal steps test (Fritz & MacKinnon 2007). As the size of the direct effect gets larger, the power to detect mediation using the causal steps approach approximates power to detect mediation by testing whether both the a and the b paths are statistically significant. It is important to note that the overall relation of X and Y represents important information for a research study, and in some stud-

ies it may be useful to require an overall X to Y relation. The point is that requiring an X to Y relation substantially reduces power to detect real mediation effects. An explanation for the low power of tests of mediation based on dividing an estimator, either $\hat{a}\hat{b}$ or $\hat{c} - \hat{c}'$, of the mediated effect by its corresponding standard error is that the resulting ratio does not always follow a normal distribution (MacKinnon et al. 2004). Resampling methods and methods based on the distribution of the product of ab address these sampling problems and are described below.

Distribution of the Product

The product of two normally distributed random variables is normally distributed only in special cases (Springer 1979), which explains the inaccuracy of methods of assessing statistical significance of mediation based on the normal distribution. For example, for two standard normal random variables with a mean of zero, the excess kurtosis is equal to six (Meeker et al. 1981) compared to an excess kurtosis of zero for a normal distribution. MacKinnon et al. (2002a, 2004a) showed that in comparison with commonly used methods, significance tests for the mediated effect based on the distribution of the product had more accurate type-I error rates and statistical power. A new program, PRODCLIN (MacKinnon et al. 2006a; program download available at **http://www.public.asu. edu/~davidpm/ripl/Prodclin/**), can now be used to find critical values of the distribution of the product and to compute confidence limits for the mediated effect.

Computer-Intensive Analysis

Computer-intensive methods use the observed data to generate a reference distribution, which is then used for confidence interval estimation and significance testing (Manly 1997, Mooney & Duval 1993, Noreen 1989). Programs to compute confidence limits of the mediated effect for bootstrap methods is described in Preacher & Hayes (2004) and Lockwood & MacKinnon (1998); the AMOS (Arbuckle 1997), EQS (Bentler 1997), LISREL (Jöreskog & Sörbom 1993), and Mplus (Muthén & Muthén 1998–2006) programs also conduct bootstrap resampling for the mediated effect.

Computer-intensive methods, also called resampling methods, for mediation are important for at least two reasons (Bollen & Stine 1990, MacKinnon et al. 2004, Shrout & Bolger 2002). First, these methods provide a general way to test significance and construct confidence intervals in a wide variety of situations where analytical formulas for quantities may not be available. Second, the methods do not require as many assumptions as other tests, which is likely to make them more accurate than traditional mediation analysis.

Assumptions of the Single-Mediator Model

There are several important assumptions for tests of mediation. For the $\hat{a}\hat{b}$ estimator of the mediated effect, the model assumes that the residuals in Equations 2 and 3 are independent and that M and the residual in Equation 2 are independent (McDonald 1997; R. Merrill, unpublished dissertation). It is also assumed that there is not an XM interaction in Equation 3, although this can and should be routinely tested. The assumptions of a correctly specified model include no misspecification of causal order (e.g., $Y \to M \to X$ rather than $X \to M \to Y$), no misspecification of causal direction (e.g., there is reciprocal causation between the mediator and the dependent variable), no misspecification due to unmeasured variables that cause variables in the mediation analysis, and no misspecification due to imperfect measurement (Holland 1988, James & Brett 1984, McDonald 1997). These assumptions may be difficult to test and may be untestable in most situations so that proof of a mediation relation is impossible. A more realistic approach is to incorporate additional information from prior research, including randomized experimental studies, theory, and qualitative methods to bolster the tentative conclusion that a mediation relation exists.

Complete Versus Partial Mediation

Researchers often test whether there is complete or partial mediation by testing whether the c' coefficient is statistically significant, which is a test of whether the association between the independent and dependent variable is completely accounted for by the mediator (see James et al. 2006). If the c' coefficient is statistically significant and there is significant mediation, then there is evidence for partial mediation. Because psychological behaviors have a variety of causes, it is often unrealistic to expect that a single mediator would be explained completely by an independent variable to dependent variable relation (Judd & Kenny 1981a).

Consistent and Inconsistent Models

Inconsistent mediation models are models where at least one mediated effect has a different sign than other mediated or direct effects in a model (Blalock 1969, Davis 1985, MacKinnon et al. 2000). Although knowledge of the significance of the relation of X to Y is important for the interpretation of results, there are several examples in which an overall X to Y relation may be nonsignificant, yet mediation exists. For example, McFatter (1979) described the hypothetical example of workers making widgets, where X is intelligence, M is boredom, and Y is widget production. Intelligent workers tend to get bored and produce less, but smarter workers also tend to make more widgets. Therefore, the overall relation between intelligence and widgets produced may actually be zero, yet there are two opposing mediational processes. A number of other resources provide examples of these inconsistent effects (Paulhus et al. 2004, Sheets & Braver 1999). Inconsistent mediation is more common in multiple mediator models where mediated effects have different signs. Inconsistent mediator effects may be especially critical in evaluating counterproductive effects of experiments, where the manipulation may have led to opposing mediated effects.

Effect Size Measures of Mediation

The raw correlation for the a path and the partial correlation for the b path are effect size measures for mediation models. Standardized regression coefficients may also serve as effect size measures for individual paths in the mediated effect. There are other effect size measures of the entire mediated effect rather than individual paths. The proportion mediated, $1 - (\frac{\hat{c}'}{\hat{c}}) = \frac{\hat{a}\hat{b}}{(\hat{a}\hat{b}+\hat{c}')}$, is often used, but values of the proportion mediated are often very small and focusing on an overall proportion mediated may neglect additional mediating mechanisms (Fleming & DeMets 1996). The proportion mediated is also unstable unless sample size is at least 500 (Freedman 2001, MacKinnon et al. 1995). Alwin & Hauser (1975) suggest taking the absolute values of the direct and indirect effects prior to calculating the proportion mediated for inconsistent models. More work is needed on effect size measures for mediation.

EXTENSIONS OF THE SINGLE-MEDIATOR MODEL

Many important extensions have addressed limitations of the mediation approach described above. First, many studies hypothesize more complicated models including multiple independent variables, multiple mediators, and multiple outcomes. These models may include hypotheses regarding the comparison of mediated effects. Second, mediation in multilevel models may be especially important, as mediation relations at different levels of analysis are possible (Krull & MacKinnon 1999, 2001; Raudenbush & Sampson 1999). Third, mediation effects may differ by subgroups defined by variables both within the mediation model and outside

the mediation model. Fourth, mediation requires temporal precedence from X to M to Y, and longitudinal mediation models have been developed (Gollob & Reichardt 1991, Kraemer et al. 2002). Finally, developments in the causal interpretation of research results (Holland 1988, Robins & Greenland 1992) provide a general framework to understand the limitations and strengths of possible causal inferences from a mediation study. Each of these extensions is described below.

Multilevel Mediation Models

Many studies measure data clustered at several levels, such as individuals in schools, classrooms, therapy groups, or clinics. If mediation analysis from these types of studies is analyzed at the individual level, ignoring the clustering, then type I error rates can be too high (Krull & MacKinnon 1999, 2001). These problems occur because observations within a cluster tend to be dependent so that the independent observations assumption is violated. The investigation of mediation effects at different levels of analysis also may be important for substantive reasons (Hofmann & Gavin 1998). For example, a mediated effect present at the therapy group level may not be present at the individual level. Similarly, it is possible that the mechanism that mediates effects at the school level, such as overall norms, may be different from the mechanism that mediates effects at the individual level.

Kenny et al. (2003) demonstrated that in some cases the a and the b paths may represent random effects. For example, assume that X, M, and Y are measured from individuals in schools and that the researcher is interested in the mediation effect, but the a, b, and c' coefficients may vary significantly across schools rather than having a single fixed effect. If a and b are random effects, they may covary, and an appropriate standard error and point estimate for the mediated effect must allow for this covariance between random effects to be applied. Kenny et al. used a resampling method to obtain a value for this covariance. Other methods that have been recently proposed to assess this covariance consist of combining Equations 2 and 3 into the same analysis (Bauer et al. 2006) and directly estimating the covariance among the random effects in the Mplus program (Muthén & Muthén 1998–2006).

Mediation with Categorical Outcomes

In some mediation analyses, the dependent variable is categorical, such as whether a person used drugs or not. In this case, Equations 1 and 2 must be rewritten for logistic or probit regression, where the dependent variable is typically a latent continuous variable that has been dichotomized in analysis. Because the residual in each logistic or probit equation is fixed, the parameters c, c', and b depend on the other independent variables in the model. Therefore, the $\hat{c} - \hat{c}'$ method of estimating mediation is incorrect because the parameter estimate of $\hat{c}'$ depends on the effect explained by the mediator and the scaling of Equations 1 and 2 (MacKinnon & Dwyer 1993). One solution to this problem is to standardize regression coefficients prior to estimating mediation (Winship & Mare 1983). If the mediator is treated as a continuous variable, a product of coefficients test of the mediated effect may be obtained using $\hat{a}$ from ordinary least squares regression and $\hat{b}$ from logistic regression. Again, better confidence limits and statistical tests are obtained if critical values from the distribution of the product or bootstrap methods are used (D.P. MacKinnon, M. Yoon, C.M. Lockwood, & A.B. Taylor, unpublished manuscript).

Multiple Mediators

Mediating processes may include multiple mediators, dependent variables, and/or independent variables. In school-based drug prevention, for example, prevention programs target multiple mediators such as resistance skills, social norms, attitudes about drugs, and communication skills. The multiple-mediator model is likely to provide a more accurate assessment of mediation effects in many research contexts. Models with more than one mediator are straightforward extensions of the single-mediator case (MacKinnon 2000). Several standard error formulas for comparing different mediated effects are given by MacKinnon (2000), and the methods are illustrated with data from a drug prevention study.

Longitudinal Mediation Models

Longitudinal data allow a researcher to examine many aspects of a mediation model that are unavailable in cross-sectional data, such as whether an effect is stable across time and whether there is evidence for one of the important conditions of causality, temporal precedence. Longitudinal data also bring challenges, including nonoptimal measurement times, omitted variables or paths, and difficult specification of the correct longitudinal mediated effect of interest (Cheong et al. 2003, Cole & Maxwell 2003, Collins et al. 1998).

There are three major types of longitudinal mediation models. The autoregressive model was described by Gollob & Reichardt (1991) and elaborated by Cole & Maxwell (2003). In the basic autoregressive model, relations that are one measurement occasion (wave) apart are specified, and the relation between the same variable over time is specified to assess stability, as are covariances among the variables at the first wave and the covariances among the residual variances of X, M, and Y at later waves. The covariances among X, M, and Y at the same wave of measurement reflect that the causal order of these measures is unknown. Only relations consistent with longitudinal mediation are estimated among the variables.

A second form of the autoregressive mediation model includes contemporaneous mediation relations among X, M, and Y, such that mediation can occur within the same wave in addition to longitudinal mediation across waves. Practically, this would occur if there were a change in the mediator that led to change in the outcome between the first and second wave of measurement. Still another form of the autoregressive longitudinal mediation model allows for cross-lagged relations among variables, where the direction of the relations among X, M, and Y are all free to vary. Freeing the directions of the relationships violates the temporal precedence specified by the mediation model but allows possible cross-lagged relations among variables to be investigated, making it a more reasonable model than assuming relations are zero among the variables. Limitations of the autoregressive models include the cross-lagged model where many true models may yield the same cross-lagged coefficients and the frequent exclusion of individual differences in mean level (see Dwyer 1983, Rogosa 1988).

Another model that can be used with longitudinal mediation data is the latent-growth modeling (LGM) or parallel-process model (Muthén & Curran 1997, Singer & Willet 2003). The LGM mediation model examines whether the growth in X affects the growth trajectory of M, which affects the growth trajectory of Y. As in the nonlatent framework, the relation between X and the growth trajectory of Y has two sources: the indirect effect via the growth of M and the direct effect. One limitation of the parallel-process model is that the mediation relation is correlational: the slope in X is correlated with the slope in M, and the slope in M is correlated with the slope in Y. The interpretation of this correlation is that change in M is related to change in Y at the same time, not that change in M is related to change in Y at a later time. An alternate way to specify the LGM mediation model is the two-stage piecewise parallel-process model (Cheong et al. 2003). In the two-stage parallel-process model, the growth of the mediator and the outcome process is modeled for earlier and later times separately, allowing the mediated effects to be investigated at different periods. Measurement invariance is very important in LGM, because changes in the measure over time will confound the interpretation of change over time.

In the difference score approach to longitudinal mediation, differences between the mediator and dependent variables scores are taken, as is the independent variable if it does not reflect assignment to treatment condition. These difference scores are then analyzed using the same equations as those used for cross-sectional models. The latent difference score (LDS) model can also be applied to three or more waves using a latent framework (Ferrer & McArdle 2003, McArdle 2001, McArdle & Nesselroade 2003). In the LDS model, fixed parameters and latent variables are used to specify latent difference scores, such that the model represents differences between waves as dynamic change. The LDS model can be especially useful in situations where it is expected there will be different predictors at different measurement occasions.

In addition to the autoregressive, LGM, and LDS models, other models can be used to analyze longitudinal mediation data, including a combination of the autoregressive and LGM models (Bollen & Curran 2004) and specification of model parameters in a continuous time metric to address the problem of different time intervals of measurement (Arminger 1986, Boker & Nesselroade 2002, Dwyer 1992).

Moderation and Mediation

The strength and form of mediated effects may depend on other variables. Variables that affect the hypothesized relation among a set of variables in such ways are known as moderators and are often tested as interaction effects (Aiken & West 1991, Baron & Kenny 1986). A nonzero XM interaction in Equation 2 discussed above is an example of a moderator effect that suggests that the b coefficient differs across levels of X. Different b coefficients across levels of X may reflect mediation as a manipulation and may alter the relation of M to Y. For example, a smoking prevention program may remove a relation between tobacco offers (M) and tobacco use (Y) because persons exposed to the program learned skills to refuse tobacco offers so that offers are significantly related to use in the control group but not in the program group (Judd & Kenny 1981a). The presence of moderator effects indicates that the modeled function changes across different levels of the moderator variable, where moderators may be either a manipulated factor in an experimental setting or a naturally occurring variable such as gender. The examination of these variables and their impact on mediation models is useful in psychological research to address the question of how an experiment achieved its effects. However, by also examining moderator effects, one is able to investigate whether the experiment differentially affects subgroups of individuals (Donaldson 2001, MacKinnon 2001, MacKinnon & Dwyer 1993, Sandler et al. 1997). Three potential models in which this examination may take place are (*a*) moderated mediation, (*b*) mediated moderation, and (*c*) mediated baseline by treatment moderation models.

Moderated mediation. The moderated mediation model is the simplest statistical model with moderator and mediation effects (Judd et al. 2001). In this model, a variable mediates the effect of an independent variable on a dependent variable, and the mediated effect depends on the level of a moderator. Thus, the mediational mechanism differs for subgroups of participants (e.g., across cohorts, ages, or sexes; James & Brett 1984).

The single-mediator version of this model consists of estimating the same mediation model for each subgroup and then comparing the mediated effect across subgroups. A statistical test of the equivalence of the mediated effect across groups was described in MacKinnon (2007), and tests of the equality of $\hat{a}$, $\hat{b}$, and $\hat{c}'$ can provide information on the invariance-of-action theory (how the program changes mediators) and conceptual theory (how mediators are related to the outcome) across groups.

The moderated mediation model is more complex when the moderator variable is continuous. Although the regression equations required to estimate the continuous moderated mediation model are the same as for the categorical case, the interpretation of results is complicated because of the large number of values of a continuous moderator. In this case, researchers may choose to analyze simple mediation effects (see Tein et al. 2004).

Mediated moderation. Mediated moderation (Baron & Kenny 1986, Morgan-Lopez & MacKinnon 2001) occurs when a mediator is intermediate in the causal sequence from an interaction effect to a dependent variable. For example, the effect of a prevention program may be greater for high-risk subjects, and the interaction effect of program exposure and risk-taking may then affect a mediating variable of social norms that then affects drug use. The purpose of mediated moderation is to determine the mediating variable(s) that explain the interaction effect. This model consists of estimating a series of regression equations where the main effect of a covariate and the interaction of the covariate and program exposure are included in both models. Morgan-Lopez & MacKinnon (2001) describe an estimator of the mediated moderator effect that requires further development and evaluation.

Mediated baseline by treatment moderation. The mediated baseline by treatment moderation model is a special case of the mediated moderation model. The substantive interpretation of the mediated effect in this model is that the mediated effect depends on the baseline level of the mediator. This scenario is a common result in prevention and treatment research, where the effects of an intervention are often stronger for participants who are at higher risk on the mediating variable at the time they enter the program

(Khoo 2001, Pillow et al. 1991). These treatment condition by baseline interactions have been found in numerous areas of research, ranging from universal prevention programs with elementary school children to selective prevention interventions with the various at-risk groups (e.g., Ialongo et al. 1999, Martinez & Forgatch 2001, Stoolmiller et al. 2000). Information provided in these models may indicate for whom an intervention is ineffective or even counterproductive and may be used to screen future participants into more effective programs based on their baseline characteristics. Various authors have outlined the equations and rationale for the mediated baseline by treatment moderator model (Baron & Kenny 1986, Morgan-Lopez & MacKinnon 2001, Tein et al. 2004).

To date, models with moderators and mediators have remained largely independent. This separation in their presentation has contributed to confusion in the understanding of each relative to the others. A critical goal of future research in this area will be to develop and test a general model in which each of the models is a special case. One such model is described in Muller et al. (2005). Another model is in development but has not yet been empirically tested in applied research (MacKinnon 2007):

$$Y = i + c_1'X + c_2'Z + c_3'XZ + b_1M$$
$$+ b_2MZ + hXM + jXMZ + e. \quad 6.$$

In this model, the XM and XMZ interactions are added to the individual mediation and moderation equations to form a general model that includes all effects (including additional c' and b effects). Here the h coefficient represents the test of whether the M to Y relation differs across levels of X, and the j coefficient represents the three-way interaction effect whereby the relations between Z and M and Y differ across levels of X. If a statistically significant j coefficient is found, further simple interaction effects and simple mediated effects are explored.

Causal Inference

Methods based on the observed regression approach to estimating mediation have been criticized based on causal analysis of the relations among variables. One of these criticisms addressed above is the equivalent model criticism. For example, if X, M, and Y are measured simultaneously, there are other models that would explain the data equally well (e.g., X is the mediator of the M to Y relationship or M and Y both cause X), and in many situations it is not possible to distinguish these alternatives without more information (Spirtes et al. 1993).

The case in which X represents random assignment to conditions improves causal interpretation of mediating variables (Holland 1988, Robins & Greenland 1992) because X precedes M and Y. Holland applied Rubin's (1974) causal model to a mediation and showed, under some assumptions, the typical regression coefficient for the group effect on test score, $\hat{c}$, and the group effect on number of hours studied, $\hat{a}$, are valid estimators of the true causal effect because of the randomization of units to treatment. The regression coefficient, $\hat{b}$, relating X to Y adjusted for M, is not an accurate estimator of the causal effect because this relation is correlational, not the result of random assignment. The estimator, $\hat{c}'$, is also not an accurate causal estimator of the direct effect.

Several new approaches to causal inference for mediation have begun to appear. One promising alternative is based on principal stratifications of the possible relations of X to M to Y where the mediated effect is estimated within these stratifications (Angrist et al. 1996, Frangakis & Rubin 2002). B. Jo (unpublished manscript) has proposed a latent class version of this model, and M.E. Sobel (unpublished manuscript) has proposed an enhancement of the Holland instrumental variable method.

The most important aspect of the causal inference methods is the illustration of the problems interpreting the M to Y relation as a causal relation. Researchers have several options in this situation. First, apply some of the new models to increase evidence for causal inference. Second, treat the results of the mediation analysis as descriptive information that may not reflect the true underlying causal mediation relation, especially for the M to Y relation, even when advanced causal inference models are applied. Third, future experimental studies (perhaps double randomization, described above) as well as qualitative and clinical information are required to validate a mediation relation. In particular, a program of research that sequentially tests predictors of the mediator theory provides the most convincing evidence for mediation.

SUMMARY AND FUTURE DIRECTIONS

There is broad and sustained interest in mediation analysis from many areas of psychology and other fields: Begg & Leung (2000), Botvin (2000), Kristal et al. (2000), Petrosino (2000). Tests for mediation differ considerably in type I error rates and statistical power (MacKinnon et al. 2002a, 2004). The recommended test of mediation assesses the statistical significance of the X to M relation, $\hat{a}$ path, and then the M to Y relation, $\hat{b}$ path. If both are statistically significant, there is evidence of mediation. Because confidence limits are important for understanding effects, confidence limits based on the distribution of the product or the bootstrap are recommended. This approach also applies to mediated effects in more complicated models. It is also important to consider opposing mediated effects and more complicated models such that overall relations may not be statistically significant yet mediation may still exist in a research study. These opposing effects or mediated effects that counteract each other resulting in a nonsignificant X to Y relation may be of substantive interest. Several effect size measures for mediation models have been proposed (A.J. Fairchild, D.P. MacKinnon, & M.P. Taborga, unpublished manuscript; Taborga et al. 1999), but these require more development.

Person-oriented approaches based on trajectory classes (Muthén & Muthén 2000) and staged responses across trials (Collins et al. 1998) represent new ways to understand mediational processes consistent with the goal of examining individual-level processes and group-level processes. Longitudinal data provide rich information for the investigation of mediation. In particular, latent growth curve and latent difference score models may be especially suited to the examination of mediation chains across multiple waves of data because of the ability to investigate the effect of prior change on later change. The usefulness of causal inference models and different alternatives to learning more about mediation are an important topic for future research. Additionally, experimental designs to investigate mediation require further development. Similarly, methods to combine qualitative as well as quantitative information about mediational processes should clarify mediation relations. These developments will advance our ability to answer mediation questions in psychology.

ACKNOWLEDGMENTS

The authors acknowledge David Kenny and Helena Kraemer for their comments on this manuscript and thank Hendricks Brown, Bengt Muthén, and other members of the Prevention Science Methodology Group for comments on presentations related to this review. This article was supported by the National Institute of Drug Abuse grant DA09757.

LITERATURE CITED

Aiken LS, West SG. 1991. *Multiple Regression: Testing and Interpreting Interactions*. Newbury Park, CA: Sage

Alwin DF, Hauser RM. 1975. The decomposition of effects in path analysis. *Am. Sociol. Rev.* 40:37–47

Angrist JD, Imbens GW, Rubin DB. 1996. Identification of causal effects using instrumental variables (with commentary). *J. Am. Stat. Assoc.* 91:444–72

Arbuckle JL. 1997. *AMOS User's Guide: Version 3.6.* Chicago: Smallwaters

Arminger G. 1986. Linear stochastic differential equation models for panel data with unobserved variables. *Sociol. Methodol.* 16:187–212

Baranowski T, Anderson C, Carmack C. 1998. Mediating variable framework in physical activity interventions: How are we doing? How might we do better? *Am. J. Prev. Med.* 15(4):266–97

Baron RM, Kenny DA. 1986. The moderator-mediator variable distinction in social psychological research: conceptual, strategic, and statistical considerations. *J. Personal. Soc. Psychol.* 51:1173–82

Bauer DJ, Preacher KJ, Gil KM. 2006. Conceptualizing and testing random indirect effects and moderated mediation in multilevel models: new procedures and recommendations. *Psychol. Methods.* 11:142–63

Begg CB, Leung DHY. 2000. On the use of surrogate end points in randomized trials. *J. Roy. Statist. Soc.* 163:15–28

Bentler PM. 1997. *EQS for Windows (Version 5.6)* [computer program]. Encino, CA: Multivar. Softw.

Bishop YMM, Fienberg SE, Holland PW. 1975. *Discrete Multivariate Analysis: Theory and Practice.* Cambridge, MA: MIT Press

Blalock HM. 1969. *Theory Construction: From Verbal to Mathematical Formulations.* Englewood Cliffs, NJ: Prentice-Hall

Boker SM, Nesselroade JR. 2002. A method for modeling the intrinsic dynamics of intraindividual variability: recovering the parameters of simulated oscillators in multi-wave panel data. *Multivar. Behav. Res.* 37:127–60

Bollen KA, Curran PJ. 2004. Autoregressive latent trajectory (ALT) models: a synthesis of two traditions. *Sociol. Methods Res.* 32:336–83

Bollen KA, Stine RA. 1990. Direct and indirect effects: classical and bootstrap estimates of variability. *Sociol. Methodol.* 20:115–40

Botvin GJ. 2000. Preventing drug abuse in schools: social and competence enhancement approaches targeting individual-level etiologic factors. *Addict. Behav.* 25:887–97

Cheong J, MacKinnon DP, Khoo ST. 2003. Investigation of mediational processes using parallel process latent growth curve modeling. *Struct. Equat. Model.* 10:238–62

Cole DA, Maxwell SE. 2003. Testing mediational models with longitudinal data: questions and tips in the use of structural equation modeling. *J. Abnorm. Psychol.* 112:558–77

Collins LM, Graham JW, Flaherty BP. 1998. An alternative framework for defining mediation. *Multivar. Behav. Res.* 33:295–312

Davis JA. 1985. *The Logic of Causal Order. Sage University Paper Series on Quantitative Applications in the Social Sciences, Series No. 07–055.* Beverly Hills, CA: Sage

Dodge KA, Bates JE, Pettit GS. 1990. Mechanisms in the cycle of violence. *Science* 250:1678–83

Donaldson SI. 2001. Mediator and moderator analysis in program development. In *Handbook of Program Development for Health Behavior Research and Practice,* ed. S Sussman, pp. 470–96. Thousand Oaks, CA: Sage

Dwyer JH. 1983. *Statistical Models for the Social and Behavioral Sciences.* New York: Oxford

Dwyer JH. 1992. Differential equation models for longitudinal data. In *Statistical Models for Longitudinal Studies of Health,* ed. JH Dwyer, M Feinleib, P Lippert, H Hoffmeister, pp. 71–98. New York: Oxford Univ. Press

Fairchild AJ, MacKinnon DP, Taborga MP. 2006. *R^2 Effect-Size Measures for the Mediated Effect*. Unpubl. manuscr.

Ferrer E, McArdle JJ. 2003. Alternative structural models for multivariate longitudinal data analysis. *Struct. Equat. Model.* 10:493–524

Fishbein M, Ajzen I. 1975. *Belief, Attitude, Intention, and Behavior: An Introduction to Theory and Research*. Reading, MA: Addison-Wesley

Fiske ST, Kenny DA, Taylor SE. 1982. Structural models for the mediation of salience effects on attribution. *J. Exp. Soc. Psychol.* 18:105–27

Fleming TR, DeMets DL. 1996. Surrogate endpoints in clinical trials: Are we being misled? *Ann. Intern. Med.* 125:605–13

Frangakis CE, Rubin DB. 2002. Principal stratification in causal inference. *Biometrics* 58:21–29

Freedman LS. 2001. Confidence intervals and statistical power of the "validation" ratio for surrogate or intermediate endpoints. *J. Statist. Plan. Inference* 96:143–53

Fritz MS, MacKinnon DP. 2007. Required sample size to detect the mediated effect. *Psychol. Sci.* In press

Gollob HF, Reichardt CS. 1991. Interpreting and estimating indirect effects assuming time lags really matter. In *Best Methods for the Analysis of Change: Recent Advances, Unanswered Questions, Future Directions*, ed. LM Collins, JL Horn, pp. 243–59. Washington, DC: Am. Psychol. Assoc.

Hebb GO. 1966. *A Textbook of Psychology*. Philadelphia, PA: Saunders. 2nd ed.

Hofmann DA, Gavin MB. 1998. Centering decisions in hierarchical linear models. Implications for research in organizations. *J. Manage.* 24:623–41

Holland PW. 1988. Causal inference, path analysis, and recursive structural equation models. *Sociol. Methodol.* 18:449–84

Holmbeck GN. 1997. Toward terminological, conceptual, and statistical clarity in the study of mediators and moderators: examples from the child-clinical and pediatric psychology literatures. *J. Consult. Clin. Psychol.* 65:599–610

Hoyle RH, Kenny DA. 1999. Statistical power and tests of mediation. In *Statistical Strategies for Small Sample Research*, ed. RH Hoyle, pp. 195–222. Newbury Park: Sage

Hyman HH. 1955. *Survey Design and Analysis: Principles, Cases, and Procedures*. Glencoe, IL: Free Press

Ialongo NS, Werthamer L, Kellam SG, Brown CH, Wang S, Lin Y. 1999. Proximal impact of two first-grade preventive interventions on the early risk behaviors for later substance abuse, depression, and antisocial behavior. *Am. J. Community Psychol.* 27:599–641

James LR, Brett JM. 1984. Mediators, moderators, and tests for mediation. *J. Appl. Psychol.* 69:307–21

James LR, Mulaik SA, Brett JM. 2006. A tale of two methods. *Org. Res. Methodol.* 9:233–44

Jo B. 2006. *Causal Inference in Randomized Trials with Mediational Processes*. Unpubl. manuscr.

Jöreskog KG, Sörbom D. 1993. *LISREL (Version 8.12)* [computer program]. Chicago: Sci. Software Int.

Judd CM, Kenny DA. 1981a. *Estimating the Effects of Social Interventions*. Cambridge, UK: Cambridge Univ. Press

Judd CM, Kenny DA. 1981b. Process analysis: estimating mediation in treatment evaluations. *Eval. Rev.* 5:602–19

Judd CM, Kenny DA, McClelland GH. 2001. Estimating and testing mediation and moderation in within-subject designs. *Psychol. Methods* 6:115–34

Kenny DA, Bolger N, Korchmaros JD. 2003. Lower-level mediation in multilevel models. *Psychol. Methods* 8:115–28

Kenny DA, Kashy DA, Bolger N. 1998. Data analysis in social psychology. In *The Handbook of Social Psychology, Volume 1*, ed. DT Gilbert, ST Fiske, G Lindzey, pp. 233–65. New York: Oxford Univ. Press

Khoo ST. 2001. Assessing program effects in the presence of treatment-baseline interactions: a latent curve approach. *Psychol. Methods* 6:234–57

Kraemer HC, Stice E, Kazdin A, Offord D, Kupfer D. 2001. How do risk factors work together? Mediators, moderators, and independent, overlapping, and proxy risk factors. *Am. J. Psychiatry* 158:848–56

Kraemer HC, Wilson T, Fairburn CG, Agras WS. 2002. Mediators and moderators of treatment effects in randomized clinical trials. *Arch. Gen. Psychiatry* 59:877–83

Kristal AR, Glanz K, Tilley BC, Li S. 2000. Mediating factors in dietary change: understanding the impact of a worksite nutrition intervention. *Health Educ. Behav.* 27(1):112–25

Krull JL, MacKinnon DP. 1999. Multilevel mediation modeling in group-based intervention studies. *Eval. Rev.* 23:418–44

Krull JL, MacKinnon DP. 2001. Multilevel modeling of individual and group level mediated effects. *Multivar. Behav. Res.* 36:249–77

Lazarsfeld PF. 1955. Interpretation of statistical relations as a research operation. In *The Language of Social Research: A Reader in the Methodology of Social Research*, ed. PF Lazarsfeld, M Rosenberg, pp. 115–25. Glencoe, IL: Free Press

Lockwood CM, MacKinnon DP. 1998. Bootstrapping the standard error of the mediated effect. In *Proceedings of the Twenty-Third Annual SAS Users Group International Conference*, pp. 997–1002. Cary, NC: SAS Inst.

MacCorquodale K, Meehl PE. 1948. Operational validity of intervening constructs. *Psychol. Rev.* 55:95–107

MacKinnon DP. 1994. Analysis of mediating variables in prevention intervention studies. In *Scientific Methods for Prevention Intervention Research: NIDA Research Monograph 139*, DHHS Pub. 94–3631, ed. A Cazares, LA Beatty, pp.127–53. Washington, DC: U.S. Dept. Health Human Serv.

MacKinnon DP. 2000. Contrasts in multiple mediator models. In *Multivariate Applications in Substance Use Research: New Methods for New Questions* ed. JS Rose, L Chassin, CC Presson, SJ Sherman, pp. 141–60. Mahwah, NJ: Erlbaum

MacKinnon DP. 2001. Mediating variable. In *International Encyclopedia of the Social and Behavioral Sciences*, ed. NJ Smelser, PB Baltes, pp. 9503–7. Oxford, UK: Pergamon

MacKinnon DP. 2007. *Introduction to Statistical Mediation Analysis*. Mahwah, NJ: Erlbaum. In press

MacKinnon DP, Dwyer JH. 1993. Estimation of mediated effects in prevention studies. *Eval. Rev.* 17:144–58

MacKinnon DP, Fritz MS, Williams J, Lockwood CM. 2006a. Distribution of the product confidence limits for the indirect effect: program PRODCLIN. *Behav. Res. Methods*. In press. Download available at **http://www.public.asu.edu/~davidpm/ripl/Prodclin/**

MacKinnon DP, Krull JL, Lockwood CM. 2000. Equivalence of the mediation, confounding, and suppression effect. *Prev. Sci.* 1:173–81

MacKinnon DP, Lockwood CM, Hoffman JM, West SG, Sheets V. 2002a. A comparison of methods to test mediation and other intervening variable effects. *Psychol. Methods* 7:83–104

MacKinnon DP, Lockwood CM, Williams J. 2004. Confidence limits for the indirect effect: distribution of the product and resampling methods. *Multivar. Behav. Res.* 39:99–128

MacKinnon DP, Taborga MP, Morgan-Lopez AA. 2002b. Mediation designs for tobacco prevention research. *Drug Alcohol Depend.* 68: S69–83

MacKinnon DP, Warsi G, Dwyer JH. 1995. A simulation study of mediated effect measures. *Multivariate Behav. Res.* 30:41–62

MacKinnon DP, Yoon M, Lockwood CM, Taylor AB. 2006b. *A Comparison of Methods to Test the Mediated and Other Intervening Variable Effects in Logistic Regression.* Unpubl. manuscr.

Manly BFJ. 1997. *Randomization and Monte Carlo Methods in Biology.* New York: Chapman & Hall. 2nd ed.

Martinez CR, Forgatch MS. 2001. Preventing problems with boys' noncompliance: effects of a parent training intervention for divorcing mothers. *J. Consult.Clin. Psychol.* 69(3):416–28

McArdle JJ. 2001. A latent difference score approach to longitudinal dynamic structural analysis. In *Structural Equation Modeling: Present and Future. A Festschrift in Honor of Karl Jöreskog*, ed. R Cudeck, S du Toit, D. Sörbom. pp. 341–80. Lincolnwood, IL: Sci. Softw. Int.

McArdle JJ, Nesselroade JR. 2003. Growth curve analysis in contemporary research. In *Comprehensive Handbook of Psychology, Vol. II: Research Methods in Psychology*, ed J Schinka, W Velicer, pp. 447–80. New York: Pergamon

McDonald RP. 1997. Haldane's lungs: a case study in path analysis. *Multivar. Behav. Res.* 32:1–38

McFatter RM. 1979. The use of structural equation models in interpreting regression equations including suppressor and enhancer variables. *Appl. Psychol. Meas.* 3:123–35

Meeker WQ, Cornwell LW, Aroian LA. 1981. The product of two normally distributed random variables. In *Selected Tables in Mathematical Statistics*, ed. WJ Kennedy, RE Odeh, JM Davenport, Vol. 7, pp. 1–256. Providence, RI: Am. Math. Soc.

Merrill R. 1994. *Treatment effect evaluation in nonadditive mediation models.* PhD thesis. Tempe: Ariz. State Univ.

Mooney CZ, Duval RD. 1993. *Bootstrapping: A Nonparametric Approach to Statistical Inference.* Newbury Park, CA: Sage

Morgan-Lopez AA, MacKinnon DP. 2001. *A mediated moderation model simulation: mediational processes that vary as a function of second predictors.* Presented at 9th Annu. Meet. Soc. Prev. Res., Washington, DC

Morgan-Lopez AA, MacKinnon DP. 2006. Demonstration and evaluation of a method to assess mediated moderation. *Behav. Res. Methods* 38:77–87

Muller D, Judd CM, Yzerbyt VY. 2005. When moderation is mediated and mediation is moderated. *J. Personal. Soc Psychol.* 89(6):852–63

Murray DM, Luepker RV, Pirie PL, Grimm RH, Bloom E, et al. 1986. Systematic risk factor screening and education: a community-wide approach to prevention of coronary heart disease. *Prev. Med.* 15:661–72

Muthén BO, Curran PJ. 1997. General longitudinal modeling of individual differences in experimental designs: a latent variable framework for analysis and power estimation. *Psychol. Methods* 2:371–402

Muthén LK, Muthén BO. 1998–2006. *Mplus: The Comprehensive Modeling Program for Applied Researchers. User's Guide.* Los Angeles, CA: Muthén & Muthén

Muthén B, Muthén L. 2000. Integrating person-centered and variable-centered analysis: growth mixture modeling with latent trajectory classes. *Alcohol. Clin. Exp. Res.* 24:882–91

Noreen EW. 1989. *Computer-Intensive Methods for Testing Hypotheses: An Introduction.* New York: Wiley

Paulhus DL, Robins RW, Trzesniewski KH, Tracy JL. 2004. Two replicable suppressor situations in personality research. *Multivar. Behav. Res.* 39:303–28

Petrosino A. 2000. Mediators and moderators in the evaluation of programs for children. *Eval. Rev.* 24(1):47–72

Pillow DR, Sandler IN, Braver SL, Wolchik SA, Gersten JC. 1991. Theory-based screening for prevention: focusing on mediating processes in children of divorce. *Am. J. Comm. Psychol.* 19:809–36

Preacher KJ, Hayes AF. 2004. SPSS and SAS procedures for estimating indirect effects in simple mediation models. *Behav. Res. Methods Instrum. Comput.* 36:717–31

Raudenbush SW, Sampson R. 1999. Assessing direct and indirect effects in multilevel designs with latent variables. *Sociol. Methods Res.* 28:123–53

Robins JM, Greenland S. 1992. Identifiability and exchangeability for direct and indirect effects. *Epidemiology* 3:143–55

Rogosa DR. 1988. Myths about longitudinal research. In *Methodological Issues in Aging Research*, ed. KW Schaie, RT Campbell, WM Meredith, SC Rawlings, pp. 171–209. New York: Springer

Rubin DB. 1974. Estimating causal effects of treatments in randomized and nonrandomized studies. *J. Educ. Psychol.* 66:688–701

Sandler IN, Wolchik SA, MacKinnon DP, Ayers TS, Roosa MW. 1997. Developing linkages between theory and intervention in stress and coping processes. In *Handbook of Children's Coping: Linking Theory and Intervention*, ed. SA Wolchik, IN Sandler, pp. 3–40. New York: Plenum

Shadish WR. 1996. Meta-analysis and the exploration of causal mediating processes: a primer of examples, methods, and issues. *Psychol. Methods* 1:47–65

Sheets VL, Braver SL. 1999. Organizational status and perceived sexual harassment: detecting the mediators of a null effect. *Personal. Soc. Psychol. Bull.* 25:1159–71

Sherman SJ, Gorkin L. 1980. Attitude bolstering when behavior is inconsistent with central attitudes. *J. Exp. Soc. Psychol.* 16:388–403

Shrout PE, Bolger N. 2002. Mediation in experimental and nonexperimental studies: new procedures and recommendations. *Psychol. Methods* 7:422–45

Singer JD, Willett JB. 2003. *Applied Longitudinal Data Analysis: Modeling Change and Event Occurrence*. London: Oxford Univ. Press

Sobel ME. 1982. Asymptotic confidence intervals for indirect effects in structural equation models. *Sociol. Methodol.* 13:290–312

Sobel ME. 1986. Some new results on indirect effects and their standard errors in covariance structure models. *Sociol. Methodol.* 16:159–86

Sobel ME. 2006. *Identification of Causal Parameters in Randomized Studies with Mediators*. Unpubl. manuscr.

Spencer SJ, Zanna MP, Fong GT. 2005. Establishing a causal chain: why experiments are often more effective than mediational analyses in examining psychological processes. *J. Personal. Soc. Psychol.* 89(6):845–51

Spirtes P, Glymour C, Scheines R. 1993. *Causation, Prediction, and Search*. New York: Springer-Verlag

Springer MD. 1979. *The Algebra of Random Variables*. New York: Wiley

Stone CA, Sobel ME. 1990. The robustness of estimates of total indirect effects in covariance structure models estimated by maximum likelihood. *Psychometrika* 55:337–52

Stoolmiller M, Eddy JM, Reid JB. 2000. Detecting and describing preventive intervention effects in a universal school-based randomized trial targeting delinquent and violent behavior. *J. Consult. Clin. Psychol.* 68:296–306

Taborga MP, MacKinnon DP, Krull JL. 1999. *A simulation study of effect size measures in mediation models*. Poster presented at 7th Annu. Meet. Soc. Prev. Res., New Orleans, LA

Tein JY, MacKinnon DP. 2003. Estimating mediated effects with survival data. In *New Developments in Psychometrics: Psychometric Society Proceedings*, ed. H Yanai, AO Rikkyo, K Shigemasu, Y Kano, JJ Meulman, pp. 405–12. Tokyo: Springer-Verlag

Tein JY, Sandler IN, MacKinnon DP, Wolchik SA. 2004. How did it work? Who did it work for? Mediation in the context of a moderated prevention effect for children of divorce. *J. Consult. Clin. Psychol.* 72:617–24

Weiss CH. 1997. How can theory-based evaluation make greater headway? *Eval. Rev.* 21:501–24

West SG, Aiken LS. 1997. Toward understanding individual effects in multiple component prevention programs: Design and analysis strategies. In *The Science of Prevention: Methodological Advances from Alcohol and Substance Abuse Research*, ed. K Bryant, M Windle, S West, pp. 167–209. Washington, DC: Am. Psychol. Assoc.

Williams J. 2004. *Resampling and distribution of products methods for testing indirect effects in complex models*. PhD thesis. Tempe: Ariz. State Univ.

Winship C, Mare RD. 1983. Structural equations and path analysis for discrete data. *Am. J. Sociol.* 89:54–110

Word CO, Zanna MP, Cooper J. 1974. The nonverbal mediation of self-fulfilling prophecies in interracial interaction. *J. Exp. Soc. Psychol.* 10:109–20

Analysis of Nonlinear Patterns of Change with Random Coefficient Models

Robert Cudeck[1] and Jeffrey R. Harring[2]

[1]Psychology Department, Ohio State University, Columbus, Ohio 43210;
email: cudeck.1@osu.edu

[2]Department of Measurement, Statistics and Evaluation, University of Maryland,
College Park, Maryland 20742; email: harring@umd.edu

Annu. Rev. Psychol. 2007. 58:615–37

First published online as a Review in
Advance on September 5, 2006

The *Annual Review of Psychology* is online at
http://psych.annualreviews.org

This article's doi:
10.1146/annurev.psych.58.110405.085520

Key Words

longitudinal data, multilevel model, hierarchical model

Abstract

Nonlinear patterns of change arise frequently in the analysis of repeated measures from longitudinal studies in psychology. The main feature of nonlinear development is that change is more rapid in some periods than in others. There generally also are strong individual differences, so although there is a general similarity of patterns for different persons over time, individuals exhibit substantial heterogeneity in their particular response. To describe data of this kind, researchers have extended the random coefficient model to accommodate nonlinear trajectories of change. It can often produce a statistically satisfying account of subject-specific development. In this review we describe and illustrate the main ideas of the nonlinear random coefficient model with concrete examples.

Contents

INTRODUCTION

The study of change and development is an essential component of research in the behavioral sciences, and in recent years the use of longitudinal designs has increased appreciably. This in turn has brought about a corresponding increase in statistical methods for the analysis of repeated measures data. Overviews of the literature, emphasizing rather distinct aspects of a growing and technical domain, have been provided by Collins (2006), DiPrete & Forristal (1994), Halaby (2004), and Raudenbush (2001).

One of the major tools for the analysis of repeated measures is the random coefficient model (RCM) (Brown & Prescott 1999, Demidenko 2004, Raudenbush & Bryk 2002, Verbeke & Molenberghs 2000). In the context of repeated measures studies, the model is based on the idea that the process of change is defined for each individual, yet also is related to the population mean trajectory. This perspective on individual change in repeated measures studies has not been widely translated into statistical practice in psychology, and the implications for research are not widely appreciated. The majority of statistical methods used in the social sciences emphasize averages, in particular the difference between population means with respect to population variances with the analysis of variance, and the assessment of mean change with structural equation models for repeated measures (Duncan et al. 1999, Ferrer & McArdle 2003, Jöreskog 1979). Although the data model of most methods is defined for a typical subject, the actual focus of the analysis is on population parameters of structural models that describe average change. At the end of the investigation, information regarding individuals is virtually unused. Although the description of average change is obviously valuable, relegating individual change to a footnote is antithetical to a science of behavior, a point that has been made often (e.g., Brown & Heathcote 2003, Hertzog & Nesselroade 2003, Rogosa & Willett 1985).

In contrast, the perspective of the RCM is appealing for the study of psychological processes within the rich behavioral tradition of individual differences. At the same time, it provides a framework for summarizing individual growth records so that persons are analytically and conceptually integrated within the larger population. The RCM is actually a collection of algebraic models and estimation methods. The large number of options is an attractive feature because an experienced researcher can generally find an interesting approach for most situations.

This review focuses on repeated measures studies in which the outcome of interest is a continuous variable and the change process is nonlinear. In many investigations, change is assumed to be steady and incremental so that a linear model is appropriate. Straight-line change is a special case of the general nonlinear model, and therefore it fits into this overall scheme entirely. However, there are numerous situations in which the form of change is not uniform but rather faster during some periods and slower in others. Over a realistic time interval, many behavioral processes exhibit differential rates of change. Verbal facility, for example, increases rapidly in childhood and reaches an optimal individual level in late adolescence. The acquisition of many skills often exhibits slow initial gain, followed by rapid improvement, and then small gains again as maximal proficiency is attained. In an intervention, response to treatment may be much stronger in one period than another. Nonlinear change is not atypical in psychological studies. Consequently the appropriate statistical method for repeated measures is a model that can handle these conditions.

EXAMPLES OF NONLINEAR CHANGE

To motivate the kind of analysis featured in this chapter, we introduce two case studies. The subject matter and research designs of the examples are quite different, and the timescale is years in one example and minutes in the other. However, the challenges of statistical analysis have many common features.

Speech Errors in Young Children

When children first begin to speak, they make a variety of syntactical and grammatical errors communicating in everyday language. As they get older, these errors decrease rapidly and are eventually eliminated. The data in

Figure 1 (Burchinal & Appelbaum 1991) were collected in a study of language development in which a sample of 43 children was observed four, five, or six times between ages six to eight using a standardized instrument of language proficiency. Approximately 40% of the cases are shown. Both the number of assessments as well as the ages of the children at the assessment points varied, so the data are not balanced. The main feature in this example is the striking individual differences, in particular, before age five. An average function is not necessarily relevant here because an average is not representative of any individual child.

Another prominent aspect is that the rate of error decrease is different at different ages, declining rapidly between ages three and four, then improving more gradually for every child in the sample until age seven or eight, when errors effectively disappear. In many developmental studies, the goal of the analysis is to understand how the behavior develops, which is essential in understanding critical periods of change and in designing interventions. At the last measurement session for each child, the researchers made an independent rating of overall speech intelligibility based on a structured interview in which scores ranged from 0 for good to 6 for unintelligible. This rating serves as a covariate to help explain differences between children in the pattern of change in the repeated measures of speech errors.

Reading Speed on the MNREAD Acuity Chart

The MNREAD Acuity Chart (Mansfield et al. 1993) is a continuous-text, reading-acuity test consisting of 19 sentences. Each sentence has 60 characters displayed on three lines, with appropriate vocabulary for third-grade readers. Print size, the independent variable, varies systematically on a logarithm scale from -0.5 to 1.3 in steps of 0.1. The size measurement, log of minimum angle of resolution (logMAR), is computed with reference to the angle subtended by the height of the lower-case letter x. The administration order of the

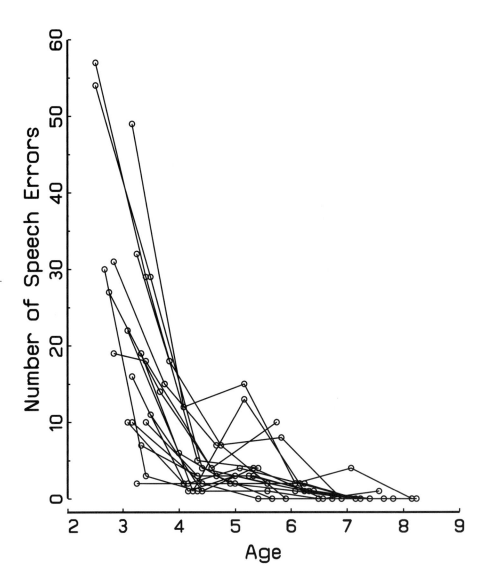

Figure 1

Decline in speech errors over the early childhood years. A subgroup of the $N = 43$ cases is shown. The ages when children were assessed varied between individuals. The rapidly decreasing pattern is generally similar for each child but differs in terms of initial level and also in the rate of decline, to some extent. Data taken from Burchinal & Appelbaum 1991.

sentences is always from largest to smallest. The last sentence at logMAR $= -0.5$ is so small that many participants with normal vision have difficulty making out the text. Reading speed is recorded as words per minute (WPM), calculated from the time required to read each sentence, including a correction for errors. **Figure 2** shows the profiles of reading speeds for 10 individuals selected from a larger sample.

Two features of the profiles are especially important scientifically and clinically. First, as is evident, WPM is relatively constant across the larger print sizes. The WPM rate that is not affected by increasing print size is called the maximum reading speed. This is a latent variable that corresponds roughly to the average WPM across the larger of the print sizes. Second, at some point in reading smaller sentences, performance deteriorates and falls off rapidly as print size decreases. The value of logMAR at the change point is another latent variable called the critical print size. It is the smallest print size that can be read with maximum reading speed. Maximum reading speed in the sample varies between approximately

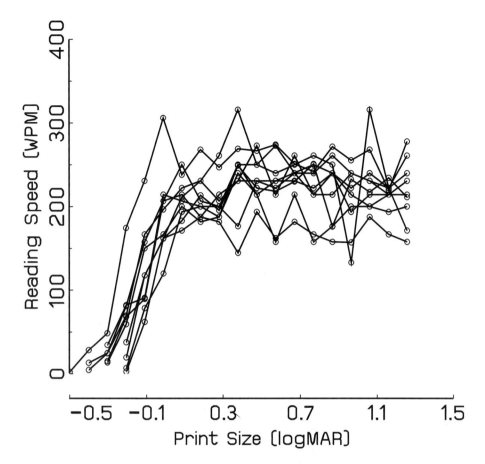

Figure 2

Reading speed in words per minute (WPM) for a subset of subjects tested on the nineteen standard sentences of the MNREAD Acuity test. The nearly constant WPM over the larger print sizes is used to determine maximum reading speed. The interpolated value of the print size at which WPM decreases is the critical print size. Data taken from Mansfield et al. 1993.

175 and 275 WPM; critical print size varies between approximately −0.1 to 0.1 logMAR. The procedure does not measure these two reading characteristics directly. One objective in describing these data quantitatively is to obtain a model-based estimate of the two latent variables (maximum reading speed and critical print size) for each person.

Common Features of the Examples

In these examples, subjects exhibit a pattern of response over the repeated measures that is similar to others, but with evident individual differences. In the first example, the pattern is a large number of speech errors when the children are young that declines in middle childhood to zero. In the second example, reading speed improves quickly and linearly until the critical print size is reached, after which it is essentially constant over the large print sizes. In both cases, individual profiles follow the generic pattern characteristic of the behavior, but vary on particular features: Peaks are somewhat higher or lower than the modal response; declines are steeper or shallower; and points of inflection are reached earlier or later. There is also within-subject variability over time, and the scatter of responses differs from person to person. The number of data points measured on the participants is unequal, and in the first example, the occasions of measurement vary as well. To satisfactorily represent these characteristics, the analytic method should accommodate them all: nonlinear patterns of change, imbalanced collections of data, within-subject variability, and especially individual differences in response.

THE NONLINEAR RANDOM COEFFICIENT MODEL

In this section, we review a version of the nonlinear RCM to illustrate its most important features. Many standard texts describe a large number of extensions (Davidian & Giltinan 1995, Fitzmaurice et al. 2004, Hand & Crowder 1996, Vonesh & Chinchilli 1997). The goal here is to introduce the main ideas conceptually. The model actually consists of three interconnected parts. The first is the nonlinear function that describes change over time in the repeated measures. This function is defined for individual subjects and employs individual coefficients. The second element is the covariance structure of the residuals, also defined as a within-subject structure. The third part is the set of models for the regression coefficients that summarize differences between persons.

Strictly speaking, the RCM refers to a model in which all coefficients of a function vary across persons. When only some coefficients are random while others are common to all, the more flexible version is known as a mixed effect model, after Laird & Ware (1982). The label RCM is especially descriptive of the essential ideas of a mixed effect model, however, so we use it throughout.

A point of contrast is relevant. A popular model conceptually related to the RCM is the latent growth curve model (LGCM) (Meredith & Tisak 1990, Bollen & Curran 2006). The theoretical underpinnings of the RCM and the LGCM are different, especially for problems that involve nonlinear change (Browne 1993, MacCallum et al. 1997). In many situations, the models give identical parameter estimates; however, the results have quite different interpretations. With other data sets, both the numerical results as well as the interpretations are entirely different. Under these circumstances, confusion between these two types of models is all but unavoidable. Such different methodologies are used in similar settings partly because the RCM arose in biostatistics in the tradition of regres-

sion, whereas the LGCM pedigree is from factor analysis and the study of latent variable change. As the research community gains experience with the distinctive features of each methodology, their similarities and differences likely will become more apparent. Here we focus on the RCM, which is based on an explicit regression function with individually varying coefficients to describe change.

Individual Function for Nonlinear Change

Several important ideas make up the RCM. One key feature is the nonlinear change pattern. The change pattern is explicit—it is a simple algebraic function that approximately describes individual improvement or decline. To be concrete, let $y_{i1}, \ldots, y_{in_i}$ be n_i measurements on the response variable y for individual i taken at the j-th design point x_{ij}. In general, n_i varies from person to person. In a longitudinal study, x_{ij} is the elapsed time from the beginning of the experiment to the j-th assessment or the age of the subject at occasion j. In the speech errors problem, for example, x_{ij} is age at occasion j, and only two children were measured at the same ages. In general, x_{ij} differs for all participants. With the MNREAD data, x_{ij} is print size of the j-th sentence. The print sizes are identical for all, but there are some missing data.

The nonlinear RCM takes its name from the assumption that measurements for the i-th case follow an individual nonlinear function with variability over time within a subject:

$$y_{ij} = f(\beta_{i1}, \ldots, \beta_{ip}, x_{ij}) + e_{ij}, j = 1, \ldots, n_i \tag{1}$$

The residuals are e_{ij}. The regression coefficients for subject i are $\beta_{i1}, \ldots, \beta_{ip}$. The algebraic function is assumed to be the same for all, but because coefficients vary between persons, the actual fitted trajectories may differ markedly.

Obviously, one of the major issues in applying the model is the choice of function used to describe change. Dozens of possibilities are presented in standard references on nonlinear regression (Bates & Watts 1988, Huet et al. 2004, Seber & Wild 1989) and the nonlinear RCM (Davidian & Giltinan 1995; Pinheiro & Bates 2000; Vonesh & Chinchilli 1997, ch. 7). We present several examples below to illustrate possibilities. The parameters of the functions are defined for a person, in keeping with the theme of the model relating to individual change. When the functions are applied to data, the coefficients produce new variables and new information about the subjects in the context of the investigation that the original data do not otherwise contain. For this reason, although one can usually consider several candidate models for any problem, it is especially helpful when the function is tailored to the study.

Exponential decline. To represent the rapid decline in the number of speech errors evident in the records of **Figure 1**, Burchinal & Appelbaum (1991) suggested a two-parameter exponential model. It was adapted for this example to be

$$f(\beta_{i1}, \beta_{i2}, x_{ij}) = \beta_{i1} \exp[\beta_{i2}(x_{ij} - 3)] \quad (2)$$

where x_{ij} is age at the j-th occasion. The basic shape of this model is similar for all the children. It exhibits a steep decline to zero errors by age eight. By including the difference $(x_{ij} - 3)$ in the exponent, the intercept, (β_{i1}), is interpreted as the number of speech errors at age three, which is approximately the mean age at first testing. The second coefficient (β_{i2}) governs the rate at which an individual trajectory decreases to zero. For β_{i1}, high values are associated with more speech errors. For β_{i2}, strong negative values indicate a steep rate of decline.

Two-phase linear model with unknown transition point. In **Figure 2**, individual repeated measures on the MNREAD test exhibit linear improvement in WPM over the smaller print sizes. At approximately logMAR = 0, a critical print size is encountered at which reading speed does not im-

prove further. We assume the maximum reading speed across the large print sizes follows a second linear function with zero slope. This basic pattern is the same for all, but maximum reading speed and critical print size vary between individuals. A function that exhibits these characteristics is the two-phase linear model with an unknown change point. Over the smaller print sizes, the function is $f_1 = \alpha_{i0} + \alpha_{i1}x_{ij}$. Beyond the critical print size (τ_i), the function is constant for all print sizes, $x_{ij} > \tau_i$: $f_2 = \gamma_{i0}$. To ensure the segments join at τ_i, we impose a restriction: $\alpha_{i0} + \alpha_{i1}\tau_i = \gamma_{i0}$. This implies that one of the coefficients is redundant and can be eliminated. We can set $\alpha_{i0} = \gamma_{i0} - \alpha_{i1}\tau_i$. The final model involves these two segments plus the unknown change point. The overall function is linear in α_{i0} and γ_{i0}, but nonlinear in τ_i and nonlinear over the print sizes

$$
f(\alpha_{i1}, \gamma_{i0}, \tau_i, x_{ij})
= \begin{cases} \gamma_{i0} + \alpha_{i1}(x_{ij} - \tau_i) & x_{ij} \leq \tau_i \\ \gamma_{i0} & x_{ij} > \tau_i \end{cases}
$$

In this function, the slope, α_{i1}, as well as the critical print size and maximum reading speed, τ_i and γ_{i0}, are important characteristics of the profile that the test does not actually measure. The model is invaluable as a way to assess these components.

This function is a type of spline model with random coefficients. It works well in a variety of settings (Naumova et al. 2001). It is straightforward to consider different patterns such as quadratic-linear or linear-exponential to allow a nonlinear trajectory in one segment and a steady-state condition in the other. The most interesting element of the function is τ_i, the value when the process shifts from the first segment to the second. When the predictor is age, τ_i marks the time when there is a distinct change of response trajectory. Morrell et al. (1995) first suggested RCMs of this kind in their study of tumor growth in cancer. Cudeck & Klebe (2002) and Harring et al. (2006) consider psychological examples. Another variant follows below.

Nonlinear model with three linear segments. The data shown in **Figure 3** are fifteen trials on the pursuit rotor task for a single individual (Fox et al. 1996). The response is time on target. The trials were taken over three days, five trial blocks per day. The interesting jump in improvement between adjacent days shows a clear reminiscence effect in which learning occurs in the absence of practice. To represent this pattern, a simple nonlinear model suggested by Dyba et al. (1997) is effective:

$$f(\alpha_{i1}, \alpha_{i2}, \alpha_{i3}, \beta_i, x_j) = \alpha_{ik}(1 + \beta_i x_j) \quad (3)$$

where the day of the experiment, $k = 1, 2$, and 3 covered the trials $1 \leq j \leq 5$, $6 \leq j \leq 10$, and $11 \leq j \leq 15$, respectively. The intercepts for each of the days are α_{i1}, α_{i2}, and α_{i3}, and β_i is a proportionality constant for the slope.

The actual slope for each day is the product $\alpha_{ik}\beta_i$. The model is linear within the five trials of each day, but nonlinear over the collection of fifteen trials and discontinuous between days. It is linear in α_{ik} but nonlinear in β_i. The function was designed to allow for the reminiscence effect between days. The function also specifies that the slope changes directly with the intercept, so an increase in intercept produces a proportionately larger slope. The model is more parsimonious than the simpler linear-linear-linear function, which has six parameters, intercept, and slope for each segment. When model (3) is fit to these data by least squares, the estimates of the coefficients are $(\hat{\alpha}_{i1}, \hat{\alpha}_{i2}, \hat{\alpha}_{i3}, \hat{\beta}_i) = (0.925, 1.36, 1.62, 0.416)$. **Figure 3** shows the fitted function, in which both the reminiscence effect and corresponding increase in slope are evident.

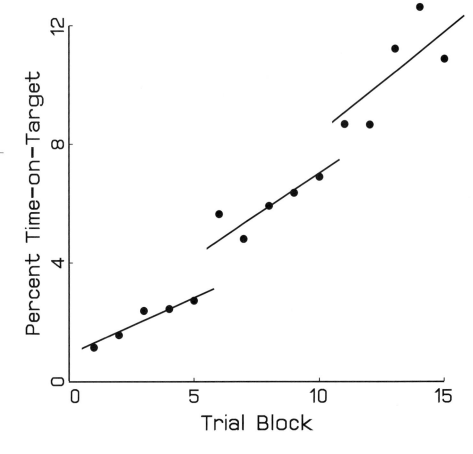

Figure 3

Fifteen time-on-target measurements taken over three days for one participant on the rotary pursuit task. The data show a reminiscence effect in which the subject improved performance in the absence of practice. The fitted function is a three-segment nonlinear model in which the slope is a proportion of the intercept. Data taken from Fox et al. 1996.

Partially nonlinear functions. Several writers (cf. Blozis & Cudeck 1999; Hand & Crowder 1996, section 8; Vonesh & Carter 1992) have reviewed a class of nonlinear functions that are quite flexible yet somewhat easier to deal with than the more general model (Model 1). These are called partially nonlinear functions because coefficients entering the function in a nonlinear fashion are assumed to be homogeneous between persons, whereas those that enter the model linearly vary between subjects. For example, Functions 2 and 3 above can be modified to be partially nonlinear models if they are specified so that the nonlinear coefficients are fixed parameters rather than individually varying coefficients:

$$f(\beta_{i1}, \beta_2, x_{ij}) = \beta_{i1} \exp[\beta_2(x_{ij} - 3)]$$
$$f(\alpha_{i1}, \alpha_{i2}, \alpha_{i3}, \beta, x_j) = \alpha_{ik}(1 + \beta x_j)$$

The linear RCM for straight-line growth is the most well-known member of this class,

$$f(\beta_{i1}, \beta_{i2}, x_{ij}) = \beta_{i1} + \beta_{i2} x_{ij}$$

because intercept and slope vary between persons, but there are no nonlinear coefficients at all.

Residuals and the Level 1 Covariance Structure

The residuals on the right-hand side of Model 1 are random variables that describe the lack of fit of the model in accounting for the responses within a subject. The statistical assumptions about the residuals make up what is known as the level 1 covariance structure. Although this structure can be elaborate, simple specifications are typical. To describe the essential ideas, let two residuals from the collection of a subject's n_i repeated measures be e_{iu} and e_{iv}. A typical assumption is that the pair is normally distributed with means of zero, variances σ_u^2 and σ_v^2, and correlation ρ_{uv}, so the covariance matrix as usual is

$$cov\begin{pmatrix} e_{iu} \\ e_{iv} \end{pmatrix} = \begin{pmatrix} \sigma_u^2 & \\ \rho_{uv}\sigma_u\sigma_v & \sigma_v^2 \end{pmatrix}$$

The most common option for the level 1 structure is to assume all variances are equal and all correlations are zero:

$$\sigma_u^2 = \sigma_v^2 = \sigma_e^2 \qquad \rho_{uv} = 0 \qquad (4)$$

Another option is to set the variances of all residuals equal but to allow autocorrelation by specifying, for example, that the correlation between every pair of residuals is the same: $\rho_{uv} = \rho$. At the other extreme from these simple structures, the variances and correlations among residuals can be specified to be functions of structural parameters, coefficients β_{ij} from the response model in Model 1, the design points, x_{ij}, and covariates. This general form is written as

$$\sigma_u^2 = g_u(\theta, \beta_{ij}, x_{ij}, c) \qquad \rho_{uv} = g_{uv}(\theta, \beta_{ij}, x_{ij}, c)$$
$$(5)$$

Virtually all covariance structures introduced for the linear RCM (Brown & Prescott 1999, ch. 10; Fitzmaurice et al. 2004, ch. 7; Verbeke & Molenberghs 2000, ch. 10) can be considered for the nonlinear RCM as well, giving a truly dizzying list of options. In some problems, the complexity of the covariance structure rivals that used for the individual nonlinear function in Model 1, even though the direct summary of the repeated measures is the major focus of attention.

The justification for the statistical investment in the covariance structure is twofold. First, the choice of covariance structure affects the fit of the model. This means that a model with a certain response function may be viewed as adequate or inadequate, depending on the form of the associated covariance structure. Second, the precision of estimation of all parameters in the composite model is affected by the covariance structure. This implies, for example, that the significance of a particular parameter is affected by choice of the within-subject, level 1 specification.

Although the full, general form of Covariance Structure 5 can be valuable in some applications, a straightforward specification such as Covariance Structure 4 often is adequate. One reason is that although a complex model may be conceptually desirable, there may not be a large enough sample or sufficiently numerous individual measurements to estimate the structure. Another reason is that when an adequate function is specified to account for the within-subject pattern of change, it often also accounts for a major proportion of the variability as well. This can be seen clearly in the linear RCM with random slopes and intercepts, in which the between-subjects covariance matrix often dominates the description of the covariance matrix among the repeated measures. Because of its importance to practice, many writers have reviewed this issue (e.g., Crowder & Hand 1990, ch. 6; Davidian & Giltinan 1995, section 5).

Individual Coefficients and the Level 2 Covariance Structure

The other set of random variables on the right-hand side of Model 1 are the individual regression coefficients, β_{ik}. In most instances, the coefficients are not measured directly, but instead are defined by their role in determining the function's shape as it accounts for the repeated measures. Thus, they are a kind of latent variable that represents scientifically important characteristics of the subjects. As the examples above illustrate, the coefficients affect the way the function changes over time, influencing such aspects of the repeated measures as the level of initial performance, level of final performance, or rate of change. A major goal of the analysis is to attempt to understand individual differences on these variables. Toward that end, a submodel is specified for each. These submodels are sometimes similar to those used in the linear RCM; however, in the nonlinear model, the random effects need not enter the model linearly, and consequently the range of forms is much wider for the latter than the former.

A basic form of the model for the regression coefficients is

$$\beta_{ik} = \beta_k + b_{ik} \tag{6}$$

The population parameter, β_k, and individual-level increment, b_{ik}, are known as fixed and random effects, respectively. The idea is that the coefficient for the i-th person is related to the fixed effect but offset by the amount b_{ik} to optimally relate the curve to the individual's data. As illustrated below, the number of individual coefficients, fixed effects, and random effects is usually unequal to allow for flexibility in the form the coefficients take. Define these, respectively, as p, q, and r.

In the population of subjects, it is almost always assumed that the random effects are normally distributed with null mean vector and covariance matrix Φ. This is called the level 2 covariance structure:

$$(b_{i1}, \ldots, b_{ir}) \sim N(\mathbf{0}, \mathbf{\Phi}) \tag{7}$$

In the specific case of $r = 2$, the covariance matrix among random effects is

$$\Phi = \begin{pmatrix} var(b_{i1}) & \\ cov(b_{i2}, b_{i1}) & var(b_{i2}) \end{pmatrix}$$

The diagonal elements of Φ are variances that summarize the extent to which the random effects cluster around zero. Off-diagonal elements of Φ describe the degree to which pairs of random effects covary. The individual coefficients often have the form of Model 6, but there are many interesting variations. Among the more useful are the following four possibilities.

Random with covariate. Covariates are included to explain between-subject differences on the coefficients. For instance, in the speech errors example, the researchers made an independent rating of speech intelligibility for each child. This variable can be used in a linear regression to examine whether β_{ik} can be accounted for by the covariate. Define the covariate as c_i. It is incorporated into the submodel for the first coefficient by writing

$$\beta_{i1} = \beta_1 + \beta_2 c_i + b_{i1} \tag{8}$$

If $\beta_2 = 0$, then the intelligibility ratings are unrelated to β_{i1}. If $\beta_2 = 0.50$, then on average β_{i1}

increases half a point for every unit increase in c_i. Another way to interpret this is to note that for all children who receive a rating of $c_i = c_0$, the mean value on the coefficient for them is $(\beta_1 + \beta_2 c_0)$. In this way the effect of a covariate is to subdivide the population into groups of individuals.

Fixed with covariate. It is sometimes found when analyzing data that one or more individual coefficients do not vary between persons. When this occurs, the random effect is excluded and the coefficient is fixed at $\beta_{i1} = \beta_1$ for all subjects, or if a covariate is included, at

$$\beta_{i1} = \beta_1 + \beta_2 c_i \qquad (9)$$

Scientifically, this means that β_{i1} is more of a universal constant than is a coefficient with random effects.

Random only. Coefficients for some models define a rate parameter or a slope. In some cases, the fixed effect for the coefficient may be zero in the population but have significant variability across individuals. This can happen in linear models on the slope coefficient when on average there is no change over time, so that $\beta_k = 0$, but performance for some subjects increases while for others it declines. The person-level coefficient is then

$$\beta_{i1} = b_{i1} \qquad (10)$$

General nonlinear function. The most general specification of an individual coefficient is a nonlinear function of fixed parameters, covariates, and random effects. With obvious analogy to the basic model itself, this is

$$\beta_{i1} = b(\beta_1, c_i, b_{i1}) \qquad (11)$$

where $b(\beta_1, c_i, b_{ik})$ is a flexible function of the arguments. Because Model 1 encompasses a large class of nonlinear functions, general forms for the coefficients in Function 11 are easily included and extend the range of the methodology significantly. For example, a coefficient in a learning experiment might be defined as the expected peak performance or

highest level of proficiency on a laboratory task. If the response is percent correct, the coefficient cannot exceed 100. To ensure the coefficient stays within bounds, one can use

$$\beta_{i1} = \frac{100 \exp(\beta_1 + b_{i1})}{\exp(\beta_1 + b_{i1}) + 1}$$

Several other examples of general nonlinear functions for the coefficients are described by Davidian & Giltinan (1995, section 4.2) and Vonesh & Chinchilli (1997, section 7.4). One major issue in developing an RCM is deciding which regression coefficients are fixed over groups of subjects, as in Function 9, and which are random, with a form similar to Functions 6, 8, 10, or 11.

CHOOSING A NONLINEAR FUNCTION

The major scientific issue when using nonlinear models is the choice of function. Occasionally a function is preferred because it has a theoretical justification based on the scientific domain and the behavior under study. Even if other alternatives perform adequately, one model may be viewed as especially satisfactory on a priori grounds, with a mathematical form and parameterization that mimics the process in important ways.

A more common situation is for a function to be selected from among several candidates because it performs well with data and gives interesting information about the response. Many functions can be expressed in equivalent ways. In some applications, two or more functions perform similarly with a given data set. When more than one candidate exists, three criteria are used to select among the contenders (see Bates & Watts 1988, section 3). The first is the ability of the function to fit data. The second is the interpretability of the parameters. The third is the behavior of the function, the characteristic shape of the trajectory and the way that the form complements the data.

Graphical displays are irreplaceable in judging whether a function is appropriate.

Because of the focus on individual change in the RCM, it is important to fit models to the data from particular individuals in a series of exploratory analyses using nonlinear least squares. In a study with a large sample, it is not possible to examine every individual with each candidate model in detail. However, a few cases can be sampled randomly to get an idea of the appropriateness of the models.

Graph Individual Data with Candidate Models

To illustrate in some detail, we consider the problem of selecting a function for the repeated measures shown in **Figure 4**. These data are from one subject who participated in an experiment conducted by Frensch et al. (1999). The Continuous Monitoring Task, the response variable in this study, requires subjects to match the size of a half-circle shown on a computer display to a target stimulus that changed in size after a specified interval. When the interval between views of the image was short, accuracy was poor. When the time interval was longer, accuracy improved. The negatively accelerating shape of the subject's accuracy scores indicates that performance was improving, but the rate of increase slowed and 100% accuracy had not been achieved, even when the time interval between views was long.

Figure 4

Measures of accuracy in the Continuous Monitoring Task as a function of speed of stimulus change for a single subject. The fitted functions are the Michaelis-Menten and hyperbolic models (*solid line*) and two forms of the quadratic (*dashed line*). The estimated coefficients of the Michaelis-Menten model (γ_0, γ_1, and γ_2) are labeled. The maximizer of the quadratic, α_x, is also marked. The Michaelis-Menten model fits well and has interpretable parameters. Data taken from Frensch et al. 1999.

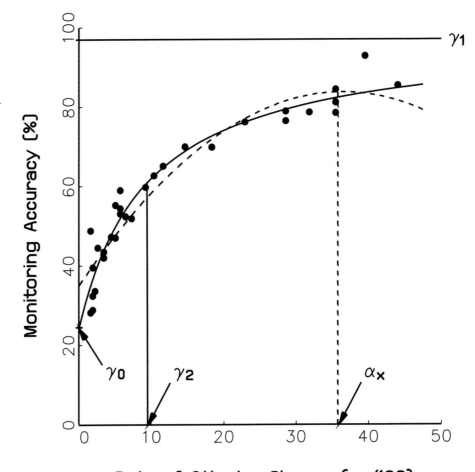

Consider four functions. First are two equivalent versions of the quadratic:

$$f_1(x) = \beta_0 + \beta_1 x + \beta_2 x^2$$
$$f_2(x) = \alpha_y - (\alpha_y - \alpha_0)(x/\alpha_x - 1)^2$$

The first of these two is the familiar polynomial form. In an appropriate range, the quadratic increases to a maximum then decreases. The second of the pair was specifically developed for this situation (Cudeck & du Toit 2002). The coefficients of f_2 have the interpretation that α_0 is initial performance, α_y is the maximum, and α_x is the maximizer; that is, $f_2(0) = \alpha_0$ and $f_2(\alpha_x) = \alpha_y$.

The next two functions are also equivalent. The most important aspect of their behavior is the increase from low accuracy for small values of x to a y-asymptote when x is large. The functions are

$$f_3(x) = \theta_0 + \frac{x}{\theta_1 + \theta_2 x}$$
$$f_4(x) = \gamma_0 + \frac{(\gamma_1 - \gamma_0)x}{\gamma_2 + x}$$

Model f_3 is known as the hyperbolic function. It has y-intercept at zero, $f_3(0) = \theta_0$, and for large x, an asymptote, $f_3(\infty) = \theta_0 + \frac{1}{\theta_2}$. Therefore, θ_0 is the initial value, and θ_2 is inversely related to maximal performance. The parameter θ_1 does not have a simple interpretation. Function f_4 is a version of the Michaelis-Menten model. It also has y-intercept, $f_4(0) = \gamma_0$, and a simple asymptote, $f_4(\infty) = \gamma_1$. The third coefficient of f_4, γ_2, is the value of the predictor at which half the total expected gain is achieved. That is, $f_4(\gamma_2) = \gamma_0 + \frac{1}{2}(\gamma_1 - \gamma_0)$. The coefficients of f_3 in terms of those of f_4 are $\theta_0 = \gamma_0$, $\theta_1 = \gamma_2(\gamma_1 - \gamma_0)^{-1}$, and $\theta_2 = (\gamma_1 - \gamma_0)^{-1}$.

Three Criteria in Model Selection

The first criterion in model selection is the ability of the function to account for data. In **Figure 4**, the fitted versions of f_1 and f_2 are the dashed line; those for f_3 and f_4 are the solid line. Although the functions follow the data relatively closely, f_3 and f_4 account for the data better than f_1 and f_2. The residual sum of squares is 620.3 versus 917.8, respectively.

The second criterion is the scientific interpretation of the parameters. By this criterion, f_2 and f_4 are preferable to f_1 and f_3. Consider the two versions of the quadratic. Each parameter of f_2 is understandable, whereas only the intercept of f_1 is. Similarly, each coefficient of the Michaelis-Menten model has a simple meaning, but only one of the parameters of f_3 does. Consequently, on the basis of meaningful parameters, f_2 is preferable to f_1, and f_4 is preferable to f_3. In **Figure 4**, the intercept of f_2 is $\hat{\alpha}_0 = 35.1$. The maximizer is shown as the dashed vertical line at $\hat{\alpha}_x = 36.4$ corresponding to the estimated maximum accuracy of $\hat{\alpha}_y = 83.7$. For f_4, the estimated parameters ($\hat{\gamma}_0 = 24.5$ and $\hat{\gamma}_1 = 97.9$) are shown on the vertical axis; $\hat{\gamma}_2 = 9.64$ is indicated on the horizontal axis.

We cannot overemphasize the value of clear interpretations of the parameters. The goal of an analysis is not just to account for data with the model, but also to gain new information about individual change. One can view a function as providing a reduction of the data by means of the model into new characteristics of the subjects. For this process to be effective, it is especially helpful when the parameters have unambiguous definitions.

Both f_2 and f_4 fit the data relatively well, although f_4 is slightly better. Both have interpretable parameters. The two sets of coefficients give different information about the data; however, both are understandable. Although the fit of the functions to data is generally satisfactory and even though the parameters are informative, the functions are not equally useful in this context.

The third consideration in model evaluation is the behavior of the function—that is, the shape and the overall trajectory—within the scientific context of the study. In this example, it is the behavior of the functions at large values of x that is salient. The behavior of f_4 is generally appropriate as a model for this variable, whereas f_2 is less suitable.

Based on knowledge of the task, monitoring accuracy clearly increases as the time between stimulus change increases. At the largest values of the predictor, this subject is still improving, approaching a maximum level of performance according to f_4 that is appropriately estimated as $\hat{\gamma}_1 = 97.9$. In contrast, f_2 reaches a maximum at $\hat{\alpha}_x = 36.4$ and declines thereafter. This behavior of f_2 does not greatly affect the fit of the model and has no bearing on the interpretability of the parameters. However, it is conceptually unsatisfactory for the function to decline at large values of x.

In summary, in this example, f_4 is clearly preferable to the other three candidates. It fits well. The parameters are understandable. The basic form of the function is appropriate given the experimental context.

One last comment is in order on f_1, the popular polynomial version of the quadratic. Although this function is the most widely used nonlinear model, and although it accounts for data relatively well, it is the least satisfactory of the four functions considered in this section. It shares the disadvantages of f_2 and has the additional liability that two of the three parameters are not interpretable (see also Pinheiro & Bates 2000, section 6.1).

Practical Issues in Model Selection

The best way to select a model is to graph data from an individual and examine the performance of candidate functions. In practice, one should study the data from a few representative subjects to ensure the function works well with all of them. In lieu of a theoretical rationale that favors a specific form, model choice is made on the basis of fit to data, interpretability of the parameters, and appropriateness of the functional form to the situation in which it is applied.

It goes without saying that this decision is subjective, and even after extensive exploration of candidate functions with a few individuals, the choice of model can be uncertain, especially if the data for individuals are highly variable within subject or if the number of repeated measures is small. In this situation, a simple function is often preferable to more complex alternatives because simple functions generally perform more reliably. When this is done, the assumption is that the model describes the major trend in the repeated measures. In some cases, after examining several possibilities, a simple model may be the best practical alternative. It is a vastly different process to carry out a thorough investigation, carefully studying several functions in many displays and then deciding on the popular linear model, for example, than just assuming linear change as a default option in an uncritical way.

TECHNICAL ISSUES

Here we briefly review two technical issues from among the many relevant ones associated with the use of the RCM. The first is a somewhat subtle matter of interpretation. This issue, although essential to a complete understanding of nonlinear change, has been neglected in virtually all discussions of models for repeated measures analysis in psychology. The second is a short catalog of options regarding estimation and computation. Obviously, this cursory treatment does not imply that the issues are unimportant.

The Subject-Specific Versus Population-Average Distinction

A major theme of the RCM is its emphasis on the individual process of change and the individual function of Model 1, $f(\beta_{i1}, \ldots, \beta_{ip}, x_{ij})$. This focus also gives the RCM several interesting statistical properties, some of which are unusual. Zeger et al. (1988) coined the term subject-specific (SS) to refer to these properties of nonlinear models for the analysis of repeated measures, and contrasted them with others that are known as population-average (PA) models. Good discussions of these ideas are presented by Davidian & Giltinan (1995, ch. 4), Fitzmaurice et al. (2004, section 13), Hand & Crowder

(1996, section 8.2), and Vonesh & Chinchilli (1997, section 7).

SS models place primary emphasis on the explicit representation of individual change. In contrast, a PA model, as its name implies, focuses on the description of the population mean change. A PA model is appropriate when primary interest centers, for example, on the average effect due to treatment compared with the average effect observed in the control condition. With a PA model, individual change is less of a specific emphasis than the main issue of accurate representation of the mean change. Conversely, an SS model is of interest if the primary issue is understanding how the treatment affects individual change. An adequate description of the mean trajectory is less important in SS models than is the accurate representation of individuals. Of course, it would be ideal if a single analysis produced both kinds of information in all situations. Unfortunately, this is not always possible, and one must sometimes choose between alternative methodologies, depending on which objective is more important for the purpose at hand.

The nonlinear RCM is SS and exhibits characteristics of this class. To illustrate one important consequence of this perspective, consider the basic form of individual coefficients in Function 6. Because the random effects have population means of zero, the fixed effects, $(\beta_1, \ldots, \beta_p)$, are the mean values of the individual coefficients

$$E(\beta_{ik}) = \beta_k$$

and are sometimes referred to as the typical values of the regression coefficients. When the nonlinear function is evaluated at the typical values, $f(\beta_1, \ldots, \beta_p, x_j)$, it gives the trajectory for an average person, a subject whose coefficients are equal to the population mean values, β_k. This is a theoretical curve for the average person because it is based on the function and uses the mean of each coefficient. In contrast, the purely data-based population mean at each occasion, x_j, is $\mu_j = E(y_{ij})$.

The pattern of change these averages follow, $\{x_j, \mu_j\}, j = 1, \ldots, n$, makes up what is called the curve of means (Hand & Crowder 1996, p. 122).

One unexpected feature of the nonlinear RCM is that the curve based on the typical values is not in general equal to the curve of means. That is,

$$f(\beta_1, \ldots, \beta_p, x_j) \neq \mu_j$$

From the perspective of popular PA models such as the structured latent curve, this result is undesirable. However, structural models for repeated measures are explicitly designed to account for the mean trajectory. In contrast, the nonlinear RCM is SS, formulated to describe individual change. It does not specifically account for the means.

A related result is that even when individual functions using individual coefficients describe individual data well, the curve of means need not follow the basic function. That is, even if the model fits data for every subject exactly so that $y_{ij} = f(\beta_{i1}, \ldots, \beta_{ip}, x_{ij})$, the same model in this ideal situation does not in general apply to the means at all, so that $\mu_j \neq f(\gamma_1, \ldots, \gamma_p, x_j)$ for any parameters $\gamma_1, \ldots, \gamma_p$. A concrete example of this fact is presented by Hand & Crowder (1996, p. 122; see also Crowder & Hand 1990, p. 147), who show that when an exponential function similar to Function 2 holds at the individual level for every subject, the model for the means is not a member of the exponential family in any form, but rather is a generalized polynomial.

Interestingly, the partially nonlinear RCM, including the important special-case linear version, enjoys both an SS as well as a PA interpretation. The individual coefficients have the desirable characteristics of SS models that account for individual-level data, and at the same time, the typical values that describe the curve of the average person also follow the curve of means. For this reason the PA-SS distinction is not relevant for understanding the partially nonlinear model—both interpretations are equally appropriate. When the model being considered is fully nonlinear, however, the nature of the model is again a consideration in interpretation.

In situations in which accounting for the empirical means using the nonlinear RCM is important, it is always possible to calculate an average over individual fitted trajectories to obtain an approximation to the curve of means. The exact function produced by the average curve is unknown, but this method can describe the mean vector well. Davidian & Giltinan (2003) argue that it may be preferable to proceed in this fashion because the attractive features of the basic SS model are maintained even as an approximation to the curve of means is computed.

The SS-PA distinction is a modern perspective on an old issue. On occasion in psychology, researchers have observed related problems empirically, notably in the learning literature in which it has been the focus of a thoughtful debate regarding the best function to represent acquisition and forgetting (Anderson & Tweney 1997, Brown & Heathcote 2003, Rubin & Wenzel 1996). The most widely used learning functions are inherently nonlinear. Thus, the inconsistency between individual curves and the corresponding mean trajectory is simply an example of the PA-SS concept. In general, there cannot be a single explicit nonlinear law of learning true both for individuals as well as the population mean trajectory. This is a consequence of the SS properties of the model.

Estimation and Computation

The nonlinear RCM is a complex structure. Theoretical and computational aspects of the model are subjects of active research. Reviews of relevant statistical theory are given by Davidian & Giltinan (1995), Demidenko (2004), Pinheiro & Bates (2000), and Vonesh & Chinchilli (1997). Davidian & Giltinan (1995, 2003) also provide an accessible treatment to computing strategies for population parameters and individual coefficients. Concepts based on the linear RCM carry over entirely to the nonlinear case, about which several excellent surveys have been recently published (Diggle et al. 1994, Fitzmaurice et al. 2004, Hand & Crowder 1996, Raudenbush & Bryk 2002, Singer & Willett 2003).

Presently, the most accessible and general programs for fitting the model are with the program NLMIXED in the SAS system (Wolfinger 1999), and the function nlme available in S-plus and R (Pinheiro et al. 2006). A library of functions, which includes the exponential in Model 2 used in the analysis of the speech errors data, is also available in LISREL (du Toit et al. 2005). RCMs can be handled quite flexibly with WinBUGS (Spiegelhalter et al. 2002). Other noncommercial programs have been distributed, such as MIXNLIN (Vonesh & Chinchilli 1997) and NLMEM (Galecki 1998).

ANALYSIS OF THE SPEECH ERRORS DATA

We return to the analysis of the speech errors data to illustrate the kind of results obtained. The number of speech errors for two children is shown in columns 2–7 of the table below. Columns 8–13 give age at the time of testing in years and months. The number of measurements for the two children are six and four, respectively. The Intelligibility variable, c_i, is used as a covariate. Missing data are marked as dots, although imbalance due to different assessment ages is the more significant feature:

Case	y_1	y_2	y_3	y_4	y_5	y_6	x_1	x_2	x_3	x_4	x_5	x_6	c
1	31	15	7	8	0	0	2–10	3–9	4–8	5–10	6–11	7–10	4
2	15	7	2	0	.	.	3–0	3–11	4–10	6–0	.	.	5

Repeating from Function 2 above, the model for the number of speech errors specifies exponential decrease with increasing age:

$$f(\beta_{i1}, \beta_{i2}, x_{ij}) = \beta_{i1} \exp\left[\beta_{i2}(x_{ij} - 3)\right]$$

The model for the coefficients is

$$\beta_{i1} = \beta_1 + \beta_3 c_i + b_{i1} \qquad \beta_{i2} = \beta_2 + \beta_4 c_i + b_{i2}$$
$$(12)$$

so $p = r = 2, q = 4$. The individual intercepts and rates both depend on a fixed coefficient, β_1 or β_2; plus a fixed coefficient for c_i, β_3 or β_4; plus random effects, b_{i1} or b_{i2}. The structure of residuals is homogeneous as in Covariance Structure 4.

The fit of the model was measured with the Akaike Information Criterion, a comparative index in which smaller values indicate better performance. For this version of the model, $AIC_1 = 1238$. Maximum likelihood estimates were calculated with SAS NLMIXED. Parameter estimates with standard error estimates in parentheses are

At age three, the estimated number of speech errors for a child with an Intelligibility score of $c_i = 0$ is $\hat{\beta}_1 = 27.0$. Intelligibility is an effective predictor of the intercept. For every increase of one unit in c_i, the number of errors at age three decreases $\hat{\beta}_3 = -2.70$. The rate of decline is $\hat{\beta}_2 = -0.908$. Because the rate is common to all, the implication is that no matter what level of speech errors existed at age three, the rate of decrease is the same thereafter. There is considerable variability in the intercepts, $\hat{\varphi}_{11} = 61.5$, and a moderate amount of scatter of the repeated measures within subject, $\hat{\sigma}_e^2 = 11.1$.

Graphs are irreplaceable at every stage of the analysis. We especially recommend three displays to accompany the presentation of results. For this example, the graphs are **Figures 1**, **5** and **6**, which are called the spaghetti plot, the swarm, and the trellis display, respectively. **Figure 1** indicates the range of patterns and the extent of the individual differences present. **Figure 5** presents the

---

$$27.3(1.7) \quad -0.776(.13) \quad -2.94(.50) \quad -0.058(.04) \quad \begin{pmatrix} 63.2(12.0) & \\ -0.18(.42) & 0.04(.03) \end{pmatrix} \quad 9.67(1.1)$$

$$\hat{\beta}_1 \qquad\qquad \hat{\beta}_2 \qquad\qquad \hat{\beta}_3 \qquad\qquad \hat{\beta}_4 \qquad\qquad\qquad \hat{\Phi} \qquad\qquad\qquad \hat{\sigma}_e^2$$

The estimated variance of the second random effect and the coefficient of the covariate for β_{i2} are both small compared to their standard errors: $\hat{\varphi}_{22} = 0.04$, $\hat{\beta}_4 = -0.058$. These results imply that c_i does not account for individual differences in slope and also that the rate of decrease in speech errors may be constant for all children.

In the second version of the model, the covariate and random effects were deleted from β_{i2}, whereas β_{i1} remained unchanged:

$$\beta_{i1} = \beta_1 + \beta_3 c_i + b_{i1} \qquad \beta_{i2} = \beta_2 \qquad (13)$$

With this modification the fit improved ($AIC_2 = 1233$), and estimates are

swarm, with the points jiggled to show the complete sample more clearly. The solid line is the curve corresponding to the estimated typical values, in this case for a child with an Intelligibility score of $c_i = 0$. Because the typical values are the means of the individual coefficients, the estimated curve should run through the middle of the point cloud.

The trellis display in **Figure 6** presents individual data with individual fitted functions. Results are presented for 16 children, selected to illustrate the range of the response patterns. Because publication space is limited, it is seldom possible to present every individual graph, unless the sample is small. However,

---

$$27.0(3.3) \quad -0.908(0.05) \quad -2.70(0.93) \quad 61.5(15.0) \quad 11.1(1.2)$$

$$\hat{\beta}_1 \qquad\qquad \hat{\beta}_2 \qquad\qquad \hat{\beta}_3 \qquad\qquad \hat{\varphi}_{11} \qquad\quad \hat{\sigma}_e^2$$

Figure 5

The curve based on the estimated typical values for the exponential model with all data from the speech errors study. The typical values are the means of the population of individual coefficients, but the corresponding curve does not estimate the curve of means.

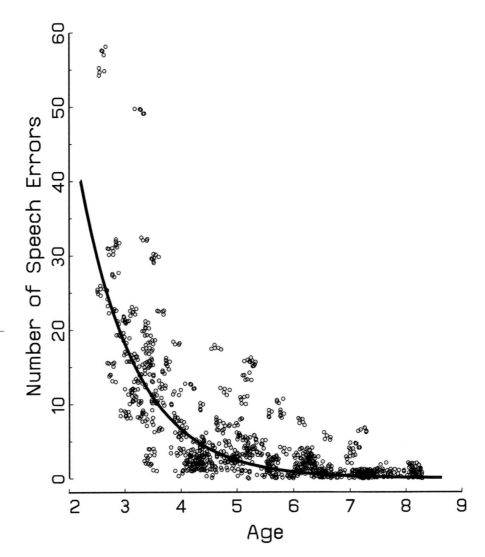

in many ways this graph is the focus of the analysis, and it is important to give information about how well the model works for several representative cases. The trellis display is a better approach to presenting the data, and for diagnosing problems, than summary statistics alone.

It is helpful to order the SS graphs of the trellis in some way to make the perception of so much information easier. There are many options, such as (*a*) best-to-worst fitting, to give an idea of the model's appropriateness; (*b*) according to values of a particular coefficient, $\hat{\beta}_{ik}$, to show clusters of individuals whose tra- jectories are similar in some way, which is use- ful for studying latent classes (Harring 2005, Jones & Rice 1992) or illustrating patterns of change for extreme values; (*c*) by groups of individuals who share similar values on the covariates, to illustrate how a particular in- crease in the covariates shifts the trajectory; or (*d*) using additional plots of candidate mod- els with data from selected individuals, similar to **Figures 3** and **4**. Also helpful are resid- ual plots, graphs of subgroups of subjects, and pairwise plots of estimated random effects. Invariably, some individuals are better fit by the model than others. If the within-subject

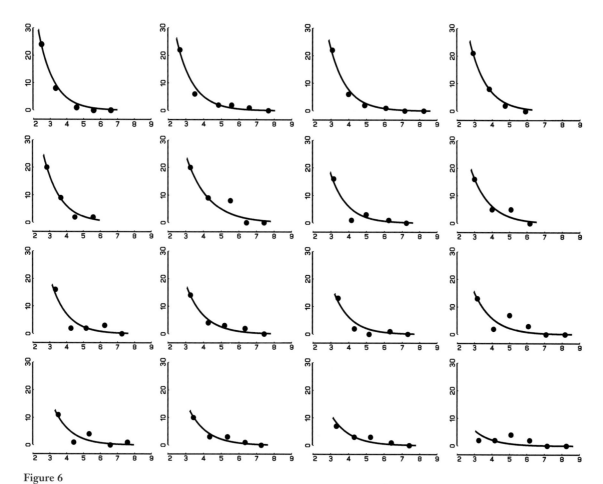

Figure 6

Trellis plot of 16 cases, with data and fitted functions from the exponential model, ordered in terms of decreasing values of the estimated intercept. The graph gives important information about the extent to which the individual-based model describes individual-level data. The heterogeneity of the response between subjects over repeated measures is evident in this display. It is also apparent that the model performs well.

variability is large, then a relatively simple model may be the best option. In this case the trellis display is an effective way to show those features of change over time that a simple model has been able to capture.

When the exponential function is used with coefficients as defined in Model 12, the overall model is nonlinear in the random effects. It is then an SS model and the proper focus is on individual change. When the model is simplified in Model 13 by specifying one coefficient as random and the other as fixed, the model becomes partially nonlinear. In the

latter case, PA and SS interpretations are both valid. Because the final model could have been 12 rather than 13 justifies the need for a general methodology that appropriately handles general nonlinear functions.

SUMMARY

Nonlinear patterns of change arise frequently in psychology in the analysis of repeated measures from longitudinal studies. The main feature of nonlinear development is that change is more rapid in some periods than in others. There typically also are strong individual differences and within-subject variability, so although a general similarity of patterns exists for different persons over time, individuals exhibit substantial heterogeneity in their behavior. To describe data of this kind, the RCM has been extended to accommodate nonlinear trajectories. Many ideas from the linear model—such as the distinction of within-subject and between-subject variability; covariates that account for individual differences in individual coefficients; and provision for imbalanced, missing, or even idiosyncratic measurement schedules—carry over completely to the nonlinear case. Nonlinear models usually account for data better than linear functions because the model can be tailored to the scientific context, and also because random effects can enter both the level 1 and level 2 submodels in a nonlinear fashion. The offsetting cost is that the model can be more difficult to specify than a simple linear model. It can be more challenging to estimate as well. There is also the subtle issue of SS versus PA models and the corresponding issues of interpretation. In spite of these considerations, the increased overhead when using the nonlinear RCM is more than compensated by the increased utility of the approach.

Arguably the most important parts of any longitudinal analysis are the graphical displays. For the RCM, three are especially helpful: the raw data plot, the plot of the curve for the typical values, and the trellis display. Graphs are also invaluable when choosing a function, when assessing the accuracy of individual fits, and when evaluating whether assumptions hold.

RCMs are so named because the function includes coefficients for each individual that essentially adapts the model to fit a person's repeated measures. The coefficients are a kind of latent variable. They give new information about the change process that is not directly measured by the data. One reason for studying repeated measures with the model is to obtain an estimate of these latent variables and also to account for the individual differences they represent. The main conceptual theme of the RCM is the focus on individual change with an individual model. This is a leitmotif of research in the behavioral sciences, and as a consequence the RCM methodology holds considerable promise for the study of growth, development, and learning in psychology.

SUMMARY POINTS

1. The study of growth and development in the analysis of longitudinal data has become one of the major research objectives of psychology.

2. Patterns of change over time are often nonlinear: At some time periods, the rate of change is much more rapid than at others. To adequately represent nonlinear development, the statistical method used should be flexible enough to describe a variety of different processes.

3. The nonlinear RCM is a generalization of regression defined for an individual's repeated measures. It is made up of three components: the fundamental nonlinear function that follows an individual's change pattern over time; the level 1 covariance structure that summarizes the variances and covariances among regression residuals; and the level 2 submodel that summarizes the individual differences between subjects on the basic regression coefficients.

4. Because the overall model is quite general, it can be challenging to develop a version that is appropriate for a given problem. In deciding on a reasonable structure, we

suggest three criteria: the fit of the model to data; the interpretability of the model parameters; and the behavior of the model in the way that it describes data.

5. The nonlinear RCM is subject-specific. It is designed to account for the repeated measures data of individuals. It does not specifically account for the population means, variances and covariances of the repeated measures.

6. Graphical displays are invaluable in all aspects of applying a RCM. Several different types of graph have been presented in this chapter. Perhaps the most important is the trellis, which shows individual data with individual fitted functions for a number of subjects.

ACKNOWLEDGMENTS

We are grateful to Thomas J. Bouchard, Margaret R. Burchinal, Gordon E. Legge, and Ulman Lindenberger for permission to use data from their research projects in the examples.

LITERATURE CITED

Anderson RB, Tweney RD. 1997. Artifactual power curves in forgetting. *Mem. Cogn.* 25:724–30

Bates DM, Watts DG. 1988. *Nonlinear Regression Analysis and Its Applications.* New York: Wiley

Blozis SA, Cudeck R. 1999. Conditionally linear mixed-effects models with latent variable covariates. *J. Educ. Behav. Stat.* 24:245–70

Bollen KA, Curran PJ. 2006. *Latent Curve Models: A Structural Equation Approach.* New York: Wiley

Brown H, Prescott R. 1999. *Applied Mixed Models in Medicine.* New York: Wiley

Brown S, Heathcote A. 2003. Averaging learning curves across and within participants. *Behav. Res. Methods Instrum. Comput.* 35:11–21

Browne MW. 1993. Structured latent curve models. In *Multivariate Analysis: Future Directions 2*, ed. CM Cuadras, CR Rao, pp. 171–98. Amsterdam: Elsevier Sci.

Burchinal M, Appelbaum M. 1991. Estimating individual developmental functions: methods and their assumptions. *Child Dev.* 62:23–43

Collins LM. 2006. Analysis of longitudinal data: the integration of theoretical model, temporal design, and statistical model. *Annu. Rev. Psychol.* 57:505–28

Crowder MJ, Hand DJ. 1990. *Analysis of Repeated Measures.* London: Chapman & Hall

Cudeck R, du Toit SHC. 2002. A nonlinear form of quadratic regression with interpretable parameters. *Multivar. Behav. Res.* 37:501–19

Cudeck R, Klebe KJ. 2002. Multiphase mixed-effects models for repeated measures data. *Psychol. Methods* 7:41–63

Davidian M, Giltinan DM. 1995. *Nonlinear Models for Repeated Measurement Data.* London: Chapman & Hall

Davidian M, Giltinan DM. 2003. Nonlinear models for repeated measurement data: an overview and update. *J. Agric. Biol. Environ. Stat.* 8:387–419

Demidenko E. 2004. *Mixed Models.* New York: Wiley

Diggle PJ, Liang KY, Zeger SL. 1994. *Analysis of Longitudinal Data.* New York: Oxford Univ. Press

DiPrete TA, Forristal JD. 1994. Multilevel models: methods and substance. *Annu. Rev. Sociol.* 20:331–57

Describes aspects of repeated measures analysis, provides data sets, and puts the nonlinear RCM into the context of other methods.

On the nonlinear RCM and review of the linear model. Coverage of statistical issues, including estimation.

Duncan TE, Duncan SC, Strycker LA, Li F, Alpert A. 1999. *An Introduction to Latent Variable Growth Curve Modeling: Concepts, Issues, and Applications*. Mahwah, NJ: Erlbaum

du Toit S, du Toit M, Mels G, Cheng Y. 2005. *LISREL for windows: SURVEYGLIM user's guide*. Chicago: Sci. Softw. Int. Inc. **http://www.ssicentral.com/lisrel/resources.html**

Dyba T, Hakulinen T, Päivärinta L. 1997. A simple nonlinear model in incidence prediction. *Stat. Med.* 16:2297–309

Ferrer E, McArdle JJ. 2003. Alternative structural models for multivariate longitudinal data analysis. *Struct. Equ. Model.* 10:493–524

Fitzmaurice G, Laird N, Ware J. 2004. *Applied Longitudinal Analysis*. New York: Wiley

Fox PW, Hershberger SL, Bouchard TJ. 1996. Genetic and environmental contributions to the acquisition of a motor skill. *Nature* 384:356–58

Frensch PA, Lindenberger U, Kray J. 1999. Imposing structure on an unstructured environment: ontogenetic changes in the ability to form rules of behavior under conditions of low environmental predictability. In *Learning: Rule Extraction and Representation*, ed. AD Friederici, R Menzel, pp. 139–62. Berlin: de Gruyter

Galecki AT. 1998. NLMEM: a new SAS:IML macro for hierarchical nonlinear models. *Comput. Methods Progr. Biomed.* 55:207–16

Halaby CN. 2004. Panel models in sociological research: theory into practice. *Annu. Rev. Sociol.* 30:507–44

Hand D, Crowder M. 1996. *Practical Longitudinal Data Analysis*. London: Chapman & Hall

Harring JR. 2005. *Nonlinear mixed effects mixture model: a model for clustering nonlinear longitudinal profiles*. PhD thesis. Univ. Minn., Minneapolis. 136pp.

Harring JR, Cudeck R, du Toit SHC. 2006. Fitting partially nonlinear random coefficient models as SEMs. *Multivar. Behav. Res.* In press

Hertzog C, Nesselroade JR. 2003. Assessing psychological change in adulthood: an overview of methodological issues. *Psychol. Aging* 18:639–57

Huet S, Bouvier A, Poursat MA, Jolivet E. 2004. *Statistical Tools for Nonlinear Regression*. New York: Springer-Verlag. 2nd ed.

Jones MC, Rice JA. 1992. Displaying the important features of large collections of similar curves. *Am. Stat.* 46:140–45

Jöreskog KG. 1979. Statistical estimation of structural models in longitudinal-developmental investigations. In *Longitudinal Research in the Study of Behavior and Development*, ed. JR Nesselroade, PB Baltes, pp. 303–52. New York: Academic

Laird NM, Ware JH. 1982. Random-effects models for longitudinal data. *Biometrics* 38:963–74

MacCallum RC, Kim C, Malarkey WB, Kiecolt-Glaser JK. 1997. Studying multivariate change using multilevel models and latent curve models. *Multivar. Behav. Res.* 32:215–53

Mansfield JS, Ahn SJ, Legge GE, Luebker A. 1993. A new reading acuity chart for normal and low vision. *Ophthalmic Vis. Opt./Noninvasive Assess. Vis. Syst. Tech. Digest* 3:232–35

Meredith W, Tisak J. 1990. Latent curve analysis. *Psychometrika* 55:107–22

Morrell CH, Pearson JD, Carter HB, Brant LJ. 1995. Estimating unknown transition times using a piecewise nonlinear mixed-effects model in men with prostrate cancer. *J. Am. Stat. Assoc.* 90:45–53

Naumova EN, Must A, Laird NM. 2001. Tutorial in biostatistics: evaluating the impact of 'critical' periods in longitudinal studies of growth using piecewise mixed effects models. *Int. J. Epidemiol.* 30:1332–41

Pinheiro J, Bates D, DebRoy S, Sarkar D. 2006. *Linear and nonlinear mixed-effects models: the nlme package*. **http://cran.r-project.org/src/contrib/Descriptions/nlme.html**

Pinheiro JC, Bates DM. 2000. *Mixed-Effects Models in S and S-PLUS*. New York: Springer-Verlag

On general issues in the study of longitudinal data, with a survey of the literature.

Raudenbush SW. 2001. Comparing personal trajectories and drawing causal inferences from longitudinal data. *Annu. Rev. Psychol.* 52:501–25

Raudenbush SW, Bryk AS. 2002. *Hierarchical Linear Models: Applications and Data Analysis Methods.* Thousand Oaks, CA: Sage. 2nd ed.

Rogosa DR, Willett JB. 1985. Understanding correlates of change by modeling individual differences in growth. *Psychometrika* 50:203–28

Rubin DC, Wenzel AE. 1996. One hundred years of forgetting: a quantitative description of retention. *Psychol. Rev.* 103:734–60

Seber GAF, Wild CJ. 1989. *Nonlinear Regression.* New York: Wiley

Singer JD, Willett JB. 2003. *Applied Longitudinal Data Analysis: Modeling Change and Event Occurrence.* New York: Oxford Univ. Press

Spiegelhalter D, Thomas A, Best N, Lunn D. 2002. *WinBUGS User Manual Version 1.4.* Cambridge, UK: MRC Biostatistics Unit. **http://www.mrc-bsu.cam.ac.uk/bugs/ overview/contents.shtml**

Verbeke G, Molenberghs G. 2000. *Linear Mixed Models for Longitudinal Data.* New York: Springer-Verlag

Vonesh EF, Carter RL. 1992. Mixed effects nonlinear regression for unbalanced repeated measures. *Biometrics* 48:1–17

Vonesh EF, Chinchilli VM. 1997. *Linear and Nonlinear Models for the Analysis of Repeated Measurements.* New York: Dekker

Wolfinger RD. 1999. Fitting nonlinear mixed models with the new NLMIXED procedure. *Proc. SAS User Group Int.* pp. 1–10. Cary, NC: SAS Inst.

Zeger SL, Liang K-Y, Albert PS. 1988. Models for longitudinal data: a generalized estimating equation approach. *Biometrics* 44:1049–60

Cumulative Indexes

Contributing Authors, Volumes 48–58

Kelman HC, 57:1–26
Kerr NL, 55:623–55
Kersten D, 55:271–304
Kessler RC, 48:191–214
Kestler L, 55:401–30
Kiecolt-Glaser JK, 53:83–107
Klin A, 56:315–36
Kolb B, 49:43–64
Kopta SM, 50:441–69
Koriat A, 51:481–537
Koutstaal W, 49:289–318
Kramer RM, 50:569–98
Krantz DS, 53:341–69
Krosnick JA, 50:537–67
Kruglanski AW, 58:291–316

L

Lachman ME, 55:305–31
Lackner JR, 56:115–47
Ladd GW, 50:333–59
Langenbucher JW, 50:79–107
Latham GP, 56:485–516
Lavie P, 52:277–303
Leary MR, 58:317–44
LeBoeuf RA, 53:491–517
Lehman DR, 55:689–714
Leiter MP, 52:397–422
Leonardo ED, 57:117–37
Lerner RM, 49:413–46
Levine B, 53:401–33
Lieberman MD, 58:259–89
Lilienfeld SO, 53:519–43
Lindenberger U, 50:471–507
Lipsey MW, 51:345–75
Loeber R, 48:371–410
Logan GD, 55:207–34
Loken B, 57:453–85
López SR, 51:571–98
Lotto AJ, 55:149–79
Lubinski D, 51:405–44
Lucas RE, 54:403–25
Lueger RJ, 50:441–69
Lussier JP, 55:431–61
Lynch EB, 51:121–47

M

MacCallum RC, 51:201–26
Maccoby EE, 51:1–27
MacCoun RJ, 49:259–87
MacKinnon DP, 58:593–614

Macrae CN, 51:93–120
MacWhinney B, 49:199–227
Maddox WT, 56:149–78
Maier SF, 51:29–57
Major BN, 56:393–421
Mamassian P, 55:271–304
Margolin G, 51:445–79
Markman AB, 52:223–47
Marshall PJ, 56:235–62
Martin A, 58:25–45
Martin RC, 54:55–89
Mashek DJ, 58:345–72
Maslach C, 52:397–422
Mayer RE, 55:715–44
Maynard A, 54:461–90
Mays VM, 58:201–25
McCeney MK, 53:341–69
McDermott C, 55:519–44
McDonald JL, 48:215–41
McFall RM, 50:215–41
McGuffin P, 54:205–28
McGuire L, 53:83–107
McGuire WJ, 48:1–30
McKenna KYA, 55:572–90
McKoon G, 49:25–42
McNally RJ, 54:229–52
Meadows EA, 48:449–80
Medin DL, 51:121–47
Meece JL, 57:487–503
Mehl MR, 54:547–77
Mellers BA, 49:447–77
Mesquita B, 58:373–403
Metzger A, 57:255–84
Miller DT, 52:527–54
Miller GA, 50:1–19
Miller RR, 48:573–607
Millis KK, 48:163–89
Mineka S, 49:377–412
Mischel W, 49:229–58;
   55:1–22
Monahan J, 56:631–59
Moore DA, 51:279–314
Morrin M, 49:319–44
Morris AS, 52:83–110
Moskowitz JT, 55:745–74
Murphy KR, 49:141–68
Myers CE, 48:481–514

N

Nader K, 48:85–114
Nairne JS, 53:53–81

Nathan PE, 50:79–107
Nezworski MT, 53:519–43
Nichols KE, 56:235–62
Niederhoffer KG, 54:547–77
Nitschke JB, 53:545–74
Norman KA, 49:289–318
Nowlis SM, 52:249–75

O

O'Brien LT, 56:393–421
Ochsner KN, 58:373–403
Oishi S, 54:403–25
Ollendick TH, 52:685–716
Olson EA, 54:277–95
Olson GM, 54:491–516
Olson JS, 54:491–516
Olson MA, 54:297–327
Orehek E, 58:291–316
Oswald FL, 51:631–64
Ozer DJ, 57:401–21

P

Paley B, 48:243–67
Palincsar AS, 49:345–75
Palmer C, 48:115–38
Paloutzian RF, 54:377–402
Pansky A, 51:481–537
Paradise R, 54:175–203
Parke RD, 55:365–99
Parks L, 56:571–600
Pashler H, 52:629–51
Pearce JM, 52:111–39
Peissig JJ, 58:75–96
Pennebaker JW, 54:547–77
Penn DC, 58:97–118
Penner LA, 56:365–92
Peplau LA, 58:405–24
Peretz I, 56:89–114
Pettigrew TF, 49:65–85
Petty RE, 48:609–47
Phelps EA, 57:27–53
Phillips SD, 48:31–59
Piliavin JA, 56:365–92
Pinder CC, 56:485–516
Pizzagalli D, 53:545–74
Plomin R, 54:205–28
Polivy J, 53:187–213
Posluszny DM, 50:137–63
Posner MI, 58:1–23
Poulos AM, 56:207–34

Weiss H, 53:279–307
Weisz JR, 56:337–63
Wells GL, 54:277–95
Wenzlaff RM, 51:59–91
Werker JF, 50:509–35
Whishaw IQ, 49:43–64
Whisman MA,
    57:317–44
Wickens TD, 49:537–57
Widiger TA, 51:377–404
Wigfield A, 53:109–32

Williams KD, 58:425–52
Willis H, 53:575–604
Wilson TD, 55:493–518
Wingate LR, 56:287–314
Winter DA, 58:453–77
Wixted JT, 55:235–69
Wood JM, 53:519–43
Wood W, 51:539–70
Woods SC, 51:255–77
Woolard JL, 50:387–418
Wulfeck B, 52:369–96

Y

Yantis S, 48:269–97
Yuille A, 55:271–304

Z

Zatorre RJ, 56:89–114
Zimmer-Gembeck MJ,
    58:119–44
Zwaan RA, 48:163–89

Chapter Titles, Volumes 48–58

Clinical and Counseling Psychology (See Also Psychopathology)

Environmental Psychology

The Environmental Psychology of Capsule Habitats	P Suedfeld, GD Steel	51:227–53
Child Development and the Physical Environment	GW Evans	57:423–51

Genetics of Behavior

See Biological Psychology

Gerontology (Maturity and Aging)

See Developmental Psychology

Health Psychology

Health Psychology: What Is an Unhealthy Environment and How Does it Get Under the Skin?	SE Taylor, RL Repetti, T Seeman	48:411–47
Health Psychology: Mapping Biobehavioral Contributions to Health and Illness	A Baum, DM Posluszny	50:137–63
Health Psychology: Psychosocial and Biobehavioral Aspects of Chronic Disease Management	N Schneiderman, MH Antoni, PG Saab, G Ironson	52:555–80

Adjustment to Chronic Diseases and Terminal Illness

Health Psychology: Psychological Adjustment to Chronic Disease	AL Stanton, TA Revenson, H Tennen	58:565–92

Health Promotion and Disease Prevention

The Psychological Aspects of Natural Language Use: Our Words, Our Selves	JW Pennebaker, MR Mehl, KG Niederhoffer	54:547–77

Personality and Coping Styles

Coping: Pitfalls and Promise	S Folkman, JT Moskowitz	55:745–74

Psychobiological Factors

Emotions, Morbidity, and Mortality: New Perspectives from Psychoneuroimmunology	JK Kiecolt-Glaser, L McGuire, TF Robles, R Glaser	53:83–107

Personality

Psychology in Other Countries

Psychopathology (See Also Clinical and Counseling Psychology)

The Effects of Stressful Life Events on Depression	RC Kessler	48:191–214
Key Issues in the Development of Aggression and Violence from Childhood to Early Adulthood	R Loeber, D Hay	48:371–410
Psychopathology: Description and Classification	PE Nathan, JW Langenbucher	50:79–107
Adult Psychopathology: Issues and Controversies	TA Widiger, LM Sankis	51:377–404
Cultural Psychopathology: Uncovering the Social World of Mental Illness	SR López, PJ Guarnaccia	51:571–98

Anxiety Disorders

Progress and Controversy in the Study of Posttraumatic Stress Disorder	RJ McNally	54:229–52

Behavioral Genetics and Psychopathology

Psychopathology in the Postgenomic Era	R Plomin, P McGuffin	54:205–28

Culture and Mental Health

Race, Race-Based Discrimination, and Health Outcomes Among African Americans	VM Mays, SD Cochran, NW Barnes	58:201–25

Disorders of Childhood

Autism in Infancy and Early Childhood	F Volkmar, K Chawarska, A Klin	56:315–36

Mood Disorders

Depression: Perspectives from Affective Neuroscience	RJ Davidson, D Pizzagalli, JB Nitschke, K Putnam	53:545–74

Personality Disorders

Assessment and Diagnosis of Personality Disorder: Perennial Issues and an Emerging Reconceptualization	LA Clark	58:227–57

Psychopathology: Various Disorders

Causes of Eating Disorders	J Polivy, CP Herman	53:187–213

Vision